T·O·U·R·I·N·G
ENGLAND

ROAD ATLAS · ILLUSTRATED MOTOR TOURS · TOWN PLANS

Colour Library Books

T·O·U·R·I·N·G
ENGLAND

Produced by the Publishing Division of the Automobile Association.

Tours compiled and driven by the Publications Research Unit of the Automobile Association.

Photographs by British Tourist Authority, J Allen Cash Photolibrary, Jarrolds Colour Library, Woodmansterne Picture Library, S & O Mathews, Barnaby's Picture Library, Association Press, Topham Picture Library, Aerofilms Ltd, J Hunter, C Molyneux, R Corbett, D Cripps, The National Trust, T Wood, J Sumner, G M Player, Yorkshire & Humberside Tourist Board, V Patel, Biofotos, H Williams, A Lawson, AA Photolibrary.

All maps by the Cartographic Department, Publishing Division, of the Automobile Association. Based on the Ordnance Survey Maps, with the permission of the Controller of HM Stationery Office. Crown Copyright Reserved.

Town plans produced by the AA's Cartographic Department. © The Automobile Association.

Filmset by Senator Graphics, Great Suffolk St, London SE1 Printed and bound by New Interlitho SPA, Milan, Italy.

This 1990 edition produced exclusively for Colour Library Books Ltd., Godalming, Surrey by The Automobile Association.

ISBN 0 86283 776 6
CLB 2473

CONTENTS

Page 1 (and cover) A Sussex Village,
painted by Edward Wilkins Waite. Bridgeman Art Library

Pages 2-3 Glastonbury Tor. Photograph Harry Williams

Pages 4-5 Alnwick Castle. Photograph Tim Woodcock

Pages 6-7 Woodbridge Tidemill. Photograph S & O Mathews

Pages 14-15 Swaledale. Photograph S & O Mathews

IN THE following pages are to be found route directions for more than 130 motor tours, information on thousands of places of interest, regional atlases, and some 130 pages of maps of important towns and cities. Together they represent the best of England's many and varied attractions.

The book is divided into four regions, each self-contained — covering the West Country, South and South East England, Central England and East Anglia, and the North Country.

Each section contains detailed route directions on motor tours with information on the most popular areas to visit in the region . . . all highlighted in the accompanying tour maps. There are descriptions of hundreds of houses open to the public, villages with delightful centuries-old streets, parks and country areas, zoos and other colourful and noteworthy places.

The atlas pages for each region show the location of most of the entries in the touring sections as well as other important features. The keymaps on pages 8 to 13 list all the town plans, motor tours and their locations, and pinpoint the areas covered by the maps on each page. In the extensive town plan sections of each region are detailed, up-to-the-minute plans of important towns and cities, with comprehensive street indexes, and brief descriptions of the towns. An index for each region lists all the entries.

USING TOURING ENGLAND

KEY TO MOTOR TOURS

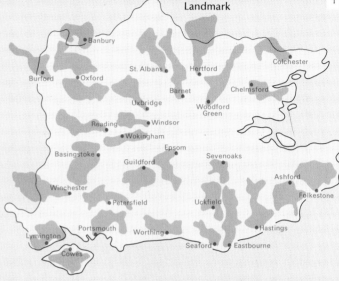

1
WEST COUNTRY
2
SOUTH AND SOUTH-EAST
3
CENTRAL AND EAST ANGLIA
4
NORTH COUNTRY

TOURING ENGLAND is divided into four convenient regional areas (see map on left). So that the motor tours are easy to find, the four areas are separated out below. The tours are arranged in alphabetical order by the name of the town in which the tour starts. It is perfectly possible to join or leave the tours at any point

MAPS
Main Tour Route
Detour
Motorway
A-class Road
B-class Road
Unclassified Road
Dual Carriageway
Road Under Construction
Airport
Battlefield
Bridge
Castle
Church as Route
Landmark

WEST COUNTRY
PAGES 40-117

SOUTH AND SOUTH EAST
PAGES 184-257

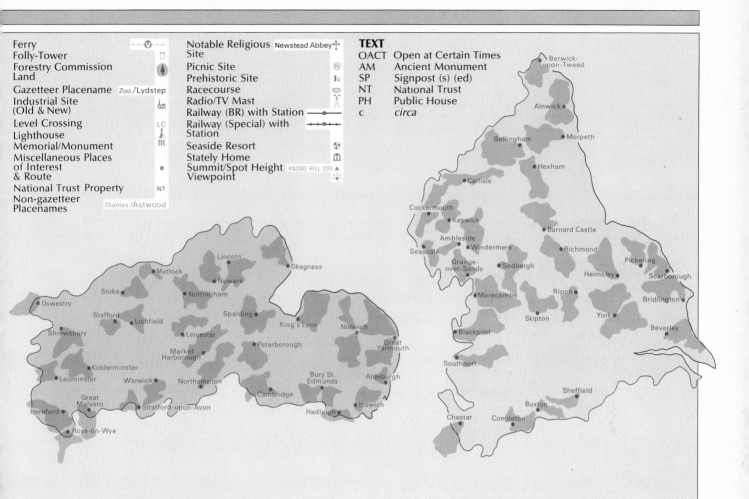

Ferry
Folly-Tower
Forestry Commission Land
Gazetteer Placename   Zoo /Lydstep
Industrial Site (Old & New)
Level Crossing   LC
Lighthouse
Memorial/Monument
Miscellaneous Places of Interest & Route
National Trust Property   NT
Non-gazetteer Placenames   Thames /Astwood

Notable Religious   Newstead Abbey
Site
Picnic Site   PS
Prehistoric Site
Racecourse
Radio/TV Mast
Railway (BR) with Station
Railway (Special) with Station
Seaside Resort
Stately Home
Summit/Spot Height   KNOWE HILL 209
Viewpoint

TEXT
OACT   Open at Certain Times
AM   Ancient Monument
SP   Signpost (s) (ed)
NT   National Trust
PH   Public House
c   *circa*

CENTRAL AND EAST ANGLIA
PAGES 328-393

NORTH COUNTRY
PAGES 472-535

KEY TO TOWN PLANS

Shown here are the locations of all the towns with plans in *Touring England*. The book is divided into four regional areas (see left), which are separated out below. Some plans of large cities have a double page-spread to themselves, but most cities and towns appear together with prominent neighbouring centres. So Poole and Christchurch appear on the same spread as Bournemouth, for example.

1
WEST COUNTRY
2
SOUTH AND SOUTH-EAST
3
CENTRAL AND EAST ANGLIA
4
NORTH COUNTRY

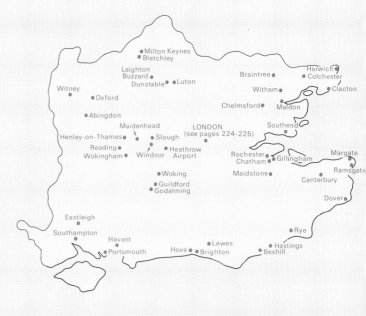

WEST COUNTRY
PAGES 120-149

SOUTH AND SOUTH-EAST
PAGES 259-289

LEGEND

Town Plan
AA recommended route
Restricted roads
Other roads
Buildings of interest
Car parks
Parks and open spaces
One way streets

Area Plan
A roads
B roads
Locations   Alton ○
Urban area

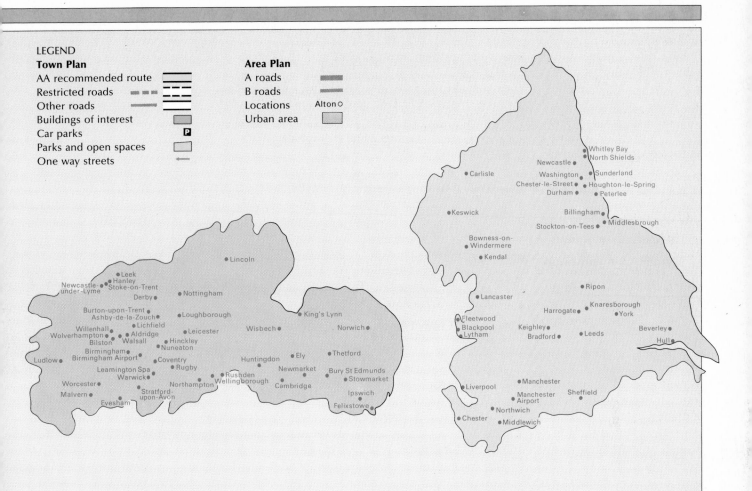

CENTRAL AND EAST ANGLIA
PAGES 395-431

NORTH COUNTRY
PAGES 537-567

KEY TO ATLAS PAGES

The atlas is divided into four parts, each of which appears at the end of one of the regional sections of the book (see left). The atlas is at the scale of three miles to the inch, and includes most roads. A great deal of additional information has been added to the mapping, as can be seen from the symbol explanations below.

4

3

2

1

1
WEST COUNTRY
2
SOUTH AND SOUTH-EAST
3
CENTRAL AND EAST ANGLIA
4
NORTH COUNTRY

Gloucester

170/171
Cardiff Bristol

172/173

164/165
Barnstaple

166/167

168/169
Salisbury

Taunton

158/159
Exeter

160/161
Weymouth

162/163
Bournemouth

Southampton

154/155

156/157
Plymouth

152/153
Truro

Northampton

314/315

316/317
Cambridge

Gloucester

306/307

308/309
Oxford

310/311

312/313
Chelmsford

Reading

LONDON
302/303

298/299
Salisbury

300/301
Guildford

304/305
Maidstone Dover

Southampton

294/295
Brighton

296/297
Newhaven

292/293
Bournemouth

WEST COUNTRY
PAGES 152-173

SOUTH AND SOUTH-EAST
PAGES 292-317

ATLAS SYMBOLS – ROAD INFORMATION

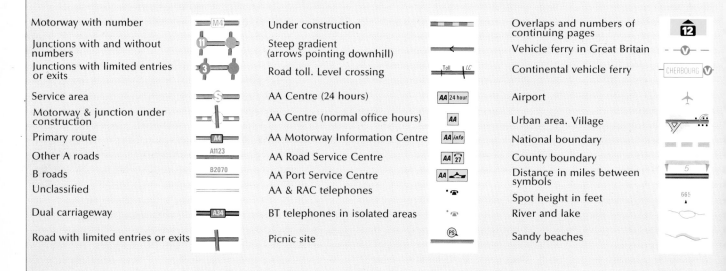

Motorway with number	Under construction	Overlaps and numbers of continuing pages
Junctions with and without numbers	Steep gradient (arrows pointing downhill)	Vehicle ferry in Great Britain
Junctions with limited entries or exits	Road toll. Level crossing	Continental vehicle ferry
Service area	AA Centre (24 hours)	Airport
Motorway & junction under construction	AA Centre (normal office hours)	Urban area. Village
Primary route	AA Motorway Information Centre	National boundary
Other A roads	AA Road Service Centre	County boundary
B roads	AA Port Service Centre	Distance in miles between symbols
Unclassified	AA & RAC telephones	Spot height in feet
Dual carriageway	BT telephones in isolated areas	River and lake
Road with limited entries or exits	Picnic site	Sandy beaches

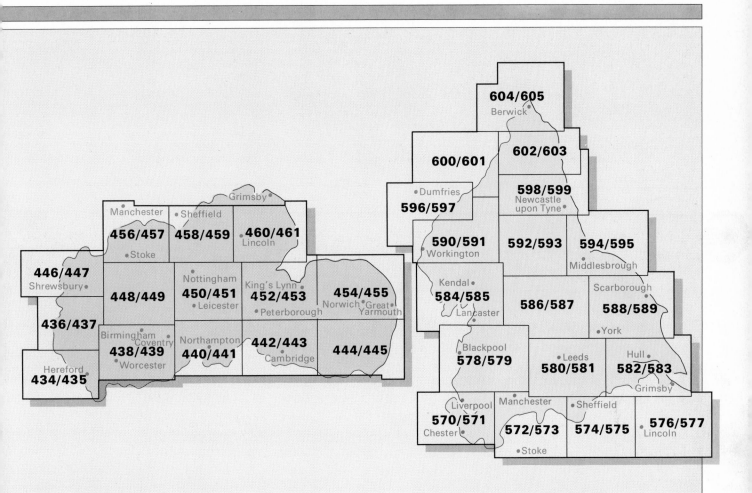

CENTRAL AND EAST ANGLIA
PAGES 434-461

NORTH COUNTRY
PAGES 570-605

ATLAS SYMBOLS – POINTS OF INTEREST

Abbey or Cathedral		Coastal Launching Site		Nature Trail	
Ruined Abbey or Cathedral		Surfing		Wildlife Park (mammals)	
Castle		Climbing School		Wildlife Park (birds)	
House and Garden		County Cricket Ground		Zoo	
House		Gliding Centre		Forest Drive	
Garden		Artificial Ski Slope		Lighthouse	
Industrial Interest		Golf Course		Tourist Information Centre	
Museum or Collection		Horse Racing		Tourist Information Centre (summer only)	
Prehistoric Monument		Show Jumping/Equestrian Centre		Long Distance Footpath	
Famous Battle Site		Motor Racing Circuit		AA Viewpoint	
Preserved Railway or Steam Centre		Cave		Other Place of Interest	
Windmill		Country Park		Boxed symbols indicate tourist attractions in towns	
Sea Angling		Dolphinarium or Aquarium			

DISCOVERING ENGLAND'S LANDSCAPES

MEN have been changing the look of England for thousands of years. Towns and villages are obviously man-made, but most country landscapes also owe their character to men. Even such wild and natural-seeming places as Dartmoor and the Lake District look as they do today because of the way men have treated them in the past. This process is continuing even now; decisions taken today will affect the look of tomorrow's England just as effectively as decisions made by Neolithic farmers, medieval husbandmen or 19th-century gentlemen farmers contributed to the England visited in the tours in this book.

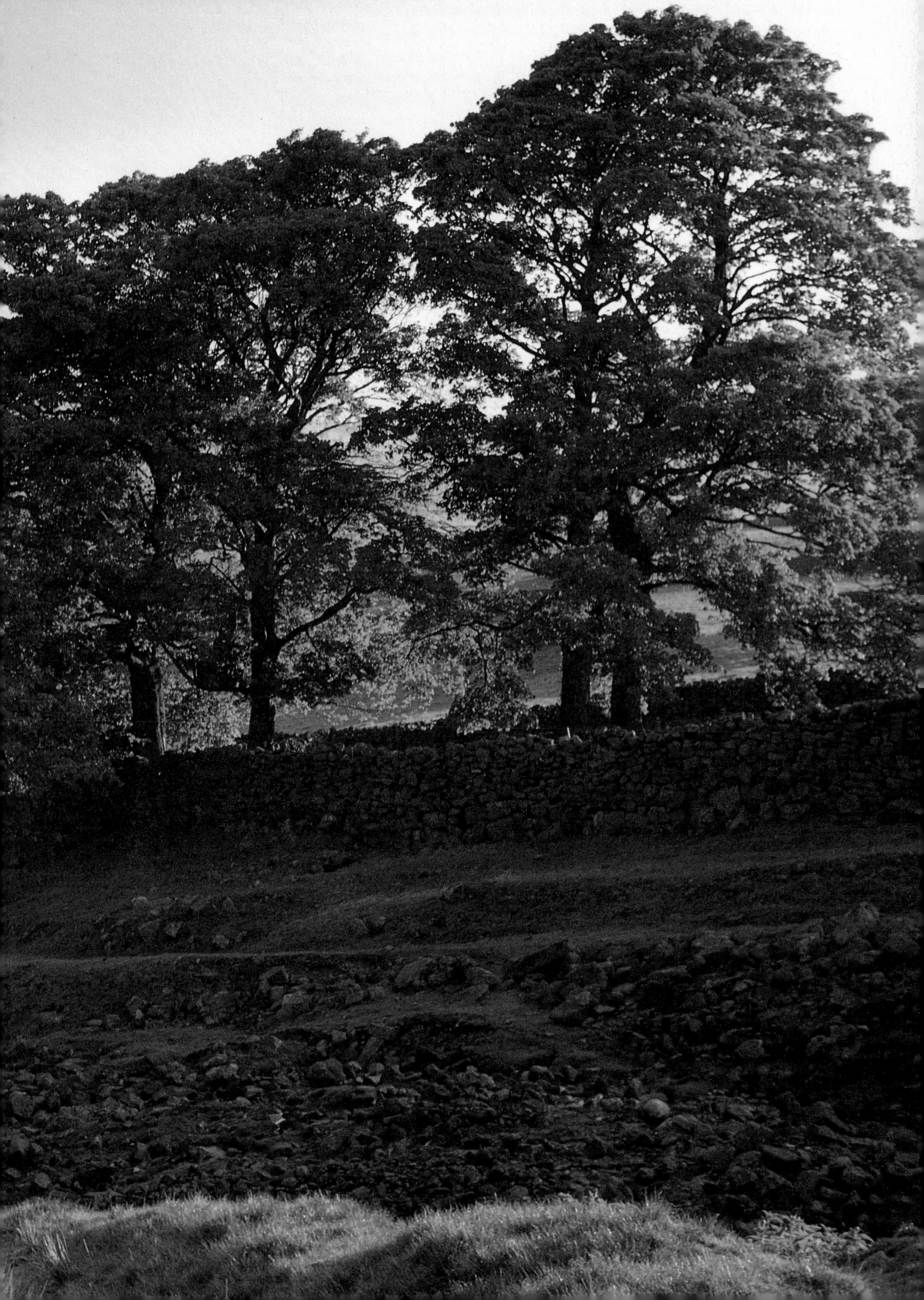

PREHISTORIC TIMES

THE STORY of the landscape of our familiar England and of its people begins with the retreat of the great ice sheets some 10,000 years ago. Much of England then would have resembled the tundra of Scandinavia — a bleak, scraped, chill land. But the end of the ice age heralded a warmer period, and forests began to grow.

Grazing animals, then present in great numbers, must have kept glades open among the forests which eventually stretched almost from seashore to mountain top. Forming part of this scene were men. The earliest of them we call Paleolithic — or Old Stone Age. All that we know about them we must learn from the few objects they left behind — principally stone tools and weapons. We do not know what impact, if any, they had on the land. They were hunter-gatherers, their lives enmeshed within the changing seasons and the movements of animals. Perhaps they were not unlike the aboriginal peoples of Australia, with an extraordinary knowledge of the foods that the country could provide. The Paleolithic Age merged almost imperceptibly with the Mesolithic, or Middle Stone Age. The tools and weapons changed in some ways, but the way of life probably changed very little. It may be that the Mesolithic people were more capable of altering their surroundings — perhaps by herding the animals. Their lives may have been rather like those of the plains Indians of North America before the arrival of the white man.

About 6,000 years ago a very different way of life began to develop. The Neolithic, or New Stone Age, was once talked of in terms of revolution, a revolution imposed by an invasion from the main part of Europe. Certainly, the way of life developed then affects us now, for it revolved around a change from the old, nomadic way to a new, settled lifestyle based on farming. But it was a much more gradual change than was previously thought.

Since their tools were still only of wood, bone and stone, the achievements of those people were incredible. They began to clear the forest cover. Those woodlands which remained were managed far more skilfully than we manage our woodlands today. Intricate patterns of fields were made based on individual farms, and larger, tribal, settlements. And monuments were built. It is these, perhaps, that most easily catch the imagination. Tombs with complex stone chambers; ceremonial avenues, sometimes miles long; huge causewayed enclosures; and most famous of all, the henge monuments.

The henge monuments were developed towards the end of the Neolithic period. That age was superseded by the Bronze Age. Again the notion of a rapid change is probably false — it is much more likely that the knowledge of metal spread gradually over a long period of time. The people of the Bronze Age further consolidated the farming landscape, more forest was felled, and an England not unlike the open one we know today came into being. The population by now was very large, indeed some areas were more thickly populated then than at any time since. Huge ranches, or estates, were laid out, the boundaries of which can still sometimes be traced.

So, for something like 3,000 years, throughout the Neolithic and Bronze Ages, men worked the land, adapting it to suit their farming practices, and populating every available area. Iron arrived very late in the prehistoric period, about 600BC, and its ascendancy coincides with that of the Celtic peoples. Originating from central Europe, the Celts seem to have imposed their ways upon the existing population in dramatic ways, but perhaps this is too simplistic a view. Maybe life did not change very much for most of the Bronze Age population. The most obvious legacies of Celtic times are the hillforts. Still dramatic, these great earthworks enclosed permanent settlements, and were not, as once thought, only used in times of emergency.

① Herefordshire Beacon, a hill-fort in the Malverns. This is possibly a late example, perhaps dating to the 2nd century BC. Some hill-forts had their origins in the late Bronze Age, although we tend to think of them as being typical of the Iron Age. Such forts had many functions, the defensive one usually being secondary

② The Sweet Track, Somerset Levels. Dating from about 4,000BC, this is the oldest of a network of tracks which have been traced in the Somerset peat. It is 1¼ miles long and consists of posts and rails on which oak planks were laid. The tracks enabled their Neolithic users to travel dryshod above the marshes

③ *Stonehenge, Wiltshire. This most famous of prehistoric monuments has a long and complex history. It began as a banked and ditched enclosure in about 3,000BC. The first stone arrangements were not added until a thousand years later, and even then it was not complete; the stones were re-arranged several times before the pattern we see today was made. Near Stonehenge are hundreds of other monuments – it was at the centre of a landscape created by a civilization whose beliefs will probably always be mysterious*

③

④

④ *Butser Hill Ancient Farm Project, Queen Elizabeth Country Park, Hampshire. Every possible piece of archaeological evidence has been used here to help re-create a prehistoric farm. The way of making hurdles (in the foreground) remains exactly the same today as it was then.*

⑤ *Bronze dagger, stone battle axe, bronze pins, incense cup. All of these objects were found in barrows close to Stonehenge, and all of them have been dated to about 1,500BC. The stone axe is perhaps the most significant item here; axes similar to it were essential in the effort to carve out the landscape. They may also have had ritual importance, since some axes were too delicate for practical use. The stone used was of many sorts, and came from places as distant as the Lake District and Ireland. Such widespread sources show that communications and trade were highly sophisticated by this time*

⑤

⑥

⑥ *Neolithic pottery vessel from Mildenhall, Suffolk. Pots such as this were an essential part of prehistoric life. They served all the functions of the different kinds of container used today*

ROMANS AND SAXONS

IMPREGNABLE as they look, the Iron Age forts were no obstacle to the Romans. Invading in 54BC, and again — permanently — in AD43, the Romans were highly organised conquerors. Celtic England was divided into tribal areas, and if anything the tribes were rivals — they did not unite to fight the Mediterranean invaders. Rome was a centralised empire in a way in which the Celtic world was not. The Romans came to exploit the rich pickings to be had, not in order to find new places to live. There were battles at the time of the invasion, and vicious uprisings 20 years later, but in our terms, the takeover was probably remarkably peaceful. For the majority of the population life went on much as before — except that the taxes were paid to a Roman overlord rather than a Celtic chieftain.

Villas of the kind we know about best — with mosaics, central heating and the rest — were fairly thinly scattered. Most of the population lived as before, in wooden huts with thatched or turfed roofs. Rome probably saw no reason to impose large change in the countryside; the British were efficient farmers who produced good crops. It was a principal reason for the invasion, after all. Large-scale drainage works were carried out in East Anglia, however, and the technology of the Romans — including heavier ploughs — enabled them to farm areas that were subsequently lost again for hundreds of years. Cities were essential to the Roman way of life, but most of the Celtic population never took to them.

At its best, the Roman era was one of the most peaceful and prosperous periods in the whole of English history. For something like 400 years there were no major upheavals. Most of what Rome introduced was good, and its central government satisfactorily stifled the rival Celtic tribal divisions. Both parties — colonists and colony — gained a good deal.

When the empire collapsed, and the Romans withdrew to defend Rome itself, nothing much appeared to change at first. As so often before in the English story, the change was more subtle than school book history allows. Rome had, in fact, been drawing in its horns for some time. So in the cities it was as if the income had been diminished. Paintwork was not renewed, broken gutters were not replaced, new buildings were not undertaken. The infrastructure gradually, imperceptibly, decayed, until there was neither the money nor the skill, nor the will power, to do anything about it.

In the countryside it was much the same, but more so. People just seemed to slip back into the old Celtic ways. The muddle, the lack of leadership, the lost organisation, was all to the advantage of the Saxons. Already here as paid mercenaries, they simply came over the Channel in larger and larger numbers. Their advance (over decades rather than days) across the country was halted for a while, but by the 8th century England was firmly divided into a series of confident Saxon kingdoms. Celtic Cornwall did not fall until the 9th century. The Welsh and Scottish in their mountain fastnesses did not fall at all.

The Saxons are credited with introducing heavier ploughs to England, and it was once popularly believed that those heavy ploughs enabled them to clear land which the light ploughs of earlier ages could not tackle. Like so much in landscape history, this view is now largely discredited. All sorts of physical factors have obliterated prehistoric sites on lower ground, giving the misleading picture of a prehistoric population confined to higher ground with lighter soil. The Saxon contribution was further consolidation of the rural landscape, and the beginning of the medieval countryside with its open-fields and nucleated villages. Both open field systems and villages are developments of the later Saxon period. Parish boundaries began to be fixed, and some ancient hedgerows along the boundaries are creations of this time.

①Burgh Castle, Norfolk. The Romans found it necessary to defend England from seaborne invaders, and so has virtually every generation since. The Roman forts of the Saxon Shore, as they are known, were built towards the end of the 3rd century AD

②Winter mosaic from Chedworth Roman Villa, Gloucestershire. This villa was at the centre of a rich farming estate

③The Fosse Way. This Roman road ran all the way from Lincoln down into Devon. It follows a straight line with only a few, short-lived deviations

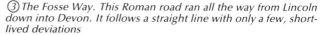

④ Silchester, Hampshire, from a painting by Alan Sorrell. Few Roman town plans can be seen in their entirety, since all but a handful now lie under the streets and buildings of modern towns and cities. After Silchester had fallen out of use it fell out of mind, and today only its substantial surrounding walls remain above ground

④

⑤ Barton-on-Humber Church, Humberside. The characteristic 'long-and-short' stonework at the corners of the tower is the clue which helps to reveal this as a Saxon church

⑥ Helmet from the Sutton Hoo Treasure, in the British Museum. The treasure of which this is part was found in a magnificent ship burial. No body was found in the excavations, but it is thought to have been the burial place of Raedwald, King of the East Angles, who died in AD624 or 625

⑥

⑤

⑦ Viking tombstone, found in St Paul's Churchyard and now in the Museum of London. London had a shadowy existence after the Romans left. This stone shows that the Vikings, at least, used it

⑧ The Alfred Jewel, Ashmolean Museum, Oxford. The inscription on this most lovely of Saxon ornaments reads 'Alfred had me made', and it may be that it did belong to the ruler of Wessex who united the Saxon kingdoms. It was made in about AD880

⑦

⑧

THE NORMANS

WILLIAM OF NORMANDY'S victory at Hastings in 1066 had dramatic consequences for the English scene. The Normans came to subjugate and to dominate; their invading army was probably little more than 10,000 strong, but their determined ruthlessness was such that they very quickly had England in thrall.

The most obvious visual legacies of Norman rule are the castles. These range in size from the largest, such as Colchester and the white keep of the Tower of London, to buildings not very much larger than a large modern house. Usually, the castles were built on earthen mounds (called mottes). Hundreds of these, now often shrouded in trees and undergrowth, are scattered across the country. Their number gives some idea of just how determined the Normans were to be seen as overlords. Most mottes never had a masonry castle built on them; the buildings would have been of timber, all traces of which have disappeared.

Even in partial ruin, the great stone castles of the Normans are awesome things. In comparison to the humble wooden houses in which most people lived they must have seemed indestructible and impregnable. Although the changes brought by the Normans were far-reaching, life for the peasants who formed the majority of the population continued much as before.

What did the English landscape look like from the castle parapets? The open field system was well established in some areas towards the end of the Anglo-Saxon period. The fields were centred upon farmsteads and villages. There were areas of woodland scattered across the landscape, but in many areas these are the selfsame woodlands that existed up until the 20th century. Although it is true that in some areas there were much larger woodlands than remain today, for the most part the ancient wildwood had been cleared long ago. In some parts of England the landscape was beginning to look very much as it does today; mid-Devon, for example, with its patterns of small, irregular fields, scattered farmsteads and deep lanes between hedges has probably changed very little. There is even an argument which suggests that the 'prairie' fields of the late 20th century are not dissimilar to the open field system. But our landscapes are very much more tidy than those, and ours lack the large numbers of people and animals which were an essential part of the medieval scene.

Domesday Book tells us a good deal about the 11th-century landscape, but it does not give a full picture. It was compiled (between 1085 and 1086) with one purpose in mind — to make taxation easier. The officials responsible for gathering its data were not concerned with those aspects of life that could not have a price put on them. Nonetheless Domesday is an extraordinary work; it reveals yet again the Norman efficiency; barely 20 years after the invasion they were able to take an inventory of what they had got. In retrospect we see the undoubted efficiency of the Normans as a good thing, but it is a view which tends to make the Anglo-Saxons seem like uncivilised oafs. They were not. For example, they had complex documents of land use and land tenure, some of which are as revealing as Domesday. And Domesday itself owes a great deal to the Saxons.

A short while after the castles came the huge Romanesque churches and cathedrals. The Saxons had built churches in stone, but they were tiny in comparison with the grand Norman designs. Again, the Normans built to impress. The greatest of their churches and cathedrals remain some of England's architectural masterpieces. Perhaps they appear sterner now than they did then, for the columns and walls were originally brightly, even garishly, painted. Such colour schemes would not be to our taste; they may not have been to the taste of the Saxons either, who may well have considered them the supreme example of Norman vulgarity.

The Bayeux Tapestry *This astonishing piece of embroidery is 320 feet long and tells the story of the build-up to the Norman invasion, the invasion itself, and the decisive battle on 14th October 1066. The story is told from the Norman point-of-view (they were the winners, after all), but the actual work of embroidery was probably undertaken by English seamstresses. Near the beginning of the story Harold is shown swearing a solemn oath to Duke William; the oath was probably that he would support William in his claim to the throne of England. Subsequently Harold was elected king on Edward the Confessor's death – and war became inevitable since both men had what they considered to be perfectly legitimate claims to the throne. The battle itself was a very close-run thing; Harold nearly won. Had he done so the story of England would have been significantly different. As well as describing great events, the tapestry depicts many quite ordinary and seemingly unrelated incidents*

①*Here the Duke of Brittany is surrendering; his stronghold is a typically Norman motte-and-bailey*

②*Harold setting out to meet William on the instructions of Edward. Obviously this was intended to be a peaceful mission, since Harold has with him his hounds and his hunting hawk*

③*As well as the main story, the top and bottom panels of the tapestry are very revealing – here ploughing and sowing are depicted*

Castles. ④ Clifford's Tower, York. The mound (or motte) here was constructed very soon after the Conquest, but the tower dates from the 13th century. ⑤ The White Tower of the Tower of London. Originally built in wood, it was rebuilt in stone between 1077 and 1097. ⑥ Colchester, Essex. The keep here is the largest the Normans built

Cathedrals ⑦ Durham. The immense columns flanking the nave are seven feet in diameter. Begun in 1093, Durham included revolutionary building techniques that had never been used before. ⑧ Lincoln. All that remains of the Norman cathedral built here at the end of the 11th century is the west front with its round-headed arches

Woodlands were vital components of medieval life. For example, they supplied food for animals, as is shown ⑨ by the illustration from a manuscript of a man hitting a tree to knock down acorns for his pigs. In the New Forest ⑩ , set aside as a hunting preserve by William the Conqueror, trees like these pollarded oaks supplied timber for houses, castles, churches, bridges and ships, etc

THE MIDDLE AGES

TOWNS AND CITIES, important to the Roman way of life, lost most of their vital function after the Roman withdrawal. They became integral parts of the country's livelihood once more during the later Anglo-Saxon period, and by the time of the Norman Conquest some were comparatively large.

Southampton is an excellent example of the increasing importance of towns in the Middle Ages. It gained a castle, of which almost nothing now remains, and it also gained a superb city wall, which stands to its original height in several places. Built into the wall were grand Norman houses, traces of which can still be seen. Inside the walls were many other fine stone houses. Nearly all have now gone, but apart from the wall, Southampton's greatest legacy from the medieval and Middle Ages are the undercrofts which were built beneath these houses. These huge, vaulted rooms seem to have fulfilled several different kinds of functions. Another of Southampton's buildings, the superb 14th-century Wool House, is a remainder of another dominant feature of life in the Middle Ages. It was built for Beaulieu Abbey to store wool from its scattered lands. An even more dramatic building belonging to the same abbey is Great Coxwell Tithe Barn, Oxfordshire. It dates from the mid 13th century and is as much a statement about the power of the Church in the Middle Ages as the castles are statements about secular power.

Before the Conquest there were about 30 monastic institutions in England; at the height of their power, in the 12th and 13th centuries, there were several hundred. They were rurally based, the majority of the orders taking their ideals from the ascetic movements of the near east, which demanded they be separate from the hurly-burly of life. The most dramatic remains of monastaries are to be found in the north and west, where the monks went in search of remote valleys in which to build. When complete, the huge churches and their ranges of buildings must have seemed even more impressive than the city cathedrals, for these immense constructions were often the only buildings of any sort for miles. The monks and their local labourers were extraordinarily industrious, not only building, but creating vast farming estates which transformed the look of the surrounding countryside.

Southampton's Wool House stored wool, and wool and sheep came to be central to the development of England's national economy for several centuries. The vast sheep walks of the monasteries were merely the beginning of a trend which at some stages seemed to fill the landscape with sheep and empty it of people.

As towns went, Southampton was undoubtedly very rich. Its ranges of stone houses were the exception; most towns and cities in the Middle Ages were still built principally of wood, mud and thatch. Growing though they were, the urban centres were very much islands in a country whose principal wealth and dominant character came from the countryside. It was a time of great expansion. But it did not last.

Towards the middle of the 14th century things started to go wrong. The population had increased dramatically, making it necessary to bring into cultivation land that had been previously abandoned as unworkable and to reclaim some land that had never been cultivated before — this included the Somerset Levels, the marshes of Kent, and some of the East Anglian Fens. But it was not enough, and some peasants lost all their land to become near-homeless and near-starving. A series of wars threatened the economy, especially affecting the export of wool. And then the weather turned sour. Season after season went by without a decent harvest being gathered. Perhaps starvation would have claimed many more lives had it not been for something which took them instead. It was the Black Death.

②Rievaulx Abbey, North Yorkshire. This is one of the best-preserved abbey ruins. Founded in 1132 by the Cistercians, but not completed until 1240, it became that order's mother church in England. The abbey's 140 monks were helped in their work by 500 lay brothers and servants. During the construction of the monastery they floated huge stones from local quarries along the River Rye, dug canals and dammed the river to provide deep water at the point of work on the abbey walls. Between them they transformed the abbey's 6,000 acres of land into a remarkably rich and efficient estate. The lay brothers (conversi) originally became part of the Cistercians' life because the monks' attendance at services left little time for manual labour. Conversi were established in 'granges' set apart from the monastery, and as well as tending Rievaulx's sheep, were involved in mining, quarrying, marsh drainage, sea-fishing and running a stud farm

①*Corfe Castle, Dorset. Set in a gap in the Purbeck Hills, Corfe represents the power and impregnability of fully developed Norman castles. It was begun in the reign of William the Conqueror, but the immense stone keep was not added until about 1100. The defences were not finally completed until near the end of the 13th century*

③*Jew's House, Lincoln. Wealthy medieval merchants built stone houses in many towns, but few are as well preserved as this*

④*Stokesay Castle, Shropshire. As society became more settled, the landed gentry built themselves homes that were not primarily defensive in function. Stokesay, built in about 1270, reflects a confidence in the times*

⑤*Sheep were vital to England's prosperity for much of the Middle Ages. At the height of its power, Rievaulx had 14,000 sheep. At first it was wool that was in most demand, but latterly English woollen cloth became the principal export*

⑥*Tithe Barn at Glastonbury, Somerset. The dedicated application of monastic communities resulted in the construction of many buildings such as this to store produce*

⑦*Bees and honey. Before the introduction of refined sugar, honey was the only form of sweetener. It was also an important preservative when used in such things as jam, and was an ingredient of the alcoholic beverage called mead*

DEATH AND RENAISSANCE

NO ONE KNOWS how many people died in the Black Death of 1348 and later years. It has been estimated that as many as 50 per cent of the population were wiped out. The effects varied from place to place, with some areas hardly touched, others with virtually no survivors. It is little wonder that images of death haunt the medieval mind. There was no comfort, no possibility of being immune.

Whole communities disappeared. Deserted villages are scattered all over England, with a concentration in the Midland counties. The reasons for the desertions are not as simple as extermination by plague, or forceful removal by landowners to make sheep walks at a later date. Undoubtedly some villages were wiped out and never re-occupied. For most it would have been a gradual decline in numbers over several generations. Some villages had been created at the height of the population expansion of the 12th century in areas that were marginal anyway; soon there was no reason to keep them going. Parts of the countryside must have had an eerie atmosphere; decaying buildings, deserted farms, landscapes slowly returning to the wild.

The peasant survivors did well, although more were picked off by further pestilences throughout the 14th century. There was now plenty of land for all, so those who had previously been landless or had lived in the badlands could claim reasonable plots for themselves. Those who had been serfs could demand decent wages, since labour was now so short. For those further up the economic scale it was much harder — fewer workers demanding more wages, the market for every kind of produce shrunk anyway. Sheep, as before, seemed the answer. Wool and, increasingly, cloth, were still principal exports. Sheep needed little looking after, so landowners tended to turn once-arable lands over to sheep pasture. Sheep and peasants prospered throughout the 15th century.

The end of the 15th century brought a decline, and it began to look as if history was repeating itself. The population grew again, but with so much land still out of production, or given over to sheep, there was not enough food to go round. There were other pressures on the countryside. Wool for cloth was still the biggest money-spinner, and magnates wanted more land for yet more sheep. Food production was another excellent investment, especially with rising urban populations, so the rich and powerful wanted land for that too. The enclosures began. Land which had always been used by all for rough grazing, or gathering fuel or wild foods began to be fenced off. Landlords began to encroach on the open fields. In fact it was generally a more productive use of the land, but it did not seem that way to the peasants who were pushed aside.

Landowners and yeomen grew rich in this period, and by the closing decades of the 15th century their wealth was becoming obvious throughout England. This was the beginning of the time that has become known as The Great Rebuilding. Thousands of the old, smelly, draughty timber and wattle dwellings were replaced by more substantial houses in a great variety of rural styles. It is largely houses of this time — late 15th to mid 17th century — which are thought of as typifying rural England. Whether they be brick and timber in the Home Counties, cob and thatch in Devon, golden limestone in the Cotswolds or whitewashed stone in the Lake District, they are the ideal to which many would-be rural dwellers of today aspire.

Some houses were not rebuilt at all, the occupants perhaps contenting themselves with minor 'modernisation' schemes. In some areas even this was not done — on the western moors there are still to be found immense stone longhouses whose form has not changed for generation after generation. Such buildings are so timeless that a casual glance cannot reveal their age. The same is often true for the landscapes around them.

① Wharram Percy deserted village, North Yorkshire. Although this village suffered badly when the Black Death reached here in 1350, it was not finally abandoned until the 15th century. Many factors besides the Black Death – including soil exhaustion, bad weather and changing economic pressures – led to hundreds of village desertions in the 14th and 15th centuries

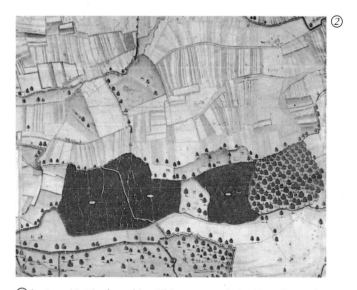

② Laxton, Nottinghamshire. This map, made in 1653, shows the medieval common field system of agriculture, with the large fields divided into strips. This way of cultivating the land, which reached its full development in the 12th century and lasted in some areas very nearly into the 19th century (and continues in Laxton), depended upon a very close co-operation between the farmers who worked the individual strips

③ *Outwood, Surrey. This post mill dates from the middle of the 17th century, but its design is the same as that used in mills since the 12th century. Windmills (and watermills) ground all the corn – so they were vital. A cross-section through a post mill and variations on the theme are shown below*

③

⑥

⑥ *Interest in new methods of improving agriculture go back a long way, as this broadsheet of 1601 shows. The publishing of new ideas helped to make the open field system seem old-fashioned and inefficient*

⑦

⑦ *The Grammar School, Market Harborough, Leicestershire. Dating from the 17th century, this school was constructed near the end of the 'Great Rebuilding', which transformed England*

④

④ *Willington Dovecote, Bedfordshire. Pigeons were a valuable source of fresh meat in winter, so cotes like this one, which was built in about 1540 and has 1,500 nesting boxes, were a sound investment*

⑤ *Bayleaf Farmhouse, Weald and Downland Open-Air Museum, Singleton, Sussex. Built in the second half of the 15th century, it is a superb example of a 'wealden' farmhouse*

⑤

⑧

⑧ *Ancient House, Clare, Suffolk. Many East Anglian villages grew in prosperity with the wool trade; when that declined they slipped into quiet retirement and seem hardly to have changed since. This fine house has the added bonus of pargetting, a kind of plaster embellishment special to East Anglia. The construction and decoration indicate that this was the home of a person of standing*

QUICKENING CHANGE

LIKE SO MANY neat phrases, the label 'Industrial Revolution' is misleading. It implies that industry was something new when it began to have a real impact during the 18th century. But this is not so; even Mesolithic men had 'factories' where flint and stone were shaped into arrowheads and other tools. Throughout history men had been tunnelling into the earth for minerals; sweating in intense heat to forge tools and utensils; expending laborious hours to produce all the things deemed necessary for life.

What the Industrial Revolution actually heralded was greater mechanisation, mass-production, and a move towards a more urban society. Previously, industry had been an integral part of the rural scene. In the Yorkshire Dales, for example, lead-mining had gone hand-in-hand with agriculture for generations. Iron was smelted wherever it was dug; for example in the Weald of Kent, which we now think of as timelessly peaceful. The countryside was full of all sorts of people pursuing all sorts of different occupations. Today's countryside would seem deserted in comparison.

Many of the early monuments of the Industrial Revolution are, indeed, in rural settings. The gaunt engine houses of the Cornish mines, the complex of buildings in the Ironbridge Gorge, the early cotton mills of Lancashire and Yorkshire, are all seen against green backdrops. Other early industrial sites were rural when they began, but are now some of our most crowded cities. It seems an obvious thing to say, but it is astonishing to realise that whole communities came into being solely to serve the new industries. Most were in the north country, where the essential raw materials were close together.

Although the look of the countryside began to change dramatically in some areas, it is perhaps the division between town and country which is the most lasting result of the Industrial Revolution. More and more people flocked to the new and expanding towns, eventually dividing the population sharply into urban and rural.

The 18th century saw the enclosure movement reaching its peak. Enclosure had been going on more or less peaceably for 300 years, but in the middle decades of the 18th century landowners took to Parliamentary Acts in order to gain the enclosures which they desired. The changes to the look of the countryside were most pronounced in the Midlands, where the open field system had been most widespread. New, neat hedges were planted in straight lines, enclosing fields of roughly equal size. The thousands of miles of hedges were most usually of one species of shrub — predominantly hawthorn. In the areas where they have not been grubbed out, these hedges can look spectacularly pretty in May, when the thorn is in bloom. However, the 'typical' hedged English landscape does not date principally from this time. Many areas had always been hedged anyway, and even in those areas where the open field system was at its most pronounced, there were hedges along parish boundaries, roadsides and other topographical features.

New hedges were only part of the changes in the countryside; enclosures went along with an explosion in farming efficiency. New crops were introduced, new ways of growing the crops were tried out; new breeds of animals appeared and farm buildings began to change to reflect changing needs. Much that was old and loved was swept away. Hundreds of books were written on every aspect of rural economy and many Georgian landowners took the ideas they contained very seriously. Usually, however, it was only the well-to-do who completely transformed their farms to the new style. Most rubbed along with the old, perhaps making a few concessions to changing taste. For the rural poor, the labourers who kept the whole system going, life probably changed very little. They had always lived close to poverty, and continued to do so.

① *Bedlam Furnace, Coalbrookdale, Shropshire. It was in this area, in 1709, that Abraham Darby first used coke to smelt iron. This furnace acquired its name because visitors thought it resembled a madhouse when in full blast*

② *Gladstone Pottery, Longton, Staffordshire. Factories like this were once common in the West Midlands; most were inspired by the pioneering pottery factories of Josiah Wedgwood*

③ *Richard Arkwright is credited with inventing a spinning machine which revolutionised the textile industry. He built the cotton mill at Cromford, Derbyshire* ④ *in 1771. It housed the new machinery, and was built in great secrecy so that the innovatory ideas should not be stolen – or the machines smashed*

⑤

⑤ *Ironbridge, Shropshire. The world's first iron bridge was designed by Abraham Darby III and opened in 1781. The iron used in its construction was made in the same furnace that Abraham Darby I had used at the beginning of the 18th century. Although the first, this elegant, much visited bridge is one of the most successful of its kind ever built*

⑥ *Stourhead, Wiltshire. At the same time that industry was transforming some parts of England, other parts were being changed just as dramatically for quite different reasons. Landscaped grounds such as Stourhead reflected a change in taste from formal gardens to 'natural' vistas – except, of course, that the views were entirely man-made. Stourhead was laid out in the years after 1740, and remains one of the finest romantic pleasure grounds in Europe*

⑥

THE 19TH CENTURY

THE YEARS between 1801 and 1901 saw more change than any time in history. In that century England established itself as the capital of an Empire which included a third of the world. The driving force of that Empire was the entrepreneurial ambition of thousands of men, and the possibilities opened up by industry. The population had been rising steadily since the 17th century, and it doubled by the first part of the 19th century, reaching 16 millions. In 1881 it was 26 millions. By the middle of the century most of that population lived in the cities. many people lived in appalling conditions; it was some considerable time before public and social services could cope with the swelling numbers.

In the countryside, the 19th century started badly. The end of the Napoleonic Wars in 1815 marked the beginning of almost 20 years of hardship and near insurrection. The price of corn fell dramatically, but rents stayed at high levels, bringing many farmers to ruin. As the farmers fell into deeper and deeper difficulties they dismissed their labourers, who joined the ranks of those who had returned from the wars with no jobs and no future. There were riots and bloodshed, and it began to look as if England might experience its own version of the French Revolution. But, in 1831, harsh measures were taken against the troublemakers; there were hangings, and hundreds were transported to Australia. The rural poor were cowed, and returned to their miserable lives.

Once stability had returned, and the rural economy began to recover in response to ever-increasing demands from the cities, improvements and new building could be undertaken. Industrial processes helped in this, and cast iron and iron parts and fittings became widespread. Corrugated iron sheeting and concrete became available in the 1860s; these materials were to have far-reaching effects on the rural scene.

Mechanisation had further impacts. The canals of the 18th century had enabled mass-produced goods to be transported ever more easily, but the railway went where the canals never had. By the 1850s railway lines were snaking everywhere. At a time when most roads were either unsuitable for heavy transport or, at best, unsuitable at certain times, the railways opened up the possibilities of moving vast quantities of goods fast.

Travel really did broaden the mind; or at least it enabled ordinary people to undertake journeys which would once have been unthinkably costly and time consuming. It also enabled people to adopt new ways of living. Before the railways, people had to live physically close to their work; now it was possible to travel to work by train. It was the beginning of commuting and of the suburbs. The railways also transformed hundreds of seaside towns and villages. Wherever the railway touched the coast, resorts began to grow to cater for the Victorian craze for seaside trips.

Agriculture went into another steep decline in the late 1870s, a decline which was to continue until the outbreak of World War I. This was partly brought about by the success of the Empire. North America, with its millions of acres of ideal corn-growing land, began to import huge quantities of cheap corn into England. There were threats from the other ex-colonial countries, too — principally cheap meat and dairy products from Australia and New Zealand.

Industry, mechanisation and new ideas were changing many rural areas. Especially affected, as ever, were those areas where the money was concentrated. In these, new buildings and new techniques made agriculture more efficient than it had ever been. Where tenants prospered, so did the labourers. In the more remote areas — principally the North and West — life went on much as it had always done. Everyone, however, no matter what their station in life, was affected by the events of the early 20th century.

①A satirical comment on the Napoleonic Wars. From 1789, when the French Revolution broke out, until 1815, when Napoleon was finally defeated at Waterloo, England went through a series of crises which came close to bringing about an English revolution. Even then the troubles were not over – at the Massacre of Peterloo in 1819 a yeomanry charge against unarmed civilians left eight dead and hundreds injured

Hundreds of miles of canal were built in England between the 1790s and the 1830s. The effects on every aspect of life were dramatic, since bulk goods – bricks, slates, grain, coal, etc – could be moved much more easily and very much more cheaply. ② Audlem locks, Shropshire Union Canal, Cheshire. The major obstacle to artificial water courses was changes in water level; the practical solution was locks. There are 15 at Audlem, raising the canal 100 feet in 1½ miles. Sometimes locks simply could not cope. The Anderton Boat Lift, Greater Manchester ③ was built in 1875 to solve a sudden 50-foot change in level

6 & 7 Cragside, Northumberland. This remarkable house was built for the 1st Lord Armstrong – inventor, scientist and industrialist. Cragside was the first house in the world to be lit by electricity derived from water power

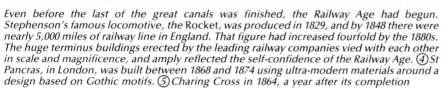

Even before the last of the great canals was finished, the Railway Age had begun. Stephenson's famous locomotive, the Rocket, was produced in 1829, and by 1848 there were nearly 5,000 miles of railway line in England. That figure had increased fourfold by the 1880s. The huge terminus buildings erected by the leading railway companies vied with each other in scale and magnificence, and amply reflected the self-confidence of the Railway Age. 4 St Pancras, in London, was built between 1868 and 1874 using ultra-modern materials around a design based on Gothic motifs. 5 Charing Cross in 1864, a year after its completion

THE 20TH CENTURY

WORLD WAR I helped agriculture, since home-produced food was obviously once more in great demand; but far more was lost than was gained. Thousands upon thousands of young men, many of whom had never left their homes before, marched off to the blood baths of France.

The respite for the countryside was short lived, since as soon as the war was over cheap imports started coming in again. English farmers could not compete, and the situation became so bad that millions of acres went out of food production altogether. A major change in the balance of land ownership was happening at this time. Throughout nearly all the historical period, land had been held by a tiny minority of owners, but between the end of the 19th century and 1939, 30 per cent of land came into the possession of owner-occupiers. Most of these were very far from being wealthy, and could not afford expensive new buildings. Nor did they have image-conscious landlords watching every development. So a remarkable assembly of do-it-yourself buildings was called into service. These included railway rolling stock, nissen huts and jerry-built constructions involving lots of corrugated iron and old bedsteads. Concrete was spreading everywhere.

The period between the two world wars was one of depression in town and country, with almost three million people out of work by the 1930s. It was a very different population from that of previous centuries; for a start, nearly all could now read and write. People lived very much longer, and, generally, lived more healthy lives. World War II was to be yet another watershed.

Despite the fact that a good many farmers started the war with outdated, decaying buildings and land in poor health, they managed to achieve a 60 per cent increase in production by 1945. They did it with no financial help from the government. Horses were still the principal means of power on most farms — and were still to be seen working until the 1950s. Only 15 per cent of cows were milked by machine in 1939, the rest being milked by hand as they always had been. To outsiders — townsfolk — it all looked just as the countryside should — dreamy and picturesque. In fact, it was very inefficient and frequently unhealthy.

Life in the big cities in the first half of the 20th century was considerably better than it had been previously, but still left much to be desired. Slums were appalling, but growing science and technology allied with improving health care, saw the end of the worst epidemics. The city infrastructure created in the 19th and early 20th centuries still keeps many of England's cities going — the sewers and water systems were built to last. The worst slums in many inner cities were bombed flat in World War II. The suburbs had grown at an astonishing rate, creating a quite new kind of community; life was lived privately, behind laurel hedges and behind net curtains.

Since World War II, both town and countryside have been totally transformed, as have the lives of the people in them. Heavy industry has shrunk away, offices have replaced factories, and high streets have been replaced by precincts and supermarkets. The old slums have all but gone — to be replaced by badly built, badly planned towers and estates which are worse in some respects.

In the 1950s and 60s immense damage was done to the hearts of hundreds of old towns and cities. It was almost as if the people wanted to complete the destruction begun in the air raids.

In parts of the countryside thousands of years of continuity have been swept aside in half a century. In part, this can be traced to the Agriculture Act of 1947, which, among other things, guaranteed farmers a minimum price for basic products. Ever-increasing efficiency and automation have rendered obsolete farming practices that

① Tractors were first used on English farms in World War I, but horses were still being used on most farms in World War II, and continued in some areas until the 1950s. When the horses went so did the need for thousands of acres of meadow and pasture to feed them on; stables were no longer needed; and the special, age-old skills of horseman, ploughman and farrier became virtually redundant

② All the world a-wheel, by Percy Spence, showing new-fangled vehicles in London's Kensington High Street. When this picture was painted in 1903, there were less than 10,000 private cars in Britain; by 1930 there were a million; today there are more than 18 million. Today's society would literally come to a halt without motorised road transport

③ Stubble burning near Cromer, Norfolk. The super-efficient agriculture of the late 20th century has a good many controversial practices – of which stubble burning is one. In areas such as East Anglia there is no use for the vast quantity of straw produced, and farmers need to dispose of it. Environmentalists say burning is wasteful and causes atmospheric pollution

③

④

⑥ Bourtonville, Buckingham shire. These houses were built in 1919. Tens of thousands like them were built between the two world wars. They promised unheard of comfort for ordinary working people

⑦ Post-war housing near Peterborough. There are now about 22 million dwellings in Britain, and some 50 per cent of families live in homes built after 1945. About half the dwellings are owner-occupied

④ Farming landscape in Hampshire. Huge machines need huge fields to work in; and in areas where no animals are kept, stock-proof hedges are sometimes seen as being unnecessary inconveniences which need expensive maintenance. Many would argue that such landscapes are sterile – wildlife and intensive farming do not seem natural bedfellows

⑤ 'Spaghetti Junction', most famous of English interchanges. Modern roads and their vehicles have not only changed the English way of life, they have also changed the look of the country. Motorways are peculiar things – although millions of people use them, hardly anyone ever visits them. This isolation has meant that some have become superb havens for wildlife

⑧ The Lloyds Building, City of London. A famous example of the Post-Modernist style, opened in 1986. Some see such buildings as the heralds of a new golden age of architecture; others think them gimmicky

⑤

Above: old and new at Pitstone, Buckinghamshire. The windmill dates back to at least 1627; the cement works is obviously modern. Both were built for purely utilitarian purposes, but will the works one day be as carefully preserved as the windmill is now?

lasted hundreds of years. At the end of World War II farmyards were complete, if run down. Today a 'traditional' farmyard is virtually impossible to find in southern England, and more and more uncommon in the west and north. Animals such as chickens and pigs have disappeared into battery houses or deep litter buildings. As more and more land has gone over to grain production, and machines have become bigger and bigger, so the fields have become bigger, eventually giving areas of the country a prairie look. It is now difficult to tell some parts of England from other parts — crops, fields and buildings all look the same. With the help of fertilizers, herbicides, pesticides, grain dryers, and all the other components of modern farming, yields have increased fantastically. With the subsidies available from the European Economic Community, farmers have been encouraged to produce more and more and more. It has led to immense surpluses.

There are now curbs to be put on over-production, and it is very likely that some land will be taken out of agricultural use altogether. Conservationists might be inclined to say that the halt has been called too late, and that it is not now possible to bring back the old — loved — landscapes.

For the facts are that in the years after World War II irreplaceable landscapes and habitats were totally destroyed. As much as 50 per cent of ancient woodlands have been grubbed up and many of those which remain are overgrown and neglected. Downlands have been reduced by 80 per cent, heathlands by 60 per cent, unspoilt lowland meadows by 95 per cent. These are habitats which are never likely to be re-created on a large scale, even supposing it were possible to do so.

It is not only natural habitats which have suffered. Intensive agricultural practices are destroying essential clues to the unravelling of the past. A classic example is the complex of ancient fields that accompanied the prehistoric village of Chysauster in Cornwall. Not long ago they were ploughed up, and the stones of their walls scattered into indecipherable heaps. It was a potential record that can now never be read. Similar things have happened all over England. It is sadly ironic that new ways of interpreting the

landscape and its history have developed at exactly the same time that the landscapes themselves are being scraped of their evidence.

As the countryside has changed, so have the people. Automation has meant that farm work which once required dozens of labourers can now be done by one man and a machine. Other jobs — such as hedge laying — which still require skill and long hours, are simply not done at all. On many a country stroll the only worker to be seen all day is likely to be a man in a tractor. The country workers who remain still live in the villages, but they are far outnumbered by newcomers. The once damp, dingy, unhealthy cottages are now expensive status symbols, far out of the reach of locals, who are likely to live on the estate on the village edge.

However, the newcomers, in many cases, have kept villages going. Without them there may well have been hundreds of 20th-century deserted village sites to baffle future archaeologists. In the last quarter of the 20th century, England is changing again. If it is not overwhelmed by misuse, then it may emerge into the 21st century ready to support and enrich the lives of its inhabitants for another 10,000 years.

The publishers acknowledge the following for the use of pictures in the Discovering England landscape chapter:

Pages 16/17: ① AA/R. Surman; ② Somerset Levels Trust; ③ Spectrum colour library; ④ AA/H Williams; ⑤ Wiltshire Archaeological & Natural History Society; ⑥ Michael Holford.
Pages 18/19: ① Dr. Richard Muir; ② AA/S & O Mathews; ③ National Monuments Record; ④ Crown Copyright H.M.S.O.; ⑤ AA/C Molyneux; ⑦ M Holford; ⑧ Ashmolean Museum Oxford.
Pages 20/21: ④ AA/R Newton; ⑤ AA/T Woodcock; ⑥ AA/R Surman; ⑦ AA/S & O Mathews; ⑧ AA/C Molyneux; ⑨ Bodleian Library; ⑩ AA/R Fletcher.
Pages 22/23: ① Spectrum colour library; ② AA/R Newton; ③ Lincoln, AA/C Molyneux; ④ Spectrum colour library; ⑤ Bodleian Library; ⑥ AA/J Wyand; ⑦ Ashmolean Library.
Pages 24/25: ① National Monuments Record; ② Bodleian Library; ③ AA/S & O Mathews; ④ AA/S & O Mathews; ⑤ AA/H Williams; ⑥ Museum of English Rural Life; ⑦ AA/T Woodcock; ⑧ AA/T Woodcock.
Pages 26/27: ① AA/R Surman; ② Spectrum colour library; ③ The Arkwright Society; ④ AA/M Adelman; ⑤ AA/R Newton; ⑥ Spectrum.
Pages 28/29: ① Bodleian Library; ② AA/R Surman; ③ AA; ④ AA/M Trelawny; ⑤ Museum of London; ⑥ Woodmansterne; ⑦ Woodmansterne.
Pages 30/31: ① Museum of English Rural Life; ② Mansell Collection; ③ AA/S & O Mathews; ④ Spectrum colour library; ⑤ West Air Photography; ⑥ AA/S & O Mathews; ⑦ AA/M Adelman; ⑧ AA/T Woodcock.
Page 32: AA/S & O Mathews;

WEST COUNTRY

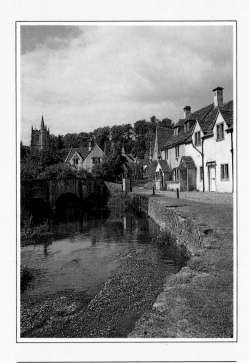

Castle Combe, Wiltshire. Genuinely picturesque, this village keeps its character despite being labelled 'the prettiest village in England'.

The delightful little cove of Chapel Porth, near St Agnes, Cornwall, takes its name from an ancient chapel which once stood in a secluded valley near the sea.

Touring the West Country

CONTENTS

INTRODUCTION

The West Country is an area of natural beauty, famed for its delightful villages, its varied coastline of tall cliffs and its long stretches of sandy beaches where surfers lie in wait for the Atlantic rollers. Wherever you go in this part of the country, there are surprising things to be seen, like daunting Dartmoor, Lorna Doone's Exmoor, the Mendips, the Forest of Dean, the Cotswolds and Thomas Hardy's Dorset. There are man-made wonders, such as Brunel's bridge over the Avon Gorge, Stonehenge, marvellous cathedrals and splendid houses. There are beautiful cities, too, from the Georgian elegance of Bath to the charm of Wells, England's smallest city.

This is truly a magnificent touring and holiday area, full of treasures just waiting to be discovered. Scattered over its moors and its tapestry of fields lie exquisite little villages linked by narrow twisting lanes, while its secluded coves and tiny harbours echo with the cries of wheeling seabirds.

Both legend and memories of the famous still live on here too. Glastonbury was the Avalon of King Arthur and Tintagel his castle, while the great Elizabethan sea captains Drake, Raleigh, Hawkins and Frobisher made their base at Plymouth where Drake played his legendary game of bowls.

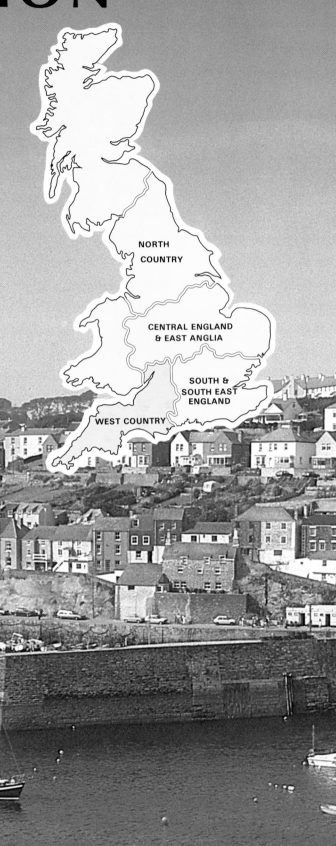

NORTH COUNTRY

CENTRAL ENGLAND & EAST ANGLIA

SOUTH & SOUTH EAST ENGLAND

WEST COUNTRY

ABOUT THE TOURS

Each tour occupies two pages and has a clear map accompanying the text. All the places described in the text are shown in **black** on the tour maps and are described as they occur on the road, linked in sequence by route directions. This precise wayfinding information is set in *italic*.

Castles, stately homes and other places of interest described in the tours are not necessarily open to the public or may be open only at certain times. It is therefore advisable to check the opening times of any place before planning a stop there. Properties administered by the National Trust and the Ancient Monument Scheme (NT and AM) are generally open most of the year, but this should be checked with the relevant organisation, as should precise opening times.

Sprawling up the cliff in typical Cornish style, Mevagissey promotes a sense of timelessness in its quaint narrow streets, colour-washed cottages and busy harbour.

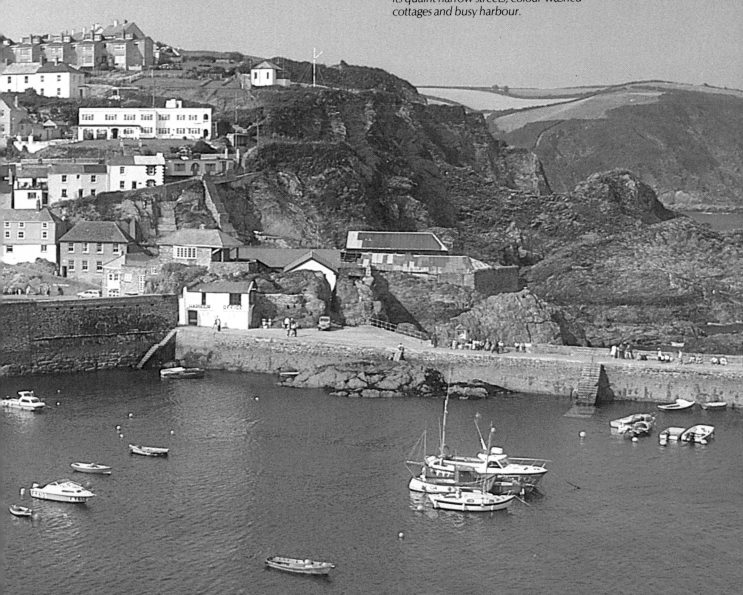

HOW TO FIND THE TOURS

All the motor tours in this part of the book are shown on the key map below and identified by the towns where they start. The tours are arranged in alphabetical order by start town name. Page numbers are also given opposite. Each tour begins at a well-known place, but it is possible to join or leave at any point if more convenient.

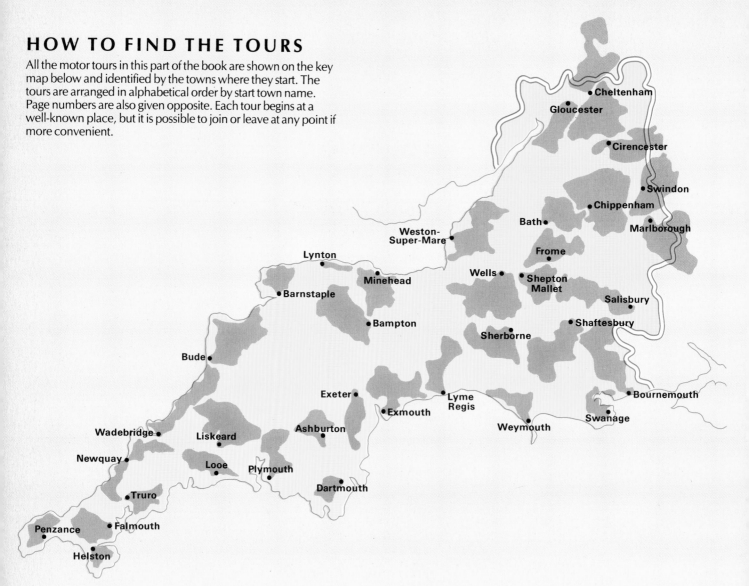

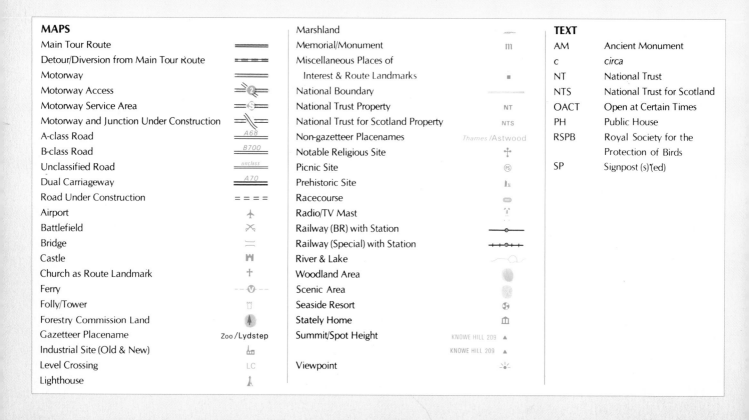

MAPS					TEXT	
Main Tour Route		Marshland			AM	Ancient Monument
Detour/Diversion from Main Tour Route		Memorial/Monument	m		c	circa
Motorway		Miscellaneous Places of			NT	National Trust
Motorway Access		Interest & Route Landmarks	■		NTS	National Trust for Scotland
Motorway Service Area		National Boundary			OACT	Open at Certain Times
Motorway and Junction Under Construction		National Trust Property	NT		PH	Public House
A-class Road	A68	National Trust for Scotland Property	NTS		RSPB	Royal Society for the
B-class Road	B700	Non-gazetteer Placenames	Thames /Astwood			Protection of Birds
Unclassified Road	unclass	Notable Religious Site	✝		SP	Signpost (s) (ed)
Dual Carriageway	A70	Picnic Site	(PS)			
Road Under Construction	= = = =	Prehistoric Site				
Airport	✈	Racecourse				
Battlefield	✕	Radio/TV Mast				
Bridge		Railway (BR) with Station				
Castle	⌘	Railway (Special) with Station				
Church as Route Landmark	✝	River & Lake				
Ferry	--V--	Woodland Area				
Folly/Tower		Scenic Area				
Forestry Commission Land		Seaside Resort				
Gazetteer Placename	Zoo /Lydstep	Stately Home	⭑			
Industrial Site (Old & New)		Summit/Spot Height	KNOWE HILL 209 ▲			
Level Crossing	LC		KNOWE HILL 209 ▲			
Lighthouse	⚲	Viewpoint	☼			

TOURING
THE WEST COUNTRY

Motor Tours
Pages 40-117

DARTMOOR NATIONAL PARK (EAST), Devon

The south-eastern edge of the vast national park that surrounds Dartmoor proper is a kinder country than the wild, high plateau farther inland. Here are wind-haunted heathlands clad with bracken and heather, where granite outcrops raise strange weathered silhouettes against the sky and the remains of prehistoric settlements survive underfoot. Country lanes strung with picturesque villages of thatch and stone lead into lush river valleys.

ASHBURTON, Devon

Once an important tin and cloth centre on a popular coaching route, Ashburton makes an ideal base from which to tour this side of the national park. Its narrow streets and old tile-hung houses impart their own particular charm to the town, and the fine local church features a characteristic Devon stair turret. The local museum includes American Indian antiques.

From Ashburton follow SP 'Buckland' along an unclassified road and shortly turn left across the River Ashburn. Ascend, and pass beneath the slopes of Buckland Beacon.

BUCKLAND BEACON, Devon

At the summit of this 1,282ft hill, which commands good all-round views, is the Ten Commandments Stone, carved by a local stonemason.
Continue to Buckland-in-the-Moor.

BUCKLAND-IN-THE-MOOR, Devon

Although visited by many people as one of the county's show villages, Buckland-in-the-Moor remains unspoilt. Its 15th- and 16th-century church contains a notable rood-screen, and the church clock has an unusual dial on which the hours are marked by the letters 'My Dear Mother' instead of numbers.

Continue and in 1 mile at a T-junction, turn left SP 'Widecombe'. Descend into the attractive East Webburn Valley and cross the river, then ascend to another T-junction. Turn right, and in 1 mile enter Widecombe-in-the-Moor.

WIDECOMBE-IN-THE-MOOR, Devon

Probably the best known and by far the most commercialized of the Dartmoor villages, Widecombe stands at 800ft and is dominated by the 120ft tower of its fine 14th-century church - often referred to as the Cathedral of the Moor. Adjacent are the Church House (NT) and the green, where the Widdecombe Fair of song fame is held on the second Tuesday in September.

Leave by the 'Bovey Tracey' road, bearing right past the green, and ascend on to open moorland. Later pass 1,560ft Rippon Tor on the right and enjoy magnificent views over South Devon to Torbay. To the left are 1,350ft Saddle Tor and the famous Haytor Rocks (1,490ft).

BELOW THE HIGH MOOR

Below the desolate summits of the high moor is a gentler country, where small rivers tumble through deep wooded valleys, and mellow old towns maintain a pace of life long gone elsewhere in England. Here were the tin, wool, and market centres of Dartmoor - the focuses of Devonshire life.

Ancient farmsteads shelter in many of Dartmoor's deep coombs.

HAYTOR ROCKS, Devon

These rocks rise 100ft above the surrounding moorland heights and form one of the most spectacular crags in the national park. They are easily accessible by car, simple to climb, and afford superb views as far as the coast and the rich, cultivated lowlands of Devon. During the 19th century stone worked from nearby quarries was loaded on to a tramway and hauled some 6 miles to a canal wharf at Teigngrace by horses. The route is still visible in places.

The church at Widecombe-in-the-Moor.

Descend to the Bovey Valley and after 3 miles at crossroads by the Edgemoor Hotel turn left, and in ½ mile turn left again on to the B3344 SP 'Manaton'. Shortly pass the Yarner Wood National Nature Reserve on the left.

YARNER WOOD NATIONAL NATURE RESERVE, Devon

This reserve protects the mature stands of oak, holly, birch, and rowan that make up an unspoilt woodland rich with birdlife. A nature trail has been laid out here, and details are available from the entrance lodge.

Continue a winding climb across the slopes of Trendlebere Down and enter dense woodland surrounding Becka Falls.

BECKA FALLS, Devon

Best seen after heavy rain, these falls are created by the picturesque Becka Brook as it leaps and plunges 70ft down a series of great boulders.
Continue on the B3344 to Manaton.

MANATON, Devon

Once the home of novelist John Galsworthy, Manaton is a scattered hamlet with a typical 15th-century church. A notable feature of the latter is its fine rood-screen, which extends right across the building. There is a pleasant green surrounded by trees and overlooked by the thatched Church House. About 1½ miles south west of Manaton is Hound Tor, where there is a medieval settlement of long houses inhabited from Saxon times to cAD1300. Bowerman's Nose, an outcrop of rock weathered into a curiously distinctive shape, can be seen ¾ mile to the south.

Continue for ¾ mile from Manaton Church and at a T-junction turn right on to the unclassifed 'North Bovey' road. Descend steeply, and after 1½ miles cross the River Bovey. Ascend into North Bovey.

NORTH BOVEY, Devon

Many people consider this east Dartmoor village to be the most picturesque in Devon. The River Bovey countryside that surrounds it is enchanting, and the unspoilt village green is complemented by the delightful Ring of Bells Inn. Inside the church is a fine screen with statuettes.

Follow SP 'Postbridge' and in ½ mile at crossroads turn left. In ¾ mile meet a T-junction and turn left on to the B3212 SP 'Princetown'. Later ascend on to open moorland, passing an unclassified left turn leading to Grimspound and 1,737ft Hameldown Tor.

GRIMSPOUND, Devon

This fine example of a Bronze-Age shepherd settlement consists of 24 small hut circles in a walled enclosure with a paved entrance. Sir Arthur Conan Doyle used the brooding atmosphere of the area in *The Hound of the Baskervilles.*

Continue on the B3212 and climb to a road summit of 1,426ft near the Warren House Inn.

WARREN HOUSE INN, Devon

A traditional welcome in the form of a peat fire that has been burning continuously for over 100 years waits here. The inn takes its name from one of the park's many rabbit warrens. A footpath leads to the headstream of the West Webburn and the remains of artificial ravines dug by tin miners long ago.
Continue to the village of Postbridge.

Bowerman's Nose stands south of Manaton.

Dartmoor

National

Park

Grimspound was home for prehistoric shepherds.

North Bovey

Manaton

Becka Falls

Edgemoor Hotel

Yarner Wood National Nature Reserve

BOWERMAN'S NOSE ▲

Grimspound

HAMELDOWN TOR 1736

HOUND TOR ▲

Warren House Inn

SUMMIT ▲ 1478

HAYTOR ROCKS 1490

SADDLE TOR ▲ 1350

Widecombe-in-the-Moor

RIPPON TOR ▲ 1560

Postbridge

Bellever

Bellever Wood

BELLEVER TOR 1455

Buckland-in-the-Moor

BUCKLAND BEACON ▲ 1281

Holne Chase

ASHBURTON

Dartmeet Bridge

Poundsgate

SHARP TOR 1260

New Bridge

River Dart Country Park

Two Bridges

West Dart River

NT

Holne

Buckfast Abbey

Dart Valley Railway

Buckfastleigh

mls 0   1   2   3

kms 0 1 2 3 4

Buckland-in-the-Moor's cottages are built to weather the roughest storms.

POSTBRIDGE, Devon
A small touring centre for the moor, Postbridge derives its name from a bridge that once carried the earliest Dartmoor post road between Exeter and south Cornwall across the East Dart River. A few yards south is the largest and by far the most impressive of Dartmoor's clapper bridges. This primitive-looking structure is massively constructed from huge granite slabs, and is thought to have been built when the inner moor was opened up for mining and farming some time during the 13th century.

Beyond the bridge a detour can be taken from the main route by turning left along an unclassified road and passing Bellever Wood to reach Bellever picnic site and nature trail.

BELLEVER, Devon
Numerous hut circles and other prehistoric monuments survive in this area. Also here are 2 fascinating nature trails laid out for visitors by the Forestry Commission.

Continue with the B3212 and reach the edge of Two Bridges.

TWO BRIDGES, Devon
An hotel and little else stands at this junction of the only 2 major routes across central Dartmoor. North east is Crockern Tor, where the so-called Tinners' Parliament met at irregular intervals to enact special laws governing the stannary towns where tin was valued and taxed. Wistman's Wood, a forest nature reserve some 1½ miles north near the West Dart River, features a mature stand of rare dwarf oaks.

Turn left on to the B3357 'Ashburton' road and after 4¼ miles descend steeply to the picturesque Dartmeet Bridge.

DARTMEET BRIDGE, Devon
Here, where the East and West Dart Rivers join forces to descend through a deep valley to Dartmouth, is one of the most popular beauty spots in the national park. Footpaths which wind through the valley allow some of the spectacular gorge-like scenery to be seen at close range.

Continue on an unclassified road and ascend (1 in 5) to the neighbourhood of 1,250ft Sharp Tor for fine views down the valley, and continue to Poundsgate. Descend steeply to cross the river at Newbridge, where there is a picnic site, and enter the woods of Holne Chase. In ½ mile turn right on to an unclassified road. (A detour from the main route to the River Dart Country Park can be made here by continuing forward for 1¾ miles).

RIVER DART COUNTRY PARK, Devon
Oak coppice, marshland, and valley bogs make up the varied landscape of this country park, which adjoins Holne Woods (NT) and occupies both banks of the River Dart.

Continue on the main route and in ½ mile turn right again to Holne.

HOLNE, Devon
In 1819 the attractive late-Georgian rectory was the birthplace of the novelist Charles Kingsley. Holne Church dates from c1300 and houses a good screen featuring a wealth of detail. An hour glass is incorporated in the carved pulpit. A fine walk leads west of the village along the Sandy Way to the source of the River Avon.

Follow SP 'Buckfastleigh' along a narrow road and in ½ mile bear right. In a further ½ mile descend (1 in 5), and at the bottom keep left. In 1½ miles meet crossroads and turn left SP 'Buckfast, Totnes'. In ¼ mile bear right then immediately left, and in ¾ mile enter Buckfast village to pass the famous abbey.

BUCKFAST ABBEY, Devon
Buckfast Abbey was founded in the 10th century, refounded 2 centuries later, and rebuilt on the old foundations by the Benedictine monks themselves between 1907 and 1938. A magnificent mosaic pavement has been laid inside the church. Near by is the House of Shells museum, which demonstrates the use of shells in arts and crafts.

Continue for ¼ mile to meet a T-junction. A short detour can be made from the main route by turning right into Buckfastleigh here.

BUCKFASTLEIGH, Devon
A long flight of steps leading to the church in this old wool town affords excellent views. Inside the church, which has an Early-English chancel, is a notable Norman font.

DART VALLEY RAILWAY, Devon
The northern terminus of this revived steam line, originally built in 1872 to serve the mining and farming industries, is in Buckfastleigh. Great Western rolling stock and a number of locomotives from that company can be seen here. The 14-mile round trip to Totnes BR station affords excellent views of the superb Dart Valley countryside.

Follow the main route by turning left at the T-junction before the detour. Cross the River Dart by Dart Bridge, turn left again, and in 1¾ miles meet a T-junction. Turn left then shortly right to re-enter Ashburton.

ALONG THE EXE VALLEY

From its wild moorland source the Exe struggles through a mile of peat before finding its deep valley to the fertile lands of North-east Devon. All along its route are little red-stone villages that burst into activity once a week when the local hunt meets.

BAMPTON, Devon
This small market town is situated by the River Batherm near its junction with the Exe. Ponies culled from the wild herds that roam the moor are sold in the October Pony Fair. The excellence of the limestone quarried to the south of the town is almost legendary. Today these quarries are of geological rather than commercial interest, and their situation affords fine views of the town. St Michael's Church, built c1300, was rebuilt with a north aisle in the 15th century. Inside are notable carved rood and tower screens and a pulpit dating from the 16th-century.

Leave Bampton on the B3222 SP 'Dulverton', and at Exe Bridge turn right A396 then almost immediately left to rejoin the B3222. Cross the River Exe and proceed through the valley of the River Barle to Dulverton.

DULVERTON, Somerset
The River Barle is spanned here by an attractive 3-arched bridge and is known for its excellent trout and salmon fishing. Dulverton itself is a shopping centre and the general administrative centre for the south-east area of Exmoor, a status that makes it a prime touring base. Everywhere is the sight and sound of water, a fact succinctly commented upon by Lord Tennyson in 1891 when he called Dulverton 'a land of bubbling streams'. Fine views of the town are available from the shade of a giant sycamore, which is some 250 years old and obscures a modest church. Local painters exhibit their works each summer in Exmoor House by the bridge.

Turn left on to the B3223 'Lynton' road and enter the Exmoor National Park.

EXMOOR NATIONAL PARK (SOUTH), Devon & Somerset
Much of this tour runs through the southern area of the Exmoor National Park, a place of dense mixed forests and wild open moors dominated in the north by the River Exe and in the south by the River Barle. Once a year the Exmoor ponies are herded and culled, some being freed and others taken to be sold at the famous local pony fairs. Pure-bred Exmoors are bay, dun, or brown, with no white or other markings of any kind, and have a characteristic oatmeal colour to the muzzle and inside ears. These animals, untainted by domestic stock, are hardy, agile creatures. The possibilities for recreation in the park are unlimited. Superb walks start from almost any point along the route, and those worried about getting lost in the vast expanse of the moor can follow specially marked trails. Care must be taken to avoid the deep, sphagnum-filled bogs; broken-in Exmoor ponies are good for trekking the moor because they know the area and recognize the smell of the boglands. The only other large herd animal found here is the red deer, a lovely, shy animal which is best sought for in secluded spots during the early morning or late evening.

Continue on the B3223. After 4½ miles reach a left turn leading to Tarr Steps for a pleasant detour from the main route.

TARR STEPS, Somerset
Tarr Steps (AM, NT) is the local name for a superb old clapper bridge. Situated on the edge of Exmoor, near Dulverton, it spans the tumbling River Barle and comprises 20 piers topped by a stone footway raised some 3ft above water level. The piers are large blocks of stone placed on the river bed, and the top is made up of several giant slabs that must have taken incredible effort to position. This fascinating monument to the ingenuity of ancient man is believed to have been built before the Norman Conquest. A car-park is provided on the approach.

Back on the main route, continue along the B3223 to reach Winsford Hill and the Caratacus Stone, on the right.

Tarr Steps' enormous slabs have been washed away many times, but have always been replaced in their original positions.

WINSFORD HILL & THE CARATACUS STONE, Somerset
Heather-clad Winsford Hill (NT) rises between Exmoor's two major rivers. Its wooded lower slopes rise to a clear summit from which the marked contrast between the River Barle woodlands and the empty slopes that rise from the Exe can be truly appreciated. The Caratacus Stone, an inscribed tablet on the hill, is

Exmoor is a beautiful mixture of rolling farmland and open moor.

thought to date from the dark ages of paganism that followed the departure of the Romans. Its inscription is ambiguous because it is incomplete, and is translated as either 'Kinsman of Caratacus' or 'Caranacus'.

Continue 1¼ miles beyond the Winsford Hill road summit to a left turn that offers a pleasant detour to Withypool.

WITHYPOOL, Somerset
Beautifully situated on the River Barle and much favoured by game anglers, this tiny village has one of the two legal commons existing in the national park (the other is at Brendon). A fine old bridge spans the river here, and nearby Withypool Hill features a stone circle among neolithic burial mounds.

Continue on the main route and after 1½ miles at crossroads turn right on to an unclassified road and descend into Exford.

EXFORD, Somerset

Hunting and horses are the bread and butter of this well-kept Exe-Valley village. The kennels of the Devon and Somerset Stag Hounds are based here, and horses are very much in evidence at all times. Exford's annual Horse Show is generally held on the 2nd Wednesday in August. The nucleus of the village is an attractive grouping of cottages, shops, and hotels around the local cricket and football field. Other buildings are dotted amid the rural outskirts, and the modest little church contains an interesting 15th-century screen.

Follow the B3224 'Lynton' road for 1 mile, rejoin the B3223, and continue to Simonsbath.

Dulverton's Market House dates from 1866.

SIMONSBATH, Somerset

Sited 1,100ft above sea level, Simonsbath is the highest village in the park and stands at the centre of what used to be the Royal Exmoor Forest. Deer were once commonplace here, but today these timid creatures are rarely seen. The 100-year-old church administers the largest parish in the park.

Turn left on to an unclassified road SP 'South Molton' and climb to 1,500ft. After 8 miles join the B3226, and in 1½ miles join the A361 and proceed to South Molton.

SOUTH MOLTON, Devon

Known to have existed as a Saxon colony cAD700, this lovely little town lies just south of Exmoor and is an agricultural centre for the region. Between the Middle Ages and the mid-19th century it became a thriving wool town; it was also a coach stop on the route to Barnstaple and Bideford, and the nearest town to the iron and copper mines of North Molton. A square of elegant Georgian houses is complemented by the town's grand 18th-century Guildhall and 19th-century Assembly Rooms, all built with the profits from wool and minerals. Disaster struck when the industries collapsed, and the town's population was reduced by half. Since 1961 it has been the centre for a busy livestock market. Opposite the square an avenue of pollarded lime trees leads to the

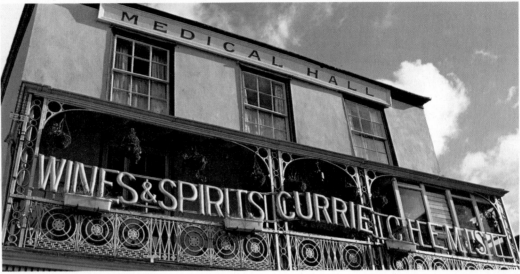

The Medical Hall in South Molton.

local church, which houses an excellently-carved pulpit and carries a 15th-century tower. A small museum behind the Guildhall displays examples of pewterware, a cider press, and an intriguing old fire engine dating from 1736. Also of interest here is the Quince Honey Farm.

Continue on the A361 'Bampton, Taunton' road and cross the rivers Mole and Yeo to Bish Mill. Branch right on to the B3221 SP 'Tiverton' and continue through woodland and hilly farming country to Tiverton.

TIVERTON, Devon

This prosperous industrial and agricultural town stands on the River Exe and its tributary, the River Lowman. After the conquest of the south-west in the 7th century it became one of the first Saxon settlements, and later during the 17th- and 18th-century heyday of the clothing industry the town became the principal industrial area in the county. Architecturally, the town has benefited greatly from the prosperity of its inhabitants. Rich wool merchants have bequeathed such fine buildings as St Peter's Church, Blundell's School, and three sets of almshouses. The church, particularly noted for the richly-carved Greenway Chapel and its organ, stands in front of a 12th-century castle (open) which preserves its towers and gateway despite being incorporated in a private house. Blundell's School is famous in having taught such illustrious persons as R D Blackmore, author of *Lorna Doone*, and Frederick Temple, Archbishop of Canterbury from 1896 to 1902. St George's Church was built in 1773 and is reputed to be one of the finest Georgian churches in Devon. Also of interest is the large and very comprehensive museum, including a GWR locomotive, housed in a 19th-century school building. The 19th-century Grand Western Canal

Exford is the most important stag hunting centre on Exmoor.

begins at the south-east edge of the town and extends for 11 miles. It was originally intended to link the Bristol Channel with the English Channel, but the project was never completed. The towpath now forms a famous scenic walk and there are horsedrawn barge trips.

From Tiverton take the A396 'Bampton' road and continue to Bolham. Turn right here for a short detour to Knightshayes Court.

KNIGHTSHAYES COURT, Devon

The 19th-century house (open) that stands here is pleasant enough to look at, but it is totally put in the shade by some of the most beautiful gardens in Devon. Protected by both the National Trust and Knightshayes Garden Trust, the grounds have a woodland theme and are particularly noted for their splendid rhododendrons.

On the main route, continue along the A396 for the return to Bampton.

THE COMBES AND GOLDEN BAYS OF NORTH DEVON

Delightful combes tumble down to the Atlantic, bold headlands guarded by lonely lighthouses jut out between sweeps of sandy beaches and everywhere in this sea-bound corner of Devon echoes with the cries of wheeling seagulls.

Combe Martin Bay

BARNSTAPLE, Devon

Onetime harbour on the estuary of the River Taw and an ancient trading centre, Barnstaple thrives now as north Devon's major market town. The wool trade brought prosperity to Barnstaple in the 18th century and its predominantly Georgian architecture reflects this period of growth. One good example is the attractive colonnaded Exchange by the river, called Queen Anne's walk. Here stands the Tome Stone where any verbal bargains struck were considered binding. Barnstaple's pleasant narrow streets are always busy, but there is an oasis of quiet at the centre. Here the large church, St Anne's Chapel and Horwood's Almshouses and School stand in the leafy churchyard. Within the Chapel is a museum of local history (OACT). On Tuesdays and Fridays the Victorian Pannier Market off the High Street bustles with traders selling delicious Devonshire produce under its high glass roof and fine wrought iron pillars.

Follow SP 'Ilfracombe A361' along the Taw estuary to Braunton.

BRAUNTON, Devon

Practically a small town, but alleged to be the largest village in England, Braunton is certainly of ancient origin. The first church was built by the Irish saint, Brannock, when a dream decreed that he must build a church wherever he first met a sow and her piglets — Braunton fitted the bill. This legend is substantiated by a carving of a sow and her litter on the church roof above the font. The church interior is high and spacious, elaborately Jacobean

with much gilt decoration. To the left of the road to Saunton lie Braunton Burrows — about 3-4 square miles of sand dunes that have been turned into a nature reserve. A nature trail runs through the dunes and a great variety of wild flowers flourish here. Backing on to the Burrows on the seaward side is Saunton Sands, where vast expanses of sand are exposed when the tide goes out.

At the traffic signals in Braunton turn left on to the B3231, SP 'Croyde', and continue through Saunton, round the headland of Saunton Down to Croyde.

CROYDE, Devon

There is a unique museum of local gems and shells at the edge of the village, and in the craft workshop demonstrations of gem cutting and polishing can be seen. To the west of the village the National Trust clifland of Baggy Point shelters the northern side of Croyde Bay, a magnificent bathing and surfing beach lying round the corner from Saunton Sands.

From Croyde village continue on the Woolacombe road to Georgeham.

GEORGEHAM, Devon

Several old thatched cottages and a stream flowing near the church make a pleasing picture in Georgeham. The church has suffered a great many changes since its first construction in the 13th century, but the Victorians were the last to tamper with it and they attempted to restore its medieval character. Interesting monuments inside include one presumed to represent Manger St

Aubyn — a 13th-century knight who fought in the 1st Crusade.

Remain on the B3231 and in 1 ¾ miles turn left on to an unclassified road, SP 'Woolacombe Steep Hill', then descend to Woolacombe and follow the Esplanade, SP 'Mortehoe', and continue to Mortehoe.

MORTEHOE, Devon

Rocky terrain characterises Mortehoe — the granite beneath emerging erratically by the roadsides. One of Thomas à Becket's murderers is reputed to have lived here prior to the bloody crime in 1170. Whether or not this is true, a relative of the murderer, Sir William de Tracy, was certainly vicar of the parish in the 14th century and he lies in a tomb-chest in the south chapel. A path from the village leads to the grassy promontory of Morte Point (NT) from where Lundy Island can be seen lying out to sea.

Continue on the unclassified road and in 2 miles join the B3343, SP 'Ilfracombe', then cross the bridge for Turnpike Cross. Here bear left, then take the next turning left B3231 SP 'Lee'. After 1 ½ miles pass the unclassified road on the left, which leads to Lee.

LEE, Devon

A picture-postcard combe opens on to Lee Bay where the rocks are veined with marble. The tiny hamlet has pretty cottages and gardens overflowing with red and purple fuchsias, but best loved is Three Old Maids Cottage — a white, thatched 17th-century 'show' cottage (not open). It was

the prototype of the many dwellings that sprang up in the 1800s as show cottages belonging to the rich.

The main tour continues to Ilfracombe.

ILFRACOMBE, Devon

In 1874 the railway came to Ilfracombe and the town's future as a holiday resort was established. It subsequently grew rapidly around the harbour and continued to straggle out to become north Devon's largest holiday town. The conical rock called Lantern Hill at the mouth of the harbour is a reminder of Ilfracombe's long history as a port. St Nicholas' Chapel has perched on top of it since the 13th century, with a light burning from its window to guide in ships.

Leave Ilfracombe on the A399 Combe Martin road and later pass the unclassified road, on the right, to Chambercombe Manor.

CHAMBERCOMBE MANOR, Devon

Set in a pretty, sheltered combe, Chambercombe (OACT), with its cobbled courtyard and uneven roofs, resembles a rambling farm building and informal romantic gardens, including a water garden, surround the house. Much of the furniture is 17th-century and there is a tiny chapel, just 10ft long, that has not been changed since it was licensed in 1404. Well in keeping with the atmosphere of the house is the tale of a corpse walled up in a secret chamber whose spirit still haunts the manor.

Continue on the A399 and in ½ mile pass Hele Mill.

This trinket at Arlington Court came from Barbados in the 19th century when shellwork was a flourishing export

The Boudoir, Arlington Court, was used by the lady of the house as a study

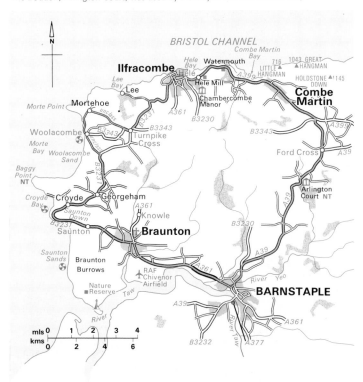

HELE MILL, Devon

Having stood derelict for over 30 years, 16th-century Hele Mill (OACT) has been restored to working order and its 18ft wheel again powers the production of wholemeal flour. Inside several items of mill machinery are on display.

Remain on the coast road and later pass Watermouth (left).

WATERMOUTH, Devon

Greatly commercialised yet still lovely is the inlet at Watermouth where yachts and small pleasure craft ride at anchor. Watermouth Castle (OACT) offers a wide range of family entertainments.

Continue into Combe Martin.

COMBE MARTIN, Devon

Combe Martin derived its name from Martin de Turribus — an adventurer who came over with William the Conqueror and won this piece of land. The village straggles along the main road running through an old mining valley, flanked by abandoned silver and lead mine workings up on the hillsides. Along the main street stands the Pack of Cards Inn, a curious place built in the 18th century by a gambling man.

The inn looks like a house of cards with its curious sloping roofs.

Continue on the A399 and after 2 miles turn right on to the B3229, SP 'Kentisbury Ford'. At Ford Cross (Kentisbury Ford) go forward on to the A39, SP 'Barnstaple'. In 1¼ miles pass, on the left, the road to Arlington Court.

ARLINGTON COURT, Devon

The Chichester family owned the estate from 1384 until 1949, when Miss Rosalie Chichester died and left it to the National Trust. This great lady spent her entire life in the house, and her tastes and personality are reflected in practically every item. She was an avid collector — not necessarily of things of any great value — but of objects that caught her fancy. Consequently the rooms are filled with fascinating treasures such as model ships, seashells from the 7 oceans of the world, birds, butterflies, fans, jewels and trinkets. All her possessions were lovingly arranged with the furniture she inherited and the Trust has sensitively preserved the individuality of her home.

Continue on the A39 which climbs to high ground before the long, gradual descent to Barnstaple.

FROM THE CITY OF ELEGANCE

High in the hills that provided the stone for Britain's most elegant city are the Cotswold wool towns. Sturdy manor houses and fine churches seem to grow from the mellow rock, and everywhere are the grass-grown scars of old quarry workings.

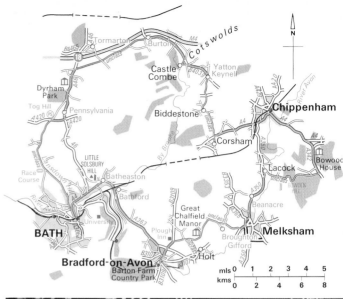

BATH, Avon

Justly spoken of as England's most elegant city, Bath is a spa resort of Georgian terraces, crescents, and squares arranged round spacious landscaped parks in the Avon Valley. Warm local stone is set off by trim lawns and mature trees, and the source of the city's prosperity still bubbles into cisterns and baths built by the Romans some 2,000 years ago. Many centuries after the invaders left *Aquae Sulis* to salvage their crashing empire, the dandified high society of Georgian England resumed the sophisticating process. Beau Nash and other arbiters of fashion came here to gossip with royalty and 'take the waters', and the legions of the wealthy occupied magnificent houses built for them by John Wood and his son. Bath today mainly reflects the cultured tastes of the 17th and 18th centuries, but it also contains relics from more distant periods. The ancient baths themselves receive half a million gallons of water at a constant 49°C each day, and their history is interestingly related in an associated museum. Overlooking the baths is the city's splendid 15th-century Abbey Church, and near by is the Pump Room (open) where people came to cure everything from boredom to gout. Rebuilt in 1795, this popular meeting place offers a choice of coffee or spa water in a genteel atmosphere heightened by chandelier lighting, chamber music, and the occasional sedan chair. The work of the Woods is everywhere, but some of the best examples can be seen in the Circus, the superb Royal Crescent (No. 1 is open), and

the Assembly Rooms (open). A very good museum of costume is housed in the latter. Several museums and similar foundations can be visited in the city, and amongst these are the Holburne of Menstrie Museum, the Victoria Art Gallery and the Bath Carriage Museum.

Leave Bath on the A4 'Chippenham' road and follow the Avon Valley to Batheaston, with views of Little Solsbury Hill to the left.

LITTLE SOLSBURY HILL, Avon

A fine Iron-Age hillfort (NT) featuring ramparts faced with dry-stone walling, stands on this flat-topped 625ft hill.

Beyond Batheaston branch right on to the A363 'Bradford-on-Avon' road. Skirt Bathford and climb along wooded slopes before crossing pleasant farmland to reach Bradford-on-Avon.

BRADFORD-ON-AVON & BARTON FARM COUNTRY PARK, Wilts

The disused Kennet and Avon Canal connects here with the River Avon, which itself is spanned by a 17th-century bridge incorporating a small contemporary lock-up. A tall but tiny Saxon church rescued from obscurity here in the 19th century has turned out to be one of the most important buildings of its age in Britain. Old weavers' cottages stand in Dutch Barton Street, and Barton Farm Country Park contains a superbly preserved 14th-century tithe barn (AM). The Park itself is an unspoilt area of country between the canal and the river.

Bradford-on-Avon's tithe barn houses a collection of agricultural machinery beneath its enormous roof timbers.

Leave the town on the B3109 'Chippenham, Corsham' road. After 1 mile reach the Plough Inn and turn right on to an unclassified road SP 'Great Chalfield, Holt'. After another 1 mile branch left on to a narrow road through attractive farmland. The road to the right offers a pleasant detour to Holt.

John Wood the Younger built Bath's magnificent Royal Crescent, which is a half-ellipse of 30 houses, between 1767 and 1774. The overall style is based on the drawings of the architect Palladio.

HOLT, Wilts

Local weavers once brought their disputes to The Courts to be settled, but this 17th-century building now enjoys a peaceful retirement amid fine gardens (NT). Features of the latter include topiary work, a lily pond, and an arboretum.

Proceed for 1 mile to Great Chalfield Manor.

GREAT CHALFIELD MANOR, Wilts

Built in the 15th century, this magnificent stone-built house (NT) features a great hall and is encircled by a moat.

Continue to a T-junction and turn right (no SP) to enter Broughton Gifford. Pass the large village green on the left, then bear left on to the 'Melksham' road. Proceed for 1¼ miles and turn left on to the B3107. After ½ mile at the edge of meet a roundabout and take the 1st exit A350 SP 'Chippenham'. For Melksham town centre take the 2nd exit.

MELKSHAM, Wilts

The River Avon is spanned here by an 18th-century bridge, and an attractive group comprising a converted tithe barn and 17th- and 18th-century houses stands near the church. Nowadays the town is an expanding industrial centre.

Continue with SP 'Chippenham A350', passing through Beanacre with 17th-century Beanacre Manor on the left. Proceed for 1¼ miles and turn right on to the unclassified 'Lacock' road to enter Lacock, then turn right SP 'Bowden Hill, Calne'.

LACOCK, Wilts

A wide architectural range from medieval times to the 18th century has been preserved in the stone, half-timbered, and thatched buildings of this delightful village (NT). Its abbey was the last religious house to be suppressed at the Dissolution in 1539, and was later converted into a private dwelling incorporating many of its medieval buildings. Over the centuries its ancient structure has acquired an octagonal Tudor tower and 17th-century gothic hall. The abbey gatehouse contains a museum of work by W H Fox-Talbot, a 19th-century pioneer of photography who once owned the abbey. Elsewhere in the village is a great tithe barn with 8 massive bays, and a small 14th-century lock-up known as the Cruck House.

About ¼ mile past Lacock Abbey cross the River Avon and begin the ascent of 580ft Bowden Hill. Proceed, with fine views of the Avon Valley, and meet a T-junction on the outskirts of Sandy Lane. Turn left on to the A342 and continue for 1½ miles to pass the entrance to Bowood House.

BOWOOD HOUSE, Wilts

The magnificent Georgian house of Bowood, with its superb art collection, is complemented by its extensive grounds, laid out by Capability Brown.

Descend to join the A4, and drive along the Avon Valley to Chippenham.

CHIPPENHAM, Wilts

Situated on the River Avon near the edge of the Cotswold Hills, this pleasant industrial town was a market centre for centuries. Several attractive half-timbered houses and an old lock-up are preserved here.

Leave Chippenham on the A4 'Bath' road, and proceed for 3½ miles. Meet crossroads and turn left on to an unclassified road for Corsham, on the edge of the Cotswold Hills.

THE COTSWOLDS

The Cotswolds extend from north of Bath to north of Oxfordshire, nowhere exceeding 30 miles in breadth but rising to 1,000ft in some places. From the 12th century the whole area benefited from the profits of wool, and a legacy of that wealth survives in the beautiful old cottages, houses, mansions, and churches which are such a feature of the district.

CORSHAM, Wilts

This developing town has an old heart of Bath limestone and a scattering of buildings from various periods. Of particular note are the 16th-century Flemish Cottages and 17th-century Hungerford Almshouses. Magnificent Corsham Court (open) was extended in Georgian times and shows work by architect John Nash and by Capability Brown, better known as a brilliant landscape gardener. Inside are good pieces of Chippendale furniture and superb paintings.

Leave Corsham with SP 'Chippenham' and after ½ mile meet crossroads. Drive forward over the A4 on to the 'Biddestone, Yatton Keynell' road, and proceed for 1¾ miles to enter Biddestone.

BIDDESTONE, Wilts

Stone houses surround an attractive green and pond in this pretty Cotswold village. The 17th-century manor house (not open) has a brick gazebo, or garden house, and can be seen from the road.

Bear right on to the 'Yatton Keynell' road and after ¾ mile cross the main road SP 'Castle Combe'. After another 1¼ miles enter Yatton Keynell, turn left on to the B4039 and follow SP 'Castle Combe'. Proceed for 1¾ miles, and turn left again on to an unclassified road for Castle Combe village. Parking in the village is severely restricted, so it is advisable to stop at one of the car parks along this road and walk.

Weathered stone houses are grouped around an ancient market cross in Castle Combe.

CASTLE COMBE, Wilts

Built of Cotswold stone deep in a stream-threaded combe, this old weaving centre is acknowledged as one of England's most picturesque villages. Numerous old buildings unalloyed by the brashness of concrete and brick present a homogeneous completeness round the canopied 13th-century market cross. Close to the centre is the 17th-century manor house, now a hotel. The village was transformed into a harbour (by means of damming the stream) for a scene in the film ''Dr. Doolittle''.

Return to the B4039 and turn left SP

Winter sunlight on Biddestone Village.

'Acton Turville'. *Proceed for 2¼ miles to pass through Burton, and at the end of the village turn left on to the unclassified 'Pucklechurch' road. Continue for 4¼ miles and meet crossroads. Turn left here on to the A46 SP 'Bath' and in ¾ mile pass on the right the entrance to Dyrham Park.*

DYRHAM PARK, Avon

Dyrham Park (NT) was built on the site of a Tudor house between 1692 and 1702 for William Blathwayt, Secretary of State and Secretary for War. Dyrham is barely glimpsed in its vale from the entrance gate, and disappears altogether as the drive descends a steep hillside of rough pasture dotted with trees before it turns along the valley floor to the house. The east front, which then greets the visitor, is a great wall of Bath stone blocking the valley with neat rows of tall, narrow many-paned windows. The interior is laid out as apartments, late 17th-century rooms of sensible and sober taste, influenced by the Dutch — William often went to the Netherlands on business. The furniture, paintings and pottery he collected are all still part of the house. A Dutch-style garden of parterres, terraces and detailed formal designs surrounded Dyrham until about 1800, when it fell to the 'modern' taste for landscaped gardens — the style of 'Capability' Brown, which survives today.

Proceed for 1¾ miles, pass through Pennsylvania, then in ½ mile meet traffic lights and turn right on to the A420 'Bristol' road. In ¾ mile reach the start of a descent, meet crossroads, and turn left on to an unclassified road (no SP). In 1 mile descend steeply, then near the top of the following ascent turn left SP 'Lansdown, Bath'. Reach the top of a 700ft ridge and pass Bath racecourse. Return to Bath.

BOURNEMOUTH, Dorset
Queen of the South Coast resorts, Bournemouth has grown into one of the largest and most popular seaside towns in the country. Its 6 miles of superb sandy beach backed by spectacular cliffs first became popular about the middle of the last century when Dr Granville recommended its mild sunny climate to invalids. Attractive parks and gardens, theatres and the world famous symphony orchestra offer a wide range of entertainment. The town also has 2 notable museums. In the Russell Coates Museum is the Henry Irving theatrical collection, a magnificent display of butterflies and moths, oriental art and a freshwater aquarium. Its geological terrace has exhibits covering 2,600 million years. Finally, the Big Four Railway Museum houses a working model railway and a large collection of nameplates and other relics.

Leave the town centre on the A338, SP 'Ringwood'. In 2¾ miles, at the roundabout, take the 3rd exit on to the A3060, SP 'Christchurch'. At the next roundabout, take the 2nd exit, SP 'Tuckton'. At the end turn left, then at the roundabout turn left again and cross the River Stour to pass Tucktonia.

TUCKTONIA, Dorset
Tucktonia (OACT) is a Britain in Miniature, containing over 200 scale models of historic buildings, all linked by a network of model railways, roads, rivers and canals. Among the models are Hadrian's Wall, London's most famous sights and a typical Cornish fishing village complete with boats.

At the next traffic signals turn right on to the A35, SP 'Lyndhurst', and at the next roundabout take the B3059 into Christchurch.

CHRISTCHURCH, Dorset
According to legend, Christ himself gave the town its name by his miraculous intervention in the building of the great Norman priory in the 12th century. Until then it had been called Twynham,

CRANBORNE CHASE AND THE AVON VALLEY
The well-wooded slopes of the lovely Avon Valley lead up to the spacious chalklands of the rolling Wiltshire Downs and on to the scattered beech woods of Cranborne Chase, a centuries-old forest where King John loved to hunt fallow deer and where, later, smugglers and poachers found refuge from the law.

Harvest time above Cranborne

an old word meaning the meeting place of 2 rivers. Near the priory, on the banks of the mill stream, stand the ruins of the Norman castle and hall, built of rough blocks of local Purbeck marble. The Red House Museum has an interesting collection of Iron-Age finds, mostly from nearby Hengistbury Head.

At the end of Christchurch High Street keep left and cross the River Avon, then at the mini-roundabout turn left B3347 into Stony Lane. At the next roundabout take the 2nd exit on to the Sopley road. Continue along the valley of the Avon to Ringwood.

RINGWOOD, Hants
The attractive, tree-clad valley of the River Avon leads to Ringwood, an old market town lying just inside the Hampshire border between 2 ancient tracts of woodland, the New Forest and the Forest of Ringwood. Among the many old houses is one called the Monmouth House (not open), where the ill-fated Duke, illegitimate son of Charles II, stayed during his rebellion against James II.

Leave on the A338 Salisbury Road. To the right of the road, beyond Blashford, is Moyles Court.

MOYLES COURT, Hants
Today a school is housed in this attractive 17th-century manor (open by appointment) with a tragic history. Two of Monmouth's rebels, fugitives from the Battle of Sedgemoor, were sheltered here by the 70-year-old lady of the manor, Dame Alicia Lisle. The bloodthirsty Judge Jeffries condemned her to be burned alive, but the sentence was commuted to the more merciful

one of beheading and her execution took place at Winchester, in September 1685.

Continue on the A338 and at Ibsley turn left SP 'Alderholt'. In ½ mile pass Harbridge church and turn left and in another ¾ mile turn right, SP 'Fordingbridge'. In 1 mile turn left on to the wooded Cranbourne road. At the edge of Alderholt bear left, and later join the Verwood road. In 1 mile turn left into Batterby Drove and continue to Verwood. Here turn right on to the B3081. In 1½ miles, turn left with the Wimborne St Giles road, and in 1¾ miles turn left again on to the B3078, SP 'Wimborne Minster'. After 1½ miles turn right SP 'Wimborne St Giles', and pass on the right Knowlton Church ruins and Knowlton Rings.

KNOWLTON RINGS, Dorset
In the quiet, wooded countryside lies a mysterious pagan site dating back to Neolithic times. Knowlton Rings consists of a number of circles and henge monuments, guarded by banks and ditches. Two of the rings can be seen clearly from the road: the Central Circle (AM) in the middle of which stand the lonely ruins of a Norman church; and to the east, the so-called Great Barrow, a 20ft mound crowned by a circle of trees.

Continue, over the River Allen, then at the T-junction turn right for Wimborne St Giles. From the village follow SP 'Cranborne' and later keep forward on to the B3081. In ½ mile turn right on to an unclassified road then in ¾ mile turn left on to the B3078 for Cranborne.

CRANBORNE, Dorset
Brick and timber houses scattered round a green, a 13th-century church with medieval wall paintings and a stone manor house make Cranborne a picturesque sight. Formerly it was the busy market centre of the Chase, to which it gave its name, and the place where the Chase Court sat. The medieval manor, Cranborne House, was rebuilt by the 1st Earl of Salisbury, who turned it into a charming Jacobean house. The lovely gardens (OACT) were laid out at the same time and there is also a garden centre.

In Cranborne turn left on to the Martin road, then in ¼ mile bear right to Boveridge. Nearly 2 miles beyond the Hampshire border at the T-junction, turn left for Martin.

MARTIN, Hants
The thatched cottages of Martin cluster in the valley of the Allen Water at the foot of the downs. To the south-west of the village, 2 ancient boundaries can be seen crossing Martin Down. The oldest

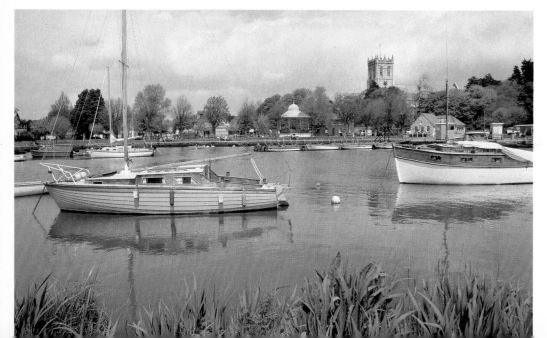

Christchurch stands between the Avon and Stour, which meet in the town's harbour

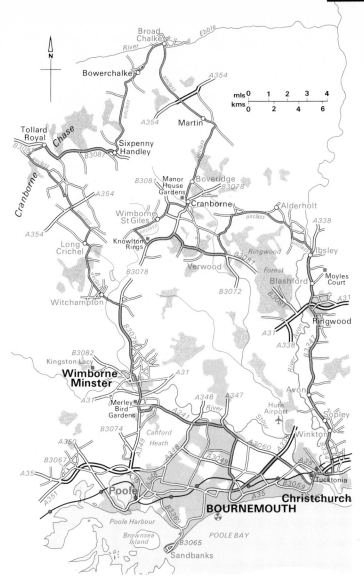

century the inn was the headquarters of a notorious smuggler, Isaac Gulliver, who had married the landlord's daughter. He and his band of 50 men successfully ran contraband from the deep chines of the Dorset coast. Deer poachers also felt safe in Sixpenny Handley and used one of the tombstones in the churchyard with impunity as a hiding place for their stolen carcases.

At Sixpenny Handley turn right on to the B3081 and continue to Tollard Royal.

TOLLARD ROYAL, Wilts
Tollard, hidden in a hollow of the downs, within the old hunting preserve of Cranborne Chase, was designated 'royal' in the 12th century by King John. His house, a lofty medieval stone building on the site of the royal hunting lodge was restored by General Sir Pitt Rivers, whose family had acquired the estate. He also laid out a charming pleasure garden, Larmer Gardens, ornamented with statues and little temples. 'Larmer' means wych elm; until 1894 there was an elm tree here which was reputed to be the place where King John's huntsmen gathered, but it has now been replaced by an oak.

At the telephone kiosk turn left, SP '13th-century church', then immediately bear right and climb on to Cranborne Chase.

CRANBORNE CHASE, Dorset & Wilts
Once a vast area of unbroken woodland, Cranborne Chase stretched across the downs from Shaftesbury in Dorset to Salisbury in Wiltshire. The Chase has long since disappeared, but many fine beech trees survive, to remind one of the vanished forest. It was a royal hunting ground even before the Normans, but it is most strongly associated with King John, who jealously guarded his right to hunt the fallow deer by stringent laws. As royalty became less addicted to hunting deer, these laws allowed the Chase to become the unsavoury haven of all kinds

of smugglers, poachers and wrongdoers, until, in 1830, Parliament put a stop to it all by a special Act.

After 1 mile, at the T-junction, turn left and re-enter Dorset. In another mile bear right and, at the next T-junction, turn right. Reach the A354, turn right then immediately left on to the Moor Crichel road. In 1½ miles, turn right for the village of Long Crichel. Here turn left, SP 'Witchampton', and at the next T-junction, turn left then immediately right, then right again for Witchampton. Later turn right on to the B3078 to Wimborne Minster.

WIMBORNE MINSTER, Dorset
The minster or 'mission' church at the centre of this old market town on the River Stour was built by the Normans on the site of a Saxon nunnery founded by St Cuthberga, sister of King Ine of Wessex. High on the outside wall of the 15th-century west tower a quarter-jack, in the form of a gaily painted Grenadier Guard, strikes the quarter hours. He is part of a 14th-century astronomical clock which can be seen inside the tower. The 16th-century Priest's House near the minster has been converted into an interesting museum of local history. To the north west is Kingston Lacy House (NT) a fine classical structure set in formal gardens and surrounded by 254 acres of parkland.

Follow signs Bournemouth A349, and cross the River Stour. After passing the Willett Arms PH the Merley Bird Gardens lie to the right of the road.

MERLEY BIRD GARDENS, Dorset
Exotic birds are housed in spacious aviaries set in the secluded walled gardens here. The house was built in the 18th century for Ralph Willett, a man who had made his fortune in the West Indies.

After another ½ mile, turn left on to the A341, SP 'Bournemouth'. In 3 miles, at the roundabout, take the 2nd exit and follow SP 'Bournemouth Town Centre'.

of these is part of Grim's Ditch, marking the southern edge of a Bronze and Iron-Age cattle ranch. More prominent is the 6ft rampart of Bokerley Dyke, a Romano-British defence against the invading Saxons.

Continue on the unclassified road and in 1½ miles cross the main road, SP 'Broad Chalke'. After entering Wiltshire climb to over 600ft, with fine downland views, then descend to Broad Chalke and follow SP 'Bowerchalke'.

BOWERCHALKE, Wilts
Watercress beds, rich emerald-green, continually fed by little trickling streams, line the approaches to this tiny downland village, tucked away on a tributary of the River Ebble. The views from here and from the road to Sixpenny Handley of the rolling downs and their belts of beech wood are particularly lovely.

Continue on the road, SP '6d Handley', to Sixpenny Handley.

One of the many monuments in Wimborne's minster: this, to Anthony Etricke, lies in the south choir aisle

SIXPENNY HANDLEY, Dorset
The famous abbreviated signpost 'To 6d Handley' conjures up an idyllic picture that the village scarcely lives up to, perhaps because it was almost totally rebuilt during 1892 in the aftermath of a disastrous fire. It is set in the lovely countryside of Cranborne Chase, however, and its history is colourful. In the 18th

BUDE, Cornwall

One of Bude's main attractions is its huge surfing beach, where strong winds that have caused hundreds of wrecks over the centuries provide a constant supply of rollers ideal for the sport. The town itself is sheltered from the full force of the weather by ridges of downland between it and the sea. Visitors interested in sun and sea bathing are catered for by Summerleaze beach, a sheltered area of sand at the mouth of the River Neet. Here a large swimming pool is naturally refilled every high tide. A notable 3-mile scenic walk extends along clifftops south of Bude, visiting Compass Point and Efford Beacon for their excellent views. Bude Castle was built in 1840 and now houses the local council offices.

Leave by the A3072 'Bideford' road. After 1¼ miles turn left on to the A39, pass the edge of Stratton, and drive to Kilkhampton.

KILKHAMPTON, Cornwall

The main feature of the village is the 12th- to 15th-century church, which contains no fewer than 157 carved bench-ends dating from the 16th century. The Norman doorway is elaborately carved, and there is a splendid barrel roof. Three miles east are the Tamar lakes with various leisure facilities.

Continue for 3 miles. A detour from the main route can be made by turning left here on to an unclassified road to reach Morwenstow.

MORWENSTOW, Cornwall

Henna Cliff rears 450ft above the waves about ¼ mile from Morwenstow village church, on the other side of a grassy coomb. It is the highest cliff in Cornwall and forms part of an awesome range that once proved useful to the wreckers, who signalled ships on to the rocks in order to plunder their cargoes. The Norman church itself stands a little aloof from the tiny village, and features attractive Romanesque zig-zag work over the porch and carved bench ends. During the 19th century the local vicar, Robert Hawker, wrote the ballad *Song of the Western Man*.

Continue on the A39 for 2 miles to Welcombe Cross. A detour can be made from the main route to reach Welcombe and Welcombe Mouth by turning left on to an unclassified road.

WELCOMBE, Devon

Situated near the Cornish border, this village stands in a remote glen that leads to a wild stretch of cliff-bound coast at Morwenstow Bay. The cliff strata here has been violently contorted by unimaginable stresses to form really spectacular coastal scenery. A fine waterfall can be seen at Marsland Mouth, and picturesque Welcombe Cove is well worth visiting.

A small stream tumbles into Bideford Bay at Buck's Mills.

NORTH DEVON CLIFFTOPS

Bude's long beach is a brief calm before the great geological storm that lies ahead. Just north are soaring cliffs violently twisted and fractured by massive forces, where small streams from the lush hinterland plunge hundreds of feet to the shore as waterfalls, or dash over boulder beds through deep wooded ravines.

Atlantic waves break constantly on Bude's magnificent beach, creating ideal conditions for surfers.

From Welcombe Cross proceed on the A39 for 1 mile to pass the West Country Inn, then branch left on to an unclassified road SP 'Elmscott'. Cross a short stretch of moorland to reach Tosberry Cross, and bear left then right for Stoke, 3 miles further on.

STOKE, Devon

Hartland's 14th-century church stands here, raising its magnificent tower 128ft into the air to form a local landmark. Inside are a carved Norman font and a fine screen.

Continue for ½ mile and descend steeply to Hartland Quay.

HARTLAND QUAY, Devon

The quay that stood here has long since been washed away by storms, but the rocky shore is a constant attraction. Some of the most exciting shorescapes of the north Devon and Cornwall coasts are formed by the strangely twisted and fractured strata of the local cliffs. The interesting Hartland Quay Museum has sections on geology, natural and coastal history, and shipwrecks. A clifftop path leads 1 mile south to Speke's Mill Mouth waterfall, perhaps the most spectacular of several cliff waterfalls in the district.

Return to Stoke and follow SP 'Hartland, Bideford'. After ½ mile a road to the left leads to Hartland Point.

HARTLAND POINT, Devon

Although only 3 miles from Hartland Quay, the beautiful 350ft cliffs here are red instead of grey. This spectacular coast has an ugly history and has been the death of many a helpless and storm-battered ship. Because of this the point carries a small white lighthouse which emits the strongest light of any on Britain's coast.

Return to Hartland.

HARTLAND, Devon

To the west of this pleasant village is the 18th-century house of Hartland Abbey. The abbey itself was founded in the 12th century and has entirely vanished. A coomb leads from here to the sea.

From Hartland proceed on the B3248 'Bideford, Clovelly' road for 3 miles and turn left on to an unclassified road. After another ¾ mile turn left again on to the B3237 and drive to the carpark for Clovelly.

CLOVELLY, Devon

Clovelly is one of the West Country's most picturesque fishing villages. No cars are allowed here because the steep cobbled street, lined with lovely old houses, descends 400ft to the sea in a series of steps. Donkeys are used to transport visitors' luggage, and zig-zag steps allow pedestrian access down the wooded cliffs to the tiny quay and a pebble beach. The idyllic surroundings of the village tend to soothe away the normal healthy respect for the open sea, but a local lifeboat station that has saved 350 lives is a sobering reminder that the tranquillity is not permanent. The village, discovered by holidaymakers in the mid-19th century, is popular with artists and enjoys a climate as mild as that of the south Devon coast. Local gardens bloom well beyond their normal season. An attractive 2-mile walk leads west from the harbour to a magnificent range of 400ft cliffs.

Return along the B3237, then in 1¼ miles turn left on to the A39 'Bideford' road to reach Buck's Cross. An unclassified road to the left leads through a wooded glen to Buck's Mills.

BUCK'S MILL, Devon

This unspoilt fishing village of thatched cottages lies at the bottom of a wooded valley, on a section of coast noted for its picturesque cliff scenery.

Continue along the A39 and in 5½ miles at a roundabout take 1st exit on to an unclassified road to reach Abbotsham.

ABBOTSHAM, Devon

Abbotsham Church features a good 15th-century barrel roof bearing trade emblems and coats of arms, and preserves carved bench-ends and a Norman font.

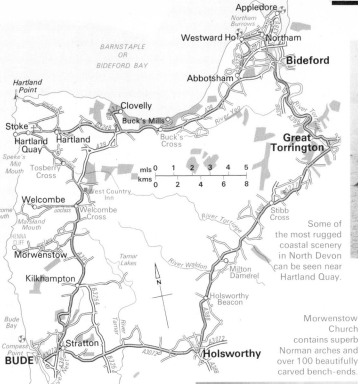

Some of the most rugged coastal scenery in North Devon can be seen near Hartland Quay.

Morwenstow Church contains superb Norman arches and over 100 beautifully carved bench-ends.

Continue and in 1¼ miles turn left on to the B3236 to reach Westward Ho!

WESTWARD HO!, Devon
Named after the famous novel by Charles Kingsley, this seaside resort offers a well-known golf course and 3 miles of sandy beach. West of the town the sands merge into rocks scattered with teeming pools, ideal ground for the infant naturalist. North-east is the 650-acre expanse of Northam Burrows, which now includes a country park and is protected from the Atlantic by a remarkable pebble ridge.

Follow signs Bideford and continue to Northam.

NORTHAM, Devon
Northam village lies close to the attractive Torridge Estuary. An inscribed stone at Bloody Corner recalls King Alfred's successful last battle againt Hubba the Dane in the 9th century.

A detour can be made to Appledore by turning left on to the A386.

APPLEDORE, Devon
Cobbled streets leading to a quay and a sandy beach contribute to the great charm of this village, which has several attractive Georgian houses and cottages. Its tranquility is somehow maintained despite the establishment in 1970 of one of Europe's largest covered shipbuilding docks, on the Torridge estuary. A maritime museum displays North Devon's shipping history.

Follow the main route on the A386 and drive to Bideford crossing the approach to the new by-pass bridge over the Torridge.

BIDEFORD, Devon
Between c1550 and 1750 this town was the principal port of north Devon and the home of a renowned

ship-building industry. Sir Richard Grenville, who obtained a charter for the town from Queen Elizabeth I, crewed his ship *Revenge* entirely with Bideford men. That brave little vessel will always be famous for its stand against 15 Spanish ships in the Azores. The mile-long, tree-lined quay remains lively, and the estuary is popular with yachtsmen and small-boat sailors. Bridgeland Road preserves evidence of a once prosperous past in the shape of 17th-century merchants' houses. Pre-dating these is the bridge over the River Torridge, a 15th-century structure unusual in that none of its 24 arches is of the same width. It has been considerably renovated and widened to take the burden of 20th-century traffic. The Royal Hotel, across the river, was originally a merchant's house and dates from 1688. It was here that Charles Kingsley wrote part of *Westward Ho!*

Leave Bideford following SP 'Torrington' and drive beside the River Torridge to reach Great Torrington.

GREAT TORRINGTON, Devon
The church in this hilltop market town was rebuilt in 1651, 6 years after it and 200 Royalist soldiers imprisoned inside were blown up by gunpowder. The tragedy was caused by Roundhead troops using the church as a gunpowder store as well as a prison. A fine 17th-century pulpit can be seen inside the building. The well-known Dartington glass is made in the town, and visitors to the factory can watch the highly skilled glassblowers at work. About 1 mile south-east of Great Torrington is Rosemoor Garden (open), where hybrid rhododendrons, eucalyptus, roses, and ornamental trees and shrubs can be seen. Within easy reach are two magnificent vantage points. The castle mound by the town centre stands on a steep hillside high above the Torridge and 1 mile north-west across a ravine the crag of Furzebeam Hill juts out above the meandering river.

From the Bideford end of the town follow SP 'Holsworthy, Bude' B3277 and cross the river into Taddiport. After 6 miles enter Stibb Cross, then forward on to the A388 for Holsworthy.

HOLSWORTHY, Devon
This bustling market town has a dubious claim to fame as the last place in England where a man was punished by being sent to the stocks. The mainly 13th-century church here has a pinnacled 15th-century tower and a carillion which plays one of a number of tunes on the hour.

Leave Holsworthy on the A3072 SP 'Bude'. Later cross the River Tamar into Cornwall and 4 miles further on reach Stratton.

STRATTON, Cornwall
An ancient town that was probably founded by the Romans, Stratton is made up of old and sometimes thatched buildings lining a steep main street. The Tree Inn was once a manor, and in 1643 it served as the home and headquarters of Sir Bevil Grenville before he led the Royalists to victory at the battle of Stamford Hill, ½ mile north-west. Features of the local church include a pinnacled 15th-century tower, a barrel roof with carved bosses, a fine 16th-century brass, and a window by the talented artist and designer Burne-Jones.

Follow SP 'Bude' on the A3072 for the return to Bude.

Clovelly is one of the most popular of Devon's picturesque fishing villages.

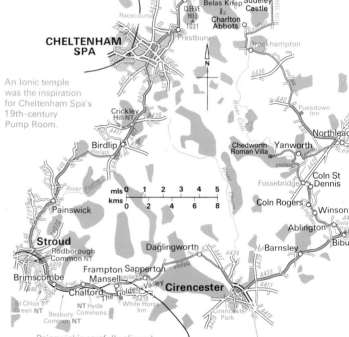

GOLD IN THE COTSWOLD COUNTRYSIDE

Here is a mature countryside, first civilized by the Romans, later smoothed by the wealth of medieval clothiers, and finally polished by Regency high fashion. Everywhere is the honey colour of Cotswold stone, giving the name of Gloucestershire's rich Golden Valley another meaning.

CHELTENHAM SPA, Glos

Cheltenham started life as a typical Cotswold village, but in 1715 a mineral spring was discovered here. A pump room was built in 1738, George III gave the place his personal approval, and within half a century architects were commissioned to design a new town. The result attracted many people of education and means, who came as much for Cheltenham's fashionable elegance and taste as for its water's vaunted medicinal properties. The architect Papworth was responsible for much that is best in Cheltenham, and Forbes built the famous Pittville Pump Room. Schools flourished too, including the Cheltenham College for Boys of 1841, and the Cheltenham Ladies' College of 1853. Composer Gustav Holst was a pupil at the town's grammar school. Each March Prestbury Park is host to the Cheltenham Gold Cup horse race.

Turn right on to the B4070, then turn left. After ¾ mile branch right on to the unclassified 'Painswick' road. In 2¼ miles meet a T-junction and turn left on to the A46. Continue to Painswick.

PAINSWICK, Glos

Years ago Painswick was an important centre of the cloth industry. This prosperity is evident in

Follow SP 'Cirencester A419' passing the wide expanse of Rodborough Common.

RODBOROUGH COMMON, Glos

Rodborough Common (NT) lies 1 mile south of Stroud. Its 240-acre site includes part of an early agricultural enclosure.

The 19th-century lines of Sudeley Castle are complemented by beautiful formal gardens.

An Ionic temple was the inspiration for Cheltenham Spa's 19th-century Pump Room.

Follow SP 'Stroud A46' then SP 'Birdlip B4070' to leave Cheltenham, then climb Leckhampton Hill. At the top meet the main road and turn right, then enter a roundabout and leave by the 1st exit on to the A417. The 2nd exit leads to delightful Crickley Hill and can be taken as a diversion from the main tour.

CRICKLEY HILL, Glos

This Country Park (part NT) comprises 36½ acres of beautiful Cotswold escarpment and an interesting Iron Age promontory fort.

Continue along the A417, with magnificent views across the Severn Valley to the Malvern Hills, and enter Birdlip.

BIRDLIP, Glos

Birdlip stands on the edge of the Cotswolds, at an altitude of 900ft. Several mosaic pavements and a well-preserved hypocaust system have been uncovered at the site of a Roman villa to the west.

its many old houses and inns, amongst which are the tall-chimneyed Court House (associated with Charles I) and 18th-century Painswick House. One of the country's few original bowling greens has been preserved at the Falcon Hotel, and a few old cloth mills have survived south of the town. St Mary's Churchyard boasts almost a hundred yews that are kept tidy in a traditional annual clipping ceremony.

Follow the Painswick Valley to Stroud.

STROUD, Glos

Situated on the modest River Frome and the Stroudwater Canal, this town was once reckoned to produce the finest broadcloth in the country. It still makes most of the baize for the world's billiard tables, and has an excellent reputation for its scarlet dyes. A number of 18th-century mills and typical Cotswold cottages have survived. The District (Cowle) Museum contains exhibits of local interest.

Painswick's carefully clipped churchyard yews were planted at the end of the 18th century.

After Rodborough Common continue along the A419 and enter Brimscombe.

BRIMSCOMBE, Glos

Most of the key buildings in Brimscombe are of relatively recent date. Holy Trinity Church was built in 1840, and both Hope Mill and Port Mill are of 19th-century origin. A few earlier buildings survive at Bourne Mill.

Continue along the pleasant Golden Valley to Chalford.

CHALFORD, Glos

Views from Chalford's steep and narrow streets encompass the fertile Golden Valley, the River Frome, and stretches of the disused Stroud Canal. An old round house which originally served as a lock-keeper's cottage now houses an interesting museum of canal relics. Thoughts of past prosperity are woken by the local mills and wool masters' houses.

THE GOLDEN VALLEY, Glos
The original Golden Valley runs from Dorstone to Pontrilas in Herefordshire. The Gloucestershire Golden Valley cradles the River Frome and, like its namesake, is known for peaceful villages and unspoilt countryside.

After 2 miles (from Chalford) reach the White Horse Inn and turn left on to an unclassified road for Frampton Mansell.

FRAMPTON MANSELL, Glos
Important buildings in this village follow Cotswold tradition by dating mainly from the years of wool prosperity. Manor Farmhouse is of the late 17th century, and St Luke's Church was built in 1844.

Continue to Sapperton.

SAPPERTON, Glos
Views from the local churchyard extend along the length of the Golden Valley. Cotswold-stone cottages in the area date back to the 17th century, and Daneway House (1 mile north-west) can claim even greater antiquity, with parts dating at least from the 13th century. The Thames and Severn Canal ran through here via a 2½-mile tunnel through which 18th- and 19th-century bargees propelled their craft by lying on their backs and pushing against the walls or roof with their feet. This was commonly known as 'legging it'.

Turn right, then meet a T-junction and turn left. After 1 mile turn right to Daglingworth.

DAGLINGWORTH, Glos
Saxon work has survived in the local church in spite of major 19th-century rebuilding.

Continue, and ½ mile beyond the village turn right on to the A417 for Cirencester.

CIRENCESTER, Glos
In Roman times Cirencester was *Corinium Dobunorum*, the second largest town in England and the focus of several major highways. When the Romans withdrew the town declined, but wool later boosted it and wool money paid for its Church of St John the Baptist, one of the largest of its kind in the country. The town's Corinium Museum contains one of the country's most comprehensive collections of Roman remains, which includes mosaic floors and Romano-British sculpture.

Follow SP 'Burford A433' to leave Cirencester. Drive to Barnsley.

BARNSLEY, Glos
The church at Barnsley was restored in the 19th century, but its 16th-century tower and two ancient carved tables survived. Sir Isaac Newton's library was discovered at Barnsley Park after it had been removed from Thame Park.

Continue to Bibury.

BIBURY, Glos
William Morris thought Bibury 'the most beautiful village in England'. Most of its stone-built houses have gardens that run down to the River Coln, and the Arlington Row (NT) of river-fronted cottages is famous. Near Arlington Mill, which houses a museum, is a bird sanctuary. Bibury Court Hotel is of Jacobean origin, and The Swan – at the end of the street – is a pleasant coaching inn.

Drive to the Swan Inn and take an unclassified road through the Coln Valley to Ablington.

ABLINGTON, Glos
This lovely River Coln community has a late 16th-century manor house with an impressive barn. There is a prehistoric long barrow near by.

After Ablington turn left to cross a river bridge over the Coln. Later turn right and continue to Winson.

WINSON, Glos
Winson Manor dates from 1740, but Manor Farm is of slightly earlier origin. Most of the village cottages are of 17th- or 18th-century date, and the church is early-Norman.

Drive through the village and turn right for Coln Rogers.

COLN ROGERS, Glos
The nave and chancel of local St Andrew's Church are Saxon. Both the Old Rectory, at the south end of the village, and Lower Farm, belong to the 17th century.

Proceed to Coln St Dennis.

COLN ST DENNIS, Glos
Coln St Dennis has a Norman church and a 19th-century rectory. The hotel at Fosse Bridge, a ¼ mile to the north-west, is also of 19th-century date. Colnpen is a 300ft long barrow near by.

Turn left for Fossebridge, left again on to the A429, then right on to an unclassified road. Follow SP 'Chedworth Roman Villa'.

CLEPWORTH ROMAN VILLA, Glos
Chedworth Roman Villa (NT) dates from the 2nd to 4th centuries, and was rediscovered in 1864. It has various rooms and two bath suites laid out around two courtyards. The site has an excellent museum.

Return for 1½ miles into Yanworth.

YANWORTH, Glos
Traces of wall paintings, fragments of medieval glass, and a Norman font can be seen in Yanworth's 12th-century church.

Continue for 2 miles to the main road. Turn left on to the A429 and drive to the outskirts of Northleach.

NORTHLEACH, Glos
Northleach stands on high ground, east of the Roman Fosse Way, between the Coln and Windrush valleys. Its attractive stone-built cottages and almshouses are dominated by a magnificent church. Nearby is the Cotswold Countryside Collection.

Continue to roundabout, turn left on to the A40 'Cheltenham' road, then after 2¾ miles pass the Puesdown Inn. After a further ¾ mile meet crossroads and turn right on to the unclassified 'Brockhampton' road. Proceed for 2¼ miles and cross the main road for Brockhampton. After ¼ mile meet crossroads and turn right SP 'Charlton Abbots'. Drive to the next crossroads, turn right SP 'Guiting Power'. Ascend and, at next crossroads, turn left along Roel Hill, passing Sudeley Castle.

SUDELEY CASTLE, Glos
Catherine Parr, the last of Henry VIII's wives, lived in this medieval castle (open). In 1858 it was reconstructed by Sir Gilbert Scott, who also designed Catherine's tomb to replace one destroyed during the Civil War.

Continue into Winchcombe.

WINCHCOMBE, Glos
Ancient Winchcombe was once capital of the Kingdom of Mercia. The site of its abbey, founded in 797 and destroyed by Henry VIII, is being excavated. Within the town hall is a Folk and Police Museum.

Mellow stone houses nestle amongst rolling Cotswold scenery at Bibury.

Follow the A46 'Cheltenham' road. After ½ mile reach an unclassified left turn leading to prehistoric Belas Knap.

BELAS KNAP, Glos
About 2 miles south-south-west of Winchcombe is the 180ft-long Belas Knap long barrow (AM). This was restored in 1930 and is considered one of the finest of its type extant.

Return and continue along the A46, with extensive views from the highest area in the Cotswolds.

CLEEVE HILL, Glos
Early 20th-century St Peter's Church shares Cleeve Hill with 17th-century Cockbury Court and 18th-century Hayes. The area is dominated by lofty Cleeve Cloud.

CLEEVE CLOUD, Glos
Overshadowing Cleeve Hill is the massive 1,031ft bulk of Cleeve Cloud, one of the highest points in the Cotswolds. Magnificent views can be enjoyed from its summit.

Continue the descent through Prestbury to Cheltenham, passing the racecourse and airfield on the way.

Several architectural styles are incorporated to glorious effect in Cirencester's parish church.

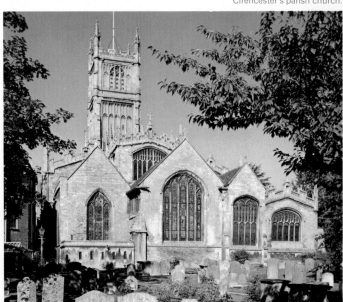

REGENCY TOWNS AND COTSWOLD VILLAGES

Cheltenham has become a byword for refinement, elegance and gentility, qualities it has managed to preserve, with its tree-lined walks, exclusive shops and graceful architecture. More rural but scarcely less elegant is Pershore in the Vale of Evesham, while Tewkesbury is a rare survival of a medieval town.

CHELTENHAM, Glos

The architects of Regency Cheltenham created a supremely elegant town where houses are arranged in patterns of leafy squares, crescents and avenues. The material used was either cream-coloured ashlar from Leckhampton quarry, or brick faced with stucco of the same delicate shade. Balconies of finely wrought iron adorn many of the buildings, adding a Continental atmosphere to the streets and squares. Cheltenham became fashionable as a spa town in the 18th century after the discovery of what is now called the Royal Old Well, and, like Bath, the whole town was designed and rebuilt during the 18th and early-19th centuries. The atmosphere is best appreciated in Lansdown Place, the Promenade, Suffolk Square,

Montpellier Walk and Montpellier Parade. The Pittville Pump Room (OACT), with its colonnaded façade, portico and beautiful interior, is a masterpiece of the Greek Revival style. South of the High Street, is Cheltenham Ladies' College, one of the oldest and most famous girls' public schools in Britain.

Leave Cheltenham on the A46, SP 'Broadway', and continue to Prestbury.

PRESTBURY, Glos

Prestbury Park, the famous steeplechase course where the prestigious Gold Cup takes place every spring, is situated just outside the village, now a residential suburb of Cheltenham. Prestbury lies at the foot of Cleeve Hill, the highest (1,082ft) point of the Cotswold Hills; from the summit the views are superb.

At the end of Prestbury turn left and climb on to Cleeve Hill, then descend to Winchcombe.

WINCHCOMBE, Glos

Many pretty gardens in the main street slope down to the River Isbourne which flows by Winchcombe. Buildings of Cotswold stone, with uneven stone roofs, preserve the charm and character of the town, once the seat of a great Benedictine Abbey, which was so thoroughly destroyed by Lord Seymour of Sudeley Castle at the time of the Reformation, that no trace of it survives. The Railway Museum (OACT) has a fine collection of relics of the steam age. Overlooking the village is Sudeley Castle, (OACT) the home of Catherine Parr — one of Henry VIII's wives who married her lover, Seymour, after the king's death. She is buried in the chapel having died a year later during childbirth. Interesting art collections, costume and furniture exhibitions can be seen in the house, which was restored in the 19th century after suffering severe damage during the Civil War. The parkland surrounding the house has an ornamental lake with a colourful assortment of wildfowl.

Continue on the A46 and after 2 miles (right) a short detour leads to the remains of Hailes Abbey.

HAILES ABBEY, Glos

The romantic ruins of the great Cistercian abbey (AM, NT), founded in 1246, stir the imagination to reconstruct the austere monastic life of medieval

times, when pilgrims came to revere the 'Blood of Hailes', a sacred phial said to contain the blood of Christ. The small museum on the site displays fragments of sculpture from the abbey.

The main tour continues on the A46. At the Toddington roundabout take the B4077, SP 'Stow-on-the-Wold'. ¾ mile farther, at a crossroads, turn left, SP 'Stanway'. Continue on this unclassified road, and in 1¼ miles keep right for Stanton.

STANTON, Glos

Beautiful villages abound in the Cotswolds, where the local golden stone blends so well with the wooded hills, but Stanton, thanks to the restoration of the 17th-century houses that line both sides of its main street, is exceptionally attractive. Village cross, church, manor house and cottages are all in harmony with the gentle countryside around.

Follow SP 'Broadway' and in ¾ mile turn right on to the A46. In 1 mile turn left for Aston Somerville, then at the T-junction turn right, SP 'Evesham'. In another mile, turn left on to the A435, SP 'Cheltenham', to reach the edge of Sedgeberrow. In 1¼ miles turn right for Ashton-under-Hill, then turn right and continue to Elmley Castle. Turn right through the village, then left, SP 'Pershore', for Little Comberton. At the crossroads turn right, SP 'Wick', and after 1½ miles turn right on to the A44, SP 'Evesham'. In 2 miles turn left on to an unclassified road for Cropthorne.

Bredon Hill — 961ft high

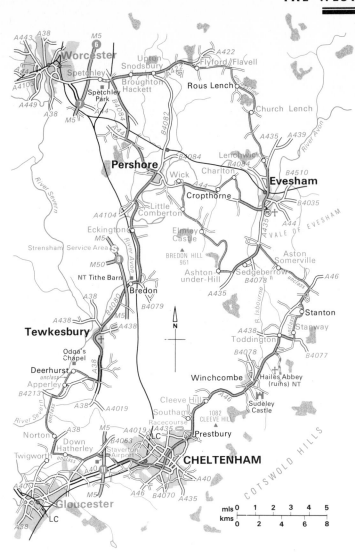

mls 0 1 2 3 4 5
kms 0 2 4 6 8

SPETCHLEY PARK, Herefs & Worcs
The house, home of the Berkeley family, is not open, but the beautiful wooded grounds (OACT) around the ornamental lake, and the garden centre, can be visited. Red and fallow deer roam the park which extends on both sides of the main road, and is linked by a graceful iron footbridge.

The main tour turns left on to the B4084, SP 'Pershore'. In 2 miles bear right, then in another 1½ miles turn left on to the A44 to reach the edge of Pershore.

PERSHORE, Herefs & Worcs
The River Avon flows past the end of the High Street of this enchanting market town in the Vale of Evesham. The land round about is celebrated for Pershore plums, which come in 2 varieties, purple and yellow. Pershore's architecture is classical Georgian, most of the elegant houses being faced with stone or stucco. The great abbey church was only partially destroyed at the Reformation, and what remains, the tower, crossing and transepts, is extremely fine.

At the edge of Pershore turn right on to the A4104, SP 'Upton', then in 2 miles turn left on to the B4080, SP 'Tewkesbury'. Cross the River Avon by a 16th-century bridge to reach Eckington. In 3 miles turn right into Bredon.

BREDON, Herefs & Worcs
Bredon, standing high above the River Avon, is a remarkably pretty village, with an impressive Norman church whose slender spire soars 160ft above the countryside around. A fine stone rectory and 2 large private residences, one Jacobean, the other Georgian, set off the church. Bredon tithe barn (NT) is a magnificent limestone structure with a steep-pitched, stone shingled roof, and dates from the 14th century.

3¼ miles beyond Bredon join the A38 to enter Tewkesbury.

TEWKESBURY, Glos
Almost all the buildings in Tewkesbury are old, timber-framed structures of considerable charm. Shortage of space in the multitude of narrow winding alleys leading off the main street has meant that the houses are tightly packed, producing a pleasing jumble of styles. It is a fascinating town to explore and Tewkesbury Abbey is one of the finest Norman buildings in the country. The interior is magnificent, particularly in the presbytery, where the roof is supported by superb vaulting. Several medieval stained-glass windows have survived, depicting the Last Judgment and the Coronation of the Virgin.

Leave Tewkesbury on the A38, SP 'Gloucester'. In 3 miles turn right on to the B4213, SP 'Ledbury', then in ½ mile bear right for Deerhurst.

DEERHURST, Glos
The village has the distinction of possessing 2 Saxon churches. St Mary's was built in the 9th and 10th centuries, while Odda's Chapel, an outstanding Saxon survival, was dedicated in 1056, as an inscribed stone, now in the Ashmolean Museum at Oxford, proves. The chapel was 'lost' for centuries, as it had been incorporated in a half-timbered farmhouse, until found in 1965.

Continue to Apperley and in 1 mile turn right on to the B4213 then take the next turning left, SP 'Norton'. Continue to Norton, and at the T-junction, turn right, then right again on to the A38, SP 'Gloucester'. In 1 mile turn left on to an unclassified road for Down Hatherley, then in another mile turn left on to the B4063, SP 'Cheltenham'. At the next roundabout join the A40 for the return to Cheltenham.

CROPTHORNE, Herefs & Worcs
Black and white cottages set in pretty gardens characterise this charming old village overlooking the River Avon. In the church are monuments to the Dingley family, whose descendants became mayors of Evesham but lost respectability in the 18th century when Samuel Dingley murdered his brother in cold blood after years of quarrels and bitter rivalry.

Continue through Cropthorne to Charlton. Turn right, then in 1½ miles turn left to rejoin the A44. In 1¼ miles, turn left on to the A435 to enter Evesham.

EVESHAM, Herefs & Worcs
The town stands in a bend of the River Avon, the hub of a fertile region of orchards in the Vale of Evesham. In the centre of the market place is the charming half-timbered Round House (Booth Hall) with overhanging upper storeys and gabled attics. It was not a market hall originally, despite its position, but one of the many attractive old inns that Evesham has preserved in its pleasant streets. From the market place an old gateway leads to the abbey gardens where there is a splendid 16th-century bell tower, once a part of the ruined abbey. Flanking the bell tower are the 2

churches of St Nicholas and All Saints.

Leave Evesham on the A435, SP 'Birmingham', and in 1½ miles turn left for Lenchwick. At the T-junction, turn left, and continue to Church Lench. Here turn right then left for Rous Lench.

ROUS LENCH, Herefs & Worcs
There are 5 little villages, all within a stone's throw of each other, that bear the name Lench. Rous Lench is the largest and prettiest of the villages. It takes its name from the Rouses, a local family, one of whom, in the late 19th century, built most of the attractive houses that stand around the shady village green. The old manor house (not open) is famous for its topiary yew garden, which dates back 300 years, and can be glimpsed from the main road.

Continue through Rous Lench and in 1 mile, at a T-junction, turn left for Flyford Flavell. In ½ mile join the A422 and continue through Upton Snodsbury to Broughton Hackett. In 1¼ miles a detour can be taken by continuing on the A422 for ¾ mile to Spetchley Park.

CHIPPENHAM, Wilts

Chippenham has been a market community since Saxon days when King Alfred stayed here and hunted in the neighbouring forests, and despite housing and industrial developments its character is essentially the same. The centre of this stone-built town is Market Place and the oldest building is the 15th century town hall.

Leave Chippenham on the A4, SP, 'Bath'. In 3½ miles turn left on to an unclassified road for Corsham.

CORSHAM, Wilts

The mellow, stone buildings of the old village centre are among the best in Wiltshire. Corsham was a weaving village in medieval times and the gabled weavers' cottages still stand in their cobbled street, as does the gabled block of the Hungerford Almshouses and School, dating from the same period. The school has kept its original seating arrangements and the master's old-fashioned pulpit desk. Near the church stands Corsham Court (OACT) — an Elizabethan stone manor house first built by 'Customer Smythe', a wealthy haberdasher from London. The present E-shaped design and pinnacled gables are a result of Paul Methuen's ownership from 1745.

Leave on the B3353, SP 'Melksham'. At Gastard, branch left by the Harp and Crown PH, SP 'Lacock', and continue to the A350 and turn right. Take the next turning left into Lacock.

LACOCK, Wilts

Lacock (NT) could stand as the pattern of the perfect English village with its twisting streets, packed with attractive buildings from the 15th to 18th centuries. Half-timbered, grey-stone, redbrick and whitewashed façades crowd together and above eye-level, uneven upper storeys, gabled ends and stone roofs blend with charming ease. Of all the outstanding buildings in the village, Lacock Abbey (NT) on the outskirts is the most beautiful. It began as an Augustinian nunnery in 1232, but after the Reformation Sir William Sharington used the remains to build a Tudor mansion, preserving the cloisters, sacristy and nuns' chapter house, and adding an octagonal tower, a large courtyard and twisted chimney stacks. It was here that W. H. Fox Talbot conducted his pioneer photographic experiments.

Turn right in Lacock, SP 'Bowden Hill', and shortly pass the entrance to Lacock Abbey. After crossing the River Avon ascend Bowden Hill, with fine views to the right. After 2 miles the tour reaches the A342. From here a detour can be made by turning left to Bowood.

BETWEEN THE COTSWOLD HILLS AND THE MARLBOROUGH DOWNS

Golden manor houses stud the countryside in the lee of the chalky heights of the Marlborough Downs and the gentler slopes of the Cotswold Hills. Between them glorious open vistas are broken only by wool towns and villages with their market crosses and stone church spires.

Silbury Hill, built c2500BC, would have taken 700 men 10 years to complete then

BOWOOD, Wilts

The magnificent Georgian house of Bowood is brilliantly complemented by its extensive gardens. The park was laid out by Capability Brown between 1762-1768 and is considered by many as the finest park in England, centring on a long narrow lake. The development of the formal gardens immediately surrounding the house and the establishment of the pleasure gardens, which cover almost a hundred acres, evolved between 1820-1850. The planting in the pleasure grounds, which began in 1820, now forms one of the great collections of trees and shrubs in England. It includes the tallest Cedar of Lebanon and poplar in the country. The whole area is mown. At the outfall from the lake are cascades and grottos, which give a sense of mystery and excitement. During May and June, a separate woodland garden is open which covers over 50 acres. The garden surrounds the family mausoleum, built in 1761 by Robert Adam. Interlinking paths wind beneath tall oaks, through banks of rhododendrons and azaleas. The house itself contains superb collections of paintings, sculpture, costumes and Victoriana. The fine library was designed by Robert Adam, and also on view is the laboratory where Dr Joseph Priestley discovered oxygen gas in 1774.

The main tour turns right, SP 'Devizes', into the village of Sandy Lane. Continue through Rowde to Devizes.

DEVIZES, Wilts

New shopping developments at Devizes have enhanced, rather than detracted from, its busy country town atmosphere. Market Square is the most attractive area and in the centre of this is the market cross, surrounded by 18th-century buildings, including the Black Swan and the Bear Hotel. Devizes, sited on the edge of Salisbury Plain, is a good centre for exploring this area rich in traces of prehistoric man.

Leave Devizes on the A361, SP 'Swindon'. In 2¼ miles turn right, SP 'Bishop's Cannings'. In ½ mile turn right SP 'Florton', into Bishop's Cannings.

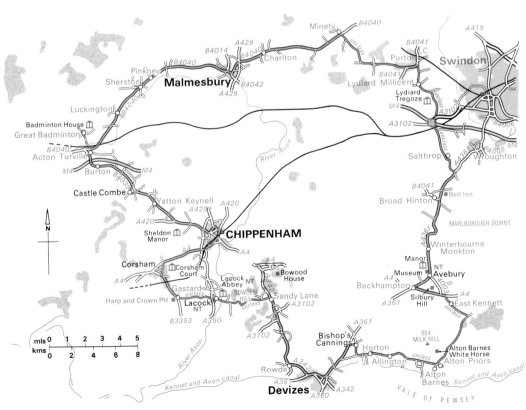

Two rows of 6 seated apostles, each with an angel flying horizontally above them, face each other inside the south porch of Malmesbury Abbey

Lacock was built with the wealth brought by the wool trade and has remained intact since the 18th century

BISHOP'S CANNINGS, Wilts
Thatched cottages lie in the shadow of St Mary's Church which was built as a parish church on the Bishop of Salisbury's estate during the 13th century. There is a curious confessional chair inside, on which an enormous hand is painted together with a number of gloomy Latin inscriptions about death and sin, such as 'The hour of death is uncertain'.

In another ½ mile, at the T-junction, turn left, SP 'Alton Priors', then cross the Kennet and Avon Canal and continue to the outskirts of Allington. After 2 miles there are views to the left of the Alton Barnes White Horse.

ALTON BARNES WHITE HORSE, Wilts
Above the twin villages of Alton Barnes and Alton Priors is a white horse carved in chalk. An unlikely local story says a man called Jack the Painter was paid £20 to cut it, but he fled with the money instead. Rough justice was later done when Jack was caught and hanged, and someone else carved the horse in 1812.

At the T-junction turn left, SP 'Marlborough'. In 2 miles turn left, SP 'East and West Kennet'. Continue through East Kennet then at the A4 turn left, SP 'Chippenham'. Later pass the prehistoric mound of Silbury Hill to the right.

SILBURY HILL, Wilts
No-one knows why this huge, mysterious conical hill (AM) was created. One fanciful theory is that the devil made it and buried beneath is a mounted warrior in gold armour. At about 130ft high, it is the highest artificial mound in Europe and covers 5½ acres.

At the Beckhampton roundabout take the A4361, SP 'Swindon', and in 1 mile keep left for Avebury.

AVEBURY, Wilts
Avebury village stands inside the outer ditch of a huge prehistoric monument — Avebury stone circle (AM). Little is known about the purpose of these famous ancient standing stones, spread over about 28 acres, but the largest ring has 100 sarsen stones left now, and what are actually the remains of 2 inner circles are scattered, seemingly at random, about the village. Avebury Manor (NT) is an Elizabethan manor house standing on the site of a small Benedictine

monastery. The gardens, bordered by stone walls, contain intricate topiary work and a large dovecot.

Continue on the Swindon road with views of the Marlborough Downs to the right. After 3½ miles pass the Bell Inn, then in another 1½ miles turn left, SP 'Wootton Bassett'. Follow this for 3¼ miles to the motorway roundabout and take the A3102, SP 'Swindon'. In ½ mile, at the next roundabout, turn left, SP 'Lydiard Millicent'. In 1 mile, to the left, lies the Lydiard Tregoze Estate.

LYDIARD TREGOZE, Wilts
Sir John St John was chiefly responsible for the spectacular monuments and decorations inside Lydiard Tregoze church which includes a splendid folding screen dedicated to his parents and an elaborate white marble monument for himself, his 2 wives and their 13 children.
The church stands in the park attached to the manor house of Lydiard Tregoze (OACT) in which the St John family lived for 4 centuries. It has been extensively restored and is mainly Georgian in appearance and interior furnishing.

Continue on the unclassified road and in ½ mile turn left, SP 'Purton', for Lydiard Millicent. At the far end of the village turn right and continue to Purton. Turn left in to the main street (B4041) and at the end of the village turn right on to an unclassified road (no SP). In 1¼ miles go over the crossroads, SP 'Minety', then ½ mile farther branch right. At the edge of Minety turn left on to the B4040, for Malmesbury.

MALMESBURY, Wilts
A tall, slender spire soars up above Malmesbury which, in turn, sits up on an isolated hill amid the surrounding water meadows. The spire belongs to the town's majestic abbey which has stood here since the 7th century. Look particularly at the splendid south porch covered in carvings and sculptures: it is one of England's best examples of Romanesque art.

Leave on the B4040, SP 'Bristol', and continue through Pinkney, Sherston and Luckington to Acton Turville. 1¼ miles to the north is Great Badminton and Badminton House.

BADMINTON HOUSE, Avon
The exciting 3-day event horse trials held annually at Badminton House have made the estate famous. Both the stables' and hunt kennels' magnificence reflect Badminton's long association with horses and hunting. At the heart of the great park is the Palladian mansion, remodelled by William Kent in about 1740. It has been the home of the Dukes of Beaufort since the 17th century. The entrance hall, hung with hunting scenes, was where the game of badminton evolved.

The main tour turns left, SP 'Chippenham'. At the Fox and Hounds PH turn left again on to the B4039. Cross the M4 and pass through Burton, then in 2½ miles turn right on to an unclassified road to Castle Combe.

CASTLE COMBE, Wilts
This village, portrayed on many a poster and picture-postcard as a haven of beauty and tranquility, well deserves its fame. A river, Bye Brook, flows through the streets under stone foot-bridges, and honey-coloured cottages — their roofs grown uneven with the passage of time — surround the market cross.

Return to the B4039, SP 'Chippenham', and turn right for Yatton Keynell. In 1¼ miles turn left on to the A420. In 1 mile, on the right, is the turning for Sheldon Manor.

SHELDON MANOR, Wilts
Terraced gardens, rose beds, water gardens and ancient yew trees encircle the Plantaganet manor house (OACT). The oldest part of the house is its 13th-century porch, still with its original stone water cistern which was fed from pipes in the roof. Within the grounds is a 15th-century detached chapel belonging to the house.

Continue on the A420 for the return to Chippenham.

COTSWOLD VALLEYS AT THE SOURCE OF THE THAMES

Stretching northwards from the infant Thames, the deep valley of the River Churn and the broader valleys of the Coln and the Leach bore into the wooded Cotswold Hills. The towns and villages of the Thames stand out amid the flat water meadows while the Cotswold valleys protect their own dreamy villages.

CIRENCESTER, Glos
This 'capital' of the Cotswolds is the epitome of an old market town, with its beautiful Tudor church dominating the busy market place. The church, built from the riches of the wool trade, has a magnificent 3-storeyed south porch with delicate fan vaulting and many interesting brasses. Around the attractive Georgian market place are a number of old streets where the stone-built houses of the wealthy Elizabethan wool merchants still stand. Cirencester stands at the meeting point of 3 Roman roads — the Fosse Way, Akeman Street, and one of the 2 Ermine Streets. Roman remains, including some fine mosaic pavements, are housed in the Corinium Museum. Cirencester Park (house not open) stands in lovely woodland and has a superb 5-mile-long avenue of chestnut trees. The 17th-century poet Alexander Pope was a frequent visitor to the house, and a rustic seat at the edge of the tree-lined avenues called the Seven Rides is named after him.

Leave on the A429, SP 'The South West' and 'Chippenham'. In 1½ miles go forward on to the A433, SP 'Bristol'. After another mile, in the meadow to the right, is the reputed source of the River Thames. Pass under a railway bridge and turn left on to an unclassified road for Kemble. Cross the main road into the village, then go over the staggered crossroads, SP 'Ewen', follow SP 'South Cerney'.

SOUTH CERNEY, Glos
Just outside South Cerney, old gravel pits have been transformed into lakes which form part of the Cotswold Water Park; the marina here is gay with sailing dinghies and motor boats on summer weekends. The village stands on the River Churn and has several attractive old streets, including one with the extraordinary name of Bow Wow.

Turn right at the war memorial into Broadway Lane. In ¾ mile pass the Costwold Water Park and in ½ mile turn right, SP 'Ashton Keynes'. In 1¼ miles turn left and shortly branch left to Ashton Keynes.

ASHTON KEYNES, Wilts
Small bridges spanning the little stream of the infant Thames lead up to the doors of several of the cottages at one end of Ashton Keynes, and at the other, a group of old stone houses form a picturesque scene with an old watermill. Just outside the village, the church and manor house look out over peaceful countryside.

At the end of the village turn left on to the Cricklade road then bear right. In 2 miles turn left on to the B4040, and in another 1½ miles turn left again to enter Cricklade. At the clock tower turn right and follow SP 'Swindon' then in ¾ mile join the A419. In 1 mile turn left on to an unclassified road for Castle Eaton. Continue on the Highworth road through Hannington and in 1¼ miles turn left on to the B4019 for Highworth. Turn left on to the A361 Stow road and after 4 miles pass a riverside park before reaching Lechlade.

LECHLADE, Glos
Just outside Lechlade, a pleasant riverside park extends along the banks of the Thames, locally referred to as (as at Oxford) as the Isis. Halfpenny Bridge leads across the river and into the Georgian market place. A delightful characteristic of the village are the many gazebos in the trim gardens of the older houses. The poet Shelley, journeying upriver from Windsor, was inspired by the calm of the river and the churchyard to write the poem *Stanzas in a Summer Evening Churchyard* while staying at the local inn. By St John's Bridge 3 shires meet — Gloucestershire, Oxfordshire and Wiltshire — and the nearby lock is an ideal picnic spot.

Leave on the A417 Faringdon road and in ¾ mile cross St John's Bridge. In 2 miles pass the grounds of Buscot Park.

BUSCOT PARK, Oxon
The Classical mansion (NT), built the Edward Loveden Townsend in 1780, is the home of a notable collection of European paintings spanning several centuries, from the Italian Renaissance to the pre-Raphaelites and 20th-century works. 18th-century paintings include a Gainsborough landscape.

The collection was begun in the 19th century by Alexander Henderson, Lord Faringdon, and continued by his descendants. The most famous portrait is by Rembrandt of Clement de Jongh. The house also contains lovely furniture of rosewood and satinwood.

Continue to Faringdon.

FARINGDON, Oxon
A traditional market town famous for its dairy produce and fine bacon, Faringdon has many interesting old inns and an 18th-century Market Hall. Faringdon House (not open) was owned by Lord Barners and the folly in the grounds was built by him during the Depression of the 1930s to relieve local unemployment. The 14th-century Radcot Bridge between Faringdon and Clanfield is said to be the oldest of the Thames bridges.

From the market square branch left on to the A4095, and after passing the church turn left. In 2½ miles cross the historic Radcot Bridge. At Clanfield go forward on to the B4020 for Alvescot. In ¼ mile turn left on to an unclassified road to Kencot and 1¼ miles beyond the village turn right into Filkins.

FILKINS, Oxon
Wistaria and clematis, for which the Cotswold villages are so famous, clamber over the pale stone of houses, barns and garden walls. Chestnut trees, laden with flower in spring, spread over the quiet main street of Filkins.

In the village turn right and after 1 mile turn right on to the A361, SP 'Stow'. In 2 miles, at the crossroads, turn left, SP 'Wildlife Park', and pass the entrance to the Cotswold Wildlife Park.

COTSWOLD WILDLIFE PARK, Oxon
In 1969, 120 acres of wooded parkland were chosen to house the animal collection of the Cotswold Wildlife Park. They have taken as their emblem one of their most attractive creatures, the chestnut-coloured Red panda, a smaller relative of the Giant panda, whose natural habitat is the high forests of the Himalayas and western China. There are

Most Roman villas had mosaic flooring such as this which can be seen at the Corinium Museum, Cirencester

many African and South American mammals, an interesting Reptile House, with crocodiles, alligators and poisonous snakes, and numerous spacious aviaries of exotic birds, including a Tropical House where sunbirds, brilliant humming birds and bluebirds hover among the blossoms of hibiscus and bougainvillea.

Continue on the unclassified road, and in ½ mile go over the crossroads, SP 'Eastleach Martin', then ½ mile later branch left and follow a narrow byroad to the twin Eastleaches.

EASTLEACH, Glos
The village consists of 2 charming Cotswold hamlets, Eastleach Martin and Eastleach Turville, standing on opposite banks of the River Leach. An old stone clapper bridge leads from one to the other, named after John Keble (founder of Keble College, Oxford), whose family were lords of the manor of Turville. The 2 old village churches were built within sight of each other; that of Eastleach Martin has 5 old sundials; that of its neighbour, a fine Norman arched doorway with a carving of Christ in Glory.

At Eastleach Turville keep right through the village on the Hatherop road. At the T-junction turn left, then in ½ mile turn right, and 2 miles farther turn right again into Hatherop. Turn left for Coln St Aldwyn. Turn left, SP 'Fairford', then cross the River Coln and ascend to Quenington.

QUENINGTON, Glos
A number of lovingly-restored 17th-century stone houses grace the village street, but it is the 12th-century village church, with its 2 beautifully carved Norman doorways that attracts visitors from miles around. The north doorway depicts in vivid detail the Harrowing of Hell and the south doorway shows Christ placing a crown on the head of the Virgin Mary.

At the green, turn left then at the end of the village recross the Coln and continue to Fairford.

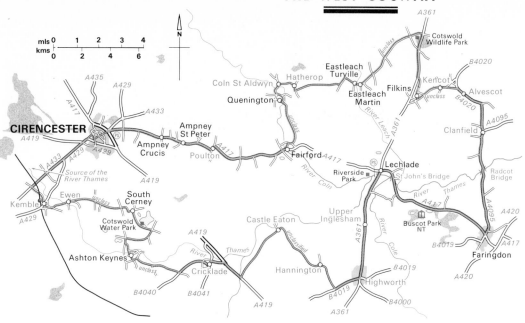

houses of all periods and, at the edge of the manor park, a picturesque stone watermill. The American air-base near Fairford was used for trials of *Concorde*.

Leave on the A417 and pass through Poulton to the villages of Ampney St Peter and Ampney Crucis.

THE AMPNEYS, Glos

Four villages all bearing the name Ampney. Ampney St Peter is generally thought to be the prettiest of them, with its village green bordered by old cottages. Ampney Crucis nearby, a pleasing blend of old and new, stands on the Ampney Brook. It takes the second part of its name from the ancient cross in the churchyard. At Down Ampney, some distance away, the composer Ralph Vaughan Williams was born.

Continue on the A417 for the return to Cirencester.

Fairford's 17th-century mill house stands beside the River Coln. St Mary's Church nearby marks the centre of the village

FAIRFORD, Glos

All the prosperity of the medieval wool trade is exemplified in the Church of St Mary at Fairford. The wool merchants, John Tame and his son Sir Edmund, paid for it to be built at the end of the 15th century and by a miracle the glorious stained-glass windows have been preserved almost intact. The church stands beside the river, overlooking the village square where houses of soft grey Cotswold stone have stood, their appearance virtually unaltered, for more than 200 years. A stroll around the streets leading off from the market place reveals old

DARTMOUTH AND THE SOUTH HAMS

The scenery of the South Hams is a landscape of rounded hills and quiet valleys, of greens and browns. In contrast are the greys and blues of the slate cliffs and the rocky outline of the coast and it is the lure of the sea which leaves the working countryside free from bustling tourism.

DARTMOUTH, Devon

Naval tradition in Dartmouth goes back to medieval times when the port was one of the busiest in England. The ships of the 2nd and 3rd Crusades anchored here on their way to the Holy Land, and in peacetime Dartmouth grew rich on the proceeds of the wine trade with France. In wartime, the town's formidable 15th-century castle could rake the estuary with cannon shot and close off the river mouth with a massive chain running across to Kingwear Castle on the opposite shore. Today the town is dominated by the Royal Naval College, designed by Sir Aston Webb and opened in 1905. Dartmouth's streets, climbing the steep wooded slope of the Dart Estuary, are intriguing to explore. Of the many ancient buildings scattered throughout the town, 14th-century Agincourt House contains a small museum, and there is another museum with a fine collection of model ships in the Butterwalk, a picturesque 17th-century market arcade. In the gardens on the quay stands what may be the world's oldest steam pumping engine, designed in 1725 by Thomas Newcomen, a native of Dartmouth. The 14th-century church of St Saviour, whose building was mainly financed by Sir John Hawley, 7 times mayor of the town, is worth a visit. The interior is richly decorated and contains an elaborate brass to Hawley and his 2 wives. Although the church door bears the date 1631, the ironwork depicting prancing leopards on the branches of a great tree belongs to the 14th century. Dartmouth has a carnival every year in July and its famous regatta is held on the Dart during late August.

Leave Dartmouth on the A379, SP 'Kingsbridge', and climb past the grounds of the Naval College. At the top turn left, SP 'Stoke Fleming' and 'Strete', and continue with occasional coastal views to Stoke Fleming.

STOKE FLEMING, Devon

Perched on the cliffs 300ft above the sea, the pretty streets of Stoke Fleming overlook a Mediterranean seascape; the white shingle of Blackpool Sands sweeping away to the south, framed by shelving headlands wooded with dark green pines. The tower of the 14th-century church served for centuries as a daymark for shipping; inside are two brasses, one, almost lifesize, to John Corp and his little grandaughter Elyenor, and one to Elias Newcomen, a 17th-century rector and ancestor of the Dartmouth born inventor, Thomas Newcomen. From the cliff path there is a fine view over Redlap Cove to the awesome Dancing Beggar rocks.

The tour skirts the cove of Blackpool Sands before ascending to Strete.

The sheltered naval town of Dartmouth

STRETE, Devon

Old stone houses set in a pleasant sheltered valley stand in peaceful contrast to the wild slate cliffs of Pilchard's Cove. Down in this cove once lived a community of fishermen, but now only the placename survives; the houses long since destroyed by the sea.

Continue on the A379 and later descend to reach Slapton Sands.

SLAPTON SANDS & SLAPTON LEY, Devon

The simple obelisk on the edge of Slapton Sands was erected to commemorate the United States troops who used this area in World War II as a training ground to practise for the Normandy landings in 1944. The long stretch of shingle beach is a good hunting ground for collectors of shells and pretty pebbles, but bathing can sometimes be dangerous. A 3-mile sandbar, carrying the road, protects the freshwater lagoon of Slapton Ley from contamination by the sea. The lake and its surrounding reedbeds are now a nature reserve for birdlife, particularly waterfowl and reed warblers.

From Slapton Sands a turning to the right may be taken to Slapton.

SLAPTON, Devon

The village lies inland from the coast road, along the steep side of the valley. Many houses in its twisting streets have had their walls rendered to hide shell damage. During the last war, villagers had to evacuate their homes when the US Army took the place over for manoeuvres. The ruined tower is all that remains of a 14th-century collegiate chantry founded by Sir Guy de Brien, one of the first Knights of the Garter and Standardbearer to Edward III.

The main tour continues with the coast road to Torcross.

TORCROSS, Devon

Pleasant old houses line the seafront along Start Bay at Torcross. Until the pilchard shoals disappeared from the south-west coast, Torcross was the most easterly fishing village to engage in this trade. The fishermen kept Newfoundland dogs who were trained to swim out to the returning boats and carry back ropes to those waiting on the shore, who hauled the laden craft to safety.

From Torcross bear right and continue inland to Stokenham.

STOKENHAM, Devon

In earlier centuries it was the duty of the inhabitants of this large hillside village to maintain a watch on the coast for shoals of fish. The fishing industry has declined, but the local fishermen still put out their pots for lobster and crab.

Turn left at Stokenham and at the next crossroads, turn left again, SP 'Start Point'. In ½ mile bear right and in just over another ½ mile pass the turning on the left to Beesands. Continue for nearly ¾ mile then bear left, and in 1 mile pass the road which leads to North Hallsands.

BEESANDS & NORTH HALLSANDS, Devon

Steep, narrow lanes lead to the two little hamlets of Beesands and North Hallsands at the southern end of Start Bay. The fierce and treacherous storms that periodically assault this part of the coast have, in the past, brought tragedy in their wake. In 1917 a former village of Hallsands, sited to the south of the present one, was completely destroyed in a storm because the Admiralty had allowed the excavation of its shingle bank. Remains of some of its houses still stand as an eerie memorial.

The main tour continues to Start Point.

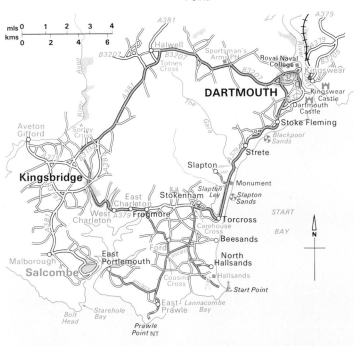

START POINT, Devon
The jagged ridge of Start Point overlooks the whole sweep of the South Hams coast and is an excellent vantage point for birdwatchers. Early migrants from the Continent alight here, and there are many native breeding colonies of seabirds. More seriously, the clifftop lighthouse warns of the Blackstone Rock on which many a ship has foundered. In 1581, a pirate was hanged in chains here as a warning to other outlaws of the ocean.

Return towards Stokenham and after 2¼ miles turn sharp left, SP 'East Prawle' and 'East Portlemouth'. In 1 mile at Cousin's Cross, bear left, then in 1¾ miles turn right. Alternatively, keep forward for the village of East Prawle and the road to Prawle Point.

PRAWLE POINT, Devon
Prawle Point (NT) is the extreme southern tip of Devon, looking west towards the Eddystone Lighthouse and east across Lannacombe Bay to Start Point. 'Prawle' comes from an old English word meaning 'look-out hill', and no name could better fit the lonely, sombre cliffs of this immemorial watching place.

The main tour continues to East Portlemouth.

Above: lobster-pots at Beesands

Right: The freshwater lagoon of Slapton Ley is separated from the sea by a shingle bar.

EAST PORTLEMOUTH, Devon
This small clifftop village looks across the Kingsbridge estuary to the lovely town of Salcombe, where pines, cypresses and palms flourish in almost Mediterranean profusion. Magnolia and fuchsia thrive here and there is an astonishing variety of wild flowers. The estuary is so sheltered that most plants bloom early and fruit ripens early. There are fine views up the many-branched estuary to Kingsbridge and beyond to the bleak expanse of Dartmoor. To the south, paths along the cliffs (NT) lead past sandy coves and weathered rocks as far as Prawle Point.

Return along the unclassified road, SP 'Kingsbridge'. In 2½ miles, at the T-junction, turn left, then in 1¾ miles go over the crossroads, SP 'Frogmore' and 'Kingsbridge'. In ½ mile descend to the hamlet of Ford and turn sharp left and in ¾ mile, at the T-junction, turn right. At the head of Frogmore Creek bear left across the bridge, then turn left on to the A379 for Frogmore.

FROGMORE, Devon
All over the South Hams district slate was used for building, both for important structures such as Dartmouth Castle and for farms and cottages. There were quarries at Frogmore and the nearby village of Molescombe, and traces of old workings, some dating back to medieval times, can be seen along Frogmore Creek.

Continue on the A379 and pass through East and West Charleton before reaching Kingsbridge.

KINGSBRIDGE, Devon
Kingsbridge, an attractive little place at the head of the estuary, offers a sheltered harbour for yachting and is also the market centre for the area. Its town hall boasts an unusual, slate hung ball clock of 1875 and the 16th-century market arcade, the Shambles, restored in the 18th century, is particularly appealing. The miniature railway on the quay carries passengers on a ½ mile trip, and the Cookworthy Museum in Fore Street commemorates William Cookworthy. Born here in 1705, he discovered china clay in Cornwall and made the first true English porcelain.

Leave by the unclassified road SP 'Totnes'. At Sorley Green Cross turn right on to the B3194 and in just over 1 mile turn left on to the A381. After 4¼ miles turn right on to the B3207, SP 'Dartmouth'. In another 4 miles, at the Sportsman's Arms PH, bear right and continue with the B3207 which later joins the A379 for Dartmouth.

DEVON'S ANCIENT CAPITAL AND THE SOUTHERN COAST

From Exeter, 2,000-year-old capital of Devon, the tour follows the contours of the southern coastline from Starcross down to colourful, Italianate Torquay. Turning inland to the wooded slopes of the Haldon Hills, it finally descends to a chequerboard farmland and back to Exeter.

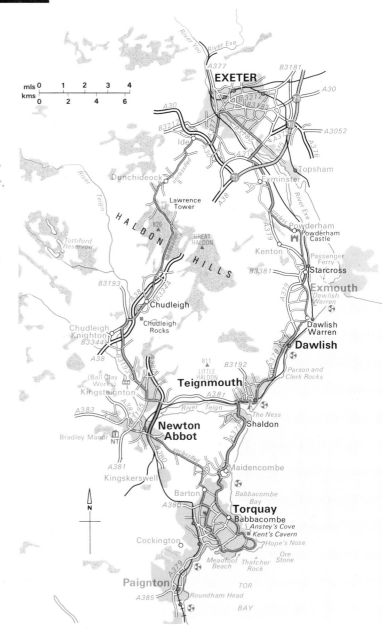

EXETER, Devon

Parts of the massive red walls of the old Roman city can still be seen, but, sadly, much of medieval Exeter was destroyed in World War II. The cathedral, with its 300ft nave, the longest span of Gothic vaulting in the world, was spared, as were the attractive old houses round the Close. The Guildhall in the High Street claims to be the oldest municipal building in England; inside, the hall is roofed with gilded beams supported by figures of bears holding staves. In Princesshay stands the entrance to a network of underground tunnels (OACT), constructed in the 13th century to carry fresh spring water around the city. Exeter's maritime traditions are well represented in the marvellous Maritime Museum on the quay which contains over 100 historic ships, from Arab dhows and Fijian outriggers to Portuguese craft and early steamships. Some are afloat on the canal and several can be boarded and explored. The handsome museum buildings have featured in the BBC television series 'The Onedin Line'.

Follow SP 'Exmouth' (A376) and at the Countess Wear roundabout, take the 3rd exit, SP 'Plymouth' (A38). Shortly cross the River Exe and the Exeter Canal, and at the next roundabout take the 1st exit on the A379, SP 'Dawlish'. Bypass Exminster and after 2½ miles turn left, SP 'Powderham Castle', and continue with views of the Exe estuary to the entrance to Powderham Castle.

POWDERHAM CASTLE, Devon

The castle (OACT), seat of the Earls of Devon, is a grand medieval fortified mansion, extended and altered in the 18th and 19th centuries but with a core some 400 years older. The somewhat flamboyantly decorated rooms are beautifully furnished and well worth a visit. Powderham sits in a magnificent deer park divided by grand avenues of cedar and ilex trees.

At the castle entrance turn left, then at the church turn right. After 1¼ miles turn left on to the A379 and continue to Starcross.

STARCROSS, Devon

Starcross, with its pretty little harbour, has kept much of its quiet village character. In the red tower of an old pumping house it preserves a relic of Brunel's short-lived atmospheric railway which ran through the village just before 1820. The engines were designed to work on the vacuum principle, using atmospheric pressure to drive the pistons, but the leather valves (there was no rubber then) leaked, and so, although trains between Exeter and Newton Abbot reached an incredible 70 mph for short stretches, the experiment failed.

Remain on the A379 for ½ mile then at the crossroads turn left on to an unclassified road, then turn left again for Dawlish Warren.

Teignmouth, seen from Shaldon across the busy estuary that separates them

DAWLISH WARREN, Devon

This promontory of sand and dune was created when a breakwater was built to protect the railway line. It has a fine golf course. On a spithead, the Warren Nature Reserve protects the vegetation, animal and birdlife in an area of just over 500 acres. It is the site of one of the estuary's high-tide wader roosts, which can be viewed from a large hide looking back up the estuary. The most exciting time for birds here is winter.

Turn right at the T-junction. In ½ mile turn left then in ¾ mile turn left again to rejoin the A379 for Dawlish.

DAWLISH, Devon

A charming 18th-century resort, Dawlish has a sandy beach framed by rocky cliffs and the main railway line from London to Penzance runs right along the sands. Through the centre of the town runs Dawlish Water, on whose banks the Lawn, a lovely

miniature garden complete with cascading waterfalls and decorative black Australian swans, was created in the 19th century.

Follow SP 'Teignmouth'.

TEIGNMOUTH, Devon

A golfcourse overlooking the town from a height of 800ft, a safe sandy beach with a sheltered harbour and a pleasant promenade, combine to make Teignmouth a perennially popular resort. To the north the bay is guarded by the Parson and Clerk stack rocks, and to the south by a small lonely lighthouse. A number of twisty old lanes wind down to New Quay, built in the 19th century for the purpose of shipping Dartmoor granite to London to rebuild London Bridge — itself replaced in 1968 and shipped to the USA. A ferry runs across the estuary to Shaldon.

Follow SP 'Torbay' and in ¾ mile, at the traffic signals, turn left and cross the River Teign for Shaldon.

Two tiers of kings, queens, saints and
angels are carved into the west front
of Exeter Cathedral. Inset: the nave

SHALDON, Devon
The French set fire to Shaldon in
1690 and burned about 100 houses
and its pretty streets now are lined
with Regency buildings. Narrow
lanes and alleys converge at
Crown Square, the old centre, and
among them the traditional Devon
cottages of whitewashed cob
(clay mixed with chopped straw)
and thatch can be seen. Shaldon
has 2 beaches; one, otherwise
cut off at high tide, is reached by a
'smugglers' tunnel.

*Turn right with the main road and
continue with some good coastal
views. In 4 miles, at the Palk Arms
PH, turn left into Hartop Road
(one-way), SP 'Babbacombe' and 'St
Marychurch'. At the end turn left
then at the mini-roundabout turn
right. At the next traffic signals turn
left into Babbacombe.*

BABBACOMBE, Devon
A model village, set in 4 acres of
perfectly landscaped miniature
gardens, is the main attraction at
Babbacombe. There are over 400
model buildings, each beautifully
made and detailed, and over
1,200ft of model railway track.
Babbacombe also has a pleasant
pebbly beach.

*Continue along Babbacombe Road
and in just over ¾ mile turn left,
SP 'Anstey's Cove', into a narrow,
one-way road. Shortly pass the car
park for Anstey's Cove.*

ANSTEY'S COVE & KENT'S CAVERN, Devon
On the heights above Anstey's
Cove is Kent's Cavern (AM), a
Palaeolithic cave dwelling. There
are 2 main caves, containing
stalagmites and stalactites and
numerous flint and bone
implements and weapons, such as
harpoons, have been found in
them, as well as traces of
prehistoric animals including the
mammoth and woolly
rhinoceros.

*From the car park descend to
Ilsham Road. (From here turn right
to visit Kent's Cavern.) The main
tour turns left and almost
immediately left again into Ilsham
Marine Drive. At the foot of the hill
turn sharp left, SP 'The Town'. In
¾ mile, at the crossroads, turn left
into Parkhill Road and continue to
Torquay.*

TORQUAY, Devon
Its white-painted villas, sub-
tropical plants and shady gardens
set among the limestone crags of
the hillside overlooking the bay,
have earned Torquay its title of
queen of the Devon coast. From
Marine Drive, which skirts the
headland, there are superb views
out across Tor Bay and inland to
the town. Torquay is the creation
of Sir Robert Palk, a governor of
Madras, who made his own
fortune in India and was left
another by a friend, General
Stinger Lawrence, which included
the hamlet of Tor Quay. He
appreciated the beauty of the site
and exploited it during the
Napoleonic Wars when the
Continent was closed to
holidaymakers: Torquay has never
looked back. Among its attractions
are Aqualand on Beacon Quay,
the largest aquarium in the West
Country, specialising in tropical
marine fish; Torre Abbey Gardens,
and the Torquay Museum in
Babbacombe Road exhibits finds
from Kent's Cavern and other
south Devon caves.

*Follow SP 'Teignmouth' A379 and
at the mini-roundabout turn left
into Hele Road. At the next
roundabout take the 3rd exit into
Barton Hill Road, SP 'Barton'.
Ascend through Barton and near
the top bear right, SP 'Newton'.
Continue with views of Dartmoor
ahead and at the T-junction turn
left. At the next roundabout take
the 3rd exit on to the A380, SP
'Exeter'. Alternatively, take the 2nd
exit for Newton Abbot.*

NEWTON ABBOT, Devon
A railway town with extensive
marshalling yards, Newton Abbot's
steep streets are lined with
stepped terraces of workmen's
cottages. All that remains of its
church is the 14th-century tower at
the town centre. Charles I once
stayed at Forde House and so,
later, did William of Orange after
he had landed at Torbay when he
came to rule England with Mary II.
Wednesday is market day, when
the town springs to life as people
crowd in from the surrounding
region. South-west of Newton
Abbot, set in the deep valley of
the River Lemon, lies Bradley
Manor (NT), a charming 15th-
century house with a gabled front
and pleasingly irregular windows.
It is considered to be one of the
best examples of a medieval
Gothic house in the West Country.

*The main tour following the bypass
crosses the River Teign then branch
left SP 'Kingsteignton', and at the
roundabout take the B3193 to
Kingsteignton. Here at the Kings
Arms PH, turn right, SP 'Exeter',
then in just over ¼ mile turn left
on to the B3193 SP 'Chudleigh'. In
3 miles cross the A38 and the River
Teign. Shortly bear right to join the
B3344, then ½ mile farther bear
right again and continue to
Chudleigh.*

CHUDLEIGH, Devon
This pleasant little hillside town is
much visited for the sake of its
Rocks, a picturesque and romantic
limestone outcrop just south of
the village. There is a pretty
waterfall here and a cavern called
the Pixie's Hole. This has a
distinctive stalagmite called the
Pope's Head. On the walls, among
countless less famous initials, are
carved those of the poet Samuel
Taylor Coleridge and his brother.

*At the war memorial in Chudleigh
branch left into Old Exeter Street.
In 1 mile go forward, SP 'Exeter',
and climb on to the Haldon Hills.*

THE HALDON HILLS, Devon
The moorland slopes and woods
of the Haldon Hills mark the start
of the switchback landscapes of
east Devon, where hill and valley
alternate in a constant upheaval.
From the tops of the hills there are
wide views of the rich red
farmland around Exeter and the
patchwork effect of the small
fields and hedges so typical of
Devon. A landmark on the hills is
Lawrence Tower, built by Sir
Robert Palk in 1788 in memory of
General Stringer Lawrence (see
Torquay).

*At the crossroads turn left, SP
'Dunchideock' and 'Ide', to follow
a high ridge. After a mile, on the
right, is Lawrence Tower and in ½
mile bear right. A long descent
then leads to Ide. At the T-junction
at the end of the village turn right,
SP 'Exeter'. At the next roundabout,
take the A377 for Exeter.*

THE HILLS OF EAST DEVON

East Devon is a mild, well-rounded collection of contrasts.
Gracious Regency coastal resorts rub shoulders with simple
picturesque villages, sub-tropical gardens grow alongside native
woodlands, and little stone farms fringe the parkland estates
of grand country houses

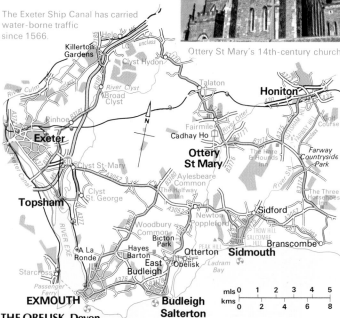

Ottery St Mary's 14th-century church.

The Exeter Ship Canal has carried
water-borne traffic
since 1566.

HAYES BARTON, Devon
1 mile west of East Budleigh is the
thatched 16th-century house of
Hayes Barton (not open), birthplace
of the famous adventurer Sir Walter
Raleigh in 1552.

*At the church turn right and shortly
rejoin the A376. Proceed to the next
crossroads, where there is an obelisk.*

EXMOUTH, Devon
Situated on the estuary of the River
Exe, this pleasant town and small
port is the oldest and one of the
largest seaside resorts in Devon.
Most of its sandy beaches offer safe
and sheltered bathing, and there are
extensive coastal views. Local tourist
facilities include swimming pools,
the town museum and the Country
Life museum. Good Georgian
houses can be seen in The Beacon,
and a picturesque group near by
includes quaint almshouses and a
tiny chapel. A passenger ferry makes
frequent estuary crossings between
Exmouth and Starcross.

A LA RONDE, Devon
This unusual circular house (open)
stands east of the Exeter road and
was built in 1798 by a Miss Jane
Parminter. Its rooms are arranged
around an octagonal hall, and the
curious Shell Gallery is imaginatively
decorated with shells, feathers, and
fascinating pictures made from a
variety of natural objects.

*Leave Exmouth on the Budleigh
Salterton road A376 and pass through
attractive woodland scenery to
Budleigh Salterton.*

BUDLEIGH SALTERTON,
Devon
During the 13th century this
Ottermouth town was a salt-panning
community supplying the local
priory. At the mouth of the river is a
shingle beach backed by red
sandstone cliffs, and less than a mile
away are the challenging fairways of

the best golf course in east Devon.
Several Georgian houses can be
seen in the town, and a small but
interesting museum called the
Fairlynch Arts Centre is in an 18th-
century thatched house.

*Keep forward through the town and
then ascend and turn left. In 2 miles at
crossroads turn left into East Budleigh.*

EAST BUDLEIGH, Devon
Typical of many Devon
communities, this charming little
village has delightful thatched
cottages and seems hardly to have
been touched by time.

A miniature railway provides a mobile
viewpoint from which to enjoy the
varied scenery of Bicton Gardens.

THE OBELISK, Devon
This curious and rather attractive
brick and stone cross is dated 1743
and carries route directions
couched in biblical terms and
phrases.

*A possible detour leads 1 mile to the
right, across the River Otter, to
Otterton.*

OTTERTON, Devon
Fine thatched cottages and a
handsome chestnut grove combine
to make this one of the most
picturesque villages in the area.
Restored Otterton Watermill is now
an interesting craft centre.

*Keep forward on the A376 and after
½ mile reach the entrance to Bicton
Park on the left.*

BICTON PARK, Devon
The gardens here are among the
most beautiful in Britain. Le Nôtre,
the designer of the superb gardens
of Versailles in France, laid out the
fine lawns of the Italian Garden in
1735 and there is an extensive
pinetum. Other features include a
narrow-gauge woodland railway,
countryside and transport
museums, the World of Tomorrow
and World of Yesterday
entertainment themes, and a large
adventure playground.

*After 1½ miles turn right on to the
A3052 and enter Newton
Poppleford. Cross the River Otter and
ascend alongside Harpford Wood.
Shortly turn right on to the B3176 SP
'Sidmouth' and skirt Bulverton Hill on
the right before descending into
Sidmouth.*

SIDMOUTH, Devon
Created as a resort from almost
nothing in the 18th century,
Sidmouth has a shingle beach
backed by spectacular red cliffs and
is still a popular holiday town. Rows
of Regency terraces are reminders of
the prosperous recent past, while
elsewhere are the more ancient Old
Chancel and Manor House. The
former incorporates medieval parts
of the old parish church, and the
latter now houses a museum. On
either side of the town are Peak Hill
to the west and Salcombe Hill to the
east, both of which offer exceptional
views of the coastline. Peak Hill
shelters the Royal Glen, a former
residence of Queen Victoria. Every
August the town is a host to a well-
known International Folk Song and
Dance Festival.

*Follow SP 'Honiton' B3175 and drive
to Sidford.*

SIDFORD, Devon
Although rebuilt and widened in
1930, Sidford's bridge still displays
the pleasing lines of the old high-
backed packhorse bridge that stood
here from c1100. Porch House,
which dates from the 16th century, is
said to have hidden Charles II after
the Battle of Worcester.

*Turn right on to the A3052 and climb
Trow Hill, which offers magnificent
views across the Sid Valley. Shortly
beyond the summit bear left then
after ¼ mile turn right on to an
unclassifed road for Branscombe.*

BRANSCOMBE, Devon

It is difficult to find the centre of this village, which sprawls along steep lanes in a wooded valley, but its situation makes it one of the loveliest in Devon. Features of the upper village include thatched roofs, an old smithy, and a Norman to later church. Some 300 acres of the beautiful Branscombe Estate is owned by the National Trust.

Pass the Mason's Arms PH then follow SP 'Beer', reach to the top of an ascent, and turn left SP 'Honiton'. Continue for 1 mile then turn left on to the A3052. After ¾ mile pass the Three Horseshoes Inn before turning right on to the B3174. After 2½ miles pass the road to the Farway Countryside Park on the right.

FARWAY COUNTRYSIDE PARK, Devon

Much of this 189-acre park is preserved in its natural state, though one or two places have been prepared as picnic sites. Attractions include pony rides, nature trails and a rare breeds farm.

In ¾ mile bear right on to an unclassified road SP 'Farway' and cross Farway Hill, with fine views into the Coly Valley on the right. After ¾ mile keep forward on the 'Honiton' road. Reach a golf course and turn left, then descend into Honiton.

HONITON, Devon

This town gave its name to Honiton lace, a material which is now produced in neighbouring villages and can still be bought in some local shops. Examples can be seen in a small museum housed in the old chapel beside the towered church. Marwood House, Honiton's oldest building, dates from 1619 and contains one of many antique shops that thrive in this acknowledged centre of the trade. A 17th-century black marble tomb to Thomas Marwood, physician to Queen Elizabeth I, can be seen in the parish church above the town. Visitors to the local pottery can watch work being thrown on the wheel and hand painted. An unusual building known as Copper Castle stands by the side of old toll gates on the eastern outskirts.

Turn left into Honiton High Street (the Exeter road), and in ¾ mile turn left on to the A375 SP 'Sidmouth'. Ascend Gittisham Hill and continue to crossroads at the Hare and Hounds Inn. Turn right on to the B3174 SP 'Ottery' and descend into Ottery St Mary.

OTTERY ST MARY, Devon

Various literary figures are associated with this pleasant River Otter town. The poet Samual Taylor Coleridge was born here in 1772, and satirist William Thackeray set his novel *Pendennis* here (though he changed the name to Clavering St Mary). The magnificent collegiate church was modelled on Exeter Cathedral by Bishop Grandisson, and dates largely from 1337. Notable features include twin 14th-

Branscombe Mouth is an unspoilt beach protected by the National Trust.

century stalls and a curious Elizabethan clock. An annual carnival is held in the town on November 5.

Go forward through the town and at the end turn right onto the B3176 SP 'Fairmile'. Cross the river to reach Cadhay House.

CADHAY HOUSE, Devon

This fine Tudor and Georgian courtyard manor house dates mainly from 1550 and is open during the summer.

Continue to Fairmile, cross the A30, and follow SP 'Clyst Hydon'. Continue through farming country to Clyst Hydon and at the end of the village turn right SP 'Cullompton'. In ¾ mile turn left on to an unclassified road. SP 'Hele' then after a further 2 miles meet a junction with the B3185 and turn left then immediately right for Hele. Pass under the M5 motorway, drive over a level crossing and the River Culm, to enter Hele

Portuguese fishing boats are displayed along with many other vessels at Exeter's Maritime Museum.

then turn left. SP 'Silverton'. In ½ mile turn left then in 1¼ miles at crossroads go forward onto the B3185 SP 'Broad Clyst' and recross the River Culm near paper mills. Skirt Killerton Gardens on the right.

KILLERTON GARDENS, Devon

The Georgian Killerton House containing a fine collection of period costumes stands in magnificent 300-acre grounds covering a hilltop. There are many ancient beech trees and a fine 15-acre garden of rare trees and shrubs.

Follow SP 'Poltimore' then 'Exeter' and descend into the city of Exeter.

EXETER, Devon

With a population of 96,000 is the county town, and administrative and commercial centre of Devon. Founded by the Romans at the lowest crossing point of the River Exe, it is one of the oldest cities in England. The cathedral, with unusual Norman twin transeptal

towers, is mainly 14th-century, and the ancient guildhall has an elaborate late 16th-century facade. The modern university is on a hilltop site on the north side of the city and, despite the depredation of wartime bombing, attractive Georgian and earlier houses may still be found in many streets. The maritime museum at the head of the Exeter Canal on the south side of the city is of great interest, as are the Royal Albert Memorial Museum, the Devonshire Regiment Museum, 15th-century Tucker's.Hall, St Nicholas's Priory (AM), Rougemont House Museum, and the underground passages. Part of the Norman Rougemont Castle has survived, and stretches of the ancient city walls can still be seen.

Recross the M5 and turn right onto the B3181 SP 'Exeter'. Proceed through Broad Clyst to Pinhoe. Keep forward SP 'Ring Road' and in 1 mile at traffic signals bear left (Exeter City Centre is to the right) and at the next roundabout take 2nd exit SP 'Torbay, Plymouth'. Keep forward to reach Countess Wear Roundabout then take 1st exit unclassified SP 'Topsham'. In 1¼ miles pass under the M5 Exe Estuary viaduct and shortly enter Topsham.

TOPSHAM, Devon

Once an important seaport, Topsham stands on the Exe estuary and features 17th- and 18th-century Dutch-gabled houses. These fine buildings, mainly in the Strand, are reminders of a flourishing trade with Holland. One of them contains a local history museum in its sail loft.

Turn left, (for town centre keep forward) go over a level-crossing then bear right. Shortly cross the River Clyst then at the George Dragon PH turn left on to the A376 and continue to reach a roundabout at Clyst St Mary, and take the 3rd exit on to the A3052 'Lyme Regis' road. In 4¾ miles reach the Halfway Inn and turn right on to the B3180 for the return over Woodbury Common to Exmouth.

COAST TO COAST

From Falmouth and the gentle southern coast where land
and sea interlace in a maze of wooded waterways; inland
to Redruth, onetime centre of tin mining and still
Cornwall's industrial pulse; then northwards to jagged
cliffs constantly struggling with the fierce Atlantic.

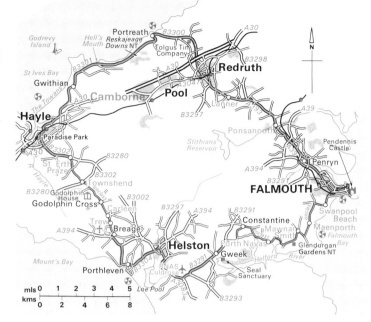

FALMOUTH, Cornwall
Falmouth has 2 distinct roles —
holiday resort and port — and
although tourism is more
prosperous now than shipping, the
harbour and docks remain busy.
The town stands at the entrance to
the Carrick Roads, a beautiful
stretch of water formed by the
merging of 7 river estuaries, and
has a huge natural harbour on one
side and sandy beaches and
gardens on the other. The port
really began to develop in the 17th
century when Falmouth was made
a Mail Packet Station, reaching its
heyday in the 19th century. At this
time it served as the hub of
communications for the British
Empire, and 39 ships were
despatching letters all over the
world. Unfortunately for Falmouth
the packet service was later
transferred to Southampton and
prosperity declined. However,
Falmouth's second role as a resort
developed rapidly when the
railway reached Cornwall and the
exceptionally mild climate assured
it year-round popularity. The long
main street of the town runs
beside the River Fal up from the
harbour and here the older, more
attractive, buildings are to be
found. The twin castles of
Pendennis (OACT) and St Mawes
(opposite Falmouth) once stood
stern guard over the entrance to
the Carrick Roads. They were built
by Henry VIII and Pendennis was
the last Royalist stronghold to fall
during the Civil War, having
valiantly withstood Cromwellian
armies for 5 months.

*Follow SP 'Beaches' and 'Helford
Passage', then 'Maenporth' and
'Mawnan'. Pass Swanpool Beach
and in ½ mile at the T-junction
turn left to Maenporth. In 1¼ miles
turn right for Mawnan Smith. At the
Red Lion Inn turn left, SP 'Helford
Passage', and in ¾ mile pass (left)
Glendurgan Gardens.*

GLENDURGAN GARDENS, Cornwall
A small, almost secret valley
descending to the Helford Passage
has been turned into an oasis of
exotic trees, flowers and shrubs.
The gardens (NT), including a
laurel maze, were originally
planted on these slopes in 1833 by
Alfred Fox. Three successive
generations continued to cultivate
the gardens which thrive in
southern Cornwall's almost sub-
tropical climate.

*Continue for nearly ½ mile then
turn right, SP 'Constantine'. After
1¼ miles turn left across a bridge,
continue to Porth Navas, and in
1½ miles turn left to Constantine.*

CONSTANTINE, Cornwall
The village of Constantine climbs
up a long, winding street and its
cottages, built of locally quarried
stone, are nearly all fronted with
neat, pretty gardens. Just to the
north, opposite Trewardrera
Manor, is an underground passage
imaginatively called Piskie Hall
(not open). It was part of a
prehistoric fortified enclosure and
is known as a fogou, the Cornish
word for cave.

*Continue through the village and
turn left, SP 'Gweek'. In 1 mile turn
right, then ½ mile farther join the
B3291 to reach Gweek.*

GWEEK, Cornwall
The tranquil banks of the Helford
River at Gweek have become a
sanctuary (OACT) for seals and
birds that have been washed up
around the Cornish coastline. Five
large open-air pools house the
animals in varying stages of
recovery and the seals in particular
are very appealing.

*Cross the Helford River and in 1¾
miles turn right on to the B3293,
then in ½ mile turn right again to
join the A3083, pass the Culdrose
Royal Naval Air Station and, in
another 1¾ miles turn left, SP
'Penzance', for Helston.*

HELSTON, Cornwall
At one time Helston, like most of
its neighbours, was a port.
However, when the Cober River
silted up in the 13th century the
town became landlocked and its
sea trading days ended. It was not
until the 18th century that Helston
gained importance once more,
this time as one of Cornwall's 4
official stannary towns, to which
all the smelted tin in the area had
to be taken for quality testing and
taxing. A stannary was a mining
district in Devon and Cornwall at
that time. Now this pleasant
market town is probably most
famous for its annual festival
called the Furry Dance, or Floral
Dance. In early May there is
continual dancing in the streets
and many people dress up in top
hats for the occasion. Folklore
claims the dance is a celebration
of the fact that no harm was done
when a dragon dropped a boulder
down on the town. Whatever its
origins, the custom certainly
stretches back thousands of years.
Among Helston's hilly streets and
grey stone houses is the Old Butter
Market, now serving as the town
museum. The small but interesting
collection here covers all aspects
of local history and includes an
old cider mill. Also of interest is the
Cornwall Aero Park and
Flambards Victorian Village, an all
weather family leisure park.
South-west of Helston is Loe Pool,
which, with a circumference of 7
miles, is Cornwall's largest lake. It
was formed about 600 years ago
when the Loe Bar cut the Cober
off from the sea. It is possible to
walk right round the lake (NT), but
the less energetic might content
themselves with a stroll through
the beautiful woodlands on the
lake's west side.

*Leave Helston on the A394
Penzance Road and then turn left
on to the B3304, SP 'Porthleven'.*

A creek of the Helford Passage

PORTHLEVEN, Cornwall
The sweep of Mount's Bay lies at the foot of this small rocky village perched above its harbour, which at one time sheltered many sea-going vessels. Now, ship-building yards are the mainstay of the village's economy.

At the harbour turn right then right again, SP 'Penzance'. In 1¼ miles turn left on to the A394 and 1 mile farther turn right, SP 'Carleen and Godolphin', to enter Breage.

BREAGE, Cornwall
Breage's church of St Breaca is of unusual interest. Built entirely of granite and dating originally from the 15th century, it contains wall paintings on the north wall depicting, amongst others, St Christopher and the Warning to the Sabbath-Breakers. Although as old as the church itself, these were not discovered until 1891. The churchyard has a sandstone 4-holed wheel cross with Saxon decoration.

At the T-junction in Breage turn left and continue through Trew and Carleen to Godolphin Cross.

GODOLPHIN CROSS, Cornwall
A Cornish family of diverse interests gave this tiny hamlet its name, and they occupied Godolphin House (OACT) from the 15th to late 18th century. Francis Godolphin was one of the first local landowners to finance tin mining; Sidney Godolphin was Queen Anne's 1st Minister for 7 years; and the 2nd Earl of Godolphin owned one of the 3 imported Arab stallions from which all British thoroughbred horses descend. The house itself is mainly 16th century and looks most impressive from the north side with its heavy colonnade. Of particular interest inside are the

Jacobean range with its fireplace and a painting of the famous Godolphin Arabian stallion.

At Godolphin Cross go over the crossroads and after ¾ mile pass Godolphin House on the left. In ½ mile bear right over the bridge and at Townshead cross the main road, SP 'Hayle'. In another 1¾ miles turn left on to the B3302 for St Erth Praze. Before entering Hayle a side road (left) may be taken to Paradise Park.

PARADISE PARK, Cornwall
Aviaries full of richly-coloured foreign birds such as the Hyacinthine Macaw and Great African Wattled Crane are the main attractions of this complex: others include a zoo for children, a miniature steam railway and a craft village.

Continue into Hayle.

HAYLE, Cornwall
During the 18th century, Cornish copper miners had to send ore to South Wales for smelting and Hayle developed as a port for this trade. Now it is mainly a light industrial town but there is a good bathing beach beyond the nearby sand dunes called The Towans.

At Hayle join the B3301 Redruth road, then in 1½ miles turn left SP 'Portreath'. Pass grass-covered sand dunes and continue to Gwithian.

GWITHIAN, Cornwall
There is no visible evidence of it in sea-facing Gwithian, but buried beneath the sands lies a small chapel, possibly dating back to Celtic Christianity when nearby Hayle was an arrival point for Irish saints. The chapel was uncovered during excavations in the last century but has sunk into oblivion once again through neglect. The present church was built in 1886.

From Gwithian the B3301 runs parallel with the coast to Portreath. There are several good viewpoints to the left within short walking distance of the road.

PORTREATH, Cornwall
At the bottom of bleak windswept cliffs nestles the small port and holiday resort of Portreath, consisting of a cluster of tiny harbour cottages around an 18th-century pier. The views from Reskajeage Downs (NT) above are spectacular.

From Portreath follow the B3300 Redruth road. After 2 miles, on the right, is the Tolgus Tin Company.

TOLGUS TIN COMPANY, Cornwall
A small part of 18th-century industrial Cornwall can still be seen at the Tolgus Tin Mill where the ancient practice of streaming — a process which involves washing the deposits of tin from the stream bed — has been carried out for generations. The

machinery which sifts and washes the extracted deposits includes the only Cornish stamps in commercial use. These heavy stamps, powered by the water mill, crush the ore so the tin can be separated from the waste. A small shop and visitor centre are open to the public.

Continue into Redruth.

REDRUTH, Cornwall
Camborne and Redruth have practically merged into one town and between them support the largest concentration of population in Cornwall. Redruth has always been at the centre of the mining industry and the town has remained primarily an industrial centre. Probably the most interesting aspects of this tradition are the engines displayed at nearby Pool. One of these is an 1887 winding engine which used to wind men as well as materials several hundred feet up and down copper and tin mine shafts. The other is an 1892 pumping engine, with a 52-ton beam used to pump water.

In Redruth turn left with the one-way traffic, then turn right and follow SP 'Falmouth' on the A393. Continue through Lanner to Ponsanooth, then in 1¾ miles go forward on to the A39 and skirt Penryn.

PENRYN, Cornwall
Almost everything that could be is built of granite here, and huge blocks of it from the Penryn quarries lie on the docks waiting to be shipped out of Cornwall. Penryn lies around the headland from Falmouth on another finger of the Carrick Roads, enjoying the same mild climate and luxuriant vegetation.

Return to Falmouth on the A39.

Hundreds of ships, including the *Nile* that cost many lives, were wrecked before Godrevy Lighthouse was built off Godrevy Point in 1859

WOOL, WEAVING AND WATER

The old wool towns and villages of Somerset and Wiltshire stud the valleys of the Rivers Frome and Avon. Blending harmoniously with the landscape is the warm-toned stone that takes its name from Bath, where it was used so effectively in the Georgian streets and squares that characterise the town.

FROME, Somerset
See page 101 for a description of this ancient wool town.

Leave Frome on the A361 Trowbridge road and continue to Beckington. Here join the A36, SP 'Bath', and continue to Woolverton. Beyond the Red Lion Inn, turn right and after ½ mile pass the Rode Tropical Bird Gardens.

RODE TROPICAL BIRD GARDENS, Somerset
Seventeen acres of trees, shrubs and lakes provide a setting for over 180 species of exotic birds. These include flamingoes, pelicans, cranes, vultures and cockatoos.

Continue and shortly pass the edge of Rode. At the crossroads turn right on to the B3109, SP Beckington, and in ¼ mile turn right again on to the A361. Pass Rode church and in just over ¼ mile turn left, SP 'Rudge' and 'Brokerswood'. In ½ mile at the T-junction, turn left. At the Full Moon PH in Rudge turn left and shortly turn left again. In ¼ mile, at the crossroads, turn right, SP 'Dilton' and 'Westbury'. Alternatively, continue with the North Bradley road to visit the Woodland Heritage Museum and Woodland Park.

WOODLAND HERITAGE MUSEUM AND WOODLAND PARK, Wilts
A lake alive with wildfowl lies in natural woodland which has been well laid out with nature walks. The natural history museum here, which includes a good forestry exhibition, provides interesting information about the park.

The main tour continues on the Westbury road and after 2 miles turn left on to the B3099, and shortly left again on to the A3098 for Westbury. Leave Westbury on the B3098, SP 'Bratton'. To the right is the Westbury White Horse.

WESTBURY WHITE HORSE, Wilts
Gleaming white on its hillside, the famous horse, carved into the chalk of Westbury Hill, dominates the landscape between Westbury and Bratton. The oldest of several in Wiltshire, this one is thought to commemorate King Alfred's victory over the Danes in AD 878. The elegant shape we see today, however, is an 18th-century remodelling of the original figure.

On the approach to Bratton turn left on to the unclassified Steeple Ashton road. After a mile, go over the crossroads and in a further ½ mile, at the T-junction, turn left and continue to Steeple Ashton.

STEEPLE ASHTON, Wilts
In medieval times, the village once had an important cloth market, and its name was originally Staple Ashton — taken from the wool staple (fibre). The market cross on the green stands next to an octagonal lock-up, where offenders were temporarily detained in the 18th and 19th centuries.

1 mile beyond the village turn left, SP 'Trowbridge', and later cross the A350 for Hilperton. Here turn left on to the A361, then take the next turning right on to the B3105. In 1¼ miles bear right and cross the Kennet and Avon Canal. Beyond Staverton turn left on to the B3107 for Bradford-on-Avon.

BRADFORD-ON-AVON, Wilts
Old houses of honey-coloured Bath stone line Bradford's steep, winding streets. The buildings range in style from late medieval to the elegant Georgian mansions erected by the wealthy cloth merchants. On the arched stone Town Bridge stands a chapel that for generations served as the town lock-up and near the river, in Barton Farm Country Park, stands a monumental 14th-century tithe barn (AM).

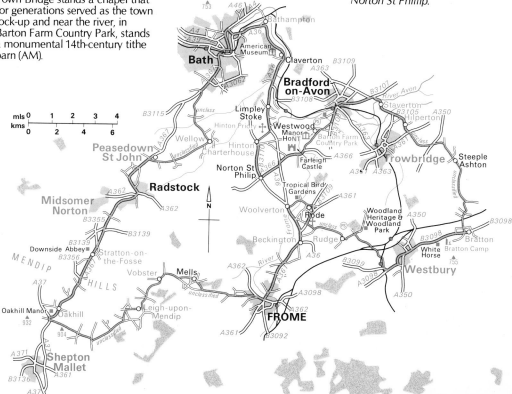

The White Horse of Westbury

From Bradford follow SP 'Frome', across the River Avon, then turn right on to the B3109. Cross the Kennet and Avon Canal, then in ½ mile branch right, SP 'Westwood'. In another ½ mile turn right to reach the edge of Westwood. At the New Inn PH turn left and to the right is Westwood Manor.

WESTWOOD MANOR, Wilts
Thomas Horton, a wealthy clothier, built the attractive stone manor house (NT) at the edge of the village in the 15th century. It contains a medieval great hall and the aptly named King's Room, whose panels are decorated with the portraits of 22 sovereigns up to Charles I. The outstanding feature of the gardens is the topiary work; one of the bushes is shaped like a cottage, and even has a doorway.

Continue along this narrow byroad for 1 mile, then turn right on to the A366, SP 'Frome', and continue to Farleigh Castle.

FARLEIGH CASTLE, Somerset
Only ruins remain of the castle (AM) built by Sir Thomas Hungerford in 1370. A later descendant, it is said, cruelly incarcerated his wife in the tower for 4 years and was himself executed for treason and 'unnatural vice' in 1540. A collection of armour and weapons is displayed in the chapel, including about 100 painted shields, a crusader's sword, and a scimitar.

Continue along the A366 and after 1 mile turn left then immediately right, SP 'Radstock', to reach Norton St Phillip.

During the 19th century it was a custom in rural America for a group of friends of a bride-to-be to weave a quilt for her trousseau. This one at Claverton Manor was made in Baltimore in 1845

NORTON ST PHILIP, Somerset
The George is one of the best preserved medieval inns in the country. Founded in the 13th century as a guesthouse for Hinton Priory, its half-timbered upper storey was added in the 15th century. The ruined priory nearby, founded in 1232, is the second oldest Carthusian house in England. Among the famous guests were the diarist Samuel Pepys, the rebel Duke of Monmouth and 'hanging' Judge Jeffreys who sentenced so many of the Duke of Monmouth's followers to death in the Bloody Assize of 1685.

At the George Inn turn on to the B3110 Bath road, and continue to Hinton Charterhouse. Here, at the 2nd crossroads, turn right (no sign). In ¾ mile, at the T-junction, turn left on to the A36 and continue to Limpley Stoke.

LIMPLEY STOKE, Wilts
The impressive arches of John Rennie's Dundas Aqueduct carry the Kennet and Avon canal across the river at Limpley Stoke. Rennie designed the canal and many of its bridges and aqueducts in the early 19th century.

Remain on the A36 and after 2 miles pass, on the left, the turning for Claverton.

CLAVERTON, Somerset
Claverton Manor (OACT), built in 1820, now houses an American museum. Period rooms and furnishings give a convincing picture of American domestic life from the 17th to the 19th century, and other exhibits include Shaker and Red Indian art.

The main tour continues along the valley of the River Avon to Bath.

BATH, Avon
Aquae Sulis to the Romans, Bath's warm, healing waters have been famous for more than 2,000 years. Parts of the original Roman baths can still be seen and the nearby museum displays a fascinating collection of Roman remains. The splendid abbey dates from the 15th century, but there has been a church here since Saxon times. Bath's heyday came in the 18th century when the dandy Beau Nash made the place fashionable. Wealthy citizens flocked to take the waters at the Pump Room and attend evening parties at the Assembly Rooms. From this period date the elegant squares, crescents and terraces that have made Bath the finest Georgian city in the country. Ralph Allen, who owned the quarries at Combe Down which provided the warm-toned Bath stone, commissioned a father and son, both named John Wood, to design Queen Square, the Circus and Royal Crescent. Later architects, including Robert Adam, who built Pulteney Bridge, completed the transformation of the city. No. 1 Royal Crescent, furnished in period, is open to the public. The Costume Museum in the Assembly Rooms displays an unrivalled collection and the Holburne of Menstrie Museum in Sydney Gardens has fine examples of china and glass.

Leave Bath on the A367, SP 'Exeter', and begin a long climb out of the city. At the roundabout at the top take the 2nd exit. In ½ mile turn left onto an unclassified road SP 'Wellow' and continue to Wellow. Turn right into the main street, SP 'Radstock', and after 3 miles turn left on to the A367 and later reach Radstock.

RADSTOCK, Somerset
This small, industrial town on a hilly site was a centre of coal-mining from the 18th to the early 20th century; the last pit closed in 1973. All that now remains of the industry are the neat rows of miners' cottages, and traces of disused railway lines and canals.

Leave on the A367 Shepton Mallet road and continue to Stratton-on-Fosse passing, on the right, Downside Abbey.

DOWNSIDE ABBEY, Somerset
The abbey was a Benedictine foundation and is now one of the leading Roman Catholic boys' public schools in England. A group of English monks, who had settled in France but were driven out during the French Revolution, founded it in 1814.

Continue on the Shepton Mallet/Yeovil road to Oakhill passing on the right Oakhill Manor.

OAKHILL MANOR, Somerset
Eight acres of attractive gardens, nestling in the Mendip Hills around Oakhill Manor (OACT), provide the setting for a magnificent miniature railway that covers ¾ mile. There is a museum here as well with numerous models of various modes of transport, all well displayed in an imaginative setting.

Remain on the A367 and in just over ½ mile turn left on to the A37, then almost immediately turn left again, SP 'Frome'. After 2 miles turn right then immediately left. In another 2 miles turn left again, SP 'Leigh-upon-Mendip. In ½ mile, at the T-junction, turn right for Leigh-upon-Mendip. Here, bear left with the Coleford/Radstock road, then keep forward, SP 'Vobster'. Enter Vobster and turn right on to the Mells road and follow SP 'Mells'.

MELLS, Somerset
Mells, with its well-kept cottage gardens, ranks as one of the prettiest villages in Somerset. The Elizabethan manor house (not open) once belonged to Abbot Selwood of Glastonbury, who, hoping to save the abbey from the Dissolution, sent the title deeds of the manor, concealed in a pie, to Henry VIII. John Horner is said to have stolen them and thus has been identified with Jack Horner of nursery-rhyme fame.

Follow SP 'Frome' and in 1¾ miles turn left. In 1 mile turn right on to the A362 for the return to the town centre.

Pulteney Bridge, Bath

GLOUCESTER, Glos

The Romans, the first to build here, created a fortified port as a springboard for their invasion of Wales, and the town later became one of the 4 *coloniae* from which Rome ruled Britain. Today Gloucester is still an inland port; a canal, opened in 1837, connects the city's docks with the River Severn and can accommodate ships of up to 1,000 tons. After the Romans left the Saxons occupied the town, and made it a *burgh*, but it was not until the Normans arrived that tangible evidence of occupation was left, for they brought with them the will and knowledge to create Gloucester Cathedral. Their church remains at the heart of the cathedral, and, as later generations added without destroying what had gone before, Gloucester preserves an unparalleled display of ecclesiastical architecture through the ages. Within the church the tomb of murdered Edward II and the glorious east window, which commemorates the Battle of Crecy in 1346, are renowned for their quality and beauty. The city retains as its main streets the 4 Roman roads which meet at the cross in the town centre. Along these ancient routes survive some old houses from Gloucester's past. A little square of medieval England remains in Northgate Street as the outer galleried courtyard of the timbered New Inn. In 1555, Bishop John Hooper spent his last night before being burnt at the stake in the house which now bears his name in Westgate Street. This splendid 16th-century building houses a superb folk museum, where trades and crafts of the past are displayed, along with numerous items of historical interest connected with the city and the county.

Leave the city centre on the A430, SP 'Bristol (A38)'. In 2¼ miles, at the roundabout, take the B4008, SP 'Quedgeley'. In ½ mile, turn right, SP 'Elmore'. After ¾ mile, at the River Severn, the famous Severn Bore can be seen during the spring and autumn high tides, when the bore waves force their way up the narrow estuary. In 1¼ miles, at the T-junction, turn right for Elmore.

ELMORE, Glos

Tucked away in the Vale of Gloucester is Elmore village, a gathering of cruck-framed barns and timbered, thatched cottages clustered about a church and a churchyard renowned for its 18th-century table tombs. Acanthus and hart's tongue fern decorate the wrought iron gates of Elmore Court (not open), a mostly Elizabethan manor with a Georgian wing. Built on ground which the Guise family has owned since the 13th century, the house is delightfully situated in a loop of the Severn.

THE VALE OF BERKELEY AND THE SEVERN VALLEY

Along the Vale of Berkeley, beside the River Severn, are flat fertile lands where cattle grew fat and lords built great houses. Higher up, on the Cotswolds, the land changes and becomes a chequerboard of stone-walled fields beneath limitless skies.

A Whooper swan taking off — just one of the 2,500-odd birds kept at the Severn Wildfowl Trust

In 1¼ miles turn left and continue to Longney. Here turn right, SP 'Saul and Frampton', then in ¾ mile, at the T-junction, turn right again for Epney. At Saul join the B4071 and in ¾ mile turn left across the swing bridge, then in ½ mile, at the crossroads, turn right to Frampton-on-Severn.

FRAMPTON-ON-SEVERN, Glos

The road splits a 22-acre village green bordered by Georgian brick houses. On the left lies 18th-century Frampton Court (not open) home of the Clifford family. In the grounds, beyond the chestnut trees which partly screen the house from the road, a delightful Gothic orangery by William Halfpenny overlooks a rectangular canal sunk in landscaped surroundings. The green ends past the duck pond and thatched and gabled houses converge towards the heart of the village. Here is the spacious church, and closeby is the Berkeley-Gloucester canal, and a canal keeper's house with a pedimented portico.

VALE OF BERKELEY, Glos

Some 700ft below the Cotswold escarpment lies the Vale of Berkeley, a great expanse of flat land beneath huge skies bounded by distant horizons: a rich area of fat cattle, orchards and old timber-framed dairy-farms. The thick deposit of clay, in places over 700ft deep, is a prime raw material for the manufacture of bricks and tiles.

Return to the B4071 and turn right, then in 1½ miles, turn right on to the A38, SP 'Bristol', and continue to Cambridge. In ¾ mile, turn right for Slimbridge. 1 mile beyond the village, cross the canal bridge for the Severn Wildfowl Trust.

SEVERN WILDFOWL TRUST, Glos

An area of flat marshland between the Gloucester and Sharpness canal and the River Severn has been reserved solely for birds. Their host is a Wildfowl Trust, founded in 1964 by Sir Peter Scott to study and preserve wildfowl throughout the world. This is one of the finest collections in the world, where some 180 species are kept out of the known 247. The Trust caters admirably for the visitor, and its real work of preservation and research has an unparalleled record which is well documented in the main hall. One example of the value of the work is the story of the Hawaiian goose. Only 42 birds were known to be alive in 1952, but since then, from 3 birds procured by Sir Peter Scott, more than 800 have been bred and either distributed to zoos or returned to their natural habitat in the wild.

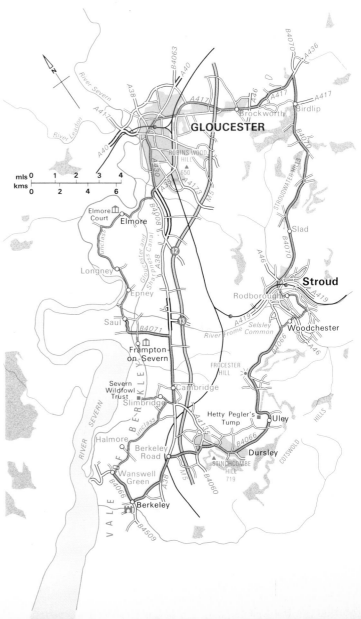

Return to Slimbridge and beyond the church turn right, SP 'Halmore', then in 1 mile, at the T-junction, turn right again. Follow a narrow byroad across flat countryside and after 2¼ miles turn left and immediately right for Wanswell Green. Here turn left on to the B4066 for Berkeley.

BERKELEY, Glos

A quiet Georgian town, Berkeley is dominated by 2 giants, Berkeley Castle from the past and an Atomic Power Station of the future. The castle (OACT) is a rugged sentinel of 900 years of English history, built in 1153 by permission of Henry I and home of the Berkeley family for centuries. It is still more a fortress than a stately home, and is best remembered for an act of violence. In 1327, Edward II was kept prisoner here and brutally murdered in the guardroom at the instigation of his wife and the Earl of Mortimer.

Follow SP 'Bristol' then keep forward, SP 'Gloucester', and in 1½ mile bear left to join the A38. At Berkeley Road turn right on to the B4066, SP 'Dursley'. In 2¼ miles turn right on to the A4135 for Dursley.

DURSLEY, Glos

Dursley's Market Hall of 1738, raised up on 12 arches of stone and graced by a statue of Queen Anne, keeps company with some elegant Georgian homes in a town which in recent years has experienced a flurry of new buildings and an influx of industry which has revitalised the community. The church has a 15th-century chapel, built of Tufa stone by a rich wool merchant, and a Gothic tower of the 1700s.

In Dursley turn left (one-way) and follow SP 'Stroud'. At the end of the town turn left on to the B4066 for Uley.

ULEY, Glos

Spilling down a hillside, distinguished houses of the 17th and 18th centuries are a legacy of Uley's success as a weaving community. Broadcloths, Spanish cloths and a blue dye of excellent quality were made here.

From Uley climb on to the Cotswolds. After 1½ miles, (left) is Hetty Pegler's Tump.

HETTY PEGLERS TUMP, Glos

Hetty Pegler's Tump (AM), is a Neolithic long barrow measuring 180ft by 90ft, where 28 people were buried in the stone-walled burial chamber. There are fine views over the Severn to the Welsh Mountains from the top.

Continue along a ridge, with good views, particularly at the Frocester Hill Viewpoint (NT). In 2¾ miles, turn right on to an unclassified road to Woodchester.

WOODCHESTER, Glos

One of the largest Roman villas found in England stood here, and in the churchyard a remarkable mosaic of Orpheus is occasionally on display, though it is mostly kept covered. The Industrial Revolution shaped the Woodchester of today and left it many fine clothiers houses, such as Southfield Mill House, and the Victorian mills which brought them prosperity.

Turn right on to the A46, then take the 1st turning left, SP 'Rodborough Common'. By the Bear Inn PH, turn left then left again, SP 'Rodborough', to cross the lofty Rodborough Common (NT). Descend through Rodborough before rejoining the A46 to enter Stroud.

STROUD, Glos

The River Frome and its tributaries powered 150 cloth mills here by 1824, and with the advent of steam, a canal was built to bring coal from the Midlands for the new machinery which brought Stroud into the forefront of England's broadcloth industry. The town still supplies most of the world's demand for greenbaize billiard table cloth. Stroud is also famous for its scarlet dyes, which were used to give the 'Redcoats' of the military their characteristic hue. Some of the old mills remain in this hilly town of narrow streets, though few of the wealthy clothiers houses have survived. The museum at Lansdown illustrates old methods of cloth weaving, many local crafts and past industries of the town. The Archaeological Room displays finds from barrows at nearby Rodborough and Nymphsfield.

Leave Stroud on the B4070, SP 'Birdlip', and gradually climb up to the Stroudwater Hills to Slad. Continue, to Birdlip. Turn right into the village then turn left on to the A417, SP 'Gloucester'. Magnificent views can be seen across the Severn Vale to the distant Malvern Hills. At the next roundabout take the 1st exit and return to Gloucester.

Above: a detail of the painting that decorates the inside of a wooden chest which belonged to Sir Francis Drake and is now kept at Berkeley Castle

Below: the cloisters of Gloucester Cathedral were built between 1351 and 1377

COVES OF THE LIZARD

Wreckers once used the jagged reefs and towering cliffs of the Lizard to cripple their prey. All round the peninsula's coast are stern little villages in rocky bays, towering stacks and pinnacles of multi-hued serpentine, and the constant boom of waves crashing into hidden caves.

HELSTON, Cornwall

In Elizabethan times Helston was one of Cornwall's 4 stannary or coinage towns, where all the smelted tin mined in the area was brought to be tested for quality and taxed. Even earlier it had been a busy port, until the Loe Bar formed across the mouth of the Cober River in the 13th century. Well-preserved Regency houses can be seen along Cross Street, and behind the early Victorian Guildhall is an interesting museum with many old implements, including a cider press. Local people would say that May 8 is the best day to visit the town, for that is the time of the Furry, or Floral Dance. From early in the morning the inhabitants dance through the winding streets and in and out of houses to celebrate the time a dragon dropped a rock on the town without causing any damage. About 1¼ miles south west of Helston, on the B3304, is a footpath leading left to Loe Pool.

CORNWALL AERO PARK & FLAMBARDS VICTORIAN VILLAGE, Cornwall

This is an award winning all-weather family leisure park with a large exhibition hall set in beautiful landscaped gardens. Flambards is an authentic life-size Victorian village. A special display covers Britain in the Blitz. The Aero Park has historic aircraft, vehicles, helicopters, Battle of Britain gallery, Concorde flight deck and an SR2 simulator.

Leave Helston on the A3083 SP 'Lizard'. Pass Culdrose Airfield and turn left on to the B3293, SP 'St Keverne'. The road to the viewing area is on the left in ½ mile.

CULDROSE ROYAL NAVAL AIR STATION, Cornwall

Navy search aircraft operate over a wide area of sea around Cornwall from this helicopter base. The public are only admitted to an aircraft viewing area.

Continue to the Mawgan Cross war memorial and branch left over crossroads on to an unclassifed road to Mawgan. Continue on the 'Manaccan, Helford' road, through St Martin's Green to Newtown. Keep left, then in 250yds turn left again. After another 1½ miles meet crossroads and go forward, then in ¾ mile turn left and descend to Helford.

HELFORD, Cornwall

This lovely little village on the wooded banks of the Helford River is a favourite haunt of anglers and yachtsmen. The river is dotted with small villages and creeks, and a passenger ferry sails from here to Helford Passage – where there is a bright, attractive inn.

Leave Helford and return along the same road for ¾ mile. Turn left for St Anthony.

The sheltered waters and hidden creeks of Helford River once made ideal bases for the secret activities of smugglers.

ST ANTHONY, Cornwall

The church of St Anthony in Meneage stands only 30yds from the creek. Its chancel and parts of the south wall are Norman, and tradition holds that it was built by shipwrecked Norman sailors as a thank-offering to St Anthony for saving them from drowning. The tranquil scenery of Gillan Creek presents a charming, timeless picture of Cornish maritime life.

Leaving St Anthony drive alongside the creek and after 1 mile turn left, SP 'St Keverne'. Climb to the edge of Gillan, keep right and follow signs for St Keverne.

A fisherman's cottage in Cadgwith.

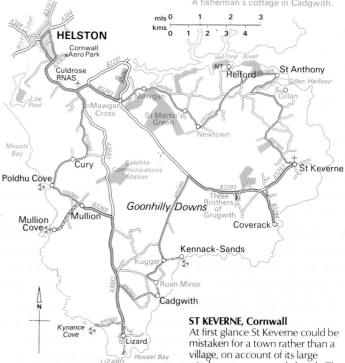

ST KEVERNE, Cornwall

At first glance St Keverne could be mistaken for a town rather than a village, on account of its large windswept square and church. The latter dates from the 15th century and carries an unusual octagonal spire which has been a welcome landmark for sailors for hundreds of years. Just 1 mile offshore are the treacherous Manacle Rocks, which have made shipwrecks a gruesome part of the village's history. Over 400 victims are buried at the church, including 126 people who died when the *Primrose* was wrecked in 1809. Two miles south-west is a Bronze-Age burial chamber known as the Three Brothers of Grugwith.

Leave St Keverne on the B3293 'Coverack and Helston' road. After 1¼ miles turn left on to an unclassified road and later join the B3294. From here descend into Coverack.

COVERACK, Cornwall

Smugglers once frequented this small fishing village, and wreckers lured unsuspecting vessels on to the Manacle Rocks to plunder their cargoes. Coverack formerly had a lifeboat station that was established after a particularly bad series of disasters. The harbour is overlooked by thatched cottages.

Climb out of Coverack on the B3294 'Helston' road, then join the B3293, and in 2½ miles at crossroads turn left on to an unclassified road SP 'Cadgwith'. Views to the right take in Goonhilly Downs Satellite Communications Station.

GOONHILLY DOWNS, Cornwall

Goonhilly Downs, a small windswept moor only about 7 square miles in area, was once covered by oak forests. Nowadays there is nothing here but a bleak stretch of gorse and heather dominated by the huge radio aerials of the Satellite Communications Station.

Drive over Goonhilly Downs for 3 miles and at Kuggar meet a T-junction. A detour from the main route leads left to Kennack Sands.

Goonhilly Downs Satellite Communications Station receives signals from all over the world.

KENNACK SANDS, Cornwall

Wide firm sands, wave-ribbed and dotted with large shallow pools at low tide, make this a perfect beach for families with children.

Turn right and in ¾ mile at crossroads, turn left for Ruan Minor. At the village turn right and make descent (1 in 4) to Cadgwith.

CADGWITH, Cornwall

Cadgwith's attractive thatched cottages overlook a stone strand dotted with beached boats and the paraphernalia of a working fishing community. All along the coast are sandy coves, and to the south is the great tidal chasm the Devil's Frying Pan. This was formed when a vast sea cave collapsed, and is at its scenic best in stormy weather.

Leave Cadgwith, continue with an unclassified road SP 'Lizard', and ascend. In ¾ mile turn right, then after another ¾ mile turn left on to the A3083 for Lizard.

LIZARD, Cornwall

A mile from Lizard is the headland of Lizard Point, the southernmost tip of a lovely peninsula that has become famous for its outstanding natural beauty (NT). In the heather and bogs of the interior rivulets and streams rise to chatter down to the beach through small valleys and, occasionally, as miniature falls over the edge of the cliffs. Many rare plants grow here, and some of the

area is leased to the Cornwall Naturalists' Trust. Splendid walks extend along the clifftops of the Point. To the east the countryside is sheltered from the full force of Atlantic gales and is lush and green, but round the Point to the west everything becomes wilder and more desolate. Much of the land on this side is pitted with holes left by people digging for the mineral serpentine, a lovely stone prized for the rich shades of greens, reds and purple released by cutting and polishing. Magnificent views from Lizard Point extend many miles along the Cornish coast to Rame Head, (near Plymouth), and when ideal conditions prevail, as far as Bolt Head in the South Hams district of Devon. This superb vantage point forms an ideal site for the Lizard Lighthouse.

Leave Lizard by returning along the A3083 SP 'Helston'. After ½ mile a detour can be made from the main route along a toll road to breathtaking Kynance Cove.

KYNANCE COVE, Cornwall

Serpentine is seen at its very best in Kynance Cove, where spectacular formations of the mineral rise in pillars, stacks, and pyramids from a flat surface of firm sand. An infinity of shades from red through to green, blue and purple lace exposed rock surfaces and ornament the insides of sea-bored caves. High above the surrealistic beach is a stark promontory that affords wonderful views along the coast. Slightly inland is a softer landscape of grass and flowers alongside small streams that eventually trickle from the cliff edge to the beach far below.

Continue with the main tour route on the A3083, and after 3½ miles turn left on to the B3296 for Mullion. From Mullion a possible detour from the main route leads left along the B3296 to lovely Mullion Cove.

Sea, rocks, and sand combine to create a spectacular seascape at Kynance Cove.

MULLION COVE, Cornwall

Almost as dramatic as Kynance, this superb cove is fringed by steep, cave-pocked cliffs that form a splendid counterpoint to rocky Mullion Island, just offshore. The small harbour (NT) here is used by local fishermen and visiting skin divers.

MULLION, Cornwall

Here the local rock changes from the colourful serpentine to greenstone, a very hard mineral that will spark when struck with steel. The village itself is large, with several shops, and boasts a fine 15th-century church. Notable bench ends inside the latter date from the 16th-century and depict a jester, a monk, Instruments of the Passion, and a few profiles.

At Mullion keep left (one-way) then turn right down an unclassified road for Poldhu Cove.

Mullion Cove is protected from Atlantic breakers by its sturdy harbour walls.

POLDHU COVE, Cornwall

A pleasant beach fringes the sheltered waters of this inlet. On top of the cliffs, which are composed of an unstable slate and clay mixture known as killas, the Marconi Memorial commemorates the first successful transatlantic radio signal in 1901. Some 22 years later this same spot was used for the testing of a short-wave beam system. At the beginning of the century the headland was covered in masts, aerials, wire, and sheds. All that remains now is the simple stone memorial and a few foundations.

Continue from Poldhu Cove, cross a bridge, and ascend to Cury.

CURY, Cornwall

The village church of St Corentin is set in a high windy churchyard and probably dates back to Norman times. It has since been added to.

Continue through the village and in ¼ mile turn left, SP 'Helston'. In 1¾ miles turn left again to rejoin the A3083. Return to Helston.

CORNWALL'S INTERIOR

Wild moorland once ridden over by highwaymen and trodden by smugglers: a landscape interrupted only by the ruins of an ancient past and lonely, forgotten mine workings: a landscape sometimes as savage or as moody as the better known coast.

LISKEARD, Cornwall
This small, busy town with several Georgian and Victorian buildings is well placed in east Cornwall as an agricultural and industrial centre. See page 77.

Leave Liskeard on the A390, SP 'Tavistock', and continue through Merrymeet to St Ive.

ST IVE, Cornwall
Eight centuries ago the Knights Templar built a hostel in St Ive and Trebeigh manor house (not open) now marks the site. They also founded the church, although the present building dates mainly from the 14th century.

Continue on the A390 then in 2¾ miles cross the River Lynher and continue to Callington. In 1½ miles pass the turning on the left to Kit Hill (toll).

KIT HILL, Cornwall
To the north of Callington is a magnificent 1,094ft viewpoint called Kit Hill. Its summit is marked by a modern radio mast and, in contrast, the old chimney stack of a derelict tin mine. Spread out below in a breathtaking panorama is the valley of the Tamar and the waters of Plymouth Sound.

There are more fine views from the A390 before reaching St Ann's Chapel. From here an unclassified road on the right leads to Cotehele House.

COTEHELE HOUSE, Cornwall
Cotehele (NT) is all a romantic, medieval house should be, and it seems suspended in that distant time. Its grey, granite walls surrounding 3 courtyards have scarcely changed since they were built between 1485 and 1627 by the Edgcumbes, nor have the furniture, tapestries and armour which grace the rooms altered. Colourful gardens of terraces, ponds and walls slope gently down to the Tamar and merge with the thick natural woodland of the valley. Cotehele Mill, the manorial water mill used for grinding corn, is here in full working order and Cotehele Quay on the banks of the river has some attractive 18th-and 19th-century boathouses.

Continue into Gunnislake. Beyond the town cross the River Tamar into Devon and climb out of the valley. In 1½ miles turn right on to an unclassified road and follow SP 'Morwellham'.

MORWELLHAM, Devon
At one time Morwellham was the busiest inland port west of Exeter and its active life spanning 900 years continued until the beginning of this century. The quays and docks on the River Tamar handled copper from nearby mines, which was then shipped to Tavistock. Now the area is preserved as an open-air industrial musuem (OACT) and an underground canal built to reach the ancient productive copper mine is just one of the fascinating things to see here amid lime kilns, waterwheels, riverside and woodland walks.

Return along the unclassified road and follow SP 'Tavistock'. On reaching the A390 turn right and continue to Tavistock.

TAVISTOCK, Devon
Tavistock's long industrial history began in the 14th century and today light industrial and timber firms keep the tradition going. Before the Dissolution, Tavistock's 10th-century Benedictine abbey was one of the richest in Devon, but little remains as evidence of this now. The town was granted to

The ancient borough of Liskeard is well-known for its monthly cattle fair

the Russell family (Dukes of Bedford), and they owned it until 1911. Of its 3 phases of industry — tin, cloth and copper — the latter had the most impact on Tavistock, although the 15th-century church was built with Devon serge profits. During the 19th-century boom the Dukes of Bedford virtually rebuilt the castellated town centre around Bedford Square and the result was a pleasant combination of architecture. With its weekly cattle and pannier market Tavistock is an attractive market town which makes an ideal touring base. Sir Francis Drake was born south of the town and a statue (of which a replica stands on Plymouth Hoe) commemorates him.

Leave Tavistock on the A384, SP 'Liskeard', and later pass the edge of Lamerton.

LAMERTON, Devon
A shady avenue of trees leads to the village church, the priest's house and the vicarage. The original church was practically destroyed by fire and the priest's house, now the church hall, was rebuilt in the 15th century. Two impressive monuments were saved from the church; one to the Tremaynes and one to the Fortescues. The Tremayne's home was Collacombe Manor (not open) — a lovely Elizabethan farmhouse just off the Launceston Road.

Continue to Milton Abbot.

Strange outcrops of granite, such as this one on Rough Tor, are scattered all over Bodmin Moor's bleak face

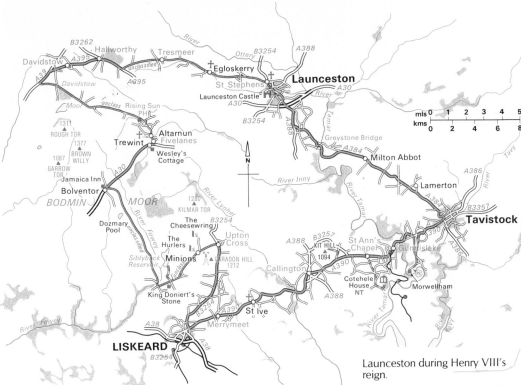

Continue to Fivelanes then turn right, SP 'Bodmin', and join the A30 to skirt the hamlet of Trewint.

TREWINT, Cornwall
John Wesley, founder of Methodism, spent some time in a small cottage here between 1744 and 1762. The cottage, restored in 1950, has been turned into a shrine to his memory and a Wesley Day Service is held here annually.

Remain on the A30 to Bolventor.

BOLVENTOR, Cornwall
On the outskirts of this tiny hamlet lies the inn made famous by Daphne du Maurier's novel *Jamaica Inn*. The lonely hostelry on the main highway across Bodmin Moor provided an ideal meeting point for smugglers in Cornwall's lawless past.

DOZMARY POOL, Cornwall
High up on Bodmin Moor, Dozmary Pool lends itself well to the many romantic legends associated with it. One of the most famous says that Sir Bedivere threw King Arthur's sword, Excalibur, into the pool at the King's request.

By the nearside of Jamaica Inn at Bolventor, turn left SP 'St Cleer'. Follow the Fowey River for 6½ miles then, at the crossroads, turn left. In ½ mile pass, on the right, King Doniert's Stone.

KING DONIERT'S STONE, Cornwall
A cross standing just off the main road bears a Latin inscription stating that 'Doniert ordered this cross for the good of his soul'. This may have been Dungarth, King of Cornwall in 875. Another Saxon cross stands next to it.

Continue on the unclassified road then in ¾ mile bear left to the village of Minions.

MINIONS, Cornwall
Near Minions, 3 stone circles make up a prehistoric monument (AM) known as the Hurlers. In the 15th century local people thought the stones were men who had been turned to stone as a punishment for hurling a ball on the Sabbath. Whatever their mysterious origin and purpose, the tops of the stones apparently needed to be on the same level. They were placed in pits of varying depths to achieve this and held in place with small granite boulders. Not more than a mile from the Hurlers on Stowe's Hill is a natural phenomenon called the Cheesewring. Encircling the summit of this strange stack of rocks is a stone rampart which once formed part of a fort — possibly Bronze Age.

Beyond Minions the tour passes a TV transmitting mast on Caradon Hill before descending to Upton Cross. Here turn right on to the B3254 for the return to Liskeard.

MILTON ABBOT, Cornwall
Tavistock Abbey used to own the village, but, like Tavistock, Milton Abbot was granted to the Russell family after the Dissolution. Similarities to the 19th-century architecture of Tavistock can be seen in the village which reflects the Russell's prosperity from copper and lead mining. Milton Green (just south) in particular has several attractive Gothic buildings, notably a Poor School and Schoolmaster's House which was a freehouse for the estate labourers' children. Endsleigh Cottage (now a hotel) is the romantically ornate house built in 1810 for the Dowager Duchess of Bedford.

Remain on the A384 and cross the River Tamar at Greystone Bridge to re-enter Cornwall. In 2 miles, turn right on to the A388. After crossing the Launceston Bypass go forward over the crossroads and enter Launceston.

13th-century ruins of Launceston Castle

LAUNCESTON, Cornwall
Arguably Cornwall's most appealing town, Launceston was the county capital until 1838. There was early settlement here because of the advantages offered by this elevated site, and the castle ruins (AM) show it to have been a Norman stronghold. The castle, erstwhile seat of William the Conqueror's brother, still has its huge round keep and from its walls great tracts of Cornish and Devonshire landscape can be surveyed. The grass below was a public execution site until 1821. Ancient, narrow streets surround the town's main square and among the many interesting Georgian buildings is Lawrence House (NT) in Castle Street. The rooms have been turned into a museum of local history now, but at one time the house was a well-known rendezvous for French prisoners on parole during the Napoleonic Wars. Narrow South Gate is the only evidence left of the town walls which encircled Launceston during Henry VIII's reign.

From the castle ruins follow SP 'Bude (B3254)'. At the bottom of the hill cross the river bridge and at the mini-roundabout go forward. At St Stephen's Church turn left SP 'Egloskerry'.

EGLOSKERRY, Cornwall
Cottages cluster around the little church which has been the village centre since Norman times. Much of the building has since been rebuilt, but the font has survived intact. On the walls hang memorials to the Specott family who lived a mile away at the large manor house called Penheale (not open) during the 17th century.

Continue along the unclassified road to Tresmeer and go forward with the Hallworthy road. In 2 miles turn right on to the A39 to reach the hamlet of Hallworthy. In 2¾ miles turn left on to the A39, then in another mile turn left again, SP 'Altarnun'. This byroad crosses Davidstow Moor with occasional views of Bodmin Moor to the right. In 5 miles, at the Rising Sun PH, bear left, then take the next turning right for Altarnun.

ALTARNUN, Cornwall
This, Cornwall's second largest parish, lies in a hollow on the edge of Bodmin Moor. Two little streams, crossed by a ford and a narrow bridge, flow through the village past the uneven stone walls of Altarnun's cottages. The church, nicknamed Cathedral of the Cornish Moors because of its size, is mainly 15th century. One of its best features is the collection of 16th-century carved bench ends depicting Tudor men and women, a piper, a jester, dancers, sheep and sheaves of corn.

LOOE, Cornwall

Now one resort, until 1883 West and East Looe were separate towns facing each other over the Looe River. Large beaches provide good bathing, surfing and angling, and Looe is Cornwall's main centre for shark fishing. The British International Sea Angling Festival is held here every autumn, and the captured sharks are subsequently chopped up and used as crab and lobster bait. West Looe has an attractive quay, and its focal point is the 19th-century church of St Nicholas, which was built mainly from the timber of wrecked ships. The tower of the church was effectively used at one time as a cage for scolding women. Nearby a 16th-century inn is renowned as a onetime haunt of smugglers. East Looe's museum is housed on the upper floor of the 16th-century guildhall (once used as a gaol), and downstairs the old town stocks and pillory can be seen. The narrow winding main street has little alleys and courts on one side leading to the quays. Near the Victorian warehouses is an aquarium which also has a stuffed shark and an old boat-building shed.

Leave on the A387 SP 'Plymouth via Torpoint'. In ½ mile branch right on to the B3253. In 3¾ miles rejoin the A387 and at Hessenford turn right on to the B3247, SP 'Seaton'. From Seaton an unclassified road on the right may be taken to the Woolly Monkey Sanctuary at Murrayton.

WOOLLY MONKEY SANCTUARY, Cornwall

South American woolly monkeys, Chinese geese, donkeys and rabbits live in this haven where there are no cages. Part of the wooded valley at Murrayton has been turned into a free-roaming sanctuary where visitors can observe these animals at close quarters (OACT).

From Seaton the main tour continues through Downderry and in 1¼ miles bears right. At Crafthole continue on the Millbrook road then in 2 miles turn right SP 'Whitsand Bay'. After 3 miles veer inland to reach the outskirts of Cawsand and Kingsand.

CAWSAND AND KINGSAND, Cornwall

As the streets of these twin villages run into each other it is hard to distinguish between them. Before the Plymouth breakwater was built, Cawsand Bay was an ideal place for the Royal Naval fleet to anchor in the 18th century and the wealth that they bought accounts for the many fine houses in the villages. The pubs too date from these prosperous times and Lord Nelson and Lady Hamilton used to stay at the Ship Inn.

SOUTH-EASTERN CORNWALL

Between Bodmin Moor and the Channel lies the high tableland of south-east Cornwall, its surface cut by deep wooded valleys branching into the sea. Two former capitals of the ancient royal Duchy lie within this peaceful region: the tiny cathedral 'city' of St Germans and the old stannary town of Lostwithiel.

Keep left and in ½ mile turn left, SP 'Millbrook'. At the top of the ascent turn left again on to the B3247. Alternatively, turn right to visit Mount Edgcumbe House and Country Park.

View from the long-distance coastal path, near Polperro

MOUNT EDGCUMBE HOUSE AND COUNTRY PARK, Cornwall

Facing Plymouth across the Sound is Mount Edgcumbe House. First built in the 16th century, it was a victim of the 1941 Plymouth Blitz and afterwards was restored as a Tudor mansion. The house, home of the Earl of Mount Edgcumbe, has fine Hepplewhite furniture, much of which came from the Edgcumbe family's original home, Cotehele. Most of the large estate has been turned into a country park and it provides scenic walks along 10 miles of beautiful coastline.

The main tour continues to Millbrook. Here turn left, SP 'Torpoint', then bear right. In 2¾ miles turn right and later descend to Antony. From here another detour can be made by turning right on to the A374 Torpoint road to Antony House.

ANTONY HOUSE, Cornwall

This dignified, silvery-grey Queen Anne mansion (NT) overlooks the Lynher River Estuary just over the water from Plymouth. The house is well known for its associations with the Cornish Carew family who played an active and often dangerous part in political affairs. Richard Carew wrote *Survey of Cornwall* in 1602, and it provides a unique record of the county during those days. The house is currently lived in by the Carew descendants and with its small, panelled rooms has more the air of a country home than a showplace.

From Antony follow the A374 Liskeard road, and continue through Sheviock to Polbathic. Here turn right on to the B3249, SP 'St Germans'. In 1 mile bear left, SP 'Saltash', to enter St Germans.

ST GERMANS, Cornwall

Until 1043 when the Cornish Bishopric merged with Exeter, this little village was Cornwall's cathedral 'city'. During the following century St Germans was recognised as an Augustinian priory and the existing church was consecrated in 1261. Much of this building has survived and stands as one of Cornwall's best examples of Norman architecture. The turreted house (not open) quite separate from the church, has been the home of the Earls of St Germans, the Eliots, since 1655. It was rebuilt about 1804 although the grounds were laid out 10 years

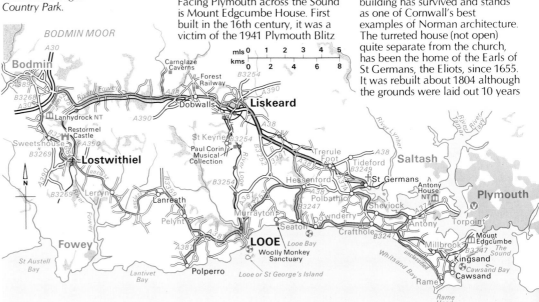

One of the Forest Railway's locos

earlier by the famous landscape gardener Humphry Repton. Of particular interest in the village itself are 6 gabled almshouses. The projecting gables stand on tall stone piers, forming a balcony which may be reached by an outside flight of steps.

At the far end of the village branch left, SP 'Liskeard'. In 1 mile go over the crossroads and in another ¾ mile turn right on to the A374. At the roundabout take the 2nd exit to join the A38. Follow this trunk road for 5½ miles before branching left on to the A390 to reach Liskeard.

LISKEARD, Cornwall
Liskeard's site across a valley accounts for its steep, narrow streets. It is a pleasant market town with a large monthly cattle fair and was one of Cornwall's 4 stannary towns. Among Liskeard's (pronounced Liscard) attractive buildings is Stuart House, where Charles I slept for a week during 1644. Well Lane is so named because a spring there, Pipe Well, was supposed to have healing properties in medieval days. Four pipes from an arched grotto produce a continual flow of water.

A 2½ mile diversion south of Liskeard leads to the Paul Corin Musical Collection at St Keyne Station. The best approach is via the B3254 and an unclassified road, SP 'St Keyne'.

PAUL CORIN MUSICAL COLLECTION, Cornwall
This fascinating collection of mechanical musical instruments founded by Paul Corin at St Keyne is housed in an old mill. Examples from all over Europe can be seen here, including fairground organs, cafe and street organs and pianos. The exhibits are all played daily, and there are European cafe orchestrations and piano performances of famous pianists to be heard.

From Liskeard the main tour follows SP 'Bodmin' and then rejoins the A38 to Dobwalls.

DOBWALLS, Cornwall
Just north of the village run 2 miles of elaborate miniature railway line. This is the Forest Railway and it is based on the steam era of the American railroad and the corresponding landscape includes lakes, forests, tunnels and canyons. In addition, the Park has an indoor railway museum, a railway walk, and play and picnic areas. Next door, in a large converted barn, is a different source of interest — the Thorburn Museum and Gallery. Here are the works of Archibald Thorburn, one of Britain's greatest bird painters (1860-1935), as well as sketches, books, letters and photographs which make up a permanent memorial exhibition to the artist.

Remain on the Bodmin road and descend into the Fowey valley. After crossing the River Fowey a road on the right, SP 'St Neot', leads to Carnglaze Slate Caverns.

CARNGLAZE SLATE CAVERNS, Cornwall
Slate has been quarried from these caves (OACT) since the 14th century and it has been traditionally used as a roofing material; now it is used more widely for all types of building. One of the caverns is 300ft high and the original tramway built to haul the stone to the surface can be seen here. Deeper into the quarry is a clear greenish-blue underground lake and lichen on the surrounding rocks reflects the light.

Continue on the A38 for 5 miles before recrossing the River Fowey. After 1½ miles, at the crossroads, turn left, SP 'Lostwithiel. In another 1½ miles turn left again on to the B3268 passing, on the left, the entrance to Lanhydrock.

LANHYDROCK, Cornwall
Lanhydrock (NT) suffered badly from a fire in 1881 so there is little of the original building left, although the house was rebuilt to the same plan. However, the charming 2-storeyed gatehouse and north wing did survive and the long gallery, 116ft long, in the latter is particularly splendid with its ceiling of intricately carved plasterwork depicting biblical scenes. The estate is approached down a long avenue of beech and sycamore, some 4 centuries old. Formal gardens lie close to the house featuring rose-beds, yew hedges and some bronze vases by Ballin, goldsmith to Louis XIV.

Remain on the B3268 Lostwithiel road and at the hamlet of Sweetshouse keep left and continue to Lostwithiel.

LOSTWITHIEL, Cornwall
Lostwithiel, with Helston, Truro and Liskeard, is another of Cornwall's 4 stannary towns, and was also the county capital in the 13th century. The former stannary offices and county treasury in Quay Street occupied a great hall and there are still remains of this 13th-century building. Overlooking the Fowey valley a mile away is Restormel Castle (OACT), where Edmund, Earl of Cornwall, ruled the county. It has been a ruin since it was abandoned in the 16th century, having been used for a time by Parliamentarian forces.

From the centre of Lostwithiel turn right into Fore Street (one-way) and at the end turn right across the River Fowey and go over the level crossing. In ¼ mile, at the crossroads, turn right for Lerryn. At the Post Office keep left, then take the next turning left, 'SP 'Polperro'. In ¾ mile go over the crossroads and follow this narrow byroad for another 1½ miles where, at the T-junction, turn left. In 2 miles turn right to enter Lanreath.

LANREATH, Cornwall
There is an extremely interesting farm museum (OACT) in Lanreath featuring farm machinery from the past. Vintage tractors, engines and

Polperro, smuggling haven during the 18th century

old farm implements, such as a turnip and cattle cake cutter and grappling irons, are just some of the things to see and sometimes there are demonstrations of traditional rural crafts including spinning and the making of corn dollies.

At the church keep left and then turn right on to the B3359 for Pelynt. In 1½ miles turn right, SP 'Polperro', then right again on to the A387 for Polperro.

POLPERRO, Cornwall
All Polperro's tiny streets and alleyways lead down to the harbour tucked into a fold in the cliffs, well protected by timber and masonry from the savage onslaught of Atlantic winter storms. Lime-washed cottages seem to grow out of the rock one on top of another, understandably attracting artists wishing to capture the true flavour of Cornwall. The Land of Legend and Model Village (OACT) gives a fascinating glimpse of old Cornwall all through the medium of animated models.

Return along the A387 to complete the tour at Looe.

LYME REGIS, Dorset

Beautiful Lyme Regis, set in lovely scenery with the River Lym running swiftly through the town, was one of the first seaside towns on the south-west coast to become a popular resort in the 18th century. Its history as a port goes back much further, however, to medieval times when the picturesque old harbour round the Cobb was first built. Lyme Regis saw the first battle of the Armada in 1588 when local ships joined Drake's fleet in a skirmish with some of the Spanish galleons. Among the town's distinguished visitors in the 18th century was Jane Austen, who loved Lyme Regis and set part of her last novel, *Persuasion,* in the old port. Shingly Lyme Bay is sheltered by cliffs rising to the magnificent Golden Cap, the highest cliff on the south coast. The area is noted for fossils and there is a fine collection in Lyme Regis museum.

Leave on the A3070 Axminster road and ascend to Uplyme.

UPLYME, Devon

Old stone cottages set in a fold of the hills behind Lyme Regis form a pleasant village street overlooked by the church, built on a hilltop from where there are glorious views westwards of the Devon landscape. In the church, near the Jacobean pulpit, is an engraved glass memorial to 2 children by the modern artist Lawrence Whistler.

In 2¼ miles turn left on to the A35 and continue to Axminster.

AXMINSTER, Devon

Some of the finest British carpets come from this delightful, busy, market town which lies on a rise of ground above the River Axe. The Axminster carpet industry was founded in 1755 by Thomas Whitty, who had made a thorough study of Turkish craftsmanship and built his factory in the town centre. Many luxurious carpets were specially woven for the great stately homes of England and the business flourished for 80 years, rivalling Wilton for its superb creations. In 1835, however; the Axminster factory went bankrupt and was bought out by a Wilton weaver. Not until 1937 was the business revived in new premises, where visitors are welcome. Bow-fronted Georgian and early Victorian houses lend charm to Axminster's bustling streets leading up to a shady green where the church looks out over the attractive town centre with its many coaching inns.

Leave on the A358 Chard road and in 3¼ miles pass through Tytherleigh and ½ mile farther turn right on to the B3167, SP 'Crewkerne'. After another 1½ miles, at the end of Perry Street, an unclassified road on the right may be taken to visit Forde Abbey.

SOMERSET TOWNS AND DEVON VILLAGES

Where the south coast cliffs sweep down to the sea around Lyme Bay and the charming seaside resort of Lyme Regis, and the ever changing vista of hills and vales reveals a pageant of historic towns and delightful villages.

The harbour at Lyme Regis

FORDE ABBEY, Dorset

Cromwell's Attorney General Sir Edmund Prideaux acquired this lovely 12th-century Cistercian monastery in 1649 and transformed it into a country house. Among its many treasures are the 5 Mortlake tapestries woven in the early 18th century to fit the walls of the saloon. The tapestries represent Raphael cartoons now in the Victoria and Albert Museum in London. Water and rock gardens are a special feature of the extensive grounds.

The main tour continues on the B3167 and in 3 miles turns right on to the A30 for Cricket St Thomas.

CRICKET ST THOMAS, Somerset

Llamas, camels, bison and wallabies roam incongruously in the landscaped parkland of a Georgian mansion, set in a secluded valley sheltered beneath the aptly named Windwhistle Ridge. Gardens and terraces lead down to a sequence of 9 lakes where flamingoes wade and black swans glide gracefully among a colourful variety of waterfowl. Cricket St Thomas is the home of the National Heavy Horse Centre and a small zoo, aviary and dairy farm add to the interest of the estate, which once belonged to the Bridport family who were connected by marriage to Lord Nelson.

DOWLISH WAKE, Somerset

Standing in the middle of the village is a thatched 16th-century barn (OACT) which belongs to Perry Bros., the famous cider producers. Here the past is recalled by a collection of farm machinery, wagons, cider presses, etc., now, sadly, replaced by more modern equipment. Cider is made on the premises during the autumn after the harvest of locally grown apples and is traditionally matured in wooden barrels under a watchful expert eye. It is for sale in the shop, together with numerous interesting gift items such as stone cider jars, corn dollies and ovenware.

The main tour continues to Ilminster. Join the A303, then branch left for the town centre.

ILMINSTER, Somerset

From the top of Beacon Hill it is said that 30 church towers and spires can be seen. That of Ilminster church, modelled on the central tower of Wells Cathedral, must be among the loveliest. Ilminster, nestling at the foot of the Black Down Hills, hides its prettiest streets away from the main roads and thatched cottages lead to a square built around a pillared market house.

Leave on the A3037 Chard road, then in 2 miles turn left on to the A358. After 1¼ miles, on the right, is Hornsbury Mill Museum.

Remain on the A30 for 2½ miles, then turn left on to an unclassified road, SP 'Ilminster'. After 3¼ miles, at the hamlet of Kingstone, bear right. Alternatively keep forward, then take the next turning left to visit Dowlish Wake.

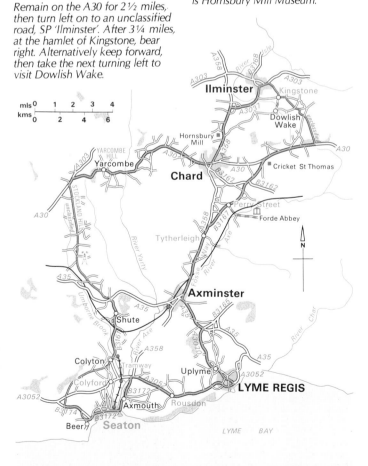

The 1,000-acre estate around Cricket House has been turned into a magnificent wildlife park

HORNSBURY MILL MUSEUM, Somerset

A splendid water wheel 18ft high dominates this 19th-century corn mill (OACT) which is kept in immaculate working order. The mill stands in attractive grounds and has a small museum of country bygones, a craft shop, and cream teas are available.

Continue on the A358 to Chard.

CHARD, Somerset

The long main street of Somerset's highest town is bordered by 2 streams, one flowing north to the Bristol Channel, the other south to the English Channel. The handsome Guildhall faces a charming Elizabethan building, once the town's manor house, where the old court room on the 1st floor can be visited. Here the infamous Judge Jeffries presided during the Bloody Assizes that followed the Duke of Monmouth's rebellion.

Leave on the A30, SP 'Exeter', and follow an undulating road to Yarcombe.

YARCOMBE, Devon

The lovely scenery of the Yarty Valley provides the setting for this graceful village. In the 15th-century church is a rare Breeches Bible (see Aylesham tour) and the carving on the bench ends is particularly fine. Almost within the churchyard, the charming village inn may well once have been the Church House.

SHUTE, Devon

A castellated 16th-century gatehouse forms the entrance to the medieval manor house of Shute Barton (NT) of which 2 wings remain. In the kitchen, the enormous hearth holds a spit large enough to roast 2 oxen. The house was once owned by Henry Grey, Duke of Suffolk and father of Lady Jane Grey, the tragic Nine Days Queen whose reign lasted from July 9 to 19 1553. She was condemned for treason and executed by order of Mary I in February 1554.

Continue on the B3161 to Colyton.

COLYTON, Devon

Pretty houses and cottages, mostly of the 17th and 18th centuries, line the narrow streets that wind up the slopes of the hillside where Colyton was founded by the Saxons in AD 700. The vicarage, the grammar school and the fine Great House, with its chequerboard frontage, all date from the Tudor period, when the manor of Colyton was bought by local inhabitants from Henry VIII. They called themselves the Chamber of Feoffees and this name has been preserved by the town authorities ever since.

At the town hall keep left, then turn right into Queen Street. Shortly turn left again on to the unclassified Sidmouth road. Nearly 3 miles farther (at Stafford Cross) go over the staggered crossroads, then at the next crossroads turn left on to the B3174, SP 'Beer', and continue to Beer.

Continue on the A30 and in 2 miles, at the A303 junction, keep left, then take the next turning left, SP 'Axminster'. Later pass the TV mast on Stockland Hill and at the A35 junction turn right, then immediately left on to the B3161 and continue to Shute.

BEER, Devon

Up on the slopes behind the seaside village of Beer runs Beer Heights Light Railway. This steam-operated passenger line travels through the Peco Modelrama park and fine views are to be had of the bay below along the way. There is even a full-size replica railway station with refreshments. Nine separate model railways are on permanent show around the house and gardens and there are souvenir and model shops to browse around.

The main tour turns left on to the B3172 to Seaton. On entering the town follow SP Sea Front. At the end of the Sea Front turn left, then turn right on to the B3172 and cross the River Axe. Follow the Axe estuary to Axmouth.

AXMOUTH, Devon

Thatched, colour-washed cottages and an old inn, grouped around the church, make up the unspoilt village scene at Axmouth. Once a busy port, situated at the point where the Roman Fosse Way crossed the river, Axmouth has seen the Axe estuary gradually silt up, today allowing passage for yachts and pleasure boats only. In 1877 the first concrete bridge in England was built across the Axe.

In 1 mile, at Boshill Cross, turn right on to the A3052 for the return to Lyme Regis.

Much of Forde Abbey's original medieval stonework can be identified in the present Tudor mansion

LYNTON, Devon

This pleasant and very popular resort is sited high on a cliff some 500ft above its sister village of Lynmouth. Tree-covered Summerhouse Hill shields it from the blustery sea gales, and a solid ring of hills protects it from the worst of Exmoor's rain. The Victorians were quick to recognize these attributes as being suited to seaside holidays, and since then the resort has attracted a constant stream of visitors. Victorian architecture predominates here, and a typical eccentricity of that era is the water-powered cliff lift. This was donated by a lawyer named George Newnes in 1890, and has been restored to working order. Newnes also built the Town Hall, behind which rise the flower-strewn slopes of viewpoint Hollerday Hill. Miles of coastline and the Exmoor hills can be seen from here. Other features of Lynton include a Catholic church containing rare and beautiful marble work, and the Lyn and Exmoor Museum in old St Vincent's Cottage. The local cliffs afford views across the Bristol Channel to Wales, and the magnificent Valley of the Rocks is accessible by footpath.

VALLEY OF THE ROCKS, Devon

The poet Robert Southey described this fantastic place of jagged tors and breathtaking coastal scenery with the words '. . . rock reeling upon rock, stone piled upon stone, a huge terrific reeling mass'.

Descend Lynmouth Hill (1 in 4) to Lynmouth and turn right on to the A39 'Barnstaple' road for Watersmeet.

WATERSMEET, Devon

As its name suggests, this National Trust beauty spot is the place where the tumbling waters of the East Lyn River converge with the Hoaroak Water, which cascades down a rocky bed in a series of waterfalls. It is best to leave the car and explore the cool beauty of this wooded gorge on foot.

Continue alongside the Hoaroak Water for ½ mile then turn left on to the B3223 SP 'Simonsbath'. Cross Hillsford Bridge, and in ¾ mile go round a hairpin bend and drive forward on to an unclassified road SP 'Brendon Valley'. Pass Brendon Church, with views of the tree-covered slopes that characterize this area, then descend through the oak-wooded valley of the East Lyn River for Brendon.

BRENDON, Devon

This picturesque village is situated on the banks of the East Lyn, which is spanned here by an attractive medieval packhorse bridge.

Continue alongside the East Lyn River to Malmsmead

MALMSMEAD, Devon

Ponies can be hired here for a 2½ - mile trek along the deep valley of Badgworthy Water, leading to the legendary Doone Country. The journey can just as easily be undertaken on foot.

INTO THE DOONE COUNTRY

Before they come here many people half believe Blackmore's romantic novel 'Lorna Doone' to be a true historical account. By the time they leave, the region's gorse and heather covered moors, wooded ravines, and exquisite little stone villages have convinced them of it.

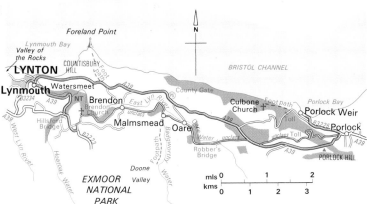

DOONE VALLEY, Devon & Somerset

R D Blackmore immortalized isolated and beautiful Hoccombe Combe as 'Doone Valley' in his famous novel *Lorna Doone*. Thanks to his brilliantly emotive style this has become one of the most romantic places in the country, and many visitors go away firmly believing that the whole tale was actually a true historical account. Tales of a villainous Doone family who terrorized the moorfolk have been told here since 1790. It appears that Blackmore seized on these as a handy base for his novel,

and although he did not concentrate on authentic landscape description, several features can be identified from his text. Lanke Combe enters the valley from the west and has miniature versions of features attributed to Doone Valley by the author, including the famous waterslide. Records show that the remains of several buildings in this area belonged to a medieval settlement, but the name Doone is not mentioned. With or without the legend, this is a beautiful area that should not be missed.

EXMOOR NATIONAL PARK (NORTH), Devon & Somerset

In its northern reaches this vast national park meets the sea with magnificent results. Rugged hogs-back cliffs stretch continuously from Lynton to Porlock, falling steeply to the waters of the Bristol Channel and affording views across to the coast of South Wales. Lush coombs wind deep into rambling moorland, scattered here and there with tiny hamlets and picturesque villages. The burgeoning life of the valleys makes a striking contrast with the remote and heather-clad wastelands through which they cut, but together these opposites form a landscape that could be nowhere else but Exmoor. Agriculture and forestry play a large part in the park's life, and the rich patchwork of farmland in areas like the Porlock Vale are sharp reminders that this is more than just a place of outstanding natural beauty. Wildlife abounds on Exmoor. The shy red deer that haunt its wooded coombs are unique in being direct descendants of the wild deer that once roamed prehistoric Britain. Common mammals thrive in a variety of habitats, and the park boasts many species of birds. Vestiges of prehistoric ages can be found in the form of earthworks, tumuli, standing stones, and barrows. Of particular note is the stone circle on Porlock Hill, but there are many other fascinating examples easily reached from Lynton.

From Malmsmead cross a river bridge into Somerset and continue to Oare.

OARE, Somerset

This tiny Oare Valley hamlet stands by the Oare Water and has strong connexions with the fiction of R D Blackmore. It was here that his heroine Lorna was married, and here that she almost met an untimely end. The village church is a lovely little 15th-century building well suited to the magical tale that has been woven around it. Inside are 19th-century boxpews and a curious piscina shaped like a man's head. Exceptionally fine coomb scenery with wooded valleys and steep screes surrounds the area.

Follow the road SP 'Oareford, Robber's Bridge' for 1¼ miles. Cross the bridge and continue the steep ascent to join the A39. Proceed along a scenic moorland road, with fine views across the Bristol Channel, and reach Porlock Hill.

PORLOCK HILL, Somerset

The notorious incline of this hill as it rises from Porlock is one of the steepest in Britain, and the breathtaking view from its summit surpasses many. A prehistoric stone circle survives close by.

Make a steep and winding descent (1 in 4) into Porlock.

Rain and mist add extra dimensions of beauty and mystery to Northern Exmoor.

PORLOCK, Somerset

Saxon Kings chose the site of this enchanting coastal village as a base from which to hunt in Exmoor Forest, and nowadays it serves as an ideal touring centre. A famous riding school is established here, and it is difficult to venture far without meeting horses and riders. Notable buildings in Porlock include 15th-century Doverhay Manor House and a mainly 13th-century red-stone church containing the tomb of one John Harrington, who is said to have fought at Agincourt. This remarkable monument is topped by almost life-size effigies of Harrington and his wife. Like many of its neighbours Porlock attracted an artistic following bent on recording its delights in paint and verse. Robert Southey the poet was obviously disenchanted with the weather when he stayed at the Ship Inn and wrote: 'Porlock, I shall forget thee not, here by the unwelcome summer rain confined . . . .'

Leave the village on the B3225 and drive to Porlock Weir.

Lynmouth Bay is overlooked by the cliff mass of Blackhead and the ancient earthworks on Wind Hill.

Culbone Church occupies a delightfully wooded position beside a stream.

PORLOCK WEIR & CULBONE CHURCH, Somerset

In years gone by Porlock was a thriving port, but all that remains today is the miniature harbour of this unique little Porlock Bay hamlet. Pleasure craft make good use of its sheltered waters, and its shingle beach is backed by cliffs cloaked with thick woodland. A pleasant walk leads from here to Culbone, where can be seen the smallest English church still in regular use. The building displays Norman and later styles, and measures only 33 by 13½ft. Inside are old benches and a 14th-century screen, while all around are woods and pits once used by a charcoal-burning community.

Return to Porlock and take the 'Lynmouth' road, then branch right on to an unclassified road SP 'Alternative Route via Toll Road' and climb gradually to open moorland. Meet a main road and turn right on to the A39, re-entering Devon at County Gate with a picnic site to the left. After another 2¼ miles reach a footpath leading right to Foreland Point.

Out of season Porlock Weir once more becomes a quiet fishing hamlet.

FORELAND POINT AND LIGHTHOUSE, Devon

The footpath to this lighthouse runs through magnificent coastal scenery (NT) and affords extensive views of the Bristol Channel.

Continue to Countisbury Hill.

COUNTISBURY HILL, Devon

Stagecoach drivers had to change horses at the ancient inn on top of this exceptionally steep hill. West of the inn prehistoric earthworks (NT) overlook the sea and superb cliff walks can be made beyond the small local church.

Descend Countisbury Hill (1 in 4) to Lynmouth.

LYNMOUTH, Devon

In 1812 the poet Shelley and his 16-year-old bride were captivated by the beautiful little fishing village that stood here. Since then tourism and a rash of boarding houses have given it a new lease of commercial life, but the basic framework of towering cliffs and swirling river valleys remains. Disastrous floods that made national headlines in 1952 swept away part of the quay, a great deal of the resort, and a curious edifice known as the Rhenish Tower. Afterwards the East and West Lyn rivers were widened, and strong walls built to prevent a recurrence of the tragedy. This tidying up included the rebuilding of the tower, which is supposed to resemble a type found in Germany and was originally constructed to store salt water for indoor bathing. The picturesque lower town is a medley of colour-washed cottages clustered amid gardens bright with roses, fuchsias, and other shrubs.

Ascend Lynmouth Hill and return to Lynton.

HIGH DOWNS AND HOCKTIDE REVELS

The bare uplands of the Marlborough and Berkshire Downs overlook open, windswept country, while the lush lowlands are dotted with small villages and noted beauty spots. At Hungerford, Hocktide is celebrated with an annual ceremony that has its origins in the pagan rites of ancient Britons.

Wansdyke, seen between Marlborough and Oare, was a 50-mile defensive earthwork thought to be built in the 1st century

MARLBOROUGH, Wilts
Marlborough's broad Georgian High Street was once a great livestock market where thousands of downland sheep were herded. Today it is a pleasant shopping centre, with a number of interesting old passages and side streets branching off on both sides. By St Peter's Church an arched gateway leads to the town's famous public school, founded in 1843 around the site of the old castle.

Leave Marlborough on the A4 Chippenham road, then turn left on to the A345, SP 'Salisbury', and continue to Oare.

OARE, Wilts
Oare sits beneath the Marlborough Downs at the head of the Vale of Pewsey, a fertile valley that separates the arid downland from the flat expanse of Salisbury Plain. The 18th-century mansion house was enlarged in the 1920s by Clough Williams-Ellis, creator of the 'Italian' seaside village of Portmeirion. He also designed other houses in the village: a T-shaped, thatched house with the unwelcoming name of Cold Blow, and a terrace of whitewashed cottages with a central archway.

Continue on the A345 to Pewsey.

A perfect combination of roses and thatch in Longparish

PEWSEY, Wilts
King Alfred's statue gazes out from the market place of Pewsey, a pleasant town sheltered by Pewsey Hill whose slopes are distinguished by a chalk white horse. The parish church rests on great sarsen stones, similar to those used at Stonehenge.

Continue on the Amesbury road, cross the River Avon and turn left, SP 'Everleigh', then immediately turn right. The outline of the Pewsey White Horse can be seen before ascending Pewsey Hill. Continue to the edge of Everleigh. Here, turn left on to the A342, SP 'Andover'. In 2 miles at the T-junction turn left then immediately right for Ludgershall.

LUDGERSHALL, Wilts
After the modern housing developments on the outskirts, the old village centre, with its almshouses, ruined castle and rambling church, comes as something of a surprise. The ruins were once a royal castle where Queen Matilda fled from King Stephen after one of their 12th-century battles.

At the T-junction turn left SP 'Andover' and continue into Hampshire. In 4¼ miles at the roundabout turn right, SP 'Thruxton'. In ¼ mile turn left, SP 'Amport'. Shortly turn right then immediately turn left across the main road for Hawk Conservancy.

THE HAWK CONSERVANCY
WEYHILL WILDLIFE PARK, Hants
Opened in 1965, the park specialises in European birds, including hawks, falcons, eagles, owls and vultures; the hawks and falcons are flown whenever weather permits. Among the other wildlife represented are many native British mammals such as polecats, squirrels, foxes and wildcats.

Continue to Amport, turn left for Monxton, then go over the crossroads and continue to Abbots Ann.

ABBOTTS ANN, Hants
The 18th-century church at Abbotts Ann contains numerous white paper garlands; more, it is said than any other village in the country. This reflects well on the morals of the inhabitants because

these used to be carried at the funerals of men and women who had died chaste and celibate.

At Abbotts Ann turn right, then left at the Eagle PH and shortly keep left then bear right. At the A343 turn left then take the next turning right SP 'The Clatfords', into Anna valley. Continue through Upper Clatford and on to Goodworth Clatford. Here, turn left, SP 'Andover', and cross the river bridge. At the A3057 junction turn right SP 'Stockbridge', then in ¼ mile turn left on to the B3420 for Wherwell . Keep left through the village and at the far end go forward on to the B3048, SP 'Longparish'. At the A303 turn right, then immediately left for Longparish.

LONGPARISH, Hants
As the name suggests, this village consists of a long main street along which are spaced a number of pretty, thatched cottages. It stands in the valley of the River Test, noted for its excellent trout fishing.

Continue along a winding road to Hurstbourne Priors. Here turn right then immediately left, SP 'Hurstbourne Tarrant', and follow the Bourne rivulet to St Mary Bourne.

ST MARY BOURNE, Hants
The Bourne valley is watered by a pretty rivulet which in a dry summer sometimes disappears, as do many of the chalk streams in this area. There is enough moisture, however, to feed the many dark green watercress beds that surround this attractive village. Its church contains a massive, carved, black marbled font from Tournai, similar to the one in Winchester Cathedral. The yew tree in the churchyard is one of the oldest in Hampshire.

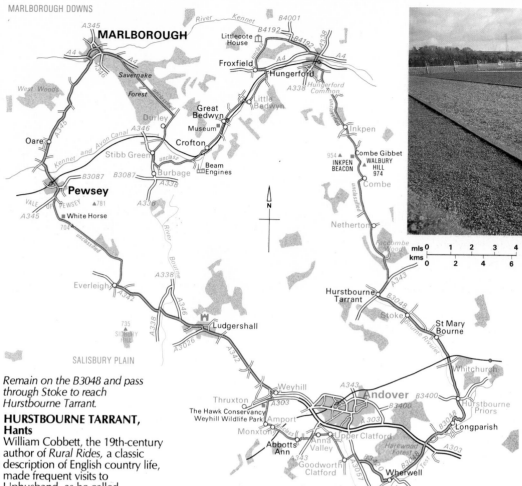

Watercress, a member of the wallflower family, is cultivated as a food crop in beds such as these at St Mary Bourne

Remain on the B3048 and pass through Stoke to reach Hurstbourne Tarrant.

HURSTBOURNE TARRANT, Hants
William Cobbett, the 19th-century author of *Rural Rides,* a classic description of English country life, made frequent visits to Uphusband, as he called Hurstbourne Tarrant.

Turn right on to the A343, SP 'Newbury' then in ½ mile turn left, SP 'Netherton'. Follow this pleasant byroad for 3¼ miles, then keep forward, SP 'Combe' and Inkpen'. Later turn sharp right to reach the edge of Combe. Keep left and continue over the shoulder of Inkpen Hill and Walbury Hill.

INKPEN HILL & WALBURY HILL, Berks
Walbury Hill, at 974ft the highest point of the Berkshire Downs, is crowned by the forbidding banks of Walbury Camp, a massive Iron-Age hill fort. Almost opposite, Inkpen Beacon tops the barren, windswept upland of Inkpen Hill. Here Combe Gibbet stands as a sinister landmark. It was erected in 1676 for the hanging of 2 local villagers who had murdered 2 of their 3 young children. The gibbet was in use until the last century.

Descend and later go over the crossroads, SP 'Hungerford', to reach Inkpen. At the T-junction turn right, then take the first turning left. In 2½ miles bear right, then continue forward, SP 'Hungerford gated road', to cross Hungerford Common. At the next T-junction turn left for Hungerford.

HUNGERFORD, Berks
Hock Tuesday, the 2nd Tuesday after Easter, is the day to visit Hungerford, for the age-old

Hocktide Ceremony, at which the town officials are elected for the coming year, takes place. Hungerford has no Mayor and Corporation, but instead, a governing body of Feoffees is elected from among the townspeople. While the elections take place, Tuttimen bearing long staves decorated with bunches (tutti) of flowers roam through the town demanding a kiss or a penny from any girl or woman they meet. In return, the Orange Scrambler, who goes with them, gives an orange. Hungerford is an attractive old town at any time of the year, and the many antique shops in its main street are fascinating.

At Hungerford turn right on to the A338. Cross the Kennet and Avon Canal, then turn left on to the A4. In ¼ mile turn right on to the B4192 SP 'Swindon'. In 1 mile keep forward, SP 'Littlecote'. After ¾ mile pass the entrance to Littlecote House.

LITTLECOTE HOUSE, Wilts
An early Tudor manor house (OACT) contains beautiful furniture, paintings and a rare example of an intact Cromwellian chapel. The magnificent Littlecote armour restored by the Royal Armouries at the Tower of London is on display in the Great Hall. Wax figures designed to appear in realistic settings to

represent the domestic scene can be found in many rooms. A farm, self-sufficient in 17th-century manner, has had its original buildings restored and workers wear costumes of the period. Continuing the theme of original style and presentation, a company of six knights and their ladies are in residence and also wear costumes of the era. Excavations in the wooded grounds have revealed a large Roman mosaic, and a miniature railway system connects this to the house, gardens and play areas.

Continue to Froxfield.

FROXFIELD, Wilts
The centrepiece of this attractive village is the group of 50 redbrick almshouses, built around a peaceful courtyard in 1694 and later enlarged. They were originally endowed by the Duchess of Somerset as a refuge for poor widows.

Turn left on to the A4 and pass the Somerset almshouses on the left. In almost ½ mile turn right, SP 'Great Bedwyn'. Cross the bridges, then turn right again to follow the Kennet and Avon Canal. At Little Bedwyn continue on the Great Bedwyn road, recross the canal and railway bridge, then turn left.

GREAT BEDWYN, Wilts
Seven generations of stonemasons have lived and worked in Great Bedwyn. Their craftsmanship is commemorated in the Stone Museum, which contains monuments, gravestones, busts and sculpture going back to the 18th century.

At Great Bedwyn turn left, then right into Church Street, SP 'Crofton'. Shortly, on the right, is the Bedwyn Stone Museum. Continue to Crofton.

CROFTON, Wilts
Crofton stands at the highest point of the Kennet and Avon Canal, about 400ft above the River Kennet. Inside the early 19th-century pumping houses (OACT) in the village are 2 beam engines, designed by Boulton and Watt, which operate a massive cast-iron beam. They were used to pump water up to the canal and have now been restored; occasionally they are powered by steam and can be seen working.

Continue on the unclassified road then cross the canal and bear right, SP 'Burbage'. In 1¾ miles, at the T-junction, turn right, then at the A346 turn right again. In ½ mile, at Stibb Green, turn right by the Three Horseshoes PH, SP 'Savernake'. After 2 miles, opposite the gateway on the right, turn left (no SP) to enter Savernake Forest. (Forestry Commission road — rough surface in places).

SAVERNAKE FOREST, Wilts
This former royal hunting forest covers more than 2,000 acres. The walks and rides radiating from the superb Grand Avenue, a 3-mile drive lined by towering beech trees, are the handiwork of Capability Brown, who was commissioned by the Marquess of Ailesbury to landscape the natural woodland.

After 3 miles turn left on to the A4 for the return to Marlborough.

MINEHEAD, Somerset

The natural beauty of its surroundings combined with its delightful situation and mild climate have made this a popular seaside resort with holidaymakers from all over the country. The Esplanade commands a wide sweep of the bay, where the sands are good and bathing is safe. A prominent feature of the high ground behind the town is North Hill, which overlooks the quaint little harbour some hundreds of feet below and affords fine views across the Bristol Channel. On the landward slope is the parish church, where years ago a light burned constantly to guide travellers on the moor and lead ships to the harbour. During these times Minehead harbour was a busy Channel port second only to Bristol, but now it is just the pleasant holiday town it appears to be. Among its attractions are the beautifully-kept Blenheim Gardens, where there is a model town which is floodlit in the evening.

WEST SOMERSET RAILWAY, Somerset

Britain's longest private line, this railway was re-opened in 1976 and runs 20 miles from the coast at Minehead to Bishop's Lydeard. Steam and diesel trains provide a nostalgic way to enjoy the scenery. Refreshments and souvenirs are available at the Minehead terminus.

Leave Minehead on the A39 'Porlock' road and enter the Exmoor National Park area. In 2¼ miles turn right on to an unclassified road and drive to Selworthy.

EXMOOR NATIONAL PARK (EAST), Somerset

East Exmoor and its associated area is a gentler landscape than the rugged central moor. Open moorland contrasts colourfully with the intensively farmed Brendon slopes, and both natural and planted forests lap occasional rocky summits that afford good all-round views. To the north is the beautiful Bristol Channel coast, while inland are National Trust villages that include some of the most picturesque communities in the entire west country.

SELWORTHY, Somerset

This charming village (NT) is one of the most frequented beauty spots in north Somerset, and is grouped round a walnut-shaped green attractively edged with flowers and overlooked by several old cottages. Also of note are the 15th-century almshouses and an old tithe barn, while over all is the sturdy square tower of the 16th-century church. This handsome building is renowned for the particularly fine wagon roof in its south aisle. Majestic Selworthy Beacon (NT) rises to 1,012ft north of the village and is a good viewpoint.

Return to the A39 'Porlock' road, turn right, and in ½ mile pass the edge of Allerford.

OVER THE BRENDON HILLS

Where Exmoor merges into the Brendon Hills the landscape changes from wild heathland to a tapestry of fields and forest. Wooded byways and patches of moor open on to panoramic seascapes fringed with busy resorts and unspoiled villages.

ALLERFORD, Somerset

Quaint cottages and the remains of a manor house can be seen here; of particular note is Allerford's much-photographed double-arched packhorse bridge.

Continue on the A39 and in ½ mile turn left on to an unclassified road SP 'Luccombe'. Pass several packhorse bridges to the right and in ¾ mile at crossroads turn right SP 'Dunkery Beacon'. A detour to Luccombe village can be taken from the main route, by keeping straight ahead.

Beyond Luccombe well-tended countryside gives way to open moorland which rises to the summit of 1,705ft Dunkery Beacon.

LUCCOMBE, Somerset

Access to this secluded little village (NT), whose name means 'closed-in combe', is by a narrow winding lane. The village church has a good tower, and the churchyard is entered through a charming lychgate.

On the main route, begin the long ascent of Dunkery Hill and bear left at the fork.

HOLNICOTE ESTATE, Somerset

The rolling moorland and dense forest round Dunkery Hill are part of the Holnicote Estate (NT), which incorporates some of the loveliest scenery in the Exmoor National Park. About half its 12,443 acres fall within the Exmoor boundaries, and the whole forms a band 6 miles deep along the Bristol Channel coastline. Features include various prehistoric remains, 4 ancient packhorse bridges, and such notable villages as picturesque Selworthy and Luccombe (both NT).

Continue the ascent of Dunkery Hill through progressively wilder scenery and reach a road summit of 1,450ft. A footpath leads from the carpark here to the 1,705 ft viewpoint of Dunkery Beacon.

DUNKERY BEACON, Somerset

Dunkery Beacon (NT), the highest point on Exmoor, is surrounded by some of the most breathtaking scenery in the national park. It was once a link in a chain of fire-beacon sites across the west country. The top is nowadays shared by a cairn commemorating the gift of the hill to the National Trust, the remains of several tumuli, and an official AA viewpoint marker. The Cloutsham Nature Trail (open all year) starts from Webber's Post and covers some 3 miles of varied habitat.

Stay on the unclassified road and descend for 2½ miles, then go forward on to the B3224 to reach Wheddon Cross. Go forward with the B3224 SP 'Taunton' and ascend on to the Brendon Hills.

BRENDON HILLS, Somerset

Undulating slopes with a rich patchwork of forest and farmland are the distinctive characteristics of this gentle range. Farmers, and more recently the Forestry Commission, have transformed the landscape from moorland into a semi-cultivated countryside of symmetrical fields bordered by beech hedges and interspersed with acres of dark conifers. In earlier times small hillside mining villages sprang up to work local deposits of iron ore, but the last Brendon iron mine closed down in 1883. Vestiges of an even earlier age can be seen along the Ridgeway, which is studded with round barrows dating from the Bronze Age.

After 1¾ miles reach Heath Poult Cross and turn right on to an unclassified road. Continue for 5 miles, along a ridge above the Exe Valley then descend into the Valley and turn left on to the A396, SP 'Tiverton'. In 2½ miles at Exebridge turn left on to an unclassified road SP 'Morebath'. After 1½ miles turn left on to the B3190 'Watchet' road, and shortly pass Morebath; 3 miles beyond the village a car park for Wimbleball Lake lies to the left.

The packhorse bridge at Allerford.

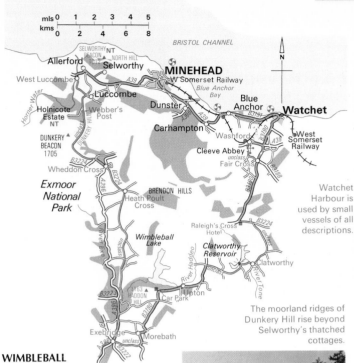

Watchet Harbour is used by small vessels of all descriptions.

The moorland ridges of Dunkery Hill rise beyond Selworthy's thatched cottages.

WIMBLEBALL LAKE
Somerset
Great care has been taken to blend this River Haddeo reservoir project with the countryside of south Exmoor. New plantations of trees native to the area have been established right down to the water's edge, and a small area of bank has been given over to leisure facilities for angling, small-boat sailing, and riding. Amenities include a carpark, a picnic area, and planned woodland walks.

Continue on the B3190 through Upton, then in 2 miles at crossroads turn right on to an unclassified road SP 'Wiveliscombe'. After a further 1 mile branch left and drive over crossroads to skirt Clatworthy Reservoir.

CLATWORTHY RESERVOIR, Somerset
Like its close neighbour Wimbleball, this beautiful upland reservoir has been integrated with the local scenery and is a haven for all kinds of wildlife. A large carpark gives access to a 10-acre public viewing area with picnic facilities.

Continue, and on the descent turn left and shortly right before crossing the River Tone and reaching Clatworthy. Keep left through the village SP 'Brompton Ralph', and after 1 mile at crossroads, turn left SP 'Raleigh's Cross', then after a further 2 miles meet a T-junction and turn left on to the B3224. Reach Raleigh's Cross Hotel and turn right on to the B3190 SP 'Watchet'. There are excellent views of the Bristol Channel at first before the long descent to crossroads at Fair Cross.
Here turn left on to an unclassified road SP 'Washford', and in 1 mile pass the entrance to Cleeve Abbey.

CLEEVE ABBEY, Somerset
Remains of this 13th-century Cistercian abbey (AM), founded in 1188, include a refectory with traceried windows, a timbered roof, and some fine wall paintings. The picturesque gatehouse and painted chamber are of particular note.

Continue to Washford, then turn right on to the A39 Bridgwater Road. In ¾ mile at crossroads turn left on to the B3190 for Watchet.

WATCHET, Somerset
Coleridge found the main character for his long, moralistic poem *The Rime of the Ancient Mariner* in this historic seaport, which now doubles as a popular resort. The Esplanade offers a grandstand view of the harbour, and the local beaches offer plenty of opportunities for the fossil hunter. Behind the town are the lofty heights of the Brendon and Quantock hill ranges.

Leave Watchet on the B3191 and continue, with views of the Bristol Channel, to Blue Anchor.

BLUE ANCHOR, Somerset
In front of this small hamlet is a clean white beach which sweeps round the alabaster rocks of Blue Anchor Bay in a brilliant arc. The area is well known for its fossils.

Continue on the B3191 to Carhampton.

The ancient village of Dunster is dominated by its romantic castle.

CARHAMPTON, Somerset
This little village dates back to 833, when it was the site of a Danish victory. Its restored church contains a magnificent painted screen which dates from the 15th century and stretches across the entire breadth of the building. Each January the villagers re-enact the old ceremony of Wassailing the Apple Trees, an ancient custom involving a toast to the largest apple tree in the cider orchards and a libation of cider thrown on its trunk. The whole procedure has more than a suggestion of ancient fertility rites. Close to the church lychgate is an old pub called the Butcher's Arms, which has the date 1638 worked in sheep's knuckle bones in the cobbled floor.

At Carhampton turn right on to the A39 'Minehead' road and after 1½ miles turn left on to the A396 SP 'Tiverton' to enter Dunster.

DUNSTER, Somerset
Dunster is a beautiful medieval village that has often been described as a 'perfect relic of feudal times'. Its unspoilt condition is largely due to its constant ownership by one family, the Luttrells, for some 600 years until 1950. The Norman castle (NT) was the family seat and is well worth visiting. Its oak-panelled halls display magnificent ceilings and fascinating relics. In the centre of the village is the octagonal Yarn Market, which was built in 1609, when Dunster was an important cloth centre. Not far away is the lovely Luttrell Arms, which is said to have stood for three centuries and was originally the house of the Abbot of Cleeve. Among its many features are an interesting 15th-century porch and a fine chamber displaying a wealth of carved oak. The parish church is by far the finest in this part of the country. Both it and its associated buildings are of particularly warm pink sandstone, and the whole harmonious group is set in a tranquil rural scene. Nearby the River Avill is spanned by the ancient Gallox packhorse bridge (AM).

Return along the A396 for ½ mile and turn left to rejoin the A39. Return to Minehead.

MORETON-IN-MARSH, Glos

Moreton-in-Marsh is a pleasant small market town under the edge of the north Cotswolds. Among many interesting old inns here are the White Hart, where Charles I slept in 1643, and the famous Redesdale Arms coaching stop. The town's curfew tower carries a 17th-century clock. Two miles north west, set in 50 acres, is the Batsford Arboretum.

Follow SP 'A44 Oxford' from Moreton-in-Marsh and continue to the Four Shire Stone, on the left of the road.

FOUR SHIRE STONE, Glos

About 2 miles east of Moreton-in-Marsh is the famous Four Shire Stone, where Gloucestershire met Oxfordshire, Warwickshire, and an isolated part of Worcestershire before the county reorganization of the 1970s.

Pass Four Shire Stone and in ¾ mile turn right on to an unclassified road for Chastleton.

CHASTLETON, Oxon

Chastleton House is of Cotswold stone and was built by wealthy wool merchant Walter Jones in 1603. His descendants are still in ownership. On the top floor of the house are state rooms and a long gallery, which contain many items of original furniture (open).

Go through Chastleton and after ½ mile turn left. Cross a cattle grid and turn right on to the A44. Pass the Cross Hands (PH) and turn left on to an unclassified road. Proceed to the Rollright Stones.

ROLLRIGHT STONES, Oxon

This important bronze-age monument (AM) comprises two configurations of stones. The circle, nicknamed 'The King's Men', measures a full 100ft across and is

IN THE VALE OF RED HORSE

Relics of ancient man dot the North Cotswold Hills above vales of almost legendary richness, where English fruit and vegetables are raised round villages that grew fat on the profits of wool. Great men lived and died here; great rivers continue to flow.

close to 'The Whispering Knights' group and an isolated outlier called the 'King's Stone'.

After ¾ mile turn left on to the A34 and descend to Long Compton.

LONG COMPTON, Warwicks

A little thatched gatehouse tops the churchyard gate at Long Compton. The church itself is of Norman and later date and preserves an old stone figure of a lady in the porch.

Continue to Shipston-on-Stour

SHIPSTON-ON-STOUR, Warwicks

Situated on the edge of the Cotswolds in the Vale of Red Horse, this old wool town has attractive Georgian houses and inns complemented by a 19th-century church incorporating the 500-year-old tower of its predecessor.

Turn left on to the B4035 'Campden' road. Proceed for 1¾ miles, cross a main road. Continue for 1¼ miles then turn right on to an unclassified road through Charingworth to Ebrington.

EBRINGTON, Glos

Delightful cottages of stone and thatch enhance the undoubted appeal of this beautiful Cotswold village. Ebrington Manor shows a great deal of restoration to its basically 17th-century structure.

Drive to the end of the village and keep right, then right again on to an unclassified road SP 'To the Hidcotes'. After 2¼ miles turn right for Hidcote Bartrim.

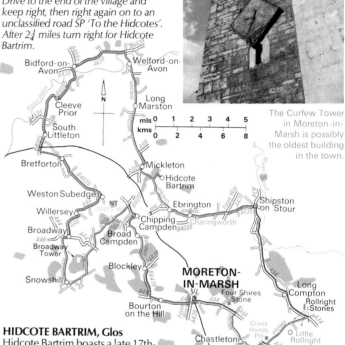

The Curfew Tower in Moreton-in-Marsh is possibly the oldest building in the town.

HIDCOTE BARTRIM, Glos

Hidcote Bartrim boasts a late 17th-century manor surrounded by lovely formal gardens (open) (NT).

Return to the T-junction and turn left, then take the next turning on the right SP 'Mickleton'. Meet the main road and turn right on to the A46 to enter Mickleton.

MICKLETON, Glos

Medford House is a superb example of Renaissance architecture, and the village itself preserves thatched and timber-framed buildings. Half a mile south east is Kingsgate Court Gardens magnificently situated, affording fine views. St Lawrence's Church dates from the 12th century.

Drive through the village and turn left. After ½ mile continue on to the unclassified road for Long Marston.

LONG MARSTON, Warwicks

King's Lodge in Long Marston has associations with King Charles II, who is said to have come here in disguise after the Battle of Worcester. The bell in the village church hangs in a turret built on great oak beams resting on the floor of the nave. The village itself is a delightful grouping of timber and thatch cottages in leafy country lanes. It has its own traditional morris dancing troupe.

Continue to Welford-on-Avon

WELFORD-ON-AVON, Warwicks

Welford-on-Avon's Norman church has an ancient lychgate and stands among charming timber-and-thatch cottages near a new maypole.

The Rollright Stones have been a Cotswolds feature for thousands of years.

Go forward and later cross the River Avon, then turn left on to the A439 and drive to Bidford-on-Avon.

BIDFORD-ON-AVON, Warwicks

Traditionally this unspoilt village was the birthplace of playwright William Shakespeare. There is little doubt that Tudor Corner House was once the Falcon Inn beloved of both Shakespeare and his contemporary Ben Jonson. Latterly the inn has served as a workhouse and as a group of cottages. A fine 15th-century bridge spans the Avon.

Turn left on to the B4085 SP 'Broadway', and cross a bridge. After ½ mile turn right for Cleeve Prior.

CLEEVE PRIOR, Herefs & Worcs

The name of this village derives from the priors of Worcester, who were once lords of the manor here. Tall chimneys and a priest's hole that once hid Charles I's banker are features of the Jacobean manor house. Stone-built cottages overlook the triangular green, and the 15th-century King's Arms still offers comfort to the traveller.

Continue to South Littleton.

SOUTH LITTLETON, Herefs & Worcs

North, Middle, and South Littleton are a picturesque group of tiny Avon Valley villages. North Littleton has a manor house, a tithe barn, and dovecote, and a church that is considered to be of great architectural merit. South Littleton boasts a beautiful early 18th-century house.

Continue along the same road for a further 1 mile, then go over a level crossing and turn left on to the unclassified 'Bretforton' road. Continue to Bretforton.

BRETFORTON, Herefs & Worcs

Three tributaries of the Avon drain the lovely countryside round this ancient village. Of particular note here are the 600-year-old Fleece Inn (NT) and medieval Grange Farm. The latter, changed greatly from its original form by successive owners, gave shelter to Prince Rupert in 1645. The country's largest collection of dovecotes survives here, including several very old examples and one that has been made into a cottage.

Join the B4035 and continue to Weston-Sub-Edge.

WESTON-SUB-EDGE, Glos

Several appealing 17th-century houses preserved in the main street of this village include Latimer's, a particularly fine example associated with the historic bishop of that name. Bank House and Riknild are also of note. Slightly later than these is the Manor House, and the 'old' Rectory was built in the 19th century.

Meet a T-junction, turn right on to the A46, and pass through Willersey.

Chipping Campden's arched Market Hall was built in 1627.

WILLERSEY, Glos

The 6 bells of Willersey's Church of St Peter were re-cast from the original 3 in 1712 and rung the following year to celebrate the Treaty of Utrecht. Various medieval styles can be seen in the building itself. Willersey House was once a farmhouse in the village, but in 1912 was dismantled and rebuilt at the top of a hill in its present enlarged form and is now the Dormy House Hotel.

Later meet a T-junction and turn right on to the A44 into Broadway.

BROADWAY, Herefs & Worcs

Broadway's wide main street is lined with fine houses and pretty cottages built in Cotswold stone. St Eadburgha's Norman and later church is somewhat self-effacingly hidden away at one end of the community, and the 17th-century Lygon Arms coaching inn shows a narrow frontage to the street.

Drive to the end of the green and turn left on to an unclassified road to Snowshill. Ascend, then bear right into the village.

SNOWSHILL, Glos

Secluded Snowshill is a hillside village of ancient Cotswold cottages grouped round a handsome 19th-century church. Its manor house (NT) dates from the 16th century, but subsequent periods have left their marks in various alterations and additions. Inside are collections of clocks, toys, and musical instruments.

Continue to the church and turn left. Ascend to the top of the incline and meet crossroads. Go forward SP 'Chipping Campden, Broadway Tower'. After 1¾ miles turn left and proceed to Broadway Tower.

BROADWAY TOWER, Herefs & Worcs

Lady Coventry built this picturesque folly tower in the 18th century, and it now forms the nucleus of a 30-acre country park. Its lofty situation at over 1,000ft gives views over several counties, and in very clear weather it is possible to pick out such landmarks as Tewkesbury Abbey, Worcester Cathedral, and Warwick.

Continue for ¼ mile, cross a main road with SP 'Mickleton', and after ¾ mile turn right. Continue for 2½ miles and meet a T-junction. Turn right on to the B4081/B4035 for Chipping Campden.

Welford-on-Avon is a picturebook village set in a pastoral landscape.

CHIPPING CAMPDEN, Glos

Wool made Chipping Campden rich, and the handiwork of the merchants who prospered here can be seen in the fine gabled stone houses, the 14th-century Woolstaplers Hall, and the 15th-century wool church. Near the church are remains of the once-beautiful Campden House, whose owner burned it down in 1645 rather than see it fall into Parliamentarian hands.

Drive through the town and turn left with the B4081 SP 'Broad Campden'. After ¼ mile turn left again on to an unclassified road for Broad Campden.

BROAD CAMPDEN, Glos

Features of this village include an 18th-century Friends' Meeting House that has been restored and the much older Chapel House – a 12th-century chapel converted into a private dwelling.

Keep right through the village then bearing right before the climb to Blockley.

BLOCKLEY, Glos

Blockley's architecture follows the usual basic pattern for the area, with a high street of 18th- and 19th-century houses complementing a Norman church.

Turn left, continue for a short distance, then turn right on to the B4479. Proceed for 1½ miles, meet a T-junction, and turn left on to the A44. Pass through Bourton-on-the-Hill.

BOURTON-ON-THE-HILL, Glos

A fine example of a Winchester bushel can be seen in Bourton's Norman and later church. The village itself stands on a hill and is made up of cottages standing in attractively-terraced gardens. Bourton House is of 18th-century date and has a superb 16th-century tithe barn.

Return to Moreton-in-Marsh.

NEWQUAY, Cornwall

Magnificent beaches', fine scenery, and a wide range of amenities for the holiday-maker have made Newquay one of the most popular seaside resorts in Cornwall. The original Iron-Age settlement was to the north east at Porth Island, where today's tourists admire the grand cliffs and splendid caves. Since the first train arrived here in 1875 tourism has been the main factor in Newquay's growth. The railway originally came to bring china clay and tin to the port, but the harbour proved too small and shallow for large cargo ships. Because of this the harbour has retained some of its original character and preserved a number of old structures. Another area of historic charm is St Columb Minor, once the mother parish of Newquay but now just a suburb. Amongst its old and attractive cottages is the church of St Columba, whose 115ft pinnacled and lichen-covered 15th-century tower is considered one of the finest in the country. Visitors can enjoy the amusement park in Trenance Garden, which also boasts the only zoo in Cornwall, and the mile-long main beach is close to the town. Between Newquay and the surfing beach at Fistral is the rock-strewn promontory of Towan Head, which affords magnificent views.

Leave Newquay on the A392 SP 'Bodmin' and continue to Quintrell Downs. Drive over a level crossing, then at roundabout SP 'St Austell' go forward on to the A3058. After ¾ mile turn right on to a narrow unclassified road SP 'Newlyn East'. Continue for 1 mile to Trerice Manor, on the right.

TRERICE MANOR, Cornwall

With its grey curving gables and E-shaped entrance front, Trerice Manor (NT) has hardly changed since it was first built by Sir John Arundell in 1573. Sir John, a member of an old and influential Cornish family, spent a great deal of time soldiering in the Low Countries. When he returned to his native Cornwall he did not entirely forget foreign parts, as the design of the house shows. Excellent plasterwork on the ceilings and fire-places is acknowledged as the most outstanding feature of the interior.

Continue for 1 mile then at crossroads turn left. In ½ mile at a T-junction turn right. A detour can be taken from the main route by turning left and driving for ½ mile to the Lappa Valley Railway.

LAPPA VALLEY RAILWAY, Cornwall

This 15-inch gauge line built on part of the former Great Western route between Newquay and Chacewater runs through a 2-mile circuit of valley scenery. A stop is made at East Wheal Rose Halt, where passengers can disembark to explore a children's leisure park and the site of an old silver and lead mine.

Continue to St Newlyn East.

ATLANTIC SEASCAPES

Long, foam-capped rollers crash on to ideal surfing beaches between the craggy headlands and promontories of Cornwall's Atlantic coast. Away from the shore is the gentle rise and fall of downland, scored by deep lanes and scattered with the beautifully decayed remains of mine buildings.

The estuary of the River Gannel opens out to form Crantock Beach.

ST NEWLYN EAST, Cornwall

Known as St Newlyn East to distinguish it from the port of Newlyn near Penzance, this attractive village was probably the original settlement of Saint Newelina, the Cornish martyr to whom the parish church is dedicated. Beautiful examples of Norman and medieval carving can be seen inside the church, including particularly fine pieces of 14th-century work.

Follow signs 'Truro', and continue for 1 mile to Fiddler's Green. Turn left, then after 1¼ miles meet crossroads. Go forward SP 'Zelah' then turn right on to the A30. Go through Zelah and in ½ mile turn left on to an unclassified road SP 'Shortlanesend'. Continue for 2 miles to reach the Shortlanesend Inn, and join the B3284 for Truro.

TRURO, Cornwall

Cathedral city of Cornwall and the county's unofficial capital, Truro stands where the rivers Allen and Kenwyn join to form the large Fal-estuary inlet known as the Truro River. Until 1752 the town was one of Cornwall's 4 stannery or coinage towns, to which all smelted tin had to be brought to be tested for quality and taxed. During this time it developed into an important centre for the export of mineral ores, and in the 18th century it became a focus of social life to rival even Bath, the country's then most fashionable town. Among the fine Georgian structures surviving from the period is the outstanding Lemon Street, which was laid out c1795 and is complemented by Walsingham Place, a beautiful early 19th-century crescent just off Victoria Place. The former Assembly Rooms date from c1770 and were the main gathering place for 18th-century society. One of Cornwall's oldest and most famous potteries, Lake's, still works in Chapel Street, and is open to visitors. Edward VII, then the Prince of Wales, laid the cathedral's foundation stone in 1880. Various types of Cornish granite were used in the building's construction, and it stands on the site of the 16th-century church of St Mary. Part of the older building is retained in the east end. The Truro Museum, in River Street, is considered to be the finest in Cornwall and has a number of exhibits depicting the history of the local mineral industries.

Leave Truro following SP 'Redruth' on the A390. In 4 miles meet a roundabout and take the 2nd exit. Continue for a further 2¼ miles to another roundabout and take the 3rd exit on to the B3277 SP 'St Agnes'. Continue to St Agnes.

One of the Wheal Coates engine houses on the cliffs at Chapel Porth near St Agnes.

ST AGNES, Cornwall

St Agnes is one of those Cornish villages that has retained its charm and character despite the burden of two centuries of mining and one century of tourism. Decaying engine houses and wildflower-covered burrows bear silent witness to the mineral booms of years gone by, and ¼ mile north is Trevaunance Cove – a lovely place with excellent sands. Many futile attempts have been made to build a harbour here, and remains of 18th-century piers from the last try can be seen at the western end of the cove. St Agnes itself fits snugly round the parish church, which was rebuilt in Cornish style during the mid-19th century but is unusual in having a slender spire. Among the pleasant streets and by-ways of the village is the quaint Stippy-Stappy, a steep and stepped row of slate-roofed cottages leading down Town Hill. The well-known beauty spot of St Agnes Beacon lies to the west. Also of interest are the St Agnes Leisure Park with five different themes, and the Little Puppet Theatre.

ST AGNES BEACON, Cornwall

It is said that 32 church towers and 23 miles of coast can be seen from 628ft St Agnes Beacon (NT), perhaps the most prominent landmark in the area. Much of the surrounding area (part NT) has been worked for minerals in times past, but the many mining scars and old buildings add a melancholy beauty rather than the sense of desecration that usually pervades industrial sites. Bolster's Dyke, a 2-mile earthwork on the Beacon, is named after a legendary giant who is supposed to have lived there in ancient times.

WHEAL COATES ENGINE HOUSE, Cornwall

One of the Wheal Coates engine houses, (NT) stands precariously on a forbidding cliff to the west of St Agnes Beacon. It contained a pumping engine for the Towanroath shaft and from a sea-cave below it is possible to look up one of the shafts beneath the pump-house.

Leave St Agnes on the B3285 Perranporth road and continue through Trevellas, then in 1 mile descend into Perranporth.

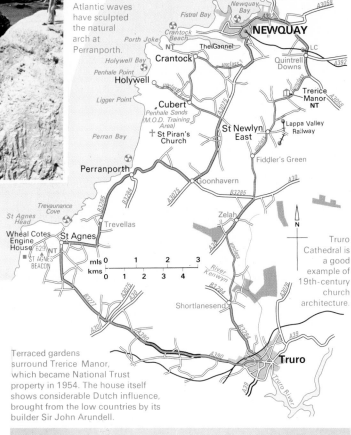

Atlantic waves have sculpted the natural arch at Perranporth.

Terraced gardens surround Trerice Manor, which became National Trust property in 1954. The house itself shows considerable Dutch influence, brought from the low countries by its builder Sir John Arundell.

Truro Cathedral is a good example of 19th-century church architecture.

PERRANPORTH, Cornwall

Terraces of hotels and guesthouses rise from the sea-level centre of this popular resort which was formerly a mining centre. Even though it lacks the quaint cottages and blue-jerseyed fishermen the public expect of the west, visitors find a more than ample attraction in the magnificent bay that sweeps away to the north. This boasts a 3-mile stretch of smooth golden sand, and is reputed to be where surfing was introduced into Britain. Penhale Point offers spectacular rock scenery, and the sands at this end of the beach have been blown into large dunes. Near by, on the road to Goonhavern, is the 2,000-year old hilltop enclosure of St Piran's Round (AM).

ST PIRAN'S CHURCH, Cornwall

Perranporth is in the parish of *Perranzabuloe* which means 'St Piran in the Sand'. St Piran is thought to have come to Cornwall from Ireland in the 6th-century, and legend has it that he wasn't always sober. However, he is said to have taught the Cornish the art of smelting and was adopted as the patron saint of tinners. He built his church north of Perranporth on the Penhale Sands, but by the 11th century shifting dunes had closed in and completely enveloped the little building. It wasn't until the 19th century that it was excavated, and nowadays it is housed in a concrete shell to protect it from further damage. The mile-long walk over easy ground to see the church is well worth the effort.

Leave Perranporth on the B3285 SP 'Newquay' and in 2 miles at Goonhavern turn left on to the A3075. In 2½ miles turn left on to an unclassified road for Cubert.

CUBERT, Cornwall

High above the sandy landscape round Cubert is the spire of the church, a local landmark. Although restored in 1852 the interior of the church preserves fine Norman and 14th-century carvings and a font. In a café in the village centre are the granite remains of a 17th-century Cornish cider press.

A pleasant detour from the main route can be taken to Holywell, some 1¼ miles beyond Cubert.

HOLYWELL, Cornwall

The large beach at Holywell Bay is quieter than most on this coastline and offers good bathing except at low tide. At the north end is a freshwater spring that gave the place its name, one of the holy wells of Cornwall. It can only be reached at low tide via steps cut into the cliff. Magnificent views can be enjoyed from Penhale Point.

Leave Cubert by the Crantock road. Continue for 1½ miles to reach Crantock.

CRANTOCK, Cornwall

A plaque records that the old stocks in the churchyard here were last used in 1817 on a 'Smuggler's son and a vagabond'. This is not surprising since the village was once notorious for its involvement in contraband. The church itself is a showpiece of Edwardian restoration. Attractive countryside (NT) lines the steep-sided estuary of the River Gannel which flows past the popular sands of Crantock Beach.

Leave Crantock on an unclassified road SP 'Newquay'. In ¾ mile turn left on to another unclassified road and continue for 1 mile to the A3075. Turn left and return to Newquay.

CORNWALL'S STERNEST COAST

Great Atlantic rollers forever pound the towering cliffs of north Cornwall, spilling their energy in roaring white surf along the wide sandy beaches which have made Newquay and Padstow such popular resorts. The calm of antiquity is reflected inland, however, where a rolling landscape gently laps the rugged edge of stark Bodmin Moor.

NEWQUAY, Cornwall
Newquay's popularity as a holiday resort stems chiefly from its magnificent sandy beaches and the superb surfing which is probably the best in Cornwall. The most attractive area of the town itself is the 17th-century harbour. Here, some of the pilot gigs which used to guide in the cargo schooners during the 19th century have been preserved. On the headland west of the harbour is another relic from Newquay's past — the Huer's Hut. In the days when pilchards provided the town with a living, a man called a huer kept watch for shoals of pilchards entering the bay. When he saw the water reddening from the mass of fish, he alerted the town by shouting. To the west lies Trenance Park and Cornwall's only full-size zoo. Eight acres of landscaped grounds effectively display wild animals, tropical birds, wildfowl, reptiles, seals and penguins and there is a pets' corner to keep children happy.

Leave Newquay on the A392, SP 'Bodmin'. In ¾ mile, turn left on to the B3276, SP 'Padstow'. Continue to Mawgan Porth.

MAWGAN PORTH, Cornwall
The small safe bay at Mawgan Porth lies at the entrance to the lovely Lanherne Valley leading up to St Mawgan. There is a wooden monument shaped like a boat in this village which commemorates the lives of 10 seamen who were shipwrecked and swept ashore at Mawgan Porth. Remains of a settlement (AM) that supported a small community of fishermen and cattle breeders from the 9th to the 11th centuries are visible near the beach and the foundations of their courtyard houses and outline of the cemetery can be discerned.

From Mawgan Porth climb to Trenance. After another mile, on the left, is the track which leads to Bedruthan Steps.

BEDRUTHAN STEPS, Cornwall
Huge lumps of granite march along this beautiful, rugged beach. The rocks were, allegedly, named Bedruthan Steps because they were thought to be the stepping stones of the giant Bedruthan. This stretch of coast (NT) is one of the most spectacular in Cornwall and the great sands are usually deserted because a steep scramble down the cliff is the only access.

Continue on the B3276 and in 1¼ miles at the T-junction turn left, then ½ mile farther turn left again for the descent to Porthcothan.

The great crags of Bedruthan Steps rise up some 200ft from the deserted sands

PORTHCOTHAN, Cornwall
The sea reaches almost to the road at Porthcothan and the great cliffs on either side are more than a match for the angry attacks of the relentless Atlantic ocean. The shelter of the rocks obviously well suited smugglers because an underground passage emerges further up the valley, and it was along here that the daredevil smugglers hid their spoils and hauled up their luggers.

Turn inland from Porthcothan and after 1 mile turn left and continue to St Merryn.

ST MERRYN, Cornwall
A newer village has developed a little way from the old church and its protective cluster of cottages. The interior pillars of the church and font are made of locally cliff-quarried Catacleuse slate. This handsome dark blue-grey stone was the only slate that could be carved easily, which is why nearly all the carved work in Cornish churches is out of this slate. Old village stocks are kept in the church porch.

At the Farmers' Arms PH in St Merryn turn left SP 'Harlyn'. In 1 mile turn right for Harlyn Bay.

Most of Newquay, north Cornwall's largest resort, has been built along the cliffs above its large, sandy beaches

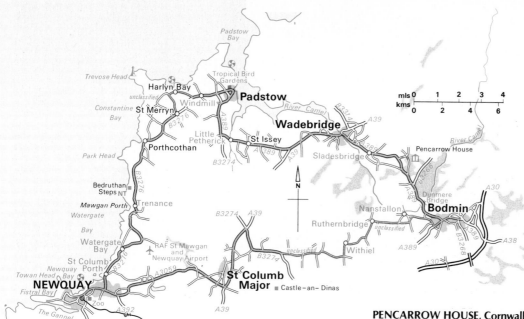

into steep granite tors, the highest being Rough Tor and Brown Willy, yet there is also a gentler aspect to the moor, of fields and wild flowers. St Petroc founded a monastery in Bodmin and his name lives on in the parish church, St Petroc's, which is the largest in Cornwall. At one time the town was renowned for its holy wells which cured eye complaints. One such well, St Guron's, stands near the church inscribed with the date 1700 and an advertisement extolling the well's powers.

Follow SP 'Redruth (A30)' and at the end of the town go forward. In ½ mile turn right, SP 'Wadebridge and Nanstallon'. In nearly another ½ mile keep left still SP 'Nanstallon'. In ¾ mile bear left, SP 'Ruthern', and go forward at the crossroads to Ruthernbridge. Here, turn left, SP 'Withiel', then in ¾ mile turn right and continue to Withiel. Here turn left, SP 'Roche', and at the church turn left again and in ½ mile turn right, SP 'St Wenn'. In 1¾ miles keep forward, SP 'St Columb', then in another mile join the B3274. In 2¼ miles turn left on to the A39 SP 'Truro', and continue along the St Columb Major bypass. From this road a detour may be made to St Columb Major.

ST COLUMB MAJOR, Cornwall
One of the chief churches in Cornwall belongs to St Columb Major. St Columba stands in a commanding position in a large churchyard and the tower has the unusual feature of 4 tiers. The good 16th-17th-century brasses inside are dedicated to the Arundell family who lived at Lanherne. Every Shrove Tuesday a local adaptation of the handball game of hurling takes place in the town's streets, using a traditional, applewood ball covered with silver. Two and a half miles south-east of St Columb Major is Castle an Dinas — an Iron-Age fort which still has 3 ramparts visible.

From the southern end of the St Columb Major Bypass the tour follows the A3059 Newquay road. In 5½ miles turn right on to the A392 for the return to Newquay.

HARLYN BAY, Cornwall
For thousands of years an Iron-Age cemetery lay hidden beneath the sands near Harlyn Bay. In 1900 it was accidentally discovered and proved to have once been the site of over 100 graves. Five of the slate slabs have been preserved on the site and a small museum nearby contains the various other finds such as brooches, tools and combs which were buried with those far-off peoples.

Cross the river bridge and in 1 mile turn left to rejoin the B3276, SP 'Padstow'. Pass through Windmill and in ¾ mile keep left, then nearly ½ mile farther turn left again for Padstow.

PADSTOW, Cornwall
Padstow is one of north Cornwall's oldest and most charming fishing towns. However, its days as a fishing and export port ended in the mid-19th century when the Camel estuary silted up, and the picturesque harbour and crooked streets now throng with holiday-makers. An annual highlight in Padstow is May Day when the Hobby Horse Dance Festival takes place. The ritual of a masked man and a bizarre hobby horse dancing through the streets welcomes summer and is supposed to be the oldest dance festival in Europe. St Petroc's Church is a reminder of the early Christianity in Padstow, dating from the 6th century when St Petroc came here from Ireland to found a monastery. (Padstow is a derivation of Petrocstowe.) The original monastic site may have been the one now occupied by Prideaux Place (not open) just above the church. This is a handsome Elizabethan house — home of the Prideaux family for several hundred years — and a monument to the Prideaux lies in

the church. Another interesting feature of Padstow is its tropical bird and butterfly gardens. A walk-in tropical house with free-flying birds and a butterfly exhibition where butterflies fly free in the summer, shows off these creatures in ideal conditions.

From the one-way system in Padstow follow SP 'Wadebridge' and ascend and at the top turn left on to the A398. In 2 miles turn left, continue through Little Petherick, and climb to St Issey.

ST ISSEY, Cornwall
About 20 figures placed in niches of Cataclewse stone stand inside St Issey's church. They were probably part of a tombchest at one time, but form part of the altar canopy now. The church tower collapsed in the last century but was rebuilt in 1873. A photograph from 1869 shows the tower falling and a policeman in a top hat looking helplessly on.

Remain on the A389 and in 2 miles turn left on to the A39 and continue to Wadebridge.

WADEBRIDGE, Cornwall
The centrepiece of this small market town is a fine medieval bridge crossing over the River Camel to Egloshayle. It was built by the vicar of Egloshayle, (the mother church of Wadebridge), because he deemed the ferry crossing to be too dangerous for his parishioners. The bridge, 320ft long, the longest in Cornwall, originally had 17 arches but 1 has since been blocked up. The foundations beneath the pillars are believed to have been based on packs of wool.

Cross the River Camel and on the far side turn right on to the A389, SP 'Bodmin'. A pleasant road then passes through Sladesbridge and after 2¼ miles a turning on the left leads to Pencarrow House.

PENCARROW HOUSE, Cornwall
Dense woods and rhododendrons cover an estate of 35 acres and in the middle hides modest, 18th-century Pencarrow House (OACT). The approach is mysterious; along a winding wooded drive and past an Iron-Age encampment ringed by dwarf oaks. Sir John Molesworth began the house in the 1700s and his descendants live there now. A great deal of the contents have been accumulated through prosperous marriages and the interior has been tastefully adapted to show the beautiful treasures off to maximum advantage.

Continue on the Bodmin road and recross the River Camel at Dunmere Bridge. A short climb then brings the tour into Bodmin.

BODMIN, Cornwall
Bodmin lies on the steep south-west edge of Bodmin Moor, equi-distant between Cornwall's north and south coasts, which makes it an ideal touring base. Approximately 12 miles square make up Bodmin Moor and very few roads cross its bleak face. The boulder-strewn slopes break out

The beach at Harlyn Bay, satellite of Newquay, is a popular bathing spot

PENZANCE, Cornwall

The most westerly town in England, Penzance enjoys a mild climate all year round. The town grew to prosperity through tin mining, and possibly smuggling, and was immortalized by Gilbert and Sullivan in *The Pirates of Penzance*. Evidence of its popularity in Regency times can be seen in the fine period buildings still standing in Chapel Street. Also here is a maritime museum with exhibits from 18th-century British warships wrecked off the Scilly Isles. There is a natural history museum in Penlee Park, and many exotic plants grow in Morab Gardens. About 2 miles inland are the Trengwainton Gardens (NT), with their exceptional collections of magnolias, rhododendrons and other shrubs. It was here that magnolias flowered for the first time in the British Isles.

MOUNT'S BAY, Cornwall

Mount's Bay curves in a series of wide coves and inlets between the Land's End peninsula in the west and The Lizard in the east. In spite of playing host to many visitors each year it is still a place of isolated bays and deserted, cliff-fringed beaches.

Leave Penzance on the A3077 'Newlyn', road skirting the harbour to Newlyn.

NEWLYN, Cornwall

This busy fishing port used to be famous for its artist colony. Many of the painters moved north to St Ives, but a few still live and work among the quaint old cottages and fish-cellars. The Passmore Edwards picture gallery shows some of the colony's work.

Cross a river bridge and immediately turn left on to an unclassified road which hugs the coast to Mousehole.

THE PENWITH PENINSULA

Storm-tumbled cliffs haunted by gulls and mermaid legends guard the wild Atlantic shoreline of Penwith. On the other side of Land's End is the great bight of Mount's Bay, where the 'nightmen' of folksong fame crept from secluded coves with 'baccy for the parson and brandy for the squire'.

The fairytale structure of St Michael's Mount dominates Mount's Bay.

MOUSEHOLE, Cornwall

Largely unchanged by time, Mousehole preserves the original character of old Cornwall in its granite houses and working harbour.

Turn left, drive to the harbour, and turn right then right again SP 'Paul', turn inland, and climb to Paul.

PAUL, Cornwall

Dorothy Pentreath, one of the last people to speak the ancient Cornish language is buried here. Inside the 15th-century church are several pieces of old armour.

Keep forward past Paul Church and after ½ mile meet a T-junction. Turn left on to the B3315 and continue for 2½ miles. A detour can be taken from the main route by turning left here on to an unclassifed road through the Lamorna Valley to Lamorna Cove.

LAMORNA COVE, Cornwall

Huge granite boulders and the rocky outcrops of this spectacular cove contrast with the gentler surrounding countryside. A granite quay and pier were built here in the last century to export granite from the quarries near by. Nowadays the cove is visited for its lovely scenery by tourists and artists.

Continue on the B3315 and in 3¼ miles, at a T-junction, turn left. Descend steeply, then climb to the edge of Treen.

TREEN, Cornwall

This tiny village lies near the fortified headland of Treryn Dinas on which stands Treen Castle (NT). Outside the local inn is a sign telling how in 1824 a nephew of Oliver Goldsmith overturned the 60 ton Logan Rock, a famous rocking stone on the headland, and how he was made to replace it at his own expense.

TREEN CASTLE (NT) Cornwall

It is believed that the defences of this excellent Iron-Age cliff castle were started between the 3rd and 2nd centuries BC. A huge bank and ditch cuts off the headland, and at the extreme tip of the rocks jutting out to sea is a bank faced with heavy masonry. Access is by footpath from Treen.

LOGAN ROCK, Cornwall

Pronounced 'loggan', the name of this curious rocking stone is derived from the Cornish verb *log*, meaning to move. It is reached by footpath from the village of Treen.

From the edge of Treen, remain on the B3315. In ¾ mile a detour from the main route can be taken by turning left on to an unclassified road for Porthcurno and the Minack Theatre.

PORTHCURNO AND THE MINACK THEATRE, Cornwall

The first transatlantic cable was brought ashore in this village. Porthcurno has an exceptionally good beach of almost white sand, and just to the south is the unique Minack Theatre — built out of living stone on the edge of the cliffs by Miss Rowena Cade in 1931. The auditorium is formed from ridges cut into the sloping rock, with the natural bedding adapted to make seats facing south and east over a stage right on the cliff edge.

Continue with the 'Land's End' road and after ½ mile turn right still with the B3315. After 2 miles turn left on to the A30 'Land's End' road, and drive to Land's End.

LAND'S END, Cornwall

Famous as England's most westerly point, Land's End is about 873 miles from the equally famous John O'Groats in Scotland. On a fine day the Isles of Scilly are visible 28 miles away to the west. A leisure and exhibition complex outlines the natural history of the area.

LONGSHIPS LIGHTHOUSE, Cornwall

Some 2 miles out to sea from Land's End the Longships Lighthouse rises 50ft high from a 60ft rock. Waves have been known to lash as high as the lantern during severe storms.

Wave torn rocks and the distant Longships Lighthouse starkly outlined against sunset at Land's End.

A short detour can be taken by turning left in St Just on to an unclassified road to Cape Cornwall.

CAPE CORNWALL, Cornwall
Features of this headland, the only 'cape' in England or Wales, include a mine chimney, prehistoric burial ground and a ruined chapel.

From St Just continue on the St Ives road B3306 to Pendeen.

On the headland at St Ives is a fishermen's chapel.

Ruined mine buildings, like the Carn Galver Mine at Morvah, add much to Cornwall's landscape.

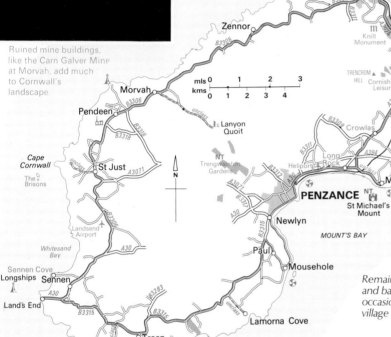

Lanyon Quoit is situated in an area rich in prehistoric remains.

Leave Land's End and return along the A30, past the 'Porthcurno' road, to Sennen.

SENNEN, Cornwall
According to legend Sennen, a small village with a past rich in local history, was the battleground for the last Cornish fight against invading Danes. The 15th-century church contains a medieval statue of the Virgin Mary and is the most westerly church in England. Sennen Cove offers good sand, excellent bathing, and superb scenery.

Continue on the A30. After 1¾ miles turn left on to the B3306, SP 'St Just' and pass Land's End Airport. After 3 miles turn left on to the A3071 and enter St Just.

ST JUST, Cornwall
Also known as St Just-in-Penwith, this village is noted for the contents of its old church. Among these is a wall painting, an interesting inscribed stone of 5th-century date, and the shaft of a 9th-century Hiberno-Saxon cross. St Just itself is enchanting.

PENDEEN, Cornwall
Around the village are derelict remains of old mine workings; one that survived until 1986, the Geevor Mine, has an impressive tin-mining museum (may not re-open after 1986). The village church is a copy of Iona Cathedral in Scotland.

Leave Pendeen and continue along the B3306 to Morvah.

MORVAH, Cornwall
This little farming and former mining village is set on the edge of the Penwith moorland. About 1 mile south of the village are Chun Castle and Chun Quoit, respectively a circular Iron-Age fort built of stone and the remains of a large Neolithic dolmen, or tomb chamber.

Shortly beyond Morvah a detour can be taken right along an unclassified road for 2 miles to Lanyon Quoit.

LANYON QUOIT, Cornwall
Perhaps the best known and most visited of Cornwall's megaliths, this neolithic tomb (NT) resembles a huge three-legged stone table.

Remain on the B3306 through rocky and barren countryside, with occasional views of the coast; skirt the village of Zennor.

ZENNOR, Cornwall
The 15th-century church in this former tin-mining community is famous for the mermaid bench end. The writers Virginia Woolf and DH Lawrence both lived in the village in the 1920s. A folk museum here is well worth visiting.

Continue on B3306 to St Ives.

ST IVES, Cornwall
Until her recent death the sculptress Barbara Hepworth was the leading light in a famous artists' community that lived in this attractive fishing port and major holiday resort. Quaint old houses, narrow streets and alleys cluster beneath the 120ft granite tower of the 15th-century church. There are two fine sandy beaches (one for surfing), and a semi-circular harbour. Of interest are the St Ives Museum (civil and maritime history) the Barnes Museum of Cinematography, Barbara Hepworth Museum and Sculpture Garden, St Ives Society of Artists Gallery, Penwith Galleries and the Bernard Leach Pottery.

Leave St Ives on the A3074 and follow SP 'Hayle'. Pass through Carbis Bay and continue into Lelant.

LELANT, Cornwall
Lelant, on the Hayle estuary has a Norman and Perpendicular-style church with a 17th-century sundial and the Cornish Heritage Leisure Park.

At Lelant turn right and in 1 mile at a roundabout take 3rd exit A30 SP 'Penzance'. One mile beyond Crowlas take 2nd exit at roundabout onto the 'Marazion' road unclassified. Shortly turn left and cross a railway bridge to Marazion.

MARAZION, Cornwall
Good bathing and fishing can be enjoyed in this ancient port, and the marshland between Marazion and Ludgvan is the habitat for many species of bird. Marvellous views of famous St Michael's Mount can be enjoyed from here.

ST MICHAEL'S MOUNT Cornwall
This little granite island (NT) rises to a 250ft summit from the waters of Mount's Bay and is accessible by foot via a causeway at low tide, or by boat, from Marazion. Its splendid castle (NT) and priory (NT), both founded by Edward the Confessor in the 11th-century, stand high above a small harbour and hamlet. Inside the 14th-century chapel is an excellent collection of armour and furniture.

Return along the unclassifed road and turn left for Long Rock to rejoin the A30 for Penzance.

PLYMOUTH AND THE WESTERN MOOR

This is the country of Drake and Raleigh, of large adventures in small boats and salty tales that the historians have somehow missed. North are the water-sculpted tors and heathy slopes of western Dartmoor, a place of vast spaces patterned with the shadows of clouds.

PLYMOUTH, Devon

Sandwiched between the estuaries of the Plym and the Tamar, this popular yachting resort and important maritime city is the venue for national sailing championships and a stop-off point for round-the-world yachtsmen. It has been a naval base since the 16th century, and in the 17th the Pilgrim Fathers sailed from its Sutton Harbour to the New World of America in the *Mayflower*. Today Sutton Harbour is busy with large and small boats, and the craft and antique shops, pubs and restaurants of the Barbican make it an exciting district of modern Plymouth as well as a fascinating historic memorial. Most of the city centre was rebuilt after appalling war damage, and the area where Royal Parade is bisected by spacious Armada Way includes a fine shopping complex. The 200ft-high Civic Centre affords excellent cross-town views from its roof deck. A prominent statue of Sir Francis Drake shares the Hoe with Smeaton's Tower (open), which is the re-erected base of the old Eddystone Lighthouse and the impressive Naval War Memorial. Near by are the 17th-century Royal Citadel (AM) and the outstanding aquarium of the Marine Biological Association. Rising from the waters of the sound, almost in front of the Hoe, is the rocky, tree-scattered hump of Drake's Island (NT). The city's Church of St Andrew is the largest in Devon and dates from the 15th century. Close by are Prysten House, the city's oldest building (open), the Victorian Guildhall and the Elizabethan Merchant's House (open). Also of interest are the Elizabethan House and Wall Mural in the Barbican, Charles Church (city war memorial) and the Museum and Art Gallery containing works by Reynolds. Across the estuary is Mount Edgcumbe, which can be reached via the Cremyll Passenger Ferry from Plymouth.

MOUNT EDGCUMBE HOUSE & COUNTRY PARK, Cornwall

This beautiful Tudor mansion (open) was severely damaged during World War II but has since been completely restored. Its lovely gardens and parkland offer extensive views of Plymouth Sound.

DEVONPORT, Devon

Although Devonport started life with an identity of its own, the establishment of the important naval dockyard on the Hamoaze in 1691 resulted in its rapid development into the navy quarter of neighbouring Plymouth. Its fine 19th-century town hall was by the architect John Foulston, and older foundations include the Gun Wharf of 1718 and the Royal Naval Hospital, also of the 18th century.

THE TAMAR BRIDGES, Devon Devon

Spanning the Tamar river north-west of Plymouth city centre are two famous bridges that have opened up the West Country to tourism. The oldest is the Royal Albert, a railway bridge designed by the brilliant engineer Brunel and completed in 1859. Close by is a modern, single-span suspension road bridge opened in 1961 with a lightness and grace that contrast sharply with the heavy solidity of its elderly neighbour.

From Plymouth follow SP 'Exeter' to reach Marsh Mills roundabout. Take 3rd exit onto the Plympton road B3416 and cross the River Plym. Shortly on the left is a road to the Plym Valley Railway then in ½ mile pass a road on the right leading to Saltram House.

Monuments to their times — these two handsome bridges span the Tamar at Saltash.

Sir Francis Drake's statue stands on Plymouth Hoe.

SALTRAM HOUSE, Devon

This fine Tudor house (NT) has an 18th-century façade and contains a saloon and dining room by designer Robert Adam. Features of the lovely garden include an 18th-century summer house and a quaint orangery dating from 1773.

Continue on the B3416 for a further ¾ mile and meet a mini-roundabout. A short detour from the main route to the centre of Plympton can be made from here by keeping forward.

PLYMPTON, Devon

In medieval times Plymouth was an insignificant little hamlet called Sutton, and Plympton an important town with a wealthy priory. Since then the elder community has

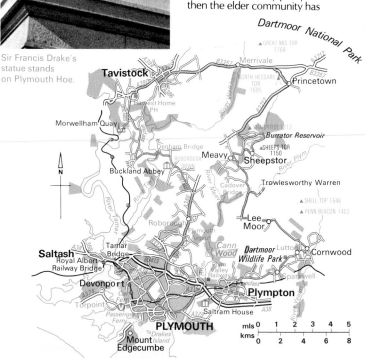

become a suburb of the successful younger. A Norman keep on a mound affords goods views. There are two medieval churches, a 16th-century guildhall, and an old grammar school where the painter Sir Joshua Reynolds, who was born in the town, was educated. At the Plym Valley Railway project (no trains running at present) a varied collection of locomotives can be seen.

From the mini-roundabout on the main route turn left SP 'Exeter', and in another ½ mile turn left again SP 'Sparkwell' and 'Cornwood'. In ¼ mile at a mini-roundabout turn right, and continue to Sparkwell. Beyond the village reach the Dartmoor Wildlife Park on the left.

DARTMOOR WILDLIFE PARK, Devon

A fine collection of British and European animals can be seen in this 25-acre zoo park. Excellent all-round views of the grounds are afforded by a tall observation tower.

Continue through Lutton to Cornwood.

CORNWOOD, Devon
The Hawns ravine on the River Yealm is a feature of this attractively situated village. Dendles Wood incorporates a national nature reserve, and there are numerous Bronze-Age enclosures and hut circles in the district. Fardell and Stert, family seats of the Raleighs and Drakes lie 1½ miles south.

At crossroads turn left SP 'Tavistock'. Begin a gradual ascent with Penn Beacon prominent on the right before skirting the industrial features of Lee Moor village.

Tunnel on the Tavistock Canal above Morwellham Quay

LEE MOOR, Devon
Colossal conical mountains of white waste dominate the landscape here, proclaiming Lee Moor as Devon's principal source of china clay.

Continue, with wide views, to a crossroads and turn right. In 1¾ miles reach Cadover Bridge on the River Plym and bear left. Trowlesworthy Warren nature trail is to the right here.

TROWLESWORTHY WARREN, Devon
This 1¾-mile nature trail flanks the south-west corner of Dartmoor alongside the River Plym. Prehistoric hut circles can be seen near the river's headwaters.

Ascend, and at the summit turn right SP 'Sheepstor, Meavy'. Descend into Meavy Valley, crossing the river to reach the edge of Meavy. A short detour can be made into the village by turning left here.

MEAVY, Devon
The stream from which this delightful village takes its name winds through woodlands over a rocky bed and pours over a small waterfall. Beside the Norman church on the village green is an ancient oak which is traditionally held to be the church's contemporary.

Cox Tor is situated north of the B3357 road between Tavistock and Merrivale.

Continue forward on the main drive SP 'Princetown' and in ½ mile turn sharp right SP 'Burrator'. In ¾ mile turn right again SP 'Sheepstor' and cross the dam of Burrator Reservoir. In another ¾ mile turn left. A short detour to Sheepstor village can be made by bearing right here.

SHEEPSTOR & THE BURRATOR RESERVOIR, Devon
This enchanting hamlet is centred round an appealing little granite church. The picturesque Burrator Reservoir offers a dramatic backcloth, its sparkling waters reflecting the height of Sheeps Tor and the wooded slopes that rise from the opposite shore.

Skirt the reservoir on a narrow road and after 3 miles turn sharp right SP 'Princetown'. Ascend, and in ¾ mile meet crossroads and turn right again on to the B3212. Climb on to the wide, open moorland of Dartmoor National Park to reach Princetown. On the approach to Princetown are views left of 1,695ft North Hessary Tor and a BBC transmitter.

DARTMOOR NATIONAL PARK (WEST), Devon
Much of this tour is in the south-western part of this vast area, and near Princetown it climbs on to the rugged uplands of the moor itself. The landscape is dramatic and full of contrast, where jagged granite tors rise, from heather and bracken-clad slopes and peat bogs constantly replenished by the highest rainfall in Devon, though here and there great plantations of conifers are helping to dry the ground and bring back the forests that once stood here. Prehistoric crosses and hut circles are common in these parts.

PRINCETOWN, Devon
Sir Thomas Tyrwhitt founded the great convict prison here in 1806 and named the town in honour of his friend, the Prince Regent. Forced labour built many of the roads that allow modern motorists to tour comfortably through remote parts of the moor, and the town church was built by prisoners in 1883.

Turn left on to the B3357 'Tavistock' road, shortly passing the prison, then in 1 mile meet a T-junction and turn left again. Great Mis Tor rises to 1,768ft to the right, and views ahead encompass the Tamar valley and Bodmin Moor. Gradually descend from Dartmoor itself and pass Merrivale Quarry in the Walkham Valley to leave the Dartmoor National Park and enter Tavistock.

Buckland Abbey contains many items connected with Sir Francis Drake, including a portrait of Elizabeth I in panelled Drake's Drawing Room.

TAVISTOCK, Devon
There is an imposing town hall and remains of an abbey founded in the 10th-century. St Eustace's church, 15th-century, has interesting monuments and there is a statue of Sir Frances Drake born at Crowndale just south of the town. Light engineering and timber-working firms in this pleasant market town continue an industrial tradition that started at least as far back as the 14th century. Despite this activity the town remains unspoilt, an ideal touring base on the western fringe of the extensive Dartmoor National Park.;

Leave Tavistock on the A390 'Liskeard' road. In 2½ miles reach the Harvest Home PH and branch left on to an unclassified road SP 'Morwellham'. In 1 mile meet crossroads and go forward, SP 'Morwellham'. Follow a long descent to Morwellham Quay.

MORWELLHAM QUAY, Devon
This quay was once a busy copper-loading port on the River Tamar. Surviving installations now form part of a major industrial museum featuring the history of the port in particular and the development of the Devon copper mines in general.

Return to the crossroads and turn sharp right SP 'Bere Alston'. Continue along a high ridge between the Tamar and Tavy valleys, and after 2¾ miles turn sharp left SP 'Denham Bridge, Plymouth'. After a long descent cross the River Tavy at Denham Bridge and immediately turn right SP 'Plymouth'. Ascend to a T-junction and turn right SP 'Buckland Abbey'. In ½ mile meet crossroads and turn right, passing the entrance to Buckland Abbey on the right, then immediately left.

BUCKLAND ABBEY, Devon
Originally built by Cistercian monks in 1278, Buckland Abbey was considerably altered and adapted as a dwelling place by the Grenville family. The present house (NT) was sold to Sir Francis Drake in 1581, and nowadays contains a Drake Museum full of relics associated with the great sailor.

In 1¾ miles drive to crossroads at the edge of Roborough Down and turn left. Meet a T-junction and turn right on to the A386 (no SP) for Plymouth. Pass through Roborough, and Plymouth Airport on the return to the city centre.

SALISBURY, Wilts
The ancient city of Salisbury first came to importance following the abandonment of nearby Old Sarum in the 13th century. The bishop's see was transferred from the old to the new site, and in 1220 the cathedral was refounded in an early-English style that made it seem to soar from the ground rather than sit solidly on it. This illusion is accentuated by numerous slim columns of Purbeck stone and a magnificent 404ft spire that was added in the 14th century and is still the tallest in the country. The Cathedral Close preserves a beauty and atmosphere all of its own, and contains fine buildings dating from the 14th to the 18th centuries. Elsewhere in the town are 16th-century Joiner's Hall (NT), the 14th-century Poultry Cross (AM), and a great number of old inns. Interesting displays illustrating local history can be seen in the Salisbury and South Wiltshire Museum.

From Salisbury follow SP 'Yeovil A30' and drive to Wilton.

WILTON, Wilts
Wilton is an interesting town best known as an important carpet-making centre. Good Georgian houses can be seen in Kinsbury Square, and a curious country cross stands near the market house of 1738. Wilton House (open) was built on the site of Wilton Abbey in the 1540s, but was completely rebuilt by Inigo Jones after a serious fire. Subsequent work includes alterations by architect James Wyatt. Features of the lovely grounds (open) include fine cedars and a Palladian-style bridge over the Nadder.

At roundabout take the 1st exit, passing Wilton House on the left. In ½ mile reach the end of the village and turn right on to an unclassified road SP 'Great Wishford'. Go forward for 2¾ miles, with Grovely Woods to the left, then turn right into Great Wishford.

ON THE WILTSHIRE DOWNS

The grandeur of this tour is in the cathedral city of Salisbury and some of the county's finest stately homes. The beauty is in its fertile river valleys, and soft downland slopes that enfold timeless villages and open up panoramic views from their tree-crowned summits.

Salisbury's cathedral has been a source of inspiration for many artists, including John Constable.

GREAT WISHFORD, Wilts
This delightful village is set in the Wylye Valley and has a church with a 15th-century crenellated tower. On Oak Apple Day (May 29) the villagers reaffirm their right to collect kindling from Grovely Woods.

Drive to the village church, turn left, and shortly afterwards turn right. Continue to Little Langford.

LITTLE LANGFORD, Wilts
Noted architect T H Wyatt rebuilt the local church in 1864, using material from the previous building. About ½ mile south west of the village is the notable iron-age hillfort of Grovely Castle.

Continue to Hanging Langford.

The bridge in the grounds of Wilton House was built in 1737 to a Palladian pattern.

HANGING LANGFORD, Wilts
Hanging Langford clings precariously to the lower flanks of hills at the edge of Grovely Wood. Some 2 miles south west of the hamlet is an earthwork that has yielded evidence of prolonged occupation.

Keep forward and drive to Wylye.

WYLYE, Wilts
Lovely flint-and-stone chequerwork cottages dating from the 17th century can be seen in this village, which stands on the Wylye River at the edge of Salisbury Plain.

SALISBURY PLAIN, Wilts
Most of the undulating 240 square miles of this windswept plateau is under cultivation, although some parts have been given over to military use. Many of its low chalk hills feature prehistoric burial mounds and other monuments. The borders of the plain are defined by the rivers Avon, Bourne, and Wylye.

From Wylye keep forward on the unclassified road SP 'Sutton Veny'. Drive along the Wylye Valley to Stockton.

STOCKTON, Wilts
Stockton boasts thatched cottages, an Elizabethan mansion, and an Elizabethan farmhouse with a great barn. Attractive almshouses are grouped round a common courtyard reached via an arched entry.

After 1 mile cross the railway line and turn right for Boyton.

BOYTON, Wilts
Flint and stone chequerwork common to this area can be seen in 13th-century and later Boyton Church, which was restored by the 19th-century architect T H Wyatt.

Drive through Corton and Tytherington, then keep left for Sutton Veny.

SUTTON VENY, Wilts
The ruined church of Sutton Veny dates from the 13th century and lies east of its 19th-century successor. Also here is a manor house dating from the 14th century.

At crossroads at the far end of the village turn left on to the B3095. Drive to Longbridge Deverill.

Overlooking the lake at Stourhead is the Pantheon, which contains casts of statues.

LONGBRIDGE DEVERILL, Wilts
John Thynne of Longleat House built the charming group of 17th-century almshouses here. His funeral helm hangs with two others in the tower of the local church.

At crossroads turn right on to the A350. In ½ mile turn left on unclassified road SP 'Crockerton' and then turn left SP 'Horningsham'. Continue through woodland passing Shear Water on the right. After 1¼ miles at T-junction turn right. Take the next turning right SP 'Longleat' to the outskirts of Horningsham. (To avoid Longleat Park toll forward through to Horningham/Bath Arms PH) turn right passing the Heavens Gate viewpoint and running alongside Longleat Estate. After 1¼ miles, before the A362 turn left to enter Longleat Park (toll).

LONGLEAT HOUSE, Wilts
This great Elizabethan mansion (open), the seat of the Marquess of Bath, stands on the site of a 13th-century priory and is a treasure house of old furniture, paintings, books, and interior decoration. It was one of England's first unified designs, and the grounds were landscaped by the brilliant 18th-century designer Capability Brown. The estate includes a large safari park (open), the first of its kind in Europe.

Leave the park with SP 'Way Out' and 'Warminster' via the Horningsham Gate.

HORNINGSHAM, Wilts
The thatched noncomformist Meeting House here, said to be one of the oldest of its kind in England, may date from the 16th century.

Drive to the Bath Arms (PH), meet crossroads, and go forward SP 'Shaftesbury' and 'Maiden Bradley'. In 1½ miles at a T-junction turn right for Maiden Bradley.

MAIDEN BRADLEY, Wilts
Wooded downland hills rise to 945ft Long Knoll above this pretty village, in which may be seen a number of attractive old houses.

At crossroads turn left on to the B3092 SP 'Mere', then pass the outskirts of Stourton.

STOURTON, Wilts
Good paintings and Chippendale furniture can be seen inside Stourhead House (NT), but this famous 18th-century mansion is best known for its superb grounds. These were laid out by Henry Hoare, who owned the estate, and show one of Europe's finest layouts of this period. In the park are classical garden temples and a delightful lake.

Continue for 1¼ miles, then turn right and then turn left SP 'Andover' to join the A303. Continue through open countryside for 3½ miles then turn right on to the B3089 SP 'Salisbury'. Continue to the A350 and turn left, then turn immediately right for Hindon.

HINDON, Wilts
Created by bishops of Winchester in the 13th century, this village was handsomely rebuilt by Wyatt after a fire and is an example of good 19th-century restoration.

Proceed from the Grosvenor Arms Hotel and turn right on to an unclassified road SP 'Tisbury'. Meet crossroads and turn right (no SP). Follow a narrow byroad to Newtown. Turn right SP 'Semley', then turn left SP 'Donhead' and 'Wardour'. Descend, and in ½ mile cross a railway. Shortly turn left SP 'Tisbury' and continue past the grounds of Wardour Castle.

WARDOUR CASTLE, Wilts
New Wardour Castle (open), the largest Georgian house in Wiltshire, was begun in 1769 for the 8th Lord Arundell. Its private chapel is larger than many a parish church, and very richly decorated.

WARDOUR OLD CASTLE, Wilts
Wardour Old Castle (AM) dates from the end of the 14th-century. It stands on a wooded bank overlooking an 18th-century artificial lake and is uniquely hexagonal in shape.

Keep forward for Tisbury.

TISBURY, Wilts
In the 7th century this village stood on an important Saxon track. Its cruciform church dates from the 12th century and shares the churchyard with a giant yew, 36ft in circumference, that is reputed to be more than 1,000 years old.

Turn right at the post office SP 'Salisbury'. Continue to the end of the village and turn right again. Proceed for ¾ mile and branch left SP 'Chilmark', passing Place Farm on the left.

PLACE FARM, Wilts
Formerly an abbey grange, this farm comprises a group of 14th to 15th-century domestic buildings. The 200ft-long tithe barn, is one of the largest in England.

Drive to Chilmark.

CHILMARK, Wilts
The creamy stone from Chilmark's quarries (closed) was used in Wilton House, Salisbury Cathedral, and the spire of Chichester Cathedral.

Turn left SP 'Salisbury', then right. Continue to the main road and turn right again, on to the B3089 for Teffont Magna. Keep right into the village, drive to the Black Horse (PH), and turn right on to an unclassified road. Continue with SP 'Tisbury' into Teffont Evias.

TEFFONT EVIAS, Wilts
Twin Teffont Magna and Teffont Evias stand close together in the beautiful Nadder Valley. The former boasts the delightful Fitz House of 1700, and the latter a Tudor mansion that was once the home of Sir James Ley, who became Lord Chief Justice of England and was immortalized by Milton in a sonnet.

In ¼ mile turn left with SP 'Salisbury' and cross a river bridge. Ascend to a main road and turn right to re-join the B3089. After ¾ mile at crossroads (the outskirts of Dinton) turn right on to an unclassified road for Fovant. A slight detour can be made to Philipps House by turning left at the crossroads.

PHILIPPS HOUSE, Wilts
Designed by Sir Jeffry Wyatville in 1816, this splendid neo-Grecian mansion (NT) stands in 200-acre Dinton Park and is let to the YWCA (open by appointment).

DINTON, Wilts
Three notable National Trust properties are to be found on the outskirts of this hillside village. Besides Philipps House there is the Tudor to 18th-century Hyde's House (not open) and ivy-covered Little Clarendon, which dates from the 15th-century (open on application).

On the main route, continue into Fovant.

FOVANT, Wilts
Huge regimental badges were cut in the chalk downs by soldiers stationed here during World War I. A memorial brass of 1492 can be seen in the local church.

Drive to the end of the village and turn right on to the A30. In ½ mile turn left on to an unclassified road SP 'Broad Chalke'. Ascend on to the downs, and after 1½ miles turn left. Drive to Broad Chalke, bear right then left through the village, and proceed to Bishopstone.

BISHOPSTONE, Wilts
Remarkable furnishings can be seen inside the local church, a beautiful cruciform building with superb stone vaulting and windows.

Continue to Coombe Bissett.

COOMBE BISSETT, Wilts
Just downstream from the fine 18th-century bridge that spans the river here is a picturesque packhorse bridge. Its wooden parapets are new, but the mounting stone is very old. Traces of every century from Norman times to the present day can be seen in the fabric of the attractive local church.

Turn left on to the A354 and return to Salisbury.

A picturesque old mill stands beside the River Ebble in Coombe Bissett.

FARMLAND AND FOREST

Gentle hills and farmland watered by several rivers characterize the fertile Blackmoor Vale. In contrast are the rolling grass and woodlands of Cranborne Chase, a vast area that was once the private hunting preserve of kings.

Gold Hill, Shaftesbury's most picturesque street, overlooks the Blackmoor Vale.

SHAFTESBURY, Dorset
Situated on the edge of a 700ft plateau, Shaftesbury is an ancient town full of quaint corners and little eccentricities. Its most famous street, cobbled Gold Hill, plunges down the hillside with a graceful abandon. Thomas Hardy used the original town name Shaston when featuring it in his novels. Shaftesbury's history began with the abbey established here c880, a foundation that became the burial place of Edward the Martyr and grew to be one of the richest in the area until destroyed at the Dissolution in the 16th century. Only slight remains now exist (AM, open sometimes), but various relics are preserved in the Abbey Ruins Museum. In the Grosvenor Hotel is the famous Chevy Chase sideboard, which was carved from a single piece of oak in the 13th century.

Take the A30 'Sherborne, Yeovil' road and descend to the Blackmoor Vale. In 5 miles at East Stour, turn left on to the B3092 SP 'Sturminster Newton' and enter the Stour Valley. Continue to Marnhull.

MARNHULL, Dorset
Thomas Hardy called this village Marlott and made it the birthplace of his heroine in *Tess of the d'Urbervilles*. The 14th-century church has an attractive pinnacled tower overlooking Blackmoor Vale.

Continue to Sturminster Newton.

STURMINSTER NEWTON, Dorset
Important livestock markets are held in this southern Blackmoor Vale town. A fine six-arched medieval bridge spans the Stour, and both Sturminster Mill and the 14th-century Fiddleford Mill one mile to the east have been restored to working order.

Sherborne Abbey has beautiful 15th-century fan vaulting in the choir.

Continue through Sturminster Newton on the 'Blandford' road. Cross a bridge and turn right on to the A357 SP 'Stalbridge' then pass through agricultural country to reach Lydlinch Common. Continue for ¾ mile and turn left on to an unclassified road SP 'Stourton Caundle'. Pass the edge of Stourton Caundle and proceed to Purse Caundle.

PURSE CAUNDLE, Dorset
Purse Caundle Manor is an excellent medieval house (open), notable for its great hall and chamber, and beautiful oriel window.

Proceed for ¼ mile and turn left on to the A30 SP 'Sherborne'. Continue to Milborne Port.

MILBORNE PORT, Dorset
Although stone is the predominant building material in this area, beautiful Venn House was brick built in Queen Anne style c1700. The local church preserves Saxon work, and a fine tympanum over the south door.

Proceed on the A30 to Sherborne. (For the town centre turn left)

SHERBORNE, Dorset
Winding streets of mellow stone-built houses dating from the 15th century onwards weave a fascinating web across this beautiful and historic town. From AD705 to 1075 Sherborne was a cathedral city, but the great church was adopted by a slightly later monastery that flourished until the Dissolution in the 16th century. Many of the foundation's buildings were adopted by other bodies and survive in a good state of preservation. Some were occupied by the famous Sherborne School, and the Abbey Gatehouse now accommodates the Sherborne Museum of local history. Over all stands the Norman to 15th-century Abbey Church, a magnificent building best known for its superb fan vaulting. The older of the town's two castles stands ½ mile east and dates from the 12th and 13th centuries. It was reduced to a picturesque heap of ruins (AM) in the Civil War. Sherborne's 16th-century castle was built for Sir Walter Raleigh, and contains fine furniture, paintings, and porcelain (open). It is set in 20-acre grounds designed by the 18th-century garden landscaper Capability Brown.

Follow SP 'Dorchester' to leave Sherborne on the A352. Pass through wooded country and continue through Middlemarsh. Make a winding ascent on the outer slopes to 860ft High Stoy to pass through a gap in the hills and reach Minterne Magna.

MINTERNE MAGNA, Dorset
Features of the attractive wild shrub garden that occupies 29 acres of ground round Minterne House (open) include bamboo-lined walks, great banks of Himalayan and Chinese rhododendrons, and a beautiful collection of azaleas.

Continue for 2 miles and branch left to enter Cerne Abbas. The turf-cut Giant can be seen to the left.

CERNE ABBAS GIANT, Dorset
This 180ft long figure (NT) is believed to be associated with fertility rites and may date from before the Roman occupation.

CERNE ABBAS, Dorset
The village of Cerne Abbas derives its name from a Benedictine abbey founded here in 987. Remains of this include a beautiful 15th-century guesthouse, and the contemporary tithe barn has been converted into a house. Early examples of heraldic stained glass can be seen in the windows of the local church.

In Cerne Abbas centre turn left on to an unclassified road, then in ¼ mile turn right on to the 'Piddletrenthide' road to reach that village.

PIDDLETRENTHIDE, Dorset
Attractive yellow-stone houses are scattered for nearly a mile along the banks of the River Piddle, or Trent. The 15th-century church has one of the finest towers in Dorset.

Turn right onto the B3143 and continue through Piddlehinton. Continue for 1¼ miles and turn left on to the Puddletown road B3142 to pass Waterston Manor and reach Puddletown.

PUDDLETOWN, Dorset
Thomas Hardy's Weatherbury in *Far from the Madding Crowd*, this village is one of the most attractive in Dorset and features a beautiful 15th-century church with an unusual panelled roof. Elizabethan and later Waterston Manor stands 2 miles northwest and was described by Hardy as Bathsheba's house in *Far from the Madding Crowd*. Between the village and Wareham are stretches of moorland that were part of the novel's Egdon Heath.

ATHELHAMPTON HOUSE, Dorset
Standing in 10 acres of formal landscape and water gardens about 1 mile east of Puddletown is the notable 15th- and 16th-century Athelhampton House, one of England's finest medieval houses (open).

Leave Puddletown by turning left on to the A354 SP 'Blandford'. Continue to Milborne St Andrew, then take an unclassifield valley road to the left and drive to Milton Abbas.

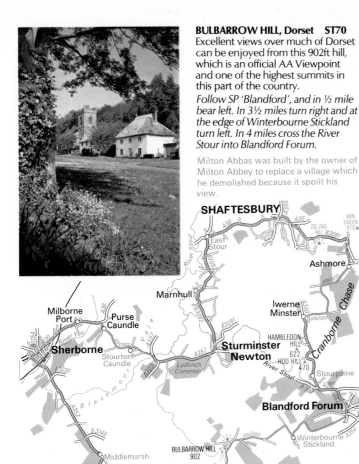

BULBARROW HILL, Dorset ST70
Excellent views over much of Dorset
can be enjoyed from this 902ft hill,
which is an official AA Viewpoint
and one of the highest summits in
this part of the country.
*Follow SP 'Blandford', and in ½ mile
bear left. In 3½ miles turn right and at
the edge of Winterbourne Stickland
turn left. In 4 miles cross the River
Stour into Blandford Forum.*

Milton Abbas was built by the owner of
Milton Abbey to replace a village which
he demolished because it spoilt his
view.

Bulbarrow Hill is situated in a part of
Dorset which is designated as an area of
outstanding natural beauty.

*Leave Blandford Forum on the B3082
then A350 SP 'Warminster'. Continue
along the Stour Valley and pass
through Stourpaine. Just past the
village on the left are the hills of
Hambledon and Hod.*

**HAMBLEDON AND HOD HILLS,
Dorset**
Grass-covered Hambledon Hill rises
to 622ft and is topped by earthworks
raised at various times between the
stone age and the Roman conquest.
Its steep flanks, worth climbing for
the tremendous views, were used by
General Wolfe to train troops before
embarking to take Quebec. To the
south east is slightly lower Hod Hill,
which features ancient earthworks
and traces of a Roman camp that
was built and manned cAD63.

Continue to Iwerne Minster.

IWERNE MINSTER, Dorset
The local Norman to 17th-century
church has an attractive stone spire.
Just outside the village is the site of a
Roman villa.

*From Iwerne Minster war memorial
turn right on to the unclassified
'Tarrant Gunville' road. Climb on to
the heights of Cranborne Chase and
turn left on to the Shaftesbury road.
Excellent views across Blackmoor
Vale can be enjoyed from this section
of route. Continue for 1¾ miles and
at crossroads turn right for Ashmore.*

ASHMORE, Dorset
Georgian houses mingle with flint,
stone, and brick cottages round a
duckpond and 19th-century church
in this charming village. The village
itself stands at 700ft in the chalk hills
of Cranborne Chase and is the
highest in Dorset. To the north is a
summit, topped by a prehistoric
earthwork, which commands views
across the Chase to the Solent
channel and the Isle of Wight.

*Keep left of Ashmore village pond
and in 1 mile join the B3081 to enter
Wiltshire for a short distance. On the
right is tree-capped Win Green, a
910ft hill which is accessible by track
and is the highest point on Cranborne
Chase. Re-enter Dorset and descend
Zig-Zag Hill to enter Shaftesbury.*

mls 0 1 2 3 4 5
kms 0 2 4 6 8

The atmosphere of rural tranquillity at
Ashmore is enhanced by a duckpond.

MILTON ABBAS, Dorset
Set in unspoilt rural surroundings,
this peaceful village of thatched and
whitewashed cottages was designed
and built from scratch during the
18th century. It was probably the first
integrally planned village in Britain.
The Brewery Farm Museum is
housed in the old brewery and
contains antique agricultural
implements, bygones, old
photographs, and other relics.

*From the foot of the village follow the
'Hilton' road past Milton Abbey.*

MILTON ABBEY, Dorset
The beautiful abbey church dates
from the 14th and 15th centuries
and stands in front of a hill
surmounted by a Norman chapel.
Next to Milton Abbey is 15th-century
Abbot's Hall, which was
incorporated in a mansion by
architects Sir William Chambers and
James Wyatt. The huge 18th-century
mansion here now is of exceptional
interest and houses a school. It is
open during the summer months.

*Reach Hilton and in ¾ mile turn right
and shortly right again for Bulbarrow
Hill.*

BLANDFORD FORUM, Dorset
All but 50 or so of the town's houses
were destroyed by a terrible fire in
1731, which explains why handsome
brick and stone architecture of the
late 18th century is so much in
evidence. Earlier survivals include the
Ryves Almshouses of 1682, Dale
House of 1689, and the early 17th-
century Old House. Much of the
countryside round Blandford is rich
arable and dairy-farming land,
watered by the beautiful River Stour
to the south and fringed by the
lovely countryside of Cranborne
Chase to the north and west.

CRANBORNE CHASE, Dorset
Now an area of rolling grasslands
scattered with fine beechwoods, the
Chase covers over 100 square miles
between Shaftesbury and Salisbury
and was once a royal hunting forest.
Subsequently the local hunting rights
passed into the hands of the earls of
Salisbury and Shaftesbury.

SHEPTON MALLET, Somerset

Shepton is short for the Saxon name Sheeptown, and Mallet was the Norman name of the lord of the manor. The wool trade brought wealth to the village in the 15th century and the magnificent church, with its high, fine tower, was built with the profits. Inside, the oak roof is lavishly decorated with 350 carved panels and about 300 carved bosses — all of different designs. In the market square stands the ornate market cross. Rebuilt in 1841, this has been the social and commercial centre of the village for 5 centuries; at one time even wives were put up for sale here, as well as more usual market goods. There is also a museum in the square where Roman relics and finds from the Mendip caves can be seen. Nearby are the medieval Shambles; these wooden market-benches were not slaughter houses (the usual meaning of Shambles) but market stalls.

Leave on the A371, SP 'Castle Cary'. After 1¾ miles turn right on to the A37, then ¼ mile farther take the A371.
Go through Prestleigh and opposite the Royal Bath and West showground, branch left on to the B3081 for Evercreech.

EVERCREECH, Somerset

Of all Somerset's beautiful Perpendicular church towers, this is perhaps the finest. An impression of great height is achieved by the tiers of tall pinnacles and bell-openings. The nave roof has 16 angels painted on its ceiling and gilded bosses. St Peter's overlooks a pleasant square with old cottages, almshouses and the village cross raised on well-worn steps.

At the crossroads turn left, SP 'Stoney Stratton', and 'Batcombe'. At the T-junction ½ mile later, turn right into Stoney Stratton, then in ¼ mile turn left, SP 'Batcombe'. After 1¾ miles bear left, then turn right, and at the next crossroads turn right again. In Batcombe, by the church, turn right on to the Bruton road and later join the B3081 for Bruton.

Superb landscaping at Stourhead

WEST SOMERSET AND THE WILTSHIRE BORDERS

The graceful spires of the great wool churches pierce the skies above the green, undulating landscape of West Somerset, and the glory of Stourhead's beautiful gardens and the excitements of Longleat's Safari Park draw visitors over the border into Wiltshire.

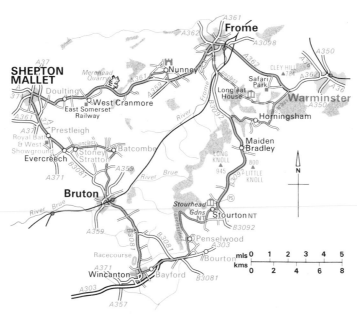

BRUTON, Somerset

Bruton was another of the chief textile towns in Somerset, and in 1290 one of the very first fulling mills in England was built on the banks of a nearby stream. The River Brue flows through the village and crossing it is the ancient packhorse bridge over which men and horses have trudged for centuries. A good view of the town is to be had from here, and several historic buildings hide among the narrow streets. There is, for instance, the 17th-century Hugh Sexey's Hospital, bequeathed to the town by a local stable boy who later found fame in London as auditor to Elizabeth I. Also of note is 16th-century King's Grammar

School which was founded by Edward VI. One of its most famous scholars was R. D. Blackmore, author of *Lorna Doone*. Bruton had a priory in the 12th century but all that remains of that now is a dovecot (NT) and part of the wall which both lie in a field behind the town.

From the one-way system in Bruton follow the B3081, SP 'Wincanton'. Continue through hilly countryside and after 4 miles pass Wincanton Racecourse before reaching Wincanton.

WINCANTON, Somerset

The town's medieval name, Wyndcaleton, came from the River Cale on which it stands on the edge of the Blackmoor Vale. Unfortunately a fire in the early 18th century destroyed most of Wincanton's buildings and left little of interest, apart from the church which has a 15th-century tower. Nevertheless it is a pleasant place with steep streets and makes an ideal base for touring the dairy hills of southern Somerset.

Turn left into Wincanton main street, SP 'Andover', and at the far end of the neighbouring village of Bayford turn left on to the A303. In 1½ miles turn left SP 'Penselwood', and in ½ mile turn left again. Later the tour bears left, SP 'Stourton', and the road gradually reaches 793ft. On the way down, after ¼ mile, turn sharp right (still SP 'Stourton'), and in 1½ miles by the ornamental lake, bear left and continue to Stourton.

Most famous of Frome's ancient lanes is Cheap Street, complete with water course

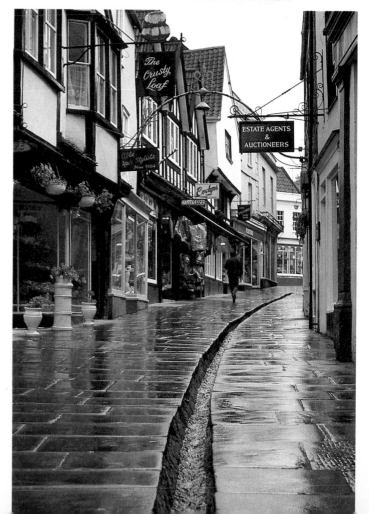

In the picture gallery ante-room at Stourhead House is *The Adoration of the Magi* — an early painting by Jan Provost

STOURTON, Wilts
Lovely Stourton (NT) lies on the edge of the Stourhead estate overlooking the lake and gardens. The village consists of an extremely pleasing group of whitewashed 18th-century cottages facing St Peter's Church standing on its smooth open lawn, an inn and the graceful medieval Bristol High Cross — brought here in 1780. Inside the church are several monuments to the Hoare family, the famous bankers and creators of Stourhead.

Continue through the village, past the entrance to Stourhead Gardens.

STOURHEAD HOUSE AND GARDENS, Wilts
During the 18th-century the Hoares built the present Palladian mansion and dammed a nearby valley to form the beautiful lake in the gardens below. The original concept of the gardens was based on 4 ingredients — water, temples, trees and green grass. It was inspired by Henry Hoare's travels through Italy and the whole is a masterpiece of landscape gardening with the lake as a glittering centrepiece. Whatever the season there is always a heady profusion of colour at Stourhead, set against the timeless backdrop of ancient beech trees, rippling water and stone temples.

Leave the gardens and in ¼ mile turn left off on to the B3092, SP 'Frome', for Maiden Bradley.

MAIDEN BRADLEY, Wilts
Bradley House, home of the Dukes of Somerset, once stood on the edge of this neat and leafy village, but apart from 1 wing, this was demolished at the beginning of the last century. At Priory Farm lie the scant remains of a former leper hospital, founded in the 12th-century for the care of female patients, and later turned into an Augustinian Priory.

2 miles beyond Maiden Bradley turn right, SP 'Horningsham' and 'Longleat', and continue to Horningsham.

HORNINGSHAM, Wilts
At the heart of the village outside The Bath Arms, huddle a group of lime trees so intertwined that their branches form a close-weave canopy overhead. There are 12 of them and are thus locally known as the Apostles. Horningsham lies under the shadow of its famous neighbour, Longleat, and its valley borders the park. Possibly it is because of Longleat that Horningsham has what could be the oldest Non-conformist chapel in England. Many think that this small, thatched meeting house was built by Sir John Thynne, builder of Longleat, for his Scottish labour force.

Remain on the Longleat road and after ¾ mile pass Horningsham Church, then in ¼ mile turn left (still SP 'Longleat'). Follow this road through attractive woodland and after 1½ miles, pass the entrance to Longleat House on the left. (Access to the Longleat estate is via a toll road. If taken, leave the grounds by following SP 'Frome' and 'The West'. Later join the B3092 and enter Frome from the south to rejoin the main tour).

LONGLEAT, Wilts
Lions have made Longleat famous, but the hub of this huge estate belonging to the Marquess of Bath, the house, deserves its own notoriety. Builder Sir John Thynne originally transformed the Augustinian priory into a comfortable house, but sadly this suffered considerable fire damage in 1567 and the existing Elizabethan mansion is mostly Robert Smythson's work. The splendid exterior is more than matched by the inside: rich tapestries, Genoese velvet and ancient Spanish leather clothe the

walls, while Italianate painted ceilings and marble fireplaces ornament the state rooms. Much of the beautiful parkland, landscaped by Capability Brown and Humphry Repton, is occupied by the Safari Park. In the drive-through open reserves many wild animals, besides the lions, roam freely. The ornamental lake is the home of sealions and hippos and in the middle lies Ape Island. A narrow-gauge railway, an adventure playground and a pets' corner are just a few of the many other attractions at Longleat.

The main tour turns left on to the A362, SP 'Frome'. (After ½ mile note the turning on the left for Longleat Safari Park). Continue on the A362 to Frome.

FROME, Somerset
The old wool town of Frome, which takes its name from the river, is a busy, thriving place whose attractive character survives the summer traffic jams. Around its market place there is a network of old narrow streets to

Nunney Castle, built by John de la Mare in 1373 with the spoils of war

be explored; paved Cheap Street, with its central water conduit, leads picturesquely to the church, where Gentle Street winds up in steps towards the top of the town. The bridge over the Frome incorporates an 18th-century lock-up and nearby stand the Bluecoat School and Blue House, an attractive almshouse, built in 1726 and recently restored.

Leave on the A361 Glastonbury road. In 3¼ miles turn right onto an unclassified road, SP 'Nunney' and continue to Nunney.

NUNNEY, Somerset
Grey-stone, red-roofed cottages cluster round Nunney Castle (AM) — the tall, grey centrepiece of the village. Really a fortified manor house built in 1373, it is a fine sight with its 4 round towers and beautiful moat. Although the castle withstood Roundhead attacks well during the Civil War, it was eventually slighted by Cromwell. A footbridge over the moat and stream leads to the village church where there are a number of elaborate stone monuments to the de la Mares, owners of the castle.

In Nunney turn left, SP 'Shepton Mallet', cross the river bridge then turn left again. A mile later, at the T-junction, turn left, then at the main road turn right on to the A361. Continue for 4¼ miles and at the crossroads turn left for West Cranmore.

WEST CRANMORE, Somerset
Near the village the East Somerset Railway Centre can be found. A new engine house has been built here by artist and railway enthusiast David Shepherd, to house his 2 locomotives — *Black Prince* and *Green Knight*.

Return to the A361 and turn left, then continue through Doulting to complete the tour at Shepton Mallet.

COUNTIES OF GOLDEN HAM STONE

Dorset, a maze of country lanes; Somerset, the land of the 'summer-farm dwellers'. Both counties a blend of patchwork fields and timeless villages, each with a glorious church built of golden Ham stone once patronised by the lords of the magnificent manor houses.

SHERBORNE, Dorset

There is a great wealth of medieval buildings in Sherborne; a legacy of its ecclesiastical importance seeded in Anglo-Saxon times when St Aldhelm was first bishop of the cathedral. From 864 to 1539 this was a monastery, and during that time Sherborne became a great centre of learning. The monks rebuilt the abbey church in the 12th and 15th centuries, the latter project producing the Ham stone roofing for which it is famous. In the abbey lie 2 Anglo-Saxon kings, Ethelbad and Ethelbert, brothers of Alfred the Great. Sherborne School, founded in 1550, took over many of the abbey buildings after the Dissolution; its chapel is the Abbot's Hall, the Abbot's Lodging has been converted into studies, and also preserved as part of the school are the library and the Abbot's kitchen. One other part of the old monastery still surviving is the monks' washhouse, now the conduit in the main shopping centre, Cheap Street. Outside the town stand Sherborne's 2 castles. The first was built by Bishop Roger in the early 12th century, but was destroyed in the Civil War by Cromwell and remains a ruin in the parkland of the other (OACT). This was built by Sir Walter Raleigh in about 1594, who found the old castle unsuitable for conversion. It is set in gardens with lakeside lawns, a cascade and an orangery in grounds landscaped by Capability Brown. Also in the garden is the seat in which it is said the thoughtful Sir Walter was sitting, quietly smoking the newly discovered tobacco, when a servant doused him with a flagon of ale thinking he was on fire.

Leave Sherborne on the A30, SP 'Yeovil'. In 2½ miles pass, on the right, Worldwide Butterflies.

WORLDWIDE BUTTERFLIES, Somerset

Compton House (OACT), an Elizabethan mansion, is the rather unlikely home of a unique butterfly farm where species from around the world are bred. These entrancing insects can be studied in all stages of their development and there is a tropical jungle where particularly exotic butterflies live. The Palm House is another oasis of luxuriant vegetation and resembles an equatorial rain forest. The Lullingstone Silk Farm also occupies Compton House and the silk from here was used for Queen Elizabeth II's wedding dress.

Continue on the A30 to Yeovil.

YEOVIL, Somerset

This is a thriving town with a definite 20th-century flavour. It suffered disastrous fires in 1499, 1623 and 1640, and air raids in World War II which destroyed many old buildings. One long-standing spectator of the town's fortunes is the Ham stone church built at the end of the 14th century. Its simplicity and size make it impressive, and its greatest possession, a 15th-century brass lectern, is also refreshingly plain. The museum in Hendford Manor displays local archaeology and history, including Roman finds and a good collection of firearms.

Leave on the A37 SP 'Bristol'. In 1 mile branch left on to an unclassified road, SP 'Tintinhull'. Later pass the edge of Chilthorne Domer to reach Tintinhull.

TINTINHULL HOUSE, Somerset

Tintinhull House (NT) stands near the village green of Tintinhull. It dates from about 1600 when it was an unassuming farmhouse, but it was suddenly given architectural distinction by the addition of the west front in 1700. The interior remains plain, the carved staircase and some fine panelling being the only notable decorative features, both dating from the early 18th century. The garden, however, is for many the chief attraction. It consists of several hedged gardens and a sunken garden cunningly designed to give the impression of many varying levels. On the north side of the house there is a large lawn, shaded by a huge cedar tree, and on the west side a forecourt, another lawn and a memorial pavilion overlook a pond.

Leave Tintinhull on the Montacute road and follow this winding lane for 2 miles. At the T-junction turn left to enter Montacute for Montacute House.

MONTACUTE HOUSE, Somerset

Edward Phelips, who became Master of the Rolls, commenced the building of Montacute House (NT) in 1588, the year of the Armada. Built to impress — houses of that period reflected the power and position of the owner — Montacute is an almost magical building, liberally endowed with gables and turrets fashioned in a rich golden stone. The Phelips family faded from power in the mid-17th century, and the house became a quiet country house in a rural backwater for almost 300 years. The great hall has splendid 16th-century panelling, heraldic glass, plaster decoration and an elaborate stone screen and the 189ft gallery is the longest of the period. The house was empty when it came to the National Trust in 1931, but has since been filled with many valuable furnishings.

After passing the house and village square turn right into Townsend. Climb through pleasant woodland before turning right. Continue to Ham Hill Country Park and descend into Stoke-Sub-Hamdon.

STOKE-SUB-HAMDON, Somerset

Churches and houses all over Somerset and Devon are built from the golden stone quarried from Ham Hill up above Stoke village. Since Roman times stone has been hewn from this hill and its summit is much ridged and terraced by the earthworks of prehistoric peoples who built their forts here. Most of the houses of the village date back to the 17th century, and are built of Ham stone with mullioned windows and charming gables. The Priory (NT) was begun in the 14th century, but only the great hall (OACT) and the screens passage remain.

At the T-junction turn left, then turn right into North Street, SP 'Martock'. Later cross the A303 and in 1 mile turn right on to the B3165 and enter Martock.

Stoke-Sub-Hamdon Priory was built in the 14th and 15th centuries of Ham stone for the priests of St Nicolas' chantry

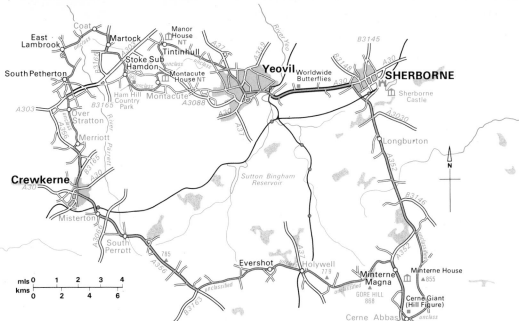

buttresses of the south transept; theories designate it either as a shrine or as a hermit's shelter. In September the town celebrates a 2-day fair, a custom centuries old and happily upheld.

Leave on the A356, SP 'Dorchester'. Pass through Misterton and South Perrott, then gradually ascend on to high ground. At the top follow an almost level road for 2 miles, then turn left on to an unclassified road for Evershot.

EVERSHOT, Dorset

This place among the hills is rather curious; it is a village yet its main street has raised pavements and old yellow and grey-stone houses, fitted with bow-fronted windows in the manner of a small town. George Crabbe, the poet, was rector of the little church here which has a rare silver Elizabethan chalice.

At the end of the village bear right. In 1¼ miles turn right then immediately left across the A37, SP 'Minterne Magna', and continue along the edge of Batcombe Hill. On reaching the A352, turn right for the hamlet of Minterne Magna.

MINTERNE MAGNA

Minterne House was built of Ham stone for Lord Digby between 1904 and 1906 by Leonard Stokes. Only the grounds are open, but, set in a lovely valley, they form a tapestry of rich colour made up of banks of rhododendrons, azaleas and magnolias.

Continue on the A352 towards Cerne Abbas. In 1¾ miles pass the Cerne Giant chalk figure (on the left), and turn left on to an unclassified road for the village centre. At the New Inn turn left, SP 'Buckland Newton'. Ascend on to high ground and at the top turn left, SP 'Sherborne'. In 3½ miles join the A352 for the return to Sherborne.

MARTOCK, Somerset

This is a charming little town enhanced by many old stone and thatched houses. The church, mainly 15th century, boasts the finest roof in the county. Virtually every inch of the tie-beam roof erected in 1513 is beautifully carved. Opposite the church is the old 14th-century manor house, one of 3 built here. The one from the 15th century lies ruined in a moated field nearby, while one from the 17th century stands close to the Georgian Market House at the end of the main street.

At the far end of the village (by the Bakers Arms PH) turn left on to an unclassified road, SP 'Coat'. At Coat turn left with the Kingsbury road, then in ¾ mile cross the river bridge and continue to East Lambrook.

EAST LAMBROOK, Somerset

In the village is East Lambrook Manor (OACT), a pretty little Tudor house with fine panelling, best known however for its gardens. These specialise in the growing of rare plants, and are laid out cottage-style as a memorial to the well-known gardener Margery Fish, as was the nursery for the propagation of rare species.

On entering the village turn left on to the South Petherton road. In 1 mile turn right for South Petherton.

SOUTH PETHERTON, Somerset

Tudor cottages, shops and villas, and a church with a roll call of vicars dating back to 1080 belong to South Petherton. Within the church walls lies the effigy of a curly-headed knight in chain mail, brought here after it was discovered by workmen digging a pit for a petrol storage tank. Also here is an extract from the diary of Richard Symonds, a Royalist soldier who stayed here in 1644, and whose writings provide a valuable insight of his contemporary world.

Branch left SP 'Illminster', and in just over ½ mile turn right on to the A303, then take the next turning left, SP 'Over Stratton'. At the far end of Over Stratton turn right then keep left and follow a pleasant byroad to Merriott. At the T-junction turn right (no sign), then at the A356 turn left and continue to Crewkerne.

CREWKERNE, Somerset

Crewkerne is a town of proud and ancient traditions, dating back to Anglo-Saxon times when it had the right of minting coins. In more recent times the town was famous for sail-making; it made sails for Nelson's *Victory*, and now does so for Americas Cup competitors. The Ham stone 15th-century church is the best building in Crewkerne, with a west front of cathedral-like proportions and glorious stained glass. An unsolved mystery are the 2 roofed-over

THE ISLE OF PURBECK

Superb views over this exceptionally beautiful peninsula can be enjoyed from high downs that drop sheer to the sea as massive limestone cliffs on the south side. East is the superb haven of Poole Harbour, which insinuates little creeks between heathery promontories and long, tree-covered spits.

THE ISLE OF PURBECK, Dorset

Most of this tour stays within the confines of the Isle of Purbeck, a wild and lovely peninsula that extends from Poole Harbour to Lulworth Cove and is crossed to the west by the Purbeck Hills. Like much of Dorset this is Thomas Hardy country, and reminders of the author and his many novels are everywhere. It is also a designated area of outstanding natural beauty.

SWANAGE, Dorset

This busy resort stands between towering downs that end as cliff-girded promontories on both sides of the sandy bay. Winding, switchback streets weave down to a shopping and amusement area concentrated on the only level piece of ground in the town – the sea front. Farther round the bay is the small pier and quay, where the Bournemouth ferry docks and anglers fish. An attractive group of old buildings clusters round the Mill Pond, off the Main Street and near the parish church is the town museum.

DURLSTON COUNTRY PARK, Dorset

Accessible from Swanage by road or a 1-mile footpath, this fascinating area of wild clifftop has many unusual features. Imposing Durlston Castle is built of Purbeck stone and occupies a lovely site near the headland. On Durlston Head itself is a 40-ton globe map of the world, fashioned from Portland stone quarried in the district, and $\frac{1}{4}$ mile away near the Anvil Lighthouse are the Tilly Whim caves – old quarries once used by smugglers.

Leave Swanage on the A351 SP 'Wareham'. In 1½ miles turn left on to the B3069 SP 'Kingston' to pass through Langton Matravers, a picturesque hillside village of local stone. At the end of the village turn left on to an unclassified road for Worth Matravers.

WORTH MATRAVERS, Dorset

This village is an enchanting combination of steep streets and stone cottages. A rough road south leads to the tiny Norman chapel and fine views on lonely St Alban's (or Aldhelm's) Head, while a toll road to the west leads to the cliff-encircled Chapman's Pool.

From Worth Matravers take the Corfe Castle road and in 1¼ miles at a T-junction turn left to rejoin the B3069. Continue to Kingston, with good views to Corfe Castle.

KINGSTON, Dorset

Features of 19th-century Kingston Church, considered one of the finest in the area, include black Purbeck marble pillars and a beautiful stone-vaulted chancel.

From Kingston a pleasant detour from the main route can be taken via a toll road to 600ft Swyre Head. In clear weather both the Isle of Portland and Isle of Wight can be seen from here. On the main route, bear right with the B3069 and make a sharp, winding descent to meet the A351. Turn left to enter Corfe Castle.

CORFE CASTLE, Dorset

Dominated by the picturesquely ruined stronghold from which it takes its name, this Purbeck-stone village owes its existence to the curiously symmetrical hill on which the castle stands. The mound rises exactly in the centre of a gap in the Purbeck Hills and was probably first fortified by King Alfred against the Danes. When the Normans came they occupied the site and began the magnificent 12th- to 15th-century castle (open) whose remains can be seen today. After the Civil War Cromwell made sure that it could never again be used against him by blowing it up with gunpowder. A river curls round the

Ammonites are the most easily identified of many fossil types found in Dorset

Corfe Castle dominates its surroundings.
The River Frome flows to the south of Wareham

base of the steep hill. On the village side is a deep moat spanned by a bridge, and in a garden off the main street is a perfect replica of the village and castle in miniature. Various old relics from the village can be seen in the local museum, and an interesting (though very informal) fossil museum occupies a shed near the castle gates.

Continue along the 'Wareham' road and just past the castle turn left on to an unclassified road and skirt the castle hill to reach Church Knowle. Drive through Church Knowle and meet crossroads. A detour can be taken from the main route by turning left and following toll roads through the estate of Smedmore House to Kimmeridge and Kimmeridge Bay.

KIMMERIDGE, Dorset

Thatched and slate-roofed cottages make up this tiny village, which is situated near the shallow bay from which it takes its name. A toll road leads to the coast.

KIMMERIDGE BAY, Dorset
Very low cliffs of black shale ring this wide, sandless bay, and the beach is littered with great chunks of rock literally packed with fossil ammonites. A condition of entry to the beach nowadays is that hammers and chisels should be left behind. A well sunk here in 1959 produces some 10,000 tons of crude oil each year.

SMEDMORE HOUSE, Dorset
Nearly all the land round Kimmeridge village and bay forms part of the Smedmore estate, and it is by permission of the big house that visitors are allowed on to the toll roads that lead to the attractive coast. The house itself (open) shows a combination of Jacobean, Queen Anne, and Georgian styles. Inside is a good collection of antique dolls.

To continue on the main route, turn right at the crossroads outside Church Knowle and cross the Purbeck Hills. Left are views of Creech Barrow and to the right is the attractive Blue Pool.

BLUE POOL, Dorset
Once an ugly scar left by the extraction of clay, this flooded pit (open) has been transformed into one of the county's most famous beauty spots by the re-establishment of coniferous woodland on its banks. Particles of clay suspended in the water make it brilliant blue when conditions are right. A short distance to the north is Furzebrook where a rail-connected terminal exports oil from the Wych Farm oil-field beside Poole Harbour.

Continue to Stoborough Green and turn left on to the A351 to reach Wareham.

WAREHAM, Dorset
Situated between the tidal River Frome and the River Trent (or Piddle), this quiet port has an ancient quay which now serves anglers and pleasure craft. In Saxon times the settlement was defended by earthworks, and their grass-covered remains still almost encircle the town. Much of Wareham was rebuilt after a great fire in 1762, which explains why so many attractive Georgian houses can be seen here. The parish church preserves original Saxon work and contains an effigy of Lawrence of Arabia. To the north of the town are the sandy heathlands and coniferous plantations of 3,500-acre Wareham Forest.

From Wareham go forward SP 'Poole' and at all roundabouts follow signs 'Poole'. After 4½ miles at the A35 roundabout take the 2nd exit SP 'Lytchett Minster B3067' and pass through Lytchett Minster to reach Upton. Here turn right on to the A350 SP 'Hamworthy'. The road ahead at this point leads to the Upton Country Park.

Continue on the A350 and pass through residential Hamworthy before crossing a bridge to reach Poole Old Town.

Kimmeridge Bay, which is famous for its fossils, is overlooked by a ruined tower that was built in the early 19th century.

POOLE, Dorset
Elizabeth I granted Poole county status which it kept until the late 19th century, and today it is a busy mixture of industrial centre and tourist resort. Its good beach and sheltered harbour have made it popular with holidaymakers, and its position close to a lovely and historic area of heaths and pinewoods makes it ideal as a touring base. Many fine old buildings stand in Poole's historic precinct, including the 18th-century Guildhall and a medieval merchant's house called Scaplen's. Both buildings contain local interest museums. Poole has a well-known pottery and also the RNLI Headquarters which has a small museum. There are also a maritime museum, aquarium, zoo and the rock and gem centre.

POOLE HARBOUR & BROWNSEA ISLAND, Dorset
Archaeological evidence suggests that Phoenician sailors were using this vast harbour as early as 800BC. It is the second largest natural harbour in the world, and has a coastline that measures over 100 miles if all its indentations are considered. Its largest island is Brownsea, which is accessible by boat from Poole Quay

and is famous as the site of Lord Baden-Powell's first scout camp. Part of its wild heath, wood, and reed-fringed marshland is protected as a nature reserve (NT) and is a haven for many forms of wildlife, including the rare red squirrel.

Follow signs 'Bournemouth' at all roundabouts and continue to follow 'Bournemouth' signs to reach the Poole Civic Centre gyratory system. From here follow signs 'Sandbanks' B3369 to skirt Poole Harbour. In 2½ miles a short detour to Compton Acres Gardens at Canford Cliffs can be made by turning left on to the B3065 and following the signs.

COMPTON ACRES GARDENS, Dorset
These famous private gardens (open) are amongst the finest in Europe and cover some 15 acres overlooking Poole Harbour, Brownsea Island and the Purbeck Hills beyond. There are seven separate and secluded gardens; English, Heather, Japanese, Italian, Roman, Rock and Water, each with its own individual beauty. Most of them contain a priceless collection of bronze and marble statues from all over the world. The careful lay-out of the gardens also include paths, bridges and stepping stones over streams and ponds.

On the main route continue with the B3369 to Sandbanks.

SANDBANKS, Dorset
The sandy beaches of this mile-long peninsula are backed by large houses and a car ferry operates from Haven Point for Studland and Swanage.

At the one-way system join the ferry lane and cross the entrance of Poole Harbour by ferry, then follow an unclassified road to Studland.

STUDLAND, Dorset
Built mainly of red brick, this village contains a fine Norman church and offers 2 miles of sandy beach sheltered by dunes. Moorland extends west from here to Wareham, and on the heathland 1 mile north west is a 500-ton ironstone rock known as the Agglestone.

BALLARD DOWNS AND OLD HARRY ROCKS, Dorset
Views from Studland Bay extend to the headland of Handfast Point and the isolated chalk stacks of the Old Harry Rocks. A little farther south the great bulk of Ballard Down dominates Swanage and offers good coastal views.

From Studland turn inland on the B3351. In 1 mile turn left on to an unclassified road SP 'Swanage' and climb round Ballard Down to return to Swanage.

The less sightly aspects of 20th-century life are softened by sunset at Poole Harbour.

IN SEARCH OF ANCIENT MAN

Near Uffington the great turf-cut figure of a horse leaps across a downland slope beneath the ramparts of a prehistoric hillfort. Elsewhere in the Vale of the White Horse are the massive stones of Wayland's Smithy, the enigmatic mound of Silbury Hill, and dozens of hilltop tumuli.

Tithe barns like the one at Great Coxwell were specially built to store the tithe, or one tenth of all produce, which was once levied from all land holders.

SWINDON, Wilts
In 1900 Old and New Swindon were combined to form Wiltshire's largest town. The small old town is still recognisable in fragments such as the remains of Holy Rood Church in the grounds of a 17th-century house, The Lawn, the old Town Hall and the Market Square. New Swindon grew out of the Great Western Railway's decision to site its repair and locomotive works here, and much of its history is detailed in the fascinating Great Western Railway Museum, the Railway Village House has been refurbished to show life at the turn of the century.

Leave the County Roundabout with SP 'Oxford A420'. In 1¼ miles after two roundabouts turn left on to the B4006 SP 'Stratton'. At traffic signals in Stratton St Margaret turn left, then turn right, and continue to Highworth.

HIGHWORTH, Wilts
Several 17th-century houses and an impressive church with a good west tower are features of this old hilltop village.

Continue on the A361. Later pass the village of Inglesham and a riverside park on the left.

INGLESHAM, Wilts
The tiny church in Inglesham stands where the River Thames meets the derelict Severn Canal and the River Coln. Inside are attractive box pews, a 15th-century screen, and a beautiful late Saxon carving of the Madonna and Child.

Wayland's Smithy is one of many outstanding prehistoric monuments which stand near the Ridgeway.

Continue on the A361. Cross the Thames via the old Halfpenny Bridge and drive into Lechlade.

LECHLADE, Glos
Lechlade marks the upper limit for large craft using the River Thames. The old Halfpenny Bridge spans the river here, and St John's Bridge stands ½ mile to the east. The local church is noted for the curious figures on its tower buttresses.

Turn right, then right again, on to the A417 Faringdon road. In ¾ mile by the nearside of the Trout Inn, turn left on to the B4449 SP 'Bampton'. A detour from the main route can be made here to Buscot village and Buscot Park by keeping forward on the A417.

BUSCOT, Oxon
Almost 4,000 acres of Buscot village and Park, including lovely woods and farmlands that run down to the Thames, are owned or protected by the National Trust. The late 18th-century house contains a noted collection of paintings, and the attractive grounds feature a water garden by landscaper Harold Peto. The Old Parsonage is an early 18th-century house in 10-acre grounds.

Continue along the unclassified road crossing the River Leach. After 1¼ miles turn right leading to Kelmscott village.

KELMSCOTT, Oxon
Poet and painter William Morris lived in Kelmscott's Elizabethan manor house and is buried in the local churchyard. The village itself is a charming collection of greystone buildings standing on the banks of the upper Thames.

Continue for a further 2¾ miles and meet a T-junction. Turn right on to the A4095 SP 'Faringdon' and shortly cross the historic Radcot Bridge.

RADCOT, Oxon
Many centuries ago the forces of Richard II and Henry IV met in battle at the 14th-century bridge here, and 300 years later Prince Rupert's cavalry defeated Cromwell's parliamentarian horsemen in nearby Garrison Field.

Continue to Faringdon.

FARINGDON, Oxon
Poet Laureate Henry Pye built Faringdon House in 1870, and Lord Berners added a folly to its park in 1935 to help relieve local unemployment. Faringdon Church lost its spire in the Civil War. The town itself is a market centre known for its dairy produce.

Follow SP 'Swindon A420', and after ¼ mile turn right into Highworth Road (B4019). After another 1¼ miles turn left on to an unclassified road for Great Coxwell.

GREAT COXWELL, Oxon
William Morris thought the great 13th-century tithe barn (NT) at Coxwell's Court Farm 'as noble as a cathedral'. Measuring 152ft long by 51ft high and 44ft wide, this huge stone building is certainly one of the finest of its kind in England today.   .

Turn left (no SP), then in ½ mile at a T-junction turn right, then turn left on to the A420. Take the 1st turning right on to an unclassified road for Little Coxwell, and continue to Fernham. Turn left on to the B4508, then in ¼ mile branch right on to an unclassified road for Uffington, in the Vale of the White Horse.

UFFINGTON, Oxon
Good views can be enjoyed from here of the 374ft-long prehistoric white horse cut into the chalk slopes of 856ft White Horse Hill.

Drive to the nearside of the village and turn right, then take the 2nd turning right SP 'White Horse Hill'. In 1 mile cross the main road and ascend White Horse Hill to reach Uffington Castle and associated monuments.

UFFINGTON CASTLE, THE RIDGEWAY, & WAYLAND'S SMITHY, Oxon
The iron-age hillfort (AM) of Uffington stands on the ancient Ridgeway above the famous White Horse in the Berkshire Downs. The Ridgeway is a pre-Roman track that follows the crest of the downs and is now the route of a long-distance footpath. Just off it in a grove of trees is the megalithic long barrow of Wayland's Smithy (AM). This excellent example has lost part of its earth mound, so its chambers are open to view. Wayland is a smith in Norse mythology, and tradition was that anyone who left a horse and coin here overnight would find his mount shod in the morning.

Follow exit signs from Uffington Castle, descend to a main road, and turn right on to the B4507 with further views of the White Horse to the right. After another 2 miles meet crossroads and turn right on to an unclassified road SP 'Lambourn'. Ascend on to the Berkshire Downs and in 4¼ miles turn right on to the B4001 for Lambourn. Continue across the Lambourn Downs to Lambourn.

LAMBOURN, Berks
Racehorses are trained on downland gallops near this lovely village, and the crystal Lambourn River is everything a chalk trout stream should be. The local cruciform church, which dates from Norman times, houses several old brasses and the village stocks.

Meet crossroads and turn right on to the B4000, then drive to the next turning left SP 'Baydon'. A short detour can be made from the main route to Ashdown House by keeping straight ahead on the B4000 for 3½ miles.

ASHDOWN HOUSE, Oxon
Ashdown House (NT) was built from chalk-rock blocks in the latter half of the 17th century. More than a quarter of its interior is taken up by a magnificent staircase.

On the main route, turn left from the B4000 on to the 'Baydon' road and in 2¼ miles meet a T-junction. Turn right and continue to Baydon.

BAYDON, Wilts
A 13th-century font can be seen in Baydon Church, which has Norman origins but acquired its west tower later. Baydon House farmhouse is of mid 18th-century date.

Turn left and continue to the downland village of Aldbourne.

ALDBOURNE, Wilts
Aldbourne, one of Wiltshire's most attractive villages, lies south east of a one-time hunting area known as Aldbourne Chase.

Turn left on to the B4192 SP 'Hungerford', then in 1¾ miles turn right on to an unclassified road and continue to Ramsbury.

It is quite likely that the exact reason for the construction of henge monuments like Avebury will never be known.

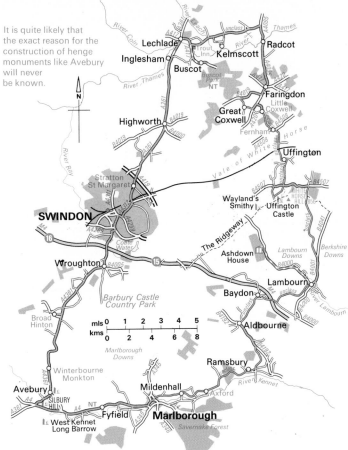

mls 0 1 2 3 4 5
kms 0 2 4 6 8

RAMSBURY, Wilts
Excellent Jacobean and Georgian buildings can be seen in this charming River Kennet village, and the church contains ancient sculptured stones.

Turn right and keep forward through the village to Axford and Mildenhall.

MILDENHALL, Wilts
Mildenhall, pronounced 'Minall', lies on the River Kennet to the north of Savernake Forest. A late Celtic vessel known as the Marlborough Bucket was unearthed at Folly Farm, which stands near by on the site of the Roman town Cunetio.

Continue to Marlborough.

MARLBOROUGH, Wilts
High downs rise to the north and south of this historic River Kennet town. Legend has it that Merlin, the magician of King Arthur's court, was buried under the town's castle mound. The town may well be old enough for this claim, but many of its more ancient foundations were damaged or destroyed by a series of bad fires and by the Civil War. Its High Street, one of the widest in England, is a reminder of the way things used to be. William Morris was a pupil at the famous 19th-century Marlborough College.

Leave Marlborough on the A4 SP 'Chippenham' and drive to Fyfield.

FYFIELD, Wilts
To the north of this attractive village is the high Fyfield Down nature reserve, which is as much protected for its prehistoric monuments as for its abundant wildlife. South of Fyfield are the sarsen stones of the Grey Wethers (NT), and about 1 mile north east of the village at Lockeridge Dene is a dolmen known as the Devil's Den.

Continue on the A4 to Silbury Hill.

SILBURY HILL & THE WEST KENNET LONG BARROW, Wilts
Situated close to the A4 road near Avebury, these superb prehistoric monuments are among the best known in Europe. Silbury Hill (AM), an enormous artificial mound that covers almost 6 acres, is still as enigmatic as when 18th-century Cornish miners employed to explore it by the Duke of Northumberland emerged baffled and empty-handed. A footpath from the A4 leads ¾ mile to the West Kennet Long Barrow (AM), the finest monument of its kind in England. Excavations during the 19th century uncovered skeletons and pottery in the tomb's passage and end chamber, but the side chambers remained undiscovered until 1955.

Drive to the Beckhampton roundabout and take the 3rd exit to leave by the A4361 SP 'Swindon'. In 1 mile keep left for Avebury.

AVEBURY, Wilts
Many experts consider Avebury the most significant prehistoric monument (AM) in Europe. It is certainly one of the largest stone circles in the world, comprising 100 standing-stone positions enclosing some 28 acres of land. Inside the large outer circle, which has quite a few gaps due to superstitious destruction in the past, are two smaller rings about 300ft in diameter. At one time a 50ft-wide avenue of stones ran 1 mile to connect with a pair of concentric circles on Overton Hill. The village itself is a collection of handsome old buildings between the stones and the banks of the monument, featuring a small museum of archaeology, the Great Barn and Museum of Wiltshire Folk and a multi-period church. Avebury Manor is a 16th-century house (open) (NT).

Continue on the 'Swindon' road to Winterbourne Monkton, with views of the Marlborough Downs to the right. Later descend to Wroughton.

WROUGHTON, Wilts
South of the village stands Barbury Castle an ancient hill fort dating from AD 566. The 130 acres of surrounding countryside is a country park.

Drive to the end of the village and turn left for the return to Swindon.

Enigmatic Silbury Hill keeps the secret of its purpose.

TRURO, Cornwall

Although it lies on the River Truro — a finger of the Fal estuary — and its history belongs to the sea, Truro serves its county now as administrative capital and cathedral city. During the Middle Ages it was important in the export of mineral ore and from the 13th to 18th centuries was one of the 4 Cornish stannary towns that controlled the quality of tin. The city's 18th-century popularity with wealthy sea merchants left a legacy of fine Georgian architecture to rival that of Bath. Truro became a fashionable focal point of society and the old theatre and assembly rooms next to the cathedral were particularly popular meeting places. However, it is in Lemon Street and Walsingham Place that the finest buildings can be seen from this elegant era. The cathedral is a relatively recent feature of Truro. For 800 years the See of Cornwall was shared with Devon, but when it was reconstituted in 1897 a new cathedral was begun. Built in early English style, it incorporated the old Church of St Mary and was completed in 1910. Inside, the main features are the baptistry, a massive Jacobean monument and the wall of the north choir. For a comprehensive picture of Cornwall's history visit the County Museum in River Street. Here too is an excellent array of Cornish minerals, together with unusual collections of porcelain and pottery. There is a small art gallery as well, containing paintings, engravings and drawings.

Leave Truro on the A39, SP 'Bodmin'. Continue through wooded country to Tresillian, situated on the creek of the Tresillian River. Cross the bridge and in 1 mile keep forward on the A390, SP 'St Austell', to Probus.

PROBUS, Cornwall

This tiny village boasts the tallest church tower in Cornwall, rising in 3 tiers to 126ft. Built during the 16th century of granite, it is richly decorated with figures, heads, animals and tracery, and lichen has given it all a pleasant greenish hue. It is strange to find this lofty tower here because the style resembles that of Somerset's churches and this ranks among the best examples.

Beyond the village pass on the right the County Demonstration Garden.

COUNTY DEMONSTRATION GARDEN AND ARBORETUM, Cornwall

Keen gardeners will find this place fascinating. Detailed displays show all aspects of gardening, including layout, the selection of plants and flowers to suit particular requirements and the effect of different weather conditions on gardens. Attractive exhibitions of fruit, herbs, flowers and vegetables

CATHEDRAL CITY BY THE SEA

In all her Georgian elegance, Truro lies demurely between shady creeks of woodland and water and the strange white moonscape of St Austell's hills of china clay. Away from these the tour runs through hidden fishing villages by way of twisting lanes, high-banked and narrow.

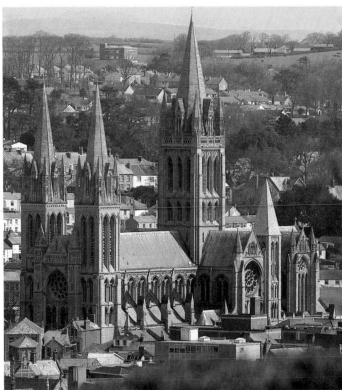

Truro Cathedral, although built in the 20th century, harmonises well with the town's Georgian architecture

illustrate a wealth of information and interest for those either with or without a garden.

Continue on the St Austell road and in ½ mile pass the entrance to Trewithen House and Gardens.

TREWITHEN HOUSE AND GARDENS, Cornwall

This simple, elegant manor house (OACT) of Pentewan stone was built for the Hawkins family in 1723. The interior is mainly Palladian yet each room has its own individuality: the oak room is panelled with oak, the dining room is decorated in grey-green and white and the drawing room is embellished with Chinese fretwork. The surrounding gardens are typical of Cornwall — huge banks of rhododendrons and magnolias ornament landscaped woodland affording frequent glimpses of sweeping parkland.

Remain on the A390 and continue through Grampound and Sticker to St Austell.

ST AUSTELL, Cornwall

White, unnatural peaks rise up to the north of St Austell, giving the moors an almost lunar appearance. They are the great spoil-heaps of white china clay which forms the basis of the

town's main industry. Before the discovery of this valuable natural resource in 1775 by William Cookworthy, St Austell was just another small tin-mining town. Clay pits were opened soon after this date and today the clay is one of Britain's major export materials. The town itself has more the appearance of a market town than an industrial one, and numbering among its pleasant buildings are the town hall, the Quaker Meeting House, the White Hart Hotel and Holy Trinity Church.

Leave St Austell on the B3273 and continue to Mevagissey.

MEVAGISSEY, Cornwall

Narrow streets wind up from the harbour of Mevagissey and colour-washed cottages cover the cliffsides haphazardly. Like many Cornish coastal villages, fishing has always provided Mevagissey with a livelihood and pilchard fishing in particular brought wealth to the village in the 18th and 19th centuries, although smuggling contributed substantially to the riches too. Besides frequent shark and mackerel fishing trips, other attractions in the village include a folk museum and a model railway. The former occupies an 18th-century boatbuilder's workshop and concentrates on local crafts, mining and agricultural equipment and seafaring relics. The latter runs through varied model terrain which includes an Alpine ski resort and a china clay pit.

Return along the B3273 and in 1 mile turn left on to an unclassified road, SP 'Gorran'. After another 1¼ miles turn left again and continue to Gorran. Beyond the village keep left, SP 'Gorran Haven', then take the next turning right and bear right again to reach Gorran Haven.

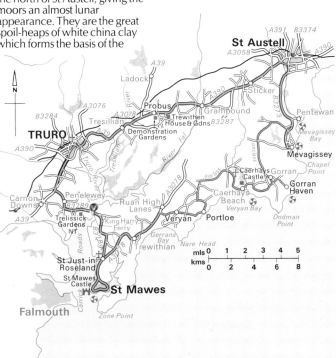

GORRAN HAVEN, Cornwall
This tiny, remote village rivalled Mevagissey in the heyday of pilchard fishing. It is a charmingly unspoilt resort now, with one village street and a pebbly beach.

Return for 1 mile to the T-junction and turn left, then in 250 yards turn left again, SP 'Caerhays'. Touch the coast again at the attractive Caerhays Beach where to the right stands Caerhays Castle.

CAERHAYS CASTLE, Cornwall
Perched above a bay, this castellated mansion (not open) looks like a fairy castle when seen from the cliff road. It was built by John Nash in 1808 for J.B. Trevannion — whose family had owned the estate since the 14th century.

A steep climb leads to St Michael's Caerhays Church. In ¾ mile take the 2nd turning left, SP 'St Mawes and Veryan', then keep left. After 1¼ miles keep left again then turn left, SP 'Veryan' and 'Portholland'. In ¾ mile turn left and nearly ½ mile farther left again, SP 'Portloe'. In just over ¼ mile bear right then descend to Portloe.

PORTLOE, Cornwall
A stream flows through this minute fishing village down to the sea. Between the steep cliffs there is a small rocky beach which is good for swimming. Traditional south Cornish beach boats work here full time, each handling about 100 crab pots.

Beyond the village ascend, then in 1 mile go over the crossroads and continue to Veryan.

VERYAN, Cornwall
Hidden in a wooded valley is the delightful inland village of Veryan. Its most distinguishing feature is its 5 Round Houses. These, placed 2 at each end of the village and 1 in the middle, are round, white-washed cottages with conical thatched roofs. A local story has it that a parson built them for his 5 daughters and he made them round so that the devil would have no corners to hide in.

Turn left, then right on to the St Mawes road. In ½ mile turn left on to the A3078. Pass through Trewithian to reach St Just in Roseland.

ST JUST IN ROSELAND, Cornwall
Tucked away up a creek of the Carrick Roads lies a tiny hamlet that more than lives up to its picturesque name; St Just was believed to be a 6th-century Celtic saint. There is little more to this place than the church, the rectory and a cottage or two, but it has one of the most beautiful churchyards in the country and it is this which has made St Just in Roseland so famous. The church lies at the bottom of a steeply wooded combe descending from the road. Enter it through a lychgate and at this point you can look down on the church tower. The way down passes through luxuriant trees and shrubs — many

familiar such as rhododendrons, hydrangeas and camelias; many not so well known — such as the Chilean myrtle, bamboos and the African strawberry tree. On either side of the path stand granite blocks inscribed with biblical verses and quotations. Another lychgate at the bottom (with an unusual granite cattle grid) leads out of the churchyard. This glorious garden is largely due to One Revd C.W. Carlyon (church rector) who began planting the shrubs in the mid-19th century.

Continue on the A3078 and in 1 mile turn right into Upper Castle Road, SP 'St Mawes via Castle'. Pass St Mawes Castle to enter the resort of St Mawes.

ST MAWES, Cornwall
St Mawes commands a fine view over the Carrick Roads and it was this strategic position which provided such an ideal site for Henry VIII's defensive castle (AM) built in the early 1540s at the

Both fishing boats and pleasure craft share Mevagissey's lively harbour

southernmost tip of the town. In fact the castle saw very little action and its great tower and battlements still stand today in excellent repair. The resort itself is smart and relatively unspoilt by tourism, backing up steeply behind the quay which was busy with sea trade in the Middle Ages.

Follow the road around the harbour and return to St Just in Roseland. Here, branch left on to the B3289 and later descend to the King Harry Ferry. On the far side climb steeply and pass Trelissick Gardens on the left.

TRELISSICK GARDENS, Cornwall
Although a house (not open) has stood here since the mid-18th century, it was not until the late 19th century that the grounds (NT) were landscaped. The Copelands, who inherited the house in 1937, continued to improve them and gave the gardens their present shape. Smooth expanses of lawn enclosed by dense shrubs and woods pierced by winding walks characterise Trelissick. Two specialities here are a collection of over 130 species of hydrangea and a dell full of giant cedar and cypress trees.

The tour continues on the B3289 and after ½ mile, at the crossroads, turn right, SP 'Truro'. Beyond Penelewey turn right again on to the A39 for the return to Truro.

BETWEEN BODMIN AND THE SEA

Majestic cliffs indented by tiny harbours are typical of north Cornwall. So also are the long sands of Bude Bay, the eerie enchantment of Arthur's Castle at Tintagel, and the dark counterpoint of Bodmin Moor rising inland.

Since the 19th century Boscastle has declined as a port but developed as a resort.

WADEBRIDGE, Cornwall
One of the finest medieval bridges in England can be seen here. Built c 1485 and widened in 1849, it spans the River Camel with 17 arches and measures 320ft long. It is thought that packs of wool may have been sunk into the river bed to make firm bases for the piers.

Leave Wadebridge on the A39 'Bude' road. Cross the bridge and turn left, then in ½ mile turn left on to the B3314 SP 'Port Isaac'. After 3 miles turn left again on to an unclassified road SP 'Rock'. In a further 1½ miles turn left into Pityme then take the next turning right SP 'Polzeath'. A detour from the main route can be made by continuing ahead for 1 mile to Rock.

ROCK, Cornwall
Rock lies opposite Padstow on the lovely Camel Estuary. The small Church of St Michael, at nearby Porthilly, was dug from drifting sand and houses a simple Norman font.

Continue along the main tour route and pass through Trebetherick to reach Polzeath.

POLZEATH, Cornwall
Safe bathing and excellent sands that offer some of the best surfing in Cornwall are the main attractions of Polzeath. The village stands on Padstow Bay and the wide Camel estuary, within easy reach of beautiful walking country (NT) round Portquin. Fine views over Portquin Bay can be enjoyed from Pentire Head, to the north.

Tintagel Castle is divided in two by a breathtaking chasm.

Leave Polzeath and ascend sharply. After 2 miles branch left SP 'Port Isaac'. In ½ mile turn left on to the B3314 for St Endellion.

ST ENDELLION, Cornwall
Although inland from sheltered Portquin Bay, St Endellion occupies an exposed site and often feels the full force of the gales for which this part of the country is known. Its beautiful compact church was built from Lundy Island granite. Inside, under the 18th-century tower arch, are several quaint bell-ringer's rhymes. A number of amusing and somewhat irreverent Georgian epitaphs can be seen on old gravestones in the churchyard.

Continue along the B3314 for 1 mile, then turn left on to the B3267 for Port Isaac.

PORT ISAAC, Cornwall
In the old part of this outstandingly picturesque fishing village the houses huddle together along a steep coombe and down to the harbour.

Turn right onto an unclassified road and descend to Port Gaverne. Pass through the village and climb inland. After 2½ miles rejoin the B3314 and continue to Delabole.

DELABOLE, Cornwall
At one time most of the roofs in Cornwall came from the ancient slate quarry in this village, which is estimated to have been worked continuously for at least 350 years. Britain's deepest man-made hole, it has a depth of 500ft and a circumference of 1½ miles.

Continue on the B3314 for 1¾ miles, then turn left on to an unclassified road SP 'Tintagel'. After ½ mile keep forward to join the B3263 then keep left. Just before the village of Trewarmet a road to the left offers a pleasant detour to Trebarwith Strand.

TREBARWITH STRAND, Cornwall
The good beach in this cove is crossed by a natural slate causeway, which leads down to the water's edge from the high-water line.

Continue through Trewarmett on the main tour route and drive to Tintagel.

TINTAGEL, Cornwall
The name Tintagel is highly evocative of the Arthurian legends, but the only King Arthur's Hall here nowadays is the modern home of the Fellowship of the Round Table. The local post office (NT) is a superb slate-built structure that dates from the 14th century and was originally a small manor house. Norman workmanship is very evident in the local church, but its origins are probably farther back in Saxon times. A Norman font and Roman milestone can be seen inside.

TINTAGEL CASTLE, Cornwall
Near Tintagel is the romantic ruined castle (AM) that, according to legend, was the birthplace of King Arthur. Its remains post-date that giant of Western folklore by some 7 centuries, but traces of a Celtic monastery (AM) founded early enough to have accommodated him can be seen close by. The castle itself was built on its wave-lashed promontory, now almost cut in half by the sea, by Reginald, Earl of Cornwall and illegitimate son of Henry I, in the 12th century. Views from here take in the entire North Cornish coast from Pentire Point to Hartland Point.

From the Wharncliffe Arms Hotel in Tintagel follow the B3263 'Boscastle' road, and shortly pass through Bossiney. Continue for another ½ mile to reach Rocky Valley.

The ancient slate post office at Tintagel.

mls 0 1 2 3 4 5
kms 0 2 4 6 8

Bodmin Moor

Rockpools are a feature of Widemouth Bay, which is situated to the south of Bude.

ROCKY VALLEY, Cornwall
Trees, stone, and water all contribute their own particular magic to the wonderful scenery of Rocky Valley, a deep cut sloping down to the sea. About 1 mile along the valley is its most magnificent feature, the 40ft waterfall of St Nectan's Kieve. Nectan (or Knighton) was a Celtic hermit saint said to have had an oratory beside the kieve (basin).

Continue on the B3263, pass through Trethevey and after 1¾ miles turn left with the B3263 SP 'Bude'. Descend steeply through a hairpin bend to Boscastle.

BOSCASTLE, Cornwall
The tiny harbour here is at the head of a deep S-shaped inlet between high cliffs, and the combined Valency and Jordan rivers meet incoming tides with dramatic effect when the moon is full and the rivers are running at full spate. Even on a calm day the sea can be impressive. A local blowhole amply demonstrates the force of the water. Boscastle itself is an attractive village arranged round a long, broad street that climbs steeply through woodland. Close to the harbour is a witches' museum of interesting (and often gruesome) relics associated with magic and witchcraft. At one time the local seal population was severely reduced by hunters, but this industry is now controlled.

Leave Boscastle, cross a river bridge, and ascend (1 in 6). After 2¾ miles turn left and immediately turn left on to an unclassified road SP 'Crackington Haven'. Later descend steeply into the village of Crackington Haven.

CRACKINGTON HAVEN, Cornwall
This tiny seaside village stands on a rugged stretch of coast and has a good surfing beach. High Cliff, to the south, drops 700ft in a series of weathered faces and terraces.

Slate from the vast quarry at Delabole has roofed buildings throughout the West Country.

Leave Crackington Haven and ascend. After 3 miles reach the village of Wainhouse Corner and turn left on to the A39 SP 'Bude'. Continue past Treskinnick Cross, then 1¼ miles farther turn left on to an unclassified road SP 'Widemouth'. After ¾ mile follow the wide sweep of Widemouth Bay to Bude.

BUDE, Cornwall
This small resort near the mouth of the River Neet was once the port for the Bude Canal which ran inland to Launceston. The town's history is displayed in the Historical and Folk Museum on the canal wharf. Also in the town was the World of Nature Exhibition covering local natural history and geology and including an aquarium.

Leave Bude on the A3072 'Bideford' road. After 1¼ miles turn left on to the A39, and in ¼ mile, turn right rejoining the A3072, SP 'Holsworthy'. Drive into Stratton.

STRATTON, Cornwall
This picturesque grouping of attractive houses and thatched cottages has a peaceful atmosphere that belies its turbulent history. In 1643 a Civil War battle was fought here and is re-enacted every May by the Sealed Knot Society. The Tree Inn was the headquarters of Sir Bevil Grenville before he led his Cavaliers to victory at Stamford Hill, just north of the village. Local legend recalls Anthony Payne, a 7ft giant who was born in the Tree Inn and was a retainer in Sir Bevil's household. The village church dates from the 15th century and houses good 16th-century brasses.

Continue on the A3072 'Holsworthy' road. After 2¾ miles at the Red Post Cross turn right on to the B3254 SP 'Launceston'.

Drive along the B3254 to Whitstone and ¾ mile beyond the village turn right on to an unclassified road SP 'Week St Mary'. Continue for 1¼ miles, meet crossroads, and drive straight on towards Canworthy Water. After 2 miles on this narrow road turn right for Canworthy Water. Here keep straight on and after 1 mile ascend to Warbstow.

WARBSTOW, Cornwall
Warbstow Bury is one of the finest Iron-Age hillforts in Cornwall. Situated at 750ft it provides extensive views in all directions except the south-west.

Continue to Hallworthy, turn right on to the A395, and in another 2¾ miles turn left on to the A39 SP 'Wadebridge'. Continue to Camelford.

CAMELFORD, Cornwall
One of the more obscure Arthurian legends places Camelford as having been the site of Camelot, the fabulous city of King Arthur and his Knights of the Round Table. Slaughter Bridge, which crosses the Camel River 1 mile north of the town, is one of several contenders for the title 'Arthur's last battleground'.

The North Cornwall Museum and Gallery contains many items on Cornish rural life.

Leave Camelford on the A39 and keep straight on. Pass through Helstone, crossing the River Allen at Knightsmill, and continue to St Kew Highway.

ST KEN HIGHWAY, Cornwall
Old stocks are preserved in the porch of the village church, and inside is a very fine Elizabethan pulpit decorated with ornamental panels. Also here is a stone inscribed with characters of the Celtic Ogham script, an ancient form of writing.

Remain on the A39 and return to Wadebridge.

WELLS, Somerset

Wells is a delightful cathedral city situated at the foot of the Mendip Hills. The west front of its fine 13th-to 15th-century cathedral is adorned with statues, and inside are a graceful branching staircase and a 14th-century clock. With its associated buildings the cathedral forms part of England's largest medieval ecclesiastical precinct. The Vicar's Close preserves picturesque 14th-century houses, and across the cathedral green is the moated Bishop's Palace (open), where Wells' famous swans ring a bell near the drawbridge for food. Other interesting old buildings include a medieval tithe barn (AM) and the 15th-century parish church. Wells Museum includes a display on the Mendip Caves.

An interesting detour from the main route to the caves of Wookey Hole can be made at Wells: leave the city on the A371 'Cheddar' road and in ¼ mile turn right on to the unclassified 'Wookey Hole' road. Continue for 1½ miles to Wookey Hole. Please note that route directions for the main tour start after the following entry.

WOOKEY HOLE, Somerset

Inhabited for some 650 years from 250BC this gigantic system was hollowed out of the Mendip limestone by the River Axe. Finds relating to the period of habitation can be seen in the associated museum. The old mill at the cave entrance demonstrates the art of paper making, and is a store for Madame Tussaud's waxwork museum and Lady Bangor's fairground collection.
Leave Wells by the A39 'Glastonbury' road and proceed to Glastonbury.

GLASTONBURY, Somerset

High above the skyline of this ancient town is the 520ft pinnacle of Glastonbury Tor, a place associated in myth with fabulous Avalon and the Celtic Otherworld. Glastonbury was probably founded in Celtic times, but according to legend it was created by Joseph of Arimathea. Other traditions connect St Patrick and King Arthur with the abbey, and it is said that Arthur is actually buried here. The well preserved remains that exist today date from the 12th and 13th centuries, and include St Mary's Church, the abbey church, and a number of monastic buildings (open). By far the best preserved is the superb Abbot's Kitchen. Features of the town itself include 2 medieval churches, the George and Pilgrim Inn, a 15th-century abbey courthouse known as the Tribunal (open) containing late prehistoric finds from lake dwellings at Meare and Godney and the Abbey Barn which houses the Somerset Rural Life Museum.

Leave Glastonbury on the B3151 'Meare' road and proceed through low-lying country to Meare.

Glastonbury Tor is reputed to be one of England's most magical places.

THE POLDEN AND MENDIP RANGES

Low-lying areas of unpopulated countryside are dominated by the bare Mendip summits and lower Polden Hills. Here are the cradle of early English Christianity, the supposed site of King Arthur's fabulous Camelot, and old battlefields that have seen decisive turning points in the country's history.

MEARE, Somerset

From c300BC to cAD100 a lake settlement of houses on stilts and brushwood existed here. Few traces of this survive, but excavations have yielded many interesting finds that are displayed in Taunton and Glastonbury Museums. A 14th-century building known as the Fish House (AM) was used by the monks of Glastonbury to house their fishermen, and the contemporary manor house was a summer residence for the abbots.

Over 400 statues survive on the west front of Wells Cathedral. They were made during the 13th century and were inspired by sculpture in Continental cathedrals.

Continue on the B3151 for 1¼ miles and turn left on to an unclassified road SP 'Shapwick'. Meet a T-junction and turn left again. Continue across level wooded countryside to Shapwick. By Shapwick Church turn right on to the 'Bridgwater' road and ascend the gradual slope of the Polden Hills.

THE POLDEN HILLS, Somerset

These low hills (part NT), rising to less than 300ft at their highest point, extend from Glastonbury to a point near Bridgwater and dominate the surrounding marshy levels.

About ¾ mile from Shapwick cross a main road, then continue for ¼ mile and turn right on to the A39. Proceed along a low ridge for 5 miles, then descend and bear sharp left over the King's Sedgemoor Drain. Cross the M5 and enter Bridgwater.

BRIDGWATER, Somerset

It was here that the Duke of Monmouth proclaimed himself King in 1685, prior to suffering a crushing defeat at nearby Sedgemoor. Of interest are the town's wide main street, the tall spire of St. Mary's church and the Admiral Blake Museum.
From Bridgwater follow SP 'Langport' on the A372 and recross the M5. Drive across Sedgemoor.

SEDGEMOOR, Somerset

In 1685 the last battle on English soil took place here when James II defeated James Duke of Monmouth. The King won a decisive victory at the expense of the lives of some 1,400 of Monmouth's followers. The rebels who survived were subsequently dealt with by the travelling 'Bloody Assize' of the notorious Judge Jeffries.

Continue through Weston Zoyland, then after another 2¼ miles skirt Middlezoy. In 1 mile turn right on to the A361 and follow SP 'Taunton to enter Othery. Continue on to Burrow Bridge.

BURROW BRIDGE & BURROW MUMP, Somerset

Wide views are afforded by the hill, or mump (NT), here; an extensive collection of Victorian engines is housed in an old pumping station (open) opposite the Mump.

Cross the River Parrett and immediately turn left (no SP) on to an unclassified road. Follow SP 'Stathe, Langport', reach Stathe, and follow SP 'Curry Rivel'. After ¾ mile branch right, and in 1 mile ascend Red Hill (NT) for excellent views over Sedgemoor. At the road summit bear right and in ¾ mile turn left on to the A378 to enter Curry Rivel. In ¼ mile turn right on to an unclassified road SP 'Drayton, Muchelney'. Proceed through Drayton to reach Muchelney.

MUCHELNEY, Somerset

The Benedictine abbey whose extensive remains (AM) survive here was not the first foundation on the site. Excavations have revealed a rare Saxon chapel, dating from around the 7th century, beneath ruined Norman monastic buildings. Priest's House is a good 14th-century thatched building (NT).

Leave Muchelney by bearing left with SP 'Langport'. Continue for 1 mile, meet a T-junction, and turn right to enter Huish Episcopi.

Wells Cathedral's 14th-century astronomical clock.

Turn right by Somerton Church into unclassified New Street SP 'Ilchester, Yeovil'. Continue for ½ mile and turn right on to the B3151. After 2¾ miles turn right then left across the A372. In 1½ miles at the edge of Ilminster reach a mini-roundabout and take the 1st exit SP 'Yeovilton'.

ILCHESTER, Somerset
In Roman times this quiet River Yeo town was an important military station. Its superb Town Hall houses a 13th-century mace - the oldest staff of office in England.

Wookey Hole was formed by the River Axe.

The Market Cross in Somerton was rebuilt in 1673.

HUISH EPISCOPI, Somerset
Glass by Burne-Jones and a fine Norman doorway are features of the local church, but its crowning glory is a 15th-century tower considered to be the finest in the county.

Turn right on to the A372 'Wincanton, Yeovil' road, and later pass the edge of Long Sutton.

LONG SUTTON, Somerset
This attractive village is grouped round a notable 15th-century church and boasts a 17th-century manor house.

In ½ mile turn left on to the B3165 SP 'Somerton', and in 2¼ miles turn right SP 'Ilchester' to enter Somerton.

SOMERTON, Somerset
Somerton was the capital of Somerset under the West Saxons and is particularly known for its attractive market place. All around the square and along the back streets are handsome old buildings, including the Town Hall of c1700 and the 17th-century Hext Almshouses. Somerton Church carries a magnificent tie-beam roof dating from the 15th century.

On the main route, continue for 1½ miles and pass the entrance to the Royal Naval Air Station for the Fleet Air Arm Museum, Yeovilton.

YEOVILTON, Somerset
Yeovilton's Fleet Air Arm Museum portrays the development of naval aviation since 1903 and displays over 40 historic aircraft.
Proceed for ¼ mile and turn right on to an unclassified road SP 'Queen Camel'. In 2½ miles go forward on to the A359 SP 'Sparkford, Frome' to enter Queen Carmel. Proceed for ¾ mile and turn right on to the A303 to enter Sparkford. Here a detour to Cadbury Castle can be taken. Proceed along the A303 for 1½ miles and turn right on to an unclassified road for South Cadbury.

CADBURY CASTLE, Somerset
Once it was thought that the myths linking this hilltop fort with King Arthur's Camelot had been disproved by excavations revealing evidence of Stone- and Bronze-Age occupation. However, digging in 1966 suggested that the site had been re-defended during Arthur's period. The Saxon King Ethelred (the Unready) established a mint here.

From Sparkford bear right to cross a railway bridge, then turn immediately left on to the A359 'Frome' road passing the Sparkford Motor Museum. Continue for 3 miles and branch left on to the B3152 SP 'Castle Cary'. Continue 1½ miles to enter Castle Cary.

CASTLE CARY, Somerset
Several fine old houses and a pretty duckpond are grouped together at the heart of this pleasant small town. The local lock-up, an unusual circular structure once used for the restriction of petty mischief makers, dates from the 18th century.
Leave Castle Cary with SP 'Bath, Bristol (A371)'. After 1 mile turn left on to the A371 SP 'Shepton Mallet'. Shortly bear right across a railway bridge, then proceed for ½ mile to the Brook House Inn and turn left on to an unclassified road SP 'Alhampton'. In 1 mile enter Alhampton and turn right SP 'Ditcheat'. Proceed to Ditcheat and at a T-junction turn left (no SP). Continue to the Manor House Inn and turn right, then shortly bear left SP 'East Pennard'. Proceed to Wraxall, and at crossroads turn right on to the A37 'Shepton Mallet' road. Ascend Wraxall Hill and after 1 mile at crossroads turn left on to an unclassified road SP 'East Pennard'. In ½ mile turn right SP 'Pilton' to reach Pilton.

PILTON, Somerset
One of the most picturesque villages in the area, lovely Pilton has an ancient cruciform tithe barn (AM) and a church with a magnificent 15th-century roof.

Meet crossroads and turn left, then descend to the church and turn left SP 'Shepton Mallet'. Meet a T-junction and turn right on to the A361. Proceed for 1 mile, then turn left on to the B3136 for Shepton Mallet.

SHEPTON MALLET, Somerset
Wool from flocks grazing the windswept Mendip Hills made the fortune of this pleasant market town. Several good 17th- and 18th-century buildings survive from this period, plus a fine church with an intricately carved nave roof.

Leave the town with SP 'Wells A371' to enter Croscombe.

CROSCOMBE, Somerset
Steep wooded hills surround this stone-built village, which has an old church containing amazing 17th-century pastoral and heraldic carvings in rich black oak.

Continue along the A371 to re-enter Wells.

WESTON-SUPER-MARE, Avon
Good beaches and lavish entertainment facilities are features of this large Bristol Channel resort. Among many places of interest are a marine lake with boating, an aquarium, and a model village. The resort's wide seafront road is lined by several public gardens and overlooks the low Flat Holme and Steep Holme offshore islands. Both these are particularly rich in birdlife. An Iron-Age earthwork (AM) can be seen 1 mile north on Worlebury Hill.

Leave Weston-super-Mare on the A370 'Bristol' road. Pass through suburbs and cross the M5 then flat countryside to reach Congresbury. Turn left, cross the River Yeo, then turn left again on to the B3133 SP 'Yatton, Clevedon'. Proceed through Yatton then cross and pass through Kenn. Cross the M5 and in ½ mile reach the Clevedon Distributor Road. For a detour to visit Clevedon Court and Clevedon Craft Centre turn right and follow signs. For a detour to Clevedon town centre keep forward.

CLEVEDON COURT, Avon
This superb 14th-century house (NT) is one of the oldest of its type to have survived anywhere in Britain. It carries an even older 13th-century tower and is considered typical of its period, with a screen passage dividing the buttery and kitchen from the great hall and the lord of the manor's living quarters. During the 18th and 19th centuries it became a popular meeting place for the avant-garde of the day. Clevedon Craft Centre lies ½ mile to the south and visitors can watch displays of wood carving and turning here at the weekends.

CLEVEDON, Avon
Situated at a junction of hill ranges, Clevedon is a quiet Severn estuary residential town and resort. The pier, designed to cope with the 40ft tidal range in this area is being restored

The main route turns left SP 'Sea Front' on to an unclassified road and in 1¼ miles turn left on to the B3130 for the front. In a further ½ mile bear left, pass the pier, and keep forward for 1½ miles to meet a T-junction, then turn left on to B3124, SP 'Portishead'. In ½ mile at the Walton-in-Gordano crossroads turn left on to an unclassified road (no SP). Continue high above the shores of the Bristol Channel, then enter a built-up area and turn left into Nore Road (no SP). Continue above the coast and in 1¼ miles pass the AA Portishead viewpoint. Pass Battery Point and descend into Portishead.

PORTISHEAD, Avon
Portishead is a residential town, small resort and former port situated on the lower slopes of a wooded hillside overlooking the Bristol Channel.

BEACHES AND GORGES
In many ways tiny Avon is the envy of much larger counties. Its port city of Bristol is one of the most historic in England, its resort offers miles of sandy beaches, and its interior is riddled by limestone cave systems that extend deep into Somerset.

Birnbeck Pier at Weston-super-Mare.

Leave Portishead on the A369 'Bristol' road. After 2¾ miles reach the M5 junction roundabout and take 4th exit SP 'Clifton' (toll) to enter hill country. Continue through Abbot's Leigh. Proceed for 1¼ miles and turn left on to the B3129 SP 'Clifton'. In ½ mile reach the Clifton Suspension Bridge.

CLIFTON SUSPENSION BRIDGE AND AVON GORGE, Avon
Here, where the sheer limestone cliffs of the Avon Gorge constrict that river to a silver ribbon some 245ft

below, is the spectacular suspension bridge by the brilliant engineer Isambard Kingdom Brunel. Started in 1836, it was not completed until 1864, 5 years after his death.
Cross the bridge and in 200yds turn left SP 'Motorway M5'. After a short distance turn left again into Clifton Down Road. After ¼ mile meet crossroads and turn left on to the B4468 SP 'Weston'. The right turn here leads to Bristol Zoo. Descend Bridge Valley Road into the Avon Gorge. At the bottom turn left on to

Clevedon Court, though much altered, preserves many 14th-century features, including the south entrance.

the A4, pass underneath the suspension bridge, and after ¼ mile keep left SP 'City Centre' to remain in Hotwell Road. Enter Bristol city centre.

BRISTOL, Avon
During the 16th century ships out of Bristol sailed to every part of the known world opening up international trading routes in a way never before imagined. In 1843 Brunel launched his SS *Great Britain*, the largest iron ship of the time, and in 1970 its rusting hulk was rescued from the Falkland Islands and returned to the Bristol dry dock in which it was originally built. Extensive renovation has restored it as a proud memorial to its great designer and the city of its birth. Nowadays the city's dock areas are at Avonmouth and Portbury which are more fitted to coping with the vast ships of 20th-century world traffic. Bristol's many lovely old buildings include a cathedral that contains examples of Norman, Early-English, Gothic and Victorian architecture. St Mary Redcliffe, one of the city's finest churches, was built and extended between the 13th and 15th centuries and carries a massive tower with a 285ft spire. The 16th-century Red Lodge (open) houses interesting work carvings and furnishings of contemporary and later date, and the Georgian House (open) features furniture from the 18th-century. Outside the Corn Exchange are the original metal 'nails' upon which merchantmen once put their payments, hence the expression 'to pay cash on the nail'. Various displays and exhibitions can be seen in St Nicholas' Church Museum and the City Museum and Art Gallery.

Other features of the Floating Harbour area are the Bristol Exhibition and Watershed Arts Complexes, the Arnolfini Gallery, National Lifeboat Museum and Bristol Industrial Museum, and the Maritime Heritage Centre.

Follow SP 'Weston (A370)' and in 1½ miles cross the impressive Cumberland Basin and Avon bridges, then keep forward to join the A370 'Long Ashton' bypass. Proceed through pleasant countryside and pass the villages of Flax Bourton and Backwell (Farleigh), then 1½ miles beyond Backwell (West Town), meet crossroads, and turn left on to an unclassified road SP 'Bristol Airport'. Ascend deep and thickly-wooded Brockley Combe, then emerge and in 1½ miles meet a T-junction. Turn right on to the A38 'Taunton' road and pass Bristol Airport on the right. Descend Red Hill, cross the River Yeo, then in ½ mile branch left on to an unclassified road SP 'Burrington, Blagdon'. Ahead are views of Beacon Batch Hill. After 1 mile turn right on to the A368 SP 'Burrington Combe' then take the 2nd turning left on to the B3134. Ascend Burrington Combe.

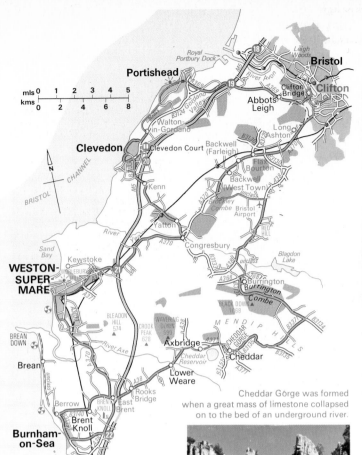

Cheddar Gorge was formed when a great mass of limestone collapsed on to the bed of an underground river.

The SS *Great Britain* at Bristol.

BURRINGTON COMBE, Somerset

High above Burrington village is 1,065ft Beacon Batch, the summit of Black Down and the highest point of the bleak Mendip range. The dramatic gorge of Burrington Combe inspired the Rev. Toplady to write the hymn *Rock of Ages*.

Climb to over 900ft, with glimpses to the left of Blagdon Lake, then cross high farmland for several miles. Meet crossroads and turn right on to the B3371 SP 'Cheddar'. Proceed through open scenery, then descend into a shallow valley and turn right on to the B3135. Make the long winding descent of Cheddar Gorge.

CHEDDAR GORGE & VILLAGE, Somerset

Every year many thousands of people come here to drive through the spectacular rock scenery of Cheddar Gorge. Curiously weathered limestone outcrops, softened in many places by the foliage of precariously rooted shrubs, hang over the road from 450ft cliffs. Underground the region is honeycombed by caves and potholes, many of which feature weird crystalline formations created by water action. Particularly good examples can be seen in Cox's and Gough's caverns (open). Various archaeological finds are displayed in the Cheddar Caves Museum.

Leave Cheddar with SP 'Bristol' and 'Weston-super-Mare' and in 1 mile turn left and immediately right on to the A371, SP 'Axbridge, Weston'. On the left is the popular yachting centre of Cheddar Reservoir. Branch left and drive into Axbridge.

AXBRIDGE, Somerset

Among many interesting and attractive old buildings in this Mendip town is King John's Hunting Lodge (NT), which dates from early Tudor times. The local manor house (not open) is also of note.

Drive to the end of Axbridge and follow SP 'Taunton, (A38)'. In ½ mile turn left on to the A38 and proceed across the flat ground of the Axe Valley. Views of 690ft Wavering Down and 628ft Crook Peak can be enjoyed to the right. Continue to Lower Weare.

LOWER WEARE, Somerset

Collections of waterfowl and a variety of small pets can be seen here at the Ambleside Water Gardens and Aviaries. Particular features of the gardens are their attractive ponds and varied shrubs.

Continue and pass through Rooks Bridge with the isolated 457ft mound of Brent Knoll increasingly prominent ahead. Cross the M5, then in $\frac{1}{4}$ mile meet a roundabout and keep left. In 1½ miles at the next roundabout take the 3rd exit on to the B3140 SP 'Burnham-on-Sea'. Proceed for 1½ miles, then meet another roundabout and keep forward to enter Burnham-on-Sea.

BURNHAM-ON-SEA, Somerset

This red-brick town is expanding to cope with holidaymakers who come to enjoy its miles of sandy beaches in larger numbers every year. Bridgwater Bay Nature Reserve lies a little to the south west.

Turn right SP 'Berrow, Brean'. After 1¼ miles reach Berrow and turn right SP 'Weston-super-Mare'. A detour from the main route to Brean can be made here by keeping forward on to an unclassified road and in ½ mile turning left.

Evening light on the vast sands at Burnham-on-Sea.

BREAN & BREAN DOWN, Somerset

At the base of 320ft Brean Down (NT), adjacent to 7 miles of sandy beaches, is the Brean Down Bird Sanctuary (open). Many species from all over the world can be seen here.

On the main route, proceed to Brent Knoll.

BRENT KNOLL, Somerset

This village takes its name from a nearby 457ft hill surmounted by an ancient camp. Inside the 15th-century church are bench ends bearing animal carvings that depict the tale of a greedy abbot who once tried to seize revenue from an unfortunate parish priest.

Meet a T-junction in the village and turn left. Skirt the base of Brent Knoll to reach East Brent, then at crossroads turn left on to the A370. Continue for 3 miles to re-enter Avon and pass the edge of Bleadon. After 2 miles meet a T-junction, turn right and return to Weston-super-Mare along the sea-front.

THOMAS HARDY'S WESSEX

Hardy's novels featured many places, thinly disguised, from his beloved Dorset. Here the visitor can find his barren island and wind-blasted heaths, earthworks overlooking thatch and stone villages from the tops of green downs, and salt lagoons held behind by giant shingle banks.

Chesil Bank stretches for 12 miles from Fortuneswell on the Isle of Portland to Abbotsbury.

WEYMOUTH, Dorset

Weymouth's early claim to fame was as the only safe port for miles around, but the town became fashionable for seaside holidays after King George III began coming here in 1789. Georgian terraces still line the wide Esplanade, and quaint little back streets wind round the old harbour. Known for years for the comings and goings of cross-Channel ferries, cargo boats, and pleasure craft, the resort offers sun and sea bathing. Among Weymouth's places of interest are the Museum of Local History and No. 3 Trinity Street. The latter is actually two 17th-century cottages with contemporary furnishings (open).

Leave Weymouth by the A354 SP 'Portland'. Cross Small Mouth, the only outlet for the waters of the Fleet, with Chesil Bank (or Beach) to the right.

CHESIL BANK, Dorset

This 20- to 30ft-high pebble ridge is 200yds wide and extends approximately 12 miles from Portland to Abbotsbury. It is separated from the mainland by a channel and tidal lagoon called the East and West Fleet, and joins the mainland at Abbotsbury. Severe storms are commonplace along the coast here, and bathing from the bank is dangerous.

Weymouth Harbour was used extensively by cargo and passenger vessels for many years.

ISLE OF PORTLAND, Dorset

Dorsetman Thomas Hardy referred to this small, almost treeless limestone peninsula as 'The Rock of Gibraltar' and used it in his novels as the 'Isle of Slingers'. Up until the 19th century it was of small importance, but then convict labour from the local prison was used to build the important naval harbour and breakwater that stand here today. The prison is now a Borstal institution. An old lighthouse on Portland Bill now serves as a bird-watching station. The interior of the island is pitted with excavations left by the extraction of the prized Portland Stone, which was used by Wren for St Paul's Cathedral. All round the coast are the deserted quays where it was loaded before road transport became a practicable possibility.

Continue on the A354 to Fortuneswell and Portland Castle.

FORTUNESWELL, Dorset

East of the village high cliffs drop to the waters of Portland Harbour. Close by is the highest spot in the peninsula, a 490ft eminence bristling with the 19th-century forts and batteries of the vast Verne Citadel.

PORTLAND CASTLE, Dorset

Built by Henry VIII in 1520, this fortress (AM) was part of a defensive chain that stretched from Kent in the east to Cornwall in the west. Its 14ft thick walls were built to absorb cannon fire.

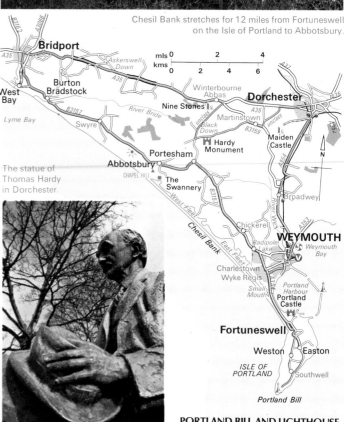

The statue of Thomas Hardy in Dorchester.

At roundabout take 2nd exit then climb steeply through Fortuneswell with SP 'Portland Bill'. Fine views can be enjoyed from the car park at the top of the ascent. Reach Easton.

EASTON, Dorset

Thatched Avice's Cottage, a 17th-century Portland Island dwelling now containing a museum, was featured as the heroine's home in Thomas Hardy's novel *The Well Beloved*. Near by is the single pentagonal tower of Bow and Arrow Castle, said to have been built by William Rufus in the 11th-century. It derives its name from the many small loopholes which pierce the walls. Pennsylvania Castle was built during the 19th century for the Governor of Portland.

Bear left unclassified and proceed to Southwell. At the Eight Kings (PH) turn left for Portland Bill.

PORTLAND BILL AND LIGHTHOUSE, Dorset

This barren mass of limestone drops to only 20ft above the sea at the southern tip of the Isle. Nearby Pulpit Rock is a pinnacle rising from the sea in a series of crags and caves. For years its labyrinthine tunnels were used by smugglers.

Return to the Eight Kings (PH) and turn left to reach Weston, passing one of the Portland stone quarries on the way.

WESTON, Dorset

Portland stone, a superb material made famous by architect Sir Christopher Wren while he was rebuilding London after the Great Fire, is quarried near this village.

Drive through Weston, climb to the top of Portland Hill, and turn left. Descend into Fortuneswell and cross to the mainland. After 1 mile turn left on to the B3157 SP 'Bridport' and proceed through Charlestown and Chickerell to reach Portesham.

PORTESHAM, Dorset
This village has an attractive green and stands at the foot of hills dotted with ancient monuments. Those nearest include burial mounds and standing stones.

Proceed on the B3157 to reach Abbotsbury.

ABBOTSBURY, Dorset
This very attractive stone-built village has a notable 15th-century tithe barn and gateway from an ancient Benedictine monastery and a 15th- to 16th-century church with a pulpit bearing the marks of Civil War bullets. Abbotsbury Gardens, 20 beautiful acres of rare sub-tropical plants are 1½ miles west of the village. Excellent views are afforded by Chapel Hill, named after the 15th-century chapel standing on its exposed summit.

ABBOTSBURY SWANNERY, Dorset
Swans, once considered a table delicacy, were bred here as long ago as 1393 to provide food for the monastery at Abbotsbury village. The swannery (open) lies ½ mile south of the village in the lagoon formed by Chesil Bank. Some 560 swans and various species of geese, ducks, and other water birds live here.

Continue on the 'Bridport' road and ascend steep Abbotsbury Hill for excellent views over low-hedged fields to the sea. Pass through Swyre to reach Burton Bradstock.

BURTON BRADSTOCK, Dorset
The restored 15th-century church in this picturesque thatched village has an embattled central tower. Unusually stratified cliffs of geological interest can be seen to the east.

Leave Burton Bradstock and proceed for 2 miles; a short detour can be made to West Bay.

WEST BAY, Dorset
A port since the 13th century, West Bay is still used for fishing but additionally caters for small cargo boats and pleasure craft. At one time it served as a harbour for Bridport, which lies 1½ miles north, but nowadays it supplements its port business with resort facilities.

Continue on B3157 to reach Bridport.

BRIDPORT, Dorset
For over 750 years Bridport has been associated with rope and net making, and it is still Europe's principal centre for the production of fishing nets, lines, and cordage. These fascinating local trades are featured in a permanent exhibition at Bridport Museum and Art Gallery. Also here are exhibits showing the archaeology, geology, and natural history of the area. After the battle of Worcester in 1651 Charles II came here to hide, rather incautiously, at the best inn in town; this is now a chemist's shop.

Excavations at Maiden Castle in 1937 revealed the bones of men killed whilst defending the fort against the Romans.

Leave Bridport on the A35 'Dorchester' road and enjoy fine views from Askerswell Down. Proceed to the Nine Stones.

NINE STONES, Dorset
This ancient stone circle (AM) beside the A35 ½ mile west of Winterbourne Abbas is the most notable of many tumuli and configurations of stones in the Dorchester area.

Continue through Winterbourne Abbas. At the end of the village bear right on to the B3159 SP 'Weymouth', then right again on to an unclassified road SP 'Hardy Monument'. Climb on to heathland and turn left to reach the monument.

Dorchester Museum displays many exhibits in elegant Victorian surroundings.

HARDY MONUMENT, Dorset
Admiral Hardy, who was beside Lord Nelson at his death during the battle of Trafalgar, is commemorated here by an obelisk on top of Black Down. Tremendous views can be enjoyed from the hill top (NT).

Continue for 2 miles to a T-junction, and turn right on to the B3159 to enter Martinstown. Drive to the end of the village and branch left on to an unclassified road. In 1¼ miles at a T-junction turn right on to A35. Continue to Dorchester.

DORCHESTER, Dorset
Thomas Hardy was born 2 miles north-east of Dorchester in a cottage (NT, open by appointment), at Higher Bockhampton. The town itself is featured in several of his novels as 'Casterbridge', and the original manuscript of *The Mayor of*

Casterbridge can be seen among other relics in the County Museum. Excellent finds from periods before and after the Romans founded their major walled town of *Durnovaria* here cAD43 are also displayed, and foundations of a Roman villa complete with tessellated pavement can be seen at Colliton Park. After the Monmouth rebellion Judge Jeffries held his notorious 'Bloody Assize' at the Antelope Hotel in 1685, sentencing 292 local men to various degrees of punishment for their treachery. Up to 74 of them were hanged in the town, and their heads were impaled on the railings of St Peter's Church as a grim warning against treason. The rest were deported. Much later in 1834 the infant trades union movement was dealt a public blow at the trial of 6 agricultural workers later to become known as the Tolpuddle Martyrs. They were tried in the courtroom of the old Shire Hall, now a Tolpuddle memorial (open), and were sentenced to transportation for joining forces to request a wage increase for local farmworkers. Also of interest in the town are the Dorset Military Museum, the Dinosaur Museum, and the 17th-century Napper's Mite almshouses.

Leave Dorchester on the A354 'Weymouth' road. An unclassified road on the right leads to Maiden Castle.

MAIDEN CASTLE, Dorset
Situated 2 miles south west of Dorchester, this vast prehistoric hillfort (AM) occupies 120 acres of land and is the finest of its kind in Britain. It was large enough to have accommodated 5,000 people, and probably developed from a simple bank and ditch defence against neighbouring tribes. After successfully storming it the Romans used the castle as a base and built a temple cAD367 within its ramparts.

Continue along the A354 and drive over downland. Pass through Broadwey and return to Weymouth.

The magnificent abbey at Bath provides a majestic backdrop to the famous Roman baths.

Key to Town Plans

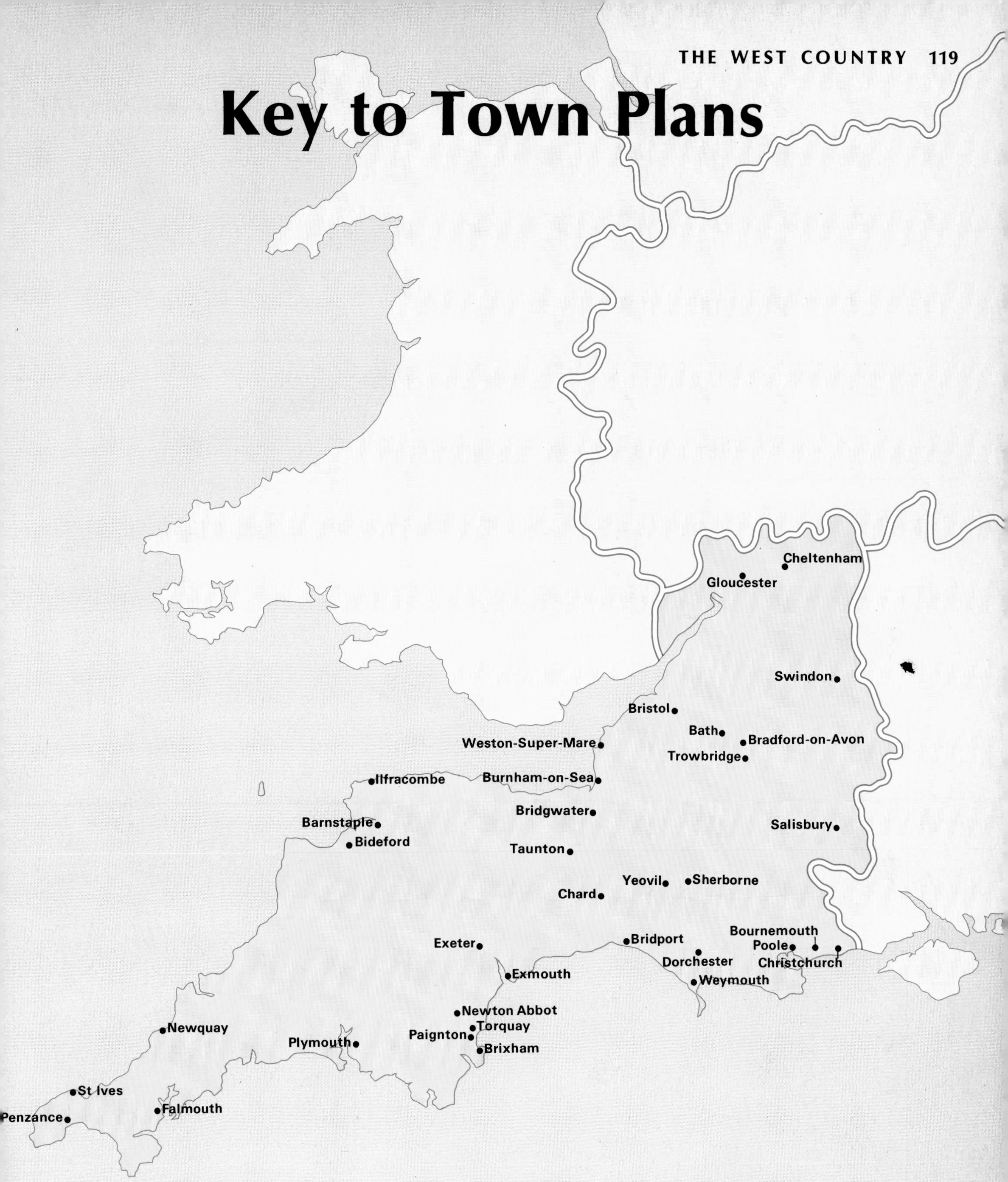

Cheltenham

Gloucester

Swindon

Bristol

Bath

Bradford-on-Avon

Weston-Super-Mare

Trowbridge

Ilfracombe

Burnham-on-Sea

Bridgwater

Barnstaple

Salisbury

Bideford

Taunton

Yeovil

Sherborne

Chard

Bridport

Bournemouth

Poole

Exeter

Dorchester

Christchurch

Exmouth

Weymouth

Newton Abbot

Newquay

Torquay

Paignton

Plymouth

Brixham

St Ives

Penzance

Falmouth

Central Barnstaple

North Devon Hospital and Maternity Hospital

LETHABY ROAD · BELMONT RD · DERBY RD · CHARLES · DART STREET · GOOD LEIGH ROAD · ASHLEIGH ROAD · ASHLEIGH CRES · BARB LA · BARBICAN ROAD · VIC. STREET · BROADFIELD ROAD · PORTLAND ST

Sports Ground

BICTON STREET · MILLER CRES · SUNFLOWER ROAD · RICHMOND STREET · HILLS VIEW · BEVAN ROAD · GLOSTER ROAD · NEWPORT ROAD · PARK LANE · ROCK AVE · ALLEN BANK · ROCK GDNS

School · FORT STREET · School

St MARY'S ROAD · VICARAGE · Health Centre · HIGH MAUDELIN STREET · NEW BLGS · BELMONT TERR · GAYDON STREET · GROS. ST · ALEX. ROAD · FORT TERRACE · Playing Field · PULCHRASS STREET · SUMMERLAND STREET · HIGHER CHURCH ST · SALEM ST · BARBICAN TERR · TRINITY PLACE · Trafalgar Lawn

Rock Park

MASEFIELD · BYRON AVE · HIGHER RALEIGH ROAD · CARL AVE · KINGSLY AVENUE · GRANV'LE AVENUE · PRINCES ST · CHARLES STREET · KING EDWARD ST · BARUM ARC. · BULLER RD · BED. ST · Penrose Almshouses · LITCHDON STREET · SOUTH WALK · Rock Park Sports Gnd

RAWLEY LAWN · PILTON LAWN · CORONATION STREET · GEORGE STREET · VIC. LAWN · BOUTPORT STREET · Queen's Hall · Pannier Mkt · Classic Cinema · QUEEN STREET · P.O. · WELLS ST · SILVER ST · DIAMOND ST · Royal Barum Pottery · TRINITY STREET · THE VALE · TAW · Leisure Centre

THE ROCK · RIDDEL AVENUE · Fire H.Q. & Station · GREEN LANE · BUTCHER'S ROW · St Anne's Chapel Mus · St Annes Chapel Mus · Guildhall · HIGH STREET · JOY ST · CROSS ST · THE SQUARE · Atheneaum & Public Library · Lorry Park · Seven Brethren Industrial Estate

BULL HILL · PILTON STREET · PILTON CAUSEWAY · Pilton Park · TULY STREET · HOLLAND STREET · Guildhall · THE STRAND · Bus Station · River · LONG BRIDGE

PRIORY CL. · ABBEY ROAD · PATHFIELD LAWN · School · BRAUNTON RD · POTTINGTON ROAD · FAIR VIEW · ROLLE STREET · MILL ROAD · NORTH WALK · Castle Mound · Cattle Market · CASTLE STREET · Castle Quay · Police Station · Civic Centre · STICKLEPATH TERRACE · CLIFFORD ST · SIGNAL TERR · Goods Depot · Barnstaple Station

School & Community Centre

N

North Devon Area

ILFRACOMBE · Hele · Combe Martin · Lynton · Lynmouth · Barbrook · Brendon · Porlock Wier · Porlock

Slade · Berrynarbor · Martinhoe · A39 · Cheriton · Malmsmead

Lee · Mortehoe · A399 · Kentisbury · A39 · Parracombe · B3223

Woolacombe · B3343 · West Down · Patchole · Blackmoor Gate · B3358 · River Exe · Exford · B3224

Pickwell · B3231 · Bittadon · East Down · Arlington · Challacombe · Simonsbath · B3223

Croyde · North Buckland · Georgeham · Milltown · Lower Loxhore · Knightacott · River Barle · Withypool · B3223

Knowle · Muddiford · Shirwell · Bratton Fleming · B3226 · North Radworthy

Saunton · Marwood · A39 · Stoke Rivers · Brayford · South Radworthy · Hawkridge

Heanton Punchardon · Ashford · Goodleigh · BARNSTAPLE · Gunn · West Buckland · Charles · Twitchen · West Anstey

Braunton · River Taw · Fremington · Bickington · Landkey Town · East Buckland · North Molton · Molland · East Anstey

Appledore · Instow · Bickleton · Swimbridge · A361 · South Molton · Bish Mill · A361 · Oldways End

Westward Ho · Northam · Westleigh · Tawstock · Bishop's Tawton · B3227 · Bishop's Nympton · B3227 · Ash Mill · Knowstone

Horwood · Newton Tracey · Hiscott · River Taw · Chittlehampton · B3226 · George Nympton · Mariansleigh · Rose Ash

BIDEFORD · Abbotsham · Woodtown · Alverdiscott · A371 · Umberleigh · Clapworthy · Alswear

Fairy Cross · Landcross · Yarnscombe · Atherington · Warkleigh

Littleham · A388 · A386 · B3227

SCALE · mls 0 · 4

Box denotes area covered by central plan

Barnstaple

During the 18th century the wool trade created a prosperity in Barnstaple to which the town's elegant Georgian buildings testify. Queen Anne's Walk, a colonnade where merchants conducted business, is both a fine example of this period and a reminder that Barnstaple has always been a trading centre. This tradition continues as today it is one of the area's busiest market towns. Of the many picturesque shopping streets Butchers Row is particularly attractive.

Ilfracombe This is North Devon's well-established "Queen of the Coast". Originally a fishing harbour, Ilfracombe evolved in the 19th century – when enterprise was all – into one of the typical seaside resorts that mushroomed all over England. Here, terraces of large Victorian hotels and houses follow the contours of the hills down to the harbour and a welter of little coves. The town is also the main departure point for Lundy Island.

Bideford South-west of Barnstaple and Ilfracombe, Bideford too has always made its living by trading and the sea. Sir Richard Grenville, a Bideford man famous for his fight against the Spaniards in the Azores, gained a charter for the town from Elizabeth I and it prospered as a port and shipbuilding centre until the 18th century. A nautical air still pervades Bideford and the long, tree-lined quay is popular.

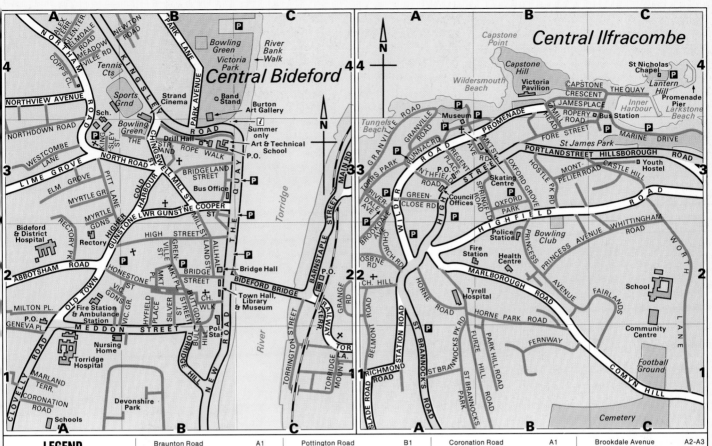

Central Bideford

Central Ilfracombe

LEGEND

Town Plan

AA recommended route
Restricted roads
Other roads
Buildings of interest Station ▣
Car parks P
Parks and open spaces
One way streets

Area Plan

A roads
B roads
Locations Patchole ○
Urban area

Street Index with Grid Reference

Barnstaple

Abbey Road	A1-A2
Alexandra Road	C3
Allen Bank	F4
Ashleigh Crescent	D4-E4
Ashleigh Road	D4
Barbican Close	D4-E4
Barbican Lane	E4
Barbican Road	D4-E4
Barbican Terrace	D3-E3
Barum Arcade	C3
Bear Street	C3-C4
Bedford Street	D3
Belmont Road	B4
Belmont Terrace	B3-C3
Bevan Road	D4
Bicton Street	B4-C4
Boutport Street	B2-B3-C3-C2

Braunton Road	A1
Broadfield Road	E4-F4
Buller Road	D3
Bull Hill	A2
Butcher's Row	C2-C3
Byron Close	A3
Carlyle Avenue	A3-B3
Carrington Terrace	B3-B4
Castle Street	C1-C2
Charles Dart Crescent	B4-C4
Charles Street	B3
Clifford Street	D1
Coronation Street	B2-B3
Cross Street	C2
Derby Road	B4
Diamond Street	D2-D3
Fair View	A1-A2
Fort Street	C3-C4-D4
Fort Terrace	C3-D3
Gaydon Street	C3
George Street	B2-B3
Gloster Road	E4-F4
Goodleigh Road	C4
Granville Avenue	A3-B3
Green Lane	B2-C2
Grosvenor Street	C4
Higher Church Street	D3
Higher Raleigh Road	A3
High Maudelin Street	B3
High Street	B2-C2
Hills View	C4
Holland Street	C1-C2
Joy Street	C2
King Edward Street	B3
Lethaby Road	B4
Litchdon Street	D2-D3-E3
Long Bridge	D2
Lower Raleigh Road	A3-A4
Magdalen Lawn	B3
Maiden Street	D2
Masefield Avenue	A3
Miller Crescent	C4
Mill Road	B1-B2
New Buildings	B3
Newport Road	E3-E4-F4
New Road	E3
Norfolk Terrace	F4
North Road	A2-A3-A4
North Walk	B1-B2
Park Lane	F4
Pathfield Lawn	A1-A2
Pilton Causeway	A2-B2
Pilton Lawn	A3
Pilton Street	A2
Portland Street	F4

Pottington Road	B1
Princes Street	B3
Priory Close	A2
Pulchrass Street	D3-D4
Queen Street	C3-D3
Raleigh Lawn	A3
Raleigh Road	A2-A3
Richmond Street	B4-C4
Riddel Avenue	A2-B2-B3
Rock Avenue	F4
Rock Gardens	F4
Rolle Street	B1-B2
St George's Road	A2-A3-A4
St Mary's Road	B4
Salem Street	D3
Signal Terrace	D1-E1
Silver Street	D3
South Walk	E3-F3
Sticklepath Terrace	D1-E1
Summerland Street	D3-D4
Sunflower Road	C4
Taw Vale	D2-D3-E3
The Rock	A2
The Square	D2
The Strand	C2-D2
Trinity Place	E3
Trinity Street	D3
Tuly Street	B2-C2
Vicarage Lawn	B3-C3
Vicrarage Street	B3-B4
Victoria Road	E4
Victoria Street	E4
Wells Street	C2-D2-D3
Yeo Vale Road	B2-B3

Bideford

Abbotsham Road	A2
Alexandra Terrace	A4
Allhalland Street	B2
Barnstaple Street	C2-C3
Bideford Bridge	B2-C2
Bridgeland Street	B3
Bridge Street	B2
Bull Hill	B1-B2
Buttgarden Street	B2
Chingswell Street	B3
Church Walk	B2
Clovelly Road	A1
Cold Harbour	B3
Cooper Street	B3
Copp's Close	A4

Ilfracombe

Avenue Road	A3-B3
Belmont Road	A1-A2

Coronation Road	A1
Elmdale Road	A4
Elm Grove	A3
Geneva Place	A1-A2
Glendale Terrace	A4
Grange Road	C2
Grenville Street	B2
Higher Gunstone	A2-B2-B3
High Street	A2-B2
Honestone Street	A2-B2
Hyfield Place	B2
Kingsley Road	A4-B4-B3
Kingsley Street	A3
Lime Grove	A3
Lower Gunstone	B3
Main Road	C3
Market Place	B2
Marland Terrace	A1
Meadowville Road	A4
Meddon Street	A1-A2-B2-B1
Mill Street	B2-B3
Milton Place	A2
Myrtle Gardens	A2-A3
Myrtle Grove	A3
New Road	B1-B2
Newton Road	A4-B4
Northam Road	A3-A4
Northdown Road	A3-A4
North Road	A3-B3
Northview Avenue	A4
Old Town	A2
Park Avenue	B3-B4
Park Lane	B4
Pitt Lane	A2-A3
Railway Terrace	C1-C2
Rectory Park	A2-A3
Rope Walk	B3
Silver Street	B2
The Quay	B2-B3-C3-C2
The Strand	B3
Torridge Hill	B1
Torridge Mount	C1
Torrington Lane	C1
Torrington Street	C1-C2
Victoria Gardens	A2-B2
Victoria Grove	A2-B2
Westcombe Lane	A3

Brookdale Avenue	A2-A3
Capstone Crescent	B4-C4
Castle Hill	C3
Church Hill	A2
Church Road	A2-A3
Comyn Hill	B1-C1
Fairlands	B2-C2-C1
Fernway	B1
Fore Street	B3-C3
Furze Hill Road	A2-A1-B1
Granville Road	A3-A4
Green Close Road	A3
Highfield Road	A2-B2-B3-C3
High Street	A2-A3-B3
Hillsborough Road	C3
Horne Park Road	A2-B2-B1
Horne Road	A2
Hostle Park Road	B3
Marine Drive	C3-C4
Market Street	B3
Marlborough Road	A2-B2
Mill Head	B3-B4
Montpelier Road	B3-C3
Northfield Road	A3
Osborne Road	A2
Oxford Grove	B3
Oxford Park	B3
Park Hill Road	B1-B2
Portland Street	B3-C3
Princess Avenue	B3-B2-C2
Promenade	B3-B4
Regent Place	A3
Richmond Road	A1
Riverdale Avenue	A3
Ropery Road	B4-C4
Runnacleave Road	A3
St Brannocks Park	A1
St Brannocks Park Road	A1-A2
St Brannocks Road	A1-A2
St James Place	B4-C4
Slade Road	A1
Springfield Road	B3
Station Road	A1-A2
The Quay	C4
Torrs Park	A3
Whittingham Road	C2-C3
Wilder Road	A2-A3
Worth Lane	C1-C2-C3

BARNSTAPLE
This ancient town stands on the Taw estuary and until the 19th century was an important port. The bridge across the river was originally built in the 1400s but has since been widened and extensively altered.

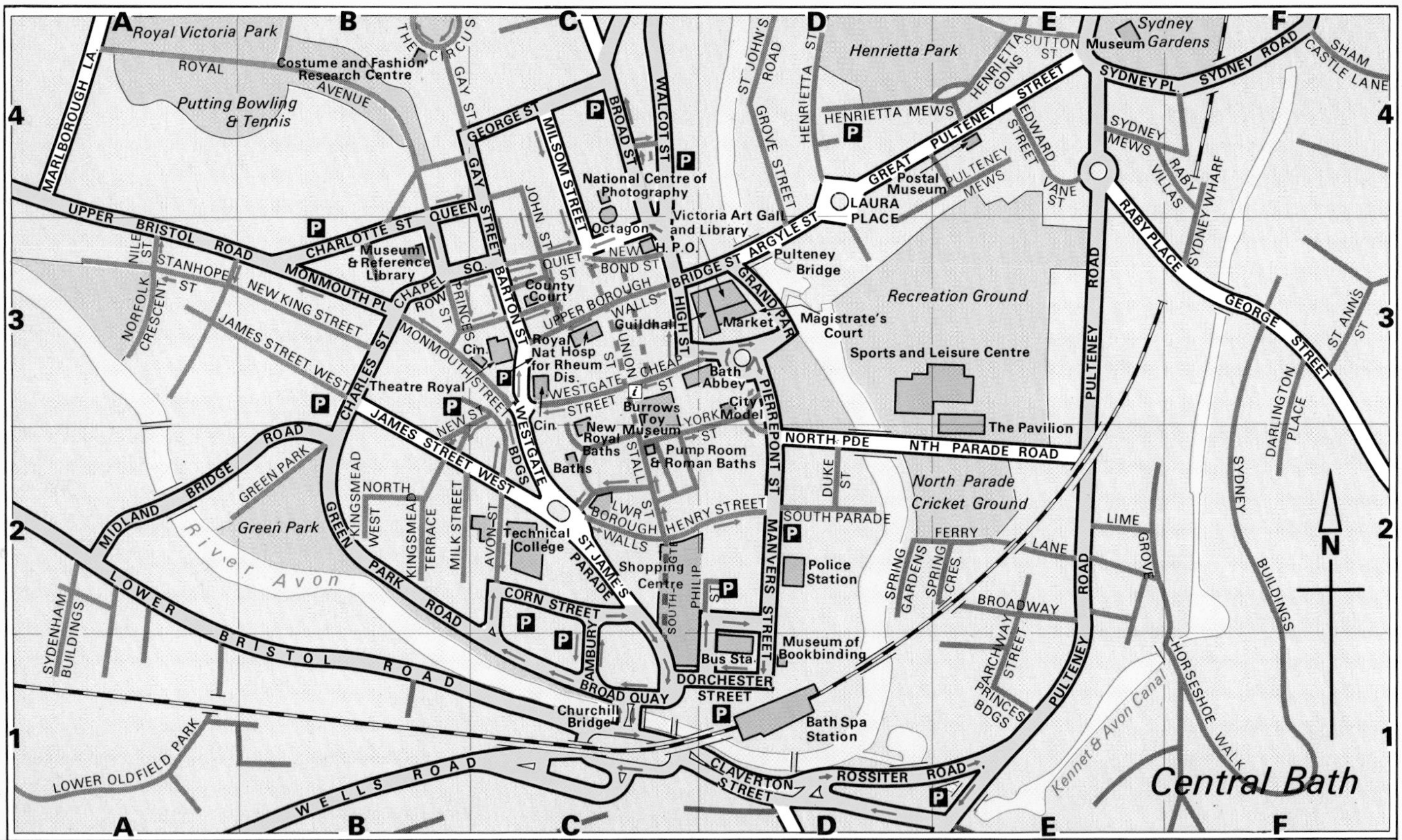

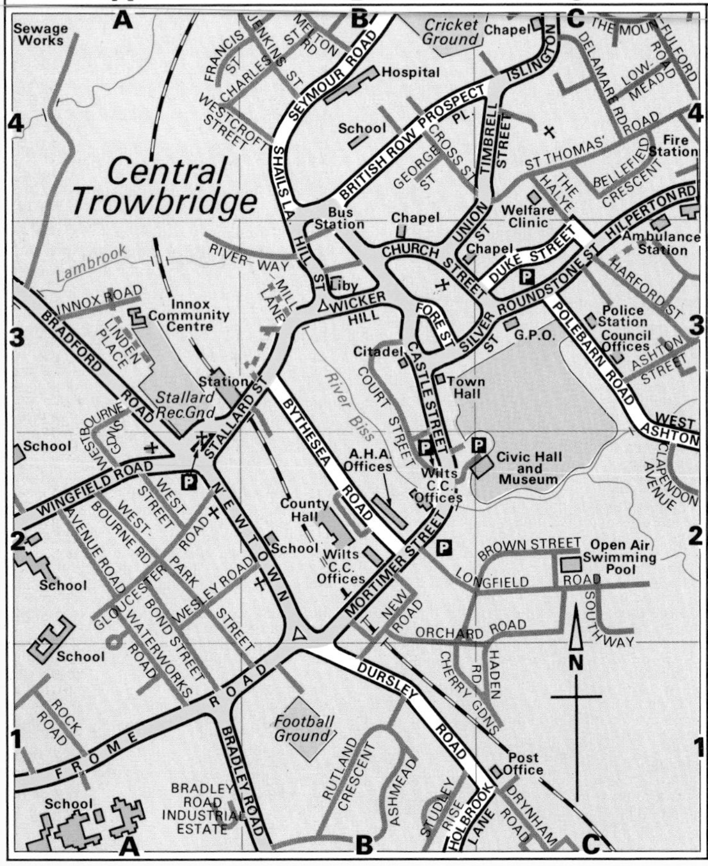

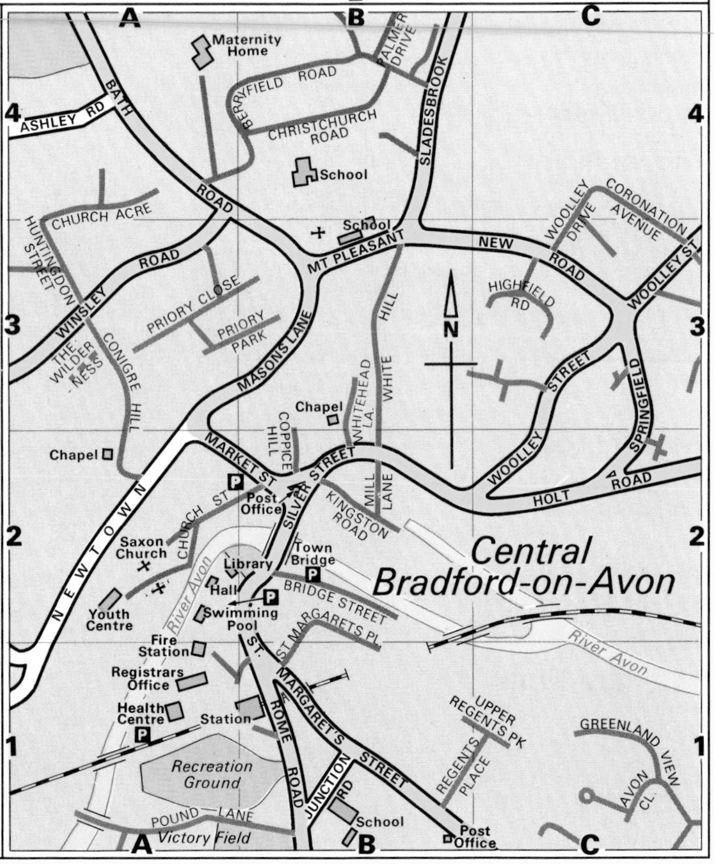

Central Bath

Central Trowbridge

Central Bradford-on-Avon

Bath

This unique city combines Britain's most impressive collection of Roman relics with the country's finest Georgian townscape. Its attraction to Romans and fashionable 18th-century society alike was its mineral springs, which are still seen by thousands of tourists who visit the Roman Baths every year. They are now the centre-piece of a Roman museum, where exhibits give a vivid impression of life 2000 years ago. The adjacent Pump Room to which the waters were piped for drinking was a focal point of social life in 18th- and 19th-century Bath.

The Georgian age of elegence also saw the building of Bath's perfectly proportioned streets, terraces and crescents. The finest examples are Queen Square, the Circus, and Royal Crescent, all built of golden local stone. Overlooking the Avon from the west is the great tower of Bath Abbey – sometimes called the "Lantern of the West" because of its large and numerous windows.

Bath has much to delight the museum-lover. Near the abbey, in York Street, is the Burrows Toy Museum – a treasure-trove of playthings spanning two centuries. The Assembly Rooms in Bennett Street, very much a part of the social scene in Georgian Bath, are now the home of the Museum of Costume, and nearby, in Circus Mews, is the Carriage Museum, which vividly recalls coaching days.

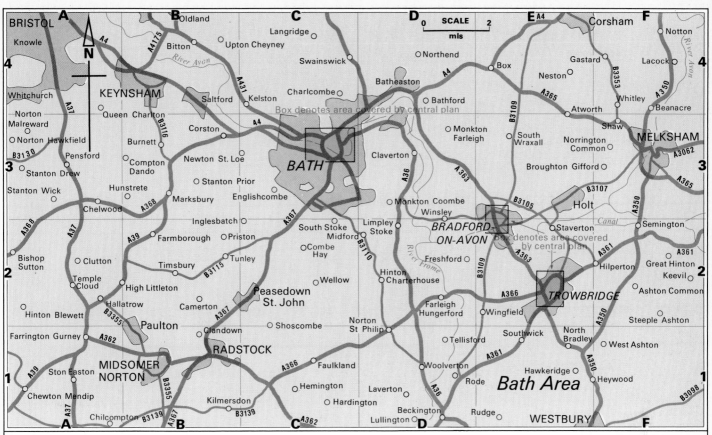

Bath Area

Key to Town Plan and Area Plan

Town Plan

A A Recommended roads
Other roads
Restricted roads
Buildings of interest   Library
Car Parks   P
Parks and open spaces
Churches   +
One Way Streets

Area Plan

A roads
B roads
Locations   Box O
Urban Area

Street Index with Grid Reference

Central Bath

Ambury	C1-C2
Archway Street	E1-E2
Argyle Street	D3-D4
Avon Street	C2
Barton Street	C3
Bridge Street	C3-D3
Broadway	E2
Broad Street	C3-C4
Broad Quay	C1
Chapel Row	B3
Charles Street	B2-B3
Charlotte Street	B3-B4
Cheap Street	C3
Claverton Street	C1-D1
Corn Street	C2
Darlington Place	F2-F3
Dorchester Street	C1-D1
Duke Street	D2
Edward Street	E4
Ferry Lane	D2-E2
Gay Street	B4-C4-C3
George Street	B4-C4
George Street	F2-F3
Grand Parade	D3
Great Pulteney Street	D4-E4
Green Park	A2-B2
Green Park Road	B1-B2-C2-C1
Grove Street	D3-D4
Henrietta Gardens	E4
Henrietta Mews	D4-E4
Henrietta Street	D4
Henry Street	C2-D2
High Street	C3
Horseshoe Walk	F1
James Street West	A3-B3-B2-C2
John Street	C3-C4
Kingsmead North	B2
Kingsmead Terrace	B2
Kingsmead West	B2
Laura Place	D3-D4
Lime Grove	E2-F2-F1
Lower Bristol Road	A2-A1-B1-C1
Lower Borough Walls	C2
Lower Oldfield Park	A1
Manvers Street	D1-D2
Marlborough Lane	A4
Midland Bridge Road	A2-B2-B3
Milk Street	B2
Milsom Street	C3-C4
Monmouth Place	B3
Monmouth Street	B3-C3
New Street	B2-B3-C3
New Bond Street	C3
New King Street	A3-B3
Nile Street	A3
Norfolk Crescent	A3
North Parade	D2
North Parade Road	D2-E2
Philip Street	C1-C2
Pierrepont Street	D2-D3
Princes Buildings	E1
Princes Street	B3
Pulteney Mews	E4
Pulteney Road	E1-E2-E3-E4
Queen Square	B3-B4-C4-C3
Quiet Street	C3
Raby Place	E4-E3-F3
Raby Villas	E4-F4
Rossiter Road	D1-E1
Royal Avenue	A4-B4
St Ann's Street	F3
St Jame's Parade	C2
St John's Road	D4
Sham Castle Lane	F4
Southgate	C1-C2
South Parade	D2
Spring Crescent	E2
Spring Gardens	D2
Stall Street	C2-C3
Stanhope Street	A3
Sutton Street	E4
Sydenham Buildings	A1-A2
Sydney Buildings	F1-F2-F3
Sydney Mews	E4-F4
Sydney Place	E4-F4
Sydney Road	F4
Sydney Wharf	F3-F4
The Circus	B4
Union Street	C3
Upper Borough Walls	C3
Upper Bristol Road	A4-A3-B3
Vane Street	E4
Walcot Street	C3-C4
Wells Road	A1-B1-C1
Westgate Buildings	C2-C3
Westgate Street	C3
York Street	C2-D2-D3

Trowbridge

Ashmead	B1
Ashton Street	C3
Avenue Road	A2
Bellefield Crescent	C4
Bond Street	A1-A2
Bradford Road	A2-A3
Bradley Road	A1-B1
British Row	B4
Brown Street	B2-C2
Bythesea Road	B2-B3
Castle Street	B2-B3
Charles Street	A4-B4
Cherry Gardens	B1-C1
Church Street	B3-C3
Clapendon Avenue	C2
Court Street	B2-B3
Cross Street	B4-C4
Delamare Road	C4
Drynham Road	C1
Duke Street	C3-C4
Dursley Road	B1-C1
Fore Street	B3
Francis Street	A4-B4
Frome Road	A1-B1
Fulford Road	C4
George Street	B4
Gloucester Road	A2
Haden Road	C1
Harford Street	C3
Hill Street	B3
Hilperton Road	C3-C4
Holbrook Lane	B1-C1
Innox Road	A3
Islington	C4
Jenkins Street	A4-B4
Linden Place	A3
Longfield Road	B2-C2
Lowmead	C4
Melton Road	B4
Mill Lane	B3
Mortimer Street	C4
New Road	B1-B2
Newtown	A2-B2
Orchard Road	B1-B2-C2-C1
Park Street	A2-A1-B1
Polebarn Road	C3
Prospect Place	B4-C4
River Way	A3-B3
Rock Road	A1
Roundstone Street	C3
Rutland Crescent	B1
St Thomas' Road	C4
Seymour Road	B4
Shails Lane	B3-B4
Silver Street	B3-C3
Southway	C2
Stallard Street	A2-A3-B3
Studley Rise	B1
The Hayle	C4
The Mount	C4
Timbrell Street	C4
Union Street	B3-B4-C4-C3
Waterwoks Road	A1-A2
Wesley Road	A2-B2
West Street	A2
West Ashton	C2-C3
Westbourne Gardens	A2-A3
Westbourne Road	A2
Westcroft Street	A4-B4
Wicker Hill	B3
Wingfield Road	A2

Bradford-on-Avon

Ashley Road	A4
Avon Close	C1
Bath Road	A3-A4-B4-B3
Berryfield Road	A4-B4
Bridge Street	B2
Christchurch Road	B4
Church Acre	A4
Church Street	A2-B2
Conigre Hill	A2-A3
Coppice Hill	B2-B3
Coronation Avenue	C3-C4
Greenland View	C1
Highfield Road	B2-B3
Holt Road	B2-C2
Huntingdon Street	A3
Kingston Road	B2
Junction Road	B1
Market Street	A2-B2
Masons Lane	A3-B3
Mill Lane	B2
Mount Pleasant	B3
Newtown	A1-A2-A3
New Road	B3-C3
Palmer Drive	B4
Pound Lane	A1-B1
Priory Close	A3-B3
Priory Park	A3-B3
Regents Place	B1-C1
Rome Road	B1
St Margaret's Place	B1-B2
St Margaret's Street	B2-B1-C1
Silver Street	B2
Sladesbrook	B3-B4
Springfield	C2-C3
The Wilderness	A3
Upper Regents Park	B1-C1
White Hill	B2-B3
Whitehead Lane	B2-B3
Winsley Road	A3-A4
Woolley Drive	C3-C4
Woolley Street	C2-C3

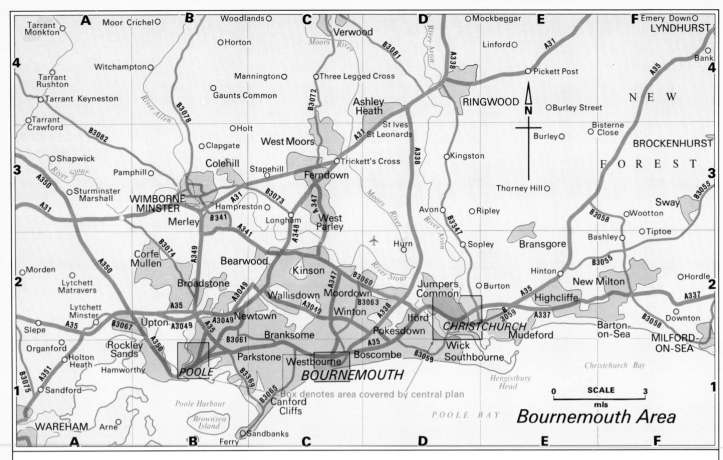

Bournemouth Area

Box denotes area covered by central plan

SCALE
mls

Street Index with Grid Reference

Bournemouth

Albert Road	C3-D3
Avenue Road	B3-C3
Bath Road	D2-E2-E3-E4-F4
Beacon Road	C1
Bodorgan Road	C4
Bourne Avenue	B3-C3
Braidley Road	B3-B4
Branksome Wood Road	A4
Cambridge Road	A2-A3
Central Drive	B4
Chine Crescent	A1-A2
Chine Crescent Road	A1-A2
Christchurch Road	F4
Cotlands Road	F4
Cranbourne Road	B2-C2
Crescent Road	A3-B3
Dean Park Crescent	C4-D4
Dean Park Road	C4
Durley Chine Road	A1-A2
Durley Gardens	A1-A2
Durley Road	A1-A2-B1
East Overcliff Drive	E2-F2-F3
Exeter Crescent	C2
Exeter Lane	C2-D2
Exeter Park Road	C2-D2
Exeter Road	C2-D2
Fir Vale Road	D3-D4
Gervis Place	C3-D3
Gervis Road	E3-F3
Glenfern Road	D3-E3-E4
Grove Road	E3-F3
Hahnemann Road	A1-B1-B2
Hinton Road	D2-D3-E2
Holdenhurst Road	F4
Lansdowne Road	E4-F4
Lorne Park Road	E4
Madeira Road	D4-E4
Marlborough Road	A2
Meyrick Road	F3-F4
Norwich Avenue	A2-A3-B3
Norwich Avenue West	A3
Old Christchurch Road	D3-D4-E4-F4
Parsonage Road	D3-E3
Poole Hill	A2-B2
Poole Road	A2
Priory Road	C1-C2

Richmond Hill	C3-C4
Russell Cotes Road	E2
St Michael's Road	B2-B1-C1
St Peter's Road	D3-E3
St Stephen's Road	B3-B4-C4-C3
Stafford Road	E4
Suffolk Road	A3-B3
Surrey Road	A3
Terrace Road	B2-C2
The Triangle	B2-B3
Tregonwell Road	B2-C2-C1
Undercliffe Drive	D1-D2-E1-E2-F2
Upper Hinton Road	D2-D3-E2
Upper Norwich Road	A2-B2
Upper Terrace Road	B2
Wessex Way	A3-A4-B4-C4-D4-E4
West Cliff Gardens	B1
West Cliff Promenade	B1-C1-D1-C1
West Cliff Road	A1-B1
Westhill Road	A2-B2-B1-C1
Westover Road	D2-D3
West Promenade	C1-D1
Wimborne Road	C4
Wootton Gardens	E3-E4
Yelverton Road	C3-D3

Christchurch

Albion Road	A4
Arcadia Road	A4
Arthur Road	B3
Avenue Road	A3-B3-B4
Avon Road West	A3-A4-B4
Bargates	B2-B3
Barrack Road	A4-A3-B2-B3
Beaconsfield Road	B2-C3
Bridge Street	C2
Bronte Avenue	B4
Canberra Road	A4
Castle Street	B2-C2
Christchurch By-Pass	B2-C2-C3
Clarendon Road	A3-B3
Douglas Avenue	A2-B2
Endfield Road	A4
Fairfield	B3
Fairmile Road	A4-B4-B3
Flambard Avenue	B4
Gardner Road	A3-A4
Gleadowe Avenue	A2-B2
Grove Road East	A3-B3

Grove Road West	A3
High Street	B2
Iford Lane	A1
Jumpers Avenue	A4
Jumpers Road	A3-A4-B4
Kings Avenue	A2-B2
Manor Road	B2
Millhams Street	B2-C2
Mill Road	B3-B4
Portfield Road	A3-B3
Queens Avenue	B1
Quay Road	B1
St John's Road	A2
St Margarets Avenue	B1
Sopers Lane	B1-B2
South View Road	A1-B1
Stony Lane	C4-C3-C2
Stour Road	B3-B2-A1-A2
The Grove	A4
Tuckton Road	A1
Twynham Avenue	B2-B3
Walcott Avenue	A4-B4
Waterloo Place	C2
Wickfield Avenue	B1-B2
Wick Lane	A1-B1-B2
Willow Drive	A1-B1
Willow Way	A1-B1
Windsor Road	A3

Poole

Ballard Road	B1-C1
Church Street	A1
Dear Hay Lane	A2-B2
Denmark Road	C3
East Quay Road	B1
East Street	B1
Elizabeth Road	C3
Emerson Road	B1-B2
Esplanade	B3
Garland Road	C4
Green Road	B2-B1-C1
Heckford Road	C3-C4
High Street	A1-B1-B2
Hill Street	B2
Johns Road	C3-C4
Jolliffe Road	C4
Kingland Road	B2-C2
Kingston Road	C3-C4
Lagland Street	B1-B2

Longfleet Road	C3
Maple Road	C3-C4
Mount Pleasant Road	C2-C3
Newfoundland Drive	C1
New Orchard	A1-A2
North Street	B2
Old Orchard	B1
Parkstone Road	C3-C2
Perry Gardens	B1
Poole Bridge	A1
St Mary's Road	C3
Seldown Lane	C2-C3
Shaftesbury Road	C3
Skinner Street	B1
South Road	B2
Stanley Road	B1
Sterte Avenue	A4-B4
Sterte Road	B2-B3-B4
Stokes Avenue	B4-C4
Strand Street	A1-B1
Tatnam Road	B4-C4
The Quay	A1-B1
Towngate Bridge	B2-B3
West Quay Road	A1-A2-B2
West Street	A1-A2-B2
Wimborne Road	B3-C3-C4

LEGEND

Town Plan

AA Recommended route	▬▬▬
Other roads	
Restricted roads	▬ ▬ ▬
Buildings of interest	☐ Town Hall
AA Centre	🅰🅰
Car Parks	🅿
Parks and open spaces	
One way streets	←

Area Plan

A roads	
B roads	
Locations	Mudeford ○
Urban area	

Bournemouth

Until the beginning of the 19th century the landscape on which Bournemouth stands was open heath. Its rise began when a scattering of holiday villas were built by innovative trend-setters at a time when the idea of seaside holidays was very new. Soon a complete village had taken shape. In the next 50 years Bournemouth had become a major resort and its population catapulted to nearly 59,000.

Today's holidaymakers can enjoy Bournemouth's natural advantages – miles of sandy beaches, a mild climate and beautiful setting, along with a tremendous variety of amenities. These include some of the best shopping in the south – with shops ranging from huge departmental stores to tiny specialist places. Entertainments range from variety shows and feature films to opera, and the music of the world-famous Bournemouth Symphony Orchestra.

Poole has virtually been engulfed by the suburbs of Bournemouth, but its enormous natural harbour is still an attraction in its own right. At Poole Quay, some 15th-century cellars have been converted into a Maritime Museum, where the town's association with the sea from prehistoric times until the early 20th century is illustrated, and the famous Poole Pottery nearby offers guided tours of its workshops.

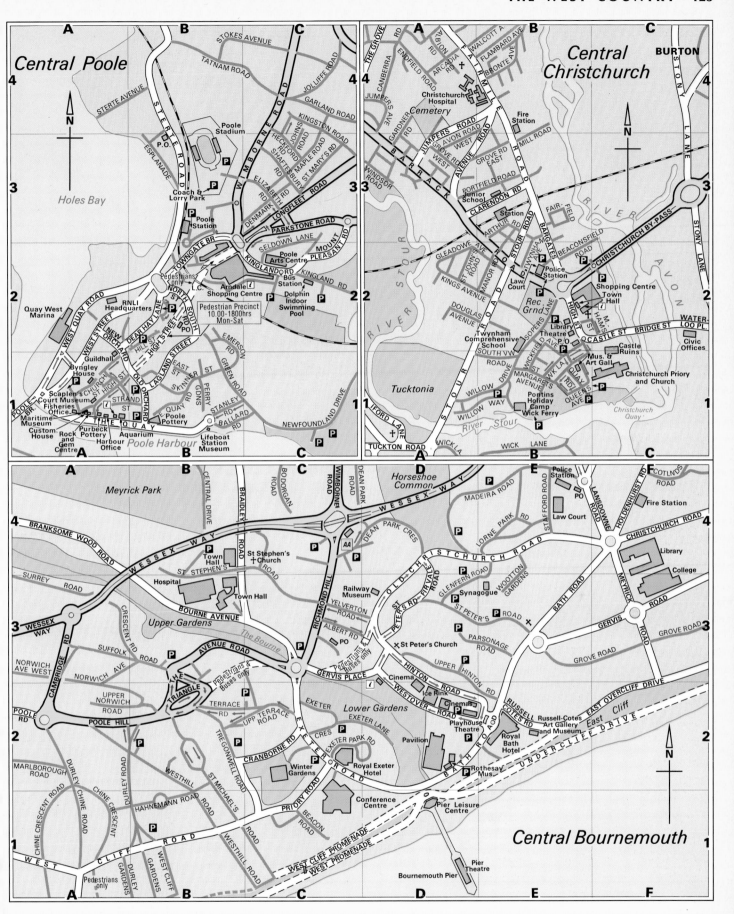

Central Poole

4

STOKES AVENUE

TATNAM ROAD

N

Holes Bay

STERTE AVENUE

STERTE ROAD

JOLLIFFE ROAD

GARLAND ROAD

KINGSTON ROAD

Poole Stadium

P.O.

ESPLANADE

WIMBORNE ROAD

Coach & Lorry Park

Poole Station

TOWNGATE BR.

NORTH ST

Pedestrians only

L.C.

HIGH ST

DENMARK RD

ELIZABETH RD

HECKFORD RD

SHAFTESBURY RD

MAPLE ROAD

ST. MARY'S RD

LONGFLEET ROAD

PARKSTONE ROAD

SELDOWN LANE

MOUNT PLEASANT RD

KINGLAND RD

KINGLAND RD

Poole Arts Centre

Arndale Shopping Centre

Bus Station

Dolphin Indoor Swimming Pool

Pedestrian Precinct 10.00-1800hrs Mon-Sat

2

Quay West Marina

WEST QUAY ROAD

WEST STREET

NEW ORCHARD

DEAR HAY LANE

HILL ST

OLD ORCHARD

RNLI Headquarters

Guildhall

Byngley House

CHURCH

HIGH ST

SOUTH RD

LAGLAND STREET

EAST ST

SKINNER ST

GREEN ROAD

EMERSON RD

PERRY GDNS

STANLEY RD

NEWFOUNDLAND DRIVE

1

POOLE BR

Maritime Museum

Custom House

Scaplen's Court Museum

Fisheries Office

Rock and Gem Centre

Purbeck Pottery

Harbour Office

THE QUAY

STRAND ST

Aquarium

QUAY

BALLARD RD

Poole Pottery

Lifeboat Station Museum

Poole Harbour

A B C

Central Christchurch

BURTON

THE GROVE

CANBERRA

ENDFIELD ROAD

WALCOTT A.

FLAMBARD AVE

BRONTE AVE

ARCADIA RD

ALBION RD

FAIRMILE ROAD

STONY LANE

JUMPER'S AVE

GARDNER ROAD

Christchurch Hospital

Cemetery

JUMPERS ROAD

GROVE AVENUE

AVON ROAD

WEST

WEST

Fire Station

WINDSOR ROAD

BARRACK ROAD

GROVE RD EAST

PORTFIELD ROAD

CLARENDON RD

Junior School

Station

FAIR-FIELD

BEACONSFIELD ROAD

CHRISTCHURCH BY-PASS

RIVER AVON

3

GLEADOWE AVE

ST JOHN'S RD

ARTHUR RD

MANOR RD

STOUR ROAD

TWYNHAM AVE

BARGATES

Police Station

KINGS AVENUE

DOUGLAS AVENUE

SOPERS LANE

Law Court

Rec. Grnd

Shopping Centre

Town Hall

HIGH ST

M.

HANTS

CASTLE ST

BRIDGE ST

WATER-LOO PL.

2

RIVER STOUR

Twynham Comprehensive School

SOUTH VW ROAD

WICKFIELD AVE

ST MARGARET'S AVENUE

WILLOW DRIVE

Theatre

P.O.

Library

WCK LA

QUAY RD

Mus. & Art Gall

Castle Ruins

Civic Offices

Christchurch Priory and Church

1

Tucktonia

IFORD LANE

WILLOW WAY

WILLOW ROAD

River Stour

WICK LANE

Pontins Holiday Camp

Wick Ferry

QUEENS AVE

Christchurch Quay

TUCKTON ROAD

WICK LA

WICK LANE

A B C

Central Bournemouth

Meyrick Park

BRANKSOME WOOD ROAD

CENTRAL DRIVE

BRADLEY RD

BODORGAN ROAD

WIMBORNE ROAD

DEAN PARK ROAD

DEAN PARK CRES

Horseshoe Common

WESSEX WAY

Madeira Rd

LORNE PARK RD

STAFFORD ROAD

Police Station

PO

LANSDOWNE ROAD

HOLDENHURST RD

COTLNDS ROAD

Fire Station

4

SURREY ROAD

WESSEX WAY

St Stephen's Church

ST STEPHEN'S ROAD

Town Hall

Hospital

Town Hall

RICHMOND HILL

AA

Railway Museum

YELVERTON ROAD

OLD CHRISTCHURCH ROAD

FIRVALE ROAD

GLENFERN ROAD

Synagogue

ST PETER'S RD

WOOTTON GARDENS

Law Court

CHRISTCHURCH ROAD

BATH ROAD

MEYRICK ROAD

Library

College

CHRISTCHURCH ROAD

3

WESSEX WAY

CAMBRIDGE RD

CRESCENT RD

SUFFOLK ROAD

NORWICH AVE

BOURNE AVENUE

Upper Gardens

The Bourne

AVENUE ROAD

ALBERT RD

PO

PETERS RD

St Peter's Church

PARSONAGE ROAD

UPPER HINTON RD

GERVIS ROAD

GROVE ROAD

GROVE ROAD

3

NORWICH AVE WEST

UPPER NORWICH ROAD

THE TRIANGLE

TERRACE RD

UPP TERRACE ROAD

Pedestrians & Buses only

GERVIS PLACE

WESTOVER ROAD

HINTON ROAD

Cinema

Ice Rink

Cinemas

RUSSELL COTES RD

Russell-Cotes Art Gallery and Museum

East Cliff

EAST OVERCLIFF DRIVE

2

POOLE RD

POOLE HILL

MARLBOROUGH ROAD

DURLEY ROAD

CHINE CRESCENT ROAD

CHINE CRESCENT

HAHNEMANN ROAD

WESTHILL

ST MICHAEL'S ROAD

CRANBORNE RD

EXETER ROAD

EXETER CRES

EXETER PARK RD

EXETER LANE

Winter Gardens

Royal Exeter Hotel

PRIORY ROAD

BEACON ROAD

Conference Centre

Pavilion

Playhouse Theatre

Royal Bath Hotel

Rothesay Mus.

UNDERCLIFF DRIVE

N

2

1

WEST CLIFF ROAD

WESTHILL ROAD

WEST CLIFF GARDENS

DURLEY GARDENS

Pedestrians only

WEST CLIFF PROMENADE

WEST PROMENADE

Pier Leisure Centre

Pier Theatre

Bournemouth Pier

1

A B C D E F

BOURNEMOUTH
The pier, safe sea-bathing, golden sands facing south and sheltered by steep cliffs, and plenty of amenities for the holiday maker make Bournemouth one of the most popular resorts on the south coast of England.

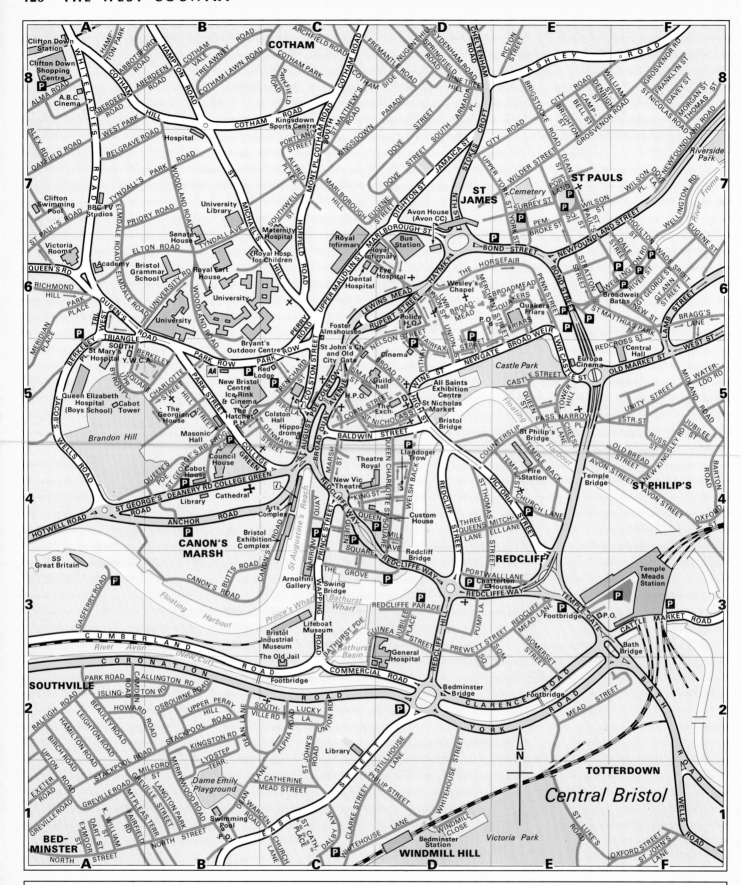

Bristol

One of Britain's most historic seaports, Bristol retains many of its visible links with the past, despite terrible damage inflicted during bombing raids in World War II. Most imposing is the cathedral, founded as an abbey church in 1140. Perhaps even more famous than the cathedral is the Church of St Mary Redcliffe. Ranking among the finest churches in the country, it owes much of

its splendour to 14th- and 15th-century merchants who bestowed huge sums of money on it.

The merchant families brought wealth to the whole of Bristol, and their trading links with the world are continued in today's modern aerospace and technological industries. Much of the best of Bristol can be seen in the area of the Floating Harbour – an arm of the Avon. Several of the old warehouses have been converted into museums, galleries and exhibition centres. Among them are

genuinely picturesque old pubs, the best-known of which is the Llandoger Trow. It is a timbered 17th-century house, the finest of its kind in Bristol. Further up the same street – King Street – is the Theatre Royal, built in 1766 and the oldest theatre in the country. In Corn Street, the heart of the business area, is a magnificent 18th-century corn exchange. In front of it are the four pillars known as the 'nails', on which merchants used to make cash transactions, hence 'to pay on the nail'.

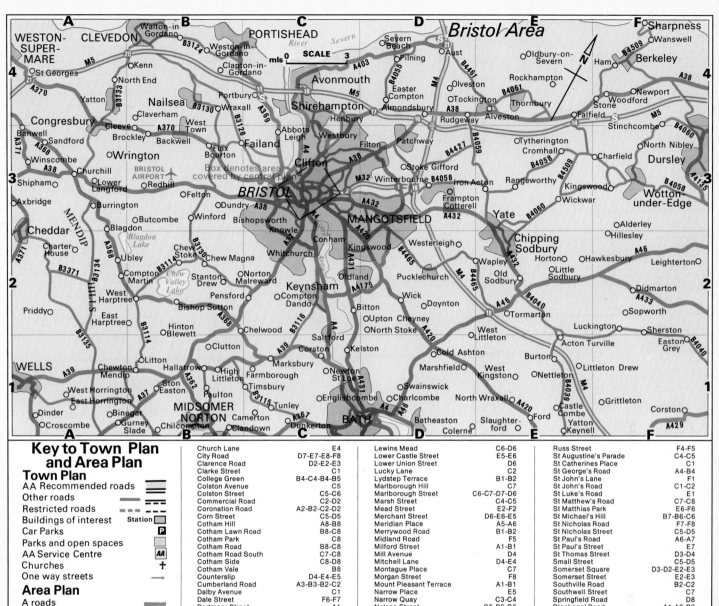

Key to Town Plan and Area Plan

Town Plan

AA Recommended roads	
Other roads	
Restricted roads	
Buildings of interest	Station
Car Parks	P
Parks and open spaces	
AA Service Centre	AA
Churches	†
One way streets	→

Area Plan

A roads	
B roads	
Locations	Hinton O
Urban area	

Street Index with Grid Reference

Bristol

Abbotsford Road	A8-B8
Aberdeen Road	A8-B8
Alexandra Road	A7
Alfred Place	C7
Allington Road	A2-B2
Alma Road	A8
Alpha Road.	C2
Anchor Road	A4-B4-C4-C5
Archfield Road	C8
Armada Place	D8
Ashley Road	E8-F8
Avon Street	E4-F4
Baldwin Street	C5-D5
Barton Road	F4-F5
Bath Road	F1-F2-F3
Bathurst Parade	C2-C3
Beauley Road	A2
Belgrave Road	A7-B7
Berkeley Place	A5-A6
Berkeley Square	A5-B5
Birch Road	A1-A2
Bond Street	D6-E6
Bragg's Lane	F6
Brighton Street	E7-E8
Brigstocke Road	E7-E8
Broadmead	D6-E6
Broad Quay	C4-C5
Broad Street	C5-D5
Broadweir	E5-E6
Butts Road	B3-C3
Camden Road	A2
Campbell Street	E8
Canon's Road	B3-C3-C4
Castle Street	E5
Catherine Mead Street	B1-C1
Cattle Market Road	F3
Charlotte Street	B5
Cheese Lane	E5
Cheltenham Road	D8
Church Lane	C1
Church Lane	E4
City Road	D7-E7-E8-F8
Clarence Road	D2-E2-E3
Clarke Street	C1
College Green	B4-C4-B4-B5
Colston Avenue	C5
Colston Street	C5-C6
Commercial Road	C2-D2
Coronation Road	A2-B2-C2-D2
Corn Street	C5-D5
Cotham Hill	A8-B8
Cotham Lawn Road	B8-C8
Cotham Park	C8
Cotham Road	B8-C8
Cotham Road South	C7-C8
Cotham Side	C8-D8
Cotham Vale	B8
Counterslip	D4-E4-E5
Cumberland Road	A3-B3-B2-C2
Dalby Avenue	C1
Dale Street	F6-F7
Dartmoor Street	A1
Davey Street	F8
Deanery Road	B4
Dean Lane	B1-C1-C2-B2
Dean Street	E7
Denbigh Street	E8
Denmark Street	B5-C5-C4
Dighton Street	D7
Dove Lane	F7
Dove Street	C7-D7-D8
Dove Street South	D7-D8
East Street	B1-C1-C2-D2
Elmdale Road	A7-A6-B6
Elton Road	A6-B6
Eugene Street	C7-D7
Eugene Street	F6-F7
Exeter Road	A1
Exmoor Street	A1
Fairfax Street	D6-D5-E5-E6
Fairfield Road	A1
Franklyn Street	F8
Fremantle Road	C8-D8
Frog Lane	B4-B5
Gasferry Road	A3
Great Ann Street	F6
Great George Street	F6
Greville Road	A1
Greville Street	A1-B1
Grosvenor Road	E7-E8-F8
Guinea Street	C2-C3-D3
Hamilton Road	A1-A2
Hampton Park	A8
Hampton Road	B8
Haymarket	D6
High Street	D5
Hill Street	B5
Horfield Road	C6-C7
Hotwell Road	A4
Houlton Street	F6-F7
Howard Road	A2-B2
Islington Road	A2-B2
Jacob's Wells Road	A4-A5
Jubilee Place	D3
Jamaica Street	D7
Jubilee Street	F5
Kingsdown Parade	C7-C8-D8
King Street	C4-D4
Kingston Road	B2
King William Street	A1
Lamb Street	F5-F6
Langton Park	B1
Leighton Road	A1-A2
Lewins Mead	C6-D6
Lower Castle Street	E5-E6
Lower Union Street	D6
Lucky Lane	C2
Lydstep Terrace	B1-B2
Marlborough Hill	C7
Marlborough Street	C6-C7-D7-D6
Marsh Street	C4-C5
Mead Street	E2-F2
Merchant Street	D6-E6-E5
Meridian Place	A5-A6
Merrywood Road	B1-B2
Midland Road	F5
Milford Street	A1-B1
Mill Avenue	D4
Mitchell Lane	D4-E4
Montague Place	C7
Morgan Street	F8
Mount Pleasant Terrace	A1-B1
Narrow Place	E5
Narrow Quay	C3-C4
Nelson Street	C5-D5-D6
Newfoundland Road	F7-F8
Newfoundland Street	E6-E7-F7
Newgate	D5-E5
New Kingsley Road	F4-F5
New Street	F6
Nine Tree Hill	D8
North Street	A1-B1
North Street	D7
Nugent Hill	D8
Oakfield Road	A7
Old Bread Street	E5-E4-F4
Old Market Street	E6-F6
Osbourne Road	B2
Oxford Street	F1
Oxford Street	F4
Parkfield Road	C8
Park Place	A6
Park Road	A2
Park Row	B6-B5-C6
Park Street	B5
Passage Street	E5
Pembroke Street	E7
Penn Street	E6
Perry Road	C5-C6
Philip Street	C1-D1
Picton Street	E8
Pipe Lane	C5
Pithay	D5
Portland Square	E7
Portland Street	C7
Portwall Lane	D3-E3
Prewett Street	D3-E3
Prince Street	C3-C4
Priory Road	A7-B7
Pump Lane	D3
Quakers Friars	E6
Queen Charlotte Street	D4-D5
Queen's Parade	B4
Queen Square	C3-C4-D4-D3
Queen's Road	A6-B6-B5
Queen Street	E5
Raleigh Road	A2
Redcliff Hill	D2-D3
Redcliff Mead Lane	E3
Redcliffe Parade	D3
Redcliff Street	D3-D4
Redcliff Way	C4-D4-D3-E3
Redcross Street	E5-E6-F6
Richmond Hill	A6
River Street	F6
Rupert Street	C6-D6
Russ Street	F4-F5
St Augustine's Parade	C4-C5
St Catherines Place	C1
St George's Road	A4-B4
St John's Lane	F1
St John's Road	C1-C2
St Luke's Road	E1
St Matthew's Road	C7-C8
St Matthias Park	E6-F6
St Michael's Hill	B7-B6-C6
St Nicholas Road	F7-F8
St Nicholas Street	C5-D5
St Paul's Road	A6-A7
St Paul's Street	E7
St Thomas Street	D3-D4
Small Street	C5-D5
Somerset Square	D3-D2-E2-E3
Somerset Street	E2-E3
Southville Road	B2-C2
Southwell Street	C7
Springfield Road	D8
Stackpool Road	A1-A2-B2
Stillhouse Lane	D1-D2
Stokes Croft	D7-D8
Straight Street	F5
Stratton Street	E6
Surrey Street	E7
Sydenham Road	D8
Temple Back	E4-E5
Temple Gate	E3
Temple Street	E4
The Grove	C3-D3
The Horsefair	D6-E6
Thomas Street	F8
Three Queens Lane	D4
Tower Hill	E5
Trelawney Road	B8-C8
Trenchard Street	C5
Triangle South	A5-A6
Triangle West	A6
Tyndall Avenue	B6-B7
Tyndall's Park Road	A7-B7
Union Road	C2
Union Street	D5-D6
Unity Street	F5
University Road	A6-B6
Upper Byron Place	A5
Upper Maudlin Street	C6
Upper Perry Hill	B2
Upper York Street	D7-E7
Upton Road	A1-A2
Victoria Street	D5-D4-E3-E4
Wade Street	F6
Wapping Road	C3
Warden Road	B1-C1
Waterloo Road	F5
Wellington Road	E6-F6-F7
Wells Road	F1-F2
Welsh Back	D3-D4-D5
West Park	A7-A8
West Street	F5-F6
Whitehouse Lane	C1-D1
Whitehouse Road	D1-D2
Whiteladies Road	A6-A7-A8
Wilder Street	D7-E7
William Street	E8-F8
Wilson Place	F7
Wilson Street	E7-F7
Windmill Close	D1
Wine Street	D5
Woodland Road	B5-B6-B7-B8
York Road	D2-E2-E2
York Street	E6-E7

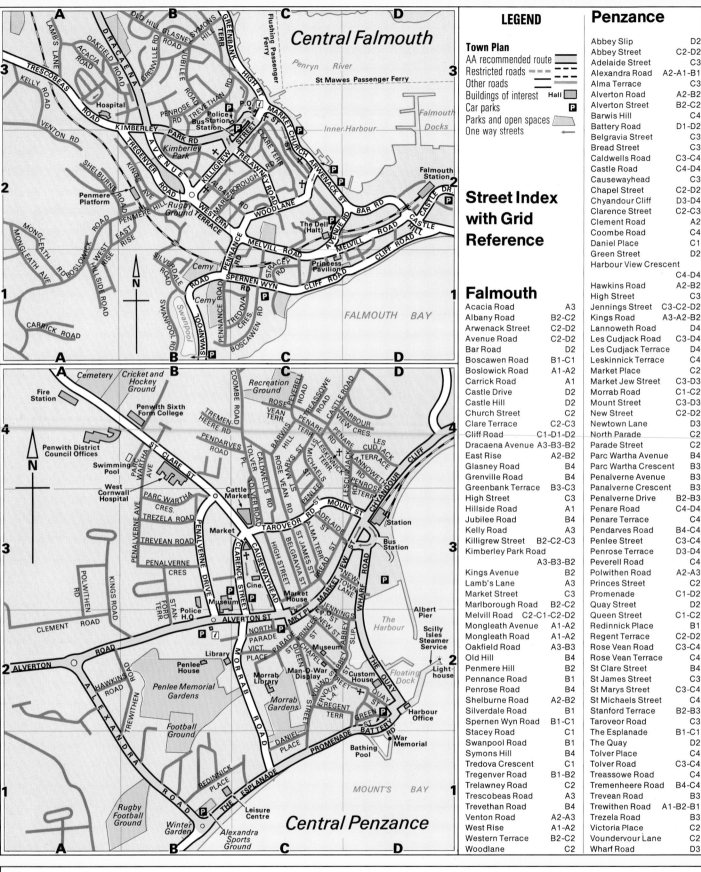

Central Falmouth

LEGEND

Town Plan
AA recommended route
Restricted roads
Other roads
Buildings of interest   Hall
Car parks   P
Parks and open spaces
One way streets

Street Index with Grid Reference

Falmouth

Acacia Road	A3
Albany Road	B2-C2
Arwenack Street	C2-D2
Avenue Road	C2-D2
Bar Road	D2
Boscawen Road	B1-C1
Boslowick Road	A1-A2
Carrick Road	A1
Castle Drive	D2
Castle Hill	D2
Church Street	C2
Clare Terrace	C2-C3
Cliff Road	C1-D1-D2
Dracaena Avenue	A3-B3-B2
East Rise	A2-B2
Glasney Road	B4
Grenville Road	B4
Greenbank Terrace	B3-C3
High Street	C3
Hillside Road	A1
Jubilee Road	B4
Kelly Road	A3
Killigrew Street	B2-C2-C3
Kimberley Park Road	A3-B3-B2
Kings Avenue	B2
Lamb's Lane	A3
Market Street	C3
Marlborough Road	B2-C2
Melvill Road	C2-C1-C2-D2
Mongleath Avenue	A1-A2
Mongleath Road	A1-A2
Oakfield Road	A3-B3
Old Hill	B4
Penmere Hill	B1
Pennance Road	B1
Penrose Road	B4
Shelburne Road	A2-B2
Silverdale Road	B1
Spernen Wyn Road	B1-C1
Stacey Road	C1
Swanpool Road	B1
Symons Hill	B4
Tredova Crescent	C1
Tregenver Road	B1-B2
Trelawney Road	C2
Trescobeas Road	A3
Trevethan Road	B4
Venton Road	A2-A3
West Rise	A1-A2
Western Terrace	B2-C2
Woodlane	C2

Penzance

Abbey Slip	D2
Abbey Street	C2-D2
Adelaide Street	C3
Alexandra Road	A2-A1-B1
Alma Terrace	C3
Alverton Road	A2-B2
Alverton Street	B2-C2
Barwis Hill	C4
Battery Road	D1-D2
Belgravia Street	C3
Bread Street	C3
Caldwells Road	C3-C4
Castle Road	C4-D4
Causewayhead	C3
Chapel Street	C2-D2
Chyandour Cliff	D3-D4
Clarence Street	C2-C3
Clement Road	A2
Coombe Road	C4
Daniel Place	C1
Green Street	D2
Harbour View Crescent	C4-D4
Hawkins Road	A2-B2
High Street	C3
Jennings Street	C3-C2-D2
Kings Road	A3-A2-B2
Lannoweth Road	D4
Les Cudjack Road	C3-D4
Les Cudjack Terrace	D4
Leskinnick Terrace	C4
Market Place	C2
Market Jew Street	C3-D3
Morrab Road	C1-C2
Mount Street	C3-D3
New Street	C2-D2
Newtown Lane	D3
North Parade	C2
Parade Street	C2
Parc Wartha Avenue	B4
Parc Wartha Crescent	B3
Penalverne Avenue	B3
Panalverne Crescent	B3
Penalverne Drive	B2-B3
Penare Road	C4-D4
Penare Terrace	C4
Pendarves Road	B4-C4
Penlee Street	C3-C4
Penrose Terrace	D3-D4
Peverell Road	C4
Polwithen Road	A2-A3
Princes Street	C2
Promenade	C1-D2
Quay Street	D2
Queen Street	C1-C2
Redinnick Place	B1
Regent Terrace	C2-D2
Rose Vean Road	C3-C4
Rose Vean Terrace	C4
St Clare Street	B4
St James Street	C3
St Marys Street	C3-C4
St Michaels Street	C4
Stanford Terrace	B2-B3
Taroveor Road	C3
The Esplanade	B1-C1
The Quay	D2
Tolver Place	C4
Tolver Road	C3-C4
Treassowe Road	C4
Tremenheere Road	B4-C4
Trevean Road	B3
Trewithen Road	A1-B2-B1
Trezela Road	B3
Victoria Place	C2
Voundervour Lane	C2
Wharf Road	D3

Central Penzance

Cornish towns

Falmouth Twin fortresses, St. Mawes and Pendennis, guard the harbour entrance and serve as a reminder of Falmouth's once vital strategic importance. Lying in the sheltered waters of the Carrick Roads and provided with one of the world's largest natural harbours, Falmouth prospered on trade until the 19th century. Today the town is popular with holidaymakers.

St Ives is one of the few British towns with a style of painting named after it, for both artists and holidaymakers are drawn to the port, with its charming old quarter known as Down-Long. Regular exhibitions of local painting, sculpture and pottery are held, and the work of sculptor Barbara Hepworth, who spent much of her creative life here, is displayed in the Hepworth Gallery.

Penzance is the first and last town in Britain — it lies at the western extremity of Mounts Bay and basks in a temperate climate and sub-tropical vegetation. Places of interest include the ornate Egyptian House (now a National Trust shop), and steamers and helicopters go to the Scilly Isles.

Newquay Favourite haunt of surfboarders for its Fistral and Watergate beaches, Newquay has a 'Huer's House' where lookouts once warned fishermen of approaching shoals of pilchards. There are fine beaches for holidaymakers, such as Towan, Lusty Glaze and Great Western.

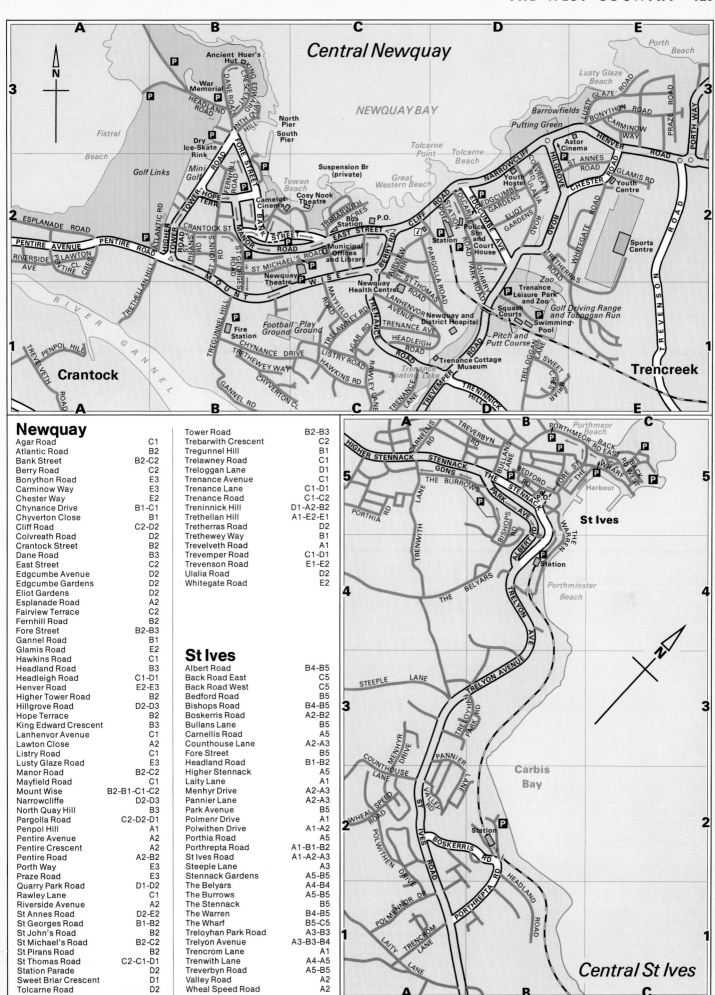

Newquay

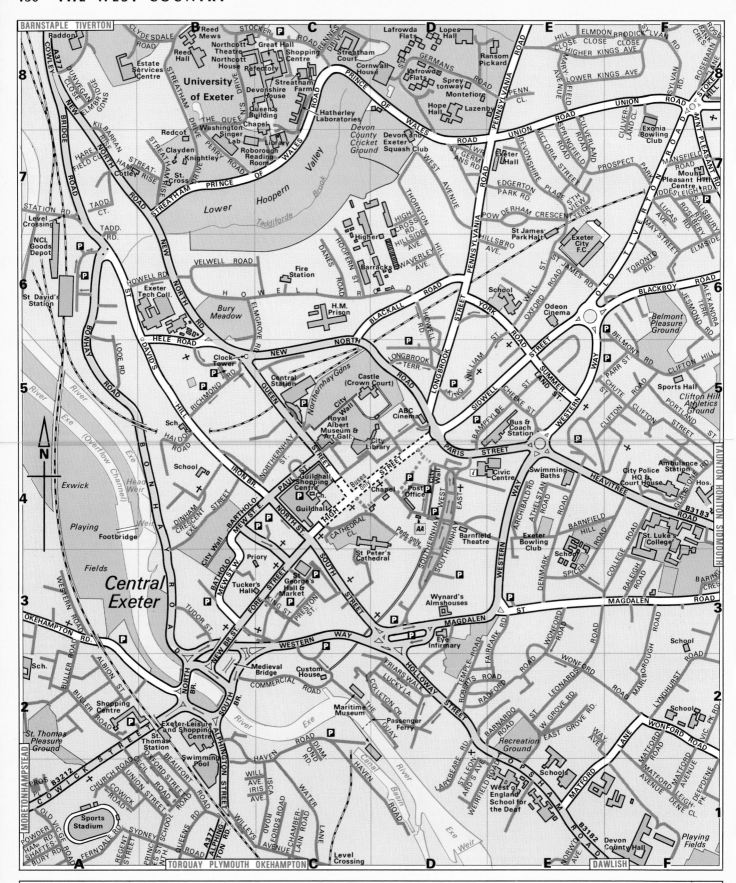

Exeter

The cathedral is Exeter's greatest treasure. Founded in 1050, but rebuilt by the Normans during the 12th century and again at the end of the 13th century, it has many beautiful and outstanding features – especially the exquisite rib-vaulting of the nave. Most remarkable, perhaps, is the fact that it still stood after virtually everything around it was flattened during bombing raids in World War II.

There are still plenty of reminders of Old Exeter, which has been a city since Roman times. Roman and medieval walls encircle parts of the city; 14th-century underground passages can be explored; the Guildhall is 15th-century and one of the oldest municipal buildings in the country; and Sir Francis Drake is said to have met his explorer companions at Mol's Coffee House. Of the city's ancient churches, the most interesting are St Mary Steps, St Mary Arches and St Martin's. Exeter is famous for its extensive Maritime Museum, with over 100 boats from all over the world. Other museums include the Rougemont House and the Royal Albert Memorial Museum and Art Gallery.

Exmouth has a near-perfect position at the mouth of the Exe estuary. On one side it has expanses of sandy beach, on another a wide estuary alive with wildfowl and small boats, while inland is beautiful Devon countryside.

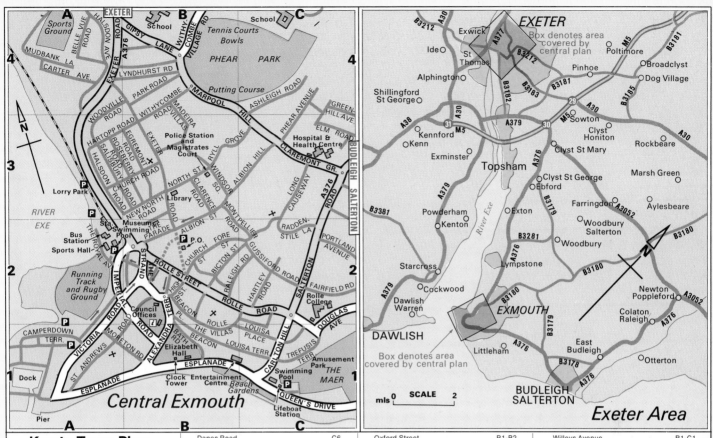

Central Exmouth

Exeter Area

Key to Town Plan and Area Plan

Town Plan
AA Recommended roads
Other roads
Restricted roads
Buildings of interset   School
Car Parks   P
Churches
Parks and open spaces

Area Plan
A roads
B roads
Locations
Urban area

Street Index with Grid Reference

Exeter

Albion Street	A2
Alexandra Terrace	F6
Alphington Road	B1
Alphington Street	B1-B2
Archibald Road	E4
Athelstan Road	E4
Bampfylde Street	D4-D5-E5
Baring Crescent	F3
Barnado Road	E2
Barnfield Hill	E4-F4
Bartholomew Street East	B4-C4
Bartholomew Street West	B3
Belmont Road	F6-F5
Blackall Road	C6-D6
Blackboy Road	F6
Bonhay Road	A6-A5-B5-B4-B3-B2
Brodick Close	F8
Buller Road	A2-A3
Cathedral Close	C4-D4
Cecil Road	A1-B1
Chamberlain Road	C1
Cheeke Street	E5
Church Road	A1-A2-B2
Chute Street	E5-F5
Clifton Hill	F5
Clifton Road	E5-F5
Clifton Street	F4-F5
Clydesdale Road	A8-B8
College Road	F3-F4
Colleton Crescent	C2-D2
Commercial Road	B2-C2
Cowick Road	A1
Cowick Street	A1-A2-B2
Cowley Bridge Road	A6-A7-A8
Culverland Close	F7-F8
Culverland Road	E7-E8

Danes Road	C6
Deepdene Park	F1
Denmark Road	F3-F4
Devonshire Place	E7
Diamond Road	C2-C1
Dineham Crescent	B4
Dunvegan Close	A8
East Grove Road	E2
Edgerton Park Road	E7
Elmbridge Gardens	A8
Elmdon Close	E8-F8
Elmgrove Road	B6-C6-B5
Elmside	F6
Exe Street	B4
Fairpark Road	E2-E3
Ferndale Road	A1
Fords Road	C1
Fore Street	B3-C3
Friars Walk	D2
Gladstone Road	F4
Haldon Road	B4-B5
Harefield Close	A7
Haven Road	B1-C1-C2-C1-D1
Heavitree Road	E4-F4
Hele Road	B6-B5
Highcross Road	D7
Higher Kings Avenue	E8-F8
High Street	C4-D4-D5
Hill Close	E8
Hillsborough Avenue	D6-E6
Hillside Avenue	D6
Holloway Street	D2
Hoopern Street	C6-C7
Howell Road	A6-B6-C6-D6-D5
Iddesleigh Road	F7
Iris Avenue	B1-C1
Iron Bridge	B4-C4
Isca Road	C1
Jesmond Road	F6-F5-F6
Kilbarran Rise	A7-A8
King Street	C3
King William Street	D5-E5-E6
Larkbeare Road	D1-D2
Leighdene Close	F1
Longbrook Street	D5-D6
Longbrook Terrace	D5
Looe Road	A5-A6
Lower Kings Avenue	E8-F8
Lower St Germans Road	D7
Lucas Avenue	F7
Lucky Lane	D2
Lyndhurst Road	F2
Magdalen Road	E3-F3
Magdalen Street	D3-E3
Mansfield Road	F7
Marlborough Road	F2-F3
Maryfield Avenue	E8
Matford Avenue	F2-F1-F2
Matford Lane	E1-F1-F2
Matford Road	F1-F2
May Street	F7-F6
Mount Pleasant Road	F8-F7
New Bridge Street─	B2-B3
New North Road	A8-A7-B7-B6-B5-C5-C6-C5-D5
North Bridge	B2
Northernhay Street	C4-C5
North Street	C4
Norwood Avenue	E1
Okehampton Road	A3-A2-B2
Old Tiverton Road	E6-F6-F7-F8
Old Vicarage Road	A1
Oxford Road	E6

Oxford Street	B1-B2
Paris Street	D5-D4-E4
Parr Street	F5
Paul Street	C4
Pennsylvania Close	E8
Pennsylvania Road	D6-D7-E7-E8
Perry Road	B7
Portland Street	F5
Powderham Crescent	D7-E7
Powderham Road	A1
Preston Street	C3
Prince of Wales Road	B7-C7-C8-D8-D7
Princes Street North	B1
Prospect Park	E7-F7
Prospect Place	A1
Queens Road	B1
Queen Street	B5-C5-C4
Radford Road	D2-E2
Raleigh Road	F3
Regent Street	A1
Rennes Drive	C8
Richmond Road	B5
Roberts Road	D2-E2
Rosebank Crescent	F8
Rosebarn Lane	F8
Rosebery Road	F6-F7
St David's Hill	A6-B6-B5-B4
St Germans Road	D8-E8
St James Road	E6
St Leonards Avenue	D1-E1
St Leonards Road	E2-E3
Salisbury Road	F7-F6
School Road	B1
Shaftesbury Road	A1
Sidwell Street	D5-E5-E6
South Bridge	B2
Southernhay East	D3-D4
Southernhay West	D3-D4
South Street	D3
South View Terrace	E7
Spicer Road	E3-E4-F4
Springfield Road	E8-E7
Station Road	A7
Stocker Road	B8-C8
Stoke Hill	F8
Streatham Drive	B7-B8
Streatham Rise	A7-B7
Summerland Street	E5
Sydney Road	A1-B1
Sylvan Road	F8
Taddiforde Court	A7
Taddiforde Road	A6-A7
Temple Road	D2-D3
The Quay	C2-D2
The Queen's Drive	B8
Thornton Hill	D7-D6
Topsham Road	E2-E1-F1
Toronto Road	F6
Tudor Street	B3
Union Road	E7-E8-F8
Union Street	A1-B1
Velwell Road	B6-C6
Victoria Park Road	F2
Victoria Street	E7
Water Lane	C1
Waverley Avenue	C6
Way Avenue	C2
Weirfield Road	D1-E1
Well Street	E6
West Avenue	D7
Western Road	A3
Western Way	E3-E4-E5, C3
West Grove Road	E2

Willeys Avenue	B1-C1
Williams Avenue	B1-C1
Wonford Road	E3-E2-F2
York Road	D6-E6-E5

Exmouth

Albion Hill	B3-C3
Albion Street	B2-B3
Alexandra Terrace	B1-B2
Ashleigh Road	C4
Bath Road	B1-B2
Beacon Place	B2
Belle View Road	A4
Bicton Street	B2-C2
Camperdown Terrace	A1
Carter Avenue	A4
Carlton Hill	C1-C2
Church Road	A3-B3
Church Street	B2
Claremont Grove	C3
Clarence Road	B3
Douglas Avenue	C1-C2
Egremont Road	B3
Elm Road	C3
Esplanade	A1-B1-C1
Exeter Road	B2-B3-B4-A4
Fairfield Road	C2
Fore Street	B2-C2
Gipsy Lane	A4-B4
Green Hill Avenue	C3-C4
Gussiford Road	C2
Halsdon Avenue	A4
Hartley Road	C2
Hartopp Road	A3-B3
Halsdon Road	A3
High Street	B2
Imperial Road	B2-A2-B2-B1
Long Causeway	C3
Louisa Place	B1-C1
Louisa Terrace	B1-C1
Lyndhurst Road	A4-B4
Madeira Villas	B3-B4
Marpool Hill	B4-B3-C3-C4
Montpellier Road	B3-B2-C2
Moreton Road	A1-B1
Mudbank Lane	A4
New North Road	B3
North Street	B3
Park Road	B4
Phear Avenue	C3-C4
Portland Avenue	C2
Queens Drive	C1
Raddenstile Lane	B2-C2
Raleigh Road	B2-C2
Rolle Road	B2-C2
Rolle Street	B2
Rolle Villas	B1-B2
Roseberry Road	A3-B3
Ryll Grove	B3-C3
St Andrews Road	A1-B1-B2
Salisbury Road	A3-B3
Salterton Road	C2-C3
The Beacon	B1-B2
The Parade	B2
The Strand	B2
The Royal Avenue	A2
Trefusis Terrace	C1
Victoria Road	A1-A2-B2
Windsor Square	B3
Withycombe Road	B3-B4
Withycombe Village Road	B4
Woodville Road	A3-A4-B4

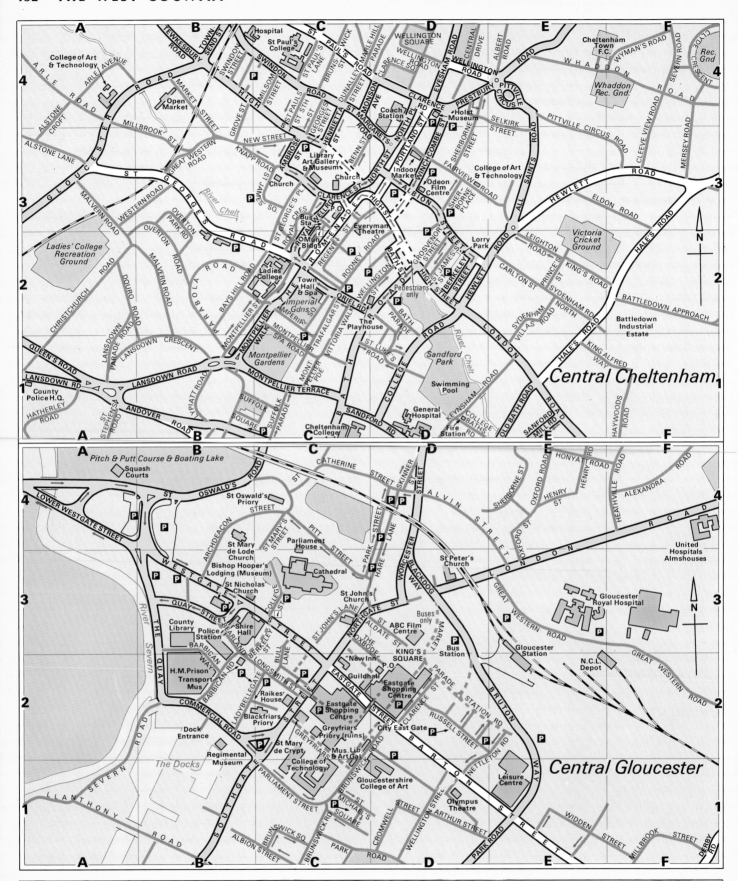

Central Cheltenham

Central Gloucester

Gloucester

Gloucester's chief asset is its beautiful Norman cathedral. Originally an abbey, the building did not become a cathedral until the reign of Henry VIII and the lovely cloisters enclosing a delightful garden epitomise the tranquil beauty of medieval monastic architecture. The city's four main thoroughfares still follow the cruciform pattern of the original Roman roads built when *Glevum* guarded the lowest Severn crossing. Since those days Gloucester has been an important inland port and today it is one of the country's major commercial and engineering centres.

Tewkesbury Black-and-white timbered buildings and ancient pubs with crooked roofs and curious names, such as *The Ancient Grudge*, lean haphazardly against each other in Tewkesbury's narrow streets. Rising above them all is the vast and beautiful abbey church, saved from destruction in the Dissolution of the Monastries by the townsfolk who bought it from Henry VIII.

Cheltenham Elegant Regency architecture arranged in squares, avenues and crescents is Cheltenham's hallmark. The whole town was purpose-built around the medicinal springs discovered in the 18th century, and, under Royal patronage, it became one of the country's most fashionable spas. The composer Gustav Holst was born here and his home is now a museum.

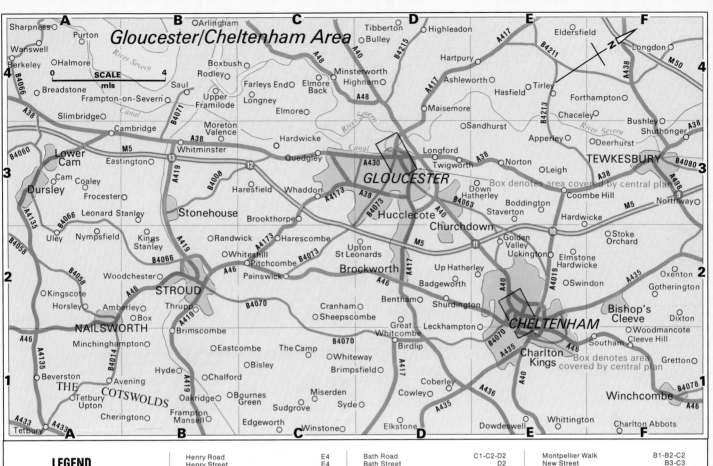

Gloucester/Cheltenham Area

LEGEND

Town Plan
AA recommended route
Restricted roads
Other roads
Buildings of interest   Station
Car parks   P
Parks and open spaces
One way streets

Area Plan
A roads
B roads
Locations   Beedon ○
Urban area

Street Index with Grid Reference

Gloucester

Albion Street	B1-C1
Alexandra Road	F4
Alvin Street	D4-E4-E3
Archdeacon Street	B3-B4-C4
Arthur Street	D1
Barton Street	D2-D1-E1
Black Dog Way	D3
Brunswick Road	C1-C2-D2
Brunswick Square	C1
Bruton Way	D3-D2-E2-E1
Bull Lane	C2-C3
Clarence Street	D2
Commercial Road	B2
Cromwell Street	D1
Derby Road	F1
Eastgate Street	C2-D2
Great Western Road	E3-F3-F2
Hare Lane	C3-D3-D4
Heathville Road	F4
Henry Road	E4
Henry Street	E4
Honyatt Road	E4-F4
Ladybellgate	B2-C2
Llanthony Road	A1-B1
London Road	D3-E3-E4-F4
Longsmith Street	B2-C2
Lower Westgate Street	A4
Market Parade	D2-D3
Millbrook Street	F1
Nettleton Road	D1-D2-E2
Northgate Street	C2-C3-D3
Oxford Road	E4
Oxford Street	E3-E4
Park Street	C3-D3-D4
Park Road	C1-D1-E1
Parliament Street	C1
Pitt Street	C3-C4
Quay Street	B3
Russell Street	D2
St Catherine Street	C4-D4
St John's Lane	C3
St Mary's Street	C4
St Michael's Square	C1
St Oswald's Road	B4-C4
Severn Road	A1-A2-B2
Sherborne Street	D4-E4
Skinner Street	D4
Station Road	D2-E2
Southgate Street	B1-C1-C2
The Quay	B2-B3
Wellington Street	D1
Westgate Street	B3-C3-C2
Widden Street	E1-F1
Worcester Street	D3-D4

Cheltenham

Albert Road	E4
Albion Street	D2-D3
All Saints Road	E3-E4
Alstone Croft	A3-A4
Alstone Lane	A3
Ambrose Street	C3
Andover Road	A1-B1
Arle Avenue	A4-B4
Arle Road	A4
Bath Parade	D1-D2
Bath Road	C1-C2-D2
Bath Street	D2
Battledown Approach	F2
Bayshill Road	B2-C2
Bennington Street	C3-D3
Berkeley Street	D2
Brunswick Street	C4
Carlton Street	E2
Central Drive	D4
Christchurch Road	A1-A2
Clarence Road	D4
Clarence Square	D4
Clarence Street	C3
Cleeve View Road	F3-F4
Clyde Crescent	F4
College Road	D1-D2
College Baths Road	D1
Douro Road	A2-B2-B1
Dunalley Street	C4
Eldon Road	E3-F3
Evesham Road	D4
Fairview Road	D3-E3
Gloucester Road	A3-A4-B4
Great Western Road	B3
Grosvenor Street	D2
Grove Street	B3-B4
Hale's Road	E1-E2-F2-F3
Hatherley Road	A1
Haywoods Road	F1
Henrietta Street	C3-C4
Hewlett Road	D2-E2-E3-F3
High Street	B4-C4-C3, D3-D2
Imperial Square	C2
Keynsham Road	D1-E1
King's Road	E2-F2
King Alfred Way	E1-F1
Knapp Road	B3-C3
Landsown Crescent	A1-B1
Lansdown Road	A1-B1
Lansdown Parade Road	A1-A2
Leighton Road	E2
London Road	D2-E2-E1
Lypiatt Road	B1
Malvern Road	A3-A2-B2
Market Street	B3-B4
Marle Hill Parade	C4-D4
Mersey Road	F3-F4
Millbrook Street	A4-A3-B3
Milsom Street	C4
Monson Avenue	C4-D4
Montpellier Parade	C1
Montpellier Spa Road	C1-C2
Montpellier Street	B1-B2-C2
Montpellier Terrace	B1-C1
Montpellier Walk	B1-B2-C2
New Street	B3-C3
North Place	D3-D4
North Street	C3-D3
Old Bath Road	E1
Oriel Road	C2
Overton Road	A2-A3-B3-B2
Overton Park Road	B2-B3
Parabola Road	B1-B2
Pittville Circus	E4
Pittville Circus Road	E4-E3-F3
Portland Street	D3-D4
Prestbury Road	D4-E4
Prince's Street	E2
Queen's Road	A1
Regent Street	C2-C3-D3
Rodney Road	C2-D2
Royal Crescent	C2-C3
Royal Well Road	C2-C3
St George's Place	C2-C3
St George's Road	A3-B3-B2-C2
St Georges Street	C3-C4
St James's Square	C3
St James's Street	D2
St Luke's Road	C1-D1
St Margarets Road	C4-D4-D3
St Paul's Lane	C4
St Paul's Road	C4-D4
St Pauls Street South	C4
St Stephen's Road	A1
Sandford Road	C1-D1
Sandford Mill Road	E1
Selkirk Street	D4-E4-E3
Severn Road	F4
Sherborne Place	D3
Sherborne Street	D3-D4
Suffolk Parade	C1
Suffolk Square	B1-C1
Swindon Road	B4-C4
Swindon Street	B4
Sydenham Road North	E2
Sydenham Villas Road	E1-E2
Tewkesbury Road	B4
The Promenade	C2-C3
Trafalgar Street	C1-C2
Townsend Street	B4
Vittoria Walk	C1-C2
Wellington Road	D4-E4
Wellington Square	D4
Wellington Street	C2-D2
Western Road	A3-B3
Whaddon Road	E4-F4
Winchcombe Street	D3-D4
Wymans Road	F4

GLOUCESTER
Gloucester Cathedral, one of the Britain's finest buildings, is a splendid example of Norman architecture. The beautiful stained-glass east window is a memorial to local men who fought at Crécy in 1346.

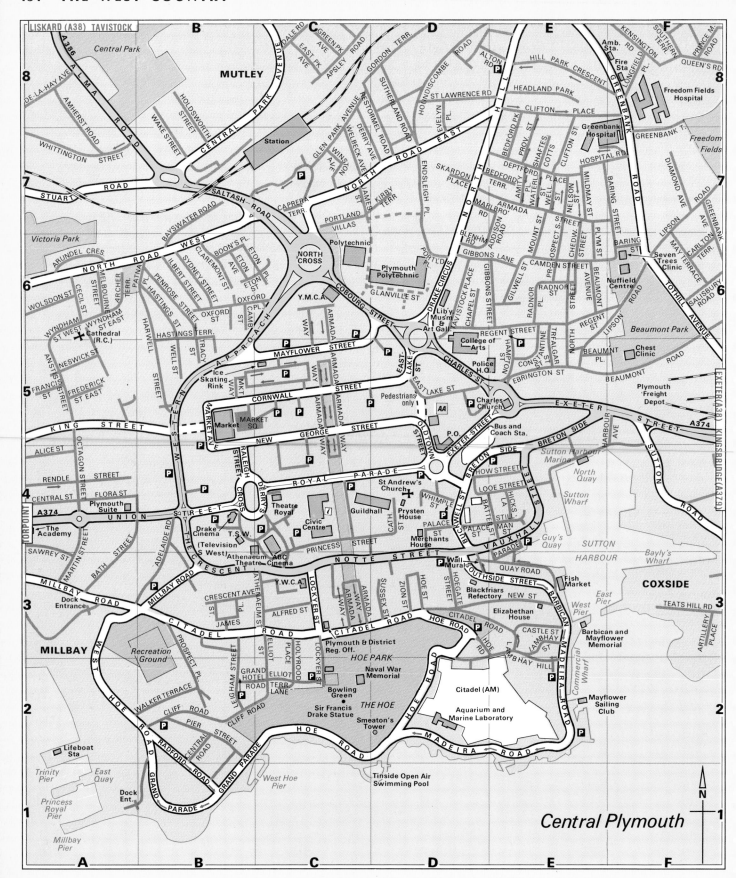

Central Plymouth

Plymouth

Ships, sailors and the sea permeate every aspect of Plymouth's life and history. Its superb natural harbour – Plymouth Sound – has ensured its importance as a port, yachting centre and naval base (latterly at Devonport) over many centuries. Sir Francis Drake is undoubtedly the city's most famous sailor. His statue stands on the Hoe – where he really did play bowls before tackling the Spanish Armada. Also on the Hoe are Smeaton's Tower, which once formed the upper part of the third Eddystone Lighthouse, and the impressive Royal Naval War Memorial. Just east of the Hoe is the Royal Citadel, an imposing fortress built in 1666 by order of Charles II. North is Sutton Harbour, perhaps the most atmospheric part of Plymouth. Here fishing boats bob up and down in a harbour whose quays are lined with attractive old houses, inns and warehouses. One of the memorials on Mayflower Quay just outside the harbour commemorates the sailing of the *Mayflower* from here in 1620. Plymouth's shopping centre is one of the finest of its kind, and was built after the old centre was badly damaged in World War II. Nearby is the 200ft-high tower of the impressive modern Civic Centre. Some buildings escaped destruction, including the Elizabethan House and the 500-year-old Prysten House. Next door is St Andrew's Church, with stained glass by John Piper.

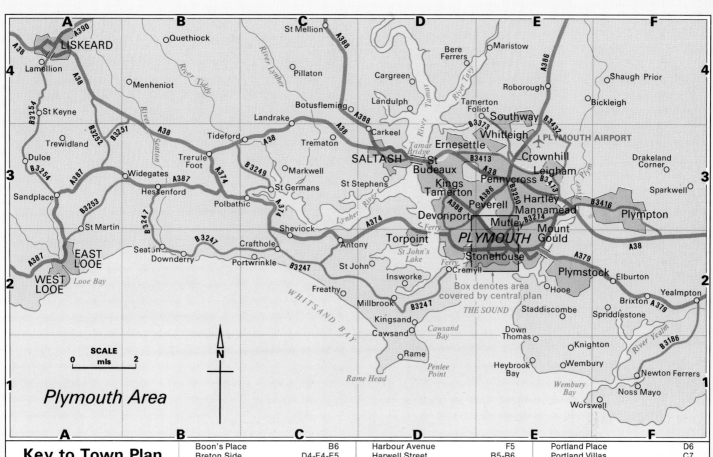

A A390 LISKEARD
Quethiock
St Mellion
Bere Ferrers
Maristow
Shaugh Prior
Lamellion
Pillaton
Cargreen
Roborough
Bickleigh
Menheniot
Landulph
Tamerton Foliot
Southway
St Keyne
Botusfleming
Whitleigh PLYMOUTH AIRPORT
Drakeland Corner
Trewidland
Landrake
Carkeel
Ernesettle
Crownhill
Tideford
Trematon
SALTASH St Budeaux
Leigham
Duloe
Trerule Foot
Markwell
Kings Tamerton
Pennycross Hartley
Sparkwell
Widegates
St Germans
St Stephens
Peverell Mannamead
Plympton
Sandplace
Hessenford
Polbathic
Devonport Mutley
Mount Gould
St Martin
Sheviock
Torpoint PLYMOUTH
EAST LOOE
Seaton Crafthole
Antony
St John's Lake
Stonehouse
Plymstock
Elburton
Downderry
Portwrinkle
St John
Cremyll
Yealmpton
WEST LOOE Looe Bay
Freathy
Insworke
THE SOUND
Staddiscombe
Brixton
Spriddlestone
Millbrook
Kingsand
Down Thomas
Knighton
Cawsand Cawsand Bay
Heybrook Bay
Wembury
Newton Ferrers
Rame
Penlee Point
Noss Mayo
Rame Head
Wembury Bay
Worswell

SCALE
0 mls 2
N

Plymouth Area

Street Index with Grid Reference

Plymouth

Addison Road	D6-D7-E7
Adelaide Road	B3-B4
Alfred Street	C3
Alice Street	A4
Alma Road	A8-A7-B7
Alton Road	D8-E8
Amherst Road	A7-A8
Amity Place	E7
Anstis Street	A5-A6
Apsley Road	C8
Archer Terrace	A6
Armada Street	D7-E7-F7
Armada Way	C3-C4-C5-C6
Artillery Place	F3
Arundel Crescent	A6
Athenaeum Street	C3
Barbican	E3
Baring Street	E7-F7-F6
Bath Street	A3-A4
Batter Street	D4-E4
Bayswater Road	B6-B7
Bedford Park	E7-E8
Bedford Terrace	D7-E7
Beaumont Avenue	E6
Beaumont Place	E5-F5
Beaumont Road	E5-F5-F6
Blenheim Road	D6

Boon's Place	B6
Breton Side	D4-E4-E5
Buckwell Street	D4
Cambridge Street	B6
Camden Street	E6
Caprera Terrace	C7
Carlton Terrace	F6
Castle Street	E3
Catherine Street	D4
Cecil Street	A6
Central Road	B2
Central Street	A4
Central Park Avenue	B7-B8-C8
Chapel Street	D6
Charles Street	D5
Chedworth Street	E6-E7
Citadel Road	B3-C3-D3-E3
Claremont Street	B6
Cliff Road	B2-C2
Clifton Place	E8-F8
Clifton Street	E7-E8
Cobourg Street	C6-D6
Constantine Street	E5-E6
Cornwall Street	B5-C5-D5
Crescent Avenue	B3-C3
Dale Road	C8
De-la-Hay-Avenue	A8
Deptford Place	D7-E7
Derry Avenue	C8-C7-D7
Derry's Cross	B4-C4
Diamond Avenue	F7
Drake Circus	D6
East Park Avenue	C8
Eastlake Street	D5
Ebrington Street	E5
Elliot Street	C2-C3
Elliot Terrace Lane	C2
Endsleigh Place	D7
Eton Avenue	B6
Eton Place	B6-C6
Eton Street	B6-C6
Evelyn Place	D7-D8
Exeter Street	D4-D5-E5-F5
Flora Street	A4
Francis Street	A5
Frederick Street East	A5
Gibbons Lane	D6-E6
Gibbons Street	E6
Gilwell Street	E6
Glanville Street	C6-D6
Glen Park Avenue	C7-C8
Gordon Terrace	C8-D8
Grand Hotel Road	B2-C2
Grand Parade	B1-B2-C2
Green Park Avenue	C8
Greenbank Avenue	F6-F7
Greenbank Road	F6-F7-F8-E8
Greenbank Terrace	F7-F8

Harbour Avenue	F5
Harwell Street	B5-B6
Hastings Street	B6
Hastings Terrace	B5-B6
Headland Park	E8
Hicks Lane	E4
Hill Park Crescent	E8-F8
Hoe Road	C2-D2-D3
Hoe Street	D3
Hoegate Street	D3
Holdsworth Street	B7-B8
Holyrood Place	C2-C3
How Street	D4-E4
Hospital Road	E7-F7
Houndiscombe Road	D7-D8
Ilbert Street	B6
James Street	C6-C7
Kensington Road	F8
King Street	A5-B5
Kirby Terrace	C7-D7
Lambhay Hill	E2-E3
Lambhay Street	E3
Leigham Street	B2-B3
Lipson Road	E5-E6-F6-F7
Lockyer Street	C2-C3
Longfield Place	F8
Looe Street	D4-E4
Madeira Road	D2-E2-E3
Marlborough Road	D7-E7
Market Avenue	B4-B5
Market Square	B5-C5
Market Way	B5
Martin Street	A3-A4
May Terrace	F6
Mayflower Street	B5-C5-C6-D5-D6
Melbourne Street	A6
Mildmay Street	E7
Millbay Road	A3-B3
Mount Street	E6-E7
Nelson Street	E7
Neswick Street	A5
New Street	D3-E3
New George Street	B4-B5-C5-D5
North Cross	C6
North Hill	D6-D7-E7-E8
North Road East	C7-D7-D8-E8
North Road West	A6-B6-B7-C7
North Street	E5-E6
Notte Street	C3-D3-D4
Octagon Street	A4-A5
Old Town Street	D4-D5
Oxford Place	B6-C6
Oxford Street	B6
Palace Street	D4
Parade	E3-E4
Patna Place	B6
Penrose Street	B6
Pier Street	B2

Portland Place	D6
Portland Villas	C7
Plym Street	E6-E7
Prince Maurice Road	F8
Princess Street	C3-C4-D4
Prospect Place	B2-B3
Prospect Street	E6-E7
Providence Street	E7-E8
Quay Road	D3-E3
Queen's Road	F8
Radford Road	B1-B2
Radnor Place	E6
Radnor Street	E6
Raleigh Street	B4
Regent Street	D6-E6-F6
Rendle Street	A4
Restormel Road	C8-D8-D7
Royal Parade	C4-D4
Stillman Street	E4
St James Place	B3
St Lawrence Road	D8-E8
Salisbury Road	F6
Saltash Road	B7-C7-C6
Sawrey Street	A3-A4
Shaftesbury Cottages	E7
Skardon Place	D7
Southern Terrace	F8
Southside Street	D3-E3
Stuart Road	A7-B7
Sussex Street	D3
Sutherland Road	D7-D8
Sutton Road	F4-F5
Sydney Street	B6
Tavistock Place	D6
Teats Hill Road	F3
The Crescent	B4-B3-C3
Tothill Avenue	F5-F6
Tracy Street	B5
Trafalgar Street	E5-E6
Union Street	A4-B4
Vauxhall Street	D3-D4-E4
Wake Street	B7-B8
Walker Terrace	A2-B2
Waterloo Street	E7
Welbeck Avenue	C7
Well Street	B5
Well Street	E7
West Hoe Road	A3-A2-B2
Western Approach	B4-B5-B6-C6
Whimple Street	D4
Whittington Street	A7
Winston Avenue	C7
Wolsdon Street	A6
Wyndham Street East	A6
Wyndham Street West	A6
Zion Street	D3

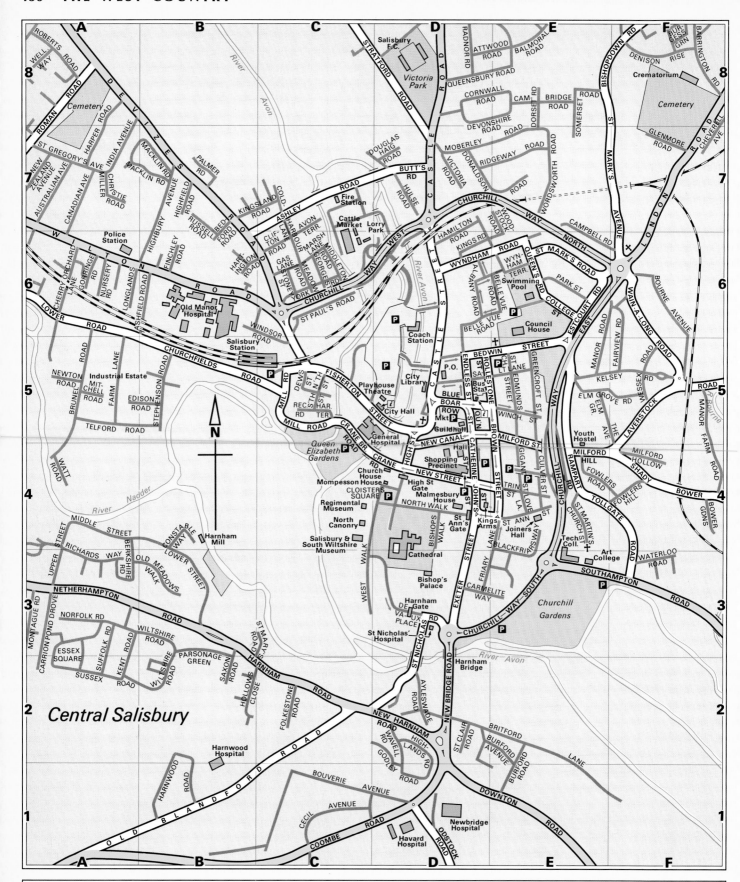

Central Salisbury

Salisbury

Its attractive site where the waters of the Avon and Nadder meet, its beautiful cathedral and its unspoilt centre put Salisbury among England's finest cities. In 1220 the people of the original settlement at Old Sarum, two miles to the north, moved down to the plain and laid the first stone of the cathedral. Within 38 years its was completed and the result is a superb example of Early English architecture.

The cloisters are the largest in England and the spire the tallest in Britain. All the houses within the Cathedral Close were built for cathedral functionaries, and although many have Georgian façades, most date back to the 13th century. Mompesson House is one of the handsome mansions here and as it belongs to the National Trust, its equally fine interior can be seen. Another building houses the Museum of the Duke of Edinburgh's Royal Regiment. At one time, relations

between the clergy and the citizens of Salisbury were not always harmonious, so the former built a protective wall around the Close.

The streets of the modern city follow the medieval grid pattern of squares, or 'chequers', and the tightly-packed houses provide a very pleasing townscape. Salisbury was granted its first charter in 1227 and flourished as a market and wool centre; there is still a twice-weekly market in the spacious square.

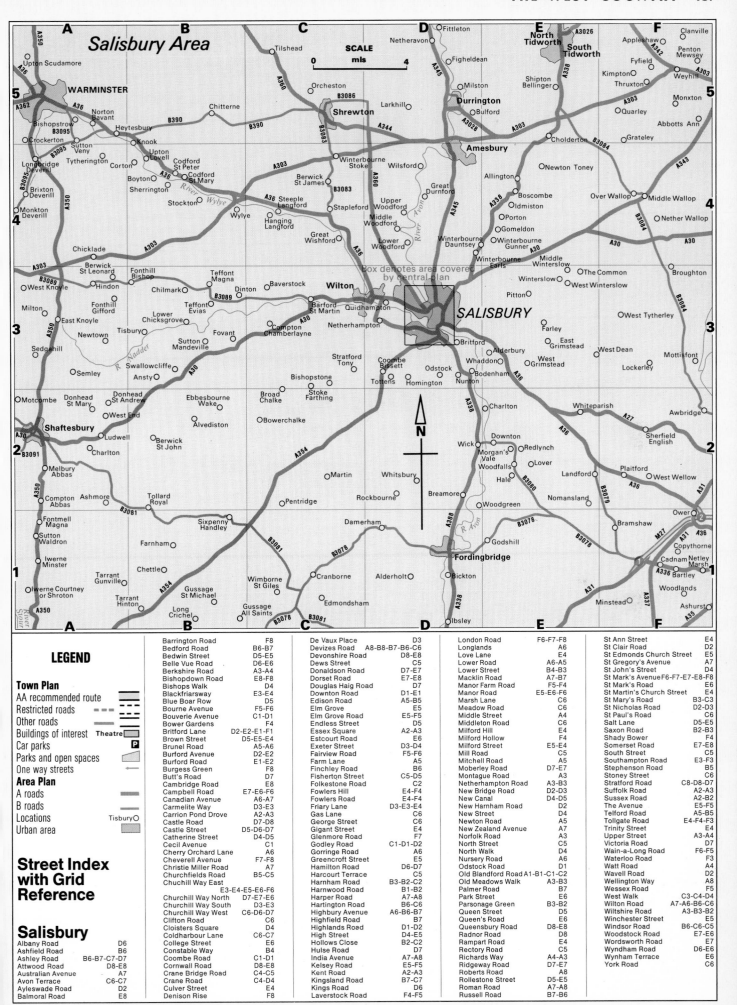

Salisbury Area

LEGEND

Town Plan
- AA recommended route
- Restricted roads
- Other roads
- Buildings of interest — Theatre
- Car parks — P
- Parks and open spaces
- One way streets

Area Plan
- A roads
- B roads
- Locations — Tisbury○
- Urban area

Street Index with Grid Reference

Salisbury

Albany Road	D6
Ashfield Road	B6
Ashley Road	B6-B7-C7-D7
Attwood Road	D8-E8
Australian Avenue	A7
Avon Terrace	C6-C7
Ayleswade Road	D2
Balmoral Road	E8
Barrington Road	F8
Bedford Road	B6-B7
Bedwin Street	D5-E5
Belle Vue Road	D6-E6
Berkshire Road	A3-A4
Bishopdown Road	E8-F8
Bishops Walk	D4
Blackfriarsway	E3-E4
Blue Boar Row	D5
Bourne Avenue	F5-F6
Bouverie Avenue	C1-D1
Bower Gardens	F4
Britford Lane	D2-E2-E1-F1
Brown Street	D5-E5-E6-E4
Brunel Road	A5-A6
Burford Avenue	D2-E2
Burford Road	E1-E2
Burgess Green	F8
Butt's Road	D7
Cambridge Road	E8
Campbell Road	E7-E6-F6
Canadian Avenue	A6-A7
Carmelite Way	D3-E3
Carrion Pond Drove	A2-A3
Castle Road	D7-D8
Castle Street	D5-D6-D7
Catherine Street	D4-D5
Cecil Avenue	C1
Cherry Orchard Lane	A6
Cheverell Avenue	F7-F8
Christie Miller Road	A7
Churchfields Road	B5-C5
Chuchill Way East	E3-E4-E5-E6-F6
Churchill Way North	D7-E7-E6
Churchill Way South	D3-E3
Churchill Way West	C6-D6-D7
Clifton Road	D4
Cloisters Square	C6
Coldharbour Lane	C6-C7
College Street	E6
Constable Way	B4
Coombe Road	C1-D1
Cornwall Road	D8-E8
Crane Bridge Road	C4-C5
Crane Road	C4-D4
Culver Street	E4
Denison Rise	F8
De Vaux Place	D3
Devizes Road	A8-B8-B7-B6-C6
Devonshire Road	D8-E8
Dews Street	C5
Donaldson Road	D7-E7
Dorset Road	E7-E8
Douglas Haig Road	D7
Downton Road	D1-E1
Edison Road	A5-B5
Elm Grove	E5
Elm Grove Road	E5-F5
Endless Street	D5
Essex Square	A2-A3
Estcourt Road	E6
Exeter Street	D3-D4
Fairview Road	F5-F6
Farm Lane	A5
Finchley Road	B6
Fisherton Street	C5-D5
Folkestone Road	C2
Fowlers Hill	E4-F4
Fowlers Road	E4-F4
Friary Lane	D3-E3-E4
Gas Lane	C6
George Street	C6
Gigant Street	E4
Glenmore Road	F7
Godley Road	C1-D1-D2
Gorringe Road	A6
Greencroft Street	E5
Hamilton Road	D6-D7
Harcourt Terrace	C5
Harnham Road	B3-B2-C2
Harnwood Road	B1-B2
Harper Road	A7-A8
Hartington Road	B6-C6
Highbury Avenue	A6-B6-B7
Highfield Road	B7
Highlands Road	D1-D2
High Street	D4-E5
Hollows Close	B2-C2
Hulse Road	D7
India Avenue	A7-A8
Kelsey Road	E5-F5
Kent Road	A2-A3
Kingsland Road	B7-C7
Kings Road	D6
Laverstock Road	F4-F5
London Road	F6-F7-F8
Longlands	A6
Love Lane	E4
Lower Road	A6-A5
Lower Street	B4-B3
Macklin Road	A7-B7
Manor Farm Road	F5-F4
Manor Road	E5-E6-F6
Marsh Lane	C6
Meadow Road	C6
Middle Street	A4
Middleton Road	C6
Milford Hill	E4
Milford Hollow	F4
Milford Street	E5-E4
Mill Road	C5
Mitchell Road	A5
Moberley Road	D7-E7
Montague Road	A3
Netherhampton Road	A3-B3
New Bridge Road	D2-D3
New Canal	D4-D5
New Harnham Road	D2
New Street	D4
Newton Road	A5
New Zealand Avenue	A7
Norfolk Road	A3
North Street	C5
North Walk	D4
Nursery Road	A6
Odstock Road	D1
Old Blandford Road	A1-B1-C1-C2
Old Meadows Walk	A3-B3
Palmer Road	B7
Park Street	E6
Parsonage Green	B3-B2
Queen Street	D5
Queen's Road	A7
Queensbury Road	D8-E8
Radnor Road	D8
Rampart Road	E4
Rectory Road	C5
Richards Way	A4-A3
Ridgeway Road	D7-E7
Roberts Road	A8
Rollestone Street	D5-E5
Roman Road	A7-A8
Russell Road	B7-B6
St Ann Street	E4
St Clair Road	D2
St Edmonds Church Street	E5
St Gregory's Avenue	A7
St John's Street	D4
St Mark's Avenue	F6-F7-E7-E8-F8
St Mark's Road	E6
St Martin's Church Street	E4
St Mary's Road	B3-C3
St Nicholas Road	D2-D3
St Paul's Road	C5
Salt Lane	D5-E5
Saxon Road	B2-B3
Shady Bower	F4
Somerset Road	E7-E8
South Street	C5
Southampton Road	E3-F3
Stephenson Road	B5
Stoney Street	C6
Stratford Road	C8-D8-D7
Suffolk Road	A2-A3
Sussex Road	A2-B2
The Avenue	E5-F5
Telford Road	A5-B5
Tollgate Road	E4-F4-F3
Trinity Street	E4
Upper Street	A3-A4
Victoria Road	D7
Wain-a-Long Road	F6-F5
Waterloo Road	F3
Watt Road	A4
Wavell Road	D2
Wellington Way	A8
Wessex Road	F5
West Walk	C3-C4-D4
Wilton Road	A7-A6-B6-C6
Wiltshire Road	A3-B3-B2
Winchester Street	E4
Windsor Road	B6-C6-C5
Woodstock Road	E7-E6
Wordsworth Road	E7
Wyndham Road	D6-E6
Wynham Terrace	E6
York Road	C6

Swindon Area

Coates
River Thames A419
A433 A419 **CIRENCESTER**
Preston
Ampney St Peter
Poulton
Fairford
Grafton
A4095
Siddington
Harnhill
A417
A419
Meysey Hampton
Radcot
A419
A429
Driffield
Down Ampney
Marston Meysey
Lechlade A417
A361
Kelmscot
River Thames
Ewen
South Cerney
Castle Eaton
Kempsford
Whelford
Inglesham
N
Eaton Hastings
Kemble
A429
Shorncote
Cerney Wick
Latton
River Thames
Upper Inglesham
SCALE 0 — 3 mls
Buscot A417
Littleworth A4095
Poole Keynes
Summerford Keynes
Hannington Wick
A420
Faringdon
A417
Oaksey
Ashton Keynes
Cricklade
A419
Hannington
Coleshill
B4019
Great Coxwell
Little Coxwell
A420
A4508
Eastcourt
Leigh
B4040
Purton Stoke
Broad Blunsdon
Highworth
B4019
Sevenhampton
River Cole
B4000
Fernham
B4508
B4040
Upper Minety
Minety
Blundson St Andrew
Stanton Fitzwarren
B4019
B4000
Watchfield
Longcot
B4509
A3
Purton
B4534
Haydon Wick
A4311
B4006
Stratton St Margaret
A361
A420
Bourton
Shrivenham
B4000
Uffington
Woolstone
Compton Beauchamp
B4507
Green Hill
B4041
B4587
A4311
B4006
South Marston
A4312 B4006
Ashbury
Cleverton
B4042
Lydiard Millicent
B4534
B4289
SWINDON
A4312
B4006
Bishopstone
Brinkworth
Callow Hill
B4042
Hook
B4534
B4553
A4289
A4259
A4006
B4000
Toothill
A3102
A4289
Wanborough
Dauntsey
M4
Grittenham
Wootton Bassett
B4005
River Ray
A4006
Box denotes area covered by central plan
Liddington
A3102
B4041
Elcombe
Wroughton
M4
A419
B4192
Tockenham Wick
A4361
B4005
Badbury
15
Lyneham
Tockenham
Chiseldon
A345
Upper Upham
B4192
Baydon
Bradenstoke
Church End
Preston
Broad Town
Uffcott
Woodsend
Aldbourne
M4
Goatacre
Bushton
Spirthill
Clyffe Pypard
Broad Hinton
Ogbourne St George
Hilmarton
A3102
Clevancy
A4041
Highway
A4361

LEGEND

Town Plan
AA Recommended roads
Other roads
Restricted roads
Buildings of interest — Museum
Car Parks — P
AA Service Centre — AA
Parks and open Spaces
One Way Streets

Area Plan
A roads
B roads
Locations — St Peter O
Urban area

Street Index – with grid reference

Swindon

Albert Street	D1
Albion Street	A2-B2-B3
Alfred Street	D4-D5
Ashford Road	C1-C2
Avenue Road	D1
Bath Road	C1-D1
Bathurst Road	D4-E4
Beatrice Road	D5-E5
Beckhampton Street	D3-E3
Belle Vue Road	D1-D2-E2
Birch Street	A3-B3
Bridge Street	C4
Bristol Street	B3-B4
Britannia Place	D1-E1
Broad Street	D4-E4
Burford Avenue	E2-F2-F3
Cambria Bridge Road	B2-B3
Campden Road	F2
Canal Walk	C3
Carfax Street	D4
Caulfield Road	E5
Chester Street	B3
Church Place	A3-B3
Clifton Street	B2-C2-C1
Colbourne Street	E5-F5
College Street	C3-D3
Commercial Road	C3-D3
Commonweal Road	C1
Corporation Street	D4-D5
County Road	E4-E5
Cricklade Road	E5
Cricklade Street	E1-E2
Crombey Street	C3-C2-D2-D3
Cumberland Road	E3-F3
Curtis Street	B2-B3-C3
Deacon Street	C2-C3
Dean Street	A3
Devizes Road	D1
Dixon Street	C2
Drake's Way	F3-F4
Drove Road	E2-E3
Dryden Street	B3-B2-C2
Dudmore Road	E3-F3
East Street	C4
Eastcott Hill	C2-D2
Eastcott Road	D1-D2
Eastern Avenue	F3
Edgeware Road	C3-D3
Edmund Street	D2
Emlyn Square	B3-B4
Euclid Street	D3-E3
Faringdon Road	B3-C3
Farnsby Street	B3-C3
Fleet Street	C3-C4
Fleming Way	C4-D4-E4
Ford Street	A3
George Street	A3
Gladstone Street	D4-D5
Globe Street	C1-C2

Swindon

Brunel's decision in 1841 to build the Great Western Railway's workshops here transformed Swindon from an agricultural village into a major industrial centre. The surviving buildings of the original railway village have been restored.

Regrettably the fortunes of the BR Engineering Ltd locomotive and other workshops (the heart of the Great Western system and renowned for locomotives such as the King George V) have declined considerably and even face complete closure — but modern Swindon has seen a remarkable revival. Plans were made in the 1950s to reduce the town's dependence on one industry, and with the combination of development aid and improved road access via the M4, Swindon has seen the arrival of a wide range of manufacturing industries and a near doubling of its population, to 150,000. Aptly chosen for the relocation of the British Rail's Western Region Headquarters from Paddington, the town now boasts a modern shopping complex, a regional theatre and the impressive Oasis Leisure Centre, while an illustrious past is recalled in the Great Western Railway Museum.

Outside Swindon are 19th-century Lydiard Mansion, standing in 150 acres of parkland, the leisure facilities of Coate Water, and a museum on naturalist and writer Richard Jeffries.

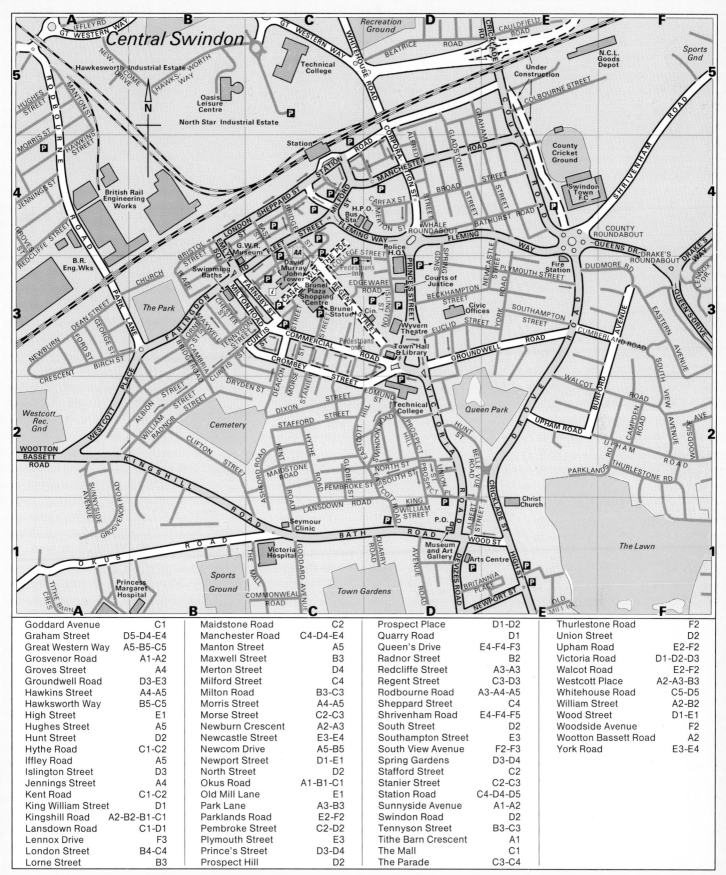

Central Swindon

N

Goddard Avenue	C1	
Graham Street	D5-D4-E4	
Great Western Way	A5-B5-C5	
Grosvenor Road	A1-A2	
Groves Street	A4	
Groundwell Road	D3-E3	
Hawkins Street	A4-A5	
Hawksworth Way	B5-C5	
High Street	E1	
Hughes Street	A5	
Hunt Street	D2	
Hythe Road	C1-C2	
Iffley Road	A5	
Islington Street	D3	
Jennings Street	A4	
Kent Road	C1-C2	
King William Street	D1	
Kingshill Road	A2-B2-B1-C1	
Lansdown Road	C1-D1	
Lennox Drive	F3	
London Street	B4-C4	
Lorne Street	B3	

Maidstone Road	C2	
Manchester Road	C4-D4-E4	
Manton Street	A5	
Maxwell Street	B3	
Merton Street	D4	
Milford Street	C4	
Milton Road	B3-C3	
Morris Street	A4-A5	
Morse Street	C2-C3	
Newburn Crescent	A2-A3	
Newcastle Street	E3-E4	
Newcom Drive	A5-B5	
Newport Street	D1-E1	
North Street	D2	
Okus Road	A1-B1-C1	
Old Mill Lane	E1	
Park Lane	A3-B3	
Parklands Road	E2-F2	
Pembroke Street	C2-D2	
Plymouth Street	E3	
Prince's Street	D3-D4	
Prospect Hill	D2	

Prospect Place	D1-D2	
Quarry Road	D1	
Queen's Drive	E4-F4-F3	
Radnor Street	B2	
Redcliffe Street	A3-A3	
Regent Street	C3-D3	
Rodbourne Road	A3-A4-A5	
Sheppard Street	C4	
Shrivenham Road	E4-F4-F5	
South Street	D2	
Southampton Street	E3	
South View Avenue	F2-F3	
Spring Gardens	D3-D4	
Stafford Street	C2	
Stanier Street	C2-C3	
Station Road	C4-D4-D5	
Sunnyside Avenue	A1-A2	
Swindon Road	D2	
Tennyson Street	B3-C3	
Tithe Barn Crescent	A1	
The Mall	C1	
The Parade	C3-C4	

Thurlestone Road	F2	
Union Street	D2	
Upham Road	E2-F2	
Victoria Road	D1-D2-D3	
Walcot Road	E2-F2	
Westcott Place	A2-A3-B3	
Whitehouse Road	C5-D5	
William Street	A2-B2	
Wood Street	D1-E1	
Woodside Avenue	F2	
Wootton Bassett Road	A2	
York Road	E3-E4	

SWINDON
Making waves at the Oasis Leisure Centre 'free-shaped' pool — under the biggest glazed dome in Britain, the water drops away gradually from inches-deep for paddling to a portholed diving area, and is fringed with tropical shrubs.

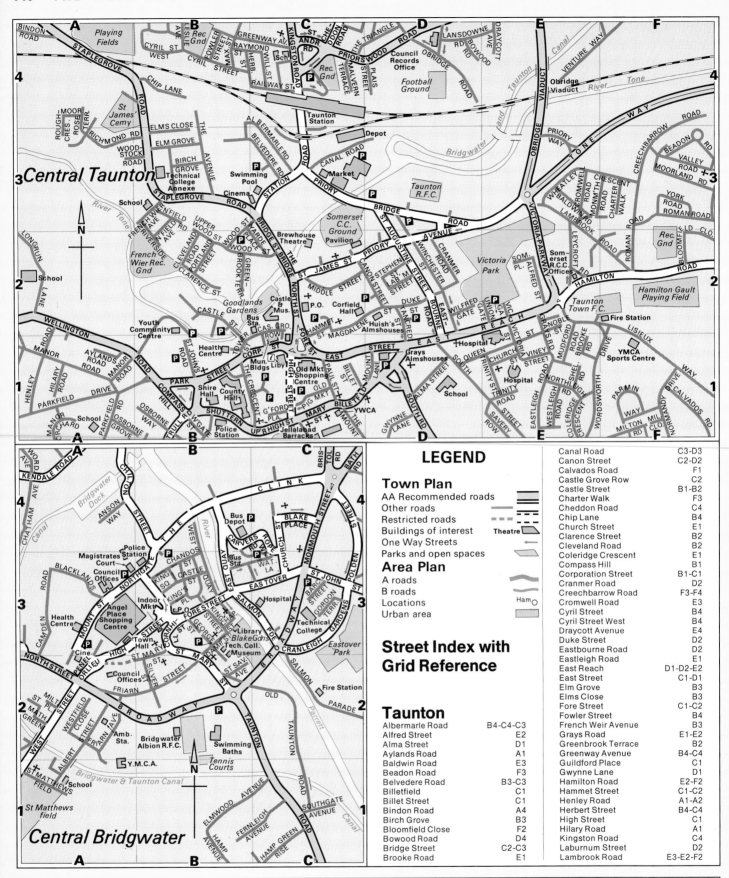

LEGEND

Town Plan

AA Recommended roads
Other roads
Restricted roads
Buildings of interest   Theatre
One Way Streets
Parks and open spaces

Area Plan

A roads
B roads
Locations   Ham○
Urban area

Street Index with Grid Reference

Taunton

Albermarle Road	B4-C4-C3
Alfred Street	E2
Alma Street	D1
Aylands Road	A1
Baldwin Road	E3
Beadon Road	F3
Belvedere Road	B3-C3
Billetfield	C1
Billet Street	C1
Bindon Road	A4
Birch Grove	B3
Bloomfield Close	F2
Bowood Road	D4
Bridge Street	C2-C3
Brooke Road	E1
Canal Road	C3-D3
Canon Street	C2-D2
Calvados Road	F1
Castle Grove Row	C2
Castle Street	B1-B2
Charter Walk	F3
Cheddon Road	C4
Chip Lane	B4
Church Street	E1
Clarence Street	B2
Cleveland Road	B2
Coleridge Crescent	E1
Compass Hill	B1
Corporation Street	B1-C1
Cranmer Road	D2
Creechbarrow Road	F3-F4
Cromwell Road	E3
Cyril Street	B4
Cyril Street West	B4
Draycott Avenue	E4
Duke Street	D2
Eastbourne Road	D2
Eastleigh Road	E1
East Reach	D1-D2-E2
East Street	C1-D1
Elm Grove	B3
Elms Close	B3
Fore Street	C1-C2
Fowler Street	B4
French Weir Avenue	B3
Grays Road	E1-E2
Greenbrook Terrace	B2
Greenway Avenue	B4-C4
Guildford Place	C1
Gwynne Lane	D1
Hamilton Road	E2-F2
Hammet Street	C1-C2
Henley Road	A1-A2
Herbert Street	B4-C4
High Street	C1
Hilary Road	A1
Kingston Road	C4
Laburnum Street	D2
Lambrook Road	E3-E2-F2

Taunton

The hub of Somerset, surrounded by the rolling, wooded Quantocks and the Blackdown Hills, Taunton lies on the River Tone in the fertile Vale of Taunton Dene. Famous for its thriving local cider industry, the town is also a lively commercial and agricultural centre whose livestock market rivals Exeter's as the most important in the West Country. In the past it was a major centre of the wool trade.

As befits a county town, Taunton is the headquarters of Somerset's entertaining and successful cricket team. It also offers National Hunt racing, has no fewer than three public schools and, somewhat improbably, the British Telecom Museum where antique telephone equipment is kept. There has been a castle in the town since Norman times: now it is home for the Somerset County and Military Museums.

Bridgwater, an industrial centre, was a busy port until Bristol overshadowed it. Twice a day a bore – a great tidal wave – surges up the River Parrett from Bridgwater Bay; the times are posted on the bridge in the town centre for those who want to see it.

In 1695 the rebel Duke of Monmouth is reputed to have surveyed the field before the Battle of Sedgemoor from the town's church tower. Dating from the 14th century, the Church of St Mary has some particularly fine Jacobean screenwork.

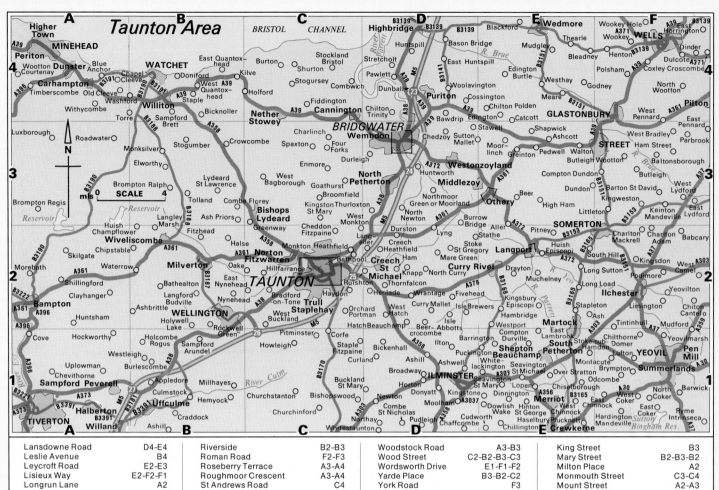

Taunton Area

Lansdowne Road	D4-E4	Riverside	B2-B3
Leslie Avenue	B4	Roman Road	F2-F3
Leycroft Road	E2-E3	Roseberry Terrace	A3-A4
Lisieux Way	E2-F2-F1	Roughmoor Crescent	A3-A4
Longrun Lane	A2	St Andrews Road	C4
Magdalene Street	C2-D2	St Augustine Street	D2-D3
Malvern Terrace	C4	St James Street	C2
Manor Orchard	A1	St John's Road	B1
Manor Road	A1	Savery Row	E1
Mary Street	C1	Shelley Road	E1
Maxwell Street	B4	Shuttern	B1
Middle Street	C2	Somerset Place	E2
Milton Close	F1	South Road	D1
Milton Road	F1	South Street	D1-E1
Monmouth Road	E3-F3	Staplegrove Road	A4-B4-B3-C3
Moorland Road	F3	Station Road	C3-C4
Mount Lane	D1	Stephen Street	D2
Mudford Road	E1-E2	Tancred Street	D1-D2
Noble Street	E2	The Avenue	B3-B4
Normandy Drive	F1	The Bridge	C2
Northfield Avenue	B2-B3	The Crescent	B1-C1
Northfield Road	B3	The Mount	C1
Northleigh Road	E1	The Triangle	C4-D4
North Street	C2	Toneway	E3-F3-F4
Obridge Road	D4	Tower Street	B1-C1-C2
Obridge Viaduct	E3-E4	Trinity Road	E1
Old Pig Market	C1	Trinity Street	E1
Osborne Grove	A1-B1	Trull Road	B1
Osborne Way	B1	Union Gate	E2
Parmin Way	F1	Upper High Street	C1
Parkfield Drive	A1	Upper Wood Street	B2-B3
Parkfield Road	A1	Valley Road	F3
Park Street	B1	Venture Way	E4-F4
Paul Street	C1	Victoria Gate	E2
Plais Street	D4	Victoria Parkway	E2-E3
Portland Street	B2	Victoria Street	E1-E2
Priorswood Road	C4-D4	Viney Street	E1
Priory Avenue	C2-D2-D3	Wellington Road	A2-A1-B1
Priory Bridge Road	C3-D3-E3	Westgate Street	B1
Priory Way	E3	Westleigh Road	E1
Queen Street	D1-E1-E2	Wheatley Crescent	E3-F3
Railway Street	C4	Wilfred Gate	D2
Raymond Street	B4-C4	William Street	C4
Richmond Road	A3-B3	Winchester Street	D2-D3

Woodstock Road	A3-B3	King Street	B3
Wood Street	C2-B2-B3-C3	Mary Street	B2-B3-B2
Wordsworth Drive	E1-F1-F2	Milton Place	A2
Yarde Place	B3-B2-C2	Monmouth Street	C3-C4
York Road	F3	Mount Street	A2-A3
		New Road	B3-C3
Bridgewater		Northgate	A3-B3-B4
		North Street	A2-A3
Albert Street	A1-A2	Old Taunton Road	B2-C2-C1
Angel Crescent	A3-B3	Penel Orlieu	A2
Anson Way	A4	Polden Street	C3-C4
Barclay Street	C3	Rope Walk	C4
Bath Road	C4	Taunton Road	B2-C2-C1
Blacklands	A3	St John Street	C3
Blake Place	C4	St Matthews Field	A1
Bristol Road	C4	St Matthews Green	A2
Broadway	A2-B2-C2-C3	St Saviors Avenue	B2
Camden Road	A3	Salmon Parade	B3-C3-C2
Carvers Road	B3-B4-C4	Silver Street	B2
Castle Street	B3	Southgate Avenue	C1
Chandos Street	B3	Taunton Road	B2-C2-C1
Chapel Street	B3	The Clink	B4-C4
Chatham Avenue	A4	Watson Lane	B3-C3
Chilton Street	A4-B4	Westfield Close	A2
Church Street	C3-C4	West Quay	B3-B4
Cornhill Street	B3	West Street	A1-A2
Cranleigh Gardens	C3	Wordsworth Avenue	A4
Dampiet Street	B3		
Eastover	B3-C3		
East Quay	B3-B4		
Elmwood Avenue	B1-C1		
Fernleigh Avenue	B1-C1		
Fore Street	B3		
Friarn Avenue	A2		
Friarn Street	A2-B2		
George Street	B3		
Gordon Terrace	C3		
Hamp Avenue	B1		
Hamp Green Rise	B1-C1		
High Street	A2-A3-B3		
Kendale Road	A4		
King's Place	B3		
King Square	B3		

TAUNTON
Taunton School, an attractive rambling building in Staplegrove Road, is one of the town's three public schools for boys. This is the largest of the three in terms of numbers of pupils and is inter-denominational.

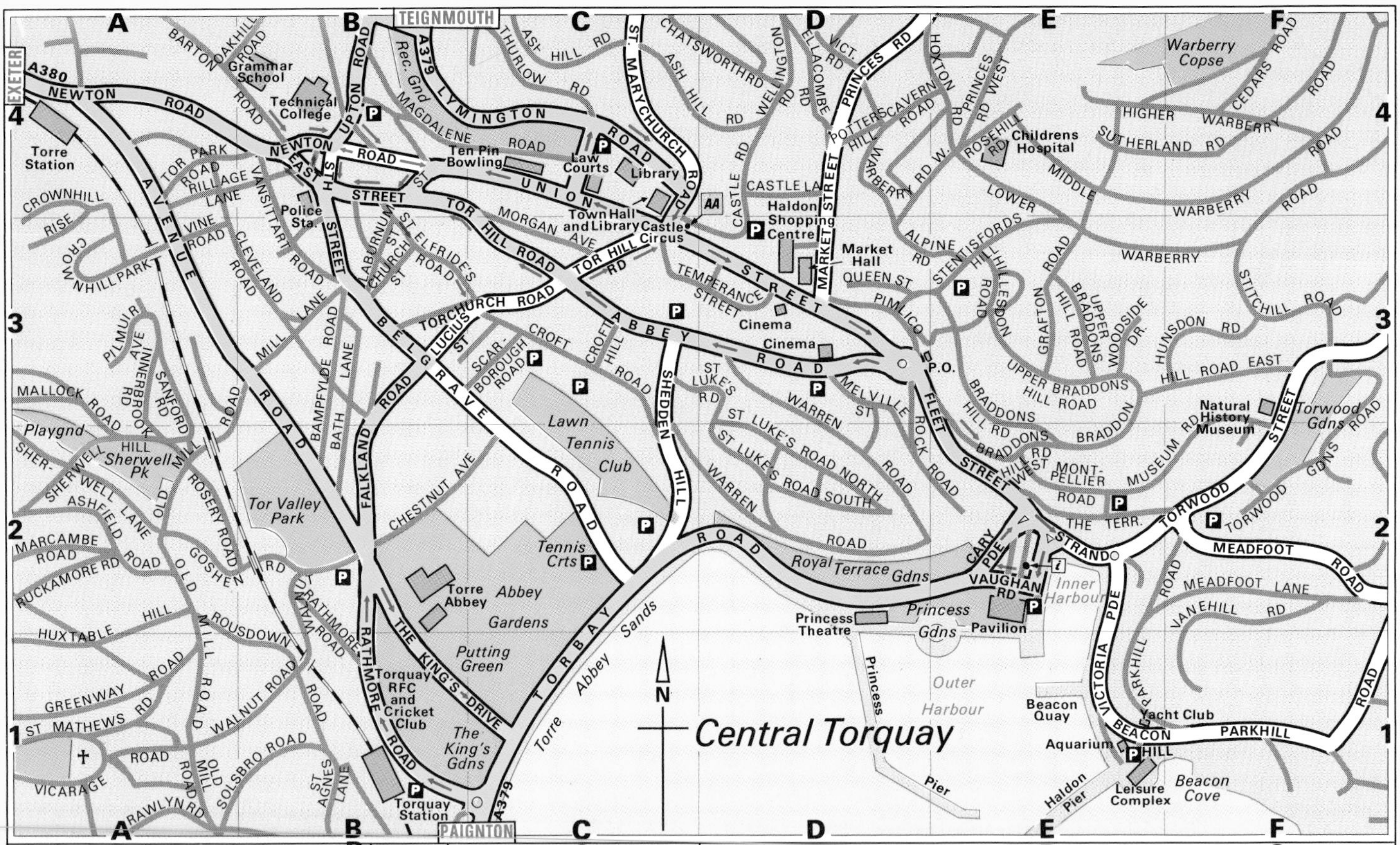

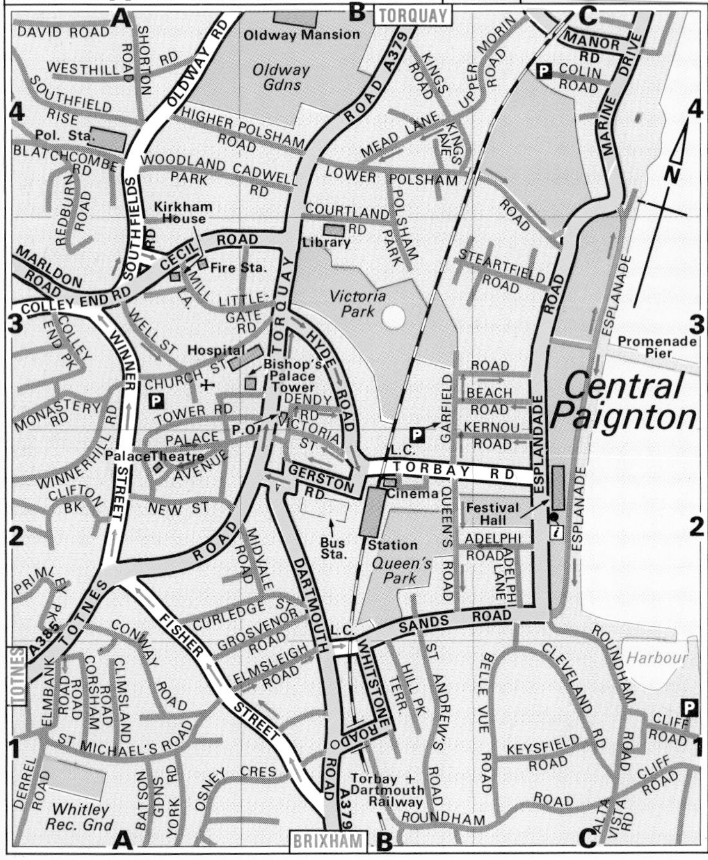

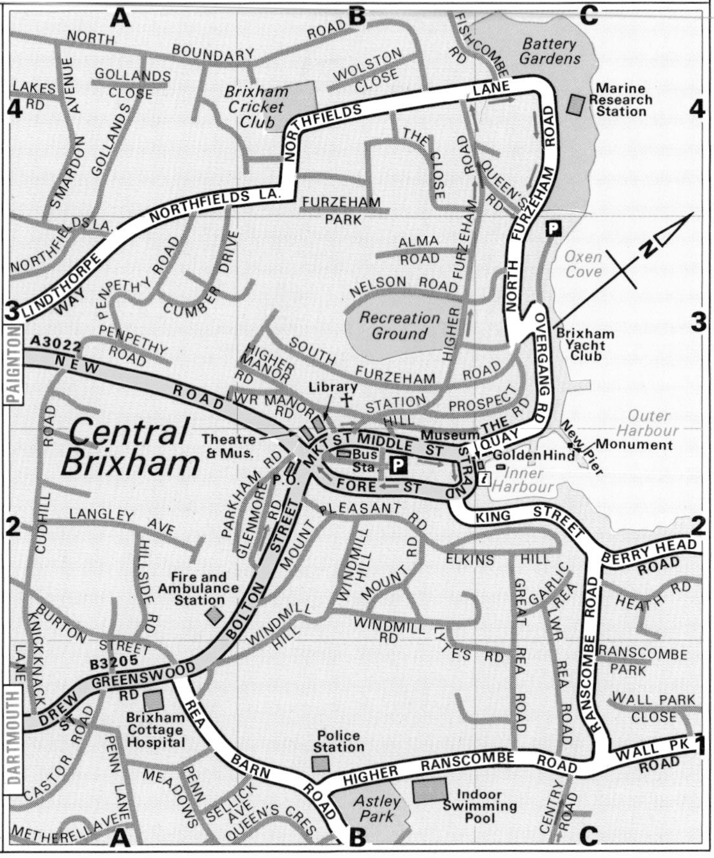

Torquay

With its sparkling houses, colourful gardens and sub-tropical plants set among the limestone crags of the steep hillside, Torquay has the air of a resort on the French Riviera – an impression strengthened by the superb views of sea and coast from Marine Drive, the 'corniche' road that sweeps around the rocky headland. Torquay is undoubtedly the queen of the Devon coast, a resort carefully planned in the early 19th century to cater for the wealthy and discriminating visitor. It had begun to be popular with naval officers' families during the Napoleonic wars when no one could travel to the continent, and this burgeoning popularity was exploited by the Palk family through two generations. Sir Robert Palk inherited an estate which included Torquay, and he and his descendants set about transforming it into the town of today.

Paignton, set on the huge sweep of Tor Bay south of Torquay, continues the range of holiday amenities and has good, sandy beaches.

Brixham, which lies a little further down the coast, falls into two parts – the old village on the hill slopes – and the fishing village half a mile below. Less commercialised than its neighbours, it is popular with holidaymakers.

Newton Abbot lies on the River Teign. It is a busy market town and has been an important railway junction since the mid 19th century.

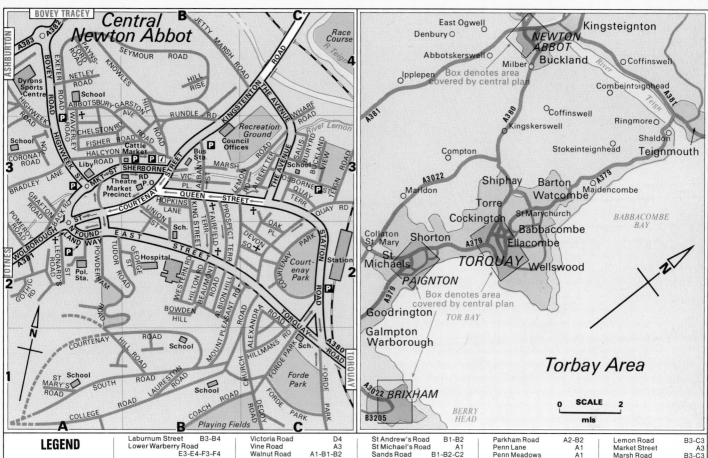

Central Newton Abbot

Torbay Area

LEGEND

Town Plan
AA recommended route
Restricted roads
Other roads
Buildings of interest   Sch
Car parks   P
Parks and open spaces

Area Plan
A roads
B roads
Locations   Coffinswell ○
Urban area

STREET INDEX WITH GRID REFERENCE

TORQUAY

Street	Grid
Abbey Road	C3-D3
Alpine Road	D3-E3
Ashfield Road	A2
Ash Hill Road	C4-D4
Avenue Road	A3-A4-B2-B3
Bampfylde Road	B2-B3
Barton Road	A4-B4
Bath Lane	B2-B3
Beacon Hill	E1-F1
Belgrave Road	B3-C2-C3
Braddons Hill Road	E2-E3
Braddons Hill Road East	E2-E3-F3
Braddons Hill Road West	E2
Cary Parade	E2
Castle Lane	D4
Castle Road	C3-D3-D4
Cavern Road	D4-E4
Cedars Road	F4
Chatsworth Road	C4-D4
Chestnut Avenue	B2-C2
Church Street	B3
Cleveland Road	A3-A4-B3
Croft Hill	C3
Croft Road	C2-C3
Crownhill Park	A3
Crownhill Rise	A3-A4
East Street	B4
Ellacombe Road	D4
Falkland Road	B2-B3
Fleet Street	D3-E2-E3
Goshen Road	A2-B2
Grafton Road	E3
Greenway Road	A1
Higher Warberry Road	E4-F4
Hillesdon Road	E3
Hoxton Road	D4-E4
Hunsdon Road	F3
Huxtable Hill	A1-A2
Innerbrook Road	A2-A3
Laburnum Street	B3-B4
Lower Warberry Road	E3-E4-F3-F4
Lucius Street	B3-C3
Lymington Road	B4-C4
Magdalene Road	B4-C4
Mallock Road	A2-A3
Marcambe Road	A2
Market Street	D3-D4
Meadfoot Lane	E2-F2
Meadfoot Road	F2
Melville Street	D2-D3
Middle Warberry Road	E4-F4
Mill Lane	B3
Montpellier Road	E2
Morgan Avenue	C3-C4
Museum Road	E2-F2-F3
Newton Road	A4-B4
Oakhill Road	A4-B4
Old Mill Road	A1-A2-A3-B3
Parkhill Road	E1-E2-F1-F2
Pimlico	D3
Pilmuir Avenue	A3
Potters Hill	D4
Princes Road	D4
Princes Road West	D4-E4
Queen Street	D3
Rathmore Road	B1-B2-C1
Rawlyn Road	A1
Rillage Lane	A4-B4
Rock Road	D2-D3-E2
Rosehill Road	E4-F4
Rosery Road	A2-B2
Rousdown Road	A2-A1-B1
Ruckamore Road	A2
St Agnes Lane	B1
St Elfride's Road	B3-C3
St Luke's Road	C3-D3
St Luke's Road North	D2-D3
St Luke's Road South	D2
St Marychurch Road	C4
St Mathews Road	A1
Sanford Road	A2-A3
Scarborough Road	C3
Shedden Hill	C2-C3
Sherwell Hill	A2
Sherwell Lane	A2
Solsbro Road	A1-B1
South Street	B3-B4
Stentisfords Hill	E3
Stitchill Road	F3
Strand	E2
Sutherland Road	E4-F4
Temperance Street	C3-D3
The King's Drive	B1-B2-C1
The Terrace	E2
Thurlow Road	C4
Torbay Road	C1-C2-D2-E2
Torchurch Road	B3
Tor Hill Road	B4-C3-C4
Tor Park Road	A4-B4
Torwood Gardens Road	F2-F3
Torwood Street	E2-F2-F3
Union Street	B4-C3-C4-D3
Upper Braddons Hill Road	E3
Upton Road	B4
Vanehill Road	F1-F2
Vansittart Road	B3-B4
Vaughan Road	E2
Vicarage Road	A1
Victoria Parade	E1-E2
Victoria Road	D4
Vine Road	A3
Walnut Road	A1-B1-B2
Warren Road	C2-C3-D2-D3
Warberry Road West	D3-D4-E4
Wellington Road	D4
Woodside Drive	E3

PAIGNTON

Adelphi Lane	C2
Adelphi Road	B2-C2
Alta Vista Road	C1
Batson Gardens	A1
Beach Road	B3-C3
Belle Vue Road	C1
Blatchcombe Road	A4
Cadwell Road	B4
Cecil Road	A3-B3
Church Street	A3-B3
Cleveland Road	C1
Cliff Road	C1
Clifton Bank	A2
Climsland Road	A1
Colin Road	C4
Colley End Park	A3
Colley End Road	A3
Conway Road	A1-A2
Corsham Road	A1
Courtland Road	B3-B4
Curledge Street	A2-B2
Dartmouth Road	B1-B2
David Road	A4
Dendy Road	B3
Derrel Road	A1
Elmbank Road	A1
Elmsleigh Road	A1-B1
Esplanade	C2-C3-C4
Esplanade Road	C2-C3-C4
Fisher Street	A1-A2-B1
Garfield Road	B2-B3-C3
Gerston Road	B2
Grosvenor Road	A1-B1-B2
Higher Polsham Road	A4-B4
Hill Park Terrace	B1
Hyde Road	B2-B3
Kernou Road	B2-C2
Keysfield Road	C1
Kings Avenue	B4
Kings Road	B4
Littlegate Road	A3-B3
Lower Polsham Road	C4-B3-B4
Manor Road	C4
Marine Drive	C4
Marldon Road	A3
Mead Road	B4
Midvale Road	B2
Mill Lane	A3
Monastery Road	A3
New Street	B2
Oldway Road	A4
Osney Crescent	A1-B1
Palace Avenue	A2-B2
Polsham Park	B3-B4
Primley Park	A2
Queen's Road	B2
Redburn Road	A3-A4
Roundham Road	B1-C1-C2
St Andrew's Road	B1-B2
St Michael's Road	A1
Sands Road	B1-B2-C2
Shorton Road	A4
Southfield Rise	A4
Southfields Road	A3-A4
Steartfield Road	B3-C3
Torbay Road	B2-C2
Torquay Road	B2-B3-B4
Totnes Road	A1-A2-B2
Tower Road	A2-A3-B3
Upper Morin Road	B4-C4
Victoria Street	B2
Well Street	A3
Westhill Road	A4
Whitstone Road	B1
Winner Street	A2-A3
Winnerhill Road	A2-A3
Woodland Park	A4
York Road	A1

BRIXHAM

Alma Road	B3
Berry Head Road	C2
Bolton Street	A1-A2-B2
Burton Street	A1-A2
Castor Road	A1
Centry Road	C1
Cudhill Road	A2-A3
Cumber Drive	A3-A4
Drew Street	A1
Elkins Hill	B2-C2
Fishcombe Road	B4-C4
Fore Street	B2
Furzeham Park	B4
Garlic Rea	C2
Glenmore Road	B2
Gollands	A3-A4
Gollands Close	A4
Great Rea Road	C1-C2
Greenswood Road	A1
Heath Road	C2
Higher Furzeham Road	B3-B4-C3-C4
Higher Manor Road	B3
Higher Ranscombe Road	B1-C1
Hillside Road	A2
King Street	B2-C2
Knick Knack Lane	A1-A2
Lakes Road	A4
Langley Avenue	A2
Lindthorpe Way	A3
Lower Manor Road	A3-B3
Lower Rea Road	C1-C2
Lyte's Road	B1-B2-C1
Market Street	B2
Metherell Avenue	A1
Middle Street	B2
Mount Road	B2
Mount Pleasant Road	B2
Nelson Road	B3-C3
New Road	A3-B3-B2
North Boundary Road	A4-B4
Northfields Lane	A3-A4-B4-C4
North Furzeham Road	C3-C4
Overgang Road	C3
Parkham Road	A2-B2
Penn Lane	A1
Penn Meadows	A1
Penpethy Road	A3
Prospect Road	B3-C3
Queen's Crescent	B1
Queen's Road	C4
Ranscombe Park	C1
Ranscombe Road	C1-C2
Rea Barn Road	A1-B1
Sellick Avenue	A1-B1
Smardon Avenue	A3-A4
South Furzeham Road	B3-C3
Station Hill	B2-B3
Strand	B2
The Close	B4
The Quay	C2-C3
Wall Park Close	C1
Wall Park Road	C1
Windmill Hill	A1-B1-B2
Windmill Road	B2-C2
Wolston Close	B4

Newton Abbot

Abbotsbury Road	A4-A3-B3
Albany Street	B3
Albert Terrace	C3
Albion Hill	B2
Alexandra Road	C1-C2
Back Road	A2-A3
Beaumont Road	B2
Bovey Road	A3-A4
Bowden Hill	B2
Bradley Lane	A3
Buckland View	C3
Chelston Road	A3-B3
Church Road	C1-C2
Coach Road	B1-C1
College Road	A1-B1
Coronation Road	A3
Courtenay Park	C2
Courtenay Road	A1-B1
Courtenay Street	A3-B3
Decoy Road	C1
Devon Square	C2
East Street	A2-B2
Exeter Road	A4
Fairfield Terrace	B2-B3
Fisher Road	A3-B3
Forde Park	C1
Garston Avenue	A4-B4-B3
George Street	B2
Gothic Road	A2
Grafton Road	A3
Halcyon Road	A3
Highweek Road	A3-A4
Highweek Street	A3
Hillmans Road	C1-C2
Hill Rise	B4
Hill Road	A1-B1
Hilton Road	B2
Hopkins Lane	B2
Jetty Marsh Road	B4-C4
Kingsteinton Road	B3-B4-C4
King Street	B2-B3
Knowles Hill Road	A4-B4-B3
Laureston Road	B1
Lemon Road	B3-C3
Market Street	A3
Marsh Road	B3-C3
Mount Pleasant Road	B1-B2-C2
Netley Road	B3
Newfoundland Way	A2
Oak Place	C2
Osborne Street	C3
Paynsford Road	A4
Pomeroy Road	A2
Powderham Road	A2-B2
Prospect Terrace	B2-B3
Quay Road	C3
Quay Terrace	C3
Queen Street	B3-C3
Rundle Road	B3-B4-C4-C3
St Leonards Road	A2
St Marys Road	A1
Salisbury Road	C3
Seymour Road	A4-B4
Sherborne Road	B3
South Road	A1-B1
Station Road	C1-C2-C3
The Avenue	C3-C4
Teign Road	C3
Torquay Road	C1-C2
Tudor Road	A2-B2
Union Street	B2-B3
Vicarage Place	B3
Waverley Road	A3-A4
Western Road	B3
Wharf Road	C3-C4
Wolborough Street	A2-A3

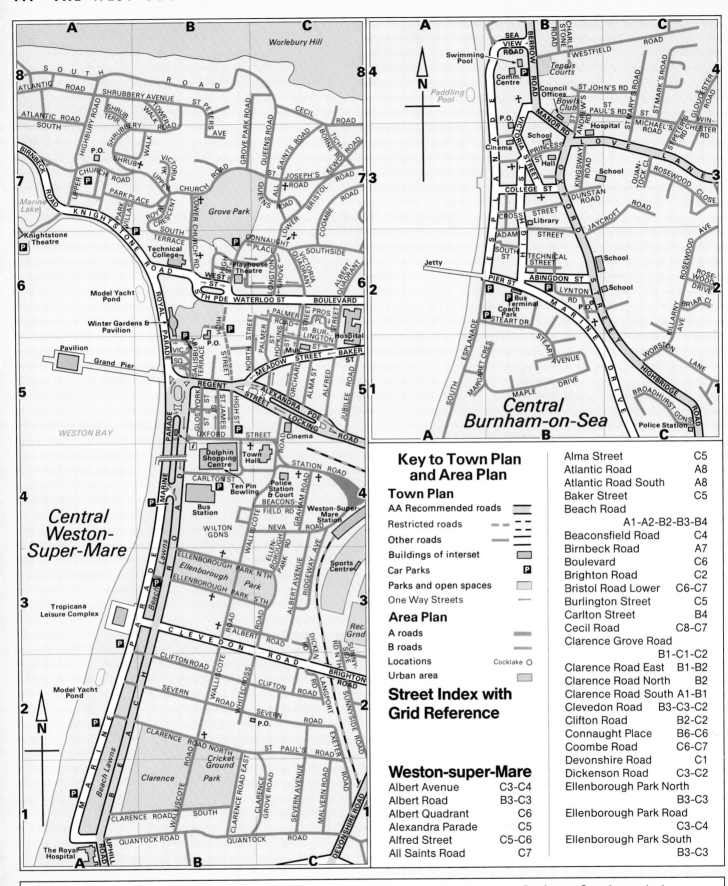

Key to Town Plan and Area Plan

Town Plan

AA Recommended roads	
Restricted roads	
Other roads	
Buildings of interset	
Car Parks	P
Parks and open spaces	
One Way Streets	←

Area Plan

A roads	
B roads	
Locations	Cocklake ○
Urban area	

Street Index with Grid Reference

Weston-super-Mare

Albert Avenue	C3-C4
Albert Road	B3-C3
Albert Quadrant	C6
Alexandra Parade	C5
Alfred Street	C5-C6
All Saints Road	C7
Alma Street	C5
Atlantic Road	A8
Atlantic Road South	A8
Beach Road	
	A1-A2-B2-B3-B4
Beaconsfield Road	C4
Birnbeck Road	A7
Boulevard	C6
Brighton Road	C2
Bristol Road Lower	C6-C7
Burlington Street	C5
Carlton Street	B4
Cecil Road	C8-C7
Clarence Grove Road	
	B1-C1-C2
Clarence Road East	B1-B2
Clarence Road North	B2
Clarence Road South	A1-B1
Clevedon Road	B3-C3-C2
Clifton Road	B2-C2
Connaught Place	B6-C6
Coombe Road	C6-C7
Devonshire Road	C1
Dickenson Road	C3-C2
Ellenborough Park North	
	B3-C3
Ellenborough Park Road	
	C3-C4
Ellenborough Park South	
	B3-C3

Weston-Super-Mare

Elegant piers, promenades and hotels mark Weston-Super-Mare's 19th-century transformation into a flourishing seaside resort. At one time nothing more than a small fishing village, the town now boasts several attractive parks and gardens, and near the beach are numerous entertainment and leisure centres.

Havens for children are the Winter Garden Complex and Tropicana, both equipped with water slides, swimming pools and solaria. Madeira Cove attracts visitors to its Marine Lake, aquarium and model village, and Knightstone Island nearby provides further entertainments.

The High Street has been turned into a pedestrian area for easy shopping, and tucked away down a cobbled street is the Woodspring Museum full of nostalgic memories of a town which still retains its character and charm.

Burnham-on-Sea enjoys two local breweries, responsible for supplying the real ales which are exclusive to the pubs in this area. Developed into a resort as early as the 18th century, Burnham-on-Sea also offers many other amenities, including a mild Somerset climate, acres of sandy beaches, a Leisure Park and a pier which was built in 1856 as a terminal for passing steamers and the railway. Live entertainment can be seen at Princess Hall.

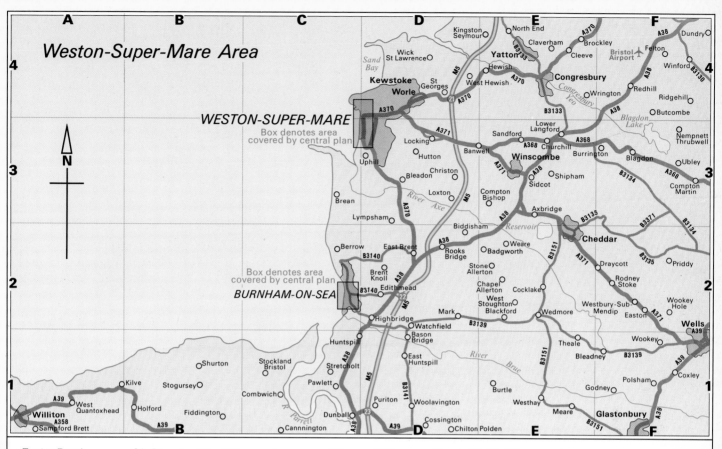

Weston-Super-Mare Area

Exeter Road	C2-C1	Royal Crescent	B7	Whitecross Road	B2-C2-C3
Gloucester Street	B5	Royal Parade	B6-B5	Wilton Gardens	B4
Graham Road	C4	St James Street	B5	York Street	B5
Grove Park Road	B7-B8-C8	St Joseph's Road	C7		
Highbury Road	A7-A8	St Paul's Road	C2-C1		
High Street	B6-B5	St Peter's Avenue	B8-B7		
Hopkin Street	C5-C6	Salisbury Terrace	B5		
Jubilee Road	C5	Severn Avenue	C1-C2		
Kew Road	C7	Severn Road	B2-C2		
Knightstone Road	A7-A6-B6	Shrubbery Avenue	A8-B8		
Langport Road	C2	Shrubbery Road	A7-B7-B8		
Locking Road	C5-C4	Shrubbery Terrace	A8		
Longton Grove	C6	Shrubbery Walk	A7-B7		
Lower Church Road	B7-B6	South Parade	B6		
Malvern Road	C1	South Road	A8-B8		
Marine Parade		Southside	C6		
	A1-A2-A3-B3-B4-B5	South Terrace	B7-B6		
Meadow Street	B5-C5	Station Road	C4		
Neva Road	B4-C4	Sunnyside Road	C2		
North Street	B5-C5-C6	Sunnyside Road North			
Orchard Street	C5-C6		C3-C2		
Oxford Street	B5-C5	Tichbourne Road	C7		
Palmer Road	C6	Tower Walk	B8		
Palmer Street	C5-C6	Upper Church Road	A7-B7		
Park Place	A7-B7	Victoria Park	B7		
Park Villas	A7	Victoria Square	B5		
Prospect Place	C6	Victoria Quadrant	C6		
Quantock Road	A1-B1-C1	Walliscote Road			
Queens Road	C7-C8		B1-B2-B3-B4-C4-C5		
Regent Street	B5-C5	Waterloo Street	B6-C6		
Ridgeway Avenue	C3-C4	West Street	B6		

Pier Street	B2
Princess Street	B3
Quantock Close	C3
Rosewood Avenue	C2-C3
Rosewood Close	C3
Rosewood Drive	C2
St Andrew's Road	B3-B4
St John's Road	B4-C4
St Marks Road	C4
St Mary's Road	C3-C4
St Michael's Road	C4-C3
St Paul's Road	B4-C4
St Peter's Road	C3-C4
Sea View Road	B4
South Esplanade	A1-A2
South Street	B2
Steart Avenue	B2-B1
Steart Drive	A2-B2
Technical Street	B2
Victoria Street	B4-B3
Westfield Road	B4-C4
Winchester Road	C4-C3
Worston Lane	C1

Burnham-on-Sea

Abingdon Street	B2
Adam Street	B2-B3
Berrow Road	B4
Briar Close	C2
Broadhurst Gardens	C1
Charlestone Road	B4
College Street	B3
Cross Street	B3
Dunstan Road	B3
Esplanade	A2-B2-B3-B4
Gloucester Road	C4
Highbridge Road	C1
High Street	B2-B3
Jaycroft Road	B2-B3-C3
Kilarny Avenue	C1-C2
Kingsway Road	B3
Love Lane	B3-C3
Lynton Road	B2
Manor Road	B4-B3
Maple Drive	B1
Margaret Crescent	A1-B1
Marine Drive	B2-B1-C1
Oxford Street	B3-B2-C2-C1

WESTON-SUPER-MARE
The piers and good beaches of Weston-Super-Mare attract over three million visitors a year, and town spectaculars such as the aircraft displays of Great Weston Air Day and the summer carnival are another powerful draw.

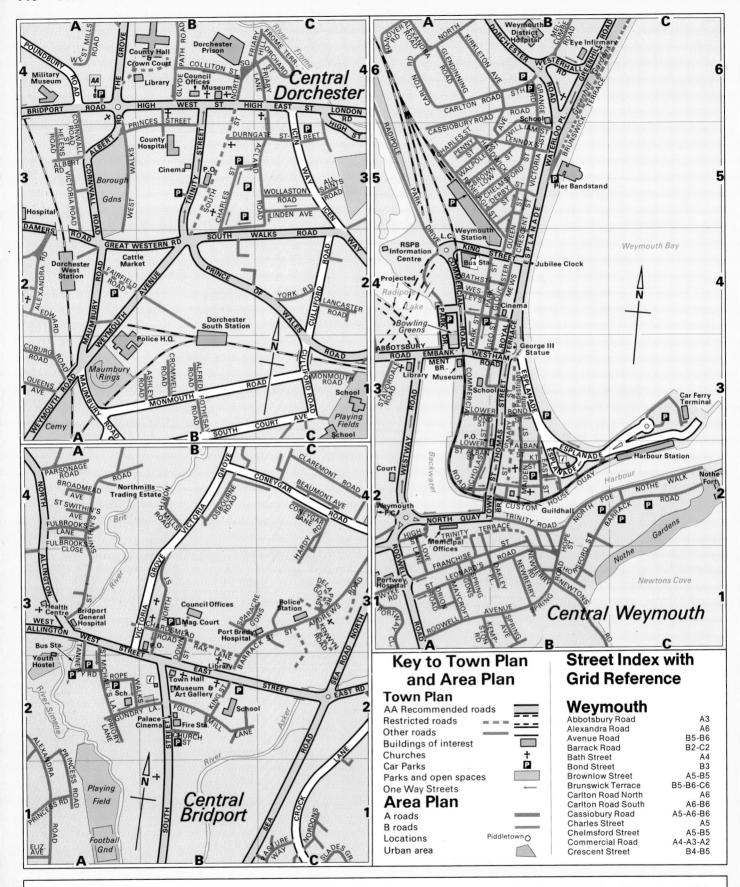

Weymouth

King George III favoured the ancient port of Weymouth and as a result the town aquired a certain fashionable status as a resort in the late 18th century. Still popular with holidaymakers, it offers good bathing, fishing and golf, and it is also a busy Channel Islands ferry port. Georgian houses – many of which have been turned into guest houses – overlook the broad esplanade, but near the harbour older buildings line narrow, picturesque streets and alleyways. One of the 17th-century houses in Trinity Street has been restored and refurnished in contemporary style, and another place of interest is the museum in Westham Road.

Dorchester is essentially still the busy market town Thomas Hardy featured in many of his novels. He was born at nearby Higher Bockhampton and several of his personal possessions are displayed in the Dorset County Museum in Dorchester. A series of fires in the 17th and 18th centuries left the town rather short of historic buildings, although St Peter's Church, which dates back to the 1400s, survived, as did the Old Shire Hall – scene of the trial of the Tolpuddle Martyrs in 1834.

Bridport's wide pavements used to be called 'ropewalks' because new ropes were laid out on them for twisting and drying. The 750-year-old industry continues to this day, and relics of the old trade are kept in the museum in South Street.

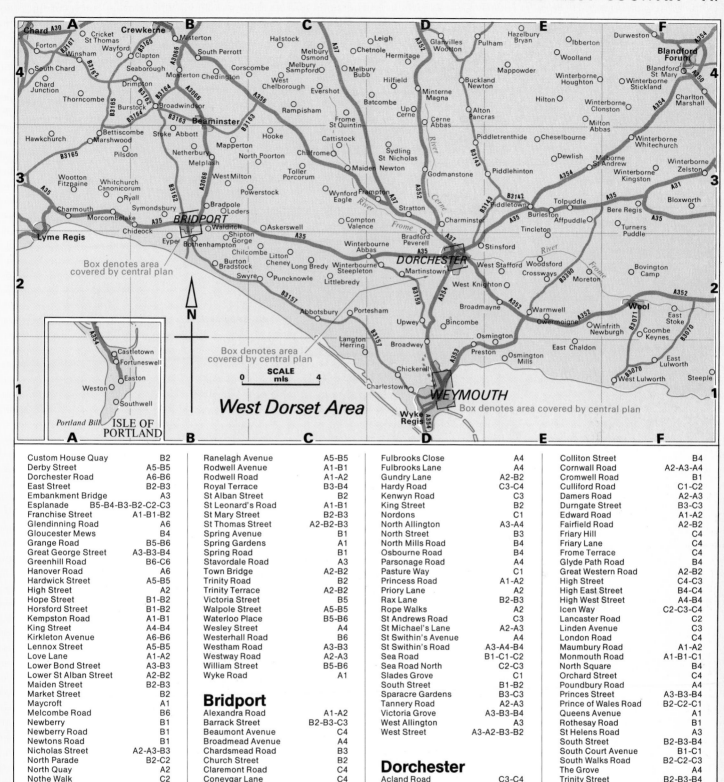

Box denotes area covered by central plan

Box denotes area covered by central plan

West Dorset Area

SCALE
mls
0   4

N

Portland Bill **ISLE OF PORTLAND**

Box denotes area covered by central plan

Custom House Quay	B2	Ranelagh Avenue	A5-B5	Fulbrooks Close	A4
Derby Street	A5-B5	Rodwell Avenue	A1-B1	Fulbrooks Lane	A4
Dorchester Road	A6-B6	Rodwell Road	A1-A2	Gundry Lane	A2-B2
East Street	B2-B3	Royal Terrace	B3-B4	Hardy Road	C3-C4
Embankment Bridge	A3	St Alban Street	B2	Kenwyn Road	C3
Esplanade	B5-B4-B3-B2-C2-C3	St Leonard's Road	A1-B1	King Street	B2
Franchise Street	A1-B1-B2	St Mary Street	B2-B3	Nordons	C1
Glendinning Road	A6	St Thomas Street	A2-B2-B3	North Allington	A3-A4
Gloucester Mews	B4	Spring Avenue	B1	North Street	B3
Grange Road	B5-B6	Spring Gardens	A1	North Mills Road	B4
Great George Street	A3-B3-B4	Spring Road	B1	Osbourne Road	B4
Greenhill Road	B6-C6	Stavordale Road	A3	Parsonage Road	A4
Hanover Road	A6	Town Bridge	A2-B2	Pasture Way	C1
Hardwick Street	A5-B5	Trinity Road	B2	Princess Road	A1-A2
High Street	A2	Trinity Terrace	A2-B2	Priory Lane	A2
Hope Street	B1-B2	Victoria Street	B5	Rax Lane	B2-B3
Horsford Street	B1-B2	Walpole Street	A5-B5	Rope Walks	A2
Kempston Road	A1-B1	Waterloo Place	B5-B6	St Andrews Road	C3
King Street	A4-B4	Wesley Street	A4	St Michael's Lane	A2-A3
Kirkleton Avenue	A6-B6	Westerhall Road	B6	St Swithin's Avenue	A4
Lennox Street	A5-B5	Westham Road	A3-B3	St Swithin's Road	A3-A4-B4
Love Lane	A1-A2	Westway Road	A2-A3	Sea Road	B1-C1-C2
Lower Bond Street	A3-B3	William Street	B5-B6	Sea Road North	C2-C3
Lower St Alban Street	A2-B2	Wyke Road	A1	Slades Grove	C1
Maiden Street	B2-B3			South Street	B1-B2
Market Street	B2	**Bridport**		Sparacre Gardens	B3-C3
Maycroft	A1	Alexandra Road	A1-A2	Tannery Road	A2-A3
Melcombe Road	B6	Barrack Street	B2-B3-C3	Victoria Grove	A3-B3-B4
Newberry	B1	Beaumont Avenue	C4	West Allington	A3
Newberry Road	B1	Broadmead Avenue	A4	West Street	A3-A2-B3-B2
Newtons Road	B1	Chardsmead Road	B3		
Nicholas Street	A2-A3-B3	Church Street	B2		
North Parade	B2-C2	Claremont Road	C4	**Dorchester**	
North Quay	A2	Coneygar Lane	C4	Acland Road	C3-C4
Nothe Walk	C2	Coneygar Road	B4-C4	Albert Road	A3-A4
Oakley Place	B1	Crock Lane	C1-C2	Alexandra Road	A2
Orion Road	A1	Delapre Gardens	C3	Alfred Road	B1
Park Drive	A3-A4	Downes Street	B2-B3	All Saints Road	C3
Park Street	A3-A4-B4	East Road	C2	Ashley Road	B1
Penny Street	A5	East Street	B2-C2	Bridport Road	A4
Portway Close	A1	Elizabeth Avenue	A1	Charles Street	B2-B3-C3
Queen Street	B4-B5	Folly Mill Lane	B2	Coburg Road	A1
Radipole Park Drive	A4-A5-A6				

Colliton Street	B4
Cornwall Road	A2-A3-A4
Cromwell Road	B1
Culliford Road	C1-C2
Damers Road	A2-A3
Durngate Street	B3-C3
Edward Road	A1-A2
Fairfield Road	A2-B2
Friary Hill	C4
Friary Lane	C4
Frome Terrace	C4
Glyde Path Road	B4
Great Western Road	A2-B2
High Street	C4-C3
High East Street	B4-C4
High West Street	A4-B4
Icen Way	C2-C3-C4
Lancaster Road	C2
Linden Avenue	C3
London Road	C4
Maumbury Road	A1-A2
Monmouth Road	A1-B1-C1
North Square	B4
Orchard Street	C4
Poundbury Road	A4
Princes Street	A3-B3-B4
Prince of Wales Road	B2-C2-C1
Queens Avenue	A1
Rothesay Road	B1
St Helens Road	A3
South Street	B2-B3-B4
South Court Avenue	B1-C1
South Walks Road	B2-C2-C3
The Grove	A4
Trinity Street	B2-B3-B4
Victoria Road	A2-A3
West Walks	A3
West Mills Road	A4
Weymouth Avenue	A1-A2-B2
Weymouth Road	A1
Wollaston Road	C3
York Road	C2

WEYMOUTH
Little has changed along the town's seafront since George III first came to the resort in the late 18th century to try out a new-fangled contraption called a bathing machine. A statue of the King stands on the esplanade.

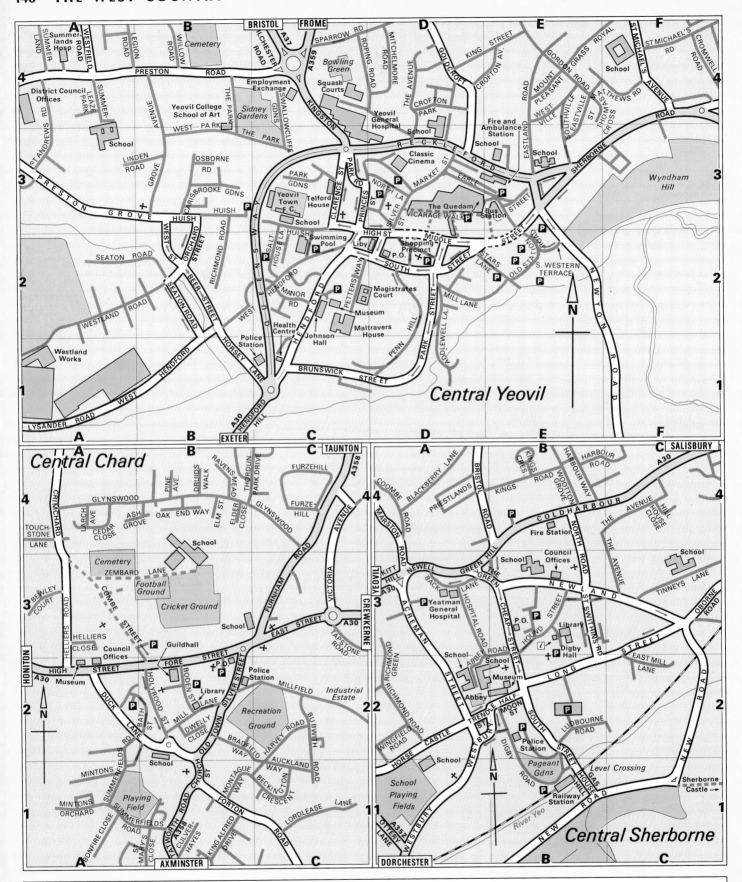

Central Yeovil

Central Chard

Central Sherborne

Yeovil

Home of the Westland helicopter and aircraft factory — as a result of which it suffered bomb damage in the Second World War — and six miles south of the Fleet Air Museum at Yeovilton, the market town of Yeovil is also known for its more homely glovemaking. There is a fine 14th-century church, and a collection of firearms and local interest items at Hendford Manor.

Sherborne Full of medieval buildings built in the golden Ham Hill stone, Sherborne has a magnificent, mainly 15th-century, abbey church. Of the town's two public schools, the 1550 boys' school occupies some of the abbey buildings, and the abbey gatehouse has a museum.

East of the town are two castles: a Norman structure which was partly destroyed after the Civil War, and the 'new' castle, a fine Elizabethan house built and occupied by Sir Walter Raleigh, and full of treasures.

Chard was the scene of one of Judge Jeffreys' Bloody Assizes, held in the courthouse (built 1590) here after the Monmouth Rebellion of 1685. The town's grammar school was founded in 1671, the Choughs Hotel is Elizabethan and the porticoed Town Hall dates back to 1834. All stand in the main street, from which streams flow north to the Bristol Channel and south to the English Channel — at 400ft (122m), this is the county's highest town.

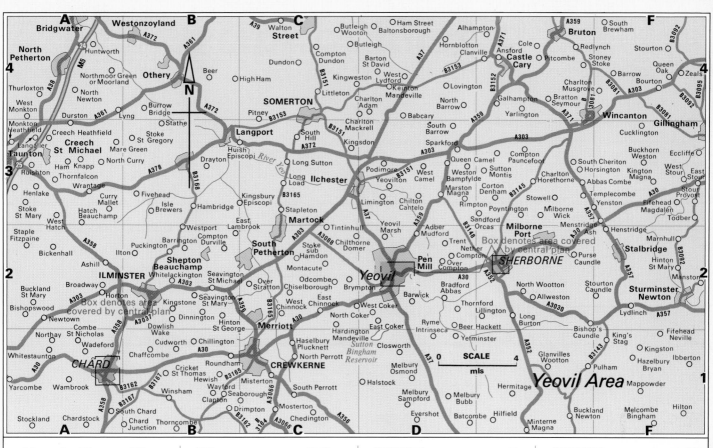

Key to Town Plan and Area Plan

Town Plan

AA Recommended roads	
Restricted roads	
Other roads	
Buildings of interest	Library
Car Parks	P
Parks and open spaces	
Churches	†

Area Plan

A roads	
B roads	
Locations	Terry's Green ○
Urban area	

Street Index

Yeovil

Addlewell Lane	D1-D2
Beer Street	B2
Brunswick Street	C1-D1
Carisbrooke Gardens	B3
Clarence Street	C3
Crofton Avenue	D4-E4
Crofton Park	D4
Cromwell Road	F4
Earle Street	D3-E3
Eastland Road	E3-E4
Eastville	E3-E4
Goldcroft	D3-D4
Gordon Road	E4
Grass Royal	E4-F4
Grove Avenue	B3-B4
Hendford	C1-C2
Hendford Hill	B1-C1
High Street	C2-D2
Horsey Lane	B2-B1-C1
Huish	B3-C3
Ilchester Road	C4
King Street	D4-E4
Kingston	C3-C4
Legion Road	A4
Linden Road	A3-B3
Lysander Road	A1
Manor Road	C2
Market Street	D3
Matthews Road	E4-F4
Middle Street	D2-E2-E3
Mill Lane	D2
Mitchelmore Road	D4
Mount Pleasant	E4
Newton Road	E3-E2-F2-F1
North Lane	C3-D3
Old Station Road	E2
Orchard Street	B2-B3
Osborne Road	B3
Queens Way	C1-C2-C3
Park Gardens	C3
Park Road	C3
Park Street	D1-D2
Penn Hill	D1-D2
Petters Way	C2
Preston Grove	A3-B3
Preston Road	A4-B4-C4
Princes Street	C3
Reckleford	C3-D3-E3
Richmond Road	B2-B3
Roping Road	C4-D4
St Andrews Road	A3-A4
St Michael's Avenue	F4
St Michael's Road	F4
St Thomas Cross	E4
Salthouse Lane	C2-C3
Seaton Road	A2-B2-B1
Sherborne Road	E3-F3-F4
South Street	C2-D2
Southville	E3-E4
South Western Terrace	E2
Sparrow Road	C4-D4
Stars Lane	D2-E2
Summerlands	A4
Summerleaze Park	A4
Swallowcliffe Gardens	C3-C4
The Avenue	D3-D4
The Park	B4-B3-C3
Vicarage Walk	D3
West Hendford	A1-B1-B2-C2
West Park	B3
West Street	B2-B3

Westfield Road	A4
Westland Road	A1-A2-B2
Westville	E4
Willow Road	B4

Chard

Ash Grove	A4-B4
Auckland Way	C1
Bath Street	A2-B2
Beckington Crescent	B1-C1
Bewley Court	A3
Boden Street	B2
Bonfire Close	A1
Bradfield Way	B2-C2-C1
Bubwith Road	C1-C2
Cedar Close	A4
Church Street	B1-B2
Combe Street	A3-B3-B2
Crimchard	A3-A4
Culverhayes	B1
Druids Walk	B4
Duck Lane	A2-B2
Dwelly Close	B2
East Street	C3
Elder Close	B4
Elm Street	B4
Fore Street	B2-B3
Forton Road	B1-C1
Furnham Road	C3-C4
Furzehill	C4
Glynswood	A4-B4-C4
Harvey Road	C1-C2
High Street	A2-B2
Helliers Close	A3
Helliers Road	A2-A3
Holyrood Street	B2
King Alfred Drive	B1
Larch Avenue	A4
Lordlease Lane	C1
Mill Lane	B2
Millfield	B2-C2
Mintons	A1
Mintons Orchard	A1
Montague Way	B1
Oak End Way	B4
Old Town	B2
Pine Avenue	B4
Ravensmead	B4
St Mary's Close	B1
Silver Street	B2-B3
Summerfields Road	A2-A1-B1

Tapstone Road	C3
Tatworth Road	B1
Thordun Park Drive	B4-C4
Touchstone Lane	A4
Victoria Avenue	C3-C4
Zembard Lane	A3-B3

Sherborne

Abbey Road	A2-B2-B3
Acreman Street	A2-A3
Back Lane	A4
Blackberry Lane	A4
Bristol Road	A4-B4
Cheap Street	B2-B3
Coldharbour	B4-C4
Coombe Road	A4
Digby Road	B1-B2
East Mill Lane	C2
Gas House Hill	B1
Green Hill	A3-B3-B4
Halfmoon Street	B2
Harbour Road	B4-C4
Harbour Way	B4
Hill House Close	C4
Horse Castle	A1-A2
Hospital Road	A3
Hound Street	B3
Kings Crescent	B4
Kings Road	A4-B4
Kitt Hill	A3
Long Street	B2-C2-C3
Ludbourne Road	B2-C2
Marston Road	A3-A4
New Road	B1-C1-C2-C3
Newell	A3
Newland	B3-B3
North Road	B3-B4
Oborne Road	C3
Ottery Lane	A1
Priestlands	A4
Richmond Green	A2-A3
Richmond Road	A2
St Swithins Road	B2-B3
South Street	B1-B2
The Avenue	C3-C4-B4-C4
The Green	A3-B3
Tinneys Lane	C3
Trendle Street	A2-B2
Westbury	A1-A2-B2
Wingfield Road	A1-A2
Wootton Grove	B4

SHERBORNE
The 'new' castle was built by Sir Walter Raleigh in 1594, and is said to be the place where a servant, horrified at the sight of smoke rising from his newfangled tobacco pipe, promptly doused him with ale to 'put out the fire'.

Legend to Atlas

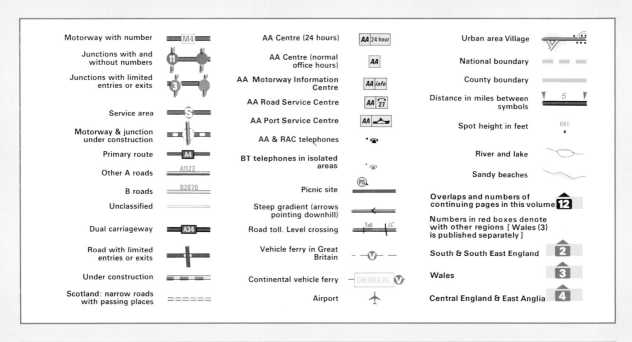

Motorway with number	AA Centre (24 hours)	Urban area Village
Junctions with and without numbers	AA Centre (normal office hours)	National boundary
Junctions with limited entries or exits	AA Motorway Information Centre	County boundary
Service area	AA Road Service Centre	Distance in miles between symbols
Motorway & junction under construction	AA Port Service Centre	Spot height in feet
Primary route	AA & RAC telephones	River and lake
Other A roads	BT telephones in isolated areas	Sandy beaches
B roads	Picnic site	Overlaps and numbers of continuing pages in this volume
Unclassified	Steep gradient (arrows pointing downhill)	Numbers in red boxes denote with other regions [Wales (3) is published separately]
Dual carriageway	Road toll. Level crossing	
Road with limited entries or exits	Vehicle ferry in Great Britain	South & South East England
Under construction	Continental vehicle ferry	Wales
Scotland: narrow roads with passing places	Airport	Central England & East Anglia

Abbey or Cathedral	Coastal Launching Site	Nature Trail
Ruined Abbey or Cathedral	Surfing	Wildlife Park (mammals)
Castle	Climbing School	Wildlife Park (birds)
House and Garden	County Cricket Ground	Zoo
House	Gliding Centre	Forest Drive
Garden	Artificial Ski Slope	Lighthouse
Industrial Interest	Golf Course	Tourist Information Centre
Museum or Collection	Horse Racing	Tourist Information Centre (summer only)
Prehistoric Monument	Show Jumping/Equestrian Centre	Long Distance Footpath
Famous Battle Site	Motor Racing Circuit	AA Viewpoint
Preserved Railway or Steam Centre	Cave	Other Place of Interest
Windmill	Country Park	Boxed symbols indicate tourist attractions in towns
Sea Angling	Dolphinarium or Aquarium	

The National Grid

The National Grid provides a system of reference common to maps of all scales. The grid covers Britain with an imaginary network of 100 kilometre squares. Each square is identified by two letters, *eg* TR. Every 100 kilometre square is then sub-divided into 10 kilometre squares which appear as a network of blue lines on the map pages. These blue lines are numbered left to right 0-9 and bottom to top 0-9. These 10 kilometre squares can be further divided into tenths to give a place reference to the nearest kilometre.

Key to Road Maps

Shetland Islands

Orkney Islands

Outer Hebrides

Stornoway

Ullapool

Portree

Thurso

Wick

Banff

Inverness

Peterhead

Aberdeen

Fort William

Pitlochry

Oban

Perth

Dundee

Edinburgh

Largs

Glasgow

Berwick

Peebles

Campbeltown

Ayr

Dumfries

Newcastle upon Tyne

Stranraer

Workington

Middlesbrough

Isle of Man

Kendal

Scarborough

Douglas

Lancaster

York

Blackpool

Leeds

Hull

Grimsby

Liverpool

Manchester

Sheffield

Caernarfon

Chester

Lincoln

Stoke

Nottingham

King's Lynn

Shrewsbury

Leicester

Norwich

Peterborough

Great Yarmouth

Aberystwyth

Birmingham

Coventry

Northampton

Cambridge

Worcester

Fishguard

Hereford

Felixstowe

Carmarthen

Gloucester

Oxford

Chelmsford

Pembroke

Swansea

170/171

172/173

LONDON

Cardiff

Bristol

Reading

Maidstone

Barnstaple

166/167

168/169

Guildford

Dover

164/165

Salisbury

Folkestone

Taunton

Southampton

158/159

160/161

162/163

Brighton

Newhaven

Exeter

Weymouth

Bournemouth

154/155

Truro

156/157

Plymouth

152/153

Scilly Isles

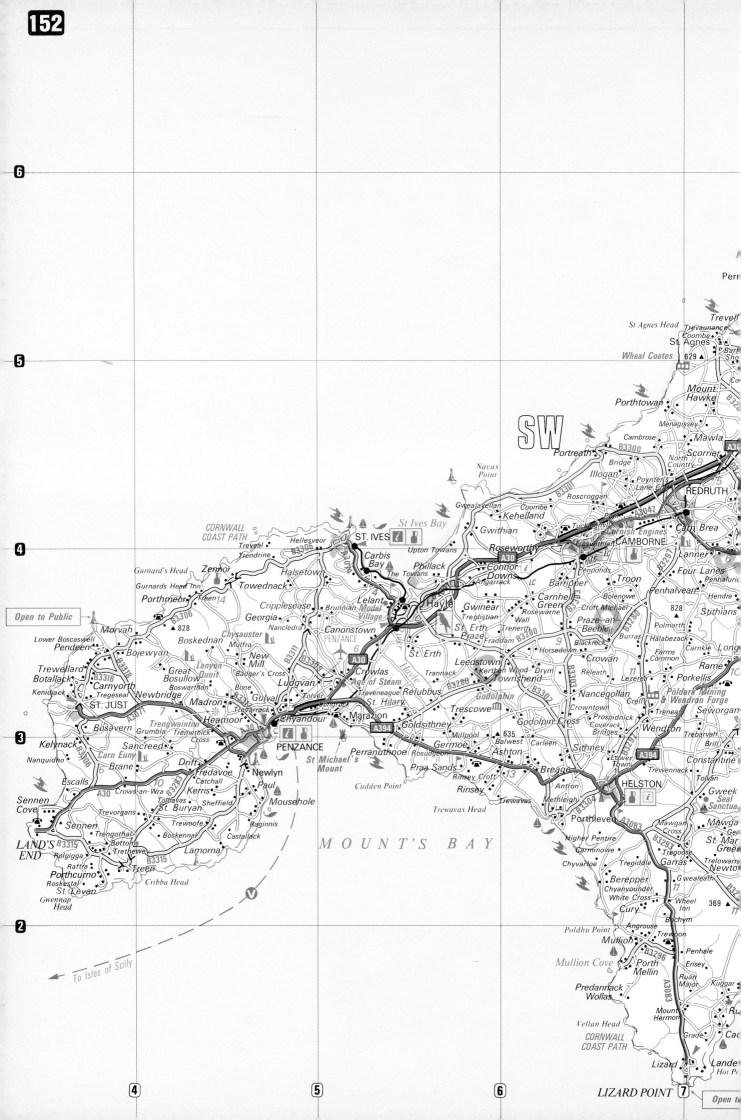

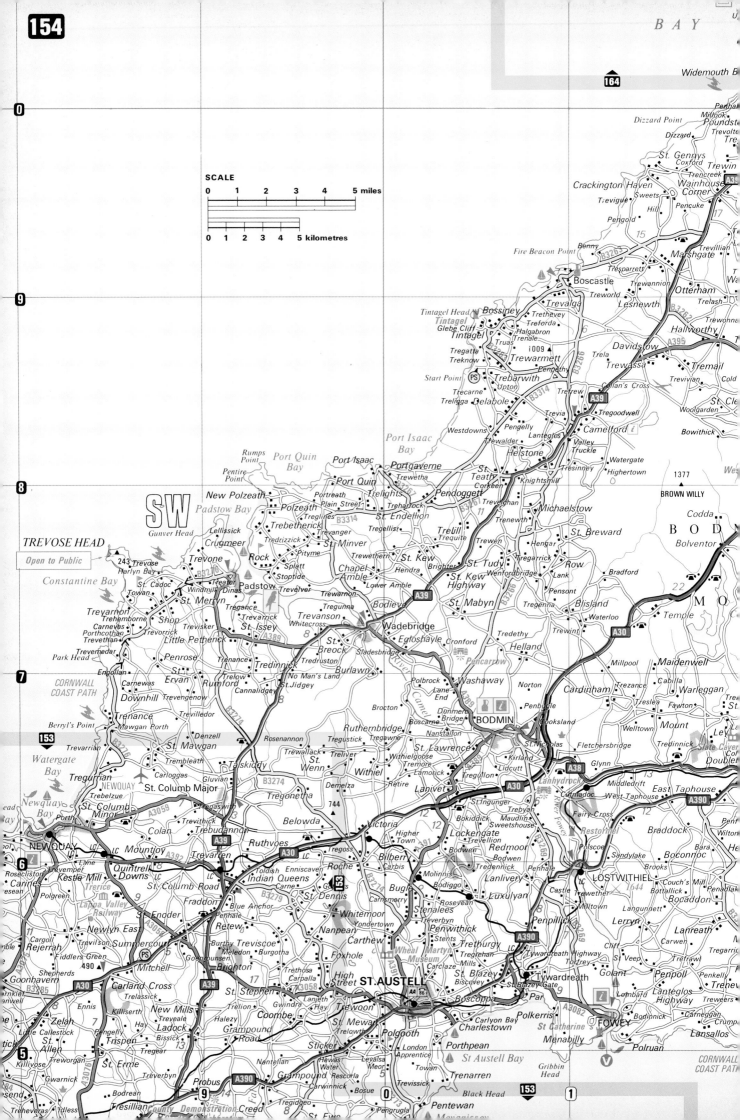

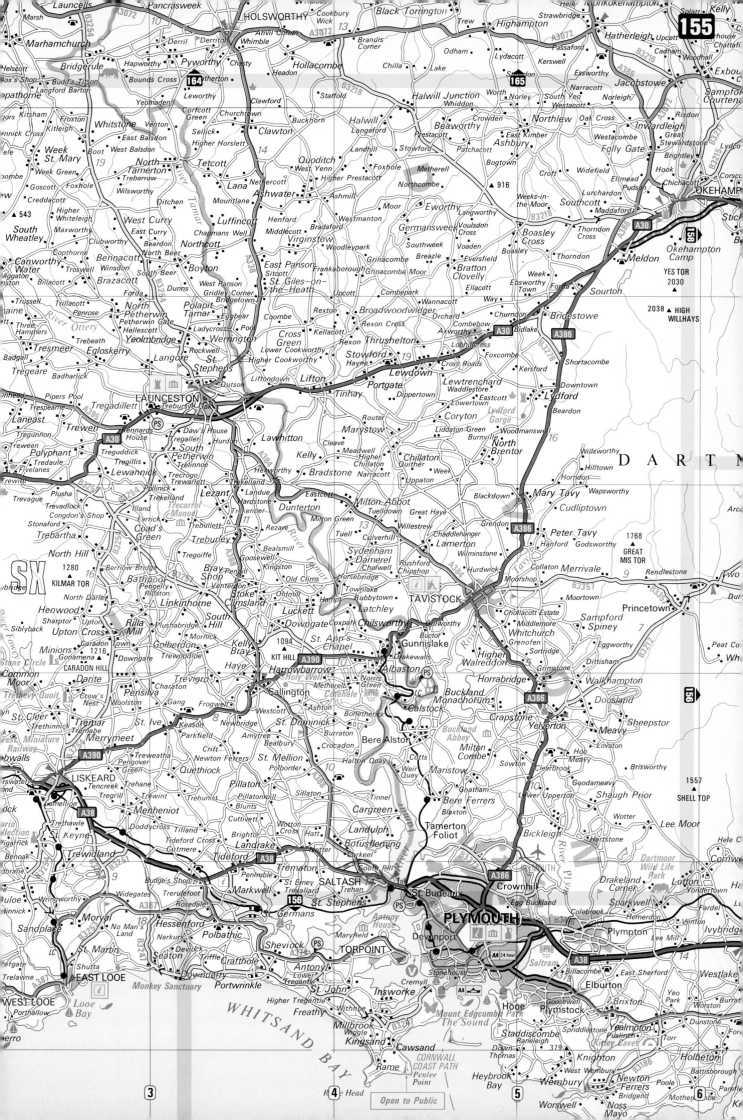

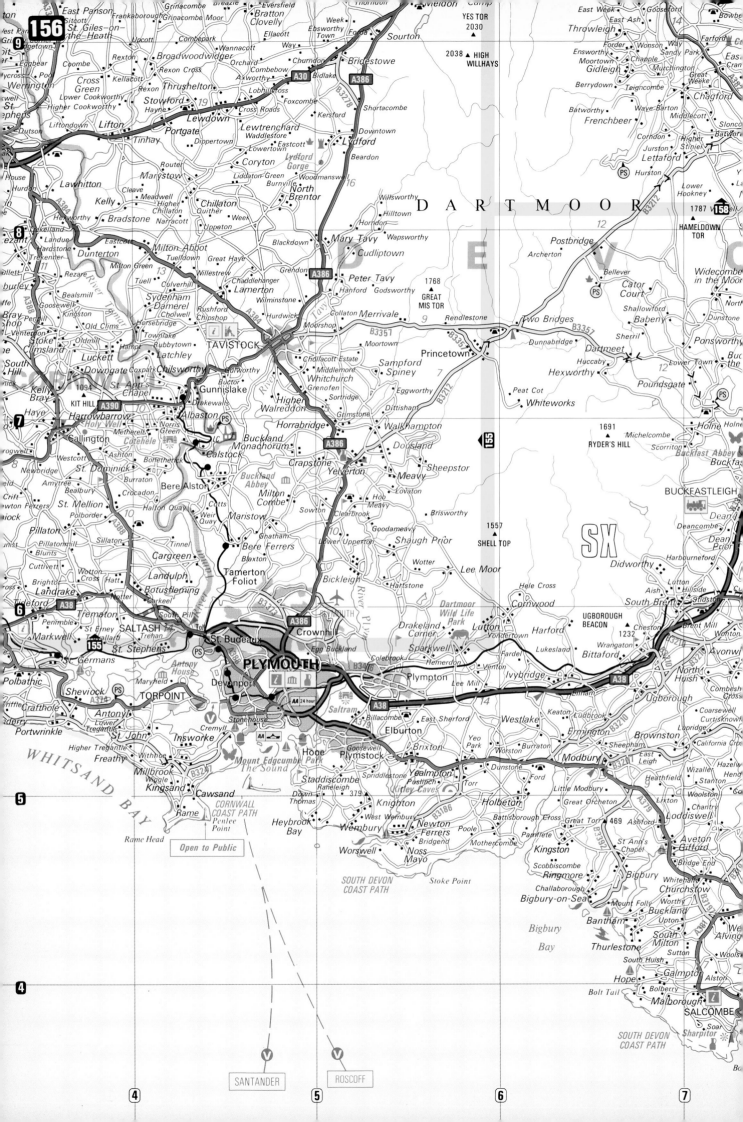

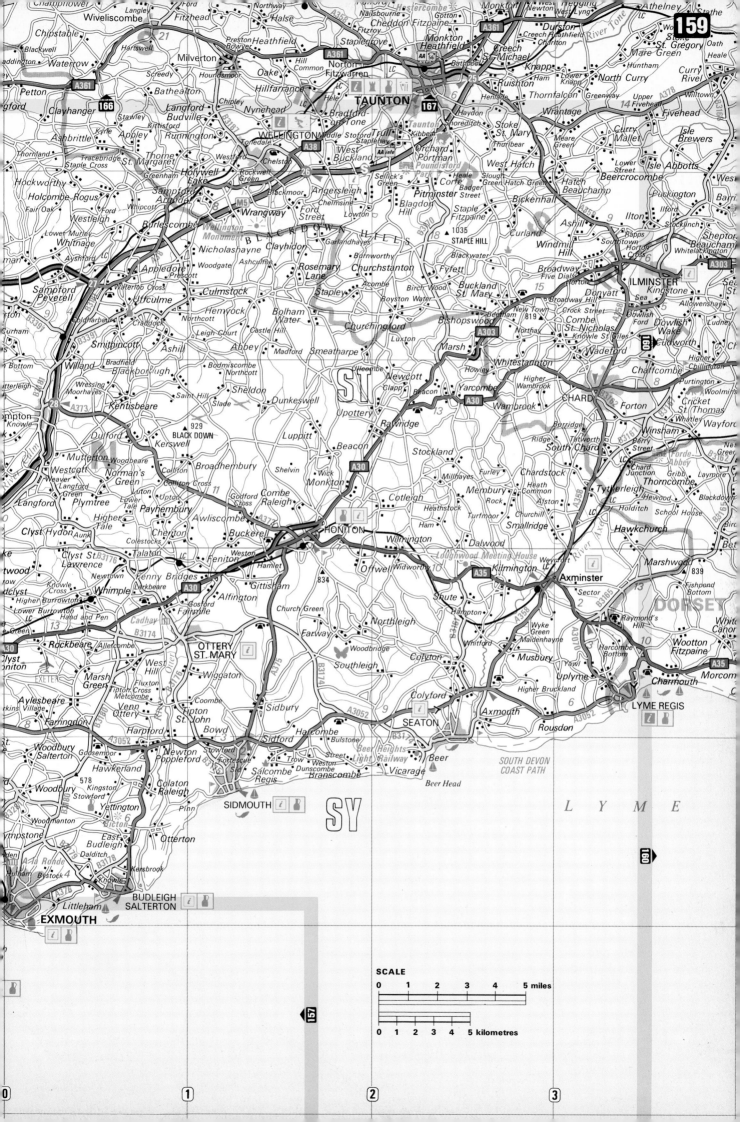

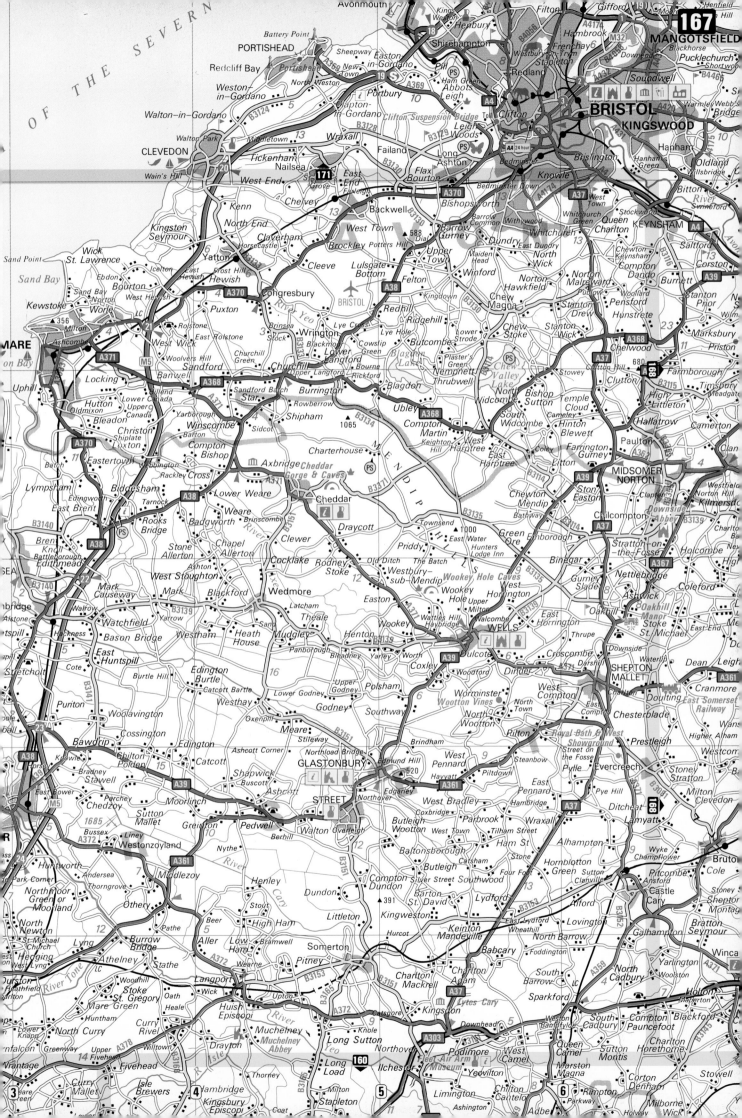

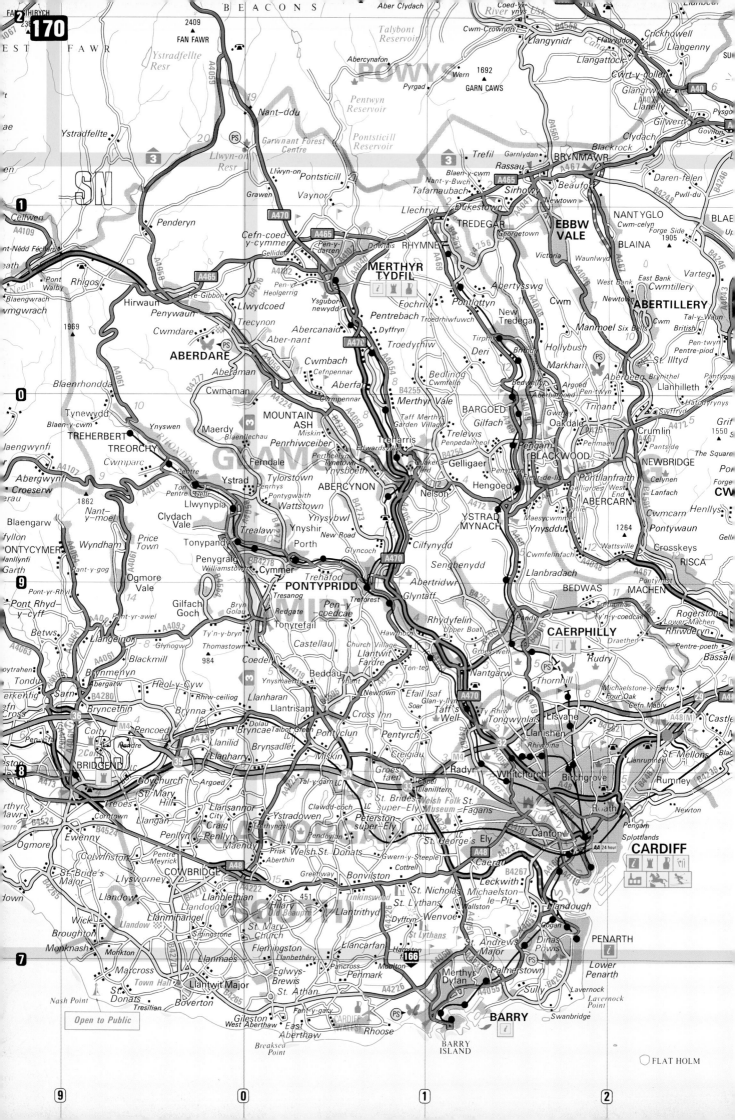

WEST COUNTRY INDEX

As well as the page number of each place name the index also includes an appropriate atlas page number together with a four figure map reference (see National Grid explanation at start of atlas section).

In a very few instances place names appear without a map reference. This is because either they are not shown on the atlas or they lie just outside the mapping area of the region. However, each tour does include a detailed map which highlights the location of all places mentioned on the route.

175

SOUTH
— AND —
SOUTH EAST

*Herstmonceux Castle, East Sussex. Built in the
15th century, the castle was partly demolished
in 1777 and not restored until the
20th century.*

The tiny church of St Thomas-a-Becket is set in isolated fields near the hamlet of Fairfield, Kent. Its interior is almost entirely of timber with box pews and a three-deck pulpit.

Touring South & South East England

CONTENTS

INTRODUCTION

At the heart of the region lies London, surrounded by a wealth of beautiful and interesting places to see. In Kent lie the orchards of the 'Garden of England', Sussex is buttressed against the sea by the line of the majestic South Downs . . . there are the New Forest, Britain's best-loved woodland, and the Chilterns to discover. Along the coast lie historic towns, ports and many popular resorts. Inland are famous cathedral cities such as Canterbury, Chichester, Winchester, the university city of Oxford; and there are castles, too, as at Arundel and Windsor along with great houses like Chartwell, Hampton Court, Hatfield and Blenheim. In London itself the pageantry and splendour of the capital city draws millions of visitors every year.

This is also the territory of Old Father Thames, where boats ply busily to and fro under elegant bridges, past church spires and stately houses.

It is a magnificent touring area with a wide variety of contrasts. While the Isle of Wight, ever popular as a tourist draw, shelters England's premier yachting centre, across the Solent Portsmouth harbours its Royal Naval Base in the shadow of the Downs. Here, too, is the 'Forest by the Sea' where the woods and heaths of the New Forest meet the Solent shore and where ponies and cattle graze on land once hunted by kings. Whether in the creeks and estuaries of the Essex coast or in the rich valleys of Kent, full of fruit orchards and the smell of growing hops, the beauty of the area is waiting to be enjoyed.

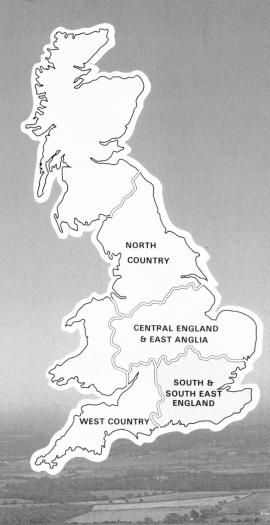

NORTH COUNTRY

CENTRAL ENGLAND & EAST ANGLIA

SOUTH & SOUTH EAST ENGLAND

WEST COUNTRY

ABOUT THE TOURS

Each tour occupies two pages and has a clear map accompanying the text. All the places described in the text are shown in **black** on the tour maps and are described as they occur on the road, linked in sequence by route directions. This precise wayfinding information is set in *italic*.

Castles, stately homes and other places of interest described in the tours are not necessarily open to the public or may be open only at certain times. It is therefore advisable to check the opening times of any place before planning a stop there. Properties administered by the National Trust and the Ancient Monument Scheme (NT and AM) are generally open most of the year, but this should be checked with the relevant organisation, as should precise opening times.

The little village of Fulking lies serenely below the north slopes of the South Downs near Devil's Dyke, a spectacular cleft in the Down's 711-foot crest.

HOW TO FIND THE TOURS

All the motor tours in this part of the book are shown on the key map below and identified by the towns where they start. The tours are arranged in alphabetical order by start town name. Page numbers are also given opposite. Each tour begins at a well-known place, but it is possible to join or leave at any point if more convenient.

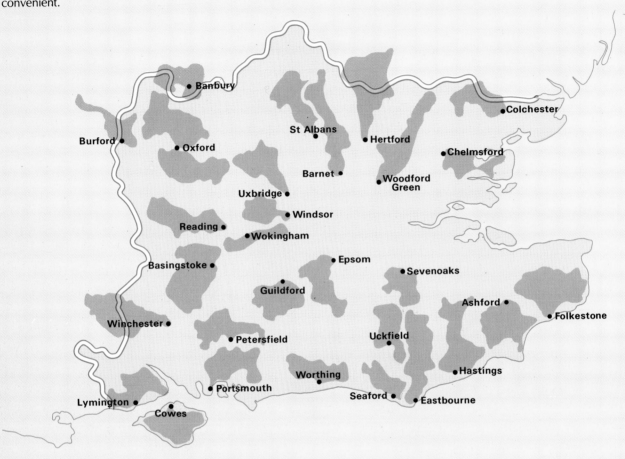

MAPS		Marshland	....	TEXT	
Main Tour Route	═══════	Memorial/Monument	m	AM	Ancient Monument
Detour/Diversion from Main Tour Route	═ ═ ═ ═	Miscellaneous Places of		c	circa
Motorway	════════	Interest & Route Landmarks	■	NT	National Trust
Motorway Access	═②═	National Boundary	....	NTS	National Trust for Scotland
Motorway Service Area	═Ⓢ═	National Trust Property	NT	OACT	Open at Certain Times
Motorway and Junction Under Construction	═╱═	National Trust for Scotland Property	NTS	PH	Public House
A-class Road	A68	Non-gazetteer Placenames	Thames /Astwood	RSPB	Royal Society for the Protection of Birds
B-class Road	B700	Notable Religious Site	✝		
Unclassified Road	unclass	Picnic Site	Ⓟ	SP	Signpost (s) (ed)
Dual Carriageway	A70	Prehistoric Site	ⓘ		
Road Under Construction	= = = =	Racecourse	⊂⊃		
Airport	✈	Radio/TV Mast	⌇		
Battlefield	⚔	Railway (BR) with Station	―●―		
Bridge	⏝	Railway (Special) with Station	┼┼┼┼		
Castle	▯	River & Lake	～		
Church as Route Landmark	✝	Woodland Area	◉		
Ferry	– Ⓥ –	Scenic Area	◉		
Folly/Tower	☗	Seaside Resort	⚓		
Forestry Commission Land	⬧	Stately Home	⌂		
Gazetteer Placename	Zoo /Lydstep	Summit/Spot Height	KNOWE HILL 209 ▲		
Industrial Site (Old & New)	⛭		KNOWE HILL 209 ▲		
Level Crossing	LC	Viewpoint	⌖		
Lighthouse	⚲				

TOURING SOUTH AND SOUTH EAST ENGLAND

Motor Tours
Pages 184-257

ASHFORD, Kent

For hundreds of years Ashford has been a market town for Romney Marsh and the Weald of Kent. Its prime situation at the meeting of the two rivers Stour (East and Great) has made it a natural focus in the past, and its proximity to London has meant new growth as a population 'overspill' town. Today it is an important shopping and touring centre a mere 14 miles from the ancient city of Canterbury and within easy reach of the south Kent beaches. The town's industrial development began in the 19th century with the establishment of large railway works, which have closed. Future development with the channel tunnel project could increase Ashford's importance as a railway interchange. Medieval, Tudor and Georgian houses have survived despite development, and the 15th-century parish church retains much of its original character. The Intelligence Corps Museum at Templar Barracks displays a fascinating array of mementos.

Leave Ashford on the A28 'Tenterden' road, after 1 mile at roundabout take 3rd exit on to an unclassified road to reach Great Chart.

GREAT CHART, Kent

A 14th-century church with a 16th-century pest house in the south corner of its churchyard can be seen here. This long, narrow structure is a timber framed building once used to isolate victims of plagues. Court Lodge, a complete 13th-century stone house, stands near the church.

Continue through the village to rejoin the A28 to Bethersden.

BETHERSDEN, Kent

Marble from this village was used for the altar stairs at Canterbury Cathedral, but many humbler buildings also display its splendour. The quarries are now worked out. Brass memorials to forbears of the 17th-century poet William Lovelace can be seen in the local 14th-century church.

Continue through High Halden to Tenterden.

TENTERDEN, Kent

Typical Wealden houses, *ie* buildings faced with tiles and weather boards, line the broad, grass-verged High Street of this delightful town. Its high situation makes its 15th-century church tower (made of the famous Bethersden marble) visible across the Weald and from many miles out to sea. At one time the tower was used as a beacon to guide shipping. In the 15th century Henry VI admitted Tenterden to the Confederation of Cinque Ports, but the course of the River Rother later changed and the town port was replaced by nearby Smallhythe. Shipbuilding became a major local concern in the 16th century. The museum has various exhibits on the history of local trades and industries. Tenterden is the terminus for the preserved Kent and East railway.

Continue on the A28, drive over a level crossing, and pass the Rolvenden station of the Kent and East Sussex Railway on the left. Drive into Rolvenden.

ROLVENDEN, Kent

Surrounded by well-wooded country, this pleasant combination of weather-boarded (Kentish clad) houses and grass verges is typical of the county. The large 14th-century church preserves two squire's pews, and the restored postmill is a perfect example. Great Maytham Hall, now converted into flats, was designed by Sir Edwin Lutyens in 1910 and stands in gardens that were laid out by landscaper Gertrude Jekyll.

AMONG THE COASTAL MARSHES

Towards the sea the Wealden hills flatten to Romney Marsh, a place of frogs and sheep where church towers can be seen for miles and the threat of flood is constant. At the sea's edge England's Napoleonic defences crumble peacefully, while massive walls repulse the ocean's eternal barrage.

Attractive gardens stretch along the banks of the River Rother at Rye.

Drive to the church and turn left on to the unclassified 'Wittersham' road. Pass through Rolvenden Layne and cross the Rother Levels. Climb on to the Isle of Oxney, an isolated area of high ground. A detour can be made from the main tour route by turning left on to the B2082 to reach Smallhythe Place. Otherwise turn right on to the B2082 and drive to Wittersham.

SMALLHYTHE PLACE, Kent

Half-timbered Smallhythe Place dates from 1480 and was once the home of actress Dame Ellen Terry. It is now a museum displaying her personal relics (NT). The adjacent 15th-century Priest's House shares its grounds with the Barn Theatre.

WITTERSHAM, Kent

Wittersham is a quiet, charming village on the central ridge of the Isle of Oxney, between the River Rother and the Royal Military Canal. During the middle ages the tower of its 14th-century church was used as a shipping beacon. Inside the church is a finely carved lectern of late medieval origin. Wealden buildings comprising a windmill, oast houses, and a timbered cottage make an attractive group 1 mile east.

Proceed on the B2082 to cross the River Rother and continue over the Rother Levels. Pass through Iden, meet the A268, and pass through Playden to reach Rye (near the Royal Military Canal).

ROYAL MILITARY CANAL

Originally a defence against an expected Napoleonic invasion, this canal between Rye and Hythe now offers peaceful towpath walks and boat-hire facilities.

RYE, E Sussex

On a small hill rising out of fenland by the River Rother, this collection of attractive old buildings and cobbled streets was one of two Ancient Towns attached to the Cinque Ports. As such it was heavily fortified against the medieval French. This maritime importance seems odd today, but at that time Rye was almost encircled by sea. Its influence declined when the harbour silted up in the 16th century, and today the sea has receded. Many historic buildings have survived here, the oldest being probably the Norman and later church, which features a 16th-century clock with an 18ft free-swinging pendulum. Near by is the 13th-century Ypres Tower, which was built as a castle and used as a prison from the 16th to 19th centuries. Nowadays it holds nothing more sinister than a museum of local history. Weather-boarded and tile-hung houses, generally with timber frames, can be seen in Mermaid Street, Church Square, Watchbell Street, and High Street. The Mermaid Inn opened in 1420 and is possibly the oldest in the country. From the same century are The Flushing Inn, Stone House, Old Hospital, and Fletcher's House. Peacock's School was built in 1636, and 18th-century Lamb House (NT) was the home of novelist Henry James. Parts of the town walls remain, but 14th-century Landgate (AM) is the only original entry. The town stands on a small hill.

A detour can be made from the main tour route to Camber Castle by taking the A259 'Hastings' road.

CAMBER CASTLE, E Sussex

This ruined 16th-century coastal defence fort was one of several built in Kent by Henry VIII as a deterrent to the French navy.

The weather-boarded buildings in Tenterden's superb High Street are typical of the Kentish Weald.

Rolvenden's painstakingly restored windmill.

DUNGENESS, Kent

This desolate shingle promontory is the site of a nuclear power station that can be seen for miles over featureless Denge Marsh. A slender lighthouse was built here in 1961 because the old one would be obscured by the power station. The original still stands, slightly inland from its successor. Much of the promontory is taken by a 12,000-acre nature reserve frequented by seabirds and shoreline wildlife.

Innumerable drainage ditches prevent Romney Marsh reverting to its natural state.

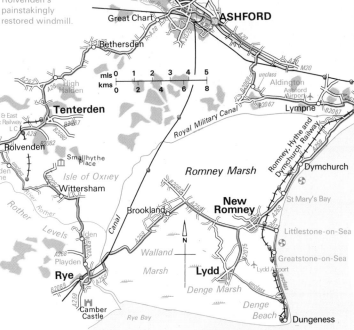

From Rye follow SP 'Folkestone A259' to reach Brookland, crossing the flat expanse of Walland Marsh on the way. Water is drained from the land by channels that crisscross the area on both sides of the route.

BROOKLAND, Kent

The 13th- to 15th-century church at Brookland displays an unusual wood and shingle belfry, and houses a Norman font thought to be unique in Britain. The latter is decorated with signs of the Zodiac and little vignettes depicting various seasonal activities.

Continue on the A259 for 1¼ miles, meet crossroads, and turn right. In 4 miles turn right again on to the B2075 'Lydd' road to reach Lydd.

LYDD, Kent

Like Rye, Lydd was once a coastal town, but it now lies a good 3 miles inland. Its 14th-century church has a 130ft tower and has been described as the 'Cathedral of Romney Marsh'. A 140-acre water sports centre is on the outskirts of the town.

Proceed to the edge of Lydd, cross a railway bridge, then branch left on to the unclassified 'Dungeness' road. Shortly turn left again. To the right of the road are Denge Marsh and Denge Beach. After 3 miles (beyond Lydd) turn right to reach Dungeness.

ROMNEY, HYTHE, AND DYMCHURCH RAILWAY, Kent

Dungeness is the southern terminus of a 13½-mile narrow-gauge line which is claimed to be the world's smallest public railway. Steam trains run from Hythe, through New Romney, and along the seaward fringe of Romney Marsh to Dungeness.

Return along the unclassified road for 1 mile, then turn right and follow SP to reach Greatstone and Littlestone-on-Sea. At Littlestone-on-Sea turn left on to the B2071 to reach New Romney.

NEW ROMNEY, Kent

One of the ancient Cinque Ports but now 1 mile inland from the sea, New Romney's harbour was destroyed in 1287 by a violent storm which changed the course of the River Rother. Thanks to William Morris the town's Norman and later church was rescued from insensitive restoration in 1878.

Continue through New Romney and turn right on to the A259 'Folkestone' road to cross Romney Marsh.

ROMNEY MARSH, Kent

Most of this 204-square-mile tract has been reclaimed from the sea by drainage work started in Roman times. Flooding is an ever-present threat, as much of the area is still below sea level at high tide, but the land is too fertile to waste and the Marsh is famous for its wool. Tulip-growing is a newly developed local industry.

Continue through St Mary's Bay to reach Dymchurch.

DYMCHURCH, Kent

Situated on the edge of Romney Marsh, this old port is guarded by an ancient sea wall and was once a centre for smugglers. It is now a resort with vast stretches of sand and a variety of historic buildings. One of several Martello towers (AM) along the coast, built as defences against Napoleon, has been restored and houses a small exhibition site.

Continue beside the sea wall to Hythe.

Amongst the steam locomotives which operate on the Romney, Hythe, and Dymchurch Railway are two miniature versions of Canadian Pacific engines.

HYTHE, Kent

This Cinque Port is now a well-known resort. Just north is Saltwood Castle, a well-preserved medieval garrison fort complete with battlement walk, undercroft, armoury, and torture chamber

Leave Hythe by the A261 'Ashford' road and in 1 mile turn left on to the B2067 'Lympne' road. Proceed to Lympne.

LYMPNE, Kent

Views over Romney Marsh and the Channel extend from Lympne Castle, which was built and variously extended from Norman times to the 15th century. The Port Lympne Zoo Park, Mansion and Gardens affords an interesting visit.

Leave Lympne on the 'Tenterden' road B2067 and in 2½ miles bear right on to the unclassified 'Aldington' road. Continue to Aldington and turn right in the village on to the B2069 'Ashford' road passing pleasant woodland and cross a railway. After ¾ mile (from the railway) turn left on to the A20. Follow SP 'Ashford' to finish the tour.

BANBURY, Oxon

'Ride a cock-horse to Banbury Cross' begins the nursery rhyme, which, with the fame of Banbury's cakes, has made the name of this town a household word. The deliciously spicy cakes first appear in town records from the 16th century, and can still be bought freshly baked here. However, the original Banbury Cross was destroyed in a Puritanical frenzy of 1602; the cross now standing in the town centre was erected in 1859. A beautiful old church went the same way — rather than restore it, the inhabitants blew it up in 1792 and replaced it with the present rather stark neo-Classical building. Similarly the old castle disappeared stone by stone, dismantled by the townsfolk to repair damage suffered by the town in 2 Civil War sieges. Despite these depredations, Banbury is a town of great charm, and although a thriving industrial, marketing and shopping centre, the character of its ancestry can be found in the twisting little medieval streets, old houses and inns — especially the gabled, half-timbered Reindeer Inn with mullion windows, in Parsons Street.

Leave Banbury on the A361 and continue to Bloxham.

BLOXHAM, Oxon

From the bridge over the stream, on whose banks grow alder and willow, ironstone houses spread up the valley walls, on one side to the 14th-century church and on the other to a hill crowned by the Victorian buildings of a public school. The old streets and houses in the centre are so closely pressed together they discourage modern additions, and so Bloxham has remained unspoilt and interesting.

At the end of the village turn left on to the Adderbury road, then left again into Milton Road. Pass the edge of Milton, then in 1 mile turn left for Adderbury. Turn left again on to the A423, then right on to the A41, SP 'Aylesbury,' and continue to Aynho.

AYNHO, Northants

On either side of the street apricot trees shade the weathered walls of stone cottages set back in unfenced gardens. The golden fruit of these trees was required by the Lord of the Manor as a toll. The recipients of the apricots were, for nearly 350 years, the Cartwright family, who lived in Aynho Park (OACT), a 17th-century mansion. Monuments to the Cartwrights feature in the church, below whose splendid tower are the village square, shops and a row of thatched cottages, built, like most of Aynho, of local limestone.

¾ mile beyond Aynho, branch left on to the B4031, SP 'Buckingham', for Croughton.

'TO BANBURY CROSS'

Cut the corners of 3 shires, Oxfordshire, Northamptonshire and Warwickshire, gathering a taste of each while passing through truly English villages — satellites to Banbury, an old country town famous for its cakes and a children's nursery rhyme.

CROUGHTON, Northants

Croughton stands on the Oxfordshire border with an American Air Force base for company. Within the peaceful church are late 13th-century wall paintings, which were not discovered until 1930. Although unfortunately damaged by an unsuccessful attempt at protecting them with a layer of wax, these famous paintings are still reasonably clear, and include illustrations of the Flight into Egypt and the Epiphany.

Continue on the B4031 for 2 miles, then turn left on to the A43 for Brackley.

BRACKLEY, Northants

Although a busy place these days, Brackley, with a long tradition of fox-hunting, has retained its pleasant country town atmosphere. In the past, a number of important visitors have stayed here; in 1215 the Barons gathered in Brackley Castle (since demolished) to discuss the Magna Carta before meeting with King John, and Simon de Montfort tried to negotiate with Henry III's messengers here. The Earl of Leicester founded the Hospital of St John and St James in the 12th century, and his heart was buried in the chapel — only to be carelessly thrown away by a 19th-century workman who discovered a lead casket and threw away the 'bit of old leather' he found inside it. The Hospital, bought by Magdalen College, Oxford, in the 15th century, is now a well-known school and the chapel is one of the oldest school chapels in Britain.

Continue through Brackley and ¾ mile beyond the town turn left, SP 'Helmdon and 'Sulgrave', and continue to Helmdon. Here cross the bridge and turn left to Sulgrave. A detour (½ mile) can be made by turning right in Sulgrave for Sulgrave Manor.

Banbury Cross is adorned by statues of Queen Victoria, Edward VII and George V

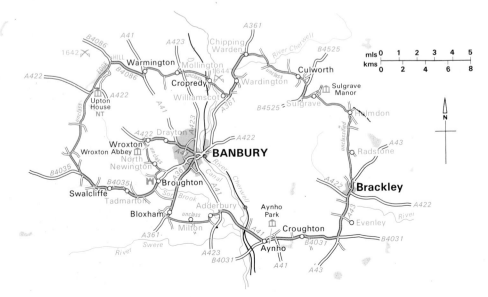

SULGRAVE MANOR, Northants
The forbears of American President George Washington lived in the Queen Anne north wing of Sulgrave Manor (OACT) between 1539 and 1610. The south wing was added in 1921, the same year the house opened its doors to the public. Carved above the porch entrance is the original American flag, 3 stars and 2 stripes, and in the hall hangs perhaps the most treasured possession of the house, an original oil painting of George Washington. Other relics include Washington's black velvet coat and a fragment of his wife's wedding dress. In the house there are great fireplaces, complete with their ancient implements; the original four-poster bed in the main bedroom; and a fascinating kitchen. The 14th-century church is closely linked to the manor and the Washington family, and includes the tomb of Laurence Washington, who built the house.

Continue on the Culworth road through Sulgrave, and in 1 mile turn right on to the B4525. In ½ mile turn left, SP 'Culworth', and at the T-junction turn left into Culworth.

CULWORTH, Northants
Culworth once had its own market and fair, but only a grocer's sign of a sugar-loaf and birch broom on a house by the green recalls these past days of importance. Charles I stayed in the village before the battle of Cropredy Bridge, and in the 18th-century the less respectable Culworth Gang, an infamous bunch of thieves, used it as their headquarters. The church has a tombstone of a negro slave who died in 1762 at the age of 16.

Continue for 1 ¾ miles, then turn right and later turn left for Chipping Warden. Join the A361 for Wardington, then in 1 mile turn right, SP 'Cropredy', and skirt the hamlet of Williamscot before reaching Cropredy.

CROPREDY, Oxon
Charles I won an early victory in Cropredy during his fight to keep the monarchy; a battle remembered by the 2 suits of armour hanging on the wall of an aisle in the spacious church. Chief among the church's treasures is the brass lectern, adorned by a glittering eagle. When the king came to fight his battle, the villagers hid the lectern in the River Cherwell for safety. Years later it was recovered, but one of the 3 brass lions which stand at the foot of the pedestal was missing. Another was made of bronze, which is why 2 lions shine brightly and the other is dull.

At the Brasenoes Arms PH in Cropredy, turn right, and in ¼ mile turn left, SP 'Mollington'. Later go over staggered crossroads into Mollington and continue to Warmington.

WARMINGTON, Warwicks
Warmington lies in rich farmland at the foot of Edgehill. Its cottages are gathered about a green, complete with a pond and sheep-dip, and nearby stands the Elizabethan gabled manor house of the village. Above the green the small brown-stone church is set on a steeply-sloping churchyard sheltered by shady pines. This was where soldiers killed in the Battle of Edgehill in 1642 were buried. The battle was the first in the Civil War between the Royalists and the Parliamentarians.

On entering Warmington bear left and cross the green and turn left on to the A41, then turn sharp right again on to the B4086, SP 'Kineton'. Continue for 2 miles with fine views from the Edge Hill plateau then turn left at a T-junction, SP 'Edge Hill'. Follow the hill for a further 1 ¾ miles before reaching the A422. From here a short detour can be made by turning left to Upton House.

A typical cottage in Culworth village

The great hall at Sulgrave Manor was part of the original house

UPTON HOUSE, Warwicks
A wealthy London merchant of James I's reign built Upton House (NT), but it was not until Lord Bearsted bought the house in 1927 and filled it with an art collection of impeccable taste that Upton became exceptional. For here are kept outstanding paintings of the Flemish and early Netherlands school, the Florentine school, and a particularly fine collection of the English 18th-century school, including works by Stubbs and Hogarth. The exquisite collections of 18th-century porcelain include Sèvres and Chelsea pieces. Upton's delightful gardens include terraces, wooded combes, a lake and a water garden.

The main tour turns right on to the A422, SP 'Stratford', then take the next turning left, SP 'Compton Wynyates'. Continue for 3½ miles to a crossroads and turn left, SP 'Banbury'. In 1 mile turn left on to the B4035 for Swalcliffe.

SWALCLIFFE, Oxon
William of Wykeham, founder of New College, Oxford (1324-1404) and a builder of cathedrals, built the lofty and buttressed tithe barn in Swalcliffe. An impressive arch of cathedral proportions opens into the massive interior, where great roof beams can be seen in the half-light. A fine church and manor house overlook the tumble of thatched cottages clustered about a hollow.

Continue on the B4035 through Tadmarton to Broughton. Here turn left, SP 'North Newington', then bear right past the entrance to Broughton Castle.

BROUGHTON CASTLE, Oxon
Broughton Castle (OACT) was last 'modernised' in about 1600, when the medieval fortified manor house of Sir John de Broughton was transformed into an Elizabethan manor by the Fiennes family. The improvements beloved by Victorians never took place because the 15th Baron was a notorious reveller and spendthrift, so no money was left for building. Indeed, the contents of the castle were auctioned to raise money in 1837, including the swans on the wide moat which surrounds the house. Across the bridge, through the battlemented gateway, great fireplaces, airy rooms, elaborate plaster ceilings and vaulted passages echo the past.

Shortly bear right again, then in ½ mile turn left for North Newington. Here turn right, SP 'Wroxton', then in 1¼ miles turn right on to the A422 and skirt the village of Wroxton.

WROXTON, Oxon
Mellowed, brown-stone cottages, many thatched, are overshadowed by Wroxton Abbey (OACT), a beautiful 17th-century house built on the foundations of a 13th-century Augustinian priory. The house possesses 3 paintings by Holbein and one by Zucchero, and of a more domestic nature, a quilt sewn by Mary, Queen of Scots.

Continue on the A422 through Drayton, then join the A41 for the return to Banbury.

BARNET, Gt London
Several charmingly-rural areas have survived here in spite of the capital's appetite for building land. Mill Hill has picturesque weather-boarded houses set neatly on the green ridge from which it takes its name. A 2-mile expanse of unspoilt countryside extends from Cockfosters to Monken Hadley, and Hadley Woods are delightful.

Leave Barnet Church with SP 'Hatfield, A1000'. After ¼ mile pass through Hadley Green.

HADLEY GREEN, Gt London
Hadley Common and Hadley Green meet at St Mary's Church, a 15th-century building of flint and ironstone, topped by an 18th-century copper beacon. Various Georgian houses and cottages cluster round the fringes of the green in a very village-like way.

Continue to Potters Bar, passing the Battle of Barnet (1471) Obelisk to the right. Meet crossroads and drive forward to pass the BBC radio station at Brookman's Park. In 2 miles bear left for Hatfield. Then forward at roundabout, in ½ mile bear left for Hatfield, at next roundabout forward passing the entrance to Hatfield House (right).

HATFIELD, Herts
Ancient Hatfield preserves many interesting buildings from its long history as a market town, not the least of which is the Tudor palace of Cardinal Moreton. Even this, however, with its Elizabeth I and Mary associations, is overshadowed by the famous and spectacular pile of Hatfield House (open). A chapel of the owners of the house, can be seen in the local church.

Proceed through Old Hatfield and meet traffic lights. Turn right here SP 'Hertford', then within ¼ mile cross a flyover and turn left to join the A414. A detour can be made from the main tour route by keeping forward on the A1000 and crossing the River Lee to Welwyn Garden City.

WELWYN GARDEN CITY, Herts
Although not the earliest of its kind in England (that honour belongs to Letchworth), Welwyn Garden City was begun in 1919 and represents an attempt to influence the living conditions of ordinary people.

Continue with the A414. In 2 miles enter a roundabout and leave by the 1st exit. After about 1 mile reach Cole Green and take the 2nd turning left on to an unclassified road SP 'Welwyn, B1000'. Continue for 1¼ miles and turn left to join the B1000. In another ¼ mile turn right on to an unclassified road across the River Mimram SP 'Archers Green'. At the end of this turn right for Tewin.

AN UNSUSPECTED COUNTRYSIDE

Major highways following ancient Roman routes carry new towns and overspill developments deep into the countryside north of London. Between them, unsuspected by their traffic, are quiet rural areas where wood and parkland insulate splendid mansions from the modern rush.

TEWIN, Herts
Tewin lies in wooded countryside above the charming River Mimram, east of the impressive 19th-century Digswell railway viaduct. Close by is beautifully-preserved Elizabethan Queen Hoo Hall.

Proceed to the green in Tewin and keep left for Burnham Green. Drive over crossroads for Woolmer Green.

WOOLMER GREEN, Herts
Local St Michael's Church, built in the late 19th century, was meant to incorporate a tower that was never erected.

Turn right on to the B197 and follow part of the old Great North Road to Knebworth.

KNEBWORTH, Herts
Several examples of the accomplished early 20th-century architect Lutyens' work can be seen in New Knebworth, including the Church of St Martin, Golf Club House, and 'Homewod'.

Meet crossroads and turn left on to an unclassified road SP 'Old Knebworth'. Pass under a railway bridge and turn right. After 1 mile Knebworth House lies to the right.

KNEBWORTH HOUSE, Herts
Among many fine paintings and relics displayed in this large house (open) are manuscripts belonging to historian Edward Bulwer Lytton, who lived here. The origins of the house itself are in the 15th century, but the building shows later influence. The grounds now form a Country Park.

Keep left with the 'Codicote' road and in ¼ mile turn right SP 'Kimpton and Whitwell'. Continue, then turn right on to the B656 SP 'Hitchin' and shortly pass the Vanstone Garden Centre on the left. Continue for 4¼ miles, passing a road on the right leading to St Ippollitts.

ST IPPOLLITTS, Herts
By all accounts St Ippollitts was a man skilled in the treatment of horses. The local church was rebuilt in 1879 from old materials.

Continue into Hitchin.

HITCHIN, Herts
Tilehouse Street and Bridge Street preserve the best of Hitchin's older houses, but many other features survive in this medieval wool town. The ancient market square and moated Hitchin Priory, the latter dating from the 1770s, are reminders of a prosperous past. Features of the town church include a fine old porch and good screenwork.

Leave the town by the A600 Bedford road. Continue to Henlow Camp.

HENLOW CAMP, Beds
Long-renowned as a flying centre, Henlow Camp is an RAF establishment situated some 2 miles south of the village from which it derives its name.

Drive to a roundabout and go forward. In 1¼ miles meet crossroads and turn right on to an unclassified road for Clifton.

CLIFTON, Beds
A large 16th-century alabaster monument to Sir Michael Fisher and his wife is in Clifton Church.

Turn left, then immediately right, SP 'Stanford'. In ¼ mile pass the church and turn left. Cross the River Ivel Navigation, proceed for ½ mile, and keep right for Stanford. Turn right on to the B658 SP 'Sandy' and keep straight on for Caldecote. Meet crossroads and turn left on to an unclassified road for Ickwell Green.

ICKWELL GREEN, Beds
Perhaps best known for the May Day revels still held round the enormous maypole that rises from its large green, this pretty village boasts several thatched cottages and a smithy where Georgian clockmaker Thomas Tompion once worked.

Turn left SP 'Old Warden' and in ¼ mile meet a T-junction. Turn right and pass Old Warden Airfield.

OLD WARDEN AIRFIELD, Beds
Historical aircraft and veteran cars can be seen in the Shuttleworth Collection at this small airfield, and flying displays are given occasionally.
Take the 'Shefford' road through Old Warden.

OLD WARDEN, Beds
The first Warden pear was grown in this pretty village. Old Warden Park house was built for Sir Joseph Shuttleworth in 1872, and is now used as an agricultural college. Nearby is the attractive Swiss Garden.
After ½ mile meet a T-junction and turn left. Continue for 1 mile, pass under a railway bridge, and turn left. Follow SP 'Shefford' and eventually rejoin the A600. Cross a river and enter Shefford village.

SHEFFORD, Beds
Southill Park, a notable Regency house to the north of Shefford, was rebuilt by Henry Holland in 1800. It was once the home of Admiral Byng, who was unjustly shot for neglect of duty after losing a battle in 1757.

Proceed to traffic signals and turn right on to the A507 SP 'Ampthill'. In 3¼ miles turn left on to an unclassified road SP 'Silsoe'. In 1 mile turn left on to the A6 for Silsoe.

SILSOE, Beds
Silsoe's church is of early 19th-century date, but is a successful attempt at a traditional English church style. Nearby is Wrest Park House and Gardens (open).
Continue to Barton-in-the-Clay.

BARTON-IN-THE-CLAY, Beds
A 16th-century painting of St Nicholas is preserved in the village church. A viewpoint known as the Clappers, including 136 acres of lovely National Trust property crowned by Clappers Wood, rises to the west.
Turn left on to the B655, SP 'Hexton'. Climb on to the Barton Hills and drive to Hexton.

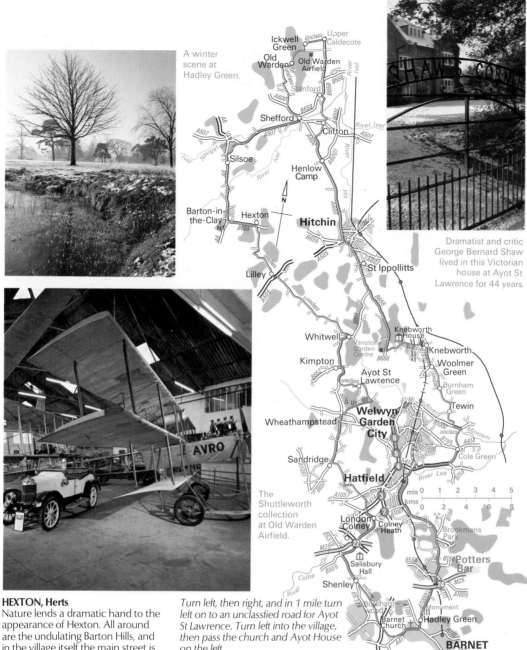

A winter scene at Hadley Green.

Dramatist and critic George Bernard Shaw lived in this Victorian house at Ayot St Lawrence for 44 years.

The Shuttleworth collection at Old Warden Airfield.

HEXTON, Herts

Nature lends a dramatic hand to the appearance of Hexton. All around are the undulating Barton Hills, and in the village itself the main street is lined with laburnums. The 19th-century St Faith's Church is guarded by giant yews.

Meet crossroads and turn right on to an unclassified road leading to Lilley.

LILLEY, Herts

Thomas Jekyll successfully copied a traditional style when he designed the attractive local church in 1870.

Keep forward over all crossroads and enter Whitwell.

WHITWELL, Herts

Brick-and-timber cottages and a charming old inn called The Bull make up this pretty village, set in unspoiled countryside.

Turn right on to the B651 SP 'St Albans', and ascend to the edge of Kimpton.

KIMPTON, Herts

The large flint Church of SS Peter and Paul stands at the north-eastern end of this village and is thought to date from the early 14th century.

Turn left, then right, and in 1 mile turn left on to an unclassified road for Ayot St Lawrence. Turn left into the village, then pass the church and Ayot House on the left.

AYOT ST LAWRENCE, Herts

Author George Bernard Shaw lived at Ayot St Lawrence from 1906 to his death in 1950 and his house – Shaw's Corner (NT) – is preserved as it was in his lifetime. His ashes were scattered in the garden.

Keep right and after 1 mile meet a T-junction. Turn right, then in a further 1½ miles meet another T-junction and turn right on to the B653. Meet a roundabout and leave by the 1st exit on the B651 into Wheathampstead.

WHEATHAMPSTEAD, Herts

Modern industry has come to Wheathampstead, and many of its old cottages are now shops. Sarah Jennings, later the Duchess of Marlborough, is said to have been born at nearby Water End Farm. Features of the village itself include a 13th-century church and the 15th-century Bull Inn.

Continue along the B651 to Sandridge.

SANDRIDGE, Herts

Roman bricks and masonry were used to build a chancel arch in the local Church of St Leonard. Also in the building is a good 14th-century stone rood screen.

Turn left on to an unclassified road SP 'Colney Heath'. In 1 mile turn left at T-junction, and in ½ mile left again. In 1 mile at roundabout forward. Then in a further mile turn right across the dual carriageway and left on an unclassified road for Colney Heath. At roundabout take the 3rd exit SP 'London Colney' and continue.

LONDON COLNEY, Herts

Situated in Salisbury Hall is the interesting Mosquito Aircraft Museum. This contains 3 Mosquitos plus 18 de Havilland aircraft plus many interesting exhibits.

At roundabout take the 2nd exit SP 'Radlett'. A detour may be made from the main tour route by leaving the last-mentioned roundabout by the 1st exit on to the B556 then driving for ½ mile to Salisbury Hall.

SALISBURY HALL, Herts

Red-brick Salisbury Hall was built by Sir John Cuttes, treasurer to Henry VIII, and is encircled by a moat.

Continue and at 2nd roundabout turn left on to the B5378 for Shenley.

SHENLEY, Herts

Nicholas Hawksmoor, the great architect, lived at Porter's Park until his death in 1736. His house now serves as a hospital. Preserved on the village green is the old parish lock-up, once used for petty criminals.

Drive to the end of the village and go forward on to an unclassified road. In 2¼ miles join one-way traffic and follow SP 'Barnet'. Cross a flyover, then turn right and in 1 mile turn left on to the A411. Return to Barnet.

The pavilion in the grounds of Wrest Park at Silsoe dates from 1709.

THE DOWNS AND TROUT STREAMS OF NORTH HAMPSHIRE

Peaceful lanes wind their way across the rolling North Hampshire Downs, then descend through strings of enchanting Saxon villages, where trout streams meander through the chalklands past green watercress beds and banks of wild flowers.

BASINGSTOKE, Hants

A town that is still expanding, Basingstoke was once a pleasant country town, but now it is surrounded by huge housing estates and the centre has been rendered unrecognisable by modern shopping precincts. The older buildings have to be sought out, but among them is the Willis Museum which is a gold mine for all those interested in Hampshire's history and archaeology. A local man, Mr Willis, founded the museum with his collection of clocks: they were his profession and his hobby.

From Basingstoke town centre, or the Ring Road, follow SP 'Aldermaston' to the Aldermaston Road Roundabout. Leave on the A340 and in 2½ miles turn right, SP 'The Vyne (NT)'. In 1½ miles, at the T-junction, turn left (no SP), or, alternatively turn right for a short detour to The Vyne.

THE VYNE, Hants

A lovely Hampshire lane leads down to The Vyne (NT) and a more charming or unpretentious country house would be hard to find. William Sandys, councillor to Henry VI, built it, and his family lived in it for the next century. Chaloner Chute was the subsequent owner and his descendants lived there until 1956. Among the best features of the house are the Gothic ante-chapel, the chapel itself with fine Flemish stained-glass and Italian glazed floor tiles, the sunny oak gallery and the neo-Classical hall and staircase decorated in pale blue and white. All the furniture and furnishings have been collected by the Chute family over several centuries. This redbrick house is set in simple but pleasant grounds; a grassy sward rolls down to the edge of a long narrow lake at the back and fields stretch away beyond. Looking somewhat out of place is the Classical portico overlooking the lake. Dating from 1650, it is the earliest example of a portico found on an English house.

The main tour continues to the edge of Bramley. Here, turn left, SP 'Silchester', and in ¾ mile turn right. In 1¼ miles, at the crossroads, turn left and in ¾ mile branch right, SP 'Silchester Ruins'. Shortly, to the right, is Silchester Calleva Museum.

SILCHESTER CALLEVA MUSEUM, Hants

This museum, housed in the grounds of Silchester rectory, was instituted in 1951 as a contribution to the Festival of Britain. It contains finds from excavations at nearby Silchester — the old Roman town called *Calleva Atrebatum*. Displays of drawings and models represent Silchester as it was in Roman times, namely a market town and a provincial administrative centre with a population of some 4,000.

Continue to the next road junction and keep left, SP 'Aldermaston'. At the end turn right, then immediately right again. In 1 mile cross the main road, then turn left and continue to Aldermaston.

ALDERMASTON, Berks

Despite the huge Atomic Research Station and accompanying housing estates on Aldermaston's doorstep, the village itself has not been marred by modern development. Its main street of colour-washed brick and timbered buildings runs uphill to Aldermaston Court which is barricaded by huge wrought iron gates known as the Eagle Gates. At the bottom of the street is the Hind's Head, an old coaching inn with a distinctive ornate black and gold clock and a gilt weather vane in the shape of a fox.

Turn right on to the A340, and at the Hind's Head PH turn left, SP 'Brimpton'. In 1¼ miles turn right, cross the River Enborne, then turn left. At Brimpton follow the Newbury road, then in 2¼ miles

Cloth used to be cleaned and thickened in the fulling mill at Alresford

turn left. In 1½ miles turn right on to the A339, then in another mile turn left, SP 'Burghclere'.

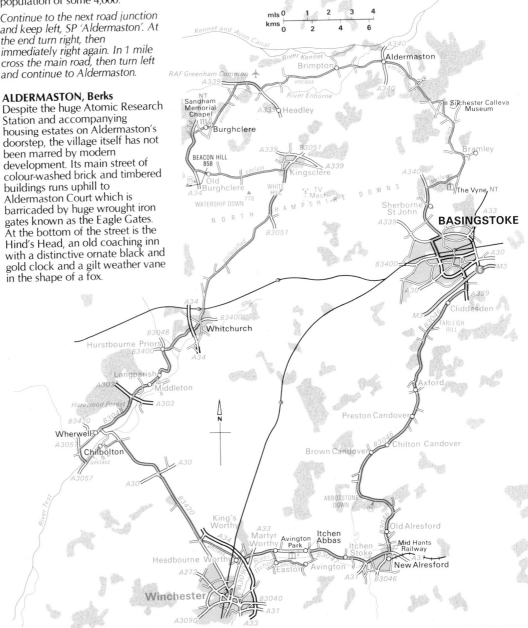

BURGHCLERE, Hants

In 1926 a chapel and 2 almshouses were built in the village of Burghclere to commemorate Henry Willoughby Sandham — a local World War I hero. The tiny Sandham Chapel (NT) is filled with visionary paintings by the English artist Stanley Spencer. Spencer served with the Royal Berkshire Regiment and the paintings here are his reflections of the war.

At the war memorial turn left and after ½ mile pass (right) the Sandham Memorial Chapel. At the A34, turn left, SP 'Winchester'. In 1¾ miles turn left, SP 'Kingsclere'. Ahead, on the A34, is Beacon Hill.

BEACON HILL, Hants

Beacon Hill rises to 858ft and is part of the chalk ridge running from Wiltshire through to Surrey and Kent. This windy, treeless viewpoint is a fine spot for picnicking and flying kites or model aeroplanes.

The main tour continues through the hamlet of Old Burghclere. In ½ mile bear right and follow a pleasant byroad along the foot of the North Hampshire Downs, with Watership Down prominent to the right, to Kingsclere. Here turn right, SP 'Whitchurch', then right again on to the B3051. Climb White Hill (to the left is a picnic area and Hannington TV mast) and continue for 5 miles, then turn left at the main road for Whitchurch.

WHITCHURCH, Hants

Anglers are familiar with the lovely trout-filled River Test and Whitchurch is one of the many villages lying along its valley. Of most interest here is the silk mill. The 18th-century brick building stands, crowned by a small bell tower, on an island in the river. Until the 1930s, when electricity deemed it redundant, water was the sole source of power. A shop (OACT) on the premises sells silk scarves, ties, shirts and so on, as well as an assortment of locally-made products.

At the mini-roundabout in Whitchurch turn right on to the B3400, SP 'Andover', and continue to Hurstbourne Priors. Here, turn left on to the B3048, SP 'Longparish', and follow a winding road along the Test valley to pass through Longparish Beyond the village, at the A303, turn right then immediately left, SP 'Wherwell'. Remain on the B3420 into Wherwell.

WHERWELL, Hants

Elfrida, Saxon queen and mother of King Ethelred, founded a priory in this exceptionally picturesque thatched village. Unfortunately fires destroyed it and the few remains of the replacement nunnery are now part of priory house. The old pronunciation of the village name is 'Orrell'.

Continue through the village on to an unclassified road ahead, SP 'Fullerton'. In 1 mile turn left on to the A3057, then ½ mile further cross the River Test and turn left on to an unclassified road for Chilbolton.

CHILBOLTON, Hants

A huge, shiny, concave disc stands on the downs above Chilbolton on the site of an old airfield. This radio-wave reflector belongs to the Chilbolton Observatory, whose purpose is to discover more about the earth's atmosphere and interplanetary space.

At the end of Chilbolton turn right, SP 'Barton Stacey', then bear left. In ½ mile turn right on to the B3420, SP 'Winchester'. At the A30 turn right, then immediately left, to follow the line of an old Roman road. After 3½ miles, at the roundabout, follow SP 'The Worthy's', for Headbourne Worthy. Here, at the green, keep left then take the next turning right. In ¼ mile turn left on to the A3090 for King's Worthy. At the far end turn left and immediately right on to the B3047, SP 'Alresford'. After a mile, turn right and cross the River Itchen to Easton. At the Cricketers PH turn left and continue to Avington Park.

AVINGTON PARK, Hants

The River Itchen flows along the parkland boundary and its water meadows provide a tranquil setting for the 17th-century mansion (OACT), enhanced by cedar trees, tulip trees and a long avenue of limes. The front of the redbrick house is broken by a large, white, Doric portico on top of which sit 3 goddesses. For several years the house was lived in by the Shelley family. John, brother of the poet Percy, was the first. A previous owner, the Marquess of Caernarvon, built an

The silk mill at Whitchurch has always been a family business employing local women to work the looms

attractive Georgian church in the park and all the woodwork — gallery, reredos, pulpit and box-pews — is carved from rich dark mahogany.

After leaving the park turn left into Avington village. In ¼ mile keep left and recross the River Itchen to reach the edge of Itchen Abbas.

ITCHEN ABBAS, Hants

Itchen Abbas is another of the lovely villages along this valley. With the old mill and the lazy brown trout in the river, it is easy to see why Charles Kingsley was inspired to write *The Water Babies* here. He used to stay at the pub, now rebuilt and called The Plough.

Leave Itchen Abbas on the B3047, SP 'Alresford', and continue to Itchen Stoke, then in 1 mile turn left on to the A31 for New Alresford.

NEW ALRESFORD, Hants

This is one of Hampshire's loveliest small towns. Its main street, appropriately called Broad Street, is flanked with lime trees and colour-washed Georgian houses. The writer Mary Mitford was born in one of them in 1787. A tributary of the Itchen flows around the town and there is a pleasant walk along its banks past an old fulling mill — a reminder of Alresford's medieval days as a wool town. Another reminder of the past is a lake at the edge of the town. In the 12th century the Bishop of Winchester dammed the village pond to form a natural harbour and make the river navigable to the sea.

MID HANTS RAILWAY, Hants

The chalk streams of Hampshire feed beds of bright green cress and provide them with ideal growing conditions. Over half the country's supply of watercress comes from Hampshire and for a long time Alresford Station was an important despatch point. The railway transported the cress all over England and came to be known as the Watercress Line. Neglected and unused for several years, enthusiasts have now restored part of the line and in summer steam trains run between Alresford and Alton.

At Alresford turn left, SP 'Basingstoke B3046', into Broad Street. At the end bear right and cross a causeway over the River Alre to Old Alresford. Cross wooded Abbotstone Down and continue through the Candover valley and down Farleigh Hill, into Cliddesden. In 1¼ miles turn left on to the A339 for the return to Basingstoke.

The lake at The Vyne was landscaped in the 18th century to enhance the view

AMONG THE COTSWOLDS

Wool and stone shaped this landscape. Mellow rock torn from hillsides cropped smooth by generations of sheep was built into great churches, houses, towns and villages by local skill applied with the profits from wool, medieval England's greatest resource.

BURFORD, Oxon

Like so many other wool towns in this part of the country, Burford is centred on a charming main street lined with honey-coloured buildings of local stone. The excellence of this building material is apparent in the fact that Sir Christopher Wren would specify no other for St Paul's Cathedral. The town's main street descends a steep hillside and crosses the River Windrush via a fine old bridge. Buildings of particular interest include 15th-century almshouses, the Great House of 1690, and basically Norman church which claims to be the second largest in Oxfordshire. Features of this splendid building include an imposing tower and spire, and somewhat macabre Civil War associations. In 1649 several Cromwellian mutineers were trapped in the building by their own forces, and on capture 3 of the imprisoned men were shot near the churchyard. The history of Burford is shown in the Torsey Museum and set in 200 acres of woodlands is the Cotswold Wildlife Park.

From the Bull Hotel in Burford follow the unclassified road to Asthall.

ASTHALL, Oxon

The banks of the Windrush afford a delightful view of Asthall Manor, a striking Elizabethan house with mullioned windows and an overall atmosphere of permanence. Alongside is the parish church, which is of Norman origin and features two interesting arches in the north chapel.

Meet a T-junction and turn right SP 'Witney'. Ascend, then turn left on to the B4047 and proceed to Minster Lovell.

MINSTER LOVELL, Oxon

Clustered stone-built cottages and the fine, partly-timbered Swan Inn nestle together to form this quaint little Windrush village. Of special note are the ruins of a 15th-century hall (AM), which boasts two gruesome legends. The first is of Lord Francis Lovell, who is supposed to have hidden in a secret room after the Lambert Simnel Rising of 1487. His whereabouts was known to only one servant, who died suddenly leaving the unfortunate Lord Francis incarcerated until his skeleton was reputedly discovered in 1718. A similar tale recounts the story of an unfortunate young Lovell bride who decided to hide in a large chest on her Christmas wedding night and became trapped.

At the White Hart Hotel turn left on to the unclassified 'Leafield' road. Descend and cross the River Windrush and continue to Leafield. Drive to the war memorial, turn left, then continue to the Fox Inn and bear right. Shortly pass the Leafield Radio Station. Continue to Shipton-under-Wychwood and turn right on to the A361 to enter the village.

The peaceful ruins of Minster Lovell Hall are haunted by macabre legends involving death by starvation and suffocation.

SHIPTON-UNDER-WYCHWOOD, Oxon

Restored Shipton Court is of Elizabethan origin and one of the finest buildings in the village; unfortunately it is closed to the public. More easily accessible is a fountain which was raised to the memory of 19 Shipton men who died in the wreck of the ship *Cosipatrick* in 1874. The Shaven Crown Inn has a Tudor gateway.

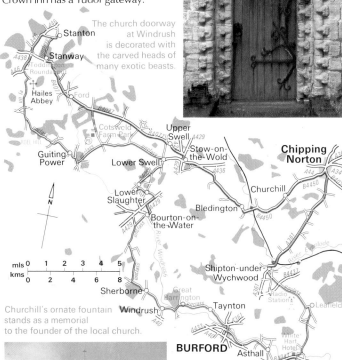

The church doorway at Windrush is decorated with the carved heads of many exotic beasts.

Churchill's ornate fountain stands as a memorial to the founder of the local church.

Cross the River Evenlode and continue to Chipping Norton.

CHIPPING NORTON, Oxon

The 'Chipping' element of this name means 'market', and for a considerable period the 'market at Norton' was the commercial centre for the Evenlode Valley. When the Cotswolds became one giant sheepwalk the town assumed new importance as a gathering place for wool merchants and other traders. Much of the town's attraction today is due to its many survivals from a prosperous past. Among these are numerous 18th-century houses and a 'wool' church that is among the finest in the county; 17th-century Almshouses, The Bliss Tweedmill of 1872, the White Hart and Crown and Cushion were once coaching inns. Four miles north-east is Chas Heton House, which contains tapestries and period furniture.

Follow the B4450 'Stow' road and drive to Churchill.

CHURCHILL, Oxon

Two famous men were born here in the 18th century – William Hastings, 1st Governor-General of India, and 'The Father of Geology' William Smith, who was the first man to map the rock strata of England and identify fossils peculiar to each layer. A restored church of 1826 crowns a nearby hilltop and displays a fine tower which can be seen for miles around. An unusual square-shaped fountain with open arches and pinnacles rising from a basin of flowing water stands as a memorial to Squire Langston, the original builder of the church.

Continue to Bledington.

BLEDINGTON, Glos

Situated near the River Evenlode, Bledington boasts its own Victorian maypole and a fine Norman church containing good examples of old glass. Nearby Maugersbury Hill forms an excellent viewpoint.

Later join the A436 for Stow-on-the-Wold.

STOW-ON-THE-WOLD, Glos

'Stow-on-the-Wold where the wind blows cold' is a local saying that aptly describes this, the highest hilltop town in the Cotswolds. It is set on a ridge between the upper valleys of the rivers Windrush and Evenlode and has an enormous market square with stocks and a 14th-century cross. This is the focal point of the town. Inside the local church is a splendid 17th-century painting of the Crucifixion by Belgian artist, de Craeyer. Hundreds of Royalists were imprisoned here after a Civil War battle fought in 1646.

Follow SP 'Tewkesbury' to join the B4077 and proceed to Upper Swell.

UPPER SWELL, Glos

This charming and unspoilt village comprises a cluster of houses and a tiny church. Its main feature is a fine manor house.

About 4¼ miles farther a road on the left leads to Cotswold Farm Park.

COTSWOLD FARM PARK, Glos

Rare breeds of British farm animals are kept here in an authentic farmyard setting in beautiful countryside on the Cotswold Hills. Major attractions include a pet's corner, young stock, and rides round the park in a pony-drawn trap.

Continue on the B4077 through Ford. Descend to Stanway.

STANWAY, Glos

Magnificent wooded hills surround this attractive small village, which has a tithe barn mentioned in the Domesday Book. Stanway House, a focal point for the community, is approached through an imposing gateway in the style of Inigo Jones.

Meet crossroads and turn right on to an unclassified road, passing the grounds of Stanway House. In 1¼ miles turn right and drive to Stanton.

STANTON, Glos

Larch woods on Shenbarrow Hill shelter this unspoilt village, which is often described as the most attractive in the Cotswolds. Elizabethan Stanton Court and 16th-century Warren House are old manor houses of particular note, and thatched barns add the softness of straw or reed to the picture. Watching over all is the homely sentinel of the restored church.

Return and in ¼ mile bear right SP 'Cheltenham'. In ¾ mile turn left on to the A46 and continue to the Toddington roundabout. Keep forward at the roundabout, then in 1 mile take the 2nd turning on the left on to an unclassified road for Hailes Abbey.

HAILES ABBEY, Glos

For many years the 13th-century Cistercian foundation was a thriving centre of learning and religion, attracting pilgrims from all over the country. Nowadays it is a collection of ruins (AM, NT) with a small site

museum in which tiles, bosses, and various early relics are preserved.

Return for 200 yds and turn left on to Roel Hill, which affords fine views of the surrounding countryside. Meet a T-junction and turn left, then turn right and continue to Guiting Power.

GUITING POWER, Glos

This picturesque village is attractively situated on the upper reaches of the River Windrush.

In ⅓ mile meet a T-junction and turn right SP 'Andoversford', then take the next turning left SP 'Stow'. Continue along a quiet country road to Lower Swell.

LOWER SWELL, Glos

Huge copper beeches and stone walls line the route into Lower Swell. In the village the small River Dikler flows past attractive bankside cottages and a working smithy. An elegant Georgian pillar topped by an urn stands on the village green and inside the local church are fine examples of Norman carving.

Turn right on to the B4068 SP 'The Slaughters', then turn left on to an unclassified road for Upper Slaughter.

UPPER SLAUGHTER, Glos

An outstanding 3-gabled Elizabethan manor house (open), with 15 tall chimneys and an avenue of mature trees, dominates this beautiful Cotswold village. Also here are a fine 17th-century parsonage and an attractive, partly Norman church.

Lower Slaughter's 19th-century brick mill contrasts sharply with the stone houses elsewhere in the village.

Pollarded willows and the enchantment of running water combine with the mellowness of old Cotswold stone in Burford's ancient river bridge, which spans the Windrush.

Drive to the end of the village and turn left, then continue to the neighbouring village of Lower Slaughter.

LOWER SLAUGHTER, Glos

As the River Eye winds its peaceful course between the rows of charming cottages which flank both its banks in this village it is spanned by many bridges, stone and wooden, and shaded by the dark-green umbrellas of stately yew trees. This scene of rural tranquillity is completed by a church with a 12th-century arcade.

Cross a bridge and turn right, then at the end of the village turn right again on to the A429. In ½ mile turn left on to an unclassified road for Bourton-on-the-Water.

BOURTON-ON-THE-WATER, Glos

This Cotswold-stone village – with its churches, shops, houses, sloping lawns alongside the River Windrush, and watermill – is reproduced at one-ninth actual size in the garden of the Old New Inn. Elsewhere in the village are the Birdland Zoo Gardens, a Village Life Exhibition and the Cotswolds Motor Museum.

Meet crossroads in the village and follow the unclassified 'Sherborne' road. Cross the river and bear right. Ascend, and in 3¼ miles turn left for Sherborne.

SHERBORNE, Glos

Number 88, a cottage on the Windrush road, was once an old chapel and retains a fine Norman doorway. Sherborne House shares extensive grounds with Lodge Park, a charming 19th-century building that was erected as a grandstand for the audiences of deer coursing.

Leave Sherborne and continue to Windrush.

WINDRUSH, Glos

This village is named after the River Windrush. The local church faces a triangular patch of green surrounded by tall trees and has a Norman doorway considered to be one of the best of its type.

Keep left and continue for ¾ mile, then meet a T-junction and turn left for Great Barrington. Drive to the war memorial and bear right for Taynton.

TAYNTON, Oxon

Taynton's thatched grey-stone houses nestle together with a 700-year-old church on timbered slopes above the River Windrush. Stone for the building of Blenheim Palace was supplied by the famous quarries in this area.

After the village keep forward for the A424, then the A361. Cross a river and re-enter Burford.

THE CREEKS AND ESTUARIES OF THE ESSEX COAST

Beautiful, unspoilt scenery surrounds the Crouch and Blackwater estuaries — sheltered waterways haunted by wildfowl and seabirds and beloved by yachtsmen. The old riverports of Burnham-on-Crouch and Maldon are redolent of the salty character of the wild and lovely Essex coast, with its deserted creeks and lonely mudflats.

Low tide at the quay in Burnham-on-Crouch, well-known for its local oyster beds

CHELMSFORD, Essex

Roman workmen cut their great road linking London with Colchester straight through Chelmsford and built a fort here, *Caesaromagus*, at the junction of the Rivers Chelmer and Cann. The town has always been an important market centre and is now the bustling modern county town of Essex. The Marconi Company, pioneers in the manufacture of wireless equipment, set up the first radio company in the world here in 1899. Exhibits of the early days of wireless can be seen in the Chelmsford and Essex Museum in Oaklands Park, as can interesting displays of Roman remains and local history.

Leave Chelmsford town centre on the A130 Southend road. At the bypass roundabout, take the 3rd exit onto the B1009. After ½ mile, turn right at the Beehive PH in Great Baddow, and at Galleywood turn left onto the B1007 before crossing Galleywood Common to reach Stock.

STOCK, Essex

A fine old tower windmill and a delightful church with a traditional Essex-style wooden belfry and spire lend character to this pleasant village of well-kept houses. Some of the timbers in the church belfry are said to have come from Spanish galleons, wrecked in the aftermath of Sir Francis Drake's defeat of the Armada.

On entering Stock turn left onto the Wickford road. (Stock Church lies ahead on the B1007). Pass the windmill on the left before reaching a T-junction. Turn right here, then after ½ mile turn left before reaching the shores of Hanningfield Reservoir. In 1 mile turn left on to the Hanningfields road and continue to South Hanningfield.

SOUTH HANNINGFIELD, Essex

The placid waters of the reservoir that has been created by damming Sandford Brook transform the scattered rural settlement of South Hanningfield into a lakeside village. Standing by the shores of the lake is the 12th-century village church whose graceful belfry is a local landmark in the flat Essex countryside.

In 1½ miles turn right on to the A130, SP 'Southend', and 2 miles farther, at the Rettendon Turnpike roundabout, take the 1st exit on to the B1012. Later skirt South Woodham Ferrers.

SOUTH WOODHAM FERRERS, Essex

The desolate marshland overlooking the sheltered creeks of the Crouch estuary, a yachtsman's paradise, was chosen by Essex County Council as the site for one of its most attractive new town schemes. At the centre is a traditional market square surrounded by pleasant arcades and terraces built in the old Essex style with brick, tile and weatherboard.

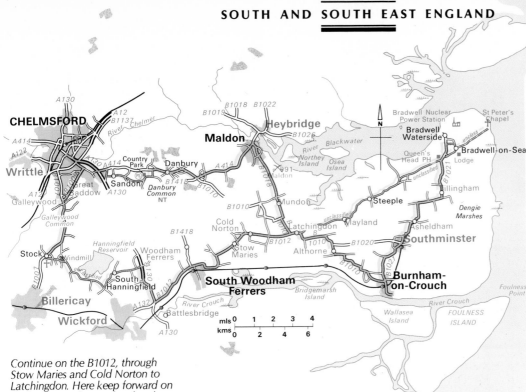

Continue on the B1012, through
Stow Maries and Cold Norton to
Latchingdon. Here keep forward on
to the B1010, then at the church
turn right. After 1½ miles turn right
again and continue through
Althorne. At the T-junction turn left
and follow a winding road to the
edge of Burham-on-Crouch. Turn
right on to the B1021 for the town
centre.

BURNHAM-ON-CROUCH, Essex
From the gaily-coloured cottages
along the quay, the town climbs
up the slopes above the seashore,
its streets lined with an assortment
of old cottages, Georgian and
Victorian houses and shops. This is
the yachting centre of Essex. In
Tudor times sailing barges
thronged the estuary where now
yachts tack jauntily to and fro.
Yachtsmen and holiday-makers
come ashore to buy provisions,
following a tradition that dates
back to the medieval era when
Burnham was the market centre
for the isolated farmsteads of
Wallasea and Foulness Islands and
the inhabitants travelled in by ferry.
The whole area was, and is to this
day, famous for its oyster beds.

Return along the B1021 and at the
end of the town keep forward on
to the Southminster road. Continue
northwards across the Dengie
Peninsula.

DENGIE PENINSULA, Essex
The salty tang of sea air, brought
inland by the east-coast winds,
gives an exhilarating flavour to the
marshlands of the Dengie
Peninsula. Like the Cambridgeshire
and Lincolnshire fens, the once
waterlogged coastal region of this
remote corner of Essex was
reclaimed from the sea by 17th-
century Dutch engineers. The
views across the marshes
encompass great sweeps of
countryside, inhabited by
wildfowl, seabirds and cattle
grazing on the saltings. The old
market town of Southminster and

the marshland villages of
Asheldham and Tillingham rise
prominently from the flat expanse
of the landscape.

In Southminster turn right at the
church, then turn left on to the
Bradwell road and at the next
T-junction turn right. A winding
road then passes through
Asheldham to Tillingham. After
another 1½ miles, at the Queens
Head PH, turn right to reach
Bradwell Waterside.

BRADWELL WATERSIDE AND
BRADWELL-ON-SEA, Essex
Overshadowing the small coastal
resort of Bradwell Waterside on
the estuary of the Blackwater
River, the massive bulk of
Bradwell Nuclear Power Station
stands as an incongruous 20th-
century intrusion on this remote
coastline. Bradwell-on-Sea, a
village now a mile or so inland
from the coast, is a cluster of
attractive cottages set about a
green leading to the church.
Bradwell Lodge (open by
appointment) a beautiful part-
Tudor, part-Georgian manor
house, has an unusually charming

Many of Tillingham's old cottages
were built by the Church

summer house. During the 18th
century the portrait painter
Thomas Gainsborough was a
frequent visitor. Not far away, on
the coast, stands the tiny 7th-
century Saxon church of St Peter-
at-the-Wall. It is one of the most
ancient churches in England and is
built across the line of the west
wall of Othona, a great 3rd-
century Roman fort.

From Bradwell Waterside return
along the B1021 and in ¾ mile
turn left for Bradwell-on-Sea
village, then in 1 mile rejoin the
B1021. At the Queens Head PH
continue on to the unclassified
Latchingdon road with occasional
views of the Blackwater estuary,
before reaching Steeple.

STEEPLE, Essex
This small village of thatched and
weather-board cottages stands on
the south bank of the Blackwater
estuary, where brightly coloured
yachts and the occasional stately
sailing barge can be seen. Around
the village stretches a rich green
countryside of fertile meadows,
patterned by lanes bordered with
banks of trees.

Continue through Mayland back to
Latchingdon. At the end of the
village turn right on to the B1010,
SP 'Maldon'. In 1 mile turn right
again on to the B1018 and
continue to Maldon.

MALDON, Essex
Just outside the fascinating old
town of Maldon lies the site of
one of the great decisive battles of
England's early history. The Battle
of Maldon was fought and lost in
991 when the English leader,
Byrthnoth, was killed by the
invading Danes after a fierce 3-day
battle. As a result of this defeat,
the English king, Ethelred the
Unready, was obliged to pay an
annual tribute of Danegeld to the
conquerors; eventually the Danes
overthrew him and Cnut became
king. Maldon itself is a charming
town, famous for its sea salt,
produced for generations as a
result of evaporating sea water.
One of its churches, All Saints, has
a unique triangular tower, and
there are many intriguing shops
and welcoming inns in its steep
winding streets.

Leave Maldon on the A414
Chelmsford road and in 3¼ miles,
at the roundabout, take the 3rd exit
and continue to Danbury.

DANBURY, Essex
It is said that this village, crowning
a high, wooded hill, takes its name
from the Danes who invaded this
part of the country in the Dark
Ages. Remains of an ancient
earthwork defence, thought to be
Danish, can still be seen around
the site of the church, which
contains 3 beautifully carved
wooden figures of knights dating
from around 1300. To the south is
Danbury Common (NT) where
acres of gorse flower in a blaze of
golden colour for much of the
year; to the west, Danbury
Country Park offers another
pleasant stretch of open country.

At the end of the village turn left
into Wells Lane. At the next
T-junction turn right, SP 'Country
Park'. Continue past Danbury
Country Park to Sandon.

SANDON, Essex
The village green of Sandon has
produced a notable oak tree,
remarkable not so much for its
height as for the tremendous
horizontal spread of its branches.
Around the green have been built
the fine church and a number of
attractive old houses, some dating
back to the 16th century when
Henry VIII's Lord Chancellor,
Cardinal Wolsey, was Lord of the
Manor of Sandon.

At Sandon bear left then
immediately right, and at the end
turn right. At the next T-junction
turn left on to the A414, then at the
roundabout go forward across the
road bridge and turn right to join
the A130 for the return to
Chelmsford.

COLCHESTER, Essex

During the 1st century, Colchester was the capital of the south-east and an obvious target for Roman invasion. The walls of their city can still be traced around the old part of the town and the huge Balkerne Gate is magnificent to this day. By the time the Normans arrived, Colchester (the name coined by the Saxons) was an important borough and they built their tremendous castle on the foundations of the Roman temple of Claudius. All that remains is part of the lofty keep — the largest ever built in Europe — and the museum it now houses provides a fine record of Roman Colchester. Profits from cloth-making, which began in the 13th century, left a substantial legacy of churches and monastic buildings to Colchester and by the 15th century there were 15 parish churches in all. Most have long since been altered and restored and some, like All Saints' housing a natural history museum and St Martin's used as a public hall, have abandoned their rightful purpose altogether. Of St John's Abbey only its 15th-century gatehouse is left, but the stone from the older abbey went into the building of Bourne Mill (NT), a Dutch-gabled fishing lodge on the banks of Bourne Pond. There are several attractive and interesting corners of Colchester with buildings spanning 6 centuries. The Minories, a Georgian house, has an art gallery, period furniture, pictures, china and silver. Another Georgian house, Hollytrees, has 18th- and 19th-century costumes and domestic craft exhibits. Aptly named Siege House bears evidence of Civil War conflict as its timbers are riddled with bullet holes. Much of Colchester's notoriety comes from its oysters and roses. Reminders of a less industrialised past are the annual oyster feast — a civic banquet worthy of royal patronage — and the annual Colchester Rose Show. Both commodities flourish today as they have done since the 18th century.

Leave Colchester on the A134, SP 'Sudbury', and at the roundabout beyond the station take the 2nd exit. Pass through Great Horkesley and gradually descend into the Stour valley.

STOUR VALLEY, Essex/Suffolk

The River Stour forms a natural boundary between Essex and Suffolk, and picturesque bridges along its route join the 2 counties. Landscape artist John Constable immortalised the valley in his famous paintings, capturing to perfection the flat water meadows, willow-lined ditches, locks and watermills.

After crossing the river into Suffolk turn left on to the unclassified Bures road. A mile later pass the turning, on the left, to Wissington.

THE STOUR VALLEY AND THE RIVER COLNE

From the ancient Roman capital of Colchester, the tour circles round the most beautiful tracts of the Essex countryside; along the Stour valley celebrated in the paintings of Constable, to the old market town of Sudbury, birthplace of Gainsborough, and across the peaceful scenery of the Colne valley.

Market day at Sudbury

WISSINGTON, Suffolk

A Norman church with a later white weather-boarded bellcote, a few thatched farm buildings and a handsome redbrick house form an attractive group in this tiny hamlet. Inside the church are fragments of some interesting 13th-century wall-paintings which depicted stories from Christ's childhood and the lives of St Margaret and St Nicholas. Wiston Hall (not open) was built in 1791 for Samuel Beechcroft — a director of the Bank of England — by architect Sir John Soane.

Continue on the unclassified road following the Stour valley to Bures.

BURES, Suffolk

In AD 855 St Edmund, East Anglian king and martyr, was crowned in a chapel above this tiny town. Below, the town full of fine half-timbered buildings, steps across both sides of the river and the boundary. An ancient thatched building called Chapel Barn once belonged to Earls Colne Priory (no longer in existence).

At the main road in Bures, turn right on to the B1508, SP 'Sudbury'. Continue along the valley and later pass through Great Cornard to reach Sudbury.

SUDBURY, Suffolk

Thomas Gainsborough, portrait painter and landscape artist, was born in Sudbury during 1727. The house, 46 Gainsborough Street (then Sepulchre Street) is now a pleasant museum and art gallery devoted to him. A bronze statue of Gainsborough, complete with brush and palette, stands in the market place. This teems with life on market days, but otherwise is only gladdened by the splendid 19th-century Corn Exchange and St Peter's Church surveying the square. The church has a piece of embroidery 5 centuries old which is still used at aldermen's funerals. Sudbury was the largest of Suffolk's wool towns and has more the stamp of a manufacturing town than most of the others. Due to the Act of Parliament passed for improving the Stour's navigation, Sudbury became an important river port. However, the railway ended the era of the flat-bottomed Stour Barge, and the last one was sold by the Canal Company in 1913.

Leave Sudbury on the A131, SP 'Chelmsford'. At Bulmer Tye turn right on to the B1058 and continue to Castle Hedingham.

CASTLE HEDINGHAM, Essex

The castle (OACT), from which the village takes its name, was one of England's strongest fortresses in the 11th century. It belonged to the powerful de Veres, the Earls of Oxford, one of whom was among the barons who forced King John to accept the Magna Carta. Some idea of the castle's great size can be gained from the impressive stone keep which remains. Although not complete, 2 of its 4 round towers are left and its walls, 12ft thick, rise up to over 100ft. A brick Tudor bridge leads to it over the moat which has long since

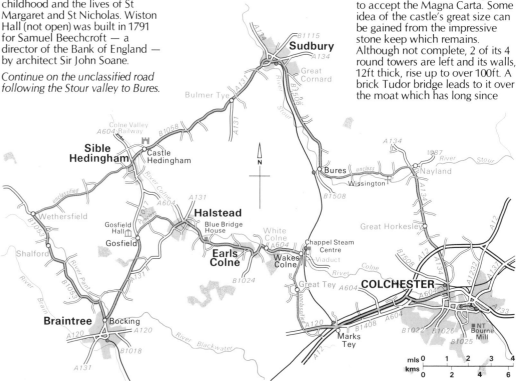

dried up. The village lying in the castle's shadow is a maze of narrow streets radiating from Falcon Square, which takes its name from the half-timbered Falcon Inn. Georgian and 15th-century houses mingle compatibly and the church, St Nicholas's, was built by the de Veres and is virtually completely Norman.

Continue on the B1058 then in ¾ mile turn left on to the A604 and enter Sible Hedingham.

SIBLE HEDINGHAM, Essex
Sir John Hawkwood was born here during the 14th century. He was one of the most famous soldiers of fortune during his time, and led mercenaries to Italy where he was eventually paid to defend Florence, where he died. There is a monument to him in the village church, decorated with hawks and various other beasts.

In Sible Hedingham turn right on to the unclassified Wethersfield road. Shortly turn right again, pass the church then turn left and continue to Wethersfield. In the village turn left on to the B1053 and follow the shallow valley of the River Pant. Pass through Shalford and after 5½ miles bear right to enter Bocking, which is combined with Braintree.

BRAINTREE AND BOCKING, Essex
Braintree was one of those ancient settlements that sprang up at the crossing point of 2 cross-country routes. Subsequent Roman occupation and development is evident from the many coins which have been found in the area. Braintree and Bocking have merged into a single town and they share the textile industry which has prospered here since the 14th century. Wool gave way to more exotic materials in the early 19th century, when the Courtauld family began the production of silk and this has been the main manufacture ever since. The other important industry here, dating from 1884, is the production of metal windows.

Courtauld's weather-boarded mill, which straddles the River Colne at Halstead

Leave on the A131 Halstead road. In 2¼ miles branch left on to the A1017, SP 'Cambridge', and continue to Gosfield.

GOSFIELD, Essex
A large lake built on the edge of Gosfield in the 18th century has been turned into a recreation centre. A paddling area has been roped off from the water-skiing area and rowing boats are available for hire. The lake and the village are all part of the Gosfield Hall (OACT) estate. It is not known for sure exactly when the Hall was built, or by whom, but it was Samuel Courtauld's (the silk manufacturing magnate) home for a time. A long Tudor gallery and some secret rooms are among the house's best features.

Tombs of 3 of the Earls of Oxford in Chapel Barn, Bures

At the far end of the village pass Hall Drive on the left (which leads to Gosfield Hall), then turn right on to the unclassified Halstead road. In 2 miles turn left on to the A131 and enter Halstead.

HALSTEAD, Essex
Through-traffic pounds along Halstead's High Street which drops down from the top of the hill to the River Colne. Here the Courtauld family established a silk factory in 1826 and it is one of the best sights in the town. The river flows beneath the mill, a low, white, weather-boarded building with rows of windows along its sides. Outside the town lies Blue Bridge House with lovely 18th-century ironwork and red and blue brickwork.

Leave Halstead on the A604 Colchester road. After 1 mile, on the left, is the Blue Bridge House. Follow the valley of the River Colne to reach Earls Colne.

EARLS COLNE, Essex
The de Veres, Earls of Oxford, and the River Colne gave the village its name. Aubrey de Vere founded a Benedictine priory here in the 12th century and both he and his wife — William the Conqueror's sister — were buried there. A redbrick Gothic mansion marks the site now. A nucleus of timbered cottages preserves the village atmosphere, although modern housing is spreading fast. Nearby Chalkney Wood, running down to the Colne, is an outstanding beauty spot.

Continue on the A604 to Wakes Colne.

WAKES COLNE, Essex
A working steam centre has been opened at Chappel and Wakes Colne station and every aspect of steam locomotion can be studied here. Locos and items of rolling stock are on display and steam hauled rides are available on some weekends.

At the crossroads on the nearside of the railway viaduct turn right on to the unclassified Great Tey road. Climb out of the valley to reach Great Tey. Continue to the A120 and turn left for Marks Tey.

MARKS TEY, Essex
Norman inhabitants gave the village its name when they came over from Marck, near Calais. The church is distinctive with its oakboarded tower, but its chief treasure is its 15th-century font. This too is made of oak and has 8 intricately carved panelled sides.

At the roundabout take the 2nd exit, SP 'Colchester', and join the A12. Later join the A604 for the return to Colchester.

COWES, Isle of Wight
This busy island port has a good harbour on the River Medina and is connected to East Cowes by floating bridge and ferry. The headquarters of the Royal Yacht Squadron is based at Cowes Castle, and the town is well known as England's premier yachting centre.

Leave Cowes following SP 'Gurnard' on the B3325. In ¾ mile keep forward on to an unclassified road for Gurnard. Reach a church and keep forward, then meet a T-junction and turn right into Lower Church Road. Continue to the next T-junction, turn left SP 'Yarmouth', and in a further 1½ miles meet another T-junction. Turn right and in another 1½ miles turn right again for Porchfield. Continue through wooded countryside and after 1½ miles turn right for Newtown.

NEWTOWN, Isle of Wight
Sited midway between Newport and Yarmouth, Newtown was created in the 13th century by the bishops of Winchester and stands on the beautiful Newtown River estuary (NT). The 18th-century Old Town Hall (NT) is notable.

In ¼ mile meet a T-junction and turn right, then in another ¾ mile meet another T-junction and turn right again on to the A3054. Proceed to Shalfleet.

SHALFLEET, Isle of Wight
Shalfleet's church displays very strong Norman features, particularly in the squat west tower and the good south doorway with its contemporary tympanum.

Continue to Yarmouth.

YARMOUTH, Isle of Wight
This Yar-estuary town is better known as a sailing centre than as a resort. Henry VIII built one of his many coastal defence forts (AM) here, and the triangular Fort Victoria of 1853 stands in the grounds of the Fort Victoria country park.

Following SP 'Freshwater', cross the Yar bridge, and in 1 mile bear right. Pass through Colwell Bay and continue to the small resort of Totland. Join the B3322 'Alum Bay' road and in ¼ mile reach a war memorial. Bear right to Alum Bay.

ALUM BAY & THE NEEDLES, Isle of Wight
Sandstone cliffs famous for their multi-coloured strata fringe this lovely bay. The isolated rock stacks of The Needles stretch out into the sea to the south-west, with Scratchell's Bay and a 200ft chalk arch beyond.

Return, and in ½ mile branch right on to an unclassified road SP 'Freshwater Bay'. To the right is Tennyson Down (NT), one of the West Wight Downs.

WEST WIGHT DOWNS, Isle of Wight
The high, gentle folds of the West Wight Downs (NT) occupy most of the island's south-west corner.

A MINIATURE LANDSCAPE

The Isle of Wight has everything offered by the mainland, but smaller. Here are high downs and soaring cliffs; long beaches fringed by farm and forestland; fishing villages and resorts popularized by royalty in the past and popular with sun seekers today.

The brass cannons overlooking the Solent at Cowes are fired to start yacht races.

Continue to Freshwater Bay and join the A3055 SP 'Chale'. Bear right and ascend, skirting Compton Bay, and drive along a beautiful clifftop road that affords some of the finest views in the island. Later pass the edge of Brook village.

BROOK, Isle of Wight
Brook House dates from the 18th century, and Brook Chine (NT) is a beautiful cleft with 40 acres of grazing and 300 yards of superb seashore.

Continue through pleasant open country with good views. In 2¼ miles pass thickly-wooded Grange Chine to the right, with Brighstone Forest to the left and Brighstone Bay to the right. St Catherine's Point and St Catherine's Hill are prominent ahead before the tour enters Chale.

CHALE, Isle of Wight
Chale Abbey preserves a 14th-century hall, and the local church commands fine views of The Needles.

Drive to Chale Church and keep forward SP 'Ventnor'. In ½ mile turn right on to the B3399 road for Blackgang. A footpath from this point leads to Blackgang Chine.

BLACKGANG CHINE & ST CATHERINE'S HILL, Isle of Wight
It is thought that this dramatic chine derived its name from a gang of smugglers, but nowadays it harbours nobody more sinister than tourists visiting the Theme Park. Inland is 773ft St Catherine's Hill (NT), which affords excellent views and features 14th-century St Catherine's Oratory.

From Blackgang Chine return to the main route and turn right on to the A3055 SP 'Ventnor'. Pass under St Catherine's Hill and continue along the undercliff to St Lawrence.

Turn right (in Niton) and continue along Undercliff to St Lawrence.

ST LAWRENCE, Isle of Wight
Old St Lawrence's was Britain's smallest church until it acquired a porch and bell tower in 1842. Tropical Bird Gardens and glass makers are situated in the 20 acres of Old Park.

Continue to Ventnor.

VENTNOR, Isle of Wight
A paper recommending the local climate for the cure of certain illnesses transformed Ventnor from a fishing village to a focus of 19th-century society. Within the Botanic Gardens is the History of Smuggling Museum.

Follow SP 'Shanklin' and ascend, with fine sea views to the right. In ¾ mile a detour can be made from the main route to the delightful village of Bonchurch by turning right on to an unclassified road.

BONCHURCH & ST BONIFACE DOWN, Isle of Wight
The writers Dickens, Thackeray, and Macaulay all stayed in this delightful village, and the poet Swinburne lived at East Dene House. The village itself stands just below the island's highest point, 785ft Boniface Down (NT), and has a Victorian church.

Continue on the main drive, pass the Landslip viewpoint to the right of the road and reach Shanklin.

SHANKLIN, Isle of Wight
A group of thatched buildings, the Crab Inn, and St Blasius's Church are all that remain of the fishing village that stood here before the seaside holiday fad took over. The town's excellent sea-bathing, superb sandy beach, and good sunshine records attract increasing numbers of visitors every year. Shanklin Chine has a spectacular 45ft waterfall.

Continue through Shanklin and Lake to Sandown.

SANDOWN, Isle of Wight
The assets that contributed to the development of Shanklin have also made Sandown a popular holiday resort. Additional attractions include the Museum of Isle of Wight Geology and a good zoo.

Turn right on to the B3395 SP 'Bembridge' and drive to Yaverland.

YAVERLAND, Isle of Wight
Yaverland Manor House (not open) is the finest 17th-century building of its kind in the island.

Meet a T-junction and turn right. In ¼ mile it is possible to make a detour from the main route by turning right to the downs of Culver and Bembridge.

Until its collapse in 1764 one of the Needles was 120ft high.

BEMBRIDGE, Isle of Wight

Yachtsmen favour the nearby natural harbour at the mouth of the Eastern Yar. Numerous displays of nautical heritage from the early days of sail to the present time, are to be found in the Maritime Museum.

Follow the B3395 'St Helens' road and in 1½ miles meet a T-junction. Turn right on to the B3330 into St Helens, then turn left SP 'Ryde' for Nettlestone. At Nettlestone branch right on to the B3340 SP 'Seaview'. On the right is the entrance to Flamingo Park. In ½ mile keep left, then meet a T-junction and turn left, then immediately left again. Turn right into Seafield Road for Seaview.

Alum Bay is famous for its multi-coloured cliffs.

Yarmouth Harbour, crowded with yachts and other sailing craft.

Whippingham's Germanic-looking church.

CULVER & BEMBRIDGE DOWNS, Isle of Wight

Covering some 104 acres of east Wight, these fine downs (NT) rise to a 343ft summit and drop sharply towards the coast. Culver Down features a bronze-age round barrow.

Continue with the main tour to skirt Bembridge Airport and at the far side meet crossroads. Turn left on to an unclassified road and in ¼ mile pass a footpath on the left leading to Bembridge Windmill.

BEMBRIDGE WINDMILL, Isle of Wight

Situated near one end of Bembridge High Street, this stone-built mill (NT) has a wooden roof and was erected c1700. Today it is the only windmill left on the island, and is maintained in working order, but last used in 1913.
Continue into Bembridge.

SEAVIEW, Isle of Wight

Much of the unspoiled fishing village is still evident in Seaview, a quiet resort offering good beaches and excellent shore angling.

Continue to a T-junction and turn right, then keep left on to an unclassified road and drive along the shoreline. In ¼ mile pass through a toll gate, and 1 mile farther turn right on to the B3330. After a short distance turn right on to the A3055 for Ryde.

RYDE, Isle of Wight

Most visitors to the island enter at Ryde, a busy port that was a small fishing and smuggling village until the 18th century.

Follow SP 'Newport' to join the A3054 and pass through Binstead.

BINSTEAD, Isle of Wight

New Quarr Abbey stands near the 12th-century remains of its predecessor at Binstead, and the local church still shows some of its 13th-century origins in spite of Victorian restoration.

Keep forward through Wootton Bridge. In 1½ miles turn right SP 'East Cowes'. Meet a T-junction and turn right on to the A3021, then in 1¼ miles turn left on to an unclassified road SP 'Whippingham Church'. Continue to Whippingham.

WHIPPINGHAM, Isle of Wight

Prince Albert built the ornate church here in 1860, and Queen Victoria was a regular member of the congregation whenever the Royal Family was in residence on the island.

Pass Whippingham Church and continue to a T-junction. Turn left into Victoria Grove, then at the next T-junction turn left again to join the A3021 for East Cowes. Return along the A3021 'Ryde' road, passing the entrance to Osborne House to the left on the outskirts of the town.

OSBORNE HOUSE, Isle of Wight

Queen Victoria and the Prince Consort built Osborne House as a retreat from the pomp and ceremony of Windsor, and Her Majesty died here in 1901. The State apartments (open) remain as they were in her day.

Continue, and in 2 miles keep right SP 'Newport', and after another ¼ mile turn right on to the A3054. Proceed to Newport.

The Indian-style Durbar Room at Osborne House was built in 1891 to accommodate state banquets.

NEWPORT, Isle of Wight

Situated at the head of the Medina estuary, this town is the capital of the island and stands on a site that has been occupied at least since Roman times. Mighty Carisbrooke Castle stands on the foundations of a Roman fort 1 mile south west. The 12th-century remains of the castle include a Norman keep and a 16th-century treadmill that used to be worked by prisoners to raise water. Today it is turned by a donkey for display purposes, and forms a fascinating exhibit in the Isle of Wight Museum.

Follow the A3020 'Cowes' road and pass Parkhurst Prison, backed by Parkhurst Forest.

PARKHURST FOREST, Isle of Wight

Parkhurst Forest is the largest stretch of woodland on the island, and one of the last British refuges of the native red squirrel.

Drive to Northwood and branch left on to the B3325. Continue to a T-junction and turn right to return to Cowes.

EASTBOURNE, E Sussex
Consistently top of the seaside sunshine league tables, the thriving resort of Eastbourne has been popular since the beginning of the 19th century.

Leave Eastbourne seafront along the B2103 'Beachy Head' road, with fine views towards the cliffs of Beachy Head. Ascend, and turn left on to an unclassified road to reach the summit of this cliff range.

BEACHY HEAD, E Sussex
Beachy Head, the vast chalk promontory that marks where the South Downs are halted by the sea, is the starting point of the South Downs Way. This path runs west to beyond South Harting on the Hampshire border.

Continue past the Belle Tout lighthouse to Birling Gap.

BIRLING GAP, E Sussex
For centuries Birling Gap was a landing place favoured by smugglers but today the rocky shingle and sand beach is more popular with bathers. Between Birling Gap and Seaford are the great chalk cliffs known as the Seven Sisters.

Follow the tour inland to Eastdean.

EASTDEAN, E Sussex
Cottages and a small shop overlook Eastdean's sloping triangular green, and the local church houses a curious copy of a Norman font.

Turn left on to the A259 'Seaford' road, ascend steeply, then at the summit turn right on to the unclassified 'Jevington' road for Friston.

FRISTON, E Sussex
This downland village lies in a hilly area now popular with glider pilots. At one time its small Church of St Mary served as a landmark for mariners and smugglers alike.

Continue, with downland to the right and Friston Forest to the left. Also to the right is 659ft Willingdon Hill. Reach Jevington.

JEVINGTON, E Sussex
A sturdy Anglo-Saxon tower is carried by Jevington's flint-built church, and in the churchyard is the copper model of a square-rigged schooner once sailed by a Chinaman buried here.

Beyond Jevington descend through Wannock, with 702ft Windover Hill to the left.

WINDOVER HILL, E Sussex
A gentle climb to the summit of this hill is rewarded by excellent views, not the least of which takes in the prehistoric Long Man of Wilmington. Nobody knows who or what this giant turf-cut figure represents.

Continue to Polegate.

POLEGATE, E Sussex
Victorian St John's Church, like much of the rest of Polegate's architecture, is unremarkable but

THE SUSSEX WEALD

Suspended between the North and South Downs is the high, broken patchwork of the Sussex Weald, a place of charming towns and villages on hillsides once cloaked by the vast, prehistoric Forest of Anderida.

homely. The most notable building here is an early 19th-century windmill with all its sails intact.

At Polegate turn left on to the A22, SP 'London'. Pass through the flat countryside of Wilmington Wood. In 2½ miles a detour from the main route is possible by turning right on to the A295 and driving to Hailsham.

HAILSHAM, E Sussex
The market at Hailsham is one of the largest in Sussex and continues a tradition that reaches back to Norman times.

In ¼ mile (beyond the Hailsham turning) turn left on to an unclassified road to Michelham Priory. Cross the River Cuckmere before reaching the priory.

MICHELHAM PRIORY, E Sussex
Remains of this small Augustinian priory (open), founded in 1229 for 12 canons and a prior, include a Tudor mansion, a 14th-century gatehouse, and an attractive bridge over the moat.

Continue and shortly turn right, and then turn immediately left, SP 'London'. Turn left on to the A22, then shortly right on to the unclassified 'Horam' road. Join the A267 and enter Horam. Continue on the 'Tunbridge Wells' road and pass through woodland scenery before reaching Cross-in-Hand, on The Weald.

Towering chalk cliffs dwarf the lighthouse at Beachy Head.

THE WEALD
The Weald is a high area of broken country suspended between the hills of the North and South Downs. Its towns and villages are rightly famous for their great character and beauty, and several wooded areas exist as reminders of the great Forest of Anderida that once cloaked these long, grassy slopes.

CROSS-IN-HAND, E Sussex
A working windmill stands in this charming village, which is sited at over 500ft on the Sussex Weald. Holy Cross Priory is partly in use as an old people's home, the house and grounds could be visited.

Cross high wooded country to Five Ashes. After ¼ mile (beyond Five Ashes), turn left on to an unclassified road. Later join the B2101 and enter Rotherfield, at the edge of Ashdown Forest.

ROTHERFIELD, E Sussex
Situated at the edge of Ashdown Forest, this village stands at 500ft near the source of the River Rother.

Keep forward, then branch right on to an unclassified road to leave by North Street. Drive to the A26. Turn right SP 'Tunbridge Wells', and pass through Eridge Green.

ERIDGE GREEN, E Sussex
Pretty estate cottages stand behind the local Victorian church, and near by is the sandstone outcrop of Bowles Rocks where trainee mountaineers practise.

Continue for 1 mile through Broadwater Forest, then turn left on to an unclassified road SP 'Groombridge'. After ½ mile turn right SP 'High Rocks', then in a further ¼ mile bear right and pass High Rocks on the right.

HIGH ROCKS, E Sussex
Perhaps the largest sandstone outcrop in the area is High Rocks, which is used extensively by climbers.

Continue for 1¼ miles. Meet crossroads and turn right on to Major York's road. On the far side of Tunbridge Wells Common turn left on to the A26 and enter Royal Tunbridge Wells.

ROYAL TUNBRIDGE WELLS, Kent
In 1606 Lord North discovered chalybeate springs in the forest that stood here. Subsequently the town of Tunbridge Wells was founded, though building did not begin in earnest until the 1630s. By the end of that century it was a flourishing spa, and has remained so to the present day. Visitors to the picturesque raised parade known as the Pantiles may still 'take the waters'.

From the town follow SP 'Eastbourne A267' and re-enter E Sussex for Frant.

FRANT, E Sussex
Houses cluster round a large green here, and the 19th-century church contains fine stained glass of earlier date.

Turn left on to an unclassified road SP 'Bells Yew Green' and at the latter turn right on to the B2169 'Lamberhurst' road. Return to Kent. Drive through woodland, then pass a left turn leading to the ruins of Bayham Abbey.

BAYHAM ABBEY, E Sussex
Claimed to be the most impressive group of monastic remains in Sussex, this picturesque ruin (NT) dates from the 13th century and comprises a church, monastery buildings, and the former gatehouse – all easily identifiable (open).

After a further ½ mile pass a left turn leading to The Owl House.

THE OWL HOUSE, Kent
Once the haunt of wool smugglers, this small half-timbered building (open) dates from the 16th century and stands in beautiful grounds. Features of the latter include woodland lakes and splendid collections of flowering shrubs.

In 1¼ miles turn left on to the B2100 and enter Lamberhurst.

LAMBERHURST, Kent
Although strung out along the busy Tunbridge Wells to Hastings road, this old village has managed to retain its own identity and features a fine 14th-century church.

About 1 mile south, off the A21, is Scotney Old Castle.

The weathered and fissured surfaces of such sandstone outcrops as Bowles Rocks, near Eridge Green, make ideal nursery faces for trainee mountaineers. All round the rocks are expanses of sand that have been worn from their surfaces.

Rudyard Kipling lived at Bateman's from 1902 until his death in 1936. The interior of the house is preserved much as he left it.

High Rocks is one of many sandstone outcrops situated near Tunbridge Wells.

SCOTNEY CASTLE, Kent

Ruins of this 14th-century tower and an attached 17th-century house (NT) stand in a landscaped and moated garden planted with trees and flowering shrubs (open). Apart from the interest of the buildings themselves, the gardens are among the finest in the country.

From Lamberhurst return along the B2100 'Wadhurst' road and re-enter E Sussex. In 3 miles turn left on to the B2099 to visit Wadhurst.

WADHURST, E Sussex

The churchyard of SS Peter and Paul features 30 iron grave slabs, a powerful indication of Wadhurst's one-time importance as an iron-smelting centre.

In 1¼ miles turn right on to an unclassified road SP 'Burwash Common'. Pass through woodland to Stonegate.

STONEGATE, E Sussex

This small village has a modern church and is attractively grouped round a junction of minor roads and lanes.

In Stonegate turn left on to the 'Burwash' road and after another ¾ mile turn right. Drive over a level crossing and cross the River Rother to enter Burwash.

BURWASH, E Sussex

In Burwash churchyard is a cast-iron grave slab that is claimed to be the oldest in the country. Pleasant old buildings in the High Street include timber-framed cottages.

Meet a junction with the A265 and turn right. Reach the war memorial and turn left on to an unclassified road SP 'Woods Corner'. In ½ mile pass a right turn leading to Bateman's.

BATEMAN'S, E Sussex

Built in 1634 for a local ironmaster, this lovely house (NT) is best known as the one-time home of writer Rudyard Kipling. Much of the neighbourhood is featured in his *Puck of Pook's Hill.*

Climb to 646ft, cross the River Dudwell, and drive through Dallington Forest. Reach Woods Corner, and at the Swan Inn turn right then left on to the 'Pont's Green' road. Later follow SP 'Ninfield' and descend. Meet the B2204 and turn right SP 'Hailsham'. Later turn right on to the A271 for Boreham Street.

BOREHAM STREET, E Sussex

This village has an appealing character enhanced by attractive houses and the White Friars Hotel. Inside the latter is a 16th-century chimney breast.

Continue through Boreham Street and in ½ mile turn left on to an unclassified road passing Herstmonceux Castle.

HERSTMONCEUX CASTLE, E Sussex

Herstmonceux Castle, a fortified 15th-century moated manor house, was for a time a ruin, before being carefully restored in the 1930's. From 1948 to the mid eighties it was the home of the Royal Greenwich

Observatory before its move to Cambridge. In the Sussex Farm Heritage Centre are some award-winning shire horses plus historic farm associated machinery.

Go forward to Wartling.

WARTLING, E Sussex

Wartling boasts a church with box pews, an 18th-century pulpit, and a wealth of fascinating Georgian monuments.

At Wartling bear right on to the 'Pevensey' road and cross the flat Pevensey Levels. Meet the A27 and turn right into Pevensey.

PEVENSEY, E Sussex

William the Conqueror disembarked here in 1066, and later built a stout castle within ancient Roman walls that had once been shaded by the

vast Forest of Anderida. The village itself preserves Tudor buildings. The old Mint House contains a small museum.

Continue along the A27 to Westham.

WESTHAM, E Sussex

It is probable that the local church was once part of the ancient Hospital of St Cross, most of which stood outside the west gate of Pevensey Castle. Close by is a pair of 15th-century houses.

Turn left on to the B2191 SP 'Eastbourne'. Drive over a level crossing and later join the A259 to return to Eastbourne.

Herstmonceux Castle was built when brick was newly fashionable in England.

THE EDGE OF THE NORTH DOWNS

Much of this is National Trust country, protected for its outstanding beauty. Valley woodlands and high, empty commons in Surrey rise to soaring outliers of the West Sussex downs, which roll summit after windy summit into the chalklands of south Kent.

EPSOM, Surrey

In the 18th century this pleasant market town was famous for the medicinal springs that gave their name to Epsom Salts; even before that it was known for horse racing. The popularity of the spa has waned, but that of the turf is still in good heart. Among the town's more notable buildings are 19th-century Durdans and 17th-century Waterloo House.

Leave Epsom from the southern end of the High Street, enter a roundabout, and take the 2nd exit to join the B280. Cross Epsom Common, with a picnic site to the right, and after 1½ miles approach traffic lights. A detour from the main tour route can be made by turning right at these lights for Chessington Zoo.

CHESSINGTON ZOO, Gt London

In 1931 Reginald Stuart Goddard founded this famous zoo in the grounds of Burnt Stub Manor, the successor to a house burned by Cromwellian troops. The grounds cover 65 acres and contain a large variety of birds, animals, and a children's zoo.

On the main route, continue forward from the traffic lights for 2 miles and turn left on to the A244 for Oxshott. Then turn right on to an unclassified road for Stoke D'Abernon.

STOKE D'ABERNON, Surrey

Preserved in the local church is Sir John d'Abernon's brass of 1277, thought to be the earliest memorial of its kind in the country. The old manor house is Tudor at heart, but received a brick face-lift sometime during the 18th century.

Turn right on to the A245 for Cobham.

A fine example of the screenwork at the church in Charlwood

COBHAM, Surrey

An inscription on the bridge here tells of an earlier structure raised by Queen Matilda, wife of Henry I, because one of her ladies drowned while crossing the pool.

At Cobham, turn left on to an unclassified road SP 'Downside and Ockham'. Cross the river bridge, then turn right and follow SP 'Ockham'.

OCKHAM, Surrey

Hidden among the trees of Ockham Park, close to the great house, is the village church. This is well known for its lovely 13th-century east window of 7 lancets, sometimes known as the Seven Sisters.

Drive to the war memorial and turn right on to the B2039. Take the next turning left on to an unclassified road. Meet crossroads and go forward for 3 miles to East Clandon.

Robert Adam was responsible for many of the fine rooms in Georgian Hatchlands, near East Clandon.

EAST CLANDON, Surrey

Timber cottages and large old barns give this place an enviable air of timelessness and peace, but the mainly 13th-century church has been poorly restored. Admiral Boscawen built 18th-century Hatchlands (NT) for his retirement, but died before he could enjoy it.

Turn left to join the A246 and continue to West Horsley.

WEST HORSLEY, Surrey

A church stood at West Horsley before the Normans came, but the massive tower dates from the 12th century. The body of the building shows traces of almost every subsequent century, including very good 15th-century screens. Sir Walter Raleigh's remains are said to lie under the south chapel.

Continue to East Horsley.

EAST HORSLEY, Surrey

The curious 19th-century mansion known as East Horsley Towers houses the Electricity Council's Staff College. Much older is the local parish church, which was altered considerably in the 13th century and restored almost out of recognition in the 19th. Beautiful recumbent figures of Thomas and Catherine Cornwallis and several old brasses can be seen inside.

Left: Leith Hill Forest is a delightful mixture of woodland and heath.
Below: 18th century Leith Hill Tower.

Continue for $\frac{1}{2}$ mile, turn right on to an unclassified road SP 'Shere', and after another $\frac{1}{2}$ mile bear left with SP 'Dorking'. Ascend through woodland to the summit of the North Downs, and after $1\frac{1}{2}$ miles meet crossroads and turn right SP 'Abinger'. Descend (1 in 6) White Downs Hill and continue for 1 mile, then turn left on to the A25. After $\frac{1}{2}$ mile turn right on to an unclassified road and ascend for $1\frac{1}{4}$ miles. A short detour can be made from the main tour route by turning sharp left to Friday Street.

NORTH DOWNS
This range of chalk hills starts near Farnham in Surrey and extends across Kent to the white cliffs of Dover, culminating in a 900ft summit near Woldingham.

FRIDAY STREET, Surrey
Old cottages and a single street leading to a lake fringed with pine and oak are the main features of this village. The Stephen Langton Inn recalls a prelate of that name who played a leading role in the signing of Magna Carta. Severell's Copse (NT) comprises 59 acres of woodland stretching from the lake to Leith Hill.

Return to the T-junction on the main route, turn left, then keep forward SP 'Leith Hill'. After $1\frac{1}{2}$ miles pass a footpath leading left to Leith Hill.

LEITH HILL, Surrey
Much of the wooded countryside south of Friday Street is protected by the National Trust, including Leith Hill, Duke's Warren, and the estate of Leith Hill Place. The hill itself carries a picturesque tower whose top is 1,029ft above sea level – the highest point in Surrey.

Continue for $1\frac{1}{4}$ miles to join the B2126, then keep left for Ockley.

OCKLEY, Surrey
The local village green is sited on the course of the great Roman Stane Street. The local church enjoys a delightful setting and its tower dates from the 18th-century and a timbered porch is of 15th-century origin.

Turn left on to the A29. After the Kings Arms turn right on to the B2126. Continue for $1\frac{1}{2}$ miles, then cross over the A24 to enter Capel. Turn right on to unclassified road SP 'Newdigate' in $\frac{1}{2}$ mile turn left then turn right and enter Newdigate.

NEWDIGATE, Surrey
Typical of Wealden villages in general, Newdigate stands in an area that was once covered by dense forest. The forest has all but disappeared, but some of the great oaks that grew hereabouts can be traced to the massive pillars and arches of the local church tower.

Turn right and drive to Rusper.

RUSPER, W Sussex
Several half-timbered and tile-hung cottages survive in this pretty village, and St Mary Magdalene's Church boasts a sturdy 16th-century tower.

Bear left SP 'Crawley', continue for $\frac{1}{4}$ mile, then turn right for Faygate. At Faygate turn left SP 'Crawley'. Meet a main road turn left on to the A264. To the right is St Leonard's Forest.

ST LEONARD'S FOREST, W Sussex
The forests of St Leonard's and Worth, along with various scattered woodlands, are among the only sizeable remnants left of the vast prehistoric Forest of Anderida.

After $2\frac{3}{4}$ miles turn left on to the A23 Crawley bypass. Follow SP 'London' through Crawley suburbs.

CRAWLEY, W Sussex
The planning of this new town is not without merit. Its industrial estates are well separated from the residential areas, and some of the worst effects of high-density building have been avoided by the imaginative use of open spaces. Some $2\frac{1}{2}$ miles north of Crawley is the Greyhound Hotel, Tinsley Green, the venue for the international marbles championship, which began as a competition between two local men for the hand of a girl in marriage.

Continue with the A23 SP 'London' to pass Gatwick Airport.

GATWICK AIRPORT, W Sussex
London's second airport after Heathrow, provides many scheduled and charter flights. The spectators' viewing area is in the terminal.

Continue for 1 mile, enter a roundabout, and leave by the 1st exit on to an unclassified road leading to Charlwood and Leigh. A detour can be made from the main tour route by taking the 3rd exit from this roundabout into Horley.

HORLEY, Surrey
A knight's effigy of c1315 and a 15th-century brass can be seen in the local church, and the half-timbered Six Bells Inn dates from the 15th-century.
Continue to Charlwood.

CHARLWOOD, Surrey
The 11th- to 15-century church in Charlwood is noted for its screen work and wall paintings. The privately-run Gatwick Zoo & Aviaries covers 10 acres, with many of the animals and birds in natural settings.
Continue to Leigh.

LEIGH, Surrey
Charming old houses in this village are complemented by a green and a 15th-century church famous for its memorial brasses. Particularly good examples of the latter are those to the Ardernes, who lived in the area during the 15th century.

Pass through Leigh and after $\frac{1}{4}$ mile turn right at the Seven Stars (PH) for Betchworth, crossing the River Mole.

The lake at Friday Street is part of the National Trust property of Leith Hill.

BETCHWORTH, Surrey
High trees border the River Mole here, and the church preserves a great Norman chest of solid oak beneath its tower.

Meet a T-junction and turn left then right SP 'Walton-on-the-Hill'. Continue to a roundabout and take the 2nd exit on to the B2032. Climb (1 in 6) Pebble Hill to the downs. At the summit turn left on to the B2033 SP 'Box Hill'. Then bear left on to an unclassified road for Box Hill Country Park and picnic site.

BOX HILL, Surrey
Named after the box trees that grow on its flanks, 563ft Box Hill (NT) is a noted viewpoint and designated area of outstanding natural beauty, including both wood and downland scenery and a Country Park.

Descend to the bottom of the hill. Approach a T-junction and turn right SP 'Mickleham' B2209. Within $\frac{1}{4}$ mile turn right again on to an unclassified road SP 'Headley'. A detour can be made from the main tour by driving ahead for Mickleham.

MICKLEHAM, Surrey
Playwright George Meredith was born here in 1864. Yews from a Druid's Grove folly stand in the grounds of 18th-century Norbury Park.

Meet a T-junction and turn right on to the B2033. Headley Heath (NT) lies away to the right. Ascend and turn left on to an unclassified road for Headley SP 'Epsom'.

HEADLEY, Surrey
Yews mark the spot where Headley's 14th-century church was pulled down in the last century, and the spire of its 19th-century successor serves as a Surrey landmark. The church bell is a good 500 years old.

After $1\frac{3}{4}$ miles meet crossroads and turn right. Pass Epsom Downs racecourse.

EPSOM DOWNS RACECOURSE, Surrey
The course here has been the home of good racing since the reign of James I, and has been the venue for the Derby since 1780 perhaps one of Britain's most famous races.

Turn left on to the B290 and return to Epsom.

Derby Day at Epsom racecourse attracts racing enthusiasts from all walks of life.

FROM THE SEA TO THE NORTH DOWNS

At Dover soaring cliffs of dazzling white chalk mark the end of the North Downs' rolling march to the sea. Inland the massive towers of Canterbury Cathedral commemorate the halt of paganism, and the rebirth of Christianity in Kent.

FOLKESTONE, Kent
A popular holiday resort and a harbour for cross-Channel ferries, this ancient port still has a fishing fleet and fish market. A wide grassy promenade known as The Leas extends along the cliff top, and attractively wooded walks slope down to the beach. Spade House, the one-time home of writer H G Wells, now contains a museum.

Follow SP 'Hythe, A259' to Sandgate.

SANDGATE, Kent
The castle here belongs to a series built by Henry VIII after his religious break with Rome, when the threat of invasion seemed very real. Shorncliffe Camp, established on the plateau above Sandgate at the beginning of the 19th century, was founded to cope with the later threat of Napoleon's navy.

Continue to Hythe.

HYTHE, Kent
This ancient Cinque Port was very prosperous in the 12th and 13th centuries; its wealth today is assured by its popularity as a resort. Near by is the Royal Military Canal, which was built in 1804 as a defence against Napoleon but nowadays serves as a valuable leisure amenity. A terminus of the Romney, Hythe, and Dymchurch narrow-gauge railway is in the town.

Follow SP 'Ashford' and 'London' to Hythe Station, past the Royal Military Canal. Return along the 'Folkestone' road, before taking the B2065 'Elham' road and climbing to high ground. Fine views of the North Downs can be enjoyed from here. Continue, and cross the M20 and at roundabout take 2nd exit B2065 to Lyminge.

LYMINGE, Kent
There has been a Christian community at Lyminge since 633, when King Ethelbert's daughter and Bishop Paulinus founded their abbey here. Fragments of walling from the original buildings are incorporated in the Church of SS Mary and Ethelburga. Most of Lyminge is Victorian; the half-timbered Old Robus and 18th-century Old Rectory are notable exceptions.

Drive to the far end of the village take 2nd left on to an unclassified road SP 'Rhodes Minnis' passing through Sibton Park. In ¼ mile (beyond Rhodes Minnis) branch left and climb through Lyminge Forest on to the North Downs. Cross the B2068 and turn right for Elmsted.

ELMSTED, Kent
Flint-built St James's Church in Elmsted is of Norman and later date and carries a medieval west tower. Inside is a late medieval half-timbered altar screen.

At Elmsted Church turn left, SP 'Wye', and continue to Hastingleigh.

HASTINGLEIGH, Kent
Norman and later St Mary's Church stands aloof from the village, half hidden from view by the fall of the downs.

Continue on the 'Wye' road to Wye Downs nature reserve.

WYE DOWNS AND NATURE RESERVE, Kent
Wye and Crundale Downs rise some 2 miles south-east of Wye and form part of the North Downs. The escarpment, covered with shrubs and woodland, is a nature reserve.

Continue to Wye.

THE NORTH DOWNS
This chalk range runs west from the White Cliffs of Dover to the Hog's Back near Guildford, and culminates in a 900ft hill at Woldingham.

WYE, Kent
Archbishop of Canterbury John Kempe founded a college of priests here in 1447, but King Henry VIII put paid to its religious teaching and it later served as a grammar school. Since 1900 it has been the agriculture school of London University. Other features of the town include a racecourse, a Georgian mill house, and 18th-century Olantigh–a venue for summer music festivals.

Follow SP 'Ashford' and cross the Great Stour River. Drive over a level crossing and turn right on to the 'Canterbury' road. After ¾ mile turn right on to the A28 and drive along the Great Stour Valley to Godmersham.

Exquisite stained glass in Canterbury Cathedral depicts Thomas à Becket and the miraculous cures associated with his name.

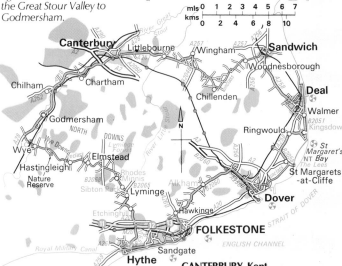

GODMERSHAM, Kent
A monument to Edward Knight, a close relative of novelist Jane Austen and owner of 18th-century Godmersham Park, can be seen in the local Norman and later church. Landscaped grounds surround the big house.

Continue to the outskirts of Chilham.

CHILHAM, Kent
Chilham village is gathered respectfully around a square at the gate of its castle, which was built for Henry II in 1174. The 300-acre grounds (open) feature wood and lakeside walks, gardens, plus medieval jousting displays.

Continue to the edge of Chartham.

CHARTHAM, Kent
This large Stour valley village is a well-known angling centre. St Mary's Church is of 13th-century date and boasts one of the oldest sets of bells in the country. East of the village is a ruined medieval chapel on a farm.

Continue to Canterbury.

CANTERBURY, Kent
When the Romans came here they took over a Belgic Stourside community and developed it into the town of *Durovernum Cantiorum*, later to become a Christian community. When the Romans left the area was swept by waves of invaders who had little time for Christianity, but in the year 597 St Augustine's mission arrived to convert King Ethelbert of Kent and restore the town's dilapidated churches. Shortly afterwards Canterbury became the Metropolitan City of the Church of England. Long stretches of the city wall survive on Roman foundations, and the present cathedral dates from 1070. This fine structure is best known as the place where Archbishop Thomas à Becket was murdered for his denial of the king's authority over the church. Canterbury Castle has the 3rd largest Norman keep in Britain. King's School is thought to be the oldest extant.

Follow SP 'Dover' then 'Sandwich' to leave Canterbury on the A257. Continue to Littlebourne.

LITTLEBOURNE, Kent
Close to the local flint church is an ancient thatched barn. Neat single-

Fishermen take aboard a net on the beach at Hythe.

A number of Chilham's ancient houses were partly refaced in brick during the 18th century.

This portrait of the 1st Earl of Sandwich hangs in the Guildhall at Sandwich.

storey cottages dating from the 17th century stand at the end of the village green.

Continue to Wingham.

WINGHAM, Kent

Interesting buildings in this town include Debridge House and Wingham Court, both of which date from the 18th century. Many of the local buildings are picturesquely half timbered, and the Red Lion dates from the 15th century.

Turn right on to the B2046 'Folkestone' road, and in 1 mile turn left on to an unclassified road SP 'Chillenden'.

CHILLENDEN, Kent

The local church retains a good many Norman features. Chillenden Windmill, built in 1868 and restored in 1958, stands $\frac{1}{2}$ mile north of the village.

Meet crossroads, turn left, and leave Chillenden by the 'Woodnesborough' road.

WOODNESBOROUGH, Kent

The church here suffered heavy restoration in the 19th century, but it retains a charming 18th-century cupola on the west tower. South-east of the church is a 17th-century brick cottage.

Continue to Sandwich.

SANDWICH, Kent

This, the oldest of the Cinque Ports, is now separated from the sea by 2 miles of sand-dunes. Among its many outstanding old buildings are the medieval Barbican, Fishgate, and a variety of houses and inns. St Bartholomew's Hospital guest house dates from the 15th century, and both the Guildhall and Manwood Court were built in the 16th. The Old House is a fine example of Tudor design. Much of the old beach between the town and Sandwich Bay is occupied by Sandwich Golf Course, which is famous the world over.

Leave Sandwich by the A258 'Dover' road and later turn left on to the A258 'Deal' road. Enter Deal.

Below: Dover's wonderfully preserved Roman lighthouse is thought to date from the 1st century. Right: the unmistakable White Cliffs of Dover would have been a familiar landmark to Roman sailors.

DEAL, Kent

Henry VIII built a castle (AM) in the shape of a six-petalled flower at Deal, though considerable protection was already offered by the notorious Goodwin Sands. These vast, shifting beds lie just 5 miles offshore and have caused hundreds of wrecks. In its early history the town was a limb of the Cinque Ports, but most of its development dates from the end of the 17th century. Local exhibits can be seen in the town museum, and collections from all over the world are shown in the Maritime Museum.

Proceed along the seafront on the 'Dover' road and branch left on to the B2057, SP 'Kingsdown'. Pass 16th-century Walmer Castle.

WALMER, Kent

The Henrian Castle (AM) here stands in attractive gardens and is the official residence of the Lord Warden of the Cinque Ports. The Duke of Wellington died here in 1852 and a number of his possessions are on display inside. Walmer Lifeboat is famous for the many rescues it has made from the Goodwin Sands.

Continue to the small resort of Kingsdown and turn inland SP 'Dover'. Drive to Ringwould, overlooking The Leas (NT).

RINGWOULD, Kent

Several bronze-age barrows can be seen near Ringwould on Free Down. The 12th- to 14th-century church has an attractive 17th-century tower.

Join the A258 'Dover' road for a short distance and turn left on to the B2058 for St Margaret's at Cliffe.

ST MARGARET'S AT CLIFFE, Kent

A variety of old buildings line the twisty main street. A haven of rural peace can be found in The Pines Garden (NT).

A short detour can be taken from the main route to St Margaret's Bay by keeping forward for 1 mile.

ST MARGARET'S BAY, Kent

This sheltered little bay, completely enclosed by towering chalk cliffs, is a popular starting point for cross-Channel swimmers. A narrow beach peters out to weed-bearded boulders and large pools in the chalk bedrock on each side.

Return to St Margaret's at Cliffe, turn left into unclassified Reach Road, and continue to a fine viewpoint overlooking Dover Harbour. Pass a footpath to the Blériot Memorial and turn left on to the A258. Enter Dover.

DOVER, Kent

Formerly the Roman walled city of *Dubris*, Dover was chief of the Cinque Ports and has a magnificent castle (AM) built on a site occupied since prehistoric times. Its strategic position gives it total command of the harbour, and successive English kings spent vast sums on its development. It was last used for military purposes during World War II. The Pharos, a surprisingly well-preserved Roman lighthouse, stands within the castle walls near the exceptionally fine Saxon Church of St Mary de Castro. Dover Town Hall incorporates the 13th-century Hall of Maison Dieu, and nearby Maison Dieu House dates from 1663. The oldest and best-preserved wall paintings north of the Alps can be seen in the Roman Painted House. A granite memorial in North Fall meadow marks the landing of Louis Blériot in 1909, after his historic cross-Channel flight.

Follow SP 'Canterbury' to leave Dover by London Road (A256). Pass a railway bridge and 1 mile farther on turn left on to the B2060 'Alkham' road, then passing Alkham, climbing through a North Downs valley to Hawkinge.

HAWKINGE, Kent

The Kent Battle of Britain Museum contains the largest and most comprehensive collection of remains of British and German aircraft from the Battle of Britain.

Return to Folkestone on the A260.

IN THE NORTH DOWNS

Some of the finest views in the south of England can be enjoyed from the great chalk ridge of the Hog's Back, which itself can be seen across miles of flat farm land scattered with small woods and copses. This is the country of the yellowhammer and skylark, of thorn-covered slopes and the gnarled creepers of old man's beard.

GUILDFORD, Surrey

Medieval kings built a great castle in this ancient town and merchants later developed it into an important centre of the wool industry. Nowadays the castle has vanished except for a 3-storey keep (open) in flower gardens, but the prosperity of wool is reflected in many fine old buildings. Charles Dickens thought the steep High Street 'the most beautiful in the kingdom'. At its summit is the 16th-century Grammar School, the contemporary Abbot's Hospital, and an 18th-century church. Farther down, the ornate clock of the 17th-century Guildhall hangs over the pavement near the Saxon tower of St Mary's Church, and the 19th-century Church of St Nicholas makes an interesting contrast at the bottom of the hill. The River Wey features an interesting 18th-century riverside crane powered by a 20ft treadmill. New buildings include Sir Edward Maufe's controversial cathedral on Stag Hill.

Leave Guildford town centre with SP 'Other Routes' and after 1 mile turn left on to the bypass SP 'Petersfield' then join the A3. After 2¼ miles drive under a road bridge, and in another mile pass the turning for Compton and Loseley House on the left. A short detour from the main route can be taken along the B3000 in the pleasant village of Compton and Loseley House.

The Hog's Back is criss-crossed by quiet country lanes.

COMPTON, Surrey

A gallery devoted entirely to Victorian painter and sculptor G F Watts displays some 200 of his works in this small village. He is commemorated by a mortuary chapel which features vivid interior decoration by his widow.

LOSELEY HOUSE, Surrey

Sir William More, a kinsman of the ill-fated Sir Thomas More, used stone from Waverley Abbey to build this magnificent Elizabethan mansion (open) near Compton. Fine ceilings are complemented by panelling from King Henry VIII's Nonsuch Palace, and every room is appointed with furniture and hangings from many periods.

Continue along the A3 for another ⅓ mile, then turn right on to the B3000 SP 'Farnham'. Proceed to Puttenham.

PUTTENHAM, Surrey

A handsomely aged church with a 15th-century tower enhances the quiet charm of this small village.

In the village turn left on to an unclassified road and continue along the southern slopes of the Hog's Back to Seale.

THE HOG'S BACK, Surrey

At its highest point this great whaleback ridge of chalk, an outlier of the North Downs, rises to 505ft above sea level. It stretches from Guildford to Farnham, with several parking areas along its length.

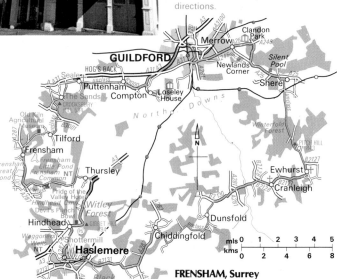

Guildford's fine 17th-century clock hangs high above the main street and can be seen for many yards in both directions.

Drive past the church in Seale and turn left. Proceed for ½ mile and meet crossroads, then turn left for The Sands. Cross a main road SP 'Tilford' and pass 534ft Crooksbury Hill on the left. Continue to crossroads and turn left again SP 'Elstead'. After a short distance turn left on to the B3001 and take the next turning right on to an unclassified road for Tilford.

TILFORD, Surrey

Features of this pleasant village include two partly medieval bridges over the River Wey, and a huge old tree known as King John's Oak. The latter is said to be many centuries old. The village is noted for its Bach music festivals. One mile west is the Old Kiln Agricultural Museum.

Cross the River Wey twice with SP 'Frensham' and after ¼ mile turn left. Continue for another 1½ miles and turn left on to the A287 SP 'Hindhead'. Proceed through Frensham.

FRENSHAM, Surrey

Frensham's lovely ponds are surrounded by woods and heathland on the Hampshire-Surrey border. The Great Pond covers 108 acres, and the Little Pond is resplendent with water lilies in late spring and summer. The 900-acre gorse and heather common (NT) features a line of large prehistoric bowl barrows, and much of the area is now protected as a country park. Frensham's restored church has a Norman font and, under the tower, a great copper cauldron reputed to be over 400 years old. Tradition holds that it belonged to a local witch called Mother Ludlam, and an 18th-century writer tells of it having been filled with ale to entertain the village 'at the wedding of poor maids'.

Cross Frensham Common to reach Frensham Great Pond and Country Park. Proceed for ¾ mile and turn left on to an unclassified road SP 'Thursley'. After 1½ miles reach the Pride of the Valley Hotel. Cross the main road and after 1¾ miles turn right for Thursley.

THURSLEY, Surrey

Old houses and charming cottages straggle along a winding lane to the village church which has a sundial on its shingled spire. A curious epitaph to an unknown sailor murdered by three ruffians at Hindhead in 1786 can be seen on a tombstone in the churchyard.

In ½ mile turn left and ½ mile further turn right on to the A3 'Hindhead' road. Drive over Hindhead Common, with the Devil's Punch Bowl on the right and Gibbet Hill, a picnic site, and Witley Forest on the left. Enter Hindhead.

Four great beams inside Thursley Church support its shingled steeple.

HINDHEAD, Surrey
Founded in the 19th century on the highest town site in Surrey, Hindhead offers some of the most beautiful surroundings in the county. The noted viewpoint of Gibbet Hill (NT) rises to 894ft in the north east, the deep combe of the Devil's Punch Bowl (NT) cuts through a sandstone ridge near by, and all around is Witley Forest. Off the B3002 1½ miles south west is the beauty spot of Waggoner's Wells (NT).

Follow SP 'Haslemere, A287' and descend to Shottermill, then keep forward on the B2131 for Haslemere.

HASLEMERE, Surrey
Haslemere stands in dense woods at the northern foot of 918ft-high Blackdown. For centuries the town has been a centre for craftsmen, and today the tradition is maintained at the Dolmetsch musical instrument workshops and museum (open). Aldworth, home of the great 19th-century poet Tennyson, stands on the slopes of Black Down. A number of 17th-century tiled houses survive behind a raised walk in the town, and the 19th-century Educational Museum of Sir John Hutchinson stands in the High Street (open). The town's annual music festival, usually held in July, is invariably devoted to the Baroque period.

Leave Haslemere on the B2131 SP 'Petworth', with Black Down (NT) on the right. After 2½ miles bear left SP 'Chiddingfold', and after a further ¾ mile meet a T-junction. Turn left on to the A283 for Chiddingfold.

Tree-shrouded Silent Pool is connected in legend with King John.

CHIDDINGFOLD, Surrey
In medieval times this large village was very famous for its fine quality glass. Despite its large size it is one of the loveliest Wealden villages. At its heart is a pretty green with a thorn tree said to be 500 years old, a pond complete with ducks and water lilies, and the delightful 14th-century Crown Inn.

Drive to the Crown Inn and turn right on to an unclassified road SP 'Dunsfold'. Reach the far side of the green and bear right, then continue for 1 mile, turn left, and proceed to Dunsfold.

DUNSFOLD, Surrey
A modern lychgate and a tunnel of clipped yews lead to Dunsfold Church, which dates from the 13th century and has an attractive Tudor porch. Its pews may be the oldest still used in England.

One mile beyond Dunsfold turn right on to the B2130 SP 'Cranleigh'. Continue for 1 mile, then bear left and after ¼ mile turn right. Drive over staggered crossroads and continue for 1¼ miles. Turn right on to the B2128 and drive into Cranleigh.

CRANLEIGH, Surrey
Cranleigh is more than a village, and yet not quite large enough to call a town. Its pleasant green has a rural aspect, but the long main street lined with maples planted by Canadian soldiers in World War I might have been borrowed from a much larger place. In 1859 a surgeon called Napper and the local rector together founded the first cottage hospital.

Clandon Park was designed by a Venetian architect in the Palladian style.

Drive to the end of the village and turn left on to the B2127. After 2¼ miles turn left again into Ewhurst.

EWHURST, Surrey
Climbers come to Ewhurst to test their mettle on Pitch Hill, a sandstone outcrop that rises 1 mile to the north of the village. Ewhurst Mill has not worked for a century and was once a haunt of smugglers.

Keep forward in Ewhurst, on to the unclassified 'Shere' road. After ¾ mile bear left and cross Pitch Hill, with Winterfold Forest on the left, and drive into Shere.

SHERE, Surrey
Situated on the River Tillingbourne under the edge of the North Downs, this enchanting village has long

proved an attraction to artists. The church, which figures in the *Domesday Book*, has a Norman tower with a medieval shingled spire. The White Horse Inn has a frame of ancient ship's timbers.

Drive to a T-junction and turn left SP 'Guildford'. Continue to the next T-junction and turn left again to join the A25. After ¼ mile, off the main road to the right, is the Silent Pool.

SILENT POOL, Surrey
According to legend King John watched a local girl bathing here. She drowned herself in a fit of shame, and anybody visiting this quiet, tree-encircled water might easily imagine that her spirit lingers here still.

Ascend to Newlands Corner.

NEWLANDS CORNER, Surrey
This famous 567ft high North Downs beauty spot offers views across the Weald to the South Downs.

At Newlands Corner keep right on the A25. Descend for 1 mile and meet crossroads. Turn left on to the A25. By keeping straight ahead a short detour can be taken from the main route to Clandon Park.

CLANDON PARK, Surrey
Built in the early 1730s, this classical mansion (NT) features noteworthy plaster decoration, and stands in gardens refashioned by Capability Brown. A famous collection of china, furniture and needlework bequeathed to the nation by Mrs Hannah Gubbay in 1969 is displayed in these elegant surroundings.

Continue on the A25 to Merrow.

MERROW, Surrey
A footpath that starts between the church and inn at Merrow runs across gentle downland to a summit which affords views into 8 or 9 counties, depending on the weather.

Forward along the A246 returning to Guildford.

HASTINGS, E Sussex

William the Conqueror ensured Hastings a firm place in English history when he assembled his army here in 1066, although the battle of Hastings actually took place at nearby Battle. His stone Norman castle now lies in ruins overlooking the town and can be reached via a cliff lift. During the Middle Ages Hastings was an important Cinque Port; until the end of the 15th century these south-east defence ports were duty-bound to supply ships and men in the event of invasion. However, when Hastings harbour silted up, the town turned to fishing for its livelihood. The Old Town to the east is the picturesque fishermen's quarter and the heart of the ancient town. Weather-boarded houses crowd down alleys to the shingle beach and the shops mostly sell sailors' bric-a-brac. Curious 3-storeyed square structures made of tarred wood stand on the beach; they are fishing net lofts and were originally built high to keep ground rent to a minimum. Fishermens' Museum which used to be the local chapel, is now packed with seafaring treasures.

Leave Hastings on the A259, SP 'Brighton', along the seafront. Pass through the neighbouring resort of St Leonards to Bexhill.

BEXHILL, E Sussex

In 1880, Lord de la Warr, member of an old Sussex family, developed this little town into a holiday resort. The rather ugly de la Warr Pavilion sitting on the sea front forms the focal point of the traditional range of seaside entertainments — concert halls, theatres, restaurants and sun lounges. Rather more attractive is the old village behind the coast line.

At Bexhill follow the A269, SP 'London', and pass through Sidley to Ninfield. Here turn right on to the Battle road and continue to Catsfield. At the end of the village turn right on to the B2095, SP 'Battle Station'. Later turn left on to the A2100 and enter Battle.

THE KENTISH WEALD TO THE CINQUE PORTS

From Hastings, where English history was made in 1066 to Rye, a smugglers' paradise in the 18th century: both vital Cinque Ports. Inland, towards the Weald, the tour passes the windmills, weather-boarding and hop fields which characterise Kent.

Above: Cranbrook's smock mill

Below: the cottage garden at Sissinghurst Castle

BATTLE, E Sussex

The Battle of Hastings took place just outside Battle, which is how the town got its name. King Harold II lost, and it was this defeat which gave the town an abbey, because William the Conqueror vowed beforehand that if he was the victor he would build one by way of thanks to God. When St Martin's Abbey was built, the high altar was placed on the spot where Harold fell. The abbey remains (OACT), actually of later buildings than William's, include a fine gateway, the monks' sleeping quarters and the cellars. In Langton House the history of Battle from Neolithic times to the present day is vividly illustrated and there are many pieces of Sussex iron from the industry which flourished over a 1,000 years ago. There is also a copy (1821) of the Bayeux Tapestry.

Remain on the A2100, SP 'London', then in 3 miles turn left on to the A21 and continue through Robertsbridge to Hurst Green. Beyond the village turn right on to the A265 and enter Kent before reaching Hawkhurst.

HAWKHURST, Kent

Hawkhurst was a onetime stronghold of the notorious Hawkhurst Gang — a group of smugglers who terrorised much of Kent and Sussex in the early 18th century. Now some way between village and town in size, the older part lies around a triangular green known as the Moor. Among the brick and weather-boarded houses around the green stands the church. Its 15th-century window tracery is particularly fine, as is the 14th-century east window.

Follow the A268, SP 'Flimwell/ Tonbridge'. A gradual climb passes through woodland into Sussex again at Flimwell. Here, at the crossroads, turn right to rejoin the A21. In 1 mile turn right on to the B2079 to reach Goudhurst.

GOUDHURST, Kent

Between the duck pond at the bottom of the hill and the church at the top, typical Kentish houses jostle each other up the main street. Goudhurst stands on a steep ridge of land and its church tower, 500ft above sea level, was used as a lookout post in both World War I and II. The church is 14th century, but the stocky tower dates from 1638, when a storm destroyed the original. Wooden painted figures inside represent Sir Alexander Colepeper and his wife and are the best of the church's many monuments.

At Goudhurst turn right on to the A262, SP 'Ashford', and in 1½ miles turn right again on to the B2085, SP 'Hawkhurst'. In 2 miles turn left, SP 'Cranbrook'. On reaching the A229 turn left, then take the next turning right on to the B2189 and enter Cranbrook.

CRANBROOK, Kent

Cranbrook was built from the profits of the cloth trade. With the streams to power fulling mills, oak trees to use as building material and fullers' earth to clean the cloth, it was an ideal centre for the industry. On the edge of the village stands one of the country's most splendid smock mills — their name supposedly coming from the resemblance to a man dressed in a smock. Built in the 18th century, its sails stretch up to nearly 100ft above the ground.

Remain on the B2189, SP 'Staplehurst', and later turn right on to the A229. In ¼ mile turn right again on to the A262, SP 'Ashford', and pass through Sissinghurst. ½ mile beyond the village a turning on the left leads to Sissinghurst Castle.

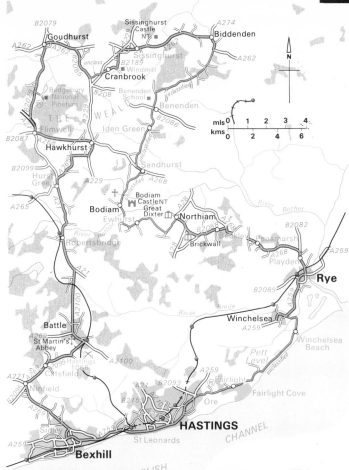

BODIAM, E Sussex
Bodiam Castle (NT) outshines its village by far. The fortress was built in the 14th century to guard this vital crossing point on the River Rother, which was a potential route inland for French invaders. Although it was not attacked at that time, the castle met its fate during the Civil War when Cromwellian armies destroyed it. Now it stands serenely as an empty shell, clearly reflected in its wide lily-covered moat.

At Bodiam turn left on to the Ewhurst road and pass the castle (left). Cross the River Rother and in ½ mile turn left, SP 'Ewhurst Green'. Pass through Ewhurst Green and follow SP 'Northiam'.

NORTHIAM, E Sussex
The gnarled old oak tree on Northiam's village green is famous because Elizabeth I dined under it in 1573. During the occasion she took her shoes off, and let the villagers keep them when she left. They are now kept at Brickwall, so named because of its high surrounding walls. Brickwall was the home of the Frewen family for 400 years and is now a boys' school. At the opposite end of Northiam is Great Dixter (OACT). Nathaniel Lloyd, architectural historian, bought the house in 1911 and commissioned Sir Edwin Lutyens to enlarge and restore it, which he did to good effect. Curiously-clipped yews are the most striking feature of the gardens.

At Northiam turn right on to the A28 Hastings road and on leaving the village branch left on to the B2088, SP 'Rye'. Pass Brickwall House (right) and continue to Beckley. At the far end turn right on to the A268 and continue to Rye.

RYE, E Sussex
Ancient, timbered and Georgian buildings, the romance of a seafaring and smuggling past in every twisting cobbled street and its perch high up on a bluff within sight and smell of the sea, give Rye its considerable charm. When the sea lapped the town walls in the 14th century, Rye was one of the most prosperous ancient ports in Sussex. However, repeated, relentless attacks and burnings by the French, together with the silting up of the harbour, were the town's undoing. One of the buildings to survive the French deflagrations was Ypres Tower — the 13th-century town fort. It is put to good use now as the town museum, containing a fascinating variety of curios from bygone days. Rye so enchanted novelist Henry James that he made his home in the Lamb House (NT) until just before he died.

Leave Rye on the A259 Hastings road. Continue for 2 miles, then cross the river bridge and bear right, then turn sharp left for Winchelsea.

WINCHELSEA, E Sussex
Like Rye, Winchelsea was also a prosperous seaport and a member of the Cinque Ports, but nevertheless the sea has always been its enemy — firstly by completely submerging the old town in the late 13th century, and then by receding and taking with it the prosperity the port bestowed. Court Hall (OACT) is one of the oldest buildings and houses a museum of the town and surrounding area.

Return down the hill and turn right, then turn right again on to the unclassified road for Winchelsea Beach. Continue to Fairlight and later turn left on to the A259 for the return to Hastings.

SISSINGHURST CASTLE, Kent
Vita Sackville-West and her husband Harold Nicolson transformed a few derelict buildings and a near wilderness into an imaginative and beautiful series of gardens, with the Tudor tower and 2 cottages as a centre-piece (NT). Each garden has an individuality of its own. There is the famous white garden (where only white or grey plants grow), the herb garden, the rose garden and many more. Redbrick walls and thick hedges divide the romantic gardens which lead naturally and enchantingly one to another. Vita Sackville-West's study — a glory-hole full of books, letters, diaries, photographs and personal mementoes — is in the tower.

The main tour continues on the A262 to Biddenden.

BIDDENDEN, Kent
Antique shops, tea shops, pubs and restaurants fill most of Biddenden's half-timbered buildings, for it is one of Kent's most popular villages. The quaint village sign depicts the 2 Maids of Biddenden — Eliza and Mary Chulkhurst. They were Siamese twins, said to be born in the 12th century although their dress on the sign is Elizabethan.

A carving of the Biddenden Maids who were joined at the hip and shoulder

At Biddenden turn right and continue on the Ashford Road, then in ¾ mile branch right, SP 'Benenden'. After 3¾ miles, at the T-junction, turn left passing Benenden School (right) and continue to Benenden. Cross the main road here and continue to Iden Green. In 2 miles turn left on' to the A268 into Sandhurst, then turn right, SP 'Bodiam', to re-enter Sussex before reaching Bodiam.

These huts at Hastings, dating from the 16th century, are still used by fishermen to dry out their nets

FAMOUS COLLEGES AND HIDDEN VILLAGES

Unspoilt villages embodying the spirit of rural England speckle the open rolling fields that separate Hertford from Cambridge. Yet it is the city of colleges and courtyards, of beauty and learning, that reigns supreme.

HERTFORD, Herts

Old houses from Jacobean to the Georgian periods mingle well with new buildings in this old county town where 3 rivers, the Lea, the Beane and the Rib meet. Little remains of the old Norman castle except for the charming 15th-century gatehouse, one of the childhood homes of Elizabeth I, standing in pleasant parkland. At the heart of the town are the famous old buildings of Christ's Hospital School, founded by the governors of the Bluecoat School in London. Several appealing figures of Bluecoat children stand on the walls and above the entrance. Lombard House (not open), a lovely Jacobean building, was the home of the judge Sir Henry Chauncy who presided over the last trial for witchcraft ever held in England (see Walkern).

The delicate vaulted ceiling of King's College Chapel, Cambridge, completed in 1515, and its lovely windows which depict Biblical tales

Leave Hertford on the B158, SP 'Wadesmill'. After 1 mile turn left, SP 'Sacombe', bear right at the fork and after 2¾ miles turn left, SP 'Watton', to join the B1001. In ½ mile turn right on to an unclassified road and continue through Sacombe to Dane End. Keep straight on and in ½ mile bear right, then keep left. In another 1¾ miles go over the crossroads, SP 'Westmill', then ¾ mile farther bear right to reach Westmill.

WESTMILL, Herts

Near to this exceptionally pretty village, complete with green and rows of tall-chimneyed cottages surrounding the church, stands one bought by the 19th-century essayist Charles Lamb. He is best know today for *Lamb's Tales from Shakespeare*, which he wrote with his sister, Mary. Button Snap is the evocative name of this thatched 17th-century cottage with tiny latticed windows, and it now belongs to the Lamb Society who have preserved and restored it (not open).

At the village green turn right, SP 'Puckeridge', and on reaching the A10 turn left for Buntingford.

BUNTINGFORD, Herts

The old Roman road of Ermine Street runs through this busy village. There is a fine range of almshouses, built in 1684 by Seth Ward who first became a distinguished scholar at Oxford, then Bishop of Exeter and finally of Salisbury.

By the nearside of the town centre turn right on to the B1038 for Hare Street. Here, turn left on to the B1368, and follow an undulating road through Barkway to Barley.

BARLEY, Herts

For more than 300 years the Fox and Hounds Inn has looked down from its hillside on the old cottages of Barley. The famous inn sign stretches right over the road; across the beam, huntsmen and hounds pursue a fox, which appears to be craftily disappearing into a hole in the roof of the inn.

Branch right, SP 'Great Chishill', to pass under the inn sign, and shortly to join the B1039. Cross into Cambridgeshire before reaching Great Chishill.

GREAT CHISHILL, Cambs

Great Chishill looks out peacefully over one of the quietest corners of Cambridgeshire. The showpiece of the village is the lofty 18th-century post mill, with white-painted timbers and a graceful fantail that turns the mill so that the sails always face into the wind.

Continue on the Saffron Walden road and after 3¼ miles turn left on to an unclassified road for Elmdon. In the village turn right on to the Ickleton road. In 3 miles, by the nearside of Ickleton village, turn left for Duxford.

DUXFORD, Cambs

Duxford's old watermill, listed in the Domesday Book, has attracted several famous visitors in the past, including Charles Kingsley, author of *The Water Babies*. Near the village, on the Battle of Britain airfield where World War II hero Douglas Bader served, is the Imperial War Museum's collection of military aircraft and armoured fighting vehicles; more than 60 historic aircraft are on view. The Duxford Aviation Society's collection of civil aircraft, including Concorde 01, is also open.

At Duxford turn right, then at the church turn left and after ¾ mile reach the junction with the A505. From here a detour can be made by turning left to visit Duxford Airfield. The main tour crosses the main road and continues to Whittlesford.

WHITTLESFORD, Cambs

The early 16th-century Guildhall, its overhanging upper storey supported on carved wooden posts, is only one of many

Westmill village green, complete with water pump

attractive buildings around the village green. In the churchyard lies the graves of many brave young airmen who served at Duxford in World War II and fought and died in the Battle of Britain.

Continue on the unclassified road and in 2½ miles, at the T-junction, turn right for Great Shelford.

GREAT SHELFORD, Cambs

Great Shelford looks out towards the gently rolling Gog Magog Hills which lie just south of Cambridge. The hills take their name from a Romano-British giant who appears in legend, sometimes as 1 person, Gogmagog, sometimes as 2, Gog and Magog. By tradition dating back to at least the 11th century, the outline of 2 gigantic figures was carved on the hillside here at Wandlebury Camp, an Iron-Age fort.

On reaching the A1301 turn left towards Cambridge. At Trumpington turn right at the traffic signals on to the A1309 and continue into Cambridge.

CAMBRIDGE, Cambs

The distinguished and beautiful architecture of Cambridge's great colleges has stamped its personality on the heart of the city even more powerfully than at Oxford. The secluded college courtyards and gardens are usually open to the public, as are the many fine college chapels. The most lovely of these is without doubt King's College Chapel, with its graceful and intricate web of fan-vaulting. Visitors can stroll peacefully along the Backs, a green, sunlit sweep of lawns leading down from St John's, Trinity, Clare, King's and Queens' colleges to the river, where in spring and summer unhurried punts drift up and down. Peterhouse is the oldest college — founded in 1284 by the Bishop of Ely — but students had settled here from Oxford in individual groups attached to monastic schools as early as the previous century. The prettiest of the colleges is held to be Queens'. Its

Mathematical bridge leading from Cloister Court to the gardens is an interesting curiosity; it was designed in 1749 on mathematical principles and originally stood without nails or similar fixings. Even more famous is the Bridge of Sighs at St John's College, so-called from the one at Venice of which it is a copy. Cambridge, as might be expected, has several interesting museums. The Fitzwilliam contains an unrivalled collection of antiquities, paintings, manuscripts and rare objects. The University Botanic Gardens, rated second only to Kew, are best visited in the afternoons when the glasshouses are open.

From the south west side of the city centre follow the A603, SP 'Sandy'. After 2 miles cross the M11 then in ½ mile turn right on to the B1046, SP 'Comberton' and 'Toft', and enter Barton. Continue, SP 'St Neots', through Comberton to Toft. In 3½ miles, at the Fox Inn, turn right and immediately left across the main road for Longstowe. In another 3 miles turn left on to an unclassified road and continue to Gamlingay.

GAMLINGAY, Cambs

The cosy row of mellow redbrick almshouses that are the focus of this appealing village were built in 1665, the year of the Great Plague. Much of the village had been destroyed by fire in 1600, but fortunately the medieval church, a fine stone building, survived.

At the crossroads in Gamlingay turn left on to the B1040 and continue to Potton. Bear right then left through the square, and at the end turn left, SP 'Biggleswade'. In 1 mile, at the crossroads, turn left on to an unclassified road for Sutton — here cross a ford by the side of the old packhorse bridge. At the end of the village go over the crossroads, SP 'Ashwell'. In 1¾ miles, at the Ongley Arms PH, turn right and ½ mile later turn left, SP 'Ashwell'. After 4½ miles, at the war memorial, turn right into Ashwell.

ASHWELL, Herts

Ash trees around the River Rhee have given this lovely village its name. It stands amid open fields, its church tower rising 176ft above the surrounding countryside. Among the many timber-framed houses scattered about its streets, the pargeted and oak-beamed cottages attached to the 17th-century Guildhall form the most charming group. The old Tythe House (AM), which was once the office of the abbots of Westminster, has been restored and preserved as the village museum, where there is a fascinating collection of village history and rural life.

In Ashwell pass the Three Tuns PH and turn left, SP 'Bygrave' and 'Baldock', then go over the crossroads, SP 'Walkern'. In 2 miles cross the main road and 4½ miles farther join the A507, then keep forward on to an unclassified road to Cromer. Here, join the B1037 for Walkern.

WALKERN, Herts

In 1712, the last trial for witchcraft ever held in England took place in Walkern. A woman called Jane Wenham was accused by a local farmer of witchcraft and was tried and sentenced to death by Sir Henry Chauncy. Queen Anne granted her a pardon and as a result of her case the barbaric laws against witchcraft were repealed in 1736.

At the end of the village go forward on to an unclassified road, SP 'Watton'. After 4 miles turn left SP 'Hertford', and enter Watton-at-Stone.

WATTON-AT-STONE, Herts

The elegant, canopied, cast-iron pump, dating from the early 19th century, and Watton Hall (not open), a house of overhanging gables, together form a traditional village group. The flint-built church, containing a wealth of medieval brasses, completes the picture.

At the roundabout take the 3rd exit on to the A602 for the return to Hertford.

LONDON
The Nation's Capital

*One of London's best known landmarks —
the Houses of Parliament, dominated by the
familiar tower of Big Ben.*

London History and London Landmarks

LONDON'S HISTORY begins in the middle of the 1st century AD when the invading troops of the Roman Emperor Claudius swept across south-east Britain to the Thames. The area was uninhabited marshland, and the Romans had to bridge the river to get to Colchester, then the most important town in the south-east. In time, they built roads converging on the bridge, river traffic increased, and a settlement grew up which they named Londinium. Its position ensured its prosperity and by the 3rd century it had become the centre of Roman administration and a prosperous walled city with a fort, a large temple, a basilica and a governor's palace. Recent excavations have shown that the present London Bridge is sited only a few hundred yards from the Roman one. Until the 17th century, London Bridge, lined on both sides with shops and houses, was the only access to the city from the south, and until the 16th century, London stayed more or less confined within the limits of the Roman walls. Southwark, on the south side of the bridge, was outside the jurisdiction of the city authorities, and by medieval times had become a refuge for criminals and the quarter where playhouses such as the Globe, forbidden within the City, could flourish.

Until after the reign of Edward the Confessor, English kings were not crowned at London. However, Edward had completed the rebuilding of Westminster Abbey just before his death, and Harold, his successor, was crowned there, as was William the Conqueror, who made Westminster his capital, at the same time conferring on London the status and privileges of a city, but also building the Tower as a symbol of his authority. London thus became truly the capital of England – but for centuries there were two centres of authority – Westminster where the monarch had his palace and where eventually parliament met, and the City where the powerful merchant guilds were supreme. Gradually wealthy landowners built themselves residences along the Strand, which linked the two centres, and the legal profession set themselves up on the site of the Temple of the Knights of St John.

From the 17th century onwards, London grew at an amazing rate, spreading far beyond the Roman and medieval walls. Even the Great Fire of 1666, to which we owe the creation of St Paul's Cathedral and many other churches designed by Wren, did not halt expansion, and surrounding villages like Chelsea, Marylebone, Islington, Kensington, Hampstead and Highgate were gradually swallowed up. The Victorian era, especially after the building of the railways, saw a phenomenal growth in size and population as trade with the Empire boomed and by 1901 the population of the capital stood at 4½ million, more than four times the number there had been in 1801.

The devastation of World War II has resulted in massive new office blocks, and whole areas of houses have been demolished to make way for high-rise or high-density flats, which have, say many, brought more problems than they have solved. Other post-war developments, such as the Barbican and the South Bank Arts Centre, have been widely acclaimed. Despite the drift of people from the centre, where housing is scarce and expensive, to the suburbs, London continues to grow and efforts are being made to attract industry back to the centre.

SURVIVOR OF THE BLITZ *St Paul's Cathedral, built after the Great Fire of 1666 as a symbol of the rebirth of the City, emerges defiantly from the smoke of a World War II bombing raid.*

WESTMINSTER'S LANDMARKS

WESTMINSTER ABBEY
Since the consecration of the abbey on 28 December 1065, the coronation of every English monarch has been held here, with the exception of the two uncrowned kings, Edward V and Edward VIII. It is also the burial place of all English monarchs from the time of Henry III, to whom we owe the rebuilding in Early English style of most of the abbey, to the reign of George III.

THE ABBEY *showing the delicacy of the fan-vaulting.*

Their tombs, particularly that of Edward the Confessor and that of Henry VII, housed in the beautiful, fan-vaulted chapel he had built in the early 16th century, are magnificent, but outnumbered by the thousand or so monuments to the great and famous. Poets' Corner is the best-known section, where many distinguished writers are remembered. Statesmen honoured include Disraeli and Gladstone, Churchill and Attlee.

WHITEHALL The old palace of Whitehall, burned down in 1698, was made the official residence of the sovereign by Henry VIII. The site is now occupied by government departments and by the Banqueting Hall, a Palladian masterpiece by Inigo Jones, which was planned as the start of a new royal palace. The ceiling of the main hall was painted for Charles I by Rubens. In the centre of the road is the Cenotaph, designed by Sir Edwin Lutyens and unveiled in 1920. Memorial services are held here every year in November. Leading off Whitehall is Downing Street, home of the Prime Minister and the Chancellor of the Exchequer.

WEST-END LANDMARKS

LEICESTER SQUARE
Devoted almost entirely to the cinema and other entertainments, the square was laid out in the 17th century on land belonging to the earls of Leicester. The streets between the square and Shaftesbury Avenue form the nucleus of London's Chinatown.

PICCADILLY CIRCUS AND SOHO The centre of London's West End and theatreland, Piccadilly Circus was once known as the hub of the Empire. At its centre is the famous statue of Eros, London's first aluminium monument, erected in 1893 to commemorate the social reformer, the 7th Earl of Shaftesbury. It represents, not Eros, but the Spirit of Christian Charity. Between Shaftesbury Avenue and its theatres and Oxford Street lies Soho, famous for its many restaurants and now notorious for sex shops and stripshows.

MARBLE ARCH Made redundant as a gateway almost as soon as it was built, Nash's imposing archway had to be moved from Buckingham Palace because it was too narrow to admit Victoria's State Coach, and was re-erected as the entrance to Hyde Park. By 1908, however, the traffic was too much for it, and it was removed to its present site, islanded by traffic on all sides, at the west end of Oxford Street, on the spot where the notorious Tyburn gallows used to stand.

POST OFFICE TOWER
Completed in 1964 and opened in 1966, the Post Office Tower, 580ft high and surmounted by a 40ft mast, is one of London's tallest buildings. At the top is a viewing platform and there used to be a revolving restaurant, but this has been closed for some years now.

ROYAL ALBERT HALL AND ALBERT MEMORIAL Much loved as the home of the Proms, the Royal Albert Hall, an immense, domed, circular structure opened in 1871, commemorates the Prince Consort, as does the elaborate Gothic memorial opposite, showing the Prince seated under a canopy and reading a catalogue of the Great Exhibition.

TRAFALGAR SQUARE
Famous for its flocks of pigeons and as a rallying point for demonstrations of all kinds, Trafalgar Square, on the site of the old Royal Mews, commemorates Lord Nelson's victory over the French in 1805. It was laid out between 1829 and 1841, but Landseer's lions, flanking Nelson's Column, were added in 1867 and the fountains, in which late-night revellers sometimes bathe, in 1948.

PICCADILLY CIRCUS *and the statue of Eros are the most famous and recognisable landmarks in London.*

CITY LANDMARKS

FLEET STREET AND THE STRAND Although many newspapers, including *The Times*, now have their offices elsewhere in London, Fleet Street is still synonymous with the power of the Press. Many of its pubs are the haunt of journalists and some, such as the Cheshire Cheese, have a long and distinguished history. The great Dr Johnson had his house in Gough Square, one of the many courts leading off the street. Fleet Street, which takes its name from the old Fleet River, runs from Ludgate to Temple

Bar, the old boundary of the City with Westminster. The archway was removed in 1878, but a memorial plinth remains. St Bride's Church, designed by Wren, is known as the Parish Church of the Press, and its spire is said to have been the inspiration for the traditional three-tier wedding cake. The Strand is the continuation of Fleet Street towards Trafalgar Square. As the name suggests, this was the river bank until the building of the Embankment. Between the Strand and the river lie two of London's four Inns of Court, the Inner and Middle

HOME OF THE PROMS *The Royal Albert Hall seats more than 5000 people in its huge, circular auditorium.*

Temple, a peaceful enclave of mostly 17th-century courts, linked by steps and alleys. The Temple Round Church, one of only five in England, dates back to the time of the Knights Templar who originally occupied this site in the 12th century. Two other famous churches, both on islands in the Strand, are St Clement Danes of nursery-rhyme fame and, since its rebuilding after the war, the RAF church, and St Mary-le-Strand, designed by James Gibbs in 1714–19.

THE BANK OF ENGLAND
This massive, windowless stone fortress stands rock-solid (whatever the state of the pound) in Threadneedle Street. Sir John Soane's original designs for the building can be seen in the Soane Museum but much of his structure was rebuilt by Sir Herbert Baker in the 1920s. Nearby are the Stock Exchange in Throgmorton Street, and Lloyds of London in Lime Street.

THE MONUMENT *offers a magnificent City panorama.*

THE MONUMENT Despite the towering office blocks, the Monument is still one of the City's most visible landmarks. Erected in 1677, it commemorates the Great Fire of 1666. From the top (202ft – the distance from its base to the place in Pudding Lane where the fire started) there are splendid views of the City.

OLD BAILEY Properly called the Central Criminal Court, the Old Bailey, crowned by the traditional figure of Justice, takes its popular name from the street where it is sited, near St Paul's. It was built where the old Newgate Prison, scene of public executions until 1868, used to stand.

THE BARBICAN London's most ambitious scheme for making the City a place to live as well as to work, the Barbican is a massive, self-contained complex west of Moorgate. Flats and tower-blocks look out on to a series of courtyards, gardens and a lake. At one end is the Museum of London at the other, an arts centre incorporating exhibition halls, a concert hall and a theatre, now the home of the Royal Shakespeare Company.

WESTMINSTER PIER AND BRIDGE Westminster Pier, just north of the bridge, is the embarkation point for many of the trips up and down the river. The bridge itself, built in the 19th century, seems to blend in with the Houses of Parliament.

THE HOUSES OF PARLIAMENT Kings from Edward the Confessor to Henry VIII lived here, but the Court had to move to St James in 1515, after a fire, and Henry VIII then built himself a new palace at Whitehall. Westminster Palace became the Houses of Parliament. In 1834 most of the old palace burnt down. Charles Barry designed the present Gothic building, and much of its intricate decoration was entrusted to Augustus Pugin. The buildings are 940ft long and include 1100 apartments and two miles of corridors. The clock tower at the north end, although smaller than the imposing Victoria Tower at the south end, is affectionately known the world over as Big Ben, although properly speaking this is the name of the 13½ ton bell that strikes the hours. Westminster Hall, 240ft long, may well be the largest Norman hall in Europe. Its magnificent hammer-beam roof dates from the reign of Richard II.

The River: Westminster to Greenwich

London owes its existence to the Thames and to the bridge the Romans built in the 1st century AD. Until less than a hundred years ago the river was busy with shipping of all kinds but nowadays even the distinctive flat-bottomed lighters have all but disappeared and the sailing barges are museum pieces.

To travel down the Thames from Westminster Pier to Greenwich in one of the many pleasure launches is to voyage past a fascinating panorama. After the splendours of Westminster, the City and the Tower of London, the scene changes to the warehouses and docks of the Pool of London and Limehouse, ending in the open spaces of Greenwich, and the Royal Naval College.

WESTMINSTER *The familiar shape of the Houses of Parliament and Westminster Bridge.*

COUNTY HALL A modern building with 750 ft of river frontage, it is the administrative headquarters of the Greater London Council.

CLEOPATRA'S NEEDLE This 69½ft-tall obelisk was given to this country in 1819 by the Viceroy of Egypt. It had been erected at Heliopolis in about 1500BC – but it has no real connection with Cleopatra.

THE SOUTH BANK COMPLEX This complex includes the Festival Hall, National Theatre and National Film Theatre, the Purcell Room, the Hayward Gallery and the Queen Elizabeth Hall.

WATERLOO BRIDGE By the 1920s John Rennie's 19th-century Waterloo Bridge was showing signs of structural weakness, and work began on this elegant replacement, designed by Sir Giles Gilbert Scott, in 1939.

SOMERSET HOUSE Elizabeth I lived in the palace that once stood on this site, and Oliver Cromwell lay in state here before his funeral. The present building dates from 1776 and a large part of it is occupied by the Registrar General's staff.

ST PAUL'S CATHEDRAL Sir Christopher Wren's magnificent Baroque cathedral replaced Old St Paul's, destroyed in the Great

THE TOWER OF LONDON *The massive keep or 'White Tower' built by William I dominates the riverside.*

Fire of 1666. Seen from the river, it retains its majesty despite surrounding office blocks. The height to the top of its cross is 365ft, and the dome is 112ft in diameter, with three galleries – the famous Whispering Gallery, the Stone Gallery and the Golden Gallery, the two latter giving fine views over London and the Thames. In the crypt are the tombs of Lord Nelson and the Duke of Wellington.

LONDON BRIDGE The medieval London Bridge was a remarkable structure, its 950ft length supported on 19 piers and bearing shops, houses and a chapel. The buildings were demolished in 1760 because of the danger of fire, and in 1831 the bridge itself was replaced by a five-arched granite bridge designed by John Rennie, and this was again replaced in 1968.

HMS BELFAST Almost opposite the Custom House is moored HMS *Belfast*, a World War II cruiser – the largest and most powerful ever built for the Royal Navy – now a museum.

THE TOWER OF LONDON In its time the Tower has been royal residence, prison, stronghold and place of execution – but it is now occupied by the Yeoman Warders, who wear picturesque Tudor costumes, the ravens, whose continued presence there is believed to guarantee its safety, and thousands of tourists who file through to see the Crown Jewels and a comprehensive collection of weapons and armour. William the Conqueror built the keep, known as the White Tower, between about 1078 and 1098, an outstanding example of Norman military architecture. Succeeding kings built and extended the defensive walls and added more towers. Many prisoners met their deaths here, including two of Henry VIII's wives, Anne Boleyn and Catherine Howard.

TOWER BRIDGE This, the most spectacular of London's bridges, was designed in the late 19th century by Sir John Wolfe-Barry. The roadway between the Gothic towers is carried on twin bascules which are raised to allow ships to enter the Pool of London; the original machinery is still in working order, though the steam engines have been replaced by electric motors for reasons of economy. A pedestrian high-level walkway has now been opened between the towers, and the original machinery can be inspected.

ST KATHARINE'S DOCK The buildings have now been adapted to a variety of uses and the docks themselves converted to marinas. The Maritime Trust's Historic Ship Collection illustrates the evolution from sail to steam and also includes the RRS *Discovery*, Captain Scott's vessel.

EXECUTION DOCK Pirates and sailors found guilty of serious crime on the high seas were hanged in chains here until three tides had washed over them. Nearby is the famous Prospect of Whitby public house.

THE GRAPES This picturesque old Limehouse pub stands near Regent's Canal Dock. Regent's Canal and the Grand Union Canal enabled goods to be shipped by barge from the Midlands to the Thames.

THE ISLE OF DOGS Charles II had his royal kennels here and this gave the island its name. Brunel's steamship *Great Eastern* was launched from a site near Millwall Docks.

GREENWICH The river gives the best view of Wren's superb Royal Naval College (originally a naval hospital). Behind them and behind the Queen's House (now part of the National Maritime Museum, rise the landscaped acres of Greenwich Park and at the top of the rise stands the Old Royal Observatory. Moored near the pier are two historic ships, *Cutty Sark*, and *Gypsy Moth IV*.

STEAM BARGES *(left) still common around Tower Bridge in the 1950s.*

THE PROSPECT OF WHITBY *is possibly the oldest of London's riverside pubs. In the foreground, the river police.*

CUTTY SARK *The only surviving example of the swift tea clippers lies in dry dock.*

Parks and Palaces

London is well-blessed with open spaces; they range from the compact green squares of residential districts to great open spaces like Hampstead Heath. Best-known, however, are the royal parks, tracts of land still owned by the Crown though the public is privileged to use them. London is also rich in royal palaces, as some past monarchs, such as Henry VIII, were keen builders. Today 'the Palace' denotes Buckingham Palace – but this has only been so for a comparatively short time, Queen Victoria being the first monarch to make her home there. The English Court remains 'the Court of St James', and it is to this that foreign ambassadors are still appointed.

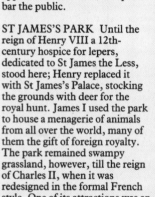

GREEN PARK Charles II purchased this extension to St James's Park, from which it is divided only by The Mall, in 1667. He was fond of walking, and Constitution Hill, which runs alongside, is thought to have been the route of his favourite 'constitutional'. Green Park differs from the other Royal Parks in having no flowerbeds and no water.

GREENWICH PARK
Greenwich Park was enclosed in 1433 to form a setting for Bella Court Palace, built there a few years earlier by the Duke of Gloucester. In Tudor times it was popular as a hunting chase, and it was not until the reign of Charles II (who had a palace there) that the present, semi-formal layout was achieved. Wide expanses of lawn, broken by avenues of trees and an ornamental pond, sweep up towards Blackheath from the Maritime Museum and the Queen's House on the riverside. Fallow deer roam in a 13-acre tract of bracken and wild flowers known as The Wilderness, and there are three bird sanctuaries. The Old Royal Observatory (now a museum) stands in the park, as does a stone bearing a strip of brass marking the Meridian – zero degrees Longitude – to which measurements made all round the world are referred.

HYDE PARK Henry VIII designed Hyde Park specifically for the purpose of hunting when the land, previously the property of the Abbey of Westminster, came into his possession at the Dissolution. In Stuart times the park was used for horse-racing, and the one-and-a-half miles of Rotten Row (a corruption of 'Route du Roi') is still popular with riders. The Serpentine Lake was formed at the instigation of Queen Caroline by damming the underground River Westbourne; it provides facilities for rowing and sailing – or even year-round bathing for the intrepid few! At the north-east corner of the park, nearest to Marble Arch, is Speaker's Corner, where anyone prepared to face the heckling of bystanders can have his say.

KENSINGTON GARDENS
Kensington Gardens were once part of Hyde Park, but when William III came to the throne in 1689 he feared the effect of Whitehall Palace's damp atmosphere on his asthma and so acquired Nottingham House, at the west end of the park. This became Kensington Palace, its grounds Kensington Gardens – more formal than Hyde Park, though now divided from it only by a road and sharing the same stretch of water. Generations of children have flocked here to see the statue of Sir James Barrie's Peter Pan, the fantastically-carved Elphin Oak and the craft of model boat enthusiasts on the Round Pond.

REGENT'S PARK Marylebone Park was renamed after the Prince Regent, later to become George IV, who was responsible for the elegant Nash residences built round its fringe; these were part of a huge neo-Classical development that would have covered the park itself had it been completed. Fortunately this was not feasible, and Nash laid out the area more or less as we know it today, with Inner and Outer Circles, artificial lake and Regent's Canal. Today there is boating on the lake, and pleasure cruises on the canal pass through London Zoo at the north end of the park. The Inner Circle encloses the rose-beds of Queen Mary's Garden, together with the Open-Air Theatre where performances of Shakespearian plays are given during the summer months.

RICHMOND PARK This, the largest of the royal parks, was originally an area of wild countryside enclosed by Charles I and used for hunting by his successors; King Henry VIII's Mound was constructed as a vantage point from which the monarch might survey the killing of his deer. The park is still fairly wild, the deer roaming freely through its coppices, but exotic shrubs have been introduced and the 18-acre Pen Ponds have been developed for fishing. Londoners owe their continued right to use the park to an 18th-century brewer called John Lewis, who opposed the Crown's attempts to bar the public.

ST JAMES'S PARK Until the reign of Henry VIII a 12th-century hospice for lepers, dedicated to St James the Less, stood here; Henry replaced it with St James's Palace, stocking the grounds with deer for the royal hunt. James I used the park to house a menagerie of animals from all over the world, many of them the gift of foreign royalty. The park remained swampy grassland, however, till the reign of Charles II, when it was redesigned in the formal French style. One of its attractions was an aviary (along the road still known as Birdcage Walk), and the islands of the ornamental lake were stocked with a collection of wildfowl.

LONDON'S ROYAL PARKS *are displayed clearly from the air as the 'lungs' of the capital.*

GREENWICH PARK *(right)* and ST JAMES'S PARK *(left) show the contrasting seasons: spring colours at Greenwich; mellow tones of autumn in St James's.*

HAMPTON COURT *The great Tudor gatehouse dates from Henry VIII's time, but the heraldic 'king's beasts' are modern.*

THE VICTORIA MEMORIAL *was erected outside the Palace at the head of the Mall in 1911.*

BUCKINGHAM PALACE, *The Mall, SW1* Buckingham Palace – formerly Buckingham House, built in 1703 for the Duke of Buckingham and Chandos – has been the principal home of the sovereign since Queen Victoria came to the throne in 1837. The original brick building was bought by George III in 1761 as a dower house for Queen Charlotte, and in the reign of George IV it was remodelled and clad in Bath Stone by John Nash. Victoria put on a new frontage, however, having Marble Arch (Nash's grand entrance) moved to Hyde Park because it was too narrow for the state coach. In 1912 the east front of the building was refaced again, being given a classical façade of Portland stone to blend with the Victoria Memorial which stands opposite the top of the Mall. Buckingham Palace is open to the public only on such occasions as investitures, though it is possible to visit the Royal Mews and the Queen's Gallery.

HAMPTON COURT PALACE, *Hampton Court Road, Kingston-upon-Thames* When Cardinal Wolsey began work on Hampton Court in 1514 he intended to become the owner of one of the most magnificent palaces in Europe; later, however, he gave it to Henry VIII in a vain attempt to curry favour. Hampton Court, in its fine riverside park, was one of the king's favourite residences. He was often there, playing Royal Tennis (today's 'real' tennis) in the enclosed court and jousting in the area where the Tiltyard Gardens are now. Five of his wives lived there, and the ghosts of two (Jane Seymour and Catherine Howard) apparently haunt it. Anne Boleyn's Gateway, a fine example of Tudor brickwork, dates from this time, surmounted by Henry's fine astronomical clock. The intricate gardens, with their famous maze, were added by Charles II and are reminiscent of Versailles. The last monarch to live there was George II, and afterwards the palace, after extensive restoration, was opened to the public. There are priceless paintings to be seen, and fine tapestries and furniture – but perhaps most impressive of all is the magnificent hammerbeam roof in the Great Hall.

KENSINGTON PALACE, *Kensington Gardens, W8* Nottingham House, the London home of the Earl of Nottingham, was purchased by William III in 1683 and was remodelled as Kensington Palace by Sir Christopher Wren. It remained the home of the reigning monarch until George II died here in 1760; it was also the birthplace of Queen Victoria, who lived here until her accession to the throne. It is now the home of Princess Margaret, but the State Apartments, where there is fine work by Wren, Grinling Gibbons and William Kent, are open.

ST JAMES'S PALACE, *St James's St., SW1* This rambling, rectangular brick mansion was built for Henry VIII. It remained the official residence of the sovereign until the time of Victoria and was the birthplace of Charles II, James II, Mary II, Queen Anne and George IV. Charles I spent his last night in its guardroom before going to the scaffold in Whitehall. All that remains of the original structure is a fine Tudor gatehouse, in front of which the Brigade of Guards parade each day. The Chapel Royal has been much altered over the centuries, but it has the original Holbein ceiling; William III, Mary II, Queen Anne, George IV, Victoria and George V were married there, and it is the setting for the annual Royal Epiphany Gifts Service. The Chapel is open to the public for services from October to Palm Sunday, though the Palace itself is not, being occupied by various Court officials.

ROYAL CEREMONIES

THE STATE OPENING OF PARLIAMENT (*Late October or early November*) After the summer recess, the new session of Parliament is opened by a speech from the monarch. The Monarch, accompanied by other members of the royal family, rides from Buckingham Palace in the Irish State Coach, a gun salute heralding their arrival at Westminster. After changing into royal robes and crown in the Robing Room, the Monarch is escorted to the Upper Chamber, where the Lords in their ceremonial robes are already assembled. The official known as Black Rod summons the Speaker and Members of the House of Commons, having first knocked three times on the door with his staff, and the Monarch then outlines the proposed government legislation for the coming session.

TROOPING THE COLOUR (*Second Saturday in June*) This ceremony takes place on Horse Guards Parade on the occasion of the sovereign's official birthday. Wearing the uniform of one of the regiments of which he or she is Colonel-in-Chief, the sovereign rides out from Buckingham Palace and takes the salute of the Brigade of Guards and the Household Cavalry. This is followed by a display of marching and the 'trooping' (display) of the 'colour' (or flag) of one of the five regiments of foot guards.

THE DISTRIBUTION OF THE ROYAL MAUNDY MONEY (*March*) Each Maundy Thursday the sovereign personally distributes alms (now purses of money, representing the original gifts of food and clothing) and, since the reign of Charles II, a purse of specially minted Maundy money, to old folk chosen from various parts of London.

London's Pageantry

Pageantry and ceremonial are colourful parts of London life, observed not only in the panoply of state and civic occasions but also in the meticulous observance of minor rituals so old that their origins have in some cases become obscured by time.

CHANGING THE GUARD *at Buckingham Palace. This daily ceremony is one of London's best-loved tourist attractions.*

DAILY CEREMONIES

THE CEREMONY OF THE KEYS (*10 pm*) Each evening the gates of the Tower of London are locked by the Chief Warder of the Yeoman Warders who is ceremonially challenged by a sentry as he nears the Bloody Tower. At 10 pm the Last Post is sounded and the Chief Warder hands over his keys to the Resident Governor and Major in the Queen's House. Applications to attend the ceremony can be made at the constable's office in the Tower.

THE CHANGING OF THE GUARD AT BUCKINGHAM PALACE (*11.30 am*) The guard, usually formed from one of the regiments of Foot Guards (the Scots, Irish, Welsh, Coldstream and Grenadier) is changed each morning. A band leads the new guard to the palace and the old one back to its barracks.

THE MOUNTING OF THE GUARD (*11 am weekdays, 10 am Sundays*) The Mounting of the Guard takes place at the Horse Guards, opposite Whitehall. The guard is formed from two units of the Household Cavalry – the Blues (identified by the red plumes on their helmets) and the Life Guards (white plumed).

CIVIC CEREMONIES

ELECTION OF THE LORD MAYOR AND LORD MAYOR'S SHOW A new Lord Mayor of London is elected every year on 29th September, Michaelmas Day. The retiring holder of the office and his aldermen attend a service at St Lawrence Jewry and then process to the Guildhall, where they make the final choice from the candidates put forward by the livery companies; the City bells ring as the old and new Lord Mayors ride to the Mansion

House together in the state coach. On 8th November, after attending a luncheon at the Mansion House, together with liverymen of their companies, they go in procession to the Guildhall, where the insignia of office are finally transferred; bells ring in all the City churches as they return to the Mansion House. The new Lord Mayor publicly assumes office on the second Saturday in November, in the 600-year-old ritual of the Lord Mayor's Show. He is flanked by a bodyguard of pikemen and musketeers as he rides to the Royal Courts of Justice in the ceremonial coach, behind a procession of colourful floats depicting some aspect of London's history. The Lord Mayor's Banquet takes place at the Guildhall on the following Monday.

PROCESSIONS In early January the Lord Mayor and his officers lead processions to the opening session of the Central Criminal Court (Old Bailey); to the first sitting of the newly-elected Court of Common Council (January) and the Church of St Lawrence Jewry for the Spital Sermon, preached by a bishop on an Easter theme (second Wednesday after Easter).

OTHER CEREMONIES

JOHN STOW'S QUILL CEREMONY (*Around 5th April*) During the memorial service for John Stow, 16th-century author of *The Survey of London*, at the Church of St Andrew Undershaft, the Lord Mayor places a new quill in the hand of Stow's statue.

ROYAL EPIPHANY GIFTS SERVICE (*6th January*) Officers of the Household offer up gold, frankincense and myrrh – the currency equivalent of the gold then being distributed to old people – at a service in St James's Chapel.

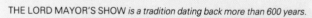

THE LORD MAYOR'S SHOW *is a tradition dating back more than 600 years.*

TROOPING THE COLOUR.

CHARLES I COMMEMORATION CEREMONY (*30th January*)

Each year, members of the Society of King Charles the Martyr and the Royal Stuart Society process from St Martin-in-the-Fields to the king's statue in Trafalgar Square to commemorate his execution on that day in 1649.

THE BLESSING OF THE THROATS (*3rd February, St Blaise's Day*)

Throat sufferers commemorate St Blaise, who, on his way to a martyr's death, saved a child who was choking on a fishbone, in a service at St Ethelreda's Church in Holborn.

CAKES AND ALE SERMON (*Ash Wednesday*)

Members of the Stationers' Company walk to St Paul's Cathedral to hear a sermon preached in accordance with the wishes of John Norton, a member of their Company who died during the reign of James I. Cakes and ale are distributed.

ORANGES AND LEMONS CHILDREN'S SERVICE (*End March*)

The children from the local primary school attend a service to commemorate the restoration of the famous bells at St Clement Danes Church in the Strand, and each receives an orange and a lemon.

HOT-CROSS BUNS SERVICE (*Good Friday*)

Morning service at St Bartholomew-the-Great, Smithfield ends with the distribution of hot-cross buns and money (provided by an ancient charity) to 21 local widows.

OAK APPLE DAY (*29th May*)

Chelsea Pensioners celebrate the escape of the founder of the Royal Hospital, Charles II, after the Battle of Worcester, decorating his statue with oak leaves in memory of the oak tree in which he hid.

CEREMONY OF THE LILIES AND ROSES (*21st May*)

Eton College and King's College, Cambridge, join in placing flowers on the spot where Henry VI, their founder, was killed in 1471.

THE KNOLLYS RED ROSE RENT (*24th June*)

In the 14th century Sir Robert Knollys was fined for building a footbridge over Seething Lane to join two of his properties. The fine was a nominal one – a red rose to be delivered to the Lord Mayor on Midsummer Day – and payment is still made by the Churchwardens of All Hallows-by-the-Tower, who carry the flower to the Mansion House.

SWAN UPPING (*Around the last Monday in July*)

The swans on the Thames between London Bridge and Henley belong to the Monarch and the Companies of Vintners and Dyers. The Monarch's Swan Keeper and the Swan Wardens and Swan Markers of the two Companies inspect the swans and mark the cygnets.

DOGGETT'S COAT AND BADGE RACE (*Late July/early August*)

Six Thames watermen row against the tide from London Bridge to Chelsea Bridge, and the winner is presented with a scarlet coat with silver buttons and badge. This is the oldest rowing event in the world, instituted in 1715.

QUIT RENTS CEREMONY (*Late October*)

In this, one of the oldest public ceremonies carried out in London, the City Solicitor makes token payment for two properties. The rents, accepted by the Queen's Remembrancer at the Royal Courts of Justice, comprise two faggots of wood, a billhook and a hatchet (for land in Shropshire) and six horseshoes and sixty-one nails (for a forge which once stood in the Strand).

PEARLY KING *at Battersea.*

WEMBLEY *Football fans.*

Calendar of Events

For Royal and Civic Occasions, see 'London's Pageantry'. Precise dates for most events may vary from year to year.

HAMPTON COURT *Henry VIII's astronomical clock.*

JANUARY
International Boat Show
(*Earl's Court*)

FEBRUARY
Cruft's Dog Show
(*Earl's Court*)

MARCH
Daily Mail Ideal Home Exhibition
(*Earl's Court*)
Druid Observance of Spring Equinox
(*Tower Hill*) around 21st
Harness Horse Parade
(*Regent's Park*) Easter Monday
Easter Parade
(*Battersea*) Easter Sunday
Oxford and Cambridge Boat Race
(*Putney to Mortlake*) end Mar/Apr

APRIL
London Marathon
Milk Cup Football Final
(*Wembley Stadium*)

MAY
May Day Procession
(*Hyde Park*) 1st May
Rugby League Cup Final*
(*Wembley Stadium*)
Summer Exhibition Opens
(*Royal Academy*)
London to Brighton Walk
(*From Westminster Bridge*)
FA Cup Final
(*Wembley Stadium*)
Chelsea Flower Show
(*Royal Chelsea Hospital*)
end May/Jun

JUNE
Cricket Test Matches
(*Lord's*)
Lawn Tennis Championships
(*Wimbledon*) end Jun/Jul

JULY
Royal Tournament
(*Earl's Court*)
AAA Championships
(*Crystal Palace*)
Royal International Horse Show
(*Wembley Arena*)
Cricket – Benson & Hedges Cup Final
(*Lord's*)
First Night of the Proms
(*Royal Albert Hall*)
Open Air Theatre Season Starts
(*Regent's Park*)

AUGUST
Greater London Horse Show
(*Clapham Common*) Bank Holiday
Cricket – Test Matches**
(*The Oval*)
Outdoor Theatre Season Starts
(*Holland Park*)
Cricket – NatWest Bank Trophy Final
(*Lord's*)

SEPTEMBER
Battle of Britain Thanksgiving Service
(*Westminster Abbey*) around 15th
Druid Observance of Autumn Equinox
(*Primrose Hill*) around 23rd
Last Night of the Proms
(*Royal Albert Hall*)

OCTOBER
Costermongers' Harvest Festival
(*St Martin's-in-the-Fields*) 1st Sunday
Horse of the Year Show
(*Wembley Arena*)
Trafalgar Day Service and Parade
(*Trafalgar Square*)

NOVEMBER
RAC London to Brighton Veteran Car Run
(*From Hyde Park*)
Remembrance Day Service
(*Whitehall – the Cenotaph*)
Sunday nearest 11th

DECEMBER
Smithfield Show
(*Earl's Court*)
International Show Jumping
(*Olympia*)
Carol Singing and Lighting of the Christmas Tree
(*Trafalgar Square*) from 16th
Switching on the Decorations
(*Regent's Street*)
New Year's Eve Celebrations
(*Trafalgar Square*)

---

* Rugby Union: Of matches involving England versus Scotland, Wales, Ireland and France, two take place at Twickenham between January and March in any given year. Matches against other foreign touring teams may also be held.
** Subject to fixtures.

Shops and Markets

Oxford Street, Bond Street, Regent Street and Knightsbridge are the traditional heart of London's shopping area, and many of the long-established department stores are found here. Charing Cross Road has its bookshops; Savile Row its high-class tailors; Soho its delicatessens; Tottenham Court Road its furniture. Street traders flourished before the days of shops, and their 'cries' are an evocative echo of Old London. Cheapside was once the centre of the City's trading ('ceap') being the Saxon word for barter or sale) but today there are markets all over the capital – large central wholesale markets and local 'village' and specialist markets.

BOND STREET Where Oxford Street is famous for department stores Bond Street is traditionally known for jewellers, art dealers and expensive boutiques. Many of the best of the latter have now colonised South Moulton Street, an attractive pedestrian way which leads off Brook Street.

KNIGHTSBRIDGE Harrods, the largest department store in Europe, lords it over the many expensive shops in Knightsbridge. Its magnificent foodhalls are a study in themselves, but every department is worth a visit, for the legend is that Harrods sells everything. For those who are daunted by the sheer size of the place, the streets round about, such as Beauchamp Place and Sloane Street, are full of interesting smaller shops and boutiques.

OUTLINED *in lights, Harrods is a world of luxury.*

OXFORD STREET Selfridges is the doyen of Oxford Street, with John Lewis, C & A, Marks and Spencer and a number of others also competing to attract the millions of shoppers who descend on the West End at weekends and, above all, at sales time.

MISSIONARY ZEAL *urges this 'man with a message' to mingle with the Oxford-Street crowds in hopes of converts.*

TRADE MARKETS

NEW COVENT GARDEN This famous flower, fruit and vegetable market is now sited at Nine Elms, Battersea, but for hundreds of years it was held in the square in front of St Paul's Church, north of the Strand. It was originally the *Convent* Garden – a walled enclosure used by the monks of Westminster Abbey. After the Dissolution the land was eventually granted to the Earls of Bedford; the fourth Earl obtained permission from Charles I to build on the site, and an Italian-style piazza surrounded by gentlemen's residences was designed by Inigo Jones. Traders were soon attracted by the central square and its covered walks, and the market was well-known by the end of the 17th century. The 19th century saw the erection of special market buildings, and the second half of the 20th century the traffic problems that brought about its removal to the Nine Elms site. The old market has become the lively centre of a revitalised area; craft goods of high quality are sold at many of the stalls in the central market area, and a host of shops and restaurants have opened in the surrounding streets.

PICCADILLY Not many shops have held their own against the tourist and airline offices that now dominate Piccadilly, but Fortnum and Mason stands firm, still supplying the finest in food and drink and a select range of fashion, from its original elegant premises. Swaine, Ardeney, Brigg & Sons specialise in riding equipment, leather goods and umbrellas. Richoux sells tempting pastries and confectionery and Hatchards, books. Facing these establishments, Burlington Arcade has many luxuries for sale, as has Jermyn Street, with its famous cheese shop, Paxton and Whitfield. Well-dressed gentlemen might order hand-

made shirts in Jermyn Street, or perfume as a gift from J. Floris, established here in 1739, on their way to wile away a peaceful afternoon at one or other of the many exclusive gentlemen's clubs that dominate Pall Mall and St James's. At the west end of Jermyn Street, in St James's Street, it is still possible to have a bowler hat made to measure at James Lock, or to have fine leather shoes made at John Lobb, a few doors away.

REGENT STREET Most of the shops are to be found near Oxford Circus, where easily the most famous are Liberty and Jaeger. Liberty, housed in a distinctive, Tudor-style building, has always

been a by-word for its beautiful fabrics. Nearby is Hamley's toyshop, a three-storey wonderland for children.

TOTTENHAM COURT AND CHARING CROSS ROADS High fashion in clothes is not to be found in either of these streets, but the best of modern furniture is displayed at Heal & Son and Habitat in Tottenham Court Road, and the whole range of bookshops, from paperback to antiquarian can be found in Charing Cross Road, where Foyles, occupying two buildings, sells not only these but very nearly all other categories of books. Music and musical instruments are also sold here.

BILLINGSGATE Billingsgate Fish Market has also been moved from its original site because of traffic congestion in the City streets. It grew up round a medieval quay just below London Bridge, probably as early as the 9th century, although it did not receive its charter until 400 years later. In 1875 an arcaded building (which still stands) was erected to bring together the sale of all kinds of fish, 'wet, dry and shell', but in 1981 the market was transferred to a new site at the less-busy West India Docks. The name of Billingsgate has long been synonymous with bad language – its tradition of colourful expletive dating back to the original fishwives who squabbled round

SMITHFIELD *(left) is the last of the famous produce markets still operating in its original premises. Covent Garden (right) has turned to new crafts.*

the quay, but ably maintained by today's hard-pressed porter, carrying anything up to a hundredweight of fish balanced on his flat-topped 'bobbing' hat.

BOROUGH MARKET This Southwark market, a direct descendant of one held on old London Bridge, occupies buildings beneath the arches on a viaduct serving London Bridge station.

SMITHFIELD Smithfield, now one of the world's largest meat markets and famous for the quality of its beef, pork and lamb, dealt originally in hay, horses, cattle and sheep; its name recalls the 'smooth field' just outside the city walls to which the animals were driven through the streets of London until the practice was restricted by statute in the middle of the 19th century. At about the same time the market was modernised, when Sir Horace Jones built the Renaissance-style Central Meat Market Arcade, capable of holding up to 400 truckloads of meat at a time.

SPITALFIELDS The name of Spitalfields Market, in the East End, like that of Covent Garden recalls earlier Church ownership of the site: in the 12th century a priory dedicated to St Mary Spital was founded here. The surrounding land was fertile, and by the time of Charles II the volume of local produce for sale was such that he granted a market charter. During the 18th and 19th centuries the area was built up with close-packed houses that subsequently deteriorated into slums, but the market continued to deal in flowers, fruit and vegetables, though no longer locally produced.

OLD STREET CRIES

Street pedlars were, even until the beginning of this century, a familiar and colourful part of London life. The Rabbit Seller (top) and the Orange Girl (above), with her barrow of fine, ripe fruit, are woodcuts from a series by Bewick and his pupils.

STREET MARKETS

BERWICK STREET MARKET, *Berwick St, W1* One of the few survivors of the old Soho, Berwick Street Market (Monday to Saturday) offers excellent value in fruit and vegetables, and there are also shellfish, clothing and household goods stalls.

BRIXTON MARKET, *Electric Avenue, SW9* Brixton (Monday to Saturday) is a general market which reflects colourfully the local community it serves. Because of the largely West Indian population, many stalls are piled with exotic fruit and vegetables, and the compelling rhythms of Caribbean music throb in the background.

CAMDEN PASSAGE MARKET, *Camden Passage, N1* This market which has grown up near the Angel, Islington, is devoted to antiques, curios and bric-à-brac of all kinds. Some of its shops and stalls open all week, but Saturday is the liveliest day.

COLUMBIA ROAD MARKET, *Shoreditch, E2* Well-known to keen gardeners, Columbia Road Market (Sunday mornings) offers a wide variety of flowers, plants and shrubs.

CAMDEN LOCK MARKET, *Camden Lock Place, NW1* Antiques, bric-à-brac, period clothes, and crafts are on sale (weekends) in this lively market which has grown up around Camden Lock in Chalk Farm.

LEADENHALL MARKET, *Gracechurch St, EC3* Specialising in meat and poultry, this City market (Monday to Friday) also offers fish, fruit and vegetables and plants. Its origins go back to the 14th century.

NEW CALEDONIAN MARKET, *Bermondsey Sq, SE1* The New Caledonian is primarily a dealers' market in antiques, though members of the public are not excluded. Much of the serious trading, however, takes place before the official opening time of 7 am on a Friday.

PETTICOAT LANE, *Middlesex St, E1* This is probably the most famous of London's street markets, typically Cockney in character and very popular with tourists. It is actually sited in Middlesex Street but was dubbed Petticoat Lane in the 17th century, when it was the place where the local poor could buy cast-off clothing of their richer neighbours. Today's market (Sunday mornings) still sells clothing of all sorts, but it also deals in most household items.

PORTOBELLO ROAD, *Notting Hill, W11* A general market during the week, with a West Indian flavour, Portobello Road assumes its distinctive character on a Saturday, when a multitude of antique stalls, arcades and shops are opened up. The items offered for sale range from expensive antiques through Victoriana to pure junk. The scene is enlivened by buskers and street entertainers.

PORTOBELLO ROAD *Bric-à-brac stalls line the street.*

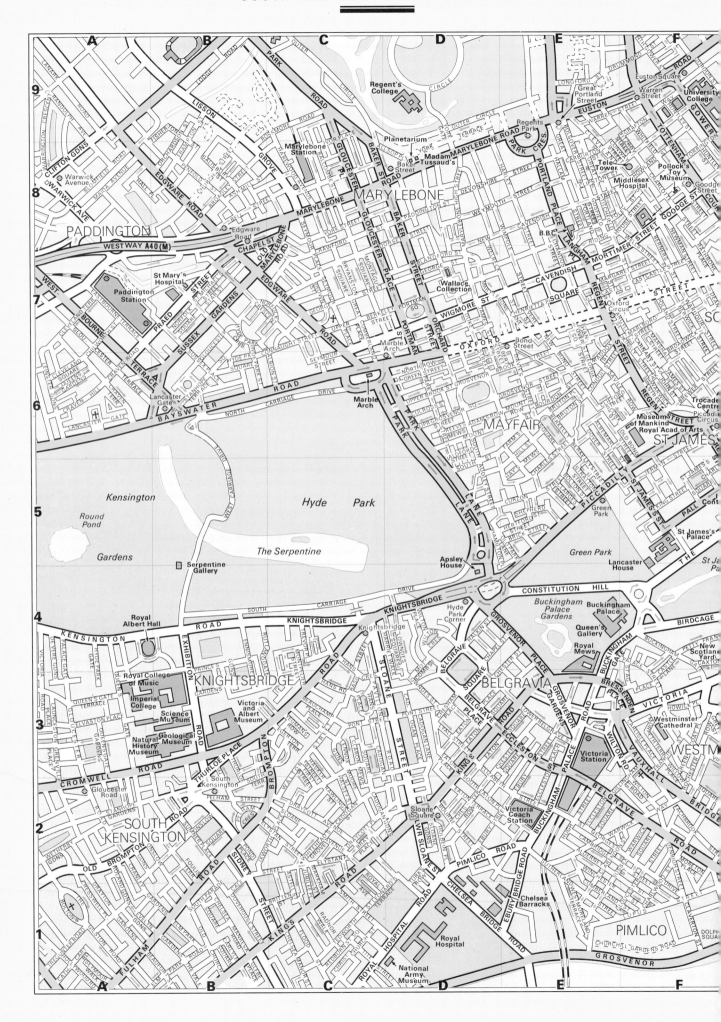

A map of central London showing Paddington, Marylebone, Mayfair, St James's, Hyde Park, Kensington Gardens, Knightsbridge, South Kensington, Belgravia, Pimlico, and Westminster.

Grid references (left): 9, 8, 7, 6, 5, 4, 3, 2, 1
Grid references (top and bottom): A, B, C, D, E, F

Labelled features include:

Parks and water: Regent's Park, Hyde Park, Kensington Gardens, Round Pond, The Serpentine, Green Park, Buckingham Palace Gardens

Districts: PADDINGTON, MARYLEBONE, MAYFAIR, ST JAMES'S, KNIGHTSBRIDGE, SOUTH KENSINGTON, BELGRAVIA, PIMLICO, WESTMINSTER

Buildings and landmarks: Regent's College, Planetarium, Madam Tussaud's, Marylebone Station, Wallace Collection, B.B.C., Tele Tower, Pollock's Toy Museum, Middlesex Hospital, University College, Great Portland Street, Warren Street, Euston Square, St Mary's Hospital, Paddington Station, Edgware Road, Marble Arch, Oxford Circus, Bond Street, Lancaster Gate, Serpentine Gallery, Apsley House, Buckingham Palace, Queen's Gallery, Royal Mews, Hyde Park Corner, Knightsbridge, Constitution Hill, Birdcage Walk, New Scotland Yard, Royal Albert Hall, Royal College of Music, Imperial College, Science Museum, Victoria and Albert Museum, Natural History Museum, Geological Museum, Sloane Square, Victoria Station, Victoria Coach Station, Westminster Cathedral, Trocadero Centre, Piccadilly Circus, Museum of Mankind, Royal Acad. of Arts, St James's Palace, Lancaster House, Chelsea Barracks, Royal Hospital, National Army Museum, South Kensington

Major roads: WESTWAY A40(M), EDGWARE ROAD, MARYLEBONE ROAD, EUSTON ROAD, PORTLAND PLACE, BAKER STREET, OXFORD STREET, PARK LANE, PARK ROAD, BAYSWATER ROAD, WEST CARRIAGE DRIVE, NORTH CARRIAGE DRIVE, SOUTH CARRIAGE DRIVE, KNIGHTSBRIDGE, PICCADILLY, PALL MALL, CROMWELL ROAD, KENSINGTON ROAD, BROMPTON ROAD, EXHIBITION ROAD, KING'S ROAD, SLOANE STREET, GROSVENOR PLACE, BUCKINGHAM PALACE ROAD, VAUXHALL BRIDGE ROAD, BELGRAVE ROAD, PIMLICO ROAD, CHELSEA BRIDGE ROAD, EBURY BRIDGE ROAD, GROSVENOR ROAD, CHURCHILL GARDENS ROAD, FULHAM ROAD, OLD BROMPTON ROAD

THE FOREST AND THE SEA

Here the woods and heaths of the New Forest meet the lovely Solent shore. Ponies and semi-wild cattle graze through oak-fringed glades where kings once hunted, and wander at will wherever there are no grids to bar them entry.

LYMINGTON, Hants
Early wealth came to Lymington from its saltworks, but these were closed in the 19th century and the town now makes a comfortable living as a busy holiday resort, yachting centre, and Isle of Wight ferry terminal. Its wide High Street, lined with 18th- and 19th- century houses, climbs from the waterfront to a church with a huge tower crowned by an exotic cupola of 18th century date.

Follow SP 'Beaulieu B3054', cross the Lymington River, and climb into the New Forest. Cross Beaulieu Heath to the pleasant picnic spot of Hatchet Pond. Turn right, then 1 mile farther turn sharp right again on to the unclassified 'Buckler's Hard' road.

BUCKLER'S HARD, Hants
This small Beaulieu River village thrived for several centuries as a shipbuilding yard. A fascinating little maritime museum recalls those times, and the deep estuary is put to peaceful use by yacht owners. The short village street of 18th-century houses was the creation of the 2nd Duke of Montagu, who planned a town and docks here to receive produce from his own extensive foreign estates.

THE SOLENT, Hants
Much of this tour is in sight of The Solent, a narrow and very busy channel that separates the coast of Hampshire from that of the Isle of Wight. It was formed by the submersion of an ancient river valley whose headstream was the Frome and tributaries the Itchen and Test. Most of the coast on the Hampshire side is designated an area of outstanding natural beauty.

Return along the 'Beaulieu' road and after 2 miles turn right on to the B3054. Enter Beaulieu.

BEAULIEU, Hants
Beaulieu's idyllic position among the woods and hills of South Hampshire is enhanced by the superb ruins of its abbey (open). Largely destroyed at the Dissolution, this important foundation retains a beauty that 'mocks the spoilers still' and preserves its great gatehouse (open) as the home of Lord Montagu. Ruined walls pierced by graceful door and window apertures surround trim lawns that were once the floors of large monastic buildings. Elsewhere in the grounds is the well-known National Motor Museum (open), which features an excellent collection of veteran and vintage cars, cycles, and motorcycles.

Continue through woodlands along the B3054 'Hythe' road for 1 mile, then turn right and immediately right again on to the unclassified 'Lepe' road, passing through woodland, and after 2½ miles enter Exbury.

Huge timbers from New Forest trees were once left to weather in the wide street at Buckler's Hard before being used to build ships.

A beech glade near Knightswood Oak.

EXBURY, Hants
The gardens of Exbury estate are famous for their magnificent rhododendron and azalea displays in late spring (house not open). The village itself stands near the creeks and saltmarshes of the Beaulieu River estuary, in an area of the Solent shore designated as being of outstanding natural beauty.

Turn left into the village and after another 2 miles bear left, with views across The Solent to the Isle of Wight. Continue along the foreshore at Lepe, now part of a country park, then turn inland. After ¾ mile turn right on to the Calshot road. Drive for another

2½ *miles, meet a T-junction, and turn right on to the B3053 to enter Calshot.*

CALSHOT, Hants
Immediately obvious in this otherwise pleasant little place is the intrusive chimney of its power station. Rather more pleasing to the eye is the low, round tower of Calshot Castle, a coastal fort built by Henry VIII. It occupies a commanding position on a promontory at the end of a long shingle beach. Calshot foreshore is part of a country park.

Return along the B3053 SP 'Southampton' and drive to the edge of Fawley.

SOUTHAMPTON WATER, Hants
Between Calshot and Eling, the route of this tour is never far from the shores of Southampton Water, a maritime highway busy with the traffic of tankers, tugs, liners, ferries and pleasure craft. Southampton port, at its head, has long been one of the most commercially and strategically important harbours in the country. The Crusaders embarked here, the *Mayflower* set sail from the local docks, and Philip II of Spain landed here on his way to marry Mary Tudor in Winchester Cathedral. Today the Water guides great vessels from all over the world into the haven of England's premier cruise passengers port.

FAWLEY, Hants
Esso's petroleum refinery, which dominates Fawley, is an unlovely building but has some claim to fame through sheer size.

Drive to the next roundabout and follow SP 'Hythe' on to an unclassified road. After 1 mile turn right into Frost Lane and descend, over a level crossing, to the shores of Southampton Water. Continue to Hythe.

HYTHE, Hants
Excellent views of Southampton docks and the shore are afforded by the Hythe ferry. Ship-spotting enthusiasts will find the village pier a handy vantage point.

Leave Hythe Pier with SP 'Totton', then after ¼ mile meet a T-junction and turn right. Continue for 2 miles, then on the nearside of the next roundabout turn sharp right on to the 'Marchwood' road. Continue through Marchwood and after 2 miles at staggered crossroads turn right on to the 'Eling' road and continue to Eling.

ELING, Hants
Situated on a creek off the head of Southampton Water, this ancient port has a toll-bridge reputed to be the smallest of its kind in Britain and a working tide mill (open).

Cross the toll-bridge and follow SP 'Lyndhurst' to join the A35, and follow to Ashurst.

ASHURST, Hants
The New Forest Butterfly Farm has an extensive display of tropical butterflies in large glasshouses.

THE NEW FOREST, Hants
This district between the River Avon and Southampton Water comprises some 92,000 acres of undulating forest and heathland threaded by small streams and scattered with ponds. Many species of trees thrive in the mixture of clays, peat, and gravels here, affording cover to various species of deer and the famous New Forest ponies. Parts of the forest are nature reserves.

Continue over heathland to Lyndhurst.

Exhibits on display at the Montagu Motor Museum include historic record-breakers.

The boats in Lymington Harbour sprout a forest of masts.

An excellent way of seeing the Solent shipping is to take the ferry from Hythe to Southampton.

The Knightswood Oak stands near Lyndhurst.

LYNDHURST, Hants
Lyndhurst is the capital of the New Forest and an extremely popular tourist centre. Woodlands lap the boundaries of the town, and it is not unusual to meet one of the area's semi-wild ponies or cows ambling through the streets. The Victorian parish church features stained glass by Burne-Jones, William Morris and others, and a large mural by Leighton. Alice Liddel, on whom the heroine of *Alice in Wonderland* was based, is buried here. West of the church is the Queen's House, where the Verderers' Court still sits to administer the forest.

Follow the 'Bournemouth' road to the Swan Inn and turn right on to the unclassified 'Emery Down' road. After ¼ mile reach the New Forest Inn and turn left SP 'Bolderwood'. Continue along one of the forest's most attractive byways. After 3 miles pass the Island Viewpoint and a common on the left, then turn sharp left (no SP) to re-enter fine woodlands along the Bolderwood Ornamental Drive. After a further 2 miles reach the Knightswood Oak on the left.

KNIGHTSWOOD OAK, Hants
The huge Knightswood Oak has a girth of more than 21ft and is thought to be 600 years old.

Keep forward from the Knightswood Oak and cross a main road to drive along the Rhinefield Ornamental Drive, bordered by fine conifers and rhododendrons. Cross heathland and pass through the outskirts of Brockenhurst. Turn left across a ford and drive to the town centre.

BROCKENHURST, Hants
Many people find this handsome, lively village an ideal base from which to explore the New Forest. The local church is of Norman origin and claims to be the oldest foundation in the forest. *Domesday* records a church on this site, and the enormous yew in the churchyard may well have been planted over 1,000 years ago. Brusher Mills, a famous New Forest snake-catcher responsible for the demise of over 3,000 adders, is buried here.

Recross the ford and follow SP 'Burley' across wide heathland with picnic areas and good views. Pass Hinchslea Viewpoint on the right and in 4¾ miles enter Burley.

BURLEY, Hants
Nearby Castle Hill rises to 300ft and affords good views over this pretty village. An intriguing collection of souvenirs, trophies, and weapons can be seen in the local Queen's Head Inn.

Take the 'Bransgore' road, cross more heathland, and reach the Crown Inn in Bransgore. Turn left here SP 'Lymington' and cross pleasant countryside. After 2 miles turn left and right across a main road, with the Cat and Fiddle Inn on the right. Drive beyond Walkford and turn left on to the A337. After ¾ mile turn right on to the unclassified 'Barton on Sea' road. Continue for ½ mile and turn left, then meet a T-junction and turn right to enter Barton on Sea.

BARTON ON SEA, Hants
This resort's low clay cliffs form part of the Barton Beds, a geological series noted for its fossil shell, bone, and shark remains. Good views from the clifftop greensward extend to the chalk stacks of the Needles, and Isle of Wight.

Reach the end of the Promenade and turn left to follow SP 'Milford on Sea' across heaths and commons. Turn right on to the B3058 and drive to Milford on Sea.

MILFORD ON SEA, Hants
A popular resort since Victorian times, Milford on Sea offers good bathing from its sand and shingle beach and excellent views across the Solent to the Isle of Wight. All Saints' Church has a picture by Perugino at the west end of the south aisle. On a promontory about 2½ miles south east is Hurst Castle.

HURST CASTLE, Hants
Built by Henry VIII in 1544, this fort (AM) was later occupied by Cromwell's forces and served as a prison for Charles I in 1648. Restoration work was carried out in 1873, and access today is by foot along a shingle promontory or by boat from Keyhaven.

From Milford on Sea, continue along the B3058 'Lymington' road and turn right on to the A337 before re-entering Lymington.

OXFORD, Oxon

This ancient and world renowned university town stands on three main waterways – the River Cherwell, the River Thames (known locally as the Isis), and the Oxford Canal. It is first mentioned in the Saxon Chronicle of 912, but all the indications are that there was a thriving community on the site at least 200 years earlier. Organized teaching has existed at Oxford since the 12th century, and the collegiate system became established in the 13th century as the various religious orders consolidated. Town and gown were often at loggerheads in medieval times, particularly when university privileges conflicted with the interests of local merchants. Charles I established his parliament here, and Oxford served as the Royalist headquarters during that troubled time of civil war. The town's street plan forms an intriguing network centred on Carfax, a junction of four streets and the centre of the old community. Perhaps the most notable of the four is High Street, which is known locally as 'The High'. At the east end is Magdalen, one of the richest colleges in Oxford, and a little closer to Carfax is St Edmund Hall – a unique r of a residential society founded for graduates in 1220. The High's centrepiece is the University Church of St Mary the Virgin, which is instantly recognizable by its beautiful 14th-century spire. Wren designed the Sheldonian Theatre, at the east end of Broad Street, and the 19th-century bulk of Ashmolean Museum displays a varied array of fascinating and often valuable collections.

From Oxford follow SP 'The East A420'. Pass through Headington.

HEADINGTON, Oxon

Stone for many of the Oxford colleges was worked in the once-famous Headington quarries. The village church dates from the 12th century and incorporates a fine Norman chancel arch. Morris dancing is a long-standing local tradition, and Headington's own troupe of dancers performs annually on Whit Monday.

Continue to a roundabout and take the 2nd exit into unclassified Bayswater Road. After ¾ mile turn right, SP 'Stanton St John'. Drive forward to a T-junction and turn right, then left, into Stanton St John.

STANTON ST JOHN, Oxon

John White, the chief founder of Massachusetts in New England, was born here in 1575. Milton's grandfather also lived here. The village has thatched farms, stone cottages, an ancient manor house, and a lovely old church.

Drive to the church, turn left, then follow SP 'Oakley'. Enter that village.

New College, Oxford, was founded by William of Wykeham in 1379. Architect James Wyatt restored the chapel buildings in the 18th century.

NORTH OF THE SPIRED CITY

Just a few miles from the city of learning and dreaming spires are the vast victory estate of Blenheim, an ancient Saxon demesne that was the playground of the high aristocracy, and the gentle contours of the Vale of Oxford.

OAKLEY, Bucks

Oakley House stands at the south end of the village and is of 17th-century date. Early 13th-century St Mary's Church contains a number of old coffin-lid monuments.

From Oakley approach a main road and turn right on to the B4011. Take the next turning left on to an unclassified road for Brill.

BRILL, Bucks

Isolated Brill is a lovely village which stands at 700ft above the Vale of Aylesbury. Its two greens are fringed with charming cottages and almshouses, and its Tudor manor house radiates the warmth of mellow red brick. Brill windmill (open) dates from 1668 and may be one of the oldest postmills to have survived anywhere in Great Britain.

Proceed to the Sun Hotel, turn left into Windmill Street, and pass the old windmill. Later ascend, then descend to join the B4011 to Blackthorn. After 1 mile turn left on to the A41 for Bicester.

BICESTER, Oxon

The site of Roman Alchester lies a mile to the south of Bicester, and the modern A421 follows the line of an old Roman road close by. No Roman remains have been found at Bicester itself, but the *castra* element in its name suggests that there was once a garrison here. If that was the case then the military tradition continues, for nowadays it is the base for one of the largest army depots in the country. Local roadsides have wide grass verges for the convenience of the many horseriders hereabouts.

Follow SP 'Oxford, A421', then turn right on to the A4095 SP 'Chipping Norton'. Proceed for 1 mile, then go forward on to the B4030 to Middleton Stoney. Cross a main road and continue to the outskirts of Lower Heyford.

LOWER HEYFORD, Oxon

Set on a slope overlooking a wide valley and the River Cherwell, Lower Heyford has a 13th-century church which carries a 15th-century tower and is entered via a 15th-century porch complete with sundial. The font dates from the 17th century.

Cross the Oxford Canal and River Cherwell. (Rousham House is on the left).

ROUSHAM HOUSE, Oxon

Near the River Cherwell is Rousham House, a 17th- and 18th-century building which boasts the only garden layout by William Kent to have survived intact (open).

Continue to the Hopcrofts Holt Hotel, and turn right on to the A423 for Deddington.

DEDDINGTON, Oxon

One of many small towns near the lovely River Cherwell, Deddington is built of honey-coloured local stone and is rich in Civil War associations. Many of these may be 'local colour', but King Charles I is reputed to have slept at 16th-century Castle Farm while in the area. The local church is of 14th-century date and has a very fine north porch. Its tower was rebuilt in 1635 after the first attempt fell down.

Turn left on to the B4031 'Chipping Norton' road and pass through Hempton. After 3 miles keep left and join the A361. After ½ mile turn left on to the B4022 SP 'Enstone'. Continue for 1 mile and turn left again on to an unclassified road for Great Tew.

GREAT TEW, Oxon

Delightful cottages of thatch and stone combine with the old village stocks here to present a truly traditional picture of rural England. A number of interesting monuments can be seen in the church, and the manor house has been rebuilt in its original gardens.

After ½ mile turn right SP 'Little Tew'. Drive to crossroads and turn left to rejoin the B4022. After a further 3 miles drive over staggered crossroads and skirt Enstone. Proceed to Charlbury.

CHARLBURY, Oxon

Set in the Evenlode Valley, Charlbury is a compact little town with many narrow streets containing 18th-century buildings, including shops and inns. Within Wychwood Forest is Cornbury Park, although the Earl of Leicester once resided here when he was a favourite of Elizabeth I, the majority of the building dates from the 17th and 18th centuries. Ditchley Park is a fine 18th-century house by James Gibb, it lies 2½ miles to the north east and is occasionally open in the summer.

Continue along the B4022, crossing the River Evenlode, with Wychwood Forest to the right. Later turn right into Witney.

WITNEY, Oxon

The name 'Witney' is synonymous with blanket making, an industry that has grown from the town's close proximity to rich wool country and the availability of ready power from the River Windrush. *Domesday* records that two mills stood here, and doubtless there were others even before that. The main street extends for almost a mile to a green set with lime trees and graced with fine houses built with the profits of wool and weaving. Prosperity is similarly mirrored in the 17th-century Butter Cross, which stands on 13 stone pillars and displays both a clock tower and a sundial. The old Blanket Hall of 1720 displays a curious one-handed clock. Witney's

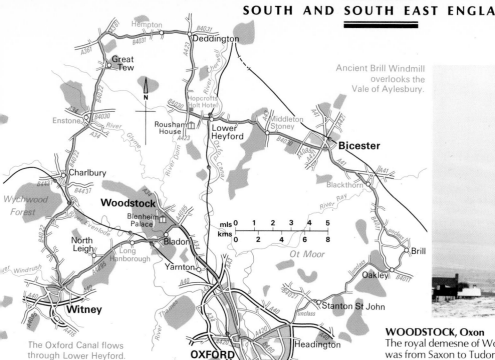

The Oxford Canal flows through Lower Heyford.

Ancient Brill Windmill overlooks the Vale of Aylesbury.

church carries a 156ft-high spire that serves as a landmark for many miles.

Return along the A4095 'Bicester' road to the outskirts of North Leigh.

NORTH LEIGH, Oxon
Features of North Leigh include a disused windmill and a church with a Saxon tower. Inside the church is a 'doom' painting and an unusual collection of coffin plates. North-east of the village are superb Roman remains (AM) on one of the best villa sites in this country.

Continue on the A4095 and pass through Long Hanborough to Bladon.

BLADON, Oxon
Sir Winston Churchill, his wife, and both his parents are buried in Bladon churchyard. The church itself is a Victorian reconstruction of a building that had previously occupied the site for many centuries.

Drive 1 mile farther and approach a roundabout. Turn left on to the A34 for Blenheim Palace and Woodstock.

BLENHEIM PALACE, Oxon
John Churchill, 1st Duke of Marlborough, won more than a victory when he crushed the French at Blenheim in 1704. Queen Anne awarded him and his heirs forever the Royal Manor of Woodstock with the Hundred of Wootton, while a no

less grateful parliament voted him half a million pounds to pay for the building of Blenheim Palace. The duchess rejected plans for the house drawn up by Wren and chose instead Sir John Vanbrugh's suitably grandiose scheme. The gardens were originally laid out by Henry Wise, and the grounds – later modified by Capability Brown – cover 2,500 acres and include a vast lake, Triumphal Way, and sunken Italian garden. The palace itself is an Eldorado of art treasures and fine furnishings. One-time prime minister and war leader Sir Winston Churchill was born here in 1874.

WOODSTOCK, Oxon
The royal demesne of Woodstock was from Saxon to Tudor times the site of a great country manor that served as the playground of royalty. Various members of the high aristocracy were born here, some installed their mistresses or hunted here, and several died here. Elizabeth I was imprisoned here by Mary for a while, but the tables were resoundingly turned when the Virgin Queen returned in triumph after her accession to the throne. Woodstock House was, unfortunately, a total casualty of the Civil War and has all but vanished. In the town itself is a grand town hall that was built in

1766 by Sir William Chambers with money donated by the Duke of Marlborough. Tradition has it that the very famous Bear Inn dates back to 1237. There are a great number of very old and attractive stone houses in the streets of Woodstock.

Return along the A34 towards Oxford. After 3½ miles meet an unclassified right turn leading to Yarnton.

YARNTON, Oxon
Yarnton's manor house was built in 1612 and has since been well restored. Above its porch are the Spencer Arms. The local church, which dates from the 13th century, carries a 17th-century tower and contains a fine Jacobean screen.

Continue along the A34 for the return to Oxford.

Blenheim Palace, which covers 3 acres of ground, was built for the Duke of Marlborough between 1705 and 1722.

OXFORD AND THE ISIS

Matthew Arnold's city of dreaming spires still enchants the visitor to Oxford, home of the oldest university in Britain. From Oxford, where the Thames is still called the Isis, the river winds its slow way through the broad green water meadows surrounding Abingdon and Dorchester.

OXFORD, Oxon

The splendour of the college architecture lends an unequalled dignity to Oxford's busy streets. Their enclosed courts and well-kept gardens (OACT) are a timeless haven from the pace of daily life outside. University, Merton and Balliol Colleges were all founded in the 13th-century and the oldest is probably Merton (1264). Edmund Hall is the only survivor of the medieval halls that pre-dated the colleges themselves. Most of the significant buildings in the city are connected with the university; The Bodleian Library's collection of rare manuscripts makes it second only in importance to the Vatican Library in Rome; the Ashmolean Museum, the oldest in the country, founded in 1683, contains opulent treasures from the Orient as well as from all the countries of Europe; the circular Sheldonian Theatre, opposite Blackwells, great rambling bookshop in the Broad, was designed in 1664 by Christopher Wren and from its cupola there are panoramic views of the city. The Broad, the Cornmarket and the High are the streets where life goes on. Here, and in the maze of side streets and winding narrow lanes that lead off, are most of the old colleges, the students' pubs, little restaurants, antique and curio shops. Eights Week, when college teams of rowing eights compete against each other in late spring, attracts hundreds of visitors to the lovely Meadows.

Leave on the A420, SP 'The West' and 'Swindon'. In 1¼ miles turn right, then at the roundabout take the 2nd exit. In ¾ mile branch left, SP 'Eynsham', then turn right on to the B4044. After crossing the picturesque Swinford Bridge (toll) go forward to the outskirts of Eynsham and turn left on to the B4449. In 2 miles turn left to Stanton Harcourt.

STANTON HARCOURT, Oxon

The majestic tombs marking generations of the Harcourt family fill the Norman church which looks down upon medieval fishponds and the lovely 17th-century parsonage. Several thatched cottages grace the village, and there is a 15th-century tower in the grounds of the old manor house (not open). The poet Alexander Pope lived here while completing his translation of Homer's *Iliad* in 1718. Also in the manor grounds is an outstanding example of a medieval kitchen, with an octagonal pyramidal roof.

Morris Dancers celebrating May morning outside the Sheldonian Theatre, Oxford

Continue to the edge of Standlake and turn left, SP 'Kingston Bagpuize'. In ½ mile turn left on to the A415, SP 'Abingdon'. Recross the Thames at Newbridge and continue to Kingston Bagpuize. Here turn left then right. In 2½ miles cross the A338, and in another 2½ miles go forward at the roundabout for the outskirts of Abingdon. Keep forward at the mini-roundabout for a diversion to Abingdon.

ABINGDON, Oxon

A mixture of Georgian houses and buildings dating back to the 13th century characterise this old Thameside town, once the county town of Berkshire, but now within Oxfordshire's boundaries. The 17th-century County Hall, standing on graceful columns, houses the Town Museum specialising in local history, and the Guildhall has a fine 18th-century Council Chamber. Several portraits line its walls, including one by Gainsborough of George III and Queen Charlotte. Down by the river stands the abbey gatehouse and a reconstructed Elizabethan theatre where plays and operas are performed in summer. Of Abingdon's 2 churches, St Helen's is the more beautiful, its elegant spire dominating the town and surrounding water meadows.

The main tour turns right on to the B4017, SP 'Drayton'. At Drayton turn left on to the B4016 for Sutton Courtenay.

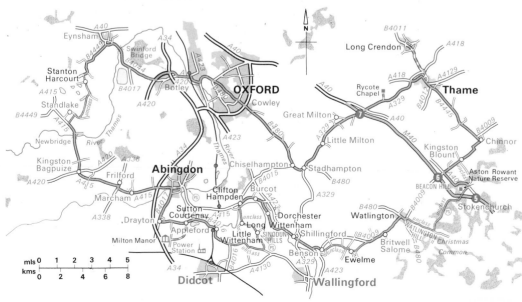

Rycote Chapel, with its fine wagon roof, has not altered since the 15th century

SUTTON COURTENAY, Oxon
One of the loveliest villages on the Thames, Sutton Courtenay's half-timbered houses and cottages are to be found along winding lanes and around a spacious green shaded by scented lime trees. In the churchyard rest the graves of Lord Asquith, who was Prime Minister at the outbreak of World War I, and Eric Blair, better known as George Orwell, author of *Animal Farm* and *1984*.

A diversion can be made to Milton Manor House by turning right in Sutton Courtenay on to an unclassified road.

MILTON MANOR, Berks
The 3-storey central portion of the Manor (OACT) was built during the 17th-century, but the 2 wings were added a century later by the Barret family. The house is remarkable for its elegant Gothic library, designed after the style of Horace Walpole's famous mansion at Strawberry Hill. The library contains a fine collection of English porcelain including Spode, Rockingham and Crown Derby.

Continue through Appleford, then go forward on to the Wallingford road. At the T-junction turn right and at the next T-junction, turn left. In ¾ mile turn left again, SP 'Little Wittenham'. Continue past the Sinodun Hills to Little Wittenham.

LITTLE WITTENHAM, Oxon
The hamlet lies in the shelter of the twin Sinodun Hills, which are crowned by a distinctive group of beech trees known as the Wittenham Clumps. A path through Wittenham Wood leads up to the ancient hill fort that commands the heights and provides superb views, westwards towards the Vale of the White Horse and eastwards to the Chiltern Hills.

In Little Wittenham turn left to reach the edge of Long Wittenham.

LONG WITTENHAM, Oxon
Half-timbered houses, an old inn and a medieval church form the long main street of this pleasant village. The Pendon Museum at the west end has fascinating detailed miniature scenes of rural life in the 1930s. Also part of the museum is the Madder Valley model railway. Built by one man, John Ahern, it pioneered the idea of setting model railways in a scenic landscape. Although Madder Valley is fictitious, many of the buildings along it are based on actual places around the country.

Continue on the Clifton Hampden road alongside the Thames. Cross the river and turn right into Clifton Hampden.

CLIFTON HAMPDEN, Oxon
By the old 6-acre bridge across the River Thames stands the Barley Mow Inn, immortalised by Jerome K. Jerome in *Three Men in a Boat*. On the other side of the river are the timbered, thatched cottages of Clifton Hampden.

In Clifton Hampden turn right on to the A415, SP 'Dorchester'. ½ mile beyond Burcot turn right on to an unclassified road for Dorchester.

DORCHESTER, Oxon
Dorchester's beautiful cobbled High Street contains a pleasing variety of interesting old buildings and the lanes leading off it are equally fascinating. In Samian Way, for example, is Molly Mop's thatched cottage; it was built in 1701 and the flint and brick walls are patterned in stripes and diamonds. The 200ft-long Abbey Church, standing on the site of a Saxon cathedral, is hidden among willow trees on a bend of the River Thame. It is famous for its magnificent sculpture and stained-glass window that traces the ancestry of the Virgin Mary.

In 1 mile turn right on to the A423 for Shillingford. In 1¼ mile turn left on to the B4009, SP 'Watlington', and enter Benson. Bear right through the village with the Ewelme road and in 1½ miles turn left, then right, into Ewelme.

EWELME, Oxon
Almost unchanged since the 15th-century when they were built, the almshouses, the old schoolhouse, and the church, form an exceptional medieval group among the brick and flint cottages of this charming village where watercress grows by the stream that runs parallel to the main street. Alice, Duchess of Suffolk, a granddaughter of the poet Geoffrey Chaucer, was responsible for them, and her imposing alabaster tomb is the most famous feature of the church. The grave of Jerome K. Jerome lies in the churchyard.

In Ewelme turn left on to the Watlington road and in 1 mile turn right on to the B4009. In 2½ miles join the B480 then turn left, SP 'Town Centre', into Watlington.

WATLINGTON, Oxon
Tucked away at the foot of the Chilterns, astride the prehistoric track known as the Icknield Way which stretches from Wiltshire up to The Wash, Watlington's Georgian architecture blends with the stone and half-timbered buildings of earlier centuries. At the centre stands the 17th-century brick market hall.

At the Market House in Watlington turn right (one-way) into Hill Road, and climb Watlington Hill, past the Watlington Mark — a chalk design cut into the hillside. At the top turn left, SP 'Kingston Blount'. After 1½ miles pass a picnic area on the right and in 1 mile cross the M40 and pass (left) the Aston Rowant Nature Reserve.

ASTON ROWANT NATURE RESERVE, Oxon
The whole of the Chiltern Hills, where the slopes and the high chalk ridges are clothed with beech woods, has been designated for preservation as an Area of Outstanding Natural Beauty. Wildlife and plants are specially protected by a number of National Nature Reserves such as Aston Rowant (OACT), which lies on one of the highest ridges of the Chilterns.

Pass the Stokenchurch Wireless Mast before turning left on to the A40 and descending wooded Beacon Hill. At the foot, turn right on to the B4009, SP 'Princes Risborough'. Continue through Kingston Blount and in 1¼ miles turn left to reach the edge of Chinnor and go forward on the B4445 to Thame.

THAME, Oxon
The architectural styles of 5 centuries are well represented at Thame, where the picturesque gabled 15th-century Birdcage Inn could have served as the model for many Christmas card and fairy story illustrations. It stands on the immensely wide High Street, the scene in autumn of the annual fair. The Spread Eagle Inn was mentioned in John Fothergill's book of country inns. *An Innkeeper's Diary*. At the north end of the street stands an old stone house (1570) which used to be Thame Grammar School, its most famous pupil was the Civil War leader John Hampden.

A detour can be made by turning right in the High Street on to the Aylesbury road. After ½ mile, at the roundabout, take the B4011 to Long Crendon.

LONG CRENDON, Bucks
In the thatched cottages of Long Crendon needle-making flourished as a cottage industry until factories took the trade away in the 1830s. A long half-timbered building (NT), the Courthouse, dating from the late 14th-century, stands near the church. Its upper storey contains one long room with an open-beamed roof, which was used as a court house in the reign of Henry V and perhaps also as a wool staple hall during the 14th and 15th centuries.

The main tour turns left in Thame on to the Oxford road. In ¾ mile, at the roundabout, take the A329. In 2 miles an unclassified road on the right leads to Rycote Chapel.

RYCOTE CHAPEL, Oxon
This outstanding example of a medieval chapel was built by the Quartermaine family from Thame and consecrated in 1449. The interior is furnished with beautiful Jacobean pews and medieval benches; the gilded stars on the ceiling were originally cut from rare European playing cards. Elizabeth I and later Charles I both visited the chapel.

Continue on the A329 through Little Milton to Stadhampton and turn right on to the B480, SP 'Oxford'. After 4 miles enter the suburbs of Oxford before crossing the Ring Road for the return to the city centre.

PETERSFIELD, Hants
In its early years Petersfield's prosperity was based on the wool trade, but as this began to decline it became an important coaching centre on the busy London to Portsmouth road. Today it is a thriving country town full of fine old houses in evocatively-named streets. A once-gilded equestrian statue of William III guards the central square, where a market is held every Wednesday and Saturday. The extensive waters of Heath Pond lie south east of the town on the B2146.

Leave Petersfield on the A3 'Guildford' road and continue to Durford Heath.

DURFORD HEATH, W Sussex
The 62-acre expanse of Durford Heath (NT) includes 4 acres of Rogate Common with its abundance of wildlife.

Continue along the A3 for ¾ mile. Reach the Jolly Drover Inn and turn right on to an unclassified road SP 'Rogate' to enter Sussex. After ¼ mile turn left on to the Fernhurst road and drive through wooded country to Milland.

MILLAND, W Sussex
Although close to the Portsmouth road, this straggling village preserves an air of remoteness and seclusion. St Luke's Church of 1878 stands in front of the primitive Old Church which it replaced.

Continue beyond Milland for 1¼ miles and turn right with SP 'The Old Cottage'. Ascend to Woolbeding and Pound Commons (NT).

WOOLBEDING COMMON, W Sussex
Woolbeding Common, part of a 1,084-acre estate (NT), includes some 400 acres of common heath and woodland open to public access.

Descend past Woolbeding's Saxon church.

Midhurst's mainly 19th-century church looks over a town that preserves beautiful buildings from many periods of architecture.

HAMPSHIRE DOWNS AND SUSSEX LANES

West of Petersfield are the rolling chalk downs of Hampshire, bare summits rising from wooded flanks watered by trout streams. East are the great wooded commons, winding lanes, and picturesque villages of Sussex.

Cowdray House was built *c*1500.

WOOLBEDING, W Sussex
Domesday describes Woolbeding as 'a perfect manor containing a church, mill, meadow, and wood.' The mill has gone, but the village is as delightful as that ancient description suggests. All Hallows' Church boasts a good Saxon nave.

Cross the River Rother, meet the A272, and turn left to enter Midhurst.

MIDHURST, W Sussex
This small market town stands on the south bank of the River Rother, at the centre of one of Sussex's most beautiful regions. South lie the downs, and north are the picturesque ruins of Cowdray House (see Easebourne).

Leave Midhurst by the A286 'Guildford' road, cross the river, and turn left through Easebourne.

EASEBOURNE, W Sussex
Formerly more important than Midhurst, immaculate Easebourne is very much an estate village. Among its many well-kept houses are Sycamore Cottage in Easebourne Lane, and The Priory, attached to the south side of St Mary's Church. Tudor Cowdray House (not open) was ruined by fire in 1793.

Leave Easebourne and climb through woodland to the 530ft Henley Common viewpoint. Continue to Fernhurst.

FERNHURST, W Sussex
Almost certainly the last stronghold of the Sussex iron-smelting industry, this large village has settled into attractive rural retirement amid the woods and valleys of the Weald.

Meet crossroads in Fernhurst and turn left on to an unclassified road. Drive through wooded country with SP 'Linchmere', and after 1 mile branch right SP 'Liphook'. Enter Linchmere.

LINCHMERE, W Sussex
Linchmere boasts a tiny green outside the enlarged hill chapel that serves as its church. Magnificent views from here extend over a deep valley flanked by steep slopes.

After Linchmere turn left on to the B2131 to re-enter Hampshire. Enter Liphook.

LIPHOOK, Hants
Most of Liphook straggles untidily along the main Portsmouth road, but here and there it preserves something of a village atmosphere. Bohunt Manor (open) stands in a lovely woodland and water garden.

A detour from the main route can be made here by turning left on to the unclassified 'Midhurst' road and driving for 1¼ miles to Hollycombe.

HOLLYCOMBE, W Sussex
The Hollycombe Working Steam Museum and Woodland Garden (open) has a remarkable collection of equipment ranging from old fairground rides to a 2ft-gauge railway through woodland banks of rhododendrons and azaleas. Attractions include traction engine rides and demonstrations of steam ploughing, threshing, and rolling.

At the Royal Anchor Hotel in Liphook (on the main route) at mini roundabouts turn right then sharp left SP 'Greatham' passing Longmoor Camp and Woolmer Forest. Continue to Greatham. In Greatham turn left on to the A325 and follow SP 'Alton'. Reach a church and after another ¼ mile turn right on to the B3006 and drive on to the east Hampshire Downs for Empshott. Continue along the B3006 to Selborne.

SELBORNE & SELBORNE HILL, Hants
It is not just the beauty of its scenery or the architectural distinction of some of its houses that have made this lovely village famous. It is also featured in Gilbert White's classic field study entitled *The Natural History of Selborne*. White, who was born in the Vicarage in 1720, made one of the first and best studies of wildlife inter-action within a defined area. He died in The Wakes, a fine house that now contains a library and the Gilbert White Museum (open). Visitors today can still see the church meadows and high beech hangers where he made many of his observations, and climb the steep Zig-Zag Path to the excellent viewpoint of Selborne Hill (NT).

In 3¼ miles turn left on to an unclassified road for Chawton. A short detour can be made from the main route here by keeping forward on the A32 to Alton.

The Gilbert
White Museum
at Selborne.

MID HANTS RAILWAY,
Hants

The original Watercress Line, as this
railway has come to be known, was
threatened with closure in 1973 and
initial efforts to keep the whole line
open were not successful. In 1975
the Winchester & Alton Railway
Company raised enough money to
open 3 miles of track between
Alresford and Ropley. All associated
buildings in the 10 miles to Alton
were also acquired.

New Alresford's Broad Street, said to be the finest
village street in Hampshire, is lined with attractive
Georgian houses and lime trees.

Jane Austen lived at Chawton Cottage
with her mother and sister.

ALTON, Hants

In years
gone by this
historic market
town grew quietly
prosperous on
brewing and the manufacture of
woollen cloth. Fine Georgian
buildings grace the main street, and
a Tudor cottage that was once the
home of the poet Spenser is in
Amery Street. Exhibits in the Curtis
Museum include a collection of craft
tools and other bygones.

*Continue back to the main tour route
and enter Chawton.*

CHAWTON, Hants

In Chawton is the unassuming 18th-
century house where novelist Jane
Austen once lived. Now a Jane
Austen Museum (open), this was her
home from 1809 till her death, and
all her later books were written here.

*Reach a roundabout at the end of
Chawton and take the 2nd exit on to
the A31. Climb to 600ft at Four Marks
continue on the A31 to roundabout,
take 3rd exit and follow into
Alresford.*

NEW ALRESFORD, Hants

During the medieval period New
Alresford grew to be one of the
10 greatest wool towns in the
country. Aptly-named Broad Street,
considered the finest village street in
Hampshire, leads downhill to
scattered Old Alresford. At the
north-west end of the village is the
large and picturesque lake.

*A short detour can be made from the
main route by turning left into Station
Road to visit the Mid Hants Railway.*

*Leave Alresford on the Winchester
road and after $\frac{1}{2}$ mile meet crossroads.
Turn left on to an unclassified road to
Tichborne.*

TICHBORNE, Hants

Tichborne is a delightful collection of
thatched 16th- and 17th-century
houses with an unspoilt little church
and a 19th-century manor house.
Some 800 years ago the ailing lady of
the manor, distressed by the poverty
of the villagers, begged her husband
to help them. Mockingly he agreed
to set aside part of his estate to
provide corn for the poor in
perpetuity, but that would be only so
much land as she could crawl round
while one torch burned. Tradition
has it that she managed to
encompass an amazing 23 acres
of ground before the flame –
and her life – expired. The land

concerned still known as The Crawls,
and every year the villages receive a
dole of 30cwt of flour blessed by the
local priest.

*Continue for 1 mile past the village,
meet a T-junction, and turn right on
to the B3046 for Cheriton. Follow SP
'Petersfield' for $\frac{1}{2}$ mile, then cross a
main road on to the unclassified
'Droxford' road. Drive through
Kilmeston, climb rolling hills, then
later turn left on to the 'Warnford'
road for a descent to the Meon Valley.
Continue to Warnford.*

WARNFORD, Hants

This beautiful Meon Valley village
has a 12th- to 17th-century church
with a massive Norman tower. Ruins
of a 13th-century building,
misleadingly known as King John's
House, is located at Warnford Park.

*Meet a T-junction and turn right on to
the A32 'Fareham' road. Cross the
River Meon and continue into
Corhampton.*

CORHAMPTON, Hants

This pleasant River Meon village
boasts a rare Saxon church with a
contemporary sundial. The walls of
the ancient nave slant crazily to the
south, but the building is quite safe.

*After another mile turn left on to the
B2150 'Waterlooville' road, then pass
the Hurdles Inn and take the next
turning left (no SP). Follow SP 'East
Meon' over crossroads and after
another $\frac{1}{2}$ mile bear left. Cross
downland to meet a T-junction and
turn left again on to the 'West Meon'
road. Continue to the slopes of Old
Winchester Hill.*

OLD WINCHESTER HILL,
Hants

Why this noted beauty spot should
be so named is a mystery, for the city
of Winchester lies a good 12 miles to
the west. The hill's windswept
summit rises to nearly 700ft,
affording excellent views over half
the county, and a 1$\frac{3}{4}$-mile nature trail
has been laid out on its flanks.

*Branch right on to a narrow road and
later turn right on to the A32. Drive
into West Meon and turn right on to
the unclassified 'East Meon' road.
Continue along the attractive Meon
Valley to the edge of East Meon.*

EAST MEON, Hants

'Father of angling' Izaak Walton once
fished here, and the village is still a
popular trout centre. The Norman
church is arguably the finest of its
kind in Hampshire.

*Follow SP 'Petersfield' and in $\frac{1}{2}$ mile
turn left on to the narrow 'Lower
Bordean' road. Later cross the A272
into the very narrow 'Colemore' road
and follow SP 'Petersfield' to a
T-junction. Turn right, descend the
attractive Stoner Hill, and return to
Petersfield.*

PORTSMOUTH, Hants

Naval tradition is everywhere in Portsmouth. The docks, founded by Richard the Lionheart at the end of the 12th century, now cover more than 300 acres. Here the most famous ship in British history, HMS *Victory*, Nelson's flagship at the Battle of Trafalgar in 1805, lies peacefully at anchor. It has been restored and fitted out to show what conditions on board ship were like. Nearby, the Royal Navy Museum has a fascinating display of model ships and figureheads, and a huge and impressive panorama representing the Battle of Trafalgar. Also in the dockyard is the Mary Rose, Henry VIII's flagship, which was raised from the seabed after a famous rescue mission. A major exhibition accompanies the restored ship. In old Commercial Road is the birthplace of Charles Dickens, which is now a museum of his life and times (OACT).

From Portsmouth city centre follow SP 'Southsea' to the seafront, then turn left along the Esplanade to Southsea.

SOUTHSEA, Hants

Henry VIII built a castle (OACT) at Southsea in 1539 to defend Portsmouth harbour. Now it houses a naval museum and archaeological exhibits. Southsea is well off for museums: Cumberland House in Easter Parade, has local natural history displays and an aquarium; the Eastney Beam-Engine House is the hub of an industrial archaeology museum and the Royal Marines Museum is to be found in Eastney Barracks.

From Southsea follow South Parade and in ¾ mile turn left into St George's Road. Pass Eastney Barracks (right) and at the roundabout, take the 2nd exit. At the next roundabout, take the A2030, SP 'Out of City'. The tour then runs alongside Langstone Harbour and in 2 miles at the roundabout, take the A27, SP 'Chichester' and continue to Emsworth.

EMSWORTH, Hants

Emsworth, tucked away between 2 of the many small creeks of Chichester Harbour, is an ancient port, famed for its oyster fisheries. Yacht building is the traditional occupation here and yachts jostle in the small, picturesque harbour. On the jetty is a majestic old tide mill.

At Emsworth turn left on to the B2148 Horndean road, pass under a railway bridge then bear left. In 1 mile turn right into Emsworth Common Road and enter Southleigh Forest. Continue to Funtington and join the B2146. In 1 mile turn right, SP 'Bosham', and pass through West Ashling. At the roundabout junction with the A27 a diversion can be made by taking the 2nd exit for Bosham.

ROYAL NAVAL BASE BENEATH THE SUSSEX DOWNS

Portsmouth, historic seat of the Royal Navy, opens the way to the hidden creeks and harbours of the Hampshire and West Sussex coasts sheltered beneath the magnificent beech hangers that cloak the South Downs.

BOSHAM, W Sussex

The village green leading from the waterfront up to the fine old church, the brick and tile-hung cottages along the strand and the sheltered harbour, all create a scene that appeals to painters and yachtsmen alike. Inhabitants of Bosham claim that it was here, and not at Southampton, that King Cnut unsuccessfully challenged the waves to withdraw. As evidence they point to the tomb that was discovered in the church about 100 years ago and said to belong to Cnut's daughter.

The main tour joins the A27 Chichester road and continues to Fishbourne.

FISHBOURNE, W Sussex

The little Sussex village of Fishbourne is outshone by the splendid Roman palace built here c AD 75. Archaeologists have unearthed a 6-acre site, the largest Roman building yet found in Britain. The north wing, with the famous 'boy on a dolphin' mosaic floor, is open, and parts of the original hypocaust (underground central heating system) and baths can also be seen. Outside, archaeologists have reconstructed the gardens as they might have been in Roman-times.

Beyond Fishbourne turn left on to the A259 and follow SP 'City Centre' into Chichester.

CHICHESTER, W Sussex

The county town of West Sussex is a delightful criss-cross of old streets, lined with handsome Georgian houses and shops. The city was founded by the Romans in AD 43, and the old Roman street plan can still be traced in North, South, East and West Streets. These divide the town in 4, meeting at the splendid octagonal market cross built in the 15th century by Bishop Story. The prettiest of the old streets are The Pallants and Little London, where an 18th-century Corn Store has been converted to the City Museum and the museum of the Royal Sussex Regiment. Chichester's great Norman cathedral contains 2 outstanding works of modern art: a dazzling tapestry by John Piper and a painting by Graham Sutherland.

From the Ring Road in Chichester follow SP 'Worthing' to the Chichester Motel Roundabout. Here follow SP 'Goodwood' and in ½ mile, at the T-junction, turn left. Later, on the right, is the entrance to Goodwood Park and House.

The cottages crowded along Bosham's quayside all have steps to their front doors to protect them from the frequent flooding of the harbour at high tide

North Street — typical of Chichester

GOODWOOD HOUSE, W Sussex

Seat of the Dukes of Richmond and Gordon, Goodwood House (OACT) was built during the late 18th century in Sussex flint. It is a treasuretrove of fine pictures, notably Vandyck's portraits and George Stubbs' paintings of racehorses; furniture; tapestries and Sèvres porcelain. Wooded parkland surrounds the house and high above on the downs is Goodwood Racecourse — once part of the estate. The glorious scenery of the downs provides a superb setting and the views are quite breathtaking.

Climb on to the South Downs to reach Goodwood Racecourse. Here turn left and later pass the entrance, on the left, to the Weald and Downland Open Air Museum just before Singleton village.

THE WEALD AND DOWNLAND OPEN AIR MUSEUM, W Sussex

All types of buildings from southern and south-eastern England have been accumulated at this open-air museum (OACT), the first of its kind to be established in this country. Here you can see, for example, a Wealden farmhouse, a charcoal burner's hut, a forge, a pottery and a smithy — just a few of the many old rural buildings from England's past.

Continue to the A286 and turn right, SP 'Midhurst', into Singleton. Continue through Cocking to Midhurst.

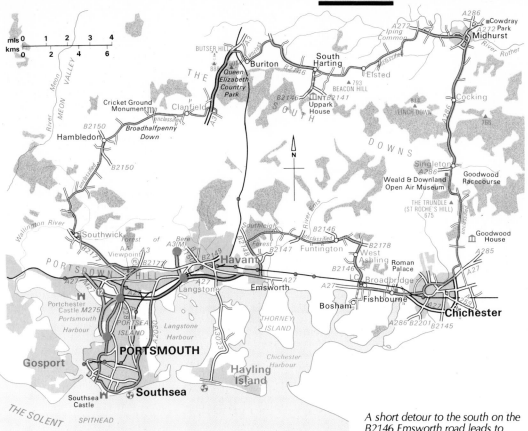

MIDHURST, W Sussex
The little town of Midhurst sits snugly in the Rother valley to the north of the downs. The quaintly named Knockhundred Row leads from North Street to Red Lion Street, where the old timbered market house stands. Of the many picturesque buildings, the half-timbered Spread Eagle Inn, dating back to medieval times, is perhaps the finest. A curfew is still rung in the church every evening at 8 p.m. in memory of a traveller who, lost in the forest long ago, followed the sound of the church bells and so was saved.

To the east of the town is Cowdray Park.

COWDRAY PARK, W Sussex
Viscount Cowdray of Midhurst bought the estate earlier this century and preserved the ruined house (OACT), once the seat of the Earls of Southampton which was destroyed by fire in 1793. The superb parkland forms an appropriate setting for the aristocratic sport of polo which was imported into England from India in the last century.

Leave Midhurst on the A272, SP 'Petersfield'. In 2½ miles turn left SP 'Elsted' and 'Harting'. Cross Iping Common, and continue through Elsted to South Harting.

SOUTH HARTING, W Sussex
The slender church spire rises out of the wooded farmland surrounding this attractive village, whose main street is lined with old houses, some of brick, some tile-hung and some of Sussex clunch — a local soft limestone. It was at Harting Grange (not open) that the 19th-century novelist Anthony Trollope spent the last 2 years of his life.

A short detour to the south on the B2146 Emsworth road leads to Uppark.

UPPARK HOUSE, W Sussex
A magnificent house in a magnificent setting on the downs, Uppark (NT) was the home of Lord Grey, 1st Earl of Tankerville, in about 1690. A later owner, Sir Matthew Fetherstonhaugh (pronounced Fanshawe) furnished it with exquisite furniture and rare carpets. His wife Sarah brought with her a wonderful Queen Anne dolls' house, complete with furniture, glass and silverware. Their extravagant and highly sociable son, Sir Harry, inherited Uppark and brought to the house a beautiful 15-year-old girl, Emma Hart, who later became Lord Nelson's Lady Hamilton. Sir Harry married his 20-year-old dairymaid when he was 70 and left her the

Bayleaf House, built in Kent between 1420 and 1480, was reconstructed at the Weald and Downland Museum in the 1970s

entire estate. The young lady spent the rest of her life conserving Uppark and it remained largely unchanged throughout the 19th century. The novelist H. G. Wells spent much of his youth here, for his mother was housekeeper.

From the Ship Inn at South Harting, follow SP 'Petersfield' along the B2146. After 2 miles re-enter Hampshire, then in just over ½ mile turn left for Buriton.

BURITON, Hants
Glorious beech hangers drop down into Buriton, whose traditional green with its duck pond is surrounded by attractive cottages, an old church, a rectory and a stone manor house. The latter was the home of famous historian Edward Gibbon, best remembered for his mammoth work, *The Decline and Fall of the Roman Empire*.

Continue through the village and in about a mile turn left on to the A3, SP 'Portsmouth'. In 2 miles, on the left, is the entrance to the Queen Elizabeth Country Park.

QUEEN ELIZABETH COUNTRY PARK, Hants
The wooded downland south of Buriton was opened by the Forestry Commission in Jubilee Year (1977) as the Queen Elizabeth Country Park (OACT). Marked trails wind through the park and there is a reconstruction of an Iron-Age settlement to be seen, as well as a craft centre displaying items used to farm the hills for the past several hundred years.

In 1 mile turn left SP 'Clanfield' then left again. At the roundabout take the 1st exit. From Clanfield cross Broad Halfpenny Down to Hambledon.

HAMBLEDON, Hants
On Broadhalfpenny Down near Hambledon, opposite the Bat and Ball Inn, stands a monument commemorating the beginning of cricket. The Hambledon Cricket Club were the first, in 1760, to play the game in an organised manner. To the west of the attractive village, on a south-facing slope, lies one of England's few successful vineyards (open by appointment), producing a white wine similar to German hock.

In Hambledon turn left on to the B2150, then in ¾ mile branch right SP 'Fareham'. After 2½ miles, at the T-junction, turn left, SP 'Southwick', at the next T-junction turn left for Southwick. Here follow SP 'Portsmouth' to join the B2177. At the roundabout at the top of Ports Down Hill take the 1st exit, SP 'Havant'. Nearly 1 mile further is an AA Viewpoint. Continue on the B2177, then shortly, turn right, SP 'Portsmouth', to join the A3. Descend to Cosham and return to Portsmouth city centre via the A3, or the M275.

BERKSHIRE'S WOODED VALLEYS AND ROLLING DOWNS

The rhythmic thud of horses hooves breaks the early-morning silence as racehorses at exercise gallop over the springy turf of the Lambourn and Berkshire Downs, high above the sheltered villages of the Kennet and Thames.

Boxford watermill on the River Lambourne

READING, Berks

The old town has all but disappeared under the impact of the 20th century, but it is still pleasant to stroll along the pretty riverside walk where the Thames runs between Reading and its quiet suburb of Caversham. In Whiteknights Park, the Museum of English Rural Life contains an interesting collection of agricultural implements and reminders of village life as it used to be. The town museum has remains from the nearby Roman fort of Silchester and the old Norman abbey, founded by Henry I who is buried in the Church of St Laurence. The Abbey Gate still stands in Forbury Street and here, from 1785-7, Jane Austen and her sister Cassandra attended a school that occupied 2 rooms above the gateway. Oscar Wilde wrote the moving *Ballard of Reading Gaol* about his imprisonment here from 1895-7.

Leave Reading on the A4, SP 'Newbury'. In 4¼ miles, at the motorway roundabout, take the 2nd exit, SP 'Theale'. At the next roundabout take the A340, SP 'Pangbourne', then turn left on to an unclassified road for Bradfield.

BRADFIELD, Berks

Set in the wooded valley of the River Pang, Bradfield, largely 18th-century, is best known for its public school, Bradfield College. It was founded in 1850 by Thomas Stevens, the local vicar, whose main concern was to train the pupils as choirboys for his church. The school has an open-air theatre, renowned for its good productions of Greek and other classical plays.

At Bradfield turn left, SP 'Bucklebury'. In 1 mile turn right through Southend Bradfield, then Chapel Row. Cross Bucklebury Common and continue to Upper Bucklebury. At the far end branch right, SP 'Cold Ash', and continue through well-wooded countryside. After 1½ miles pass the outskirts of Cold Ash, then in ¾ mile go over the crossroads and descend to Ashmore Green. Here, branch right into Stoney Lane (no SP) and continue to the suburbs of Newbury. At the T-junction turn right, then turn left on to the B4009 and continue to the edge of Newbury. For the town centre take the 3rd exit at the roundabout.

NEWBURY, Berks

This old market town is nowadays best known for its racecourse where major steeplechase and hurdling events are held in the winter season. In the past, the town was noted for its weaving industry and its most famous resident was Jack of Newbury, John Smalwoode, who started life in the Tudor period as a penniless apprentice and became an immensely wealthy clothier. In 1513 he led 100 men to fight at the Battle of Flodden, and was important enough to act as host to Henry VIII. He paid for the building of the beautiful Tudor church of St Nicholas, where a brass (1519) commemorates him. The remains of his house can be seen in Northbrook Street, and the 17th-century timbered cloth hall now houses the town museum.

At Newbury the main tour joins the bypass, SP 'Hungerford A4'. At the next roundabout take the B4494, SP 'Wantage', and in nearly ¾ mile pass on the left the turning to Donnington Castle.

DONNINGTON CASTLE, Berks

The gatehouse and the massive round towers of the gateway of Donnington Castle (AM) stand as a reminder of the 2 Civil War battles of Newbury. The Royalist leader Sir John Boys beat off 2 attacks in 1643 after the first battle, even though his castle was pounded almost to rubble by cannon shot. Again in 1644, after the second battle, Donnington played its part by defending the king's retreat to Oxford, but the castle gradually fell into picturesque ruin.

Continue on the B4494 and in ¼ mile bear left (still SP 'Wantage'), then gradually climb over the well-wooded Snelsmore Common — now a country park. In 1 mile, before the motorway bridge, turn left on to an unclassified road for Winterbourne. At the far end of the village turn right, SP 'Boxford', and later descend into the Lambourn valley to Boxford.

BOXFORD, Berks

Old, weathered cottages and a lovely gabled watermill standing on a clear, bubbling stream make an idyllic rural picture in this charming Berkshire village set in the Lambourn valley.

Turn left and cross the river bridge, then keep left. At the main road turn right by the Bell Inn, SP 'Easton' and 'Welford', and continue to Great Shefford. Here, join the A338, then keep forward on to the unclassified Lambourn road and later skirt East Garston.

EAST GARSTON, Berks

Under the shelter of the Berkshire Downs nestle a medley of old brick and timber cottages, some thatched, some tiled. On the street that leads up to the church is an appealing group of black and white cottages, each with its own little bridge across the river.

Continue along the valley, through Eastbury for Lambourn.

LAMBOURN, Berks

Horses could be said to outnumber people in Lambourn, where almost every house has its own block of stables, and on the springy turf of Lambourn Down strings of highly bred racehorses can be seen at exercise against an exhilarating backdrop of open countryside. The village itself, in its downland setting, makes an attractive sight, especially around the medieval church where there are old almshouses and an ancient village cross.

At the crossroads turn right on to the B4001, SP 'Wantage', and cross the Lambourn Downs. After 6 miles, at the crossroads, turn right on to the B4507 for Wantage.

WANTAGE, Berks

The statue of King Alfred in the market place at Wantage commemorates the fact that this pleasant old town in the Vale of the White Horse was his birthplace in 849. No Saxon relics survive, but the town contains a number of attractive Georgian buildings.

Follow SP 'Newbury B4494' and climb on to the Berkshire Downs. After 4 miles turn left on to an unclassified road for Farnborough. Continue across the downs to West Ilsley and then East Ilsley.

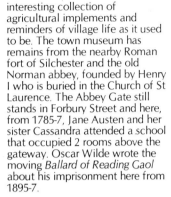

Count Gleichen's statue of King Alfred, a tribute to a great warrior who united Saxon England, stands in Wantage market

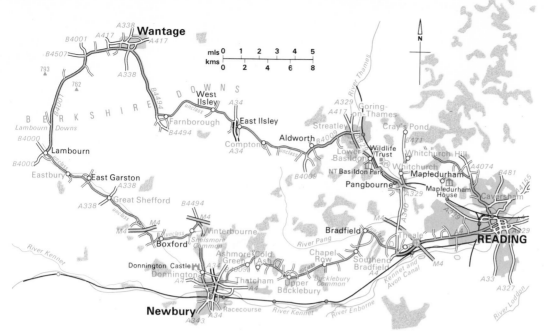

At the mini-roundabout in Pangbourne turn left, then left again on to the B471, SP 'Whitchurch'. Cross the Thames by a toll bridge and enter Whitchurch. After ¾ mile, at Whitchurch Hill, turn right, SP 'Goring Heath'. Nearly 1½ miles farther turn right again, SP 'Reading', then in 2½ miles pass on the right the turning for Mapledurham.

MAPLEDURHAM, Oxon
Wooded hills surround this peaceful little village where pretty cottages, 17th-century almshouses and an old watermill, the last one on the Thames to preserve its wooden machinery, are attractively grouped by the river. Mapledurham House (OACT) is a lovely brick manor house built in the reign of Elizabeth I by Sir Michael Blount, who entertained her here. Two of his descendants, the sisters Mary and Martha Blount, were friends of the 18th-century poet and satirist Alexander Pope, who wrote in a poem addressed to one of them: 'She went from Op'ra, park, assembly, play/To morning walks and pray'rs three hours a day;' John Galsworthy chose the village for the site of Soames Forsyte's country house in the *Forsyte Saga*.

Continue on the Reading road then in ¾ mile turn right on to the A4074 and later descend into Caversham. At the traffic signals turn right and recross the Thames for the return to Reading.

WEST AND EAST ILSLEY, Berks
At these twin villages the traveller stands in the heart of the Berkshire Downs, amid a seemingly endless panorama of superb country. East Ilsley seems to exist solely for the training of horses. There are stables everywhere and fenced-off rides cover the surrounding hills.

At East Ilsley bear left for Compton. Continue on the Pangbourne road then in 2¼ miles turn left on to the B4009, SP 'Streatley', and skirt the village of Aldworth.

ALDWORTH, Berks
The 9 'giants' of Aldworth were all members of the de la Beche family. Three of them are nicknamed John Long, John Strong and John Never-Afraid. A fourth one, John Ever-Afraid, has disappeared, but according to legend he was buried halfway up the church wall to fulfil an oath — he swore that the devil could have his soul if he was buried inside or outside the church. The village well, now disused, has the distinction of being one of the deepest (372ft) in the country.

The tour descends into the Thames valley to reach Streatley. At the traffic signals turn right on to A329, SP 'Reading'. Beyond Lower Basildon pass Basildon Park (right).

BASILDON PARK, Berks
This imposing 18th-century house, built by John Carr of York, was used by troops in both World War I and II but otherwise stood empty from 1910 until Lord and Lady Ilife bought it. After lovingly restoring the house, they gave it to the National Trust in 1977. The splendid plasterwork inside is attributed to William Roberts of Oxford.

½ mile further, on the left, is the Child Beale Wildlife Trust.

CHILD BEALE WILDLIFE TRUST, Berks
Colourful exotic birds, including ornamental pheasants, peacocks and flamingoes, strut around this unusual garden. A lake, a river and garden statuary provide an attractive setting for walking, and there is a special area for children.

Mapledurham, one of England's largest Elizabethan houses, was the home of the Blount family for 12 generations

Continue alongside the River Thames to Pangbourne.

PANGBOURNE, Berks
Kenneth Graham, author of *The Wind in the Willows*, lived and died at Pangbourne, and it is easy to imagine his characters Mole and Rat rowing up and down the river here, where the Thames meets the Pang. Above Pangbourne's pleasant houses is the Nautical College, founded in 1917 by Sir Thomas Devitt.

EXOTIC ANIMALS IN THE CHILTERNS

Just a stone's throw from Hertfordshire's densely populated towns lie unsuspected areas of wooded countryside hiding Whipsnade's and Woburn's free-roaming wild animals — creatures as much at home here in the Chilterns as in their far-off native lands.

ST ALBANS, Herts

The remains of *Verulamium,* once the most important Roman town in Britain, lie across the River Ver to the west of the present city of St Albans. Here stand the ruins of the great amphitheatre and part of a hypocaust (underground heating system). The Verulamium Museum contains some spectacular mosaic pavements and many other fascinating relics. Modern St Albans takes its name from the first Christian martyr in Britain, Alban, a Roman convert who lived in *Verulamium.* The mighty abbey was founded in 793 on the hill where he is thought to have been killed, and contains his shrine. Made of Purbeck marble, the shrine was lost for years; it was discovered in the last century, shattered into fragments, and restored by Sir Giles Gilbert Scott. The only English Pope to date, Nicholas Breakspear, was a native of St Albans, son of an abbey

tenant. He was elected in 1154 and took the name of Adrian IV. Several old streets meander around the town centre where the 15th-century curfew tower rises 77ft high, and there are a number of historic houses to be found. The Old Fighting Cocks Inn claims to be one of Britain's oldest pubs, and on the site of the Fleur de Lys Inn, in French Row, the King of France was held prisoner after the Battle of Poitiers in 1356. Other places of interest are the Kingsbury Watermill Museum, where the 'Handmeade' is preserved — a working watermill of the 16th century; the Organ Museum; the City Museum which houses part of the Salaman Collection of craft implements, and the beautiful gardens of the National Rose Society where more than 1,650 sorts of roses bloom.

Leave St Albans on the A1081, SP 'Harpenden'.

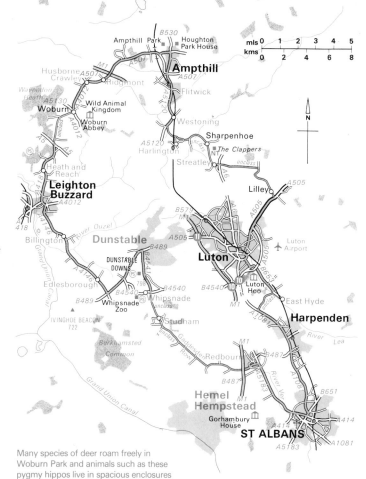

Many species of deer roam freely in Woburn Park and animals such as these pygmy hippos live in spacious enclosures

HARPENDEN, Herts

Harpenden means 'spring or valley of the harpers', and this pleasant small town set in lovely, wooded countryside, is much sought after by London commuters. Its High Street is full of interesting and attractive old houses and shops, and the common, bright with gorse, looks out over the peaceful slopes of the Harpenden valley.

Continue on the Luton road and in 1¾ miles pass the Fox PH, then ¼ mile farther turn right, SP 'New Mill End'. In another 1½ miles turn left on to the B653 SP 'Luton'. Later, to the left, pass Luton Hoo.

LUTON HOO, Beds

The colourful Edwardian diamond magnate Sir Julius Wernher, decided to have Robert Adam's Classical 18th-century stone-built mansion remodelled in 1903 to suit his own extravagant tastes. His fabulous collection of art treasures includes Faberge jewels and Imperial robes worn at the court of the Russian Tsars, paintings by Titian and Rembrandt, rare tapestries and old porcelain (OACT).

Continue into Luton.

LUTON, Beds

Luton is now Bedfordshire's largest town, a thriving centre of light industry and famous for its international airport. In the past, however, it was famed for the making of pillow-lace and the elegant straw-plaited hats worn by ladies to protect their complexions from the sun. Exhibits in the Wardown Museum illustrate the history of these crafts from a bygone era.

Leave on the A505, SP 'Hitchin', and after 3¾ miles pass the Silver Lion PH, then branch left, SP 'Lilley', and turn left into Lilley.

LILLEY, Beds

This quiet little village on the prehistoric track called the Icknield Way was the home of a 19th-century eccentric, John Kellerman. He claimed to be the last descendant of the medieval alchemists and to possess the secret of turning base metal into gold. The family crest of the Salusburys, local landowners, is carved on many of the cottages.

Continue on the unclassified road and in nearly 2 miles turn left, SP 'Streatley'. In another 2 miles cross the main road for Streatley. Here, turn right and continue to Sharpenhoe.

SHARPENHOE, Beds

A footpath winds from Sharpenhoe, a tiny village nestling at the foot of a steep hill, to a lovely area of high woodland known as the Clappers (NT). The views from the top explain why John Bunyan chose this for the 'Delectable Mountain' of *Pilgrim's Progress*.

Capability Brown landscaped the formal gardens of Luton Hoo which houses the splendid Wernher art collection

Turn left, SP 'Harlington', and in 1¾ miles turn on to the Westoning road and skirt the village of Harlington. After another 1¼ miles turn right on to the A5120, SP 'Ampthill', and continue through Westoning to Flitwick. Here, cross the railway bridge and turn left to reach Ampthill.

AMPTHILL, Beds

Sheltered by low hills, Ampthill presents a charming mixture of thatched cottages, Georgian houses, old coaching inns and a parish church set in a pretty square. Ampthill Park (house not open), is famous for the ancient oak trees in its grounds. Catherine of Aragon, first wife of Henry VIII, was dismissed to Ampthill when the king decided to divorce her.

A short detour can be made to visit the ruins of Houghton Park House, 1 mile north of the town.

HOUGHTON PARK HOUSE, Beds

The 17th-century mansion (AM) that was once the home of the Countess of Pembroke, sister of Sir Philip Sidney, fell into ruins nearly 200 years ago. This is thought to have been the 'House Beautiful' of *Pilgrim's Progress*, the book that John Bunyan wrote while a prisoner in Bedford gaol. The hill on which the gaol stands is thus his 'Hill of Difficulty'.

At Ampthill the main tour turns left on to the B530 SP 'Woburn'. In ¾ mile turn right on to the A507. Pass through Ridgmont and at Husborne Crawley join the A4012. In 1¾ miles turn left for Woburn

WOBURN, Beds

The village of Woburn has a number of attractive buildings dating from the post-coach era, and is filled with antique shops and boutiques catering for the thousands of visitors drawn to

Woburn Abbey (OACT), seat of the Dukes of Bedford. This most flamboyant of all Britain's stately homes is famous for its Wild Animal Kingdom. Herds of rare species of deer and numerous other exotic animals are housed in the beautiful 3,000-acre park and there are many other attractions, to suit the whole family. The abbey itself is a spacious 18th-century mansion designed by Henry Holland and contains a notable collection of paintings by Canaletto, Velasquez, Gainsborough and Van Dyck.

At Woburn turn right, SP 'Leighton Buzzard'. In 2 miles turn left and then right on to the A418 and continue through Heath and Reach to reach Leighton Buzzard.

LEIGHTON BUZZARD, Beds

A graceful 5-sided market cross with 2 tiers of arches holding carved figures, erected in 1400, stands at the centre of the market town. One of the attractive old buildings nearby, the Wilkes Almhouses, is the scene of a curious ceremony which takes place annually in May: while portions of the founder's will are read aloud, a choirboy stands on his head. As Leighton Buzzard has now been joined to Linslade on the opposite bank of the Ouzel, the town is sometimes called Leighton-Linslade. From Pages Park station, the Leighton Buzzard Light Railway, converted from industrial track, runs through nearly 4 miles of lovely wooded countryside.

Leave on the A4146, SP 'Hemel Hempstead'. Pass through Billington into Buckinghamshire, then continue to Edlesborough. In 1 mile turn left on to the B489, SP 'Dunstable'. Occasional views of the Whipsnade White Lion cut into the hillside can be seen on the right before reaching the outskirts of Dunstable. Here, at the mini-roundabout, turn right on to the B4541, SP 'Whipsnade', and climb on to the Dunstable Downs.

DUNSTABLE DOWNS, Beds

Rising dramatically from the surrounding farmland, Dunstable Downs, a steep scarp of the Chiltern Hills, is an ideal centre for gliding. Part of the downs, an area of woods and common land where many species of wildflowers grow, belongs to the National Trust. Two ancient highways cross the hills: the great Roman road of Watling Street, and the Icknield Way, a much older prehistoric track that may have been named after the tribe of the Iceni, whose queen, Boudicca, was eventually defeated by the Romans. Five Knolls, just outside Dunstable, is a group of round barrows where several Bronze-Age skeletons, knives and weapons have been excavated.

Near the top of the climb pass a picnic area and bear right. In 1¼ miles, at the crossroads, go forward SP 'Studham'. Alternatively, turn right on to the B4540 to visit Whipsnade Zoo.

WHIPSNADE ZOO, Beds

Over 2,000 wild animals roam the large paddocks of the 500-acre park set in the beautiful Chiltern countryside. Lions, tigers, bears and rhinos can be seen in almost natural conditions and there are many rare birds too. A passenger railway drawn by steam locomotives takes visitors through several of the paddocks, including the White Rhino enclosure. Special features include the dolphinarium and the children's zoo and farm.

The main tour continues to Studham. At the clock tower keep forward, SP 'Gaddesden Row', and in ½ mile go over the crossroads then bear left. Pass through Gaddesden Row and at the Plough PH bear left. In 2 miles turn left, SP 'Redbourn'. Later pass under the motorway bridge and turn left for Redbourn. Here turn right and at the roundabout take the 2nd exit on to the A5183, SP 'St Albans'. After 3 miles, near the Pré Hotel, a drive on the right leads to Gorhambury House.

GORHAMBURY HOUSE, Herts

Sir Francis Bacon, the Elizabethan writer and scholar who some believe to have been the real author of Shakespeare's plays, was born here. He rose to be Lord Chancellor of England under James I but was finally disgraced and impeached for embezzlement. His memorial stands in St Michael's Church, St Albans, a life-size marble figure showing the great philosopher alseep in a chair. The Tudor manor where Bacon lived is now partly ruined, but the present 18th-century house (OACT) contains relics of the Bacon family as well as a fine collection of Chippendale furniture.

Continue on the A5183 for the return to St Albans.

LEWES AND THE SOUTH DOWNS

Two lovely river valleys cut through the downs on their way to the sea with its high white cliffs. In between, low-lying water meadows and wooded lanes hide dignified manor houses and medieval hamlets with historic Lewes at their heart.

SEAFORD, E Sussex

A flat, exposed stretch of land — once wild and empty but now covered with buildings — separates Seaford from the sea. The port lost its importance as long ago as the 16th century when the River Ouse changed its course after a particularly violent storm and flowed into the sea at Newhaven instead. East of Seaford, high white cliffs of chalk stretch away from Seaford Head to Beachy Head. On the promontory of Seaford Head, beside the clifftop path to Cuckmere Haven, lie remains of an Iron-Age hill fort. During excavations broken flint axes, saws and arrowheads were found buried in 2 small pits; they were probably religious offerings.

From Seaford, follow the A259 Eastbourne road. Cross the Cuckmere River by the Exceat bridge, then in ¼ mile turn left on to the unclassified Litlington road. To the right of the A259 at this junction is the Seven Sisters Country Park.

SEVEN SISTERS COUNTRY PARK, E Sussex

Nearly 700 acres of downland and marshland have been turned into the Seven Sisters Country Park. Nature trails wind through the countryside and fishing is available along the Cuckmere valley. An old barn at Exceat houses the park information centre, and here there are interesting permanent displays of local history and temporary exhibitions.

Continue on the Litlington road and after nearly ½ mile pass the turning for Westdean (right).

WESTDEAN, E Sussex

Westdean village sits peacefully at the end of a No Through Road and seems remote from the hectic 20th century. Its cottages, mostly flint, cluster round a pond, a dovecot (AM) and the ruins of the medieval manor house (AM). Inside the Church of All Saints is a Jacob Epstein bronze bust of Lord Waverley, Home Secretary during World War II. It is possible that the site of this little village may be where Alfred the Great first met Asser, the monk who later became Bishop of Sherborne and wrote an account of the king's life.

Continue on the Litlington road and after another ½ mile, pass Charleston Manor on the right.

CHARLESTON MANOR, E Sussex

Only the grounds of this part-Norman, part-Tudor and part-Georgian manor house are open. However, the romantic gardens, full of bulbs and flowering shrubs contained by yew hedges and flint walls, are exceptionally pretty. Particularly interesting are the huge restored tithe barns, one thatched, the other tiled, and the medieval dovecot with its conical roof and revolving ladder.

Continue through Litlington and after ¾ mile turn left, SP 'Alfriston'. In another ¾ mile, turn left to recross the Cuckmere River. At the next T-junction, turn left for Alfriston.

ALFRISTON, E Sussex

The High Street of this tiny market town runs south from its square. Here stands the old market cross, shaded by the branches of a massive chestnut tree. On either side of the High Street are timbered buildings, some hung with tiles, some with weather-boarding, but virtually all are pre-18th century. Among the finest buildings are the 3 inns: The George, The Market Cross and The Star. The latter is most famous, both for its external carvings and the brightly coloured ship's figurehead which stands outside, and for its associations with smugglers. Alfriston was a well-known hideout for these outlaws in the early 19th century as it was on their route up the Cuckmere valley from the sea 3 miles away. Behind the High Street, overlooking the river and a large green known as the Tye, is Alfriston's church. Named Cathedral of the Downs because of its size, the cruciform church is particularly lovely and has some of the best flintwork in the country. On the edge of the green is the Clergy House (NT). This 14th-century building was, in 1896, the first to be bought by the newly formed National Trust.

By the 1800s Alfriston's Clergy House was being used as labourers' cottages

Return along the unclassified Dicker road and after 1 mile pass Drusillas Zoo Park on the right.

DRUSILLAS ZOO PARK, E Sussex

Hiding in the heart of the Cuckmere's low-lying water meadows and sleepy villages is Drusillas Zoo Park. Apart from the zoo itself, there are a great variety of different attractions here. These include a butterfly house, a farm, an adventure playground, a bakery selling its own freshly baked bread and a railway to take passengers on a round trip through the park.

On reaching the main road turn left at the roundabout and take the A27, SP 'Lewes'. After 4½ miles a detour to the left may be taken to West Firle.

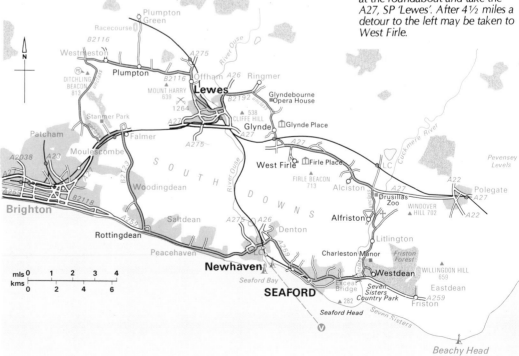

Anne of Cleves House, 16th-century, stands in Southover High Street, Lewes

WEST FIRLE, E Sussex
Such is the feudal atmosphere of West Firle (curiously there is no East Firle) that it still seems to be part of the estate attached to Firle Place (OACT). The village hides on the edge of the parkland and the Gage family crest over the inn confirms its connection with the great house. The Gages have owned Firle Place ever since the 15th century, and the main part of the house dates from that time. No alterations of any consequence were made to it until 1774, when the front was rebuilt to incorporate a gallery for the 1st Viscount's splendid art collection. Half an hour's walk away from the village is Firle Beacon, a magnificent viewpoint with distant views of the sea.

Continue on the A27 and in ½ mile turn right on to an unclassified road for Glynde.

GLYNDE, E Sussex
Like Firle, the small village of Glynde has a great house on its doorstep, Glynde Place (OACT). The present Elizabethan manor was built of flint and Caen stone in 1569, but the impressive stable block was added in the 18th century. The stable buildings surround a delightful courtyard of smooth lawn, roses and climbing plants. Bronzes, needlework and a pottery can be seen at Glynde Place, but one of its most prized possessions is a drawing by Rubens. This was a study for the painted ceiling of the Banqueting House at Whitehall.

At the far end of the village pass Glynde Place, and in ¾ mile bear left, SP 'Ringmer'. After 1 mile pass Glyndebourne Opera House.

GLYNDEBOURNE, E Sussex
When John Christie, onetime science master at Eton, inherited his ancestral home at Glyndebourne, he decided to indulge his great love of opera and build an opera house in the grounds of his Tudor mansion. Since opening in 1934, Glyndebourne has become internationally famous for its opera festivals performed from May to August. The idyllic setting, the elaborate champagne picnics on the beautiful lawns and the elegance of evening dress, combine to produce a magical atmosphere at Glyndebourne that is unforgettable.

Continue, and on reaching the B2192 turn left, SP 'Lewes'. At the A26 turn left to reach Lewes.

LEWES, E Sussex
With the downs rising up around it and the River Ouse flowing through it, Lewes was an ideal site on which to build a defensive fort and the Normans made full use of it. William de Warenne, husband of William the Conqueror's daughter Gundrada, originally built his castle of wood on 2

Although sheep still graze the chalky slopes of the South Downs, many acres are now being used for arable farming instead

artificial mounds. Later a stone keep was built but little except this and the gateway remain, however, because in 1620 the castle was demolished and the stone sold off as building material for 4d a load. The imposing outer gatehouse, called Barbican House, is 14th century and a museum of Sussex archaeology is kept here now. Wide views from the top of the keep encompass Offham Hill. It was there that Henry III unsuccessfully fought Simon de Montfort in 1264 at the Battle of Lewes. East Sussex's charming country town of steep streets, little alleyways and neat, red-roofed Georgian houses covers no more than a square mile. Nearly every building is of interest; Anne of Cleves House — so called because it was one of the properties Henry VIII gave Anne as payment for divorcing him — is open as a folk museum. There is another museum in Regency House and this is devoted to military heritage and includes a short history of the

British army. Traditionally, every November 5 the streets throng with torch-lit processions and bonfires blaze in celebration of Guy Fawkes.

Leave the town centre on the A275, SP 'East Grinstead'. Pass through Offham then in almost ½ mile turn left on to the B2116, SP 'Hassocks'. Continue along the foot of the South Downs to Plumpton.

PLUMPTON, E Sussex
A church, a post office, an inn, an old rectory and Plumpton Place make up the old village of Plumpton; the modern village, 2 miles away, is called Plumpton Green and lies handy to Plumpton Racecourse. Plumpton Place (not open) a half-timbered, E-shaped house, was restored by Sir Edwin Lutyens after World War II. Above the village a V-shaped group of fir trees commemorate Queen Victoria's Golden Jubilee.

Continue to Westmeston. Here, turn left on to an unclassified road, SP 'Underhill Lane'. At the next crossroads turn left and climb to the summit of Ditchling Beacon (813 ft) — one of the highest points on the South Downs. 2½ miles later, turn left, SP 'Moulsecombe'. In another 1¼ miles turn left on to the A27 and pass Stanmer Park (the site of the University of Sussex). Branch left then turn right on to the B2123, SP 'Rottingdean', and pass through Woodingdean to reach Rottingdean.

ROTTINGDEAN, E Sussex
Flint and brick cottages brighten up the High Street of this onetime smuggling town which has the salty flavour of the sea. Rudyard Kipling, author of *Jungle Book*, stayed here as a boy with his uncle, the painter Sir Edward Burne-Jones. Some of Burne-Jones' glasswork can be seen in the church, which overlooks a green with a pond — a particularly attractive corner of the town. A Georgian house, remodelled by Sir Edwin Lutyens, contains the library, an art gallery and a museum with some Kipling exhibits and a good toy collection.

At Rottingdean turn left on to the A259, SP 'Newhaven', and continue along the coast road through Saltdean and Peacehaven to Newhaven.

NEWHAVEN, E Sussex
Well-known as a cross-channel departure point to France, Newhaven teems with passengers both coming and going to the Continent. The town was called Meeching until the 1560s, when the Ouse changed its course (see Seaford) and Newhaven seemed more appropriate.

From Newhaven follow SP 'Eastbourne' and remain on the A259 for the return stretch to Seaford.

THE WEALD OF WEST KENT

Since medieval times the wealthy have come to West Kent to build their great houses amongst the woods and weathered rocks of the High Weald. Below is a different world of rich valleys full of twisty lanes, fruit orchards, and the smell of growing hops.

SEVENOAKS, Kent

Tradition has it that this town was named from a clump of 7 oaks that once grew here. The original trees have long gone, but in 1955 new ones were taken from Knole Park and planted on the common. It was Knole Park that brought prosperity to Sevenoaks in the 15th century when Archbishop Bourchier acquired it and rebuilt the manor house (NT) as a palace for archbishops of Canterbury. Nowadays the town is largely residential, with an air of confident ease typical of long-established communities. Cricket has been played on The Vyne wicket since 1734.

Leave Sevenoaks with SP 'Westerham' (A25). After 1 mile turn left on to the A25. There are fine views towards the steep wooded escarpment of the North Downs to the right. Continue into the village of Sundridge.

SUNDRIDGE, Kent

Sundridge's pride is the 15th-century timbered hall-house in its main street. The great hall is several storeys high, and its original stone hearth is still to be seen. The house was restored in 1923. Nearby Ovenden House dates from 1745, and 13th-century Sundridge Church contains a number of good brasses.

Keep forward and enter Brasted.

BRASTED, Kent

In spite of traffic the main village street still retains much of its character. At one point it opens on to a small green fringed by half-timbered houses. Brasted Place, in a fine park adjoining the village, was built by Robert Adam in 1784 and subsequently became the home of Napoleon III. About 1½ miles south of the village is 600-acre Brasted Chart (NT), which offers pleasant walks and drives.

Continue along the A25 to Westerham, passing Quebec House on entering the village.

QUEBEC HOUSE, Kent

On the eastern outskirts of Westerham village is early 17th-century Quebec House (NT), famous as the boyhood home of General Wolfe. Relics of this hero of the Battle of Quebec, who died winning the victory that made Canada British, are preserved inside the house. His statue stands in Westerham High Street.

Continue into Westerham village.

WESTERHAM, Kent

General Wolfe was born in the vicarage here in 1727. He stayed at the George and Dragon in 1758, during what was to prove his last visit to the town. Another famous person with Westerham connexions

was Sir Winston Churchill, whose statue stands on the tiny green. Westerham Hill is an 800ft- high viewpoint crossed by the Pilgrims' Way.

Continue on the 'Redhill' road. At the end of the village turn left on to the unclassified road for Squerryes Court.

SQUERRYES COURT, Kent

The Warde family have lived in this 17th-century mansion from the time of General Wolfe to the present day, and it was here in 1741 that Wolfe received his commission. A room is set aside for Wolfe mementos, and other parts of the house feature fine paintings and tapestries.

This statue of General Wolfe stands on the green in Westerham.

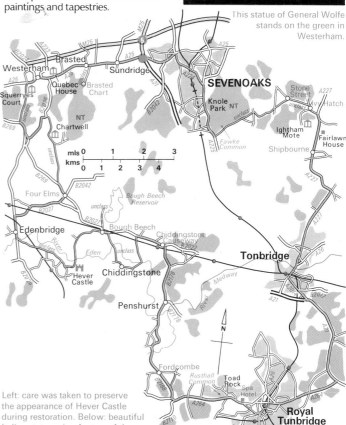

Left: care was taken to preserve the appearance of Hever Castle during restoration. Below: beautiful Italian statuary is a feature of the grounds at Hever Castle.

Ascend through thickly-wooded country and turn left on to the B269 'Edenbridge' road, with fine views across the Weald. In ¾ mile turn left on to the B2026 'Westerham' road. Climb on to wooded Crockhamhill Common. After the common turn right on to an unclassified road to Chartwell.

CHARTWELL, Kent

Chartwell will always be associated with Winston Churchill. It was his country home from 1922 until his death, and part of it now houses a Churchill museum. Other rooms are arranged much as they must have been in his lifetime. The Churchilliana on display include photographs illustrating every stage of his life, gifts given to him by other world leaders, and his Nobel Prize. A good many of his paintings are to be seen in the house, and in his studio at the end of the garden.

Beyond Chartwell descend to the Eden Valley and turn left on to the B269 'Tonbridge' road. At Four Elms turn right on to the B2042 SP 'Edenbridge', and shortly join the B2027. After 1½ miles turn left on to the B2026 into Edenbridge, and drive along the main street.

EDENBRIDGE, Kent

Several old buildings survive in Edenbridge main street, particularly between the 16th-century Crown Hotel and the bridge over the River Eden. The mainly 13th-century church carries a massive tower crowned by a spire of later date.

Cross the River Eden, take the first turning on the left, and proceed along an unclassified road to Hever Castle.

HEVER CASTLE, Kent

In Tudor times 13th-century Hever Castle was the home of the Boleyns, whose daughter Anne married Henry VIII and bore him the future Queen Elizabeth I. The building began life as a fortified farmhouse, but was made into a crenellated mansion at the beginning of the 15th century. The fortunes of the house waned with the fall of the Boleyns, and by the beginning of this century it had once more reverted to use as a farmhouse. It took a wealthy American, William Waldorf Astor, to restore it to its present magnificence. The superb gardens feature Tudor-style flower beds and a 35-acre lake. Both house and gardens are open to the public.

Leave the castle and continue to Bough Beech. A detour can be made from here to Bough Beech Reservoir: turn left on to the B2027, cross a railway bridge, then turn right on to an unclassified road to the reservoir.

BOUGH BEECH RESERVOIR, Kent

This reservoir is the haunt of migrant waders, ducks, wintering divers, grebe and geese. Access is by written permission only.

Leave Bough Beech and join the B2027 for 200 yards, then turn right on to the unclassified 'Chiddingstone' road. Drive to crossroads and turn left for Chiddingstone. Ahead, at the crossroads, is the entrance to Chiddingstone Castle.

CHIDDINGSTONE, Kent

Chiddingstone, a National Trust village, has a beautifully preserved street lined with half-timbered 16th- and 17th-century houses that were probably built with iron-industry money. At the top of the street is 19th-century Chiddingstone Castle. The Chiding Stone, from which the village takes its name, is a large sandstone rock behind the street. Nagging wives were once brought here to be chided by the assembled village population.

After ¼ mile (beyond the village) branch left. In 1¾ miles turn right on to the B2027 for Chiddingstone Causeway. Pass the local church and turn right to follow the B2176. Enter Penshurst.

PENSHURST, Kent

At the centre of Penshurst, behind a screen of tall trees, is 14th-century Penshurst Place. The Sidney family and their descendants have lived here for more than 400 years, and Sir Philip Sidney – diplomat, courtier, and poet – was born here in 1554. The family became Earls of Leicester, and the village contains the original Leicester Square.

Leave Penshurst and follow the B2188 'Tunbridge Wells' road through the Medway Valley to Fordcombe.

FORDCOMBE, Kent

This 19th-century picture village of half-timbered and tile-hung cottages is grouped round a pleasant green. It was built at the instigation of Lord Hardinge, whose seat was near by at South Park.

Beyond Fordcombe turn left on to the A264. Cross Rusthall Common and note a left turn leading to Toad Rock.

TOAD ROCK, Kent

Amongst the many eroded sandstone outcrops in the Tunbridge Wells area is Toad Rock, on Rusthall Common, which has been weathered to look like a toad. Other unusual rock formations are to be found at nearby Happy Valley.

In ¼ mile reach the Spa Hotel and turn right on to Major York's road. Proceed to the far side of the common (carpark for the Pantiles) and turn left on to the A26 into Royal Tunbridge Wells.

ROYAL TUNBRIDGE WELLS, Kent

Extensive parks and gardens impart a quiet charm to this elegant Regency town. The 17th-century Church of St Charles the Martyr is the oldest here and Holy Trinity dates from the 19th century. The latter was built by Decimus Burton, who also laid out lovely Calverley Park. Medicinal waters discovered by Lord North in 1606 – the main reason for the foundation of the town – may still be drunk at the Pantiles, an 18th-century raised promenade fringed with lime trees.

Leave the town with SP 'Hastings' to join the A264. Later turn left on to the A21 'Sevenoaks' road. Pass woodland and branch left on to the A2014. Later turn right and enter Tonbridge.

TONBRIDGE, Kent

A settlement has existed here at least since Anglo-Saxon times. The River Medway played an important part in the town's early prosperity, and the later introduction of the railway increased its importance as a centre of communication. Today Tonbridge is a mixture of market town and rail depot built round a ruined Norman to 14th-century castle on a mound.

Cross the River Medway and follow SP 'Gravesend, A227'. Ascend to Shipbourne.

The variety of architectural styles in the houses at Chiddingstone creates a beautiful village landscape.

SHIPBOURNE, Kent

Most of the Victorian village that makes up Shipbourne lies to the west of the green. St Giles' Church was reconstructed in the 1880s.

Beyond the village pass Fairlawne House.

FAIRLAWNE HOUSE, Kent

Situated just ¾ mile north of Shipbourne, this splendid house (unfortunately not open to the public) dates from the 18th century and features a Great Room designed by the architect Gibbs.

Pass Fairlawne House and ascend. At the top of the hill turn left on to an unclassified road SP 'Ivy Hatch'. Take the next turning left and descend a narrow lane to Ightham Mote.

IGHTHAM MOTE, Kent

Medieval Ightham Mote, a small manor house set in lovely meadowland, is considered to be the most complete of its kind in Britain (open at certain times). Its low bulk is encircled by a moat, and its fine wooded grounds feature a tree-fringed lake. Peacocks are kept in the gardens.

Return to Ivy Hatch and keep left on the 'Seal' road. After a short way turn left again and drive to the village of Stone Street. Bear left on the 'Fawke Common, Riverhill' road and continue through heaths and woodland. Later cross Fawke Common, meet a main road and turn right on to the A225. Descend, and reach the entrance to Knole Park on the right.

KNOLE PARK, Kent

In 1456 Thomas Bourchier, then Archbishop of Canterbury, bought an ordinary manor house called Knole Park. He and his successors developed this humble beginning into a great palace, but when Archbishop Warham died in 1532 Henry VIII seized the estate for himself. Elizabeth I granted it to Sir Thomas Sackville in 1566, who died while improvement work on the interior of the house was still in progress. Knole Park (NT) (open) looks much as it must have done then.

Return to Sevenoaks.

Kent is renowned for oast houses like this one near Bough Beech.

UCKFIELD, E Sussex
Standing on a hillside above the valley of the River Ouse, Uckfield looks towards the great sweep of the downs. Traditional Sussex houses, brick and tile-hung, or weather-boarded, line its attractive main street.

Leave Uckfield on the Eastbourne Road. In 2½ miles cross the A22, SP 'Isfield', and 1¼ miles farther keep left on the Ringmer road to shortly pass the entrance to Bentley Wildfowl Gardens.

BENTLEY WILDFOWL GARDENS, E Sussex
A succession of ponds, surrounded by luxurious belts of trees and bushes, create an ideal habitat for many varieties of interesting wildfowl; spectacular flocks of rose-coloured flamingoes, black swans and ornamental pheasants bring a blaze of exotic colour to the Sussex countryside.

At the T-junction 2 miles later, turn left on to the B2192, SP 'Halland', then in 1½ miles turn right on to an unclassified road for Laughton.

LAUGHTON, E Sussex
Between wooded countryside to the north and the flat marshlands of Glynde Level to the south, stands the little village of Laughton. A curious buckle emblem can be seen on the church tower, on the ruined tower of Laughton Place south of the village, and on several buildings round the area. This was the badge of the Pelhams and dates back to the Battle of Poitiers in 1356, when Sir John Pelham captured the French King and was awarded the Badge of the Buckle of the King's Swordbelt by a grateful Edward III.

Turn left on to the B2124, SP 'Hailsham'. On reaching the A22 turn right then take the next turning left, SP 'Chiddingly'. In ¾ mile turn left again for Chiddingly.

CHIDDINGLY, E Sussex
The tall church spire soars above the cottages of this small, quiet village. From the church, you can see for miles over the downs, and on a clear day it is possible to pick out the chalky outline of the Long Man of Wilmington — a giant figure cut out of the turf above Wilmington. Inside the church is an outsize monument to members of the Jefferay family, with 2 large standing figures in elaborate Elizabethan dress.

Turn left in the village, SP 'Whitesmith', and in 1 mile at the T-junction, turn right, SP 'Waldron'. Continue for 2 miles, then turn right and immediately left on to the Heathfield road. In 1½ miles, at the crossroads, turn left SP 'Blackboys'. On reaching the main road turn left then immediately right, SP 'Buxted'. After 1¾ miles turn left and continue to Buxted.

ASHDOWN FOREST AND THE FOREST WEALD

Never far from the quietly civilised villages of East Sussex and the Kent borders are the woods and heathlands of Ashdown Forest — a tame fragment of the vast primeval wilderness that covered much of south-east England in ancient times.

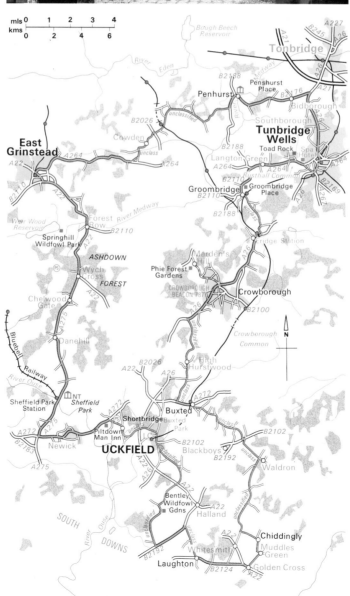

BUXTED, E Sussex
Hogge House, a 16th-century black and white timbered building at the gates of Buxted Park, was the home of Ralph Hogge, a local iron-master, the first man to cast an iron cannon in 1543. The old village that he knew was allowed to fall into ruins during the 19th century because Lord Liverpool, the owner of Buxted Park (not open) wanted to improve the view from his mansion. Consequently Liverpool moved the village to its present site near the station. The parish church still stands in the park. It is dedicated to St Margaret of Scotland and her emblem, the marguerite, is carved around the pulpit and embossed on the ceiling.

At Buxted turn left on to the A272 and skirt the grounds of Buxted Park. After ¾ mile turn right on to an unclassified road and continue to High Hurstwood. Bear left into the village, then ascend to skirt part of the Ashdown Forest. On reaching the A26 turn right, passing over Crowborough Beacon (792ft), and enter Crowborough.

Weather-boarding, typical of Kentish cottages, like these in Groombridge, was added to give extra protection

CROWBOROUGH, E Sussex
Crowborough has grown up around a triangular green, and climbs up over the slopes of the 796ft Beacon Hill from where there are superb views. A relatively modern town — its oldest house dates from the 19th century — it owes its charm to its position on the eastern edge of Ashdown Forest. Nearby the Phie Forest Gardens are a favourite place for country walks and picnics.

Remain on the A26 and in 3 miles pass Eridge Station, then immediately turn left on to an unclassified road for Groombridge.

GROOMBRIDGE, E Sussex/Kent
Groombridge spans the county border between East Sussex and Kent. The old part of the village, in Kent, is exceptionally pretty, with 18th-century brick and tile-hung cottages grouped around a triangular green which leads to the gates of Groombridge Place, (not open) a delightful Jacobean moated manor house set in lovely gardens (open by appointment).

In Groombridge turn right on to the B2110, SP 'Tunbridge Wells'. Pass the grounds of Groombridge Park (right), then in 1¼ miles turn right, on to the A264. Continue through Langton Green and after crossing Rusthall Common, a side road on the left may be taken to visit the curious Toad Rock, so called because of its distinctive shape. Continue on the A246 and in ¼ mile at the Spa Hotel, turn right, SP 'Brighton'. On the far side of the common turn left on to the A26 to enter Tunbridge Wells.

TUNBRIDGE WELLS, Kent

This delightful town owes its existence to Lord North who, in 1606, discovered the medicinal springs in what was then a sandstone outcrop in the Forest of Ashdown. Many of its houses date from the late 17th and 18th centuries, by which time it had become a fashionable spa. The famous Pantiles, an elegant colonnaded walk lined with fashionable shops and shaded by trees, takes its name from the large roofing tiles, 15 of which survive, laid to appease Queen Anne who had protested at the muddy state of the ground. The town museum contains a fascinating collection of Tunbridge Ware — small boxes and trinkets decorated with a mosaic of tiny pieces of wood — and Victorian paintings, toys and dolls.

Leave Tunbridge Wells on the A26, SP 'Tonbridge' and 'London'. Pass through Southborough, then in 1 mile turn left on to the B2176, SP 'Penshurst'. Continue through Bidborough to Penshurst.

PENSHURST, Kent

The pretty village of Penshurst lies between the Rivers Medway and Eden. Around the approach to the churchyard is a charming group of timbered cottages, the central one raised up on pillars to form an archway. Penshurst Place (OACT) was the home of the gallant Elizabethan soldier-poet Sir Philip Sidney who, when dying after the Battle of Zutphen, gave the water offered to him to an enemy soldier, saying: 'Thy necessity is greater than mine'. The manor house, set in lovely 17th-century gardens, was originally built in the 15th century by Sir John de Pulteney, 4 times Lord Mayor of London, and his magnificent medieval great hall survives. Descendants of Sidney, the de L'Isle family, still live at Penshurst.

Branch left on to the B2188, and in ¾ mile turn right, SP 'Chiddingstone'. After 1½ miles, at the T-junction, turn right, and ¾ mile farther keep left, SP 'Cowden'. In another mile turn left, then in 1½ miles cross the main road to reach Cowden. Go through the village and turn right on to the East Grinstead road. On reaching the A264 turn right for East Grinstead.

EAST GRINSTEAD, W Sussex

The old centre of East Grinstead, originally a small market town, remains unspoilt, and in the main street are many Tudor half-timbered buildings. The most attractive group is Sackville College (OACT): gabled, 17th-century almshouses built around a quiet courtyard with the dignified air of an Oxford college.

Leave on the A22 and continue to Forest Row. Springhill Wildfowl Park lies 1½ miles to the west.

SPRINGHILL WILDFOWL PARK, E Sussex

Rare varieties of ducks and wild geese, flamboyant peacocks, graceful swans, flamingoes and cranes inhabit this 10-acre forest garden that surrounds an attractive 15th-century farmhouse on the borders of Ashdown Forest.

Continue on the Eastbourne road into part of the Ashdown Forest.

ASHDOWN FOREST, E Sussex

Ashdown Forest, lying between the North and South Downs, covers more than 14,000 acres. Extensive though it is, Ashdown is merely a remnant of the vast primeval Forest of Anderida which cut Sussex off from the rest of the country. It remained a wild and dangerous area until Elizabethan times when the great trees were felled to provide fuel for the forges of the Wealden iron industry.

A collection of toys and games can be seen in the stable block of Penshurst Place

At Wych Cross turn right on to the A275, SP 'Lewes'. Continue through Chelwood Gate and Danehill to Sheffield Park.

SHEFFIELD PARK, E Sussex

The gardens (NT) of the elegant 18th-century house (OACT) built by Wyatt for the Earl of Sheffield, are one of the great showplaces of Sussex. The original landscape design, featuring broad, curving lakes was carried out by Capability Brown and his pupil Humphry Repton. Two more lakes were added later, and around the

Careful planting at Sheffield Park ensures a blaze of colour all year round

4 stretches of water A. G. Soames, who bought the property in 1909, created gardens and walks of rhododendrons, azaleas, maples, birches and other trees.

THE BLUEBELL RAILWAY, E Sussex

At Sheffield Park station you can take a step back into the past by travelling on the famous Bluebell line, where vintage steam trains trundle along the old East Grinstead to Lewes track, through 5 miles of glorious Sussex countryside to Horsted Keynes.

Continue on the A275 and 2 miles later turn left on to the A272. Pass through Newick to reach Piltdown.

PILTDOWN, E Sussex

Between Newick and Uckfield stands an inn called the Piltdown Man. Its name and the inn sign which depicts on one side an apelike skull and on the other a club-wielding caveman, commemorate one of the greatest archaeological hoaxes of all time. In 1912 a respectable young lawyer called Charles Dawson caused a sensation by announcing his discovery of the skull of a creature that was joyfully hailed as evidence of the 'missing link' between *homo sapiens* and the great apes. Piltdown Man remained a 'fact' for more than 40 years, until scientific dating techniques established in 1953 that the skull had been cobbled together from the jaw of an orangutan and the deformed cranium of a medieval skeleton.

After passing the Piltdown Man Inn turn right, SP 'Shortbridge'. At Shortbridge, cross the river and turn left for the return to Uckfield.

THE BUCKINGHAM CHILTERNS

Great rounded hills crowned with beeches enfold valleys where pure chalk streams are home to the speckled trout. Here and there steeples rise dark against the green flanks, proclaiming downland villages famous for their beauty.

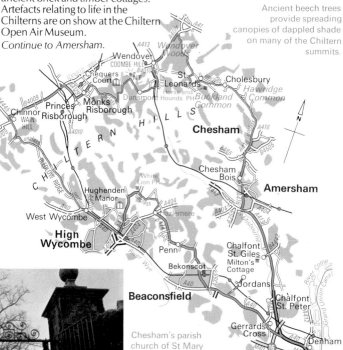

UXBRIDGE, Gt London
Uxbridge stands on the banks of the River Colne and the Grand Union Canal. Its Old Crown and Treaty House featured in an historic meeting between Charles I and Parliament in 1645. St Margaret's Church dates from the 14th and 15th centuries, but its tower was rebuilt in 1820. The Market House dates from 1789.

Follow SP 'Denham' then 'Beaconsfield' to leave Uxbridge on the A4020, crossing the Grand Union Canal and the River Colne. Proceed to the Denham roundabout and take the 3rd exit on to the A40. Denham village lies off the road to the right.

DENHAM, Bucks
Denham is a most attractive village of fine houses, old inns, and ancient brick and timber cottages. St Mary's Church, which dates from the 15th century, contains wall paintings of the Day of Judgement and a 13th-century font. The local Wesleyan Chapel was built in 1820. At the end of the main street is 17th-century Denham Place, which stands in grounds landscaped by Capability Brown. Savay Farm is a 14th-century hall house.

Continue for 2 miles, with the River Misbourne to the right of the road, and meet traffic signals. Turn right on to the A413, SP 'Amersham' and proceed for 2¼ miles. Go forward to skirt Chalfont St Peter.

Go forward to skirt Chalfont St Giles. A detour from the main route to Milton's Cottage can be made by driving to the Pheasant Inn and turning left on to an unclassified road.

MILTON'S COTTAGE, Bucks
Milton lived in this timber-framed and brick cottage (open) during the plague year of 1665. He completed *Paradise Lost* here and began *Paradise Regained.*

CHALFONT ST GILES, Bucks
St Giles' Church has a 13th-century heart in Victorian dress. The village has a small green bordered by ancient brick and timber cottages. Artefacts relating to life in the Chilterns are on show at the Chiltern Open Air Museum.
Continue to Amersham.

Ancient beech trees provide spreading canopies of dappled shade on many of the Chiltern summits.

CHESHAM, Bucks
Chesham stands in the Chess Valley, with attractive Chiltern countryside to the north-west. Georgian houses and cottages exist here. The George Inn in the High Street dates from 1715. A charter granted by King Henry III in 1257 gave Chesham its market, held every Wednesday.

In Chesham bear left then right with one-way traffic SP 'Berkhamsted'. Meet a roundabout, drive forward for about a ¼ mile, and turn right. Continue to a T-junction and turn left. Within ⅓ mile keep forward to an unclassified road SP 'Tring'. In 1¾ miles bear left to climb on to the Chilterns.

THE CHILTERN HILLS
Wooded in the west but mostly windswept and bare near Ivinghoe in the east, the Chiltern Hills extend in a majestic line from Goring in the Thames Valley to a point near Hitchin, and culminate in 835ft Coombe Hill above Wendover. Many of the chalk 'downs' are crowned with ancient beech groves. The North Bucks Way, a 30-mile walk from Wolverton to Chequers, is open for public use.

Keep forward to Hawridge Common and continue to Cholesbury.

CHALFONT ST PETER, Bucks
A complete contrast in building styles is offered by two local churches. One is a Victorianized 18th-century structure and the other a 20th-century creation. The once-fashionable gothic-revival style is evident in Chalfont House, which was built for General Churchill.

AMERSHAM, Bucks
Amersham is a lovely collection of old houses, quaint cottages, and ancient inns in the Misbourne Valley. Sir William Drake built the Town Hall in 1682, some 15 years after the almshouses bearing his name. Beech woods grace the Chiltern countryside around the town.

Chesham's parish church of St Mary dates mainly from the 19th century, but retains details from earlier periods.

mls 0 1 2 3 4 5
kms 0 2 4 6 8

Meet traffic signals by the Crown Hotel and turn right into Church Street. Within 1 mile approach more traffic signals and turn left on to the A416 for Chesham Bois.

CHESHAM BOIS, Bucks
St Leonard's at Chesham Bois is a 19th-century restoration, but the arch of its south entrance may have been part of a medieval church. Memorial brasses can be seen inside.

Continue on the A416 to Chesham.

CHOLESBURY, Bucks
Cholesbury Common boasts a fine tower windmill which started life as a smock mill in 1863. Its form was revised after it had been declared unsafe in 1884, and it has now been converted into a private house. Iron-age Cholesbury Camp covers 15 acres near by.

Continue to Buckland Common, then drive to the Horse and Hound (PH) and keep left. Take the next turning right to St Leonards.

ST LEONARDS, Bucks

The Church of St Leonard, rebuilt after the Civil War and restored in 1845, has plastered walls and carries a squat bell turret surmounted by a spire.

Follow the 'Aston Clinton' road. Descend Aston Hill through Wendover Woods T-junction A4011. Turn left and continue along the A4011 to Wendover.

WENDOVER, Bucks

Many delightful brick and timber cottages survive here, plus a collection of quaint inns which includes the Red Lion Hotel, where Oliver Cromwell slept in 1642. Bosworth House, in the main street, is of 17th-century origin. Both the local windmill and a watermill have been converted into houses. The ancient Icknield Way crosses the Chilterns near by on its way from east to south-west England.

Turn left on to the A413 SP 'Amersham'. Within ¼ mile turn left again, then continue for 1½ miles and turn right on to an unclassified road. Ascend to Dunsmore, go forward with SP 'Kimble', and follow the narrow road over a shoulder of Coombe Hill.

COOMBE HILL, Bucks

About 1½ miles west of Wendover is Coombe Hill (NT) – 106 acres of downland in the highest part of the Chilterns. Excellent views include Aylesbury and the Chequers Woods.

Descend to Chequers Court.

CHEQUERS COURT, Bucks

Chequers is a notable 16th-century house that was given to the nation by Lord Lee of Fareham, as a thank-offering for the ending of World War I. About 3 miles from Princes Risborough in hundreds of acres of parkland, it is the Prime Minister's official country residence and contains valuable Cromwellian relics.

Turn left SP 'Great Missenden'. In 1¼ miles turn sharp right SP 'Princes Risborough', and in 1 mile descend Longdown Hill. Turn left on to the A4010 for Monks Risborough.

MONKS RISBOROUGH, Bucks

A well-known local landmark is the 80ft chalk cross cut on a slope overlooking the Icknield Way. Its upkeep was traditionally the duty of the earls of Buckingham.

Continue to Princes Risborough.

PRINCES RISBOROUGH, Bucks

Among several picturesque old houses surviving here is a 17th- and 18th-century manor house (NT).

At roundabout take 3rd exit A4129 SP 'Thame'. In 1 mile at roundabout turn left on to the B4009. Proceed to Chinnor along the line of the Icknield Way.

Above: this pastel of John Milton at the age of 62 hangs in Milton's Cottage. Right: this picturesque, creeper hung cottage is where the poet ended his days in blindness and loneliness, a disillusioned old man.

CHINNOR, Oxon

A Chiltern village with a cement works sounds incongruous, even to 20th-century ears, but Chinnor has just such an industry. Its moated manor house and attractive church are more typical of the area.

Meet crossroads and turn left, then within ¼ mile go forward along an unclassified road with SP 'Bledlow Ridge'. Wain Hill viewpoint lies to the left.

WAIN HILL, Bucks

Cut into the solid chalk slope of Wain Hill is the 75ft-long Bledlow Cross, one of two turf-cut crosses in the county.

In ½ mile ascend Chinnor Hill and turn sharp left for the climb to Bledlow Ridge.

BLEDLOW RIDGE, Bucks

The climb to Bledlow Ridge is steep, but well worth the effort for it commands breathtaking views.

Descend to West Wycombe.

WEST WYCOMBE, Bucks

This town has a beautifully-preserved main street (NT) which enshrines architecture dating from the 15th to 19th centuries. The town's Church of St Laurence stands isolated on a 600ft-high hill at the site of a village which has long gone. Artificial chalk caves in the area once housed the notorious Hell Fire Club founded by Sir Francis Dashwood who owned the mansion in West Wycombe Park (NT). Nearby is a small motor museum.

Join the A40 and drive through the village to High Wycombe.

HIGH WYCOMBE, Bucks

High Wycombe has been important since Roman times, and once earned a very good living from wool and lace. It is now well known for the manufacture of furniture, particularly chairs, and has a museum dealing solely with the craft in Castle Hill House. The Guildhall and octagonal Little Market House are scheduled as Ancient Monuments.

Leave High Wycombe following SP 'Great Missenden, A4128' and cross the River Wye. Within 1½ miles reach Hughenden Manor on the left.

HUGHENDEN MANOR, Bucks

Hughenden Manor was the home of Disraeli, Prime Minister of Great Britain under Queen Victoria. It was remodelled in 1862 but his study still remains as he left it.

After about ¼ mile turn right. Ascend for ¾ mile and approach the White Lion (PH). Turn right again into unclassified Cryers Hill Lane and proceed to a T-junction. Turn left SP 'Penn' and in 1 mile turn right. In ½ mile approach traffic signals at Hazlemere and drive straight over crossroads on to the B474 SP 'Beaconsfield'. Go forward to Penn.

PENN, Bucks

Penn is in one of the loveliest parts of the Chilterns. Village inn and church stand side by side overlooking the green in the company of fine Georgian houses, and the view from the churchyard is exceptional.

Continue through Penn to the outskirts of Beaconsfield and Bekonscot Model Village.

BEKONSCOT MODEL VILLAGE, Bucks

Situated in Warwick Road, Beaconsfield New Town, this model has cottages, churches, waterways, a railway, an airport, farms, and fields, at the scale of one inch to one foot.

Continue into Beaconsfield.

BEACONSFIELD, Bucks

Beaconsfield has a green bordered by roads of Queen Anne and Georgian houses, and ancient inns with notable histories. The half-timbered Royal Saracen's Head was once a coaching stop. Although St Mary's Church is medieval in origin it wears a Victorian face; the poet Edmund Waller lies buried here.

At roundabout turn left A40 SP 'London'. Continue for ½ mile, enter a roundabout, and leave by the 1st exit. After another ½ mile at roundabout the unclassified left turn leads to Jordans.

JORDANS, Bucks

The most famous of all Quaker Meeting Houses stands here. It was built in 1688 and is only a few years younger than Old Jordans Farm, where Quaker meetings were held prior to its completion.

Continue along the A40 to the outskirts of Gerrards Cross.

GERRARDS CROSS, Bucks

This largely residential district has a Byzantine-style church of 1859 and a few Georgian houses.

Continue along the A40 and enter Denham roundabout. Leave by the A4020 exit and return to Uxbridge.

A painted ceiling dominates the Blue Drawing Room in 18th-century West Wycombe Park.

SANCTITY IN STONE

Centuries before Christianity the primitive peoples of England raised the huge megaliths of Stonehenge. Much later came the cathedrals, the Norman permanence of Winchester and soaring early-English completeness of Salisbury.

WINCHESTER, Hants
Venta Belgarum to the Romans, this one-time capital of Wessex boasts an 11th-century and later cathedral that is the second longest in Europe. Inside are richly-carved chantry chapels, the oldest iron grille in England, and coffins holding the bones of Saxon kings. Survivals from the distant 13th century include excellent stretches of the city walls, the hall of Pilgrims' School, and the 13th-century and later Deanery. Winchester College, founded by William of Wykeham in 1382, retains much of its original structure and stands near the ruined Bishop's Palace of Wolvesey Castle. Castle Hall dates from the 13th century, and 16th-century Godbegot House stands on the site of a palace built by King Canute. Close to the centre of town the River Itchen rushes through a lovely old mill (NT) of 1744 before winding through attractive gardens alongside the medieval walls.

Follow SP 'Stockbridge' to leave Winchester on the A272, and in 4¾ miles reach the Rack and Manger Inn. Turn right on to an unclassified road SP 'Crawley'. After another 1 mile reach a pond and turn left into Crawley village.

CRAWLEY, Hants
Almost too perfect to be true, this picture-book village has timber-framed cottages, an old pub, and a duckpond. Its homely church has Norman features, and its Court dates from the late 19th century.

Drive to the far end of the village and keep left, then in 1¼ miles turn right to rejoin the A272. Proceed to Stockbridge Down.

STOCKBRIDGE DOWN, Hants
Situated on the north side of the A272, this lovely area of open downland (NT) features a group of bronze-age round barrows and the south-west ditch and rampart of iron-age Woolbury Camp hillfort.

Later descend and enter the Test Valley, then continue to the edge of Stockbridge.

STOCKBRIDGE, Hants
People from all over the world come here to fish the Test, one of the most sought-after game rivers in the country. Stockbridge itself is a one-street town of mainly Victorian buildings. The Town Hall, the Grosvenor Hotel, and the White Hart Inn are all early 19th-century, and only the 13th-century chancel of the old church remains.

Meet a roundabout and take the 2nd exit on to the A30, then drive to the next roundabout and branch left on to the A3057 SP 'Andover'. In 1 mile turn left on to an unclassified road SP 'Longstock', then cross a bridge and cross the River Test to Longstock.

LONGSTOCK, Hants
Thatched cottages strung out along a narrow, winding lane form the spine of this pretty village. Medieval tiles can be seen behind the altar of the 19th-century church, which is also notable for its beautiful chancel arch.

Turn left, then at the end of the village turn right (no SP) on to a narrow by-road. In ¾ mile meet a T-junction and turn right. Continue across open downland, then in another ¾ mile keep forward SP 'Grateley'. Pass Danebury Ring on the left.

DANEBURY RING, Hants
At the top of a 469ft hill is Danebury Ring, an iron-age camp that has been thoroughly excavated in recent years. It has been acquired by the County Council as a Heritage Site and public amenity area.

In 2 miles meet a main road and turn left on to the A343. Pass the Army Aviation Museum, then after 1½ miles reach Middle Wallop. Meet crossroads and turn right on to the B3084 for Over Wallop.

OVER WALLOP, Hants
Although St Peter's Church in Over Wallop displays 12th- and 13th-century traces, much of its old structure has been hidden by Victorian restoration.
Inside is a 15th-century font.

In 2¼ miles enter Grateley, keep forward on the B3084 passing Quarley Hill on the right, in 1¾ miles at a T-junction turn left on to the A303 SP 'Amesbury'. After ¾ mile at a roundabout take 2nd exit A303 SP 'Amesbury and Exeter', join the dual carriageway and after 5 miles bypass Amesbury before reaching a roundabout.

Danebury Ring consists of three lines of ramparts and ditches and encloses 13 acres.

In Saxon times Winchester was the capital of England.

The church at King's Somborne.

AMESBURY, Wilts
At Amesbury the Avon is crossed by a five-arched Palladian bridge which complements the stately flow of the river. Amesbury Abbey is of the 19th century and stands in a park in which beech clumps have been planted to represent the positions of English and French ships at Trafalgar. The Church of SS Mary and Melor is a flint-built Norman structure containing a contemporary font fashioned from Purbeck marble.

At the roundabout keep forward then in 1¾ miles turn right on to the A344 SP 'Devizes'. Continue to Stonehenge.

Stonehenge is probably the most famous prehistoric monument in the world.

STONEHENGE, Wilts
Almost nothing is known about this most famous of all prehistoric megalithic monuments. From time to time the public imagination is caught by theories of sun-worship rites and primitive astronomical computers, but it is likely that these have as little factual base as the neo-druidical ceremonies enacted here every Midsummer's Night Eve. Originally Stonehenge (AM) comprised an encircling ditch and bank dating from the stone age, but this simple base was later developed into circles of sarsen stones around a horseshoe of trilithons enclosing the enigmatic Welsh bluestones. Several stones still stand where they were first erected thousands of years ago, and the largest measures almost 30ft high from its deeply buried base to its top. Much of the surrounding land belongs to the National Trust.

Continue on the A344 and in 1¾ miles turn left on to the A360 SP 'Salisbury'. In 1 mile meet a roundabout and keep forward, passing Normanton Down.

NORMANTON DOWN, Wilts
In the Normanton Down area there are no fewer than 26 round barrows of various types, and a single long barrow dating from an earlier period. Excavations of this remarkable group have shown them to be Wessex Graves dating from the early bronze age. Hundreds of other examples survive near Stonehenge.

Follow an undulating road across part of Salisbury Plain, and after 3 miles meet crossroads. Turn left on to an unclassified road SP 'The Woodfords'. Continue to Middle Woodford.

MIDDLE WOODFORD, Wilts
Most of Middle Woodford Church was rebuilt in Victorian times, though the great flint and rubble tower is a survival from earlier days. Heale House, where Charles II once hid and from which he rode forth to view Stonehenge, only the eight acre gardens are open.

At Middle Woodford meet a T-junction and turn right to follow the River Avon to Lower Woodford.

LOWER WOODFORD, Wilts
High downs rise on either side of this tiny village, which is the lowest of three Woodfords strung along the Avon Valley. The only building of any real note here is the manor house (not open), but the local countryside is enchanting.

In 2 miles cross a river bridge and turn left, then immediately right and shortly pass the earthworks of Old Sarum.

OLD SARUM, Wilts
In Roman times this important centre was linked by the Port Way to *Calleva Atrebatum*, a significant garrison town near Silchester in Hampshire. After a while Old Sarum became the site of a great cathedral, but a combination of water shortage, military troubles, and exposure to inclement weather prompted a move to Salisbury in 1220. The cathedral was demolished in 1331 and the materials transported to the new site for the superb building that stands today.

The River Test is renowned for its trout fishing.

Reach the main road and turn right on to the A345. Continue to Salisbury.

SALISBURY, Wilts
Salisbury's 404ft cathedral spire, the tallest in England, dominates most approaches to this lovely city. The cathedral itself is a perfect example of early-English architecture, set amid an enchanting medley of houses in the ancient cathedral close. Many other old buildings survive in the city.

From Salisbury follow SP 'Southampton' to leave on the A36. In 2¼ miles at the start of the dual carriageway, turn right on to an unclassified road SP 'Alderbury', continue into Alderbury.

ALDERBURY, Wilts
Alderbury House is said to be built of stone from the old belfry of Salisbury Cathedral. The small farm at nearby Ivychurch is on the site of a Norman priory, and local St Mary's Church is of Victorian date.

At Alderbury continue to the end of the village, cross bridge and follow SP 'West Grimstead'. Drive to that village and keep forward SP 'West Dean', and in 3 miles meet a junction and turn right for West Dean.

WEST DEAN, Wilts
Half hidden among trees at the top of a hill are remains of the old St Mary's Church of West Dean. New St Mary's was built of flint and brick in 1866. Close to the ruins is a good 16th-century barn.

Turn right SP 'Lockerley', then beyond East Dean go over a level crossing and continue to Lockerley. In ½ mile bear right, and ¼ mile farther pass under a railway bridge. Drive to the nearside of a green and turn left SP 'Dunbridge'. At Dunbridge turn left on to the B3084 and drive over a level crossing and river bridge. In ½ mile turn right on to an unclassified road SP 'Mottisfont Village'. Meet a T-junction and turn right. Pass the entrance to 18th-century Mottisfont Abbey.

MOTTISFONT, Hants
Remains of a 12th-century priory are incorporated in 18th-century Mottisfont Abbey (NT), which houses an excellent collection of paintings by Rex Whistler.

Cross the River Test then later meet the main road and turn left on to the A3057. Follow the Test Valley to King's Somborne.

KING'S SOMBORNE, Hants
A ring of bells in the Church of SS Peter and Paul is inscribed 'completed in the Jubilee Year of Queen Victoria, 1887'. The building itself is of ancient foundation but was much restored in 1885. The architect Sir Edwin Lutyens designed modern Marsh Court.

In King's Somborne turn right on to an unclassified road SP 'Winchester', then take the next turning left. After another ¾ mile turn right SP 'Farley Mount' then climb through well-wooded country to Farley Mount. This country park has an excellent picnic site. Meet a fork junction and bear left to follow a pleasant by-road. Go forward over all crossroads for 3 miles, then turn left on to the A3090 to re-enter Winchester.

WINDSOR, Berks

The largest inhabited castle in the world rambles over 13 acres on a chalk bluff above the River Thames. Windsor Castle has been a royal residence since Henry 1's reign and every subsequent ruling English monarch has made additions to it. However, George IV contributed most and he was responsible for the distinctive multi-towered skyline of today. The parts of the castle open to the public are St George's Chapel, burial place of kings and queens; Queen Mary's Dolls' house, designed by Sir Edwin Lutyens and exquisitely perfect to the tiniest detail; the state apartments, full of outstanding paintings, carvings, furniture and porcelain; and the enormous Round Tower which surveys 12 counties. Most of the town's architecture is a mixture of Victorian and Georgian with the notable exception of the Guildhall (OACT). Sir Christopher Wren, whose father was Dean of Windsor, completed it in 1689 and it now displays various exhibits of local history, with portraits of kings and queens lining the walls.

WINDSOR GREAT PARK, Berks

Stretching south of the castle from the river to Virginia Water are some 4,800 acres of glorious open parkland, dense beech woods and beautiful formal gardens. Both Home Park, the private land around the castle, and the Great Park, are dissected by the Long Walk. This magnificent avenue of chestnut and plane trees leads from the castle to Snow Hill. Here, at the park's highest point, stands a towering equestrian statue of George III. Savill Gardens and the Valley Gardens within the park are both woodland areas of great beauty. Rhododendrons, azaleas, roses, camelias and magnolias are just some of the lovely flowers and shrubs that provide colour in them all year round.

Leave Windsor on the A308, SP 'Maidenhead'. In 4 miles pass under the motorway bridge and turn right on to the B3028 for Bray.

BRAY, Berks

The song called *The Vicar of Bray* has made the village name familiar. Just which vicar it refers to is uncertain, but Simon Aleyn of Tudor times seems to be the most popular candidate. The almshouses are a particularly attractive feature of this Thameside village. They were founded by William Goddard in 1627 and a figure of him stands over the gateway. A pretty lane leads from the main street to the churchyard, which is entered through a timber-framed gatehouse. This may have been the chantry house, for the chantry Chapel of St Mary stands inside the churchyard. It was used as a small school in the early 17th century.

REACHES OF THE THAMES AND ROYAL WINDSOR

The stern towers of Windsor's mighty castle look down in royal splendour on the ever-changing life of the Thames, where boats ply busily to and fro between leafy banks and beneath elegant bridges.

At the end of the village bear right, continue for 1 mile to the edge of Maidenhead then turn right on to the A4 (no SP) and shortly cross Maidenhead Bridge.

MAIDENHEAD, Berks

Maidenhead, so near to London and on one of the loveliest stretches of the Thames, has become a popular residential commuter town. The town first began to grow in the 13th century around the bridge which was replaced in 1772 by a fine stone one. During the Civil Wars and the 17th century Revolution Maidenhead was a strategic point. The Henry Reitlinger Bequest Museum in Oldfied House (OACT) by the bridge is filled with glass, pictures, ceramics and sculptures, as well as numerous other treasures. Just upstream is Boulters Lock Inn — a popular stopping place for river navigators since the 18th century.

After crossing the Thames continue for nearly ½ mile, then turn left on to an unclassified road, SP 'Wycombe'. After 2 miles, on the left, is the entrance to Cliveden.

In the 1820s Windsor Castle was transformed from a hotch-potch of apartments to a magnificent palace at a cost of about £1,000,000

CLIVEDEN, Berks

A house has stood at Cliveden (NT) since 1666, but it has not been the present one. Two fires burnt down the original and its successor, and this third house, built in the 19th century, is largely the work of Sir Charles Barry. Between the wars it was owned by the Astors and was a popular meeting place for influential politicians and social celebrities. The grounds are exceptionally beautiful, due to natural terrain as much as design. The site slopes down to a part of the Thames called Cliveden Reach and the views from the back of the house are superlative. Here, the huge terrace drops down to a great carpet of lawn patterned with low box hedges, and beyond lies the Italian Garden. Other features of the grounds include woodland walks, a monumental Victorian fountain, an elaborate water garden with a Japanese pagoda and glades of dark green ilex trees that provide an ideal setting for the stone statues scattered within them.

Continue on the unclassified road and in just over ¼ mile turn left, SP 'Bourne End'. In ¾ mile turn left still SP 'Bourne End'. Nearly ½ mile farther turn left on to the A4094, SP 'Cookham', and later cross the River Thames for Cookham.

Marlow's suspension bridge, built in 1831, and the 19th-century Church of All Saints — one of the town's 3 churches

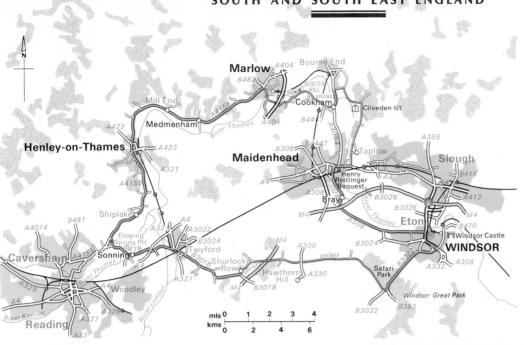

today, with its groups of cottages, 15th-century manor house and 16th-century inn with dormer windows.

Continue on the A4155 to Henley.

HENLEY-ON-THAMES, Oxon
Henley is the most famous of the Thames resorts due to the prestigious annual regatta held here in July. The first inter-varsity race took place here in 1829 and within 10 years it was a recognised national event enjoying royal patronage. The graceful bridge in Henley is 18th century, appropriately decorated with the faces of Father Thames and the goddess Isis. Apart from the boating available throughout the summer and the pleasant walks along the towpaths, there are lots of interesting shops, inns and teashops in Henley. Most of the inns are old coaching houses with squares that were once the scene of bull and bear fights. Kenton theatre, completed in 1804, is the 4th oldest theatre in England.

Leave Henley on the A4155, SP 'Reading'. In 2 miles pass the Shiplake war memorial, and after another 2½ miles, at the Flowing Spring PH, turn left (one-way), SP 'Sonning'. At the end turn left again on to the B478 (no SP) for Sonning.

SONNING, Berks
Eleven arches form the 18th-century bridge across the Thames at Sonning. The village is pretty and unspoilt, with little streets of cottages, grander Georgian houses and a lock gaily bedecked with flowers. The Bishops of Salisbury lived here centuries ago, but the only sign of their palace is a mound in the grounds of Holme Park.

Bear left through the village and at the roundabout take the 2nd exit on to the A3032, SP 'Twyford'. In Twyford turn right on to the A321, SP 'Bracknell'. After crossing the railway bridge keep forward on to the B3018 and remain on it to Shurlock Row. Turn left on to an unclassified road, SP 'Maidenhead', into the village, and at the far end turn right on to the Hawthorn Hill road. Later pass over the M4 and in 1¼ miles cross the A330, SP 'New Lodge'. In 4 miles turn left on to the B3022, SP 'Windsor', then turn left again and shortly pass Windsor Safari Park and Seaworld (left).

WINDSOR SAFARI PARK AND SEAWORLD, Berks
This was one of the first Safari parks to spring up in Britain. Apart from the fascinating drive-through reserves, aviaries and caged animals, there is a modern dolphinarium too. Here, bottle-nosed dolphins perform their incredible tricks, vying for popularity with the killer whale.

Continue on the B3022 for the return to Windsor.

Looking upstream at Henley towards the 16th-century tower of St Mary's Church, distinguished by its flint and stone chequerwork and 4 octagonal turrets

COOKHAM, Berks
The modern painter, Stanley Spencer, was a native of Cookham. More people throng the streets and river since his days, but the redbrick cottages facing the green and the river scenes are easily identified in many of his paintings. Several of Spencer's works can be seen in the King's Hall Gallery in the unspoilt High Street. One of the boathouses along the river acts as the office of the Keeper of the Royal Swans. He is in charge of the annual ceremony of Swan Upping — the counting and marking of all cygnets on the Thames.

Turn right into the main street (B4447), SP 'Cookham Dean'. In almost ½ mile, before the White Hart Inn, turn right, SP 'Winter Hill Golf Club'. ¼ mile beyond the viewpoint of Winter Hill turn right, then right again, and descend through thick beech woods. At the next T-junction, turn right and cross the Thames for Marlow.

MARLOW, Bucks
The jewel of this busy town is its fine suspension bridge which was renovated to mint condition in 1966. It spans the river near a cascading weir and the beautiful beech trees of Quarry Wood form a backdrop for this, the lock and the lock house. By the bridge is the Compleat Angler Hotel, named after Izaak Walton's book about the delights of fishing as a pastime. Marlow's broad main

street and West Street are full of unspoilt buildings from the 16th to 18th centuries, among which was the home of Shelley and his wife.

At the end of Marlow High Street turn left on to the A4155, SP 'Henley' and continue to Medmenham.

MEDMENHAM, Bucks
A clique of roisterers in the 18th century came to be known as the Hellfire Club and their headquarters were at Medmenham. The leader, Sir Francis Dashwood, was a Chancellor of the Exchequer, and he rebuilt the Norman abbey here in which to hold his scandalous parties. Finally, public exposure and disgrace ended the club's activities for good. There is little sign of those revelries in the village

ROYAL PARKS AND HAMPSHIRE WOODS

Close to Windsor is the semi-cultivated countryside of royal parkland; farther away, near the Duke of Wellington's country estate, are dark ranks of conifer plantations and the lighter greens of oak and birch tangled with honeysuckle.

WOKINGHAM, Berks
Wokingham boasted a bell foundry in the 14th century, and the silk industry flourished here in Elizabethan days. Rose Street preserves timbered houses and the Rose Inn, where poets Dean Swift, Pope, and Gay spent a wet afternoon together. Gay utilized the time in composing verses to the landlord's daughter, Molly Mog. Several almshouses exist in and around the town, and Lucas Hospital of 1665 – at Luckely – is considered particularly fine.

Follow SP 'Reading, A329' to leave Wokingham via Broad Street. In ¼ mile approach the clock tower, then turn left on to the B3349 SP 'Arborfield' and go over a level crossing. After 2¼ miles turn right for Arborfield Cross.

ARBORFIELD CROSS, Berks
To the left of Arborfield Cross, off the A327, is Arborfield Garrison. Within the complex is the Royal Electrical and Mechanical Engineers Museum, which is open to the public most weekdays.

Turn right and immediately left on to an unclassified road SP 'Swallowfield'. Continue for 2 miles and turn right. Swallowfield Park is on the right.

SWALLOWFIELD PARK, Berks
Swallowfield Park lies almost on the Hampshire border, at the meeting of the rivers Loddon and Blackwater. Swallowfield Park house was rebuilt in the late 17th century and remodelled by William Atkinson in 1820.

At the park gates turn left across the Blackwater River to reach Swallowfield. Turn left SP 'Basingstoke', at T-junction turn left on to the main road B3349 for Risely. Bear right and in ½ mile at T-junction turn right and at roundabout take 1st exit SP 'Basingstoke' A33. A detour from the main route can be made by taking 2nd exit unclassifield road for 2 miles at T-junction turn left and left again for entrance, for Stratfield Saye Park. Then return to the main route.

STRATFIELD SAYE PARK, Hants
This rather unstately stately home (open) was built in the reign of Charles I and purchased by the 1st Duke of Wellington in 1817. The duke intended to use the £600,000 voted to him by a grateful nation to build a new house in the superb park, but funds did not permit this and so the great soldier set about making the existing building as comfortable and convenient as he could. Central heating was installed in the passageways, and there were 'new-fangled' water closets of blue-patterned china in every room. It has been the home of the dukes of Wellington ever since.

Eversley's ancient origins are suggested by the picturesque nameplate on its village green.

On the main route, drive to the Wellington Monument and turn left on to an unclassified road, SP 'Hook & Eversley', cross Heckfield Heath, and continue for ½ mile. At roundabout take 2nd exit B3011, then after ½ mile branch left on to an unclassified road. Continue, cross the River Whitewater, then after 2½ miles meet crossroads and drive forward. A short detour can be made to the village of Eversley by turning left here and continuing for ½ mile.

EVERSLEY, Hants
St Mary's Church at Eversley was built in the 18th century, and is distinguished in having had naturalist Charles Kingsley as rector. The north aisle was built in his memory. Bramshill House, a Jacobean mansion regarded as one of the finest in the country, is now the Police Staff College.

Join the A327 for Eversley Cross and drive to The Chequers (PH). Turn left on to the B3016 SP 'Wokingham' and continue to Finchampstead.

FINCHAMPSTEAD, Berks
Finchampstead's pride is the splendid avenue of Wellingtonia pines which runs 1 mile east to Crowthorne. Its church has a white-painted body of Norman date and carries an 18th-century tower built in red brick. The whole building stands on a prehistoric earthwork, as if aloof from the village.

Turn right, then after ¼ mile meet a war memorial and turn right on to the B3348 SP 'Crowthorne'. Pass Finchampstead Ridges on the right.

FINCHAMPSTEAD RIDGES, Berks
This 60-acre heather and woodland National Trust property offers excellent views over Berkshire, Hampshire, and Surrey countryside.

Continue, enter a roundabout, and take the first exit on to the A321. After 1 mile at roundabout take 3rd exit B3430 on to Nine Mile Ride.

NINE MILE RIDE, Berks
Nine Mile Ride follows the line of a Roman road through delightfully wooded country. At the Bracknell end, to the south, is the 20-acre iron-age hillfort of Caesar's Camp, part of which is now a public recreation ground with a picnic site.

After 2¾ miles at roundabout take 2nd exit SP 'Bagshot'. Continue passing Caesar's Camp (see Nine Mile Ride) and at roundabout take 2nd exit on to the A322. Proceed for 1½ miles on to the A332 'Ascot' road. Continue for 1¾ miles and bear right. Approach a roundabout and leave by the 3rd exit on to the A329, with Ascot racecourse on the left, and enter Ascot.

ASCOT, Berks
Ascot has strong Queen Anne connections. It was she who instituted the Royal Ascot race meeting in 1711, a fashionable event still held in June and patronized by members of the Royal Family. The Ascot Gold Cup was presented for the first time in 1807.

Continue to Virginia Water, which can be seen on the left.

VIRGINIA WATER, Surrey
This 1½-mile-long artificial lake, laid out by Thomas Sandby for George III, is situated at the south-east corner of Windsor Great Park and is well known for its beauty. Colonnades brought from the Roman port of Leptis Magna stand on its bank in contrast to a 100ft totem pole set up in 1958 to mark the centenary of British Columbia. The nearby Valley Gardens are most inviting.

Continue at T-junction and turn left on to the A30. Pass the Wheatsheaf Hotel and proceed for 1¼ miles, then turn left on to an unclassified road for Savill Gardens (left).

THE SAVILL GARDENS, Berks
Windsor Great Park is noted for its magnificent horticultural areas, but none is more popular than the wooded 20-acre Savill Gardens. Its variety of flowers provide a wealth of colour throughout the seasons.

Continue to The Sun (PH) and go forward for ½ mile before turning right for Englefield Green.

ENGLEFIELD GREEN, Surrey
This large residential district lies within easy reach of delightful Windsor Great Park. Its 250-year-old Barley Mow Inn was once a popular coaching stop. Late 19th-century Royal Holloway College stands among gardens and playing fields between Englefield Green and the railway. It was one of the first women's colleges ever built and became a constituent college of London University in 1900.

Cross a main road and pass a left turn to Cooper's Hill RAF Memorial.

Windsor Castle has dominated its surroundings ever since William the Conqueror started it in the 11th century.

An equestrian statue of George III by sculptor Richard Westmacott stands on a granite base at the end of the Long Walk in Windsor Great Park.

Return along the A308 SP 'Windsor'. In 1 mile meet a roundabout and take the 3rd exit to pass Runnymede.

RUNNYMEDE, Surrey

About $\frac{1}{2}$ mile north-west of Egham are the 60-acre riverside meadows of Runnymede. It was here in 1215 that King John was prevailed upon by his barons to seal the draft of Magna Carta, from which seed – almost by accident – grew the English ideal of personal liberty. Overlooking the meadows is Cooper's Hill, which is crowned by the RAF Memorial and has the American Bar Association's Magna Carta Memorial at its foot. Halfway up its slopes is a memorial to the assassinated US President, John F Kennedy.

Continue through Old Windsor.

OLD WINDSOR, Berks

Old Windsor parish stretches from the River Thames to Virginia Water, including the semi-wild countryside

An immense variety of trees and shrubs is displayed in the magnificent formal landscapes which surround Virginia Water.

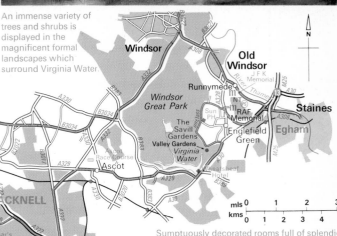

Sumptuously decorated rooms full of splendid furniture are features of the seat of the dukes of Wellington, at Stratfield Saye Park.

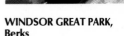

COOPER'S HILL RAF MEMORIAL, Surrey

The Commonwealth Air Forces Memorial on Cooper's Hill commemorates 20,000 allied airmen who died, with no known grave, in World War II. The site, which gives views of Windsor Castle and seven counties, overlooks Runnymede.

Return to main route then after 300 yards bear left and descend Tite Hill to the edge of Egham. Enter a roundabout and leave by the 1st exit to rejoin the A30. After another ¾ mile enter another roundabout and leave by the 3rd exit on to the A308. Continue to Staines.

STAINES, Surrey

The old market town of Staines, at the junction of the rivers Colne and Thames, is entered via a superb road bridge built by Rennie and opened by William IV. The by-pass & M25 crosses by a modern bridge. West of the local church the London Stone marks the limit of the City of London's former jurisdiction. Sir Walter Raleigh was brought here to be tried because at that time London was in the grip of the plague.

of the Great Park and parts of Windsor Forest. Edward the Confessor had his palace here before the new Windsor of today existed, and William the Conqueror held a Great Council (Witan) here in 1070 – just 4 years after the Norman invasion of Britain.

At roundabout take 1st exit A308; to the left lies Windsor Great Park. Later enter a roundabout and leave by the 3rd exit, into King's Road, to enter Windsor.

WINDSOR, Berks

Windsor is a largely Georgian and Victorian town that owes its existence to its magnificent castle. William the Conqueror first appreciated the site's strategic importance over Old Windsor and built a palisaded fort within a moat. Practically every English monarch who has taken the throne in the 900 years since then has contributed to its development, and today it is the largest inhabited castle in the world.

Leave the town with SP 'Bagshot A332', to return along King's Road. In ¾ mile enter a roundabout and leave by the 2nd exit to enter Windsor Great Park.

WINDSOR GREAT PARK, Berks

Within the boundaries formed by Home Park and the castle to the north, and by all that remains of Windsor Forest's royal chase to the south and west, Windsor Great Park encompasses an area of almost 5,000 acres. Ancient King's Oak, near Forest Gate, is claimed to be the largest in the park. Legend has it that antlered Herne the Hunter meets here with his ghastly pack before chasing across the night skies. Most of the park is accessible by well-kept footpaths.

Continue for 4 miles before bearing right, then turn left SP 'Ascot'. After another ¼ mile meet crossroads and

turn right on to the B3034 SP 'Winkfield'. After ¾ mile turn left on to the A330 SP 'Ascot'. After ¼ mile turn right on to the B3034, then go forward over all crossroads to join the A3095. Continue for ¼ mile then turn left to rejoin the B3034 and continue for 1 mile. Cross a humpback bridge, keep left, and enter Binfield.

BINFIELD, Berks

Alexander Pope sang in the choir of the local church as a boy. Among the church's treasures is a fine old hour glass.

Approach crossroads and turn left on to an unclassified road. After ½ mile bear right. Continue, at T-junction turn right on to the B3408, in 1 mile at roundabout take 2nd exit A329 to return to Wokingham.

EPPING AND THE VILLAGES OF ESSEX

Most of the great forest that covered West Essex in Norman times has been cut down, though Epping and Hatfield remain. The magic of Essex today is its village life, which has a timeless quality that echoes the tranquillity of forest communities in ancient days.

WOODFORD GREEN, Gt London

Sir Winston Churchill was MP for Wanstead and Woodford from 1924 to 1964. His statue on Woodford Green is by David McFall.

From Woodford Green follow the A104 'Epping' road and in ¾ mile turn left on to the A110 SP 'North Chingford'. In another ¾ mile turn right on to an unclassified road into Forest Side. Continue to a T-junction and turn right into Ranger's Road (A1069) to pass the Royal Forest Hotel and Queen Elizabeth's Hunting Lodge.

QUEEN ELIZABETH'S HUNTING LODGE, Gt London

Queen Elizabeth's Hunting Lodge is a wood-and-plaster building thought to have been erected towards the end of the 15th century so that the sovereign of the day could enjoy a grandstand view of the chase. After having served as a keeper's lodge for a number of years it now houses the Epping Forest Museum.

EPPING FOREST, Essex

Epping Forest owes its creation to the Norman Conquest. It was maintained as a royal hunting area through the reigns of various monarchs, and in the reign of King Charles I its bounds were fixed to embrace some 60,000 acres. In 1882 what was left of it was formally opened as a publicly-owned area by Queen Victoria.

Enter Epping Forest and in 1 mile meet a T-junction. Turn left on to the A104 and in 1¼ miles meet a roundabout. Leave by the 1st exit on to an unclassified road SP 'High Beach', then bear right SP 'King's Oak' for High Beach.

HIGH BEACH, Essex

It is arguable whether this village is named 'Beech' after the area's principal tree or 'Beach' denoting a gravel bank. Either would seem to be appropriate. The poet Tennyson spent his early manhood here.

Beyond the King's Oak (PH) the Epping Forest Conservation Centre lies to the right. Continue to the next road junction and turn left, then descend and in ¾ mile cross the main road. Continue for 1 mile and turn right SP 'Epping' to pass through Upshire. Ascend to re-enter the forest, then meet a T-junction and turn left to join the B1393. Continue to Epping.

EPPING, Essex

Epping lies outside the forest and has managed to retain its own identity as a small market town of some charm, despite the proximity of London. Winchelsea House and Epping Place, in the High Road, are both of 18th-century date.

Drive to the green at the end of the town and branch left on to the B181, SP 'Roydon'. In 1¼ miles bear right. After ¾ mile, having passed over Cobbin's Brook, reach a T-junction and turn left. Continue through Epping Green to Roydon.

ROYDON, Essex

About 1½ miles south-west of Roydon are the ruins of Tudor Nether Hall, a Manor house that belonged to the Coltes family. It was here that Thomas More came to woo and win the elder daughter of John Coltes. Preserved in the village itself are the old parish cage, stocks, and a whipping post.

Turn left with SP 'Hertford' and shortly

This superb brass is one of 15 preserved in Sawbridgeworth's 14th-century church.

cross the River Stort and a level crossing to enter Hertfordshire. In ¾ mile turn right with SP 'Chelmsford' to join the A414. After 3 miles go forward on unclassified road through High Wych, and at T-junction turn left on to the A1184 to Sawbridgeworth.

SAWBRIDGEWORTH, Herts

A number of fine Georgian and older buildings survive in this small town, and to the south is Pishiobury – a fine house built by James Wyatt in 1782 and now a school. Ancient brasses are preserved in St. Mary's Church.

Meet crossroads and turn right on to unclassified road SP 'Chelmsford'. Turn right onto the A1060 then turn left on to the B183 SP 'Takeley' for Hatfield Broad Oak.

The two upper floors of Queen Elizabeth's Hunting Lodge were originally designed without infilling between the beams, thus enabling an uninterrupted view of the hunt.

HATFIELD BROAD OAK, Essex

Notable features in this markedly-pretty village include a Norman and later church, 18th-century almshouses, and several distinctive Georgian houses.

Keep left and in 1¼ miles turn left on to an unclassified road SP 'Hatfield Forest'. In ¾ mile keep forward and skirt the Hatfield Forest Country Park.

HATFIELD FOREST, Essex

Once a part of the ancient Royal Forests of Essex, 1,049-acre Hatfield Forest is now protected by the National Trust and offers splendid woodland walks along its chases and rides. Additional amenities include boating and fishing.

Continue, and later turn right on to the A120 for Takeley.

TAKELEY, Essex

Takeley, on the line of the old Roman Stane Street, has an interesting Norman and later church with Roman masonry in the fabric of its walls. Inside is a modern font surmounted by a 6ft-high medieval cover. Good timbered houses and 17th-century barns can be seen in the village.

Drive to traffic signals and turn left off the A120 on to an unclassified road SP 'Broxted'. In 1¼ miles note Stansted Airport to the left. In another 1¼ miles turn right into Molehill Green. Continue with SP 'Thaxted' and pass through Broxted.

BROXTED, Essex

Broxted's church shows a happy blend of 13th- and 15th-century styles, with the nave and chancel from the earlier period and a belfry and north aisle from the later. Church Hall is of late 16th- to mid 17th-century date.

Beyond the village join the B1051 for Thaxted.

THAXTED, Essex

Many old houses survive to remind the visitor that this was once a very prosperous town. The 15th-century church was clearly built by a community with a great deal of money to spend. The timbered Guildhall dates from the 16th century and incorporates an earlier ancient lock-up. Several old almshouses and a tower windmill can be seen in the area.

Turn left on to the B184 and continue through the village. At the end meet the Fox and Hounds (PH) and turn right on to the B1051 for Great Sampford.

GREAT SAMPFORD, Essex

This pretty village has attractive gabled houses, and opposite the Bull Inn is an Elizabethan manor house. A large pond and three-cornered green complete the picture.

Turn right again on to the B1053 and continue to Finchingfield.

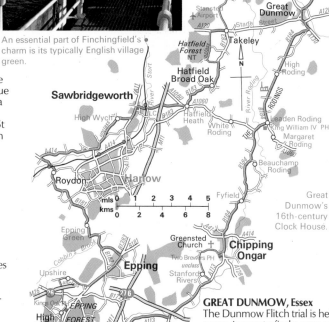

FINCHINGFIELD, Essex

Possibly the most photographed village in Essex, Finchingfield is a picture-book community complete with a church on a hill, a picturesque windmill, quaint old cottages, and a charming green enlivened by the noisy population of its duckpond. St John's Church has a sturdy Norman tower that indicates its origins, but the main body is an attractive mixture of styles. One mile north west is Spains Hall and Gardens.

Drive to the war memorial and turn right on to the B1057 for Great Bardfield.

An essential part of Finchingfield's charm is its typically English village green.

GREAT BARDFIELD, Essex

A major feature of this old market town is a restored windmill that goes by the name 'Gibraltar'. A pleasant mixture of old cottages and shops complemented by the mainly 14th-century church is surveyed by a timber-framed 16th- and 17th-century hall from its hill above the River Pant.

Turn right SP 'Dunmow' and continue to Bran End. After 2½ miles turn left on to the A130 and continue to Dunmow.

Epping Forest's many acres of varied scenery provide one of East London's most valuable leisure amenities.

The massive timbers of Greensted Church are a unique survival.

Great Dunmow's 16th-century Clock House.

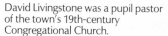

GREAT DUNMOW, Essex

The Dunmow Flitch trial is held here every 4 years to find a man and wife who have not had a domestic brawl or wished to be unmarried for 12 months and a day. A flitch of bacon is presented to the couple able to prove this enviable state of affairs. The town, a quiet enough place even without this incentive, boasts a large church and a rather small square.

Turn left again SP 'Chelmsford', then in ¾ mile turn right on to the B184 SP 'Ongar'. Continue to High Roding and Leaden Roding.

THE RODINGS, Essex

A number of attractive villages in the Roding Valley share this suffix. These include High Roding, with its thatched and gabled cottages and a 13th-century church, and Leaden Roding.

Reach the King William IV (PH) in Leaden Roding and turn right on to the A414. In 1 mile turn left on to the B184 for Fyfield. From Fyfield drive for 2½ miles, enter a roundabout, and leave by the 2nd exit on to the A128 into Chipping Ongar.

CHIPPING ONGAR, Essex

Chipping Ongar began as a market town beneath the walls of a Norman castle. Only the mound and moat of the castle remain, but the contemporary Church of St Martin of Tours still flourishes. Explorer

David Livingstone was a pupil pastor of the town's 19th-century Congregational Church.

Drive to the end of the High Street and turn right on to an unclassified road SP 'Greensted'. Pass the Two Brewers (PH) and after 1 mile pass Greensted Church on the right.

GREENSTED CHURCH, Essex

St Andrew's Church is famous as the only surviving example of a Saxon log church extant. The body of King Edmund is known to have been rested here in 1013, but the building is probably much older than that.

In a further ½ mile turn left SP 'Stanford Rivers' and follow a narrow road, then in 1¼ miles meet crossroads and turn left again. Drive to a T-junction, turn right on to the A113 SP 'London', and in 3 miles enter a roundabout. Leave by the 2nd exit for Abridge and continue to Chigwell.

CHIGWELL, Essex

Novelist Charles Dickens used the 17th-century King's Head in Chigwell as The Maypole in his book *Barnaby Rudge*. The town's grammar school was founded in 1629 by Archbishop Harsnett, whose memorial brass can be seen inside local St Mary's Church.

After another 1¾ miles meet a T-junction and turn right, then in ¾ mile meet traffic signals and turn right again on to the A1009 SP 'Woodford Green'. Return to Woodford Green.

RESORTS AND DOWNLAND VILLAGES

High above the bright, mercurial resorts of the Sussex coast are the tranquil hamlets of the South Downs. Here change is gradual, a process to be approached with the caution born from centuries of experience.

WORTHING, W Sussex
Until the 1760s Worthing was little more than a fishing hamlet, but by the end of that century the patronage of George III's family had encouraged the smart set and the inevitable speculators to take an interest in the new town. Sadly there were no lasting major developments of any great merit, although the usual 18th-century terraces preserve something of the old gentility. Today Worthing is a popular seaside resort with a pier and an extensive pebble beach.

Leave Worthing by the A259 'Brighton' road, with occasional views of the sea to the right. Pass through South Lancing and by Shoreham Airport. Cross the River Adur and enter Shoreham-by-Sea.

SHOREHAM-BY-SEA
W Sussex
Sand at low tide, good fishing in the River Adur, and a busy harbour are features of this popular seaside town. Saxon workmanship can be seen in the mainly Norman structure of St Nicholas' Church. An old chequered-flint house in the town contains the Marlipins Museum of local relics.

Continue on the A259 to Southwick.

SOUTHWICK, W Sussex
Situated on the eastern part of Shoreham Harbour, with the South Downs to the north, Southwick forms part of the Shoreham conurbation and has all but lost its own identity. Roman artefacts excavated from a villa ¼ mile north of the station can be seen in the museum at Hove.

Continue along the A259 to Portslade-by-Sea.

PORTSLADE-BY-SEA, E Sussex
The 'by Sea' part of Portslade is a fairly recent seaside development of the original village, which lies 1 mile inland and has a church with Norman origins. North of the churchyard are remains of a 12th-century flint-built manor house.

Continue along the A259 to Hove.

HOVE, E Sussex
Elegant Hove is so much a part of Brighton these days. It has a good beach, several excellent Regency terraces, a museum and art gallery and the British Engineerium with a Victorian water pumping station.

Continue into Brighton.

BRIGHTON, E Sussex
This famous resort developed as a result of the 18th-century health fad for sea bathing. Its success was assured by the patronage of George IV in 1784, and the many superb terraces preserved there today prove its continued prosperity. As with all playgrounds of the wealthy the town has a number of eccentricities. The most impressive of these is the Royal Pavilion, a magnificent Oriental-style palace built for the Prince Regent by Henry Holland in 1787. Various museums, galleries, and theatres exist in the town, and visitors are offered all the usual distractions of the British seaside holiday. An excellent aquarium can be visited near Palace Pier, and the Volk's Electric Railway – the first of its kind in the world – runs from here to the Black Rock area. Old Brighton is preserved in the winding streets of The Lanes, which contrast with the new conference centre and up-to-the-minute marina development.

Return along the seafront towards Hove, passing the King Alfred Sports Centre, and meet traffic lights. Turn right here into Hove Street and follow SP 'London'. After 1 mile cross over main A27 and in another ¾ mile at West Blatchington turn right on the A2030.

WEST BLATCHINGTON, E Sussex
An early 18th-century windmill and 19th-century St Peter's Church are all that remain of the village that originally stood in this highly-developed area.

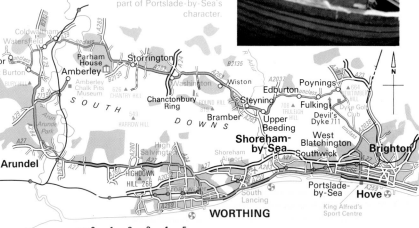

Warehouses and sea-going vessels of all descriptions are an integral part of Portslade-by-Sea's character.

Brighton's elegant pier dates from the 19th century.

Brighton Pavilion has been remodelled several times since it was first built. Architect John Nash was largely responsible for its final appearance.

Continue to ascend the A2038. Meet crossroads and turn left on to an unclassified road SP 'Devil's Dyke'. After ¼ mile keep left and ascend through open downland to Devil's Dyke.

DEVIL'S DYKE, W Sussex
Devil's Dyke is a cleft in the 711ft crest of the South Downs (see below). According to local legend the devil tried to carve a large nick to let the sea in, but failed. The spot has become popular with hang-glider enthusiasts.

THE SOUTH DOWNS
Stretching west from Beachy Head into Hampshire, the South Downs range is all that remains of a huge chalk backbone that connected England with the Continent. Some 7,000 years ago the Atlantic forced its way through to join up with the North Sea. Access for rambling and riding is available via numerous footpaths and bridleways.

Return, and after ½ mile turn left SP 'Poynings' to pass the Dyke Golf Club. After ¾ mile turn left, with views of 664ft Newtimber Hill on the right. After a further ¼ mile turn sharp left and descend into Poynings.

Mosaic pavements are a feature of the Roman remains at Bignor.

POYNINGS, W Sussex
Poynings is a charming downland village with an old church that was endowed by Michael de Poynings, who died in 1369. The Rectory is of early 19th-century date.

Turn left and follow the foot of the South Downs to Fulking.

FULKING, W Sussex
Flocks of sheep graze the sides of the downland fold in which this ancient hamlet stands, and slake their thirsts at a chalk spring. A like service is offered to humankind by the pleasant Shepherd and Dog Inn.

Continue to Edburton.

EDBURTON, W Sussex
A spectacularly sheer downland escarpment towers above this tiny place, making it seem even smaller than it is. The village boasts a privately-owned craft pottery and a salmon-smoking concern. Prehistoric Castle Rings stands on Edburton Hill.

Leave Edburton with 708ft Truleigh Hill to the left and continue to the A2037. Turn left on to the A2037 for Upper Beeding.

UPPER BEEDING, W Sussex
Upper Beeding lies at the north end of a gap in the downs made by the River Adur. It has a narrow main street lined with old cottages.

Leaving Upper Beeding, turn right on to the unclassified road SP 'Steyning', and cross the River Adur into Bramber.

BRAMBER, W Sussex
Before the River Adur silted up this place was a large port. Its massive Norman castle was dismantled after the Civil War, leaving only a gateway and easily-traceable sections of wall (NT). An unusual museum is the House of Pipes, which features some 35,000 tobacco pipes from all over the world.

Continue to Steyning.

STEYNING, W Sussex
Steyning enjoys a magnificent position at the foot of the South Downs and has a late-Norman church. In Mouse Lane is a 15th-century poorhouse, and an old market house stands in the High Street. The Grammar School of 1614 can be seen in Church Street.

Leave Steyning to join the A283. On the left is Steyning Round Hill, which gives views over the Adur Valley. Continue skirting Wiston Park and Wiston.

WISTON, W Sussex
It is well worth stopping in this lovely village at the foot of downland near Chanctonbury. Unfortunately its 14th-century church was badly treated by the 19th-century restorers, but the overall atmosphere of peaceful antiquity.

Continue on the A283. In 1 mile pass an unclassified left turn leading along a wooded glade to the footpath for Chanctonbury Ring.

CHANCTONBURY RING, W Sussex
The extensive prehistoric earthworks of Chanctonbury Ring occupy a 783ft downland summit which affords views over some 30 miles of countryside.

Continue along the A283 to the edge of Washington, enter a roundabout, and leave by the 2nd exit for Storrington. Left of the road are 626ft Chantry Hill and 549ft Harrow Hill.

STORRINGTON, W Sussex
Kithurst Hill rises to 697ft above this straggling village and forms an excellent viewpoint. Celtic field patterns are preserved on its slopes, is the 28-acre Sullington Warren (NT). A large tithe barn of 1685 stands at Manor Farm.

In 1 mile pass an unclassified left turn leading to Parham House.

The nave of Steyning's parish church is a superb example of Norman architecture.

PARHAM HOUSE, W Sussex
This delightfully unpretentious Elizabethan house has a 158ft long gallery and contains fine furnishings and pictures (open).

Continue on the A283 for 1 mile farther then turn left on to an unclassified road SP 'Greatham'. In 2¼ miles cross the River Arun to Coldwaltham. Turn left on to the A29 into Watersfield, then in ½ mile turn right on to the B2138 'Petworth' road. Take the next turning left on to an unclassified road for West Burton, then turn right for Bignor.

BIGNOR, W Sussex
Several notable old houses here include the famous Old Shop, an unusual yeoman's house of the 15th century. The Roman villa sites here are one of the largest and best known in the country.

Return to West Burton then, turn left SP 'Bury' and in 1 mile turn right on to the A29 SP 'Bognor'. Ascend Bury Hill, meet a roundabout and take 1st exit into Amberley.

AMBERLEY, W Sussex
The old lime quarries now have a new lease of life as the Chalk Pits Museum, with many attractions on its industrial past.

Return to roundabout take 1st exit A284 SP 'Littlehampton'. Skirt the grounds of Arundel Park and in 2¼ miles turn left on to an unclassified road to enter Arundel.

ARUNDEL, W Sussex
Looming large over Arundel to guard a gap made in the downs by the River Arun valley is ancient and much-restored Arundel Castle, seat of the Duke of Norfolk. Behind its heavy grey walls are rooms rich in furnishings and art treasures, many of which are open to the public. A prominent town existed here before the Norman conquest, but comparatively few ancient houses remain. The only real rivals to the castle are the 14th-century Church of St Nicholas and the superb Church of Our Lady and St Philip Neri.

Continue on the A27 'Worthing' road, and in 5 miles pass an unclassified right turn to Highdown Hill.

HIGHDOWN HILL, W Sussex
Between the South Downs and the sea, about 1 mile south of the A27, is 266ft Highdown Hill (NT). This 50-acre site is of great archaeological importance for its late bronze-age, early iron-age and Saxon cemeterys, nearby is Highdown Hill Gardens.

Continue on the A27 towards Worthing. Meet a roundabout and take the 2nd exit. After ¾ mile meet another roundabout and take the 3rd exit for the return to Worthing.

Arundel Castle, one of the most impressive Norman and medieval strongholds in the south of England, is the home of the dukes of Norfolk, hereditary Earls Marshal of England.

Key to Town Plans

Milton-Keynes
Bletchley

Leighton Buzzard
Dunstable
Luton
Braintree
Colchester

Witney
Oxford
Witham
Maldon
Chelmsford

Abingdon

Maidenhead
Henley on Thames
Slough
LONDON
Southend
Reading
Windsor
Wokingham
Heathrow
Airport
Rochester
Chatham
Gillingham
Margate
Ramsgate

Woking
Maidstone
Canterbury

Godalming
Guildford

Dover

Eastleigh
Rye
Southampton
Lewes
Havant
Hove
Brighton
Bexhill
Hastings
Portsmouth

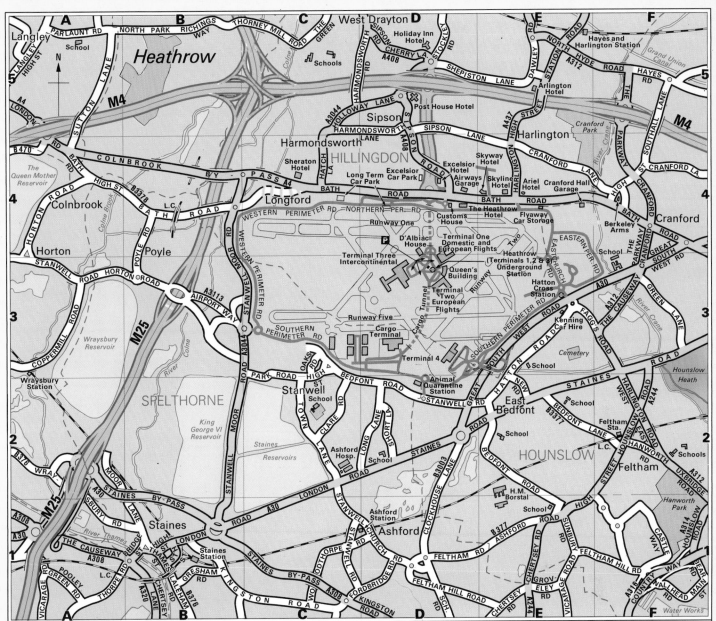

Heathrow Airport

Biggest and busiest airport in the United Kingdom, handling more international traffic than any other airport in the world, Heathrow broke its own records on 31 August 1980, when 112,880 passengers passed through. 1983 saw a total of 26,749,200 travellers, assisted by the 45,000-strong staff of the British Airports Authority and the 74 airline companies from 68 countries which operate scheduled services from the airport. Aircraft go to over 90 countries, and Heathrow's No 1 runway, 2.42 miles (3.9km) in length, is the longest used by civilian aircraft in the United Kingdom.

It all began when the site was transferred from the Air Ministry to the Ministry of Civil Aviation on 1 January 1946. On 31 May 1946, it opened as London (Heathrow) Airport, superseding the Airport of London at Croydon, established in 1928. This resulted in the operation of direct services between the United Kingdom and the United States of America. On 16 December 1955, the first three permanent buildings were opened by the Queen, and all three passenger terminals are now interlinked by pedestrian subways with moving walkways. The terminals are situated in the central area of the airport, and are also linked to the M4. A fourth terminal is under construction on the south-eastern side of the airport.

Terminal 1 is used by United Kingdom and Irish airlines for domestic and European flights, and for British Airways flights to and from certain destinations in North America. Terminal 2 is used by other European airlines except for the Irish airlines. Terminal 3 is the one used by intercontinental airlines going to Africa, America, Asia and Australia.

In 1966, the newly appointed British Air Authority took over the responsibility for both Heathrow and the second airport at Gatwick (the two are linked by a frequent daily helicopter service). Direct rail access came in 1977 when the Underground's Piccadilly Line was extended and in the same year, Heathrow Central Station opened.

Today the Queens Building Roof Gardens and viewing gallery allow visitors to admire the aircraft and to watch the airport at work. There is a small admission charge for this.

Visitors who have come to the Queens Building Roof Gardens can also take refreshments there, at one of the many restaurants to be found throughout the airport. All three passenger terminals have licensed restaurants where full meals are served, and there are also grill bars providing hot meals. Light refreshments can also be bought.

Multi-storey car parks are sited at each of the passenger terminals for short term car parking. Heathrow also has long term car parks, situated on the northern perimeter road. A free coach carries passengers between the long term car parks and the terminals. During the night (from midnight to 6am), passengers wanting this service can contact the coach base on the special direct line telephones which are in use at the pick-up points.

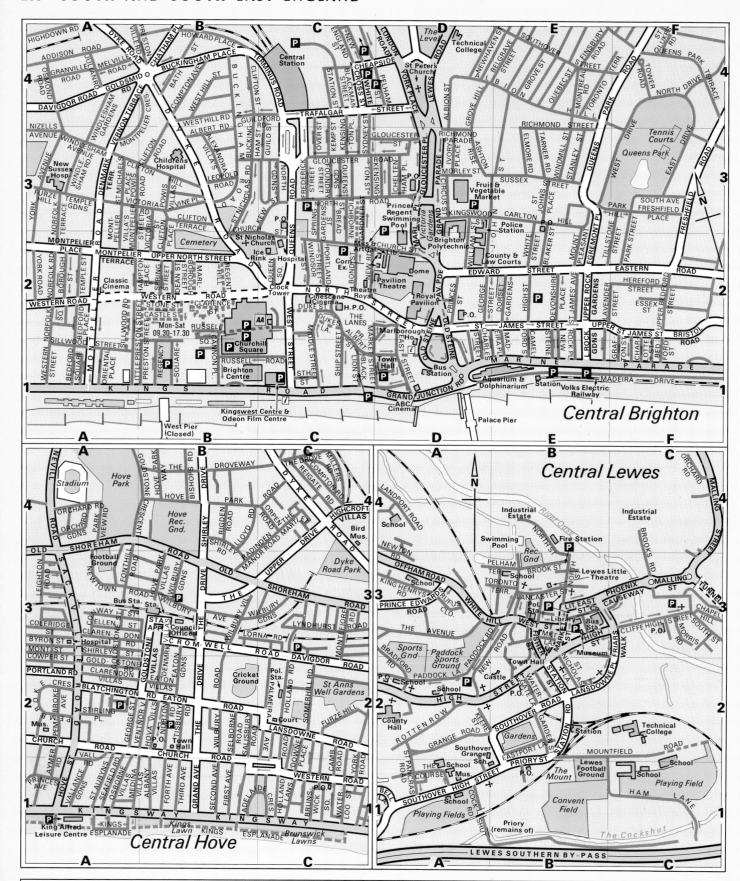

Central Brighton

Central Hove

Central Lewes

Brighton

Dr Richard Russell, from nearby Lewes, created the resort of Brighton almost singlehandedly. And he did it not by building houses or hotels, but by writing a book. His book, which praised the health-giving properties of sea-bathing and sea air, soon came to the attention of George, then Prince Regent and one day to become King George IV. He stayed at Brighthelmstone – as it was then known –

in 1783 and again in 1784. In 1786 the Prince rented a villa on the Steine – a modest house that was eventually transformed into the astonishing Pavilion. By 1800 – its popularity assured by royal patronage – the resort was described in a contemporary directory as 'the most frequented and without exception one of the most fashionable towns in the kingdom'.

Perhaps the description does not quite fit today, but Brighton is a perennially popular seaside

resort, as well as a shopping centre, university town and cultural venue. The Pavilion still draws most crowds, of course. Its beginnings as a villa are entirely hidden in a riot of Near Eastern architectural motifs, largely the creation of John Nash. Brighton's great days as a Regency resort *par excellence* are preserved in the sweeping crescents and elegant terraces, buildings which help to make it one of the finest townscapes in the whole of Europe.

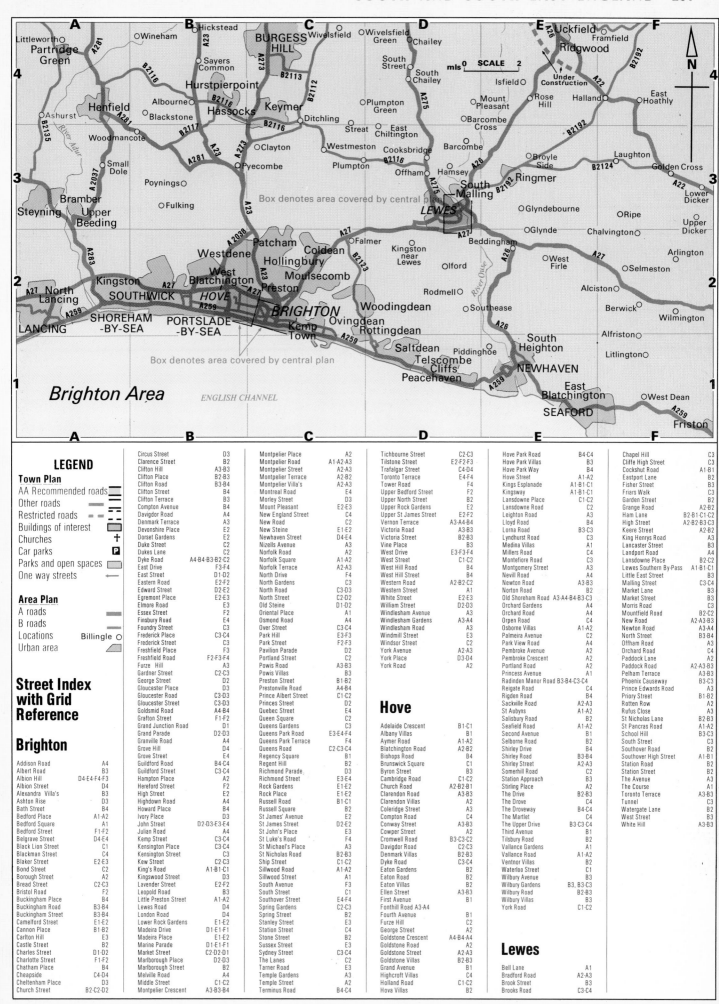

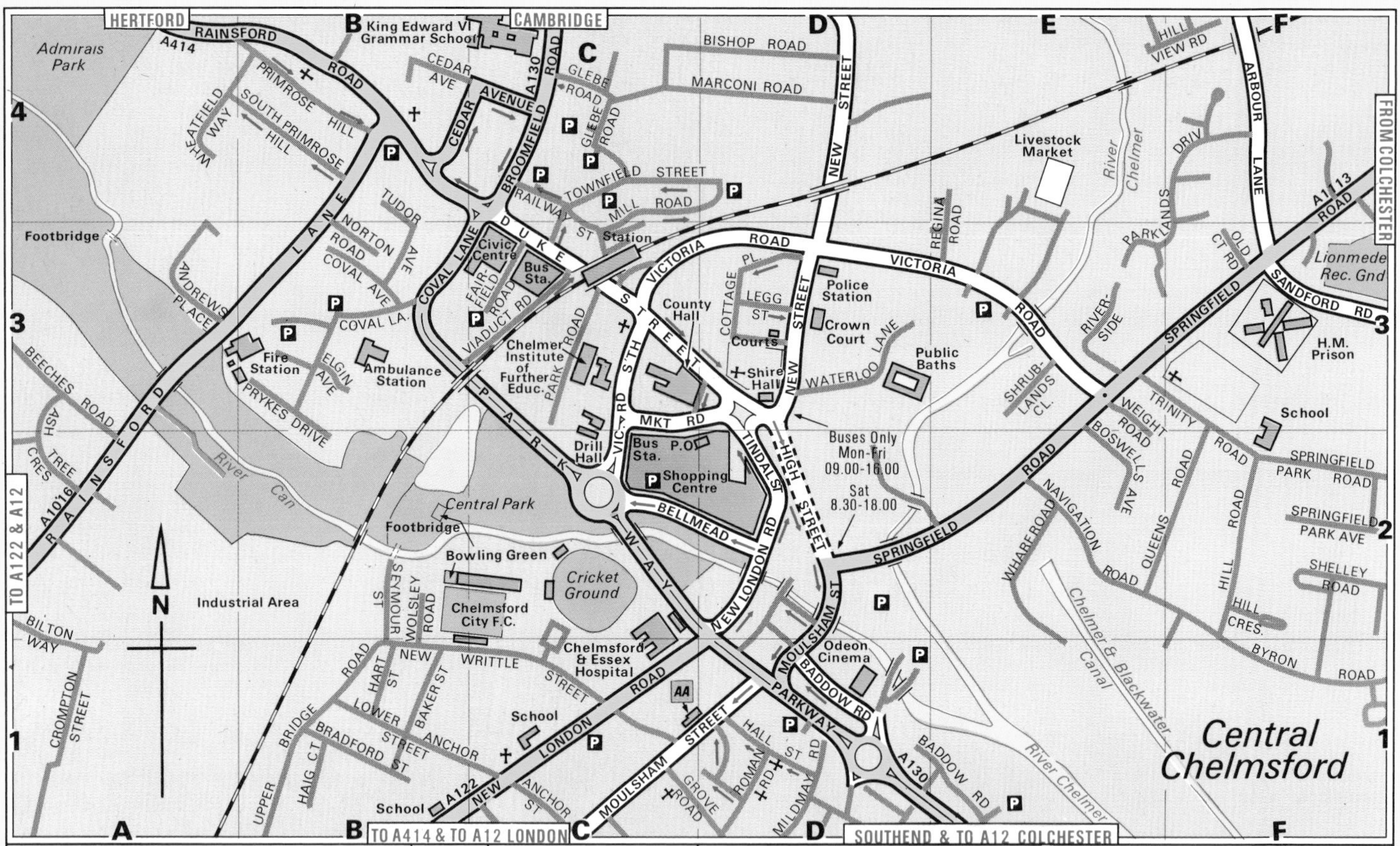

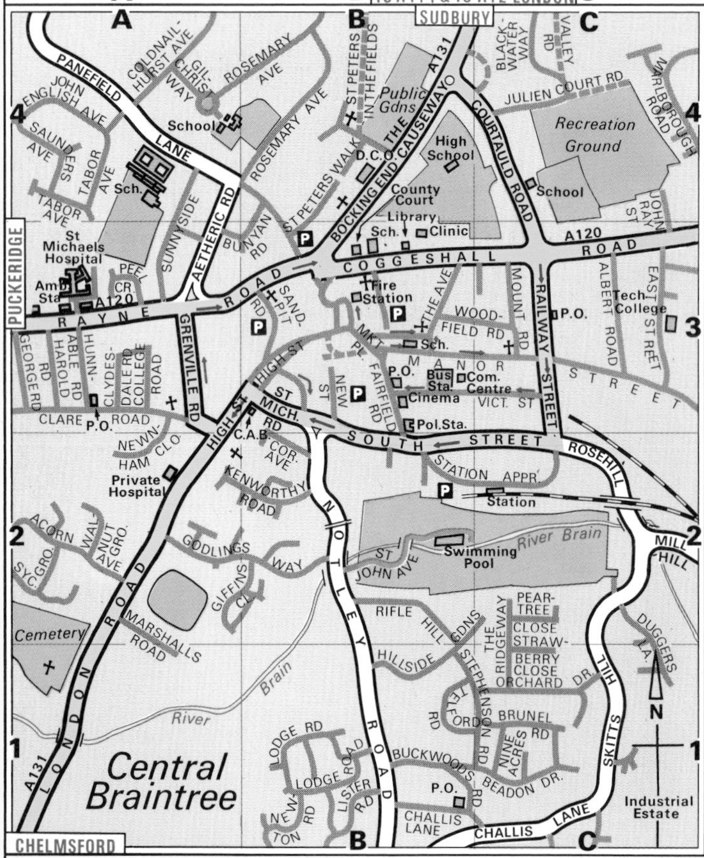

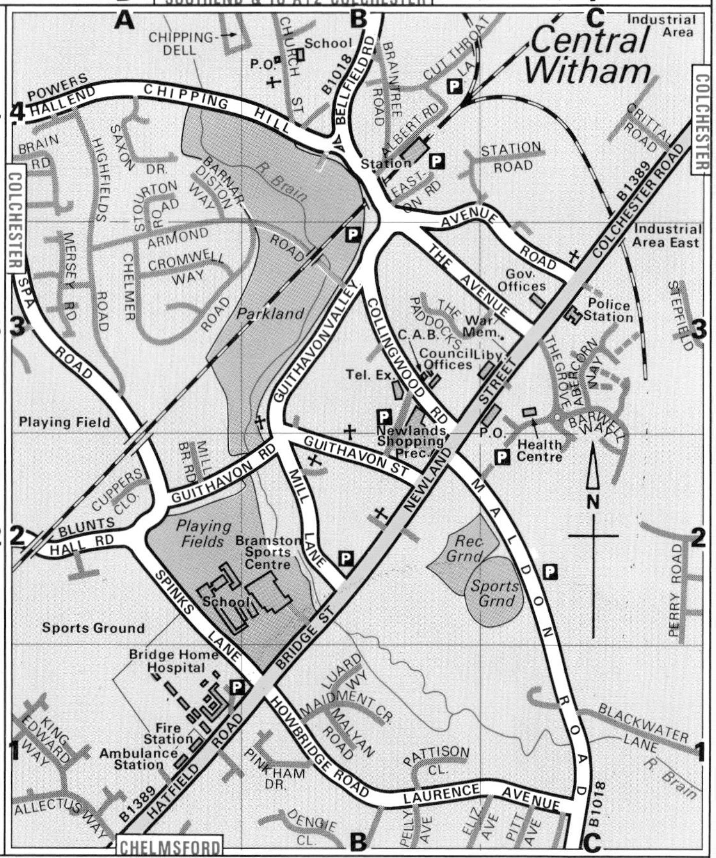

Chelmsford

Important since Roman times, this county town of Essex has undergone a good deal of expansion and development in recent years, providing it with good shopping and leisure facilities. Older buildings are concentrated in the Tindal Street area, notably the Shire Hall and the Cathedral, which dates from the 15th century. The cattle market (now on a modern site) has been going since Elizabethan days, and other places of interest include the Chelmsford and Essex Museum, which also houses the Museum of the Essex Regiment.

Braintree has been concerned with textile making since the early Middle Ages, and still keeps up the connection with the Courtaulds Group, associated with the area since the 19th century.

Maldon has retained a fascinating old quarter around All Saints Church, at the top of the High Street. A river port which has seen some industrialisation, it remains popular with holidaymakers for its position at the junction of the Blackwater and Chelmer rivers, and offers good facilities for boating along the river banks.

Witham's recent Town Development Scheme has brought expansion, incorporating housing estates, offices and factories for this ancient town on the River Brain. It has nevertheless retained some fine Georgian buildings, and several old coaching inns can be seen in the main street.

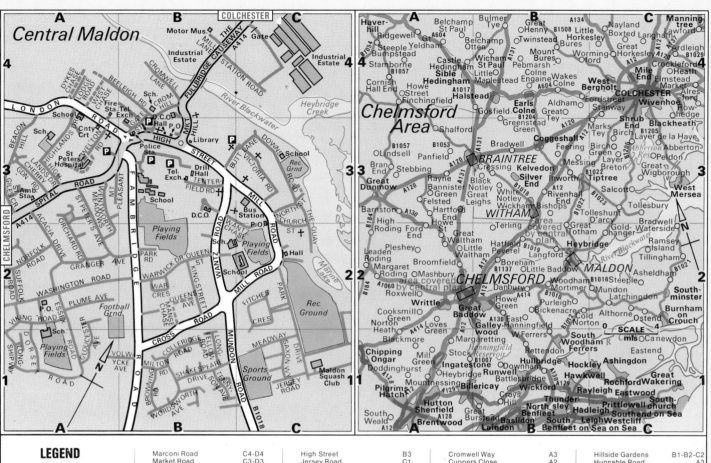

LEGEND

Town Plan

AA recommended route
Restricted roads
Other roads
Buildings of interest   Theatre ▣
Car parks   P
Parks and open spaces   ▨

Area Plan

A roads
B roads
Locations   Notley○
Urban area   ◯

Street Index with Grid Reference

Chelmsford

Anchor Street	C1
Andrews Place	A3
Arbour Lane	F4-F3
Ash Treet Crescent	A3-A2
Baddow Road	D1-E1
Baker Street	B1
Beeches Road	A3-A2
Bellmead	C2-D2
Bilton Way	A2-A1
Bishops Road	C4-D4
Boswells Avenue	E3-E2
Bradford Street	B1
Broomfield Road	C4
Byron Road	F2-F1
Cedar Avenue	B4-C4
Cottage Place	D3
Coval Avenue	B3
Coval Lane	B3-C3
Crompton Street	A1
Duke Street	C4-C3-D3
Elgin Avenue	B3
Fairfield Road	C3
Glebe Road	C4
Grove Road	C1-D1
Haig Court	B1
Hall Street	D1
Hart Street	B1
High Street	D3-D2
Hill Crescent	F2
Hill Road	F2
Hill View Road	E4-F4
Legg Street	D3
Lower Anchor Street	B1-C1
Marconi Road	C4-D4
Market Road	C3-D3
Mildmay Road	D1
Mill Road	C4-D4
Moulsham Street	C1-D1-D2
Navigation Road	E2
New London Road	B1-C1-D1-D2
New Street	D3-D4
New Writtle Street	B1-C1
Norton Road	B3
Old Court Road	F3
Parklands Drive	E3-F3-F4
Park Road	C3
Parkway	B3-C3-C2-D2-D1-E1
Primrose Hill	B4
Prykes Drive	B3-B2
Queens Road	E2-F2-F3
Railway Street	D3
Rainsford Lane	A2-A3-B3-B4
Rainsford Road	A4-B4
Regina Road	E3-E4
Riverside	E3
Roman Road	D1
Sandford Road	F3
Seymour Street	B2-B1
Shelley Road	F2
Shrublands Close	E3
South Primrose Hill	A4-B4
Springfield Park Avenue	F2
Springfield Park Road	F2
Springfield Road	D2-E2-E3-F3-F4
Tindal Street	D3-D2
Townfield Street	C4-D4
Trinity Road	E3-F3-F2
Tudor Avenue	B4-B3
Upper Bridge Road	B1
Viaduct Road	B3-B4
Victoria Road	C3-D3-E3
Victoria Road South	C2-C3
Waterloo Lane	D3
Weight Road	E3-E2
Wharf Road	E2
Wheatfield Way	A4-B4
Wolsey Road	B1-B2

Maldon

Acacia Drive	A3-A2
Beacon Hill	A3-A4
Beeleigh Road	A4-B4
Browning Road	B1
Butt Lane	B3-C3
Cherry Garden Road	A3
Church Street	C2
Colleridge Road	B1
Cromwell Hill	B4
Cromwell Lane	B4
Cross Road	B1-B2
Dorset Road	A2-A1
Downs Road	C3
Dykes Chase	A4
Essex Road	A2-A1
Fambridge Road	B3-B2-B1
Fitches Crescent	C2
Fullbridge	B4
Gate Street	B3-B4
Gloucester Avenue	A1-A2
Granger Avenue	A2-B2
Highlands Drive	A3-A4
High Street	B3
Jersey Road	C1
King Street	B2
Lodge Road	A4
London Road	A4-A3-B3
Longfellow Road	B1
Longship Way	A1
Manse Chase	B2
Market Hill	B3-B4
Meadway	C1
Mill Lane	B4
Mill Road	B2-C2-C3-B3
Milton Road	B1
Mount Pleasant	A3
Mundon Road	B2-B1-C1
Norfolk Road	A2
North Street	C3
Orchard Road	A3-A2
Park Drive	C2-C1
Park Road	B2
Plume Avenue	A2
Queens Avenue	B2
Queen Street	B2
St Giles Crescent	A3
St Peter's Avenue	A3-B3
Saxon Way	C1
Shakespeare Drive	B1
Spital Road	A3-B3
Station Road	B4-C4
Suffolk Road	A2
The Causeway	B4-C4
The Quay	C3-C2
Tennyson Avenue	B1
Tenterfield Road	B3
Victoria Road	C3
Viking Road	A1-A2
Volwycke Avenue	A1-B1
Wantz Chase	B3-C3-C2
Wantz Road	B2-B3
Warwick Crescent	B2
Warwick Drive	C2
Washington Road	A2-B2
Wellington Road	A3
Wentworth Meadows	A4
West Chase	A4
Wordsworth Avenue	B1

Witham

Abercorn Way	C3
Albert Road	B4
Allectus Way	A1
Armond Road	A3-B3
Avenue Road	B4-B3-C4-C3
Barnadiston Way	A4
Barwell Way	C3-C2
Bellfield Road	B4
Blackwater Lane	C1
Blunts Hall Road	A2
Brain Road	A4
Braintree Road	A4
Bridge Street	B1-B2
Chelmer Road	A3-B3
Chippingdell	A4-B4
Chipping Hill	A4-B4
Church Street	B4
Colchester Road	C3-C4
Collingwood Road	B3
Crittal Road	C4

Cromwell Way	A3
Cuppers Close	B1
Cut Throat Lane	B4-C4
Dengie Close	B1
Easton Road	B1
Elizabeth Avenue	B1-C1
Guithavon Road	B3-B2
Guithavon Street	B3-B2
Guithavon Valley	B2
Hatfield Road	A1-B1
Highfields Road	A4-A3
Howbridge Road	B1
King Edward Way	A1
Laurence Avenue	B1-C1
Luard Way	B1
Maidment Crescent	B1
Maldon Road	B2-C2-C1
Malyan Road	B1
Mersey Road	A3
Millbridge Road	A2
Mill Lane	B2
Newland Street	B2-B3-C3
Pattison Close	B1
Pelly Avenue	B1
Perry Road	C2
Pinkham Drive	B1
Pitt Avenue	C1
Powers Hall End	A4
Saxon Drive	A4
Spa Road	A3-A2
Spinks Lane	A2-A1-B1
Station Road	B4-C4
Stepfield	C3
Stourton Road	A3-A4
The Avenue	B3-C3
The Grove	C3
The Paddocks	B3-C3

Braintree

Acorn Avenue	A2
Albert Road	C3
Aetheric Road	A3-A4
Beadon Drive	C1
Blackwater Way	C4
Bocking End	B3-B4
Brunel Road	C1
Buckwoods Road	C4
Bunyan Road	A3-B3-B4
Challis Lane	B1-C1
Clare Road	A3
Clydesdale Road	A3
Coggeshall Road	B3-C3
Coldnailhurst Avenue	A4
College Road	A3
Coronation Avenue	B2
Courtauld Road	B4-C4-C3
Duggers Lane	C2-C1
East Street	C3
Fairfield Road	B3
George Road	A3
Giffins Close	A2-B2
Gilchrist Way	A4
Godlings Way	A2-B2
Grenville Road	A3
Harold Road	A3
High Street	A2-A3-B3

Hillside Gardens	B1-B2-C2
Hunnable Road	A3
John English Avenue	A4
John Ray Street	C4-C3
Julien Court Road	C4
Kenworthy Road	A2-B2
Lister Road	B1
Lodge Road	B1
London Road	A1-A2
Manor Street	B3-C3
Market Place	B3
Marlborough Road	C4
Marshalls Road	A2-A1
Mill Hill	C2
Mount Road	C3
Newnham Close	A2-A3
New Street	B3
Newton Road	B1
Nine Acres	C1
Wotley Road	B2-B1
Orchard Drive	C1
Panefield Lane	A4
Peartree Close	C2
Peel Crescent	A3
Railway Street	C3
Rayne Road	A3-B3
Rifle Hill	B2
Rosehill	C2
Rosemary Avenue	A4-B4
St John Avenue	B2
St Michaels Road	B3
St Peters in the Fields	B4
St Peters Walk	B3-B4
Sandpitt Road	B3
Saunders Avenue	A4
Skitts Hill	C1-C2
South Street	B3-B2-C2
Station Approach	B2-C2
Stephenson Road	B1-C1
Strawberry Close	C1
Sunnyside	A3-A4
Sycamore Grove	A2
The Avenue	B3
The Causeway	B2
The Ridgeway	C1-C2
Tabor Avenue	A4
Telford Road	B1
Valley Road	C4
Victoria Street	B3-C3
Walnut Grove	A2
Woodfield Road	B3-C3

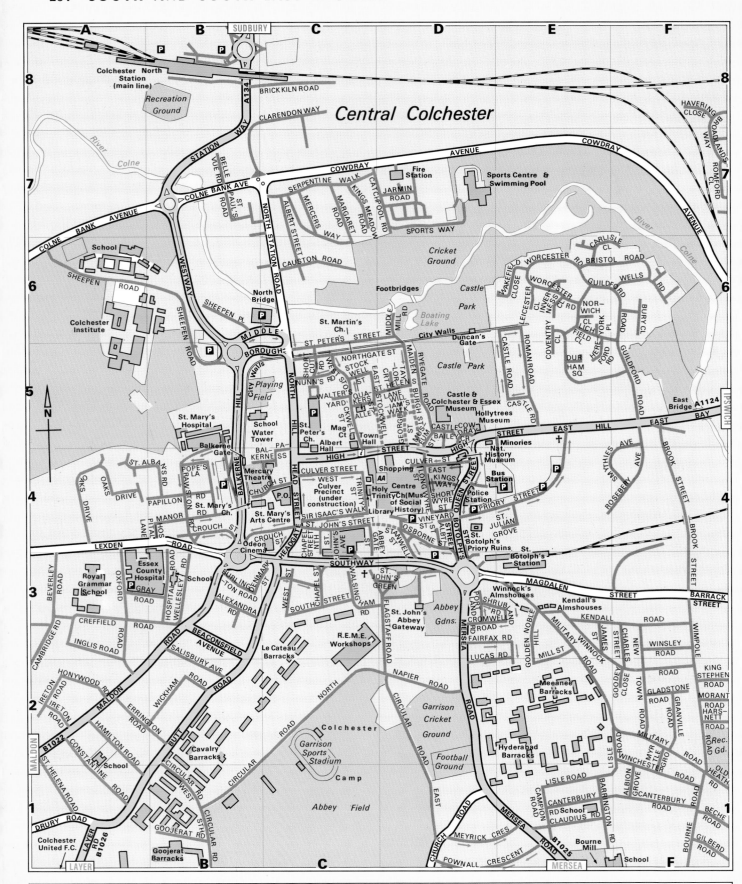

Colchester

The oldest recorded town in England, Colchester was also a Roman capital and the great walls built by the invaders stand to this day. Remains of one of their massive gateways, Balkerne Gate, have also survived. Colchester's Norman castle keep, the largest in Britain, retains an air of dark medieval menace, although it now houses nothing more sinister than the Colcester and Essex Museum

where many Roman antiquities can be seen. Colchester's proximity to the continent led to the arrival of Flemish refugees during the 16th century, and they revived the cloth trade that had flourished here in the Middle Ages. Many of their attractive gabled and colour-washed houses line West Stockwell Street, known as Dutch Quarter. In contrast, much of the town centre has been turned into a modern shopping precinct.

In the High Street is Hollytrees Museum, an

early 18th century house containing collections of costumes and toys, etc. Two of the town's churches have become museums in recent years; Holy Trinity is a museum of social history and All Saints houses a natural history museum.

The town hall is one of Colchester's most striking buildings; dating from the end of the 19th century, it has an ornate exterior and a 162ft tower. Colchester's other tall tower is more famous. Known as 'Jumbo', it is a vast water tower built in 1882.

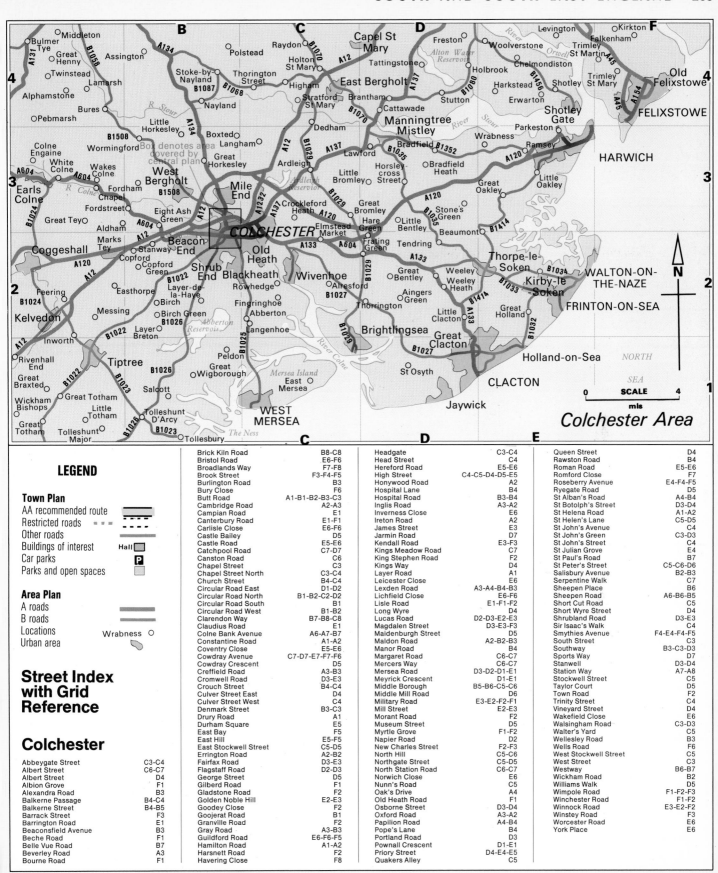

Colchester Area

LEGEND

Town Plan

AA recommended route	
Restricted roads	
Other roads	
Buildings of interest	Hall
Car parks	P
Parks and open spaces	

Area Plan

A roads	
B roads	
Locations	Wrabness ○
Urban area	

Street Index with Grid Reference

Colchester

Abbeygate Street	C3-C4
Albert Street	C6-C7
Albert Street	D4
Albion Grove	F1
Alexandra Road	B3
Balkerne Passage	B4-C4
Balkerne Street	B4-B5
Barrack Street	F3
Barrington Road	E1
Beaconsfield Avenue	B3
Beche Road	F1
Belle Vue Road	B7
Beverley Road	A3
Bourne Road	F1

Brick Kiln Road	B8-C8
Bristol Road	E6-F6
Broadlands Way	F7-F8
Brook Street	F3-F4-F5
Burlington Road	B3
Bury Close	F6
Butt Road	A1-B1-B2-B3-C3
Cambridge Road	A2-A3
Campian Road	E1
Canterbury Road	E1-F1
Carlisle Close	E6-F6
Castle Bailey	D5
Castle Road	E5-E6
Catchpool Road	C7-D7
Canston Road	C6
Chapel Street	C3
Chapel Street North	C3-C4
Church Street	B4-C4
Circular Road East	D1-D2
Circular Road North	B1-B2-C2-D2
Circular Road South	B1
Circular Road West	B1-B2
Clarendon Way	B7-B8-C8
Claudius Road	E1
Colne Bank Avenue	A6-A7-B7
Constantine Road	A1-A2
Coventry Close	E5-E6
Cowdray Avenue	C7-D7-E7-F7-F6
Cowdray Crescent	D5
Creffield Road	A3-B3
Cromwell Road	D3-E3
Crouch Street	B4-C4
Culver Street East	D4
Culver Street West	C4
Denmark Street	B3-C3
Drury Road	A1
Durham Square	E5
East Bay	F5
East Hill	E5-F5
East Stockwell Street	C5-D5
Errington Road	A2-B2
Fairfax Road	D3-E3
Flagstaff Road	D2-D3
George Street	D5
Gilberd Road	F1
Gladstone Road	F2
Golden Noble Hill	E2-E3
Goodey Close	D3-D4
Goojerat Road	B1
Granville Road	F2
Gray Road	A3-B3
Guildford Road	E6-F6-F5
Hamilton Road	A1-A2
Harsnett Road	F2
Havering Close	F8

Headgate	C3-C4
Head Street	C4
Hereford Road	E5-E6
High Street	C4-C5-D4-D5-E5
Honywood Road	A2
Hospital Lane	B4
Hospital Road	B3-B4
Inglis Road	A3-A2
Inverness Close	E6
Ireton Road	A2
James Street	E3
Jarmin Road	D7
Kendall Road	E3-F3
Kings Meadow Road	C7
King Stephen Road	F2
Kings Way	D4
Layer Road	A1
Leicester Close	E6
Lexden Road	A3-A4-B4-B3
Lichfield Close	E6-F6
Lisle Road	E1-F1-F2
Long Wyre	D4
Lucas Road	D2-D3-E2-E3
Magdalen Street	D3-E3-F3
Maidenburgh Street	D5
Maldon Road	A2-B2-B3
Manor Road	B4
Margaret Road	C6-C7
Mercers Way	C6-C7
Mersea Road	D3-D2-D1-E1
Meyrick Crescent	D1-E1
Middle Borough	B5-B6-C5-C6
Middle Mill Road	D6
Military Road	E3-E2-F2-F1
Mill Street	E2-E3
Morant Road	F2
Museum Street	D5
Myrtle Grove	F1-F2
Napier Road	D2
New Charles Street	F2-F3
North Hill	C5-C6
Northgate Street	C5-D5
North Station Road	C6-C7
Norwich Close	E6
Nunn's Road	C5
Oak's Drive	A4
Old Heath Road	F1
Osborne Street	D3-D4
Oxford Road	A3-A2
Papillon Road	A4-B4
Pope's Lane	B4
Portland Road	D3
Pownall Crescent	D1-E1
Priory Street	D4-E4-E5
Quakers Alley	C5

Queen Street	D4
Rawston Road	B4
Roman Road	E5-E6
Romford Close	F7
Roseberry Avenue	E4-F4-F5
Ryegate Road	D5
St Alban's Road	A4-B4
St Botolph's Street	D3-D4
St Helena Road	A1-A2
St Helen's Lane	C5-D5
St John's Avenue	C4
St John's Green	C3-D3
St John's Street	C4
St Julian Grove	E4
St Paul's Road	B7
St Peter's Street	C5-C6-D6
Salisbury Avenue	B2-B3
Serpentine Walk	C7
Sheepen Place	B6
Sheepen Road	A6-B6-B5
Short Cut Road	C5
Short Wyre Street	D4
Shrubland Road	D3-E3
Sir Isaac's Walk	C4
Smythies Avenue	F4-E4-F4-F5
South Street	C3
Southway	B3-C3-D3
Sports Way	D7
Stanwell	D3-D4
Station Way	A7-A8
Stockwell Street	C5
Taylor Court	D5
Town Road	F2
Trinity Street	C4
Vineyard Street	D4
Wakefield Close	E6
Walsingham Road	C3-D3
Walter's Yard	C5
Wellesley Road	B3
Wells Road	F6
West Stockwell Street	C5
West Street	C3
Westway	B6-B7
Wickham Road	B2
Williams Walk	D5
Wimpole Road	F1-F2-F3
Winchester Road	F1-F2
Winnock Road	E3-E2-F2
Winsley Road	F3
Worcester Road	E6
York Place	E6

COLCHESTER
The castle keep, all that remains of Colchester's great fortress that once stretched from the High Street to the north wall of the town, was built round the masonry platform of the Roman Temple of Claudius.

Central Margate

N

Lighthouse
The Harbour
The Bay

Winter Gardens
FORT HILL
FORT CRESCENT
Pol. Sta.
TRINITY SQUARE
TRINITY SQUARE
Caves
ZION PLACE
NORTHDOWN ROAD
Tudor House
THE PARADE
KING STREET
MKT ST
MARINE DRIVE
NEW ST
HIGH STREET
HAWLEY STREET
DANE HILL
DANE RD
CECIL SQ.
UNION ROW
P.O.
UNION CRES.
Council Offices & Library
ADDINGTON STREET
ADDINGTON ROAD
School
VICTORIA ROAD
School for the Deaf
Casino Amusements
MARINE TERRACE
Clock Tower
MARINE GDNS
CENTRE Precinct
BELGRAVE ROAD
GROSVENOR PLACE
HIGH STREET
CHURCHFIELDS
MILL LA.
LAUS ANNE TERR
CHAR SQ
ST. PETER'S FOOTPATH
Twin Cinema's & Squash Courts
Bembom Brothers Amusements Park
Plaza Cinema
CHURCHFIELDS PLACE
VICARAGE PLACE
GROS. GDNS
Fire Sta.
CH. ST PETER'S School
COWPER MILTON ROAD AVE
Margate Station
ALL SAINTS AVE
ALL SAINTS AVE
QUEENS AVE
VICTORIA RD
Golf Course
TIVOLI PARK
TIVOLI ROAD
PARK AVENUE
MARLBORO ROAD
BUCKINGHAM ROAD
CONNAUGHT ROAD
ST PETER'S RD
RAMSGATE RD
Swimming Pool
Hantsdown Park
Tivoli Industrial Estate
ALEXANDRA ROAD
Sports Centre
Thanet United F.C.
Tivoli Park

Central Canterbury

A B C

West Station
ROPER RD
ST STEPHEN'S RD
ST. STEPHEN'S ROAD
NOTLEY ST
NEW RUTTINGTON LANE
ST DUNSTAN'S STREET
STATION RD WEST
NORTH LANE
POUND LANE
ST PETER'S LA.
ST RADIGUNDS STREET
UNION ST
ARTILLERY STREET
MILITARY ROAD
St John's Hospital
Amb Station
ORCHARD ST
L.C.
Westgate Museum
Westgate Hall
Sidney Cooper Centre
Blackfriars Refectory
Marlowe's Th.
Weavers King's
BOROUGH
BROAD
OLD RUTTINGTON LANE
LANE
HOLMES RD
King's School
City Walls
WHITEHALL ROAD
WESTGATE GARDENS
LINDEN GROVE
ST PETER'S PLACE
BLACK GRIFFIN LANE
ST PETER'S ST
THE FRIARS
BEST LANE
Hospital
P.O.
Art Gallery Library & Museums
Cathedral
Teacher's Training College
RHEIMS WAY
Greyfriars Friary
Poor Priests Hospital & Her. Centre
ST PETER'S GROVE
STOUR STREET
HIGH ST
Christ Church Gateway
Chequers of the Hope
Roman Pavement
MONASTERY ST
St Augustine's Abbey
LONGPORT
Great Stour
Queen Elizabeth's Guest Chamber
HAWK'S LANE
GUILDHALL ST
MARGARET'S ST
BURGATE
CH. ST
LWR BRIDGE ST
St Augustine's College
Castle
STOUR STREET
ST JOHN'S LANE
MARY'S ST
WATLING ST
ROSE LA.
ST GEORGE'S ST
ST GEORGE'S PLACE
LOWER CHANTRY LA.
IVY LANE
Bus Station
Mag. Ct.
ABC Cinema
Fire Station
Dane John
CASTLE ST
CASTLE ROW
PIN HILL
RHODAUS TOWN
UPP. BRIDGE ST
DOVER ST
NEW DOVER ROAD
Police Station
SIMMONDS ROAD
GORDON ROAD
East Station
STATION ROAD EAST
RHODAUS CLOSE
LANS-DOWN ROADS
COSSINGTON ROAD
OATEN HILL
WINCHEAP
YORK ROAD
MARTYR'S FIELD ROAD
LIME KILN
CAMBRIDGE ROAD
NUNNERY FIELDS
NUNNERY ROAD
PROS-PECT PL.
PUCKLE LANE
RAY MOND AVE
VICTORIA RD
HEATON RD
GUILDFORD RD
ZEALAND RD
NORMAN ROAD
N

Central Dover

A B C

GUSTON ROAD
UPPER ROAD
Bleriot Memorial
JUBILEE ROAD
To Eastern Docks
Terminal Building
AA Port Service Centre
Connaught Park
CONNAUGHT ROAD
Castle Walls
Dover Castle
CASTLE AVENUE
CASTLEMOUNT ROAD
School
St Mary's Church & The Pharos
Castle Walls
CASTLE HILL ROAD
EAST CLIFF
MARINE PARADE
Youth Hostel
SALISB ROAD
PARK AVE
GODWYNE ROAD
LEYBURNE RD
HAROLD ST
TASWELL STREET
VICTORIA PARK
LAURESTON PLACE
Health Centre
MAISON DIEU ROAD
Pol. Sta.
College of Technology
Bus Sta.
WOOLCOMBER
Sports Centre & Swimming Pool
Fire Sta.
LADYWELL PK
PENCESTER ROAD
Pencester Gardens
CASTLE ST
RUSSELL ST
THE GATEWAY
MARINE PARADE
N
BIGGIN ST
Town Hall & Museum & Library
Hosp.
CANNON ST
YORK STREET
Bureau de Change
TOWN WALL ST
EFFINGHAM ST
H.P.O.
Dover College
LANC RD
ALBANY PLACE
Roman Painted House
DURHAM HILL
CAMBRIDGE RD
FOLKESTONE ROAD
Priory Station
Cowgate Cemetery
WATERLOO CRESCENT
Wellington Basin
SNARGATE
Central Dover
CLARENDON PLACE
CLARENDON ST
NORTH MILITARY ROAD
Walls
AA Hire Services
CENTRE ROAD
KNIGHTS TEMPLARS
UNION STREET
THE VIADUCT
Granville Basin
Prince of Wales Pier
Terminal Building
Hovercraft Terminal North Pier
Tidal Basin
Western Docks South Pier
LORD WARDEN SQUARE
SOUTH MILITARY ROAD
CITADEL ROAD
CHANNEL VIEW
LIMEKILN ST
Walls
Walls
Citadel H.M. Borstal
ARCHCLIFFE ROAD
B.R. Car Ferry Reception Area
Marine Station
Admiralty Pier

Key to Town Plan and Area Plan

Town Plan
AA Recommended roads
Restricted roads
Other roads
Buildings of interest — Art Gallery
Car Parks — P
Churches — †
Parks and open spaces
One Way Streets →

Area Plan
A roads
B roads
Locations — Womenswold ○
Urban area

Street Index with Grid Reference

Margate

Addington Road	C3
Addington Street	C2-C3
Alexandra Road	B1-C1
All Saints Avenue	A2
Belgrave Road	B2
Buckingham Road	B1-C1
Cecil Square	B3
Cecil Street	B3-C3
Charlotte Square	C2
Churchfields	C2
Churchfields Place	B3-C3-C2
Church Street	C2
Connaught Road	C1
Cowper Road	C2
Dane Hill	C3-C4

Dover

Travellers tend to rush through Dover – it is one of the busiest passenger ports in England – and by so doing miss an exciting town with much of interest. Outstanding is the castle. Its huge fortifications have guarded the town since the 12th century, but within its walls are even older structures – a Saxon church and a Roman lighthouse called the Pharos. In the town itself, the town hall is housed within the walls of a 13th-century guest house called the Maison Dieu. The Roman Painted House in New Street consists of substantial remains of a Roman town house and include the best-preserved Roman wall paintings north of the Alps.

Canterbury is one of Britain's most historic towns. It is the seat of the Church in England, and has been so since St Augustine began his mission here in the 6th century. The cathedral is a priceless work of art containing many other works of art, including superb displays of medieval carving and stained glass. Ancient city walls – partly built on Roman foundations – still circle parts of the city, and a wealth of grand public buildings as well as charming private houses of many periods line the maze of lanes in the shadow of the cathedral.

Margate and **Ramsgate** both grew as commercial ports, but for many years they have specialised in catering for holidaymakers who like safe, sandy beaches and excellent facilities.

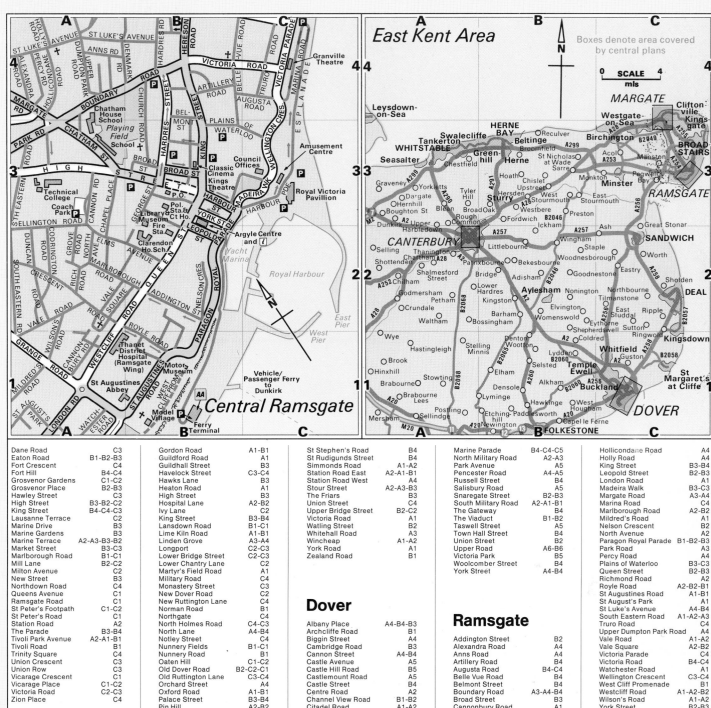

Dane Road	C3	Gordon Road	A1-B1
Eaton Road	B1-B2-B3	Guildford Road	A1
Fort Crescent	C4	Guildhall Street	B3
Fort Hill	B4-C4	Havelock Street	C3-C4
Grosvenor Gardens	C1-C2	Hawks Lane	B3
Grosvenor Place	B2-B3	Heaton Road	A1
Hawley Street	C3	High Street	B3
High Street	B3-B2-C2	Hospital Lane	A2-B2
King Street	B4-C4-C3	Ivy Lane	C2
Lausanne Terrace	C2	King Street	B3-B4
Marine Drive	B3	Lansdown Road	B1-C1
Marine Gardens	B3	Lime Kiln Road	A1-B1
Marine Terrace	A2-A3-B3-B2	Linden Grove	A3-A4
Market Street	B3	Longport	C2-C3
Marlborough Road	B1-C1	Lower Bridge Street	C2-C3
Mill Lane	B2-C2	Lower Chantry Lane	C2
Milton Avenue	C2	Martyr's Field Road	A1
New Street	B3	Military Road	C4
Northdown Road	C4	Monastery Street	C3
Queens Avenue	C1	New Dover Road	C2
Ramsgate Road	B3	New Ruttington Lane	C4
St Peter's Footpath	C1-C2	Norman Road	B1
St Peter's Road	C1	Northgate	C4
Station Road	A2	North Holmes Road	C4-C3
The Parade	B3-B4	North Lane	A4-B4
Tivoli Park Avenue	A2-A1-B1	Notley Street	C4
Tivoli Road	B1	Nunnery Fields	B1-C1
Trinity Square	C4	Nunnery Road	B1
Union Crescent	C3	Oaten Hill	C1-C2
Union Row	C3	Old Dover Road	B2-C2-C3
Vicarage Crescent	C1	Old Ruttington Lane	C3-C4
Vicarage Place	C1-C2	Orchard Street	A4
Victoria Road	C2-C3	Oxford Road	A1-B1
Zion Place	C4	Palace Street	B3-B4
		Pin Hill	A2-B2
		Pound Lane	A4-B4
		Prospect Place	C1
		Puckle Lane	C1
Canterbury		Raymond Avenue	C1
		Rheims Way	A2-A3
Artillery Street	C4	Rhodaus Town	B1
Best Lane	B3	Roper Road	A4
Black Griffin Lane	A3	Rose Lane	B2-B3
Borough	B4-C4	St Dunstan's Street	A4
Broad Street	C4-C3	St Georges Lane	A4
Burgate	B3-C3	St George's Place	C2
Cambridge Road	A1-B1	St George's Street	B3-B2
Castle Row	A2-B2	St John's Lane	B2
Castle Street	A2-B2	St Margaret's Street	B2-B3
Church Street	C3	St Mary's Street	A2-B2
Cossington Road	C2-C1	St Peters Grove	A3-B3
Dover Street	C2	St Peter's Lane	B4
		St Peter's Place	A3
		St Peter's Street	A3-B3

St Stephen's Road	B4	Marine Parade	B4-C4-C5
St Rudigunds Street	B4	North Military Road	A2-A3
Simmonds Road	A1-A2	Park Avenue	A5
Station Road East	A2-A1-B1	Pencester Road	A4-A5
Station Road West	A2	Russell Street	B4
Stour Street	A2-A3-B3	Salisbury Road	A5
The Friars	B3	Snaregate Street	B2-B3
Union Street	C4	South Military Road	A2-A1-B1
Upper Bridge Street	B2-C2	The Gateway	B4
Victoria Road	A1	The Viaduct	B1-B2
Watling Street	B2	Taswell Street	A5
Whitehall Road	A3	Town Hall Street	B4
Wincheap	A1-A2	Union Street	B2
York Road	A1	Upper Road	A6-B6
Zealand Road	B1	Victoria Park	B5
		Woolcomber Street	B4
		York Street	A4-B4

Dover

Albany Place	A4-B4-B3
Archcliffe Road	B1
Biggin Street	A4
Cambridge Road	B3
Cannon Street	A4-B4
Castle Avenue	B5
Castle Hill Road	B5
Castlemount Road	A5
Castle Street	B4
Centre Road	A2
Channel View Road	B1-B2
Citadel Road	A1-A2
Clarendon Place	A2-A3
Clarendon Road	A3
Connaught Road	A5-A6
Durham Hill	A3-A4
East Cliff	C5
Effingham Street	A4
Folkestone Road	A3-A4
Godwyne Road	A5
Guston Road	A6
Harold Street	A5
Jubilee Road	C6
Knights Templars	A2
Ladywell Park Road	A4-A5
Lancaster Road	A4
Laureston Place	B5
Leyburne Road	A5
Limekiln Street	B1-B2
Lord Warden Square	C1-C2
Maison Dieu Road	A5-B5

Ramsgate

Addington Street	B2
Alexandra Road	A4
Anns Road	A4
Artillery Road	B4
Augusta Road	B4-C4
Belle Vue Road	B4
Belmont Street	B4
Boundary Road	A3-A4-B4
Broad Street	B3
Cannonbury Road	A1
Canon Road	A3
Chapel Place	A2-A3
Chatham Street	A3
Church Road	B3-B4
Codrington Road	A2
Crescent Road	A2
Denmark Road	A4-B4
Duncan Road	A2
Ellington Road	A2-A3
Elms Avenue	A2-B2
Esplanade	C3-C4
George Street	B3
Grange Road	A1
Grove Road	A2
Harbour Parade	B3-C3
Harbour Street	B3
Hardres Street	B3-B4
Hereson Road	B4
High Street	A3-B3

Hollicondane Road	A4
Holly Road	A4
King Street	B3-B4
Leopold Street	B2-B3
London Road	A1
Madeira Walk	B3-C3
Margate Road	A3-A4
Marina Road	C4
Marlborough Road	A2-B2
Mildred's Road	A1
Nelson Crescent	B2
North Avenue	A2
Paragon Royal Parade	B1-B2-B3
Park Road	A3
Percy Road	A4
Plains of Waterloo	B3-C3
Queen Street	B2-B3
Richmond Road	A2
Royle Road	A2-B2-B1
St Augustines Road	A1-B1
St August's Park	A1
St Luke's Avenue	A4-B4
South Eastern Road	A1-A2-A3
Truro Road	C4
Upper Dumpton Park Road	A4
Vale Road	A1-A2
Vale Square	A2-B2
Victoria Parade	C4
Victoria Road	B4-C4
Watchester Road	A1
Wellington Crescent	C3-C4
West Cliff Promenade	B1
Westcliff Road	A1-A2-B2
Wilson's Road	A1-A2
York Street	B2-B3

DOVER
The famous White Cliffs of Dover provide exhilarating coastal walks with views out across the Channel. Paths to the north-east lead to Walmer and to the south-east, to Folkestone.

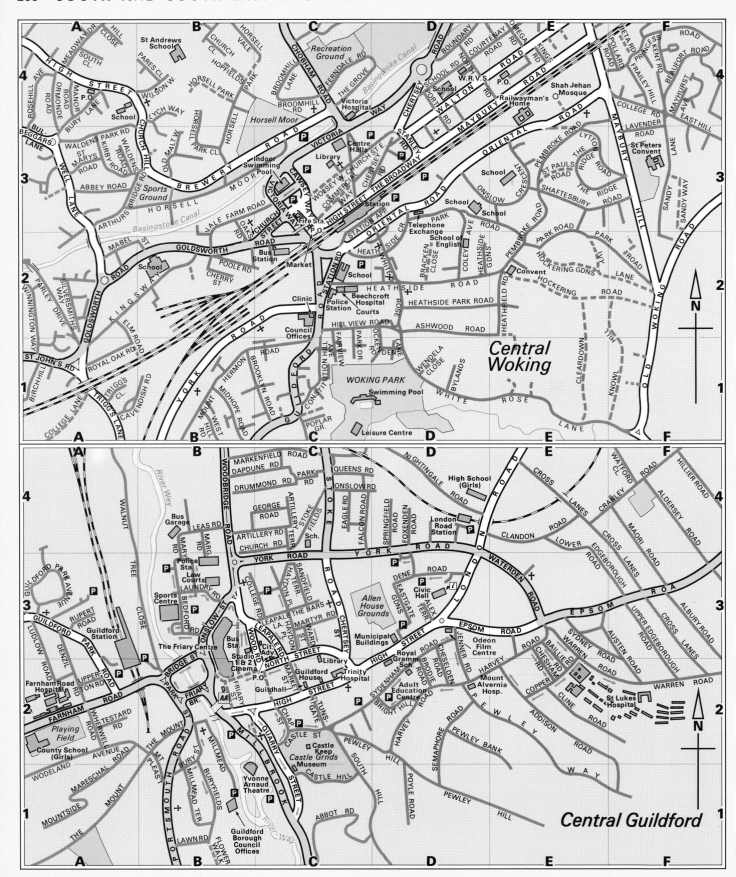

Guildford

Guildford's impressive modern redbrick Anglican cathedral, consecrated in 1961, looks down on the county town of Surrey from its hill-top setting on the outskirts. Nearby are the differently-styled modern buildings of the University of Surrey. Another example of modern architecture is the Yvonne Arnaud Theatre, which opened in 1958 on the banks of the River Wey. Despite being a busy modern shopping centre the town retains many old buildings and its steep, partly-cobbled High Street has an unchanging Georgian character. Most prominent is the Guildhall with its hexagonal bell-turret and gilded clock overhanging the pavement. All that remains of the city's castle, just off the High Street, is the 12th-century keep built by Henry II, but close by the Castle Museum has a comprehensive range of local antiquities.

Godalming An important staging post on the London to Portsmouth road in stagecoach days, this attractive North Downs town still has several old coaching inns as well as a number of other 16th-century buildings. Local artefacts can be found in the Borough Museum.

Woking A residential and commuter town on the disused Basingtoke Canal, Woking developed as a direct result of the arrival of the railway in the 1830s. Its most distinctive feature is its large Mosque, built in 1889.

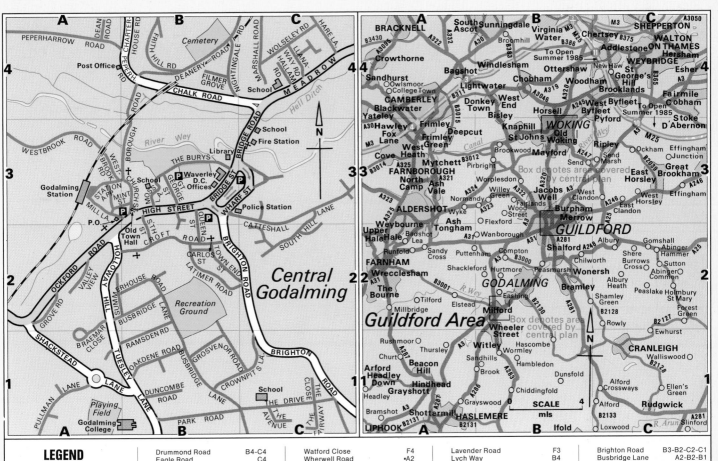

Central Godalming

Guildford Area

SCALE
mls

LEGEND

Town Plan

AA recommended route
Restricted roads
Other roads
Buildings of interest   Station
Car parks
Parks and open spaces
One way streets

Area Plan

A roads
B roads
Locations   Fairlands
Urban area

Street Index with Grid Reference

Guildford

Abbot Road	C1
Addison Road	E2-F2-F1
Albury Road	F2-F3
Aldersey Road	F2-F3
Alexandra Terrace	D3
Artillery Road	B4-C4
Artillery Terrace	C4
Austen Road	E3-F3-F2
Baillie Road	E2-E3
Bedford Road	B2
Bridge Street	B2-B3
Bright Hill	D2
Brodie Road	D2
Buryfields	B1
Bury Street	B1-B2
Castle Hill	C1
Castle Street	C2
Chapel Street	C2
Chertsey Street	C2
Cheselden Road	D2-D3
Chesham Road	E2-E3
Church Road	B3-B4-C4
Clandon Road	D4-E4
Cline Road	E2-F2
College Road	B3-C3
Copper Road	E2
Cranley Road	E4-F4
Cross Lanes	E4-F4-F3-F2
Dapdune Road	B4-C4
Dene Road	D3
Denzil Road	A2-A3

Drummond Road	B4-C4
Eagle Road	C4
Eastgate Gardens	D3
Epsom Road	D3-E3-F3
Falcon Road	C4
Farnham Road	A2-B2
Flower Walk	B1
Foxenden Road	D4
Friary Bridge	A2-B2
Friary Street	B2
George Road	B4-C4
Guildford Park Avenue	A3
Guildford Park Road	A2-A3
Harvey Road	D2-E2-E3
Haydon Place	C3
High Street	B2-C2-D2-D3
Hillier Road	F4
Jenner Road	D2-D3
Laundry Road	B3
Lawn Road	B1
Leapale Lane	C3
Leapale Road	C3
Leas Road	B4
London Road	D3-D4-E4
Lower Edgeborough Road	E4-E3-F3
Ludlow Road	A2-A3
Maori Road	F4-F3
Mareschel Road	A1-A2
Margaret Road	B3-B4
Markenfield Road	B4-C4
Market Street	C2
Martyr Road	C3
Mary Road	B3-B4
Millbrook	B2-C2-C1
Millmead	B1-B2
Millmead Terrace	B1
Mount Pleasant	B1-B2
Mountside	A1
Nightingale Road	D4
North Street	C2-C3
Onslow Road	C4-D4
Onslow Street	B3
Park Road	C4
Park Street	B2
Pewley Bank	D2-E2-E1
Pewley Hill	C2-D2-D1-E1
Pewley Way	D2-E2-E1-F1
Portsmouth Road	B1-B2
Poyle Road	D1
Quarry Street	C2-B3-C3
Queens Road	C4-D4
Rupert Road	A3
Sandfield Terrace	C3
Semaphore Road	D1-D2
South Hill	C2-C1-D1
Springfield Road	D4
Stoke Fields	C3
Stoke Road	C3-C4
Sydenham Road	C2-D2-D3
Sydney Road	E3-F3-E2
Testard Road	A2
The Bars	C3
The Mount	A1-B1-B2
Tunsgate	C2
Upper Edgeborough Road	F2-F3
Upperton Road	A2
Walnut Treet Close	B2-B3-A3-A4
Ward Street	C3
Warren Road	E3-E2-F2
Waterden Road	D3-E3

Watford Close	F4
Wherwell Road	A2
Woodbridge Road	B4-B3-C3-C2
Wodeland Avenue	A1-A2-B2
York Road	B3-C3-C4-D3-D4

Woking

Abbey Road	A3
Arthurs Bridge Road	A3-B4
Ashwood Road	D2-E2
Beaufort Road	F4
Beta Road	F4
Birch Hill	A1
Boundary Road	D4
Bracken Close	D2
Brewery Road	B3-C3-C4
Brooklyn	B1-C1
Broomhill Lane	C4
Broomhill Road	C4
Bulbeggars Lane	A3
Bury Lane	A3-A4
Bylands	D1
Cavendish Road	A1-B1
Cawsey Way	C3
Cherry Street	B2
Chertsey Road	C3-D3-D4
Chobham Road	C4
Church Close	B4
Church Hill	B3-B4
Church Street	C2-C3
Church Street East	C3-D3
Cleardown	E1-E2
Coley Avenue	D2-D3
College Lane	A1
College Road	F4
Commercial Way	C3
Constitution Hill	C1
Courteney Road	D4-E4
Elm Road	A2-A1
East Hill	F3-F4
Fairview Avenue	C1-C2
Ferndale Road	C4
Frailey Hill	F4
Goldsworth Road	A1-A2-B2-C2
Guildford Road	B1-C1-C2
Heathfield Road	E2
Heathside Crescent	C2-D2-D3
Heathside Gardens	D2
Heathside Park Road	C2-D2-E2
Heathside Road	C1-D1-E1
Heathside Road	E2
High Street	A3-B4
High Street	C3
Hill Close	A4
Hill View Road	C2-D2
Hockering Gardens	E2
Hockering Road	E2-F2
Hopfields	D2
Horsell Moor	A3-B3-C3
Horsell Park	B3-B4-C4
Horsell Park Close	B3-B4
Horsell Vale	B4-C4
Ivy Lane	E2-F2
Kent Road	F4
Kings Road	E4
Kings Way	A1-A2-B2
Kirby Road	A3
Knowl Hill	F1-F2

Lavender Road	F3
Lych Way	B4
Lytton Road	E3-F3
Mabel Street	A2-B2
Manor Road	A4
Maybury Hill	E4-F4-F3-F2
Maybury Road	D3-D4-E4
Mayhurst Avenue	F4
Meadway Drive	A4
Midhope Road	B1
Mount Hermon Road	B1-C1
North Road	D4-E4
Oaks Road	B2-B3
Ockenden Road	D1-D2
Old Malt Way	B3
Old Woking road	F1-F2-F3
Omega Road	E4
Onslow Crescent	D3-E3
Oriental Road	C2-C3-D2-D3-E3-E4
Ormonde Road	A3-A4
Pares Close	A4-B4
Park Drive	C1-C2
Park Road	D3-E3-E2-F2
Parley Drive	A1-A2
Pembroke Road	E2-E3-E4
Pollard Road	F4
Poole Road	B2-C2
Poplar Grove	C1
Port Road	D3-D4
Princes Road	F4
Rosehill Avenue	A4
Royal Oak Road	A1
St Johns Road	A1
St Marys Road	A3
St Pauls Road	E3
Sandy Lane	F2-F3-F4
Sandy Way	F4
School Road	D1
Shaftesbury Road	E3-F3
Silversmiths Way	A2
South Close	A4
Stanley Road	B4
Station Approach	C2-C3-D3
Station Road	C2
The Broadway	D3
The Grove	C4-D4
The Ridge	E3-F3
Trigg's Close	A1
Trigg's Lane	A1
Vale Farm Road	B2-B3-C3
Victoria Way	C2-C3-C4-D4
Waldens Park Road	A3
Waldens Road	A3
Walton Road	D3-D4-E4
Well Lane	A3
Wendella Close	D1
West Hill Road	B1
White Rose Lane	D2-D1-E1-F1
Winnington Way	A1-A2
Wilson Way	B4
Wolsey Way	C3
York Road	B1-B2-C2

Godalming

Borough Road	B3-B4
Braemar Close	A1-A2
Bridge Road	B3-C3-C4
Bridge Street	B3
Brighton Road	B3-B2-C2-C1
Busbridge Lane	A2-B2-B1
Carlos Street	B2
Catteshal Lane	B3-C3-C2-C3
Chalk Road	B4-C4
Charterhouse Road	B4
Church Street	B3
Croft Road	B2
Crownpits Lane	B1-C1
Dean Road	A4
Deanery Road	B4
Duncombe Road	B1
Filmer Grove	B4
Frith Hill Road	B4
Great George Street	B3
Grosvenor Road	B1-C1
Grove Road	A2
Hallam Road	C4
Hare Lane	C4
High Street	B3
Holloway Hill	A2
Latimer Road	B2
Llanaway Road	C4
Marshall Road	C4
Meadrow	C4
Mill Lane	B1
Mint Street	A3-B3
Moss Lane	B3
Nightingale Road	B4-C4
Oakdene Road	B1
Ockford Road	A2-A3-B2-B3
Park Road	B1
Peperharow Road	A4-B4
Pullman Lane	A1
Queen Street	B3-B2
Ramsden Road	A1-B1-B2
Shackstead Lane	A2-A1-B1
South Hill	C2-C3
South Street	B2-B3
Station Approach	A3
Summerhouse Road	A2-B2
The Avenue	C1
The Burys	B3
The Close	C1
The Drive	C1
The Fairway	C1
Town End Street	B2-C2
Tuesley Lane	A2-A1-B1
Valley View	A2
Westbrook Road	A3
Wharf Street	B3-C3
Wolseley Road	C4

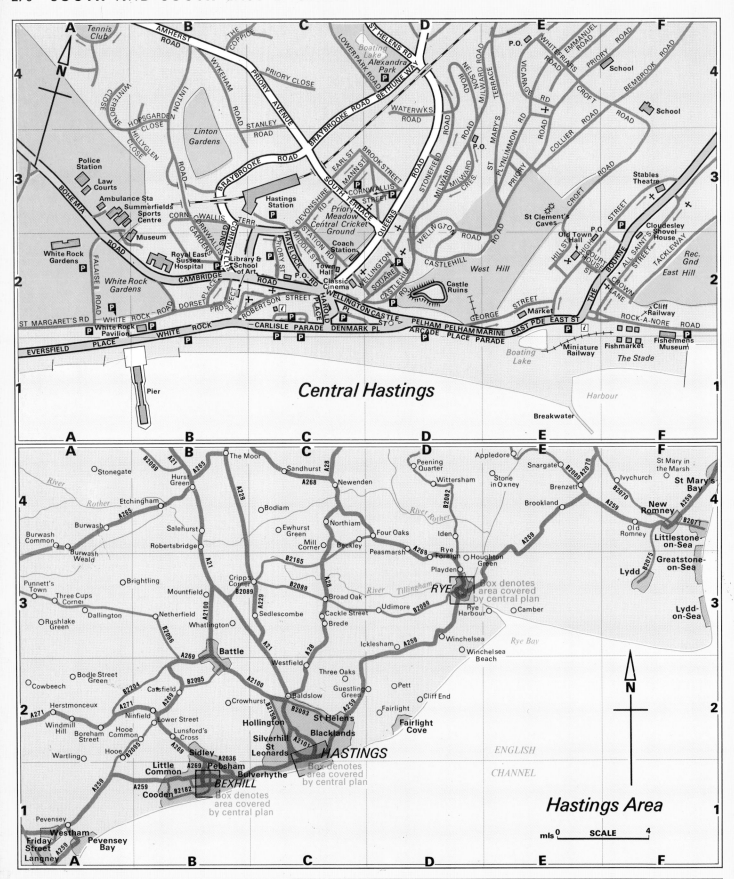

Central Hastings

Hastings Area

mls 0 SCALE 4

Hastings

Overlooking the beach of this popular resort are the remains of a castle established by William the Conqueror; Battle Abbey, the actual site of the great conflict of 1066, lies to the north of the town on the A2100. The Hastings Embroidery, which was commissioned in 1966 to commemorate the battle's 900th anniversary and depicts 81 memorable events in British history, can be seen at the Town Hall.

Rich in historical associations, Hastings also has a historic Old Town — a pleasant jumble of ancient buildings and narrow streets, and site of the local fish market and Fisherman's Museum. Theatres, pubs and amusement areas fill the main resort, which has all the amenities expected of a major holiday centre.

Bexhill offers the entertainment facilities of the De La Warr Pavilion, which overlooks the sands,

and a good range of outdoor activities can be enjoyed in nearby Egerton Park. Manor Gardens, in the older part of the town, contains the Manor Costume Museum and the ruins of the manor house.

Rye is an atmospheric town of cobbled streets and half-timbered houses. A gang of smugglers had its headquarters at the 15th-century Mermaid Inn, and other places of interest include the Baddings Tower Museum, the Rye Town Model and the old harbour, which is now a nature reserve.

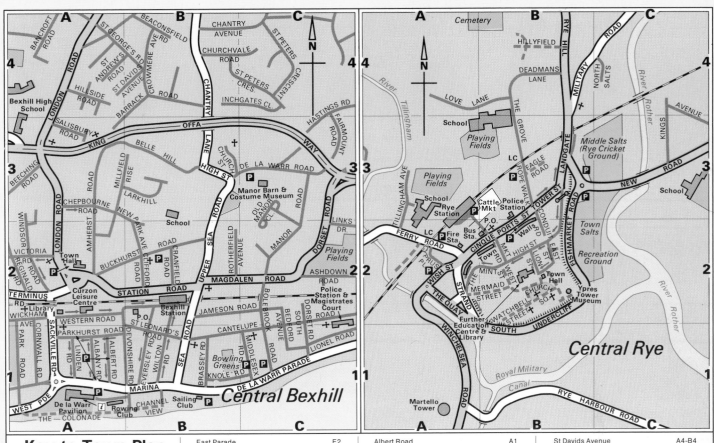

Central Bexhill

Central Rye

Key to Town Plan and Area Plan

Town Plan
AA Recommended roads
Restricted roads
Other roads
Buildings of interest   Castle ▣
Car Parks   P
Churches   ✝
Parks and open spaces
One Way Streets →

Area Plan
A roads
B roads
Locations   Kingston ○
Urban area

Street Index with Grid Reference

Hastings

Amherst Road	B4
All Saints Street	F2-F3
Bembrook Road	F4
Bethune Way	D4
Bohemia Road	A3-A2-B2
Braybrooke Road	B3-C3-C4-D4
Brook Street	C3-D3
Cambridge Road	B2-C2
Carlisle Parade	C2
Castlehill Road	D2-E2-E3
Castle Street	D2
Collier Road	E3-E4-F4
Cornwallis Gardens	B3-B2
Cornwallis Street	C3-D3
Cornwallis Terrace	B3-C3
Courthouse Street	E2
Croft Road	E4-F4-F3-E3
Crown Lane	F2
Denmark Place	C2-D2
Devonshire Road	C3
Dorset Place	B2
Earl Street	C3

East Parade	E2
East Street	E2
Emmanuel Road	E4
Eversfield Place	A1
Falaise Road	A2
George Street	D2-E2
Harold Place	C2
Havelock Road	C2
High Street	E2-F2-F3
Hill Street	E2
Hillyglen Close	B3
Hopsgarden Close	B3-B4
Linton Road	B4-B3
Lower Park Road	C4-D4
Mann Street	C3-D3
Marine Parade	D2-E2
Middle Street	C2
Milward Crescent	D3
Milward Road	D3-D4-E4
Nelson Road	D4
Pelham Arcade	D2
Pelham Place	D2
Plynlimmon Road	E3-E4
Priory Avenue	B4-C4-C3
Priory Close	C4
Priory Road	E3-E4-F4
Priory Street	C2
Prospect Place	B2
Queens Road	C2-D2-D3-D4
Robertson Street	B2-C2
Rock-a-Nore Road	F2
St Helens Road	D4
St Margaret's Road	A2
St Mary's Terrace	E3-E4
South Terrace	C3-D3
Stanley Road	B3-C3-C4
Station Road	C2-C3
Stonefield Road	D3-D4
Tackleway	F2-F3
The Coppice	B4-C4
The Bourne	E2-F2
Vicarage Road	E4
Waterworks Road	D4
Wellington Place	C2-D2
Wellington Road	D3-D2-E2
Wellington Square	D2
White Rock	B1-B2
White Rock Road	A2-B2
Whitefriars Road	E4
Winterbourne Close	A3-A4
Wykeham Road	B4-B3-C3

Bexhill

Albany Road	A1
Albert Road	A1
Amherst Road	A2-A3
Ashdown Road	C2
Bancroft Road	A4
Barrack Road	A3-B4
Beaconsfield Road	B4
Bedford Avenue	C2-C1
Beeching Road	A3
Belle Hill	B3
Bolebrook Road	C2-C1
Brassey Road	B1
Buckhurst Road	A2-B2
Cantelupe Road	B1-C1-C2
Channel View	B1
Chantry Avenue	B4-C4
Chantry Lane	B4-B3
Chelsea Close	C2
Chepbourne Road	A3
Church Street	B3
Churchvale Road	B4-C4
Clifford Road	B2
Cornwall Road	A2-A1
Cranfield Road	B2
Crowmere Avenue	B4
De la Warr Parade	B1-C1
De la Warr Road	C3
Devonshire Road	A1-B1
Dorset Road	C2-C3
Dorset Road South	C2-C1
Eversley Road	B1
Fairmount Road	C3-C4
Hastings Road	C4-C3
High Street	B3
Hillside Road	A4
Inchgates Close	B4-C4
Jameson Road	B2-C2
King Offa Way	A3-B3-C3
Knole Road	B1-C1
Larkhill	A3-B3
Linden Road	A1
Links Drive	C2
Lionel Road	C1
London Road	A4-A3-A2
Magdalen Road	B2-C2
Manor Road	C2-C3
Marina	A1-B1
Middlesex Road	C1
Millfield Rise	A3-B3
New Park Avenue	A3-B3-B2
Old Manor Close	C2-C3
Park Road	A1-A2
Parkhurst Road	A1
Reginald Road	A2
Rotherfield Avenue	B2
St Andrew's Road	A4-B4

St Davids Avenue	A4-B4
St George's Road	A4-B4
St Leonard's Road	B2-B1
St Peters Crescent	B4-C4
Sackville Road	A2-A1
Salisbury Road	A3
Sea Road	B1-B2
Station Road	A2-B2
Terminus Road	A2
The Colonade	A1
Upper Sea Road	B2-B3
Victoria Road	A2
West Parade	A1
Western Road	A2
Wickham Avenue	A2
Wilton Road	B1
Windsor Road	A3-A2

Rye

Church Square	B2
Cinque Ports Street	A2-B2-B3
Conduit Road	B3-B2
Cyprus Place	A2
Deadmans Lane	B4
Eagle Road	B3
East Street	B2
Ferry Road	A2
Fishmarket Road	B2-B3
High Street	B2
Hillyfield	B4
Kings Avenue	C3-C4
Landgate	B3
Lion Street	B2
Love Lane	A4-B4
Market Road	B2
Mermaid Street	A2-B2
Military Road	B4-C4
New Road	B3-C3
North Salts	C4
Rope Walk	B3
Rye Harbour Road	B1-C1
Rye Hill	B4
South Undercliff	B1-B2
Strand	A2
The Grove	B4-B3
The Mint	A2-B2
The Quay	A2
Tillingham Avenue	A2-A3
Tower Street	B3
Watchbell Street	B2
West Street	B2
Winchelsea Road	A1-A2
Wish Street	A2

HASTINGS
Although the harbour of this one-time Cinque Port silted up centuries ago, fishing boats are still winched up on the shingle beach, and fishermen's net-drying huts at the foot of the cliff railway are a distinctive feature.

Luton Area

A422 Beachampton, Thornton, B4033, Thornborough, Whaddon, Nash, Great Horwood, Little Horwood, Adstock, A413, Addington, Mursley, Winslow, Granborough, Hoggeston, Dunton, North Marston, Oving, Pitchcott, Quainton, Hardwick, Weedon, Waddesdon, A41, Quarrendon, Upper Winchendon, Stone, AYLESBURY, Walton, Southcourt, Bedgrave, Aston Clinton, Bishopstone, Stoke Mandeville, Dinton, Ford, North Lee, Haddenham, A4010, Wendover, Wigginton

MILTON KEYNES, Wavendon, Aspley Guise, A5130, A421, Walton, Bow Brickhill, Bletchley, Fenny Stratford, B4034, Newton Longville, Drayton Parslow, Stewkley, B4032, Swanbourne, Linslade, South End, LEIGHTON BUZZARD, Wing, Ledburn, Mentmore, Wingrave, Horton, Cheddington, Rowsham, Hulcott, Bierton, Marsworth, Wilstone, Buckland, Tring, Aldbury, B4506, Little Gaddesden, Great Gaddesden, Potten End, Gadebridge, HEMEL HEMPSTEAD, Berkhamsted, Dudswell, A41(M), Halton, A4011

Brogborough, Ridgmont, A507, Steppingley, Husborne Crawley, Woburn, Woburn Sands, Little Brickhill, Great Brickhill, Stoke Hammond, North End, Soulbury, A4146, A4012, Church End, Tingrith, Mitton Bryan, Toddington, Heath and Reach, Hockliffe, Eggington, Tilsworth, Stanbridge, Billington, Eaton Bray, Totternhoe, Church End, Edlesborough, Whipsnade, Dagnall, Ringshall, Hindnall, Water End

Ampthill, Maulden, Flitton, Silsoe, Greenfield, Eversholt, Pulloxhill, Westoning, Harlington, Streatley, Upper Sundon, Sundon Park, Marsh Farm, DUNSTABLE, Houghton Regis, Caddington, Kensworth, Slip End, Kensworth Common, A5, Holywell, Studham, Flamstead, Markyate, A5, Jockey End, Redbourn, New Greens, Highfield, ST ALBANS

Clophill, Meppershall, Upper Gravenhurst, Shillington, Apsley End, Lower Stondon, Holwell, Barton-le-Clay, Hexton, Pirton, B655, Limbury, Leagrave, Stopsley, LUTON, Luton Airport, Park Town, Peter's Green, Pepperstock, Blackmore End, Ayot St Lawrence, Batford, Harpenden, Wheathampstead, Lemsford, Sandridge, Marshalswick, A414, Hatfield

Henlow, Church End, Arlesey, Radwell, A507, Ickleford, LETCHWORTH, HITCHIN, Gosmore, Great Offley, Kings Walden, St Ippollitts, Preston, Cockernhoe, Breachwood Green, Whitwell, Kimpton, Codicote, Welwyn, Digswell, WELWYN GARDEN CITY, The Ryde

Ashwell, Stotfold, Weston, Great Wymondley, Little Wymondley, Graveley, Old Town, STEVENAGE, B656, St Paul's Walden, Knebworth, Woolmer Green, Oaklands, B197, BALDOCK, A505, A1(M), B197

N

Box denotes area covered by central plan

Central Leighton Buzzard

BROOMHILLS RD, PLANTATION, WINSTON CLO., OAKLEY GREEN, CHURCHILL ROAD, NELSON ROAD, CLARENCE ROAD, HEATH ROAD, RIVERSIDE, PENNIVALE CL., HEDGE, ROOSEVELT AVE, School, Cemy, KING ST, DIGBY ST, ASHWELL ST, MILL ROAD, PLUMTREE LA, EAST ST, ATTERBURY AVE, MILES AVENUE, VANDYKE ROAD, QUEEN ST, CHURCH ST, BAKER, Health Centre, WEST SIDE, BEDFORD ST, LAMMAS WALK, Council Offices, GEORGE ST, REGENT ST, Pol. Sta. Mag. Ct, HOCKCLIFFE ROAD, THE MARTINS DRIVE, BOSSINGTON LA, ROTHSCHILD RD, LIME GRO., N, Union Canal, Mill Race, WINDSOR AVE, BASSETT RD, ODGLEY ST, School, RELIEF STREET, HOCKCLIFFE RD, HARTWELL CRES., ALBANY ROAD, WOODMAN CL., BROOKLANDS DRIVE, VIMY RD, Council Offices, WEST STREET, The Bossard Centre, HIGH ST, MKT SQ., LAKE ST, DUDLEY ST, STEPPING STONE WALK, SOUTH STREET, OLD RD, NEW RD, CH. RD, SHIP RD, WING RD, Schools, P.O., PULFORD RD, CHURCH AVE, Fire Station, Liby, School, Rec. Gnd, GROVE RD, HARROW RD, STANBRIDGE ROAD, MENTMORE ROAD, CAMBERTON RD, Meml Playing Fields, Clipstone Brook, Sports Ground, GROVEBURY ROAD, BILLINGTON ROAD

N

Central Dunstable

WESTFIELD ROAD, LORING ROAD, BOWER AVE, MAIDEN ROAD, Chiltern Radio, PARK ST, CROFT GREEN, BEECH GREEN, VICTORIA ST, WATERLOW RD, CLIFTON RD, GEORGE ST, ASHTON RD, Baths, BEECROFT, WORTHING TON ROAD, BENNING AVE, UNION STREET, WEST PARADE, STUART ST, EDWARD ST, WINFIELD ST, School, Council Depot, Health Centre, P.O., Council Offices, VERNON PL., Library, Recreation Centre, Dunstable Park, Vauxhall Motors, Queensway Hall, College, COURT DRIVE, KINGSCROFT AVE, Ambulance Station, LEIGHTON CT, Sports Ground, PRINCES ST, ALBION ST, MATT ST, NORTH ST, AA, School, HIGH STREET SOUTH, KINGS WAY, Mineral Line, Fairview Trading Estate, WEST STREET, Cemy, KIRBY ROAD, BURR ST, Sch. ST, NIELD ST, Pol. Sta., ASHTON SQ., CHURCH STREET, PRIORY RD, ST PETERS RD, ST ALFRED, CANESWORDE RD, Recreation Ground, OSBORNE RD, FIRST AVE, BULL PND, FRIARS WALK, BRITAIN ST, LOVERS WALK, RICHARD ST, ENGLANDS LANE, GREAT NORTHERN ROAD, CANESWORDE ROAD, LANGDALE ROAD, APPLEBY GDNS, ENNERDALE, KESWICK, MERE CL., AGGRAS CL., DALE CL., PATTERDALE, AVENUE, Rugby Club, PENRITH AVE, Cricket Ground, HAWTHORN CL., GARDEN ROAD, KING ST, PARK RD, GROVE ROAD, DOWNS ROAD, School, HILTON AVE, TARNSIDE CL., KIRKSTONE, CARTMEL DRIVE, STAVELY ROAD, FURNESS AVE, BRAMPTON RISE, PERIWINKLE LA., Water Works, HOWARD RD, HALF MOON LA., BLOWS RD, ALLEN CT, Spts Gnd

N

Luton

Huge numbers of people go to Luton each year; for most the stay is very brief since it is the starting-off point for holidays on the Mediterranean and all over Europe. The airport has become Luton's best-known feature, but the town prospered for a long time before the advent of aeroplanes. Straw plaiting and straw hat making were the mainstays of its fortunes from the 19th century onwards, and even today hats are still made here. In the town's museum and art gallery, at Wardown Park, are exhibits of the hat trade, and of the pillow lace trade, another of the town's traditional industries. Also in the museum are exhibits devoted to natural history and local life, including a 'Luton Life' gallery complete with reconstructed street scene. St Mary's is the parish church. It is a huge building – one of the largest churches in England – containing much of interest. It dates principally from the 13th to 15th centuries, and has a spectacular font of Purbeck marble, along with many monuments and excellent carving in stone and wood. Just to the south of the town is Luton Hoo, a palatial mansion built to the designs of Robert Adam. It contains a notable collection of pictures and tapestries and sumptuous Fabergé jewellery. The mansion is surrounded by a magnificently landscaped 1,500-acre park laid out by Capability Brown in the 18th century.

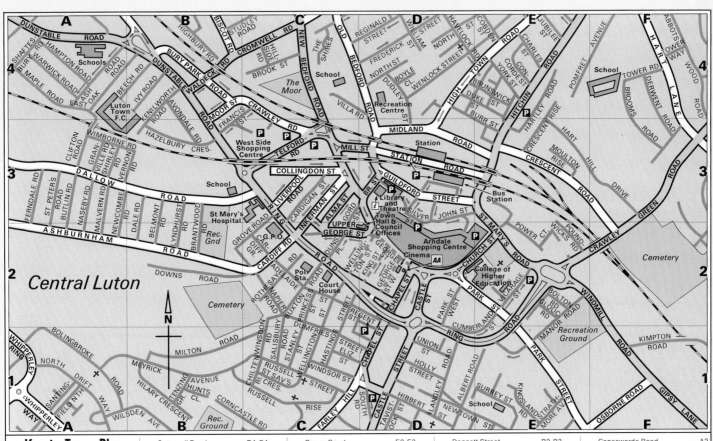

Central Luton

Key to Town Plan and Area Plan

Town Plan

AA Recommended roads
Other roads
Restricted roads
Buildings of interest — Library
Churches — †
Car Parks — P
Parks and open spaces
AA Service Centre — AA
One way street — →

Area Plan

A roads
B roads
Locations — Kensworth ○
Urban area

Street Index

Luton

Abbots Wood Road	F4
Adelaide Street	C2
Albert Road	D1-E1
Alma Street	C2-C3
Ashburnham Road	A3- 2-B2-C2
Ash Road	A4
Avondale Road	B4-B3
Beech Road	A4-B4
Belmont Road	B2-B3
Biscot Road	B4
Bolingbroke Road	A1
Bolton Road	E2
Boyle Close	D4
Brantwood Road	B2-B3
Bridge Street	D3
Brook Street	C4
Brooms Road	F3-F4
Brunswick Street	D4-E4
Burr Street	D4-D3-E4
Bury Park Road	B4
Butlin Road	A2-A3
Buxton Road	C2
Cardiff Grove	C2
Cardiff Road	C2
Cardigan Street	C3
Castle Street	D1-D2
Charles Street	E4
Chapel Street	D1-D2
Chilton Rise	C1
Church Street	D2-E2
Clifton Road	A3
Cobden Street	E4
Collingdon Street	C3
Concorde Street	E4
Corncastle Road	B1-C1
Crawley Green Road	E2-F2-F3
Crawley Road	C3-C4
Crescent Rise	E3-E4
Crescent Road	E3-F3-F2

Cromwell Road	B4-C4
Cumberland Street	D1-E1-E2
Dale Road	B2-B3
Dallow Road	A3-B3-C3
Derwent Road	F3-F4
Downs Road	B2-C2
Dudley Street	D3-D4
Duke Street	D4-E4
Dumfries Street	C2-C1-D1
Dunstable Place	C2
Dunstable Road	A4-B4-B3
Elizabeth Street	C1-D1
Farley Hill	C1
Ferndale Road	A3
Francis Street	B3-B4-C4
Frederick Street	D4
George Street	D2
George Street West	D2
Gipsy Lane	F1
Gloucester Road	E2
Gordon Street	C2-C3-D3
Granville Road	A3
Grove Road	B2-C3-C3
Guildford Street	D3
Hampton Road	A4
Hart Hill Drive	E3-F3
Hart Lane	F3-F4
Hartley Road	E3-E4
Hastings Street	C1-C2
Havelock Road	D4-E4
Hazelbury Crescent	B4
Hibbert Street	D1
Highbury Road	B4
Hightown Road	D3-D4-E4
Hilary Crescent	B1
Hillside Road	C4
Hitchin Road	E3-E4
Holly Street	D1
Hunts Close	B1
Inkerman Street	C2-C3
Ivy Road	B4
John Street	D3
Jubilee Street	E4
Kenilworth Road	B3-B4
Kimpton Road	F1
Kingsland Road	E1
King Street	D2
Langley Road	D1
Liverpool Road	C3
Lyndhurst Road	B2-B3
Malvern Road	A2-A3
Manor Road	E1-E2
Maple Road East	A4
Meyrick Avenue	A1-B1-C1
Midland Road	D3-E3
Mill Street	C3-D3
Milton Road	B1-C1
Moor Road	B3-B4-C4
Moulton Rise	E3
Napier Road	C2
Naseby Road	A2-A3
New Bedford Road	C3-C4
Newcombe Road	A2-A3-B3
Newtown Street	D1-E1
North Drift Way	A1
North Street	D4-E4
Oak Road	A4-B4
Old Bedford Road	C4-D4-D3
Osborne Road	E1-F1
Park Street	D2-E2-E1
Park Street West	D2
Pomfret Avenue	E4-F4
Poundwicks Road	E2-E3

Power Court	E2-E3
Princess Street	C2
Regent Street	C2-D2
Reginald Street	C4-D4
Ring Road	C3-C2-D2-D1-E1-E2
Rothesay Road	C2
Russel Rise	C1
Russell Street	C1
St Mary's Road	E2-E3
St Peter's Road	A2-A3
St Saviors Crescent	C1
Salisbury Road	C1-C2
Santingfield North	A1
Shaftesbury Road	A4
Shirley Road	A3
Silver Street	D2-D3
South Road	D1
Stanley Street	C1-C2
Station Road	D3-E3
Strathmore Avenue	E1
Studley Road	B4-C4
Surrey Street	E1
Tavistock Street	D1
Telford Road	C3
Tenzing Grove	B1
The Shires	C4
Tower Road	F4
Tower Way	F4
Union Street	D1
Upper George Street	C2-D2
Vernon Road	A3-B3
Vicarage Street	E2
Villa Road	C4-D4
Waldeck Road	B4
Warwick Road	A4
Wellington Street	C1-C2-D2
Wenlock Street	D4
Whipperley Ring	A1
Whipperley Way	A1
William Street	D4
Wilsden Avenue	A1-B1
Wimborne Road	A3-B3
Windmill Road	E2-F2-F1
Windsor Street	C1
Winsdon Road	C1-C2
York Street	E4

Leighton Buzzard

Albany Road	C2
Ashwell Street	B3
Atterbury Avenue	C3
Baker Street	B3
Bassett Road	A2-B2-B3
Beaudesert	B3-C3
Bedford Street	B3
Billington Road	C1
Bossington Lane	A2-A3-A4
Bridge Street	A2-B2
Brooklands Drive	C2
Broomhills Road	B4-C4
Camberton Road	A1
Church Avenue	B2
Church Road	A2
Churchill Road	C4
Church Square	B2
Church Street	B2
Clarence Road	B4-C4
Digby Street	B3

Doggett Street	B2-B3
Dudley Street	B2-C2
East Street	B3-C3
Garden Hedge	B3-B4-C4
George Street	C3
Grovebury Road	B1-C1
Grove Road	B1-B2
Harrow Road	C1
Hartwell Crescent	B2-C2
Heath Road	B3-B4
High Street	B2
Hockcliffe Road	C2-C3
Hockcliffe Street	B2-C2
King Road	B3
Lake Street	B2-B1-C1
Lammas Walk	B2-B3
Leighton Road	A2
Lime Grove	A3
Market Square	B2
Mentmore Road	A1
Miles Avenue	C3
Mill Road	B3
Nelson Road	C4
New Road	A2
North Court	B4
North Street	B2-B3
Oakley Green	C4
Old Road	A2
Pennivale Close	B3-B4
Plantation Road	B3-B4
Plumtree Lane	B3-C3
Pulford Road	B2
Queen Street	B3
Regent Street	C3
Relief Road	B2
Riverside	B4
Rothschild Road	A3
Roosevelt Avenue	C4
Ship Road	B2
South Street	C1-C2
Stanbridge Road	C1
Steppingstone Place	C2
Stoke Road	A2-A3-A4
The Martins Drive	A4
The Paddock	A4
Vandyke Road	C2-C3-C4
Vimy Road	A2
West Side	B3
West Street	A2-B2
Windsor Avenue	A3-B3
Wing Road	A1-A2
Winston Close	B4-C4
Woodman Close	C2

Dunstable

Albion Street	B3
Alfred Street	C2
Allen Close	C1
Appleby Gardens	A1-A2
Ashton Road	B4
Ashton Square	B2-B3
Beech Green	A4
Beechcroft Way	A4
Benning Avenue	A3-A4
Blows Road	C1
Borough Road	C1
Brampton Rise	A1-B1
Britain Street	B2-C2
Bull Pond Lane	B1-B2
Burr Street	A3-A2-B2

Canesworde Road	A2
Cartmel Drive	A1
Chiltern Road	A3-A4-B4
Church Street	B3-C3-C2
Clifton Road	A4-B4
Court Drive	B3-C3
Croft Green	A4
Downs Road	C1
Edward Street	B3-B4
Englands Lane	C2
Ennerdale Avenue	A2
First Avenue	A2-B2
Friars Walk	B2
Furness Avenue	B1
Garden Road	B1
George Street	B4
Grasmere Close	A1-A2
Great Northern Road	B1-C1-C2
Grove Road	C1
Half Moon Lane	C1
Hawthorn Close	B1
High Street North	B3-B4
High Street South	B3-B2-B1-C1
Hilton Avenue	A1
Howard Place	C1
Icknield Street	B2-B3
Keswick Close	A1-A2
Kingscroft Avenue	C3
Kingsway	C3
King Street	B1-C1-C2
Kirby Road	A2-A3
Kirkstone Drive	A1
Langdale Road	A1-A2
Leighton Court	A3
Loring Road	A4
Lovers Walk	B2-C2
Maidenbower Avenue	A1
Matthew Street	B3
Osborne Road	A2
Park Road	C1
Park Street	B4
Patterdale Close	A1
Penrith Avenue	A2-B2-B1
Periwinkle Lane	B1
Princes Street	A4-A3-B3
Priory Road	C2
Richard Street	C2
St Peter's Road	C2
Stavely Road	A1
Stuart Street	B4
Tarnside Close	A1
Union Street	A4-B4
Vernon Place	B3
Victoria Street	A4-B4-B3
Waterlow Road	A4-B4
Westfield Road	A4
West Parade	A3
West Street	A3-B3
Winfield Street	B4
Worthington Road	A4

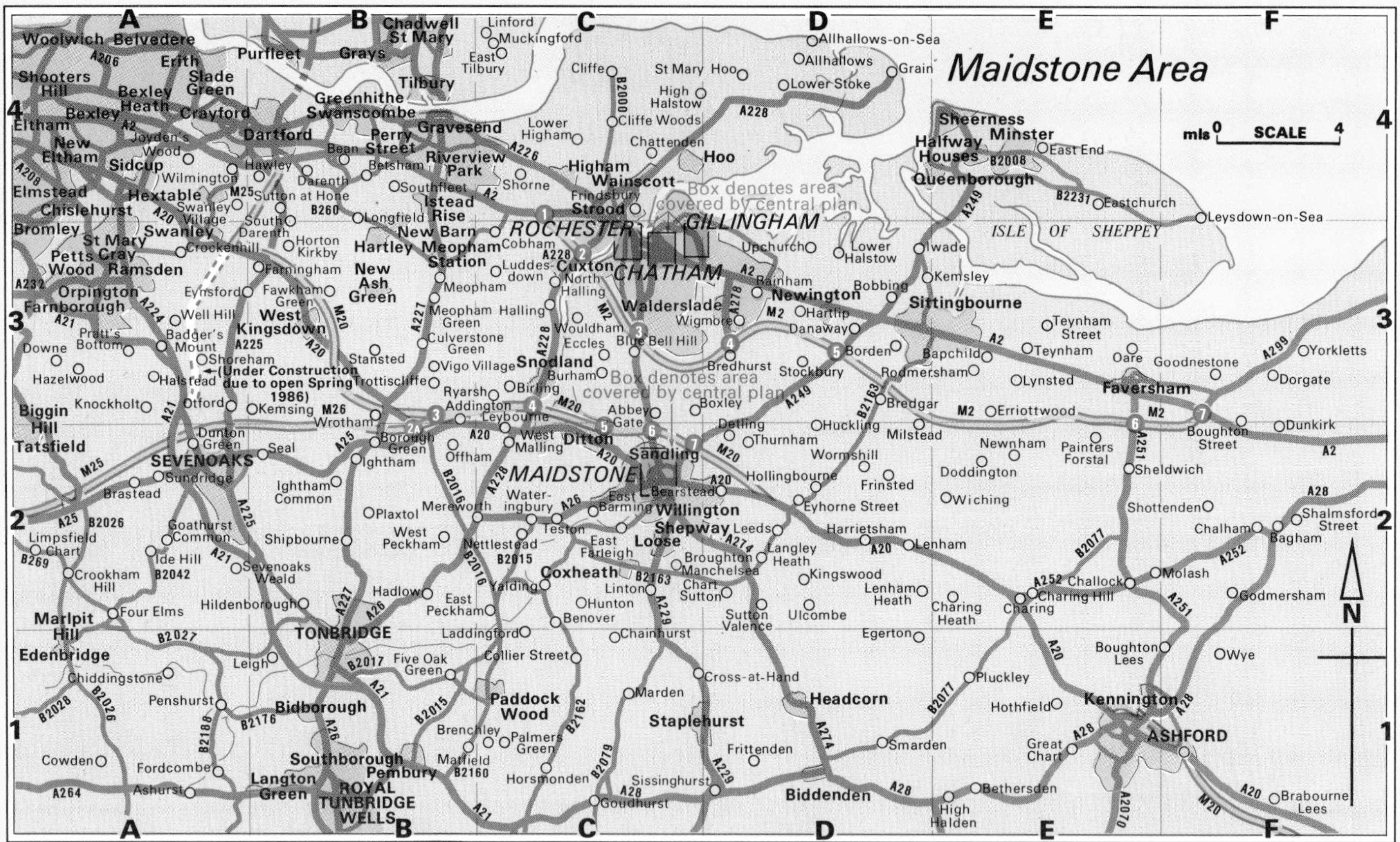

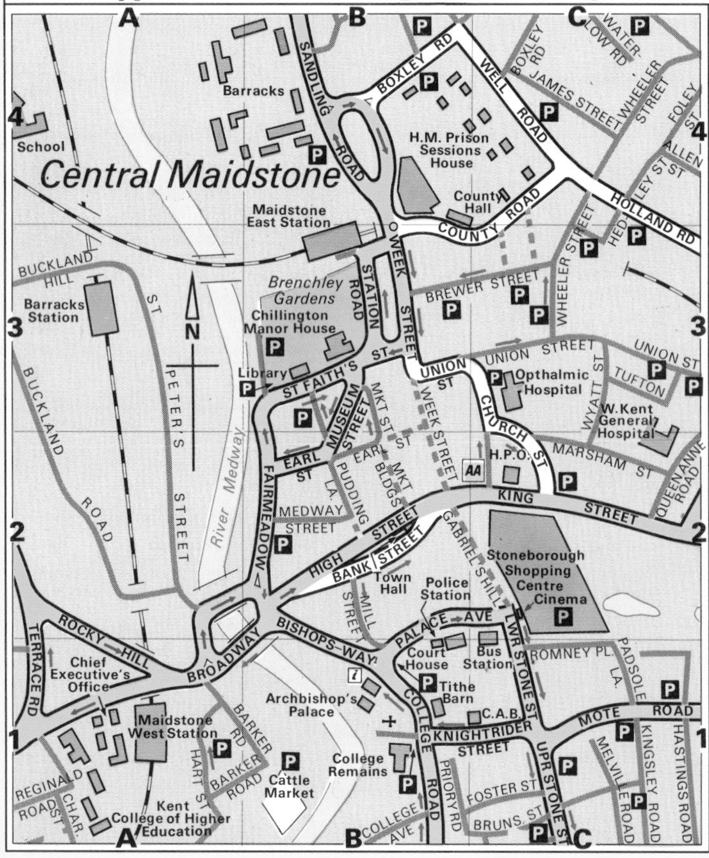

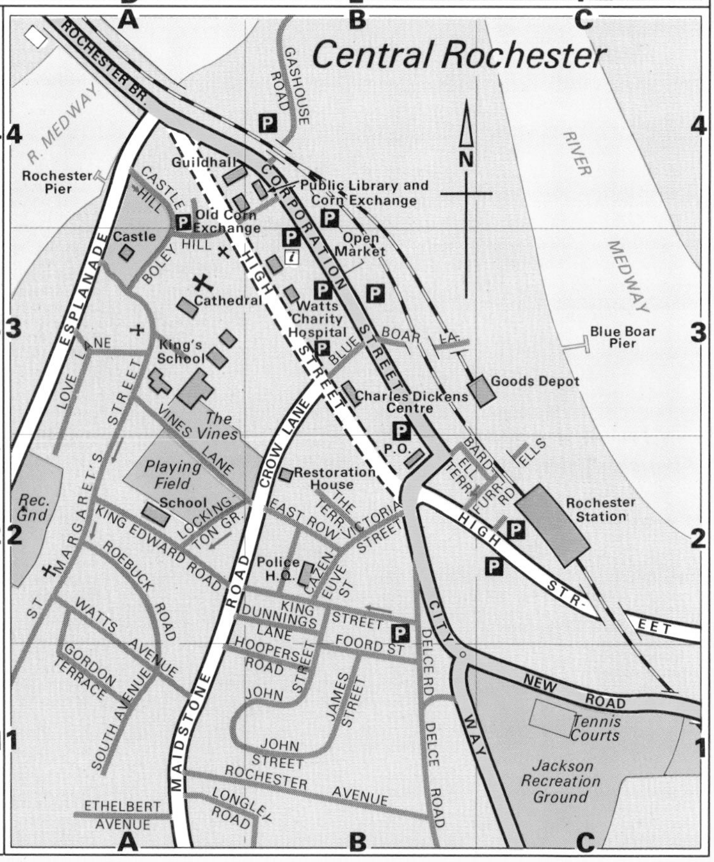

Maidstone Area

ISLE OF SHEPPEY

Box denotes area covered by central plan

Box denotes area covered by central plan

SCALE

N

Central Maidstone

N

Central Rochester

N

RIVER MEDWAY

Maidstone

County town of Kent, Maidstone has long been a place of importance. The ruins of the 14th-century Archbishop's Palace overlook the River Medway, and Allington Castle dates from the 13th century. Maidstone Museum and Art Gallery explores the town's extensive history; also of interest is the Tyrwhitt-Drake Museum of Carriages, housed in the Palace stables.

Rochester Medieval walls enclose the Norman castle and cathedral of this attractive and historic town, but its quaint old shops, inns and tea shops give it a distinctly Victorian flavour. Charles Dickens spent much of his life in the area and featured Rochester in his novels: justly proud of its associations with the great man, the town boasts an award-winning Charles Dickens Centre.

Gillingham has been associated with the nearby Royal Naval Dockyard since Tudor times and it continues the tradition with the Royal Naval Barracks and the Royal School of Military Engineering, both situated in the Brompton area.

Chatham Home of the Royal Naval Dockyard since the 16th century, Chatham today is dominated by the office tower block which crowns the Pentagon Centre, a shopping and entertainments complex. Pleasant riverside gardens have been laid out on the site of the old Gun Wharf, and the Medway Heritage Centre is in Dock Road.

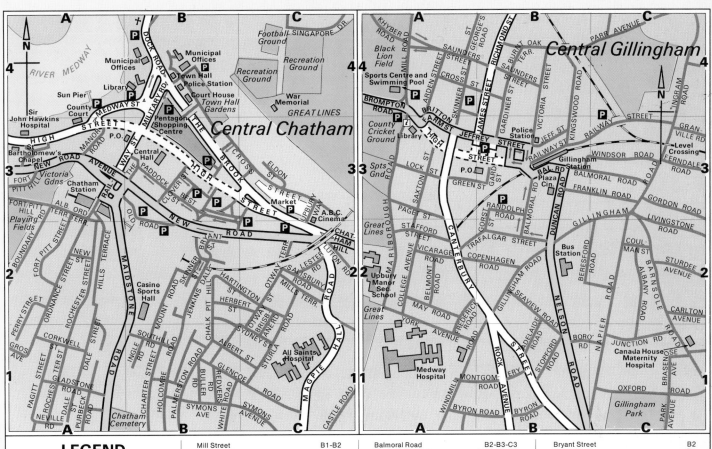

LEGEND

Town Plan
AA Recommended roads
Restricted roads
Other roads
Buildings of interest — Station
Churches — +
Parks and open spaces
Car Parks — P
One Way Streets — ↳

Area Plan
A roads
B roads
Locations — Muckingford ○
Urban area

Street Index with Grid Reference

Maidstone

Allen Street	C4
Bank Street	B2
Barker Road	A1-B1
Bishops Way	B1-B2
Boxley Road	B4-C4
Brewer Street	B3-C3
Broadway	A1-B1-B2
Brunswick Street	C1
Buckland Hill	A3
Buckland Road	A2-A3
Charles Street	A1
Church Street	C2-C3
College Avenue	B1
College Road	B1
County Road	B4-B3-C3-C4
Earl Street	B2-B3
Fairmeadow	B2-B3
Foley Street	C4
Foster Street	B1-C1
Gabriel's Hill	B2-C2
Hart Street	A1
Hastings Road	C1
Hedley Street	C3-C4
High Street	B2
Holland Road	C3-C4
James Street	C4
Kingsley Road	C1
King Street	B2-C2
Knightrider Street	B1-C1
Lower Stone Street	C1-C2
Market Buildings	B2
Market Street	B2-B3
Marsham Street	C2
Medway Street	B2
Melville Road	C1
Mill Street	B1-B2
Mote Road	C1
Museum Street	B2-B3
Padsole Lane	C1
Palace Avenue	B1-B2-C2
Priory Road	B1
Pudding Lane	B2
Queen Anne Road	C2
Reginald Road	A1
Rocky Hill	A1-A2
Romney Place	C1
St Faith's Street	B3
St Peter's Street	A2-A3
Sandling Road	B4
Station Road	B3
Terrace Road	A1-A2
Tufton Street	C3
Union Street	C1
Upper Stone Street	C1
Waterlow Road	C4
Week Street	B2-B3
Well Road	B4-C4
Wheeler Street	C3-C4
Wyatt Street	C2-C3

Rochester

Bardell Terrace	B2-C2
Blue Boar Lane	B3
Boley Hill	A3
Castle Hill	A3-A4
Cazeneuve Street	B2
City Way	B2-B1-C1
Corporation Street	A4-B4-B3-B2
Crow Lane	B2-B3
Delce Road	B1-B2
Dunnings Lane	A2-B2
East Row	B2
Esplanade	A2-A3-A4
Ethelbert Avenue	A1
Foord Street	B1
Furrells Road	B2-C2
Gashouse Road	B4
Gordon Terrace	A1
High Street	A4-A3-B3-B2-C2
Hoopers Road	A1-B1
James Street	B1
John Street	B2-B1-A1-B1
King Edward Road	A2
King Street	B2
Lockington Grove	A2-B2
Longley Road	A1-B1
Love Lane	A2-A3
Maidstone Road	A1-A2-B2
New Road	B1-C1
Rochester Avenue	A1-B1
Rochester Bridge	A4
Roebuck Road	A1-A2
St Margaret's Street	A1-A2-A3
South Avenue	A1
The Terrace	B2
Victoria Street	B2
Vines Lane	A3-A2-B2
Watts Avenue	A1-A2

Gillingham

Adelaide Road	B1-B2
Albany Road	C1-C2
Arden Street	A4
Balmoral Road	B2-B3-C3
Barnsole Road	C1-C2-C3
Belmont Road	A2
Beresford Road	C2-B2-C2
Borough Road	B1-C1
Brasenose Avenue	C1
Britton Farm Street	A3-A4
Brompton Road	A4
Burnt Oak Terrace	B4
Byron Road	A1-B1
Canterbury Street	A3-A2-B2-B1
Carlton Avenue	C2
College Avenue	A2
Copenhagen Road	A2-B2
Coulman Street	C2
Cross Street	A4-B4
Duncan Road	B2-B3
Ferndale Road	C3
Franklin Road	B3-C3
Frederick Road	A1-A2
Gardiner Street	B3-B4
Gillingham Road	B2-B3-C2
Gordon Road	C3
Gorst Street	B2-B3
Granville Road	C3
Green Street	A3-B3
High Street	A3-B3
Ingram Road	C3-C4
James Street	A3-B3-B4
Jeffery Street	A3-B3
Junction Road	C1
Khyber Road	A4
Kingswood Road	B3-B4
Lester Road	C2-C3
Livingstone Road	C2-C3
Lock Street	A3
Marlborough Road	A2-A3-A4
May Road	A2
Mill Road	A4
Montgomery Road	A1-B1
Napier Road	B1-C1-C2-C3
Nelson Road	B2-B1-C1
Oxford Road	C1
Paget Street	A3
Park Avenue	C1
Parr Avenue	B4-C4
Railway Street	B3-C3
Randolph Road	B3
Richmond Street	B4
Rock Avenue	B1-B2
St George's Road	A4-B4
Saunders Street	A4-B4
Saxton Street	A2-A3
Seaview Road	B1-B2
Skinner Street	A3-A4
Stafford Street	A2
Stopford Road	B1
Sturdee Avenue	C2
Trafalgar Street	A2-B2
Vicarage Road	A2
Victoria Street	B3-B4
Windmill Road	A1-B1-B2
Windsor Road	B3-C3
York Avenue	A1-A2

Chatham

Albany Terrace	A3
Albert Street	B1-C1
Best Street	B3
Boundary Road	A2-A3
Brisbane Road	C1-C2
Bryant Street	B2
Buller Road	B1
Castle Road	C1
Chalk Pit Hill	B1-B2
Charter Street	B1
Chatham Hill	C2
Clover Street	B3
Corkwell Street	A1
Cross Street	B3-C3
Dale Street	A1-A2
Dock Road	B4
Eldon Street	C3
Fort Pitt Hill	A3
Fort Pitt Street	A2-A3
Gladstone Road	A1
Glencoe Road	B1-C1
Grosvenor Avenue	A1
Hartington Street	B2-C2
Herbert Street	B2-C2
High Street	A3-B3-C3
Hills Terrace	A2
Holcombe Road	B1-B2
Ingle Road	B1
Jenkins Dale	B2
Lester Road	C2
Luton Road	C2
Magpie Hall Road	C1-C2
Maidstone Road	A3-A2-B2-B1-A1
Manor Road	A3
Medway Street	A3-A4-B4
Military Road	B3-B4
Mills Terrace	C2
Mount Road	B1-B2
Neville Road	A1
New Road	B3-B2-C2
New Road Avenue	A3-B3
New Street	A2
Old Road	A3-B3-B2
Ordnance Street	A1-A2-A3
Ordnance Terrace	A3
Otway Street	C1-C2
Otway Terrace	C2
Pagitt Street	A1
Palmerston Road	B1
Perry Street	A1-A2
Purbeck Road	A1
Railway Street	A3-B3
Redvers Road	B1
Rochester Street	A1-A2
Salisbury Road	C2
Singapore Drive	C4
Skinner Street	B2
Southill Road	B1
Sturla Road	C1-C2
Sydney Street	B2-C2-C1
Symons Avenue	B1-C1
The Brook	B4-B3-C3
The Paddock	B3
Upbury Way	C2-C3
White Road	B1

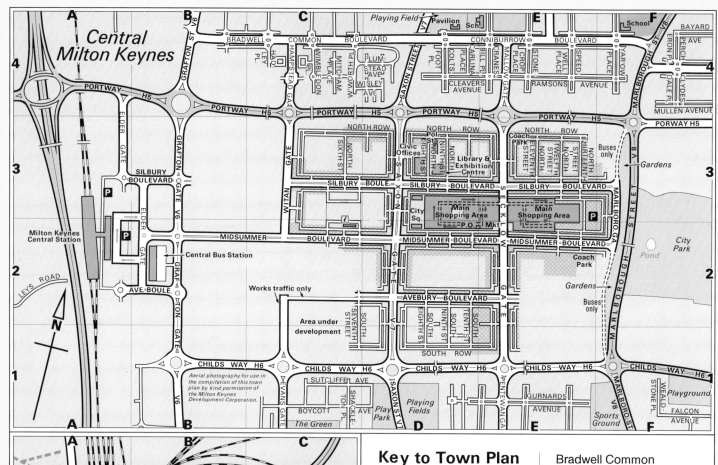

Central Milton Keynes

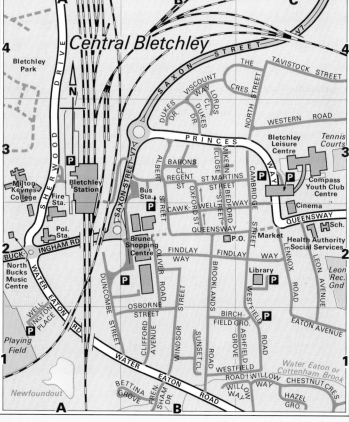

Central Bletchley

Key to Town Plan and Area Plan

Town Plan

AA Recommended roads	
Other roads	
Restricted roads	
Buildings of interest	Library
Parks and open spaces	
Car parks and car parking areas	P
One Way Streets	

Area Plan

A roads	
B roads	
Locations	Stanford O
Urban area	

STREET INDEX- with grid reference

Milton Keynes

Avebury Boulevard
            A2-B2, C2-D2-E2
Bayard Avenue   F4
Boycott Avenue   C1-D1

Bradwell Common
Boulevard   B4-C4-D4
Carlina Place   D4
Childs Way
            B1-C1-D1-E1-F1
Cleavers Avenue   D4-E4
Clydesdale Place   F4
Coltsfoot Place   D4
Conniburrow Boulevard
            D4-E4-F4
Cranesbill Place   E4
Elder Gate A4-A3, B3-B2
Evans Gate   C1
Falcon Avenue   F1
Grafton Gate   B1-B2-B3
Grafton Street   B4
Gurnards Avenue   E1
Hadley Place   C4
Hampstead Gate   C4
Leys Road   A2
Mallow Gate   E4
Marlborough Gate F2-F3
Marlborough Street
            F1-F2-F3-F4
Midsummer Boulevard
            B2-C2-D2-E2-F2

Milton-Keynes

The most famous of Britain's New Towns, Milton Keynes was officially opened in 1973. The new city was carefully and considerately planned to integrate with the existing towns and villages and countryside, and yet provide a self-sufficient community where industry, business and housing could develop.

Milton Keynes borough covers some 22,000 acres of North Buckinghamshire, including the towns of Bletchley, Stony Stratford and Wolverton, but the hub of the region is Central Milton Keynes. Here, one of the largest and most attractive shopping areas in Britain can be found. All the shops are under cover and are reached from tall glass-walled arcades paved with marble and lined with exotic trees and shrubs.

The variety of modern housing in Milton Keynes is another of the city's exciting attractions.

Purpose-built homes have been imaginatively planned to suit all ages, and the residential areas have generous areas of green open spaces.

Recreational facilities are also an integral part of the city's concept. Bletchley – one of three leisure centres – has a huge multi-purpose sports hall where international events are held, and an exotic free-form swimming pool. Here, beneath the tinted glass of the pyramidal building, real palm trees create a Mediterranean atmosphere.

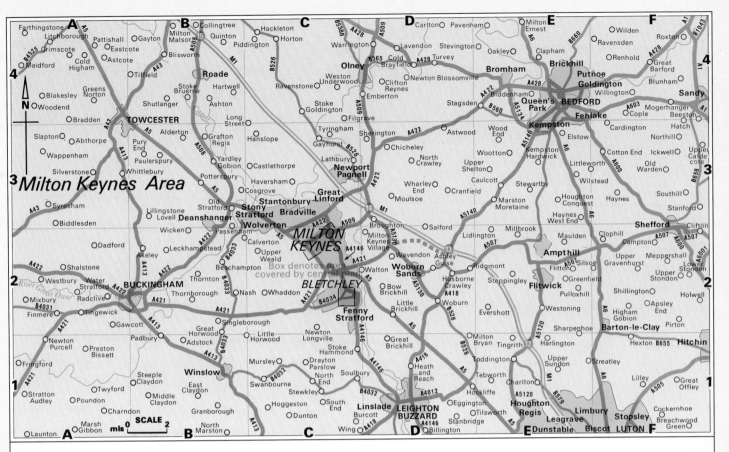

Map of **Milton Keynes Area** with grid references A–F (columns) and 1–4 (rows). Labelled places include: Farthingstone, Litchborough, Gayton, Collingtree, Hackleton, Milton Malsor, Quinton, Piddington, Horton, Warrington, Carlton, Pavenham, Milton Ernest, Wilden, Ravensden, Roxton, Pattishall, Eastcote, Gayton, Cold Brayfield, Lavendon, Stevington, Oakley, Clapham, Brickhill, Renhold, Great Barford, Grimscote, Bliss worth, Olney, Turvey, Bromham, Putnoe, Goldington, Blunham, Maidford, Cold Higham, Tiffield, Roade, Hartwell, Weston Underwood, Clifton Reynes, Newton Blossomville, Stagsden, Biddenham, Queen's Park, BEDFORD, Willington, Sandy, Blakesley, Greens Norton, Shutlanger, Ashton, Ravenstone, Stoke Goldington, Emberton, Astwood, Wood End, Kempston, Fenlake, Cardington, Cople, Mogerhanger, Beeston, Woodend, Stoke Bruerne, Long Street, Filgrave, Tyringham, Sherington, Chicheley, North Crawley, Elstow, Kempston Hardwick, Hatch, Northill, Upper Caldecote, Bradden, TOWCESTER, Alderton, Grafton Regis, Hanslope, Gayhurst, Lathbury, Newport Pagnell, Upper Shelton, Wootton, Cotton End, Ickwell, Old Warden, Slapton, Abthorpe, Pury End, Yardley Gobion, Castlethorpe, Haversham, Great Linford, Wharley End, Cranfield, Caulcott, Stewartby, Houghton Conquest, Wilstead, Haynes, Southill, Wappenham, Paulerspury, Pottespury, Stantonbury, Bradville, Moulsoe, Marston Moretaine, Haynes West End, Stanford, Silverstone, Whittlebury, Old Stratford, Stony Stratford, MILTON KEYNES, Broughton, Salford, Millbrook, Maulden, Clophill, Campton, Shefford, Clifton, Syresham, Lillingstone Lovell, Deanshanger, Wolverton, Milton Keynes Village, Lidlington, Ampthill, Upper Gravenhurst, Meppershall, Upper Stondon, Lower Stondon, Biddlesden, Dadford, Wicken, Passenham, Calverton, Upper Weald, Woburn Sands, Husborne Crawley, Ridgmont, Steppingley, Flitton, Silsoe, Greenfield, Shillington, Holwell, Westbury, Water Stratford, Beachampton, Thornton, Nash, Whaddon, Walton, Bow Brickhill, Flitwick, Pulloxhill, Apsley End, BUCKINGHAM, Radclive, Thornborough, BLETCHLEY, Little Brickhill, Woburn, Evershott, Westoning, Higham Gobion, Pirton, Barton-le-Clay, Mixbury, Finmere, Tingewick, Gawcott, Padbury, Singleborough, Fenny Stratford, Great Horwood, Little Horwood, Newton Longville, Stoke Hammond, Milton Bryan, Tingrith, Harlington, Sharpenhoe, Hexton, Hitchin, Newton Purcell, Preston Bissett, Adstock, Drayton Parslow, Heath and Reach, Toddington, Upper Sundon, Streatley, Fringford, Mursley, Swanbourne, Stewkley, North End, Soulbury, Tebworth, Charlton, Lilley, Great Offley, Stratton Audley, Twyford, East Claydon, Steeple Claydon, Winslow, Middle Claydon, Hoggeston, Dunton, South End, Wing, Linslade, LEIGHTON BUZZARD, Hockliffe, Eggington, Tilsworth, Houghton Regis, Leagrave, Limbury, Stopsley, Cockernhoe, Breachwood Green, Poundon, Charndon, Granborough, North Marston, Burcott, Billington, Stanbridge, DUNSTABLE, Biscot, LUTON.

Scale: mls 0 — 2

Box denotes area covered by central plan

Mitcham Place	C4
Mullen Avenue	F4
North Eighth Street	D3
North Eleventh Street	E3
North Ninth Street	D3
North Row	C3-D3-E3
North Sixth Street	C3
North Thirteenth Street	E3
North Twelfth Steet	E3
Pentewan Gate	E1
Percheron Place	F4
Plumstead Avenue	C4-D4
Portway	A4-B4-C4-D4-E4-E3-F3-F4
Ramsons Avenue	E4-F4
Saxon Gate	D1-D2-D3
Saxon Street	D1, D4
Secklow Gate	E1-E2-E3
Shackleton Place	C1
Silbury Boulevard	A3-B3, C3-D3-E3-F3
South Eighth Street	D1-D2
South Ninth Street	D1-D2
South Row	D1-E1
South Seventh Street	C1-C2
South Tenth Street	D1-D2
Speedwell Place	E4
Stonecrop Place	E4
Sutcliffe Avenue	C1-D1
Wandsworth Place	C4
Wealdstone Place	F1
Wimbledon Place	C4
Wisley Avenue	C4-D4
Witan Gate	C2-C3
Yarrow Place	F4

Bletchley

Albert Street	B2-B3
Ashfield Grove	C1
Barons Close	B3
Bedford Street	B2-B3
Bettina Grove	A1-B1
Birchfield Grove	B1-C1
Brooklands Road	B1-B2
Buckingham Road	A2
Cambridge Street	C2-C3
Cawkwell Way	B2-C2
Chestnut Crescent	C1
Clifford Avenue	B1
Dukes Drive	B3
Duncombe Street	A2-A1-B1
Eaton Avenue	C1
Findlay Way	B2-C2
Frensham Drive	B1
Hazel Grove	C1
Lennox Road	C1-C2
Leon Avenue	C1-C2
Lords Close	B3-B4
Mikern Close	B3
North Street	C3-C4
Oliver Road	B1-B2
Osborne Street	A1-B1
Oxford Street	B2-B3
Princes Way	B3-C3
Queensway	B2-C2
Regent Street	B3
St Martins Street	B3-C3
Saxon Street	A3-A2-B2-B3-B4-C4
Sherwood Drive	A2-A3-A4
Sunset Close	B1
Tavistock Street	C4
The Crescent	B4-C4
Viscount Way	B4
Water Eaton Road	A2-A1-B1-C1
Wellington Place	A1-A2
Western Road	C3
Westfield Road	B1-C1-C2
Willow Way	B1-C1
Windsor Street	B1-B2

MILTON KEYNES
Huge industrial estates and modern factories were built in Milton Keynes during the 1970s to provide employment for the people who moved to the New Town from London as a result of the capital's housing problems.

Central Witney

Central Abingdon

Oxford Area

Oxford

From Carfax (at the centre of the city) round to Magdalen Bridge stretches High Street, one of England's best and most interesting thoroughfares. Shops rub shoulders with churches and colleges, alleyways lead to ancient inns and to a large covered market, and little streets lead to views of some of the finest architecture to be seen anywhere. Catte Street, beside St Mary's Church (whose lovely tower gives a panoramic view of Oxford), opens out into Radcliffe Square, dominated by the Radcliffe Camera, a great round structure built in 1749. Close by is the Bodleian Library, one of the finest collections of books and manuscripts in the world. All around are ancient college buildings. Close to Magdalen Bridge is Magdalen College, founded in 1448 and certainly not to be missed. Across the High Street are the Botanical Gardens, founded in 1621 and the oldest such foundation in England. Footpaths lead through Christ Church Meadow to Christ Church College and the cathedral. Tom Tower is the college's most notable feature; the cathedral is actually its chapel and is the smallest cathedral in England. Among much else not to be missed in Oxford is the Ashmolean Museum, whose vast collections of precious and beautiful objects from all over the world repay many hours of study; perhaps the loveliest treasure is the 9th-century Alfred Jewel.

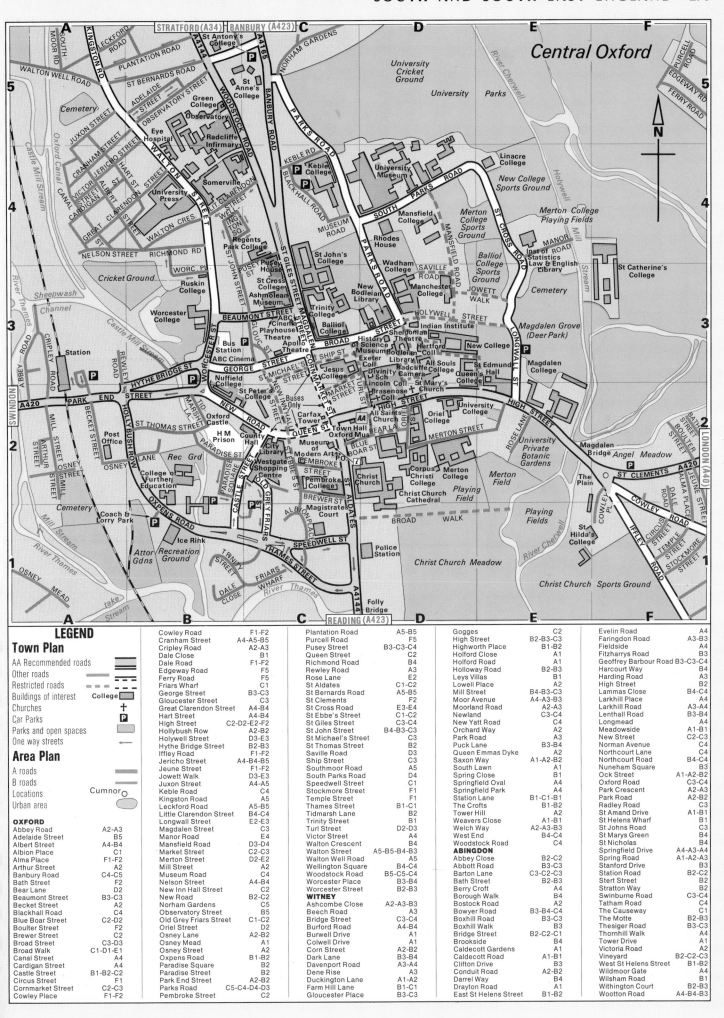

Central Oxford

LEGEND

Town Plan

AA Recommended roads	
Other roads	
Restricted roads	
Buildings of interest	College
Churches	+
Car Parks	P
Parks and open spaces	
One way streets	←

Area Plan

A roads	
B roads	
Locations	Cumnor ○
Urban area	

OXFORD

Abbey Road	A2-A3
Adelaide Street	B5
Albert Street	A4-B4
Albion Place	C1
Alma Place	F1-F2
Arthur Street	A2
Banbury Road	C4-C5
Bath Street	F2
Bear Lane	D2
Beaumont Street	B3-C3
Becket Street	A2
Blackhall Road	C4
Blue Boar Street	C2-D2
Boulter Street	F2
Brewer Street	C2
Broad Street	C3-D3
Broad Walk	C1-D1-E1
Canal Street	A4
Cardigan Street	A4
Castle Street	B1-B2-C2
Circus Street	F1
Cornmarket Street	C2-C3
Cowley Place	F1-F2

Cowley Road	F1-F2
Cranham Street	A4-A5-B5
Cripley Road	A2-A3
Dale Close	B1
Dale Road	F1-F2
Edgeway Road	F5
Ferry Road	F5
Friars Wharf	C1
George Street	B3-C3
Gloucester Street	C3
Great Clarendon Street	A4-B4
Hart Street	A4-B4
High Street	C2-D2-E2-F2
Hollybush Row	A2-B2
Holywell Street	D3-E3
Hythe Bridge Street	B2-B3
Iffley Road	F1-F2
Jericho Street	A4-B4-B5
Jeune Street	F1-F2
Jowett Walk	D3-E3
Juxon Street	A4-A5
Keble Road	C4
Kingston Road	A5
Leckford Road	A5-B5
Little Clarendon Street	B4-C4
Longwall Street	E2-E3
Magdalen Street	C3
Manor Road	E4
Mansfield Road	D3-D4
Market Street	C2-C3
Merton Street	D2-E2
Mill Street	A2
Museum Road	C4
Nelson Street	A4-B4
New Inn Hall Street	C2
New Road	B2-C2
Norham Gardens	C5
Observatory Street	B5
Old Grey Friars Street	C1-C2
Oriel Street	D2
Osney Lane	A2-B2
Osney Mead	A1
Osney Street	A2
Oxpens Road	B1-B2
Paradise Square	B2
Paradise Street	B2
Park End Street	A2-B2
Parks Road	C5-C4-D4-D3
Pembroke Street	C2

Plantation Road	A5-B5
Purcell Road	F5
Pusey Street	B3-C3-C4
Queen Street	C2
Richmond Road	B4
Rewley Road	A3
Rose Lane	E2
St Aldates	C1-C2
St Bernards Road	A5-B5
St Clements	F2
St Cross Road	E3-E4
St Ebbe's Street	C1-C2
St Giles Street	C3-C4
St John Street	B4-B3-C3
St Michael's Street	C3
St Thomas Street	B2
Saville Road	D3
Ship Street	C3
Southmoor Road	A5
South Parks Road	D4
Speedwell Street	C1
Stockmore Street	F1
Temple Street	F1
Thames Street	B1-C1
Tidmarsh Lane	B2
Trinity Street	B1
Turl Street	D2-D3
Victor Street	A4
Walton Crescent	B4
Walton Street	A5-B5-B4-B3
Walton Well Road	A5
Wellington Square	B4-C4
Woodstock Road	B5-C5-C4
Worcester Place	B3-B4
Worcester Street	B2-B3

WITNEY

Ashcombe Close	A2-A3-B3
Beech Road	A3
Bridge Street	C3-C4
Burford Road	A4-B4
Burwell Drive	A1
Colwell Drive	A1
Corn Street	A2-B2
Dark Lane	B3-B4
Davenport Road	A3-A4
Dene Rise	A3
Duckington Lane	A1-A2
Farm Hill Lane	B1-C1
Gloucester Place	B3-C3

Gogges	C2
High Street	B2-B3-C3
Highworth Place	B1-B2
Holford Close	A1
Holford Road	A1
Holloway Road	B2-B3
Leys Villas	B1
Lowell Place	A2
Mill Street	B4-B3-C3
Moor Avenue	A4-A3-B3
Moorland Road	A2-A3
Newland	C3-C4
New Yatt Road	C4
Orchard Way	A2
Park Road	A3
Puck Lane	B3-B4
Queen Emmas Dyke	B3
Saxon Way	A1-A2-B2
South Lawn	B1
Spring Close	B1
Springfield Oval	A4
Springfield Park	A4
Station Lane	B1-C1-B1
The Crofts	B1-B2
Tower Hill	A2
Weavers Close	A1-B1
Welch Way	A2-A3-B3
West End	B4-C4
Woodstock Road	C4

ABINGDON

Abbey Close	B2-C2
Abbott Road	B3-C3
Barton Lane	C3-C2-C3
Bath Street	B2-B3
Berry Croft	A4
Borough Walk	B4
Bostock Road	A2
Bowyer Road	B3-B4-C4
Boxhill Road	B3-C3
Boxhill Walk	B3
Bridge Street	B2-C2-C1
Brookside	B4
Caldecott Gardens	A1
Caldecott Road	A1-B1
Clifton Drive	A4
Conduit Road	A2-B2
Darrel Way	B4
Drayton Road	A1
East St Helens Street	B1-B2

Evelin Road	A4
Faringdon Road	A3-B3
Fieldside	A4
Fitzharrys Road	B3
Geoffrey Barbour Road	B3-C3-C4
Harcourt Way	B4
Harding Road	A3
High Street	B2
Lammas Close	B4-C4
Larkhill Place	A4
Larkhill Road	A3-A4
Lenthall Road	B3-B4
Longmead	A4
Meadowside	A1-B1
New Street	C2-C3
Norman Avenue	C4
Northcourt Lane	C4
Northcourt Road	B4-C4-C4
Nuneham Square	B3
Ock Street	A1-A2-B2
Oxford Road	C3-C2-C4
Park Crescent	A2-A3
Park Road	A2-B2
Radley Road	C3
St Amand Drive	A1-B1
St Helens Wharf	B1
St Johns Road	C3
St Marys Green	B4
St Nicholas	B4
Springfield Drive	A4-A3-A4
Spring Road	A1-A2-A3
Stanford Drive	B3
Station Road	B2-C2
Stert Street	B2
Stratton Way	B2
Swinburne Road	C3-C4
Tatham Road	C4
The Causeway	C1
The Motte	B2-B3
Thesiger Road	B3-C3
Thornhill Walk	A2
Tower Drive	A1
Victoria Road	A1
Vineyard	B2-C2-C3
West St Helens Street	B1-B2
Wildmoor Gate	A4
Wilsham Road	B1
Withington Court	B2-B3
Wootton Road	A4-B4-B3

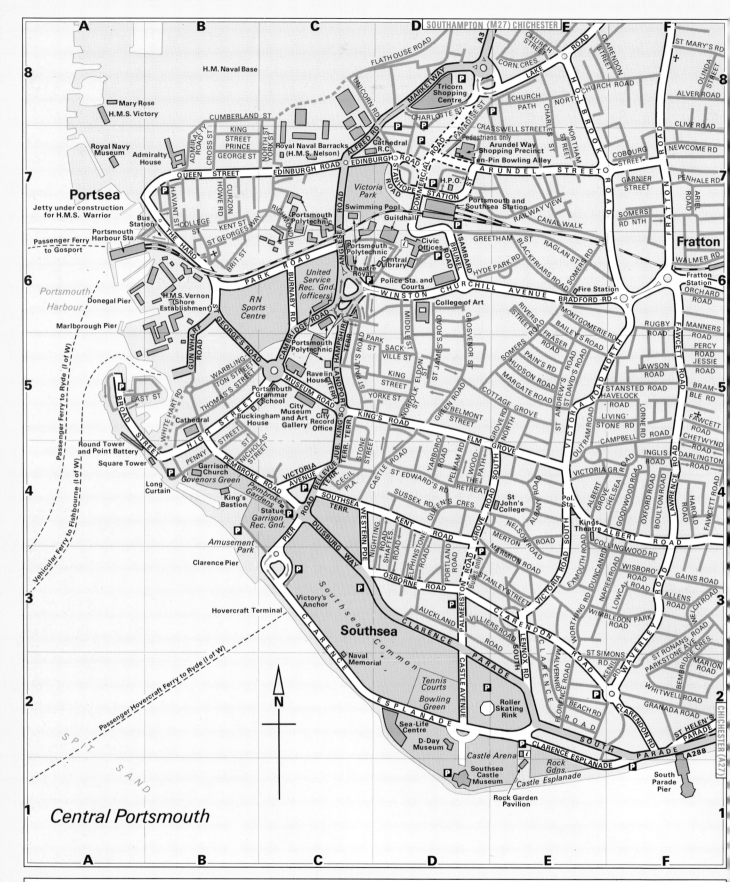

Central Portsmouth

Portsmouth

Richard the Lionheart first recognised the strategic importance of Portsea Island and subsequently ordered the first docks, and later the town of Portsmouth, to be built. Over the centuries, succeeding monarchs improved the defences and extended the docks which now cover some 300 acres – as befits Britain's premier naval base. Of the defensive fortifications, Fort Widley and the Round Tower are the best preserved remains. Two famous ships rest in Portsmouth; HMS Victory and the Mary Rose. The former, Lord Nelson's flagship, has been fully restored and the adjacent Royal Naval museum houses numerous relics of Trafalgar. The Mary Rose, built by Henry VIII, lay on the sea bed off Southsea until she was spectacularly raised in 1982. She has now been put on display and there is an exhibition in Southsea Castle of artefacts that have been recovered from her. Portsmouth suffered greatly from bombing in World War II and the centre has been almost completely rebuilt. However, the old town, clustered around the harbour mouth, escaped severe damage and, now restored, forms an attractive and fashionable area of the city.

Southsea, Portsmouth's near neighbour, developed in the 19th century as an elegant seaside resort with fine houses and terraces, an esplanade and an extensive seafront common.

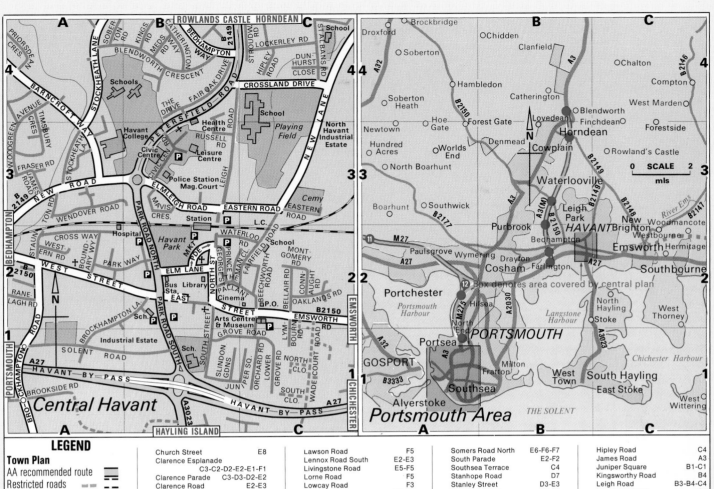

Central Havant

Portsmouth Area

LEGEND

Town Plan

AA recommended route
Restricted roads
Other roads
Buildings of interest   Station
Car parks
Parks and open spaces
One way streets

Area Plan

A roads
B roads
Locations   O Lovedean
Urban area

Street Index with Grid Reference

Portsmouth

Admiralty Road	B7-B8
Albany Road	E4
Albert Grove	E4-F4
Albert Road	E4-F4
Alfred Road	C7-D7-D8
Allens Road	F3
Alver Road	F8
Anglesea Road	C6-C7
Ariel Road	F7
Arundel Street	D7-E7-F7
Auckland Road	D3-E3-E2
Bailey's Road	E5-E6
Beach Road	E2
Bellvue Terrace	C4
Belmont Street	D5
Bembridge Crescent	F2-F3
Blackfriars Road	E6
Boulton Road	F4
Bradford Road	E6-F6
Bramble Road	F5
Britain Street	B6
Broad Street	A5-A4-B4
Burnaby Road	C6
Cambridge Road	C5-C6
Campbell Road	E4-F4-F5
Canal Walk	E6-E7
Castle Avenue	D2-D3
Castle Road	C4-D4-D5
Cecil Place	C4
Charles Street	E7-E8
Charlotte Street	D8
Chelsea Road	F4
Chetwynd Road	F4-F5
Church Path	E8
Church Street	E8
Clarence Esplanade	C3-C2-D2-E2-E1-F1
Clarence Parade	C3-D3-D2-E2
Clarence Road	E2-E3
Clarendon Road	D3-E3-E2-F2
Clarendon Street	E8-F8
Clive Road	F7-F8
Cobourg Street	F7
College Street	B6-B7
Collingwood Road	E4-E3-F3
Commercial Road	D6-D7-D8
Cornwallis Crescent	E8
Cottage Grove	D5-E5
Crasswell Road	D7-E7
Cross Street	B7-B8
Cumberland Street	B8-C8
Curzon Howe Road	B7
Darlington Road	F4
Duisburg Way	C3-C4
Duncan Road	E3-F3-F4
East Street	A5-B5
Edinburgh Road	C7-D7
Eldon Street	D5
Elm Grove	D5-D4-E4
Exmouth Road	E3-E4
Fawcett Road	F4-F5-F6
Elphinstone Road	D3-D4
Flathouse Road	C8-D8
Florence Road	E2
Fraser Road	E5-E6
Fratton Road	F6-F7-F8
Gains Road	F3
Garnier Street	F7
Goodwood Road	F4
Granada Road	F2
Green Road	D5
Greetham Street	D6-E6
Grosvenor Street	D5-D6
Grove Road North	E5
Grove Road South	D4-E4
Gun Wharf Road	B5-B6
Hampshire Terrace	C5-C6
Harold Road	F4
Havant Street	B7
Havelock Road	E5-F5
High Street	B4-B5-C5
Holbrook Road	E7-F7-E8
Hudson Road	F4
Hyde Park Road	D6-E6
Inglis Road	F4
Isambard Brunel Road	D6-D7
Jessie Road	F5
Jubilee Terrace	C4-C5
Kenilworth Road	F2
Kent Road	C4-D4
Kent Street	B7
King Street	B7-C7
King Street	C5-D5
King's Road	C5-D5
King's Terrace	C5
Lake Road	D8-E8
Landport Terrace	C5
Lawrence Road	F4-F5

Lawson Road	F5
Lennox Road South	E2-E3
Livingstone Road	E5-F5
Lorne Road	F5
Lowcay Road	F3
Malvern Road	E2-E3
Manners Road	F5-F6
Margate Road	E5
Marion Road	F2
Market Way	D8
Marmion Road	D4-D3-E3
Merton Road	D4-E4
Middle Street	D5-D6
Montgomerie Road	E6-E5-F5
Museum Road	C5
Napier Road	E3-F3-F4
Nelson Road	D4-E4-E3
Newcombe Road	F7
Nightingale Road	D4-D5
Norfolk Street	D5
North Street	C7-C8
Northam Street	E7
North Church Road	E8-F8
Olinda Street	F8
Orchard Road	F6
Osborne Road	C3-D3
Outram Road	E4-E5
Oxford Road	F4
Pain's Road	E5
Palmerston Road	D3
Paradise Street	D7-D8
Park Road	B6-C6
Park Street	C5-D5
Parkstone Avenue	F2-F3
Pelham Road	D4-D5
Pembroke Road	B4-C4
Penhale Road	F7
Penny Street	B4-B5
Percy Road	F5
Pier Road	C3-C4
Portland Road	D3-D4
Prince George Street	B7-C7
Queen's Crescent	D4
Queen Street	B7
Raglan Street	E6
Railway View	D7-E7
Richmond Place	C6-C7
Rivers Street	E6
Rugby Road	F6
St Andrew's Road	E4-E5-E6
St David's Road	E5
St Edward's Road	D4
St George's Road	B6-B5-C5
St Georges Way	B6-B7-C7
St Helen's Parade	F2
St James's Road	D5-D6
St Mary's Road	F8
St Nicholas' Street	B4-B5
St Paul's Road	C5-C6
St Ronans Road	F2-F3
St Simons Road	E2-F2
Sackville Street	D5
Shaftesbury Road	D3-D4
Somers Road	D5-E5-E6

Somers Road North	E6-F6-F7
South Parade	E2-F2
Southsea Terrace	C4
Stanhope Road	D7
Stanley Street	D3-E3
Stansted Road	E5-F5
Station Street	D7
Stone Street	C4-C5
Sussex Road	D4
The Hard	B6-B7
The Retreat	D4
Thomas's Street	B4-B5-C5
Unicorn Road	C8-D8
Victoria Avenue	C4
Victoria Grove	E4-F4
Victoria Road North	E4-E5-F5-F6
Victoria Road South	E3-E4
Villiers Road	D3-E3
Walmer Road	F6
Warblington Street	B5
Waverley Road	F2-F3-F4
Welch Road	F3
Western Parade	C3-C4
White Hart Road	B4-B5
Whitwell Road	F2
Wimbledon Park Road	E3-F3
Winston Churchill Avenue	C6-D6-E6
Wisborough Road	F3
Woodpath	D4
Worthing Road	E2
Yarborough Road	D4-D5
York Street	C7-C8
Yorke Street	C5-D5

Havant

Barncroft Way	A3-A4
Bedhampton Way	B4
Beechworth Road	C2
Bellair Road	C2
Blendworth Crescent	A4-B4
Brockhampton Lane	A1-A2-B2
Brockhampton Road	A1-A2
Brooksidé Road	A1
Boundary Way	A2
Catherington Way	B4
Civic Centre Road	B3
Connaught Road	C2
Cross Way	A2
Crossland Drive	C4
Dunhurst Close	C4
East Street	B2-C2
Eastern Road	B3-C3
Elm Lane	B2
Elmleigh Road	B3
Emsworth Road	C2
Fairfield Road	B2-C2-C3
Fair Oak Drive	B4
Fraser Road	A3
Grove Road	B1-C1
Havant By-Pass	A1-B1-C1

Hipley Road	C4
James Road	A3
Juniper Square	B1-C1
Kingsworthy Road	B4
Leigh Road	B3-B4-C4
Lockerley Road	C4
Lower Grove Road	C1
Lymbourn Road	C1-C2
Manor Close	B2-C2
Market Parade	B2
Mavis Crescent	B3
Medstead Road	B4
Montgomery Road	C2
New Lane	C3-C4
New Road	A3-B3
North Close	C1
North Street	B2
Oaklands Road	C2
Orchard Road	C1
Park Road North	B2-B3
Park Road South	B1-B2
Park Way	A2-B2
Petersfield Road	B3-B4
Prince George Street	B2
Priorsdean Crescent	A4
Ranelagh Road	A2
Russell Road	B3
St Albans Road	C4
Slindon Gardens	B1
Solent Road	A1-B1
Soberton Road	A4
South Close	C1
South Street	B1-B2
Staunton Road	A2-A3
Stockheath Lane	A3-A4
Stroudwood Road	C4
The Drive	B4
The Pallant	B2-C2
Timsbury Crescent	A3-A4
Wade Court Road	C1-C2
Waterloo Road	B2-C2
Wendover Road	A3-B3
West Street	A2-B2
Western Road	A2
Woodgreen Avenue	A3-A4

Central Reading

LEGEND

Town Plan

AA recommended route
Restricted roads
Other roads
Buildings of interest   School
Car parks   P
Parks and open spaces
One way streets

Area Plan

A roads
B roads
Locations   Wilsden○
Urban area

Reading

Shopping and light industry first spring to mind when thinking of Reading, but the town actually has a long and important history. Its rise to significance began in 1121 when Henry I founded an abbey here which became the third most important in England. However, after the Dissolution of the Monasteries, only a few ruins were left. Reading also used to be one of the major centres of the medieval cloth trade, but, already declining in the early 17th century, this source of income was reduced still further as a result of Civil War disturbances.

A fascinating collection of all types of farm implements and domestic equipment can be found in the extremely comprehensive Museum of English Rural Life, situated in the University Campus at Whiteknights Park. The town's own museum has major displays about nearby Silchester – the powerful Roman town of *Calleva*.

Henley-on-Thames, famous for its annual rowing regatta, is a lovely old town, well-provided with old coaching inns, Georgian façades and numerous listed buildings.

Wokingham has been a market town for centuries and over the years has been known for its silk industry and its bell-foundry. Half-timbered gabled houses can be seen in the town centre, although modern development surrounds it.

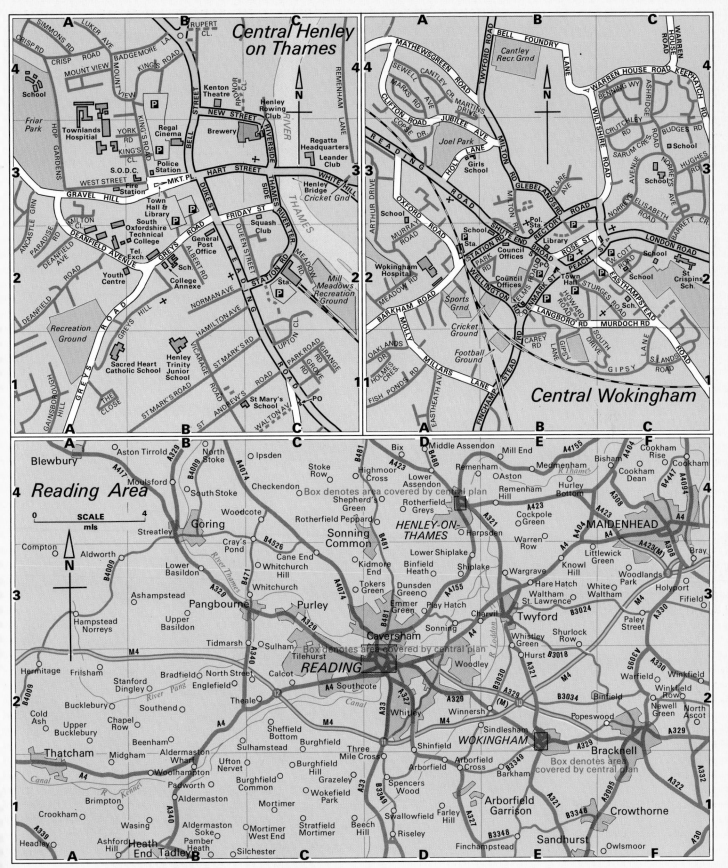

READING
Whiteknights, which consists of 300 acres of landscaped parkland, provides Reading's modern university with an incomparable campus setting and includes a conservation area and a biological reserve for research purposes.

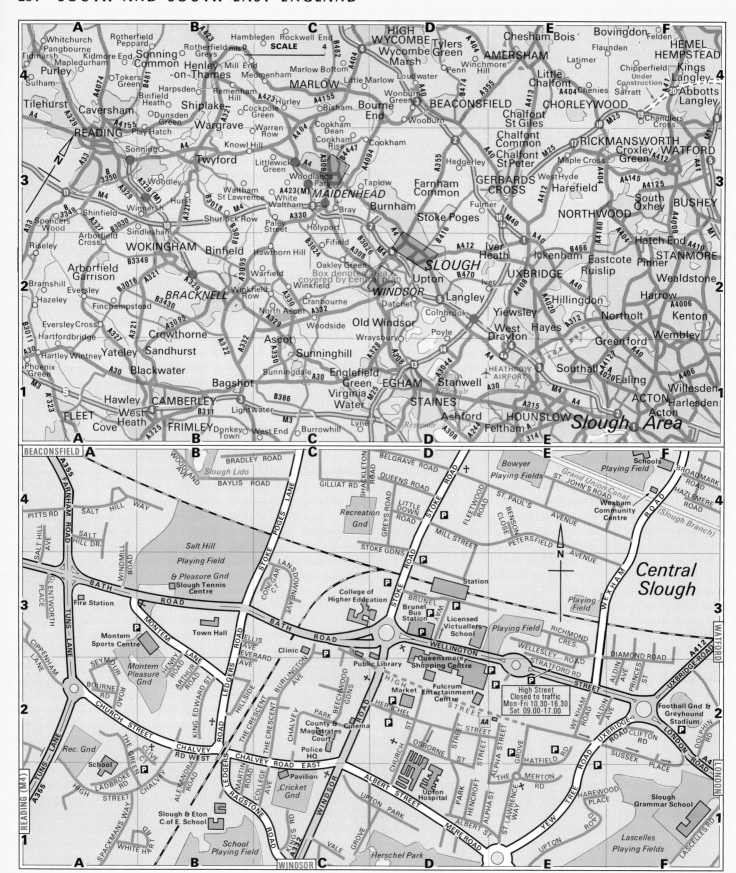

Slough

The town is something of a non-starter as far as architectural beauty or historical interest is concerned. However, it is a good shopping centre and has plenty of sports and leisure facilities.

Windsor The distinctive outline of the castle's towers and battlements above the Thames completely dominates the town. First built by the Normans to guard the approaches to London, it has been altered and added to at different times by various kings, but Henry III and Edward III contributed most to its present haphazard shape. The State Apartments are magnificent, as is St George's Chapel, with its superb fan-vaulted ceiling. Queen Mary's Dolls' House is an exquisite model house of the 1920s, complete down to the last detail. The town itself, squeezed between the castle walls and the river, has several attractive streets graced with fine buildings. One 17th-century colonnaded building by Sir Christopher Wren contains a small museum of local interest, and a recent new attraction is the Madame Tussaud's Royalty and Railways Exhibition.

Maidenhead used to be an important stage-post on the London to Bath road and is now a prosperous Thameside residential town. Oldfield House, near the ancient bridge designed by Brunel, contains the Henry Reitlinger Bequest Museum, specialising in glass and ceramics.

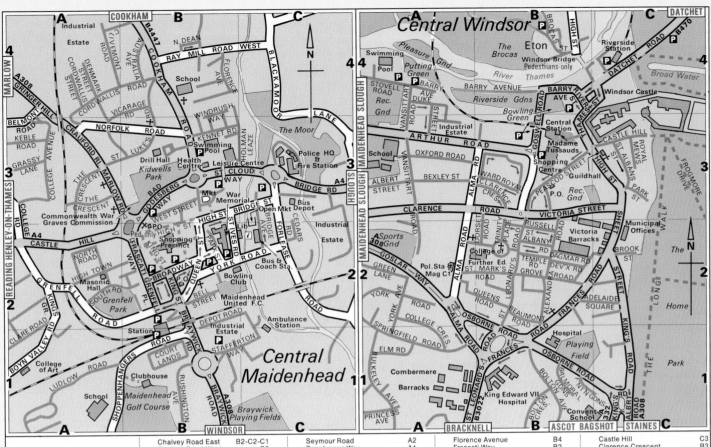

LEGEND

Town Plan

AA recommended route
Restricted roads
Other roads
Buildings of interest
Car parks   Station ☐P
Parks and open spaces
One way streets →

Area Plan

A roads
B roads
Locations   Hightown○
Urban area

Street Index with Grid Reference

Slough

Albert Street	C1-D1-E1
Aldin Avenue	E2-F2
Alexandra Road	B1-B2
Alpha Street	D1-E1-E2
Arthur Road	B2
Bath Road	A3-B3-C3
Baylis Road	B4-C4
Beechwood Gardens	C2
Belgrave Road	D4
Benson Close	E4
Bourne Road	A2
Bradley Road	B4-C4
Broadmark Road	F4
Brunel Way	D3
Burlington Avenue	C2-C3
Chalvey Park	C2
Chalvey Road East	B2-C2-C1
Chalvey Road West	B2
Church Street	A2-B2
Church Street	D1-D2
Cippenham Lane	A2-A3
Clifton Road	F2
Clive Court	A2-B2-B1
College Avenue	C1
Conegar Court	C3
Diamond Road	E3-F3-F2
Dolphin Road	F2
Ellis Avenue	B3-C3
Everard Avenue	B3-B2-C2
Farnham Road	A3-A4
Fleetwood Road	D4
Gilliat Road	C4
Glentworth Place	A3
Greys Road	D4
Harewood Place	E1
Hatfield Road	E1-E2
Hazlemere Road	F4
Hencroft Street	D1-D2
Henry Road	B2-B3
Herschel Street	D2-E2
High Street	D2-E2
High Street Chalvey	A2-A1-B1-B2
Hillside	B2
King Edward Street	B2
Kings Road	C1
Ladbroke Road	A1
Landsdowne Avenue	C3
Lascelles Road	F1
Ledgers Road	B1-B2-B3
Little Down Road	D4
London Road	F1-F2
Martin Road	B1
Mere Road	D1
Merton Road	E1
Mill Street	D4
Montem Lane	A3-B3-B2
Osborne Street	D1-D2
Park Street	D1-D2
Petersfield Avenue	E4-E3-F3
Pitts Road	A4
Princes Street	F2
Queens Road	D4
Ragstone Road	B1-C1
Richmond Crescent	E3
St John's Road	E4-F4
St Lawrence Way	E1
St Paul's Avenue	D4-E4-F4
Salt Hill Avenue	A3-A4
Salt Hill Drive	A4
Salt Hill Way	A4-B4
Shackleton Road	C4

Seymour Road	A2
Spackmans Way	A1
Stoke Gardens	C4-D4
Stoke Road	D3-D4
Stoke Poges Lane	B3-C3-C4
Stratford Road	E2-E3
Sussex Place	E2-F2-F1
The Crescent	B2-C2
The Green	A2-A1-B1
The Grove	E1-E2
Tuns Lane	A1-A2-A3
Upton Park	C1-D1
Upton Road	E1
Uxbridge Road	E2-F2-F3
Vale Grove	C1-D1
Wellesley Road	E3
Wellington Street	D2-D3-E3-E2-F2
Wexham Road	E2-E3-F3-F4
White Hart Road	A1-B1
Windmill Road	A3-A4
Windsor Road	C1-C2-D2-D3
Woodland Avenue	B4
Yew Tree Road	E1-E2

Maidenhead

Australia Avenue	B4
Bad Godesberg Way	B3
Bell Street	B2
Belmont Road	A3-A4
Blackamoor Lane	C3-C4
Boyn Valley Road	A1-A2
Braywick Road	B1-B2
Bridge Avenue	C2-C3
Bridge Road	C3
Bridge Street	B3-C3
Broadway	B2
Castle Hill	A2
Cedars Road	C2-C3
Clare Road	A1-A2
Clivemont Road	A4-B4
College Avenue	A3
College Road	A2-A3
Cookham Road	B3-B4
Cordwallis Road	A3-A4-B4
Cordwallis Street	A4
Court Lands	B1
Crauford Rise	A3
Denmark Street	A4
Depot Road	B1-B2-C2
Forlease Road	C2-C3

Florence Avenue	B4
Frascati Way	B2
Grassy Lane	A3
Grenfell Place	B2
Grenfell Road	A2-B2
Gringer Hill	A4
High Street	B2-B3
High Town	A2-B2
Holman Leaze	B3-C3
Keble Road	A3
Kennet Road	B3
King's Grove	A2
King Street	B2
Ludlow Road	A1
Marlow Road	A3-B3
Norfolk Road	A3-B3
North Dean	B4
North Road	A2
Park Street	B2-B3
Queen Street	B2-B3
Ray Mill Road West	B4-C4
Rushington Avenue	B1
St Cloud Way	B3-C3
St Ives Road	B2-B3
St Luke's Road	A3-B3-B4
Shoppenhangers Road	A1-B1
South Road	A2-B2
Stafferton Way	B1-C1
The Crescent	A3
Vicarage Road	A3-A4-B4
West Street	B3
Windrush Way	B3-B4
York Road	B2-C2

Windsor

Adelaide Square	B2-C2
Albany Road	B2
Albert Road	C1
Albert Street	A3
Alexandra Road	B2-B3
Alma Road	B3-A3-A2-A1-B1
Arthur Road	A3-B3
Balmoral Gardens	B1
Barry Avenue	A4-B4
Beaumont Road	B2
Bexley Street	A3
Bolton Avenue	B1
Bolton Crescent	B1
Brocas Street	B4
Brook Street	C2
Bulkeley Avenue	A1

Castle Hill	C3
Clarence Crescent	B3
Clarence Road	A3-B3
College Crescent	A1-A2
Dagmar Road	B2
Datchet Road	B4-C4
Devereux Road	B2
Dorset Road	B2-B3
Duke Street	A3-A4
Elm Road	A1
Fountain Gardens	B1-C1
Frances Road	B1-B2-C2
Frogmore Drive	C3
Goslar Way	A2
Goswell Road	B3-B4
Green Lane	A2
Grove Road	B2
High Street	B4
High Street	B3-C3
King's Road	C1-C2
Osborne Road	A2-B2-B1-C1
Oxford Road	A3
Park Street	C3
Peascod Street	B3
Princess Avenue	A1
Queens Road	A2-B2
River Street	B4
Royal Mews	C3
Russell Street	B2
St Albans Street	C3
St Leonard's Road	A1-B1-B2
St Mark's Road	A2-B2
Sheet Street	C2-C3
Springfield Road	A1-A2
Stovell Road	A4
Temple Road	B2
Thames Street	B3-B4-C4
The Long Walk	C1-C2-C3
Trinity Place	B2-B3
Vansittart Road	A2-A3-A4
Victoria Street	B3-C3
Ward Royal	B3
York Avenue	A1-A2
York Road	A2

SLOUGH

Salt Hill Park in the centre of Slough features a bowling green, tennis courts and a children's play area, as well as pleasant walks through landscaped gardens. This is one of several recreational areas scattered throughout the town.

Southampton

In the days of the great ocean-going liners, Southampton was Britain's premier passenger port. Today container traffic is more important, but cruise liners still berth there. A unique double tide caused by the Solent waters, and protection from the open sea by the Isle of Wight, has meant that Southampton has always been a superb and important port. Like many great cities it was devastated by bombing raids during World War II. However, enough survives to make the city a fascinating place to explore. Outstanding are the town walls, which stand to their original height in some places, especially along Western Esplanade. The main landward entrance to the walled town was the Bargate – a superb medieval gateway with a Guildhall (now a museum) on its upper floor. The best place to appreciate old Southampton is in and around St Michael's Square. Here is St Michael's Church, oldest in the city and founded in 1070. Opposite is Tudor House Museum, a lovely gabled building housing much of interest. Down Bugle Street are old houses, with the town walls, pierced by the 13th-century West Gate, away to the right. At the corner of Bugle Street is the Wool House Maritime Museum, contained in a 14th-century warehouse. On the quayside is God's House Tower, part of the town's defences and now an archaeological museum.

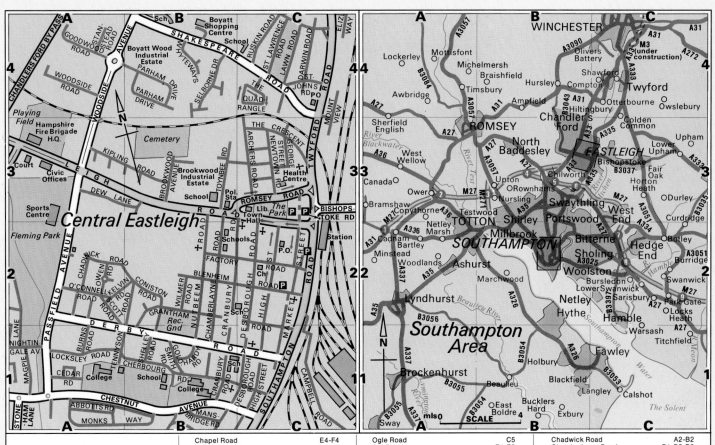

Key to Town Plan and Area Plan

Town Plan

A.A. Recommended roads	
Other roads	
Restricted roads	
Buildings of interest	Cinema
A A Service Centre	AA
Car Parks	P
Parks and open spaces	
One way streets	→

Area Plan

A roads	
B roads	
Locations	Ower ○
Urban Area	

SOUTHAMPTON

Above Bar	C5
Above Bar Street	C5-C6-C7-C8
Albert Road North	F3-F4
Albert Road South	F2
Anderson's Road	F3-F4
Anglesea Terrace	F4
Argyle Road	E8-F8
Back of the Walls	C1-C2-D2-D3-D4
Bargate Street	C4
Bedford Place	B8-C8
Bernard Street	C3-D3-E3
Blechynden Terrace	A7
Boundary Road	E2-F2
Briton Street	C2-D2
Britons Road	D8-E8-E7
Broad Green	D6
Brunswick Place	C8-D8
Brunswick Square	D2-D3
Bugle Street	C2-C3
Canal Walk	D3-D4
Canute Road	E2-F2
Castle Way	C2-C3-C4
Central Bridge	E3-F3
Central Road	E1-E2
Chantry Road	F3

Chapel Road	E4-F4
Chapel Street	E4
Charles Street	E3
Charlotte Place	D8
Civic Centre Road	B6-C6
Clovelly Road	D8-E8-F8
Coleman Street	E5-F5
College Street	E3
Commercial Road	A7-B7-C7
Cook Street	E4
Cossack Green	D5-D6
Cumberland Place	B7-B8-C8
Cunard Road	D1-E1
Derby Road	F7-F8
Devonshire Road	B8
Duke Street	E3
Durnford Road	F8
East Road	F2
East Street	C4-D4
East Park Terrace	D6-D7-D8
Eastgate Street	D3-C3-C4-D4
Evans Street	E4
Exmoor Road	E8
French Street	C2
Glebe Road	F3-F4
Golden Grove	E6-F6-F5
Granville Street	F4
Grosvenor Square	B8
Handel Road	A8-B8
Handel Terrace	A8
Hanover Buildings	C5-C4-D4
Hartington Road	F7-F8
Havelock Road	B6-B7
Herbert Walker Avenue	A3-B3-B2
High Street	C1-C2-C3-C4
Houndwell Place	D4-D5
James Street	E5-F5
John Street	E2-E3
Kingsway	E6-E7
King Street	D3-D4
Kings Park Road	C8
Latimer Street	E2-E3
Lime Street	D4-E4
London Road	C8
Lower Canal Walk	D1-D2
Manchester Street	B6-C6
Marsh Lane	E3-E4
Melbourne Street	F4-F5-F6
Melbury Road	E1
Morris Road	A7-A8-B8
New Road	E6-D6-D7
Newcombe Road	A8
Nichols Road	E7-E8
North Brook Road	E8-E7-F7
North Front	D6
Northam Road	E6-E7-F7
Northumberland Road	F7-F8

Ogle Road	C5
Old Road	E1-E2
Orchard Lane	D3-D4
Orchard Place	D2-D3
Oriental Terrace	C2-D2
Oxford Avenue	D8-E8-F8
Oxford Street	D3-D2-E2
Paget Street	F4
Palmerston Road	D5-D6
Park Walk	C6-C7
Platform Road	D2-E2
Porters Lane	C2
Portland Street	C5
Portland Terrace	B6-B5-C5-C4
Pound Tree Road	C5-D5
Queens Terrace	D2-E2
Queen's Way	D2-D3-D4
Radcliffe Road	F7-F8
Richmond Street	E3
Royal Crescent Road	F2-F3
St Andrews Road	D7-D8
St Marks Road	E7
St Mary's Place	E4-E5
St Mary's Road	D8-D7-E7
St Mary's Street	E4-E5-E6
Salisbury Street	C8
Saltmarsh Road	F2-F3
Simnel Street	C3
South Front	D5-E5-E6-D6
Sussex Road	C5-C6
The Polygon	A8-A7-B7-B8
Terminus Terrace	E2-E3
Threefield Lane	E3-E4
Town Quay	B2-C2-C1-D1
Trinity Road	D7-E7
Upper Bugle Street	C3-C4
Vincents Walk	C5
West Marlands Road	C6-C7
West Road	D1-D2-E2
West Park Road	A7-B7
West Quay Road	A5-A4-B4-B3
Western Esplanade	B2-B3-B4-B5-B6-A6
Windsor Terrace	C6
Winkle Street	C1-C2
Winton Street	D6-E6
Wolverton Road	F7
Wyndham Place	A7
York Buildings	C4-D4

EASTLEIGH

Abbots Road	A1
Archers Road	C3
Blenheim Road	B2-C2
Brookwood Avenue	B3
Burns Road	A1
Campbell Road	C1
Cedar Road	A1

Chadwick Road	A2-B2
Chamberlayne Road	B1-B2-B3
Chandlers Ford By-pass	A4
Cherbourg Road	A1-B1-C1
Chestnut Avenue	A1-B1-C1
Coniston Road	B2
Cranbury Road	C1-C2-C3
Darwin Road	C4
Cranbury Road	C1-C2-C3
Darwin Road	C4
Derby Road	A2-A1-B1-C1
Desborough Road	B1-C1-C2
Dew Lane	A3-B3
Elizabeth Way	C4
Factory Road	B2-C2
George Street	C3
Goldsmith Road	B1
Goodwood Road	A4
Grantham Road	B1-B2-C2-C1
High Street	C1-C2
Kelvin Road	A2-B2
Kipling Road	A3-B3
Lawn Road	C4
Leigh Road	A3-B3-C3-C2
Locksley Road	A1-A2
Magpie Lane	A1-A2
Mansbridge Road	B1
Market Street	C1-C2-C3
Monks Way	A1-B1
Mount View	C3-C4
Newtown Road	C3
Nightingale Avenue	C3
Nutbeem Road	B1-B2-B3
O'Connell Road	A2
Owen Road	A2
Parnham Drive	A4-B4
Passfield Avenue	A1-A2-A3
Romsey Road	B3-C3
Ruskin Road	C4
Stanstead Road	A4
Stoneham Lane	A1
St John's Road	C4
St Lawrence Road	C4
Scott Road	A2
Selborne Drive	B4
Shakespeare Road	B4-C4
Shelley Road	B1
Southampton Road	C1-C2
The Crescent	C3
The Quadrangle	C4
Tennyson Road	A1-A2-B2
Toynbee Road	B3
Twyford Road	C3-C4
Whyteways	B4
Wilmer Road	B2
Woodside Avenue	A3-A4
Woodside Road	A4

SOUTHAMPTON
Although liners still use Southampton's docks which handled all the great ocean-going passenger ships before the age of air travel replaced sea travel, the port is chiefly used by commercial traffic today.

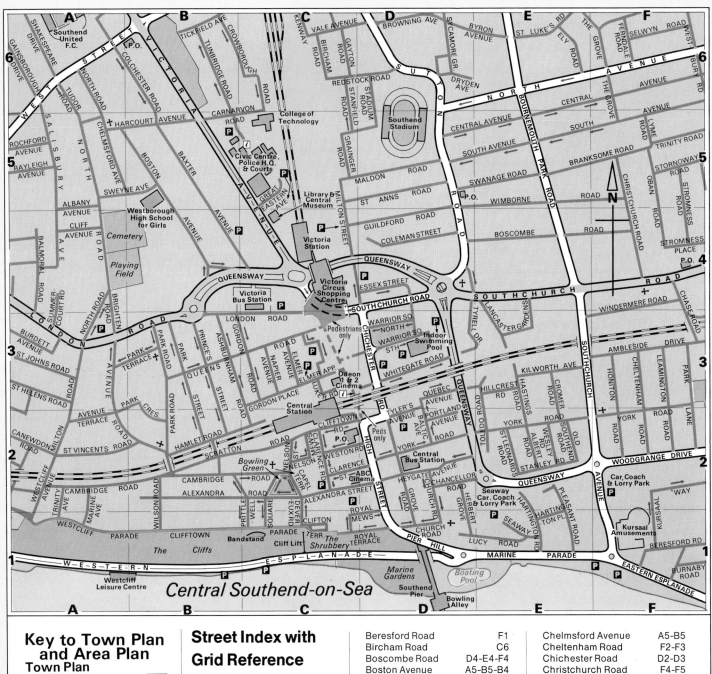

Central Southend-on-Sea

Key to Town Plan and Area Plan

Town Plan

A A Recommended roads	
Other roads	
Restricted roads	
Buildings of interest	Pavilion
Car Parks	P
Parks and open spaces	
Churches	+
One Way Streets	→

Area Plan

A roads	
B roads	
Locations	Parkston O
Urban area	

Street Index with Grid Reference

Southend-on-Sea

Albany Avenue	A5
Albert Road	E2
Alexandra Road	B2-C2
Alexandra Street	C2-D2
Ambleside Drive	E3-E4
Ashburnham Road	B3-C3-C2
Avenue Road	A3-A2-B2
Avenue Terrace	A2
Balmoral Road	A4
Baltic Avenue	D2-D3
Baxter Avenue	B5-B4-C4

Beresford Road	F1
Bircham Road	C6
Boscombe Road	D4-E4-F4
Boston Avenue	A5-B5-B4
Bournemouth Park Road	E4-E5-E6
Branksome Road	E5-F5
Brighten Road	A3-A4
Browning Avenue	D6
Burdett Avenue	A3
Burnaby Road	F1
Byron Avenue	D6-E6
Cambridge Road	A2-B2-C2
Canewdon Road	A2
Capel Terrace	C2
Carnarvon Road	B5-C5-C6
Central Avenue	D5-E5-E6-F6
Chancellor Road	D2
Chase Road	F3-F4

Chelmsford Avenue	A5-B5
Cheltenham Road	F2-F3
Chichester Road	D2-D3
Christchurch Road	F4-F5
Church Road	D1-D2
Clarence Road	C2
Clarence Street	C2-D2
Cliff Avenue	A4
Clifftown Parade	B1-C1
Clifftown Road	C2
Clifton Terrace	C1
Colchester Road	A6-B6-B5
Coleman Street	D4
Cromer Road	E2-E3
Crowborough Road	B6-C6
Devereux Road	C1-C2
Dryden Avenue	D6
Eastern Esplanade	F1
Elmer Approach	C3

Southend

The longest pleasure pier in the world and brilliant illuminations along the seafront in autumn are just two of the attractions of this thriving, immensely popular seaside resort, which offers the visitor every facet of the traditional holiday. Dance halls, theatres, amusement arcades and funfairs fill the Marine Parade area, with Peter Pan's Playground next to the pier and the

Kursall Amusement Park at the eastern end of the seafront both attracting crowds of visitors. The Pier itself offers entertainments (not least a wax museum housed in the replica of Sir Francis Drake's *Golden Hind* which lies alongside) and its 1¼ mile length is usually liberally dotted with fishermen. The most popular beaches are at Westcliffe and Thorpe Bay, while Leigh-on-Sea, linked to Southend by a lengthy promenade, makes a peaceful contrast to the main seafront area.

Places of interest include the village of Prittlewell, on the northern edge of town, with its 12th-century Priory and 13th-century church, 13th-to 14th-century Southchurch Hall (a timber-framed manor house with period furniture and beautiful grounds) and the Central Museum, which traces the history of south-east Essex back to the Romans. Good shopping and sports facilities, pleasant parks, professional cricket and football, and greyhound racing are other features of the town.

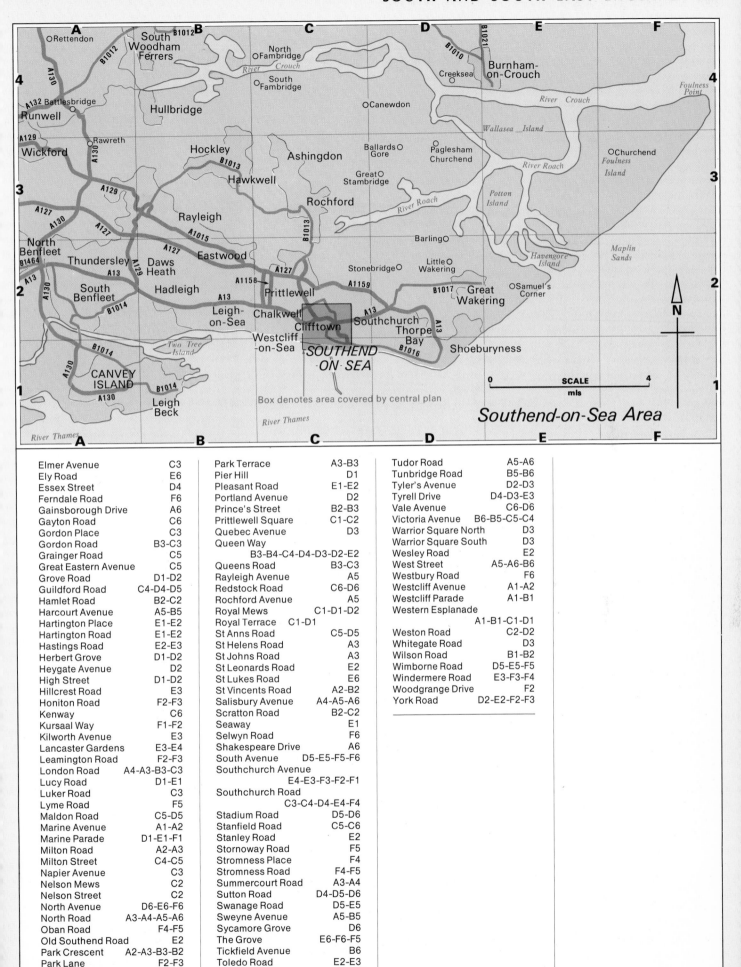

Southend-on-Sea Area

Box denotes area covered by central plan

Elmer Avenue	C3	Park Terrace	A3-B3	Tudor Road	A5-A6
Ely Road	E6	Pier Hill	D1	Tunbridge Road	B5-B6
Essex Street	D4	Pleasant Road	E1-E2	Tyler's Avenue	D2-D3
Ferndale Road	F6	Portland Avenue	D2	Tyrell Drive	D4-D3-E3
Gainsborough Drive	A6	Prince's Street	B2-B3	Vale Avenue	C6-D6
Gayton Road	C6	Prittlewell Square	C1-C2	Victoria Avenue	B6-B5-C5-C4
Gordon Place	C3	Quebec Avenue	D3	Warrior Square North	D3
Gordon Road	B3-C3	Queen Way		Warrior Square South	D3
Grainger Road	C5		B3-B4-C4-D4-D3-D2-E2	Wesley Road	E2
Great Eastern Avenue	C5	Queens Road	B3-C3	West Street	A5-A6-B6
Grove Road	D1-D2	Rayleigh Avenue	A5	Westbury Road	F6
Guildford Road	C4-D4-D5	Redstock Road	C6-D6	Westcliff Avenue	A1-A2
Hamlet Road	B2-C2	Rochford Avenue	A5	Westcliff Parade	A1-B1
Harcourt Avenue	A5-B5	Royal Mews	C1-D1-D2	Western Esplanade	
Hartington Place	E1-E2	Royal Terrace	C1-D1		A1-B1-C1-D1
Hartington Road	E1-E2	St Anns Road	C5-D5	Weston Road	C2-D2
Hastings Road	E2-E3	St Helens Road	A3	Whitegate Road	D3
Herbert Grove	D1-D2	St Johns Road	A3	Wilson Road	B1-B2
Heygate Avenue	D2	St Leonards Road	E2	Wimborne Road	D5-E5-F5
High Street	D1-D2	St Lukes Road	E6	Windermere Road	E3-F3-F4
Hillcrest Road	E3	St Vincents Road	A2-B2	Woodgrange Drive	F2
Honiton Road	F2-F3	Salisbury Avenue	A4-A5-A6	York Road	D2-E2-F2-F3
Kenway	C6	Scratton Road	B2-C2		
Kursaal Way	F1-F2	Seaway	E1		
Kilworth Avenue	E3	Selwyn Road	F6		
Lancaster Gardens	E3-E4	Shakespeare Drive	A6		
Leamington Road	F2-F3	South Avenue	D5-E5-F5-F6		
London Road	A4-A3-B3-C3	Southchurch Avenue			
Lucy Road	D1-E1		E4-E3-F3-F2-F1		
Luker Road	C3	Southchurch Road			
Lyme Road	F5		C3-C4-D4-E4-F4		
Maldon Road	C5-D5	Stadium Road	D5-D6		
Marine Avenue	A1-A2	Stanfield Road	C5-C6		
Marine Parade	D1-E1-F1	Stanley Road	E2		
Milton Road	A2-A3	Stornoway Road	F5		
Milton Street	C4-C5	Stromness Place	F4		
Napier Avenue	C3	Stromness Road	F4-F5		
Nelson Mews	C2	Summercourt Road	A3-A4		
Nelson Street	C2	Sutton Road	D4-D5-D6		
North Avenue	D6-E6-F6	Swanage Road	D5-E5		
North Road	A3-A4-A5-A6	Sweyne Avenue	A5-B5		
Oban Road	F4-F5	Sycamore Grove	D6		
Old Southend Road	E2	The Grove	E6-F6-F5		
Park Crescent	A2-A3-B3-B2	Tickfield Avenue	B6		
Park Lane	F2-F3	Toledo Road	E2-E3		
Park Road	B2-B3	Trinity Avenue	A1-A2		
Park Street	B2-B3	Trinity Road	F5		

Legend to Atlas

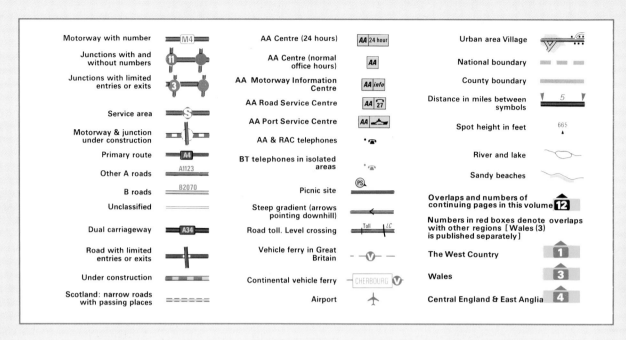

Motorway with number	M4	
Junctions with and without numbers		
Junctions with limited entries or exits		
Service area	S	
Motorway & junction under construction		
Primary route	A4	
Other A roads	A1123	
B roads	B2070	
Unclassified		
Dual carriageway	A34	
Road with limited entries or exits		
Under construction		
Scotland: narrow roads with passing places		

AA Centre (24 hours)	AA 24 hour
AA Centre (normal office hours)	AA
AA Motorway Information Centre	AA info
AA Road Service Centre	AA 27
AA Port Service Centre	AA
AA & RAC telephones	
BT telephones in isolated areas	
Picnic site	PS
Steep gradient (arrows pointing downhill)	
Road toll. Level crossing	Toll LC
Vehicle ferry in Great Britain	V
Continental vehicle ferry	CHERBOURG V
Airport	

Urban area Village	
National boundary	
County boundary	
Distance in miles between symbols	5
Spot height in feet	665
River and lake	
Sandy beaches	
Overlaps and numbers of continuing pages in this volume	12
Numbers in red boxes denote overlaps with other regions [Wales (3) is published separately]	
The West Country	1
Wales	3
Central England & East Anglia	4

Abbey or Cathedral	Coastal Launching Site	Nature Trail
Ruined Abbey or Cathedral	Surfing	Wildlife Park (mammals)
Castle	Climbing School	Wildlife Park (birds)
House and Garden	County Cricket Ground	Zoo
House	Gliding Centre	Forest Drive
Garden	Artificial Ski Slope	Lighthouse
Industrial Interest	Golf Course	Tourist Information Centre
Museum or Collection	Horse Racing	Tourist Information Centre (summer only)
Prehistoric Monument	Show Jumping/Equestrian Centre	Long Distance Footpath
Famous Battle Site	Motor Racing Circuit	AA Viewpoint
Preserved Railway or Steam Centre	Cave	Other Place of Interest
Windmill	Country Park	Boxed symbols indicate tourist attractions in towns
Sea Angling	Dolphinarium or Aquarium	

The National Grid

The National Grid provides a system of reference common to maps of all scales. The grid covers Britain with an imaginary network of 100 kilometre squares. Each square is identified by two letters, *eg* TR. Every 100 kilometre square is then sub-divided into 10 kilometre squares which appear as a network of blue lines on the map pages. These blue lines are numbered left to right 0 - 9 and bottom to top 0 - 9. These 10 kilometre squares can be further divided into tenths to give a place reference to the nearest kilometre.

Key to Road Maps

Shetland
Islands

Orkney
Islands

Outer
Hebrides

Stornoway

Thurso

Wick

Ullapool

Portree

Banff

Inverness

Peterhead

Aberdeen

Fort
William

Pitlochry

Oban

Perth

Dundee

Edinburgh

Largs

Glasgow

Peebles

Berwick

Campbeltown

Ayr

Dumfries

Stranraer

Newcastle
upon Tyne

Workington

Middlesbrough

Kendal

Scarborough

Isle of
Man

Lancaster

York

Douglas

Blackpool

Leeds

Hull

Grimsby

Liverpool

Manchester

Sheffield

Caernarfon

Chester

Lincoln

Stoke

Nottingham

King's Lynn

Shrewsbury

Leicester

Norwich

Aberystwyth

Birmingham

Coventry

Northampton

Peterborough

Great
Yarmouth

316/317

Worcester

314/315

Cambridge

Fishguard

Carmarthen

Hereford

Felixstowe

Pembroke

Swansea

Gloucester

306/307

308/309

Oxford

310/311

312/313

Chelmsford

Cardiff

Bristol

Reading

LONDON

302/303

Maidstone

304/305

Barnstaple

298/299

300/301

Guildford

Dover

Folkestone

Salisbury

Taunton

Southampton

294/295

Brighton

296/297

Newhaven

292/293

Exeter

Weymouth

Bournemouth

Truro

Plymouth

Scilly
Isles

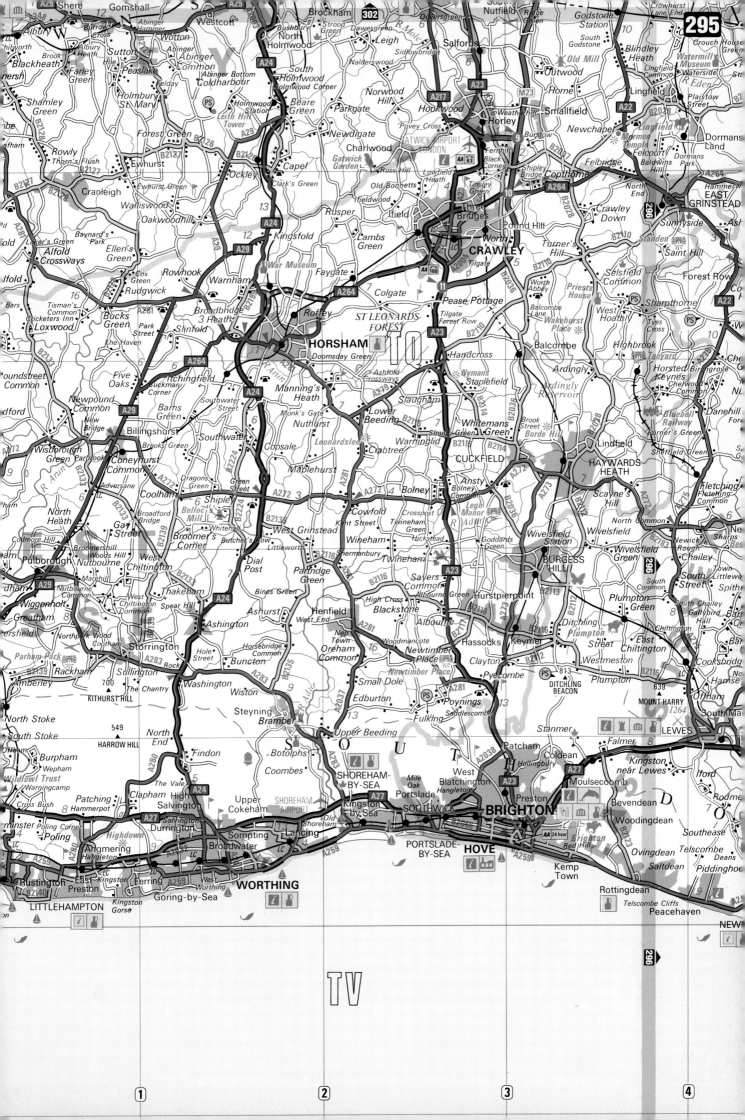

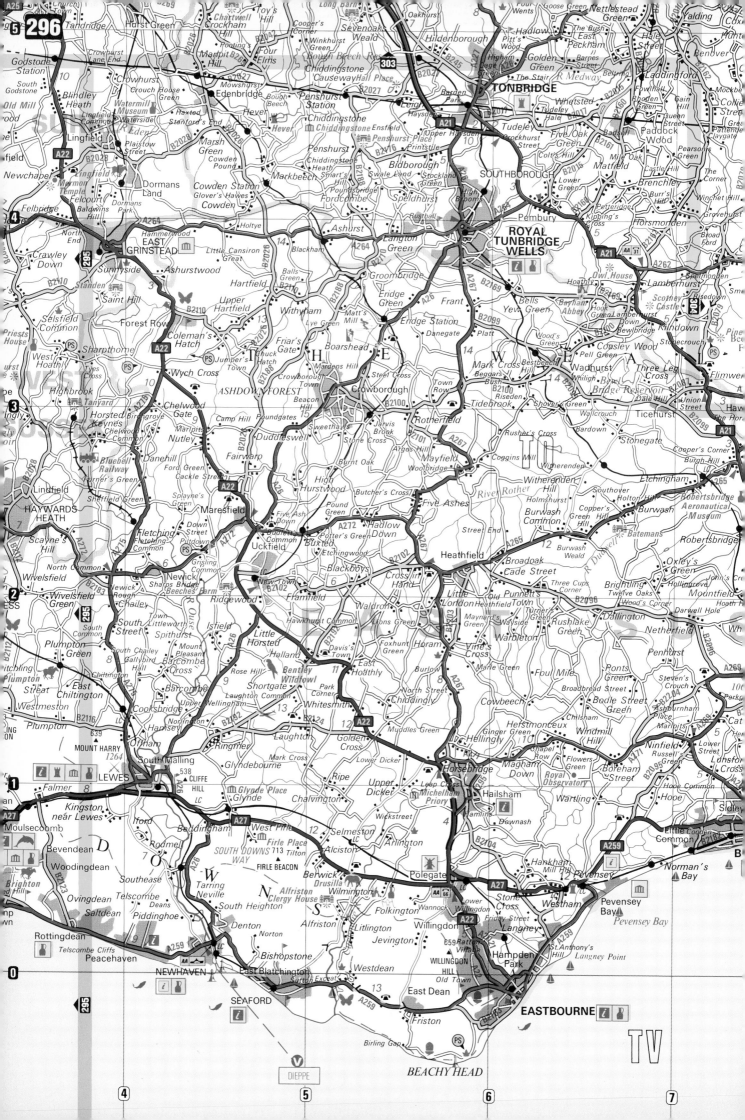

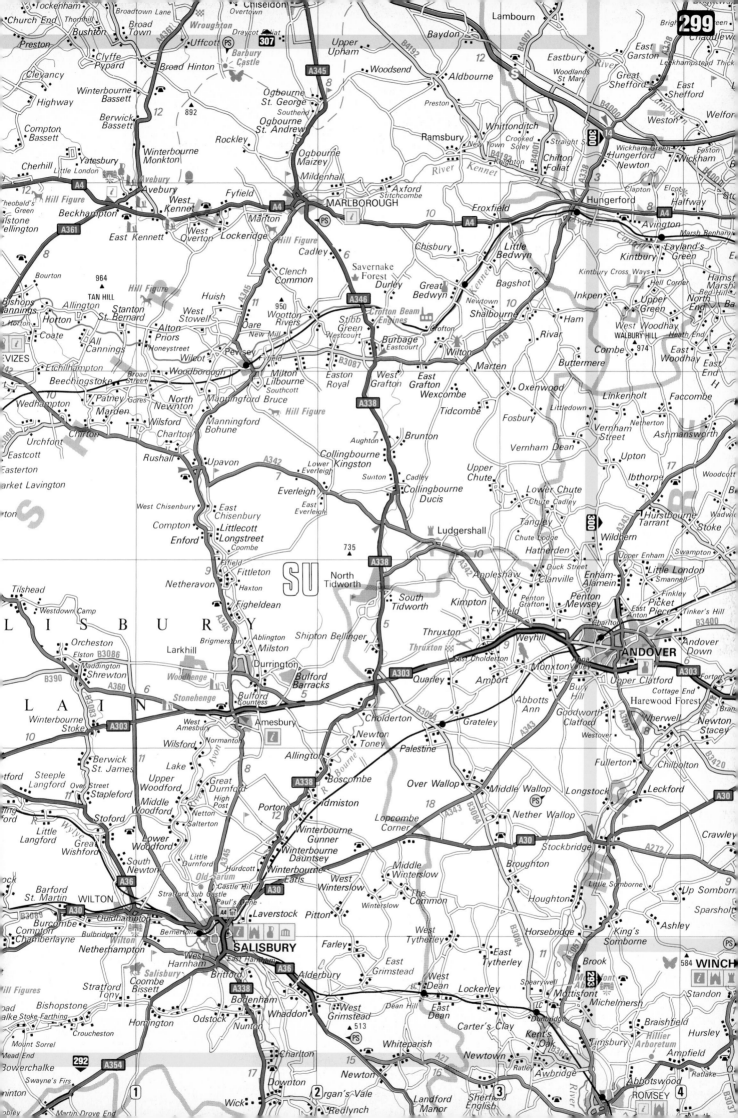

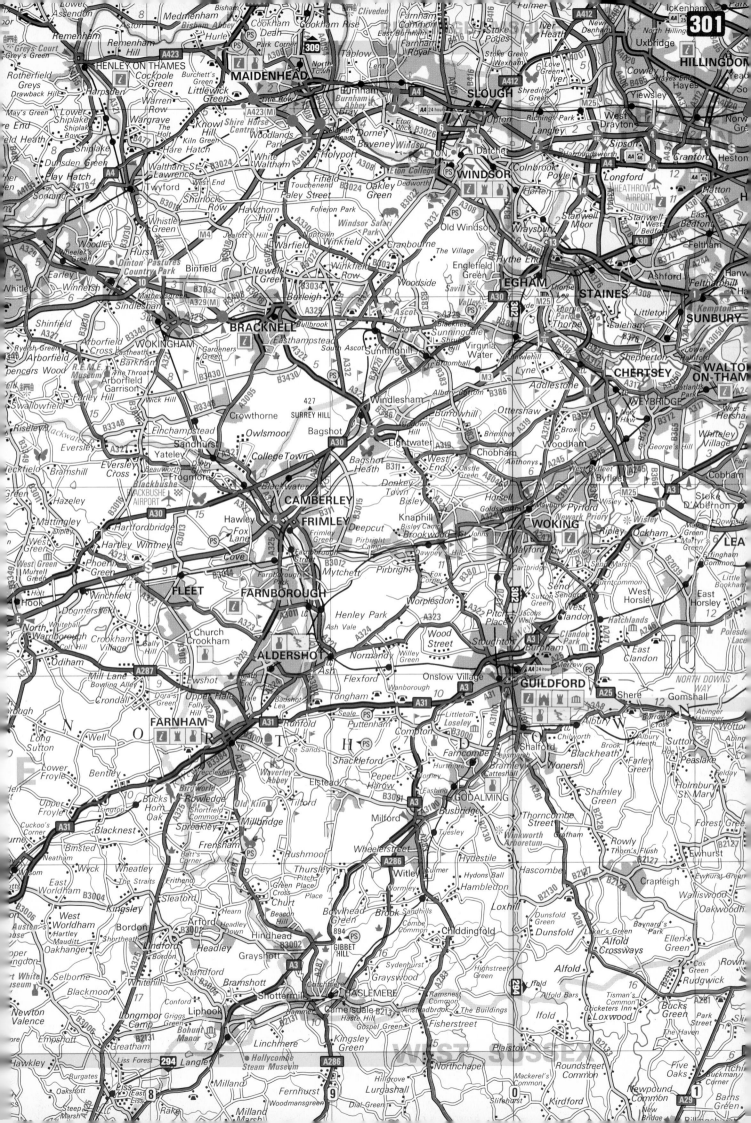

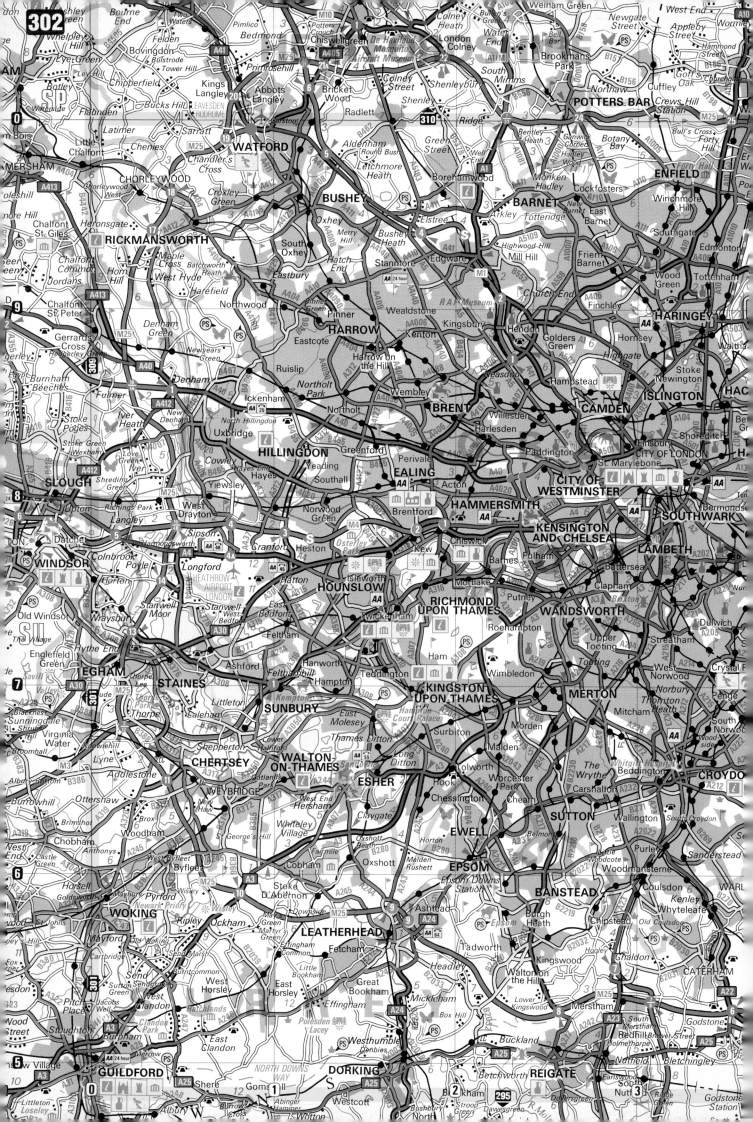

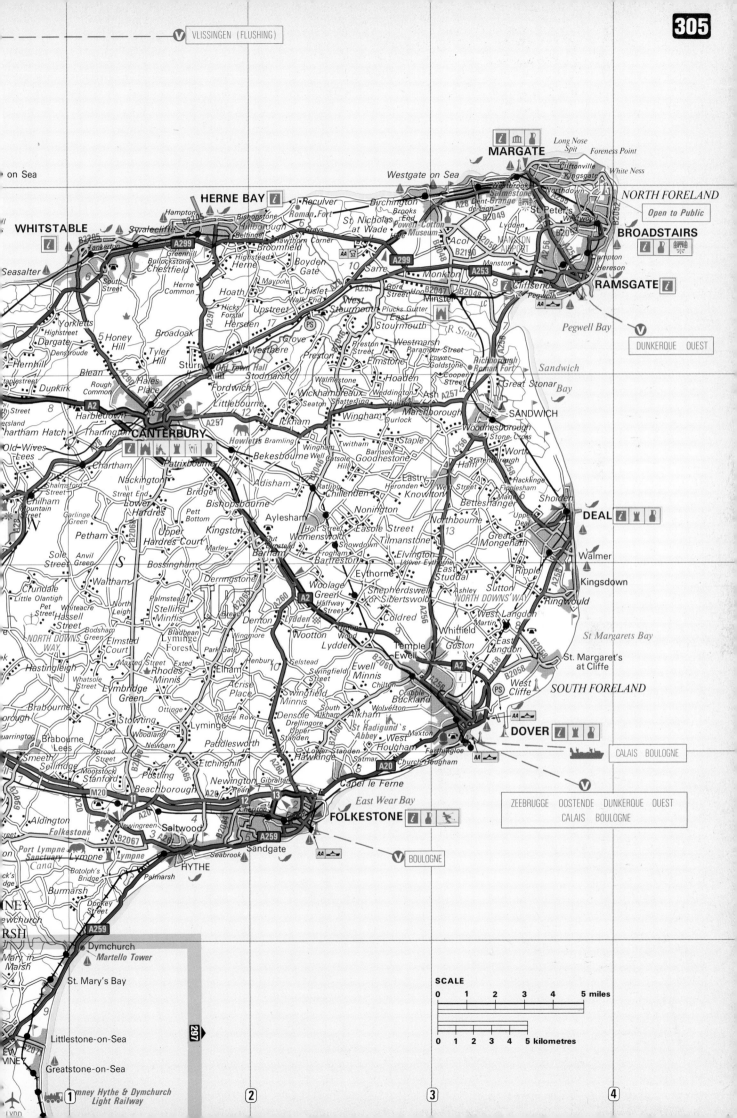

VLISSINGEN (FLUSHING)

MARGATE

Long Nose
Spit
Foreness Point

NORTH FORELAND

Open to Public

Westgate on Sea

Cliftonville
Kingstate
White Ness

HERNE BAY

Reculver
Roman Fort

Birchington

Brooks
End

Westbrook
Solmestone
Northdown
Dent-Grange
de-lion
St. Peter's
Westwood

BROADSTAIRS

Hampton
Swalecliffe

Bishopstone
Beltinge
Hillborough

St. Nicholas
at Wade

Powell-Cotton
Museum

Lydden

WHITSTABLE

Tankerton
Greenhill

Hawthorn Corner
Highstead

Sarre

Acol

MANSTON
AIRPORT

Manston

RAMSGATE

Seasalter

South
Street

Chestfield
Bullockstone

Broomfield

Herne

Boyden
Gate

Maypole

Chislet

West
Stourmouth

Monkton

Minster

Cliffsend
Pegwell

Pegwell Bay

DUNKERQUE OUEST

Hernhill

Honey
Hill

Broadoak

Herne
Common

Hoath

Hicks
Forstal
Hersden

Walk End

Glove

Grove

Preston
Street

East
Stourmouth

Westmarsh
Paramour Street
Lower
Goldstone

Richborough
Roman Fort

Sandwich

Great Stonar
Bay

Dunkirk

Blean

Rough
Common

Hales
Place

Sturry
Fordwich
Littlebourne

Westbere

Stodmarsh

Wickhambreaux
Seaton
Shattering

Walmestone
Weddington
Gull

Elmstone

Hoaden

Ash

Cooper
Street

SANDWICH

Harbledown

A2

Thanington

CANTERBURY

Ickham

Wingham

Marshborough

Woodnesborough
Stone Cross

Worth

Old-Wives
Lees

Chartham

Patrixbourne

Howletts

Bramling

Wingham
Well

Twitham

Staple

Goodnestone

Ham

Statenborough

Hacklinge
Finglesham

Sholden

DEAL

Shalmsford
Street

Chilham
Mountain
Street

Nackington
Street End
Lower
Hardres

Bridge
Bishopsbourne

Adisham

Ratling

Chillenden

Knowlton

West
Street

Northbourne

Great
Mongeham

Walmer

Garlinge
Green

Pett
Bottom

Aylesham

Holt Street

Easole Street

Tilmanstone

Kingsdown

Petham

Upper
Hardres Court

Kingston

Marley

Snowdon

Womenswold

Elvington
Lower Eythorne

Upper
Deal

Sole
Street

Anvil
Green

Bossingham

Barham
Denstone

Frogham
Barfreston

Eythorne

East
Studdal

Sutton

Ripple

Waltham

Derringstone

Woolage
Green

Shepherdswell
or Sibertswold

Ashley

Ringwould

NORTH DOWNS WAY

Little Olantigh
Pet
Street
Hassell
Street

North
Leigh

Palmstead
Stelling
Minnis

Half-way
Street

Coldred

Whitfield

West Langdon
Martin

St Margarets Bay

Crundale

Whiteacre
Street
Bodsham
Green

Breach

Denton
Lydden

Upper
Wood
Lydden

A256

Guston

East
Langdon

St. Margaret's
at Cliffe

NORTH DOWNS
WAY

Elmsted
Court

Bladbean

Wingmore

Wootton

Temple
Ewell

SOUTH FORELAND

Hastingleigh
Whatsole
Street

Maxted Street
Rhodes
Minnis

Park Gate

Henbury

B2060

Ewell
Minnis

Chilton

Crabble
Buckland

West
Cliffe

Elmbridge
Green

Exted
Elham

Selsted

Swingfield
Street

Wolverton

Brabourne
borough

Ottinge

Acrise
Place

Swingfield
Minnis

South
Alkham

Alkham

Maxton

West
Hougham

DOVER

CALAIS BOULOGNE

Stowting

Lyminge

Ridge Row

Densole
Drellingore
Upper
Standen

St Radigund's
Abbey

Farthingloe

Brabourne
Lees

Woodland
Newbarn

Paddlesworth

C Lower Standen

Church Houghham

Smeeth
Sellindge

Broad
Street
Etchinghill

Hawkinge

A20

ZEEBRUGGE OOSTENDE DUNKERQUE OUEST
CALAIS BOULOGNE

Moorstock
Stanford

Postling
Beachborough

Newington
Pean

Gibraltar

Capel le Ferne

Aldington

M20

A20

Beachborough

Enbrook

East Wear Bay

Folkestone

Newingreen

Saltwood

B2064

A259

Sandgate

FOLKESTONE

B2067

Lympne

Lympne

Seabrook

BOULOGNE

Port Lympne
Sanctuary

Canal

Botolph's
Bridge

HYTHE

Palmarsh

Burmarsh

Donkey
Street

NEY

Dymchurch

Martello Tower

St Mary in
Marsh

RSH

A259

St. Mary's Bay

Littlestone-on-Sea

297

Greatstone-on-Sea

SCALE

0   1   2   3   4   5 miles

0 1 2 3 4 5 kilometres

Romney Hythe & Dymchurch
Light Railway

1   2   3   4

SOUTH AND SOUTH-EAST
INDEX

As well as the page number of each place name the index also includes an appropriate atlas page number together with a four figure map reference (see National Grid explanation at start of atlas section).

In a very few instances place names appear without a map reference. This is because either they are not shown on the atlas or they lie just outside the mapping area of the region. However, each tour does include a detailed map which highlights the location of all places mentioned on the route.

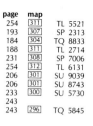

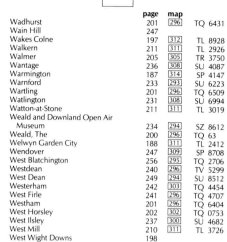

CENTRAL
—AND—
EAST ANGLIA

*Worcester Cathedral. Much of the cathedral
dates from the 11th century, although most of
the exterior is a clever Victorian restoration.*

Standing 46ft above the Suffolk countryside with its sails spanning almost 55 feet, the finely-preserved Saxtead Green Windmill is recognised as one of the finest post mills in the county.

Touring Central England & East Anglia

CONTENTS

INTRODUCTION

At the heart of this colourful region lies the West Midlands, cradle of the Industrial Revolution, and all around are marvellous things to discover. Here are Shakespeare's Stratford-upon-Avon, Staffordshire's porcelain, the beauty of the Peak District and the wide expanse of the Fenland, where the towers of medieval churches and old windmills rise from the low-lying landscape. In the west, Marcher fortresses guard the once turbulent borderlands between England and Wales, while in the east around Spalding are the bulb fields of the Fens. Between is Sherwood — a forest echoing with the legends of Robin Hood and his outlaw band. The region is also rich with historic towns like the beautiful stone town of Stamford and the ancient port of King's Lynn. It offers great opportunities to wander in the medieval streets of Norwich, Shrewsbury and Ludlow, to enjoy the scholarly atmosphere of Cambridge, and to marvel at the majestic towers of Lincoln's cathedral. There are also mighty castles, such as Warwick and Belvoir, and magnificent houses like Chatsworth and the royal residence of Sandringham.

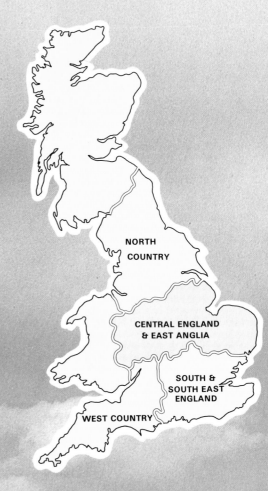

NORTH COUNTRY

CENTRAL ENGLAND & EAST ANGLIA

SOUTH & SOUTH EAST ENGLAND

WEST COUNTRY

ABOUT THE TOURS

Each tour occupies two pages and has a clear map accompanying the text. All the places described in the text are shown in **black** on the tour maps and are described as they occur on the road, linked in sequence by route directions. This precise wayfinding information is set in *italic*.

Castles, stately homes and other places of interest described in the tours are not necessarily open to the public or may be open only at certain times. It is therefore advisable to check the opening times of any place before planning a stop there. Properties administered by the National Trust and the Ancient Monument Scheme (NT and AM) are generally open most of the year, but this should be checked with the relevant organisation, as should precise opening times.

Near the Staffordshire village of Gnosall the Shropshire Union Canal, which links the Mersey to the Severn, is splashed with brightly coloured boats.

HOW TO FIND THE TOURS

All the motor tours in this part of the book are shown on the key map below and identified by the towns where they start. The tours are arranged in alphabetical order by start town name. Page numbers are also given opposite. Each tour begins at a well-known place, but it is possible to join or leave at any point if more convenient.

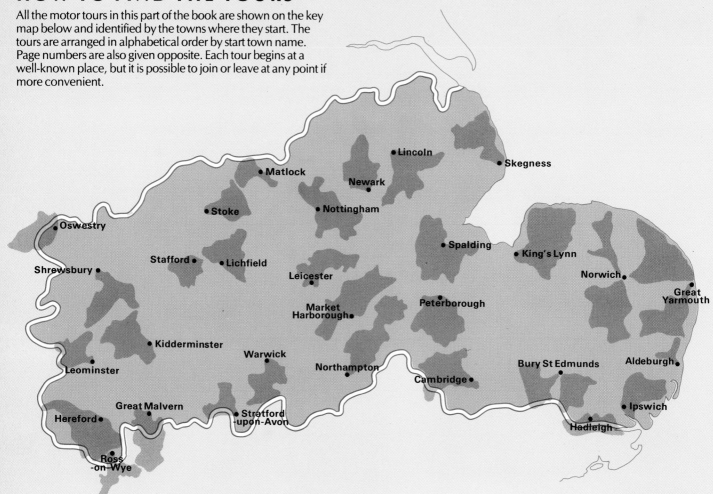

MAPS		Marshland		**TEXT**	
Main Tour Route		Memorial/Monument	m	AM	Ancient Monument
Detour/Diversion from Main Tour Route		Miscellaneous Places of		c	*circa*
Motorway		Interest & Route Landmarks	■	NT	National Trust
Motorway Access	②	National Boundary		NTS	National Trust for Scotland
Motorway Service Area	⑤	National Trust Property	NT	OACT	Open at Certain Times
Motorway and Junction Under Construction	A68	National Trust for Scotland Property	NTS	PH	Public House
A-class Road	A68	Non-gazetteer Placenames	*Thames /Astwood*	RSPB	Royal Society for the
B-class Road	B700	Notable Religious Site	✝		Protection of Birds
Unclassified Road	unclass	Picnic Site	ⓟ	SP	Signpost (s) (ed)
Dual Carriageway	A70	Prehistoric Site			
Road Under Construction	= = = =	Racecourse			
Airport	✈	Radio/TV Mast			
Battlefield	✕	Railway (BR) with Station			
Bridge		Railway (Special) with Station	++++		
Castle	⊭	River & Lake			
Church as Route Landmark	✝	Woodland Area			
Ferry	--Ⓥ--	Scenic Area			
Folly/Tower		Seaside Resort			
Forestry Commission Land		Stately Home	🏛		
Gazetteer Placename	Zoo /Lydstep	Summit/Spot Height	KNOWE HILL 209 ▲		
Industrial Site (Old & New)			KNOWE HILL 209 ▲		
Level Crossing	LC	Viewpoint			
Lighthouse	⚐				

TOURING CENTRAL ENGLAND AND EAST ANGLIA

Motor Tours
Pages 328-393

ALDEBURGH, Suffolk

There is more to this small, salt-laden town with its long, straight, somewhat desolate shingle beach than at first meets the eye. The musicians Benjamin Britten and Peter Pears made their homes here and an annual music festival, founded by Benjamin Britten, takes place every June and focuses on the Maltings at Snape, just west of the town along the broad Alde estuary. One of Britten's most popular works is *Peter Grimes,* which is set against the background of Aldeburgh's Moot Hall. This is the town's most striking building, with its 2 tall Jacobean chimneys, dating back to the time of Henry VIII, and now standing defiantly facing the advancing sea. The council chamber (open to the public in summer) is on the upper floor, where visitors can see old maps, prints and objects of local interest. *Peter Grimes* was inspired by the work of the poet George Crabbe. He lived in the town during the 17th century when its fortunes had considerably declined since its earlier heyday as a port and ship-building centre: the Dutch Wars, the transition of shipbuilding to the Blackwall yard, and sea damage had taken their toll. At least half this Tudor town has now been destroyed by the encroachment of the sea.

Leave Aldeburgh on an unclassified road for Thorpeness.

THORPENESS, Suffolk

The building of Thorpeness began just 70 years ago and was deliberately planned as a resort of quiet and refinement. A large boating lake, called the Meare, was created and a number of pleasant houses were built

VILLAGES OF EASTERN SUFFOLK

The coastline from Aldeburgh to the vanished city of Dunwich is an area of haunting bleakness that is the prelude to an extremely varied tour through Suffolk's most delightful villages, past several bird sanctuaries, some splendid churches and a historic castle.

The curious House in the Clouds and the post mill at Thorpeness

between this and the sea. One of the town's most distinctive buildings is the extraordinary House in the Clouds. It looks like a mock-Tudor building, but beneath the facade is a water tower on stilts. The post windmill standing beside it was brought from Aldringham so the tower could use it as a pump.

At Thorpeness turn inland and follow the B1353 to Aldringham. Here turn right on to the B1122 for Leiston.

LEISTON, Suffolk

Leiston is distinguished by having one of the most advanced schools in the country — Summerhill. It was founded by educationalist A. S. Neill as an experiment in self-education and has proved very successful. The surrounding marshes were first drained between 1846 and 1850 by the Garretts of Leiston Iron Works. Richard Garrett created a portable steam engine and threshing machine and a bust of him can be seen in the town's Victorian church.

Leave on the B1122, SP 'Yoxford', and in 1 mile pass the remains of Leiston Abbey.

LEISTON ABBEY, Suffolk

Leiston Abbey (AM) was first founded on the Minsmere Marshes in 1182, and was moved to its present site in 1363 and then rebuilt by Robert de Ufford, Earl of Suffolk. The ruins incorporate an octagonal brick gate-turret which was added when it was converted into a diocesan retreat during Tudor times.

Continue to Theberton and ½ mile beyond the village turn right on to the B1125 for Westleton.

WESTLETON, Suffolk

Farmland and heathland surround the village of Westleton which consists of a variety of attractive buildings — redbrick and colour-washed. A shaded duck pond lies at one end of the village green where every summer a week-long fair is held featuring races and general festivities. Westleton used to have 2 windmills, but one, the smock mill, has been converted into a house and the other, a tower mill, is derelict.

At the end of the village turn right on to the unclassified Dunwich road and shortly pass the Minsmere Bird Sanctuary on Westleton Heath.

THE MINSMERE BIRD SANCTUARY, Suffolk

This is one of the Suffolk reserves where avocets — a rare black and white wading bird — breed, and the public are allowed access to some parts of the reserve as well as to several hides. The sanctuary covers 1,500 acres and the varied habitats it provides include reed beds, woodland and heathland.

Continue to Dunwich.

DUNWICH, Suffolk

Dunwich was a city about the size of Ipswich in the 12th century, but everything from those days has all gradually been washed away by savage sea storms. It was still an important port in Roman times, but the sea started its onslaught in 1326 and by the 16th century most of the city lay on the sea bed. It is said that church bells can be heard ringing out across the lonely beach. All that remains now beneath the crumbling cliffs is a scattering of cottages, an inn and a general store. However, a dramatic idea of the city's former glory and importance can be gained by studying the relics and pictures in the museum in St James' Street. North-east of this lonely and evocative place is the extensive Dunwich Forest where there is an excellent picnic site.

Leave on the Blythburgh road and pass through Dunwich Forest. In 1½ miles, at the crossroads, turn right on to the B1125. In 1 mile a detour may be taken by turning right on to the B1387 to Walberswick.

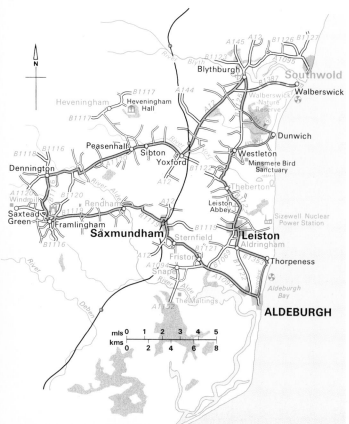

Blythburgh's church tower was crowned by a spire until 1577 when it fell through the roof, killing a man and a boy

WALBERSWICK, Suffolk

Walberswick's ruined church tower stands proudly as a landmark to those at sea. The pleasant houses around the village green have attracted artists over many years and it was a favourite spot of the artist Wilson Steer earlier this century. Just across the estuary (crossed by ferry) is the smart little town of Southwold (see page 339) with brick and colour-washed Georgian houses. A national nature reserve, overlooking the Blythe estuary, is home to an interesting variety of waders and rare birds.

The main tour keeps forward on the B1125 into Blythburgh.

Aldeburgh is famous for its 'long-shore' herring and the best sprats in England are caught here in November and December

BLYTHBURGH, Suffolk

The collapse of the fishing trade along the east coast contributed to Blythburgh's decline from a prosperous town to the village it is today. The huge and magnificent church rising up above the marshes is the only reminder of the town's importance in the 15th century when there was a mint here, a gaol, crowded quays and 2 annual fairs. It is a light and spacious building with a great wooden roof decorated with carved angels and painted flowers. Another notable feature of the church is the bench-ends depicting the 7 deadly sins, and a wooden clock with a quarter jack.

At Blythburgh turn left on to the A12 Ipswich road for Yoxford.

YOXFORD, Suffolk

Locally known as 'The garden of Suffolk', because it is surrounded by the parkland of 3 country houses (not open), Yoxford is packed with attractive timbered houses featuring balconies and bow-windows. Cockfield Hall was originally a magnificent Tudor house built during Henry VIII's reign; it was altered in the 19th century, but is still most impressive and has a thatched Victorian lodge in the village.

Turn right on to the A1120, SP 'Stowmarket', for Sibton.

SIBTON, Suffolk

Sibton stands at the junction of 2 Roman roads in the Minsmere valley. It is a pretty place, with a group of cottages and small 18th-century bridges cross the Drain, a ditch that drains the farmland along its length. Romantic, overgrown ruins of Sibton Abbey, the only Cistercian house in Suffolk, lie in the woods near the village. It was founded in 1150 but was never prosperous and fell into neglect after the Dissolution.

Continue to Peasenhall.

PEASENHALL, Suffolk

Trickling through the village is a little stream that brings an air of serene tranquility to the cluster of houses on its banks; the stream is actually part of the Drain. Peasenhall's claim to fame is that the Suffolk seed drill was originally manufactured here. The Wool Hall has been discovered and restored only recently. About 4 miles to the north of the village stands Heveningham Hall (see page 339), a lovely Palladian house set in magnificent grounds landscaped by Capability Brown.

Remain on the A1120 for Dennington.

DENNINGTON, Suffolk

Treasures which fill the 14th-century church at Dennington include an extremely rare altar canopy, some beautiful screens and, on a bench-end on the south side, a curious carving of a giant with a webbed foot.

At the church branch left on to the B1116 for Framlingham.

FRAMLINGHAM, Suffolk

The Earls of Norfolk used to own the impressive castle in this lively market town. The castle (AM) was destroyed in 1639, but before that it was the home of Mary Tudor during her attempts to gain the throne. The ruins of the original castle are extensive and are an unusual example of the 12th-century style, using square towers rather than round ones. Next door to the castle is the church with its memorials to the Norfolk family and one of the most splendid wooden church roofs in Suffolk. The rest of the old town consists of many attractive cottages, and historic buildings, centred on the market square. Saxted Green lies 2 miles to the east of Framlingham and is the site of a famous windmill (AM). It is a very good example of an 18th-century post mill — the oldest type of windmill — where the body carrying the sails and machinery rotates on an upright post.

Leave Framlingham on the B1119, SP 'Saxmundham'. In 4 miles pass through Rendham, then in another 2¾ miles reach the outskirts of Saxmundham. Here, turn left then right, and at the T-junction turn right on to the A12 for the town centre.

SAXMUNDHAM, Suffolk

One of the more modern towns in this part of Suffolk, its origins actually go back to the 13th century when there was a market here occupying 7 acres. However, most of the existing buildings in the main street are 19th century.

Continue on the Ipswich road for 1 mile and turn left on to the B1121, SP 'Aldeburgh'. Pass through Sternfield and Friston, then later join the A1094 for the return to Aldeburgh.

EAST ANGLIAN HEARTLANDS

The last king of East Anglia ruled from Bury St Edmunds in the 9th century. Today the town is an important market centre for east Suffolk, a focal point for farming communities made rich by a flourishing wool trade in medieval times.

Once a rich and splendid monastery, the abbey at Bury St Edmunds is now an extensive ruin.

BURY ST EDMUNDS, Suffolk

Edmund, the last king of the East Angles, was killed by the Danes c869 and was subsequently hailed by his people as a martyr. In 903 his body was moved from its resting place at Hoxne to Bury, then known as *Beodricsworth*, which became an important religious centre and place of pilgrimage. The abbey that grew here prospered until it was burned by the townsfolk in 1465. Its rebuilding resulted in one of the architectural glories of England, but it became too powerful and, like many of its contemporaries, was broken at the Dissolution. Today its former splendour can be judged by extensive ruins that form a focal point for a country park. Two gates still stand, and the precincts are made splendid by the Cathedral Church of St James. A large graveyard separates this fine building from 15th-century St Mary's Church, which is known for its magnificent hammerbeam roof and the grave of Mary Tudor. Mary's life is illustrated in a window given by Queen Victoria. Bury St Edmunds itself is an attractive market town which retains its 11th-century street plan and many fine old buildings. Moyse's Hall dates from the 12th century and contains a museum, and the lovely Guildhall and Cupola House are both of 15th-century origin. Excellent Georgian shop fronts are preserved in some streets, and the Town Hall of 1771 was designed by Robert Adam. Also from this period are a brick-built Unitarian chapel with an exceptionally well-preserved interior, and the Angel Corner (NT) is a Queen Anne house, now containing a collection of clocks and watches. The Theatre Royal (NT) build in 1819 is a rare example of a Georgian playhouse. The 18th-century Angel Hotel was the scene of Mr Pickwick's meeting with Sam Weller in Charles Dickens' *Pickwick Papers*.

Some 2½ miles south west of the town, off the A143, is Ickworth House.

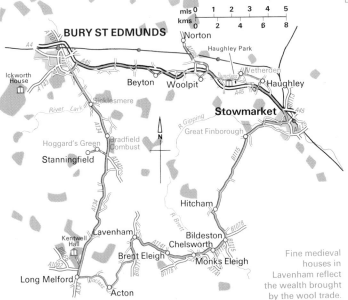

Fine medieval houses in Lavenham reflect the wealth brought by the wool trade.

ICKWORTH HOUSE, Suffolk

Started by Frederick Harvey, 4th Earl of Bristol and the Bishop of Derry, this 18th-century house (NT) is one of the most remarkable in England and an apt memorial to its builder's eccentricity. The Earl Bishop intended to fill it with works of art collected during his extensive travels, but in Rome he was imprisoned by Napoleonic troops and his enormous collection confiscated. He died in 1803, with only half his dream actually realized in bricks and mortar. Visitors today can see the full glory of the strange elliptical rotunda that grew from plans by the Italian architect Asprucci. Inside the house is a fine collection of 18th-century and French furniture. Part of the 2,000-acre grounds (NT) were landscaped by Capability Brown.

Leave Bury St Edmunds on the A134 'Sudbury' road. Drive through the villages of Sicklesmere and Bradfield Combust, and ¾ mile beyond the latter pass an unclassified right turn leading through Hoggards Green to the village of Stanninglield. This offers a pleasant detour from the main route.

STANNINGFIELD, Suffolk

Stanningfield Church has two fine Norman doorways, one within a timbered porch, and the 13th-century chancel preserves notable features. West of the village is Elizabethan Coldham Hall, which has a dovecote of the same period.

Continue on the A134 and approach Long Melford with the grounds of Kentwell Hall to the right.

KENTWELL HALL, Suffolk

Access to this mellow Elizabethan manor (open) is through a 300-year-old avenue of lime trees and over a moat. The combination of water, tree-shaded grass, and old brick forms a tranquil beauty that is a rarity in the 20th century.

LONG MELFORD, Suffolk

Perhaps the stateliest village in Suffolk, Long Melford has an impressive main street lined by fine old buildings and dominated by a magnificent church. The latter dates from 15th-century reconstruction and occupies the site of a Roman temple. Its many windows give the interior an airiness accentuated by soaring columns and slender pillars. The Lady Chapel of 1496 can almost be considered as separate from the main building, though attached in mortar if not in style to the east end. The well-proportioned tower is a sensitive addition dating from 1903. Interesting monuments include a carved 15th-century piece in the Clopton Chantry and a number of contemporary brasses that illustrate clothing and hairstyles of the period. Leading down towards the village from the church is a triangular green fringed by the 18th-century wall of the Congregational churchyard, the 15th-century Bull Hotel and 16th-century Trinity Hospital. The latter was founded by Sir William Cordell and greatly restored in the 19th century. Dominating the village is Melford Hall (NT), one of the finest Elizabethan manors in England. It occupies three sides of a lovely old courtyard and carries a splendid array of turrets.

Drive to the Bull Inn and turn left on to the unclassified 'Lavenham' road. In 1¼ miles continue forward to Acton.

ACTON, Suffolk

Inside Acton Church is an excellent brass, the most famous military memorial of its type in the country. It was raised to Sir Robert de Bures c1302 and depicts a knight in chain mail holding a shield. A notable sculpture of a reclining man with his wife at his feet carries the date 1722 and has been attributed to Thomas Green of Camberwell.

From Acton turn left with SP 'Lavenham'. In 2¼ miles join the B1071 and continue to Lavenham.

LAVENHAM, Suffolk

Easily one of the most outstanding villages in East Anglia, Lavenham has hardly changed in appearance since its heyday as an important wool town in the 14th and 15th centuries. Its dozens of immaculately preserved buildings include timber-framed houses, the Guildhall (NT), and the Wool Hall. Slightly apart from the village is the local church, a superb building that is considered a complete work of art in itself. It carries a 141ft tower resplendent with shiny knapped flint, and was built with money donated by a family of clothiers. Other reflections of prosperous times are 15th-century Little Hall, the old Town Cross (AM), and The Priory. An 18th-century hand-operated fire engine is preserved in the village.

Leave Lavenham on the A1141 'Hadleigh' road. After 2 miles turn left on to an unclassified road and enter Brent Eleigh.

One of the many superb old buildings preserved in Long Melford is Elizabethan Melford Hall.

BRENT ELEIGH, Suffolk

Fine wall paintings have been discovered in the 14th-century Church of St Mary here, and Jacobean woodwork is much in evidence on the pulpit, south door, and box pews. Elizabethan Brent Eleigh Hall has modern additions by architect Sir Edwin Lutyens.

Return to the A1141 and turn left for Monks Eleigh.

MONKS ELEIGH, Suffolk

This pleasant little village has a good church with a notable tower and a carved pulpit. An attractive weatherboarded mill and Georgian millhouse stand near by.

Drive to the end of the village and bear left on to the B1115 'Stowmarket' road. Continue to Chelsworth.

CHELSWORTH, Suffolk

An attractive double hump-backed bridge spans the small River Brett here, and the village features many lovely timber-framed houses.

Stay on the B1115 and turn left for Bildeston.

Moated Kentwell Hall dates from the 16th century and stands in lovely grounds about 1 mile north of Long Melford.

BILDESTON, Suffolk

Many notable half-timbered cottages survive here, and the village church is reached by a footpath across pleasant farming country.

From Bildeston continue on the B1115 to Hitcham.

HITCHAM, Suffolk

A 15th-century hammerbeam roof can be seen in Hitcham Church, which is comfortable rather than outstanding and forms a natural focus for this delightful village. Many of the local cottages are half timbered.

Continue on the B1115 and drive through Great Finborough to reach Stowmarket.

STOWMARKET, Suffolk

Poet John Milton visited this busy Gipping Valley market town many times to see his tutor Thomas Young, who lived at the vicarage. Most of the buildings are of fairly recent date, like the good Georgian and Victorian houses round the market square. Inside the town church, which displays a variety of styles, are an old organ and a rare wigstand. A large open-air museum relating to East Anglian Life has an attractive riverside setting here, with frequent demonstrations from craftsmen.

Leave the town on the A1302 'Bury St Edmunds' road. In ¾ mile join the A45, and after another 1¾ miles branch left on to an unclassified road. Continue to the village of Haughley.

HAUGHLEY, Suffolk

A Norman castle that once stood here has entirely vanished, but its mound remains as a monument to the village's previous importance. There are 30 18th-century leather buckets in the church porch, possibly a hangover from early fire precautions, and the nave has a good roof. New Bell's Farm is an experimental station of the Soil Association.

In Haughley turn left and continue to Wetherden. In the latter village turn left again, then in a further ½ mile turn right and pass the grounds of Haughley Park on the left.

HAUGHLEY PARK, Suffolk

Characteristic stepped gables and elegant octagonal chimneys are dominant features of this lovely old house, built in 1620 and restored in recent years. It stands in beautiful grounds and is open to the public on Tuesdays May to September.

After 1¼ miles rejoin the A45. In ½ mile branch left, then turn left on to an unclassified road. A short detour can be made from the main route to passing over the A45 to join the A1088 'Thetford' road and driving for 2½ miles.

NORTON, Suffolk

Excellent examples of old woodcarving, including misericords and a notable font, can be seen inside the local church. Nearby is the partly 18th-century Rectory and The Norton Bird Gardens set in 4 acres of gardens with a variety of species.

On the main route, continue to Woolpit.

WOOLPIT, Suffolk

At one time wolves were brought here to be destroyed and buried, hence the name. A local legend tells of the Green Children, a boy and girl who suddenly appeared in some obscure period of village history and were remarkable for their distinctive colour. The story goes on to say that they claimed to be from underground St Martin's Land, a place of perpetual twilight, and that the boy died but the girl married and had a family. The local church boasts a rare brass-eagle lectern and double-hammerbeam roof.

Leave Woolpit on the unclassified 'Bury St Edmunds' road and in ¾ mile rejoin the A45. In 1¼ miles turn left for Beyton.

BEYTON, Suffolk

Good Norman features of Beyton Church include a pleasing round tower and an attractively simple doorway.

After village rejoin the A45 for the return to Bury St Edmunds.

BURY ST EDMUNDS, Suffolk

'Shrine of a King, cradle of the Law' runs the city motto, which refers to the 2 great events of the city's history. St Edmund was buried here 33 years after his death in 869 at the hands of the Danes. The monastery where he lay was given abbey status in 1032 by King Crut, eager to please his new subjects. The 'Law' in the motto refers to an event in 1214 when King John's barons swore on the high altar of the abbey church to force the king to accept the Magna Carta. The best preserved remains of the abbey are 2 gatehouses, one 12th-century, the other 14th-century. Two churches stand at the edge of the abbey precincts, St Mary's, a 15th-century church with a fine hammerbeam roof, and St James', built a little later. The rest of the town follows the rectangular plan set out by Bishop Baldwin in the 11th century, but the houses are essentially Georgian, or appear so; Bury kept up with fashion, often not by rebuilding, but by adding new façades in the latest style to the fronts of existing buildings. Angel Hill is a fine example, it is a square surrounded by some of Bury's best houses — including Angel Corner (OACT), a Queen Anne Mansion which houses one of the largest collections of clocks and watches in Britain. The oldest Norman house in East Anglia is claimed to be Moyse's Hall (OACT), c1180, in the Butter Market. It is now a museum displaying Bronze-Age weapons, medieval relics and other items of Suffolk archaeology and natural history.

Leave on the A143, SP 'Sudbury', then 'Haverhill'. At Horringer is the entrance to Ickworth.

ICKWORTH, Suffolk

The centre of this most unusual house (NT) is a great rotunda with 2 arms curving away which end in square blocks, each the size of a substantial country house. The interior of the rotunda is lit by a glass dome 100ft above the floor, and the odd-shaped rooms, hung with paintings by Titian, Velasquez, Hogarth, Reynolds and Gainsborough, are furnished with fine 18th-century English and French furniture. Earl-Bishop Frederick Hervey designed the house to hold a collection of choice artefacts (now at Ickworth), collected on his European tours but sadly he died abroad before the house was finished. Capability Brown landscaped the surrounding parkland which features majestic oak and cedar trees.

Continue on the A143 and pass the edge of Chedburgh. In 3 miles, at the Plumbers Arms PH, turn right, SP 'Lidgate'. In ¾ mile bear left then turn right on to the B1063 Newmarket Road, and continue to Lidgate.

HORSES AND KINGS

From Bury St Edmunds, shrine of a martyred king, to Newmarket, the headquarters of horse racing in Britain since the 17th century — but the glamour of the sport of kings soon gives way to the continuity of tradition — lands and buildings owned by the same families for centuries.

Ickworth's central feature, the great rotunda, was built in the 1790s

LIDGATE, Suffolk

Suffolk House (not open), brick-gabled and timber-fronted, was the birth-place of the poet John Lydgate, who was born c1370 and lived as a Benedictine monk at Bury. He imitated Chaucer in his work and although he became a court poet, he died in poverty. In the mainly 14th-century church there is a brass of a cleric, said to be Lydgate.

In 1¼ miles keep forward on to the B1085 Kentford road to Dalham.

DALHAM, Suffolk

Thatched cottages set back from the road in their own gardens line both banks of the River Kennet, and woods climb an escarpment to the church at the north end of the village. Paintings inside depict the building of the steeple in 1625 There is a monument of Sir Marten Stukeville and his 2 wives: Stukeville was probably with Sir Francis Drake on his last fateful voyage.

Turn left across the bridge, SP 'Moulton', and ascend past a windmill. At Moulton turn left, beyond the post office, on to the Newmarket road. Gradually ascend Warren Hill, passing several racing stables on either side of the road. There are good views of Newmarket and the surrounding country on the descent into the town. At the bottom turn right, then at the clock tower turn left to enter Newmarket.

NEWMARKET, Suffolk

Newmarket, the home of English horse racing. James I often came here, hunting and tilting, and organised the first recorded horse race in 1619. The High Street, which follows the ancient road, has Jubilee Clock tower at one end, and at the other the Cooper Memorial Fountain. In between are many fine houses and hotels, including the headquarters of the Jockey Club formed in 1750. Next door is the National Horseracing Museum telling the story of horseracing development in this country. The racecourse itself has been painted by many great artists — the wide downland, high elevation and magnificent views creating a memorable setting, enhanced by the massive Anglo-Saxon earthwork known as Devil's Dyke.

Leave Newmarket on the A1304, and in ¾ mile turn left on to the B1061, SP 'Haverhill'. Shortly bear right, then go over a level crossing into Cambridgeshire. In 1 mile cross the Devil's Dyke, marked by a line of trees. Continue to Dullingham then in 1 mile turn left and pass through Burrough Green. Continue to Great Bradley.

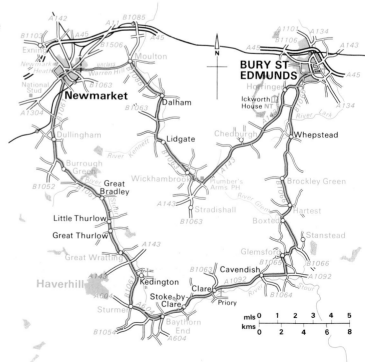

Cavendish, once the ancestral village of the Dukes of Devonshire

GT BRADLEY, Suffolk
The church at Great Bradley — a village set in meadowland beside the River Stour — is reputed to have the best brick porch in Suffolk: its bricks made by the 'King's own brickmaker' in early Tudor times. The tower, built in the early 14th century, retains one of its original bells and also has a fire-place, which may have been used in the preparation of the holy wafers used in communion.

Continue on the B1061 to Little and Great Thurlow.

The best of Britain's horses compete on the famous Newmarket turf, the centre of the English horse racing world

LITTLE & GT THURLOW, Suffolk
The 2 villages are so close together as to be almost one. Great Thurlow has a fine Georgian Hall and a Perpendicular church, originally Norman, in which there is a sanctuary chair where criminals could claim safe refuge. Little Thurlow has a past dominated by the Soames family, who built the almshouses and grammar school in the 1600s.

Continue to Great Wratting, then at the main road turn right, then left, on to the B1061 and shortly skirt Kedington.

KEDINGTON, Suffolk
Kedington possesses one of the foremost churches in Suffolk. Stepping on to the uneven brick floor, seeing the ancient pews and monuments that have not changed in centuries, is like stepping back in time. There are separate little pews for boys and girls, and another angled so that the overseers could keep an eye on their charges, a triple-decker pulpit, and the Barnardister pew. The Barnardister family was one of Suffolk's most important and oldest families, stretching back for 27 generations in an unbroken line.

Continue on the B1061 and at Sturmer turn left on to the A604. Follow the River Stour round to Baythorn End, then turn left on to the A1092 Clare road and recross the river into Suffolk to reach Stoke-by-Clare.

STOKE-BY-CLARE, Suffolk
Strung out along the road in the Stour valley, is Stoke-By-Clare, with houses of the 15th-19th centuries, some of which are timber-framed or plastered and decorated with chevrons or fish-scale patterns. Near the church stands a tall Tudor dovecot, resembling a gatehouse, which belonged to a college of priests who were transferred from a priory in Clare in 1124. A Queen Anne house, now a private school, has the remains of the old priory built into it. In 1948 wall-paintings were revealed in the church; they are thought to be some of the last executed before the Reformation.

Continue to Clare.

CLARE, Suffolk
Clare is an ancient little market town on the River Stour with a history centred upon its Norman castle of which only the 53ft-high motte and some masonry remains. Lady Elizabeth Clare, who founded Clare College, Cambridge, in the 14th century, lived here occasionally, and in those days the castle was large enough to house her 250-strong retinue and several hundred horses. The Augustinians founded their first priory in England here in 1248, and there are extensive remains still visible near the river. The Prior's house was turned into a dwelling house after the Dissolution and is complete. Among the many old houses in the town is the Ancient House, c1473. This timber-framed building is renowned for the fine plaster-work, or pargetting, on its exterior walls. Also of interest is the Swan Inn, which has a remarkable carved bracket of a swan with a crown round its neck.

Leave on the A1092, SP 'Sudbury' and continue to Cavendish.

CAVENDISH, Suffolk
Cavendish is one of Suffolk's show-pieces. A noble church rises above half-timbered thatched cottages around a village green. By the pond is the Old Rectory, a 16th-century building which was used by Sue Ryder as a home for concentration-camp victims. St Mary's Church dates from the 13th and 14th centuries and has within it 2 lecterns; one is a brass 16th-century eagle, the other is a wooden lectern with 2 17th-century books chained to it.

In 1 mile turn left on to the B1065 for Glemsford. Follow SP 'Bury St Edmunds' through the village and ¾ mile beyond the church turn left on to the B1066, following the attractive Glem valley to Boxted. Beyond the village the road becomes more winding and hilly and passes through Hartest and Brockley to Whepstead.

WHEPSTEAD, Suffolk
Set in splendid rolling country, Whepstead possesses the only church dedicated to St Petronilla, and its fair share of Suffolk manor houses (not open); Plumpton Hall, where 2 of Cromwell's brothers-in-law lived; Doveden (pronounced Duffin) Hall, moated with Tudor chimneys, and Manston Hall, red-brick, half-timbered and now a farmhouse.

3½ miles beyond Whepstead turn right on to the A143 for the return to Bury St Edmunds.

CAMBRIDGE, Cambs

This famous and attractive university town started life as a small Celtic settlement on the marshy banks of the Cam. In 1209 a split in the Oxford community resulted in a migration of students and scholars to Cambridge, and the establishment of a university that was to rival its unwilling parent in wealth and prestige. Traces of the first foundation – which was Peterhouse in 1284 – are largely disguised by later work, but 14th-century Clare College occupies buildings that were part of a 12th-century nunnery. Most of the other colleges show similar mixtures. King's College, founded by Henry VI in 1441, has an outstanding chapel that overlooks the Cam and is famous for some of the finest gothic fan vaulting in Europe. Corpus Christi is unique in having been founded by two town guilds, and lovely half-timbered Queens' of 1346 is by far the most picturesque. Much more can be learned about the university and its superb buildings, and the interested visitor is advised to invest in a guide booklet. The town itself is a delightful collection of old streets and houses alongside the river. Peaceful lawns and meadows slope down to the water's edge as grassy quays for summer punters, in marked contrast to the busy activity of the excellent shopping areas in the middle of town. Not surprisingly the city has several good museums. Extensive art and archaeological collections are housed in the Fitzwilliam, the Scott Polar Research Institute has many relics relating to famous expeditions, and the Sedgwick displays fossils from many different parts of the world. Cambridge and County Folk Museum is packed with domestic and agricultural bygones.

Leave Cambridge on the A1303 'Bedford' road and drive for 2½ miles to reach Madingley Postmill.

BETWEEN THE OUSE AND THE CAM

West of Cambridge and the willow-shaded Cam a countryside of orchards and pasture stretches flatly to low Fenland horizons. Here and there the skyline is interrupted by a windmill or church tower, the roofs of an ancient riverside town, or the bushy crown of an occasional copse.

Trinity College Bridge in Cambridge leads to the famous 'Backs'.

MADINGLEY POSTMILL, Cambs

The body of this restored windmill pivots on a central post so that the sails can be turned into the wind. Originally from Huntingdonshire, this interesting industrial relic was moved to its present site in 1936.

Continue for ¼ mile to reach the American Cemetery.

AMERICAN CEMETERY & CHAPEL, Cambs

The War Memorial Chapel that stands here is a striking example of modern architecture. Inside is a 540-square-foot map showing Atlantic sea and air routes used by American forces during World War II.

Continue and at roundabout take 4th exit on to an unclassified road to reach Madingley.

MADINGLEY, Cambs

Just outside this attractive village is Madingley Hall, a fine Elizabethan house that stands in a wooded park and serves as a hostel for university students. Both Edward VII and George VI lived here when they were undergraduates at Cambridge.

Continue to the A604 and turn left. Proceed for 4 miles, turn right on to an unclassified road, and drive to Swavesey.

SWAVESEY, Cambs

Attractively situated close to fenland, this long, narrow village has a good 14th-century church with notable window tracery. Inside the building are bench-ends with animal carvings.

Proceed to Over.

OVER, Cambs

This pretty fenland village stands in orchard country to the east of the River Ouse, a popular venue for boating and angling. Its pleasant church contains a bell that was cast some 600 years ago.

Drive to Willingham.

WILLINGHAM, Cambs

The local windmill and the impressive tower of Willingham's 14th-century church are prominent landmarks in the flat farmlands that surround this village. The church nave has a notable 15th-century hammerbeam roof adorned with over 50 carved angels.

Turn left on to the B1050 and reach the River Ouse. Follow the river and turn left on to the A1123 to enter the village of Earith. Continue through Needingworth, and after 1¾ miles turn left on to the A1096 to enter St Ives.

ST IVES, Cambs

In 1110 King Henry I granted St Ives the right to hold a fair. The town grew up around its fairground and its annual market became established as one of the largest in England. The River Ouse runs through the town and is spanned here by a narrow 6-arched bridge (AM) that dates from the 15th century. The Norris Museum situated in the Broadway contains a comprehensive collection of Huntingdonshire history.

Follow the A1096 south and cross the river. After ½ mile turn right on to an unclassified road and continue to Hemingford Grey.

HEMINGFORD GREY, Cambs

A moated mansion in this lovely village dates back to the 12th century and is thought to be the oldest inhabited dwelling in England. The 12th-century church is picturesquely sited in a bend of the River Ouse.

Turn left and shortly right, proceed to Hemingford Abbots, and follow SP 'Huntingdon' to join the A604. Drive for 1 mile and branch left. Meet a roundabout and turn right on to an unclassified road to reach Godmanchester.

GODMANCHESTER, Cambs

The site of this ancient town was once occupied by a Roman military station. Nowadays it is a treasure-house of varied architectural styles. Island Hall is a mid-18th-century mansion set in a tranquil riverside setting (open).

Turn right on to the B1043, crossing a 14th-century bridge (AM), and enter Huntingdon.

HUNTINGDON, Cambs

Both Oliver Cromwell and the diarist Samuel Pepys were born here and attended the town's former grammar school. Parts of the building date back to Norman times, and today it houses a museum of Cromwellian relics.

Leave Huntingdon on the A141 'Kettering' road and drive to Hinchingbrooke House.

King's College Chapel, a medieval masterpiece, is one of the principal glories of Cambridge.

HINCHINGBROOKE HOUSE, Cambs

Now restored and in use as a school, this Tudor and later mansion (open) has been home to the Cromwells and the Earls of Sandwich. It incorporates parts of a medieval nunnery.

Continue on the A141 'Kettering' road to Brampton.

BRAMPTON, Cambs

Pepys House in Brampton is a lovely old gabled cottage that was the home of the diarist's parents, and was owned by him from 1664 to 1680. The stalls in the local church display excellent carving.

Leave Brampton and in 2 miles join the A1 for the outskirts of Buckden.

The Great Ouse at Hemingford Grey.

Britain's oldest surviving postmill at Bourn resembles those seen in illuminated manuscripts.

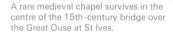

BUCKDEN, Cambs

Considerable remains of Buckden Palace, a former residence of the bishops of Lincoln, comprise a fine Tudor tower and an inner gatehouse of c1490 (open). The buildings are well restored and in use as a school. The local church is known for its notable spire and carvings.

Continue to a roundabout on the A1 and take the B661 'Kimbolton' road to reach Grafham Water.

GRAFHAM WATER, Cambs

This 2½-square-mile reservoir supplies drinking water for 1½ million people and is a valuable leisure amenity offering long bankside walks and facilities for boating and trout fishing. Several picnic sites have been laid out around the edge.

Continue to Great Staughton.

GREAT STAUGHTON, Cambs

Opposite 14th-century and later Great Staughton Church, which has a fine tower and contains good monuments, is a mansion with a pair of picturesque timber-framed barns. The village cross dates from the 17th century and features a sundial.

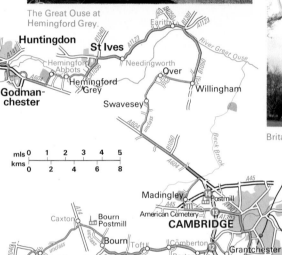

A rare medieval chapel survives in the centre of the 15th-century bridge over the Great Ouse at St Ives.

At Great Staughton turn left on to the A45 and continue for 4 miles, crossing the A1. Cross the River Ouse and enter St Neots on the B1428.

ST NEOTS, Cambs

The great charm of this ancient market town is its compactness. Interesting old inns can be found in many of its secretive back streets, and attractive buildings cluster round three sides of the Ouse-side market square.

Leave St Neots by turning right on to the B1043 crossing the A45 and after 3 miles join the A1. Turn left on to the B1042 and drive through Sandy.

SANDY, Beds

Low wooded hills that rise to the east of this large River Ivel village make a pleasant change from the flat countryside crossed by much of the tour. About 1 mile east is the 100-acre Lodge Nature Reserve, which is the HQ of the Royal Society for the Protection of Birds. A nature trail offers public access.

Continue along the B1042 and pass a TV mast to the left before reaching Potton. At Potton take the B1040 'St Ives' road through Gamlingay to Waresley, then drive forward on to an unclassified road for Great Gransden. Turn right, then shortly left into the village. Follow SP to Caxton and turn right then left for 'Bourn' to reach Bourn Postmill.

BOURN POSTMILL, Cambs

Although the working parts of this remarkable windmill have been replaced from time to time, the base and outer structure date back at least to 1636. It is claimed to be the oldest example in England.

Continue for 1 mile, meet a T-junction and turn right to reach Bourn.

BOURN, Cambs

Red-brick Bourn Hall has Jacobean origins but has been restored. Between it and the attractive little Bourn Brook is a church with a fine 13th-century tower.

Drive through Bourn and join the B1046. Continue through Toft and Comberton to reach Barton, and turn left on to the A603. Proceed for 1 mile, at roundabout take 3rd exit on to the unclassified 'Trumpington' road, and continue to Grantchester.

GRANTCHESTER, Cambs

Rupert Brooke immortalized this beautiful village of thatched and lime-washed cottages in his poem *The Old Vicarage, Grantchester*. He lived here for a while after leaving King's College in nearby Cambridge, and wrote of the village as 'the lovely hamlet'.

Cross the Cam and continue to Trumpington.

TRUMPINGTON, Cambs

Inside the elaborate local church is England's second oldest memorial brass. It is dated 1289 and was raised to Sir Roger de Trumpington, whose local associations are obvious in the name. Other features of the village include a 16th-century inn and two 18th-century halls.

Join the A1309 and return to Cambridge.

THE MALVERN HILLS AND THE VALE OF GLOUCESTER

The stark outlines of the Malvern Hills, an ancient natural rampart, are never far from view as the tour follows the pleasant valley of the River Leadon and skirts the fringe of the Royal Forest of Dean, before turning northwards to run through the Vale of Gloucester and the broad valley of the Severn.

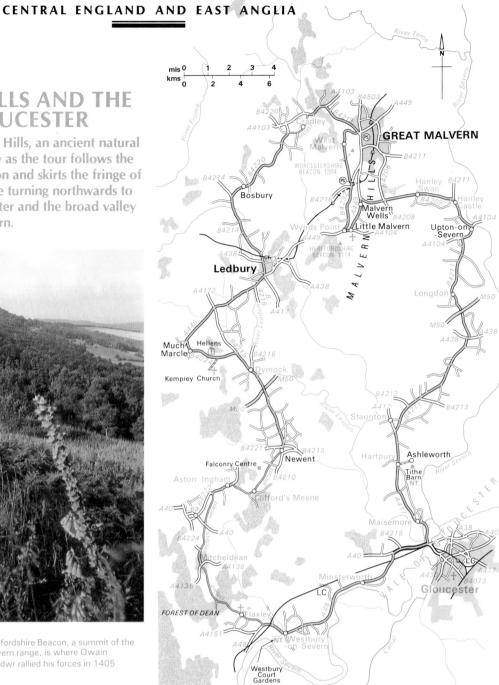

GT MALVERN, Herefs & Worcs
The distinctive character of this busy holiday centre was established in the Victorian and Edwardian periods when people came to take the waters and promenade in the Winter Gardens. Great rambling houses looking out across the town towards Worcester cling precariously to the steep slope of the dramatic Malvern Hills. The town itself clusters around the ancient priory church, a magnificent building which contains exquisite 15th- and 16th-century stained glass and beautiful tiles from the same period. Above the main street of the town by the Mount Pleasant Hotel, a steep flight of steps leads up to St Anne's Well, the source of the pure water for which visitors flocked to Malvern. Among many distinguished residents, the most famous was the composer Sir Edward Elgar, in whose memory an annual festival is held. George Bernard Shaw was a frequent visitor, and several of his plays received their world premiere at the festival.

Herefordshire Beacon, a summit of the Malvern range, is where Owain Glyndwr rallied his forces in 1405

THE MALVERN HILLS, Herefs & Worcs
The Malvern Hills rise abruptly from the broad, flat valley of the River Severn, an impressive 9-mile range of wild, upland country, from where 14 counties can be seen on a clear day. The Worcestershire Beacon at the northern end is the highest (1,395ft) point and the entire length of the ridge can be walked to the Herefordshire Beacon (1,114ft) at the south. The banks of a great Iron-Age fort, known as the British Camp, crown this hill, which Elgar used as the setting for *Caractacus*.

Leave Great Malvern on the B4219, SP 'Worcester' then 'Hereford'. In 2 miles turn left on to the A4103 and in 1 mile turn left on to an unclassified road for Cradley. Beyond the village turn right, SP 'Bromyard', and later turn left on to the B4220, SP 'Ledbury', and continue to Bosbury.

BOSBURY, Herefs & Worcs
Bosbury stands on the banks of the River Leadon, in the centre of a fertile hop and fruit growing region. The village has a charming street of black and white houses around an imposing Norman church with a detached tower. Inside the church, 2 remarkable 16th-century monuments to members of the Harcourt family face each other in baroque splendour.

¾ mile beyond Bosbury turn left on to the B4214, and continue past hop fields to Ledbury.

LEDBURY, Herefs & Worcs
An unspoilt town with a wealth of 16th- and 17th-century black and white buildings, Ledbury is set in a lovely corner of the English countryside where rich green meadows are watered by slow-moving streams. The main street, lined with old houses, leads to the market place where the 17th-century market house, timbered in a herringbone pattern, stands on pillars of oak. Here the Feathers Hotel rubs shoulders with the medieval chapel of St Katherine's Hospital, and a narrow cobbled lane where the houses project over the street takes the visitor straight back to Elizabethan England. At the end of the lane, St Michael's Church displays the grandeur of a small cathedral. Inside is a formidable collection of monuments of every period from the medieval to the 19th-century. Elizabeth Barrett Browning's stern father, Edward Moulton Barrett, lies in the north aisle.

At the crossroads in Ledbury turn right on to the A449, SP 'Ross', and continue to Much Marcle.

MUCH MARCLE, Herefs & Worcs

Cider-making has been a local industry around Much Marcle for nearly 400 years and in the 19th century a local firm was one of the first to build a cider factory. There are 2 manor houses in this attractive black and white village: Homme House (not open) and Hellens, a lovely old brick house (OACT) whose ancestry goes back to Norman times, although the present building is mostly 16th century. The church contains some exquisitely sculptured tombs, including a rare 14th-century oak figure of a man carved from a single block of wood.

Turn left on to the B4024, SP 'Newent'. After 1½ miles a detour can be taken to Kempley Church by turning right on to an unclassified road.

KEMPLEY CHURCH, Glos

The village, whose inhabitants once attended services in Kempley Church, has moved away to Kempley Green, leaving the old vicarage and 17th-century farmhouse isolated beside the Norman Church of St Mary. This small building is unique in England for the series of frescoes in the chancel painted between 1130 and 1140. The centre-piece shows Christ seated on a rainbow, surrounded by sun, moon, stars and the emblems of the Evangelists. Other figures include the Virgin Mary, St Peter and the Apostles.

The main tour continues on the B4024. In 1 mile, turn right on to the B4215 for Dymock, pleasantly situated in the Leadon valley. In 3½ miles turn right, then left, into Newent.

NEWENT, Glos

This small, essentially Georgian, town lies in the heart of an intensely rural part of Gloucestershire. The crooked main street has some well-kept 18th-century houses and a few older, timber-framed buildings, including a market house standing on posts, whose one large upper room is approached by outside stairs.

In the town turn right on to an unclassified road , SP 'Cliffords Mesne'. After 1¼ miles pass the Falconry Centre.

FALCONRY CENTRE, Glos

The ancient art of falconry can be studied at this fascinating centre (OACT) which specialises in birds of prey. There is an interesting museum with many photographs and displays about birds of prey; a wide variety of birds in aviaries; a falcon flying ground and a Hawk Walk where hawks are kept.

Continue through Cliffords Mesne SP 'Ashton Ingham', and in ¾ mile keep left to join the B4222, SP 'Ross', to Aston Ingham. In 1 mile keep forward, SP 'Mitcheldean'. In 1½ miles cross the main road, then in another 1½ miles join the B4224 into Mitcheldean which lies at the northern edge of the Forest of Dean.

THE FOREST OF DEAN, Glos

The Forest of Dean is one of the most ancient royal forests in Britain. For centuries this was an important industrial area, as a vast coalfield underlies the woodland, and iron ore has been worked here since Roman times. Weapons for the Crusades were forged here, and in Tudor times trees were felled to provide timber for warships. These days the Forest has been made more accessible by nature trails, picnic sites and way-marked routes.

At the far end of Mitcheldean go over the crossroads, SP 'Flaxley and Westbury', to follow a pleasant byroad, passing Flaxley. In 1½ miles turn left on to the A48, SP 'Gloucester', and at Westbury-on-Severn pass Westbury Court Gardens.

WESTBURY COURT GARDENS, Glos

Very few of the formal water gardens, modelled in the 17th-century after the Dutch style, survived the 'landscaping' craze of the 18th-century. However, Westbury Court Gardens (NT) lay forlorn and derelict for years, its hedges overgrown, its canals silted up, and its lawns covered with weeds and so remains as one of the best examples of its time. Ten years of devoted work and replanting have restored its elegant design, and the charming colonnaded pavilion has been rebuilt. Plants that are known from records to have flourished there originally have been replanted, including old roses, quince and morello cherry trees.

Continue on the A48, following the River Severn before reaching Minsterworth, a good viewpoint for the famous Severn Bore tidal wave. In 2 miles, at the roundabout, join the A40. There are distant views of Gloucester, with its cathedral, before the tour turns left on to the A417, SP 'Ledbury'. Follow the River Severn through Maisemore to Hartpury, where there is a fine, old tithe barn near the church. A detour can be taken by turning right to Ashleworth.

ASHLEWORTH, Glos

The pretty cottages in this charming little village, tucked away down a country lane, are grouped about a green. Another lane leads to Ashleworth Quay, down by the River Severn, where a church, a manor house (not open) and a great 16th-century tithe barn (NT) make up an outstanding group of medieval limestone buildings. The barn is 125ft long and has a magnificent roof.

The main tour continues on the A417. In 1¼ miles turn right on to the B4211, SP 'Upton-on-Severn'. In 5 miles, at the T-junction, turn right then left, continuing to Longdon with views of the distant Malvern Hills to the left. In 2¼ miles turn right on to the A4104 for Upton-on-Severn.

UPTON-ON-SEVERN, Herefs & Worcs

A delightful reminder of country towns as they used to be, with old-fashioned shops, old inns and streets where it is a joy to stand and look around. Looking out over the meadows of the River Severn, the old church tower, crowned with an 8-sided cupola, is the sole remnant of the original parish church. Locally known as the 'Pepperpot' it is now a Heritage Centre showing the development of the town and the Civil War battle of Upton Bridge.

In Upton-on-Severn turn left, then keep forward on the B4211, SP 'Malvern', to Hanley Castle. Turn left again on to the B4209, SP 'Malvern Wells', to pass through Hanley Swan, and continue to Malvern Wells.

MALVERN WELLS, Herefs & Worcs

Malvern Wells is a continuation of Great Malvern, liberally sprinkled with the gracious villas of a bygone age. In the churchyard of St Wulstan's Church at Little Malvern where primroses and violets flower among the graves in spring, is the simple tombstone to the composer Sir Edward Elgar and his wife.

At Malvern Wells turn left on to the A449, SP 'Ledbury', and 'Ross', and ascend to Wynds Point, a notable viewpoint beneath the Herefordshire Beacon. At the British Camp Hotel turn right on to the B4232, SP 'West Malvern', along Jubilee Drive. In 2¼ miles turn right, then left, and skirt the Worcestershire Beacon to West Malvern. Continue on the B4232 for the return to Great Malvern.

GREAT YARMOUTH AND HER HINTERLAND

Something for everyone; traditional seaside entertainment is to be had at lively Yarmouth, with its pier, arcades and illuminations. Southwold offers the homely attractions of a small fishing town (as well as fresh seafood), and for those who prefer to get away from it all, and admire unspoilt coastal scenery, there is Covehithe.

GT YARMOUTH, Norfolk
Three rivers, the Yare, the Bure and the Waverley, flow into the sea at Great Yarmouth which stands on the long spit of land separating the fresh and salt waters. For over 1,000 years Yarmouth has been a great herring fishing port, but its fleet has dwindled during this century and the tourism which began in the 18th century has overtaken it. A promenade runs along the seaward side of the town and behind there are entertainments of every kind: bowling greens, tennis courts, boating lakes, theatres, amusement arcades and piers which are brilliantly illuminated during the summer season. Although air raids in World War II devastated much of the old town, there are still remains of its medieval town walls and a part of the Rows, a complex grid-iron pattern of narrow streets which grew up within the walls. The Old Merchants House (AM) in Row 117 is a 17th-century house typical of those owned by merchants not quite rich enough to live in the great houses on the quayside. A museum of local history is sited in the Tolhouse (OACT) in Tolhouse Street, a 13th-century building said to be the oldest civic building in Britain. On South Quay the rich merchants had their houses, such as the Customs House of 1720 where John Andrews lived, the most famous of herring merchants, and the Elizabethan House (OACT), a 16th-century house which had a new façade added in the 19th-century. In one corner of the market place is the attractive Fishermen's Hospital, founded in 1702, and next to it is Sewell House (OACT) (1646), where Anna Sewell, authoress of Black Beauty, was born in 1820.

Leave Yarmouth on the A12. At the roundabout at the edge of Gorleston-on-Sea, take the 3rd exit, SP 'Burgh Castle'. In 2 miles turn right for the village of Burgh Castle.

BURGH CASTLE, Norfolk
The village is named after the Roman fort (AM) here, which was one of a chain the invaders built along the east coast. After the Romans left, St Fursey, an Irishman, built a monastery within the fort walls, but the site was later used again as a castle by the

Normans. In later centuries stone from the castle was used for building in the village. The substantial walls and bastions, still held together by Roman mortar, give an idea of the scale of the fort, built in about AD 300.

From Burgh Castle follow the Belton road and in 1½ miles, at the T-junction, turn left, SP 'Yarmouth'. In 1 mile turn left on to the A143, then immediately right, SP 'Blendeston'. In 1½ miles turn right, SP 'Somerleyton', then after another mile turn left. Later pass (left) Somerleyton Hall.

SOMERLEYTON HALL, Suffolk
The Victorian railway entrepreneur Sir Morton Peto had this Anglo-Italian mansion (OACT) built around an old Elizabethan hall in 1844. He also had the church, school and cottages of the village built to complement it. The house stands among magnificent trees and shrubs, and of particular interest is the clipped yew maze. The oak parlour in the house has beautiful carved panelling by Grinling Gibbons, and the dining room is hung with paintings by old masters. The game trophies proudly displayed throughout the house are the victims of the sporting Crossley family, who bought the house in 1866.

At the next T-junction turn right on to the B1076 and continue to St Olaves. From here a short detour can be made by turning right on to the A143 to visit Fritton.

FRITTON, Suffolk
The church here has a Saxon tower and a chancel showing the work of Norman stone masons. There are several notable wall-paintings, and a trap door under the thatched roof of the chancel is said to have been used by smugglers whom prudence required them to lie low. Near the partly-ruined St Olave's Priory (AM), is the Fritton Decoy, a long, wooded lake used to trap wildfowl.

At St Olaves the main tour turns left on to the A143. Cross the River Waveney and continue through Haddiscoe to Tofts Monks. In 2¼ miles, at the roundabout, take the A146. After 1 mile turn right on to the A145 into Beccles.

The superbly restored post mill at Holton: the mill is pivoted on a central post and turns with the wind

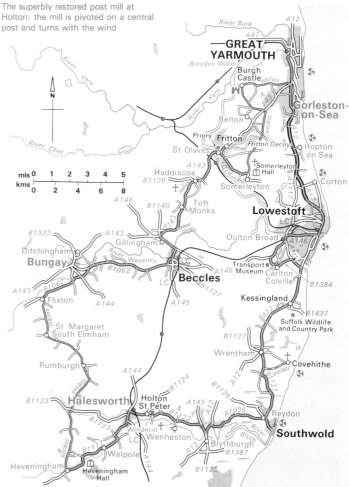

The River Blythe at Southwold

The main tour continues to Wrentham. Here turn right on to the A12 and continue to Kessingland.

KESSINGLAND, Suffolk
The village is mainly in 2 parts; near the coast road, from where the church's 13th-century tower has served for centuries as a landmark for sailors; and the popular beach and caravan site by the sea. Nearby is the Suffolk Wildlife and Country Park, (OACT) a small, attractive zoo with a mixed collection of animals, including lions, tigers, a walk-through aviary, monkeys, badgers and a lake full of waterfowl.

Remain on the A12 for another 2 miles, than at the roundabout take the A1117, SP 'Great Yarmouth'. At the next roundabout take the B1384. In ¾ mile turn right, SP 'Beccles', then at the T-junction turn left and shortly pass the East Anglia Transport Museum at Carlton Colville.

EAST ANGLIA TRANSPORT MUSEUM, Suffolk
The museum covers 3 acres which can be seen from a tramway and narrow-gauge railway, and exhibits include historic cars, commercial vehicles, trams, buses and trolleybuses as well as collections of curios connected with the historical development of transport.

Continue to the A146 and turn right to reach Oulton Broad. At the traffic signals turn right with the A146 and continue into Lowestoft.

LOWESTOFT, Suffolk
During the 14th century Lowestoft was an important fishing port, valuable to the nation, and although the fleets are now a shadow of their former glory, the town is a lively place, and the trawlers docking and unloading their catch to be cleaned and gutted on the quayside ready for the busy fish market, is an exciting spectacle. South Town is the tourist section, with many seaside lodgings giving it a traditional seaside atmosphere, and a long esplanade runs alongside the beach to Claremont Pier. At one end is a children's corner, a boating lake and a miniature steam railway. The northern limit of the old town is marked by the Upper Lighthouse, open at weekdays. A feature of this part of the town are the 'Scores', narrow alleys which cut steeply down from the High Street to the shore, where the fish-houses for curing herring used to stand, few of which still survive.

Leave on the A12. In 5 miles re-enter Norfolk and later skirt Gorleston-on-Sea before the return to Great Yarmouth.

Southwold — a pleasant seaside resort with the character of a fishing port

BECCLES, Suffolk
Beccles quay on the River Waveney is an ideal centre for exploring the network of local waterways, and the boats provide a colourful scene in the summer months. The 14th-century chapel is unusual in having a separate 92ft-high bell tower, holding a peal of 10 bells.

Leave Beccles on the B1062, and follow the Waveney valley to the outskirts of Bungay
Here, turn left on to the B1062, SP 'Diss'. In ½ mile go over the staggered crossroads and continue to Flixton. Pass the Buck Inn and at the next road junction turn left, SP 'St Margarets', and in 1¾ miles turn left into St Margaret South Elmham. Continue to Rumburgh and in 1 mile turn right, SP 'Cookley', then in 1 mile bear right, SP 'Heveningham'. In another mile go over the staggered crossroads and continue to Heveningham. Turn left into the village and join the B1117, SP 'Halesworth', and in 1 mile pass the entrance to Heveningham Hall.

HEVENINGHAM HALL, Suffolk
In 1777 Sir Gerald Vanneck MP commissioned Sir Robert Taylor to enlarge the family's Queen Anne house, Heveningham Hall. Taylor built an impressive

Palladian mansion; he screened the north front with Corinthian columns and added a wing to either side. Then James Wyatt took over, his task being to oversee the interior decoration. Biagio Rebecca, an Italian artist, was employed to do the house painting. The result is a magnificent Georgian house typical of all that is fine of the period. The grounds were landscaped by Capability Brown, and include one of Suffolk's finest 'crinkle-crankle' walls (curves in and out to give plants' protection) and a beautifully-proportioned orangery by Wyatt.

Continue through Walpole and in 2 miles join the A144 for Halesworth. At the end of the main street turn right on to the B1132, SP 'Southwold', and continue to Holton-St-Peter.

HOLTON ST PETER, Suffolk
An attractive village which takes the latter half of its name from the Church of St Peter. This has a round Norman tower, a Norman doorway, a 15th-century octagonal font and a 16th-century linenfold pulpit. Overlooking the village from a hillside is a post mill situated among pine woods.

At the edge of the village bear right, then in 3½ miles turn right on to the A145. At the next T-junction turn left on to the A12, then skirt an inland lake formed by the River Blyth before turning right on to the A1095. Continue through Reydon to Southwold.

SOUTHWOLD, Suffolk
Southwold, perched on cliffs overlooking the North Sea, has flint, brick and colour-washed cottages, a church and a market place. There are 7 spacious greens which resulted from a disastrous fire in 1659, because as the herring trade declined, there was less money for rebuilding, and the damaged areas were left as open spaces. There is, however, evidence of Dutch influence in the buildings that did arise, as can be seen in the gabled cottages in Church Street, and the museum in Bartholomew Green (OACT). The museum displays relics of the Southwold Railway (1879-1929), and illustrates local history, including an archaeological collection.

The tour returns to Reydon and turns right on to the B1127, SP 'Wrentham'. After 3 miles a byroad (right) may be taken to visit Covehithe.

COVEHITHE, Suffolk
This delightful, unspoilt village has a stretch of sandy beach that is often empty. The beach is backed by cliffs and the village dominated by the ruins of a huge 14th-15th century church. Judging by the size of the church, Covehithe must once have been a prosperous place; the church fell into disrepair in the 17th century.

Chinese ring-necked pheasants in John Gould's *Book of Birds*, which can be seen in the library of Somerleyton Hall

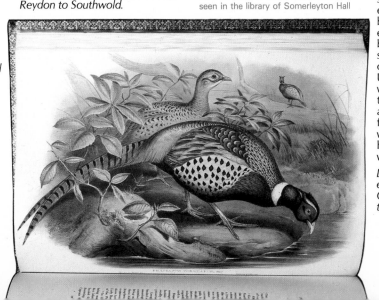

HADLEIGH, Suffolk

Many fine Georgian and Victorian houses are preserved in this River Brett market town, and the High Street shows a remarkable architectural mixture of timber, brick, and plaster-faced buildings. Some of the plasterwork has been raised in decorative relief, known as pargetting, and most of the structures are excellent examples of their type. The fine 15th-century Guildhall (open) has two overhanging storeys and has been a school and an almshouse. Also of note is the imposing Deanery Tower, a remnant of the medieval palace of Archdeacon Pykenham. Features of the local 14th- to 15th-century church include a bench-end that depicts the legend of a wolf which found and guarded the decapitated head of St Edmund.

Leave Hadleigh on the A1071 'Sudbury' road. At the edge of the town turn right on to the A1141 'Kersey, Lavenham' road and follow the shallow valley of the River Brett for 1¼ miles. Meet crossroads and turn left on to an unclassified road for Kersey.

CONSTABLE LANDSCAPES

Here is the country of John Constable, who immortalized much of its rural beauty in his paintings. Here also are the ragged estuaries of the Stour and Orwell, which carve the coastline into a confusion of small bays, sheltered shingle beaches, and reed-covered marshes.

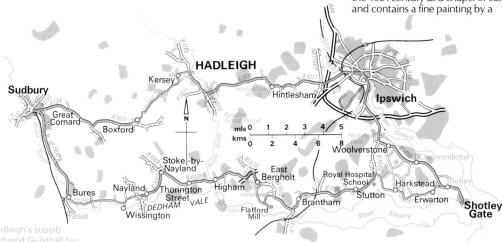

Hadleigh's superb timbered Guildhall has been well restored and extended. The ground floor originally formed almshouses.

Wildlife of all kinds and restored Thames barges co-exist on the Orwell estuary.

KERSEY, Suffolk

Shakespeare mentioned the cloth once made in this beautiful old weaving centre in his plays *Measure for Measure* and *Love's Labours Lost*. Nowadays Kersey's Brett Valley position, sloping streets, and numerous half-timbered buildings make it known as one of the most picturesque places in Suffolk. The local church is a gem of 14th- and 15th-century architecture on a site mentioned in the *Domesday Book*.

Drive to the church in Kersey and follow the 'Boxford' road. Continue to Boxford.

BOXFORD, Suffolk

This quaint old village takes its name from an attractive stream that runs close to its timber-framed cottages. Its church features an unusual wooden porch that may be the earliest of its kind in the country, and contains an unusual 17th-century font with doors.

Leave Boxford on the A1071 'Sudbury' road and continue for 2½ miles. Turn right on to the A134 and drive to Sudbury.

SUDBURY, Suffolk

Sudbury stands on the River Stour and is famous as the birthplace of painter Thomas Gainsborough in 1727. His house at 46 Gainsborough Street is now a local arts centre and museum containing a selection of his work, and he is commemorated by a bronze statue on Market Hill. Novelist Charles Dickens referred to the town as 'Eatanswill' in *Pickwick Papers*. St Peter's Church was built in the 15th century as a chapel of ease and contains a fine painting by a local artist named Robert Cardinall. St Gregory's is much older, having been built on the foundations of an old college by the Archbishop of Canterbury c1365. In 1381 he was brutally murdered in the Peasants' Revolt, and his skull is preserved as his memorial in the vestry. Other features of the building include beautifully carved choir stalls and one of the finest 15th-century font covers in the country. Also in the town is the notable Corn Exchange, containing the Quay Theatre and Arts Centre.

Leave Sudbury on the B1508 SP 'Bures' and continue to Great Cornard.

GREAT CORNARD, Suffolk

Although almost a suburb of nearby Sudbury, the nucleus of this village is still centred on its charming church and preserves an identity entirely separate from its large neighbour.

Stay on the B1508 and drive through the Stour Valley to Bures.

BURES, Suffolk

Fine half-timbered houses and an elegant church dating from the 13th to 15th centuries are the main features of this pretty little village, which stands on the banks of the River Stour. Inside the church is a font adorned with painted shields and a private chapel containing a monument dated 1514. Chapel Barn is an ancient thatched building that was once attached to the former Earl's Colne Priory.

Drive to Bures Church and turn left on to an unclassified road SP 'Nayland'. Follow the Stour Valley for 3¾ miles to reach a right turn that can be taken as a short detour to Wissington.

WISSINGTON, Suffolk

Many people come to this attractive village to see the famous series of 13th-century wall paintings in St Mary's Church, a well preserved Norman building with later additions. Close by is an 18th-century house built by architect Sir John Soane.

On the main route, continue with the 'Nayland' road and in 1 mile meet staggered crossroads. Drive across on to the B1087 to enter Nayland at the start of Dedham Vale.

The Chapel Barn near Bures preserves several alabaster tomb chests.

NAYLAND, Suffolk

Alston Court, an attractive half-timbered courtyard house, is one of many 15th-century buildings to be seen in this River Stour village. John Constable painted the altar piece in the local church.

DEDHAM VALE, Essex

This area of outstanding natural beauty stretches from Nayland village to Flatford Mill, and is familiar to many people through the paintings of John Constable.

From Nayland continue on the B1087 to reach Stoke-by-Nayland.

STOKE-BY-NAYLAND, Suffolk

Visitors who are also lovers of John Constable's paintings will recognise the lofty 120ft tower of Stoke-by-Nayland's handsome church. Entry to the south end of the building is through magnificently carved doors, and inside are many notable monuments. Close by are the timber-framed Maltings and the Guildhall, both superb survivals from the 16th century.

Leave Stoke-by-Nayland on the B1068 'Ipswich' road and drive to Thorington Street.

THORINGTON STREET, Suffolk

Early 18th-century additions are evident in the mainly 16th-century structure of Thorington Hall (NT), a fine house that completely dominates this tiny village.

Continue on the B1068 and later cross the River Brett to enter Higham.

HIGHAM, Suffolk

Attractive St Mary's Church and 19th-century Higham Hall preside over this pleasant little village, which has a number of good timber-framed cottages.

Leave Higham on the B1068 and after 2 miles meet the A12. Turn left then in ¼ mile turn left again onto the B1070 'East Bergholt' road. Continue for 1 mile into East Bergholt.

EAST BERGHOLT, Suffolk

In 1776 the great landscape painter John Constable was born here, and speaking of the area he once said 'These scenes made me a painter.' Clustered round the 14th-century church are mellow Elizabethan cottages set amid beautiful gardens. Separated from the church but close by is a unique timber-framed belfry. Stour, home of the late Randolph Churchill, stands near by in the gardens which he created (open).

Drive to East Bergholt Church and bear right to reach Flatford Mill.

FLATFORD MILL, Suffolk

Perhaps the most famous and admired of all Constable's landscape subjects, Flatford Mill (NT) is picturesquely situated on the River Stour and serves as a field-study centre. Both it and nearby Willy Lott's Cottage (NT) attract legions of artists every summer.

Leave Flatford Mill and bear right along a one-way street. After ¾ mile meet crossroads and turn right. Continue for ½ mile to meet the B1070 'Manningtree' road, then drive forward and continue for another 1½ miles to the A137. Turn left here SP 'Ipswich' to reach Brantham.

BRANTHAM, Suffolk

Inside Brantham Church is an altar-piece with a painting by John Constable.

Leave Brantham on the A137. Continue for 1 mile, reach the Bull Inn, and turn right on to the B1080 'Holbrook' road. Continue to Stutton.

STUTTON, Suffolk

Architecture from many periods survives in the church, and there are a number of notable private houses in the neighbourhood. Among these is Stutton Hall (not open), which dates from 1553.

Drive forward for 1 mile and pass through the grounds of the Royal Hospital School.

ROYAL HOSPITAL SCHOOL, Suffolk

An impressive tower with a white stone pinnacle that can be seen for miles around marks the location of the Royal Hospital School, which was founded in 1694 for the sons of seamen. The present group of buildings was occupied when the school moved from Greenwich in the early part of this century.

From the school continue for ½ mile and turn right on to an unclassified road for Harkstead.

Dark-framed and pastel-tinted weavers' houses line Kersey's pretty main-street, which runs down to a small ford.

HARKSTEAD, Suffolk

Notable features of this solitary 14th-century church are its contemporary tower and fine Easter Sepulchre. The building as a whole is an interesting example of medieval architecture.

Continue on the winding 'Shotley' road and drive through Erwarton.

ERWARTON, Suffolk

Red-brick almshouses are a striking feature of this pretty village, which also has an Elizabethan hall with a fine gateway.

Leave Erwarton and pass the gatehouse of Erwarton Hall. Continue to Shotley and turn right on to the B1456 for Shotley Gate.

SHOTLEY GATE, Suffolk

Views of the busy shipping traffic into Harwich and Felixstowe can be enjoyed from this promontory. Close by is the former naval training centre HMS Ganges.

Return along the B1456 'Ipswich' road, pass through Chelmondiston, and reach Woolverstone.

The scene at Flatford Mill has changed little from the days when it was the subject of Constable's famous pictures.

WOOLVERSTONE, Suffolk

Imposing Woolverstone Hall, built in the 18th century by William Berners, is beautifully situated overlooking the attractive Orwell estuary. It now houses a school.

Continue along the B1456 beside the River Orwell, then later turn right on to the A137 and drive to Ipswich.

IPSWICH, Suffolk

Modern commercial development has made this major port and agricultural centre into the largest town in Suffolk. In spite of this it has managed to preserve a number of historic buildings.

Leave Ipswich with SP 'Colchester', then join the A1071 'Sudbury' road. Cross the River Gipping and proceed to Hintlesham

HINTLESHAM, Suffolk

The Great Hall was recently owned by the the internationally famous chef Robert Carrier, but is now a Hotel. The building itself has an Elizabethan core behind a fine Georgian acade and features a drawing room with an exceptional filigreed plaster ceiling. Inside the local church are notable monuments to the Timperley family.

Leave Hintlesham on the A1071 and return to Hadleigh.

HEREFORD, Herefs & Worcs
Once the capital of Saxon West Mercia, this ancient town is at the centre of a rich agricultural district and is especially noted for the production of cider. There has been a cathedral in the city since the 7th century, but the present building dates mainly from the 12th and shows a variety of later alterations. It is dedicated to St Mary and to St Ethelbert, a king of East Anglia who was murdered near Hereford in AD 794. His tomb later became a famous shrine. Other notable relics in the cathedral are the 14th-century *Mappa Mundi* (Map of the World), King Stephen's 800-year-old chair, the best library of chained books in the country, and many monuments and tombs. Cloisters leading to the ancient Bishop's Palace contain a rare 12th-century timbered hall, and the College of Vicars Choral dates from the 15th century. There is another chained library in All Saints Church. The 11th-century St Peter's Church is the oldest in Hereford. A wealth of half-timbered buildings is preserved here, including the outstanding early-15th-century Old House, now a museum. In Widemarsh Street is the St John Coningsby Museum, which incorporates a 12th-century chapel and hall with 17th-century almshouses. Preserved main-line steam locomotives are maintained at the Bulmers Railway Centre. The lovely Wye flows under the ancient Wye Bridge, past the cathedral grounds and castle ruins. Also to be seen are the Museum and Art Gallery, the Churchill Gardens Museum in a fine Regency house, the Cider Museum with a reconstruction of a cider factory, and the Waterworks Museum containing a collection of pumping engines. There are also some remains of the medieval city walls.

Leave Hereford on the A438 SP 'Brecon'. After 5 miles reach The Weir on the left.

THE WEIR, Herefs & Worcs
Fine views of the Wye and the Black Mountains can be enjoyed from this steeply sloping riverside garden (NT, open). The house (not open) dates from the 18th century.

Continue to Letton, with occasional views of the Wye, and 1¾ miles beyond the village turn left and pass through Willersley and Winforton. Proceed to Whitney-on-Wye.

Follow the Wye to enter the Welsh county of Powys. Continue, with views of the Black Mountains to the left, to reach the outskirts of Clyro.

CLYRO, Powys
Francis Kilvert the diarist was curate of this quiet little village between 1865 and 1872. His notes and records paint a highly detailed picture of life in the Radnorshire hills during the 19th century, and have been the subject of a television series. The local church was rebuilt in 1853 but

RIVERS OF THE SOUTH

After looping from its mid-Wales source the magical Wye swings in great curves down to Hay, Ross, and the cathedral city of Hereford. West of the Wye the River Dore flows gently through its fertile valley to join the Monnow, a Wye tributary overlooked by ruined border fortresses.

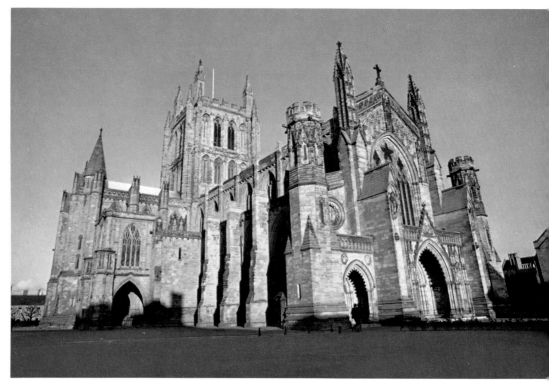

Hereford Cathedral's massive sandstone tower was designed and built at the beginning of the 14th century.

retains some of its original 13th-century structure. There are slight remains of a Norman castle, and to the east, of a Roman fort.

Turn left on to the B4351, shortly cross the Wye, then turn right into Hay-on-Wye.

HAY-ON-WYE, Powys
Book lovers are in their element here, for Hay has more than its fair share of book shops. Narrow streets winding through the old town are full of fascinating small shops, and on market day are alive with bustling activity. William de Braose, one of the most ruthless of the Marcher Lords, built a castle here to replace one burned down by King John. Folk hero Owain Glyndwr destroyed the later castle during the 15th century, but a fine gateway, the keep, and parts of the wall remain. Alongside the ruins is a Jacobean house.

At the Blue Boar Inn turn left on the B4348 'Peterchurch' road and re-enter England. After 2¼ miles turn right SP 'Ross' and continue to the edge of Dorstone.

Winding its way from its mountain source, the River Wye sweeps in great loops into the rolling farm and pasture lands at How Caple.

DORSTONE, Herefs & Worcs
Thomas de Brito, one of the four knights who murdered Thomas à Becket in Canterbury Cathedral, founded the local church. Although largely rebuilt in 1889 it retains a 13th-century tower arch. A lane from Dorstone leads 1 mile north to Arthur's Stone, a prehistoric tomb (AM) dating from c 2000 BC. The view from here is magnificent.

Continue and in ¼ mile at crossroads turn right. Drive along the Golden Valley to Peterchurch.

PETERCHURCH, Herefs & Worcs
Situated in the heart of the lush Golden Valley, Peterchurch has a large and exceptionally well-preserved Norman church. A wooden panel representing a fish with a chain round its neck hangs over the south door. Wellbrook Manor (not open) is one of the best examples of a 14th-century hall-house in the country.

After 2 miles turn right on to the B4347 SP 'Pontrilas', still following the River Dore; later enter Abbey Dore.

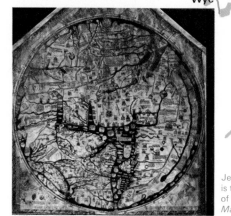

ABBEY DORE, Herefs & Worcs
The meadows and orchards of the Golden Valley surround this little village, which is famous for its parish church. In 1174 an abbey was founded here, but after the Dissolution of the Monasteries its buildings were neglected. In 1633 Lord Scudamore commissioned the brilliant craftsman John Abel to rebuild the church. Much of the original fabric was restored; additions by Abel included the fine wooden screen. Court Gardens (open) across the river have 4 acres of walled and river gardens and exotic plants.

Continue to Ewyas Harold.

EWYAS HAROLD, Herefs & Worcs
An important Norman castle stood here during the 13th century, but only the mound has survived to the present day. The church, partly rebuilt in 1868, retains its impressive 13th-century tower.

Bear left over a river bridge. After ¾ mile cross the A465 and the River Dore, then turn right SP 'Monmouth'. After 1½ miles turn right to re-enter Wales and ascend to Grosmont.

GROSMONT, Gwent
This small old-world town, set amid beautiful scenery by the River Monnow, was a borough until 1860. Inside its massively towered church is a huge, flat-faced stone knight of ancient origin. The castle (AM) here was one of 3 erected in the vicinity to protect the border between England and Wales, the others being Skenfrith and White Castle. It is quite likely that the first on this site was built as early as

c 1070, but it was largely rebuilt during the reign of Henry III. Owain Glyndwr, the Welsh partisan, took the castle in 1410 but was ousted by Harry Monmouth (who was later to become King Henry V). This was Glyndwr's last recorded battle.

Continue through pleasant hill country and after 4¼ miles turn left on to the B4521 SP 'Ross'. Reach the edge of Skenfrith.

Jerusalem is the centre of the world on the *Mappa Mundi*, in Hereford Cathedral.

The craggy ruins of Skenfrith Castle stand near the River Monnow.

SKENFRITH, Gwent
Remains of 13th-century Skenfrith Castle (AM, NT), one of a trio built to defend the English border, include a central keep enclosed by a four-sided curtain wall and a moat. In its western range is a flight of stone steps leading down to a central room which contains a fireplace with beautifully carved capitals. The local church also dates from the 13th century and has an impressive partially-timbered tower.

Cross the River Monnow, re-enter England, and after 1¾ miles at Broad Oak crossroads turn right on to an unclassified road SP 'Welsh Newton'. After 1¼ miles reach the entrance to Pembridge Castle.

PEMBRIDGE CASTLE, Herefs & Worcs
Dating originally from the 13th

century, this castle (not open) has a 16th-century chapel and a 17th-century hall. Some of the structure was restored during this century, and the buildings are partly used by a local farmer.

Continue and in 1 mile reach the A466, and turn right into Welsh Newton. Take the next turning left on to an unclassified road SP 'Llangarren' and after 1¾ miles turn right to enter Llangrove. Continue and descend into Whitchurch.

WHITCHURCH, Herefs & Worcs
Roman remains were found on the outskirts of this village in the 19th century. The Church of St Dubricius is set beside the River Wye and contains a Norman font. Nearby are the Jubilee Maze and Museum of Mazes.

Follow SP 'Ross' to join the A40 and continue through Pencraig, with occasional views of the Wye. Later reach Wilton.

WILTON, Herefs & Worcs
The splendid bridge and nearby buildings here are described in tour from Ross-on-Wye.

At the roundabout take 3rd exit B4260 into Ross.

Ross-on-Wye is dominated by its 13th-century church.

Prehistoric Arthur's Stone is situated near Dorstone.

ROSS ON WYE, Herefs & Worcs
A handsome market hall standing in the centre of this town is just one of many attractive buildings preserved here. Overlooking all is the fine 13th-century church.

Follow SP 'Ledbury' and after 1 mile at roundabout take 2nd exit on to the A449. At the next roundabout take 1st exit SP 'Worcester'. After 1¾ miles branch left to join the B4224 SP 'Hereford'. In ¼ mile turn left and proceed to Fownhope.

FOWNHOPE, Herefs & Worcs
Wooded hills, leafy lanes with grassy verges, and old timbered buildings exist in a magical combination in and around this picturesque Wye-side village. The church has a Norman tower and preserves a contemporary tympanum which depicts the Virgin and Child.

Continue to Mordiford

MORDIFORD, Herefs & Worcs
Parts of the beautiful bridge that spans the Lugg here date from the 14th century. Near by, making a delightful group, are the partly-Norman church and a Georgian rectory. The Palladian mansion of Sufton Court to the north is open occasionally.

Keep left and cross the River Lugg and continue through Hampton Bishop to re-enter Hereford.

FARMLANDS OF SUFFOLK

This corner of rural Suffolk is the England of the romantics, an ideal of pastoral beauty hauntingly captured in the paintings of John Constable. It is a place of rolling meadows and tiny rustic villages, where life moves at an easy pace and the air of timelessness can almost be touched.

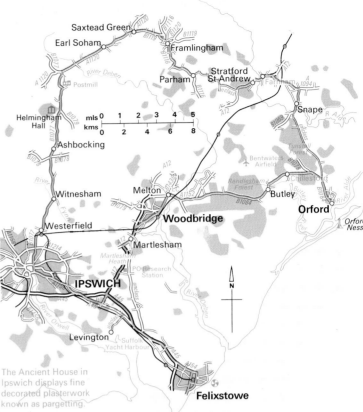

The Ancient House in Ipswich displays fine decorated plasterwork known as pargetting.

This rare old mill on the river Deben at Woodbridge is operated by the rise and fall of water between tides. Records of East Anglian mills worked in this way date back as far as the 12th century.

IPSWICH, Suffolk

Centuries of development have made this major port the largest and one of the most successful towns in Suffolk. It is the main centre of employment in the eastern part of the county, and despite continued expansion has managed to keep many relics of its eventful past intact. A red-brick gateway bearing royal arms survives from the unfinished Cardinal College of St Mary, which was founded by Cardinal Wolsey – a native of the town – in the 16th century. The Ancient or Sparrowe's House of 1567 stands in the Buttermarket and is noted for its exterior decoration of intricate patterns and features carved in plaster, an outstanding example of the East Anglian art of pargetting. Original oak panelling and heavy carved beams can be seen by visitors to the bookshop which it now houses. Close by are the Great White Horse Hotel, which features in Charles Dickens' *Pickwick Papers*, and many old streets lined with well-preserved timber-framed houses. Christchurch Mansion (open) was built by a Tudor merchant and is isolated in an oasis of parkland near the centre of town. It contains fine collections of furniture and paintings. Exhibits relating to local history and wildlife can be seen in the Ipswich Museum of Archaeology and Natural History, which stands in the High Street. The number of good

churches in the town reflects its former importance and prosperity. Among the best are: St Margaret's, with a fine hammerbeam roof; St Peter's, with an impressive black Tournai font; and St Mary-le-Tower, which boasts a lovely pulpit carved by Grinling Gibbons. A remarkable 16th-century Unitarian Meeting House stands in Friar Street.

Leave Ipswich on the A1156 with SP 'Felixstowe' and in 5 miles reach an unclassified right turn leading to Levington. A short detour can be taken to Levington from here.

LEVINGTON, Suffolk

This attractive small village stands on the banks of the Orwell and is the base for the Suffolk Yacht Harbour. Its church dates from the 16th century.

On the main route, continue along the A45 and after 5 miles follow SP 'Town Centre' to enter Felixstowe.

FELIXSTOWE, Suffolk

Towards the end of the 19th century this sheltered spot on the Suffolk coast was developed as a seaside resort. It attracted fashionable society, including the German Kaiser, and acquired a 2-mile length of promenade bordered by delightful flower displays and beautifully tended lawns. Long before this a 16th-century stronghold which became the Landguard Fort (AM) was defending the sea approach to

Harwich. A later period of insecurity this time generated by Napoleon's hold on Europe, resulted in the building of a Martello tower c1810. Felixstowe Dock is an important container port. A modern leisure centre offers all year round entertainment.

Leave Felixstowe on the A45 'Ipswich' road and in 7 miles turn right on to the A12 SP 'Woodbridge' and 'Gt Yarmouth'. After 4 miles reach a roundabout and go forward, passing the Post Office Research Station on Martlesham Heath. In ¾ mile turn right on to the A12 to reach Martlesham.

MARTLESHAM, Suffolk

Martlesham village is picturesquely sited on a creek of the River Deben and features a church with an unusual 7-sided wagon roof. The local Red Lion Inn displays a curious sign that was taken from a Dutch ship in 1672.

Continue on the A12 to the end of Martlesham, drive under a railway bridge, then turn right on to the B1438 to reach Woodbridge.

WOODBRIDGE, Suffolk

Attractive houses of major historical interest surround the old market square round which this port has grown. Many date from the 16th century, and the entire group is centred on the superb Shire Hall, which features work from the 16th to 19th centuries and picturesque Dutch-style gables. Multi-period Woodbridge Church carries a tall, flint-flushwork tower and contains a seven sacrament font. One old mill, a rare example which depends on the tide, is open. The port's status as a busy centre of ocean trade declined a long time ago, but today it is a popular sailing centre with a fine riverside park at Kyson Hill (NT).

From Woodbridge continue on the B1438 to Melton.

MELTON, Suffolk

A small colour-washed brick building known as Friar's Dene was once the village gaol. Melton Church has a handsome tower with an attractive broach spire.

From Melton turn right on to the A1152 SP 'Orford'. Cross the railway line and the River Deben, then bear left and in ¾ mile keep forward on to the B1084. After a short distance enter part of Rendlesham Forest, which contains a picnic site, and continue to Butley.

BUTLEY, Suffolk

An Augustinian priory founded here in 1171 has vanished but its superb 14th-century gatehouse has survived as one of the finest medieval buildings of its kind in Suffolk. Particularly notable are the heraldic designs cut into its stonework.

Leave Butley, remaining on the B1084, then skirt part of Tunstall Forest and pass through Chillesford. In 1¾ miles meet crossroads and turn right to reach Orford.

The finely-preserved postmill at Saxtead Green is typical of many in Suffolk.

ORFORD, Suffolk

In 1165 Henry II built a moat-encircled castle with an 18-sided keep here in an attempt to establish Norman power over the peoples of East Anglia. Today the building (AM) that developed from these early beginnings contains a collection of arms and affords excellent views of the picturesque houses and fishermen's cottages below its walls. On the seaward side of the village the River Alde is separated from the sea by Orford Ness.

ORFORD NESS, Suffolk

This long strip of coastal marshland is occupied by the Orford Ness and Havergate national nature reserve, one of the few places in England where the rare avocet can be seen.

From Orford return along the B1084 and in 1¼ miles drive forward on to the unclassified 'Snape' road. Skirt another part of Tunstall Forest for nearly 4 miles and join the B1069. Pass The Maltings, cross the River Alde, and enter Snape.

Tudor Helmingham Hall's moat is spanned by two drawbridges.

SNAPE, Suffolk

The magnificent Maltings concert hall, built on the site of old maltings where barley was stored prior to export, is the yearly venue for the famous Aldeburgh Music Festival. Its situation on the banks of the River Alde adds an extra dimension to its pleasing architecture. Snape Church houses a richly carved 15th-century font, and close to the village are slight remains of an ancient Benedictine priory.

Leave Snape, continue for ¾ mile, then meet the A1094 'Ipswich' road and turn left. In 2 miles turn left on to the A12 and pass through Farnham for Stratford St Andrew.

STRATFORD ST ANDREW, Suffolk

Close to this pleasant little village is 17th-century Glemham Hall (open), an impressive red-brick mansion standing in 350 acres of beautiful parkland. Inside are panelled rooms appointed with fine paintings and Queen Anne furniture. The village church contains Norman workmanship and houses a 13th-century font.

Remain on the A12 and in 1 mile, at an entrance to Glemham Hall, turn right on to the unclassified 'Parham' road. In a further 1 mile turn right, then in a short distance turn left and continue to Parham.

PARHAM, Suffolk

Tranquilly set in the upper valley of the River Alde, this little village has a church where the village stocks and a beautiful 14th-century screen are preserved. Just to the south-east is 16th-century Moat Hall, a picturesque timber-framed house that is encircled by a moat and nowadays serves as a farm.

Leave Parham on the B1116 and continue to Framlingham.

FRAMLINGHAM, Suffolk

Framlingham's superb Norman castle (AM) was started in 1190 and represented an important advance in castle design. Fragments of the Great Hall are incorporated in picturesque 17th-century almshouses, and the towers carry distinctive Tudor chimneys. Monuments to the Howard family, who took possession in the 15th century, can be seen in the local church. The town itself is a historic market centre with many old houses and a well-known college.

From Framlingham follow the B1119 SP 'Stowmarket' to reach Saxtead Green.

Thames barges moored on the Orwell estuary near Ipswich are reminiscent of a maritime past when the elegance of sail was commonplace.

SAXTEAD GREEN, Suffolk

One of the finest postmills (AM) in Suffolk with its wooden superstructure and brick round house stands here. Stones and machinery inside are in excellent working order. It was first recorded in 1706 and substantially rebuilt at least twice during its working life. Today it stands 46ft high and carries sails with a span of almost 55ft.

Leave Saxtead Green on the A1120 'Stowmarket' road and continue to Earl Soham.

EARL SOHAM, Suffolk

Old cottages and Georgian houses face rows of allotments across a long street in this somewhat rambling village. The local church carries a 15th-century tower and contains several good monuments.

Drive to the end of Earl Soham village and turn left, then in 3 miles turn left again on to the B1077 'Ipswich' road. In 1 mile pass another fine windmill on the left, then in a further 1¼ miles reach Helmingham Hall on the right.

HELMINGHAM HALL, Suffolk

Every night the two drawbridges that span the moat to this lovely manor house are raised, though more for the sake of tradition than against rival lords or jealous monarchs. Home of the Tollemache family since the 16th century, the hall has Georgian additions with crenallations by John Nash and stands amid beautiful gardens (open) in an ancient deer park. More than 500 red and fallow deer share the estate with herds of Highland cattle. Visitors may recognise parts of the grounds from John Constable's great landscape painting *Helmingham Dell*.

Continue to Ashbocking.

ASHBOCKING, Suffolk

The medieval church in this village carries a 16th-century tower which is contemporary with Ashbocking Hall, an attractive timber-framed building near by.

Continue to Witnesham.

WITNESHAM, Suffolk

Situated near a tributary of the River Deben, this peaceful little village has an Elizabethan hall and a good church. The hall includes a few Victorian additions and the church, which contains an 8-sided font, has an excellent hammerbeam roof.

Continue on the B1077 to Westerfield.

WESTERFIELD, Suffolk

Westerfield Hall is a 17th-century building with attractive Dutch gables. The local church dates from c1300 and features a nave window in which pieces of a Norman doorway have been re-used. The roof in both the chancel and nave is of hammerbeam construction.

Leave Westerfield and drive through built-up areas to re-enter Ipswich.

KIDDERMINSTER, Herefs & Worcs
Carpets were the foundation of Kidderminster's prosperity, and the carpet-weaving industry that was introduced here in 1735 continues to be a major concern. The town's architecture is homely rather than distinguished, although handsome St Mary's Church and the cluster of Georgian buildings in Church Street have much to offer the eye.

Leave Kidderminster on the A456 'Leominster' road and shortly reach the West Midlands Safari Park.

WEST MIDLANDS SAFARI PARK, Herefs & Worcs
Giraffes, elephants, and many other exotic beasts can be seen in the 200 acres of this interesting wildlife park. Other attractions include a pets' corner for the children, a 'boat safari', bird gardens, and a complete dolphinarium.

Cross the River Severn via Telford's bridge and enter Bewdley.

BEWDLEY, Herefs & Worcs
Telford's fine bridge spanning the Severn at Bewdley was built in 1795. Severnside is a beautiful street lined with 17th- and 18th-century houses. An elegant parade of Georgian and earlier buildings line both sides of Load Street, which is eventually closed off by a large Georgian house and 18th-century St Anne's Church. Bewdley's more distant history is represented by several excellent half-timbered buildings. Past industries of the town are demonstrated at the museum housed in 18th-century buildings called The Shambles, and

ANCIENT TOWNS

From Kidderminster this tour visits the handsome Georgian streets of Bewdley, the purpose-built canal town of Stourport, and delightful Ludlow — an ancient gem in the English landscape. Scattered between are villages, each one unique in its character.

a craft centre in Lax Lane specialises in brassrubbing. Overlooking the town is Tickenhill House, and period mansion refaced in 1738 and incorporating a royal palace.

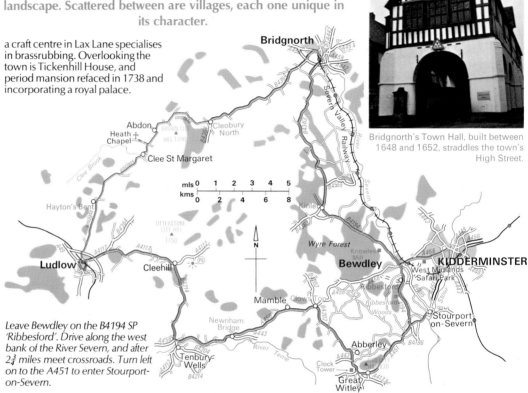

Bridgnorth's Town Hall, built between 1648 and 1652, straddles the town's High Street.

Leave Bewdley on the B4194 SP 'Ribbesford'. Drive along the west bank of the River Severn, and after 2¾ miles meet crossroads. Turn left on to the A451 to enter Stourport-on-Severn.

STOURPORT-ON-SEVERN, Herefs & Worcs
After the opening of the Staffordshire and Worcestershire Canal, built by the engineer James Brindley in 1766, Stourport became a major canal port. It has survived to the present day as the only example of a purpose-built canal town in England.

Return along the A451 SP 'Great Witley' and recross the River Severn. After 4½ miles reach Great Witley.

GREAT WITLEY, Herefs & Worcs
Entry into Great Witley's Chapel of St Michael transports the visitor from the English countryside to some remote part of Italy. Rich rococo decoration completely alien to rural Britain assaults the eye — not unpleasantly — from skilfully-patterned walls and painted ceiling panels. Close to the chapel, which was consecrated in 1735, is the ruined shell of 17th-century and later Witley Court.

At the end of the village turn right on to the A443. SP 'Ludlow'. After 1 mile branch right on to the B4202 SP 'Cleobury Mortimer'. Shortly reach the edge of Abberley.

Winter holds the canal basin at Stourport-on-Severn in an icy grip. A Georgian warehouse stands in the background.

ABBERLEY, Herefs & Worcs
Overlooked by 930ft Abberley Hill, this peaceful little village is centred on the ruins of a Norman church that was replaced by a handsome Victorian successor. The clock tower of Abberley Hall is visible for miles.

Continue, and gradually ascend to Clows Top for good all-round views. Meet crossroads and turn left on to the A456 SP 'Leominster'. Descend with distant views into Mamble.

MAMBLE, Herefs & Worcs
Mamble's church dates almost entirely from the beginning of the 13th century and carries an unusual timber bell turret.

Continue to Newnham Bridge and turn right then follow the Teme Valley to the edge of Tenbury Wells.

TENBURY WELLS, Herefs & Worcs
Mineral springs discovered here in 1839 brought instant fame as a spa town to Tenbury, and the Pump Room and Baths from this period can still be seen. 'Taking the waters' has long since ceased to be fashionable, and nowadays the town fulfils a quiet rôle as a little market centre for the surrounding countryside. Half-timbered buildings make a pleasant contrast with two fine churches dating from the 19th century.

Take 2nd main turning on to the B4214 SP 'Cleehill' and proceed through hilly country to Cleehill.

CLEEHILL, Salop
Just east of Cleehill on the A4117 is an AA viewpoint which affords superb views to the east and south. North is 1,750ft Titterstone Clee Hill, whose bare slopes rise to a summit crowned by the vast 'golf ball' of a satellite tracking station.

Turn left on to the A4117 and descend then cross the bypass into Ludlow.

LUDLOW, Salop SO57
Ludlow is a latterday Camelot on the banks of the Corve and Teme, among the gentle Shropshire hills. High above the town's roof tops soars the 135ft tower of the parish church, while on the ground the lovely River Teme adds its own enchantment to the picture-book quality of Ludlow Castle. The church, mainly of 15th-century date, is the largest in the county and preserves contemporary choir stalls. The ashes of poet A E Housman are kept here. Near by are the beautiful black-and-white Reader's House (open on application), and the 17th-century Feathers Hotel. These are possibly the best of many half-timbered buildings preserved in the town. Georgian architecture testifies to the continued popularity of Ludlow and is epitomized in the elegant Butter Cross, which now houses a museum. Broad Street, lined with many fine dwellings from the same period, extends from the Butter Cross to Ludlow's sole surviving medieval gate, the Broad Gate. The town's earliest structure is, of course, the castle. From as early as 1085 this occupied a strategic position in the contentious England/Wales border country known as the Marcher Lands. The town was actually planned round the castle in the 12th century. John Milton's 'Comus' was given its first performance here in 1634. Ludford Bridge (AM) spans the Teme and is of medieval origin.

To leave Ludlow return along the A4117 'Kidderminster' road and pass under a railway bridge. Immediately turn left into unclassified Fishmore Road. After 1 mile branch right SP 'Hayton's Bent'. Ascend, with views to Corve Dale, Wenlock Edge, and the Clee Hills, and follow SP 'Clee St Margaret' to reach that village.

CLEE ST MARGARET, Salop
Remotely set in the Clee Hills by the Clee Brook, this little village is built mainly of stone and is centred on a church with a Norman nave.

Cross a ford and turn left SP 'Abdon'. After ½ mile meet crossroads; a detour (SP 'Bouldon') may be taken left from here across pleasantly rural Shropshire countryside to visit Heath Chapel.

Scenes such as this, of the steam-operated Severn Valley Railway, were once commonplace throughout Britain.

HEATH CHAPEL, Salop
This simple, barn-like building stands on its own in a field and is a perfect example of Norman ecclesiastical architecture. It contains a Norman font and various furnishings dating from the 17th century.

Continue on the main route to Abdon.

ABDON, Salop
Bracken-covered slopes rise from this village to Abdon Burf, a tract of rough country that culminates in the dominating eminence of 1,790ft Brown Clee Hill. Excellent views across to Wenlock Edge are afforded by this high region.

Turn right SP 'Ditton Priors' and after 1 mile turn left then in ¾ mile bear right SP 'Cleobury North'. Skirt the north side of Brown Clee Hill, and after 1½ miles turn left and descend to a T-junction. Turn right and continue for ½ mile, then turn left on to the B4364 SP 'Bridgnorth'. Enter Cleobury North.

CLEOBURY NORTH, Salop SO68
Wooded Burwarton Park adds much to the charm of this village, which boasts a large and picturesque Norman church that was carefully restored by architect Sir Gilbert Scott in the 19th century.

Continue on the B4364 to the

The impressive remains of Ludlow's castle are reflected in the waters of the River Teme near 15th-century Dinham Bridge.

outskirts of Bridgnorth, then turn right on to the A458 to enter the town.

BRIDGNORTH, Salop
Shropshire has more than its fair share of lovely old towns, and Bridgnorth vies with the best of them. It is divided into two parts — Upper Town and Lower Town — by a steep ridge which is negotiated by a twisty road, several flights of steps, and a funicular railway with a breathtaking gradient of 1 in 2. In Lower Town is Bishop Percy's House, a fine half-timbered building of 1580 which is possibly the oldest structure in Bridgnorth. Upper Town is on the site of the original settlement and though much of it burned down during the Civil War the High Street is still straddled by its picturesque town hall (AM). The half-timbered upper storey of this building was made from a barn after the old town hall became a battle casualty. Many fine inns can be found in the High Street as it leads to the ancient North Gate, and at the other end are the elegant Georgian houses of East Castle Street. A precariously leaning tower (AM) is all that remains of Bridgnorth Castle. Nearby St Mary Magdalene's Church was built by engineer and architect Thomas Telford in 1794, and St Leonard's Church stands at the heart of a charming mixture of buildings dotted among grassy verges. The Hermitage (AM) is one of several local caves inhabited until fairly recent times. The station and engine shed at the northern terminus of the Severn Valley Railway provide much interest. East of the town on the Stourbridge road the Midland Motor Museum has over 90 exhibits.

THE SEVERN VALLEY RAILWAY, Salop
Steam locomotives operate between Bridgnorth and Kidderminster over one of Britain's best preserved railways, following the Severn Valley and providing a mobile viewpoint through the beautiful countryside of the area. Trains run most months in the year.

Leave Bridgnorth on the B4364 'Cleobury Mortimer' road and drive to Kinlet. Turn left on to the B4363 SP 'Bewdley', then shortly meet a T-junction and turn left on to the B4194. Continue through Wyre Forest.

WYRE FOREST, Salop, Herefs & Worcs
This one-time royal hunting forest covers an extensive area of mixed heath, scrub, and woodland. During the spring its many wild cherry trees make a picture of white blossom, and in summer the forest is a great attraction to walkers and picnickers. Knowles Mill, a National Trust property set in an orchard, stands close by off the B4194.

Enter Bewdley and turn left for the return to Kidderminster.

SALTINGS ON THE WASH

Along the sweeping coastline of the Wash are wide sandy bays backed by wild salt marshes populated by wildlife suited to the open surroundings. Here and there the flint tower of a medieval village church breaks the skyline, providing a landmark for travellers on both land and sea.

The creek at Burnham Overy Staithe is very popular with yachtsmen.

Dutch influence is evident in King's Lynn's charming Custom House.

KING'S LYNN, Norfolk
Two markets were founded here in Norman times, medieval merchants came here to build warehouses on the River Ouse, and 20th-century industry has continued the town's long history of commercial significance. Everywhere are survivals from periods that the settlement has grown through, and its medieval buildings are some of the finest in the country. Traces of the ancient walls show how the town has expanded since the troubled times in which they were built, and the superb Hanseatic Warehouse of 1428 recalls full-sailed barques laden with exotic goods. To complement the two market places are two guildhalls, both of which date from the early 15th century. The biggest of these (NT) is the largest medieval guildhall extant and is now used as a theatre. The other contains old town regalia, including a 14th-century vessel known as King John's Cup. Both the last-mentioned building and the much more recent Town Hall of 1895 display a striking flint-chequerwork design. The superb Custom House, perhaps the most outstanding building in the town, was built by architect Henry Bell while he held office as mayor in 1683. Many other of the town's old buildings have ancient roots but have been changed over the centuries. Clifton House dates originally from the 14th century but has later additions; Hampton Court shows period work from the 14th to 18th centuries; and Dutch-gabled Thoresby College of c1500 now reflects the tastes of the 17th century. The huge parish church contains two outstanding memorial brasses that are the biggest and most famous in England. Red Mount Chapel of c1485 is an octagonal building with beautiful fan vaulting.

Leave King's Lynn by the A47 'Swaffham' road and continue to Middleton.

MIDDLETON, Norfolk
Major Everard-Hutton, one of the famous Six Hundred who fought at Balaclava, is commemorated by a memorial in the local church. Some 3 miles north west is Middleton Tower, a splendid red-brick gatehouse of mainly 19th-century date.

Pass Walton Common, then cross the River Nar to enter Narborough.

NARBOROUGH, Norfolk
Several fine brasses and a standing effigy can be seen in the local church.

Continue, and later pass Swaffham Heath to reach Swaffham.

SWAFFHAM, Norfolk
Legend tells of the 'Pedlar of Swaffham', who travelled to London to throw himself into the Thames but was dissuaded by a man he met on London Bridge. This stranger related a dream in which he found treasure in a remote village garden – a garden that the pedlar recognised as his own. He hastened home to find two pots of gold; an image of the pedlar is now incorporated in the town sign. The triangular market place has a domed rotunda built by the Earl of Oxford in 1783 as a market cross. Features of the local church include a splendid angel-carved double-hammerbeam roof and a fine 16th-century west tower.

Leave Swaffham on the A1065 'Cromer' road. In 2¾ miles turn left on to an unclassified road for Castle Acre.

CASTLE ACRE, Norfolk
This aptly-named village lies within the outer bailey of an 11th-century castle, of which only the earthworks and a 13th-century gateway remain. Impressive ruins of an 11th-century Cluniac priory, including fine Norman arcading (AM) and a Tudor gatehouse, can be seen near by.

Continue through the village and turn right SP 'Newton'. Rejoin the A1065 'Cromer' road and drive to Weasenham.

WEASENHAM, Norfolk
Prehistoric barrows in all shapes and sizes, including bell, bowl, disc, and saucer types, can be seen in the countryside round Weasenham Plantation.

Continue to East Raynham.

EAST RAYNHAM, Norfolk
Raynham Hall, a magnificent 17th-century building which has been ascribed partly to Inigo Jones, was once the home of the agricultural innovator nicknamed Turnip Townshend.

In 2¼ miles turn right SP 'Town Centre' for Fakenham.

FAKENHAM, Norfolk
This attractive market town dates from Saxon times and was a Royal Manor until the 17th century. Its Market Place has two old coaching inns, both showing traces of earlier work behind Georgian façades, and the parish church has a commanding 15th-century tower.

From Fakenham town centre follow SP 'King's Lynn' to join the A148. In ¼ mile turn right on to the B1105 SP 'Walsingham' and descend into East Barsham.

EAST BARSHAM, Norfolk

East Barsham is known for its brick and terracotta manor house, a splendid example of early Tudor work. Fine chimneys typical of the style rise high above the rooftops, and the approach is guarded by an imposing two-storeyed gatehouse.

Continue for 1 mile to Houghton St Giles.

HOUGHTON ST GILES, Norfolk

On the far side of the Stiffkey river, about 1 mile south west of this attractive village, is the last in a chain of wayside chapels which once lined the Walsingham Way. It is known as the Slipper Chapel because pilgrims to the shrine of Our Lady at Walsingham would remove their shoes here before completing their journey barefoot. It is now the official Roman Catholic Shrine of Our Lady.

Continue to Walsingham, also known as Little Walsingham.

The legendary Pedlar of Swaffham is commemorated by the town sign.

WALSINGHAM, Norfolk

The shrine at Walsingham, a place of paramount importance to the pilgrims of the middle ages, was founded in the 11th century. Virtually every English king from Richard I to Henry VIII came here, and the last-named had the shrine robbed when he dissolved the monasteries. In the 19th century the pilgrimages were revived, and a new Shrine of Our Lady was built for the Anglican Church in the early part of the 20th century. Remains of what was once a giant concourse of buildings date mainly from the 13th and 14th centuries, and include the superb east wall of the priory.

Continue on the B1105 'Wells' road and skirt Wighton to meet the A149. Turn left, then right, with SP 'The Beach'. Enter Wells-next-the-Sea.

WELLS-NEXT-THE-SEA, Norfolk

Old houses and the picturesque quayside make a charming group in this small resort and port. Bathing may be enjoyed in a nearby creek.

Leave the resort on the A149 'Hunstanton' road and drive to Holkham.

The Marble Hall in the Palladian mansion of Holkham exemplifies William Kent's lavish style.

HOLKHAM, Norfolk

Holkham Hall (open), a vast Palladian mansion, is one of the show-pieces of the county. The present house was rebuilt in the 18th century to plans by William Kent, who also designed much of the furniture to be seen inside. Experts consider the entrance into the wonderful alabaster hall to show Kent's genius at its peak, and all the rooms are sumptuously decorated in the fashion of the day. An impressive art collection is displayed in the house, and the library has an excellent collection of 18th-century books. The lake-watered grounds were laid out by Capability Brown in 1762.

Continue to Burnham Overy Staithe.

BURNHAM OVERY STAITHE, Norfolk

Close to this tiny village are a water mill (NT) and tower windmill (NT), both in a good state of preservation. Neither is open to the public at time of publication.

After a short distance cross the River Burn and continue to Burnham Deepdale.

BURNHAM DEEPDALE, Norfolk

Inside the local church, which carries a rare Saxon round tower, is an outstanding Norman font.

Continue to Brancaster Staithe.

BRANCASTER STAITHE, Norfolk

A boat service operates from here to Scolt Head Island, where there is a bird sanctuary (NT) and nature reserve.

Continue for $\frac{1}{2}$ mile to Brancaster.

BRANCASTER, Norfolk

This one-time Roman station is now a golfing resort. A lane leads from the church to a pebble beach which, though not as attractive as its large sandy neighbour, is far safer for bathing.

Continue through Titchwell to Thornham.

THORNHAM, Norfolk

A rectangular earthwork on a slope overlooking the waters of the Wash here was excavated in 1960, revealing the remains of an iron-age village. The complex, thought to date from cAD40, measures 133 by 175ft and includes a defensive ditch cut into the soft chalk.

Drive through Old Hunstanton and $\frac{1}{2}$ mile farther turn right on to an unclassified road SP 'Sea Front'. Continue into Hunstanton.

A peaceful atmosphere pervades Wells-next-the-Sea.

HUNSTANTON, Norfolk

Hunstanton is the largest seaside resort in west Norfolk and the only East Anglian coastal town to face west. Great stretches of sand are backed by cliffs of mixed chalk and sand rising 60ft above the beach.

Pass the Pier, bear right into Westgate, and in $\frac{1}{4}$ mile meet a roundabout. Take the 1st exit SP 'King's Lynn', then meet the main road and turn right on to the A149 to reach the outskirts of Heacham.

HEACHAM, Norfolk

Pocahontas, the Red Indian princess who married John Rolfe at Heacham Hall in 1614, is commemorated in both the village sign and a memorial in the local church. Her son founded a line which was to include the wife of US president Woodrow Wilson.

Continue to Snettisham.

SNETTISHAM, Norfolk

One of the finest churches in Norfolk stands here. Its lofty spire can be seen for many miles across the flat local countryside, and its superb west front is reminiscent of Peterborough Cathedral. Also in the village is attractive Old Hall, an 18th-century house with Dutch gables.

Continue through Ingoldisthorpe to Dersingham. Turn left on to the B1440 SP 'Sandringham'. Ascend through wooded country and in $\frac{1}{2}$ mile pass the gates of Sandringham House.

SANDRINGHAM, Norfolk

Included in this 7,000-acre estate, owned by the Royal Family, are a 19th-century house and museum (open), the farms and woodlands of 7 parishes, and a 300-acre country park. The park church is of exceptional note and contains an organ that was the last gift of King Edward VII. Many superb royal memorials enrich the interior, and the nave is roofed in English oak.

In 1 mile turn right on to the B1439 into West Newton. Continue to the main road and turn left to rejoin the A149. In 1 mile turn right on to an unclassified road for Castle Rising.

CASTLE RISING, Norfolk

The sea has long withdrawn from this one-time port, but the Norman castle (AM) built to protect it still stands. It occupies a Roman site and has a great keep in which a fascinating sequence of rooms, galleries, and minor stairs are reached by a single dramatic staircase. The local Church of St Lawrence is famous for its Norman west front, which has a fine doorway on the lower level and houses a richly carved square font on a circular shaft. Bede House or Trinity Hospital dates from the 17th century and is an almshouse charity for elderly ladies.

Continue to South Wootton, meet traffic signals, and drive over crossroads. After another $1\frac{1}{4}$ miles meet a T-junction, turn right, and return to King's Lynn.

LEICESTER, Leics
Situated on the River Soar and Grand Union Canal, this county town and university city has been a thriving centre at least since Roman times. Relics from its very early history include Roman pavements under the former Central Station and below a shop fronting St Nicholas' Church. Other traces of the occupation have been found at the Jewry Wall site, including remains of 2nd-century Roman baths and the wall itself. Various relics from ancient times to the middle ages can be seen in the Jewry Wall Museum and site. The Leicestershire Museum and Art Gallery stands in New Walk, a delightful promenade of elegant houses, mature trees, and carefully preserved Victorian lamp-posts. An ancient city gateway known as The Magazine houses the museum of the Royal Leicestershire Regiment, and the Newarke Houses Museum offers a vivid insight into social history from the 16th century to Victorian times. It is housed in an interesting old Chantry House of 1511, and its immediate neighbour dates from c1600. Wygston's House Museum of Costume is laid out in a 15th-century house, and the Leicestershire Museum of Technology preserves various items of industrial interest in the apt surroundings of Abbey Pumping Station. Among many interesting churches in Leicester is St Martin's, which stands on a Saxon site that was previously occupied by a Roman temple and now enjoys cathedral status. It was largely rebuilt in the 19th century and has a well proportioned tower and spire. Good Norman work is retained by the Church of St Mary de Castro. The city's Guildhall is a fine late 14th-century building with magnificent timbering, and the 17th-century Court House incorporates fragments of a Norman hall. There is also a Norman castle, but very little of it survives. Close to the university is a fine public park and cricket ground, and the University Botanic Gardens are of note.

Leave Leicester on the A46 'Newark' road and after 3 miles branch left on to the B667 into Thurmaston.

THE CRAGS OF CHARNWOOD

Charnwood Forest is a huge upthrusting of rock whose wind-blasted heaths dominate miles of Leicestershire's gentle farming country. Now treeless and pitted with great quarries, it is an eerie place where open moorland flows round fascinating outcrops of rock and the lines of ancient forts.

The small brook at Rearsby is spanned by a quaint medieval bridge.

THURMASTON, Leics
This large suburb of Leicester stands on the east bank of the River Soar and has a number of developing industries. In its older quarter is a fine church with distinctive 13th century nave arcades.

Continue through the town on the B667, reach a roundabout at the far end, and take the 2nd exit on to the A607 SP 'Melton'. Drive through Syston.

SYSTON, Leics
The tower buttresses of Syston Church display curious sculptures of a man and two women, possibly representations of the founder and his wives. Many of the houses in the area are brick-built structures of 18th-century date.

Continue to Rearsby.

REARSBY, Leics
Situated on a tributary of the River Wreake, this village has a good 13th- and 14th-century church with an unusual drum-shaped font. To the east of the church is an attractive 6-arched medieval bridge, and a gabled house of 1661 stands in Mill Road.

Turn right on to the B674 for Gaddesby.

GADDESBY, Leics
One of the largest and most beautiful of Leicestershire's many lovely village churches can be seen here. Its south side is richly decorated with stone carvings, and the south aisle is a showpiece. Inside is an equestrian statue of Colonel Cheney at Waterloo.

Charnwood Forest's windswept character is well appreciated from Beacon Hill.

Stay on the B674, and within 1 mile turn left on to an unclassified road to Great Dalby. Meet a T-junction and turn right into Great Dalby. Pass the village church, turn right on to the B6047, and proceed to Twyford. Turn left on to the unclassified 'Burrough' road and proceed to Burrough-on-the-Hill.

BURROUGH-ON-THE-HILL, Leics
Breached ramparts of an iron-age fort at Burrough Hill are thought to mark the site of a pre-Roman capital. The local church dates from the 13th century and has a good tower.

Continue to Somerby, meet a T-junction, and turn left SP 'Pickwell' and 'Melton'. In 2¼ miles cross the A606 and follow SP for Stapleford. To the right, on the approach to Stapleford, is Stapleford Park.

STAPLEFORD PARK, Leics
Home of Lord and Lady Gretton, this fine old house (open) has an early wing dating from 1500 and was restored in 1633. Its exterior decoration includes an exceptional collection of stone sculptures depicting scenes from history, the scriptures, and legend; inside are rooms that have been attributed to John Webb. As well as fine pictures, tapestries and furniture, the house contains the famous Thomas Balston collection of Victorian Staffordshire pottery figures (NT). In the grounds are a lake with an island bird sanctuary, a miniature steam passenger railway, and many other diversions for both children and adults.

From Stapleford proceed north and after a short distance turn left to join the B676. A short detour from the main route to the village of Saxby can be made by turning right here on to the B676.

SAXBY, Leics
An ancient Saxon cemetery has been discovered at Saxby, and the local rectory and church both date from 1789.

On the main route, continue along the B676 to Melton Mowbray.

MELTON MOWBRAY, Leics
No matter what various sections of public opinion feel about hunting it is still a thriving tradition, and nowhere is it in better health than at Melton Mowbray. Three famous packs meet here, and the district is often loud with the noise of horns, hounds, and horses. The town is internationally famous for Stilton cheese and pork pies, and its attractive situation on the River Eye makes it a popular goal for summer visitors. St Mary's is arguably the stateliest and most impressive of all the county's churches, and beautifully illustrates the early-English, decorated, and perpendicular architectural periods. Anne of Cleves House is of ancient origin. The Melton Carnegie Museum depicts the making of Stilton cheese and pork pies. Attractive parks and gardens border the river.

Leave Melton Mowbray on the A6006 'Loughborough' road, pass Asfordby, and in 3¼ miles turn left on to the B676. After 1½ miles pass beneath the A46, which follows much of the course of the ancient Fosse Way.

FOSSE WAY

Certain stretches of this famous Romanized road are mere tracks, but much of its diagonal route across England from Axminster to Lincoln is followed by modern main roads. Excavations have shown that the courses of earlier paths were adopted by the Roman engineers who plotted the road.

Continue to Burton-on-the-Wolds, turn left on to an unclassified road, then shortly join the B675 and drive to Barrow-upon-Soar.

BARROW-UPON-SOAR, Leics

This attractive and popular village stands on the east bank of the River Soar and has a curious village sign that depicts an aquatic prehistoric reptile. Good local buildings include an old hospital of 1694 and almshouses of 1825.

Drive to the end of Barrow-upon-Soar, at roundabout take 2nd exit then cross a river bridge. Turn right into Quorndon.

QUORNDON, Leics

Valuable Tudor relics are preserved in the 14th-century Farnham Chapel of Quorndon's fine granite church, which also has a good Norman doorway. The village gives its name to the most famous hunt in England, and has a station on the Great Central Railway. The latter runs 5 miles between Loughborough and Rothley and a 3-mile extension to Birstal is currently undergoing reconstruction.

CHARNWOOD FOREST,

Once an important hunting ground, the bracken-covered summits of Charnwood Forest thrust their bare crags of ancient rock high above the fertile wooded plains of Leicestershire. Their presence in the generally unspectacular Midlands countryside is a startling scenic contradiction, and the fascinating range of geological beds that make

Kirby Muxloe Castle, unfinished since the 15th century.

Old John Tower in Bradgate Park is an 18th-century folly built on a 700ft hill.

up their bulk is a constant source of interest to geologists. Fine views can be enjoyed from the forest, and its sweeping barrenness gives an invigorating sense of freedom.

At Quorndon, turn left on to the A6 and drive for 200 yards, then turn right on to the unclassified 'Cropston' and 'Anstey' road to skirt Hawcliff Hill and Buddon Wood, on the edge of Charnwood Forest. After 2¼ miles meet crossroads and turn right towards Swithland. After a short distance cross the end of lovely Swithland Reservoir, a noted local beauty spot. Ascend through the village of Swithland.

SWITHLAND, Leics

An attractive village associated with the traditional industry of slate cutting, Swithland stands near the eastern edge of Charnwood Forest in pleasantly wooded surroundings. Good monuments can be seen in the local church.

Drive 1 mile beyond Swithland and turn left for Woodhouse Eaves.

WOODHOUSE EAVES, Leics

Several of the cottages in this picturesque hill village are made of rough stone taken from the slate pits at Swithland. To the west is 818ft Beacon Hill, an AA viewpoint and the site of an iron-age encampment.

Drive to the end of the village and turn left on to the B591; in 1¼ miles pass the Beacon Hill carpark and viewpoint, then in a short distance at crossroads turn left on to the B5330 and meet crossroads. Drive forward on to the unclassified road for Newtown Linford, and pass the main entrance for Bradgate Park on the approach to the village.

BRADGATE PARK, Leics

The 850 acres of untouched heath and woodland that make up this superb country park were given to the city and county of Leicester in 1928 as permanent public space. The area, which extends from Cropston Reservoir to Newtown Linford, offers excellent walks through stands of cedar and oak, and alongside the course of a tiny stream. Bradgate House, now in ruins, was completed c1510. In 1537 it was the birthplace of the unfortunate Lady Jane Grey, who was the uncrowned Queen of England for nine days before being beheaded by order of Mary Tudor. At the highest point of the park is an 18th-century folly tower known as Old John, which was erected to the memory of a retainer who was killed by a falling flagpole.

Continue into Newtown Linford.

NEWTOWN LINFORD, Leics

This village stands on the borders of Bradgate Park and has some attractive old houses, but it is a little too close to the suburbs of Leicester for comfort. Its 18th-century church features painted royal arms.

Follow the B5327 'Leicester' road to Anstey.

ANSTEY, Leics

The 5-arched packhorse bridge that spans Rothley Brook in this Charnwood village is considered one of the finest in England. It dates from the 14th or 15th century and is complemented by some fine old cottages. Anstey was the birthplace of Ned Ludd, who as an apprentice initiated the infamous Luddite riots of 1812 by wrecking machinery that had been introduced to take over his job.

Meet a roundabout and turn right, crossing Rothley Brook with the old packhorse bridge to the right. Continue for 200 yards and turn right on to the unclassified 'Glenfield' road, then after a further 1 mile meet a roundabout and keep forward to enter Glenfield.

GLENFIELD, Leics

Victorian St Peter's was built to replace the old Glenfield Church, which stands in ruins near by. Several architectural features salvaged from the interior of the older structure can be seen inside.

From Glenfield follow SP 'Kirby Muxloe' to Kirby Muxloe.

KIRBY MUXLOE, Leics

Considered an excellent example of its type, this moat-encircled fortified manor (AM) was begun by Lord Hastings in 1480 – towards the end of the Wars of the Roses. The wars ended before the house was completed, and Hastings was executed for treason.

Meet roundabout at the edge of Kirby Muxloe and turn left towards Leicester. In 1 mile meet a roundabout and turn left on to the A47 for the return to Leicester.

HEREFORD'S QUIET VALLEYS

Great Marcher fortresses like Ludlow Castle were built by the Normans to subdue the turbulent Welsh. Fierce battles have left no scars on these mild green hills and fertile valleys which epitomize the serenity and certainties of the rural way of life in one of the few remaining true pastoral regions of England.

LEOMINSTER, Herefs & Worcs
Hop gardens and orchards flourish around Leominster, one of the great wool towns of England from medieval times until the 18th century. Narrow medieval streets with their tightly-packed jumble of timber-framed houses contrast with the more spacious layouts of the Georgian era, best seen in Broad Street. A grey-stone priory church of 3 naves, stands amid green lawns shaded by trees. According to tradition it was founded in the 11th century by Earl Leofric, husband of Lady Godiva. A medieval ducking stool, last used to punish a nagging wife in the early 19th century, is on view in the church. Nearby, Grange Court, a delightful brick and timber house built in 1633 by John Abel, was moved to this site in 1855. It was originally the town hall and stood at the crossroads in the centre of Leominster. In Etnam Street is a folk museum devoted to the local history of the area.

Follow the A44, SP 'Rhayader', to Eardisland.

EARDISLAND, Herefs & Worcs
The village of Eardisland presents an exquisite picture in an idyllic setting among the green meadows bordering the River Arrow. Half-timbered black and white façades stand out among the old brick and colour-washed cottages that represent a medley of traditional styles of building. Near the old bridge over the river stands a 14th-century yeoman's hall, Staick House, and the old school house and village whipping post face the 17th-century manor house (not open) in whose garden stands a tall, 4-gabled dovecot of unusually charming design.

Continue on the A44 to Pembridge.

PEMBRIDGE, Herefs & Worcs
Pretty black and white timbered houses, their upper storeys drunkenly overhanging the pavements, are the keynote of this appealing village. Behind the New Inn, in the tiny market square, the old market house is raised on 8 oak columns. In the centre of the main street, weathered stone steps lead steeply uphill to a church with an unusual detached bell tower dating from the 14th century.

In 4½ miles pass the edge of Lyonshall and continue to Kington.

KINGTON, Herefs & Worcs
Sheltered by Hergest Ridge and Rushock Hill, Kington is an ancient town famous for its sheep markets. Offa's Dyke, the old Mercian defence against the Welsh, crosses Rushock Hill to the north. West of the town, the house called Hergest Court (not open) and for generations the home of the Vaughan family, was reputedly haunted by the ghost of 'Black Vaughan' until a 17th-century exorcism was said to have transformed his evil spirit into a bluebottle.

Crowning the height of Ludlow Hill is one of England's finest Norman castles

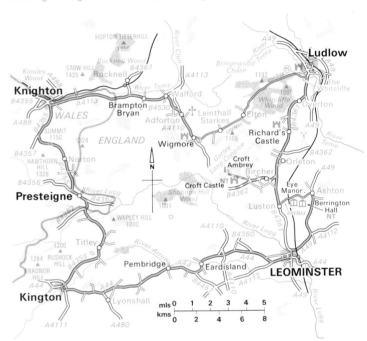

Turn right SP 'Presteigne' to join the B4355. After 6 miles cross the border into Wales and shortly enter Presteigne.

PRESTEIGNE, Powys
Presteigne stands on the bank of the River Lugg, at this point the boundary between England and Wales, in the rich green countryside of hill and vale so characteristic of the Welsh Marches. A priest hole, where a Roman Catholic priest remained hidden from persecution for 2 years, can be seen in the 17th-century Radnorshire Arms. In the churchyard is the grave of Mary Morgan, hanged in 1805 aged 17 for the murder of her illegitimate child. Her lover, who was a party to the crime and gave her the knife with which to do it, then sat as a member of the jury that condemned her. A royal pardon was granted but, sadly, arrived too late to save her.

Continue on the B4355 and at the end of the town turn right, SP 'Knighton'. Cross the River Lugg to reach Norton then ascend past Hawthorn Hill to 1,150ft before a long descent to the edge of Knighton.

KNIGHTON, Powys
In 1971 the Offa's Dyke Path was officially opened by Lord Hunt of Everest at a ceremony held in Knighton's riverside park. The earthworks of Offa's Dyke, the ancient frontier between England and Wales, built by King Offa of Mercia in the 8th century, are clearly visible on the west of the town, and Knighton stands at about the half-way point of the walk. The central Wales railway line, one of only 2 railways surviving in mid Wales, passes through Knighton at an enchanting neo-Gothic railway station. It owes its design to the owner of the land who, when he sold it to the railway, insisted in approving the plans of all the buildings.

Pembridge — typical Hereford architecture

These splendid bow-windows, known as oriels, belong to the Angel Hotel — one of Ludlow's many memorable buildings

At the near edge of Knighton turn right on to the A4113, SP 'Ludlow', to follow the Teme valley, later recrossing the border into England.

BRAMPTON BRYAN,
Herefs & Worcs
The name of the village derives from Bryan de Brampton who built a massive fortress here in the 13th century. Two great round towers, the gatehouse and hall survive, standing in the grounds of the manor house (not open). De Brampton's daughter, Margaret, married Robert Harley, and one of their descendants became a Lord Mayor of London. Harley Street, fashionable West End home of many exclusive medical practices, is named after him.

In 1½ miles at Walford turn right on to the B4530, SP 'Hereford'. In 1 mile turn right on to the A4110, and continue through Adforton to Wigmore.

WIGMORE, Herefs & Worcs
Between the manor house (not open) and the church lie the delightful half-timbered cottages of Wigmore. Little remains of the moated 14th-century castle, owned by the Mortimer family, which was dismantled during the Civil War in 1643, but near Adforton are the picturesque ruins of an Augustinian abbey founded in 1179.

Turn left on to the Ludlow road, and pass through Leinthall Starkes and Elton. After the descent through Whitcliffe Wood there is a magnificent view of Ludlow before reaching Ludford Bridge. To reach Ludlow town centre turn left on to the B4361, cross the River Teme and ascend into the town.

Delightfully delicate 17th-century stucco work at Eye Manor

LUDLOW, Shrops
The tour climbs from the River Teme up the steep hillside whose summit is crowned by the mighty walls of Ludlow Castle (OACT), one of the great Marcher fortresses, constructed in 1085 by the Earl of Shrewsbury. It was to Ludlow Castle that Prince Arthur, elder son of Henry VII, brought his young Spanish bride Catharine of Aragon, and had gardens laid out for her in a series of pleasant walks. He died here and his younger brother not only ascended to the throne as Henry VIII, but also married his brother's widow. The town is a feast of old buildings, from the black and white Feathers Inn, its façade ornamented with rich carving, to the restrained elegance of Georgian town houses. Broad Street, leading up from the river to the castle, is said to contain no building later than the 15th century. Near the top, Broad Gate, the only one of the original town gates that remains, leads to the 18th-century stone Butter Cross where the town museum is housed. The great 15th-century church of St Lawrence bears a graceful spire 135ft high. The interior is famous for the exquisitely carved misericords of the choir stalls, and for its lovely east window which depicts the life and miracles of the saint in 27 separate scenes.

The main tour turns right on to the B4361, SP 'Leominster', and in 1½ miles turns right again, SP 'Presteigne', to reach Richard's Castle.

RICHARD'S CASTLE,
Herefs & Worcs
A steep path leads north-west from the village through woodland to the earthworks of the ancient castle. It was built in the reign of Edward the Confessor and is one of only 2 in the county that pre-date the Norman Conquest.

Continue on the B4361, passing the edge of Orleton. The main tour continues south on the B4361, but from here a detour can be made to Croft Castle. Turn right on to the B4362, SP 'Presteigne', and in ½ mile bear right into Bircher. In 1 mile turn right for the entrance to Croft Castle and footpaths to Croft Ambrey.

CROFT CASTLE, Herefs & Worcs
Apart from a break of 173 years, from 1750 to 1923, this splendid Marcher castle (NT) has been the home of the Croft family ever since the medieval period. Walls and towers date from the 14th century, but the magnificent interior, with its superb collection of Gothic furniture, belongs to the 18th and early 19th centuries. The outstanding features of the extensive park, planted with many varieties of rare trees and shrubs, are the avenues of beech, oak and Spanish chestnut. The chestnut trees are particularly ancient — thought to be more than 350 years old. Close to the castle stands the church, with a monument to Sir Richard Croft. His finely carved armour represents the suit he wore at the Battle of Tewkesbury (1471).

Return to the B4361 and turn right to rejoin the main tour. At the edge of Luston turn left, SP 'Ashton', to reach Eye Manor.

CROFT AMBREY,
Herefs & Worcs
This Iron Age fort is situated at 1,000ft on the edge of Leinthall Common. It covers an area of 24 acres and was occupied from 400 BC to 50 AD. The climb to the top is rewarded with wide views of several counties.

EYE MANOR, Herefs & Worcs
This Carolean manor house (not open) is renowned for its elaborate superbly moulded and painted plaster ceilings. The finest are those of the great parlour and the dining hall. Eye Manor originally belonged to a Barbados sugar planter and slave trader, Ferdinando Gorges.

Continue, passing in 1½ miles on the right, Berrington Hall.

BERRINGTON HALL,
Herefs & Worcs
When the estate was bought by London banker and former Lord Mayor Thomas Harley, 3rd son of the 3rd Earl of Oxford, in 1775, he employed Capability Brown to create the park and choose the site for the house. Brown's son-in-law, Henry Holland, designed Berrington Hall (NT) as a neo-Classical building, completed in 1781. The style of the interior echoes the Classical theme: its outstanding features are the marble hall and the staircase hall.

At the A49 turn right, (care required), for the return alongside Berrington Park to Leominster.

IN THE WOODLANDS OF CANNOCK CHASE

Nowadays the great chase, or hunting ground, of Cannock is a protected area of woodland famous for its superb stands of mature oak and birch. All around are the quaint black-and-white villages typical of the area, guardians of tradition.

LICHFIELD, Staffs

A city of great age and architectural distinction, Lichfield has a fine red sandstone cathedral which carries three tall spires popularly known as the Ladies of the Vale. They form a well-known local landmark easily discernible above the rooftops of the town, and the grand west front of the building carries no less than 113 statues within its arcades and panels. Before the Commonwealth this type of decoration was reasonably common, but Cromwellian troops tracking down the sin of idolatry smashed such work wherever they could. Inside the building is preserved the 7th-century manuscript book of the *St Chad Gospels*, a rare treasure indeed. Other features include beautiful windows, a sculpted group by Chantrey, and numerous good memorials. The Bishop's Palace of 1687 is a lovely old example of its type, and restored Lichfield House dates from the 16th century. An old house in the Market Square was the birthplace of Dr Johnson and now serves as a Johnsonian Museum featuring, amongst other relics, his favourite silver teapot. The Lichfield Heritage Exhibition and Treasury is housed in the ancient Guild church of St Mary's, included is an audiovisual on the Civil War and siege of Lichfield and examples of the silversmith's craft.

Leave Lichfield with SP 'Tamworth A51', passing the Barracks to the left on Whittington Heath.

WHITTINGTON BARRACKS, Staffs

The official museum of the Staffordshire Regiment can be visited at Whittington Barracks, themselves evidence of Lichfield's long association with the military.

Pass a TV mast on the right and descend past Hopwas Hays Wood to Hopwas, then continue to Tamworth.

TAMWORTH, Staffs

Tamworth's fine castle (open) displays an intriguing mixture of architectural styles ranging from the original Norman to the charming pretence of the 19th century. The 10ft-thick walls of the keep are typically Norman, but the less massive warden's lodge and beautiful banqueting hall both show the delicacy of Tudor workmanship. A frieze of 55 oak panels in the state dining room, which is in the north wing, is painted with the arms of the lords of the castle up to 1718. A museum of local history is housed in the castle. Tamworth Church has a unique square tower with a double-spiral staircase at one corner, and the red-brick Town Hall of 1701 is one of the prettiest in the country.

Follow the A513 'Burton' and 'Alrewas' road, and after 4 miles pass an unclassified left turn that can be taken as a detour from the main route to Elford village.

Rich furnishings in Lichfield Cathedral include an ornate choir screen.

TRENT & MERSEY CANAL, Staffs

Designed by the great engineer Brindley to service the industrial heartlands of England, this canal was begun in the late 18th century and was the first safe means by which fragile goods could be transported from the Potteries district. Josiah Wedgwood, owner of one of the more famous Staffordshire china industries, worked in association with Brindley to produce this undoubted advantage to his interests. Just beyond Alrewas the canal actually joins the Trent by lock, and leaves the river by the same method after 250 yards.

In 1¾ miles at junction turn left on to the B5016 for Barton-under-Needwood. Continue forward SP 'Yoxall', then in 1 mile reach The Bell (PH) and turn right on to the unclassified 'Tutbury' road. In 3 miles cross a main road and continue to Tutbury.

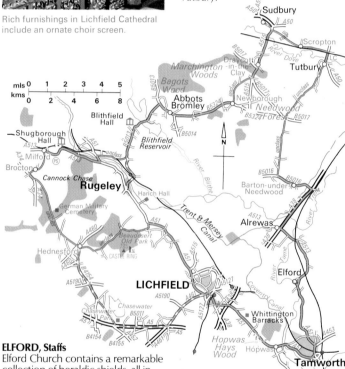

Tranquillity reigns today on the Trent and Mersey Canal, formerly an important route for the pottery trade.

ELFORD, Staffs

Elford Church contains a remarkable collection of heraldic shields, all in excellent condition, and the evocative monument to a child who is said to have been killed after being hit on the temple by a tennis ball in 1460. Many other fine memorials can be seen here.

On the main route, continue along the A513 to Alrewas.

ALREWAS, Staffs

Famous for its River Trent eel fishing and basket-weaving industries, this charming little village of thatched black-and-white Tudor cottages is considered one of the prettiest in the county. Its 13th- and 14th-century church contains a fine font, and its situation on the Trent and Mersey Canal offers fine towpath walks.

Turn right on to the A38 SP 'Burton', and in 1 mile cross the River Trent before continuing alongside the canal.

TUTBURY, Staffs

This picturesque old town stands on the banks of the River Dove and claims to have the finest Norman church in the Midlands. The west front of the building is certainly magnificent. Mary Queen of Scots was twice imprisoned in Tutbury Castle (open), and led a thoroughly miserable existence in the cramped surroundings of a high tower that still stands. Nowadays this sad place is visited for the outstanding views it affords over Needwood Forest. Other remains of the castle, dramatically situated on an isolated outcrop of rock, include 14th-century John of Gaunt's Gateway. The most striking building in the main street of the town is the old Dog and Partridge Inn.

Drive forward into the A50 High Street and cross the River Dove. Continue over a level crossing, then turn left on to an unclassified road SP 'Scropton' and 'Sudbury'. Continue for 2 miles beyond Scropton and turn left on to the A515. A short detour from the main route to attractive Sudbury can be made by turning right here on to the A515, then left on to an unclassified road leading to the village of that name.

Tutbury Castle offers excellent views over Needwood Forest.

SUDBURY, Derbys
Built largely in the 17th century, this village is an excellent early example of unified design being applied to a community rather than being allowed to develop in its own random fashion. Sudbury Hall (NT), seat of the Vernon family, contains exceptional carving by the sculptor Grinling Gibbons. A stained glass window given by Queen Victoria can be seen in the village church.

On the main route, continue along the A515 and recross the River Dove. Reach Draycott-in-the-Clay and ascend, then in ¾ mile meet crossroads and turn right on to an unclassified road for Newborough. Continue to Newborough and turn right on to the B5324 SP 'Abbots Bromley', then cross rolling countryside and turn right on to the B5014 to enter Abbots Bromley.

ABBOTS BROMLEY, Staffs
People from all over the country come to Abbots Bromley on the Monday after September 4, when the curious and ritualistic Horn Dance is performed through the streets and surrounding country lanes. Six of the twelve dancers carry ancient reindeer antlers on their shoulders, a seventh rides a hobby horse, a fool capers along the route in multi-coloured costume, and the entourage is completed by a young girl alongside a boy carrying a bow and arrow. The dance as it is seen today is thought to commemorate the granting of hunting rights to the local people by the Abbot of Bromley in the 12th century. However, it is likely to have been derived from a pagan ceremony with roots far back in prehistoric times. Features of the town itself include many half-timbered houses and a market place with an old butter cross. The 16th-century Church House and Bagot Almshouses are of particular note.

Continue along the B5014 and in ¼ mile turn left on to the B5013 SP 'Rugeley'. In 1 mile cross the extensive Blithfield Reservoir.

BLITHFIELD RESERVOIR, Staffs
The Queen Mother opened this 4,000 million gallon reservoir in 1953, and today it has become naturalized to such an extent that it is a valuable sanctuary for wildlife. Views can be enjoyed from the road, but a permit is required to visit the banks.

Pass a viaduct to reach Blithfield Hall on the right.

BLITHFIELD HALL, Staffs
Set graciously in the peaceful Blithe Valley, this estate has been the home of the Bagot family and their ancestors for 900 years and includes a fine old house of Elizabethan origin. Additions from later periods are evident in the design of the building, and inside is a magnificent staircase in carved oak. Of particular interest is a unique collection of relics from the Stuart period. Herds of black-necked Bagot goats roam the park.

Continue along the B5013 and in 1¾ miles turn right on to the unclassified 'Stafford' road. A short detour from the main route to the village of Rugeley can be made by keeping forward along the B5013 for a further 2¼ miles.

RUGELEY, Staffs
During the 19th century this village became nationally famous as the home of notorious Dr William Palmer, who was found guilty of poisoning a bookmaker to whom he owed money. On its own this act is not sensational, but it appears that this unfortunate victim was the last in a long line of poisonings by Palmer, including many relatives and friends. The grave of the bookmaker, John Cook, can be seen in the local churchyard. The actual town is a pleasant little place that easily lives down its connexion with the Prince of Poisoners. About 4 miles south-south-east is Hanch Hall of 13th-century origin. House and gardens (open).

On the main route, continue along the unclassified 'Stafford' road and in 1½ miles meet crossroads. Turn left, then left again to join the A51, then cross the River Trent and at roundabout take 2nd exit A513 SP 'Stafford'. Follow the Trent Valley and pass the entrance to Shugborough Hall on the right before reaching Milford.

SHUGBOROUGH HALL, Staffs
Now run by Staffordshire County Council and housing the county museum, this great white mansion (NT) stands in beautiful grounds on the River Sow and contains fine collections of furniture and period bric-à-brac. Access to the gardens is by a bridge over a lovely ornamental lake, and the grounds are scattered with superb classical monuments and follies. The most notable of the latter are the Doric Temple and the Tower of the Winds.

Continue to Milford and turn left on to the unclassified 'Brocton' road. At Brocton drive forward SP 'Stafford', then meet a main road and turn left on to the A34 SP 'Cannock'. In ¼ mile turn left on to the unclassified 'Hednesford' road and climb to Cannock Chase.

CANNOCK CHASE, Staffs
Once the private hunting ground of the kings of England, the 26 square miles of wooded Cannock Chase form a designated area of outstanding natural beauty that is available for everybody to enjoy. Several pine and spruce plantations have been established in the area by the Forestry Commission, but a few of the majestic oaks that were once commonplace can still be seen in Brocton Coppice. The feather-like plumes of birches grace Black Hill, and to the west the bracken-clad forest glades give way to heather and gorse. Among many wild creatures to be seen here are deer and the rare native red squirrel. Good views are afforded by the hilltops of Seven Springs, which culminate in 795ft Castle Ring; the latter is crowned by the ramparts of a good iron-age hillfort.

Sudbury Hall is a typical example of 17th-century elegance.

Continue along the unclassified 'Hednesford' road and pass a German military cemetery on the left. Meet crossroads and ascend, then meet more crossroads and drive forward into the colliery district round Hednesford. In ¼ mile drive forward, descend to crossroads, and keep forward to cross a railway bridge. Turn right on to the A460, drive under a railway bridge, and turn left on to an unclassified road SP 'Rawnsley' and 'Hazelslade'. An alternative return to Lichfield, taking in the Chasewater Park Railway at Brownhills, can be taken by continuing with the A460 and following the route indicated on the tour map. On the main route, continue along the unclassified road and after ¾ mile turn left. Drive over a level crossing and climb through thick woodland to crossroads. Turn right into Startley Lane and descend. Continue, with Castle Ring rising from Cannock Chase to the right, and meet a main road. Turn right on to the A51 for the return to Lichfield.

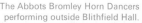
The Abbots Bromley Horn Dancers performing outside Blithfield Hall.

LINCOLN AND THE WITHAM VALLEY

The proud triple towers of Lincoln Cathedral can be seen for many miles across the flat lands of the Witham Valley, a fertile area of farms and fens whose threatened monotony is relieved by picturesque villages of honey-coloured stone.

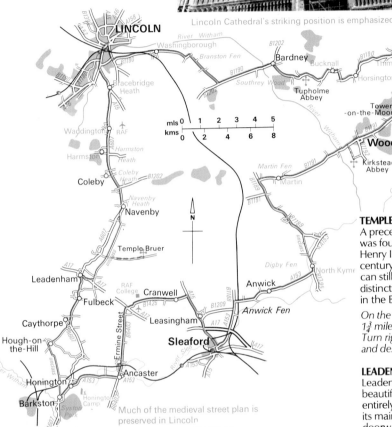

Lincoln Cathedral's striking position is emphasized by its impressive west front.

LINCOLN, Lincs

Historic Lincoln rises majestically from the north banks of the River Witham, on a slope crowned by its beautiful triple-towered cathedral. This splendid building, the third largest of its type in England, completely dominates the city and overlooks miles of countryside. Its 11th-century origins are largely hidden by extensions and additions from subsequent periods, and its many ancient treasures include the best preserved of four existing copies of *Magna Carta*. In the Library are first editions of *Paradise Lost, Don Quixote*, and part of Spenser's *Faerie Queen*. Amongst many other interesting churches in the city are St Benedict's and St Peter at Gowt's, both of which include a great deal of Saxon work. Newport Arch (AM), the only surviving Roman gateway to span an English street, is a relic of the ancient walled city of *Lindum Colonia*. The Close, also known as Minster Yard, contains a superb collection of buildings including a fine tithe barn of 1440 and the ancient Bishop's Palace (AM). Lincoln Castle was founded by William the Conqueror in 1068 and over the centuries has grown into the impressive structure that occupies some 6 acres of city ground today. Its main features include 14th-century Cobb Hall, which was once a place of punishment, the Observatory Tower, and a fine Norman keep. Other old buildings in

the city include the Jew's House, a fine example of 12th-century domestic architecture, and nearby Aaron's House – a product of the prosperous wool age and the oldest inhabited dwelling in England. Timber-framed 16th-century houses line the High Street as it crosses High Bridge, preserving in miniature the appearance of old London Bridge before it was destroyed in the Great Fire that razed the capital in 1666.

From Lincoln follow SP 'Sleaford A15' and ascend to Bracebridge Heath. Turn right on to the A607 SP 'Grantham' and after a short distance pass the large RAF base at Waddington on the left. Continue past Harmston Heath (on the left) and the village of Harmston in attractively wooded countryside to the right. After a short distance pass Coleby on the right, with Coleby Heath stretching away to the left.

Much of the medieval street plan is preserved in Lincoln

COLEBY, Lincs

Interesting old buildings in this pleasant village include the church and 17th-century Coleby Hall. The former is of Norman date and incorporates a Saxon tower, and the latter shares attractive grounds with the Temple of Romulus and Remus, by Sir William Chambers.

Continue on the A607 into Navenby, with Navenby Heath on the left.

NAVENBY, Lincs

Stone and pantiled houses form charming architectural groups in this pleasant little village, and the restored church rises grandly above their rooftops to complete the picture. Inside the church is a notable Easter Sepulchre decorated with carved figures.

Beyond Navenby turn left on to an unclassified road SP 'Ancaster, Sleaford'. Continue for 2¼ miles and meet crossroads. A detour from the main route can be made here by turning left and driving for 2¼ miles to Temple Bruer; access is via a road through Temple Farm.

TEMPLE BRUER, Lincs

A preceptory of the Knights Templar was founded here during the reign of Henry II, and the restored 13th-century tower (AM) of their church can still be seen. Very few of their distinctive round churches survive in the British Isles.

On the main route, continue for 1¾ miles and meet more crossroads. Turn right on to the A17 SP 'Newark' and descend into Leadenham.

LEADENHAM, Lincs

Leadenham Old Hall (not open) is a beautiful building of c1700 built entirely of golden ironstone. One of its main features is a delightful rustic doorway. The village itself is dominated by its lovely church spire and boasts a 19th-century drinking fountain beneath a hexagonal canopy.

Meet traffic lights in Leadenham and turn left on to the A607 SP 'Grantham'. Continue to Fulbeck.

FULBECK, Lincs

A delightful combination of woods and farmland surrounds this pretty village. The hall, dating from 1773, contains fine period furniture and is set in an 11-acre garden.

Proceed on the A607, passing the edge of Caythorpe.

CAYTHORPE, Lincs

The characteristically utilitarian appearance of Caythorpe's village architecture is lifted by the mellow gold of local ironstone. Notable Ivy House dates from 1684 and has projecting wings with gables. The local church features a good tower.

Drive ¼ mile beyond the Caythorpe crossroads and turn right on to an unclassified road for the village of Hough-on-the-Hill.

HOUGH-ON-THE-HILL, Lincs
As its name suggests, this village occupies a lofty site that makes it an excellent viewpoint. The local church is noted for its tower, which features a curious Saxon turret containing a newel stairway.

Beyond the local church turn left SP 'Barkston, Grantham' and proceed to Barkston.

BARKSTON, Lincs
Barkston Church features a good ironstone tower. Close by is a group of almshouses that reflect a style uniformly applied to the buildings of the local Belton estate.

From Barkston turn left on to the A607, with Syston Park ahead. After ¾ mile drive forward on to the A153, skirting Honington.

North Kyme Fen typifies the Kesteven area of Lincolnshire

HONINGTON, Lincs
About ¾ mile south-east of this village is Honington Camp, one of the few major hillforts built in this part of the country. It is of iron-age date and was probably manned to defend the Ancaster Gap. During the 17th century an urn of Roman coins was found here, which seems to suggest that the inhabitants of nearby Ancaster found the camp useful. Honington Church contains some good Norman work.

Continue on the A153, passing Honington Camp, and proceed for 2½ miles. Turn left on to the B6403 to Ancaster.

ANCASTER, Lincs
Sited on the old Roman road of Ermine Street, this village is set in pleasantly wooded countryside and stands near the site of Roman *Causennae*. Remains of this ancient camp and posting station can be seen near by, and relics excavated from the area can be seen in Grantham Museum – including mosaic flooring and an altar. Some 2 miles south of the village are quarries where the famous Ancaster stone was worked for many of Lincolnshire's beautiful churches.

Proceed along a modern road that follows the line of Ermine Street.

ERMINE STREET, Lincs
This Roman road, built about 1,900 years ago between London and Lincoln, allowed the occupying forces to reach trouble spots in eastern England with comparative ease. The name is derived from a Saxon tribe who lived near by.

Drive for 3¾ miles beyond Ancaster and turn right on to the A17, then left on to the B1429 SP 'Cranwell', passing the RAF College. Continue to Cranwell.

CRANWELL, Lincs
Traces of Saxon workmanship can be seen in Cranwell's mainly Norman church, which houses a fine old screen. West of the village is the well-known RAF college, which was founded in 1920 and includes a number of well-designed buildings.

In ¾ mile turn right on to the A15 'Sleaford' road and pass the edge of Leasingham.

LEASINGHAM, Lincs
Notable buildings in this old village include the Ancient House of 1658, the 17th-century Old Hall, and Georgian Leasingham Manor. Later additions include Leasingham Hall and Roxholme Hall, both of the 19th century. The local church has a lofty west tower crowned by a spire.

Proceed along the A15 to Sleaford.

SLEAFORD, Lincs
Charmingly situated on the banks of the peaceful River Slea, this pleasant little market town is dominated by a 12th- to 15th-century church with one of the earliest stone spires in England. The building's outstanding window tracery is arguably the best in the country. Early structures in the town include a 15th-century timber-framed vicarage and the Black Bull Inn; a carved stone at the latter is dated 1689 and 1791, and illustrates the old sport of bull baiting. Most of the town's workaday buildings date from the 19th century, including the Sessions House, and the Carre's Hospital.

Leave Sleaford on the A153 'Horncastle' road. After 2¾ miles turn right and proceed to Anwick.

Little survives to tell of the wealth and prestige that came to Bardney Abbey before its downfall and ruin.

ANWICK, Lincs
Just south of Anwick's medieval church are adjoining cottages in the romantic gothic style. One houses the post office and the other is a smithy.

Continue with Anwick Fen on the right, and drive through the village of North Kyme. Beyond North Kyme continue forward on to an unclassified road SP 'Walcot', skirting Digby Fen on the left. In 1¼ miles turn left on to the B1189; proceed for 4 miles and turn right on to the B1191 SP 'Woodhall Spa', driving through Martin and later passing Martin Fen on the left. Cross the River Witham at Kirkstead Bridge, and after another ¾ mile pass a right turn leading to Kirkstead Abbey. It is worth making the short detour to this historic place.

KIRKSTEAD ABBEY, Lincs
Scant remains of a rich Cistercian abbey founded by Hugo Brito in 1139 can be seen here, but the site is most famous for the 13th-century architectural gem of St Leonard's Chapel. This was built outside the abbey gates for lay worshippers, and has survived in a remarkably good state of preservation. Its wooden screen is thought to be the second oldest in England and includes timber work dating from 1210.

Like many of Sleaford's buildings, Carre's Hospital, in Eastgate, dates from the mid-19th century.

Continue along the main route and enter Woodhall Spa.

WOODHALL SPA, Lincs
In Victorian and earlier times this inland resort was famous for its natural springs, and a fine pump room and bathing establishment remain from this period. Nowadays the town is well known as a golfing centre, with Lincolnshire's only championship-standard course.

Continue along the B1191 to Tower on the Moor.

TOWER ON THE MOOR, Lincs
This impressive 60ft tower dominates the local countryside and is a well-known (if enigmatic) landmark. It is thought to have been built in the 15th century.

Continue along the B1191 to Horncastle.

HORNCASTLE, Lincs
Roman *Banovallum*, the 'walled place on the River Bain', stood on the site now occupied by this pleasant little market town. Remains of the ancient fort that guarded the settlement have been incorporated in the modern town library. The local church dates from the 13th century and contains the fine Dymoke Brass of 1519, plus a 17th-century chest and various other relics. A 10-day horse fair was held in Horncastle every August and is featured in George Borrow's *Romany Rye*.

Leave Horncastle on the A158 'Lincoln' road and in ½ mile turn left on to the B1190 SP 'Bardney'. Drive through Thimbleby, Horsington, and Bucknall, later passing Tupholme Abbey to the left.

TUPHOLME ABBEY, Lincs
Remains of a religious house that was founded c1160 can be seen here, including part of the refectory.

Continue along the B1190 for 1½ miles and turn left into Bardney.

BARDNEY, Lincs
Ethelred, King of Mercia, founded a Benedictine abbey here in the 7th century. It was rebuilt in Norman times by the Earl of Lincoln, and grew to become one of the country's most powerful centres of religion and education. Excavations conducted amongst the extensive ruins in 1912 uncovered many interesting relics, some of which can be seen in the local church. The town itself is a typical fenland community on the River Witham, in an agricultural area.

Leave Bardney and cross the railway and the River Witham. Continue along the B1190, with Branston Fen to the right, and shortly bear right to skirt the Lincoln Edge. In 3 miles reach the Plough Inn and bear right SP 'Lincoln', then drive through Washingborough and return to Lincoln.

INSIDE OLD RUTLAND

Tiny Rutland has vanished in name but survives in fact. The towering spires of its churches rise from typically-clustered cottages of thatch and ironstone, and some of England's richest pasture is grown where the stag and hart were hunted in ancient times.

Market Harborough's old grammar school was founded in the 17th century and is a fine example of its type.

MARKET HARBOROUGH, Leics

A market was held here as early as 1203, and over the centuries the town has grown and prospered to become the mature community that exists today. The most recent developments have been industrial, but these have not been made at the expense of many fine buildings from previous, less intrusive periods. The most famous is the former grammar school, a lovely timbered and gabled building of 1614 that stands on wooden pillars above street level. The Three Swans is the largest of many old local inns and displays one of the finest wrought-iron signs in England. The parish church dates from the 13th to 15th centuries and is known for its tower, a beautiful structure crowned by a broach spire that is visible for miles around. Every November the church bells are rung to commemorate the rescue of a merchant lost in the Welland marshes in 1500, and the ringers traditionally receive one shilling for beer. Much of the town's present prosperity is due to the Symington family, who made liberty bodices in a Victorian factory behind the church.

Leave the town on the A427 'Corby' road to reach Dingley.

Rockingham Castle's Panel Room is part of a rich collection of treasures.

DINGLEY, Northants

The most impressive feature of this small village is Dingley Hall (not open), an unforgettable building with a south gateway flanked by polygonal towers.

Continue, and in about 2¼ miles pass the village of Stoke Albany to the left.

STOKE ALBANY, Northants

Features of the fine local church, which dates from the 13th century, include good doorways and windows.

Continue along the A427 beyond East Carlton, then turn left on to the B670 and proceed to Rockingham.

Naseby was the scene of a decisive Civil War battle.

ROCKINGHAM, Northants

Set on a steep hillside overlooking the River Welland, this lovely village of flint-built thatched cottages has a number of new houses that have been built of traditional materials to harmonize with the whole. The summit of the hill is occupied by Rockingham Castle, which was originally built by William the Conqueror, and affords views into 4 counties. The site of the keep is now a rose garden surrounded by yew hedges, but surviving fragments of the old structure include the moat, foundations of the Norman hall, and the twin towers of the gatehouse. King John used the castle both as a fortress and as a hunting lodge for Rockingham Forest, a vast blanket of wood and heathland that once covered much of Leicestershire. The mainly Elizabethan house that stands here today (open) contains collections of paintings and furniture.

Turn left on to the A6003 'Uppingham' road, crossing the River Welland. (To enter Rockingham village turn right here into the A6003 main street.) Continue to Caldecott and drive forward on to the B672, then in 4½ miles pass under the Welland railway viaduct.

WELLAND VIADUCT, Northants

This 82-arch railway viaduct dates from 1874 and is a notable example of 19th-century industrial

architecture. It spans the complete width of the Welland Valley and is a well-known landmark.

In 2 miles turn right, then left, to join the A6121; continue to Ketton.

KETTON, Leics

One of the largest and most attractive of old Rutland's villages, this picturesque collection of butter-coloured buildings is a noted quarrying centre. The local stone is greatly prized as a building material and has been worked at least since Roman times. St Mary's Church has an exquisite spire that rises high above the village's sepia roofs of Collyweston slate, perfectly complementing one of the finest examples of church architecture in the east Midlands. The west front of the building is an excellent example of late 12th-century work, and the rest of the structure dates almost entirely from the 13th century.

Continue along the A6121 and drive through Tinwell to Stamford.

STAMFORD, Lincs
Justly considered one of England's most beautiful towns, stone-built Stamford has a long history that can be traced back as far as the time of Danish settlement. In the 13th and 14th centuries it was important enough to have its own university, and the powerful influence of early Christianity is evident in many fine churches and other ecclesiastical buildings. All Saints' Place is the visual centre of the town and is noted for its outstanding, multi-period architecture. Browne's Hospital has been described as one of the finest medieval almshouses surviving in England, and includes a beautiful Jacobean hall and chapel. Close to the Welland are the ancient Burghley Almshouses. The George Hotel was a coaching inn in the 14th century, and among fine buildings from many periods in St George's Square is a house that has been continuously inhabited since c1350. Even older than that is the Bastion in West Street, a section of the old town wall that has been untouched for 700 years. Close to the town is Elizabethan Burghley House (open) where the well-known Burghley Horse Trials are held. The house itself is considered one of England's greatest mansions and contains many superb rooms. It boasts over 100 works of art and antique furnishings.

Follow SP 'Grantham' and then 'Oakham' to leave Stamford by the A606. Continue to Empingham.

EMPINGHAM, Leics
Dominating this large attractive village is the handsome tower and spire of St Peter's Church, a well-proportioned building with a good west front. Features of the interior include fragments of ancient glass and considerable remains of medieval colour.

Continue, and 1 mile beyond Whitwell reach Rutland Water on the left. Turn right here on to the unclassified 'Exton' and 'Cottesmore' road, entering an avenue of trees. After 1¼ miles reach a right turn that offers a pleasant detour to Exton. The main route skirts Exton Park.

EXTON, Leics
Situated in one of the largest ironstone extraction areas in Britain, this charming village of thatched limestone cottages is well worth the small diversion needed to visit it. The ruined Old Hall, probably built during the reign of Elizabeth I, was burned down in 1810; the New Hall replaced it some 40 years later. Exton's parish church is noted for its remarkable range of monumental sculpture, which illustrates the progress of this art form in England from the 14th to 18th centuries.

On the main route, drive to Cottesmore and turn left on to the B668. Continue to Burley.

This gateway forms an imposing entrance to the mansion at Burghley.

BURLEY, Leics
Burley-on-the-Hill (not open) is considered by many to be the most beautiful country house in the county. Its fine colonnades and exquisitely restrained detail, the work of Joseph Lumley between 1694 and 1705, ornament a small hill that was once an ancient earthwork. The building is best appreciated from the south, looking down a long avenue of trees to the fine lines of the front.

Descend into Oakham.

OAKHAM, Leics
Once the capital of the tiny and now defunct county of Rutland, this well-known hunting centre preserves memories of its former status in the Rutland County Museum. This is housed in the late 18th-century indoor riding school of the Rutland Fencibles. The town's church dates from the 12th to 15th century and features unusual nave capitals. It shares its churchyard with the original grammar school, which was founded in 1584. Remains of Oakham Castle include a beautiful Norman hall (open), where a unique collection of horseshoes is nailed to the wall. These were traditionally contributed to the household by members of the royalty or peerage visiting the lordship for the first time. An old butter cross with stocks has been preserved in the town.

Follow SP 'Melton Mowbray', drive over a level crossing, and turn left then left again on to an unclassified road for Braunston.

BRAUNSTON, Leics
This lovely ironstone village stands on a hillside above the valley of the little River Gwash. Inside its distinctive church are traces of a previous building dating from the 12th and 13th centuries.

From Braunston follow the 'Leicester' road, and in 4¾ miles pass 755ft Whatborough Hill to the right. Access to the summit is by a nearby track. Continue to Tilton.

TILTON, Leics
The early-English and later church in this high village is noted for its strange gargoyles.

Join the B6047 'Market Harborough' road and in 2 miles drive over a main road. After another 3 miles reach the top of an ascent and turn right on to an unclassified road SP 'Carlton, Kibworth'. Continue to Kibworth Harcourt.

KIBWORTH HARCOURT, Leics
Examples of architecture from many periods can be seen in this village. Among the most notable are the Old House of 1678, the 18th-century Congregational Church, and 19th-century Kibworth Hall. Close to the village is the imposing tower of St Wilfred's Church.

Follow SP 'Leicester' to join the A6, then take the 1st unclassified road on the left SP 'Kilby, Wistow'. Cross the Grand Union Canal at a series of locks, continue to crossroads, and turn left for Fleckney and Saddington. Drive to Saddington, turn right, and continue to Mowsley. At Mowsley turn right and right again with SP 'Leicester'. In 1 mile turn left on to the A50, and after a further 1¼ miles turn right on to the B5414. Drive to North Kilworth and turn right on to the A427, then turn left with the B5414 for South Kilworth.

SOUTH KILWORTH, Leics
South Kilworth's church is mainly of 19th-century design, although Norman and 14th-century work from a previous building can be seen inside. The font is of 12th- or 13th-century date.

Beyond South Kilworth pass Stanford Reservoir on the left, then turn left on to the unclassified 'Stanford on Avon' road. Descend to Stanford on Avon, passing Stanford Hall and Stanford Park on the right.

STANFORD ON AVON, Leics
Divided between Leicestershire and Northamptonshire by the River Avon, this pleasant village has a good church with a pinnacled 15th-century tower. Stanford Hall (open) is impressively sited in open pasture and stands on the site of an earlier house. The present building dates from the reign of William and Mary, and has an imposing facade that adds a touch of grandeur to its pleasing design. Its rooms contain collections of costumes and furniture, and there is a motor museum in the stable.

In ¼ mile turn left on to the 'Cold Ashby' road and later re-cross the Grand Union Canal. In 1¼ miles climb 690ft Honey Hill. Continue to Cold Ashby and turn left on to the B4036, then drive to Naseby.

NASEBY, Northants
A stone column 1½ miles north of this village marks the field where the Battle of Naseby was fought in 1645. The Cromwellian victory heralded a new era of British government and sealed the fate of King Charles I. The Naseby Battle Museum at Purlieu Farm displays layouts of the battleground and various local relics. In Naseby Churchyard is a huge copper ball that is said to have been brought back from the Siege of Boulogne in 1544.

At Naseby turn left then right on to the unclassified 'Sibbertoft' road, and in 1 mile pass the site of the Battle of Naseby on the left. Reach Sibbertoft and turn right for the 'Theddingworth' road, and after 1 mile bear right to Marston Trussell. Return to Market Harborough via Lubenham and the main A427.

PEAK DISTRICT NATIONAL PARK

Some of England's wildest and most beautiful scenery is protected and made accessible to millions of people in the 542 square miles of this national park, which is mainly divided between the counties of Derbyshire, Cheshire, and Staffordshire. The high, craggy northern region includes gritstone Kinder Scout and various other lofty peaks, but in the south are gentler limestone landscapes that have been sculpted by water and softened by valley woodlands. The undulating White Peak area has thinly-grassed pastures separated by snaking limestone walls, and the lovely River Dove flows through its deep ravine past pinnacles, buttresses, and spires of weathered stone. East are the gritstone uplands and ridges of Millstone Edge, Froggat Edge, and Stanton Moor.

MATLOCK, Derbys

This River Derwent spa town is situated on the eastern edge of the national park, in a high area of gritstone moors and ridges. During the 19th century it was a resort for people following the fashion for taking the waters, and a great hydropathy centre was built at Matlock Bank. This impressive building now houses Derbyshire County Council. Along the banks of the Derwent stretch lovely Hall Leys Gardens.

A detour can be taken from the main route to Matlock Bath by leaving Matlock on the A6 SP 'Derby' and continuing south for 1¼ miles.

MATLOCK BATH, Derbys

Regency visitors popularized the medicinal springs of Matlock Bath, and although the resort declined in Victorian times it remains one of the district's many attractive touring centres. Its Petrifying Wells are very famous and are hung with various objects left by visitors to turn to stone. Every autumn a parade of illuminated and decorated boats is staged on the River Derwent. The resort's charming setting among tree-covered hills is overlooked by the 1,000ft Heights of Abraham, which were worked for lead in Roman times. The Victorian Prospect Tower, on the crest of the heights commands excellent views. In the town is the Peak District Mining Museum, which traces the history of the Derbyshire lead industry.

On the main tour, leave Matlock on the A6 'Buxton' road and drive to Darley Dale.

DARLEY DALE, Derbys

Stone from the quarries near here has long been prized as a building and sculpting material, and can be seen to advantage in many of Britain's large towns. The village church preserves ancient stone coffins and sections of an unusually decorated Saxon cross.

Leave Darley Dale and continue on the A6 to reach Rowsley.

HILLS OF THE SOUTHERN PEAK

This part of the Peak District national park is of gentle aspect, a region of undulating limestone hills scored by the beautifully-wooded Derwent Valley and trout-rich races of the Wye. Curtains of rich foliage screen weathered outcrops, curious stone spires, and the dark mouths of caves.

ROWSLEY, Derbys

Local examples of 17th-century domestic architecture include a fine old bridge over the River Wye and the pleasant Peacock Inn of 1652 More recent survivals include two obsolete station buildings, one of which was designed by Sir Joseph Paxton in 1849.

Drive 1¼ miles beyond Rowsley and turn left on to the B5056 'Ashbourne' road. A pleasant detour from the main route to Haddon Hall can be made by keeping straight ahead on the A6 for ½ mile.

HADDON HALL, Derbys

Medieval architecture can be seen at its best in the peaceful lines of this romantic old house (open). Parts of it date from the 12th century, and although it was originally built as a fortified manor house it has never seen military action. Among its many treasures is a chapel with a Norman font and lovely 15th-century wall paintings, and a long gallery with a painted ceiling and outstanding panelling. Terraced rose gardens are a striking feature of the grounds.

On the main tour, continue along the B5056 'Ashbourne' road and in 1 mile bear right on to an unclassified road SP 'Youlgreave'. A detour to Winster and the Nine Ladies stone circle can be made by driving along the B5056 for a further 2¾ miles, then turning left on B5057 to Winster.

WINSTER, Derbys

Set in the main street of this delightful village is a stone built 17th-18th-century market house (NT).

Return and in 1¾ miles turn right on to an unclassified road, through Birchover to Stanton Moor.

STANTON MOOR, Derbys

The most remarkable of several fascinating prehistoric sites on the moor is the Nine Ladies stone circle (AM), which stands 900ft above sea level in an area that affords splendid views into the Derwent Valley.

On the main tour, continue along the unclassified 'Youlgreave' road, enter the Bradford Valley, and after ¾ mile pass the village of Alport to the left.

Dovedale is said to be the most beautiful of the Derbyshire Dales.

ALPORT, Derbys

Pleasantly sited on a tumbling tributary of the River Bradford, attractive Alport is typical of the area and preserves a number of old houses. The oldest is 16th-century Monk's Hall.

Leave Alport and continue to attractive Youlgreave.

YOULGREAVE, Derbys

Every June, on the Saturday nearest St John the Baptist's Day, the springs and wells of this charming village are dressed with flower pictures as part of an ancient Derbyshire tradition. Today the ceremony is Christian, but it is likely that the ornamentation was once intended to appease the spirits of the springs.

Leave Youlgreave on the 'Ashbourne' road for 4½ miles and meet the A5012. Turn right here, then turn left to join the A515 and continue to the Newhaven Hotel.

NEWHAVEN HOTEL, Derbys

This building, a black-and-white structure with 5 bays, was built by the Duke of Devonshire in the 18th century. About 2½ miles north is the outstanding prehistoric stone circle of Arbor Low (AM).

Continue along the A515 to Alsop Plantation, with lovely Dovedale to the west of the road.

ALSOP PLANTATION, Derbys

The plantation on Alsop Moor is protected by the National Trust and extends alongside the main A515, below a 1,253ft summit. Its presence is an attractive addition to the local limestone scenery.

In 1½ miles pass the edge of Dovedale to the right.

DOVEDALE, Derbys & Staffs

Here the lovely River Dove flows through a 2-mile ravine where spectacular limestone scenery of craggy buttresses and curiously weathered outcrops is clothed and softened by carpets of lush vegetation. Perhaps the most famous of many beauty spots in the national park, the dale (NT) is also noted for trout fishing.

In 2¾ miles turn left on to an unclassified road and continue to the village of Tissington.

TISSINGTON, Derbys

Greystone houses line two sides of the attractive triangular green on which this exceptionally beautiful village is centred; the third side is occupied by a fine Norman and later church. Features of the latter include a good Norman font, an unusual 2-decker pulpit dating from the 18th century, and various monuments. Traditional Derbyshire well-dressing ceremonies are enacted at five different wells on Ascension Day.

Leave Tissington and turn right, then drive through attractive parkland to meet the A515. Turn left and continue to Fenny Bentley.

Beautiful gardens surround romantic Haddon Hall.

MIDDLETON TOP, Derbys

An Engine House with beam engine built in 1829.

Return to main route, then descend through the attractively wooded Via Gellia for Cromford.

Many Derbyshire wells, such as this example at Tissington, are decorated for thanksgiving ceremonies.

Richard Arkwright's original cotton mill at Cromford was two storeys taller than the present building.

Crich Museum houses many historic trams in working order.

SOUTH WINGFIELD MANOR, Derbys

Extensive remains can be seen of a fine 15th-century manor house where Mary Queen of Scots was imprisoned in 1584. Access to ruins is through the Manor Farm.

Continue along the B5035 to Crich and branch right on to an unclassified road SP 'Holloway' for the Crich Tramway Museum.

CRICH TRANWAY MUSEUM, Derbys

Vintage tramcars from all over Britain have been restored to working order and are on display in this fascinating museum, which occupies a disused quarry. An air of authenticity is created by a period setting comprising the reconstructed façade of Derby's Georgian Assembly Rooms and a collection of Victorian Street furniture. An exhibition illustrates the history of lead mining in Derbyshire.

FENNY BENTLEY, Derbys

Features of this pleasant village include the successful amalgamation of a 15th-century manor house with the remains of an ancient tower, and a good Derbyshire church. Inside the latter is a macabre monument commemorating Thomas Beresford, his wife, 16 sons, and 5 daughters.

Leave Fenny Bentley, drive for ½ mile, and turn left on to the B5056 SP 'Bakewell'. Continue to Grangemill. At crossroads turn right on to the A5012 continue for 1¾ miles to reach a right turn B5023. A detour can be made by turning right then sharp left to Middleton. At crossroads turn right and right again for Middleton Top.

CROMFORD, Derbys

The world's first mechanized textile factory was built here by Richard Arkwright, a native of the village, in 1771 (open). The mill is gradually being restored by the Arkwright Society. One of the key figures in England's industrial revolution, he lived in Willersley Castle and built the church in which he is buried. A fine old bridge that spans the River Derwent here carries a rare 15th-century bridge chapel (AM).

Leave Cromford and turn left, then turn right on to the A6 SP 'Derby'. Pass Cromford Canal on the left, then reach Shining Cliff Wood on the right.

SHINING CLIFF WOOD, Derbys

This attractive area of woodland (NT) occupies 200 acres on the west bank of the River Derwent, and is a haven for many forms of wildlife.

Continue along the A6 to reach Ambergate and turn left on to the A610 SP 'Ripley'. Follow the Amber Valley, and after 2 miles turn left on to the B6013 SP 'Chesterfield'. In 3 miles turn left again on to the B5035 to reach South Wingfield Manor.

CRICH STAND, Derbys

High above the Crich Tramway Museum is the 940ft summit of Crich Stand, a lofty vantage point crowned by a monument to the Sherwood Foresters – the Nottingham and Derby Regiment.

Descend to Holloway. Turn right SP 'Riber' and 'Tansley', then in ½ mile meet crossroads and drive straight on. In 2 miles meet a T-junction and turn left SP 'Riber Village', and after ¼ mile keep left to reach the Riber Castle Fauna Reserve on the right.

RIBER CASTLE FAUNA RESERVE, Derbys

Near-natural surroundings are provided for comprehensive collections of European birds and animals in the 20 acres of this excellent reserve. Special features include a colony of lynx, and many breeds of domestic animals that have died out elsewhere. Picturesque ruins of 19th-century Riber Castle dominate 853ft Riber Hill.

Descend steeply through hairpin bends, turn right at the bottom, and in ¾ mile turn left on to the A615. Return to Matlock.

THROUGH THE DUKERIES

The open countryside of the Trent valley gives way to the ancient woodlands of Sherwood Forest, the traditional hunting ground of Robin Hood and his merry men. Here, a series of palatial estates known as the Dukeries were created in the 18th and 19th centuries by 4 dukes.

Mighty Newark Castle was 'slighted' by Cromwell's soldiers in the Civil War

NEWARK-ON-TRENT, Notts

At the centre of the old market town whose ruined castle walls are reflected in the river, is the old cobbled market place surrounded by attractive buildings. Most famous is the 14th-century timbered White Hart Inn, its façade adorned by figures of angels. Nearby stands the Clinton Arms, where William Gladstone, who became Prime Minister in the late 19th century, gave his first public political speech. In the streets around the market place fine Georgian buildings lend character to the town, and opposite the castle is a remarkable Victorian extravaganza, the Ossington Coffee Palace, built by Lady Ossington to promote the cause of temperance. The castle (AM), of which only the west wall, towers and north gateway remain, was where King John died of a surfeit of food and drink at the end of the disastrous journey during which he lost the crown jewels in the Wash. The castle, held for the king during the Civil War, proved impregnable to siege, but its commander surrendered after King Charles had given himself up to the Scots, and Cromwell's troops destroyed it. The church of St Mary Magdalen is remarkably beautiful and has a soaring 240ft slender spire.

Leave Newark on the A46, SP 'Lincoln'. In 2½ miles, at the roundabout, turn left on to the A1133, SP 'Gainsborough', and continue to Collingham.

COLLINGHAM, Notts

A plaque on the village cross records that in 1795 the River Trent burst its banks and swept through the village causing a flood 5ft deep. In the following century there was another flood almost as bad, but the Trent has since been diverted and its old course through Collingham is followed now by the River Fleet, which is no threat to this pleasant village strung out along the eastern river bank.

At the end of the village turn right on to the South Scarle road, then in ¼ mile turn left. Later, at the T-junction, turn right into South Scarle. Follow the Swinderby road, then shortly turn left, SP 'Eagle'. In ½ mile bear right and later, at the T-junction, turn right. In another ½ mile turn left, SP 'Lincoln', and ¾ mile further turn left again. Pass through Eagle and after 1½ miles turn left, SP 'Doddington', then in ¾ mile turn left again to reach Doddington.

DODDINGTON, Lincs

The focal point of the village of Doddington is its lovely Elizabethan mansion (OACT), owned by the Jarvis family. Portraits by Reynolds, Lawrence and Lely decorate the walls, and the rooms contain fine period furniture, porcelain and ceramics. Among the curiosities on show is a medieval scold's bridle — a fearsome contraption put on a nagging wife to stop her talking.

Go forward on to the B1190. In 3¼ miles turn left on to the A57, and in just over ¼ mile turn left on to the Worksop road. Continue past Newton On Trent and Dunham, then in 1¾ miles turn right, SP 'East Drayton'. In 1 mile at the T-junction, turn left for East Drayton. At the church turn right and continue to Stokeham. Here, turn right then left on to the Leverton road. After 1¼ miles turn left into Treswell, then turn right for South Leverton and North Leverton.

NORTH & SOUTH LEVERTON, Notts

Dutch-gabled houses dating from the 17th and 18th centuries give these 2 villages a distinct resemblance to Holland. At North Leverton, a trim tower windmill, 3 storeys high and still in working condition, also echoes the atmosphere of the Netherlands. The mill, erected in 1813, is known as a subscription mill because all the neighbouring farmers banded together to finance it.

Continue on the unclassified road to Sturton-le-Steeple. From here a detour can be made by turning right to visit Littleborough.

LITTLEBOROUGH, Notts

As its name suggests, this is a tiny village with an even tinier Norman church. It was here that King Harold and the Saxon army crossed the Trent in 1066 on their desperate march south to Hastings to stop the Norman invasion. A drought in 1933 lowered the river level to reveal a paved ford, which has been in existence since the village was built.

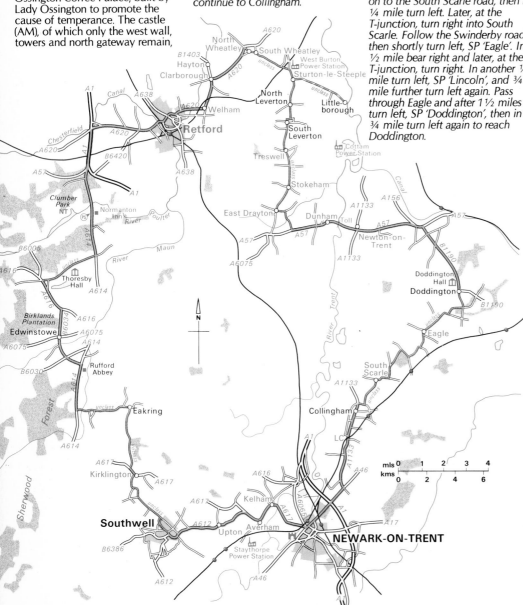

Southwell minster; unique in having pyramidal roofs to its towers

The entrance to Thoresby Hall

At Sturton-le-Steeple, follow SP 'Gainsborough', then 'Wheatley', to pass near West Burton Power Station. Beyond South Wheatley turn left into North Wheatley and at the end of the village turn left again on to the A620 and continue through Retford, SP 'Worksop'. In 3¾ miles turn left, SP 'Newark', to join the A1. Later, at the roundabout, take the A614 to enter Sherwood Forest and the area known as the Dukeries.

THE DUKERIES, Notts
The name Dukeries was given to the northern part of Sherwood Forest because, in the 18th and 19th centuries, no less than 4 dukes and several earls and marquises bought estates in the area. Most of the forest had been completely denuded of trees in the aftermath of the Civil War, and the land was desolate. It was not until the Dukes of Norfolk, Kingston, Newcastle and Portland began to establish plantations of woodland that the forest regained something of its traditional appearance. Three of the ducal estates remain: Clumber Park, Thoresby Hall and Welbeck Abbey; Rufford Abbey, an estate of the Earls of Shrewsbury is just outside the boundary of the Dukeries proper.

After 1¼ miles cross the River Poulter, with Clumber Park to the right.

CLUMBER PARK, Notts
The Duke of Newcastle created this 3,400-acre park (NT), one of the original Dukeries, in the 18th century. It was planted with noble trees, the showpiece of which is the 3-mile avenue of lime trees called the Duke's Drive. Near the ornamental lake stands an elegant 19th-century church in red and white sandstone, built by the 7th Duke as a private chapel. The imposing ducal mansion was, however, demolished in the 1930s when the estate was sold.

Continue past the Normanton Inn and in 1½ miles, at the crossroads, turn right on to the unclassified Thoresby Hall road.

THORESBY HALL, Notts
This gigantic Victorian mansion (OACT), home of the Countess Manvers, is the third stately home to stand on the 12,000-acre Dukeries park. It was designed by Anthony Salvin, who restored Windsor Castle, and is probably the largest Victorian house in England, with 29 main apartments and 78 bedrooms. The interior is lavishly decorated, and there are statues of Robin Hood and Little John in the library, carved by a Mansfield woodcarver. The estate was originally enclosed in the 17th century by the 1st Earl of Kingston. The park was laid out around beautiful ornamental lakes surrounded by avenues of chestnut trees. On the edge of the lake stands a 'model' village, built in 1807, and on the hillside above it is a folly called Budby Castle.

After 2½ miles turn left and join the A616, then in 1½ miles turn right on to the B6034 and continue to Edwinstowe.

EDWINSTOWE, Notts
This substantial colliery village is the biggest of the villages in the Dukeries area. The Birklands plantation, the oldest part of Sherwood Forest, comes right up to the edge of the village. Birklands means birch, and silver birch and oak trees are the main species in the estate. Part of Birklands is now the Sherwood Country Park and here the Major Oak stands. Named after a local historian, Major Rooke, the oak is the oldest tree in the forest, with a girth of 30ft around its hollow trunk. Although damaged by a storm in recent years, its massive branches spread a circumference of 270ft. This is said to have been Robin Hood's hideout for his outlaw band, and there is a local tale that Robin Hood and Maid Marion were married in Edwinstowe Church.

Continue on the B6034, and in 1 mile, at the traffic signals, go forward, then in ½ mile turn right on to the A614 to pass the entrance to Rufford Abbey.

RUFFORD ABBEY, Notts
A Cistercian abbey stood here from medieval times until the Dissolution of monasteries in Henry VIII's reign, when the estate was given to the Earl of Shrewsbury. It later passed into the hands of his daughter-in-law, Bess of Hardwick, who built a great mansion on the site which over the centuries has fallen in ruins. Her descendant, Sir George Savile, planted most of the oak and ash woodlands in the 18th century, and the estate is now a country park (OACT) with a lake and formal gardens.

Continue along the A614 for 1¾ miles, then turn left on to an unclassified road to Eakring.

EAKRING, Notts
Oil was first struck near this surprisingly rural village in 1939, which today stands at the centre of the Nottinghamshire oilfield. The village church contains a brass to the Revd William Mompesson who came here as vicar in 1670 from plague-ridden Eyam in Derbyshire. When he arrived in Eakring, however, his parishioners still feared the plague and at first refused to let him enter the village; a stone cross on the outskirts marks the place where he preached his sermons. Eventually all was well, and he remained in Eakring till his death in 1708.

Leave Eakring on the Kirklington road then ascend. On the descent there are good views before turning left on to the A617 for Kirklington. By the nearside of the village turn right on to the Southwell road. After 2½ miles turn right for Southwell town centre.

SOUTHWELL, Notts
The glory of Southwell is its great minster, a 12th- and 13th-century building with a Romanesque nave and transept. In the octagonal chapter house are exquisite carvings of foliage — oak, hawthorn and vine leaves. Vicar's Court, in the precinct, is a delightful group of 17th-century houses with hipped roofs. King Charles I spent his last night as a free man at the Saracen's Head, an old coaching inn in the town.

Leave Southwell on the A612 Newark road, and continue through Upton to Kelham then cross the Trent and return to Newark.

NORTHAMPTON, Northants
One of the largest market towns in England, Northampton is the administrative centre of its county and is noted for its high number of fine churches. Among the finest is Holy Sepulchre, a rare round church that was founded in 1110 and has been variously adapted through the ages. Inside is a 6ft-tall brass which dates from the 17th century and is one of the largest in England. Other old buildings include 17th-century Haselrigg House, the 16th-century Welsh House. Abington Park has landscaped surroundings, and a 15th- to 18th-century house containing a museum. The Northamptonshire Record office is housed in Delapre Abbey, a 19th-century building on the site of a Cluniac nunnery. The main industry of the town used to be shoe manufacturing whose history is displayed in the Museum of Leathercraft. One of the Eleanor Crosses erected by Edward I, can be seen on the town's southern outskirts.

Leave Northampton on the A4500 'Wellingborough' road and drive to Ecton.

ECTON, Northants
Features of this village include a 13th- and 14th-century church, a gothic-revival hall, and an elegant 17th-century manor house.

From Ecton drive for 1¼ miles and turn right on to the B573. Enter Earls Barton.

EARLS BARTON, Northants
The magnificent Saxon church tower here was built about 1,000 years ago and may once have been incorporated in the defences of a nearby Norman castle.

Continue through Great Doddington and in 1½ miles meet traffic signals. Continue forward to Wellingborough.

WELLINGBOROUGH, Northants
Situated at the junction of the rivers Ise and Nene, this old market centre is now a rapidly developing town serving numerous light industries.

The Welland Valley near Harringworth is dominated by a stupendous railway viaduct.

NORTHAMPTONSHIRE RIVERLANDS

Between the meanderings of the Welland and Nene are forests and farms, water meadows loud with the calls of wildfowl, and villages of stone and thatch clustered round elegant church spires. Much of the countryside was once held by squires, and many of their sturdy farms survive.

Follow SP 'Peterborough' to join the A510, and continue to Finedon.

Fotheringhay's church is an imposing survival of a much larger structure.

FINEDON, Northants
Curiously decorated ironstone houses and cottages gather beneath the graceful 133ft spire of an ironstone church in this large village. The church dates from the 14th century, but most of the houses were built by the village squire in Victorian times.

Proceed for 3¼ miles and turn right on to the A604. In 3¼ miles cross the River Nene into Thrapston.

THRAPSTON, Northants
The device from which the American Stars and Stripes were derived can be seen on a tablet to Sir John Washington in the village church. A nephew of Washington emigrated to America and was the great-grandfather of the first US president.

Return across the River Nene and turn right on to the A6116 to reach Islip.

ISLIP, Northants
Brasses re-created by the Reverend H Macklin, author of a standard book on this type of memorial, can be seen in Islip Church.

Proceed to Lowick.

LOWICK, Northants
Lowick's notable church has a 15th-century tower and 14th-century windows featuring 16 beautiful figures worked in stained glass.

Drive through Sudborough and on approaching Brigstock turn right on to a narrow unclassified road SP 'Lyveden'. Proceed for 2¼ miles; ½ mile to the right of the road is Lyveden New Bield.

LYVEDEN NEW BIELD, Northants
When Sir Thomas Tresham's family became involved in the Gunpowder Plot he had to stop building this ambitious house, which was begun in 1600 and still remains as a shell (NT). Its plan was meant to symbolize the Passion of Christ.

Continue for 2⅓ miles and turn right on to the A427 to enter Oundle.

OUNDLE, Northants
Set in pleasant countryside by the River Nene, this stone-built town is a place of narrow streets and alleys between rows of old houses broken by the occasional tiny cottage or inn. Its well-known public school was founded in the 16th century by William Laxton, a grocer who was born here and eventually became Lord Mayor of London. Latham's Hospital dates from 1611. The Norman and later St Peters' has a magnificent 280-foot spire.

Leave Oundle and follow the 'Peterborough' road for 1¼ miles, then turn left on to an unclassified road SP 'Fotheringhay' and pass Cotterstock village on the left.

COTTERSTOCK, Northants
The poet John Dryden wrote his *Fables* in an attic room of 17th-century Cotterstock Hall while staying with his cousin, who owned it. Beautiful gardens lead from the house to the banks of the River Nene. In the village are a fine church, a 14th-century rectory, and an 18th-century mill with later mill cottages.

Drive through Tansor and continue to Fotheringhay.

FOTHERINGHAY, Northants
A mound here once carried the grim castle in which Mary Queen of Scots was imprisoned before her execution in 1587. Nowadays the mellow old cottages and willow-hung banks of the Nene create a tranquillity in which such macabre associations become difficult to believe. The imposing church was a gift from Edward IV.

Take the 'King's Cliffe' road and pass through Woodnewton to reach Apethorpe.

APETHORPE, Northants
Stone-built Apethorpe boasts a very large Tudor and later hall, and an imposing 13th- and 17th-century village church, now a museum.

Proceed to King's Cliffe.

KING'S CLIFFE, Northants
Features of this beautiful little village include 17th-century almshouses, a church with a Norman tower and 13th-century spire, and lovely surroundings.

Turn right to follow the 'Stamford' road and later turn left on to the A47. In ¾ mile turn right on to an unclassified road and drive to Collyweston.

COLLYWESTON, Northants
Stone roofing slates have been quarried here for many years. The church has a Saxon chancel wall, and a Dovecote dates from the 16th century.

Turn left on to the A43; and at roundabout take 3rd exit then shortly left into Duddington.

DUDDINGTON, Northants
Thatched cottages and a medieval 4-arched bridge across the River Welland help to make this one of the prettiest villages in the area. The picture is completed by a 17th-century watermill and mansion.

Drive through Duddington to rejoin the A43. In ¾ mile turn right on to the unclassified 'Wakerley' and 'Harringworth' road. Drive past extensive ironstone workings to reach Harringworth.

HARRINGWORTH, Northants
A spectacular feature of this village is the 82-arch brick-built railway viaduct that spans the Welland Valley here. This magnificent feat of engineering was built between 1874 and 1879.

Proceed south to Gretton.

GRETTON, Northants
Stocks and a whipping post still stand on the green in this attractive hilltop village, and fine views extend into the Welland Valley. A few 17th-century houses and a church with Norman origins are reminders of its long history.

Drive along the 'Weldon' road for 1½ miles and turn left. In ¾ mile a detour may be made from the main route by turning left; this leads to Kirby Hall in ¾ miles and Deene Park in 2¼ miles.

Duddington's famous watermill was built in 1664

KIRBY HALL, Northants
This magnificent old house (AM) was begun in 1572 and bought by Sir Christopher Hatton, a favourite of Queen Elizabeth I. In the 17th century its appearance was completely changed by the architect Inigo Jones.

DEENE PARK, Northants
A little farther along the detour route from Kirby Hall is the 16th-century mansion of Deene Park (open), which stands in a lake-watered estate known for its rare trees.

Proceed along the main tour route to Weldon.

WELDON, Northants
The fine lantern tower carried by Weldon Church was once an invaluable landmark for travellers in thickly-wooded Rockingham Forest. An old lock-up once used for petty criminals stands on the green.

On entering Weldon turn right into Chapel Road then right at T-junction. At roundabout take 1st exit A43 for Geddington. Meet crossroads and turn left on to an unclassified road to enter the village.

Edward I erected this cross at Geddington in 1290, as a memorial to Queen Eleanor.

GEDDINGTON, Northants
One of the three surviving Eleanor Crosses stands in the main square of this lovely stone and thatch village, a reminder of the grief experienced by Edward I at the loss of his queen some 7 centuries ago. Of later date is the medieval bridge that spans the River Ise here, and ¾ mile south is 15th-century Boughton House (open), a monastery enlarged to its present magnificent proportions in the 16th and 17th centuries. Inside are art collections and sumptuous old furnishings, while all around are beautifully planned and tended gardens.

Return to the crossroads and drive forward on to the unclassified 'Newton' and 'Rushton' road. After Newton turn right then left under a railway. Continue to Rushton.

RUSHTON, Northants
Triangular Lodge (AM), a famous curiosity in the grounds of 15th-century Rushton Hall, is far more than a mere folly. Its peculiar design, in which the number three is depicted time and again, is a devout symbolization of the Trinity, disguised to fool religious persecutors during a time of repression. The village is a cluster of golden ironstone houses on the banks of the River Ise.

In Rushton turn right SP 'Desborough'; at Desborough turn left on to the A6 to reach Rothwell.

It is thought that Inigo Jones may have been responsible for the ornamental garden gateway of Kirby Hall.

ROTHWELL, Northants
Inside the mainly 13th-century church of this old industrial town is a charnel containing thousands of bones. The centre of Rothwell is graced by the elegant 16th-century Market House (AM).

Turn right on to the B576 and proceed to Lamport.

LAMPORT, Northants
Mainly 17th- and 18th-century Lamport Hall (open) is set in an attractive park featuring an early alpine rock garden. Inside the house are paintings by Van Dyck and other artists, and an excellent collection of china and furniture.

In Lamport turn left on to the A508 and drive to Brixworth.

BRIXWORTH, Northants
Local Roman buildings were cannibalized to provide materials for a fine church raised here in the 7th century. The skill of the Saxon builders has been well proved, because today the church survives as one of the finest of its type.

Pass the Red Lion (PH) and turn left on to the unclassified 'Sywell' road. Later cross the Pitsford Reservoir into Holcot, meet crossroads and turn right SP 'Northampton' to reach Moulton. In Moulton turn left and shortly right onto the A43 to return to Northampton.

NORWICH, Norfolk

Once an important centre of the worsted trade, this county town stands on the River Wensum and boasts a cathedral with one of the finest interiors in the country. It dates from Norman times and contains the oldest bishop's throne still used in England. Other major features include a fine presbytery, a beautiful cloister, and a magnificent nave roof featuring many of the 800 roof bosses to be found in the cathedral. Access to the building is by two fine gates, the Erpingham of 1420 and St Ethelbert's of 1272 (both AM). Close to a former water gate on the river are Pull's Ferry and the Barge Inn, two reminders of the city's antiquity, and amongst the many other fine old buildings are no less than 30 parish churches. The largest and finest of these is St Peter Mancroft, which carries a notable tower, but all the others have particular details that make them worth a visit. St Andrew's dates from the 15th century and displays a remarkable series of carved shields, and St Michael-at-Coslany has fine flintwork in the Thorpe Chapel. Norwich Castle (open) was started c1130, but its Norman origins have been heavily disguised by 19th-century refacing. Survivals from the medieval city and later are many. Flint-faced Bridewell is a 14th-century merchant's house that now contains a museum; the Cow Tower (AM) dates from the same period and formed part of a defensive system along the river bank. Slightly later is the St Peter Hungate Church, a 15th-century building which carries a fine hammerbeam roof and now houses a museum. In the 1920s a chapel was converted to house the well-known Maddermarket Theatre. The most famous of the city's many picturesque streets is Elm Hill, a cobbled road lined with old colour-washed shops and houses, while the most outstanding of its lay buildings are the 15th-century Suckling House and chequered-flint Guildhall. In 1978 the supermarket magnet Sir Robert Sainsbury presented the University the Sainsbury Centre for Visual Arts, which is housed in an outstanding modern building. The colourful open-air market has been a weekday occurrence since Norman times.
Leave Norwich on the A47 'Yarmouth' road and pass through Thorpe St Andrew to Blofield.

BLOFIELD, Norfolk

Blofield Church, an impressive building that forms a landmark visible for miles round the village, is noted for its tall west tower. Inside is an 8-sided font ornamented with various scenes in relief.
Continue to Acle.

ACLE, Norfolk

This well-known touring centre is within easy reach of the lovely Norfolk Broads and is a good base from which to explore the area. Its unusual church has a picturesque thatched roof and a round tower

AMONG THE NORFOLK BROADS

Close to the great cathedral city of Norwich are marshlands, meres, and lakes in a landscape dotted with the stark shapes of old wind pumps. Hidden canals link vast acreages of water drained from the local countryside, offering ideal highways by which to explore the broadlands.

Norwich Castle rises high above the city from a landscaped hilltop.

that dates from the 12th century. East of the village, on the tour route, are several windpumps that have survived from the days when many such machines were built to pump excess water from the reclaimed marshlands.
Continue along the A47 to Great Yarmouth.

GREAT YARMOUTH, Norfolk

Holiday amenities in this important oil and fishing port include 5 miles of seafront fringed by excellent sands and backed by colourful gardens. Its situation on Breydon Water, the combined estuaries of the Bure, Waveney and Yare, gives it an aspect that suits both the holidaymakers and the busy maritime traffic that uses its harbour. The town is very old and has managed to retain many historic features. Most of these can be seen in the South Quay area, where there are remains of the town walls and the notable Custom House. Leading from the town wall to the quay are the Rows, a number of narrow lanes where the 300-year-old Merchant's House (AM) can be seen. Close by is the 14th-century Greyfriar's Cloister (AM). The Elizabethan House Museum has a largely 16th-century interior disguised by a Georgian façade. Exhibits include furniture from that and later periods, and a fascinating collection of Victorian toys. The 13th-century building that houses the Tollhouse Museum is one of the oldest in Great Yarmouth and incorporates ancient dungeons. Close to England's largest parish church is Anna Sewell House, a 17th-century building that was the birthplace of the authoress of *Black Beauty*. The House of Wax museum features various historical figures and scenes , and the Maritime Museum of East Anglia illustrates life saving and marine oil exploration. Near Wellington Pier in an acre of landscaped garden is the quaint Merrivale Model Village.
Leave Great Yarmouth on the A149 SP 'Caister'. In 2 miles meet a roundabout and drive forward to enter Caister.

CAISTER-ON-SEA, Norfolk

Remains of town walls and a gateway (AM) survive from the time when this popular little resort was a Roman settlement. Much more recent is the 15th-century castle (open), whose remains now house a museum of veteran and vintage cars.
From the town centre turn left on to the A1064 'Acle' road and pass the remains of Caister Roman Town on the right. Meet a roundabout and take the 2nd exit. In ¾ mile turn right on to an unclassified road SP 'Great Ormesby', and in 1 mile turn left on to the A149 to enter Ormesby St Margaret – at the edge of the Broads country.

THE BROADS, Norfolk

More than 30 large and very beautiful sheets of water, often linked by navigable channels, are contained in a triangular area between Norwich, Lowestoft, and Sea Palling. These, together with many rivers, lakes, and canals, provide some 200 miles of water for cruising and sailing. The essential character of the Broads can only be properly appreciated from a boat, and there are hire firms and tour operators in such centres as Wroxham, Horning and Potter Heigham. Angling permits are available from tackle shops in these and other towns.
A short and very pleasant detour from the main route can be made by staying on the A149 and continuing to Ormesby Broad.

ORMESBY BROAD, Norfolk

The main road between Ormesby St Margaret and Rollesby crosses this vast expanse of water and offers some of the best broadland views available to the motorist.
On the main route, drive to the war memorial in Ormesby St Margaret and turn right on to an unclassified road alongside the green, SP 'Scratby'. Meet a T-junction and turn right SP 'Hemsby'. At Hemsby, drive to the end of the village and turn left on to the B1159 SP 'Mundesley'. Continue along a winding road to Winterton.

Ormesby, one of Broadland's loveliest stretches of water.

WINTERTON-ON-SEA, Norfolk
Much of the countryside round this little fishing village is included in a 260-acre nature reserve.

Continue to West Somerton.

WEST SOMERTON, Norfolk
Situated at the weedy eastern end of Martham Broad, this quiet village is an excellent angling base and a good place to see how the marshes were drained. A maze of streams and man-made ditches still carries excess water into the main broads, and two windpumps that were used to pump from one level to another can be seen near by.

Continue with SP 'Cromer' to Horsey Mere.

Horsey Church is noted for its thatched roof and unusual stained-glass windows.

HORSEY MERE, Norfolk
Access to this important breeding ground for marshland plants and animals is restricted to naturalists and permit holders. The mere's drainage windmill (NT) was built in 1912 and has been well restored.
Continue to Horsey.

HORSEY, Norfolk
Despite frequent incursions of the sea since it was built, the thatched village church has retained its Norman round tower.
Continue to Sea Palling, then in 1¾ miles turn left B1151 to Stalham.

STALHAM, Norfolk
Two miles south east of Stalham is the Sutton windmill, the tallest windmill in the country built in 1789 it has nine floors plus a cap floor, and a museum.
Return to B1159 turn left and continue to Lessingham, then Happisburgh.

HAPPISBURGH, Norfolk
Offshore shipping is warned away from the treacherous Haisboro' Sands by a lighthouse, but the same drifts provide sun and sea bathers with a superb dune-backed beach. The name of this pretty little fishing village is pronounced Hazeborough.
In 1¼ miles meet crossroads and turn right for Walcott. Continue to Bacton.

BACTON, Norfolk
Easy access to the broad local beach of shingly sand and pebbles is via a high sea wall. The village itself is an attractive little place that grew up alongside Broomholm Priory, a 12th-century foundation that claimed to possess a piece of the True Cross and became a great centre of pilgrimage. Remains of the priory, which was mentioned by Chaucer, include the gatehouse, north transept, chapter house, and refectory.

Drive past a windmill to Mundesley.

West Somerton was the haunt of smuggling gangs in the 18th century.

The best way to appreciate the Norfolk Broads is by boat.

The best way to appreciate the Norfolk Broads is by boat.

MUNDESLEY, Norfolk
This quiet resort has a gently shelving sand beach backed by cliffs. It is associated with the poet William Cowper.

Continue to Trimingham.

TRIMINGHAM, Norfolk
Some of the highest cliffs in Norfolk overlook a good bathing beach here. A painted screen can be seen in the local church.

Continue to Overstrand.

OVERSTRAND, Norfolk
Pleasant cliff walks lead from here to the nearby resort of Cromer, and safe bathing can be enjoyed from the local sands. The 14th-century Church of St Martin was built after the old parish church fell into the sea.

Continue to Cromer.

CROMER, Norfolk
Although a bustling resort mainly occupied with the needs of holidaymakers, Cromer still has a small fishing fleet and has the reputation for supplying the best crabs in England. Its sandy beach is backed by lofty cliffs, and its many amenities include a zoo and boating pool. The 15th-century parish church carries one of the tallest towers in Norfolk. Close to Cromer is Felbrigg Hall (NT), a fine house that dates from the 17th century.

Leave Cromer on the A149 'Norwich' road and in 2¼ miles bear left SP 'North Walsham'. Continue to Thorpe Market and North Walsham.

NORTH WALSHAM, Norfolk
Homely buildings and winding little lanes make this beautiful market town well worth a pause in any journey. Its fine church is given an air of gothic mystery by a ruined tower that fell in 1724. Inside are a painted screen, a tall 15th-century font cover, and various monuments. The local grammar school was founded in the early 17th century.

Follow SP 'Norwich' on the B1150. Pass Westwick Park and drive beneath an arched gateway which spans the road; continue to Coltishall.

COLTISHALL, Norfolk
This shooting and angling centre is situated on the River Bure and enjoys a genteelly relaxed atmosphere imparted by many 18th-century buildings.

Cross the River Bure to Horstead.

HORSTEAD, Norfolk
Horstead Church carries a slender west tower that dates from the 13th century. The delightful village mill stands opposite the miller's house.

Drive through wooded countryside and return to Norwich.

NORWICH AND THE WAVENEY VALLEY

South of the fine old cathedral city of Norwich lies an area of lovely wooded countryside that stretches down to the Suffolk border, where the River Waveney meanders through a tranquil valley of great beauty.

NORWICH, Norfolk
East Anglia's capital city is full of curious old streets and alleys, antique and curio shops, with interesting buildings at almost every turn. Elm Hill, a narrow cobbled lane, pretty, and crowded with ancient shops and courtyards, is the best known of all the old streets, but there are many more around the market place. Every day, except Sunday, there is a large bustling market beside the old Guildhall, built in the 15th century of local knapped flints. Not far away on St Andrew's Street, Strangers' Hall museum is a fascinatingly-preserved medieval merchant's house, its rooms furnished in the style of different periods. Nearby, in a little alley off Bedford Street stands the Bridewell Museum of local crafts, and near to it is a Dickensian-looking mustard shop and small museum run by Colmans, who still manufacture mustard in Norwich. The castle, a square Norman keep raised high on a mound overlooking the centre, is now the city museum and art gallery, with a fine collection of pictures by John Crome and John Sell Cotman, leaders of the Norwich School of painters who flourished in the last century. Undoubtedly the finest sight in Norwich, however, is the beautiful Norman cathedral, whose slender spire rises above the water meadows of the River Wensum. Work on the cathedral began in 1069 and continued for over 50 years. There are 2 medieval gates to the precincts, the Ethelbert and the Erpingham; just inside the latter stands Norwich School, founded in 1316, at which Horatio Nelson was a pupil for a short time. The lovely walled cathedral Close, bordered by elegant 18th-century houses, stretches down to the river where a charming 16th-century house known as Pull's Ferry (not open) is portrayed in many local paintings and postcards. Apart from the great Norman cathedral, Norwich has a Roman Catholic cathedral and 32 medieval churches; once there were even more and it was said that the city had a church for every week of the year, but a pub for every day.

Leave Norwich on the A11, SP 'Thetford'. In 9 miles turn right, SP 'Town Centre', into Wymondham.

WYMONDHAM, Norfolk
This small country town, pronounced Windham, is a delightful jumble of old cottages, traditional shops, timbered inns and 18th-century houses. At the centre of the old streets is an ornate half-timbered Butter Cross, raised on wooden pillars. The spectacular abbey church, with 2 great towers at each end, was once shared by the monks of the priory (now ruined) and the townspeople. As a result of a quarrel with the town, the monks built a wall to isolate their part of the church and so the townsfolk built the great square west tower for themselves. The monks' part of the church was later destroyed, leaving only the tower.

Leave Wymondham on the B1135, and continue to Kimberley, then turn left on to the B1108 for Hingham.

HINGHAM, Norfolk
The large number of elegant redbrick Georgian houses in this attractive village show that it was once a thriving market town. Hingham was the birthplace of one Samuel Lincoln, who emigrated to America in 1637 and there raised a family whose most famous descendant, 2 centuries later, was Abraham Lincoln, who became president of the United States. The bust of Lincoln in the imposing village church was presented by the people of Hingham, Massachusetts, the New World town in which Samuel Lincoln had settled.

Continue on the B1108 and later pass Scoulton Mere (right) before reaching Scoulton. 1½ miles beyond the village turn left on to the B1077, SP 'Attleborough'. In 2 miles, at the T-junction, turn left. The B1077 leads through Great Ellingham to Attleborough.

ATTLEBOROUGH, Norfolk
Although not a particularly attractive town, there is a fine church with a famous and beautiful 15th-century rood screen. The countryside round here is celebrated for the rearing of fine turkeys and ducks and until recently there was a vast annual turkey fair at Attleborough.

Leave Attleborough on the B1077 Diss road and continue to Old Buckenham.

OLD BUCKENHAM, Norfolk
The village green is so enormous that the groups of cottages round the edges have remained as separate little hamlets, each with its own delightful name — Hog's Snout, Puddledock and Loss Wroo are just a few examples.

1½ miles beyond the village turn left on to the B1113 to visit New Buckenham.

NEW BUCKENHAM, Norfolk
'New' is a relative term, for this charming village is at least 8 centuries old and preserves a street plan laid out in medieval times. Its pretty cottages lead up to a village green, near which stands a 17th-century market house supported on wooden posts. The one at the centre served in bygone days as a whipping post. A little way outside the village is the castle mound with the ruins of the castle built in 1145.

Return along the B1113 and follow the Stowmarket road to Banham.

BANHAM, Norfolk
The village of Banham is exceptionally pretty with elm trees round its green. Nearby, Banham Zoo and Monkey Sanctuary is famous for its colony of woolly monkeys, one of only 6 in the whole of Europe. Woolly monkeys came originally from the rain forests of the Amazon Basin in South America, and are a delicate breed, difficult to rear in our climate. Many other species of monkeys from Africa and Asia can be seen here too, as well as other types of animals and birds of prey. Also within the zoo grounds is Lord Cranworth's motor museum. Racing cars, motorcycles and children's pedal cars dating from the 1920s to the 1960s are all displayed in an imaginative setting.

Continue on the B1113 to Kenninghall, and at the end of the village turn left for North Lopham. In 1 mile, at South Lopham, turn left on to the A1066. Later (right) are Bressingham Gardens.

Colman's Mustard Shop in Bridewell Alley, Norwich, has a small museum

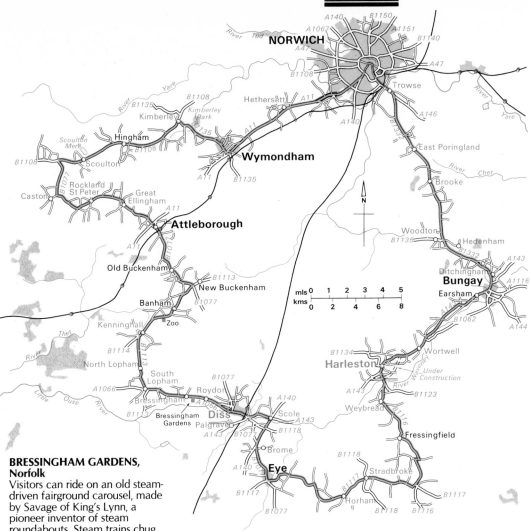

EARSHAM, Norfolk

In 1965 naturalist Philip Wayre set up an Otter Trust (OACT) on the banks of the Waveney at Earsham, and now it has the largest collection of otters in the world. As well as British otters, European, North American and Asian otters are bred here in semi-natural conditions. There are also large lakes with a variety of waterfowl and a pleasant walk can be taken alongside the river.

Continue on the A143 to Bungay.

BUNGAY, Suffolk

Bungay is a fascinating place, with a history that goes back long before the Norman Conquest. There was a massive castle here in Norman times, and in a part of the ruins, traces of an old mining gallery can be seen. This is thought to date from the days of Henry II, when the lord of the castle, Hugh Bigod, defied the king, and an attempt was made to undermine the castle walls by tunnelling. The castle in fact survived many years after this, only to be demolished by local entrepreneurs looking for good building stone. Bungay has many fine buildings, including an outstanding 17th-century Butter Cross, built to keep the butter cool on market days, surmounted by the figure of Justice. Printing and leather-working have been the town's major industries since the 18th century.

Follow SP 'Norwich' to join the B1332. Continue through Brooke and Poringland and in 3 miles, at the traffic signals, turn left on to the A146 for the return to Norwich.

BRESSINGHAM GARDENS, Norfolk

Visitors can ride on an old steam-driven fairground carousel, made by Savage of King's Lynn, a pioneer inventor of steam roundabouts. Steam trains chug along 2 miles of track through the beautiful countryside of the Waveney valley, and the 6 acres of gardens specialising in alpine plants and hardy perennials, are a delightful spectacle at all seasons of the year.

Remain on the A1066 and beyond Roydon bear right to reach Diss. Leave on the A1066 and at the end of the town join the A143 for Scole. Here, turn right on to the A140, SP 'Ipswich'. Cross the River Waveney into Suffolk then in 1½ miles turn left on to the B1077 for Eye.

EYE, Suffolk

The church at Eye, with its wonderful tower of superb Suffolk flushwork, rising over 100ft, is the pride of this enchanting little place, but its appealing streets are packed with interesting old buildings of all periods. The timber-framed Guildhall dates from the 16th century and there are a number of fine houses in the streets leading up to the ruins of the Norman castle.

At Eye branch left, then left again on to the B1117. Follow a winding road to Horham, where the road bears left and continues to Stradbrooke. In 2¾ miles turn left on to the B1116, SP 'Harleston', and later pass through Fressingfield.

FRESSINGFIELD, Suffolk

This attractive village, deep in the Suffolk countryside, is a mecca for gourmets who come from all over the country to dine at the Fox and Goose Inn, a charming timber-framed building, once the Guildhall of the village.

Remain on the B1116 to Weybread and later cross the River Waveney back into Norfolk. On reaching the main road turn right and enter Harleston. Continue on the A143 Yarmouth road, which follows the Waveney valley through Wortwell to Earsham.

The delightful village green at Banham, overlooked by church and Guildhall

GREAT HOUSES OF NORFOLK

From Norwich, the beating heart of Norfolk, the tour
meanders to the peaceful seaside resorts of Cromer and
Sheringham, through a landscape of broad fields and
slumbering villages overlorded by churches of medieval
splendour and great manor houses.

NORWICH, Norfolk
Onetime centre of the worsted
trade, Norwich is now a county
borough, port, industrial centre
and cathedral city. The charm of
Norwich lies in its combination of
antiquity and modernity and the
history that has made it one of
Britain's most flourishing cities.
See page 366 or 368.

*Leave Norwich on the A140, SP
'Cromer', and beyond the Airport
continue to the edge of Marsham.
In 1 mile, at the roundabout, go
forward on to the B1145 into
Aylsham.*

AYLSHAM, Norfolk
This is a charming little market
town with many old buildings,
brick-built and Dutch-gabled.
Wherries — light flat-bottomed
rowing boats — sailing up the
Bure, now no longer so navigable,
brought wealth in the Middle Ages
to this town noted for its worsted
cloth and linen. John of Gaunt is
said to have held the manor at
Blickling, and to have founded the
church in 1380. The church has
altered little since his day, and
contains a fine font and, of
particular interest, a copy of the
Breeches Bible of 1611; so called
for the passage in Genesis which
reads 'they sewed fig leaves
together and made themselves
breeches'. The famous landscape
gardener Humphry Repton
(1752-1818) is buried in the
churchyard.

*In Aylsham turn left, SP
'Saxthorpe', on to the B1354. In
1½ miles (right) is Blickling Hall.*

BLICKLING HALL, Norfolk
Yew hedges (15ft across) planted
in the late 17th century line velvet
lawns either side of the driveway
which sweeps up to the pleasingly
symmetrical Jacobean front of
Blickling Hall (NT). Between 2 tall
turrets a Dutch-gabled roofline
culminates in a central domed
turret, beneath which mullioned
windows complete the picture of a
perfect English country house. The
house was begun in 1616 within a
dry moat on the side of an old hall
in which Anne Boleyn was born.
The Jacobean exterior hides a
Georgian interior; much was
remodelled by the 2nd Earl of
Buckinghamshire during the 18th
century, although the long gallery
still keeps its splendid plaster
moulded ceiling of the 1620s.

*Return along the B1354 for ½
miles then turn left, SP 'Cromer'. In
1 mile turn left and cross the River
Bure into Ingworth and in 1½
miles turn left on to the A140.
At Roughton turn left on to the
B1436 which leads to Felbrigg.*

FELBRIGG, Norfolk
The Felbrigg estate lies on top of a
ridge, now divorced from the
village of Felbrigg which may have
been moved as a result of the
plague and re-established in its
present position to avoid further

infection. The Jacobean entrance
front of Felbrigg Hall (NT) was
built in the 1620s, and in 1665 a
new brick wing was added to the
south. Then in the 18th century
William Windham II had the
house refurbished in
contemporary style, after the
completion of his Grand Tour of
Europe, creating a new dining
room, staircase and a Gothic
library. The glorious plaster ceiling
in the dining room was left
untouched and dates from 1687.

*½ mile beyond the entrance to
Felbrigg Hall turn right on to the
A148 for Cromer.*

The garden at Blickling Hall has a long
history, but the main flower beds and
lawns seen here date from the 1930s

CROMER, Norfolk

The splendid Perpendicular church tower, 160ft high, of this ancient fishing village served as a lighthouse before the construction of a purpose-built one. The old village survives in the midst of a Victorian seaside resort born of the railway age. The impressive seafront is backed by high cliffs topped by hotels which are reached by steep stone steps. The crabs along this coast are the best in England and Cromer crab is renowned. It is the chief catch here, and the boats used are a special small double-ended broad-beamed variety — a version of the Shetland boats which came down this coast after herring. There is no harbour here, and the boats are launched and landed from the beach.

Traditional gardens in Heydon

Leave on the A149, SP 'Sheringham', and pass through East and West Runton to Sheringham.

SHERINGHAM, Norfolk

Sheringham, like Cromer, was also established as a resort during the railway age, and the old flint village is still discernible within the Victorian brick town. Crab is also the main catch here, but when the weather is bad the fishermen collect the pebbles from the beach which are then ground down to make glazes for the local pottery. Sheringham Hall (open by appointment) is a Regency building in a beautiful park (OACT), both the work of Humphry Repton. The highlight of the estate is perhaps the mile-long rhododendron drive which was planted in the 19th century. Sheringham Station is the headquarters of the North Norfolk Railway and steam-hauled trains operate. There is also rolling stock and a museum.

Leave on the A1082, SP 'Holt'. Climb through wooded country then turn right on to the A148, SP 'King's Lynn', and continue to Holt.

HOLT, Norfolk

The town of Holt has a well-kept appearance and there is nothing to offend the eye. Here and there among the smartly painted walls the flintwork shows itself to advantage, indicating that this stone is the main building material of the area. Most famous of its buildings is Gresham's School, founded by Sir John Gresham who was born here in 1519. Gresham became Lord Mayor of London and also founded the Royal Exchange there.

From the town centre follow the unclassified Baconsthorpe road and continue to Baconsthorpe.

BACONSTHORPE, Norfolk

Baconsthorpe Castle (AM) stands sadly forgotten among muddy Norfolk farmland which now has greater importance than the castle itself. It was a fortified manor house built by Sir Henry Heydon in 1486. The gatehouse stands well preserved, as do the curtain walls, the remains of a 17th-century dwelling hall and an 18th-century Gothic mansion, built in front of the castle largely from stone taken from the original building.

Follow SP 'North Walsham' to Plumstead. ½ mile beyond the village, at the crossroads, turn right on to the Saxthorpe road. In 3¼ miles keep forward on to the B1149 into Saxthorpe. Cross the River Bure and turn right, SP 'Heydon', then immediately turn left at the Dukes Head Inn. In 2 miles, at the T-junction, turn left. In ½ mile, at the crossroads, turn left again into Heydon.

HEYDON, Norfolk

This is an extremely pretty village of pleasant houses centred around a charming village green. Heydon Hall (open by appointment) begun in 1581 but much enlarged since, is the home of the Bulwer family, of whom Lord Lytton, author of *The Last Days of Pompeii* was a member. The house has an E-shaped 3-storey front and the grounds include an ice-house and a lookout tower.

Return to the crossroads and turn left, SP 'Cawston'. In 1 mile turn right and continue to the edge of Cawston. Turn right on to the B1145 Bawdeswell road, and in 1½ miles pass the turning on the right leading to Salle.

SALLE, Norfolk

The tiny village of Salle is the unlikely site of a cathedral-like church full of rich treasures, totally out of proportion to the almost non-existent parish which it serves. It was built by 3 immensely wealthy local families; the Briggs, the Fountaynes, and the Boleyns. Anne Boleyn (wife of Henry VIII) is said to be buried here, but it is more likely her remains lie in the Tower of London where she was beheaded. Over the west door are 2 lovely feathered angels carrying censers. Within is an unusual font on which the symbols of the 7 sacraments are carved.

Continue along the B1145 into Reepham.

REEPHAM, Norfolk

This little 18th-century town has outdone other similar East Anglia towns with 2 parish churches sharing the same churchyard, because Reepham has 3. Hackford parish church burnt down in 1543, and only a ruined wall remains, but the other 2 are still standing. St Mary's is the parish church of Reepham and contains an especially delicate altar-tomb to Sir Roger de Kerdiston, who died in 1337. Nearby St Michael's has an excellent Jacobean pulpit.

Cromer's Victorian seafront. The tower of the old village church soaring above the 19th-century town was used as a lighthouse in days gone by

At the crossroads turn right with the B1145 for Bawdeswell.

BAWDESWELL, Norfolk

This village lies on an ancient route once used by pilgrims on their way from Norwich to the shrine of Our Lady of Walsingham. A timber-framed house in the village street, called Chaucer House, recalls that the reeve in Chaucer's *Canterbury Tales* came 'from Norfolk, near a place called Bawdeswell.'

At the end of the village turn left on to the A1067, SP 'Norwich'. In 2¼ miles pass, (left), the Norfolk Wildlife Park.

NORFOLK WILDLIFE PARK, Norfolk

The well-known naturalist Philip Wayre opened the Norfolk Wildlife Park and Pheasant Trust in 1961, which was originally his private collection. It boasts the largest collection of European animals in the world, but the zoo breeds more animals than it takes from the wild, and where possible returns animals bred in captivity to their natural habitat to boost the native population. The zoo has a remarkable breeding record, and is dedicated to the conservation of endangered species. Animals which are kept here range from the European beaver to the European bison, stone curlews to European eagle owls. This 50-acre site is also the home of the Pheasant Trust. This was started in 1959 to begin the captive breeding of endangered species of wild pheasants in order that natural populations could be restocked, a policy carried out with outstanding success.

Follow the A1067 through the Wensum valley and pass through Great Witchingham (Lenwade) before the return to Norwich.

NOTTINGHAM, Notts

The growth of this ancient city was influenced by the Saxons, Danes, and Normans, but it was the industrial revolution that made it a thriving commercial centre famous for fine lace. Early prosperity was aided by the natural highway provided by the River Trent, a strategic advantage that may have prompted William the Conqueror to build a strong castle here soon after his invasion of Britain. It was destroyed in the reign of Stephen, rebuilt by Henry II, and throughout the turmoil of the Wars of the Roses remained loyal to the cause of the Yorkists. When the Tudors came to the throne it fell into a slow decline and was reduced to ruins by the time it was bought by the Duke of Newcastle in 1651. The duke converted the soundest parts of the building into a house, but this was gutted by Reform Bill rioters in 1831. Nowadays the castle is the property of the Corporation and houses a museum and art gallery. Among several good churches in Nottingham is St Mary's, a splendid example of 15th-century architecture with excellent windows and a glorious Madonna and Child painted by Bartolommeo. Other notable buildings include the 18th-century Shire Hall, the partly-medieval Trip to Jerusalem Inn, and a wealth of Georgian domestic architecture. The city's natural history museum is in Wollaton Hall, a 16th-century building that stands close to the university campus.

Leave the city with SP 'Loughborough A60' and cross the River Trent. A pleasant detour from the main route to Holme Pierrepont can be made by turning left on to the A6011.

HOLME PIERREPONT, Notts

This early Tudor hall (open) was built to a medieval design c1500 and contains a fine collection of 17th-century English oak furniture. Its grounds include a formal courtyard garden of Victorian date, a country park, and a national and international competition and training centre for water sports.

On the main route, continue along the A60 and pass Ruddington and Bradmore to reach Bunny.

Victorian Belvoir Castle dominates the surrounding landscape.

THE FORESTS OF SHERWOOD

Away from the industry of the coalfields is a picturesque countryside of forests, farms, and villages thick with legends of Robin Hood and his outlaw band. Great oaks grow in Sherwood, and fertile countryside follows the meandering course of the River Trent.

BUNNY, Notts

A great deal of this village was designed in the 17th century by Thomas Parkyns, who did as much as he could to improve the living conditions of his tenants by rebuilding farms and providing four charming almshouses. He lived at Bunny Hall, and his great love for sporting combat earned him the title The Wrestling Baron. This passionate interest is evident in his book *The Cornish Hugg*, and his self-designed graveyard monument shows him in an aggressive stance at the start of a bout. The local church dates from the 14th century and contains several good monuments.

Beyond Bunny turn right on to an unclassified road SP 'Gotham, East Leake' and skirt wooded Bunny Hill. Reach a railway bridge and after another ¼ mile turn left. Continue to East Leake, meet a T-junction, and turn right for East Leake Church.

EAST LEAKE, Notts

Inside the partly Norman church at East Leake is an unusual vamping horn, a type of trumpet that was once used during choir services to 'vamp up' or encourage the singers.

Return to the centre of East Leake and keep straight on to Costock. Cross a main road, continue through Wysall to Keyworth, then turn right and drive to Widmerpool.

WIDMERPOOL, Notts

Some of the county's loveliest woodland scenery makes a perfect setting for this charming little village. The picturesquely ruined church has a 19th-century body with a 14th-century tower and contains an exquisite marble sculpture.

On the nearside of Widmerpool turn left SP 'Kinoulton', and in 1½ miles cross two main roads. The 2nd of these follows the old Fosse Way.

FOSSE WAY

Much of this ancient Romanized track is followed by modern main roads, though parts are still foot and bridle paths.

In a short distance descend and keep forward into Kinoulton.

KINOULTON, Notts

Glorious views over the rich Vale of Belvoir and mature woodlands known as the Borders can be enjoyed from this high village, which claims to have one of the best cricket grounds in the county. The local church, built in brick by the Earl of Gainsborough c1793, stands opposite a forge.

Meet a T-junction and turn right to Hickling, then drive forward along a winding road for Nether Broughton. Continue with SP 'Melton' to turn left on to the A606, and in 1¼ miles climb Broughton Hill at the northern end of the Leicestershire Wolds. Meet crossroads, turn left on to the unclassified 'Eastwell' road, then in ½ mile keep forward and meet a T-junction. Turn left SP 'Eastwell', and after 4 miles meet crossroads and turn left again, SP 'Harby'. After a short distance descend 524ft Harby Hill, and continue to Harby. Turn right SP 'Bottesford', and in 4 miles pass a right turn leading to Belvoir Castle. A worthwhile detour can be made from the main route to this historic building.

BELVOIR CASTLE, Leics

Nowadays the superb site overlooking the Vale of Belvoir is occupied by a 19th-century 'castle' by architect James Wyatt, but originally this windy ridge was guarded by a strong medieval fortress that was occupied by the Manners family in the 16th century. This original castle was built in the late 11th century by Robert de Todeni. His coffin is on display in the present castle. The old castle was twice remodelled and finally much of it was destroyed by fire in the 19th century. Its rebuilding and refurbishment were supervised by Sir John Thoroton, friend and chaplain to the Manners family. The present structure (open) is renowned for its pictures, superb Gobelin Tapestries, and a regimental museum of the 17th/21st Lancers. The attractive grounds of the castle contain a number of interesting features including several statues, a mausoleum and a temple.

Continue to Bottesford.

BOTTESFORD, Leics

The church in this village is one of the best in the county and contains an outstanding collection of monuments. Old stocks and a whipping post are preserved near the remains of an old cross, and attractive Fleming's Bridge dates from the 17th century.

In Bottesford turn left on to the A52 and continue to Bingham.

Bottesford still retains its old stocks and whipping post.

BINGHAM, Notts

The most notable building in this village is the church, which boasts a fine tower capped by a spire. Some of its windows date from the 14th and 15th centuries.

Meet traffic signals and turn right on to the B687 SP 'Newark'. In 1 mile meet a roundabout and take the 2nd exit on to the A6097, then after a further 1 mile pass East Bridgford on the right.

EAST BRIDGFORD, Notts

Several good Georgian cottages and houses can be seen in this village, which occupies an attractively wooded site above the River Trent.

Descend and cross the River Trent, then meet a roundabout and take the 2nd exit to skirt Lowdham. In 1¼ miles turn left on to the unclassified 'Woodborough' road. Continue to Woodborough.

WOODBOROUGH, Notts

The broad upper windows in the terraced cottages of this village were once filled by the frames of stocking knitters, for whom the terraces were originally built. Inside the attractive 14th-century church is later monumental sculpture and carving.

Drive to the end of Woodborough, turn left to reach high ground, and in 1½ miles turn right on to the B684. After another 1½ miles turn right on to the A614, then in 3½ miles turn left on to the unclassified 'Kirkby-in-Ashfield' road to enter Sherwood Forest.

SHERWOOD FOREST, Notts

All that remains of the 100,000-acre wood and pasture land that surrounded Nottingham in the 13th century are a few tracts between that city and the Dukeries District. The area is inextricably meshed with the legend of Robin Hood, the philanthropic outlaw who is popularly thought to have been born in Locksley c1160. Tradition has it that Robin of Locksley was the true Earl of Huntingdon, and the legend is perpetuated by many local

Magnificent old oak trees still survive in Sherwood Forest, part of which is now a country park.

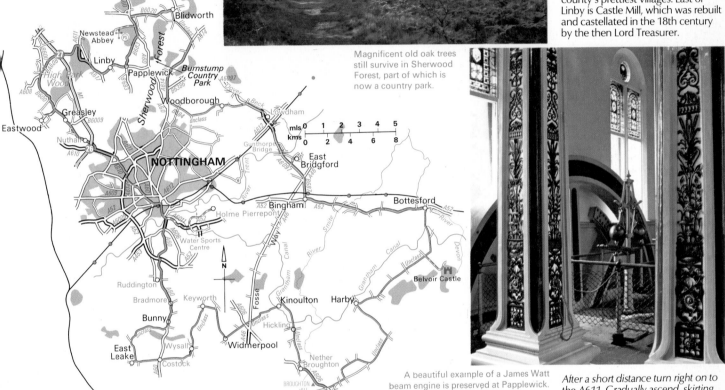

A beautiful example of a James Watt beam engine is preserved at Papplewick.

PAPPLEWICK, Notts

Papplewick Pumping Station is a fine Victorian building situated in a landscaped park. It contains two Boulton and Watt beam engines and is open most Sundays. On seven weekdays during the year, the boilers are steamed with engines working.

Turn right on to the B6011 SP 'Linby'; continue to Linby.

LINBY, Notts

The combination of red-roofed stone cottages with two crosses and a small stream flowing on each side of the main street makes this one of the county's prettiest villages. East of Linby is Castle Mill, which was rebuilt and castellated in the 18th century by the then Lord Treasurer.

After a short distance turn right on to the A611. Gradually ascend, skirting the southern part of Sherwood Forest, and after 1¼ miles turn left on to the A608. Ascend, cross the M1 motorway, then after another 1½ miles join the B600 SP 'Nottingham' and continue through wooded country. In 2¼ miles pass an unclassified right turn offering a detour to Eastwood.

EASTWOOD, Notts

The house in which D H Lawrence was born in 1885 in this old mining town, has been restored and furnished to depict working class life in Victorian times (open). The sharp contrast between pithead and countryside are reflected in many of his novels.

On the main route, continue along the B600 to Greasley.

GREASLEY, Notts

Handsome Greasley Church has a tall 15th-century tower that serves as a landmark for many miles around.

Drive into a built-up area, then meet a T-junction in Nuthall and turn left. After a short distance meet a roundabout and go forward on to the A610 for the return to Nottingham.

references. An old oak known as Robin Hood's Larder stands within the boundaries of Sherwood, but the oldest tree in the forest is claimed to be Green Dale Oak, which stands south of Welbeck Abbey and is also said to be the largest in the district. Part of the area has been preserved as the Burntstump Country Park.

In 1½ miles turn right SP 'Blidworth', and after a further ¼ mile turn left on to the B6020 SP 'Sutton-in-Ashfield', passing through the edge of Blidworth.

BLIDWORTH, Notts

Tradition has it that this colliery village was the home of Friar Tuck and Maid Marian, characters that add the essential ingredients of humour and romance to the Robin Hood legend. The fellow outlaw and friend of Robin, Will Scarlet, is said to be buried in the local churchyard.

In 2¼ miles meet crossroads and turn left on to the A60 to pass the entrance of Newstead Abbey on the right.

The superb lake provides a perfect setting for Newstead Abbey.

NEWSTEAD ABBEY, Notts

An abbey founded here in the 12th century was converted into a house in 1550 and later was to be the ancestral home of the poet Lord Byron. In 1931 the house (open) was given to the city of Nottingham, and today it provides a fitting setting for

relics of the poet, and of the explorer Dr Livingstone – who stayed here in 1864. Surviving features of the religious foundation include the west front of the priory church, the cloisters, and the Chapter House.

Continue along the A60 and in ½ mile turn right on to the B683. Continue to Papplewick.

OSWESTRY, Shrops

Sometimes in England, sometimes in Wales, Oswestry was for centuries a battleground between the 2 countries, until the Act of Union in 1535 permanently established the border to the west of the town. Three times ravaged by fire, and by plague in 1559, when nearly a third of the inhabitants perished, few of Oswestry's medieval buildings have survived. Among those which have, Llwyd Mansion, a black and white timbered building in the centre of the town, bears the double-headed eagle of the Holy Roman Empire on one wall. The crest was granted to the Lloyd family in recognition of its services during the Crusades. Other noteworthy ancient buildings include the row of cottages near the church which originally housed Oswestry Grammar School. This was founded in 1407 and is thought to be the oldest secular foundation in the country. In Morda Road, the Croeswylan Stone, or Cross of Weeping, marks the place to which the market was shifted during the plague. Oswestry supported the Royalist cause in the Civil War, but Cromwell's forces took the town and destroyed the castle, of which only a grassy mound and a few fragments of masonry survive. King Oswald's Well sprang up, according to legend, on the spot where an eagle dropped one of the limbs of King Oswald of Northumbria, slain at the Battle of Maserfield by King Penda of Mercia in 642. The parish church is dedicated to Oswald, and Oswestry is a corruption of his name.

Leave Oswestry on the A483 Wrexham road, and in 1 mile pass (left) Old Oswestry.

THE WELSH MARCHES AND THE BERWYN MOUNTAINS

The turbulent history of the borderlands between England and Wales resulted in a series of magnificent Norman castles. The tour leads from the Border town of Oswestry, to Chirk, through the delightful woodlands of the Ceiriog valley, across the foothills of the wild Berwyn Mountains and along the Cain and Vynrwy valleys.

The coat of arms decorating the wrought iron gates of Chirk Castle belongs to the Myddleton family, who have lived in the castle since 1595

OLD OSWESTRY, Shrops

On a ridge a little to the north of Oswestry lie the remains of a massive Iron-Age hill fort, known in English as Old Oswestry and in Welsh as Yr Hen Dinas, 'the old fort'. It dates from about 250BC, when the first lines of defence, 2 great banks and ditches, were constructed. At a later date a third bank was added and the whole site was enclosed by a formidable double rampart. The fort was inhabited for more than 300 years, until the Romans destroyed it in AD75.

Continue on the A483 and at Gobowen turn left at the roundabout on to the A5, SP 'Llangollen'. In 2 miles descend into the Ceiriog valley where the Chirk Aqueduct can be seen ahead. Cross the river into Wales and ascend to the edge of Chirk.

CHIRK, Clwyd

Chirk is an attractive small town with streets of pleasant houses shaded by trees. A short footpath leads west from Chirk to the stone arched aqueduct built by Thomas Telford between 1796 and 1801. Its 10 great arches carry the Shropshire Union Canal high over the Cairiog valley. Alongside runs the railway viaduct, built in 1848.

A detour can be taken by keeping forward with the A5, then take the next turning left on to an unclassified road to Chirk Castle.

CHIRK CASTLE, Clwyd

The Welsh name of the castle, Castell y waun, meaning 'meadow castle' aptly describes its beautiful setting. Built by Edward I in 1310, Chirk (NT) is a fine example of a border stronghold — a rectangular stone fortress with massive, round drum towers at the 4 corners. In 1595 it became the home of Sir Thomas Myddelton, later Lord Mayor of London. His son held the castle for Parliament during the Civil War, and relics of that period can be seen in the courtyard. Later, the family supported Charles II, and the magnificent long gallery contains portraits and furniture dating from the Restoration. There is a beautifully decorated and furnished suite of 18th-century rooms, whose elegance is echoed by the graceful wrought iron gates at the entrance to the park. These, with their delicate tracery of foliage, were the work of Robert and John Davies, 2 brothers who lived near Wrexham. Through the park runs a part of Offa's Dyke, which for many centuries after King Offa's death in AD796, marked the boundary between England and Wales. There is a walk to Llangollen from here.

The main tour turns left at the edge of Chirk on to the B4500, SP 'Glyn Ceiriog'. Follow the Ceiriog valley, through Pontfadog, to Glyn Ceiriog.

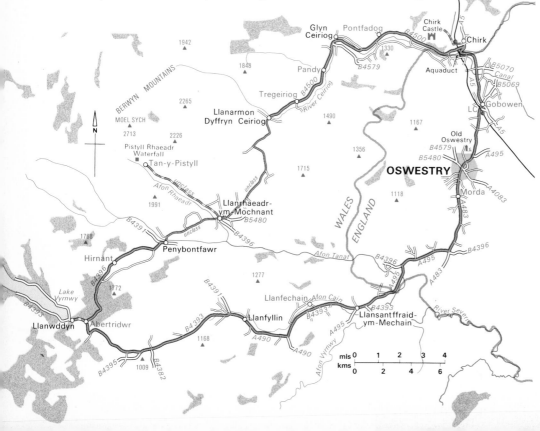

The dramatic waterfall of Pistyll Rhaeadr is the highest in Wales

GLYN CEIRIOG, Clwyd

Llansantffraid Glyn Ceiriog, to give the village its full name, stands on the swift-flowing River Ceiriog and is the main centre for exploring the lovely Ceiriog valley. Quarrying was once a major industry and in the Village Institute there are relics of the narrow-gauge tramway that ran from the quarries to the canal at Chirk.

Continue on the Llanarmon road for the gradual climb through the narrowing valley, passing the villages of Pandy and Tregeiriog and approaching the foothills of the Berwyn Mountains, to Llanarmon Dyffryn Ceiriog.

LLANARMON DYFFRYN CEIRIOG, Clwyd

Situated at the head of the Ceiriog valley, Llanarmon, a secluded village hidden in the foothills of the Berwyn Mountains, makes an excellent centre for walkers and for riding holidays. Penybryn, just above the village, was the birthplace of the great lyric poet John Ceiriog Hughes (1832-87). A farm labourer, who later became stationmaster at Glyn Ceiriog, Hughes wrote in Welsh but is, paradoxically, best remembered among the English for the translation of one of his less accomplished poems, *God Bless the Prince of Wales.*

Go forward over the crossroads, SP 'Llanrhaeadr', and climb out of the valley. In 1 ¾ miles, at the top, turn left and descend following a hilly, narrow byroad to Llanrhaeadr-ym-mochnant.

LLANRHAEADR-YM-MOCHNANT, Clwyd

This large market village has grown up around a tiny square where the 17th-century inn and the solid, square tower of the parish church make a pleasant group. The village was the birthplace in 1540 of William Morgan, later Bishop of St Asaph, who made the first translation of the Bible into Welsh, thus helping to preserve the language from extinction. It was published in 1588 by permission of Elizabeth I, who revoked a decree of Henry VIII which had officially banned Welsh.

A detour can be taken by turning right in the village to Tany-y-pistyll and the remarkable Pistyll Rhaeadr waterfall.

PISTYLL RHAEADR, Clwyd

The falls of Pistyll Rhaeadr, rightly considered to be one of the Seven Wonders of Wales (see Llangollen tour), cascade down a tree-covered gorge high up in the Rhaeadr valley. The water falls for 200ft, then pours through a natural rock arch to tumble down a further 100ft in a series of leaps and rocky pools.

The main tour continues through the village. Cross the river bridge and by the Three Tuns PH, go forward for Penybontfawr.

PENYBONTFAWR, Powys

Its picturesque setting amid the Berwyn Mountains is the charm of this small village on the Afon Tanat. As with many hill villages, church, vicarage, school and terraced houses were all built in the 19th century and only the outlying farms date from an earlier period. To the north-east of the village rises the bleak summit of the 3,713ft-high Moel Sych.

At the T-junction turn right then left on to the B4396, SP 'Lake Vyrnwy', and follow a winding narrow road to Llanwddyn.

LLANWDDYN, Powys

This is a new, model village, built in the 1880s when the Afon Vyrnwy valley was drowned to form Lake Vyrnwy. The old village, which lies at the bottom of the lake, originally grew up around the church of a 6th-century Celtic saint, Wddyn. Later it became part of the principality of Powys and in the 13th century was acquired by the Jerusalem Knights of St John.

Leave Llanwddyn on the B4393 Llanfyllin road, passing through rolling hill scenery. In 7 ¾ miles turn right on to the A490 to enter Llanfyllin.

LLANFYLLIN, Powys

This little market town on the River Cain centres on a pleasant square where the town hall used to stand. In olden days, Llanfyllin had a dubious reputation for strong ale — Old ale fills Llanfyllin with young widows — ran the saying. During the Napoleonic Wars French prisoners were quartered here and a room in the chemist's shop still displays frescoes painted by them during their captivity.

Follow the Welshpool road and in 2 miles turn left on to the B4393, SP 'Llansantffraid' and 'Oswestry'. Continue along the Cairn valley then in 3 ¾ miles turn left on to the A495 to enter Llansantffraid-ym-mechain.

LLANSANTFFRAID-YM-MECHAIN, Powys

The village strays along the main road in 3 stages. First comes the church, with vicarage, school hotel and timbered brick cottages gathered close around it. Next, a group of new houses spread out around the flour mill, and finally set around the 18th-century arched bridge stands a collection of tidy Victorian houses.

Follow the Vyrnwy valley before crossing the border into Shropshire. Later, at the T-junction turn right, then in 2 ¼ miles turn left on to the A483 for the return to Oswestry.

THE FEN COUNTRY

For centuries farmers have been draining the fens and creating new fields, but Oliver Cromwell, the farmer's son who became Lord Protector of England, would still recognise the broad horizons of the Cambridgeshire-Northamptonshire border, his old school in Huntingdon, and his family home — Hinchingbrooke House.

PETERBOROUGH, Cambs

Factories, office blocks and extensive housing estates have turned the ancient settlement of Peterborough into a 'New Town', unfortunately with little charm. Until the 19th century and the development of the railway, it was a peaceful river port on the Nene with an outstanding cathedral. The latter, built of local Barnack stone, is still magnificent and the triple-arched front is its chief glory. Catherine of Aragon and Mary, Queen of Scots were buried here, although Mary's body was subsequently reburied in Westminster Abbey by James I. Another fine building still standing is the old Guildhall in Market Place. It was built to commemorate the Restoration of Charles II and at one time was used as a Butter Market. A few old stone houses have also survived such as those in Preistgate and among them is the Museum and Art Gallery. Here there are bone carvings made by French prisoners during the Napoleonic Wars.

From Peterborough city centre follow SP 'Leicester (A47)' and cross the railway bridge. In 1¾ miles, at the roundabout, take the unclassified road for Longthorpe.

LONGTHORPE, Cambs

Longthorpe Tower (AM) was added to the village manor house in the 14th century as fortification. On one floor of the square tower there are some rare wall-paintings dating from about 1330, but they were not discovered until after World War II. The paintings represent religious and allegorical

tales such as the Three Living and the Three Dead, and the Wheel of the Five Senses, figured as animals.

Beyond the village, at the T-junction, turn right. At the roundabout take the A47, SP 'Leicester', and continue to Castor.

CASTOR, Cambs

When the Romans occupied Britain they built *Durobrivae* by the Nene and took over the potteries at Castor, and Castor ware was subsequently sent to all corners of their Empire. The Normans built the village church, using Roman remains, and it is the only one in England dedicated to St Kyneburgha, the sister of King Peada who founded Peterborough Abbey.

After 3 miles cross the A1 then turn left on to the A6118 for Wansford.

WANSFORD, Cambs

Crossing the River Nene at Wansford is a medieval 10-arched bridge which links the village on either side of it. Wansford is sometimes known as Wansford in England, and this dates from the 17th century when a traveller called Drunken Barnabee arrived at the village inn (now called Haycock Inn) and, finding a plague sign on the door, slept on a haycock. During the night the Nene swept him downstream and when he awoke people said to him: 'Whereaway, from Greenland?' to which he replied: 'No; from Wansford Brigs in England.'

Continue on the B671, then in 3½ miles turn right on to the A605, SP 'Oundle', and enter Elton.

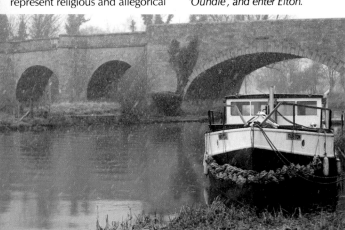

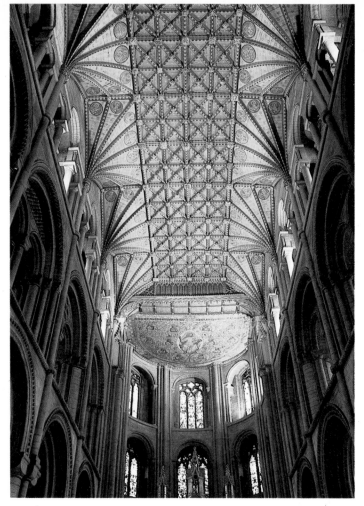

The 15th-century roof of the presbytery and chancel in Peterborough Cathedral

ELTON, Cambs

Along the village's 2 main streets — Over End and Middle Street — are ranked stone-built cottages and houses, many with mullioned windows. All Saints Church has 2 Saxon crosses in its churchyard which indicates there may have been a church on this site since the 10th century. Elton Hall (OACT) in Elton Park, dates from the 15th century but has had 18th- and 19th-century alterations

Continue on the A605 to Oundle.

OUNDLE, Northants

This lovely old county town has been unspoilt by time; alleyways thread their way past ancient inns, tall stone houses with steep roofs and tiny cottages with the smallest of windows. Oundle's famous public school was founded in 1556 by William Laxton, a grocer of the town who became Lord Mayor of London; the school is still owned by the Grocers' Company. The Nene flows round the town, making it a very popular sailing centre with beautiful views of the surrounding countryside.

Leave by the Kettering road. Cross the river and pass Barnwell Country Park. Join the A605 then in 1¾ miles (on right) is the turning for Lilford Park.

Wansford Bridge has been added to over the years which accounts for its irregular arches

LILFORD PARK, Northants

The 4th Baron Lilford, a keen ornithologist and naturalist, focused attention on Lilford Park at the end of the last century through the aviaries and gardens he built here. These have been restored or rebuilt, and the gardens are stocked with hundreds of birds, including the Lilford crane, named after the baron, and the Little owl, which Lilford introduced to Britain from Europe by releasing breeding pairs from aviaries in this park. The grounds, covering about 240 acres, offer a range of attractions for the whole family, including a children's farm, a craft and museum centre and an antique centre. The 17th-century house, Lilford Hall, is only open for special events such as motor shows and craft markets.

Continue on the A605 and in 1 mile pass the edge of Thorpe Waterville, then in another mile turn left on to an unclassified road for Titchmarsh.

TITCHMARSH, Northants

There is a splendid Perpendicular tower on the village church, which has a ha-ha (sunken ditch which cannot be seen from a distance) as a boundary. Two painted monuments inside the church are by Mrs Elizabeth Creed, cousin of John Dryden, the poet. The delightful thatched almshouses which stand to the south of the church and green, were provided by the Pickering family in 1756.

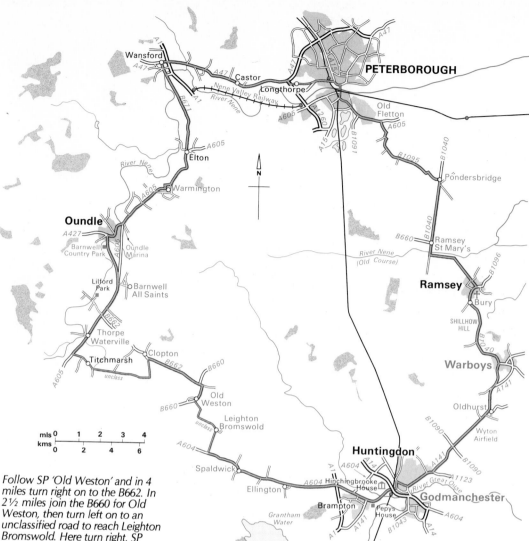

From the Ring Road (one way) follow the A141, SP 'March'. Pass RAF Wyton before reaching the edge of Oldhurst. In ½ mile turn left on to the B1040, SP 'Ramsey'. Pass through Warboys and Bury before entering Ramsey.

RAMSEY, Cambs

Ramsey Abbey, built in 969 on a tiny island in the marshland of the Fen country, prospered to become one of the 13th century's most important abbeys. As a result of this prosperity a town grew up around it. The Dissolution, however, brought an end to both: the abbey was destroyed and the lands sold off. Thereafter a series of misfortunes befell the town: the Parliamentarians destroyed many buildings during the Civil War; the Great Plague struck in 1666, and a series of devastating fires ravaged the town in the 17th and 18th centuries. All that remains of the abbey now is the gatehouse (NT) which looks across the smooth lawns of Abbey Green. A few 18th-century houses surround the green, but the rest of Ramsey is mostly 19th century. Great Whyte is the town's wide, main street, built in 1852 over Bury Brook which flowed through the town.

Turn left to continue on the B1040, SP 'Pondersbridge'. In 2¾ miles turn right and cross the river bridge then at Pondersbridge turn left on to the B1095, SP 'Peterborough'. In 4 miles turn left on to the A605 and pass through Old Fletton before the return to Peterborough.

Follow SP 'Old Weston' and in 4 miles turn right on to the B662. In 2½ miles join the B660 for Old Weston, then turn left on to an unclassified road to reach Leighton Bromswold. Here turn right, SP 'Huntingdon', and descend, then in 1 mile turn left on to the A604. Nearly 6 miles farther, at the roundabout, take the 2nd exit, then join the A141 before reaching the edge of Brampton.

BRAMPTON, Cambs

Among the reddish-yellow cottages in Brampton is the gabled house once owned and lived in by diarist Samuel Pepys's family (open by appointment). It is said that Pepys buried his money here when an invasion from Holland was feared.

At the roundabout go forward and in 1 mile pass (left) Hinchingbrooke House.

HINCHINBROOKE HOUSE, Cambs

A medieval nunnery was the foundation of Hinchinbrooke House (OACT), the remains of which were given to Oliver Cromwell's grandfather in 1538, but it was Oliver's father who began to adapt the ruins and build a country home. The house was damaged by fire in 1830 but afterwards restored by Edward Bore. One of the best features of the interior is the 17th-century carved staircase, which was installed during the 1950s from a house in Essex (now demolished). Hinchinbrooke has been used as a school since 1962.

Continue into Huntingdon.

HUNTINGDON, Cambs

Once a county town, Huntingdon has ancient origins, its history stretching back to Roman times — coins and pottery of that era have been found here. By the end of the 10th century a market and a mint were established, and the town grew in prosperity. However, the Black Death of 1348 drastically reduced the population, and the town sank into obscurity. Always a centre for local agriculture, Huntingdon survived the setback, and was again a substantial little market town by the 18th century, when the impressive town hall was built. In 1599 Oliver Cromwell was born here, and both he and Samuel Pepys attended the grammar school (OACT), now a museum of relics associated with Cromwell. The famous poet William Cowper lived in Cowper House in 1765. Most of the town is Georgian, but the George and Falcon inns are fine examples of 17th-century building and the finest medieval bridge in the county links the town with Godmanchester.

The George Inn in Huntingdon retains its courtyard, galley and external staircase of the 17th century.

ROSS-ON-WYE, Herefs & Worcs

High above the roofs of this attractive town rises the splendid 208ft spire of St Mary's Church, the topmost part of which was rebuilt in the 17th century with money donated by the philanthropic John Kyrle. Inside the main church, which dates mainly from the 13th century, are numerous interesting monuments. An important feature of the High Street is the red-sandstone Market Hall (AM) of 1670, which features a Charles II medallion set into the gable overlooking Man of Ross House – where Kyrle lived. The most conspicuous reminder of Kyrle's many benefactions is the Prospect – a garden with excellent views over the river. Several ancient and attractive groups of buildings are preserved in the town, including a number of almshouses and the 16th-century Wilton Bridge.

Leave Ross-on-Wye by the B4260 SP 'Monmouth (A40)'. After ¾ mile cross the River Wye into Wilton.

WILTON, Herefs & Worcs

The splendid 16th-century bridge that spans the Wye here features a curiously inscribed sundial which was added in the 18th century. Near by are a group of old buildings and the picturesquely overgrown ruins of a 13th-century castle.

At the roundabout take 1st exit A40 and in 2 miles ascend to Pencraig. Continue for ½ mile, then turn left on to an unclassified road. Proceed to Goodrich.

GOODRICH, Herefs & Worcs

Imposing ruins of moated Goodrich Castle (AM), built in the 12th century as a defence against Welsh raiders, stand on a wooded hill overlooking the beautiful River Wye.

Branch right with SP 'Symond's Yat' then turn right on to the B4229. After ¾ mile turn left on to an unclassified road SP 'Symond's Yat East' and cross Huntsham Bridge. After 1 mile keep left and steeply ascend a narrow road to reach Symond's Yat Rock.

SYMOND'S YAT, Herefs & Worcs

This famous beauty spot lies in a narrow loop of the River Wye. An AA viewpoint at the summit of 473ft Yat Rock affords magnificent views over the Yat (gap or 'gate') itself, and of the river as it winds through the rich woodlands of its deep valley.

Join the B4432 SP 'Coleford' and continue to Christchurch, then turn right on to the B4228. After ½ mile meet crossroads and turn right on to the A4136 SP 'Monmouth'. Proceed to Staunton.

STAUNTON, Glos

Fine views of the Wye Valley can be enjoyed from many vantage points around this old village. The local

THE FOREST OF DEAN

Carpets of daffodils in spring and a leafy canopy in summer provide a backcloth for the one-man craft industries for which the forest is famous. West are the silvery coils of the majestic River Wye, which borders this outstanding region and divides England from Wales.

The Forest of Dean is a place of beauty and interest at all times of the year.

church has Norman origins and is often referred to as the 'Mother Church of the Forest of Dean'. An isolated rock known as the Buckstone makes a fine viewpoint. It used to move to the touch, but after having been dislodged in 1885 it was firmly fixed in its original position.

Descend into Wales through beautifully wooded scenery and after 4½ miles turn left on to the A466 SP 'Chepstow'. A short detour to Monmouth can be made by remaining on the A4136.

MONMOUTH, Gwent

Strategically placed where the rivers Wye and Monnow meet, this ancient town played a vital role in subjugating South Wales from the Roman period till the Middle Ages. The outstanding reminder of these troubled times is a unique

fortified bridge (AM) which has spanned the Monnow and guarded the town since 1260. The once-powerful castle (birthplace of Henry V) preserves an interesting 12th-century building among its remains. Near by is the Great Castle House (exterior AM), a 17th-century structure noted for its fine interior decorations. Other historic buildings include a ruined priory, several fine churches, an 18th-century shire hall, and venerable houses of the Tudor and Georgian periods. The Monmouth Museum in the Market Hall contains notable Nelson relics. East of the town is wooded Kymin Hill (NT), an excellent viewpoint which carries an 18th-century Naval Temple at its summit.

Shots from a cannon called Roaring Meg battered Goodrich Castle into submission during the Civil War.

Continue along the Wye Valley and pass through Redbrook, where the river forms part of the border between England and Wales. East of the road are traces of Offa's Dyke.

OFFA'S DYKE, Gwent etc

King Offa of Mercia constructed the banks and ditches of these extensive earthworks some time during the 8th century. The dyke, broken in places, stretches from Chepstow to Prestatyn and for many centuries was accepted as the boundary between England and Wales.

Cross Bigsweir Bridge and drive through Llandogo. Continue to Tintern Abbey.

TINTERN ABBEY, Gwent

Set amid the soft hills of Gwent and surrounded by the remains of ancient monastic buildings is the beautiful roofless church of Tintern Abbey. This once-important Cistercian foundation was created in 1131, and its size gradually increased along with its influence and importance – mainly in the 13th and 14th centuries. Close by is the little village of Tintern Parva.

Continue along the A466 and after 3 miles pass a path on the right leading to Wyndcliff Viewpoint. Drive through St Arvans and pass Chepstow Racecourse on the left. At the roundabout take the first exit into Chepstow.

CHEPSTOW, Gwent

Spectacularly perched above a bend of the Wye are the extensive remains of Chepstow Castle (AM), a massive fortification that was begun in stone only a year after the Norman invasion of England. The quaint old town, includes many old houses. A fine 18th-century house contains the town's museum, and the West Gate (AM) of the town wall still survives.

Leave Chepstow on the A48 SP 'Gloucester' and cross the River Wye into England. Ascend, and after ¼ mile at crossroads turn left on to the B4228, SP 'Coleford'. Continue to the edge of Hewelsfield.

HEWELSFIELD, Glos

Norman workmanship is evident in the fabric of Hewelsfield Church, which is said to be one of the oldest in the Forest of Dean.

Continue, with views of the River Severn to the right, and later turn left into St Briavels.

ST BRIAVELS, Glos

During the Middle Ages this quiet little village was the administrative centre for the Forest of Dean. Its church was built in 1089 and maintains a custom in which small cubes of bread and cheese are distributed among the parishioners after evening service on Whit Sunday. This practice is probably 700 years old. St Briavels Castle, now a youth hostel, has a magnificent 13th-century gatehouse and a 12th-century great hall.

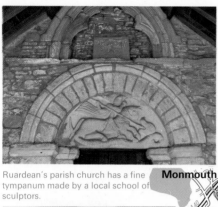

Ruardean's parish church has a fine tympanum made by a local school of sculptors.

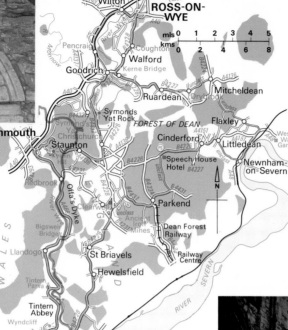

Chepstow was one of the earliest stone castles to be built in Britain.

The tower on Monnow Bridge was built as a fortified entrance to Monmouth.

The writer C S Lewis was so moved by the majestic roofless ruin of Tintern Abbey that he wished all churches were open to the sky.

Keep forward through St Briavels and after ¼ mile reach crossroads and turn left rejoining the B4228. After 1¾ miles turn left on to the B4231 and after ¼ mile turn right to rejoin the B4228. After ¾ mile turn right on to an unclassified road SP 'Parkend', and after 1 mile meet a T-junction. Turn right on to the B4431 and continue to Parkend.

PARKEND, Glos
This rather undistinguished village has an interesting 'gothicky' church dating from 1822. Close by is the Dean Forest Railway.

DEAN FOREST RAILWAY, Glos
Plans are underway to open a working steam railway from Lydney to Parkend in the near future. A collection of locomotives and rolling stock is kept at the Norchard Railway Centre north of Lydney.

Continue on the B4431, and after 1¼ miles turn left on to an unclassified road SP 'Speech House'. Approach Speech House through the Forest of Dean.

FOREST OF DEAN, Glos
Within the boundaries of this historic area – the first National Forest Park to be created in England – is some of the finest woodland scenery to be found anywhere in Britain. Since 1016 the forest has been Crown property (although it is now cared for by the Forestry Commission) and it is

famous for a number of privately run industries, including coal mining and traditional charcoal burning. Specially laid-out forest trails and a forest drive help visitors appreciate the best that the area has to offer.

SPEECH HOUSE HOTEL, Glos
This handsome building succeeded St Briavels to become the administrative centre for the Forest of Dean, on its completion in 1676 it now serves as an hotel, but the old Verderers Court of Foresters is still held there.

Turn right on to the B4226 and pass a picnic site on the left. Continue to the edge of Cinderford.

CINDERFORD, Glos
Typical of early 19th-century development, this village was largely created to house the workforce required to operate the Forest Vale Ironworks.

Continue on the B4226 and ascend. After ¾ mile turn right on to the A4151 SP 'Gloucester' and proceed to Littledean.

LITTLEDEAN, Glos
Features of this small place include an attractive old church, an 18th-century gaol which now serves as a police station, and Littledean Hall (open), incorporating Roman, Saxon and Norman work, with a museum, watergardens and a large Roman temple.

At the T-junction turn right SP 'Newnham' on to an unclassified road. Descend to Newnham-on-Severn.

NEWNHAM-ON-SEVERN, Glos
Many old houses survive in this pleasant little town, which has a grassy bank down the centre of its high street. The local church affords enchanting views across the River Severn to the Cotswold Hills.

Turn left on to the A48 'Gloucester' road. After 2 miles turn left on to an unclassified road SP 'Mitcheldean'. Continue to Flaxley.

FLAXLEY, Glos
Unspoilt Flaxley is a cluster of houses with an unpretentious church and an historic abbey. The latter was originally created in the 12th century, but after a great fire in 1777 much of the monastic complex was rebuilt in the Georgian style. It is now used as a private dwelling.

Continue and in 1 mile turn right. Two miles farther cross a main road to enter Mitcheldean.

MITCHELDEAN, Glos
The beautiful 18th-century spire of Mitcheldean Church rises grandly over the roofs of much older half-timbered cottages in the village.

At Mitcheldean Church turn left for Drybrook. At Drybrook crossroads go straight across, then keep left. In ¾ mile meet a T-junction and turn right on to the B4227. Continue to Ruardean.

RUARDEAN, Glos
Above the inner doorway of Ruardean's notable church is a beautifully-preserved Norman tympanum depicting St George's battle against the dragon.

Bear right and descend, and after 1½ miles turn right on to the B4228 SP 'Ross'. Follow the River Wye and drive through Kerne Bridge to reach Walford.

WALFORD, Herefs & Worcs
This Wye-side village has a 13th-century church and stands on the site of a Roman camp.

Continue on the B4228 to return to Ross-on-Wye.

POETRY AND SHROPSHIRE IRON

Inspiration lives in the Shropshire hills and along Wenlock Edge. Housman captured its essence in the lovely poems of 'A Shropshire Lad', and the early ironmasters distilled it in a graceful bridge that was to herald the industrial revolution.

SHREWSBURY, Salop

Superbly set in a huge loop of the Severn, this beautiful and unspoilt town is famous for its half-timbered buildings and picturesque streets. Also here are many excellent examples of 18th- and 19th-century architecture. Traditionally founded during the 5th century by the Romans, Shrewsbury has been occupied by various peoples interested in its strategic position. Two notable 18th-century bridges span the Severn into the town centre, and the remains of a castle that defended the vulnerable north-eastern entrance dominate the imposing railway station. Fortification of the castle site was begun in the 11th century, but the remains date mainly from the 13th and were incorporated in a private house about 200 years ago. Near by are the 17th-century buildings of old Shrewsbury School, which now houses the civic library. Outstanding churches in Shrewsbury include the Norman and later Abbey Church, 12th- to 17th-century St Mary's, and mainly 18th-century St Julian's, with its ancient towers. Amongst the outstanding buildings are Rowley's Mansion, which houses a museum of local history and art; Whitehall of 1582; the gateway of the Council House; the Lion Coaching Inn; and the small complex of 14th-century cottages, shops and fine old hall called Bear Steps.

Leave Shrewsbury on the A49 'Leominster' road, and ½ mile beyond Baystonhill turn left on to an unclassified road to reach Condover.

CONDOVER, Salop

Pink sandstone was the predominant material used to build both the 17th-century local church and Condover Hall (open on application), a splendid example of Elizabethan architecture.

At Condover turn left SP 'Pitchford' and after ⅓ mile bear left. After 1½ miles meet crossroads and turn right to enter Pitchford.

PITCHFORD, Salop

Half-timbered Pitchford Hall (not open) is a perfect example of a 16th-century black-and-white building, and the adjacent church retains good Norman details.

Continue to Acton Burnell.

ACTON BURNELL, Salop

Edward I held what is said to have been the first English parliament here in 1283. Ruined Acton Burnell Castle (AM) dates from the 13th century and was built by Robert Burnell, Bishop of Bath and Wells, partly as a castle and partly as a palace.

Meet crossroads, turn right SP 'Church Stretton', and after 2 miles bear right. Enter Longnor.

LONGNOR, Salop

In a grove of trees here is a perfect 13th-century church with 18th-century furnishings. Longnor Hall (not open) stands in a large deerpark and dates from 1670. Near by is black-and-white Moat House.

Continue, and after a short way turn left on to the A49. Enter Leebotwood.

Winter sunshine on Wenlock Edge.

LEEBOTWOOD, Salop

The finest of several half-timbered buildings in this village is the thatched Pound Inn. A 1,236ft hill known as The Lawley rises high above the village nearby.

Continue, with Caer Caradoc Hill to the left and the Long Mynd moorland to the right.

CAER CARADOC HILL, Salop

Earthworks of an iron-age hillfort said to have been defended by King Caractacus crown this miniature mountain, which is only 1,500ft high.

Amongst Shrewsbury's many beautiful half-timbered buildings is the Old Council House gateway.

THE LONG MYND, Salop

Rising like the armoured back of some prehistoric monster from the ordered fields of lowland Shropshire, the Long Mynd is a heather-covered mass of ancient grits and shales, largely owned and protected by the National Trust. Where the moorland hills fall towards Church Stretton they are scored by numerous ravines; the lovely Cardingmill Valley is possibly the most beautiful.

Continue and meet crossroads. Turn right on to the B4371 SP 'Town Centre' and enter Church Stretton.

CHURCH STRETTON, Salop

During the late 19th century the district around Church Stretton became known as 'Little Switzerland', and the town itself developed into a popular inland resort. Red-brick and half-timbered Victorian villas mingle with older black-and-white buildings to create a pleasant character complemented by the Church of St Lawrence, which has been adapted through many periods. Above the Norman north doorway is a Celtic fertility symbol. There are three Strettons in the valley – Church Stretton at the centre, All Stretton to the north, and Little Stretton to the south. The latter has many half-timbered buildings.

Return to crossroads and turn left on to the B4370. Pass through the pretty village of Little Stretton. Turn right on to the A49, and continue to Craven Arms.

CRAVEN ARMS, Salop
Originally the hamlet of Newton, this 19th-century town development was renamed after a coaching inn that just preceded its expansion. Today it is an important centre for livestock auctions.

A detour of ¾ mile from the main tour route can be made by continuing on the A49 to Stokesay Castle.

STOKESAY CASTLE, Salop
Wooden beams, overhanging walls, steep roofs, and decorated woodwork, make Stokesay a picture-book castle. It is of the oldest surviving examples of a fortified manor house set in a romantic setting with a quaint Elizabethan gatehouse and dating from c 1280. The castle (AM) owes its superb condition to a singularly uneventful history. Beyond the moat is a church that was damaged during the Civil War and subsequently refurbished during the Commonwealth. Interior furnishings and fittings of that time remain intact.

Leave Craven Arms on the B4368 SP 'Bridgnorth' and enter Corve Dale. Shortly reach Diddlebury.

DIDDLEBURY, Salop
Diddlebury enjoys a picturesque setting beside the river in Corve Dale, beneath the high ridge of beautiful Wenlock Edge. Saxon masonry in the local church includes attractive herringbone work on the north wall.

Continue to the White House at Aston Munslow.

THE WHITE HOUSE, Salop
Many periods are represented in the complex of buildings associated with this mansion, and the house itself has a 14th-century hall and 16th-century cross-wing. A fascinating museum of country life accommodated here displays a variety of farm relics.

Continue through Munslow, with Wenlock Edge to the left and the River Corve to the right. Reach Shipton.

SHIPTON, Salop
Famous and beautiful Shipton Hall (open) is the focal point of this Corve Dale village. Built in c 1587 and enlarged at the back during the mid-18th century, it comprises a large range of buildings, including a fine stable block which dates from the 18th century.

At Shipton bear left on to the B4378 SP 'Much Wenlock' and continue to Much Wenlock.

MUCH WENLOCK, Salop
Poet A E Housman celebrated the beauty of this region in his collection *A Shropshire Lad*. The town is a charming little market centre with

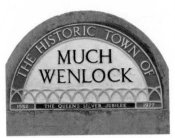

The traceried stonework of Wenlock Priory is echoed in the symbolic design of Much Wenlock's attractive town nameplate.

many excellent half-timbered and other buildings, including such notable examples as Raynald's Mansion, the Manor House, and the Guildhall. Remains of Wenlock Priory (AM), which was founded in the 7th century and became a Cluniac house in 1080, include beautiful interlocking Norman tracery. Near by is splendid Priors Lodge of 1500.
Leave Much Wenlock on the A458 'Bridgnorth' road and continue to Morville.

MORVILLE, Salop
Morville Hall (NT) was rebuilt in the 18th century, and the local church contains a wealth of details from many periods.
Continue and later at roundabout take the 1st exit to join the B4364 and enter Bridgnorth.

BRIDGNORTH, Salop
Bridgnorth is an ancient town, with many interesting buildings.
Leave Bridgnorth on the B4373 and after 5½ miles bear right SP 'Wellington'. Descend into the Severn Gorge and cross the river to reach a T-junction. Turn left and in ¼ mile at roundabout join the A4169 to enter Ironbridge.

IRONBRIDGE, Salop
Across the River Severn here is a splendid iron bridge that was built in

Right: Abraham Darby designed the revolutionary bridge at Ironbridge in the 18th century, unconsciously creating a memorial to the British industrial revolution. Below: a detail of the bridge's ironwork.

1779, the first of its kind in the world. This must surely be the most beautiful monument there is to the industrial revolution, which had its birth in this area. The Ironbridge Gorge Museum, covering six square miles, includes a reconstructed Victorian village and museums of iron and steel making and of the Coalport China Company and a visitor centre. The streets and buildings of Ironbridge itself cling to the sides of the Severn Gorge.
Beyond Ironbridge keep forward on to the B4380 SP 'Shrewsbury'. Continue to Buildwas.

BUILDWAS, Salop
Concrete cooling towers looming from a local power station otherwise hidden by trees make a controversial counterpoint to the 12th-century remains of Buildwas Abbey (AM), near the River Severn. Stone from the ruin was incorporated in the local church. North of the hamlet is the 1,334ft bulk of The Wrekin.
Continue through Leighton, along the Severn Valley, to the edge of Wroxeter.

WROXETER, Salop
During Roman times the important town of *Uriconium* stood here. Excavated remains (AM) include the baths and fragments of other buildings. Near by is a church which incorporates Roman bricks and masonry in its fabric, and displays architectural features from many ages. Inside are several very fine monuments and memorials.
Continue on the B4380 and after ¾ mile turn left on to the A5. Enter Atcham.

ATCHAM, Salop
Spacious wooded parklands and two 18th-century bridges are the main features of this pretty village which also has a church uniquely dedicated to St Eata. The Myton and Mermaid Inn is of Georgian origin, and Longer Hall was built in 1803 to designs by John Nash. Humphrey Repton laid out the grounds of both Longner and nearby Attingham Hall (NT) (open), a magnificent house of 1785.
Cross the Severn and return to Shrewsbury.

SKEGNESS, Lincs
In 1863 a rail service was begun at Skegness, with trains running to and from the teeming towns of the industrial Midlands. The result was a boom in seaside tourism, and the holiday crowds of today continue to enjoy the excellent sands and bathing facilities that prompted the transformation of this one-time fishing village into one of the east coast's most popular resorts. Magnificent seafront gardens border a long promenade where, in simpler days, Lord Tennyson and his brothers strolled to take the bracing sea air. A vast swimming pool, the Natureland Zoo, and various first-class entertainments vie for attention with 6 miles of sandy beach. The Church Farm Museum has the Farmhouse and cottage furnished as it would have been in the 19th century. At the southern end of the beach is Gibraltar Point, where there is a nature reserve and bird observatory.

Leave Skegness on the A158 'Lincoln' road and drive to Burgh-le-Marsh.

BURGH-LE-MARSH, Lincs
One of the main features of this area is a fine 5-sailed tower windmill that is still in working order. The impressive local church has two porches and a tower with 16 iron crosses. Inside is a restored screen.

Drive for 2¾ miles beyond the village and approach a roundabout with Gunby Hall to the left.

GUNBY HALL, Lincs
Lord Tennyson described this imposing red-brick building (NT) as 'a house of ancient peace'. It was built c1700 by Sir William Massingberd and shows the influence of Sir Christopher Wren. Features of the interior include an oak staircase, wainscoted rooms containing portraits by Reynolds, and various pieces of fine furniture. The house and its formal gardens are open by prior written appointment.

Continue along the A158 and drive through Candlesby, with Welton High Wood to the right. Proceed to Scremby.

SCREMBY, Lincs
Notable features of the good 18th-century church in Scremby include a panelled chancel and a monument to Charles Brackenbury.

Beyond Scremby meet crossroads and turn right on to an unclassified road to Skendleby.

SKENDLEBY, Lincs
Attractively set in the Lincolnshire Wolds, this pleasant village features a partly greenstone church and a mid 18th-century hall. Near by is a prehistoric site known as the Giant's Hill, where there are two long barrows. The most prominent measures 200ft long and stands 5ft high; the other has been severely reduced by ploughing.

Drive to the end of Skendleby and bear right SP 'Willoughby', then

BETWEEN THE WOLDS AND THE SEA

Attractive resorts and beaches of fine sand are interspersed with charming little fishing villages on Lincolnshire's holiday coast. Inland are picturesque hamlets clustered round greenstone churches, hills crowned by solitary windmills, and the enchanting lanes of the Wolds country.

Skegness prepares for the holiday season.

ascend to cross a main road. Descend, and in 1¾ miles turn left on to the B1196 SP 'Alford'. Approach Alford, with Well Vale to the left, and turn sharp left on to an unclassified road to enter the village of Well.

WELL, Lincs
Set on the eastern slopes of the Wolds, in the pastoral beauty of Well Vale, this tiny village takes its name from a spring that bubbles from the chalk to fill two lakes in a closely-wooded valley. Close to the village the beautiful Georgian red-brick building of Well Vale Hall stands in 170 acres of fine parkland.

Return to the B1196 and turn left to enter Alford.

ALFORD, Lincs
One of Lincolnshire's finest windmills can be seen here. Its 6-storey brick tower carries five sails and is topped by an ogee cap. It dates from 1813 and, although intact, is no longer in use. Merton Lodge is a good example of the many Georgian and later houses to be seen in the town.

Leave Alford on the A1104 'Louth, Lincoln' road and ascend. Reach Ulceby; cross a roundabout and take the 2nd exit on to the A16, then in ⅓ mile turn right on to the unclassified 'Harrington' road. Continue, with panoramic views, into Harrington.

HARRINGTON, Lincs
Harrington Hall (open) was rebuilt in 1673 and features a good Elizabethan facade and contains fine 17th- and 18th-century paintings, china and furniture and beautiful gardens.

Continue through pleasantly wooded countryside to Somersby.

Burgh-le-Marsh church clock urges a greater regard for time.

SOMERSBY, Lincs
The poet Alfred Lord Tennyson was born in this tiny Wolds village. His house, which still stands but is not open to the public, was adapted by his father to include a dining room with high gothic windows that entirely suited that era of romanticism. Various memorials to the Tennyson family can be seen in the local church, and a fine carved cross stands in the churchyard.

Keep forward into a narrow road for Salmonby and turn left SP 'Horncastle'. Continue for 2 miles, then meet crossroads and turn right SP 'Belchford'. Climb to a road summit of 455ft, with good all-round views, then descend into Belchford and turn right SP 'Alford'. After a short distance ascend Belchford Hill and meet a T-junction. Turn left SP 'Louth' and continue, with magnificent views, to a road summit of 487ft. In 3¼ miles meet crossroads and turn right on to the A153, passing the entrance to Caldwell Park Motor Cycle Racing Circuit on the right. In ¾ mile branch right (no SP) on to an unclassified road and continue to Tathwell.

TATHWELL, Lincs
Attractively situated in a sheltered position above a lake, this village has a good church that features a Norman tower and contains various interesting monuments.

Beyond Tathwell meet crossroads and drive forward SP 'Legbourne'. A short detour from the main route can be taken by turning right at the crossroads and driving to Bully Hill.

BULLY HILL, Lincs
Some of the finest prehistoric barrow groups to have survived in the whole county of Lincolnshire can be seen here. The largest of seven measures 60ft in diameter by 10ft high, and they are thought to date from the late stone or early bronze age.

On the main route, drive 1¼ miles beyond the crossroads and turn right on to the A16. After another 1¼ miles turn left on to the unclassified 'Little Cawthorpe' road, descend through Maltby and Haugham Woods, and turn right at Little Cawthorpe. Reach the village church and turn left (no SP), then pass through a ford and meet a T-junction. Turn right, and in ½ mile turn right again on to the A157. Continue to the end of Legbourne and bear right, then turn left on to the unclassified 'Manby' road. Continue to Little Carlton, turn left to reach Manby village.

Few windmills are as well preserved as this tower mill at Burgh-le-Marsh. It was built in 1833 and is in good working order.

The solid Norman tower of St Vedast's Church, Tathwell, is well sheltered from the elements.

Gunby Hall's austere face conceals a wealth of fine decoration.

MANBY, Lincs
The greenstone church of this pleasant little village has a tall tower and contains a remarkably well-preserved Saxon slab decorated with a distinctive rope design.

Meet crossroads beyond Manby and turn right on to the B1200. Continue to Saltfleetby.

SALTFLEETBY, Lincs
Close to St Peter's Church in Saltfleetby is the isolated tower of a church that the present greenstone building replaced. The recent building incorporates a few early-English fragments from its predecessor.

Meet a junction with the A1031, turn right, and continue to Theddlethorpe St Helen.

THEDDLETHORPE ST HELEN, Lincs
This tiny coastal village is near a scrub-covered foreshore that forms part of a national nature reserve and is one of the few remaining habitats of the Natterjack toad. This curious amphibian runs instead of hops, and is easily identifiable by the pale stripe down its back. Signposts and warning flags mark the site of an RAF bombing range on the sands.

Proceed along the A1031 for 3 miles, then turn left on to the A1104 into Mablethorpe.

MABLETHORPE, Lincs
Thanks to a highly expensive system of groynes this popular resort boasts a beautiful beach of firm golden sand. In normal weather swimmers can enjoy safe bathing here, but rough conditions make the water treacherous and red flags are flown to warn people away. Low tide reveals old stumps that are the sole remains of a woodland village swamped by the sea in 1289. All that survived was the fine old Church of St Mary, which contains various medieval relics. Today the town is guarded by a concrete promenade.

Leave Mablethorpe on the A52 'Skegness' road and continue to Trusthorpe.

TRUSTHORPE, Lincs
Fine sands and good bathing facilities make this a popular resort, but it is also the base for Humber Radio – an important Post Office link with ships and oil rigs in the North Sea. The tall radio mast dominates the village.

Continue on the A52 and drive into Sutton-on-Sea.

SUTTON-ON-SEA, Lincs
Safe bathing and a level sandy beach are the main features of this little coastal resort. The 4,500-year-old stumps and roots of a forest that was flooded by the sea can be seen at low tide.

From Sutton-on-Sea it is possible to take a pleasant detour from the main route, along the shore below the Sea Bank Dyke. In 1 mile meet a roundabout and turn left on to the unclassified road to Sandilands and drive straight on beside the sea wall. Reach Chapel St Leonards and turn left across a river bridge, then turn right with SP 'Skegness' to rejoin the A52 before Ingoldmells. On the main route, continue along the A52 to Huttoft.

HUTTOFT, Lincs
A tall windmill of the tower type can be seen here, with an interesting early-Victorian grain store.

Continue along the A52 and drive through Mumby to Ingoldmells.

INGOLDMELLS, Lincs
This little resort offers 3 miles of firm golden sand and a host of holiday diversions, including a funfair. Remains of an early iron-age salt-panning site between Ingoldmells and Chapel St Leonards include various structures that can only be seen at low tide.

Continue along the A52 for the return to Skegness.

BULB FIELDS IN THE FENS

Spring in the Fens is an explosion of colour. Daffodils, tulips, and hyacinths cover acre after flat acre of reclaimed land, stretching away from the bulb towns in gloriously-variegated carpets reminiscent of the Dutch countryside rather than rural England.

SPALDING, Lincs

This historic fenland town stands on the banks of the Welland in an area of drained marshland where market gardeners and bulb growers raise crops in soil of almost legendary richness. In springtime the district is glorious with tulips, daffodils, narcissi, and hyacinths that form a carpet of blazing colour comparable only with the bulb fields of Holland. Every May the town holds a spectacular Flower Festival that attracts visitors from all over the country. On the eastern outskirts are the beautiful Springfield Gardens, 25 acres of lawns and water features designed to show over a million bulbs to their best advantage. In summer the early freshness of the bulbs is replaced by the mature beauty of more than 80 species of rose in the magnificent Summer Rose Garden. The town itself has many old buildings in charming streets on both banks of the river, including several good examples of 18th-century design. One of the oldest is the greatly restored Ayscoughfee Hall, which dates from the 15th century and now houses a museum of local history. Its mellow stone and graceful lines are complemented by well-kept lawns enclosed by yew hedges. A small museum in Broad St (open by appointment) was founded by the Gentleman's Society in 1710. Spalding has many good churches, but the best is the late 13th-century Church of SS Mary and Nicholas. This has an angel-carved hammerbeam roof in the nave and was extensively restored by the Victorian architect Sir G G Scott.

Leave Spalding on the A16 'Boston' road and drive to Pinchbeck.

PINCHBECK, Lincs

Situated on the River Glen in a bulb-growing district, this village has preserved its old wooden stocks and has a restored church with a leaning tower. A fine 18th-century group of buildings includes the rectory and a stable block.

Continue on the A16 to Surfleet.

The area around Spalding is ablaze with tulips in the spring.

SURFLEET, Lincs

The spire on the church in this fenland village leans 6ft out of true – considerably more than the tower at Pinchbeck. Naturalist Gilbert White described a local heronry in his early work *Natural History*, but this has since been abandoned.

Cross the River Glen and proceed along the A16 to Gosberton.

GOSBERTON, Lincs

An outstanding feature of this pleasant little village is its cruciform church, which displays a curious tower gargoyle fashioned in the shape of an elephant.

Fleet Fen is part of Lincolnshire's extensive 17th-century drainage works.

Leave Gosberton, keep forward on the A152, and continue to Donington.

DONINGTON, Lincs

In Roman times the area around Donington was drained in the first of many attempts to reclaim agricultural land from the Fens. Much later the town was a centre of the flax and hemp industry, and nowadays it is a popular touring base. Its cobbled market square is surrounded by pleasant Georgian buildings, and its church carries a fine tower surmounted by an elegant spire. Inside is a tablet commemorating Captain Matthew Flinders, a great sailor who was born in Donington and travelled with Captain Bligh after the *Bounty* mutiny. He became a pioneer of Australian exploration and wrote a book about his voyages. He died in 1814, on the day that his book was published.

Continue through fenland along the A52.

THE LINCOLNSHIRE FENS, Lincs

The Fens of Lincolnshire covered an area that is barely above sea level and have been reduced by centuries of land reclamation. The Romans built the first sea wall here and drained the land behind it; in subsequent centuries their work was continued, and much later the expertise of Dutch engineer Vermuyden was used to make many acres of ground into rich arable land. A giant reclamation scheme begun in the 17th century used the talents of such famous men as Rennie and Telford, and was largely responsible for the shape of the landscape as it exists today. Everywhere the flat fields and pastures are criss-crossed by drains and dykes that stretch away to an almost treeless horizon.

Continue along the A52, with Swaton Fen on the right and Horbling Fen to the left. In 4 miles turn left on to the B1177 'Bourne' road and proceed to Horbling.

HORBLING, Lincs

Spring Well, situated a little way north of Horbling's Norman and later church, was once a communal washing trough. The village itself is a charming collection of mainly Georgian houses.

Proceed along the B1177 to Billingborough.

BILLINGBOROUGH, Lincs

The local church carries a 150ft spire that can be seen for a long way over the surrounding flat countryside. An unusual façade is displayed by the George and Dragon Inn, which dates from the 17th century.

Continue for ¾ mile by Billingborough Fen and pass a track leading right to the site of Sempringham Abbey.

SEMPRINGHAM ABBEY, Lincs

Sir Gilbert of Sempringham founded the Gilbertine order here c1130. He was the son of the local lord, and the Gilbertines were the only monastic order to have been founded in Britain. Close to the site an uneven area of grassland covers the remains of the village, but the superb Norman church survives as an outstanding example of its period.

Continue along the B1177 and drive through Pointon to Dowsby.

DOWSBY, Lincs

Dowsby Hall was built c1603, and the local church contains many fine moulded arches.

Stay on the B1177 through Dunsby, passing Dowsby Fen and Dunsby Fen on the left. Join the A15, with Bourne North Fen to the left, and continue to Bourne.

The beautiful water gardens near Peakirk are the home of various water birds, including trumpeter swans.

Large stone warehouses testify to Market Deeping's former prosperity, which has left a fine architectural heritage.

BOURNE, Lincs
Bourne is an ancient market town and reputedly the birthplace of Hereward the Wake, the last Saxon to resist the invading Norman army. The town was the former manufacturing base of the BRM racing car and is renowned for the purity of its water. The many watercress beds in the area are ample proof of the latter. Good domestic architecture in the town includes attractive Tudor cottages in South Street and a generous scattering of Georgian houses and shops. The Burghley Arms Hotel was the birthplace of Sir William Cecil, Lord High Treasurer to Elizabeth I, in 1520. Other famous natives of the town include Frederick Worth, founder of the House of Worth in Paris, and Robert Mannying, who founded an Augustinian abbey here in the 13th century. Remains of the monastic buildings are incorporated in the nave of the parish church. A Roman canal known as the Car Dyke runs close to the town, and castle earthworks can be seen a little way south.

Continue along the A15 'Peterborough' road and drive through Thurlby. Cross the River Glen and continue through Baston and Langtoft to Market Deeping.

MARKET DEEPING, Lincs
Several fine old houses testify to the one-time prosperity and importance of this ancient market town, situated on the River Welland at the edge of the Fens. Its restored church has an unusual rood loft doorway, and the 13th-century parish rectory is thought to be the oldest inhabited parsonage in England.

Leave Market Deeping on the A15, cross the River Welland, and pass the village of Northborough. Proceed to Glinton.

GLINTON, Cambs
Among the pleasant stone cottages of this attractive village is a fine 17th-century manor house; the entire group is centred on the slender spire of the local church.

Leave Glinton and turn left on to the B1443 'Thorney' road. Continue to Peakirk.

PEAKIRK, Cambs
A rare 14th-century lectern and numerous paintings can be seen in Peakirk's church, the only one in Britain dedicated to St Pega. Close to the village is the Wildfowl Trust gardens.

Leave Peakirk and continue east for 4 miles, then turn left on to the A1073. After another 2 miles turn left again on to an unclassified road and drive into Crowland.

CROWLAND, Lincs
One of the most interesting features of this pleasant little town is its unique Triangular Bridge (AM), which was built in the 14th century to span several streams of the River Welland. Its three arches, which meet at an angle of 120 degrees, now stand on dry land. In 1720 a carved figure of the Virgin Mary was taken from the partly ruined abbey that now serves as the parish church and placed on the bridge. The original abbey was founded in 716 by King Ethelbald in memory of St Guthlac.

From Crowland follow the B1040 to Thorney.

THORNEY, Cambs
It was here that the Saxon hero Hereward the Wake made his last stand against the invading Norman armies under William the Conqueror. Remains of a 12th-century abbey built by William after his victory can be seen near by, and the restored abbey church shows Norman and later workmanship. Abbey House is a largely 16th-century building with 17th-century additions. A good 18th-century windmill stands in the grounds.

From Thorney turn left on the A47 'Wisbech' road and in 1½ miles turn left again on to the B1167 SP 'Gedney Hill'. Continue for 4½ miles, then turn left on to the B1166 to Gedney Hill. At Gedney Hill turn left and continue to Holbeach Drove, then turn right on to the B1168 with Fleet Fen to the right. Meet crossroads 1 mile beyond Holbeach St Johns and turn right on to the B1165 for Sutton St James. Drive to the end of this village, turn left on to the B1390 to Long Sutton.

LONG SUTTON, Lincs
Many different architectural periods are represented in the fabric of this pretty market town's church, but the main feature is its detached, 162ft tower. This has a lead and timber spire that is considered one of the finest in Britain.

Leave Long Sutton on the A17 SP 'Sleaford', passing Gedney to the left.

Whaplode Church never came to the attention of 19th-century restorers, whose enthusiasm often outstripped their ability.

GEDNEY, Lincs
The fine marshland church in Gedney features a notable west tower and contains a 14th-century brass. Also inside are a number of alabaster effigies.

Leave the village and in a short distance turn left on to the A151 'Spalding' road, passing through Fleet Hargate into Holbeach.

HOLBEACH, Lincs
One of the county's major bulb-growing centres, this ancient market town boasts many good Georgian houses and a 14th-century church with a lofty spire and fine traceried windows. William Stukely, a founder of the Society of Antiquaries, was born here in 1718.

Proceed along the A151 to Whaplode.

WHAPLODE, Lincs
The splendid Norman and later church in this little marshland village has a presence that is out of all proportion to the size of the community that it serves. Inside is a notable 17th-century monument to Sir Anthony Irby.

Continue along the A151 for the return to Spalding.

STAFFORD, Staffs

New buildings encircle the county town, but despite this the old centre retains its dignified character. In Greengate Street stands the aptly named High House, 4 storeys high, and a beautiful example of timberframe construction. St Chad's is a fine Norman church with carvings said to have been the work of Saracens brought back to England after the Crusades by Lord Biddulph. The parish church, St Mary's, contains a monument to Izaak Walton, the noted angler, who was born at Stafford in 1593. Noel's Almshouses in Mill Street, a group of stone houses round a spacious courtyard, date from 1660. The William Salt Library in Eastgate Street is a remarkable collection of old deeds, drawings and books on Staffordshire history amassed by William Salt.

Leave on the A518, SP 'Telford' and 'Newport', and pass through Haughton for Gnosall.

GNOSALL, Staffs

Gnosall's church has a superb Norman interior, featuring massive pillars and decorated arches. An interesting item near the altar, in the pavement of the south aisle, is the rough carving of a pair of sheep-shearer's shears, no doubt a tribute to the importance of the wool trade. High on the tower outside can be seen a mason's mark of shield and hammer.

WHERE A HUNTED KING FOUND REFUGE

The capital of the Black Country is, unexpectedly, the gateway to the leafy woodlands and deer-haunted glades of Cannock Chase — noble remnant of a royal forest — and to the quiet pleasures of Staffordshire's unassuming countryside, where a succession of stately homes once gave shelter to the exiled Charles II.

Continue to Newport.

NEWPORT, Shrops

A town of great charm, Newport's broad main street passes on either side of its imposing church, whose 14th-century tower looks out on a vista of handsome 18th-century houses. There is a famous grammar school near the church, founded by William Adam in the Commonwealth period, that still has its original 17th-century clock. One of its most famous pupils was Sir Oliver Lodge, who was one of the pioneer experimenters in wireless telegrams.

Turn left then right, still SP 'Telford', to remain on the A518. In 2 miles turn left on to an unclassified road and enter Lilleshall. In 1¼ miles turn left, SP 'Lilleshall Abbey', and pass the remains in 1 mile (left).

LILLESHALL ABBEY, Shrops

Lilleshall Abbey (AM) now consists of graceful ruined arches and walls but some idea of its former magnificence can be gained by looking through the west front down the length of the ruins to the east window. It was founded in 1148 and after the Dissolution Henry VIII gave the abbey to the Leveson family, who were local landowners at that time. It stands in the grounds of the Hall that has now been turned into the National Sports Centre, which is where the English team trained before winning the World Cup in 1966.

In 2 miles turn left on to the B4379, then turn right, SP 'London'. Later cross the A41 to join the B5314. In another 2 miles turn left on to the A5, then take the next turning right on to an unclassified road and pass the entrance to Weston Park.

WESTON PARK, Staffs

This Classical 17th-century house (OACT) has been the family home of the Earls of Bradford for 300 years. The rooms are mainly of 18th and 19th-century inspiration, and the tapestry room, lined with rose-pink Gobelin tapestries, is particularly notable. However, the real treasure of Weston is the magnificent collection of paintings, which includes portraits of the Bradfords and works by leading Dutch, Italian and French masters.

Continue along the unclassified road to Tong.

TONG, Shrops

Thatched cottages, a distant mock-castle, wooded slopes and an ancient church give Tong its charm and character. When Charles Dickens wrote *The Old Curiosity Shop* he had this village in mind as the final haven of Little Nell and her grandfather. The red sandstone church, with unusual battlements, has one of the most splendid arrays of monuments in the Midlands. Many are of Lady Elizabeth Pembruge — who founded the church in the early 15th century — and her husband. Others include effigies of the Vernon family, including Sir Richard, Speaker of the House of Commons in 1428.

The Shropshire Union Canal at Gnosall, which links the Mersey to the Severn

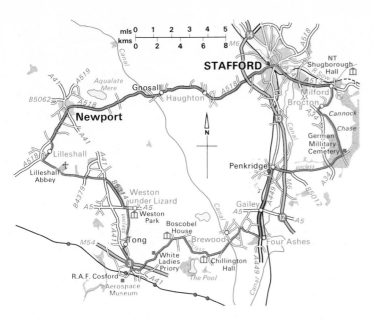

At the church turn left, then shortly turn left again on to the A41. In almost 1 mile, at the start of the dual-carriageway, turn left on to an unclassified road (no SP). Alternatively, turn right to visit the Aerospace Museum.

AEROSPACE MUSEUM, Shrops
Two hangars within the grounds of Cosford RAF station house the museum. One hangar concentrates on rockets, ranging from the earliest German model to more modern ones. The other hangar has over 50 aircraft, including a World War II Lincoln Bomber which is being meticulously restored by teams of volunteers. Here too is a prototype of the TSR2 — a new fighter-plane which Harold Wilson cancelled because it was costing too much money. Each exhibit has a placard describing its history, and outside there are picnic sites and a souvenir shop.

The main tour later joins a narrow byroad, SP 'Shackley', and continues to Boscobel House.

BOSCOBEL HOUSE, Shrops
Built in 1600 for the Roman Catholic Gifford family, Boscobel House (AM) was amply provided with secret hiding places to shelter priests, and it was here that Charles II, defeated and weary, found refuge in 1651 after the Battle of Worcester. Hunted high and low by soldiers, he spent the day in an oak tree near the house hidden by the loyal Penderel family, who were Boscobel's tenants. The present oak tree, although ancient, is not the original, but grew from one of its acorns. Whiteladies nearby, is a ruined 12th-century nunnery where the king also sheltered from pursuit.

At the T-junction turn right, then branch left on to another byroad (no SP). In ¾ mile turn right and 1¼ miles farther pass (right) Chillington Hall.

CHILLINGTON HALL, Staffs
For 800 years, Chillington Hall (OACT) has belonged to the Gifford family through direct male descent, but it was not until 1724 that Peter Gifford began to build the existing redbrick mansion. He demolished part of the Tudor house and bought in Francis Smith of Warwick as the architect. Later, in about 1750, Sir John Soane built the east front and one of the most interesting rooms is Soane's saloon, which replaced the Tudor great hall. It has an oval ceiling which leads up to an oval lantern and over the chimneypiece is the Gifford family arms. Capability Brown landscaped the grounds in the 18th century and formed the beautiful ornamental lake that occupies 75 acres.

After passing the main gateway turn left then in 1 mile turn left again. In ¾ mile go over the crossroads, SP 'Four Ashes', then in another ¾ mile, at the T-junction, turn left. At the next T-junction turn right and cross the river bridge then turn right again, still SP 'Four Ashes'. In 1¼ miles turn left on to the A449, SP 'Stafford', then at the Gailey roundabout take the 2nd exit and continue to Penkridge.

PENKRIDGE, Staffs
Of the several pleasing old buildings in this quiet little town near the River Penk, the old stone and timber deanery, dating from the 16th century is the most outstanding. The large parish church is packed with interesting monuments and was once the collegiate church of the area which maintained a dean and 4 canons. North of the church is the timber-framed Old Deanery.

At Penkridge turn right on to the unclassified road, SP 'Cannock', then turn right again. Cross the M6 then in ½ mile turn left, SP 'Rugeley'. In 2 miles cross the A34 and enter Cannock Chase.

CANNOCK CHASE, Staffs
Conifers, silver birches, heathland and little valleys cover a wide area of countryside that was for centuries the royal hunting forest of Cannock Chase. Fallow deer, descendants of the vast herds that roamed the Chase in medieval and Tudor times, graze among the surviving areas of oakwood, and in marshy areas the rare sundew flourishes. Soaring up above the treeline, the Post Office tower looks down on the German Military cemetary where the dead of 2 wars lie buried, including the crew of the first Zeppelin shot down in World War I.

At the next crossroads turn left, SP 'Brocton' and 'Stafford', and pass the German Military cemetary. Descend to the A34 and turn right. In ¼ mile, at the crossroads, turn right into Brocton, then continue to Milford. From here a short diversion to the right along the A513 leads to Shugborough Hall.

SHUGBOROUGH HALL, Staffs
The white, colonnaded mansion (NT) set in beautiful grounds has been the home of the Anson family, Earls of Lichfield, since the 17th century. The fortune of

The dining room fireplace and a portrait of Admiral Lord Anson at Shugborough

George Anson, the celebrated admiral and circumnavigator of the world, paid for much of the splendour of house and park. Mementoes of the admiral's voyages and victories are an outstanding feature of the house, which also contains fine paintings and 18th-century furniture. In the park, the flamboyant Triumphal Arch, modelled on that of the Emperor Hadrian at Athens, commemorates Admiral Anson's victory over the French in 1747. Other particularly charming features are the elegant little Tower of the Winds and, on an island in the lake, the Cat's Monument in memory of a favourite pet of the Admiral that sailed round the world with him. The Staffordshire County Museum and Farm Park are also contained in the grounds of Shugborough Hall. Museum exhibits include social history, crafts and agricultural subjects, and the park has rare farm livestock.

The main tour leaves Milford on the A513 and later joins the A34 for the return to Stafford.

STAFFORDSHIRE'S VALLEYS

Three valleys, Dovedale, the Manifold and the Churnet, offer some of the loveliest scenery to be found anywhere England. Often, and unfairly, dismissed for the industrial sprawl of the Potteries, the countryside of north Staffordshire changes from a patchwork of small, hedged fields to the bleak grandeur of the open moors.

A piece of 'jasperware' pottery made by Wedgwood in Stoke-on-Trent

STOKE-ON-TRENT, Staffs

In 1910, the towns known as the Potteries — Hanley, Burslem, Tunstall, Fenton, and Longton — were amalgamated and named Stoke-on-Trent. Pots dating from before the Roman era have been discovered in the area, but the great English porcelain companies, Wedgwood, Minton, Spode and Doulton, were all established in the late-18th and early-19th centuries. Most of the factories organise conducted tours and the Gladstone Pottery Museum in Longton, with its carefully restored and preserved traditional bottle-shaped kilns has practical demonstrations of the craft as well as exhibitions. Hanley's City Museum contains one of the finest collections of pottery and porcelain in the world. Novelist Arnold Bennet, who wrote books about the Potteries, or 5 Towns was born in Hanley in 1867. Drawings, manuscripts, letters and other relics of the writer can be seen in the City Museum. Another native of the Potteries represented in the museum is the aeronautical engineer R J Mitchell who designed the first 'Spitfire' aeroplane in 1936 which became famous as a World War II fighter. Also near Cobridge is Ford Green Hall (OACT), a 16th-century timber-framed mansion built for the Fords, a family of yeoman farmers, which contains English furniture and domestic items of the 16th to 18th centuries. Some idea of the development of mining technology can be gained from the Chatterley Whitfield Mining Museum near Tunstall. Guided tours take you 700ft below the ground around the workings and there is a colliery lamphouse exhibition and museum

From the city centre at Hanley follow SP 'Burslem A50', and in ¾ mile turn right on to the A53. Pass through Baddeley Green and Endon then in 1¼ miles turn left, SP 'Rudyard', into Dunwood Lane, and continue for 2½ miles to Rudyard.

RUDYARD, Staffs

This charming little village was made famous by the parents of the novelist and poet Rudyard Kipling, whom they named after the place where they had spent many holidays, and where it is said Lockwood Kipling proposed to Alice Macdonald. The lake lies in a deep wooded valley surrounded by high moors, and along the shores of the nearby reservoir are pleasant walks, with picnic sites.

Turn right on to the B5331. In 1 mile, at the T-junction, turn right on to the A523 then take the next turning left, SP 'Meerbrook'. In ½ mile turn left again and later skirt Tittesworth Reservoir before reaching Meerbrook.

MEERBROOK, Staffs

A lonely village surrounded by bleak moorland, Meerbrook lies in the shadow of Hen Cloud (1,250ft). Nearby are the Staffordshire Roaches, a forbidding outcrop of dark millstone grit rocks rising to 1,658ft which have been weathered over the ages into fantastic shapes.

Turn right at the church, SP 'Blackshaw Moor' and 'Leek' and in 1¼ miles turn left on to the A531. In 2 miles go forward over a crossroads then turn right, SP 'Longnor'. A long descent leads to the Manifold valley and Longnor.

LONGNOR, Staffs

Longnor is the market centre of the far north of Staffordshire, a charming stone-built place surrounded by superb hill scenery, whose narrow streets and alleys end abruptly in magnificent views of the Peak District.

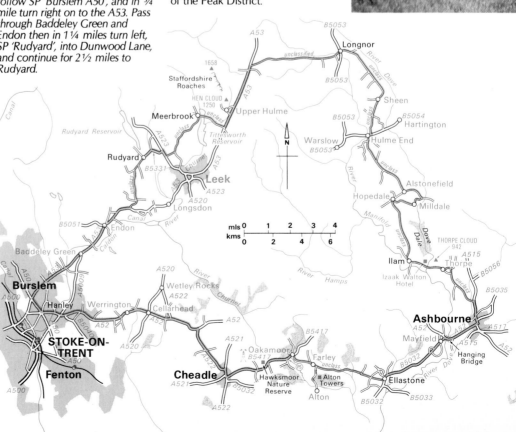

Dovedale's alpine scenery has earned it the title Little Switzerland

Follow SP 'Bakewell' and in ½ mile branch right, SP 'Hulme End'. Continue, through Sheen, then in 1½ miles turn right on to the B5054 into Hulme End, and at the Light Railway Hotel turn left on to the unclassified road for Alstonefield. Here keep left, SP 'Ashbourne', and in 1¼ miles turn sharp right (care needed) SP 'Milldale'. At Milldale, turn right and ascend a narrow gorge to Hopedale. At the Watts Russell Arms turn left, SP 'Ilam', and in 100 yds turn left again. After 2 miles descend into Ilam.

ILAM, Staffs
Ilam owes its delightful and unique appearance to the 19th-century manufacturer Jesse Watts Russell, who bought the village and estate. The cottages he built are completely different in design from the traditional Staffordshire style, with steep-pitched, gabled roofs covered with dark red, shaped tiles. Ilam Hall is now a youth hostel, but the spacious park in the lower reaches of the Manifold valley belongs to the National Trust.

At the war memorial turn left, SP 'Dovedale, Thorpe'. In ¾ mile, by the entrance to the Izaak Walton Hotel, a short detour can be made by turning left to reach a car park at the entrance to Dovedale (reached on foot).

DOVEDALE, Staffs
Dovedale, at the southern edge of the Peak District National Park, is one of the most beautiful valleys in England. The River Dove, the boundary between Staffordshire and Derbyshire, runs through a deep, wooded limestone gorge, where high white cliffs,

Below: 150 years ago Alton Towers was no more than a bare and rocky wasteland

honeycombed with caves, have been weathered into distinctive shapes — the 12 Apostles, Dovedale Castle, Lion's Head, and so on. At the southern end of the valley, annual sheepdog trials draw crowds at the end of August from all over the region.

Cross the River Dove into Derbyshire then skirt the village of Thorpe and in ½ mile, at the Dog and Partridge Hotel, turn right, SP 'Ashbourne'. In 2 miles turn right on to the A515 to enter Ashbourne.

ASHBOURNE, Derbys
Ashbourne has some fine architecture, particularly in Church Street, where 2 sets of almshouses, an Elizabethan grammar school, a mansion house and an old inn make a pleasing group. The parish church, St Oswald's, is considered one of the best examples of Early English style in the North Midlands. Ashbourne holds a traditional football game on Shrove Tuesday, when the inhabitants of the 2 banks of Henmore Brook compete in a riotous game with few rules and unlimited numbers. The locally famous Ashbourne gingerbread is still made to a secret recipe, taught to the town's bakers by French soldiers held prisoner during the Napoleonic Wars.

Leave on the A52, SP 'Uttoxeter (B5032)', and in 1½ miles cross the Hanging Bridge.

HANGING BRIDGE, Staffs
The Hanging Bridge leads the way from Derbyshire across the River Dove to the small stone-built village of Mayfield, clinging to the Staffordshire bank. The name is said to commemorate the hanging of Jacobite supporters of Bonnie Prince Charlie in 1745 — his army had reached Derby on the march south, but then retreated back to Scotland. Records show, however, that the name is much older than the 18th century.

Beyond the bridge turn immediately left on to the B5032. Continue through Mayfield following the Dove valley, to reach Ellastone.

ELLASTONE, Staffs
Robert Evans, father of the novelist George Eliot (Mary Ann Evans), worked as a carpenter here for a time, and the village features in her novel *Adam Bede* under the name Hayslope. Not far from the village, Wootton Lodge (not open) looks out over the Churnet valley. A tall, graceful building, it is one of the finest examples of Jacobean architecture in the county.

Turn left in the village then in ¼ mile turn right on to an unclassified road. In ½ mile go forward over crossroads and in another ½ mile turn left. In 1½ miles, at the edge of Farley, a detour can be made by turning left, 'SP 'Alton', for Alton Towers.

ALTON TOWERS, Staffs
The 15th Earl of Shrewsbury, whose family had acquired vast estates in Staffordshire, came to Alton in the early 19th century and fell in love with the rugged scenery of the Churnet valley. The 600-acre gardens of Alton Towers (OACT) are the result of his work. Thousands of trees and flowering shrubs — rhododendrons, azaleas, Japanese maple, cedars, dwarf and giant conifers, tulip trees — cover the hillsides and set off a series of gardens, ornamental ponds and fountains, connected by winding paths designed to offer an ever-changing succession of views. Soaring above the gardens, the towers and pinnacles of Alton Towers seem like something from a fairy tale. Most of the house, built by the 16th Earl, is just a shell, but the chapel, with its splendid roof designed by the Victorian architect, Pugin, is intact and now houses a superb model railway. Other modern innovations include a miniature scenic railway, an aerial cable car and numerous amusements for children.

The main tour continues into Farley. At the end of the village turn left, SP 'Oakmoor', and in 1 mile turn left again on to the B5417. Cross the River Churnet into Oakmoor and later pass (right) the Hawksmoor Nature Reserve.

HAWKSMOOR NATURE RESERVE, Staffs
This part of the Churnet valley, between Oakmoor and Cheadle, was presented to the National Trust in 1926 by J. R. B. Masefield, a well-known Staffordshire naturalist and cousin of the poet John Masefield. Several rare varieties of tree, such as the lodge pole pine and the red oak flourish alongside the native plants, and many birds — curlews, pheasants, redstarts, nightjars and warblers — have found refuge in the woodland. Nature trails are well marked.

Continue on the B5417 to Cheadle.

CHEADLE, Staffs
High moorland surrounds this small market with a high street of pleasant 18th-century and Victorian buildings, but dominating it all is the massive Roman Catholic church whose lofty spire (200ft) is a landmark for miles around. The church was built in 1846 by Pugin and is regarded as one of his masterpieces. The interior is a magnificent tableau of rich colour, creating an atmosphere of 19th-century opulence.

At the town centre turn right on to the A522, SP 'Leek', and in 2¼ miles turn left on to the A52 for Cellarhead, Werrington and Bucknall. At the traffic signals beyond Bucknall turn right, then at the next traffic signals go forward on the A5008 for the return to Hanley (Stoke-on-Trent).

SHAKESPEARE AND THE HEART OF ENGLAND

Among the winding lanes of Warwickshire and Worcestershire a wealth of timber, thatch and stone, seen in country cottage, village church and stately home, revives the atmosphere of Tudor England. From the interplay of forest and farmland, garden and park, Shakespeare drew the stirring imagery of his writing.

STRATFORD-UPON-AVON, Warwicks

Sir Hugh Clopton's 14-arched medieval stone bridge is still, as it has been since Shakespeare's day, the main gateway to Stratford. The house in Henley Street, where the poet was born on 23 April 1564, is a substantial timber-framed building preserved by the Shakespeare Birthplace Trust (OACT) as a museum, but the house he bought after becoming successful, New Place, was wantonly destroyed by an 18th-century owner. The foundations remain, however, and a delightful Elizabethan knot garden has been planted on the site. Hall's Croft, where the poet's daughter Susanna lived with her husband, Dr John Hall, contains a fascinating collection of Elizabethan medical implements. The most elaborate timbered house in Stratford is Harvard House, built in 1596 by the grandparents of John Harvard, who sailed to America, and on his death left £799 17s 2d with which to found Harvard University. The Royal Shakespeare Theatre, built in 1932, dominates the riverside, striking a startlingly modern note amid the old buildings of the town. It incorporates a museum and art gallery. Holy Trinity Church is Shakespeare's burial place: he died in 1616 and lies under the chancel with Susanna and John Hall. As a change from the Shakespearean connections of Stratford, the Motor Museum is a superb evocation of 1920s motoring history, specialising in sports and touring cars. There are several gardens laid out on the banks of the Avon which provide a welcome respite from the bustle of the town.

Leave Stratford on the A439, SP 'Evesham'. After ½ mile a short detour to the right may be taken along Shottery Road to the hamlet of Shottery.

The Tudor gatehouse of Coughton Court dominates the 18th-century west front that was built around it

SHOTTERY, Warwicks

Tourists flock to this pretty little hamlet across the fields from Stratford to see the idyllic thatched and timbered cottage (OACT) where Anne Hathaway lived and where Shakespeare came to woo her. Original Tudor furniture and fascinating domestic items are displayed in the old rooms. The Hathaway family lived in the house from 1470 until 1911, when it was acquired by the Shakespeare Birthplace Trust.

The main tour continues on the A439 along the shallow valley of the River Avon and later skirts Bidford-on-Avon.

A fascinating array of rural bygones can be seen in the barns belonging to Mary Arden's cottage in Wilmcote

BIDFORD-ON-AVON, Warwicks

Shakespeare's connection with Bidford was the Falcon Inn, a handsome gabled building which still stands, though it is now a private house. The poet is known to have enjoyed many a drinking bout at the Falcon, and is popularly supposed to have composed the 4 lines of doggerel that end: 'Dodging Exhall, Papist Wixford, Beggarly Broom and drunken Bidford'.

Remain on the Evesham road and in 3 miles turn right on to an unclassified road to enter Harvington. Here turn right, SP 'The Lenches', then at the end of the village cross the main road and continue to Church Lench.

THE LENCHES, Herefs & Worcs

Five villages with the name Lench are dotted about the countryside north of Evesham, and 2 of them, Church and Rous Lench, lie on the route. Lench comes from an old English word meaning 'hill', and this part of the country, near the old Warwickshire border is an area of little hills. Each has a distinctive charm, but Rous Lench is perhaps the most interesting

At Church Lench turn right to reach Rous Lench. Continue on the Inkberrow road and in 1 mile, at the T-junction, turn right, SP 'Alcester'. In another 1½ miles turn left for Abbots Morton.

ABBOTS MORTON, Herefs & Worcs

Often described as the most perfect village in the country, Abbots Morton is rich in black and white timbered cottages of all shapes and sizes. Its lovely 14th-century stone church stands surrounded by trees on a small mound overlooking the village, while on the green stands a thatched letterbox.

Bear right into the village and ¾ mile further, at the T-junction, turn left. In 1½ miles turn right on to the A441, then in another ½ mile, turn left on to the A435, SP 'Birmingham'. Later pass the entrance to Ragley Hall.

RAGLEY HALL, Warwicks

A stately Jacobean mansion of 15 bays, built between 1680 and 1690 by Robert Hooks for the 1st Earl of Conway, Ragley Hall (OACT) is one of the finest houses in England. Much of the sumptuous interior, however, was designed in the 18th century by James Gibbs for the 2nd Baron Conway, later created Earl, the Marquess of Hertford. Showpiece of the house is the great hall, 70ft long, 40ft wide and 40ft high, decorated with exquisite rococo plasterwork. Paintings by great European masters such as Reynolds and Hoppner, and collections of fine porcelain are on display.

Continue to Alcester.

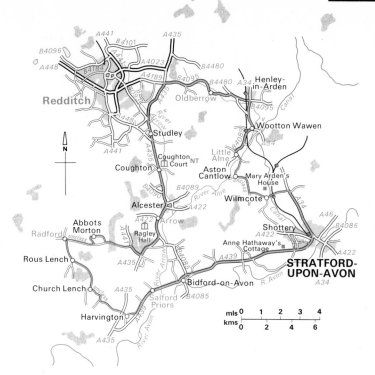

Malt Mill Lane in Alcester is lined by a remarkable collection of ancient houses which were renovated in 1975

ALCESTER, Warwicks
This attractive little market town (pronounced Olster) lies at the confluence of the Rivers Arrow and Alne. Its oldest building is the Old Malt House, a gabled, half timbered structure dating from 1500, but the narrow streets contain many charming Jacobean and Georgian houses; Butter Street in particular is a delight, with its rows of picturesque old cottages. Tudor cottages cluster about the parish church with its 14th-century west tower, the nave and aisles having been rebuilt in the 18th-century. It contains the fine alabaster tomb of Fulke Greville, the grandfather of the Elizabethan poet who was his namesake. Alcester Mop is a pleasure fair held in the town each October.

Leave on the A435 Birmingham road and continue to Coughton.

COUGHTON, Warwicks
The influence of the Throckmortons predominates in the 16th-century church, where monuments and brasses commemorate generations of this staunchly Roman Catholic family. Coughton Court (NT) was the family home, its Tudor stone gatehouse flanked by warm-toned stucco giving entrance to a courtyard with 2 timbered wings. As befits a Roman Catholic house, there is a hidden chapel, reached by a rope ladder, in one of the turrets, and many Jacobite relics. The Throckmortons were implicated in the 1605 Gunpowder Plot, and it was at Coughton that the family and friends of the conspirators waited anxiously for news. In the saloon is the famous Throckmorton coat, made for a bet in 1811 from wool sheared at sunrise and woven into a coat by sunset of the same day.

Continue through Studley.

STUDLEY, Warwicks
Pleasant countryside surrounds this small town which is possibly the largest centre of needle-making in Europe. Since 1800, when steam power was introduced, the industry has been mechanised, but the tradition goes back for more than 300 years, and there are many old houses dating from the 17th century.

At the end of the town go forward at the roundabout, SP 'Birmingham'. Nearly 2 miles farther turn right on to the B4095 and continue to Henley-in-Arden.

HENLEY-IN-ARDEN, Warwicks
Once, as the last part of the name suggests, Henley lay in the great Forest of Arden. Its ¾ mile-long broad main street is bordered by timbered houses and inns of all periods and makes a charming picture. Many of the inns date from the great coaching age of the 18th-century when Henley was served daily by a mail coach and 4 post coaches.

Leave on the A34 Stratford Road to reach Wootton Wawen.

WOOTTON WAWEN, Warwicks
The fine village church exhibits features of almost every style of English architecture, from Anglo-Danish to the late Middle Ages. Parts of the crossing tower are the most ancient, but there are examples of Norman, early English, Decorated and Perpendicular styles as well as features of the 17th, 18th and 19th centuries. The village is attractive, with a graceful 17th-century hall (not open) which was the childhood home of Mrs Fitzherbert whom the Prince Regent, later George IV, loved and with whom he illegally contracted a secret marriage in 1785.

Leave on the B4089 Alcester Road. In 2 miles branch left, SP 'Aston Cantlow'. Cross the river bridge and turn right for Aston Cantlow.

Ragley Hall commands sweeping views over its parkland to the distant Cotswolds

ASTON CANTLOW, Warwicks
This church is very probably the one in which John Shakespeare and Mary Arden, Shakespeare's parents, were married in 1557, though the church records begin only in 1560. The Victorian architect William Butterfield designed the pretty cottages, vicarage, school and master's house near the church, and the rest of the village is a pleasing mixture of black and white timbered houses offset by terraces of red brick. The name Cantlow comes from the Cantelupe family, and Thomas Cantelupe, rector of the village church later became Chancellor of England and Bishop of Hereford. In 1282 he died while on pilgrimage to Rome and was subsequently (1320) canonized, the only Warwickshire rector to be so honoured and the last Englishman to be canonized until after the Reformation.

Go forward through the village, then turn left, SP 'Wilmcote'. In 1 mile turn left again for Wilmcote.

WILMCOTE, Warwicks
The highlight of Wilmcote is the lovely timbered farmhouse that was the home of Mary Arden, Shakespeare's mother. Simply furnished, in period, the old timbered house, surrounded by a charming old-fashioned cottage garden, retains a strong sense of atmosphere, enhanced by the collection of old Warwickshire agricultural implements housed in the stone barns belonging to the house (OACT).

Turn left, SP 'Stratford', then in 1 mile turn right on to the A34 for the return to Stratford-upon-Avon.

WARWICK, Warwicks

Imposing Warwick Castle is one of the finest medieval strongholds in Europe. It stands on a Saxon site above this compact River Avon town, and its exceptional Norman and later structure hides an interior completely rebuilt during the 17th century. The castle is still occupied, but visitors have access to the state rooms, torture chamber, silver vault, ghost tower, and Avon-side grounds that were landscaped by Capability Brown. Also in the town are the remains of town walls, two gates, and a great number of building styles ranging from half-timbered to the conscious starkness of the 20th century. Lord Leycester's Hospital was founded as a guildhall in 1383 and converted to almshouses in 1571 (open), and the 18th-century Shire Hall is considered an excellent example of its type. Elizabeth Oken's House contains a Doll Museum, and 17th-century St John's House features both a museum of crafts, costume, and furniture, and the Museum of the Royal Warwickshire Regiment. The 18th-century Court House is an Italianate building.

Leave Warwick on the A425 'Banbury' road and continue for 2¼ miles to join the A41. Proceed for 1¼ miles and turn right on to the B4087 SP 'Wellesbourne'. Continue to Wellesbourne.

A magnificent collection of armour is housed in Warwick Castle.

WELLESBOURNE, Warwicks

Georgian houses and a Hall dating from c1700 are the main features of this pleasant village.

Follow SP 'Stratford B4086' for 1 mile and turn right on to the B4088 SP 'Charlecote' to reach the village of Charlecote.

CHARLECOTE, Warwicks

Charlecote Park (NT) is a fine Elizabethan house with a great hall and museum. The Avon flows through grounds where Shakespeare is said to have been caught poaching deer. Attractive old cottages survive in the village.

In Charlecote turn left on to the unclassified 'Hampton Lucy' road and cross the River Avon. Continue to Hampton Lucy.

SHAKESPEARE COUNTRY

England's heartlands are watered by the Avon and Stour, great rivers that wind through charming Elizabethan villages, country estates graced by stately houses, and historic towns where Shakespeare drew inspiration from the comedy and tragedy in the lives of his contemporaries.

The River Avon formed an essential aspect of Warwick Castle's defences.

HAMPTON LUCY, Warwicks

Of particular interest here is a cast-iron bridge that was built in 1829.

On entering Hampton Lucy bear left SP 'Stratford'. Proceed for 1¼ miles, bear left again, and in ¾ mile turn left on to the A46 for Stratford.

STRATFORD-UPON-AVON, Warwicks

William Shakespeare was born here in 1564. His childhood home contains a museum relating to his life, and the old Guildhall that housed his school still stands. A picturesque Elizabethan knot garden can be seen near the foundations of New Place, where he died, and his remains lie in Holy Trinity Church. A lovely thatched and timbered cottage (open) in the nearby village of Shottery is where his wife Anne Hathaway was born, and gabled Hall's Croft (open) was the home of their daughter Susanna. Many of the great man's works are staged in the Royal Shakespeare Theatre, which was built on an Avon-side site in 1932; it incorporates a museum and picture gallery (open). Among many 15th- and 16th-century buildings preserved in the town are several lovely half-timbered houses and the 14-arch Clopton Bridge over the Avon. Harvard House was the home of the grandparents of John Harvard, founder of the US university of the same name. The World of Shakespeare specializes in scenes from Elizabethan England, the Motor Museum preserves a number of veteran and vintage cars, and an Arms and Armour museum exhibits some 800 pieces.

Leave the town by the A34 'Oxford' road and later pass Alscot Park to the right. Proceed to Alderminster.

ALDERMINSTER, Warwicks

Views across the Stour valley to Meon Hill and the Cotswolds can be enjoyed from the 13th-century church here.

The Guildhall schoolroom, where the poet and dramatist William Shakespeare took his first steps in learning.

Remain on the A34 to reach Newbold-upon-Stour. At the end of that village turn right on to an unclassified road and drive to Armscote. Turn right and continue to Ilmington.

ILMINGTON, Warwicks

Situated at the east foot of the Cotswolds, this village has several picturesque cottages and an old tithe barn. The rectory and manor house both date from the 16th century. Above the village is 854ft Ilmington Down, one of the highest points in Warwickshire.

Turn left and follow SP 'Campden' to climb Ilmington Down. Descend, meet crossroads, and turn left to reach Ebrington.

EBRINGTON, Glos

Delightful stone and thatched cottages complement a church with a fine Norman doorway in this lovely Cotswold village.

Join the B4035 and drive to Shipston-on-Stour.

SHIPSTON-ON-STOUR, Warwicks

Once one of the most important sheep markets in the country, this mainly Georgian town lies at the edge of the Vale of Red Horse.

Follow SP 'Banbury', cross the River Stour, and proceed for ¾ mile to crossroads. Turn left on to the unclassified 'Honington' road, then in ¾ mile turn right SP 'Tysoe' and proceed for 2¾ miles. Meet crossroads and drive forward. In ¾ mile a detour from the main route can be made by turning right to reach Compton Wynyates.

COMPTON WYNYATES, Warwicks

The estate in which this exceptional Tudor house stands has been in the same family since the 13th century. Sir William Compton built the magnificent red-brick extravagance that stands here today, and the interior has remained largely unaltered since Tudor times (not open). Close to the house the wild hillside parkland has been cultivated as a modern topiary garden.

Continue to Upper Tysoe.

UPPER TYSOE, Warwicks

One of a trio of villages named from the Norse God Tiw, this little place has a 16th-century manor house and stands in the Vale of Red Horse. The Vale itself derives its name from a turf-cut figure on Rising Hill, due east of Lower Tysoe. Until 1800 this was scoured annually, but it is now scarcely visible.

In Upper Tysoe turn left SP 'Kineton', then right SP 'Shenington' and 'Banbury'. Ascend Tysoe Hill, meet crossroads, and turn left to follow the ridge of Edgehill. Continue for 2 miles and drive forward on to the A422. A short detour from the main route can be made by continuing on the A422 for ½ mile to Upton House.

The superb Tudor architecture of Compton Wynyates.

Anne Hathaway's Cottage at Shottery.

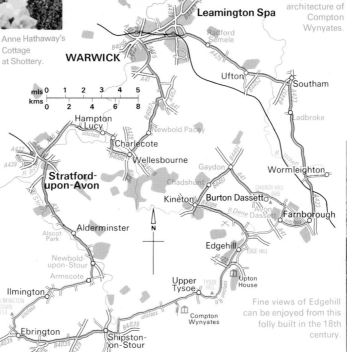

Fine views of Edgehill can be enjoyed from this folly built in the 18th century.

UPTON HOUSE, Warwicks

Good views can be enjoyed from the lovely terraced gardens of this impressive 17th-century house (NT). Inside are collections of porcelain, pictures, and various pieces of 18th-century furniture.

On the main route, continue for $\frac{1}{4}$ mile after joining the A422 and bear left on to an unclassified road for Edgehill village.

EDGEHILL, Warwicks

An 18th-century folly which now forms part of a pub in the village affords extensive views over the countryside. North, on private ground by the B4086, is the field where the first major battle of the Civil War was fought in 1642. Here the horizon is dominated by the attractively wooded 700ft ridge of Edgehill, which extends for 3 miles.

Leave Edgehill village and in 1 mile bear left on to the B4086 SP 'Kineton'. Descend to Kineton with the Edgehill battlefield to the left.

KINETON, Warwicks

Near Kineton station are the remains of a motte and bailey castle, and $\frac{3}{4}$ mile north west is a sail-less tower windmill. The church has a splendid 13th-century doorway.

Turn right on to the B4451 SP 'Southam' and proceed to Gaydon. Turn right on to the A41 SP 'Banbury'. Proceed for 2 miles and turn left on to the unclassified 'Fenny Compton' road, then keep forward SP 'Burton Hills'. Ascend the Burton Hills (a country park) and pass the isolated village of Burton Dassett to the right.

BURTON DASSETT, Warwicks

Church Hill rises to 689ft above this pretty village and is surmounted by a lookout tower that may once have been part of a medieval windmill. The hill's summit, used as a beacon site during the Battle of Edgehill in 1642, is now a country park.

Continue for 1 mile to reach crossroads and turn right to descend to Avon Dassett. Drive to the end of the village and keep forward. Enter Farnborough.

FARNBOROUGH, Warwicks

Notable Farnborough Hall (NT) dates from the 17th and 18th centuries and features excellent rococo stucco-work with panels of scrolls, rays, shells, fruit and flowers. Delightful grounds include landscaped terraced lawns which afford superb views to the ridge of Edgehill. A classical air is given the gardens by a small Ionic temple and an oval pavilion.

Keep left through Farnborough and at the end of the village turn left on to the A423 SP 'Coventry'. In 2 miles it is possible to make a detour from the main route to Wormleighton by turning right on to an unclassified road.

WORMLEIGHTON, Warwicks

Prince Rupert slept at Wormleighton Manor the night before he gave battle to parliamentarian cavalry at Edgehill. The reputedly lovely house was destroyed later in the Civil War, but the imposing gateway survives, complete with its carved crests.

On the main route, proceed on the A423 to the edge of Southam.

SOUTHAM, Warwicks

At one time this ancient town was famed for a mineral spring and healing well which were both claimed to have wide-ranging medicinal powers. The Reverend Holyoake, a rector of the local 15th- and 16th-century church, compiled the first dictionary of the English language.

At the edge of Southam turn left on to the A425 SP 'Leamington' to reach Ufton.

UFTON, Warwicks

Views from this 380ft-high village extend beyond the ancient Fosse Way and River Avon to the distant Malvern Hills, known for their mineral springs. Inside the village church, which dates from the 13th century but has been extensively restored since, is a good 16th-century memorial brass.

Continue and pass through Radford Semele to reach Leamington Spa.

LEAMINGTON SPA, Warwicks

In the 18th century it was claimed that mineral springs in this lovely old town were beneficial in the treatment of various complaints. As the high-society fashion for taking the waters blossomed so also did Leamington, and today it boasts many grand old buildings that recall the prosperity of those times. The Pump Room of 1814, rebuilt in 1925, is an excellent focus for the terraces of Regency, Georgian, and Victorian houses that grace the streets around it. Between the buildings are wide parks and open spaces, the carefully tended Jephson Gardens, and the vagrant windings of the River Lea. The Warwick Art Gallery and Museum exhibits a good selection of paintings and examples of 18th-century glass.

Continue along the A425 and return to Warwick.

Key to Town Plans

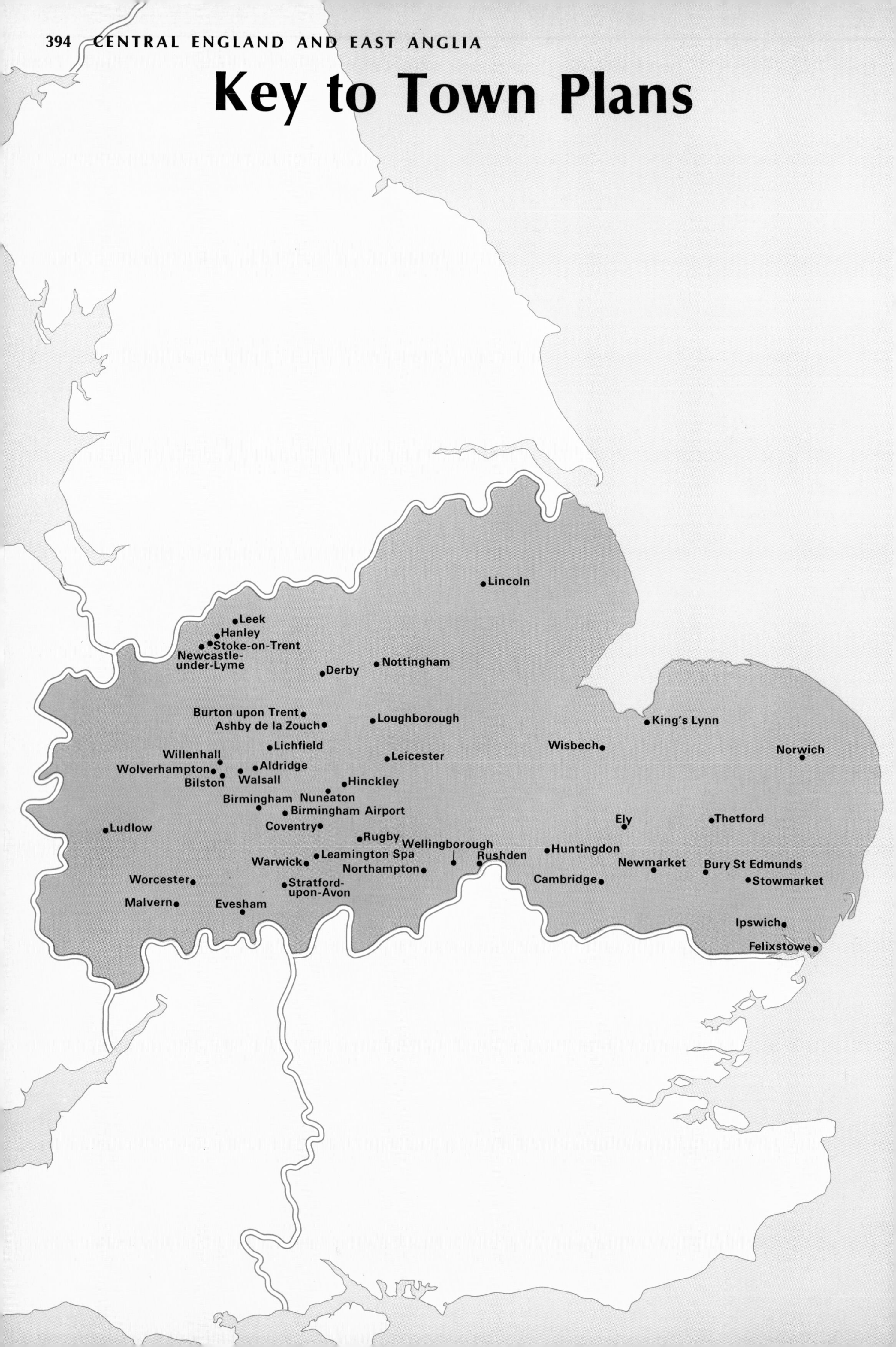

Lincoln

Leek
Hanley
Stoke-on-Trent
Newcastle-
under-Lyme

Derby

Nottingham

Burton upon Trent
Ashby de la Zouch

Loughborough

King's Lynn

Lichfield

Leicester

Wisbech

Norwich

Willenhall
Wolverhampton
Bilston

Aldridge
Walsall

Hinckley

Birmingham Nuneaton
Birmingham Airport

Ely

Thetford

Ludlow

Coventry

Rugby

Wellingborough

Huntingdon

Warwick

Leamington Spa

Rushden

Newmarket

Bury St Edmunds

Northampton

Cambridge

Stowmarket

Worcester

Stratford-
upon-Avon

Malvern

Evesham

Ipswich

Felixstowe

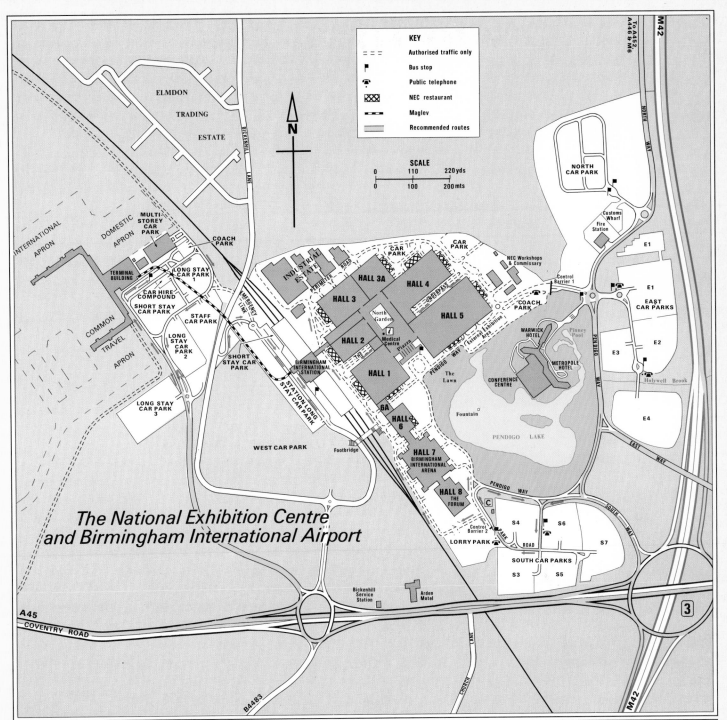

The National Exhibition Centre and Birmingham International Airport

KEY

- = = = Authorised traffic only
- Bus stop
- Public telephone
- NEC restaurant
- Maglev
- Recommended routes

SCALE

0 — 110 — 220 yds
0 — 100 — 200 mts

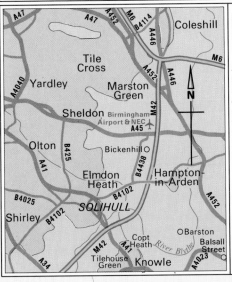

Birmingham International Airport and NEC

Situated just nine miles east of the city, Birmingham International Airport is a short distance from the M6 and M42 motorways, and provides quick and easy access from most parts of the country. This is a popular embarkation point for charter flights to a wide range of European holiday destinations, and it also provides a comprehensive network of scheduled flights to many British and European destinations.

A special viewing area with its own shop and buffet is situated on the third level, with its own access at the front of the terminal building. The airport's choice of buffets and licensed bars also includes the 150-seater Landside Restaurant, and all of them are open to the general public as well as to passengers. Multi-storey and surface car parking is available, while Birmingham International Station offers an 80-minute rail link

with London (Euston), and connections to other British cities. The airport is also the site of the Maglev transit system, which sweeps travellers in 90 seconds from the three-storey airport terminal to the Birmingham International Railway Station, and to the National Exhibition Centre. The Maglev has three unmanned cars (each taking up to 32 passengers with their luggage), suspended by magnetic levitation 15mm above guidance tracks and driven without friction by linear induction motors, along a 600 metre elevated track.

National Exhibition Centre The new centre was opened by HM the Queen in February 1976 and lies about eight miles east of Birmingham city centre. The 10 exhibition halls have an interior area of 105,085 square metres and the landscaped setting covers 310 acres. The central feature of the complex — the Piazza — has shops, banks, medical and visitor services, including the Birmingham Convention and Visitor Bureau. The International Area is a multi-purpose hall for conventions, concerts and sporting events, with seating for up to 12,000, and the Forum is designed specifically for presentations and product launches.

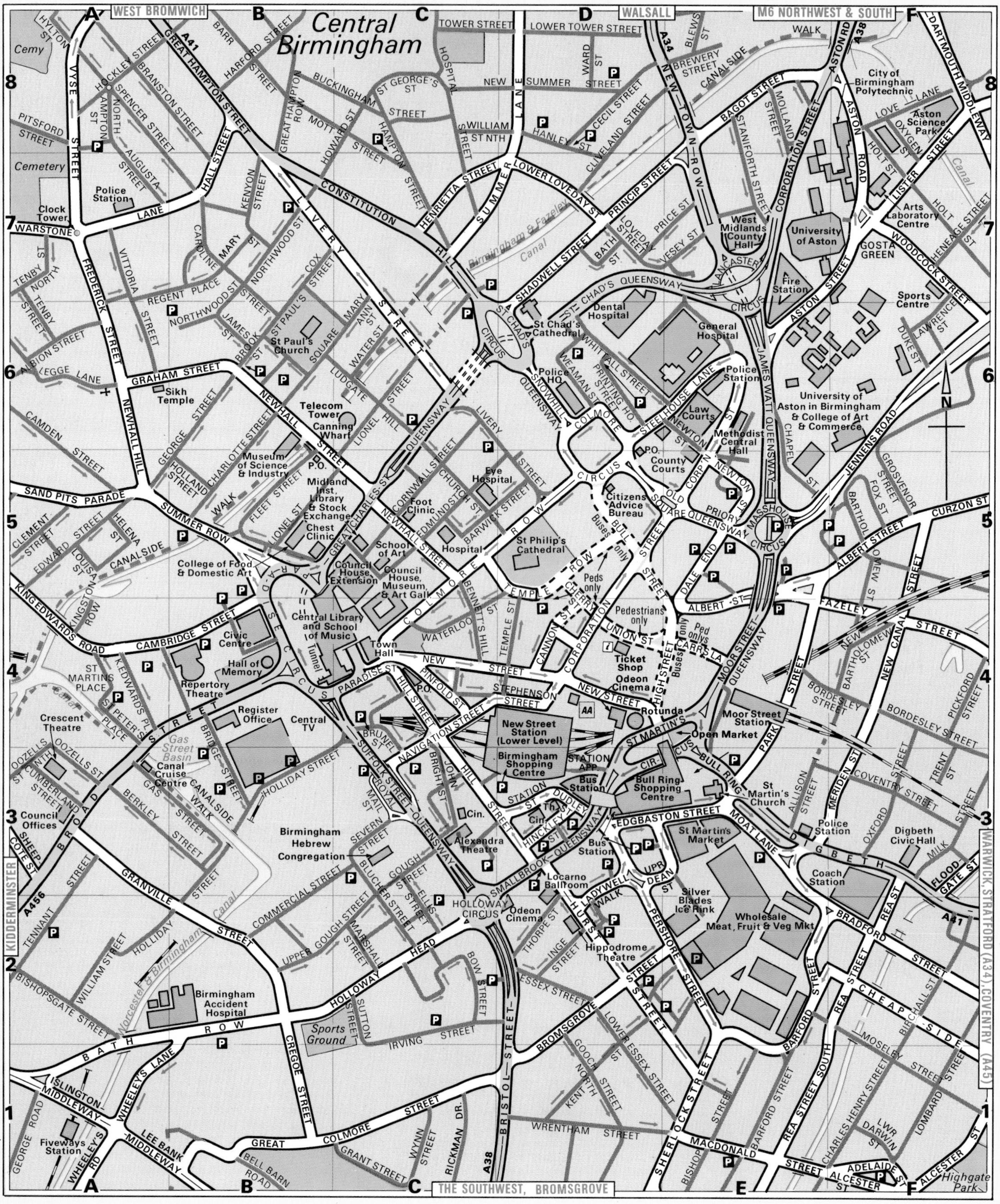

Central Birmingham

Birmingham

It is very difficult to visualise Birmingham as it was before it began the growth which eventually made it the second-largest city in England. When the Romans were in Britain it was little more than a staging post on Icknield Street. Throughout medieval times it was a sleepy agricultural centre in the middle of a heavily-forested region. Timbered houses clustered together round a green that was eventually to be called the Bull Ring. But by the 16th century, although still a tiny and unimportant village by today's standards, it had begun to gain a reputation as a manufacturing centre. Tens of thousands of sword blades were made here during the Civil War. Throughout the 18th century more and more land was built on. In 1770 the Birmingham Canal was completed, making trade very much easier and increasing the town's development dramatically. All of that pales into near insignificance compared with what happened in the 19th century. Birmingham was not represented in Parliament until 1832 and had no town council until 1838. Yet by 1889 it had already been made a city, and after only another 20 years it had become the second largest city in England. Many of Birmingham's most imposing public buildings date from the 19th century, when the city was growing so rapidly. Surprisingly, the city has more miles of waterway than Venice.

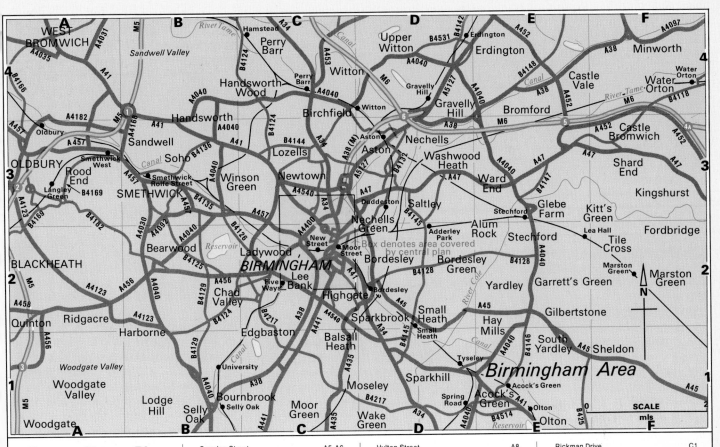

Key to Town Plan and Area Plan

Town Plan

AA Recommended roads	≡
Restricted roads	≡
Other roads	≡
Buildings of interest	Station ▢
AA Centre	AA
Car Parks	P
Parks and open spaces	▬
Churches	†

Area Plan

A roads	▬
B roads	▬
Locations	Meer End ○
Urban area	▭

Street Index with Grid Reference

Birmingham

Adelaide Street	F1
Albert Street	E4-E5-F5
Albion Street	A6
Alcester Street	F1
Allison Street	E3
Aston Road	F8-E8-F8-F7
Aston Street	E6-E7-F7-F8
Augusta Street	A7-A8
Bagot Street	E8
Barford Street	E1-E2-F2
Barr Street	B8
Bartholomew Street	F4-F5
Barwick Street	C5-D5
Bath Row	A1-A2-B2
Bath Street	D7
Bell Barn Road	B1
Bennett's Hill	C4-C5
Berkley Street	A3-B3
Birchall Street	F1-F2
Bishop Street	E1
Bishopsgate Street	A2
Blews Street	E8
Blucher Street	C2-C3
Bordesley Street	E4-F4-F3
Bow Street	C2
Bradford Street	E3-E2-F2
Branston Street	A8-B8-B7
Brewery Street	E8
Bridge Street	B3-B4
Bristol Street	C1-D1-D2-C2
Broad Street	A2-A3-A4-B4
Bromsgrove Street	D1-D2-E2
Brook Street	B6
Brunel Street	C3-C4
Buckingham Street	B8-C8
Bull Ring	E3
Bull Street	D5-E5-E4
Cambridge Street	A4-B4-B5

Camden Street	A5-A6
Cannon Street	D4
Caroline Street	B6-B7
Carrs Lane	E4
Cecil Street	D8
Chapel Street	E5-E6
Charles Henry Street	F1
Charlotte Street	B5-B6
Cheapside	F1-F2
Cherry Street	D4-D5
Church Street	C6-C5-D5
Clement Street	A5
Cliveland Street	D7-D8-E8
Colmore Circus	D5-D6
Colmore Row	C4-C5-D5
Commercial Street	B2-B3-C3
Constitution Hill	B7-C7
Cornwall Street	C5-C6
Corporation Street	D4-D5-E5-E6-E7-E8-F8
Coventry Street	E3-F3
Cox Street	B7
Cregoe Street	B1-B2
Cumberland Street	A3
Curzon Street	F5
Dale End	E4-E5
Dartmouth Middleway	F7-F8
Digbeth	E3-F3
Dudley Street	D3
Duke Street	F6
Edgbaston Street	D3-E3
Edmund Street	C5-D5
Edward Street	A5
Ellis Street	C2-C3
Essex Street	D2
Fazeley Street	E5-E4-F4
Fleet Street	B5
Floodgate Street	F3
Fox Street	F5
Frederick Street	A6-A7
Gas Street	A3-B3
George Road	A1
George Street	A5-B5-B6
Gooch Street North	D1-D2
Gosta Green	F7
Gough Street	C3
Graham Street	A6-B6
Grant Street	C1
Granville Street	A3-A2-B2
Great Charles St Queensway	B5-C5-C6
Great Colmore Street	B1-C1-D1
Great Hampton Row	B8
Great Hampton Street	A8-B8
Grosvenor Street	F5-F6
Hall Street	B7-B8
Hampton Street	C7-C8
Harford Street	B8
Hanley Street	D7-D8
Helena Street	A5
Heneage Street	F7
Henrietta Street	C7-D7
High Street	D4-E4
Hill Street	C4-C3-D3
Hinckley Street	D3
Hockley Street	A8-B8
Holland Street	B5
Holliday Street	A2-B2-B3-C3-C4
Holloway Circus	C2-C3-D3-D2
Holloway Head	B2-C2
Holt Street	F7-F8
Hospital Street	C7-C8
Howard Street	B7-C7-C8
Hurst Street	D3-D2-E2-E1

Hylton Street	A8
Inge Street	D2
Irving Street	C2-D2
Islington Middleway	A1
James Street	B6
James Watt Queensway	E5-E6
Jennens Road	E5-F5-F6
John Bright Street	C3-C4
Kent Street	D1-D2
Kenyon Street	B7
King Edward's Place	A4
King Edward's Road	A4-A5
Kingston Row	A4
Ladywell Walk	D2-D3
Lancaster Circus	E6-E7
Lawrence Street	F6-F7
Lee Bank Middleway	A1-B1
Legge Lane	A6
Lionel Street	B5-C5-C6
Lister Street	F7-F8
Livery Street	B7-C7-C6-D6-D5
Lombard Street	F1-F2
Louisa Street	A5
Love Lane	F8
Loveday Street	D7
Lower Darwin Street	F1
Lower Essex Street	D2-D1-E1
Lower Loveday Street	D7
Lower Tower Street	D8
Ludgate Hill	B6-C6
Macdonald Street	E1-F1
Marshall Street	C2
Mary Street	B7
Mary Ann Street	C6-C7
Masshouse Circus	E5
Meriden Street	E3-F3
Milk Street	F3
Moat Lane	E3
Molland Street	E8
Moor Street Queensway	E4-E5
Moseley Street	E2-F2-F1
Mott Street	B8-C8-C7
Navigation Street	C3-C4
New Street	C4-D4
New Bartholomew Street	F4
New Canal Street	F4-F5
Newhall Hill	A5-A6
Newhall Street	B6-B5-C5
New Summer Street	C8-D8
Newton Street	E5
New Town Row	D8-E8-E7
Northampton Street	A8
Northwood Street	B6-B7
Old Square	D5-E5
Oozells Street	A3-A4
Oozells Street North	A3-A4
Oxford Street	F3-F4
Oxygen Street	F7-F8
Paradise Circus	B4-B5
Paradise Street	C4
Park Street	E3-E4
Pershore Street	D3-D2-E2
Pickford Street	F4
Pinfold Street	C4
Pitsford Street	A8
Price Street	D7-E7
Princip Street	D7-E7-E8
Printing House Street	D6
Priory Queensway	E5
Rea Street	E2-F2-F3
Rea Street South	E1-F1-F2
Regent Place	A7-B7

Rickman Drive	C1
Royal Mail Street	C3
St Chad's Circus	C7-C6-D6
St Chad's Queensway	D6-D7-E7
St George's Street	C8
St Martin's Circus	D3-D4-E4-E3
St Martin's Place	A4
St Paul's Square	B7-B6-C6
St Peter's Place	A4
Sand Pits Parade	A5
Severn Street	C3
Shadwell Street	D6-D7
Sheepcote Street	A3
Sherlock Street	D1-E1-E2
Smallbrook Queensway	C3-D3
Snow Hill Queensway	D6
Spencer Street	A8-A7-B7
Staniforth Street	E7-E8
Station Approach	D3
Station Street	D3
Steelhouse Lane	D6-E6
Stephenson Street	C4-D4
Suffolk Street Queensway	B4-C4-C3
Summer Row	A5-B5
Summer Lane	C7-D7-D8
Sutton Street	C2
Temple Row	C5-D5
Temple Street	D4-D5
Tenby Street	A6-A7
Tenby Street North	A7
Tennant Street	A2-A3
Thorpe Street	D2-D3
Tower Street	C8-D8
Trent Street	F3-F4
Union Street	D4
Upper Dean Street	D3-E3
Upper Gough Street	B2-C2-C3
Vesey Street	D7-E7
Vittoria Street	A6-A7
Vyse Street	A7-A8
Ward Street	D8
Warstone Lane	A7-B7
Water Street	C6
Waterloo Street	C4-C5-D5
Weaman Street	D6
Wheeley's Lane	A1-B1-B2
Wheeley's Road	A1
Whittall Street	D6-E6
William Street	A2
William Street North	C8-D8
Woodcock Street	F6-F7
Wrentham Street	D1-E1
Wynn Street	C1

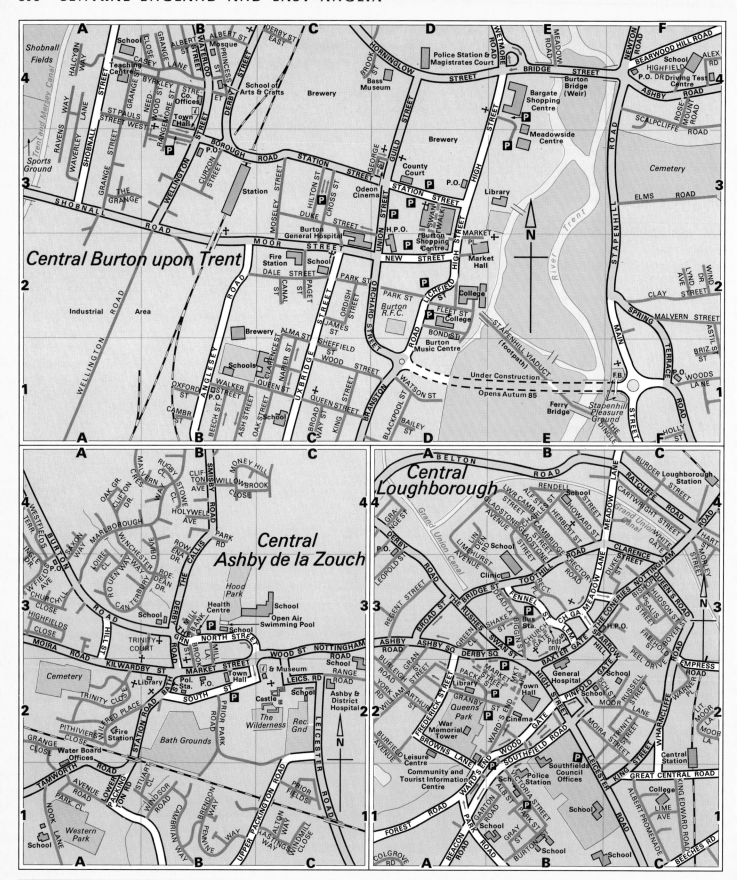

Burton upon Trent

Beer has been brewed here since medieval times and is still prevalent in the town, even though the number of breweries has diminished. The Bass Museum traces the history of the local brewing industry, and other places of interest include the Meadowside Centre, with its fine facilities for sports and the arts. Interesting old buildings can be seen, especially around Horninglow Street, and the Market Hall (now the new shopping centre) dates from the 19th century.

Loughborough Forty-seven locally-made bells ring out from the Queens Park Carillon Tower every Sunday during the summer, and many of Britain's churches have bells from Loughborough's John Taylor Foundry. A busy market and university town situated on the River Stour, Loughborough is also known for its colleges of technology and physical education. Its facilities include a modern Leisure Centre, and amongst local places of interest are the Parish Church of All Saints, dating from the 14th century, the much-restored Old Rectory, and Loughborough Central Station, where steam trains operate most weekends.

Ashby-de-la-Zouch Soap, crisp and biscuit making are the chief present-day concerns of this pleasant market town. The remains of the 15th-century castle are preserved near the centre of the town.

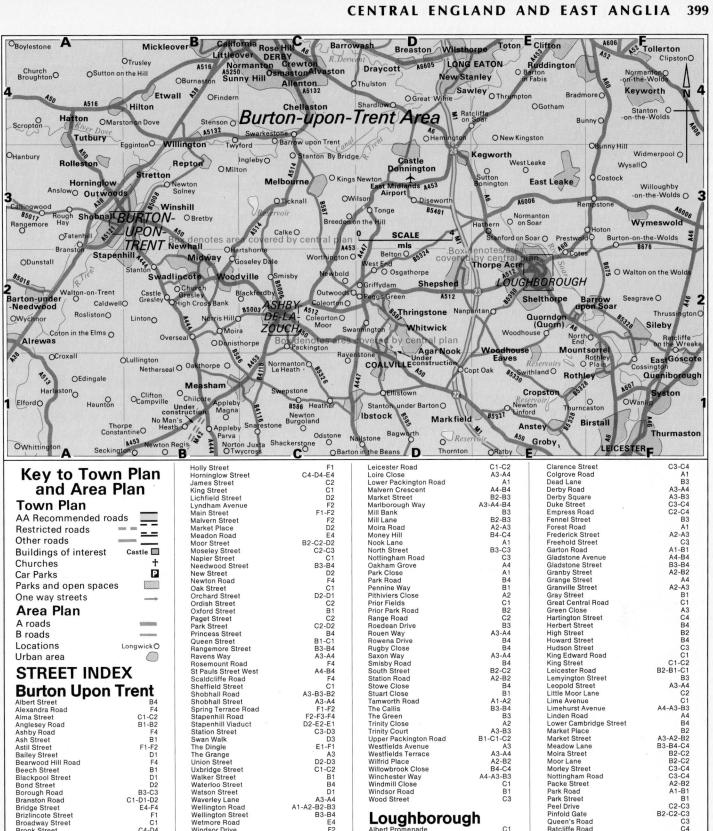

Key to Town Plan and Area Plan

Town Plan

AA Recommended roads	
Restricted roads	
Other roads	
Buildings of interest	Castle 🔲
Churches	✝
Car Parks	🅿
Parks and open spaces	
One way streets	→

Area Plan

A roads	
B roads	
Locations	Longwick ○
Urban area	

STREET INDEX
Burton Upon Trent

Albert Street	B4
Alexandra Road	F4
Alma Street	C1-C2
Anglesey Road	B1-B2
Ashby Road	F4
Ash Street	B1
Astil Street	F1-F2
Bailey Street	D1
Bearwood Hill Road	F4
Beech Street	B1
Blackpool Street	D2
Bond Street	D2
Borough Road	B3-C3
Branston Road	C1-D1-D2
Bridge Street	E4-F4
Brizlincote Street	F1
Broadway Street	C1
Brook Street	C4-D4
Byrkley Street	A4-B4
Cambridge Street	B1
Canal Street	C2
Casey Lane	A4-B4
Clarence Street	C1-C2
Clay Street	F2
Cross Street	C3
Curzon Street	B3
Dale Street	B2-C2
Derby Street	B3-B4-C4
Derby Street East	C4
Duke Street	C3-C2-D2
Elms Road	F3
Fleet Street	D2
George Street	D3
Grange Close	A4-B4
Grange Street	A3-A4
Green Street	D1-D2
Guild Street	D3-D4
Halcyon Way	A4
Highfield Drive	F4
High Street	D2-D3-E3-E4
Hilton Street	C3
Holly Street	F1
Horninglow Street	C4-D4-E4
James Street	C2
King Street	C1
Lichfield Street	D2
Lyndham Avenue	F2
Main Street	F1-F2
Malvern Street	F2
Market Place	D2
Meadon Road	E4
Moor Street	B2-C2-D2
Moseley Street	C2-C3
Napier Street	C1
Needwood Street	B3-B4
New Street	D2
Newton Road	F4
Oak Street	C1
Orchard Street	D2-D1
Ordish Street	C2
Oxford Street	B1
Paget Street	C2
Park Street	C2-D2
Princess Street	B4
Queen Street	B1-C1
Rangemore Street	B3-B4
Ravens Way	A3-A4
Rosemount Road	F4
St Pauls Street West	A4-B4
Scaldcliffe Road	F4
Sheffield Street	C1
Shobhall Road	A3-B3-B2
Shobhall Street	A3-A4
Spring Terrace Road	F1-F2
Stapenhill Road	F2-F3-F4
Stapenhill Viaduct	D2-E2-E1
Station Street	C3-D3
Swan Walk	D3
The Dingle	E1-F1
The Grange	A3
Union Street	D2-D3
Uxbridge Street	C1-C2
Walker Street	B1
Waterloo Street	B4
Watson Street	D1
Waverley Lane	A3-A4
Wellington Road	A1-A2-B2-B3
Wellington Street	B3-B4
Wetmore Road	E4
Windsor Drive	F2
Woods Lane	F1
Wood Street	C1-D1

Ashby De La Zouch

Alton Way	C1
Avenue Road	A1
Bath Street	B2
Brendon Way	B1
Brook Street	B2-B3
Burton Road	A4-A3-B3
Cambrian Way	B1
Canterbury Way	A3-B3-B4
Churchill Close	A3
Clifton Drive	A4
Derby Road	B2-B3
Grange Close	A2
Hastings Way	C1
Highfields Close	A3
Hill Street	A3
Holywell Avenuue	B4
Ingle Drive	A3-A4
Kilwardby Street	A2-B2

Leicester Road	C1-C2
Loire Close	A3-A4
Lower Packington Road	A1
Malvern Crescent	A4-B4
Market Street	B2-B3
Marlborough Way	A3-A4-B4
Mill Bank	B3
Mill Lane	B2-B3
Moira Road	A2-A3
Money Hill	B4-C4
Nook Lane	A1
North Street	B3-C3
Nottingham Road	C3
Oakham Grove	A4
Park Close	A1
Park Road	B4
Pennine Way	B1
Pithiviers Close	A2
Prior Fields	C1
Prior Park Road	B2
Range Road	C2
Roedean Drive	B3
Rouen Way	A3-A4
Rowena Drive	B4
Rugby Close	B4
Saxon Way	A3-A4
Smisby Road	B4
South Street	B2-C2
Station Road	A2-B2
Stowe Close	B2
Stuart Close	B1
Tamworth Road	A1-A2
The Callis	B3-B4
The Green	B3
Trinity Close	A2
Trinity Court	A3-B3
Upper Packington Road	B1-C1-C2
Westfields Avenue	A3
Westfields Terrace	A3-A4
Wilfrid Place	A2-B2
Willowbrook Close	B4-C4
Winchester Way	A4-A3-B3
Windmill Close	C1
Windsor Road	B1
Wood Street	C3

Loughborough

Albert Promenade	C1
Albert Street	B1
Alfred Street	B4
Arthur Street	A2
Ashby Road	A3
Ashby Square	A3
Baxter Gate	B2-B3
Beacon Road	A1
Beeches Road	C1
Belton Road	A4-B4-C4
Biggin Street	B3
Bishop Street	C3
Boyer Street	B3
Bridge Street	A3-B3
Brook Street	A3
Browns Lane	A1-A2
Burder Street	A2
Burfield Avenue	A2
Burleigh Road	A2-A3
Burton Road	B1
Cambridge Street	B4
Cartwright Street	C4
Charles Street	B4
Church Gate	B3

Clarence Street	C3-C4
Colgrove Road	A1
Dead Lane	B3
Derby Road	A3-A4
Derby Square	A3-B3
Duke Street	C3-C4
Empress Road	C2-C4
Fennel Street	B3
Forest Road	A1
Frederick Street	A2-A3
Freehold Street	C3
Garton Road	A1-B1
Gladstone Avenue	A4-B4
Gladstone Street	B3-B4
Granby Street	A2-B2
Grange Street	A4
Granville Street	A2-A3
Gray Street	B1
Great Central Road	C1
Green Close	A3
Hartington Street	C4
Herbert Street	B4
High Street	B2
Howard Street	B4
Hudson Street	C3
King Edward Road	C1
King Street	C1-C2
Leicester Road	B2-B1-C1
Lemyington Street	B3
Leopold Street	A3-A4
Little Moor Lane	C2
Lime Avenue	C1
Limehurst Avenue	A4-A3-B3
Linden Road	A4
Lower Cambridge Street	B4
Market Place	B2
Market Street	A3-A2-B2
Meadow Lane	B3-B4-C4
Moira Street	B2-C2
Moor Lane	B2-C2
Morley Street	C3-C4
Nottingham Road	C3-C4
Packe Street	A2-B2
Park Road	A1-B1
Park Street	B1
Peel Drive	C2-C3
Pinfold Gate	B2-C2-C3
Queen's Road	C3
Ratcliffe Road	C4
Rectory Place	B3
Regent Street	A3
Rendell Street	B4
Russell Street	C2
Salisbury Street	C3
School Street	B2-C2
Shakespeare Street	B3
Southfield Road	B1-B2
Sparrow Hill	B3-C3
Swan Street	B2-B3
The Coneries	B3-C3
The Rushes	A3
Toothill Road	B3-B4
Trinity Street	C2
Victoria Street	B1
Ward's End	A1-A2-B2
Warner Place	C2
Wharncliffe Road	C1-C2-C3
White Gate	C4
William Street	A2
Wood Gate	B2
York Road	A2

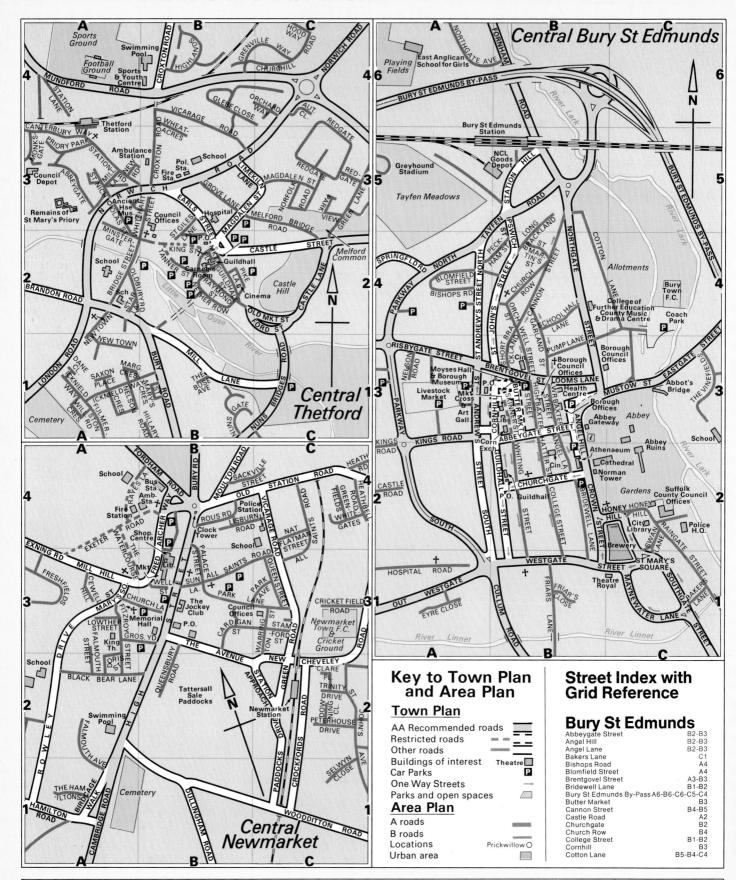

Central Bury St Edmunds

Central Thetford

Central Newmarket

Key to Town Plan and Area Plan

Town Plan

AA Recommended roads	
Restricted roads	
Other roads	
Buildings of interest	Theatre
Car Parks	P
One Way Streets	
Parks and open spaces	

Area Plan

A roads	
B roads	
Locations	Prickwillow ○
Urban area	

Street Index with Grid Reference

Bury St Edmunds

Abbeygate Street	B2-B3
Angel Hill	B2-B3
Angel Lane	B2-B3
Bakers Lane	C1
Bishops Road	A4
Blomfield Street	A4
Brentgovel Street	A3-B3
Bridewell Lane	B1-B2
Bury St Edmunds By-Pass	A6-B6-C6-C5-C4
Butter Market	B3
Cannon Street	B4-B5
Castle Road	A2
Churchgate	B2
Church Row	B4
College Street	B1-B2
Cornhill	B3
Cotton Lane	B5-B4-C4

Bury St Edmunds

This is one of the architectural gems of East Anglia with its streets of Georgian and earlier houses on the Norman grid pattern. The Norman Abbey ruins are set in attractive grounds with a magnificent gateway, and the cathedral church of St Edmunds-bury is adjacent to a massive Norman tower. Also worth seeing are the Guildhall (13th-century and later), the Athenaeum, the colonnaded Corn Exchange (1862) and the 1711 Pentecostal Church. Moyses Hall and Borough Museum goes back to the 12th century and the rebuilt Market Cross and Art Gallery to the 17th. Angel Corner has a fine display of clocks and watches, and St Mary's Church holds Mary Tudor's tomb.

Newmarket Headquarters of British horse racing, breeding and training for nearly 400 years, this is the home of the Jockey Club (founded 1750), the National Stud and the National Horseracing Museum. The racecourse has the world's longest 'straight'.

Thetford was once a Saxon cathedral city and seat of early kings. London overspill sparked off expansion in the 1960s, but Georgian and medieval buildings can still be seen in the town, as well as a Norman castle mound, 12th-century priory remains and Iron Age earthworks. *Rights of Man* author Thomas Paine was born here in 1737. The 15th-century Ancient House offers local history exhibits and the Museum of Childhood Treasures.

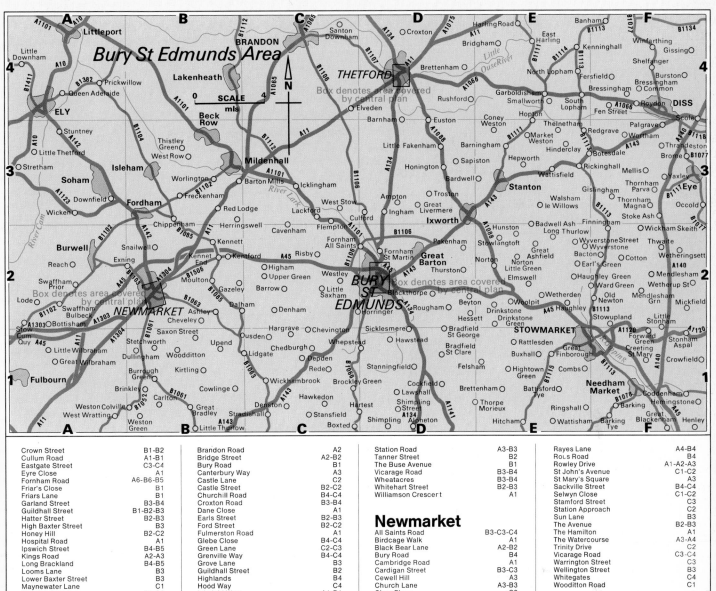

Bury St Edmunds Area

BRANDON

THETFORD

NEWMARKET

BURY ST EDMUNDS

Crown Street	B1-B2
Cullum Road	A1-B1
Eastgate Street	C3-C4
Eyre Close	A1
Fornham Road	A6-B6-B5
Friar's Close	B1
Friars Lane	B1
Garland Street	B3-B4
Guildhall Street	B1-B2-B3
Hatter Street	B2-B3
High Baxter Street	B3
Honey Hill	B2-C2
Hospital Road	A1
Ipswich Street	B4-B5
Kings Road	A2-A3
Long Brackland	B4-B5
Looms Lane	B3
Lower Baxter Street	B3
Maynewater Lane	C1
Mustow Street	B3-C3
Nelson Road	A3
Northgate Avenue	A6-B6
Northgate Street	B3-B4-B5
Orchard Street	B4
Out Westgate	A1
Parkway North	A3-A4
Parkway South	A1-A2-A3
Peckham Street	A4-B4
Pump Lane	B3
Raingate Street	C1-C2
Risbygate Street	A3
St Andrew's Street North	A3-A4
St Andrew's Street South	B1-B2-A2-A3
St John's Street	B3-A3-A4-B4
St Martin's Street	B4
St Mary's Square	C1
School Hall Lane	B4
Short Brackland	B3-B4
Skinner Street	B3
Southgate Street	C1
Springfield Road	A4
Station Hill	B5
Swan Lane	C1-C2
Tayfen Road	A4-A5-B5
The Vinefields	C3
Well Street	B3-B4
Westgate Street	B1-C1
Whiting Street	B1-B2-B3

Thetford

Abbeygate	A3
Autumn Close	C4

Brandon Road	A2
Bridge Street	A2-B2
Bury Road	B1
Canterbury Way	A3
Castle Lane	C2
Castle Street	B2-C2
Churchill Road	B4-C4
Croxton Road	B3-B4
Dane Close	A1
Earls Street	B2-B3
Ford Street	B2-C2
Fulmerston Road	A1
Glebe Close	B4-C4
Green Lane	C2-C3
Grenville Way	B4-C4
Grove Lane	B3
Guildhall Street	B2
Highlands	B4
Hood Way	C4
Icknield Way	A1-B1
King Street	B2
Limekiln Lane	B3-C3
London Road	A1-A2
Magdalen Street	B2-B3-C3
Margarets Crescent	A1
Market Place	B2
Melford Bridge Road	B3-C3-C2
Mill Lane	A3
Mill Lane	B2-B1-C1
Minstergate	A2-A3
Monksgate	A3
Mundford Road	A4-B4
Nelson Crescent	A1
Nether Row	B2
New Road	A3
New Town	A1-A2
Norfolk Road	C3
Norwich Road	A2-A3-B3-C3-C4
Nuns Bridges Road	B1-C1-C2
Nuns Gate	B1
Oldbury Road	A2
Old Market Street	B2-C2
Orchard Way	C4
Park View	C3
Pike Lane	B2
Priory Park	A3
Raymond Street	B2
Redgate	C3-C4
St Giles Lane	B2-B3
St Mary's Crescent	B1
St Nicholas Street	A2-A3
Saxon Place	A1
Star Lane	A2
Station Lane	A4

Station Road	A3-B3
Tanner Street	B2
The Buse Avenue	B1
Vicarage Road	B3-B4
Wheatacres	B3-B4
Whitehart Street	B2-B3
Williamson Crescent	A1

Newmarket

All Saints Road	B3-C3-C4
Birdcage Walk	A1
Black Bear Lane	A2-B2
Bury Road	B4
Cambridge Road	A1
Cardigan Street	B3-C3
Cewell Hill	A3
Church Lane	A3-B3
Clare Place	C2
Cricket Field Road	C3
Crockfords Road	C1-C2
Doris Street	A2-A3
Downing Close	C2
Dullingham Road	B1
Exeter Road	A3-A4-B4
Exning Road	A3-A4
Falmouth Avenue	A1-A2
Falmouth Street	A2-A3
Fitzroy Street	A2-A3
Fordham Road	A4-B4
Fred Archer Way	B3-B4
Freshfields	A3
Greenfields	C4
Green Road	C2-C3
Grosvenor Yard	A3-B3
Hamilton Road	A1
Heatherbell Road	C4
Heath Road	C4
High Street	A1-A2-B2-B3-B4
Lisburn Road	B4-C4
Lowther Street	A3
Mill Hill	A3
Moulton Road	B4
Nat Flatman Street	C4
New Cheveley Road	C2-C3
Old Station Road	B4-C4
Paddocks Drive	C1-C2
Palace Street	B3-B4
Park Avenue	B3-C3
Park Lane	B3-C3
Peterhouse Drive	C2
Queensbury Road	B2-B3
Queen Street	C3

Rayes Lane	A4-B4
Rous Road	B4
Rowley Drive	A1-A2-A3
St John's Avenue	C1-C2
St Mary's Square	A3
Sackville Street	B4-C4
Selwyn Close	C1-C2
Stamford Street	C3
Station Approach	C2
Sun Lane	B3
The Avenue	B2-B3
The Hamilton	A1
The Watercourse	A3-A4
Trinity Drive	C2
Vicarage Road	C3-C4
Warrington Street	C3
Wellington Street	B3
Whitegates	C4
Wooditton Road	C1

BURY ST EDMUNDS
Overlooked by Moyses Hall, market stalls still crowd the Cornhill and Buttermarket twice a week, and have been a feature of the town for several centuries.

Central Cambridge

BEDFORD · MADINGLEY ROAD · HUNTINGDON · NEWMARKET

Lucy Cavendish Collegiate Society
Westminster College Theological and Cheshunt College
St John's College Sports Ground
School of Pythagoras
Kettle's Yard
LA Magdalene College
CHESTERTON
Jesus Green
Midsummer Common
River Cam
KIMBERLEY RD · DE FREVILLE AVE · AYLESTONE ROAD · BELVOIR
Peterhouse Ground
Trinity College Ground
CLARKSON ROAD
ADAMS ROAD
Robinson College
HERSHEL ROAD
Clare Hall
University Rugby Football Ground
CRANMER ROAD
Selwyn College
University Library
Clare Memorial Court
King's School Playing Field
King's College Fellows Garden
WEST ROAD
Institute of Criminology
University Arts Faculties
Harvey Court
THE BACKS
River Cam
St John's College
Bridge of Sighs
St John's Bridge
Trinity Bridge
Garret Hostel Bridge
Trinity Hall
Clare Bridge
King's Bridge
Queen's Bridge
Queen's College
St Cath's Coll
Corpus Christi College
Pembroke College
University Centre
SILVER STREET
MILL LANE
PEMBROKE ST
Trinity College
Gonville & Caius College
Sen. Ho.
Old Schools
Guildhall
King's College & Chapel
Arts Th'tre
St Bene't's
Mkt Pl.
Victoria Cinema
University New Museums Site
ABC Cinema
Museum's
TENNIS CT RD
DOWNING STREET
CORN EXCH. ST
St John's St
Sidney Sussex College
Wescott House Theol.
Arts Cinema
Christ's College
Christ's Pieces
Emmanuel College
Brass Rubbing Centre
Bus Station
Library
P.O.
School
Melbourne Place
Work Terrace
Emmanuel College
Parker's Piece
Police H.Q. & Fire Station
Parkside Indoor Swimming Pool
Grafton Shopping Centre
Lion Yard Shopping Centre
Peter's Field
G.P.O. Sorting Office
College of Arts & Technology New Building
NEWMARKET
CHELMSFORD
SANDY
Jesus College
Wesley House Theological
Butts Green
PARK PARADE
JESUS LANE
VICTORIA AVENUE
MAIDSCAU SEWAY
MADINGLEY ROAD
NORTHAMPTON ST
BRIDGE ST
MAGDALENE ST
SIDNEY ST
EMMANUEL ROAD
PARKER STREET
ST ANDREWS STREET
PARK TERRACE
PARKSIDE
EAST ROAD
MILL RD
WILLIS ROAD

Cambridge Area

Box denotes area covered by central plan

Sawtry · Upwood · Great Raveley · Warboys · Coveney · ELY · Prickwillow · Lakenheath · THETFORD · Elveden · Barnham
Hamerton · Woodwalton · Abbots Ripton · Wistow · Somersham · Mepal · Witcham · Witchford · Stuntney · Thistley Green · West Row · Beck Row · Mildenhall · Icklingham
Upton · Alconbury Weston · Little Stukeley · Broughton · Old Hurst · Pidley · Sutton · Wentworth · Little Thetford · Worlington · Freckenham · Barton Mills · West Stow · Ampton
Buckworth · Alconbury · Great Stukeley · Woodhurst · Colne · Earith · North Hill · Stretham · Isleham · Red Lodge · Tuddenham · Lackford · Flempton · Ingham
Barham · Kings Ripton · Bluntisham · Haddenham · Wilburton · SOHAM · Downfield · Chippenham · Herringswell · Cavenham · Culford · Hengrave · St Martin
Spaldwick · Easton · Ellington · HUNTINGDON · Houghton · ST IVES · Needingworth · Over · Willingham · Wicken · Fordham · Snailwell · Kennett · Risby · Higham · Fornham All Saints · BURY ST EDMUNDS
Grafham Water · Brampton · Hemingford Abbots · Hemingford · Holywell · Fenstanton · Fen Drayton · Cottenham · Burwell · Exning · Kennet End · Kentford · Gazeley · Barrow · Dalham · Denham · Westley · Little Saxham · Horringer
Grafham · Buckden · Offord Cluny · Offord D'arcy · Graveley · Papworth St Agnes · Swavesey · Rampton · Landbeach · Waterbeach · Reach · Swaffham Prior · NEWMARKET · Moulton · Gazeley · Cheveley · Saxon Street · Upend · Ousden · Lidgate · Depden · Rede · Chedburgh · Brockley Green · Hawstead · Chevington
West Perry · B661 · Hilton · B1040 · Conington · Boxworth · Elsworth · Dry Drayton · Girton · Impington · Milton · HISTON · A45 · Lode · Swaffham Bulbeck · Bottisham · Stow cum Quy · Teversham · Little Wilbraham · Great Wilbraham · Dullingham · Stetchworth · Wooditton · Kirtling · Cowlinge · Denston · Hawkedon · Stansfield · Shimpling Street
Great Staughton · Hail Weston · Little Paxton · Toseland · Caxton · Bourn · Highfields · Coton · Hardwick · Madingley · Comberton · CAMBRIDGE · Grantchester · Trumpington · Fen Ditton · Teversham · Fulbourn · West Wratting · Weston Colville · Carlton · Great Bradley · Little Thurlow · Stradishall · Stansfield · Hartest · Boxted · Shimpling
Eaton Socon · ST NEOTS · Croxton · Eltisley · Great Gransden · Longstowe · Toft · Barton · Little Eversden · Great Eversden · Haslingfield · Harlton · Orwell · Haxton · Harston · Great Shelford · Stapleford · Sawston · Babraham · Little Abington · Great Abington · Hildersham · Horseheath · West Wickham · Great Thurlow · Withersfield · Barnardiston · Hundon · Chilton Street · Glemsford · Poslingford · Cavendish · Long Melford
Wyboston · Little Barford · Abbotsley · Kingston · Longstowe · Great Eversden · Pampisford · Whittlesford · Duxford · Hinxton · Ickleton · Great Chesterford · Little Chesterford · Linton · HAVERHILL · Shudy Camps · Castle Camps · Helions Bumpstead · Steeple Bumpstead · Birdbrook · Stoke by Clare · Ashen · Belchamp St Paul · Belchamp Otten · Belchamp Walter · Bulmer
Roxton · Tempsford · Gamlingay · Waresley · Great Gransden · Longstowe · Barrington · Newton · Foxton · Foxton · Shepreth · Meldreth · Fowlmere · Thriplow · Hadstock · Bartlow · Ashdon · Little Walden · Wixoe · Sudbury
Blunham · Gransden · Everton · Hatley St George · East Hatley · Arrington · Shingay · Whaddon · Wrestlingworth · Wendy · MELBOURN · Hinxton · Little Chesterford · Kedington · Pentlow · Foxearth · Belchamp
Sandy · Potton · Croydon · Guilden Morden · Steeple Morden · Litlington · Bassingbourn · Kneesworth · ROYSTON · Great Chishill · Stanstead
Mogerhanger · Beeston · Dunton · Eyeworth · Sutton · Abington Pigotts · Shingay
Northill · Upper Caldecote · Old Warden · Southill · Langford · Edworth · Hinxworth · Ashwell
Ickwell · BIGGLESWADE · Broom · Stanford · Caldecote
Old Warden · A600

SCALE
mls 0   2

A1 · A14 · A141 · A142 · A10 · A1101 · A11 · A134 · A143 · A604 · A505 · A1307 · A1304 · A1303 · A45 · M11 · A428 · A603 · A1123 · B1040 · B1050 · B1049 · B1102 · B1104 · B1112 · B1106 · B1065 · A1065 · B1382

Grafham Water · R Great Ouse · R Cam · Old Bedford River · Cam

Cambridge

Few views in England, perhaps even in Europe, are as memorable as that from Cambridge's Backs towards the colleges. Dominating the scene, in every sense, is King's College Chapel. One of the finest Gothic buildings anywhere, it was built in three stages from 1446 to 1515.

No one would dispute that the chapel is Cambridge's masterpiece, but there are dozens of buildings here that would be the finest in any other town or city. Most are colleges, or are attached to colleges, and it is the university which permeates every aspect of Cambridge's landscape and life. In all there are 33 university colleges in the city, and nearly all have buildings and features of great interest. Cambridge's oldest church is St Bene't's, with a Saxon tower; its most famous is the Church of the Holy Sepulchre, one of only four round churches of its kind.

Huntingdon and *Ely* are both within easy driving distance of Cambridge. Oliver Cromwell and Samuel Pepys were pupils at Huntingdon Grammar School. The building is now a Cromwell museum. Ely also has strong Cromwellian connections – he and his family lived here for ten years. Ely's outstanding feature is the cathedral, a Norman foundation crowned by a stately octagonal lantern tower which contains the Stained Glass Museum.

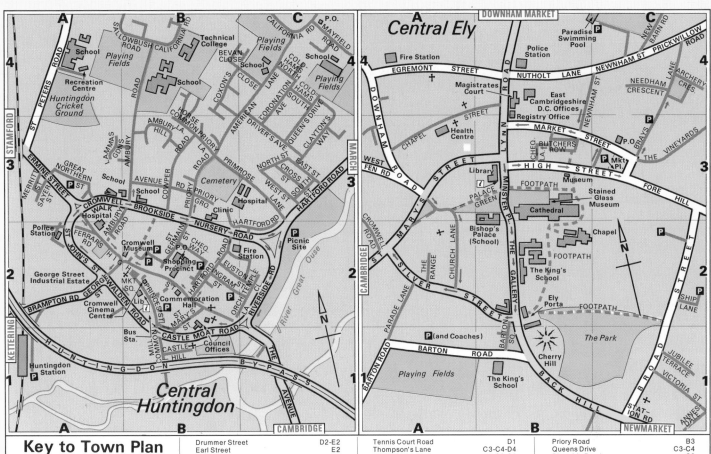

Central Huntingdon

Central Ely

Key to Town Plan and Area Plan

Town Plan
AA Recommended roads
Restricted roads
Other roads
Buildings of interest — College
Car Parks — P
Parks and open spaces
One Way Streets

Area Plan
A roads
B roads
Locations — Haslingfield ○
Urban area

Street Index with Grid Reference

Cambridge

Adam and Eve Street	F1-F2
Adams Road	A2-A3
Auckland Road	F3
Aylestone Road	F4
Belvoir Road	F4
Benet Street	C1-C2-D2
Bridge Street	C3-D3
Broad Street	F1
Brunswick Terrace	F3
Brunswick Walk	F3
Burleigh Street	F2
Castle Street	C4
Chesterton Lane	C4-D4
City Road	F2
Clarendon Street	E1-E2
Clarkson Road	A3-A4
Corn Exchange Street	D1-D2
Cranmer Road	A1
De Freville Avenue	F4
Downing Street	D1
Drummer Street	D2-E2
Earl Street	E2
East Road	F1-F2
Eden Street	F2
Elm Street	E2-F2
Emmanuel Road	E2
Emmanuel Street	D1-D2-E2
Fair Street	F2-F3
Fitzroy Street	F2
Gold Street	F2
Grange Road	A1-A2-A3-A4
Green Street	C2-D2-D3
Hershel Road	A2
Hobston Street	D2-D3
James Street	F2-F3
Jesus Lane	D3-E3
John Street	F2
Kimberley Road	F4
King's Parade	C1-C2
King Street	D3-E3
Lady Margaret Road	B4
Lower Park Street	D3-D4
Madingley Road	A4-B4
Magdalene Street	C4
Maids Causeway	E3-F3
Malcolm Street	D3
Manor Street	D3-E3
Market Street	D2
Melbourne Place	E1-E2-F2
Mill Lane	C1
Mill Road	F1
Napier Street	F2-F3
Newmarket Road	F3
New Park Street	D4
New Square	E2-F2
Northampton Street	B4-C4
Orchard Street	E2-F2
Paradise Street	F2
Parker Street	E1-E2
Park Parade	D4
Parkside	E1-F1
Park Street	D3
Park Terrace	E1
Parsonage Street	F3
Pembroke Street	C1-D1
Pound Hill	B4-C4
Prospect Row	F1-F2
Queens Road	B1-B2-B3-B4
St Andrew's Street	D2-D1-E1
St John's Lane	D4
St John's Street	C3-D3
St Peter's Street	B4-C4
Short Street	E2-E3
Sidney Street	D2-D3
Silver Street	B1-C1

Tennis Court Road	D1
Thompson's Lane	C3-C4-D4
Trinity Street	C2-C3
Victoria Avenue	E3-E4
Victoria Street	E2
Warkworth Terrace	F1
West Road	A1-B1
Willis Road	F1

Huntingdon

Ambury Hill	B3
Ambury Road	A2-A3-B3-B4
American Lane	B3-B4-C4
Avenue Road	B3
Bevan Close	B4-C4
Brampton Road	A2
Brookside	B2-B3
California Road	B4-C4
Castle Hill	B1
Castle Moat Road	B1-B2
Chequers Way	B2
Clayton's Way	C3-C4
Coldhams North	C4
Coldhams South	C4
Coronation Avenue	C3-C4
Cowper Road	B3
Coxon's Close	B4
Cromwell Walk	A3-B3
Cross Street	C3
Driver's Avenue	C3-C4
East Street	C3
Ermine Street	A3
Euston Street	B2-C2
Ferrars Road	A2
George Street	A2
Great Northern Street	A3
Hartford Road	B2-C2-C3
High Street	A2-B2
Horse Common Lane	B3
Huntingdon Bypass	A2-A1-B1-C1
Ingram Street	B2-C2
Lammas Gardens	A3-B3
Market Square	B2
Mayfield Road	C4
Merritt Street	A3
Mill Common	B1
North Street	C3
Nursery Road	B3-B2-C2
Orchard Lane	B2-C2
Primrose Lane	B3-C3
Princes Street	B2
Priory Grove	B3
Priory Lane	B3

Priory Road	B3
Queens Drive	C3-C4
Riverside Road	C2
St Germain Street	B2
St John's Street	A2-A3
St Mary's Street	B1-B2
St Peters Road	A3-A4
St Sayer Street	A3
South Street	C3
Swallowbush Road	A4-B4
The Avenue	C1
Temple Close	C2
Walden Road	A2-B2-B1
West Street	C3

Ely

Annesdale	C1
Archery Crescent	C4
Back Hill	B1-C1
Barton Road	A1-B1
Barton Square	B1-B2
Brays Lane	C3-C4
Broad Street	C1-C2-C3
Butchers Row	B3
Chapel Street	A3-A4-B4
Chequers Lane	B3
Church Lane	A2-A3
Cromwell Road	A2-A3
Downham Road	A3-A4
Egremont Street	a4-B4
Fore Hill	C3
High Street	B3-C3
Jubilee Terrace	C1
Lynn Road	B3-B4
Market Place	C3
Market Street	B3-C3
Minster Place	B2-B3
Needham Crescent	C4
New Barn Road	C4
Newnham Street	B3-B4-C4
Nutholt Lane	B4
Palace Green	A3-B3
Parade Lane	A1-A2
Prickwillow Road	C4
St Mary's Street	A2-A3-B3
Ship Lane	C2
Silver Street	A2-B2
Station Road	C1
The Gallery	B2
The Range	A2
The Vineyards	C3
Victoria Street	C1
West Fen Road	A3

CAMBRIDGE
Behind the gracious university college buildings beautiful lawns and gardens known as the Backs sweep down to the River Cam which, spanned by little bridges and shaded by willows, provides an idyllic setting for punting.

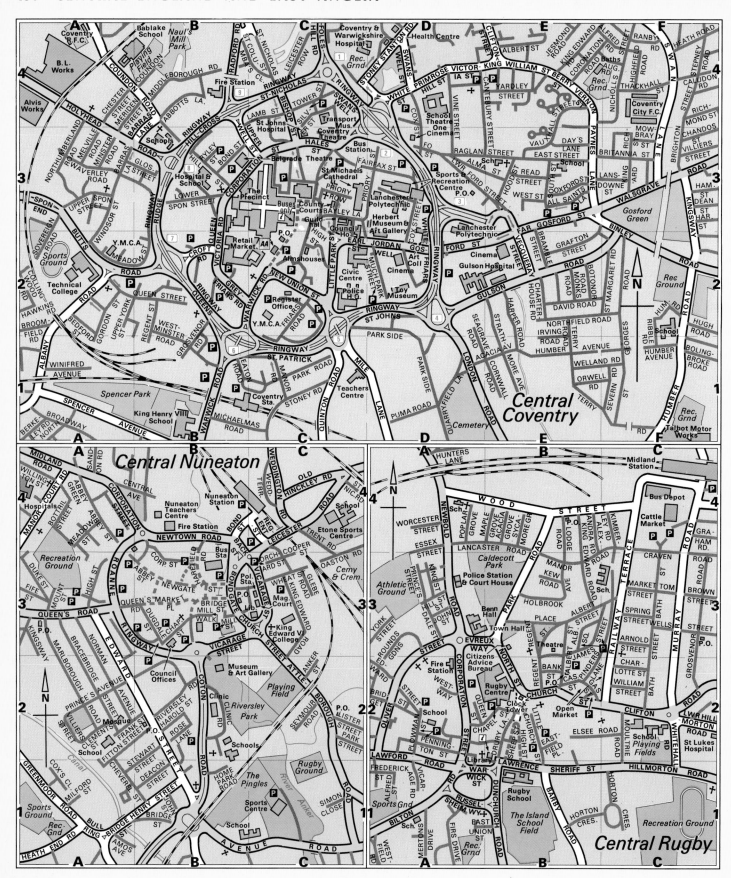

Central Coventry

Central Nuneaton

Central Rugby

Coventry

Few British towns were as battered by the Blitz as Coventry. A raid in November 1940 flattened most of the city and left the lovely cathedral church a gaunt shell with only the tower and spire still standing. Rebuilding started almost immediately. Symbolising the creation of the new from the ashes of the old is Sir Basil Spence's cathedral, completed in 1962 beside the bombed ruins.

A few medieval buildings have survived intact in the city. St Mary's Guildhall is a finely restored 14th-century building with an attractive minstrels' gallery. Whitefriars Monastery now serves as a local museum. The Herbert Art Gallery and Museum has several collections. Coventry is an important manufacturing centre – most notably for cars – and it is also a university city with the fine campus of the University of Warwick some four miles from the centre.

Nuneaton is an industrial town to the north of Coventry with two distinguished old churches – St Nicholas' and St Mary's. Like Coventry it was badly damaged in the war and its centre has been rebuilt.

Rugby was no more than a sleepy market town until the arrival of the railway. Of course it did have the famous Rugby School, founded in 1567 and one of the country's foremost educational establishments. The railway brought industry – still the town's mainstay.

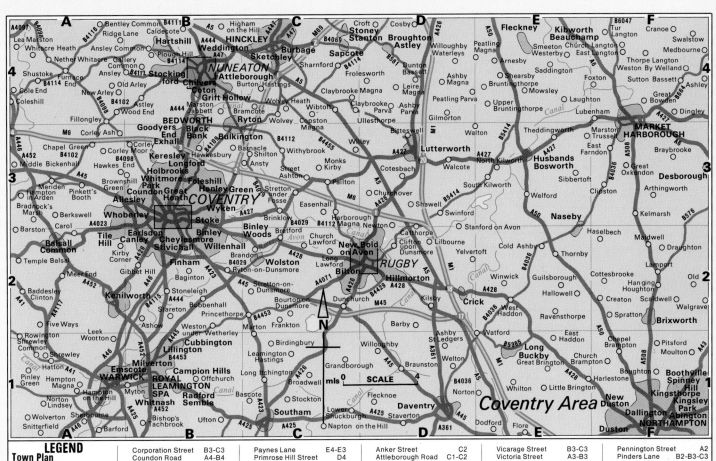

LEGEND

Town Plan

AA Recommended roads	
Restricted roads	
Other roads	
Buildings of interest	Sta.
Car parks	P
Parks and open spaces	
One way streets	←

Area Plan

A roads	
B roads	
Locations	Shitton ○
Urban area	

Street Index with Grid Reference

Coventry

Abbotts Lane	B4
Acacia Avenue	D1-E1
Albany Road	A1-A2
Albert Street	D4-E4
Alfred Road	E4-F4
All Saints Lane	E3
Alma Street	D3-E3
Augustus Road	E4-F4
Barras Lane	A3-B3-B4
Bayley Lane	C3
Bedford Street	A2
Berkeley Road North	A1
Berry Street	E4
Binley Road	E3-F3-F2
Bishop Street	C3-C4
Bolingbroke Road	F1
Bond Street	B3
Botonor Road	E2
Bramble Street	E2-E3
Brighton Street	F3-F4
Britannia Street	E3-F3
Broadway	A1
Broomfield Road	A2
Butts Road	A3-A2-B2
Canterbury Street	D4-D3-E3
Chandos Street	F3
Charterhouse Road	E2
Chester Street	A4
Clifton Street	D4-E4
Colchester Street	E4
Collingwood Road	A2
Cornwall Road	E1
Coronation Road	E4-F4
Corporation Street	B3-C3
Coundon Road	A4-B4
Coundon Street	B4
Cox Street	D2-D3-D4
Caludon Road	F4
Croft Road	B2
David Road	E2
Days' Lane	E3
Dean Street	F3
Eaton Road	B1
Earl Street	C2
East Street	E3
Fairfax Street	C3-D3
Far Gosford Street	E2-E3
Foleshill Road	C4
Ford Street	D3
Friars Road	C1-C2
Gloucester Street	A3-B3
Gordon Street	A1-A2
Gosford Street	D2
Grafton Street	E2-E3
Greyfriars Road	B2
Grosvenor Road	B1-B2
Gulson Road	D2-E2-E3
Hales Street	C3
Hamilton Street	F3
Harley Street	F2-F3
Harper Road	E1-E2
Hawkins Road	A2
Heath Road	F4
High Street	C2-C3
Highfield Road	F4
Hill Street	B3
Holyhead Road	A4-A3-B3
Hood Street	E3
Hugh Road	F2
Humber Avenue	E1-F1
Humber Road	F1-F2
Irving Road	E1-E2
Jesmond Road	E4
Jordan Well	D2
King Edward Road	E4
King Richard Street	F3
King William Street	D4-E4
Kingsway	F2-F3
Lamb Street	B4-C4
Lansdowne Street	E3-F3
Leicester Row	C4
Little Park Street	C2
London Road	D1-D2
Lower Ford Street	D3-E3
Lower Spon Street	B3
Manor Road	C1
Meadow Street	A2-B2
Melville Road	A2
Meriden Street	A3-A4-B4
Michaelmas Road	B1-C1
Middlesborough Road	B4
Mile Lane	C1-D1
Minster Road	A3
Monks Road	E2
Mowbray Street	F3
Much Park Street	D2
New Union Street	C2
Nicholls Street	F4
Northfield Road	E2-F2
Northumberland Road	A3-A4

Orwell Road	E1-F1
Oxford Street	E3
Park Road	C1
Park Side	C2-D2-D1

Paynes Lane	E4-E3
Primrose Hill Street	D4
Priory Row	C3
Priory Street	C3-D3
Puma Road	D1
Quarryfield Lane	D1
Queen Street	A2-B2
Queen Victoria Road	B2-B3
Quinton Road	C1
Radford Road	B4
Raglan Street	D3-E3
Ranby Road	F4
Read Street	E4
Regent Street	B1-B2
Ribble Road	F1-F2
Richmond Street	F4
Ringway Hill Cross	B3-B4
Ringway Queens	B2
Ringway Rudge	B2-B3
Ringway St Johns	C2
Ringway St Nicholas	B4-C4
Ringway St Patrick	C1
Ringway Swanswell	C4
Ringway Whitefriars	D3-D2
Ryley Street	B3
St Columba's Close	B4-C4
St Georges Road	F1-F2
St Margaret Road	F2
St Nicholas Street	C4
Seagrave Road	D2-D1-E1
Severn Road	F1
Silver Street	C4
South Street	E3
Sovereign Road	A2-A3
Spencer Avenue	A1-B1
Spon End	A3
Stepney Road	F4
Stoney Road	C1
Stoney Stanton Road	C4-D4
Strathmore Avenue	E1-E2
Swan Lane	F3-F4
Swanswell Street	D4
Terry Road	E2-E1-F1
Thackhall Street	F4
Tower Street	C4
Upper Spon Street	A3-B3
Upper Well Street	B4-B3-C3
Upper York Street	B1
Vecqueray Street	E2
Vernon Street	E4
Victoria Street	D4
Villiers Street	F3
Vine Street	D4-D3
Walsgrave	F3
Warwick Road	B1-B2-C2
Waverley Road	A3
Welland Road	E1-F1
West Street	E3
Westminster Road	B2-B1
Weston Street	D4
White Street	D4
Windsor Street	A2-A3
Winifrid Avenue	A1
Yardley Street	D4-E4

Nuneaton

Abbey Green	A4
Abbey Street	A4-A3-B3
Alexandra Street	A3
Amos Avenue	A1
Anker Street	C2
Attleborough Road	C1-C2
Avenue Road	B1-C1
Back Street	B4-B3
Bond Gate	B3
Bond Street	B4-C4
Bottril Road	A4
Bracebridge Street	A2-A3
Bridge Street	A1-B1, B3
Bull Ring	A1
Broad Street	A3
Central Avenue	A4-B4
Chapel Street	B3
Cheverel Street	A1-B1
Church Street	B3-C3-C2
Clements Street	A2
Clinic Road	B2
Cooper Street	C2
Corporation Street	A4-B4-B3
Coton Road	B1-B2
Cox's Close	A1
Deacon Street	B1
Dugdale Street	B3-B2
Duke Street	A3
Edward Street	A3-A2-B2-B1
Fife Street	A3
Fitton Street	A1-A2-B2
Frank Street	A2-B2
Glebe Road	C3
Greenmoor Road	A1-A2
Harefield Road	B3-B4
Harold Street	B2
Heath End Road	A1
Henry Street	A1-B1
High Street	A3
Home Park Road	B1
Inner Ring Road	B3
John Street	B1
King Edward Road	C2-C3
Kingsway	A3
Leicester Road	B3-C3-C4
Lister Street	C2
Manor Court Road	A4
Marlborough Road	A2-A3
Market Place	B3
Meadow Street	A4
Midland Road	A4
Milford Street	A1
Mill Street	B3
Mill Walk	B3
Mount Street	A3
Newdegate Street	B3
New Town Road	A4-B4
Norman Avenue	A2-A3
Oaston Road	C3-C4
Old Hinckley Road	C4
Orchard Street	C3
Park Street	C2
Prince's Avenue	A2
Queen's Road	A3-B3
Regent Street	C4
Ringway	A3-B3-B2
Riversley Road	B2
Rose Lane	B2
Roxanne	A3-A4
St Nicholas Road	C4
Sandon Road	A4
Seymour Road	C2
Simon Close	B2
Stewart Street	A1-B1-B2
Trent Road	C3-C4

Vicarage Street	B3-C3
Victoria Street	A3-B3
Villiers Street	A2
Weddington Road	C4
Weddington Terrace	C4
Wheat Street	C3
Willington Street	A4

Rugby

Acacia Grove	B4
Albert Square	B3
Albert Street	B2-B3-C3
Alexandra Road	B4
Alfred Street	A1
Arnold Street	C3
Bank Street	B2
Barby Road	B1
Bath Street	C2-C3-C4
Bilton Road	A1
Bridget Street	A2
Castle Street	B2
Chapel Street	A2-B2
Charlotte Street	C2
Church Street	B1-B2
Clifton Road	C2
Corporation Street	A2-A3-A1
Craven Road	C3-C4
Dale Street	A3
Drury Lane	B2
Dunchurch Road	B1
Eastfield Place	B2
East Union Street	A1-B1
Edward Street	A2
Elsee Road	B2-C2
Essex Street	A3-A4
Evreux Way	A3-B3
Firs Drive	A1
Frederick Street	A1
Gas Street	B2
Graham Road	C4
Grosvenor Road	C2-C3
High Street	B2
Hill Street	A3
Hillmorton Road	C1
Holbrook Avenue	B3
Horton Crescent	B1-C1
Hunters Lane	A4
James Street	B3-C3
Kew Road	B3
Kimberley Road	C4
King Street	A3
King Edward Road	B3-B4
Lancaster Road	A4-B4
Lawford Road	A4
Lawrence Sherriff Street	B1-B2
Little Church Street	B1-B2
Lodge Road	B3-B4
Lower Hillmorton Road	C2
Manor Road	B3-B4-C4
Maple Grove	B4
Market Street	C3
Mertons Drive	A1
Moultrie Road	C1-C2
Murray Road	C2-C3-C4
Newbold Road	A4-A3
North Street	B2-B3
Oliver Street	A2-A3
Park Road	B3-B4

Pennington Street	A2
Pinders Lane	B2-B3-C3
Plowman Street	A2
Poplar Grove	A4
Prince's Street	A2
Queen Street	A2
Railway Terrace	C2-C3-C4
Regent Place	B3
Regent Street	B2-B3
Russelsheim Way	A1-B1
Rounds Gardens	A2-A3
St John Street	A3
Sheep Street	B2
Spring Street	C3
Sycamore Grove	B4
Tom Brown Street	C3
Vicarage Road	A1
Warwick Street	A1-B1
Wells Street	C3
Westfield Road	A1
Westway	A2
Whitehall Road	C1-C2
William Street	C2
Wood Street	A4-B4-C4
Worcester Street	A4
York Street	A3

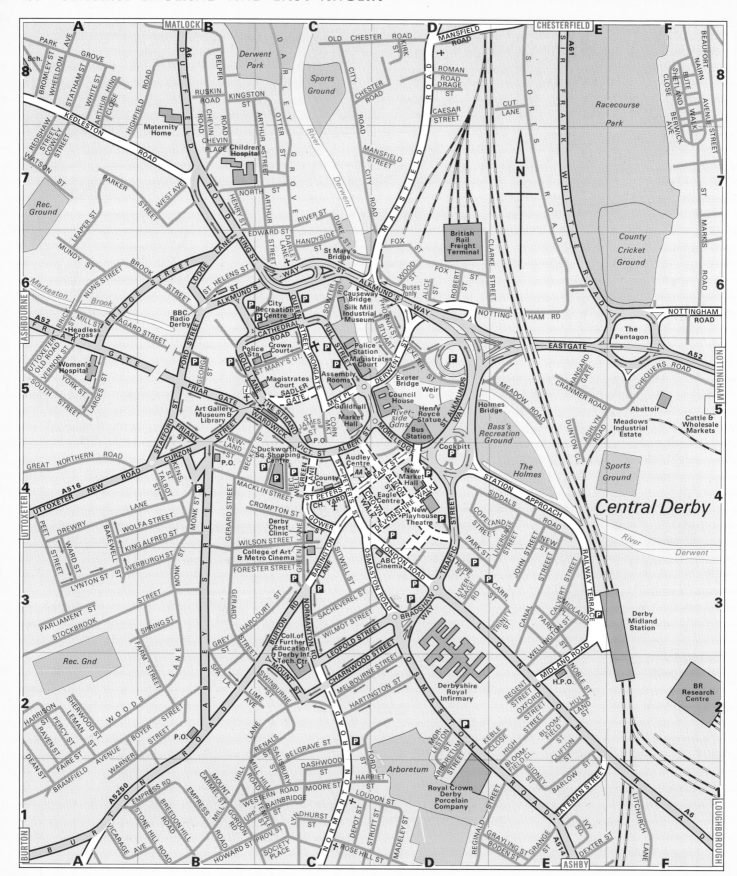

Central Derby

Derby

Present-day Derby, designated a city in 1977, is a product of the Industrial Revolution. During the 19th century the Midland Railway made its headquarters in the ancient country town, bringing with it prosperity and considerable new building. Around the old Market Place stand the Guildhall, which is now used as a concert hall, the Market Hall, and the façade of the old Assembly Rooms

which burnt down in 1963. Later Rolls-Royce established its car manufacturing works here and one of the company's founders, Sir Henry Royce, is commemorated in the Arboretum, laid out by Joseph Loudon. Rolls-Royce aero engines can be seen in the Industrial Museum, appropriately housed in England's first silk mill, set up in 1717 on the banks of the Derwent.

Despite this strong industrial influence, for many people Derby means only one thing –

porcelain. The Royal Crown Derby Porcelain Company produced work of such excellence that George III granted it the right to use the Crown insignia. A museum on the premises houses a treasure-trove of Crown Derby.

Derby's cathedral, All Saint's, was built during Henry VIII's reign but, except for its 178ft-high pinnacled tower, was rebuilt in 1725 by James Gibb. The tomb of Bess of Hardwick, who died in 1607, can be seen inside.

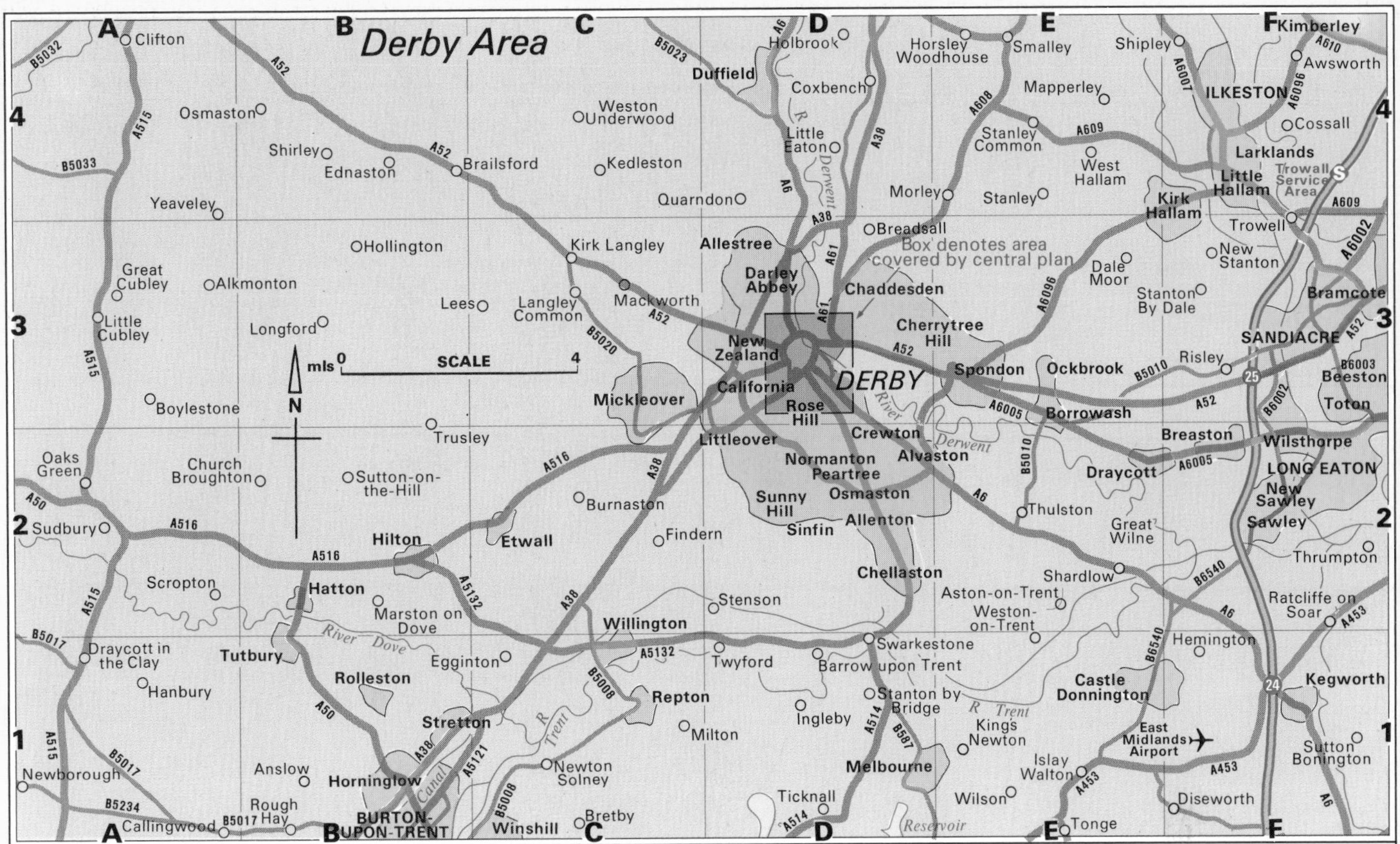

Derby Area

(Map area plan showing Derby and surrounding region with grid references A–F and 1–4)

Map locations include: Clifton, Osmaston, Shirley, Ednaston, Brailsford, Yeaveley, Great Cubley, Alkmonton, Hollington, Kirk Langley, Weston Underwood, Kedleston, Quarndon, Duffield, Holbrook, Coxbench, Little Eaton, Horsley Woodhouse, Smalley, Shipley, Kimberley, Awsworth, Cossall, ILKESTON, Larklands, Trowall Service Area, Little Hallam, Kirk Hallam, Trowell, New Stanton, Bramcote, SANDIACRE, Beeston, Toton, Risley, Breaston, Draycott, Wilsthorpe, LONG EATON, New Sawley, Sawley, Thrumpton, Ratcliffe on Soar, Kegworth, Sutton Bonington, Diseworth, Tonge, Wilson, Islay Walton, Kings Newton, Castle Donnington, East Midlands Airport, Hemington, Weston-on-Trent, Aston-on-Trent, Shardlow, Great Wilne, Chellaston, Stenson, Willington, Twyford, Barrow upon Trent, Swarkestone, Stanton by Bridge, Ingleby, Ticknall, Melbourne, Bretby, Winshill, BURTON-UPON-TRENT, Newton Solney, Milton, Repton, Stretton, Horninglow, Anslow, Rolleston, Egginton, Hatton, Marston on Dove, Tutbury, Hanbury, Draycott in the Clay, Newborough, Callingwood, Rough Hay, Scropton, Sudbury, Oaks Green, Church Broughton, Hilton, Etwall, Burnaston, Findern, Sutton-on-the-Hill, Trusley, Longford, Boylestone, Little Cubley, Mackworth, Langley Common, Lees, New Zealand, Mickleover, California, Rose Hill, Littleover, Sunny Hill, Sinfin, Allenton, Osmaston, Peartree, Normanton, Crewton, Alvaston, Thulston, DERBY, Spondon, Ockbrook, Borrowash, Chaddesden, Cherrytree Hill, Darley Abbey, Allestree, Breadsall, Morley, Stanley, Stanley Common, West Hallam, Dale Moor, Stanton By Dale, Mapperley, Woodhouse

Box denotes area covered by central plan

SCALE 0 mls 4 N

LEGEND

Town Plan
- AA recommended route
- Restricted roads
- Other roads
- Buildings of interest — Station
- Car parks — P
- Parks and open spaces
- One way streets

Area Plan
- A roads
- B roads
- Locations — Niwton○
- Urban area

Street Index with Grid Reference

Derby

Abbey Street	B2-B3-B4
Agard Street	A6-B6-B5
Albert Street	C4-C5-D5
Albion Street	D4
Alice Street	D6
Arboretum Street	D1-D2
Arthur Hind Close	A7-A8
Arthur Street	B8-C8-C7-C6
Ashlyn Road	E4-E5-F5
Babington Lane	C3-C4
Bakewell Street	A4-A3
Barlow Street	E1-E2
Bateman Street	E1
Beaufort Street	F8-F7
Becket Street	B4-B5-C5
Becket Well	C4
Belgrave Street	C1-C2
Belper Road	B8-B7
Berwick Avenue	F8-F7
Bloomfield Close	E1
Bloomfield Street	E2
Boden Street	D1-E1
Bold Lane	B5-C5
Boyer Street	A2-B2
Bradshaw Way	D3
Bramfield Avenue	A1-A2
Breedon Hill Road	B1
Brick Street	A6
Bridge Street	A5-A6-B6
Bromley Street	A8
Brook Street	A6-B6
Burton Road	A1-B1-B2-C2-C3
Bute Walk	F8-F7
Caesar Street	D8
Calvert Street	E3
Canal Street	E3-E4
Carrington Street	D3-E3
Cathedral Road	B5-B6-C5-C6
Charnwood Street	C2-D2-D3
Chester Road	C8-D8
Chequers Road	F5
Chevin Place	B7
Chevin Road	B8-B7
City Road	C8-C7-D7-D6
Clarke Street	D6-E6
Clifton Street	E1-E2
Copeland Street	D4-E4
Corn Market	C5
Cowley Street	A7-A8
Cranmer Road	E5-F5-F5
Crompton Street	B4-C4
Crown Walk	C4-D4
Curzon Street	B4-B5
Cut Lane	E8
Darley Grove	C8-C7
Darley Lane	C6-C7
Dashwood Street	C1
Dean Street	A2-A1
Depot Street	C1
Derwent Street	D5-D6
Devonshire Walk	D4
Dexter Street	E1-F1
Drage Street	D8
Drewry Lane	A4-B4
Duke Street	C7-C6
Duffield Road	B8-B7
Dunton Close	E5-E4
Eastgate	E5
East Street	C4-D4
Edward Street	B7-C7
Empress Road	A1-B1
Exeter Street	D5
Faire Street	A1-A2

Farm Street	A3-B3-B2
Ford Street	B5-B6-C2-C1-D1
Forester Street	B3-C3
Fox Street	D6
Friar Gate	A6-A5-B5
Friary Street	B5
Full Street	C6-C5
George Street	B5
Gerard Street	B2-B3-B4
Gordon Road	B1
Gower Street	C4
Grange Street	E1
Grayling Street	D1-E1
Great Northern Road	A4
Green Lane	C3-C4
Grey Street	B3
Handyside Street	C6
Hansard Gate	E5
Harcourt Street	B3-C3
Harriet Street	C1-D1
Harrison Street	A2
Hartington Street	C2-D2
Henry Street	B7
Highfield Road	A7-A8-B8
High Street	E1-E2
Hope Street	D3
Howard Street	B1
Hulland Street	E2
Iron Gate	C5
Ivy Square	E1
John Street	E3-E4
Keble Close	D2-E2
Kedleston Road	A8-A7-B7
Kensington Street	B4
King Alfred Street	A3-B3-B4
Kingston Street	B8-C8
King Street	B6-C6
Kirk Street	D8
Larges Street	A5
Leaper Street	A6-A7
Leman Street	A2
Leopold Street	C2-C3-D3
Lime Avenue	B2-C2
Litchurch Lane	F1
Liversage Road	D3
Liversage Street	E3-E4
Lodge Lane	B6
London Road	D4-D3-E3-E2-F2-F1
Loudon Street	C1-D1
Lyndhurst Street	C1
Lynton Street	A3
Macklin Street	B4-C4
Madeley Street	D1
Mansfield Road	D6-D7-D8

Mansfield Street	C7-D7
Market Place	C5
Meadow Road	E5
Melbourne Street	C2-D2
Midland Place	E3
Midland Road	E2-E3
Mill Hill Lane	B1-B2-C2
Mill Hill Road	B1-C1
Mill Street	A6
Monk Street	B3-B4
Moore Street	C1
Moreledge	D4-D5
Morleston Street	D1-D2
Mount Street	C2
Mount Carmel Street	B1
Mundy Street	A6
Nairn Avenue	F7-F8
New Street	E4
Newland Street	B4
Noble Street	E2
Normanton Road	C1-C2-C3
North Street	B7-C7
Nottingham Road	D6-E6-F6
Nuns Street	A6
Old Chester Road	C8-D8
Osmaston Road	E1-D1-E2-D2-D3-C3-C4
Otter Street	C7-C8
Oxford Street	E2
Parker Street	A7-B7
Park Grove	A8
Park Street	D4-D3-E3
Parliament Street	A3
Peet Street	A3-A4
Percy Street	A2
Phoenix Street	D6
Provident Street	C1
Queen Street	C5-C6
Railway Terrace	E3-E4
Raven Street	A1-A2
Redshaw Street	A7-A8
Regent Street	D2-E2
Reginald Street	D1-E1
Renals Street	B2-C2
River Street	C7
Robert Street	D6
Roman Road	D8
Rose Hill Street	C1-D1
Ruskin Road	B8
St Alkmund's Way	B6-C6-D6-D5
St Helens Street	B6
St James Street	C5
St Mark's Road	F6-F7
St Mary's Gate	C5

St Peters Church Yard	C4
St Peter's Street	C4
Sacheverel Street	C3
Sadler Gate	C5
Salisbury Street	C1-C2
Sherwood Street	A2
Shetland Close	F8
Siddals Road	D4-E4
Sidney Street	E1
Sir Frank Whittle Road	F6-E6-E7-E8
Sitwell Street	C3
Society Place	C1
South Street	A5
Sowter Road	C6
Spa Lane	B2-B2
Spring Street	B3
Stafford Street	B4-B5
Statham Street	A8
Station Approach	D4-E4
Stockbrook Street	A2-A3-B3
Stone Hill Road	A1-B1
Stores Road	E6-E7-E8
Strutt Street	D1
Stuart Street	D5-D6
Swinburne Street	C2
Talbot Street	B4
Temple Street	C1
The Strand	C5
Traffic Street	D3-D4
Trinity Street	E3
Upper Bainbridge Street	B1-C1
Uttoxeter New Road	A4-B4
Uttoxeter Old Road	A5
Vicarage Avenue	A1-B1
Victoria Street	A5
Vernon Street	A5
York Street	A5
Ward Street	A3-A4
Warner Street	A1-A2-B2
Wardwick	B5-C5-C4
Watson Street	A7
Wellington Street	E2-E3
Werburgh Street	A3-B3
West Avenue	B7
Western Road	B1-C1
Wheeldon Avenue	A8
White Street	A8
Wilmot Street	C3-D3
Wilson Street	B3-B4-C4
Wolfa Street	A4-B4
Woods Lane	A2-B2-B3
Wood Street	D6

DERBY
The 1907 Silver Ghost, one of Rolls Royce's first cars, was produced just before the company moved its factory to Derby. Cars were their sole product until World War I when the first aero engine was designed.

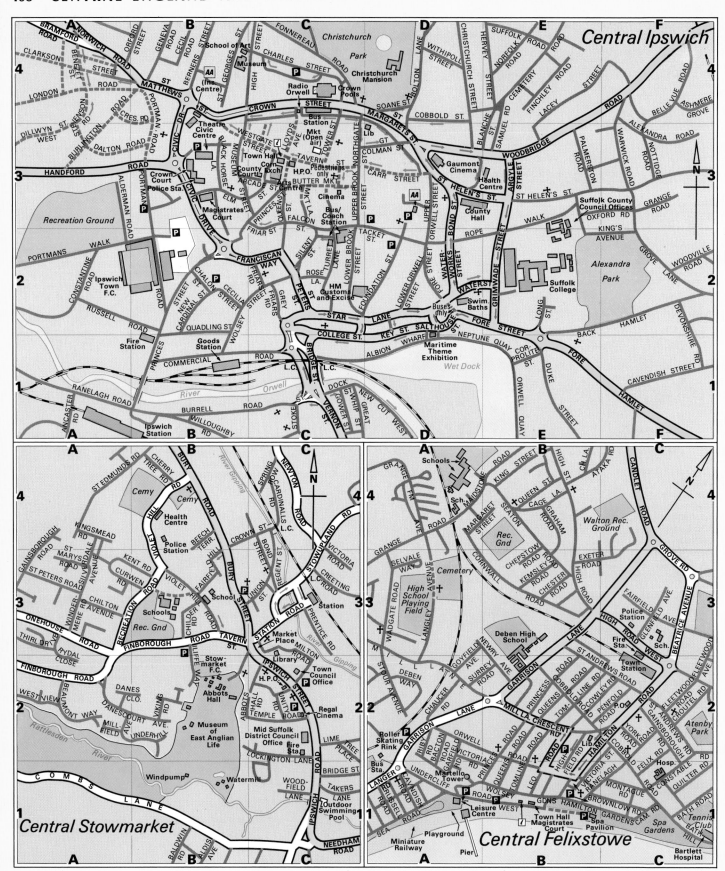

Central Ipswich

Central Stowmarket

Central Felixstowe

Ipswich

In the Middle Ages England became rich from wool, and East Anglia in particular prospered. Ipswich shared in the wealth, being the port from which wool was exported to Europe. Twelve medieval churches survive in Ipswich, a remarkable number for a town of its size, and all of them have features of beauty and interest. Of the town's nonconformist chapels, the 17th-century Unitarian is outstanding. Unfortunately, many of Ipswich's ancient secular buildings were swept away during the 1960s fever for clearances, precincts and redevelopment; however, some of the finest survive. Best is Ancient House, dating back to 1567 and embellished on the outside with complex decorative plasterwork. Other fine buildings can be seen in Lower Brook Street and Fore Street. Christchurch Mansion dates from 1548 and now houses a museum.

Felixstowe is a seaside resort with Edwardian characteristics, a commercial centre, and a container port. Its handsome promenade is nearly two miles long.

Stowmarket has an excellent country life museum – the Museum of East Anglian Life. Among its exhibits are reconstructed buildings, agricultural machinery and domestic items. The town itself is a shopping and market centre for the rich arable farmlands of Central Suffolk.

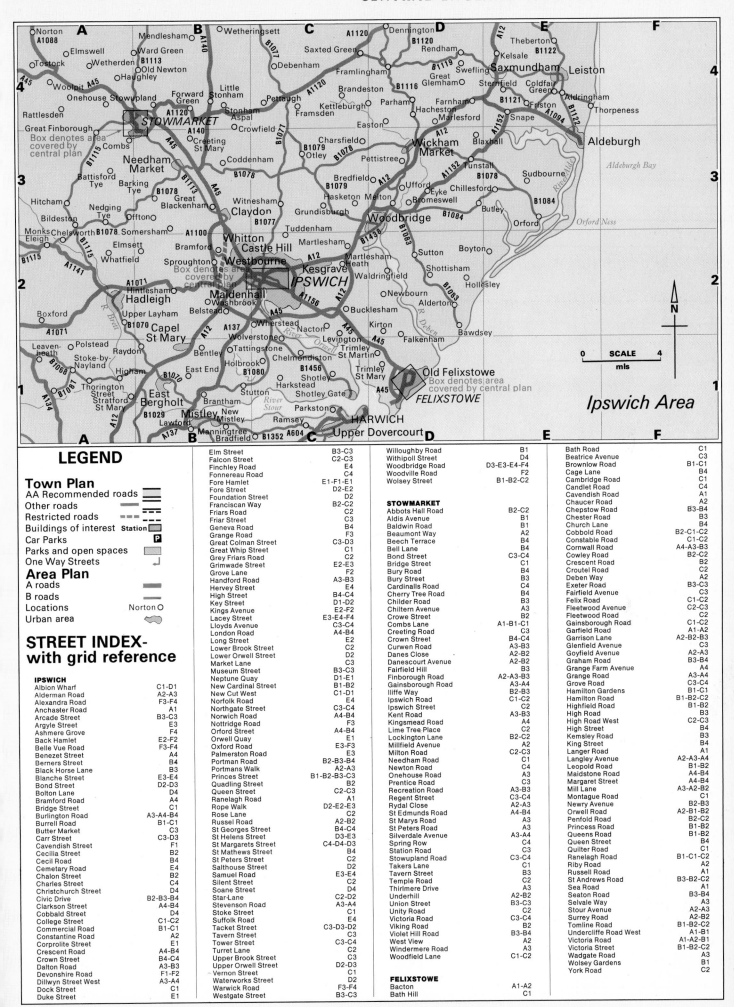

Ipswich Area

LEGEND

Town Plan
AA Recommended roads
Other roads
Restricted roads
Buildings of interest **Station**
Car Parks **P**
Parks and open spaces
One Way Streets

Area Plan
A roads
B roads
Locations Norton○
Urban area

STREET INDEX-
with grid reference

IPSWICH

Albion Wharf	C1-D1
Alderman Road	A2-A3
Alexandra Road	F3-F4
Anchaster Road	A1
Arcade Street	B3-C3
Argyle Street	E3
Ashmere Grove	F4
Back Hamlet	E2-F2
Belle Vue Road	F3-F4
Benezet Street	A4
Berners Street	B4
Black Horse Lane	B3
Blanche Street	E3-E4
Bond Street	D2-D3
Bolton Lane	D4
Bramford Road	A4
Bridge Street	C1
Burlington Road	A3-A4-B4
Burrell Road	B1-C1
Butter Market	C3
Carr Street	C3-D3
Cavendish Street	F1
Cecilia Street	B2
Cecil Road	B4
Cemetary Road	E4
Chalon Street	B2
Charles Street	C4
Christchurch Street	D4
Civic Drive	B2-B3-B4
Clarkson Street	A4-B4
Cobbald Street	D4
College Street	C1-C2
Commercial Road	B1-C1
Constantine Road	A2
Corprolite Street	E1
Crescent Road	A4-B4
Crown Street	B4-C4
Dalton Road	A3-B3
Devonshire Road	F1-F2
Dillwyn Street West	A3-A4
Dock Street	C1
Duke Street	E1
Elm Street	B3-C3
Falcon Street	C2-C3
Finchley Road	E4
Fonnereau Road	C4
Fore Hamlet	E1-F1-E1
Fore Street	D2-E2
Foundation Street	D2
Franciscan Way	B2-C2
Friars Road	C2
Friar Street	C3
Geneva Road	B4
Grange Road	F3
Great Colman Street	C3-D3
Great Whip Street	C1
Grey Friars Road	C2
Grimwade Street	E2-E3
Grove Lane	F2
Handford Road	A3-B3
Hervey Street	E4
High Street	B4-C4
Key Street	D1-D2
Kings Avenue	E2-F2
Lacey Street	E3-E4-F4
Lloyds Avenue	C3-C4
London Road	A4-B4
Long Street	E2
Lower Brook Street	C2
Lower Orwell Street	D2
Market Lane	C3
Museum Street	B3-C3
Neptune Quay	D1-E1
New Cardinal Street	B1-B2
New Cut West	C1-D1
Norfolk Road	E4
Northgate Street	C3-C4
Norwich Road	A4-B4
Nottridge Road	F3
Orford Street	A4-B4
Orwell Quay	E1
Oxford Road	E3-F3
Palmerston Road	E3
Portman Road	B2-B3-B4
Portmans Walk	A2-A3
Princes Street	B1-B2-B3-C3
Quadling Street	B2
Queen Street	C2-C3
Ranelagh Road	A1
Rope Walk	D2-E2-E3
Rose Lane	C2
Russel Road	A2-B2
St Georges Street	B4-C4
St Helens Street	D3-E3
St Margarets Street	C4-D4-D3
St Mathews Street	B4
St Peters Street	C2
Salthouse Street	D2
Samuel Road	E3-E4
Silent Street	C2
Soane Street	D4
Star-Lane	C2-D2
Stevenson Road	A3-A4
Stoke Street	C1
Suffolk Road	E4
Tacket Street	C3-D3-D2
Tavern Street	C3
Tower Street	C3-C4
Turret Lane	C2
Upper Brook Street	C2
Upper Orwell Street	D2-D3
Vernon Street	C1
Waterworks Street	D2
Warwick Road	F3-F4
Westgate Street	B3-C3

Willoughby Road	B1
Withipoll Street	D4
Woodbridge Road	D3-E3-E4-F4
Woodville Road	F2
Wolsey Street	B1-B2-C2

STOWMARKET

Abbots Hall Road	B2-C2
Aldis Avenue	B1
Baldwin Road	B1
Beaumont Way	A2
Beech Terrace	B4
Bell Lane	B4
Bond Street	C3-C4
Bridge Street	C1
Bury Road	B4
Bury Street	B3
Cardinalls Road	C4
Cherry Tree Road	B4
Childer Road	B3
Chiltern Avenue	A3
Crowe Street	B2
Combs Lane	A1-B1-C1
Creeting Road	C3
Crown Street	B4-C4
Curwen Road	A3-B3
Danes Close	A2-B2
Danescourt Avenue	A2-B2
Fairfield Hill	B3
Finborough Road	A2-A3-B3
Gainsborough Road	A3-A4
Iliffe Way	B2-B3
Ipswich Road	C1-C2
Ipswich Street	C2
Kent Road	A3-B3
Kingsmead Road	A4
Lime Tree Place	C2
Lockington Road	B2-C2
Millfield Avenue	A2
Milton Road	C2-C3
Needham Road	C1
Newton Road	C4
Onehouse Road	A3
Prentice Road	C3
Recreation Road	A3-B3
Regent Street	C3-C4
Rydal Close	A2-A3
St Edmunds Road	A4-B4
St Marys Road	A3
St Peters Road	A3
Silverdale Avenue	A3-A4
Spring Row	C4
Station Road	C3
Stowupland Road	C3-C4
Takers Lane	C1
Tavern Street	B3
Temple Road	C2
Thirlmere Drive	A3
Underhill	A2-B2
Union Street	B3-C3
Unity Road	C3
Victoria Road	C3-C4
Viking Road	B2
Violet Hill Road	B3-B4
West View	A2
Windermere Road	A3
Woodfield Lane	C1-C2

FELIXSTOWE

Bacton	A1-A2
Bath Hill	C1

Bath Road	C1
Beatrice Avenue	C3
Brownlow Road	B1-C1
Cage Lane	B4
Cambridge Road	C1
Candlet Road	C4
Cavendish Road	A1
Chaucer Road	A2
Chepstow Road	B3-B4
Chester Road	B3
Church Lane	B4
Cobbold Road	B2-C1-C2
Constable Road	C1-C2
Cornwall Road	A4-A3-B3
Cowley Road	B2-C2
Crescent Road	B2
Croutel Road	C2
Deben Way	A2
Exeter Road	B3-C3
Fairfield Avenue	C3
Felix Road	C1-C2
Fleetwood Avenue	C2-C3
Fleetwood Road	C2
Gainsborough Road	C1-C2
Garfield Road	A1-A2
Garrison Lane	A2-B2-B3
Glenfield Avenue	C3
Goyfield Avenue	A2-A3
Graham Road	B3-B4
Grange Farm Avenue	A4
Grange Road	A3-A4
Grove Road	C3-C4
Hamilton Gardens	B1-C1
Hamilton Road	B1-B2-C2
Highfield Road	B1-B2
High Road	B3
High Road West	C2-C3
High Street	B4
Kemsley Road	B3
King Street	B4
Langer Road	A1
Langley Avenue	A2-A3-A4
Leopold Road	B1-B2
Maidstone Road	A4-B4
Margaret Street	A4-B4
Mill Lane	A3-A2-B2
Montague Road	C1
Newry Avenue	B2-B3
Orwell Road	A2-B1-B2
Penfold Road	B2-C2
Princess Road	B1-B2
Queens Road	B1-B2
Queen Street	B4
Quilter Road	C1
Ranelagh Road	B1-C1-C2
Riby Road	A2
Russell Road	A1
St Andrews Road	B3-B2-C2
Sea Road	A1
Seaton Road	B3-B4
Selvale Way	A3
Stour Avenue	A2-A3
Surrey Road	A2-B2
Tomline Road	B1-B2-C2
Undercliffe Road West	A1-B1
Victoria Road	A1-A2-B1
Victoria Street	B1-B2-C2
Wadgate Road	A3
Wolsey Gardens	B1
York Road	C2

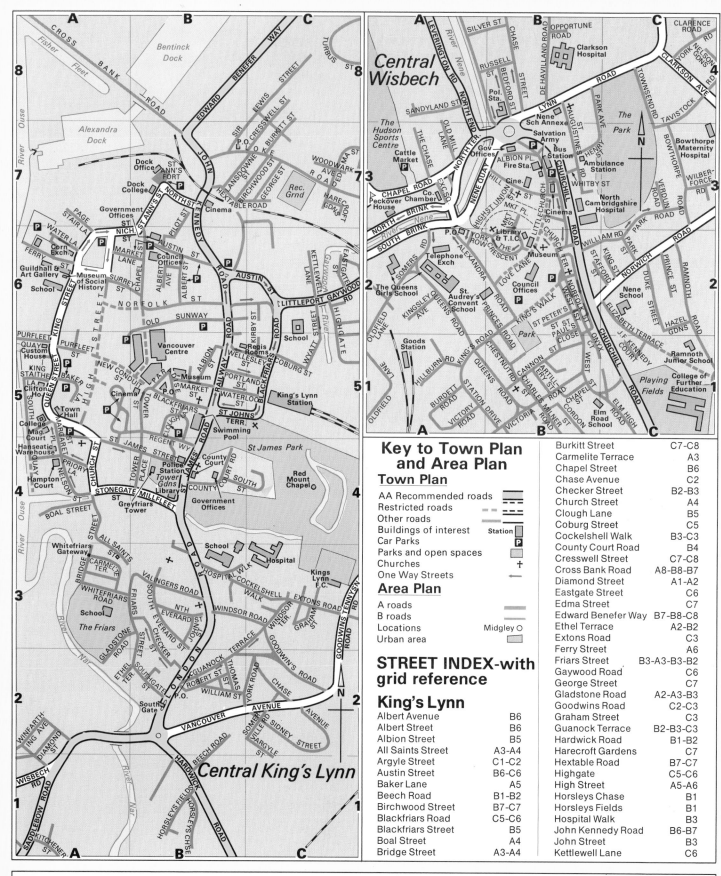

Key to Town Plan and Area Plan

Town Plan

AA Recommended roads	▬▬▬
Restricted roads	▬ ▬ ▬
Other roads	▬▬▬
Buildings of interest	Station ▯
Car Parks	P
Parks and open spaces	
Churches	+
One Way Streets	←

Area Plan

A roads	▬▬▬
B roads	▬▬▬
Locations	Midgley O
Urban area	▭

STREET INDEX-with grid reference

King's Lynn

Albert Avenue	B6
Albert Street	B6
Albion Street	B5
All Saints Street	A3-A4
Argyle Street	C1-C2
Austin Street	B6-C6
Baker Lane	A5
Beech Road	B1-B2
Birchwood Street	B7-C7
Blackfriars Road	C5-C6
Blackfriars Street	B5
Boal Street	A4
Bridge Street	A3-A4
Burkitt Street	C7-C8
Carmelite Terrace	A3
Chapel Street	B6
Chase Avenue	C2
Checker Street	B2-B3
Church Street	A4
Clough Lane	B5
Coburg Street	C5
Cockelshell Walk	B3-C3
County Court Road	B4
Cresswell Street	C7-C8
Cross Bank Road	A8-B8-B7
Diamond Street	A1-A2
Eastgate Street	C6
Edma Street	C7
Edward Benefer Way	B7-B8-C8
Ethel Terrace	A2-B2
Extons Road	C3
Ferry Street	A6
Friars Street	B3-A3-B3-B2
Gaywood Road	C6
George Street	C7
Gladstone Road	A2-A3-B3
Goodwins Road	C2-C3
Graham Street	C3
Guanock Terrace	B2-B3-C3
Hardwick Road	B1-B2
Harecroft Gardens	C7
Hextable Road	B7-C7
Highgate	C5-C6
High Street	A5-A6
Horsleys Chase	B1
Horsleys Fields	B1
Hospital Walk	B3
John Kennedy Road	B6-B7
John Street	B3
Kettlewell Lane	C6

King's Lynn

Pilgrims on their way to Walsingham would stop at the 15th-century Red Mount Chapel in the Walks at King's Lynn, and commercial prominence really began here as far back as the 13th century, when this Great Ouse port had connections with the German trading towns of the Hanseatic League. Prosperity continued until well into the 18th century, and although modern expansion has brought new shopping, sports and entertainment facilities to the town centre, a number of medieval buildings survive, including the Guild Hall of St George (now a theatre) and the Guild Hall of Holy Trinity. St Margaret's Church still has portions of its Norman tower. The Lynn Museum in Old Market Street looks at the history of the area, and is complemented by the Museum of Social History in King Street.

Wisbech is at the heartland of soft fruit cultivation, and is especially known for its strawberries. Set in the low-lying fens and linked to the Wash by the River Nene, it has some fine examples of Georgian architecture in the North and South Brinks which line the river on either side. Eighteenth-century Peckover House now belongs to the National Trust; also of interest is the Clarkson Memorial in Bridge Street, erected in memory of Thomas Clarkson, who campaigned for the abolition of slavery.

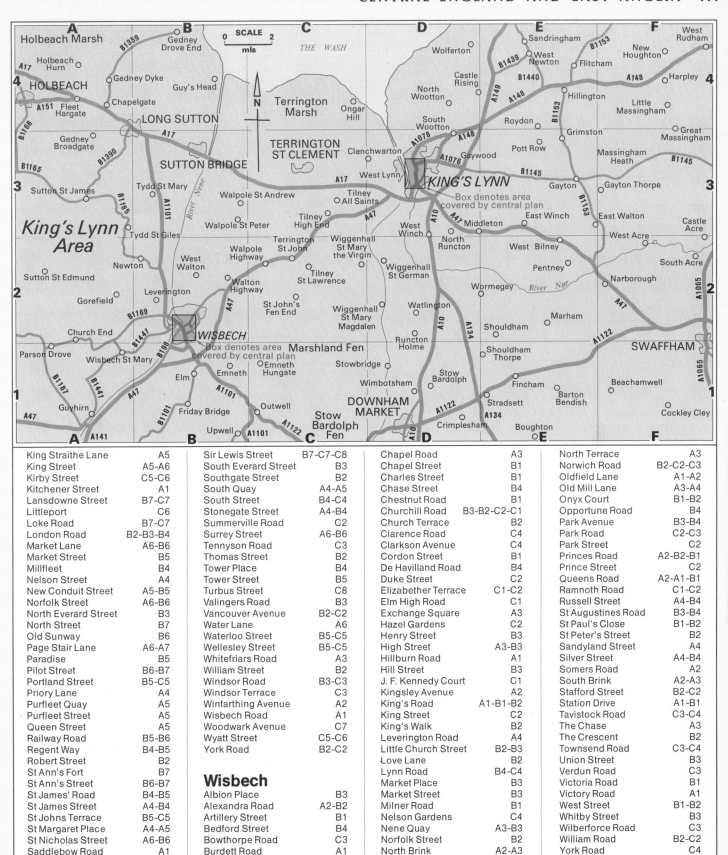

King Straithe Lane	A5
King Street	A5-A6
Kirby Street	C5-C6
Kitchener Street	A1
Lansdowne Street	B7-C7
Littleport	C6
Loke Road	B7-C7
London Road	B2-B3-B4
Market Lane	A6-B6
Market Street	B5
Millfleet	B4
Nelson Street	A4
New Conduit Street	A5-B5
Norfolk Street	A6-B6
North Everard Street	B3
North Street	B7
Old Sunway	B6
Page Stair Lane	A6-A7
Paradise	B5
Pilot Street	B6-B7
Portland Street	B5-C5
Priory Lane	A4
Purfleet Quay	A5
Purfleet Street	A5
Queen Street	A5
Railway Road	B5-B6
Regent Way	B4-B5
Robert Street	B2
St Ann's Fort	B7
St Ann's Street	B6-B7
St James' Road	B4-B5
St James Street	A4-B4
St Johns Terrace	B5-C5
St Margaret Place	A4-A5
St Nicholas Street	A6-B6
Saddlebow Road	A1
Sidney Street	C2

Sir Lewis Street	B7-C7-C8
South Everard Street	B3
Southgate Street	B2
South Quay	A4-A5
South Street	B4-C4
Stonegate Street	A4-B4
Summerville Road	C2
Surrey Street	A6-B6
Tennyson Road	C3
Thomas Street	B2
Tower Place	B4
Tower Street	B5
Turbus Street	C8
Valingers Road	B3
Vancouver Avenue	B2-C2
Water Lane	A6
Waterloo Street	B5-C5
Wellesley Street	B5-C5
Whitefriars Road	A3
William Street	B2
Windsor Road	B3-C3
Windsor Terrace	C3
Winfarthing Avenue	A2
Wisbech Road	A1
Woodwark Avenue	C7
Wyatt Street	C5-C6
York Road	B2-C2

Wisbech

Albion Place	B3
Alexandra Road	A2-B2
Artillery Street	B1
Bedford Street	B4
Bowthorpe Road	C3
Burdett Road	A1
Cannon Street	B1

Chapel Road	A3
Chapel Street	B1
Charles Street	B1
Chase Street	B4
Chestnut Road	B1
Churchill Road	B3-B2-C2-C1
Church Terrace	B2
Clarence Road	C4
Clarkson Avenue	C4
Cordon Street	B1
De Havilland Road	B4
Duke Street	C2
Elizabether Terrace	C1-C2
Elm High Road	C1
Exchange Square	A3
Hazel Gardens	C2
Henry Street	B3
High Street	A3-B3
Hillburn Road	A1
Hill Street	B3
J. F. Kennedy Court	C1
Kingsley Avenue	A2
King's Road	A1-B1-B2
King Street	C2
King's Walk	B2
Leverington Road	A4
Little Church Street	B2-B3
Love Lane	B2
Lynn Road	B4-C4
Market Place	B3
Market Street	B3
Milner Road	B1
Nelson Gardens	C4
Nene Quay	A3-B3
Norfolk Street	B2
North Brink	A2-A3
North End	A3-A4

North Terrace	A3
Norwich Road	B2-C2-C3
Oldfield Lane	A1-A2
Old Mill Lane	A3-A4
Onyx Court	B1-B2
Opportune Road	B4
Park Avenue	B3-B4
Park Road	C2-C3
Park Street	C2
Princes Road	A2-B2-B1
Prince Street	C2
Queens Road	A2-A1-B1
Ramnoth Road	C1-C2
Russell Street	A4-B4
St Augustines Road	B3-B4
St Paul's Close	B1-B2
St Peter's Street	B2
Sandyland Street	A4
Silver Street	A4-B4
Somers Road	A2
South Brink	A2-A3
Stafford Street	B2-C2
Station Drive	A1-B1
Tavistock Road	C3-C4
The Chase	A3
The Crescent	B2
Townsend Road	C3-C4
Union Street	B3
Verdun Road	C3
Victoria Road	B1
Victory Road	A1
West Street	B1-B2
Whitby Street	B3
Wilberforce Road	C3
William Road	B2-C2
York Road	C4
York Row	A2

KINGS LYNN
Designed by local architect Henry Bell and dating back to 1683, the elegant Old Customs House bears witness to a longstanding importance as a trading centre serving both the Midlands (via inland waterways) and Europe.

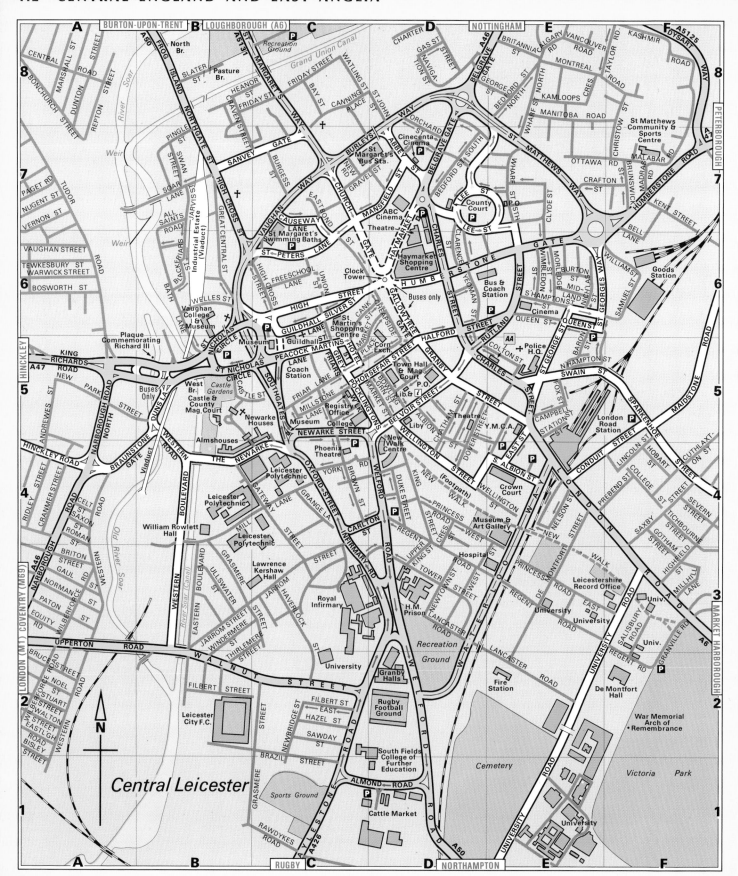

Central Leicester

Leicester

A regional capital in Roman times, Leicester has retained many buildings from its eventful and distinguished past. Today the city is a thriving modern place, a centre for industry and commerce, serving much of the Midlands. Among the most outstanding monuments from the past is the Jewry Wall, a great bastion of Roman masonry. Close by are remains of the Roman baths and

several other contemporary buildings. Attached is a museum covering all periods from prehistoric times to 1500. Numerous other museums include the Wygston's House Museum of Costume, with displays covering the period 1769 to 1924; Newarke House, with collections showing changing social conditions in Leicester through four hundred years; and Leicestershire Museum and Art Gallery, with collections of drawings, paintings, ceramics, geology and natural history.

The medieval Guildhall has many features of interest, including a great hall, library and police cells. Leicester's castle, although remodelled in the 17th century, retains a 12th-century great hall. The Church of St Mary de Castro, across the road from the castle, has features going back at least as far as Norman times; while St Nicholas's Church is even older, with Roman and Saxon foundations. St Martin's Cathedral dates mainly from the 13th to 15th centuries and has a notable Bishop's throne.

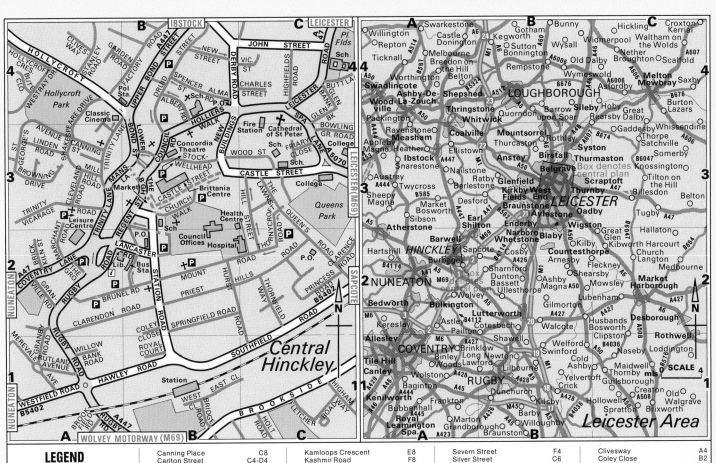

LEGEND

Town Plan

AA Recommended route	▬▬▬
Restricted roads	▭▭▭
Other roads	▬▬▬
Buildings of interest	▬
Car parks	**P**
Parks and open spaces	▬

Area Plan

A roads	▬▬
B roads	▬▬
Locations	Creaton○
Urban area	▭

Street Index with Grid Reference

Leicester

Abbey Street	D7
Albion Street	D4-D5
All Saints Road	B7
Almond Road	C1-D1
Andrewes Street	A4-A5
Aylestone Road	C1-C2
Baron Street	E5-E6
Bath Lane	B5-B6
Bay Street	C8
Bedford Street North	E8
Bedford Street South	D7
Belgrave Gate	D7-D8-E8
Bell Lane	F6-F7
Belvoir Street	D5
Bisley Street	A1-A2
Blackfriars Street	B6
Bonchurch Street	A7-A8
Bosworth Street	A6
Bowling Green Street	D5
Braunstone Gate	A4-B4-B5
Brazil Street	C1-C2
Britannia Street	E8
Briton Street	A3
Brown Street	C4
Bruce Street	A2
Brunswick Street	F7
Burgess Street	C7
Burleys Way	C7-D7-D8
Burton Street	E6
Calgary Road	E8
Campbell Street	D5
Cank Street	C6-D6

Canning Place	C8
Carlton Street	C4-D4
Castle Street	B5-C5
Celt Street	A4
Central Road	A8
Charles Street	D7-D6-D5-E5
Charter Street	D8
Chatham Street	D4-D5
Cheapside	D5-D6
Christow Street	F7-F8
Church Gate	C7-C6-D6
Clarence Street	D6-D7
Clyde Street	E6-E7
College Street	F4
Colton Street	D5-E5
Conduit Street	E4-F4-F5
Crafton Street	E7-F7
Cranmer Street	A4
Craven Street	B7-B8
Crescent Street	D4
Cuthlaxton Street	F4-F5
De Montfort Street	E3-E4
Dover Street	D4-D5
Duke Street	D4
Duns Lane	B5
Dunton Street	A8
Dysart Way	F7-F8
East Bond Street	C6-C7-D6
East Street	E4-E5
Eastern Boulevard	B3-B4
Eastleigh Road	A2
Equity Road	A3
Filbert Street	B2-C2
Filbert Street East	C2
Fox Street	E5
Freeschool Lane	C6
Friar Lane	C5
Friday Street	B8-C8
Frog Island	B8
Gallowtree Gate	D6
Gas Street	D8
Gateway Street	B4-C4-C3
Gaul Street	A3
George Street	D8-E8
Gotham Street	F3-F4
Granby Street	D5-E5
Grange Lane	C4
Granville Road	F2-F3
Grasmere Street	B4-B3-C3-C2-C1-B1
Gravel Street	C7-D7
Great Central Street	B6-B7
Greyfriars	C5
Guildhall Lane	C6
Halford Street	D5-D6-E6
Haverlock Street	C2-C3
Haymarket	D6-D7
Hazel Street	C2
Heanor Street	B8-C8
High Cross Street	B7-B6-C6
Highfield Street	F3
High Street	C6-D6
Hinckley Road	A4
Hobart Street	F4
Horsefair Street	C5-D5
Hotel Street	C5
Humberstone Gate	D6-E6
Humberstone Road	F7
Infirmary Road	C4-C3-D3
Jarrom Street	B3-C3
Jarvis Street	B7

Kamloops Crescent	E8
Kashmir Road	F8
Kent Street	F7
King Richards Road	A5
King Street	D4-D5
Lancaster Road	D3-E3-E2
Lee Street	D6-D7-E7
Lincoln Street	F4-F5
London Road	E5-E4-F4-F3
Madras Road	F7
Maidstone Road	F5-F6
Malabar Road	F7
Manitoba Road	E8-F8
Mansfield Street	C7-D7
Market Place	C5-C6-D6
Market Street	D5
Marshall Street	A8
Midland Street	E6
Mill Hill Lane	F3
Mill Lane	B4-C4
Millstone Lane	C5
Morledge Street	E6
Montreal Road	E8-F8
Narborough Road	A3-A4
Narborough Road North	A4-A5
Navigation Street	D8
Nelson Street	E4
Newarke Street	C5
Newbridge Street	C2
New Park Street	A5-B5
New Road	C7
Newtown Street	D3
New Walk	D4-E4-E3-F3
Nicholas Street	E6
Noel Street	A7
Northampton Street	E5
Northgate Street	B7-B8
Norman Street	A3
Nugent Street	A7
Orchard Street	D7-D8
Ottawa Road	E7-F7
Oxford Street	C4
Paget Road	A7
Paton Street	A3
Peacock Lane	C5
Pingle Street	B7
Pocklingtons Walk	C5-D5
Prebend Street	E4
Princess Road East	E3-F3
Princess Road West	D4-E4
Queen Street	E6
Rawdykes Road	B1-C1
Regent Road	D4-D3-E3-F3-F2
Repton Street	A7-A8
Ridley Street	A4
Roman Street	A4
Rutland Street	D5-E5-E6
St George Street	E5-E6
St Georges Way	E6-F6
St John Street	D8
St Margaret's Way	B8-C8-C7
St Martins	C5
St Mathews Way	E7
St Nicholas Circle	B6-B5-C5
St Peters Lane	C6
Salisbury Road	F2-F3
Samuel Stuart	F6
Sanvey Gate	B7-C7
Sawday Street	C2
Saxby Street	F4
Saxon Street	A4

Severn Street	F4
Silver Street	C6
Slater Street	B8
Soar Lane	B7
South Albion Street	E4
Southampton Street	E6
Southgates	C5
Sparkenhoe Street	F4-F5
Station Street	E5
Stuart Street	A2
Swain Street	E5-F5
Swan Street	B7
The Newarke	B4-C4
Taylor Road	E8-F8
Tewkesbury Street	A6
Thirlemere Street	B2-B3-C3
Tichbourne Street	F3-F4
Tower Street	D3
Tudor Road	A5-A6-A7-A8
Ullswater Street	B3
Union Street	D6
University Road	E1-E2-E3-F3
Upper King Street	D3-D4
Upperton Road	A3-B3-B2
Vancouver Road	E8
Vaughan Way	C6-C7
Vaughan Street	A6
Vernon Street	A6-A7
Walnut Street	B3-B2-C2
Walton Street	A2
Warwick Street	A6
Waterloo Way	D2-D3-E3-E4
Watling Street	C8
Welford Road	D1-D2-D3-D4
Welles Street	B6
Wellington Street	D4-E4-D5
Western Boulevard	B3-B4
Western Road	A1-A2-A3-A4-B4-B5
West Street	D3-E3-E4
Wharf Street North	E7-E8
Wharf Street South	E7
Wilberforce Road	A2-A3
William Street	F6
Wimbledon Street	E6
Windermere Street	B2-B3-C3
Yeoman Street	D6
York Road	C4

Hinckley

Albert Road	B4
Alma Road	B4
Bowling Green Road	C3
Brick Kiln Street	A2
Bridge Road	B1
Brookfield Road	A1
Brookside	B1-C1
Browning Drive	A4
Brunel Road	A2-B2
Bute Close	A4
Butt Lane	C4
Canning Street	A3
Castle Street	B3-C3
Charles Street	C4
Church Walk	B3
Clarence Road	C4
Clarendon Road	A2-B2
Cleveland Road	A3

Clivesway	A4
Coley Close	B2
Council Road	B3
Coventry Lane	A2
Derby Road	B4
Druid Street	B3-B4
East Close	B1-C1
Factory Road	A4-B4
Fletcher Road	C1
Friary Close	C3
Garden Road	A4-B4
Glen Bank	C4
Granby Road	A1-A2
Granville Road	A2
Hawley Road	A1-B1
Higham Way	C1
Highfields Road	C4
Hill Street	C2-C3
Holliers Walk	B3-B4
Hollycroft	A4
Hollycroft Crescent	A4
Holt Road	C1
Hurst Road	B2-C1-C2
John Street	C4
Lancaster Road	A2-B2
Leicester Road	C4
Linden Road	A3
Lower Bond Street	B3-B4
Mansion Lane	A3-B3
Marchant Road	A2-A3
Merevale Avenue	A1
Mill Hill Road	A3
Mount Road	B2-C2
New Buildings	B3-B4
New Street	B4
Priest Hills Road	B2-C2
Princess Road	C4
Queens Road	C2-C3
Regent Street	A2-B2-A3-B3-A4
Royal Court	B1
Rugby Road	A2-A1-B1
Rutland Avenue	A1
St George's Avenue	A3-A4
Shakespeare Drive	A3-A4
Southfield Road	B1-C1-C2
Spa Lane	C3-C4
Spencer Street	B4
Springfield Road	B2
Stanley Road	A4
Station Road	B1-B2
Stockwellhead	B3
The Borough	B3
The Grove	A2
The Lawns	C3
Thornfield Way	C2
Thornycroft Road	B4
Trinity Lane	A2-A3-A4-B4
Trinity Vicarage Road	A3
Upper Bond Street	B4
Victoria Street	C4
West Close	B1
Westray Drive	A4
Westfield Road	A1
Willow Bank Road	A1
Wood Street	B3-C3

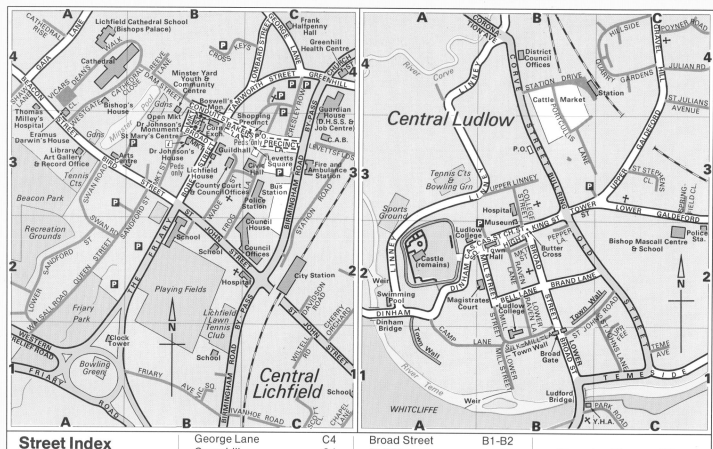

Street Index with Grid Reference

Lichfield

Bakers Lane	B3-C3
Beacon Street	A3-A4
Bird Street	A3-B3
Birmingham Road By-Pass	B1-B2-C2-C3-C4
Bore Street	B3
Broad Market	B3
Cathedral Close	A4-B4
Cathedral Rise	A4
Chapel Lane	C1
Cherry Orchard	C1-C2
Church Street	C4
Conduit Street	B3-B4
Cresley Row	C3-C4
Crosskeys	B4-C4
Dam Street	B4
Davidson Road	C2
Dean's Walk	A4-B4
Friary Avenue	B1
Friary Road	A1-B1
Frog Lane	B2-B3-C3
Gaia Lane	A4

George Lane	C4
Greenhill	C4
Ivanhoe Road	B1-C1
Lombard Street	C4
Lower Sandford Street	A1-A2
Levettsfields	C3
Market Street	B3-B4
Precinct Lane	C3
Queen Street	A2
Reeve Lane	B4
St John Street	B3-B2-C2-C1
Sandford Street	A2-B2-B3
Scott Close	C1
Shaw Lane	A4
Station Road	C2-C3
Swan Road	A2-A3
Tamworth Street	B3-B4-C4
The Friary	A2-B2-B3
Vicars Close	A4
Victoria Square	B1
Wade Street	B2-B3
Walsall Road	A1-A2
Western Relief Road	A1
Westgate	A3-A4
Wittell Road	C1

Ludlow

Bell Lane	B2
Brand Lane	B2-C2

Broad Street	B1-B2
Bull Ring	B3
Camp Lane	A2-A1-B1
Castle Square	A2-B2
Castle Street	B2
College Street	B2-B3
Coronation Avenue	A4-B4
Corve Street	B3-B4
Dinham	A2
Gravel Hill	C4
High Street	B2
Hillside	C4
Julian Road	C4
King Street	B2-B3
Linney	A2-A3-B3-A3-A4-B4
Lower Broad Street	B1
Lower Galdeford	C2-C3
Lower Mill Street	B1
Lower Raven Lane	B1-B2
Market Street	B2
Mill Street	B1-B2
Old Street	B3-B2-C2-C1
Park Road	B1-C1
Pepper Lane	B2
Portcullis Lane	B4-B3-C3
Poyner Road	C4
Quarry Gardens	C4
Raven Lane	B2
St Johns Lane	C1-C2
St Johns Road	B1-B2-C2
St Julians Avenue	C4
St Stephens Close	C3

Silk Mill Lane	B1
Springfield Close	C3
Station Drive	B4
Teme Avenue	C1
Temeside	B1-C1
Tower Street	B3-C3
Upper Fee	C1-C2
Upper Galdeford	C3-C4
Upper Linney	B3

Key to Town Plan

AA Recommended roads	▬▬▬
Restricted roads	▭▭▭
Other roads	▬▬
Buildings of interest	Cinema
Parks and open spaces	◢
Car Parks	P
Churches	†

Lichfield Three graceful spires known as the 'Ladies of the Vale' soar up from Lichfield's Cathedral of St Mary and St Chad. Constructed in the 13th century and combining early English and decorated Gothic styles, the Cathedral is the most outstanding feature of this attractive city, which has retained a distinctly rural appearance despite a good deal of industrial expansion.

Most distinguished son of Lichfield is Dr Samuel Johnson and his father's 18th-century house in Market Square (which served the family as a dwelling and a bookshop) has been restored and converted into a museum. Johnson's birthday (18 September) is commemorated on the nearest Saturday by a procession from the Guild Hall.

Ludlow, built on a steep hill washed on two sides by the Rivers Corve and Teme, has, since earliest times, been recognised as a strategic site, and the Normans were quick to take advantage of this. Their castle, now an impressive ruin crowning the hilltop, looks out over the Welsh Marches. The town beneath is a charming mixture of wide Georgian streets and narrow medieval alleyways where 18th-century brick and stucco rubs shoulders with half-timbered Tudor buildings with leaning walls and steeply-pitched roofs. The most famous of all the timbered buildings is the Feathers Hotel, although it has plenty of competitors, and the dignified stone Butter Cross houses the town's museum.

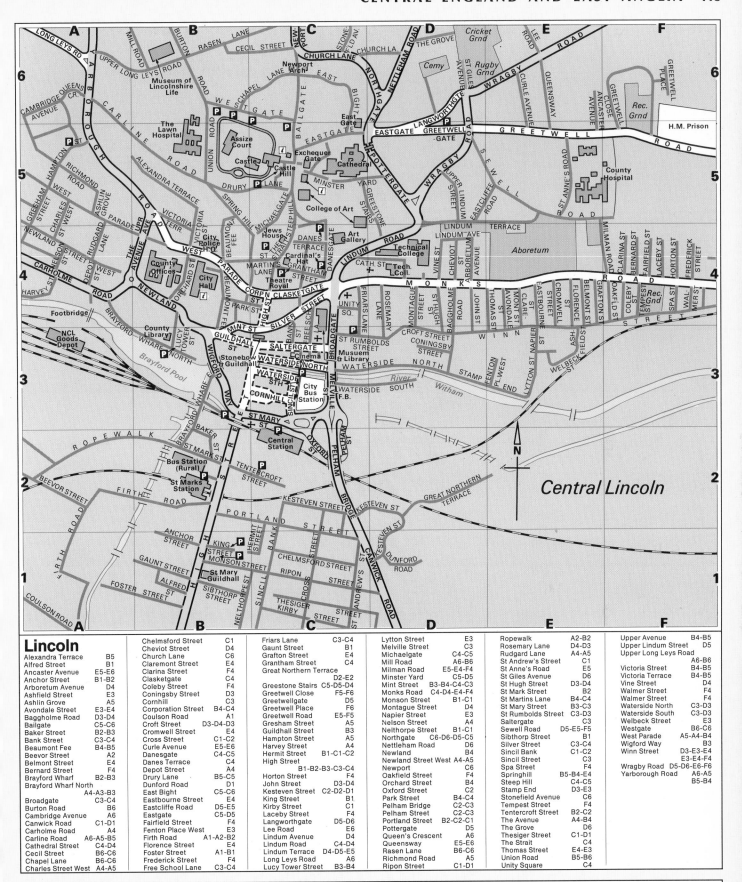

Central Lincoln

Lincoln

The striking triple-spired cathedral of Lincoln, the third largest in England, dominates the countryside for miles. Its impressive west front, decorated with many statues, is all that remains of the first cathedral the Normans built, and most of the rest dates from the 13th century. Among its treasures is one of the four extant original copies of Magna Carta.

Built on a rugged limestone plateau above the River Witham, the cobbled streets of the medieval city straggle down the sides of the hill past old houses built from the same local honey-coloured limestone as the cathedral. Modern Lincoln owes much to engineering industries, but few tentacles of change have crept into the heart of the city where the oldest inhabited house in England, Aaron's House, can be found. Other places of interest include the quaintly-named Cardinal's Hat

– thought to be named after Cardinal Wolsey who was Bishop of Lincoln for one year. Newport Arch, at the end of the picturesque street called Bailgate, is a relic from the Roman city of Lincoln – *Lindum Colonia*. It is the only Roman gateway in the country still open to traffic. Complementing the cathedral in size if not in majesty is the Norman castle. It is possible to walk along the battlements and the old prison chapel provides a grim insight into the punishment meted out in less enlightened times.

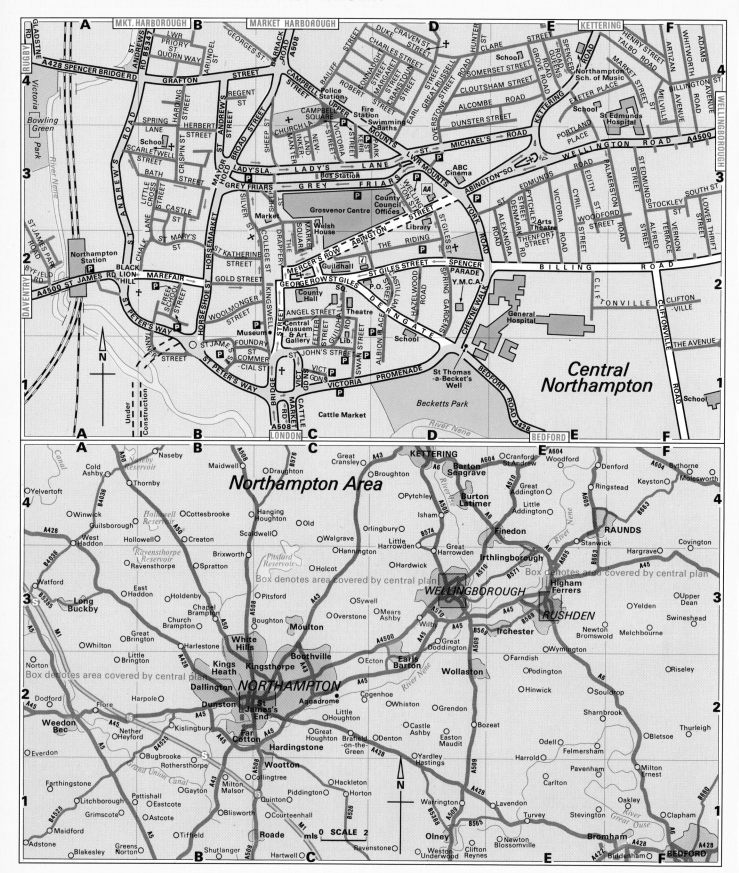

Northampton

The town's long connection with the boot and shoe trade started during the Civil War when Northampton made footwear for Cromwell's army. Now, although still internationally famous for this commodity, it is also an important light industry and distribution centre. Predictably, both the town's museums contain shoes, and include Queen Victoria's wedding shoes and Nijinsky's ballet shoes among their exhibits.

Northampton has a long and important history and its castle became a resting place for every English king from Henry I to Edward III. However, due to Charles II's destruction of the castle and the town walls, and a devastating fire in 1675, little remains of the medieval town. The vast market square — one of the largest in the country — dates from the days of the cattle drovers when Northampton was an important market centre, and many of the street names — such as Horsemarket and Mercer's Row — reflect the town's history.

Wellingborough stands in the valley of the River Nene; like Northampton, the manufacture of footwear is a well-established industry. The two churches of the town form an interesting contrast; All-Hallows retains traces of medieval workmanship and has a 17th-century house as well as a church hall, whilst St Mary's is a modern building designed by Sir Ninian Comper.

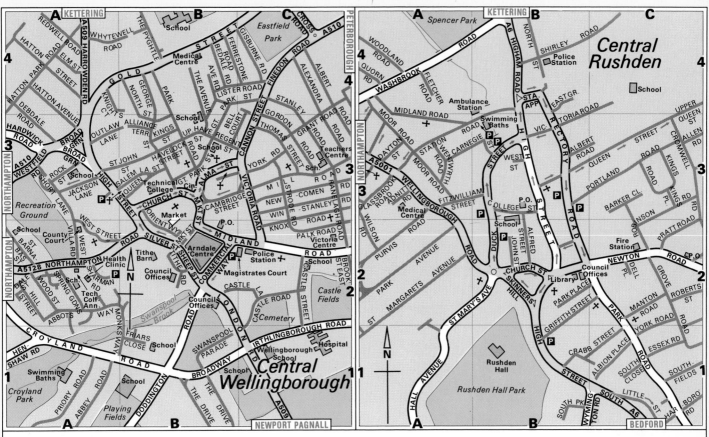

Central Wellingborough

Central Rushden

LEGEND

Town Plan

AA recommended route
Restricted roads
Other roads
Buildings of interest   Library
Car parks   P
Parks and open spaces

Area Plan

A roads
B roads
Locations   Winfarth O
Urban area

Street Index with Grid Reference

Northampton

Abington Square	D3-E3
Abington Street	C2-D2-D3
Adams Avenue	F4
Albion Place	D1-D2
Alcombe Road	D4-E4
Alexandra Road	E2-E3
Alfred Street	F2-F3
Angel Street	C2
Artizan Avenue	F3-F4
Arundel Street	B4
Bailiff Street	C4
Barrack Road	C4
Bath Street	A3-B3
Bedford Road	D1-E1
Billing Road	E2-F2
Billington Street	F4
Black Lion Hill	A2
Bridge Street	C1-C2
Broad Street	B3-B4-C4
Byfield Street	A2
Campbell Square	C4
Campbell Street	C4
Castle Street	B3
Castillian Street	D2
Cattle Market Road	C1
Chalk Lane	B2-B3
Charles Street	C4-D4
Cheyne Walk	D1-D2
Church Lane	C3-C4
Clare Street	D4-E4
Cliftonville	E2-F2
Cliftonville Road	F1-F2
Cloutsham Street	D4-E4
College Street	C2
Commercial Street	B1-C1

Connaught Street	C4-D4
Cranstoun Street	D4
Craven Street	D4
Crispin Street	B3
Cyril Street	E2-E3
Denmark Road	E2-E3
Derngate	C2-D2-D1
Duke Street	C4-D4
Dunster Street	D3-D4-E4
Earl Street	D3-D4
Edith Street	E3
Exeter Place	E4-F4
Fetter Street	C1-C2
Free School Street	B2
Foundry Street	B1-C1
George Row	C2
Georges Street	B4-C4
Gladstone Road	A4
Gold Street	B2-C2
Grafton Street	B4-C4
Great Russell Street	D4
Greyfriars	B3-C3-D3
Grove Road	E4
Guildhall Road	C1-C2
Harding Street	B4
Hazelwood Road	D2
Henry Street	F4
Herbert Street	B3
Horsemarket	B2-B3
Horseshoe Street	B1-B2
Hunter Street	D4
Inkerman Terrace	C3
Kerr Street	C3-C4
Kettering Road	E3-E4
Kingswell	C1-C2
Lady's Lane	B3-C3-D3
Little Cross Street	B3
Lower Mounts	D3
Lower Priory Street	B4
Lower Thrift Street	F2-F3
Marefair	A2-B2
Margaret Street	D4
Market Square	C2-C3
Market Street	E4-F4
Mayor Hold	B3
Melville Street	F4
Mercers Row	C2
Newland	C3
Overstone Road	D3-D4
Palmerston Road	F3-F4
Park Street	C3
Portland Place	E3-E4
Pytchley Street	E3
Queens Road	E4
Quorn Way	B4
Regent Street	B4
Robert Street	C4-D4
St Andrews Road	A2-A3-A4-B4
St Andrews Street	B3-B4
St Edmunds Road	D3-E3-F3
St Edmunds Street	F3
St Giles Square	C2
St Giles Street	C2-D2-D3
St James Road	A2
St James Park Road	A2-A3
St James Street	B1
St John's Street	C1
St Katherine Street	B2-C2
St Mary's Street	B2
St Michael's Road	D3-E3
St Peter's Way	A2-B2-B1-C1

Scarletwell Street	A3-B3
Sheep Street	C3-C4
Silver Street	B3-C3
Somerset Street	D4-E4
South Street	F3
Spencer Road	E4
Spencer Bridge Road	A4
Spencer Parade	D2
Spring Gardens	D2
Spring Lane	A4-B4-B3
Stockley Street	F3
Swan Street	C1-C2
The Avenue	F1
The Drapery	C2-C3
The Riding	C2-D2
Tanner Street	B1-B2
Talbot Road	E4-F4
Thenfoot Street	E2-E3
Upper Mounts	C4-C3-D3
Vernon Terrace	F2-F3
Victoria Gardens	C1
Victoria Promenade	C1-D1
Victoria Road	E2-E3
Victoria Street	C3-C4
Wellington Road	E3-F3
Wellington Street	D3
Whitworth Road	F3-F4
Woodford Street	E3-F3
Woolmonger Street	B2-C2
York Road	D3-D2

Wellingborough

Abbey Road	A1
Abbotts Way	A2
Albert Road	C3-C4
Alexandra Road	C3-C4
Alliance Terrace	B3
Alma Street	B3
Avenue Road	B4
Bedale Road	B4
Bell Court	B3-C3-C4
Broad Green	A3
Broadway	B1-C1
Brook Street East	C2
Cambridge Street	B3-C3
Cannon Street	C3-C4
Castle Lane	B2-C2
Castle Road	C1-C2
Castle Street	C2
Church Street	B3
Commercial Way	B2
Cross Road	C4
Croyland Road	A2-A1-B1
Dale Street	A2
Debdale Road	A3-A4
Doddington Road	B1-B2
Ferrestone Road	B4-C4
Finedon Road	C4
Friars Close	B1
George Street	B3-B4
Gisburne Road	C4
Gold Street	A4-B4-C4
Gordon Road	C3
Grant Road	C3-C4
Great Park Street	B3-B4-C4
Hardwick Road	A3

Harrowden Road	A3-A4
Hatton Avenue	A3-A4
Hatton Street	A4
Hatton Park Road	A4
Havelock Street	B3
Henshaw Road	A1
High Street	A3-B3-B2
Hill Street	A2
Irthlingborough Road	C1-C2
Jackson Lane	A3
Kings Street	B3
Knights Court	A4-B4
Knox Road	C2-C3
Lister Road	B4-C4
London Road	B1-B2-C2-C1
Market Street	B2-B3
Midland Road	B2-C2
Mill Road	C3
Monks Way	A1-B1-B2
Newcomen Road	C3
North Street	B3-B4
Northampton Road	A2-B2
Orient Road	C2-C3
Outlaw Lane	A3-B3
Palk Road	C2
Park Road	B3-B4
Priory Road	A1
Queen Street	B3
Ranelagh Road	C2-C3
Redwell Road	A4
Regent Street	B3-C3
Rock Street	A3
St Barnabas Street	A2
St John Street	A3-B3
Salem Court	A3-B3
Sharman Road	A2
Sheep Street	B2
Short Lane	A3
Silver Street	B2
Spring Gardens	A2
Stanley Road	C3-C4
Strode Road	C2-C3
Swanspool Parade	B1
The Avenue	B3-B4
The Drive	B1
The Pyghtle	B4
Thomas Street	C3
Tithebarn Road	B2
Upper Havelock Street	B3
Victoria Road	C2-C3
West Street	A2
Westfield Road	A3
West Villa Road	A2
Whytewell Road	A4-B4
Winstanley Road	C3
Wood Street	A2
York Road	C3

Rushden

Adnitt Road	A2-A3
Albert Road	B3-C3
Albion Place	C1
Alfred Street	B2-B3
Allen Road	C3
Barker Close	C3
Carnegie Street	A3-B3

Church Street	B2
College Street	B3
Crabb Street	B1-C1
Cromwell Road	C2-C3
Dayton Street	A3
Dell Place	C2
Duck Street	B2-B3
East Grove	B4
Essex Road	C1
Fitzwilliam Street	A3-B3
Fletcher Road	A4
Glassbrook Road	A3
Griffith Street	B1-B2-C2
Grove Road	C1-C2
Hall Avenue	A1
Harborough Road	C1
High Street	B2-B3-B4
High Street South	B2-B1-C1
Higham Road	B4
John Street	B2
Kings Road	C3
Kings Place	C3
Little Street	C1
Manton Road	C2
Midland Road	A3-A4
Moor Road	A3-A4
Newton Road	C2
North Street	B4
Park Avenue	A2
Park Place	B2-C2
Park Road	C2-C1
Pemberton Street	A3-A4
Portland Road	B3-C3
Pratt Road	C2-C3
Purvis Road	A2-A3
Queen Street	B3-C3
Quorn Road	A4
Rectory Road	B2-B3-B4
Roberts Street	C2
Robinson Road	C2-C3
St Margarets Avenue	A1-A2
St Mary's Avenue	A1-A2-B2
Shirley Road	B4-C4
Skinners Hill	B2
South Close	C1
South Park	B1
Southfields	C1
Station Approach	B4
Station Road	A3-B3-B4
Upper Queen Street	C3-C4
Victoria Road	B3-B4-C4
Washbrook Road	A4-B4
Wellingborough Road	A3-A2-B2
Wentworth Road	A3
West Street	B3
Wilson Road	A2-A3
Woodland Road	A4
Wymington Road	B1-C1
York Road	C1-C2

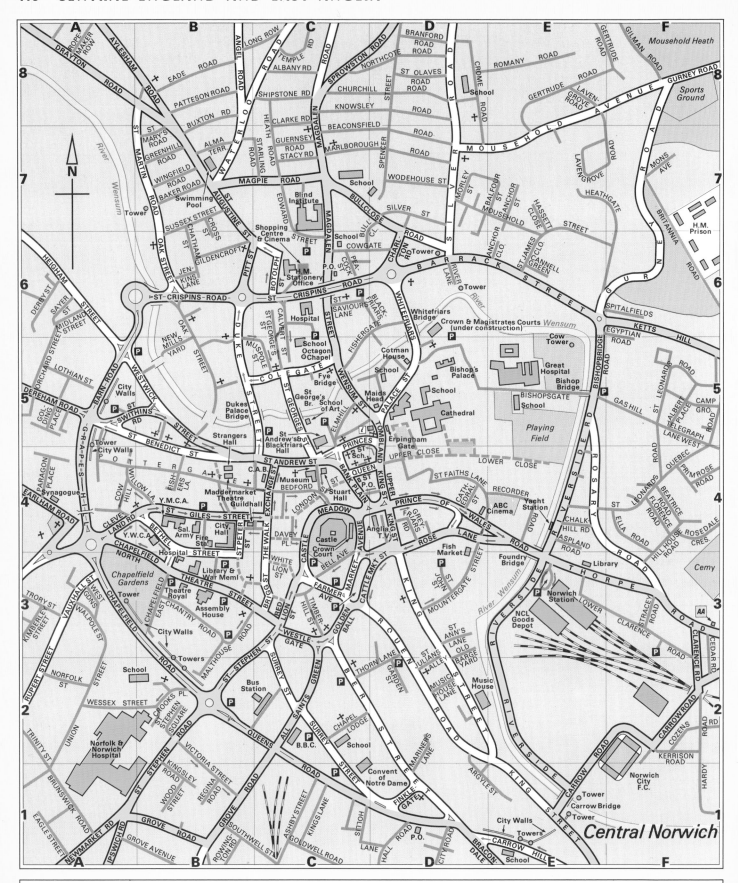

Central Norwich

Norwich

Fortunately the heart has not been ripped out of Norwich to make way for some bland precinct, so its ancient character has been preserved. Narrow alleys run between the streets – sometimes opening out into quiet courtyards, sometimes into thoroughfares packed with people, sometimes into lanes which seem quite deserted. It is a unique place, with something of interest on every corner.

The cathedral was founded in 1096 by the city's first bishop, Herbert de Losinga. Among its most notable features are the nave, with its huge pillars, the bishop's throne (a Saxon survival unique in Europe) and the cloisters with their matchless collection of roof bosses. Across the city is the great stone keep of the castle, set on a mound and dominating all around it. It dates from Norman times, but was refaced in 1834. The keep now forms part of Norwich Castle Museum –

an extensive and fascinating collection. Other museums are Bridewell Museum – collections relating to local crafts and industries within a 14th-century building – and Strangers' Hall, a genuinely 'old world' house, rambling and full of surprises, both in its tumble of rooms and in the things which they contain. Especially picturesque parts of the city are Elm Hill – a street of ancient houses; Tombland – with two gateways into the Cathedral Close; and Pull's Ferry – a watergate by the river.

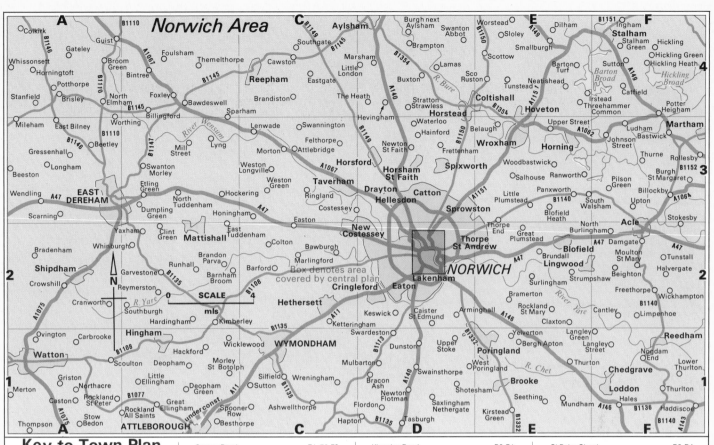

Norwich Area

Box denotes area covered by central plan

NORWICH

Key to Town Plan and Area Plan

Town Plan
AA Recommended roads
Restricted roads
Other roads
Buildings of interest — School
AA Service Centre — AA
Car Parks — P
Parks and open spaces
One Way Streets →

Area Plan
A roads
B roads
Locations — East Rushton○
Urban area

Street Index with Grid Reference

Norwich

Albany Road	C8
Albert Place	F5
All Saints Green	C2-C3
Alma Terrace	B7
Anchor Close	E6
Anchor Street	E7
Angel Road	B8
Argyle Street	D2-D1-E1
Ashby Street	C1
Aspland Road	E4
Aylesham Road	A8-B8
Baker Road	B7
Balfour Street	E7
Bank Plain	C4
Barn Road	A5
Barrack Street	D6-E6
Beaconsfield Road	C7-D7
Beatrice Road	F4
Bedford Street	C3
Bell Avenue	C3
Ber Street	C3-C2-D2-D1
Bethel Street	B4-B3
Bishopbridge Road	E5-E6
Bishopsgate	D5-E5
Blackfriars	C6-D6
Botolph Street	C6
Bracondale	D1-E1
Branford Road	D8
Brigg Street	C3
Britannia Road	F7-F6
Brunswick Road	A1
Bull Close	C6-C7-D7
Bull Close Road	C7-D7-D6
Buxton Road	B7-B8
Calvert Street	C6-C5
Camp Grove	F5
Cannell Green	E6
Carrow Hill	D1-E1

Carrow Road	E1-E2-F2
Castle Meadow Street	C3-C4
Cathedral Street	D4
Cattle Market	C3-D3
Cedar Road	F3-F2
Chalkhill Road	E4
Chantry Road	B3
Chapelfield East	B3
Chapelfield North	A4-A3-B4-B3
Chapelfield Road	A3-B3-B2
Chapel Lodge	C2
Churchill Road	C8-D8
Charlton Road	D6
Chatham Street	B7-B6
City Road	D1
Clarence Road	F3-F2
Clarke Street	C7-C8
Cleveland Road	A4-B4
Colegate	B5-C5
Cowgate	C6-D6
Cow Hill	A4
Cozens Road	F2
Crome Road	D8-D7
Crooks Place	B2
Cross Street	B7-B6
Davey Place	C4
Derby Street	A6
Dereham Road	A5
Drayton Road	A8-B8
Duke Street	B6-B5-C5-C4
Eade Road	B8
Earlham Road	A4
Esdelle Street	B7-C7
Edward Street	C7-C6
Egyptian Road	E6-F6-F5
Ella Road	F4-F3
Elmhill	C5
Exchange Street	C4
Farmer Avenue	C3
Finklegate	D1
Fishergate	C5-C6-D6
Fishers Lane	B4
Florence Road	F4
Garden Street	D2
Gas Hill	E5-F5
Gertrude Road	E7-E8-F8
Gildencroft	B6
Gilman Road	F8
Golden Ball	C3
Golding Place	A5
Goldwell Road	C1
Grapes Hill	A5-A4
Greenhill Road	B7
Greyfriars Road	D4
Grove Avenue	A1-B1
Grove Road	A1-B1-C1-C2
Gurney Road	E6-F6-F7-F8
Guernsey Road	C7
Hall Road	D1
Hardy Road	F1-F2
Hassett Close	E7
Heathgate	E7-F7
Heath Road	C8-C7
Heigham Street	A6-A5
Hill House Road	F3-F4
Hollis Lane	C1-D1
Ipswich Road	A1
Jenkins Lane	B6
Kerrison Road	F2
Ketts Hill	E6-F6-F5
Kimberley Street	A3
Kings Lane	C1

Kingsley Road	B2-B1
King Street	D4-D3-D2-E2-E1
Knowsley Road	C8-D8
Lavengrove Road	E8-E7-F7
London Street	C4
Long Row	B8-C8
Lothian Street	A5
Lower Clarence Road	E3-F3-F2
Lower Close	D4-E4
Magdalen Road	C7-C8
Magdalen Street	C7-C6-C5
Magpie Road	B7-C7
Malthouse Road	B2-B3
Mariners Lane	D1-D2
Market Avenue	C3-C4
Marlborough Road	C7-D7
Midland Street	A5-A6
Mons Avenue	F7
Morley Street	D7
Mountergate Street	D3-D4
Mousehold Avenue	D7-E7-E8-F8
Mousehold Street	D7-E7-E6-F6
Music House Lane	D2
Muspole Street	B5-C5
Newmarket Road	A1
New Mills Yard	B5
Norfolk Street	A2
Northcote Road	C8-D8
Oak Street	B6-B5
Old Barge Yard	D2-D3
Orchard Street	A5-A6
Palace Street	D5
Paragon Place	A4
Patteson Road	B8
Peacock Street	C6
Pitt Street	B6-C6
Pottergate	A4-B4
Prince of Wales Road	D4-E4-E3
Primrose Road	F4
Princes Street	C4-C5-D5
Quebec Road	F4-F5
Queens Road	B2-C2-C1
Queen Street	C4-D4
Recorder Road	E4
Red Lion Street	C3
Regina Road	B1
River Lane	D6
Riverside	E3-E2-E1
Riverside Road	E3-E4-E5
Romany Road	D8-E8
Ropemaker Row	A8
Rosary Road	E5-E4-F4-F3
Rosedale Crescent	F4
Rose Lane	D3-D4-E4
Rouen Road	C3-D3-D2
Rowington Road	B1
Rupert Street	A2-A3
St Andrew Street	C4
St Ann's Lane	D5
St Augustine Street	B7-B6
St Benedict Street	A5-B5-B4
St Crispins Road	B6-C6-D6
St Faiths Lane	D4
St George's Street	C6-C5-C4
St Giles Street	B4-C4
St James Close	E6
St John Street	D3
St Juliens Alley	D2-D3
St Leonards Road	E4-F4-F5
St Martin Road	A8-B8-A7-B7
St Mary's Road	B7
St Olaves Road	D8

St Peter Street	B3-B4
St Saviours Lane	C6
St Stephen Road	A1-B1-B2
St Stephen Street	B2-B3-C3
St Stephen Square	B2
St Swithins Road	A5-B5
Sayer Street	A6
Shipstone Road	C8
Silver Road	D6-D7-D8
Silver Street	D7
Southwell Street	B1-C1
Spencer Street	D7-D8
Spitalfields	E6-F6
Sprowston Road	C8-D8
Stacy Road	C7
Starling Road	B7-C7
Stracey Road	F3
Surrey Street	C3-C2-C1-D1
Sussex Street	B6-B7
The Walk	C3-C4
Telegraph Lane West	F5-F4
Temple Road	C8
Theatre Street	B3-C3
Thorne Lane	C2-D2-D3
Thorpe Road	E3-F3
Timberhill Street	C3
Tombland	D5-D4
Trinity Street	A2-A1
Trory Street	A3
Union Street	A1-A2-A3
Upper Close	D4
Upper King Street	D4
Vauxhall Street	A3
Victoria Street	B2-B1
Walpole Street	A3
Waterloo Road	B7-B8-C8
Whitefriars	D6-D5
White Lion Street	C3
Willow Lane	A4-B4
Wingfield Road	B7
Wensum Street	C5-D5
Wessex Street	A2-B2
West Gardens	A3
Westle Gate	C3
Westwick Street	A5-B5-B4
Wodehouse Street	D7
Wood Street	B1

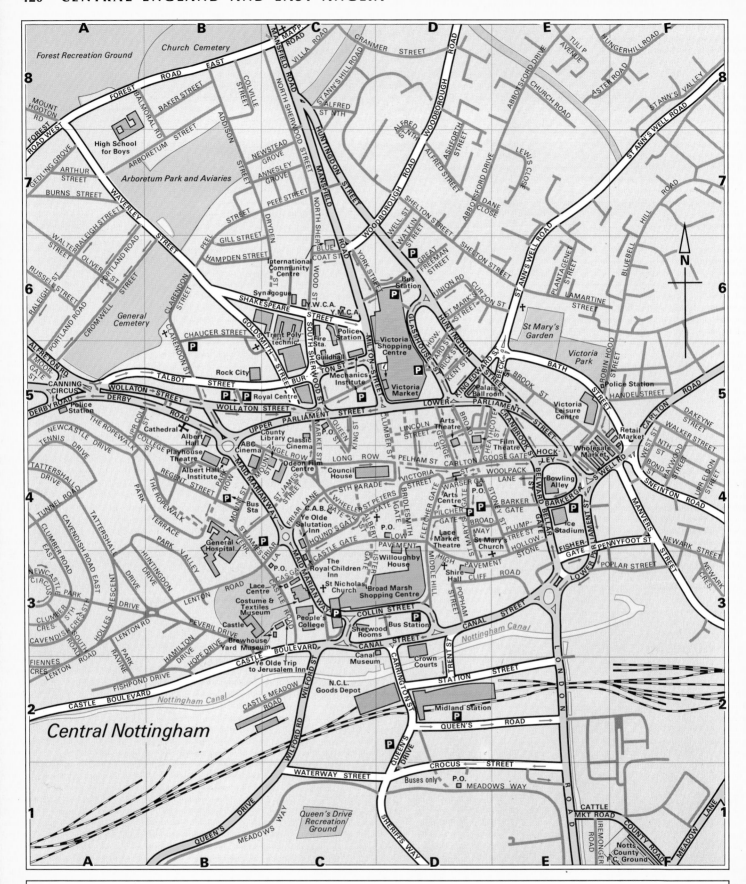

Central Nottingham

Nottingham

Hosiery and lace were the foundations upon which Nottingham's prosperity was built. The stockings came first – a knitting machine for these had been invented by a Nottinghamshire man as early as 1589 – but a machine called a 'tickler', which enabled simple patterns to be created in the stocking fabric, prompted the development of machine-made lace. The earliest fabric was produced in 1768, and an example from not much later than that is kept in the city's Castlegate Costume and Textile Museum. In fact, the entire history of lacemaking is beautifully explained in this converted row of Georgian terraces. The Industrial Museum at Wollaton Park has many other machines and exhibits tracing the development of the knitting industry, as well as displays on the other industries which have brought wealth to the city – tobacco, pharmaceuticals, engineering and printing. At Wollaton Hall is a natural history museum, while nearer the centre are the Canal Museum and the Brewhouse Yard Museum, a marvellous collection which shows items from daily life in the city up to the present day. Nottingham is not complete without mention of Robin Hood, the partly mythical figure whose statue is in the castle grounds. Although the castle itself has Norman foundations, the present structure is largely Victorian. It is now a museum.

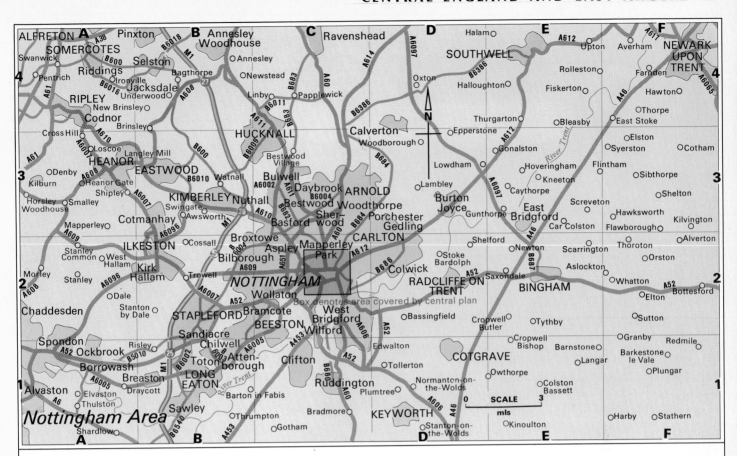

Key to Town Plan and Area Plan

Town Plan

AA Recommended roads	
Restricted roads	
Other roads	
Buildings of interest	Theatre
Car Parks	P
Parks and open spaces	
Churches	†
One Way Streets	→

Area Plan

A roads	
B roads	
Locations	BagthorpeO
Urban area	

Street Index with Grid Reference

Nottingham

Abbotsford Drive	D7-D7-E7-E8
Addison Street	B7-B8
Albert Street	C4
Alfred Street	D7
Alfred Street North	C8, D7-D8
Alfreton Road	A5-A6
Angel Road	B5-B4-C4
Annesley Grove	B7-C7
Ashford Street	D7-D8
Aster Road	E8-F8
Arboretum Street	A7-B7-B8
Arthur Street	A7
Baker Street	B8
Balmoral Road	A8-B8-B7
Barker Gate	E4
Bath Gate	E5-F5
Beck Street	E5
Bellar Gate	E4
Belward Street	E4
Bluebell Hill Road	F6-F7
Bluecoat Street	C6
Bond Street	F4
Bridlesmith Gate	D4
Broad Street	D4-D5
Broadway	D4-E4
Brook Street	E5
Burns Street	A7
Burton Street	C5

Canal Street	C3-D3-E3
Canning Circus	A5
Carlton Road	F5
Carlton Street	D4
Carrington Street	D2-D3
Castle Boulevard	A2-B2-B3-C3
Castle Gate	C3-C4
Castle Market Road	E1-F1
Castle Meadow Road	B2-C2
Castle Road	C3
Cavendish Crescent South	A3
Cavendish Road East	A3-A4
Chaucer Street	B5-B6
Church Road	E8
Clarendon Street	B5-B6
Cliff Road	D3-E3
Clumber Crescent South	A3
Clumber Road East	A3-A4
Clumber Street	D4-D5
College Street	A5-B5-B4
Collin Street	C3-D3
Colville Street	B8
County Road	F1
Cranbrook Street	E4-E5
Cranmer Street	C8-D8
Crocus Street	D1-E1
Cromwell Street	A5-B6-C6
Curzon Street	D6-E6
Dane Close	D7-E7
Dakeyne Street	F5
Derby Road	A5-B5
Dryden Street	C6-C7
Fieness Crescent	A2
Fishergate	E3-E4
Fishpond Drive	A2-B2
Fletcher Gate	D4
Forest Road East	A8-B8-C8
Forest Road West	A7-A8
Friar Lane	C3-C4
Gedling Grove	A7
George Street	D4-D5
Glasshouse Street	D5-D6
Gill Street	B6-C6
Goldsmith Street	B6-C6-C5
Goose Gate	D4-E4
Great Freeman Street	D6
Hamilton Drive	B2-B3
Hampden Street	B6-C6
Handel Street	E5-F5
Haywood Street	F4-F5
High Pavement	D4-D3-E3
Hockley	E4
Holles Crescent	A3
Hollowstone	E3-E4
Hope Drive	B2-B3
Hound's Gate	C4

Howard Street	D5-D6
Hungerhill Road	E8-F8
Huntingdon Drive	A4-A3-B3
Huntingdon Drive	C8-C7-D7-D6-D5-E5
Huskisson Street	C6
Iremonger Road	E1
Kent Street	D5
King Edward Street	D5-E5
King Street	C4-C5
Lamartine Street	E6-F6
Lenton Road	A2-A3-B3
Lewis Close	E7
Lincoln Street	D5
Lister Gate	C3-C4
London Road	E1-E2-E3
Long Row	C4-D4
Lower Parliament Street	D5-E5-E4-E3
Low Pavement	C4-D4
Maid Marion Way	B4-C4-C3
Mansfield Street	C6-C7-C8
Manvers Street	F3-F4
Mapperley Road	C8
Market Street	C4-C5
Meadow Lane	F1
Meadows Road	B1-C1-D1-E1
Middle Hill	D3-D4
Milton Street	C6-C5-D5
Moorgate Street	A5
Mount Hooton Road	A8
Mount Street	B4-C4
Newark Crescent	F3
Newark Street	F3-F4
Newcastle Circus	A3
Newcastle Drive	A4-A5
Newstead Grove	B7-C7
North Street	F4-F5
North Sherwood Street	C6-C7-C8
Oliver Street	A6
Park Drive	A3-B3
Park Ravine	A2-A3
Park Row	B4
Park Terrace	A4-B4
Park Valley	A4-B4-B3
Peel Street	B6-B7-C7
Pelham Street	D4
Pennyfoot Street	E4-F4
Peveril Drive	B3
Pilcher Gate	D4
Plantagenet Street	E6
Plumptree Street	E4
Popham Street	D3
Poplar Street	E3-F3
Portland Road	A5-A6-A7
Queen's Drive	B1-C1, D1-D2
Queen's Road	D2-E2
Queen Street	C4-C5

Releigh Street	A6-A7
Regent Street	B4
Rick Street	D5
Robin Hood Street	E5-F5-F6
Russell Street	A6
St Ann's Hill Road	C8
St Ann's Valley	F7-F8
St Ann's Well Road	E5-E6-E7-F7-F8
St James Street	C4
St James Terrace	B4-B3-C3
St Mark's Street	D6
St Peters Gate	C4-D4
Shakespeare Street	B6-C6
Shelton Street	D7-D6-E6
Sherriffs Way	D1
Sneinton Road	F4
South Parade	C4-D4
South Road	A3
South Sherwood Street	C5-C6
Southwell Road	E4-F4
Station Street	D2-E2
Stony Street	D4-E4
Talbot Street	A5-B5-C5
Tattershall Drive	A4-A3-B3
Tennis Drive	A4-A5-A4
The Robewalk	A5-A4-B4
Trent Street	D2-D3
Tulip Avenue	A8
Tunnel Road	A4
Union Road	D6
Upper College Street	A5-B5
Upper Eldon Street	F4
Upper Parliament Street	B5-C5-D5
Victoria Street	D4
Villa Road	C8
Walker Street	F4-F5
Walter Street	A6-A7
Warser Gate	D4
Waterway Street	C1-D1
Watkin Street	D6-D7
Waverely Street	A8-A7-B7-B6
Wellington Street	D6-D7
West Street	F4-F5
Wheeler Gate	C4
Wilford Road	C1-C2
Wilford Street	C2-C3
Wollaton Street	A5-B5-C5
Woodborough Road	C6-C7-D7-D8
Woolpack Lane	D4-E4
York Street	C6-D6

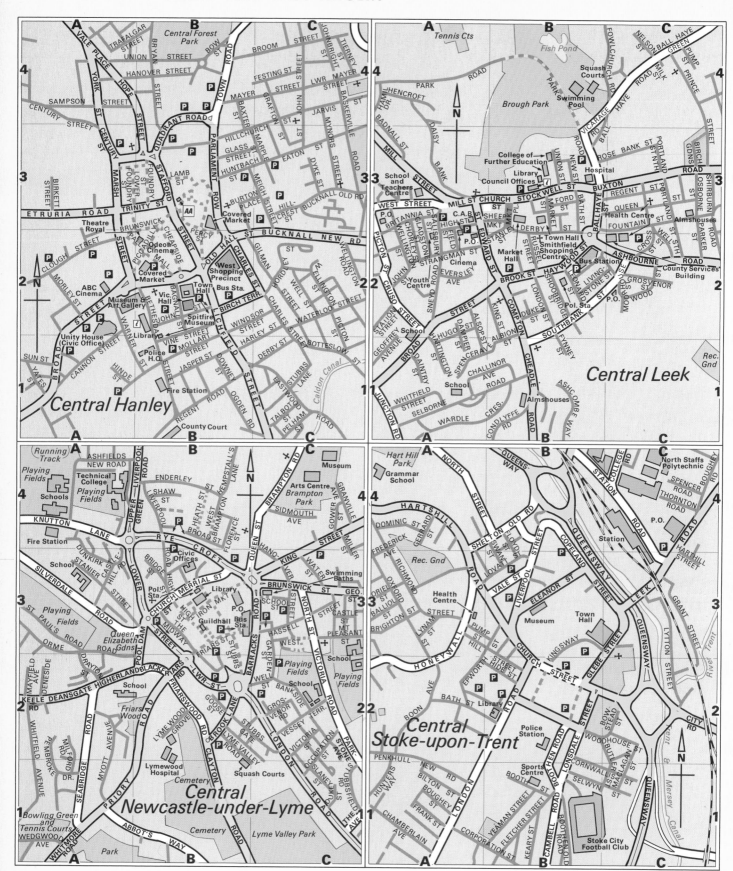

Central Hanley

Central Leek

Central Newcastle-under-Lyme

Central Stoke-upon-Trent

Stoke-on-Trent

Wedgwood, Spode and Royal Doulton are among the names that spring to mind with the mention of Stoke-on-Trent. Renowned for many years as the capital of the pottery industry, the town has numerous museums dealing with the industry's history as well as with leading figures involved in it, and tours of pottery factories can be arranged. On the sporting side, Stoke City, the local football team, which plays in the Canon League, boasts Sir Stanley Matthews amongst its former players.

Hanley is the birthplace of Arnold Bennet, who immortalised the Potteries in his stories about the 'Five Towns'. Born here too was Spitfire designer Reginald Mitchell, and the town has a museum devoted to his life and work. Another great attraction of Hanley for many is the fine woodland expanse of 90-acre Central Forest Park.

Leek was once renowned for silk and dye, but now attracts visitors to its antique shops. Amongst its interesting older buildings, Brindley Mill and Museum specialises in the work of 18th-century canal builder James Brindley.

Newcastle-under-Lyme boasts a fine old Guildhall and several inns dating from the 17th and 18th centuries. Keele University, to the south-west, has contributed to the town's cultural activities in recent years.

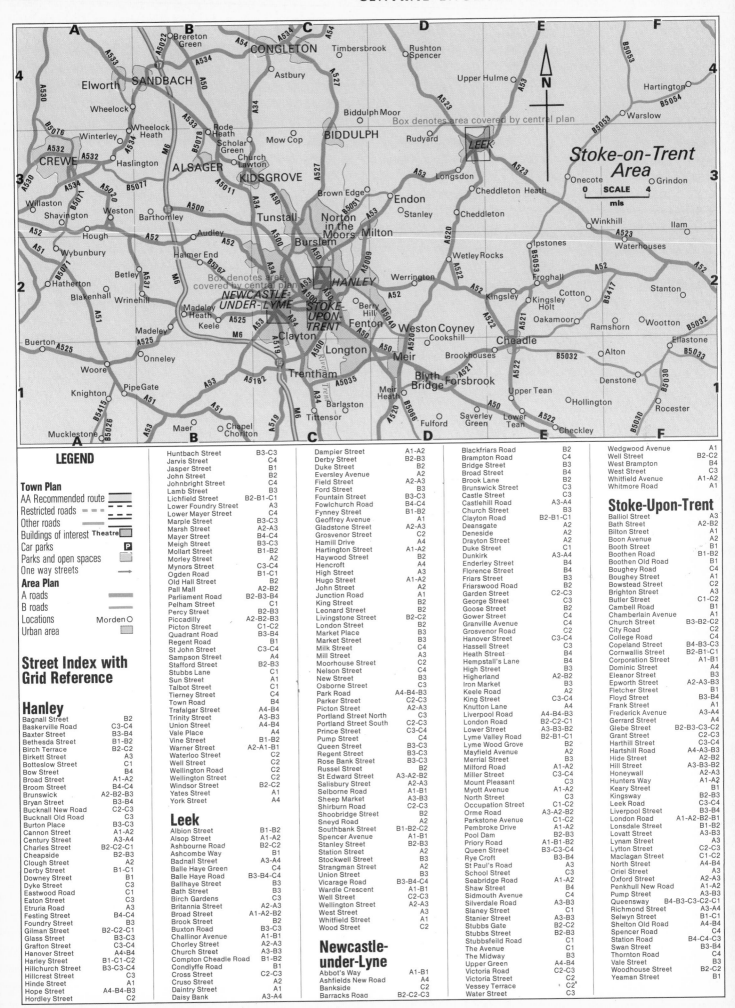

LEGEND

Town Plan

AA Recommended route
Restricted roads
Other roads
Buildings of interest Theatre
Car parks
Parks and open spaces
One way streets

Area Plan

A roads
B roads
Locations Morden○
Urban area

Street Index with Grid Reference

Hanley

Bagnall Street	B2
Baskerville Road	C3-C4
Baxter Street	B3-B4
Bethesda Street	B1-B2
Birch Terrace	B2-C2
Birkett Street	A3
Botteslow Street	C1
Bow Street	B4
Broad Street	A1-A2
Broom Street	B4-C4
Brunswick	A2-B2-B3
Bryan Street	B3-B4
Bucknall New Road	C2-C3
Bucknall Old Road	C3
Burton Place	B3-C3
Cannon Street	A1-A2
Century Street	A3-A4
Charles Street	B2-C2-C1
Cheapside	B2-B3
Clough Street	A2
Derby Street	B1-C1
Downey Street	B1
Dyke Street	C3
Eastwood Road	C1
Eaton Street	C3
Etruria Road	A3
Festing Street	B4-C4
Foundry Street	B3
Gilman Street	B2-C2-C1
Glass Street	B3-C3
Grafton Street	C3-C4
Hanover Street	B3
Harley Street	B1-C1-C2
Hillchurch Street	B3-C3-C4
Hillcrest Street	C3
Hinde Street	A1
Hope Street	A4-B4-B3
Hordley Street	C2

Huntbach Street	B3-C3
Jarvis Street	C4
Jasper Street	B1
John Street	B2
Johnbright Street	C4
Lamb Street	B3
Lichfield Street	B2-B1-C1
Lower Foundry Street	A3
Lower Mayer Street	C4
Marple Street	B3-C3
Marsh Street	A2-A3
Mayer Street	B4-C4
Meigh Street	B3-C3
Mollart Street	B1-B2
Morley Street	A2
Mynors Street	C3-C4
Ogden Road	B1-C1
Old Hall Street	B2
Pall Mall	A2-B2
Parliament Road	B2-B3-B4
Pelham Street	C1
Percy Street	B2-B3
Piccadilly	A2-B2-B3
Picton Street	C1-C2
Quadrant Road	B3-B4
Regent Road	B1
St John Street	C3-C4
Sampson Street	A4
Stafford Street	B2-B3
Stubbs Lane	C1
Sun Street	A1
Talbot Street	C1
Tierney Street	C4
Town Road	B4
Trafalgar Street	A4-B4
Trinity Street	A3-B3
Union Street	A4-B4
Vale Place	A4
Vine Street	B1-B2
Warner Street	A2-A1-B1
Waterloo Street	C2
Well Street	C2
Wellington Road	C2
Wellington Street	C2
Windsor Street	B2-C2
Yates Street	A1
York Street	A4

Leek

Albion Street	B1-B2
Alsop Street	A1-A2
Ashbourne Road	B2-C2
Ashcombe Way	B1
Badnall Street	A3-A4
Balle Haye Green	C4
Balle Haye Road	B3-B4-C4
Ballhaye Street	B3
Bath Street	C3
Birch Gardens	B1
Britannia Street	A2-A3
Broad Street	A1-A2-B2
Brook Street	B2
Buxton Road	B3-C3
Challinor Avenue	A1-B1
Chorley Street	A2-A3
Church Street	A3-B3
Compton Cheadle Road	B1-B2
Condlyffe Road	B1
Cross Street	C2-C3
Cruso Street	A2
Daintry Street	A1
Daisy Bank	A3-A4

Dampier Street	A1-A2
Derby Street	B2-B3
Duke Street	B2
Eversley Avenue	A2
Field Street	A2-A3
Ford Street	B3
Fountain Street	B3-C3
Fowlchurch Road	B4-C4
Fynney Street	B1-B2
Geoffrey Avenue	A1
Gladstone Street	A2-A3
Grosvenor Street	C2
Hamill Drive	A4
Hartington Street	A1-A2
Haywood Street	B2
Hencroft	A4
High Street	A3
Hugo Street	A1-A2
John Street	B2
Junction Road	A1
King Street	B2
Leonard Street	B2
Livingstone Street	B2-C2
London Street	B2
Market Place	B3
Market Street	B3
Milk Street	C4
Mill Street	A3
Moorhouse Street	C2
Nelson Street	C4
New Street	B3
Osborne Street	C3
Park Road	A4-B4-B3
Parker Street	C2-C3
Picton Street	A2-A3
Portland Street North	C3
Portland Street South	C2-C3
Prince Street	C3-C4
Pump Street	C4
Queen Street	B3-C3
Regent Street	B3-C3
Rose Bank Street	B3-C3
Russel Street	B3
St Edward Street	A3-A2-B2
Salisbury Street	A2-A3
Selborne Road	A1-B1
Sheep Market	A3-B3
Shirburn Road	C2-C3
Shoobridge Street	B2
Sneyd Road	A2
Southbank Street	B1-B2-C2
Spencer Avenue	A1-B1
Stanley Street	B2-B3
Station Street	A2
Stockwell Street	B3
Strangman Street	A2
Union Street	B3
Vicarage Road	B3-B4-C4
Wardle Crescent	A1-B1
Well Street	C2-C3
Wellington Street	A2-A3
West Street	A3
Whitfield Street	A1
Wood Street	C2

Newcastle-under-Lyne

Abbot's Way	A1-B1
Ashfields New Road	A4
Bankside	C2
Barracks Road	B2-C2-C3

Blackfriars Road	B2
Brampton Road	C4
Bridge Street	B3
Broad Street	B2
Brook Lane	B2
Brunswick Street	C3
Castle Street	C3
Castlehill Road	A3-A4
Church Street	B3
Clayton Road	B2-B1-C1
Deansgate	A2
Deneside	A2
Drayton Street	C1
Duke Street	A3-A4
Dunkirk	A3-A4
Enderley Street	B4
Florence Street	B4
Friars Street	B3
Friarswood Road	B2
Garden Street	C2-C3
George Street	C3
Goose Street	B2
Gower Street	C4
Granville Avenue	C4
Grosvenor Road	C2
Hanover Street	C3-C4
Hassell Street	C3
Heath Street	B4
Hempstall's Lane	B4
High Street	B3
Higherland	A2-B2
Iron Market	B3
Keele Road	A2
King Street	C3-C4
Knutton Lane	A4
Liverpool Road	A4-B4-B3
London Road	B2-C2-C1
Lower Street	A3-B3-B2
Lyme Valley Road	B2-B1-C1
Lyme Wood Grove	B2
Mayfield Avenue	A2
Merrial Street	B3
Milford Road	A1-A2
Miller Street	C3-C4
Mount Pleasant	C3
Myott Avenue	A1-A2
North Street	C4
Occupation Street	C1-C2
Orme Road	A3-A2-B2
Parkstone Avenue	C1-C2
Pembroke Drive	A1-A2
Pool Dam	B2-B3
Priory Road	A1-B1-B2
Queen Street	B3-C3-C4
Rye Croft	B3-B4
St Paul's Road	A3
School Street	C3
Seabridge Road	A1-A2
Shaw Street	B4
Sidmouth Avenue	A2
Silverdale Road	A3-B3
Slaney Street	C1
Stanier Street	A3-B3
Stubbs Gate	B2-C2
Stubbs Street	B2-B3
Stubbsfield Road	C1
The Avenue	C1
The Midway	B3
Upper Green	A4-B4
Victoria Road	C2-C3
Victoria Road	C2
Vessey Terrace	C2*
Water Street	C3

Wedgwood Avenue	A1
Well Street	B2-C2
West Brampton	B4
West Street	C3
Whitfield Avenue	A1-A2
Whitmore Road	A1

Stoke-Upon-Trent

Balliol Street	A3
Bath Street	A2-B2
Bilton Street	A1
Boon Avenue	A2
Booth Street	B1
Boothen Road	B1-B2
Boothen Old Road	B1
Boughey Road	C4
Boughey Street	A1
Bowstead Street	C2
Brighton Street	A3
Butler Street	C1-C2
Cambell Road	B1
Chamberlain Avenue	C4
Church Street	B3-B2-C2
City Road	C2
College Road	C4
Copeland Street	B4-B3-C3
Cornwallis Street	B2-B1-C1
Corporation Street	A1-B1
Dominic Street	A4
Eleanor Street	B3
Epworth Street	A2-A3-B3
Fletcher Street	B1
Floyd Street	B3-B4
Frank Street	A1
Frederick Avenue	A3-A4
Gerrard Street	A4
Glebe Street	B2-B3-C3-C2
Grant Street	C2-C3
Harthill Street	C3-C4
Hartshill Road	A4-A3-B3
Hide Street	A2-B2
Hill Street	A3-B3-B2
Honeywall	A2-A3
Hunters Way	A1-A2
Keary Street	B1
Kingsway	B2-B3
Leek Road	C3-C4
Liverpool Street	B3
London Road	A1-A2-B2-B1
Lonsdale Street	B1-B2
Lovatt Street	A3-B3
Lynam Street	A3
Lytton Street	C2-C3
Maclagan Street	C1-C2
North Street	A4-B4
Oriel Street	A3
Oxford Street	A2-A3
Penkhull New Road	A1-A2
Pump Street	A3-B3
Queensway	B4-B3-C3-C2-C1
Richmond Street	A3-A4
Selwyn Street	B1-C1
Shelton Old Road	A4-B4
Spencer Road	C4
Station Road	B4-C4-C3
Swan Street	B3-B4
Thornton Road	C4
Vale Street	B3
Woodhouse Street	B2-C2
Yeaman Street	B1

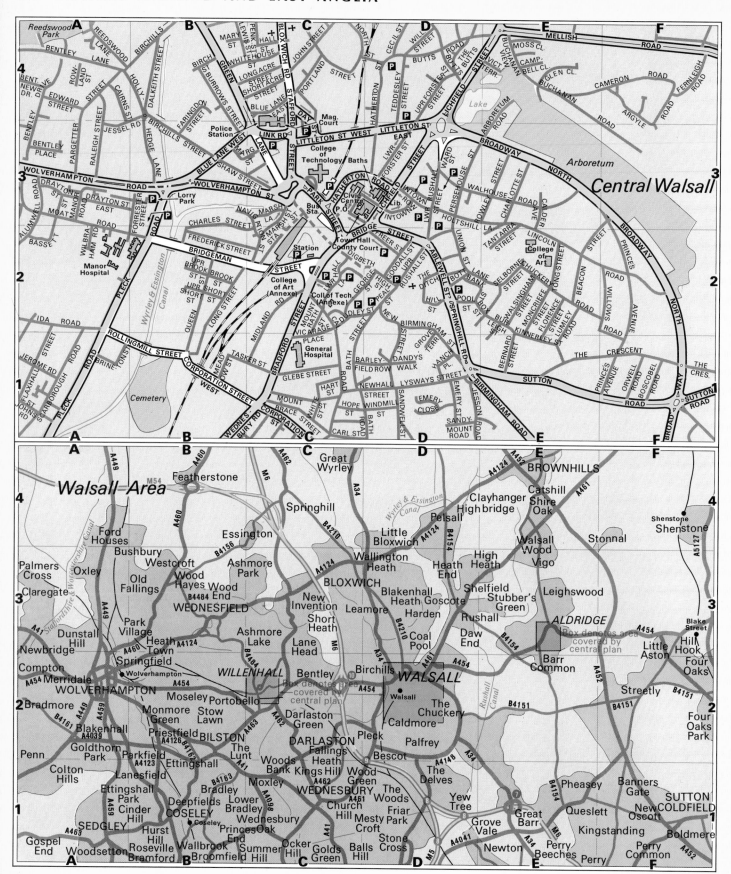

Central Walsall

Walsall Area

Walsall

Affectionately known as the 'Town of 100 Trades' because of its diversity of industries, Walsall is nevertheless a specialist in one area — leather manufacture. Saddles have been produced here since the 19th century, and all the British Army's saddles in World War I were Walsall-made.

A conservation area has been established at Church Hill, covering the Parish Church of St

Matthew (which dates back to the 12th century), and part of the town centre where Italian Renaissance style Taylor's Music Shop is just one of several fine Victorian buildings to be seen. Other places of interest are the Central Library's Local History Gallery, Belsize House, the birthplace of Jerome K. Jerome (now a museum dealing with his life and work) and the Garman Ryan Collection which has art donated by Lady Kathleen Epstein, widow of sculptor Sir Jacob. The

Walsall Illuminations appear each September.

Aldridge enjoys the contrasts of an industrial town set in pleasant rural surroundings. The oldest part of town, around the Parish Church, has been declared a conservation area.

Willenhall has kept its old 'Black Country' character, and the market place area is being restored in 19th-century style. A reputation for lock and key making is recalled in the local library's Lock Museum.

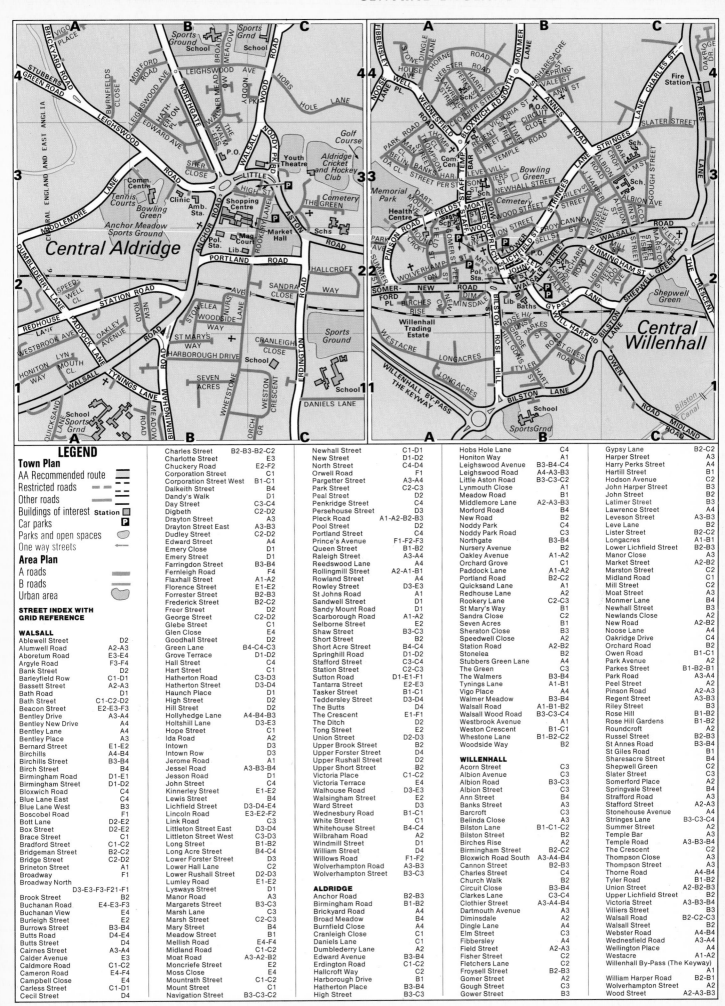

Central Aldridge

Central Willenhall

LEGEND

Town Plan

AA Recommended route	
Restricted roads	
Other roads	
Buildings of interest	Station ▣
Car parks	Ⓟ
Parks and open spaces	
One way streets	←

Area Plan

A roads	
B roads	
Urban area	

STREET INDEX WITH GRID REFERENCE

WALSALL

Ablewell Street	D2
Alumwell Road	A2-A3
Aboretum Road	E3-E4
Argyle Road	F3-F4
Bank Street	D2
Barleyfield Row	C1-D1
Bassett Street	A2-A3
Bath Road	D2
Bath Street	C1-C2-D2
Beacon Street	E2-E3-F3
Bentley Drive	A3-A4
Bentley New Drive	A4
Bentley Lane	A4
Bentley Place	A3
Bernard Street	E1-E2
Birchills	A4-B4
Birchills Street	B3-B4
Birch Street	B4
Birmingham Road	D1-E1
Birmingham Street	D1-D2
Bloxwich Road	C4
Blue Lane East	C4
Blue Lane West	B3
Boscobel Road	F1
Bott Lane	D2-E2
Box Street	D2-E2
Brace Street	C1
Bradford Street	C1-C2
Bridgeman Street	B2-C2
Bridge Street	C2-D2
Brineton Street	A1
Broadway	F1
Broadway North	D3-E3-F3-F2I-F1
Brook Street	B2
Buchanan Road	E4-E3-F3
Buchanan View	E4
Burleigh Street	E2
Burrows Street	B3-B4
Butts Road	D4-E4
Butts Street	D4
Cairnes Street	A3-A4
Calder Avenue	E3
Caldmore Road	C1-C2
Cameron Road	E4-F4
Campbell Close	E4
Carless Street	C1-D1
Cecil Street	D4

Charles Street	B2-B3-B2-C2
Charlotte Street	E3
Chuckery Road	E2-F2
Corporation Street	C1
Corporation Street West	B1-C1
Dalkeith Street	B4
Dandy's Walk	D1
Day Street	C3-C4
Digbeth	C2-D2
Drayton Street	A3
Drayton Street East	A3-B3
Dudley Street	C2-D2
Edward Street	A4
Emery Close	D1
Emery Street	D1
Farringdon Street	B3-B4
Fernleigh Road	F4
Flaxhall Street	A1-A2
Florence Street	E1-E2
Forrester Street	B2-B3
Frederick Street	B2-C2
Freer Street	D2
George Street	C2-D2
Glebe Street	C1
Glen Close	E4
Goodhall Street	D2
Green Lane	B4-C4-C3
Grove Terrace	D1-D2
Hall Street	C4
Hart Street	C1
Hatherton Road	C3-D3
Hatherton Street	D3-D4
Haunch Place	D1
High Street	D2
Hill Street	D2
Hollyhedge Lane	A4-B4-B3
Holtshill Lane	D3-E3
Hope Street	C1
Ida Road	A2
Intown	D3
Intown Row	D3
Jerome Road	A1
Jessel Road	A3-B3-B4
Jesson Road	D1
John Street	D2
Kinnerley Street	E1-E2
Lewis Street	B4
Lichfield Street	D3-D4-E4
Lincoln Road	E3-E2-F2
Link Road	C3
Littleton Street East	D3-D4
Littleton Street West	C3-D3
Long Street	B1-B2
Long Acre Street	B4-C4
Lower Forster Street	D3
Lower Hall Lane	C2
Lower Rushall Street	D2-D3
Lumley Road	E1-E2
Lysways Street	D1
Manor Road	A3
Margarets Street	B3-C3
Marsh Lane	C3
Marsh Street	C2-C3
Mary Street	B4
Meadow Street	B1
Mellish Road	E4-F4
Midland Road	C1-C2
Moat Road	A3-A2-B2
Moncriefe Street	E2
Moss Close	E4
Mountrath Street	C1-C2
Mount Street	C1
Navigation Street	B3-C3-C2

Newhall Street	C1-D1
New Street	D1-D2
North Street	C4-D4
Orwell Road	F1
Pargetter Street	A3-A4
Park Street	C2-C3
Peal Street	D2
Penkridge Street	C4
Persehouse Street	D3
Pleck Road	A1-A2-B2-B3
Pool Street	D2
Portland Street	C4
Prince's Avenue	F1-F2-F3
Queen Street	B1-B2
Raleigh Street	A3-A4
Reedswood Lane	A4
Rollingmill Street	A2-A1-B1
Rowland Street	A4
Rowley Street	D3-E3
St Johns Road	A1
Sandwell Street	D1
Sandy Mount Road	D1
Scarborough Road	A1-A2
Selborne Street	E2
Shaw Street	B3-C3
Short Street	B2
Short Acre Street	B4-C4
Springhill Road	D1-D2
Stafford Street	C3-C4
Station Street	C2-C3
Sutton Road	D1-E1-F1
Tantarra Street	E2-E3
Tasker Street	B1-C1
Teddersley Street	D3-D4
The Butts	D4
The Crescent	E1-F1
The Ditch	D2
Tong Street	E2
Union Street	D2-D3
Upper Brook Street	B2
Upper Forster Street	D4
Upper Rushall Street	D2
Upper Short Street	B2
Victoria Place	C1-C2
Victoria Terrace	E4
Walhouse Road	D3-E3
Walsingham Street	E2
Ward Street	D3
Wednesbury Road	B1-C1
White Street	C1
Whitehouse Street	B4-C4
Wilbraham Road	A2
Windmill Street	D1
William Street	D4
Willows Road	F1-F2
Wolverhampton Road	A3-B3
Wolverhampton Street	B3-C3

ALDRIDGE

Anchor Road	B2-B3
Birmingham Road	B1-B2
Brickyard Road	A4
Broad Meadow	B4
Burnfield Close	A4
Cranleigh Close	C1
Daniels Lane	C1
Dumbleberry Lane	A2
Edward Avenue	B3-B4
Erdington Road	C1-C2
Hallcroft Way	C2
Harborough Drive	B1
Hatherton Place	B3-B4
High Street	C3

Hobs Hole Lane	C4
Honiton Way	A1
Leighswood Avenue	B3-B4-C4
Leighswood Road	A4-A3-B3
Little Aston Road	B3-C3-C2
Lynmouth Close	A1
Meadow Road	B1
Middlemore Lane	A2-A3-B3
Morford Road	B4
New Road	B2
Noddy Park	C4
Noddy Park Road	C3
Northgate	B3-B4
Nursery Avenue	B2
Oakley Avenue	A1-A2
Orchard Grove	C1
Paddock Lane	A1-A2
Portland Road	B2-C2
Quicksand Lane	A1
Redhouse Lane	A2
Rookery Lane	C2-C3
St Mary's Way	B1
Sandra Close	C2
Seven Acres	B3
Sheraton Close	B3
Speedwell Close	A2
Station Road	A2-B2
Stonelea	B2
Stubbers Green Lane	A4
The Green	C3
The Walmers	B3-B4
Tynings Lane	A1-B1
Vigo Place	A4
Walmer Meadow	B4
Walsall Road	A1-B1-B2
Walsall Wood Road	B3-C3-C4
Westbrook Avenue	A1
Weston Crescent	B1-C1
Whetstone Lane	B1-B2-C2
Woodside Way	B2

WILLENHALL

Acorn Street	C3
Albion Avenue	C3
Albion Road	B3-C3
Albion Street	C3
Ann Street	B4
Banks Street	A3
Barcroft	C3
Belinda Close	B4
Bilston Lane	B1-C1-C2
Bilston Street	B2
Birches Rise	A2
Birmingham Street	B2-C2
Bloxwich Road South	A3-A4-B4
Cannon Street	B2-B3
Charles Street	C4
Church Walk	B2
Circuit Close	B3-B4
Clarkes Lane	C3-C4
Clothier Street	A3-A4-B4
Dartmouth Avenue	A3
Diminsdale	A2
Dingle Lane	A4
Elm Street	C3
Fibbersley	A4
Field Street	A2-A3
Fisher Street	C2
Fletchers Lane	C2
Froysell Street	B2-B3
Gomer Street	A2
Gough Street	C3
Gower Street	B3

Gypsy Lane	B2-C2
Harper Street	A3
Harry Perks Street	A4
Hartill Street	B1
Hodson Avenue	C2
John Harper Street	B3
John Street	B2
Latimer Street	B3
Lawrence Street	A4
Leveson Street	A3-B3
Leve Lane	B2
Lister Street	B2-C2
Longacres	A1-B1
Lower Lichfield Street	B2-B3
Manor Close	A3
Market Street	A2-B2
Marston Street	C3
Midland Road	C1
Mill Street	C2
Moat Street	A3
Monmer Lane	B4
Newhall Street	B3
Newlands Close	A2
New Road	A2-B2
Noose Lane	A4
Oakridge Drive	C4
Orchard Road	B2
Owen Road	B1-C1
Park Avenue	A2
Parkes Street	B1-B2-B1
Park Road	A3-A4
Peel Street	A2
Pinson Road	A2-A3
Regent Street	A3-B3
Riley Street	B3
Rose Hill	B1-B2
Rose Hill Gardens	B1-B2
Roundcroft	A2
Russel Street	B2-B3
St Annes Road	B3-B4
St Giles Road	B1
Sharesacre Street	B4
Shepwell Green	C2
Slater Street	C3
Somerford Place	A2
Springvale Street	B4
Strafford Road	A3
Stafford Street	A2-A3
Stonehouse Avenue	A4
Stringes Lane	B3-C3-C4
Summer Street	A3
Temple Bar	A3
Temple Road	A3-B3-B4
The Crescent	C2
Thompson Close	A3
Thompson Street	A3
Thorne Road	A4-B4
Tyler Road	B1-B2
Union Street	A2-B2-B3
Upper Lichfield Street	B3
Victoria Street	A3-B3-B4
Villiers Street	B3
Walsall Road	B2-C2-C3
Walsall Street	B2
Webster Road	A4-B4
Wednesfield Road	A3-A4
Wellington Place	A4
Westacre	A1-A2
Willenhall By-Pass (The Keyway)	A1
William Harper Road	B2-B1
Wolverhampton Street	A2
Wood Street	A2-A3-B3

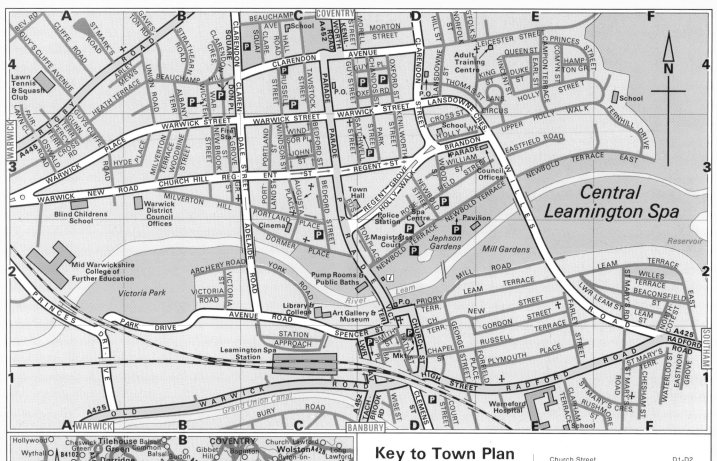

Central Leamington Spa

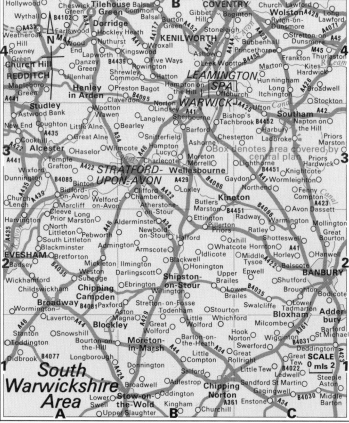

South Warwickshire Area

Key to Town Plan and Area Plan

Town Plan

AA Recommended roads	▬▬▬
Other roads	▬▬▬
Restricted roads	- - - -
Buildings of Interest	Baths
Car Parks	P
Parks and open Spaces	◢

Area Plan

A roads	▬▬
B roads	▬▬
Locations	Wimpstone○
Urban area	◢

Street Index with Grid Reference

Leamington Spa

Adelaide Road	C2-C3
Albany Terrace	B3-B4
Archery Road	B2-C2
Arley Mews	A4-B4
Augusta Place	C3
Avenue Road	B2-C2-C1
Bath Place	D1
Bath Street	D1
Beaconsfield Street	F2
Beauchamp Avenue	C4
Beauchamp Hill	B4
Bedford Street	C2-C3
Beverley Road	A4
Brandon Parade	D3-E3
Bury Road	C1-B1
Campion Terrace	E4
Chandos Street	D4
Chapel Street	D1
Chesham Street	F1
Church Hill	B3
Church Street	D1-D2
Church Terrace	D1-D2
Clapham Terrace	E1
Clarendon Avenue	C4-D4
Clarendon Crescent	B4
Clarendon Place	B3-B4-C4-C3
Clarendon Square	B4-C4
Clarendon Street	D3-D4
Clemens Street	D1
Cliffe Road	A4
Comyn Street	E4
Court Street	D1
Cross Road	A3
Cross Street	D3
Dale Street	B3-C3
Dormer Place	C2
Duke Street	E4
Earl Street	E4
Eastfield Road	E3
Eastnor Grove	F1
Euston Place	C3.D2
Fairlawn Close	A3-A4
Farley Street	E1-E2
Fernhill Drive	F3-F4
Forfield Place	D1-E1
Gaveston Road	B4
George Street	D1-D2
Gordon Street	E1-E2
Grove Street	B3
Gunnery Terrace	A3
Guy Place	C4-D4
Guy Street	C4-D4
Guys Cliffe Avenue	A4
Guys Cliffe Road	A3-A4
Hall Road	C4
Hampton Grove	
Heath Terrace	A3-A4-B4
High Street	D1-E1
Hill Street	D4
Holly Walk	C2-D2-D3-E3
Holly Street	E4
Hyde Place	A3-B3
John Street	C3
Kenilworth Road	C4
Kenilworth Street	D3-D4
King Street	E4
Lansdowne Circus	E3-E4
Lansdowne Crescent	D4-E4-E3
Lansdowne Street	D4
Leam Street	F2
Leam Terrace	D2-E2

Warwick

The old county town of the shire, Warwick lies in the shadow of its massive, historic castle which occupies the rocky ridge above the River Avon. Thomas Beauchamp and his son built the huge towers and curtain walls in the 14th century, but it was the Jacobean holders of the earldom, the Grevilles, who transformed the medieval stronghold into a nobleman's residence. In 1694,

the heart of the town was almost completely destroyed by fire and the few medieval buildings that survived lie on the outskirts of the present 18th-century centre. Of these Oken House, now a doll museum, and Lord Leycester's Hospital, almshouses dating back to the 14th century, are particularly striking.

Stratford-upon-Avon, as the birthplace of William Shakespeare, England's most famous poet and playwright, is second only to London as a

tourist attraction. This charming old market town is a living memorial to him; his plays are performed in the Royal Shakespeare Theatre which dominates the river bank, a waxwork museum specialises in scenes from his works, and his childhood home in Henley Street is a museum.

Leamington Spa, an inland spa on the River Leam, gained the prefix 'Royal' after Queen Victoria had visited it in 1838, and the town has been a fashionable health resort ever since.

Central Warwick

Central Stratford-upon-Avon

WARWICK
These pretty brick and timbered cottages standing in the shadow of the great medieval towers of Warwick Castle are among the few buildings in the town that survived a devastating fire in the late 17th century.

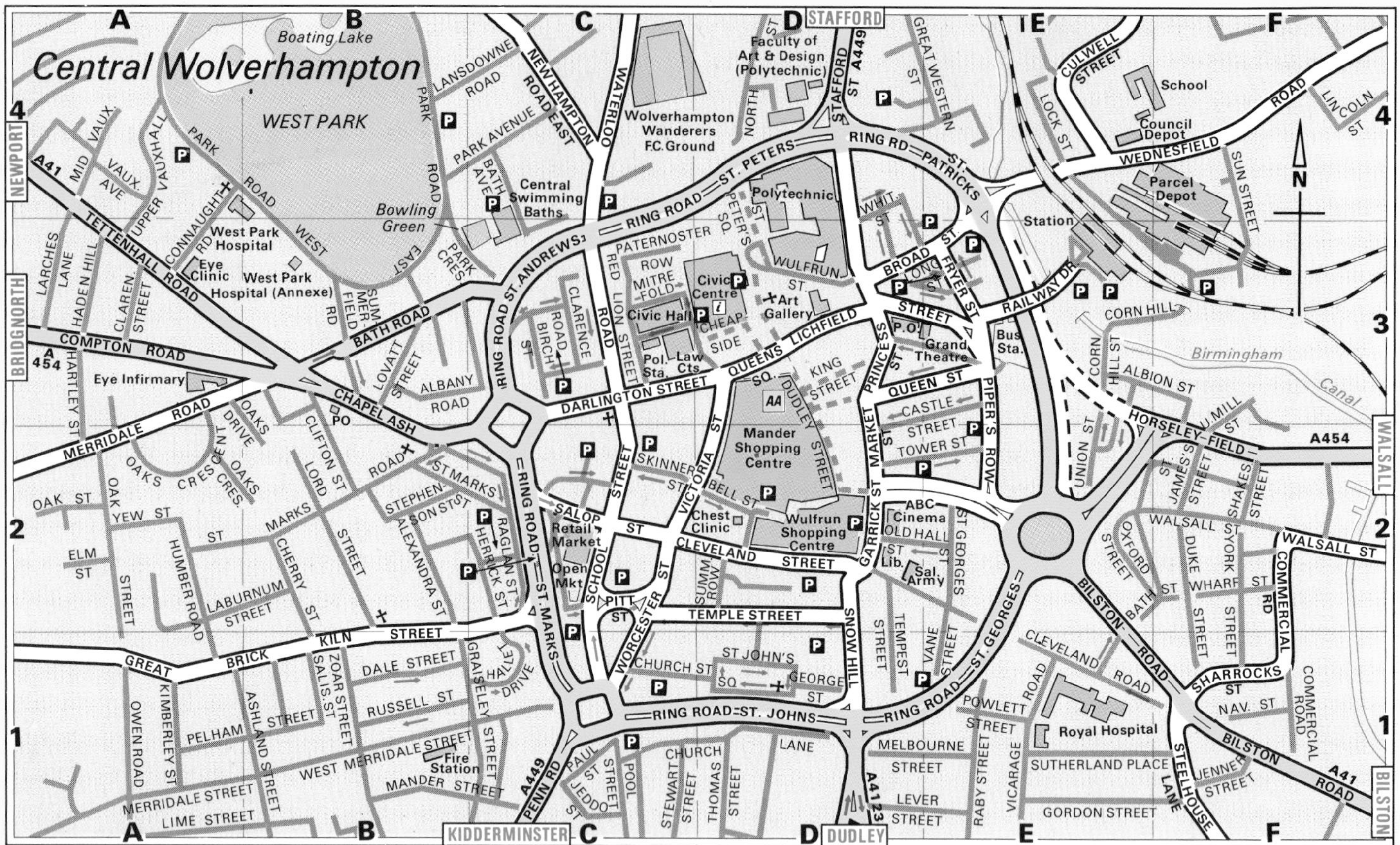

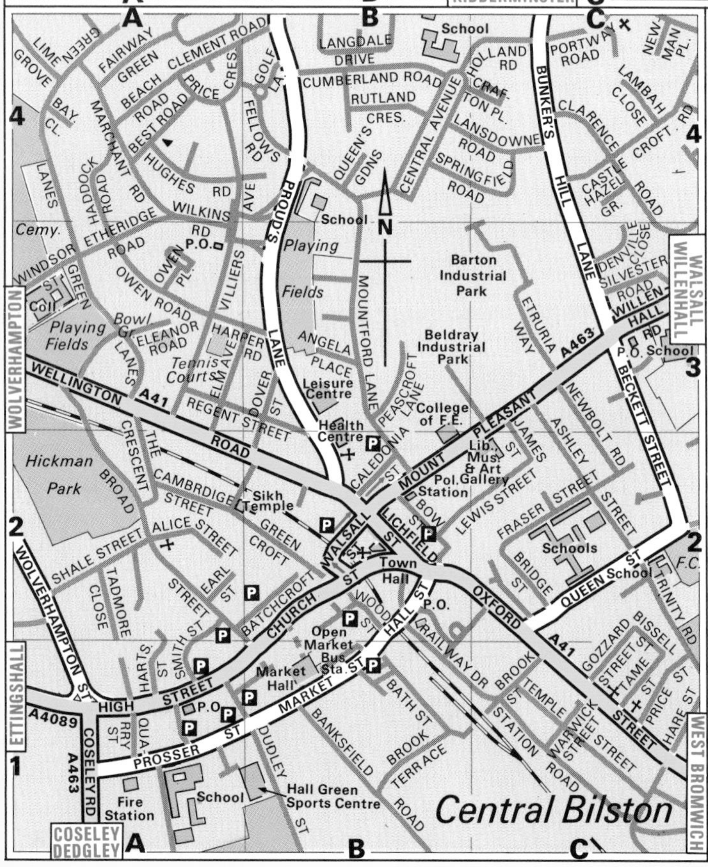

Central Wolverhampton

(Map of Central Wolverhampton with grid references A–F, 1–4)

Central Bilston

(Map of Central Bilston with grid references A–C, 1–4)

Key to Town Plan and Area Plan

Town Plan

AA Recommended roads
Other roads
Restricted roads
Buildings of interest — Library
Car Parks — P
Parks and open spaces
Churches — †
One Way Streets

Area Plan

A roads
B roads
Locations — Springhill O
Urban area

Street Index With Grid Reference

Wolverhampton

Street	Grid Reference
Albany Road	B3-C3
Albion Street	E3-F3
Alexandra Street	B2
Ashland Street	A1-B1
Bath Avenue	C3-C4
Bath Road	B3-C3
Bath Street	E2-F2
Bell Street	D2
Bilston Road	E2-E1-F1
Birch Street	C3
Broad Street	D3-E3-E4
Castle Street	D2-D3-E3
Chapel Ash	B3-B2-C2
Cheapside	D3
Cherry Street	B1-B2
Church Lane	C1-D1
Church Street	C1-D1
Clarence Road	C3
Clarendon Street	A3
Cleveland Road	D2-E2-E1-F1
Cleveland Street	C2-D2
Clifton Street	B2-B3
Commercial Road	F1-F2
Compton Road	A3-B3
Connaught Road	A3-A4
Corn Hill	E3-F3
Corn Hill Street	E3
Culwell Street	E4
Dale Street	B1
Darlington Street	C3-D3
Dudley Street	D2-D3
Duke Street	F1-F2
Elm Street	A2
Fryer Street	E3
Garrick Street	D2
George Street	D1
Gordon Street	E1-F1
Graiseley Street	B1-C1-B1
Great Brick Kiln Street	A1-B1-B2-C1-C2
Great Western Street	D4-E4
Haden Hill	A3
Hallet Drive	C1
Hartley Street	A2-A3
Herrick Street	B2-C2
Horseley Field	E3-F3-F2
Humber Road	A1-A2
Jeddo Street	C1
Jenner Street	F1
Kimberley Street	A1
King Street	D3
Laburnum Street	A2-B2
Lansdowne Road	B4-C4
Larches Lane	A3-A4
Lever Street	D1-E1
Lichfield Street	D3-E3

Wolverhampton

Present-day Wolverhampton, capital of the Black Country, is a large and efficient town that belies its ancient origins. It was referred to as 'Heantun' in a 10th-century Royal charter, and the town coat of arms includes a cross ascribed to the Anglo-Saxon King Edgar.

In Victorian times Wolverhampton was widely known for its manufacture of chains, locks and nails, although the workshops were often tiny sheds in people's back yards. Today, many kinds of brass and iron products, as well as aircraft components, leave Wolverhampton's factories. Some different, but no less traditional, products of Midland craftsmen are displayed in the museum inside 19th-century Bantock House. These include japanned tin and papier-maché articles and painted enamels, as well as early Worcester porcelain.

Pre-dating Wolverhampton's industrial history by several hundred years is the carved shaft of Dane's Cross in St Peter's churchyard. Standing 14ft high, near a holed Bargain Stone, it was supposed to commemorate the defeat of the Danes in a local battle. The church mostly dates from the 15th century, and has a panelled tower and fine stone pulpit. There was an earlier monastery on the site, refounded in 994 by Lady Wulfruna, whose charter can now be seen in the vestry.

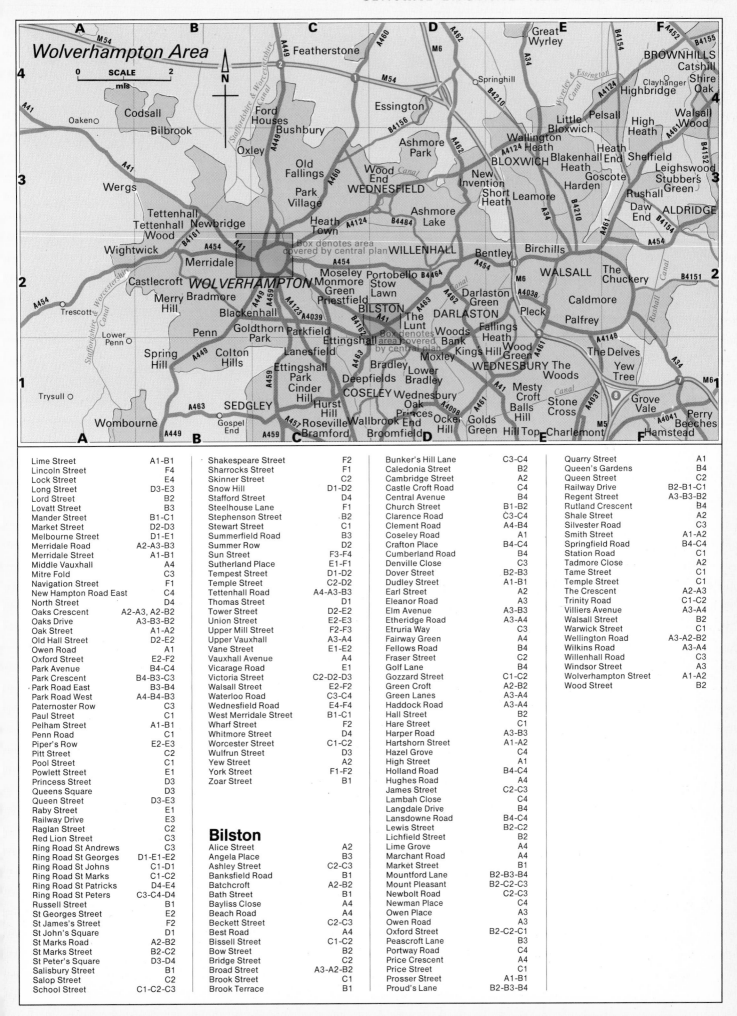

Wolverhampton Area

Lime Street	A1-B1
Lincoln Street	F4
Lock Street	E4
Long Street	D3-E3
Lord Street	B2
Lovatt Street	B3
Mander Street	B1-C1
Market Street	D2-D3
Melbourne Street	D1-E1
Merridale Road	A2-A3-B3
Merridale Street	A1-B1
Middle Vauxhall	A4
Mitre Fold	C3
Navigation Street	F1
New Hampton Road East	C4
North Street	D4
Oaks Crescent	A2-A3, A2-B2
Oaks Drive	A3-B3-B2
Oak Street	A1-A2
Old Hall Street	D2-E2
Owen Road	A1
Oxford Street	E2-F2
Park Avenue	B4-C4
Park Crescent	B4-B3-C3
Park Road East	B3-B4
Park Road West	A4-B4-B3
Paternoster Row	C3
Paul Street	C1
Pelham Street	A1-B1
Penn Road	C1
Piper's Row	E2-E3
Pitt Street	C2
Pool Street	C1
Powlett Street	E1
Princess Street	D3
Queens Square	D3
Queen Street	D3-E3
Raby Street	E1
Railway Drive	E3
Raglan Street	C2
Red Lion Street	C3
Ring Road St Andrews	C3
Ring Road St Georges	D1-E1-E2
Ring Road St Johns	C1-D1
Ring Road St Marks	C1-C2
Ring Road St Patricks	D4-E4
Ring Road St Peters	C3-C4-D4
Russell Street	B1
St Georges Street	E2
St James's Street	F2
St John's Square	D1
St Marks Road	A2-B2
St Marks Street	B2-C2
St Peter's Square	D3-D4
Salisbury Street	B1
Salop Street	C2
School Street	C1-C2-C3

Shakespeare Street	F2
Sharrocks Street	F1
Skinner Street	C2
Snow Hill	D1-D2
Stafford Street	D4
Steelhouse Lane	F1
Stephenson Street	B2
Stewart Street	C1
Summerfield Road	B3
Summer Row	D2
Sun Street	F3-F4
Sutherland Place	E1-F1
Tempest Street	D1-D2
Temple Street	C2-D2
Tettenhall Road	A4-A3-B3
Thomas Street	D1
Tower Street	D2-E2
Union Street	E2-E3
Upper Mill Street	F2-F3
Upper Vauxhall	A3-A4
Vane Street	E1-E2
Vauxhall Avenue	A4
Vicarage Road	E1
Victoria Street	C2-D2-D3
Walsall Street	E2-F2
Waterloo Road	C3-C4
Wednesfield Road	E4-F4
West Merridale Street	B1-C1
Wharf Street	F2
Whitmore Street	D4
Worcester Street	C1-C2
Wulfrun Street	D3
Yew Street	A2
York Street	F1-F2
Zoar Street	B1

Bilston

Alice Street	A2
Angela Place	B3
Ashley Street	C2-C3
Banksfield Road	B1
Batchcroft	A2-B2
Bath Street	B1
Bayliss Close	A4
Beach Road	A4
Beckett Street	C2-C3
Best Road	A4
Bissell Street	C1-C2
Bow Street	B2
Bridge Street	C2
Broad Street	A3-A2-B2
Brook Street	C1
Brook Terrace	B1

Bunker's Hill Lane	C3-C4
Caledonia Street	B2
Cambridge Street	A2
Castle Croft Road	C4
Central Avenue	B4
Church Street	B1-B2
Clarence Road	C3-C4
Clement Road	A4-B4
Coseley Road	A1
Crafton Place	B4-C4
Cumberland Road	B4
Denville Close	C3
Dover Street	B2-B3
Dudley Street	A1-B1
Earl Street	A2
Eleanor Road	A3
Elm Avenue	A3-B3
Etheridge Road	A3-A4
Etruria Way	C3
Fairway Green	A4
Fellows Road	B4
Fraser Street	C2
Golf Lane	B4
Gozzard Street	C1-C2
Green Croft	A2-B2
Green Lanes	A3-A4
Haddock Road	A3-A4
Hall Street	B2
Hare Street	C1
Harper Road	A3-B3
Hartshorn Street	A1-A2
Hazel Grove	C4
High Street	A1
Holland Road	B4-C4
Hughes Road	A4
James Street	C2-C3
Lambah Close	C4
Langdale Drive	B4
Lansdowne Road	B4-C4
Lewis Street	B2-C2
Lichfield Street	B2
Lime Grove	A4
Marchant Road	A4
Market Street	B1
Mountford Lane	B2-B3-B4
Mount Pleasant	B2-C2-C3
Newbolt Road	C2-C3
Newman Place	C4
Owen Place	A3
Owen Road	A3
Oxford Street	B2-C2-C1
Peascroft Lane	B3
Portway Road	C4
Price Crescent	A4
Price Street	C1
Prosser Street	A1-B1
Proud's Lane	B2-B3-B4

Quarry Street	A1
Queen's Gardens	B4
Queen Street	C2
Railway Drive	B2-B1-C1
Regent Street	A3-B3-B2
Rutland Crescent	B4
Shale Street	A2
Silvester Road	C3
Smith Street	A1-A2
Springfield Road	B4-C4
Station Road	C1
Tadmore Close	A2
Tame Street	C1
Temple Street	C1
The Crescent	A2-A3
Trinity Road	C1-C2
Villiers Avenue	A3-A4
Walsall Street	B2
Warwick Street	C1
Wellington Road	A3-A2-B2
Wilkins Road	A3-A4
Willenhall Road	C3
Windsor Street	A3
Wolverhampton Street	A1-A2
Wood Street	B2

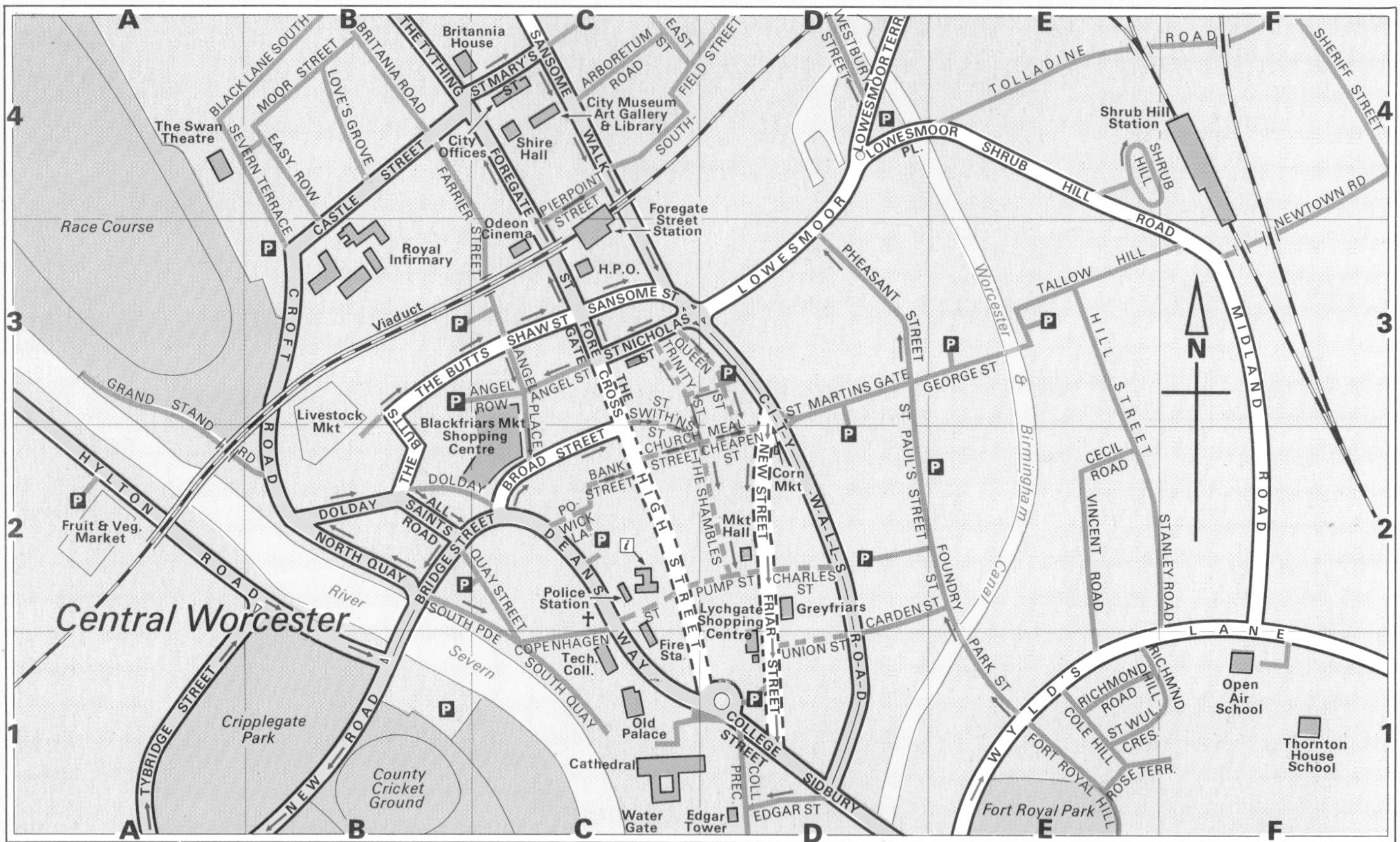

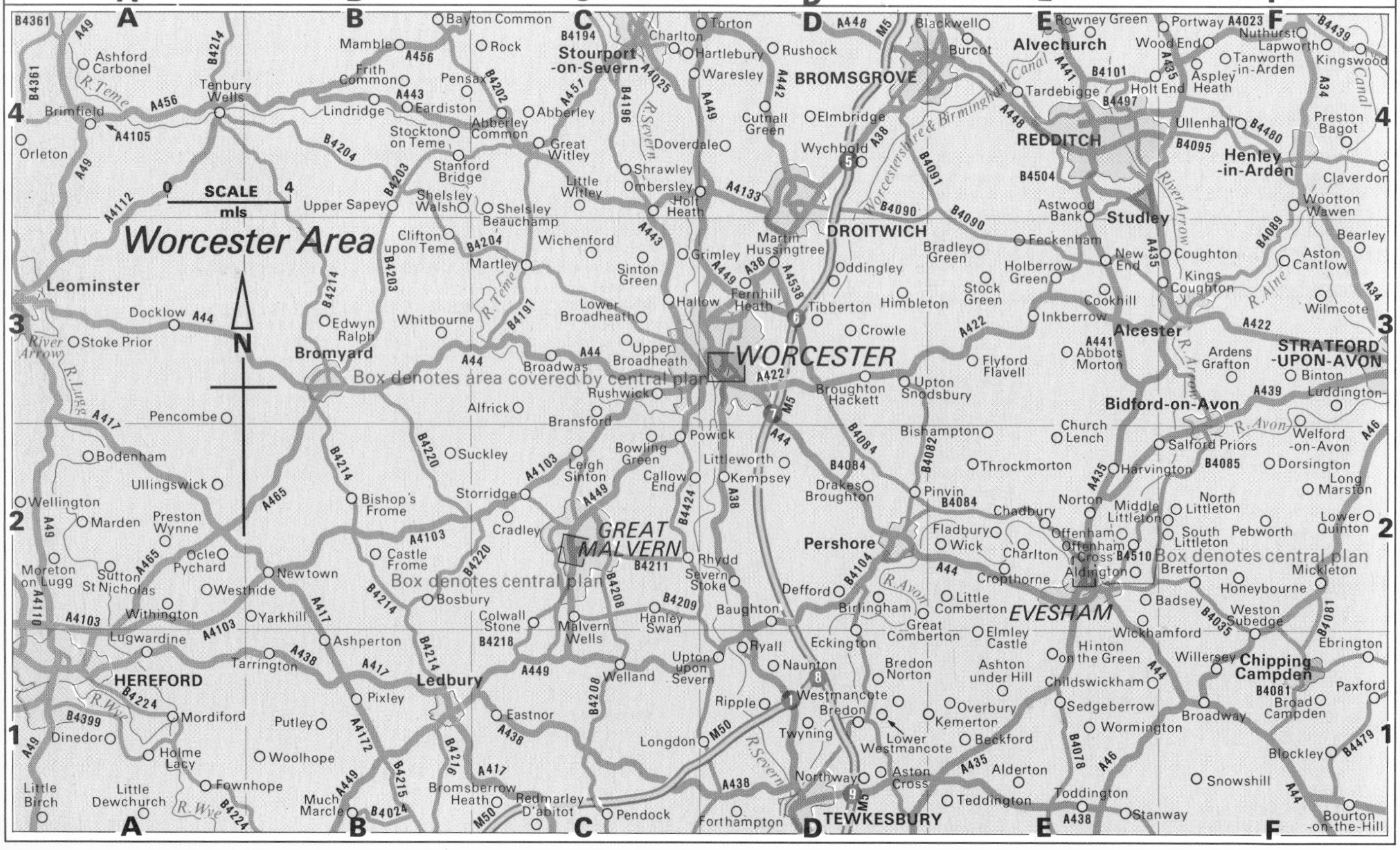

Worcester

County town and cathedral city, Worcester stands on the banks of the Severn in an area of rich agricultural land. Sadly, during the 1960s, the city suffered somewhat from ruthless redevelopment, but there is still much to interest the visitor, including The Commandery and the Tudor House, 15th-century buildings which both house museums. The cathedral, Worcester's oldest building, overlooks the river and the county cricket ground. It is one of the venues of the Three Choirs Festival, alternating with Gloucester and Hereford Cathedrals.

Worcester has become famous for its porcelain industry which was founded during the 18th century as an alternative to the ailing cloth trade. An exquisite collection of 'Royal Worcester' can be seen in the Dyson Perrins Museum.

Evesham is surrounded by the orchards that flourish in the fertile Vale of Evesham. It is an ancient market and light industrial town with two churches, a 16th-century bell-tower and the ruins of a Norman abbey all sharing the same grounds.

Malvern, famous for its mineral water, nestles at the foot of the Malvern Hills which are designated an Area of Outstanding Natural Beauty. Visitors have been drawn to this attractive town since Victorian times, and it retains much of the genteel elegance associated with bygone days.

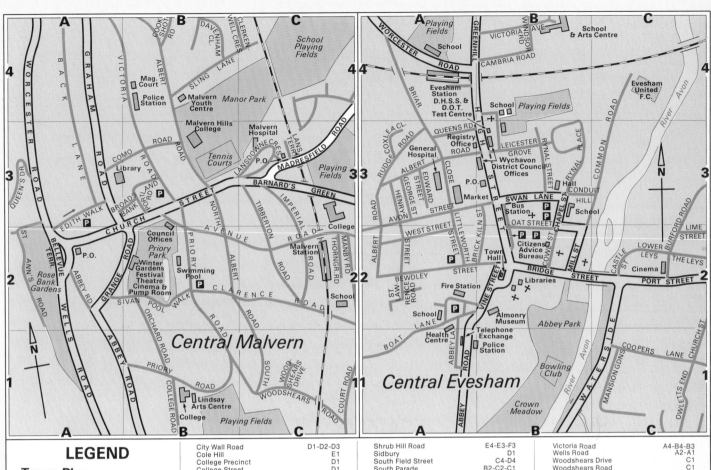

LEGEND

Town Plan

AA Recommended roads	
Restricted roads	
Other roads	
Buildings of interest	Cinema ▣
Car Parks	ℙ
Parks and open spaces	
One Way Streets	→

Area Plan

A roads	
B roads	
Locations	Suckley ○
Urban area	

Street Index with Grid Reference

Worcester

All Saints Road	B2
Angel Place	C2-C3
Angel Row	B3-C3
Angel Street	C3
Arborteum Road	C4
Bank Street	C2
Black Lane South	A4-B4
Bridge Street	B2-C2
Britania Road	B4
Broad Street	C2-C3
Carden Street	D2-E2
Castle Street	B3-B4
Cecil Road	E2
Charles Street	D2
Church Street	C2

City Wall Road	D1-D2-D3
Cole Hill	E1
College Precinct	D1
College Street	D1
Copenhagen Street	C1-C2
Croft Road	B3-B2
Deans Way	C1-C2
Dolday	B2-C2
East Street	C4
Easy Row	B4
Edgar Street	D1
Farrier Street	B4-C4-C3
Foregate	C3
Foregate Street	C4-C3
Fort Royal Hill	E1
Foundry Street	E2
Friar Street	D1-D2
George Street	D3-E3
Grand Stand Road	A3-A2-B2
High Street	C2-C1-D1
Hill Street	E2-E3
Hylton Road	A3-A2-B2-B1
Love's Grove	B4
Lowesmoor	D3-D4
Lowesmoor Place	D4-E4
Lowesmoor Terrace	D4
Meal Cheapen Street	D2
Midland Road	F2-F3
Moor Street	D2-D3
New Road	B1
New Street	D2-D3
Newton Road	F3-F4
North Quay	B2
Park Street	E1-E2
Pheasant Street	D3
Pierpoint Street	C4
Powick Lane	C2
Pump Street	C2-D2
Quay Street	B2-C2-C1
Queen Street	C3-D3
Richmond Hill	E1-F1
Richmond Road	E1
Rose Terrace	E1-F1
St Martin's Gate	D3
St Mary's Street	B4-C4
St Nicholas Street	C3
St Paul's Street	D3-D2-E2
St Swithuns Street	C2-C3
St Wulstans Crescent	E1-F1
Sansome Street	C3
Sansome Walk	C3
Severn Terrace	A4-B4-B3
Shaw Street	C3
Sheriff Street	F4
Shrub Hill	E4-F4

Shrub Hill Road	E4-E3-F3
Sidbury	D1
South Field Street	C4-D4
South Parade	B2-C2-C1
South Quay	C1
Stanley Road	E2-F2
Tallow Hill	E3-F3
The Butts	B2-B3-C3
The Cross	C3
The Shambles	D2
The Tything	B4
Tolladine Road	E4-F4
Trinity Street	C3-C2
Tybridge Street	A1-A2-B2-B1
Union Street	D1
Vincent Road	E1-E2
Westbury Street	D4
Wyld's Lane	E1-F1-F2

Malvern

Abbey Road	A2-A1-B1
Albert Road South	B2-C2-C1
Albert Road North	B4-B3-B2
Avenue Road	B3-B2-C2
Back Lane	A4-A3
Barnard's Green	C3
Bellevue Terrace	A2
Broads Bank	A3-A4
Church Street	A3-A2-B2-B3
Clarence Road	B2-C2
Clerkenwell Crescent	B4-C4
College Road	B1
Como Road	A3-B3
Cookshot Road	B4
Court Road	C1
Davenham Close	B4
Edith Walk	A2-A3
Graham Road	A4-A3
Grange Road	A2-B2
Imperial Road	C2-C3
Lansdowne Crescent	C3
Lansdowne Terrace	C3
Madresfield Road	C3-C4
Orchard Road	B1-B2
Portland Road	B3
Priory Road	B3-B2-B1
Queen's Drive	A3
St Ann's Road	A2-A3
Sivan Pool Walk	A3-B3
Thorn Grove Road	C2
Tibberton Road	C3-C2

Victoria Road	A4-B4-B3
Wells Road	A2-A1
Woodshears Drive	C1
Woodshears Road	C1
Worcester Road	A4-A3-A2

Evesham

Abbey Road	A1-A2
Albert Road	A2-A3-B3
Avon Street	A2-A3-B3
Bewdley Street	A2-B2
Boat Lane	A1-A2-B2
Briar Close	A4-A3
Brick Kiln Street	B2-B3
Bridge Street	B2-C2
Burford Road	C2-C3
Cambria Road	B4
Castle Street	C2
Chapel Street	B2-B3
Church Street	C1-C2
Coopers Lane	C1
Common Road	B3-C3-C4
Conduit Hill	B3-C3
Cowl Street	B2
Coxlea Close	A3
Edward Street	A3
George Street	A3
Greenhill	A3-A4
Henry Street	A2-A3
Leicester Grove	B3
Lime Street	C2
Littleworth Street	A2-A3
Lower Leys	C2
Mansion Gardens	C1
Mill Street	B2-B3
Oat Street	B2
Owletts End	C1
Port Street	C2
Queens Road	A3
Rudge Road	A3
Rynal Place	B3
Rynal Street	B3
St Lawrence Road	A2
Swan Lane	B3
The Leys	C2
Victoria Avenue	B4
Vine Street	A2-B2
Waterside	B1-C1-C2
West Street	A2
Windsor Road	B4
Worcester Road	A4

WORCESTER
Worcester Cathedral, set high on the banks of the Severn with views across the Malvern Hills, has dominated the city for centuries. The chapter house, with its massive central column, is considered one of the finest in Britain.

Legend to Atlas

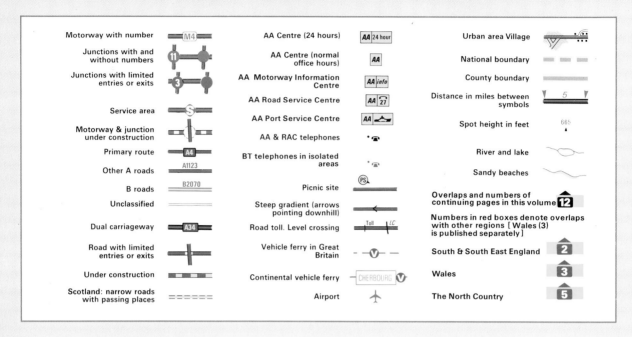

Motorway with number — M4
Junctions with and without numbers — 11
Junctions with limited entries or exits — 3
Service area — S
Motorway & junction under construction
Primary route — A4
Other A roads — A1123
B roads — B2070
Unclassified
Dual carriageway — A34
Road with limited entries or exits
Under construction
Scotland: narrow roads with passing places

AA Centre (24 hours) — AA 24 hour
AA Centre (normal office hours) — AA
AA Motorway Information Centre — AA info
AA Road Service Centre — AA 27
AA Port Service Centre — AA
AA & RAC telephones
BT telephones in isolated areas
Picnic site — PS
Steep gradient (arrows pointing downhill)
Road toll. Level crossing — Toll LC
Vehicle ferry in Great Britain — V
Continental vehicle ferry — CHERBOURG V
Airport

Urban area Village
National boundary
County boundary
Distance in miles between symbols — 5
Spot height in feet — 665
River and lake
Sandy beaches
Overlaps and numbers of continuing pages in this volume — 12
Numbers in red boxes denote overlaps with other regions [Wales (3) is published separately]
South & South East England — 2
Wales — 3
The North Country — 5

Abbey or Cathedral
Ruined Abbey or Cathedral
Castle
House and Garden
House
Garden
Industrial Interest
Museum or Collection
Prehistoric Monument
Famous Battle Site
Preserved Railway or Steam Centre
Windmill
Sea Angling

Coastal- Launching Site
Surfing
Climbing School
County Cricket Ground
Gliding Centre
Artificial Ski Slope
Golf Course
Horse Racing
Show Jumping/Equestrian Centre
Motor Racing Circuit
Cave
Country Park
Dolphinarium or Aquarium

Nature Trail
Wildlife Park (mammals)
Wildlife Park (birds)
Zoo
Forest Drive
Lighthouse
Tourist Information Centre
Tourist Information Centre (summer only)
Long Distance Footpath
AA Viewpoint
Other Place of Interest
Boxed symbols indicate tourist attractions in towns

The National Grid

The National Grid provides a system of reference common to maps of all scales. The grid covers Britain with an imaginary network of 100 kilometre squares. Each square is identified by two letters, *eg* TR. Every 100 kilometre square is then sub-divided into 10 kilometre squares which appear as a network of blue lines on the map pages. These blue lines are numbered left to right 0-9 and bottom to top 0-9. These 10 kilometre squares can be further divided into tenths to give a place reference to the nearest kilometre.

Key to Road Maps

Thurso •
Wick •

Stornoway •

Outer
Hebrides

Ullapool •

Portree •

Banff •

Inverness • Peterhead •

Aberdeen •

Fort
William •

Pitlochry •

Oban •

Perth • Dundee •

Edinburgh •

Largs • Glasgow •

Peebles •

Berwick •

Campbeltown • Ayr •

• Dumfries

Newcastle
upon Tyne •

Stranraer •

Workington •

Middlesbrough •

Kendal •

Scarborough •

Isle of
Man

Douglas •

Lancaster •

York •

Blackpool •

Leeds • Hull •

Liverpool •

Grimsby •

Manchester • Sheffield •

456/457 **458/459** **460/461**
Lincoln •

Caernarfon • Chester •

Stoke •

446/447
Shrewsbury •

Nottingham •
450/451 King's Lynn • **454/455**
448/449 Leicester • **452/453** Norwich •
• Peterborough Great
436/437 Yarmouth

Aberystwyth •

Birmingham • Northampton •
Coventry • **442/443** **444/445**
438/439 **440/441** Cambridge •
Worcester •

Fishguard • Carmarthen •

434/435
Hereford • Felixstowe •

Pembroke • Swansea • • Gloucester Chelmsford •

Cardiff • Bristol • Oxford •

LONDON •
Reading •

Maidstone •

Barnstaple • Guildford • • Dover
Salisbury • Folkestone •

Taunton • Southampton •
Brighton • Newhaven •

Exeter • Weymouth • Bournemouth •

Truro • Plymouth •

Scilly
Isles

Shetland
Islands

Orkney
Islands

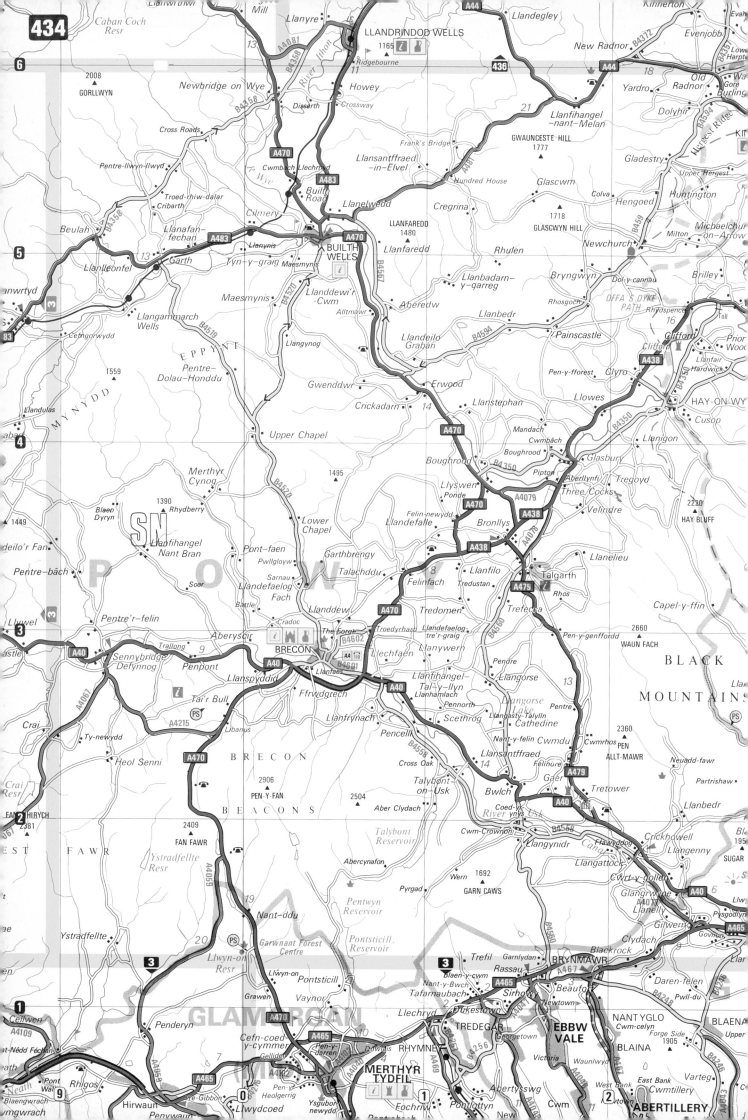

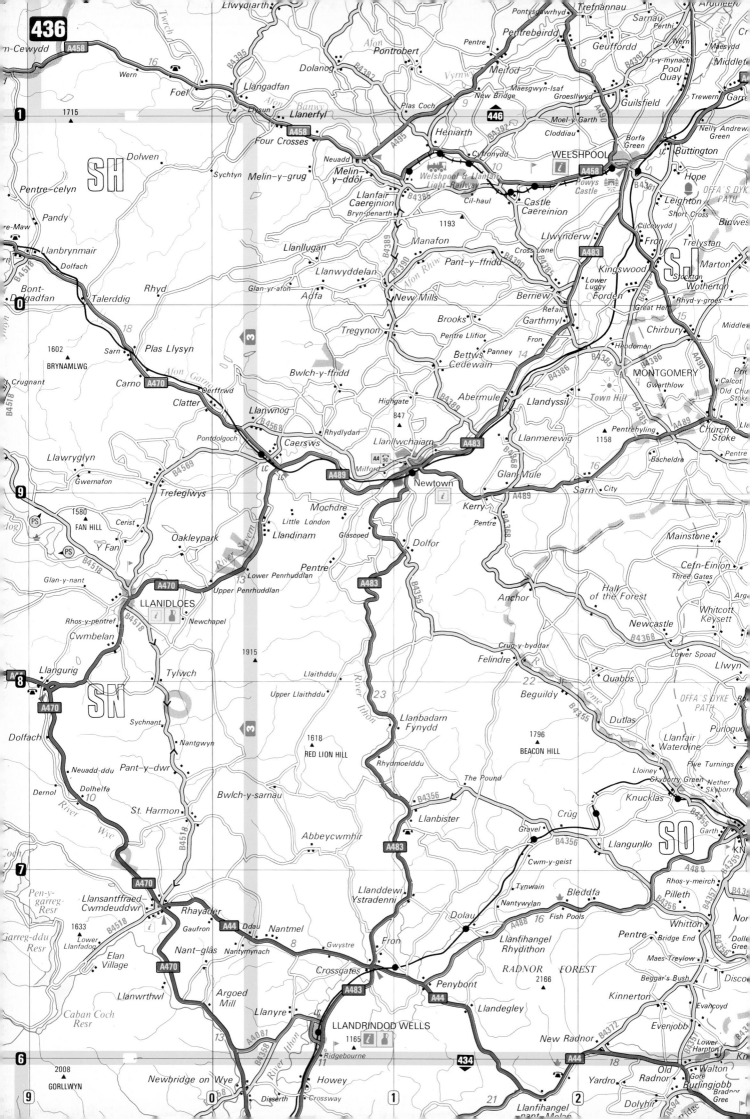

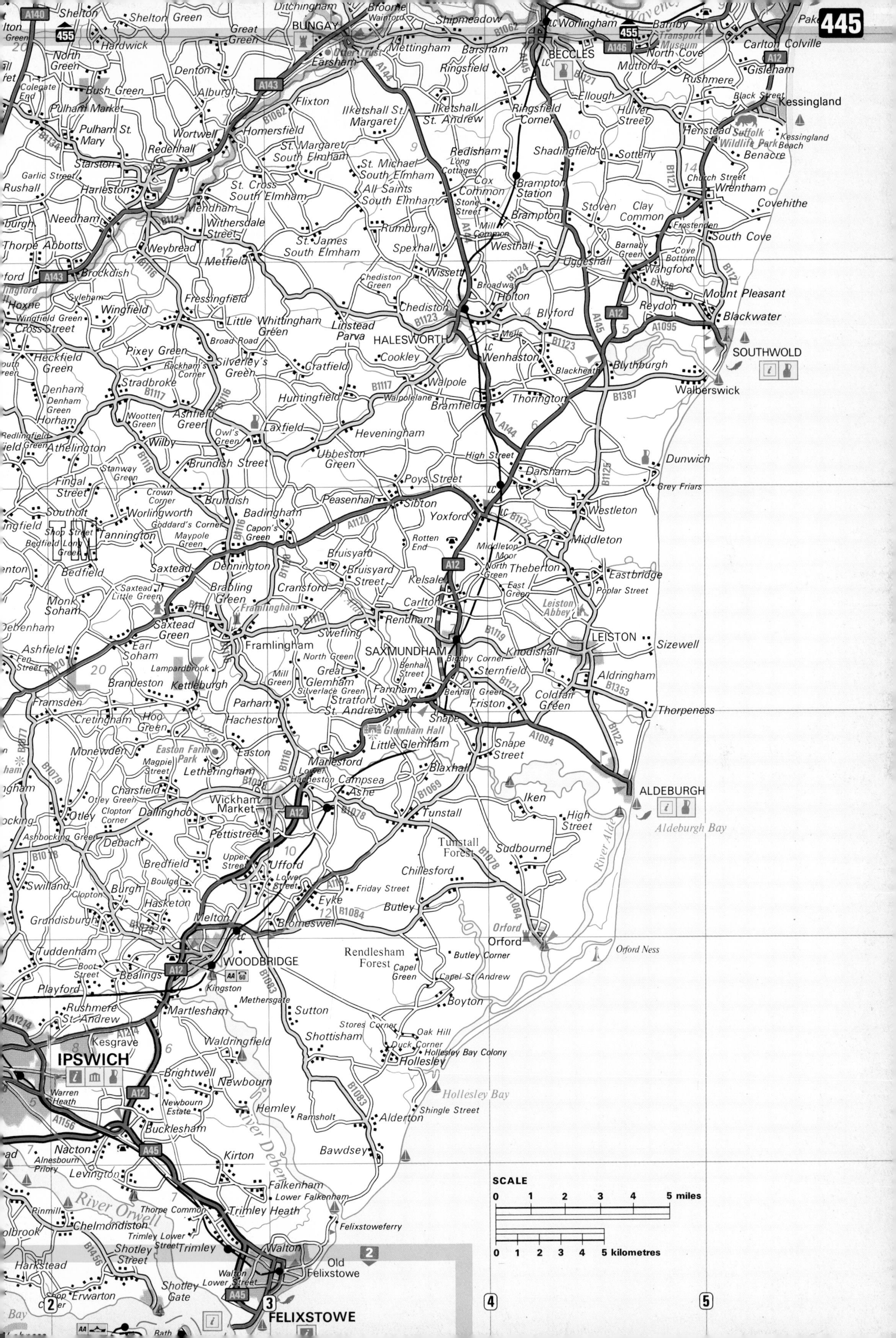

A140 · Shelton · Shelton Green · Ditchingham · Broome · Shipmeadow · Worlingham · Barnby · Pake
455 · Hardwick · Great Green · BUNGAY · Wainford · A146 · BECCLES · North Cove · Carlton Colville · A12 · Gisleham
North Green · Denton · Alburgh · Earsham · Mettingham · Barsham · Ringsfield · Mutford · Rushmere
Colegate End · Bush Green · Flixton · A143 · A144 · Ilketshall St. Margaret · Ilketshall St. Andrew · Ringsfield Corner · Ellough · Black Street · Kessingland
Pulham Market · Pulham St. Mary · Wortwell · Homersfield · B1062 · St. Michael South Elmham · Redisham · Shadingfield · Sotterly · Henstead · Suffolk Wildlife Park · Kessingland Beach
B1134 · Redenhall · St. Margaret South Elmham · All Saints South Elmham · Long Cottages · Cox Common · Brampton Station · Stoven · Clay Common · Benacre
Starston · Harleston · Mendham · St. Cross South Elmham · Stone Street · Brampton · Church Street · Wrentham
Garlic Street · Rushall · Needham · B1123 · Withersdale Street · Rumburgh · Mill Common · Barnaby Green · Covehithe
Thorpe Abbotts · Weybread · St. James South Elmham · Spexhall · Westhall · Uggeshall · Cove Bottom · South Cove
A143 · Brockdish · Syleham · Metfield · B1116 · St. Andrew · Wissett · Broadway · Holton · B1124 · Wangford · Wangford
Hoxne · Wingfield Green · Wingfield · Fressingfield · Little Whittingham Green · Linstead Parva · Chediston Green · Chediston · Blyford · A145 · A12 · Reydon · Mount Pleasant · Blackwater
Cross Street · Heckfield Green · Pixey Green · Broad Road · Cookley · Wenhaston · B1123 · A1095 · SOUTHWOLD
Denham · Denham Green · Horham · Stradbroke · B1117 · Silverley's Green · Cratfield · Walpole · Blackheath · Blythburgh · B1387 · Walberswick
Redlingfield Green · Athelington · Wootten Green · Ashfield Green · Owl's Green · Laxfield · Huntingfield · Walpole lane · Bramfield · Thorington · Dunwich · Grey Friars
Fingal Street · Stanway Green · Wilby · Brundish Street · Ubbeston Green · Heveningham · High Street · Darsham · B1125 · Westleton
Southolt · Worlingworth · Crown Corner · Brundish · Peasenhall · Poys Street · Sibton · Yoxford · LC · B1122 · Middleton
Shop Street · Tannington · Goddard's Corner · B1116 · Capon's Green · Bruisyard · Rotten End · Middleton Moor · Middleton
Bedfield Long Green · Bedfield · Maypole Green · Saxtead · Dennington · Bruisyard Street · Kelsale · North Green · Theberton · Eastbridge
Monk Soham · Saxtead Little Green · Brabling Green · Cransford · Carlton · East Green · Poplar Street
Ashfield Fen Street · Earl Soham · Saxtead Green · A1120 · Framlingham · Swefling · Rendham · B1119 · Leiston Abbey · Sizewell
B1120 · Brandeston · Kettleburgh · Lampardbrook · North Green · SAXMUNDHAM · Bigsby Corner · Sternfield · Knodishall · LEISTON
Framsden · Cretingham · Hoo Green · Parham · Mill Green · Great Glemham · Benhall Street · Benhall Green · B1121 · Coldfair Green · Aldringham · B1353
Monewden · Easton Farm Park · Hacheston · Silverlace Green · Stratford St. Andrew · Farnham · Friston · Thorpeness
Charsfield · Easton · Letheringham · Marlesford · Glemham Hall · Little Glemham · Snape · A1094 · ALDEBURGH
Otley Green · Magpie Street · Lower Hacheston · Campsea Ashe · Little Glemham · Snape Street · Aldeburgh Bay
Swilland · Clopton Corner · Dallinghoo · Wickham Market · Blaxhall · Iken · High Street
Ashbocking Green · Debach · Pettistree · A12 · Tunstall · Sudbourne
Clopton · Hasketon · Bredfield · Upper Street · Ufford · Tunstall Forest · Chillesford · B1078
Grundisburgh · Burgh · Boulge · Lower Street · Friday Street · Butley · B1084 · Orford
Tuddenham · Melton · Bromeswell · Eyke · Butley Corner · Orford
Boot Street · Bealings · Kingston · WOODBRIDGE · AA 60 · Rendlesham Forest · Capel Green · Capel St Andrew · Orford Ness
Playford · Rushmere St Andrew · Martlesham · Methersgate · Sutton · Boyton
IPSWICH · Kesgrave · A1214 · Waldringfield · Shottisham · Stores Corner · Oak Hill · Hollesley Bay Colony
Warren Heath · Brightwell · Newbourn · Newbourn Estate · Duck Corner · Hollesley
A12 · Bucklesham · Hemley · Ramsholt · Shingle Street · Alderton
Nacton · Kirton · Falkenham · Lower Falkenham · Hollesley Bay · Bawdsey
Alnesbourn Priory · A45 · Thorpe Common · Trimley Heath · Felixstoweferry
Rinmil · Chelmondiston · Trimley Lower Street · Trimley · Walton · FELIXSTOWE
Harkstead · Shotley Street · Shotley Gate · Walton Lower Street · Old Felixstowe · A45

SCALE
0 1 2 3 4 5 miles
0 1 2 3 4 5 kilometres

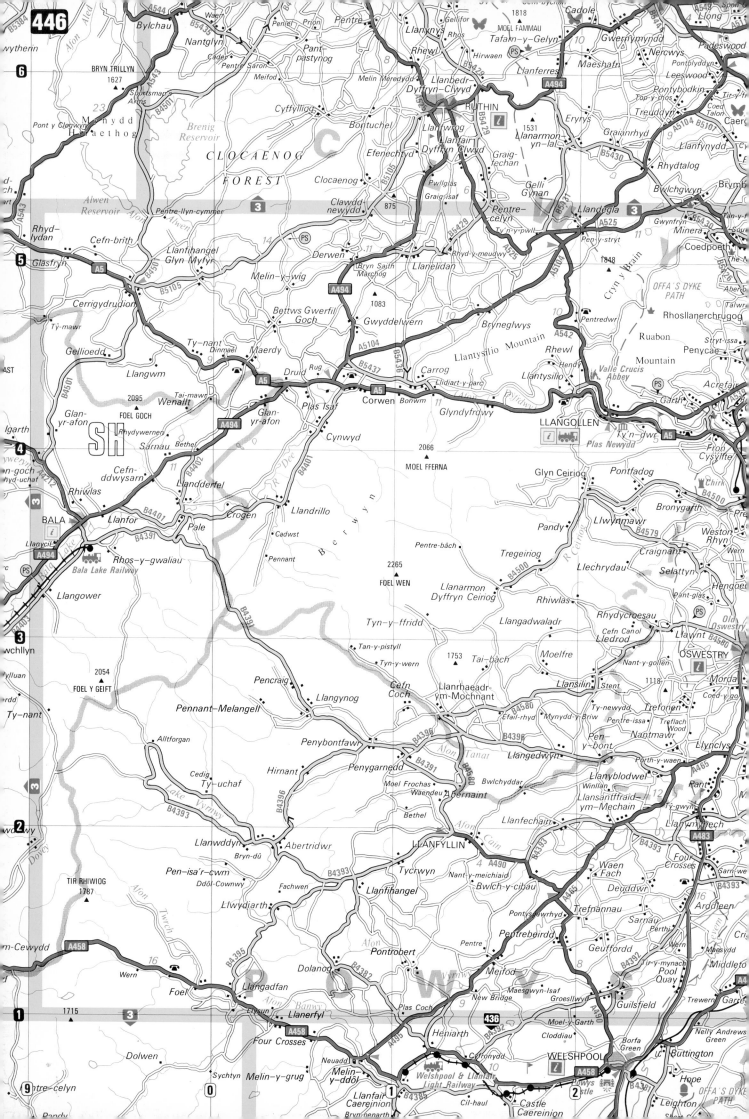

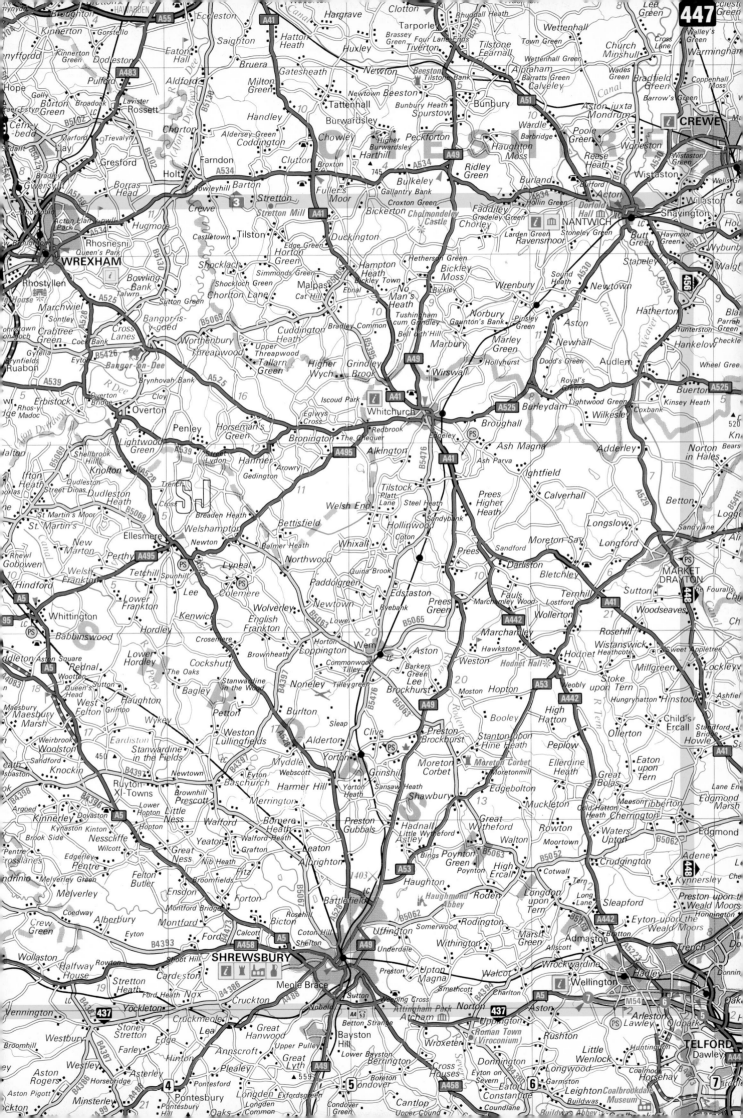

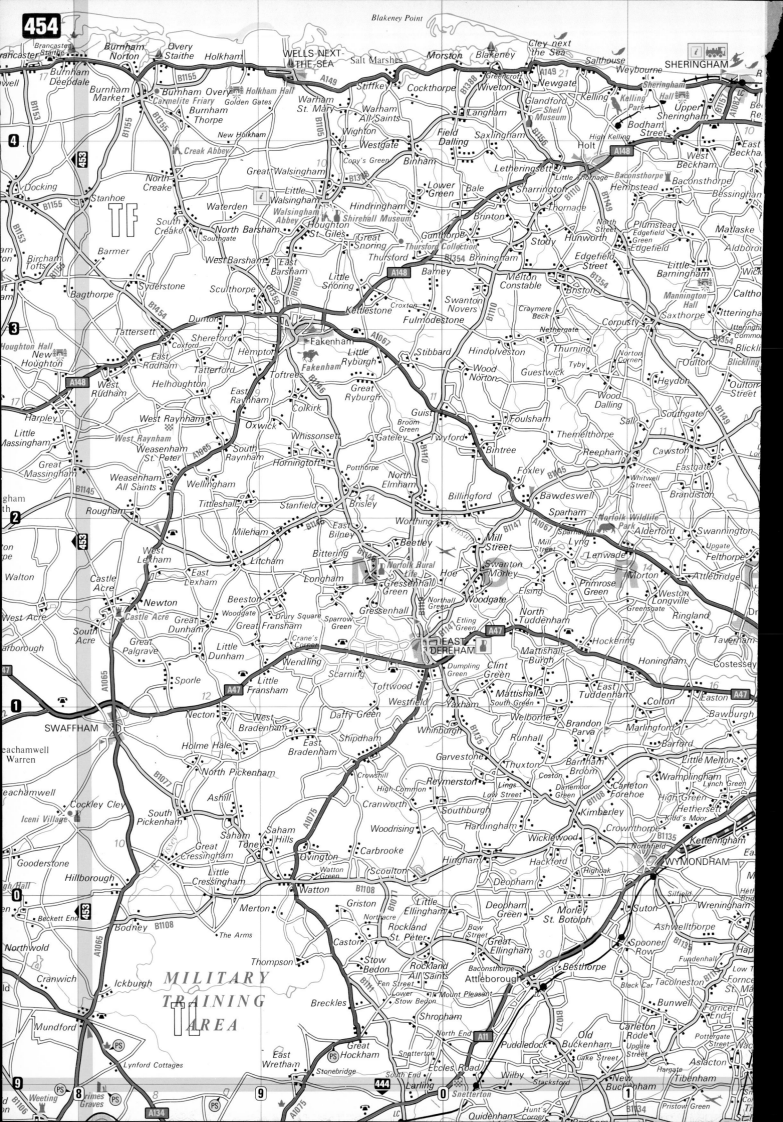

SCALE

0 1 2 3 4 5 miles

0 1 2 3 4 5 kilometres

West Runton East Runton CROMER *Open to Public*

Overstrand Sidestrand

A149 A148 A140 B1159

Aylmerton Felbrigg Felbrigg Hall Crossdale Street Northrepps Trimingham Gimingham Mundesley

Gresham Roughton Southrepps Lower Street Trunch Paston Bacton Green Bacton

Sustead Metton Thorpe Market Bradfield Knapton Old Hall Street Keswick Walcott

Hanworth Thurgarton Antingham Stow Mill B1145 B1159

Alby Hill Erpingham Swafield Edingthorpe Pollard Street Ridlington Happisburgh

Colby Suffield Edingthorpe Green Witton Ridlington Street Whimpwell Green

Ingworth Felmingham Spa Common Crostwight Happisburgh Common Eccles on Sea

Banningham Trungate NORTH WALSHAM Meeting House Hill Honing Hempstead Sea Palling

Aylsham Tuttington Westwick Bengates Briggate East Ruston Lessingham Ingham Corner Waxham

Silvergate Burgh next Aylsham Worstead Stalham Hickling Ingham

Marsham Skeyton Swanton Abbot Dilham Stalham Green Hickling Green Horsey Corner Horsey

Brampton Sloley Smallburgh Low Street Calthorpe Street Hickling (Heath) Hill Common

Buxton Lamas Oxnead Scottow Fairstead Tunstead Sutton Wood Street Horsey Mere

Stratton Strawless Little Hautbois Market Street Pennygate Barton Turf Catfield Drainage Windmill Somerton

Hevingham Sco Ruston St. James Beeston Hall Neatishead Irstead Potter Heigham Winterton-on-Sea

Waterloo Horstead Coltishall Threehammer Common Ludham Martham Hemsby Hembsy Hole

New Hainford Hainford Belaugh Hoveton Horning A1062 Johnson's Street Cess Newport

St. Helena Frettenham B1354 Wroxham Upper Street Ludham Bridge Bastwick Repps Rollesby

Newton St. Faith Crostwick Woodbastwick Upper Street Thurne Burgh St Margaret Ormesby St. Margaret Scratby

Horsham St. Faith Spixworth Rackheath Salhouse Panxworth Ranworth Clippesby Filby Ormesby St. Michael California East End

NORWICH AIRPORT New Rackheath Little Plumstead Pilson Green Fairhaven Gargate Green Billockby Roman Town Caister-on-Sea

Sprowston Thorpe End Garden Village Hemblington South Walsham Upton Thrigby Mautby Caister

Hellesdon New Costessey Blofield Heath North Burlingham Acle Stokesby West End West Caister

NORWICH Great Plumstead Lingwood Damgate Runham Great Yarmouth

Bowthorpe Thorpe St Andrew Blofield Beighton Stracey Arms Wind Pump A47 Runham

Colney Postwick Brundall South Burlingham Tunstall Cobholm Island GREAT YARMOUTH

Eaton Trowse Newton Surlingham Strumpshaw Moulton St. Mary Halvergate Southtown Gorleston on Sea

Lakenham Kirby Bedon Steam Museum Southwood Berney Arms Station Burgh Castle Bradwell

Arminghall Bramerton Buckenham Freethorpe Berney Arms Burgh Browston Green Belton Hobland Hall

Framingham Pigot Rockland St. Mary Hassingham Wickhampton Freethorpe Common Pettitts Rural Industries Hopton on Sea

Framingham Earl Hellington Cantley Limpenhoe Witton Green Reedham Fritton Lound

Stoke Holy Cross Yelverton Claxton Langley Street Hardley Street Nogdam End St Olaves Priory Herringfleet Blundeston

Swainsthorpe Upper Stoke East Carleton Bergh Apton Ashby St. Mary Thurton Chedgrave Norton Subcourse Lower Thurlton St Olaves Somerleyton Corton

Bracon Ash Newton Flotman Howe Hawe's Green High Green Loddon Hales Thurlton Thorpe Haddiscoe Oulton Lowestoft End

Shotesham Brooke Mundham Seething Raveningham Maypole Green LOWESTOFT

Tasburgh Kirstead Green Thwaite St. Mary Hales Hall Kirby Cane Bull's Green Burgh St Peter Oulton Broad

Upper Tasburgh Saxlingham Nethergate Saxlingham Green Hempnall Woodton Hedenham Toft Monks Wheatacre Aldeby Kirkley Pakefield

Stratton St. Michael Hempnall Green Topcroft Stockton Gillingham Oulton Corton

Fritton Topcroft Street BUNGAY Broome Wainford Shipmeadow Worlingham Barnby Transport Museum Carlton Colville

Long Stratton Morningthorpe Shelton Shelton Green Great Green Ditchingham Mettingham Barsham BECCLES North Cove Gisleham

Hardwick North Green Denton Earsham Ringsfield Mutford

River Waveney A143 A146 A12 A1117 A1065 A1067 A140 A11 A47 A146

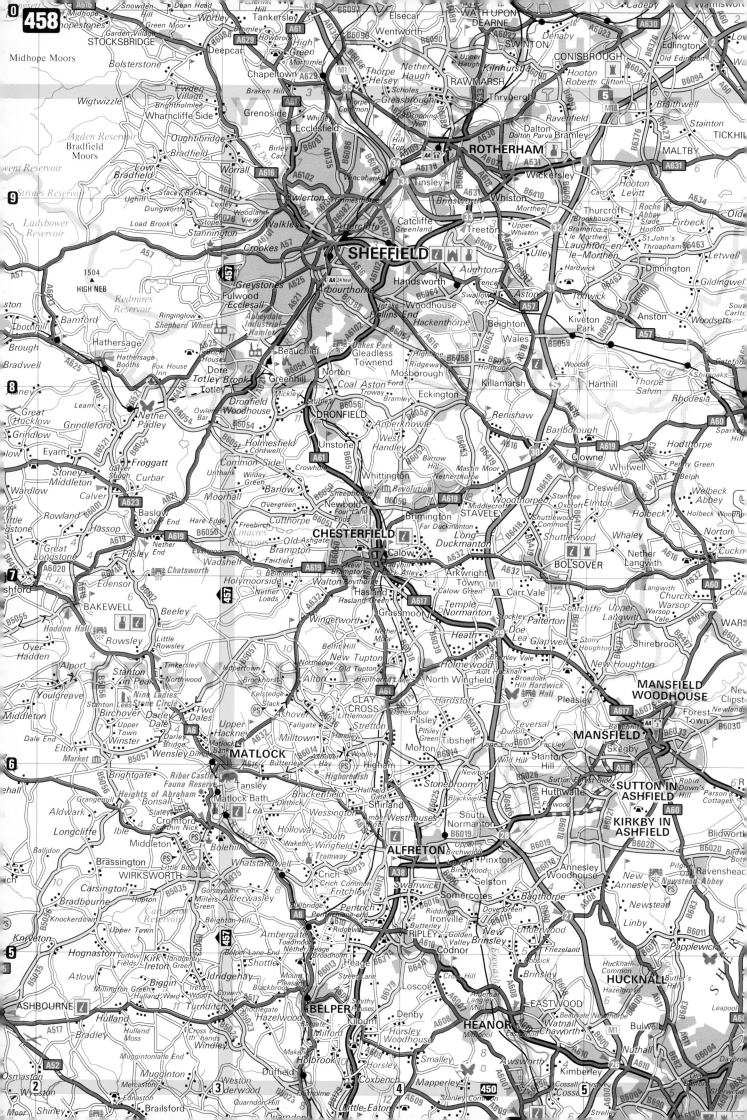

As well as the page number of each place name the index also
includes an appropriate atlas page number together with a four figure
map reference (see National Grid explanation at start of atlas section).

In a very few instances place names appear without a map reference.
This is because either they are not shown on the atlas or they lie just
outside the mapping area of the region. However, each tour does
include a detailed map which highlights the location of all places
mentioned on the route.

464

NORTH COUNTRY

Monsale Dale Viaduct, Derbyshire. Improving the view was not what the builders of this viaduct had in mind – but that is what they achieved.

The jagged, timeless ruins of Whitby Abbey, founded by St Hilda in 657, rise majestically above the town on the East Cliff and provide an impressive landmark for miles along the coast.

Touring the North Country

CONTENTS

INTRODUCTION

The North has lots of variety and contrasts, an area of huge industrial conurbations and a countryside of outstanding natural beauty. There are the beautiful Yorkshire Dales and Moors, and the magnificent Lake District of Wordsworth, with its dramatic panoramas. To the far north-east, Northumberland rolls away in exhilarating abandon to the Scottish border. Here, faint echoes of Border battles still linger around fortresses rising dramatically above the sea.

The region's cities are exquisite: York with its medieval walls and Minster, or Chester, with its unique 'Rows'. In surprising contrast are the holiday playgrounds of the north and those utterly English traditional seaside resorts such as Blackpool and Morecambe.

To the far north lies the boundary of an ancient empire — Hadrian's Wall. This extraordinary monument undulates across the rocky spine of Britain still proclaiming after centuries the rights of the Roman Empire. Here too, can be found the ruins of abbeys where medieval monks once found peace and solitude, while perhaps the region's newest man-made wonder, the largest single-span suspension bridge in the world, spans the Humber near Hull.

NORTH COUNTRY

CENTRAL ENGLAND & EAST ANGLIA

SOUTH & SOUTH EAST ENGLAND

WEST COUNTRY

ABOUT THE TOURS

Each tour occupies two pages and has a clear map accompanying the text. All the places described in the text are shown in **black** on the tour maps and are described as they occur on the road, linked in sequence by route directions. This precise wayfinding information is set in *italic*.

Castles, stately homes and other places of interest described in the tours are not necessarily open to the public or may be open only at certain times. It is therefore advisable to check the opening times of any place before planning a stop there. Properties administered by the National Trust and the Ancient Monument Scheme (NT and AM) are generally open most of the year, but this should be checked with the relevant organisation, as should precise opening times.

The tranquility of a traditional hay meadow at Muker in Upper Swaledale contrasts with the spectacular scenery of its setting in the remote Yorkshire Dales.

HOW TO FIND THE TOURS

All the motor tours in this part of the book are shown on the key map below and identified by the towns where they start. The tours are arranged in alphabetical order by start town name. Page numbers are also given opposite. Each tour begins at a well-known place, but it is possible to join or leave at any point if more convenient.

Berwick-upon-Tweed

Alnwick

Morpeth

Bellingham

Hexham

Carlisle

Cockermouth
Keswick
Barnard Castle

Seascale
Ambleside
Richmond

Windermere
Sedbergh
Pickering
Scarborough

Grange-over-Sands
Helmsley

Morecambe
Ripon
Bridlington

Skipton
York

Blackpool
Beverley

Southport

Sheffield

Buxton
Chester
Congleton

MAPS		Marshland	⸽⸽⸽⸽⸽	**TEXT**	
Main Tour Route	═══	Memorial/Monument	₥	AM	Ancient Monument
Detour/Diversion from Main Tour Route	▪▪▪▪	Miscellaneous Places of Interest & Route Landmarks	▪	c	circa
Motorway	═══			NT	National Trust
Motorway Access	②≋	National Boundary		NTS	National Trust for Scotland
Motorway Service Area	⑤≋	National Trust Property	NT	OACT	Open at Certain Times
Motorway and Junction Under Construction	≋≋	National Trust for Scotland Property	NTS	PH	Public House
A-class Road	A68	Non-gazetteer Placenames	Thames /Astwood	RSPB	Royal Society for the Protection of Birds
B-class Road	B700	Notable Religious Site	✝		
Unclassified Road	unclass	Picnic Site	Ⓟ	SP	Signpost (s) (ed)
Dual Carriageway	A70	Prehistoric Site	ᴫ		
Road Under Construction	= = = =	Racecourse	⬭		
Airport	✈	Radio/TV Mast	🗼		
Battlefield	⚔	Railway (BR) with Station	━●━		
Bridge	⟂	Railway (Special) with Station	┿┿●┿┿		
Castle	♜	River & Lake	◠◡		
Church as Route Landmark	✝	Woodland Area	🌳		
Ferry	— Ⓥ —	Scenic Area	▒		
Folly/Tower	♜	Seaside Resort	⚓		
Forestry Commission Land	▲	Stately Home	⌂		
Gazetteer Placename	Zoo /Lydstep	Summit/Spot Height	KNOWE HILL 209 ▲		
Industrial Site (Old & New)	⛏		KNOWE HILL 209 ▲		
Level Crossing	LC	Viewpoint	☀		
Lighthouse	⚲				

TOURING
THE NORTH COUNTRY

Motor Tours
Pages 472-535

ALNWICK, Northumb

This attractive and historic town is a convenient touring centre situated in attractive countryside only 4 miles from the coast. Its splendid castle was once a stronghold of the dukes of Northumberland, and over hundreds of years has been extended to cover some 7 acres of ground. It was founded by the Percy family in the 12th century, but was ruined during a particularly violent phase of border warfare and was not restored to military effectiveness until the 14th century. The major features of its design date from this time, although a great deal of maintenance work was carried out in the 18th and 19th centuries, and today it ranks as one of the most magnificent buildings of its type in the country. The gateway is guarded by an impressive barbican, and the outline of its massive keep, walls and towers completely dominates the town's horizon. Parts of the castle open to visitors are the armoury in Constable's Tower, a museum of British and Roman antiquities in the Postern Tower, the keep, and many of its beautifully furnished state rooms. The town itself has several good churches and several good Georgian buildings. St Michael's echoes the castle with its battlemented tower and is said to preserve some of the best 15th-century workmanship in the county. Among the treasures inside are numerous fine monuments and a Flemish carved chest that dates from the 14th century. Remains of Alnwick Abbey stand on the northern outskirts of the town and include a well-preserved 14th-century gatehouse. The 18th-century Town Hall has shops in its arcaded ground floor. The annual Alnwick fair is held on the last Sunday in June, when the townsfolk dress in period costumes. The fair lasts for 7 days. Some 3 miles north-west of Alnwick in Hulne Park are the remains of 13th-century Hulne Priory.

Follow SP 'Morpeth', then 'Bamburgh B1340' and cross the River Aln via Denwick Bridge. Pass through Denwick, turn right on to an unclassified road SP 'Longhoughton', and after 2¾ miles turn left to join the B1339. Enter Longhoughton, then after another 1 mile turn right and in ½ mile drive forward on to an unclassified road SP 'Howick'. Continue for 1 mile to pass the entrance to Howick Hall, then turn right and after another ¾ mile keep left to reach the edge of Howick.

HOWICK, Northumb

Situated where the Great Whin Sill outcrop meets the sea in 120ft cliffs of black rock, this hamlet is also a good base from which to tour the fine 18th-century mansion (open) standing in beautiful grounds (open).

In 1¼ miles meet crossroads and turn right through an archway to the fishing village of Craster.

AN UNDISCOVERED COAST

Much of Northumberland's coast is unvisited and unspoiled. North of Alnwick it is designated an Area of Outstanding Natural Beauty, while to the south the lovely River Coquet meets the sea after winding past the religious foundations and mighty castles of bygone ages.

Crabbing boats at Craster are still built to the traditional Northumbrian design.

CRASTER, Northumb

Craster is known for its oak-smoked kippers and splendid cliff scenery. The former can be sampled at many places in the district, and the latter is best appreciated from a 1¼-mile walk leading to Dunstanburgh Castle. Above the village is the Georgian house of Craster Tower, which incorporates the remains of a medieval building from which it takes its name.

Restoration in the 19th century preserved Bamburgh Castle's imposing presence on the Whin Sill outcrop.

DUNSTANBURGH CASTLE, Northumb

The great rocky promontory that juts into the sea here would be impressive in any circumstances, but crowned with the picturesque ruins of Dunstanburgh Castle it is magnificent. Remains of this essentially 14th-century structure (AM, NT) cover 11 acres of ground and are enclosed by massive defensive walls. This particular section of coast is in a designated area of outstanding natural beauty.

Return from Craster for ½ mile and turn right SP 'Embleton'. In another ¾ mile meet a T-junction and turn right for Embleton.

EMBLETON, Northumb

One of the main buildings in this pretty village is the 14th-century fortified vicarage, which incorporates a pele tower. Military precautions in buildings ideologically devoted to peace are not uncommon in this area which was racked by war between Scots and English for centuries.

Keep left and drive to the church, then turn right on to the B1339. In 1¼ miles keep forward on to the B1340, and 1¼ miles farther turn right. In another 1½ miles meet crossroads and turn right again for Beadnell.

BEADNELL, Northumb

Close to this small fishing village are several 18th-century lime kilns (NT). Safe bathing and a sandy beach make it attractive as a resort, and the surrounding countryside is beautiful.

Continue to Seahouses.

SEAHOUSES, Northumb

During the late 19th century a harbour was built here to serve north Sunderland, and the village that grew up to house the port workers has changed little to the present day. It is a pretty place with plenty of boat traffic, including a service that runs to the offshore Farne Islands.

FARNE ISLANDS, Northumb

It is said that St Aidan came to this group of 25 small islands (NT) to meditate in the 7th century, and that St Cuthbert stayed in a little hermitage here until he was reluctantly persuaded to become Bishop of Lindisfarne in the same period. Nowadays the group is best known for its bird sanctuary, and ornithologists of the Bird Observatory study from a converted 16th-century pele tower.

At Seahouses turn right, reach a war memorial, and turn left to follow the coast road to Bamburgh.

BAMBURGH, Northumb

Grace Darling was born in this unspoilt fishing village in 1815, and is buried in the graveyard of the mainly 13th-century church. She became instantly famous in 1838 when she sailed with her father from a lighthouse on Longstone Island, in the teeth of a gale, to rescue survivors from the wrecked ship *Forfarshire*. The RNLI has founded a local museum to her memory. Immediately obvious to the visitor is Bamburgh's huge Norman castle (open), once the seat of the kings of Northumbria now restored to its original magnificence, it includes the Armstrong Museum of Industrial Archaeology. During the 18th century it became a charitable institution, with schools, accommodation for shipwrecked sailors, and a hospital.

Branch right on to the B1342 SP 'Belford' and in 2½ miles meet a T-junction. Turn left, then after another 1¾ miles reach Belford Station and drive over a level crossing. In 1 mile cross over the A1 on to the B6349 for Belford.

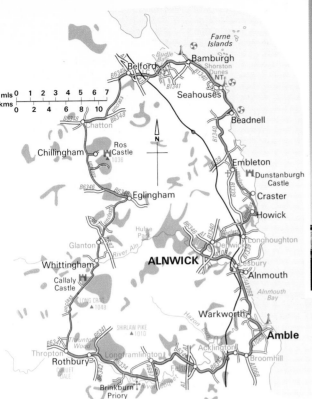

Statues guard the barbican at Alnwick Castle.

ROTHBURY, Northumb
The Victorian Cragside House was the first house in the world to be lit by electricity generated by water power (open), it stands in a 900-acre country park. The surrounding area is rich in various prehistoric remains.

Keep forward and in ½ mile bear right on to the B6334 SP 'Morpeth'. After 3½ miles it is possible to take a short detour from the main route by turning right to Brinkburn Priory.

BRINKBURN PRIORY, Northumb
Beautifully set in a loop of the River Coquet, and is surrounded by rhododendrons in a wooded setting, this 12th-century foundation was created by Augustinian Canons and has one of the best priory buildings (AM) in the country. This status is largely due to sensitive 19th-century restorers.

On the main route, continue for 1½ miles and turn left on to the A697 SP 'Coldstream'. Reach the edge of Longframlington and turn right on to the B6345, then continue to Felton. Cross the River Coquet, keeping on the B6345 SP 'Amble'. After another 1¾ miles turn left and continue through Acklington. Turn left again at Broomhill village on to the A1068 for Amble.

AMBLE, Northumb
North of this attractive little resort is a stretch of coast that has been designated an area of outstanding natural beauty. Eider ducks breed on Coquet Island, which lies offshore from Amble.

Turn left and follow SP 'Alnwick', then in 1½ miles meet a T-junction and turn right into Warkworth.

WARKWORTH, Northumb
At the top of the main street in Warkworth are the impressive remains of a 12th-century and later castle (AM) that was probably built by the 1st Earl of Northumberland. Its keep, gatehouse, and hall are particularly notable. The view along the main street as it climbs towards the ruins between buildings of many periods is unforgettable. The mainly Norman Church of St Lawrence has an outstanding stone spire which is one of only two ancient examples to be found in the county, and the famous Warkworth Hermitage is a rock-cut chapel (AM) dating from the 14th century.

In 3¼ miles meet a roundabout and drive forward. A short diversion can be made from the main route by taking the 3rd exit from the roundabout and visiting Alnmouth.

ALNMOUTH, Northumb
This holiday resort was once a major grain-shipping port, but nowadays it deals mainly with yachtsmen and other small-boat sailors.

On the main drive, return along the A1068 via Lesbury to Alnwick.

BELFORD, Northumb
In coaching days this small market town on the Great North Road was a popular stop where passengers could stretch their legs and take refreshment at local inns. Belford Hall (not open) is a large building designed by James Paine in 1756.

Continue on the B6349 SP 'Wooler', and after another ¾ mile turn left again on to an unclassified road SP 'Chatton'. In 3 miles meet a T-junction and turn right on to the B6348, then descend from Chatton Moor to reach Chatton village. Drive to the end of the village and turn left on to an unclassified road SP 'Chillingham'. After another 1½ miles reach Chillingham Post Office and turn left; cross a ford into the village.

CHILLINGHAM, Northumb
During the summer months the grounds of 14th- and 17th-century Chillingham Castle (not open) are accessible for people wishing to see the remarkable Chillingham wild cattle. The animals in this herd are the descendants of wild oxen believed to have been trapped when the park was created in 1220.

Return to Chillingham Post Office and turn left, then pass an unclassified left turn leading to Ros Castle. This offers a pleasant detour from the main route.

ROS CASTLE, Northumb
Local people will insist, with some justice, that the views from this 1,036ft hill (NT) are better than any others in the county. The magnificent panorama stretches east to the coast and the Farne Islands, west to the Cheviot Hills, and embraces the romantic medieval outlines of both Bamburgh and Dunstanburgh Castles.

On the main tour, continue for 3 miles and drive forward to join the B6346 for Eglingham.

EGLINGHAM, Northumb
The multi-period church in Eglingham is a charming, if heavily restored, asset to the villagescape. Eglingham Hall (not open) dates from the early 18th century.

On the nearside of Eglingham turn right on to an unclassified road SP 'Beanley' and 'Powburn', then in 1 mile bear left SP 'Glanton'. After another 2½ miles cross a main road for Glanton, then turn right and take the next turning left for Whittingham.

Atlantic seals bask under Longstone lighthouse in the Farne Islands, offshore from Bamburgh.

WHITTINGHAM, Northumb
Attractively grouped on both banks of the River Aln, this pretty village was once famous as the location of a large fair. A lovely stone bridge spans the river, and the local church shows evidence of Saxon origins in its tower and nave. A 15th-century pele tower survives here.

Cross the River Aln, turn right SP 'Callalay', and after 2 miles skirt the grounds of Callalay Castle.

CALLALAY CASTLE, Northumb
The Callalays are the last of three families to have successively owned this estate since Saxon times, and the manor house is one of the best in the county. Most of the present building (open) dates from the 17th to 19th centuries, but the 15th-century pele tower which it incorporates is evidence of a much earlier building.

In 2¼ miles turn left SP 'Thropton', ascend, then descend into Coquet Dale at the edge of Thropton. Meet a T-junction and turn left on to the B6341 for Rothbury.

AMBLESIDE, Cumbria

This popular tourist centre of grey slate houses stands near the northern end of Lake Windermere and is popular with anglers, fell walkers, and climbers. The waters of the lake are alive with fish large enough to satisfy the most discriminating fishermen, and the rugged countryside of the Coniston Fells is only 3 miles away. The beautiful scenery of the lake shores is best appreciated from the water, and regular boat tours can be joined at Waterhead. In the town library are various relics discovered on the site of a 2nd- to 4th-century Roman fort excavated in Borrans Park. Tiny 18th-century Bridge House contains a National Trust information centre. About 1 mile south of Ambleside is the enchanting woodland garden of Stagshaw (NT) (open) with superb views of the lake from informal surroundings. In early times the floors of domestic and public buildings were covered with dried rushes that were replaced as they became soiled, and every July the town has a rush-bearing ceremony as a reminder of the days when everybody in the community collected rushes for the church floor. This very practical idea may have stemmed from Roman harvest thanksgiving celebrations.

Leave Ambleside with SP 'Keswick' to join the A591 and drive through pleasant mountain scenery to reach Rydal, near the Rydal Water.

RYDAL, Cumbria

Close to Rydal is the little River Rothay, which links the east end of peaceful Rydal Water with the vast expanse of Lake Windermere. The poet William Wordsworth lived at Rydal Mount (open) from 1815 until his death in 1850, and must have been inspired by the glorious views over two beautiful lakes that can be enjoyed from the 4½-acre gardens. Nowadays the house is a sort of historical shrine to the poet, preserving many personal relics from his lifetime. Dora's Field was given by Wordsworth to his daughter, and is famous for its daffodils. Nearby Nab Cottage is associated with the writers Thomas de Quincey and Hartley Coleridge. The whole area is dominated by the rugged heights of Nab Scar and Loughrigg Fell.

Leave Rydal and drive past the shores of Rydal Water and Grasmere, with Rydal Fell rising to the right. Continue for ¼ mile beyond Grasmere to reach Dove Cottage.

DOVE COTTAGE, Cumbria

After William Wordsworth had lived in this tiny 17th-century cottage from 1799 to 1808 it became the home of the writer Thomas de Quincey, who occupied it for 26 years. A Wordsworth Museum which now adjoins the house preserves several manuscripts and first editions of the poet's work.

Leave Dove Cottage and turn left on to the B5287 to reach Grasmere.

HIGH LAKELAND PASSES

Fell and dale scenery at its most impressive can be enjoyed from this route, but it should be remembered that the roads in this part of Lakeland are particularly severe. Hard Knott and Wrynose passes have gradients up to 1 in 3 and should not be attempted unless both car and driver are fit.

GRASMERE, Cumbria

The idyllic setting for this tiny stone village is between the tranquil waters of Grasmere Lake and the jagged heights of Helm Crag and Nab Scar. Close by is a beautiful natural arena where the famous Grasmere Sports are staged every August, perpetuating such traditional events as Lakeland wrestling and the guides footrace. The latter follows an arduous course up a steep crag and along a ridge before descending through rough country to end in the arena. Important sheepdog trials are held in the village at about the same time, and the two events make a colourful high spot to the summer. A local rush-bearing ceremony involves the carrying of elaborately decorated bundles of rushes to the church, after which each of the bearers is rewarded with a piece of delicious local gingerbread.

Tranquil Rydal Water contrasts with the constant bustle and activity of Lake Windermere. Both waters are renowned for their excellent fishing, and are the homes of many wildfowl.

In Grasmere turn left on to an unclassified road SP 'Langdale' and follow a winding, bumpy road along the west side of Grasmere Lake. In 1¼ miles begin the ascent of Red Bank passing through woodland, and climb to the summit. Turn right here, descend through picturesque moorland, and at Chapel Stile bear right SP 'Dungeon Ghyll' to join the B5343. Drive along Great Langdale, passing through magnificent mountain scenery below cliffs that tower high above the road. Ahead are Langdale Pikes.

Dove Cottage in Grasmere, once the simple home of poet William Wordsworth, is now a museum containing examples of his work and various personal belongings.

Among the many traditions preserved in Grasmere is that of gingerbread making.

LANGDALE PIKES, Cumbria

Harrison Stickle and Pike O'Stickle soar to respective heights of 2,403ft and 2,323ft above the secluded green dales and sparkling little tarns of the area. Collectively known as Langdale Pikes, they are separated by a deep cleft which contains the roaring waters of Dungeon Ghyll Force. This spectacular Lakeland feature is well worth a visit and can be easily reached by footpath from the New Hotel.

Drive ¾ mile beyond the New Hotel and turn sharp left on to an unclassified road. Continue through a narrow pass with several steep climbs and a number of hairpin bends. Views from the road extend back to Great Langdale, and the lovely waters of Blea Tarn can be seen from the summit of the pass. Descend steeply, with views of the picturesque Little Langdale Valley, then turn very sharp right to climb the steep Wrynose Pass.

WRYNOSE PASS, Cumbria

All around this high pass are the steep sloping peaks of the Cumbrian Mountains. Just below the 1,281ft summit is the Three Shires Stone, where the boundaries of Lancashire, Cumberland, and Westmorland used to meet before the national county reorganization. The summit itself affords spectacular views over the surrounding hills and moors.

CUMBRIAN MOUNTAINS, Cumbria

Lakeland's highest passes cross the ancient Cumbrian Mountains, a range made up of several major groups separated by deep lake and river-filled valleys. At the geographical centre of the district are 3,210ft Scafell Pike, which is the highest mountain in England, the 3,162ft bulk of Sca Fell, and 2,960ft Bow Fell. To the north-west rise the Great Gable and Pillar groups, and Langdale Pikes to the east. Climbing parties test their skills on many of the peaks, and the high country holds many scenic rewards for the energetic fell walker.

Descend sharply from the summit of Wrynose Pass. Views ahead extend over the valley to Hard Knott Pass, where the mountain road can be seen snaking across ridges and dropping away into hidden folds in the landscape. Continue along Wrynose Bottom alongside the River Duddon, with steep scree slopes on either side.

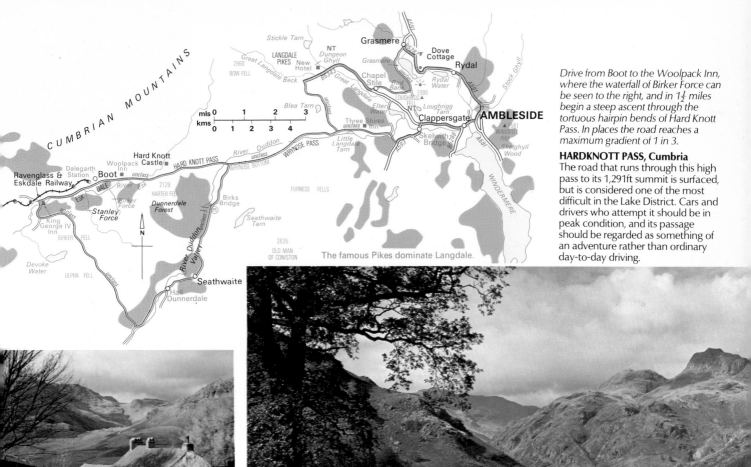

Drive from Boot to the Woolpack Inn, where the waterfall of Birker Force can be seen to the right, and in 1½ miles begin a steep ascent through the tortuous hairpin bends of Hard Knott Pass. In places the road reaches a maximum gradient of 1 in 3.

HARDKNOTT PASS, Cumbria
The road that runs through this high pass to its 1,291ft summit is surfaced, but is considered one of the most difficult in the Lake District. Cars and drivers who attempt it should be in peak condition, and its passage should be regarded as something of an adventure rather than ordinary day-to-day driving.

The famous Pikes dominate Langdale.

A typical Lakeland cottage at Blea Tarn, one of the wilder and less frequented areas of Lakeland.

RIVER DUDDON VALLEY, Cumbria
Close to the Three Shires Stone in Wrynose Pass is the source of the River Duddon, a beautiful water that chatters down to Wrynose Bottom, through Seathwaite and the Dunnerdale villages to Ulpha. Its entire course is through attractive scenery immortalized by Wordsworth in no less than 35 individual sonnets.

In 2 miles turn left SP 'Broughton, Duddon Valley', with 2,129ft Harter Fell prominent to the right. Continue past a deep river gorge on the right. Pass the Dunnerdale Picnic Area, with the 2,631ft Old Man of Coniston to the left, and continue to Seathwaite.

DUNNERDALE FOREST, Cumbria
Walks from a riverside carpark provided by the Forestry Commission lead through the lovely and secluded countryside of Dunnerdale Forest, a haven for many different species of wildlife. A particularly scenic path leads to 2,129ft Harter Fell, providing excellent views over the Duddon Valley, Eskdale, and the Hard Knott Pass from its high route. Just below Birk's Bridge the Duddon flows through an impressive gorge.

SEATHWAITE, Cumbria
A remote Dunnerdale village in attractive surroundings, Seathwaite is well known as a walking centre and was beloved of the poet Wordsworth. His *Excursion* describes both the village and its 18th-century parson Robert Walker, whose grave can be seen in the local churchyard. About ½ mile north of Seathwaite is the Walna Scar Track, which leads 5 miles across the fells to Coniston.

Leave Seathwaite and continue, passing the peak of 1,735ft Caw on the left, to reach Hall Dunnerdale. At Hall Dunnerdale turn right and drive under a thickly wooded ridge, then in 1¼ miles at Ulpha turn right with SP 'Eskdale' and ascend through more thick woodland. Follow a narrow winding road over Birker Fell for magnificent views to Sca Fell, Scafell Pike, Bow Fell, and the cone-shaped bulk of Harter Fell. Reach the King George IV Inn and turn sharp right with SP 'Boot, Langdale'. Follow the picturesque valley of Eskdale to reach Dalegarth Station, on the Ravenglass and Eskdale Railway.

RAVENGLASS AND ESKDALE RAILWAY, Cumbria
Established in 1875 to carry iron ore, this fascinating little narrow-gauge railway has been revived to carry passengers through 7 miles of enchanting countryside between Dalegarth in Eskdale to Ravenglass, on the coast. Other stations allow the line to be joined at Eskdale Green and Beckfoot. The railway operates both steam and diesel locomotives, and provides a very convenient way by which to enjoy some of the district's best scenery.

ESKDALE AND STANLEY FORCE, Cumbria
At its lower end this beautiful valley has a pastoral aspect, with bankside footpaths following the course of the River Esk through gentle farmlands. Beyond the villages of Eskdale Green and Boot it turns north and becomes wilder as it forges between the rocky flanks of Sca Fell and Bow Fell. Opposite Dalegarth Station is the starting point for the Stanley Gill Nature Trail, which leads to a lush valley and the stunning 60ft cascade of Stanley Force. Many of the paths in the dale are more suited to climbing than walking.

Leave Dalegarth Station and continue on an unclassified road to Boot.

BOOT, Cumbria
A good starting point for walks along the heathery foothills of Eskdale, this beautifully situated village is surrounded by some of the highest mountains in the Lake District. Lovely Dalegarth Hall is a quaint old farmhouse with round chimney stacks that were once typical of the Lakeland region in general.

HARDKNOTT CASTLE, Cumbria
Just before the summit of Hardknott Pass are the remains of a Roman fort (AM) known as Hardknott Castle. Built in the 2nd century AD, the ruins include surviving fragments of corner watchtowers and a bath house. It was sited in this improbable and isolated position to guard a route from the port of Ravenglass.

Begin the steep descent from the summit of the pass, negotiating very sharp hairpin bends, and in 1 mile bear left and drive along Wrynose Bottom before climbing over the steep Wrynose Pass. Descend, with excellent views over Little Langdale, and follow the valley with Little Langdale Tarn visible to the right. Pass the Three Shires Inn, and in 1 mile meet a T-junction and turn right SP 'Coniston'. In ¼ mile turn left on to the A593 SP 'Ambleside', and drive through Skelwith Bridge to reach Clappersgate.

CLAPPERSGATE, Cumbria
Magnificent views are afforded by the White Craggs Garden (limited opening) in Clappersgate, and in the gardens are splendid displays of heathers, rhododendrons, azaleas and many other plants.

Leave Clappersgate and cross the river bridge, then turn left for the return to Ambleside.

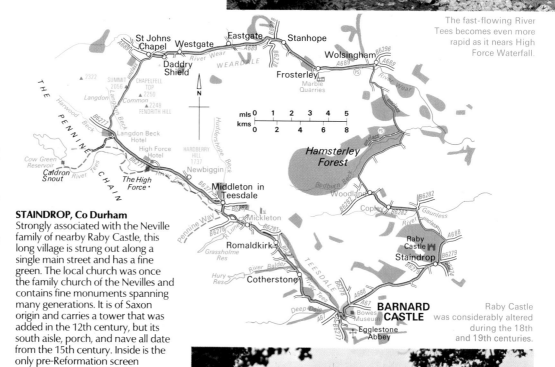

THROUGH WEARDALE AND TEESDALE

Deep in the wooded outriders of the eastern Pennines are beautiful river valleys and spectacular waterfalls, attractive little dales villages, and the stream-fed waters of placid reservoirs. Everywhere is the sound of water falling from ledges, tumbling over boulders, and cascading down hillsides.

The fast-flowing River Tees becomes even more rapid as it nears High Force Waterfall.

BARNARD CASTLE, Co Durham

The town of Barnard Castle stands in a picturesque setting on a clifftop overlooking the River Tees and is an ideal base from which to explore the lovely countryside of Teesdale. The first castle to stand here was built in the 12th century by Guy de Balliol, but this was rebuilt by his nephew Bernard – hence the Barnard element of the town name – and adapted throughout the centuries by various owners. During the Civil War it fell to the Cromwellian army, after which it was left to crumble away in peace. Today the site covers 6½ acres, and the extensive remains (AM) include the 3-storey keep and parts of a 14th-century great hall. In the town itself is a medieval bridge that is still in use, and many old houses and inns. It is thought that Charles Dickens may have written *Nicholas Nickleby* while staying here. Close to the town is the fascinating Bowes Museum of Art and the local countryside is dotted with picturesque little villages.

A short detour before the main route begins can be taken to Egglestone Abbey by driving south on the B6277 and turning off with SP on an unclassified road.

Egglestone Abbey is now a romantic ruin.

EGGLESTONE ABBEY, Co Durham

These lovely ruins (AM) date from the 12th century and occupy a beautiful rural site beside the River Tees. Close by the Thorsgill Beck is spanned by a medieval packhorse bridge and an attractive 18th-century road bridge.
On the main tour, leave Barnard Castle with SP 'Bishop Auckland' and at the edge of the town turn left to follow the A688 to Staindrop.

STAINDROP, Co Durham

Strongly associated with the Neville family of nearby Raby Castle, this long village is strung out along a single main street and has a fine green. The local church was once the family church of the Nevilles and contains fine monuments spanning many generations. It is of Saxon origin and carries a tower that was added in the 12th century, but its south aisle, porch, and nave all date from the 15th century. Inside is the only pre-Reformation screen surviving in County Durham.

Turn left by Staindrop Church and after 1 mile reach the entrance to Raby Castle.

RABY CASTLE, Co Durham

This impressive pile stands in a 270-acre deer park and exactly matches the popular conception of what a castle should look like, right down to its moat and nine great towers. It is known to have been in existence in one form or another from 1016, but its present distinctive appearance is largely due to 14th-century rebuilding and extension. Over the centuries Raby has played a major role in the politics of Britain. The huge Baron's Hall was the scene of plotting aimed at putting Mary Queen of Scots on the English throne instead of Elizabeth I, but when the scheme failed the castle was forfeited and passed into the hands of the Neville family. Later it became the property of the Vanes, Lords of Barnard; nowadays it is a valuable national asset which attracts many visitors each year. Inside are fine collections of furniture, paintings and ceramics, and among the many fine chambers is a curious octagonal drawing room. The kitchens display 14th-century rib vaulting and preserve a smoke-driven spit, while outside in the stables is a collection of carriages.

Leave Raby Castle and continue along the A688 for ¼ mile. Turn left on to an unclassified road SP 'Cockfield' and after ¼ mile keep straight on SP 'Butterknowle'. After another 2¼ miles turn left on to B6282 for Copley and continue to Woodland. Meet a T-junction and turn left, then after 300 yards turn right on to an unclassified road SP 'Hamsterley'. Descend, with good views over Hamsterley Forest.

HAMSTERLEY FOREST, Co Durham

Fast becoming known as one of the most beautiful countryside recreation areas in the county, this large state forest is crossed by a road that is open to motorists. It can be explored via dozens of footpaths,

and parking space is virtually limitless. Visitors are catered for with three picnic sites, drinking water, forest picnic furniture, and a visitors' centre. A special woodland trail has been laid out to help children identify various species of plants and animals, and the glades away from the busy areas are the homes of roe, fallow, and red deer.

After 3 miles turn left SP 'Wolsingham' and descend, then in ¾ mile meet a T-junction and turn left again to cross Bedburn Beck. After a short distance pass a left turn that gives access to Hamsterley Forest, and drive through woodland before emerging into open countryside and descending into Weardale. Cross the River Wear and continue to the edge of Wolsingham.

Raby Castle was considerably altered during the 18th and 19th centuries.

WOLSINGHAM, Co Durham
A good base from which to explore beautiful Weardale, this typical Durham town of stone-built houses holds a precarious balance between the needs of industry and the preservation of its charm. The result is the type of contrast seen between giant steelworks on the outskirts and the historic 12th-century tower of St Mary's Church, more towards the centre of the town. North of Wolsingham is the lovely Tunstall Reservoir, which was formed by the constriction of Waskerley Beck and has become the home of many water birds and other wild creatures with a liking for aquatic surroundings.

Turn left on to the A689 SP 'Stanhope' and continue to Frosterley.

FROSTERLEY, Co Durham
A local stone known as Frosterley marble is much prized for building and monumental sculpture, but centuries of quarrying have almost exhausted the supply. What little is left is being saved for purposes considered important enough for such a rare material. Many of the county's churches have fonts, memorials, pillars, and various other features fashioned from the stone, which is not really marble but a grey limestone that becomes black and reveals hundreds of tiny fossils when polished. A particularly fine example of the material can be seen near the door of the local church, bearing the inscription 'This Frosterley marble and limestone, quarried for centuries in this parish, adorns cathedrals and churches throughout the world'.

Leave Frosterley and continue along the A689 to Stanhope.

An unusual feature of Stanhope Church-yard is the fossilized stump of a tree.

STANHOPE, Co Durham
Stanhope churchyard features the fossilized stump of a tree that grew some 150 million years ago. The church itself dates from 1200 and contains a number of fascinating relics, including a Saxon font, two wooden plaques and a painting all thought to be Flemish. Close to the churchyard gate is the old town cross. West of Stanhope, in the high Weardale moorland, is a wooded gorge containing the famous Heathery Burn Cave. Bronze-age weapons and various artefacts proving the early domestication of horses in England were found here, and are now on display in London's British Museum.

Leave Stanhope on the A689 'Alston' road and continue to Eastgate.

The drama of Caldron Snout is well worth the difficult approach.

EASTGATE, Co Durham
Attractive Frosterley marble is shown to advantage by the font in Eastgate's 19th-century parish church. A feature of the beautiful moorland countryside around the village is the Low Linn Falls, where a burn tumbles over rocks in an area that is of particular interest to geologists and botanists.

Leave Eastgate and continue along the A689 beside the River Wear to reach Westgate.

WESTGATE, Co Durham
Both Westgate and Eastgate derived their names from the entrances to Old Park, which was once the hunting residence of the bishops of Durham. The village has a 19th-century church and an attractive watermill, and was once well known as a cock-fighting centre. Nowadays it has a strange claim to fame as the only place where a medieval thimble has been found.

Continue to Daddry Shield.
The high moorland of Weardale is within easy reach of Stanhope.

DADDRY SHIELD, Co Durham
Another old centre of cock fighting, this attractive Weardale village stands just north of a mountain rescue post.

Continue to St John's Chapel.

ST JOHN'S CHAPEL, Co Durham
This ancient market centre takes its name from the Church of St John the Baptist. The original foundation was probably created many hundreds of years ago, but the present building dates from 1752.

Turn left on to an unclassified road SP 'Middleton-in-Teesdale' and climb to 2,056ft on Langdon Common, part of the Pennine Chain.

THE PENNINE CHAIN
Popularly known as the Backbone of England, this great upland mass of hills, moorland, and mountains stretches north from Kinder Scout in Derbyshire to the Cheviot foothills on the Scottish border. A 250-mile footpath known as the Pennine Way traverses the range from end to end.

Descend into Teesdale, meet a T-junction, and turn left on to the B6277. In ½ mile reach the Langdon Beck Hotel, where a short detour can be made from the main route by turning right and driving along a rough track to the picnic area at Cow Green Reservoir. A private road (locked) and footpath (open) lead from here to the waterfall of Caldron Snout.

CALDRON SNOUT, Co Durham
More of a tiered cascade than a proper waterfall, beautiful Caldron Snout tumbles 200ft down a natural staircase formed by a hard rock known as dolerite. It used to be fed by a long winding pool called the Well, but this has now been incorporated in the Cow Green Reservoir. Downstream from the cascade is the spectacular High Force waterfall, and between the two are the remains of a slate mill.

Continue along the B6277 and after 2¼ miles meet the High Force Hotel. A footpath opposite the hotel leads to the High Force waterfall.

HIGH FORCE, Co Durham
Here one of England's loveliest waterfalls plunges 70ft over the menacing black cliff of the Great Whin Sill, to be caught in a deep pool surrounded by shrubs and rocks.

Continue along the B6277 through Newbiggin to reach the town of Middleton-in-Teesdale

MIDDLETON-IN-TEESDALE, Co Durham
Strong Quaker influence is evident in the no-frills orderliness of this stern little town. This is because local lead mines, the mainstay of Middleton's economy until they were closed at the start of this century, were run by that denomination. The local church dates from the 19th century and shares its churchyard with various remains of a predecessor.

Leave Middleton-in-Teesdale and turn right on to a road SP 'Scotch Corner'. Cross the River Tees and in ½ mile keep left SP 'Barnard Castle'. Continue for ¾ mile, rejoin the B6277, and continue through Mickleton and attractive Romaldkirk.

ROMALDKIRK, Co Durham
The attractive houses of this perfect little Teesdale village are interspersed with greensward that transforms an already good villagescape into a splendid one.

Leave Romaldkirk and continue along the B6277 to Cotherstone.

COTHERSTONE, Co Durham
Beautiful and dramatic scenery surrounds this pleasant village, which stands at the junction of Balder Beck and the River Tees. Close to the watersmeet are slight remains of a Norman castle.

Leave Cotherstone, recross the River Tees, and return to Barnard Castle.

Bewcastle's ancient cross is decorated with intricate carvings and Runic inscriptions.

AMONG THE BORDER FORESTS

The fascinating remains of Hadrian's Wall can be seen at their best over the vast coniferous plantations and wild moorlands of the Kielder and Redesdale Forests, parts of the Border Forest Park. Special Forestry Commission roads allow motorists to enjoy this area right up to the Scottish Border.

BELLINGHAM, Northumb

The focus of life in North Tynedale, this small market town once had a flourishing iron industry but nowadays is best known as a gateway to the great moors and forests of Nortumberland. Its ancient Church of St Cuthbert has a unique roof, barrel vaulted with six-sided stone ribs instead of the usual timber, probably as a precaution against fire. In the churchyard is a well whose waters are traditionally held to have healing powers.

Leave Bellingham on the B6320 with SP 'Hexham', and in ⅓ mile turn left and cross a river bridge. Take the next turning right on to an unclassified road SP 'Kielder', then drive through picturesque North Tynedale.

NORTHUMBERLAND NATIONAL PARK, Northumb

Extending from Hadrian's Wall in the south to the Cheviot Hills in the north, this 400-square-mile national park occupies the whole western corner of Northumberland and joins the Border Forest Park along its western boundary. Much of the district is high moorland, with rugged hills and summits that afford superb views of the local countryside, but towards the east its character changes to a gentler landscape where the valleys of the Coquet, Redesdale, and North Tyne meander through beautiful woodland. Walking and pony-trekking are two popular ways in which visitors explore the park.

Continue for 4 miles, cross a river bridge, then turn right and continue to Stannersburn. After a while enter the Kielder Forest and drive to Kielder Reservoir.

KIELDER FOREST, Northumb

Really part of the Border Forest Park, this great sea of conifers blankets the slopes of the Cheviot Hills with the varied greens of larch, spruce, Scots pine, and lodgepole pine. It was planted by the state to meet the needs of industry and has matured as a valuable addition to the Northumbrian landscape.

BORDER FOREST PARK, Northumb, Borders

So called because it crosses the border into Scotland, this vast area of woodland incorporates three forests and is the largest area of its type in Britain. In the east its vast landscapes merge with the open moorland horizons of the Northumberland National Park, making a staggering 600 square miles

of beautiful, wild, and essentially unspoiled countryside in all. Both parks are crossed by the 250-mile Pennine Way footpath, and the Kielder, Redesdale, and Wauchope forests offer many planned walks and nature trails. Various leisure activities are catered for.

KIELDER RESERVOIR, Northumb

The largest reservoir in Western

Europe, situated in the heart of the Border Forest Park, offers a variety of activities. Within Tower Knowe is a Water Authority's Information Centre.

Continue through the Kielder Forest to the village of Kielder.

Much of the Border Forest Park has been planted with softwood species to supply the timber industries. Their dark ranks echo the forests of the past.

KIELDER, Northumb

This and several other villages were developed as the area's forestry industry became established, and nowadays they make handy bases from which to explore the local countryside. Kielder Castle is an 18th-century shooting lodge that now serves as a Border Forest Park information centre and a Forest Museum.

Continue for 3 miles and cross the Scottish border, then in 3¼ miles turn left on to the B6357 SP 'Newcastleton' and follow the attractive Liddel Water. In 6¼ miles reach a junction with the B6399. A detour from the main route to Hermitage Castle can be made by turning right on to the B6399, driving for 4 miles, then turning left on to an unclassified road.

HERMITAGE CASTLE, Borders

Romantically associated with Mary Queen of Scots, this brooding castle (AM) punctuates the desolate moorland landscape with four great towers and grim walls that entirely suit their windswept situation. It was a stronghold of the Douglas family in the 14th century, and much later became the property of Mary's lover Bothwell.

On the main route, bear left with the B6357 to reach Newcastleton.

NEWCASTLETON, Borders

Before the forestry industry became such an important influence on local life this attractive village was a flourishing weaving centre. Its position affords views of beautiful Liddesdale from almost anywhere in or around the village, and beyond Newcastleton Forest are the magnificent 1,678ft Larriston Fells. This part of the Border Forest Park was planted in 1921.

Drive to the far end of the village and turn left on to an unclassified road (no SP). Cross a river bridge and turn right SP 'Brampton', then after 3 miles cross Kershope Burn to enter the English county of Cumbria. Ascend a winding road through the Kershope Forest, then after ¾ mile reach the Dog and Gun Inn and turn left SP 'Carlisle'. In 4 miles turn right, and in another ¾ mile drive forward on to the B6318. Take the next turning left on to an unclassified road and drive to Bewcastle.

BEWCASTLE, Cumbria

Several ancient remains can be seen in the bleak open moorland that surrounds Bewcastle. Materials from a Roman fort that was once an outpost of Hadrian's Wall were used to build a castle (AM) here, but this too has succumbed to the ravages of time and cottage builders, leaving just a few fragments. In the village churchyard is the famous Bewcastle Cross, which dates from the 7th century and is intricately carved with Runic inscriptions and patterns.

At Bewcastle turn right (no SP) and cross a river bridge. In 5 miles cross the B6318, and in 2¼ miles meet a T-junction. Turn left SP 'Birdoswald' and follow the line of Hadrian's Wall for ½ mile to reach Banks.

HADRIAN'S WALL, Northumb, Cumbria

This mighty engineering achievement was built in the 2nd century AD and is the most impressive monument to the Roman occupation in Britain. It runs for 73 miles across the entire width of northern England and is remarkably well preserved along several sections. It was part of a complex defence system designed to keep the marauding Scottish tribes out of the Romanized south, and included two broad ditches and a series of milecastles interspersed with turrets and signal towers. The Romans finally abandoned the wall in AD 383, but it survived in a reasonably complete state until quarried by road builders in the 18th century. Well-preserved forts can be seen at Chesters, Housesteads, Vindolanda, and Birdoswald, while the most complete section of wall stands to the west of the River North Tyne. Walks along the wall are most enjoyable and can be very instructive.

The northern frontier of Roman Britain still forms a barrier as it follows the high ridges of Whin Sill.

One of the best-preserved of the original 17 Hadrian's Wall forts has been excavated at Housesteads, revealing many facets of Roman life.

BANKS, Northumb

A turret (AM) on the Roman wall here was once manned by troops garrisoned at the nearest milecastle. A footpath leads east to the Pike Hill signal tower, part of a beacon system by which a warning of attack could be sent the length of the wall with surprising speed. One mile south west lies the Augustinian, Lanercost Priory (AM) which was founded in 1166 and its nave is still in use. In the rebuilt Abbey Mill, is a craft workshop for the handicapped.

Continue to Birdoswald.

BIRDOSWALD, Cumbria

Large and impressive outer defences of a Roman fort (AM) known as *Camboglanna* can be seen here beside the River Irthing, and well-preserved sections of Hadrian's Wall (AM) extend east and west. Close by are the substantial remains of Harrow's Scar Milecastle (AM).

In ½ mile ascend, then turn right on to the B6318 SP 'Gilsland' and in 1 mile turn right to reach Gilsland.

GILSLAND, Northumb

Sulphur and chalybeate springs brought brief fame to this small place as a spa resort, but it is much better known for its excellent Roman remains. Hadrian's Wall runs south of the village and includes the Poltross Burn Milecastle (AM), a fascinating and well-preserved survivor from the occupation. Close to the village is an attractive waterfall.

From Gilsland turn left along the B6318 and in 2 miles meet a junction and turn left to enter Greenhead.

GREENHEAD, Northumb

Close to Greenhead is a dramatic series of ravines known as the Nine Nicks of Thirlwall. Near by are the ruins of Thirlwall Castle, which was built in the 14th century, and the route of a Roman track known as the Maiden Way runs through the area.

Turn left on the B6318, ascend, and in 5 miles reach the Twice Brewed Inn.

TWICE BREWED INN, Northumb

Slightly away from the site of the original building, this famous inn now houses a useful Northumberland National Park information centre. Close by, at Winshields, the Roman wall (AM) reaches its highest point of 1,230ft above sea level.

Continue along the B6318 to reach Housesteads, where there is a reasonable carpark.

HOUSESTEADS, Northumb

The best-preserved fort (AM, NT) on Hadrian's Wall can be seen here. Once known as *Vercovicium*, it follows the typical Roman pattern of rectangular walls with rounded corners, and was built to house up to 1,000 infantrymen. Relics found during excavations in the area are displayed in a well laid-out museum, and close to Housesteads the wall itself reaches its highest point as it follows the high ridges of the Great Whin Sill rock outcrop. Marvellous views from the ridge extend west and take in several little lakes, including the lovely Crag Lough.

Continue for 5 miles to reach Carrawborough.

CARRAWBOROUGH, Northumb

One of the very few Mithraic temples to be found in Britain has been excavated here. Probably dating from the 3rd century, it was a very small building containing three dedicatory altars to the deity Mithras, and a figure of the Mother Goddess. Close by is the Roman fort known as *Brocolitia*.

Continue along the B6318 to reach Chollerford.

CHOLLERFORD, Northumb

Housesteads may be the best preserved of the Roman wall's forts, but *Cilurnum* (or Chesters) is by far the most interesting and best excavated. It was a large stronghold housing 500 troops. Digging has revealed fascinating details of the fort itself, plus the remains of a bath house and central heating system. Relics from this and other sites can be seen in the interesting local museum, and traces of the Tyne bridge that the fort was built to guard have been found downstream of the present 18th-century crossing.

Meet a roundabout and take the 1st exit on to the B6320 SP 'Wark, Bellingham'. Enter the North Tyne Valley to reach Wark.

WARK, Northumb

Access to this picturesque huddle of cottages and houses is by an iron bridge over the River North Tyne. The woodlands of Wark Forest stretch away to the west.

Continue along the B6320 for the return to Bellingham.

PEACE IN THE BORDER LANDS

Green rounded hills and unspoilt miles of coastline betray nothing of the centuries of human violence that once made this lovely area a place to avoid. Now the only battles are between nesting gulls, and the only invasions are of migrant birds seeking the haven of a largely unpopulated countryside.

BERWICK-UPON-TWEED, Northumb

A busy seaport and now England's northernmost town, Berwick was alternately held by Scottish and English forces during the bitter border struggles that began with the Romans and persisted until the 15th century. Remains of a castle built here by the Normans in the 12th century include three towers and ancient sections of wall that were later incorporated in the medieval town defences. During Elizabethan times the town walls (AM) were restored to full defensive effectiveness, and they have survived as a complete 2-mile circuit round old Berwick. Their rebuilding was done with gun warfare very much in mind, and in their present condition they represent the earliest examples of their type in northern Europe. The approach to the town itself is dominated by three famous and attractive bridges over the River Tweed. Berwick Bridge dates from the 17th century and has 15 elegant arches, the Royal Border Bridge of 1880 was built to carry a railway into the town, and the Tweed Road Bridge is a good example of modern architecture dating from 1928. It is said that the town has more buildings scheduled for preservation than any other place of comparable size in England, and a walk round the lovely old streets would certainly seem to confirm that. The parish

church, one of the few to be built during Cromwell's Commonwealth, is of exceptional architectural interest and was extended in the 19th century. In 1717 Vanbrugh built Britain's earliest barracks here, and today these incorporate the well laid out Museum of the King's Own Scottish Borderers. The Georgian period is represented by the Town Hall (open by arrangement) and several fine houses attractively sited by the quay. Relics from the town's past can be seen with collections of paintings and ceramics in Berwick Museum, and the lovely local countryside includes a coastal area of outstanding natural beauty. Every May Day the traditional ceremony of Riding the Bounds, reaffirming the parish boundaries, takes place here.

Leave Berwick on the A1167 with SP 'Edinburgh', and in ½ mile bear left on the A6105 SP 'Kelso'. In a further ½ mile turn left A1 then after ½ mile turn right B6461 after 1 mile enter the old Scottish county of Berwickshire. In ¾ mile keep left, and after another 1½ miles turn left on to an unclassified road SP 'Norham'. Later cross the River Tweed by the Union Suspension Bridge and re-enter Northumbeland. In ½ mile meet a T-junction and turn right, then in 1¼ miles turn right again and continue to Norham.

Berwick's 17th-century bridge was built across the estuary in 1611 to connect the town with Tweedmouth.

NORHAM, Northumb

One of the two triangular greens in this attractive village features a 19th-century cross, and together they form a focal point for the solid little stone-built houses that surround them. At the east end of the main street the massive Norman keep of a 12th-century castle (AM) towers above the River Tweed from a rocky outcrop, proclaiming a strength that resisted the efforts of Scottish forces for many hundreds of years. The army of Robert the Bruce unsuccessfully assaulted its walls for nearly a year, and 12 months later the castle resisted a siege that was immortalized by Sir Walter Scott in the poem *Marmion*. The hero of the occasion was Sir William Marmion, an English knight who accepted a lady's challenge to take command of the most dangerous place in Great Britain as proof of his love. On February 13 the opening of the salmon season is marked by a ceremony known as the Blessing of

the Nets, after which the Tweed can be fished for salmon by anyone with the right or money to do so.

Leave Norham, meet a main road, and turn left on to the B6470 SP 'Cornhill'. In ½ mile turn right on to an unclassified road, then in ¾ mile turn right again on to the A698. After a further 2 miles cross (with care) the picturesque Twizel Bridge.

The keep of Norham Castle dates from *c*1160.

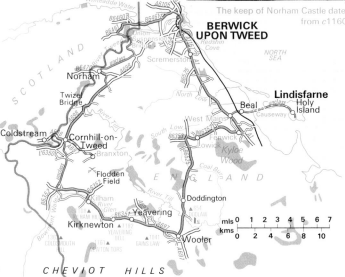

TWIZEL BRIDGE, Northumb

This beautiful 15th-century bridge spans the River Till with a single elegant arch of 90ft. Views from the bridge into the deep wooded glen are enchanting, and the ivy-covered folly of Twizel Castle enhances the scene from a nearby ridge. Many such 18th-century conceits were left unfinished, but this was genuinely never completed.

Leave Twizel Bridge and continue to Cornhill-on-Tweed.

CORNHILL-ON-TWEED, Northumb

The Scottish poet and folk hero Robert Burns entered England for the first time when he crossed the River Tweed here in 1787. This and other events are recorded on a plaque at nearby Coldstream.

A detour can be made from the main route to Flodden Field from Cornhill: meet a roundabout in the village and take the 1st exit on to the A697, then after 1½ miles turn right on to an unclassified road and proceed to Branxton for Flodden Field.

FLODDEN FIELD, Northumb

In 1513 one of the bloodiest battles ever witnessed on English soil was fought at Flodden Field, just a few hundred yards south of Branxton village. A monument inscribed 'To the brave of both nations' now marks the spot where James IV of Scotland was killed when the English army of 26,000 defeated a huge invading force of 40,000. Both sides suffered appalling casualties, with as many as 1,600 deaths between them.

A second detour from the main route at Cornhill to the village of Coldstream can be followed by taking the 2nd exit at the roundabout on to the A697 and driving for 1¾ miles.

COLDSTREAM, Borders

John Smeaton built the 5-arched bridge over the River Tweed here in 1766 to replace a ford that had been used for many hundreds of years, often by the armies of Scotland and England. A plaque on the bridge records the poet Burns' first crossing of the river into England, and one near the market commemorates the raising of the Coldstream Guards to fight in Cromwell's New Model Army.

On the main tour, meet the roundabout in Cornhill and take the 2nd exit on to the A697. Take the first turning left on to an unclassified road SP 'Learmouth', then in 1¼ miles meet crossroads and drive forward. Take the 2nd turning left SP 'Yetholm' and in 2½ miles meet crossroads. Turn left on to the B6352 SP 'Wooler' and in ¼ mile bear right to follow the Bowmont Water, then 2 miles farther turn right on to the B6351. Cross a river bridge, meet a T-junction, and turn left to follow the foot of the Cheviot Hills. Pass the edge of Kilham and drive to Kirknewton.

KIRKNEWTON, Northumb

Kirknewton's church has a chancel and south transept that were obviously built for defensive as well as religious purposes, a reminder of the centuries of unrest suffered by this and many other border villages. The valley of the College Burn leads from the village to the 2,676ft summit of The Cheviot via a narrow constriction known as Hen Hole. The lovely countryside hereabouts is best appreciated on foot.

Continue along the B6351 to Yeavering.

YEAVERING, Northumb

The Saxon King Edwin had his capital here in the 7th century, and excavations in a field near the River Glen have revealed traces of wooden halls and amphitheatres from his ancient town. It was Edwin who, according to tradition, allowed the monk Paulinus to convert the people of Northumbria to Christianity. One of the largest hillforts in the border country can be seen to the south of the village, on the 1,182ft summit of Yeavering Bell.

From Yeavering continue along the foot of the Cheviot Hills.

Winter in the Cheviot Hills can be a beautiful but lonely season.

THE CHEVIOT HILLS, Northumb

Much of this lonely range forms the border between Scotland and England. Its grassy flanks and mountainous summits are cropped smooth by the famous Black Face and Cheviot sheep, hardy breeds that can find food in the most unlikely places and survive with the minimum of interference from man. The countryside between the hills and Hadrian's Wall forms part of the Northumberland National Park, and the arduous northern section of the 250-mile Pennine Way brings the footpath to an end here. North-east of The Cheviot itself lies the picturesque College Valley, and the equally attractive Harthope Valley lies to the east. Auchope Cairn, rising to 2,382ft, straddles the border between England and Scotland.

After 1¼ miles turn right on to the A697 to reach the edge of Wooler.

WOOLER, Northumb

Situated north-east of the Cheviot, this attractive little place makes a natural base from which to explore the open landscapes of the Cheviot Hills. Close to the village is a stone which commemorates the Battle of Hamildon Hill, when an English army led by Henry Percy defeated a huge Scottish army under the command of the Earl of Douglas.

Leave Wooler, turn left on to the B6525 SP 'Berwick' and continue to the village of Doddington.

The Priory at Holy Island was an important religious centre for centuries.

DODDINGTON, Northumb

Features of this village include a ruined pele tower of 1584 and a 13th-century church containing a Norman font. The local countryside is very rich in prehistoric remains, including earthworks and stones bearing the enigmatic cup-and-ring marks of ancient cultures. South is the iron-age hillfort of Dod Law, where a natural crag known as the Lateral Stone features curious carvings and vertical grooves. Below this is a cave known as Cudy's Camp; Rowting Lyn Camp is situated in a miniature gorge near by.

Leave Doddington and drive forward for 5 miles, then branch right on to the B6353 to reach Lowick. Pass Fenwick, meet the A1, and turn left to reach the Plough Hotel in West Mains; a detour from the main route can be taken by following a side road to the right by the hotel and driving to the village of Beal.

BEAL, Northumb

Most of the beautiful coastline near Beal is included in a national nature reserve, and the horizon to the south-west is dominated by the low summits of the gentle Kyloe Hills. A causeway exposed at low tide leads to Holy Island, but visitors should take careful note of the tide tables displayed all round the village to avoid being cut off.

To continue the detour, cross to the Holy Island of Lindisfarne via a causeway that is exposed for about 2 hours before and from approximately 3½ hours after high tide.

HOLY ISLAND (LINDISFARNE), Northumb

Historically known as Lindisfarne, this Cradle of Christianity is only an island at high tide but offered sufficient isolation to please the missionaries who were led here from Iona by St Aidan in the 7th century. About 150 years later their monastic foundation was sacked and destroyed by Danish marauders, but in 1082 the Benedictine order built a fine priory on the same site. Its gaunt ruins (AM) still stand today, and various relics found during excavations can be seen in a local museum. The island's restored 16th-century castle (NT) contains antique oak furniture. Examples of the needlework for which the islanders are justly famous can be seen in the 13th-century parish church. Christianity has been at Lindisfarne for a long time, but a reminder of more ancient days is the Petting Stone. A legend attached to this was that brides who jumped over the stone would have a happy marriage – a tradition with more than a hint of paganism. The nature reserve on Holy Island is an important haven for an enormous variety of wildfowl and wading birds.

On the main tour, leave the Plough Hotel in West Mains and continue along the A1. Passing Scremerston, at roundabout take 2nd exit A1167 and return to Berwick-upon-Tweed.

BEVERLEY, Humberside

The gothic completeness of medieval Beverley Minster has won it acclaim as one of the most beautiful churches in Europe. Its lovely twin bell towers can be seen for miles across the flat Humberside pastures, and its interior is packed with the monumental art of some 700 years. Here can be seen the full blossoming of the 14th-century stonemason's skill in the magnificent Percy Tomb, the ingenuity of 15th-century glassmakers in the great east window, and the craft of local men in the rich extravagance of carved wood. At the far end of the Main Street is St Mary's Church, a beautiful building that was started in the 12th century as a chapel for its more famous neighbour. Over the years it has been enlarged, with a wealth of excellent architectural detail, and is now independent. One of its more notable features is a 15th-century ceiling painting of the English kings. In early times the town was an important market centre and the capital of the East Riding of Yorkshire, a status that it had to defend with a stout wall pierced by five gates. Subsequent periods saw the community outgrow these confines, and all that remains today is the 15th-century North Bar. Evidence that much of the expansion was in the 18th and 19th centuries can be seen in the many Georgian houses and shopfronts that survive. The ornate market cross dates from c1714, and the Guildhall of 1762 displays a wealth of plasterwork and wood carving by local men. Inside 18th-century Lairgate Hall (open), which houses the council offices, is a Chinese Room with hand-painted wallpaper. Beverley's Art Gallery and Museum displays pictures and relics of local interest.

Leave Beverley and follow SP 'Hessle, A164'. Later reach Skidby Windmill.

SKIDBY WINDMILL, Humberside

Well-preserved Skidby Windmill was built in 1821 and is the only example to have remained intact north of the River Humber and east of the Pennine Chain. Its black-tarred tower and white cap form a striking combination that makes it a prominent local landmark. An agricultural museum has been established inside (open).

At the windmill turn left on to an unclassified road SP 'Cottingham'. Later turn right on to the B1233 to reach Cottingham.

COTTINGHAM, Humberside

Several halls of residence for the students from Hull University are established in this village, which is grouped round a large square. Inside the local church is a fine brass dating from the 14th century.

Continue along the B1233 and drive over a level crossing. Keep forward through 2 roundabouts, then ¼ mile beyond the University of Hull turn right on to the A1079. Proceed to the centre of Hull.

HUMBERSIDE AND HOLDERNESS

Between the River Humber and the sea is a flat peninsula famous for its magnificent churches, whose towers and spires stand high above the surrounding countryside of marshlands and drainage canals. Fishing fleets put out from Hull, and many of the coastal villages have become holiday resorts.

HULL, Humberside

This major industrial and commercial centre is an international port and a fishing base for deep-sea vessels. As such it suffered badly in World War II, but its rebuilding has included a fine shopping precinct scattered with flowerbeds and interspersed with parks and gardens. Docks stretch for a full 7 miles along the north side of the Humber, joined here by the little River Hull, and one of the world's longest suspension bridges at 4,626ft/1,410m — The Humber Bridge. Despite these extensive new developments the city centre still has a few old buildings untouched by bombs or town planning, including the largest parish church in England and 18th-century Maister House (NT). An early 17th-century mansion in which the MP and anti-slavery campaigner William Wilberforce was born in 1759 is now preserved as the William Wilberforce Historical Museum. The Town Docks Museum relates to fishing and shipping, and the Transport Museum has a collection of vehicles including a steam Train Locomotive of 1882. The Archaeology and Natural History Museum has several interesting displays and contains The Hasholme Boat, the biggest surviving prehistoric logboat in the country.

Leave Hull on the A165 with SP 'Hornsea' and 'Bridlington'. In 3½ miles reach a roundabout. Keep forward to another roundabout and take the 3rd exit on to the B1238 SP 'Aldbrough'. Continue for 1¼ miles and keep forward to reach Sproatley.

SPROATLEY, Humberside

This village is in the heart of the Holderness area, where vast fields, golden with corn in summer, stretch flatly to the horizon or lap the fringes of small copses. Its 19th-century church, given an air of mystery by a cloak of ivy, contains an inscribed coffin lid of the 13th century.

Bear right, drive to the end of the village, and turn left on to an unclassified road to reach Burton Constable Hall.

BURTON CONSTABLE HALL, Humberside

Grand 18th-century state rooms and 200 acres of parkland enchantingly landscaped by Capability Brown are features of this attractive Elizabethan house (open). Lakes covering some 22 acres provide plenty of scope for boating, venue for several rallies and fairs during the summer months.

Return to Sproatley and turn right to return along the B1238. Meet a war memorial and branch left on to the B1240 to Preston. At Preston turn left again to reach Hedon.

The Proud Pharisee is one of many carvings in the nave of magnificent Beverley Minster.

HEDON, Humberside

At one time this small town was a major port connected to the Humber Estuary by canals. It was rich enough to start building the magnificent King of Holderness in the 12th century, and subsequent work on this church shows the prosperity to have lasted at least until the 15th century. Trade has long since filtered away to Hull, but the huge pinnacled tower of the 'King' remains in all its glory. Near by, the Ravenspur Cross commemorates a long vanished village of that name, where Bolingbroke (later Henry IV) landed in 1399 to claim the English throne for the House of Lancaster.

Turn left on to the A1033 SP 'Withernsea'. Pass through flat agricultural countryside crisscrossed by drainage canals to reach Keyingham.

KEYINGHAM, Humberside

An attractive medieval church can be seen in this village, and just to the north west is a tower that was once a windmill.

Drive through Ottringham and continue to the edge of Winestead.

WINESTEAD, Humberside

Features from the Norman and Jacobean periods jostle for attention with others less easy to define in Winestead Church. A good 16th-century brass can be seen inside.

Continue to Patrington.

PATRINGTON, Humberside

Hedon's superb church has a rival here in the Queen of Holderness, a magnificent cruciform building in the decorated style of architecture. Its tower and spire are considered outstanding, and excellent craftsmanship of many kinds can be seen inside. At one time the village was an important market town in the manor administered by the archbishops of York.

A pleasant detour can be taken from the main route by following the B1445 from Patrington to Easington (where there is a natural gas pipe terminal), and continuing through Kilnsea to Spurn Head and the Humber Shore.

St Patrick's Church in Patrington has the grandeur of a small cathedral.

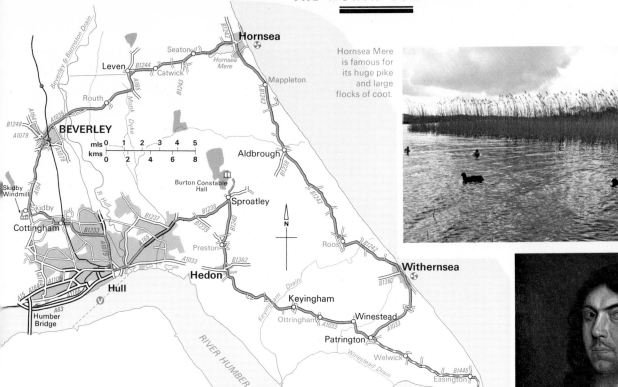

Hornsea Mere is famous for its huge pike and large flocks of coot.

The poet Andrew Marvell was MP for Kingston upon Hull from 1658 until his death in 1678.

Spurn Head Nature Reserve attracts huge numbers of migrant birds, as well as flocks of waterfowl and waders.

SPURN HEAD, Humberside

Between the North Sea and the Humber estuary is Spurn Head, a narrow hook of sand and shingle that lengthens by about a yard each year as silt from the Humber and aggregate from the Holderness cliffs is deposited at its tip. At present it is about 3½ miles long and is gradually being stabilized by the tough roots of marram grass. Many migrant species of bird rest in the sanctuary at the end of the peninsula, and their comings and goings are watched from a special observatory. Centuries ago a beacon was burned here to guide shipping through the Humber estuary, but nowadays the steady beam of a lighthouse provides a more dependable warning. A road stretches for about three-quarters of the peninsula's length; the rest, except parts of the bird sanctuary, can be explored on foot.

On the main route, drive from Patrington on the A1033 and continue to Withernsea.

WITHERNSEA, Humberside

This quiet resort offers donkey rides, a reasonable sand and shingle beach, paddling and boating pools, a playground, and various amusement arcades – in fact, many of the diversions associated with family seaside holidays. Sports facilities include bowling greens, a putting course, and an open-air swimming pool. Inland the white 127ft bulk of a disused 19th-century lighthouse rises from a street of houses, and a quirky castellated gateway survives from a pier that stood here in the Victorian heyday of seaside holidays.

Drive to the Spread Eagle (PH) in Withernsea and turn left into Hull Road. Drive to the old lighthouse and turn right on to the B1242 SP 'Roos' and 'Hornsea'. Pass through Roos and in ⅓ mile turn left. Continue for a further ¼ mile, then turn right and proceed to Aldbrough.

Withernsea lighthouse is now disused but still provides a focal point in this small resort.

ALDBROUGH, Humberside

About 1½ miles from this small village is a pleasant sand and shingle beach backed by small eroded cliffs. In the village itself is a 13th- to 15th-century church with a Norman arch and a sundial bearing a Saxon inscription.

Continue along a flat, winding road and pass through Mappleton to reach Hornsea.

HORNSEA, Humberside

Hornsea has become very well known through its fine pottery, which is made in Rolston Road and can be bought from a seconds shop. More can be learned about the processes and skills involved from a conducted tour, and the company has a special playground and mini-zoo for the children. The resort itself is popular with families and offers excellent sands divided from gardens and amusements by the fine Promenade. Behind the narrow streets and clustered houses of the old village is Hornsea Mere, a 2-mile lagoon formed during the ice ages. Today it is a popular boating venue with a reserve for wildfowl and a 5-mile walk round its wood and reed-fringed banks.

Skirt Hornsea Mere on the B1244 with SP 'Beverley'. Pass through Seaton and Catwick to reach Leven.

LEVEN, Humberside

Between Leven and the River Hull is a 3-mile stretch of canal built in 1802. At one end of the waterway is the Canal House, a fine 3-bay building which incorporates a grand Georgian doorway from a house at Hull. Inside the dignified village church is the shaft of a Saxon cross.

Turn left on to the A165 then after 1 mile meet a roundabout and take the 2nd exit on to the A1035 SP 'Beverley'. Pass through rather featureless countryside and cross the River Hull, and the adjacent Beverley and Barmston drain; re-enter Beverley.

BEACHES AND THE BOWLAND FELLS

Blackpool is more than the most popular holiday resort in the north; it is also an ideal place from which to tour the rolling, windmill-dotted landscape of the Fylde, its austere little villages, and the high wild moors of the Forest of Bowland.

The packhorse bridge near Hurst Green.

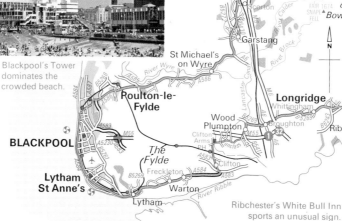

Blackpool's Tower dominates the crowded beach.

BLACKPOOL, Lancs

Every summer Lancashire shuts down its industry for the annual wake, or holiday, and for a brief period Blackpool's resident population of about 152,000 is swelled by an influx of 8 million trippers eager to be entertained. Until the seaside-holiday vogue of the 18th century the town was little more than a cluster of cottages, but it has developed from these small beginnings to become one of the premier resorts in Great Britain. Everything is geared up to the boisterous, fun-fair atmosphere of high summer, and the natural asset of a beautiful sandy beach is supplemented by three fine piers and the splendid dominance of the famous 519ft tower. In the latter are a ballroom that is often the scene of dance festivals and beauty contests, undersea world, amusements, and various facilities for children. The traditional heart of the 7-mile Promenade is the famous Golden Mile, a bewildering collection of novelty shops, ice-cream vendors, and seafood stalls. Blackpool Zoo is one of the most modern in Britain, featuring a unique free-flight bird hall. Some of the other animal enclosures can be visited by miniature railway, and the entire complex is laid out to the best advantage of both visitors and animals. The East Drive area is well known for its richly-planted gardens, and the town's many other parks and public open spaces are green islands of peace amongst the bustle and noise of streets packed with tourist and local traffic. Sporting events held here every year include county cricket, league football, and various other championships associated with the amenities available.

Leave Blackpool and follow the A584 SP 'Lytham St Anne's' along the coast to reach Lytham St Anne's.

LYTHAM ST ANNE'S, Lancs

No less than four championship courses make this popular seaside resort a mecca for golfing enthusiasts. Sand yachting and safe bathing are offered by 6 miles of sandy beach, and the British Sand Yachting Championships are held here every May. The residential part of the resort is laid out on garden-city lines, with many beautiful parks and gardens between streets of pleasant houses. Ashton Gardens and Lowther Gardens are of particular note, and the fascinating Alpine Gardens offer fine walks in landscaped surroundings where little bridges span water and cool hollows. In and between these gardens are many good half-timbered buildings, including the attractive 18th-century structure of Lytham Hall.

Drive through the town to Lytham.

LYTHAM, Lancs

Lytham and St Anne's are incorporated in the borough of Lytham St Anne's, but this is where the similarity stops. The former is a quiet residential town with few of the holiday amusements and entertainments offered by the St Anne's area. A white windmill on picturesque Lytham Green near the shore is typical of many that once operated in the area.

Ribchester's White Bull Inn sports an unusual sign.

THE FYLDE, Lancs

Between the Wyre estuary north of Blackpool and the Ribble estuary in the south is a flat, wind-blown area of land known as the Fylde. This area was once known for its many windmills, and several of these fascinating old structures have survived intact.

Continue along the A584 SP 'Preston' to reach Warton.

WARTON, Lancs

There is a small aerodrome here, and the town has a good church of Victorian date.

Continue along the A584 to Freckleton, then in 2¾ miles meet traffic signals and turn left on to the A583. Take the first turning right on to an unclassified road SP 'Clifton'. Skirt Clifton, and in 2 miles reach the Clifton Arms (PH). Turn right SP 'Broughton' and cross the Lancaster Canal. In 1¼ miles meet a T-junction and turn right, then after another ¼ mile turn left. In 1¼ miles join the B5411 and continue to Woodplumpton.

WOODPLUMPTON, Lancs

The 20th-century navigator Henry Foster was born in this village, and his memorial can be seen in the local church. This warm, honey-coloured building is mainly of 15th- to 19th-century date.

Drive to the end of the village and turn right SP 'Broughton', then in a short distance turn right again on to the B5269. Continue to Broughton, meet traffic signals, and drive forward SP 'Longridge'. Proceed through Whittingham to Longridge.

LONGRIDGE, Lancs

High above the roof tops of this pleasant village is the fine steeple of 19th-century St Wilfrid's Church, a symmetrical counterpoint to the nearby craggy bulk of 1,148ft Longridge Fell.

Leave Longridge on the B6243 SP 'Clitheroe' and in ½ mile turn right with the B6245 SP 'Blackburn'. Later bear left into Ribchester.

RIBCHESTER, Lancs
In Roman times the wild country hereabouts was guarded by a fort that stood on this site for 300 years. Known as *Bremetennacum*, its large remains have been excavated and many of the finds installed in the local Museum of Roman Antiquities. A model displayed here shows what the building must have looked like in its complete state, and among the exhibits are gold coins, pieces of pottery, brooches, oil lamps, and a rare bronze parade helmet. Other remains from the same period have been incorporated in some of the village buildings. Two Roman columns support the oak gallery in 13th-century St Wilfred's Church, and the pillars at the entrance of the White Bull Inn are said to have come from a Roman temple. Just to the north of Ribchester is the Norman Stydd Chapel and a neat row of attractive 18th-century almshouses.

A detour from the main route can be made to Longridge Fell by leaving the centre of Ribchester on an unclassified road SP 'Chipping', then driving for $3\frac{1}{2}$ miles to the excellent road summit and viewpoint of the fell. On the main tour, leave Ribchester by continuing along the B6254 and in $\frac{1}{2}$ mile turn left on to an unclassified road SP 'Hurst Green'. In $1\frac{3}{4}$ miles reach the top of an ascent and turn right on to the B6243 'Clitheroe' road and continue to Hurst Green.

HURST GREEN, Lancs
An attractive feature of this village is the Church of St John the Evangelist, which was built in 1838 and has a castellated tower in keeping with the romantic leanings of the period. In magnificent grounds close to Hurst Green is the imposing building of Stonyhurst, a famous school that was founded in the 16th century.

Leave Hurst Green and continue along the B6243. In $1\frac{3}{4}$ miles cross the River Hodder, with a 16th-century packhorse bridge visible to the right. In $1\frac{1}{4}$ miles meet a junction with the unclassified 'Bashall Eaves' road. A short detour can be taken from the main route to Clitheroe by turning right here and driving along the B6243.

CLITHEROE, Lancs
After the Civil War the small Norman keep of Clitheroe Castle (open) was presented to General Monk, and today it still stands in a dominant position on a limestone knoll above the town. Inside is an important collection of fossils from the surrounding district. The town itself is an industrial centre that grew to prosperity through cotton, and at one time it was full of the clatter and noise of textile milling. Sinister Pendle Hill, associated with the notorious trial of several Lancashire women who were said to be witches and accordingly executed, rises to 1,831ft on the east side of Clitheroe. Ironically the founder of the Society of Friends claims to have drawn his inspiration from the same hill.

Refreshing solitude is discovered near Blaze Moss in the Trough of Bowland.

On the main tour, keep forward at the junction and follow the unclassified road to Bashall Eaves. After 1 mile drive over crossroads and follow the Hodder Valley, with Longridge Fell on the left. To the right are views of 1,296ft Waddington Fell and 1,300ft Easington Fell. At Bashall Eaves keep forward, then after 1 mile reach Browsholme Hall.

BROWSHOLME HALL, Lancs
Altered and extended during the 18th century, this basically Tudor mansion contains fascinating collections of tapestry work, armour, furniture, and pictures. It is open by appointment and stands in beautiful gardens that were landscaped in honour of the Prince Regent and Mrs Fitzherbert.

Continue for 1 mile and turn right SP 'Whitewell' via Hall Hill. After $\frac{1}{4}$ mile an unclassified right turn offers a short detour which ascends for 1 mile to a 960ft viewpoint.

VIEWPOINT, Lancs
One of the best parts of the tour, this high road summit affords magnificent views south to the Hodder Valley, Longridge Fell, and Pendle Hill, with the dark peaks of the Pennine Range in the distance. North and west are the hills of the Forest of Bowland, with 1,629ft Totridge Fell and 1,415ft Burn Fell particularly prominent.

On the main tour, climb to a road summit of 750ft and descend into the Hodder Valley at Whitewell. Turn right SP 'Lancaster' and enter the Forest of Bowland.

FOREST OF BOWLAND, Lancs
In the days when the word 'forest' meant 'hunting ground' this area was the preserve of the kings of England, who regarded the local deer as their own property and were particularly hard on anybody caught poaching. Today the forest is a largely treeless expanse of moorland and steep-sided fells which has been designated as being of outstanding natural beauty. It lies partly in Lancashire and partly in what used to be the West Riding of Yorkshire, and offers excellent riverside walks.

Cross the River Hodder and Langden Brook. Drive through Dunsop Bridge into a deep, narrow valley and climb to the Trough of Bowland.

TROUGH OF BOWLAND, Lancs
Here the road climbs to more than 1,000ft above sea level via steep gradients (1 in 6) through lonely moorland that was once the haunt of highwaymen. Views from the summit encompass 1,383ft Blaze Moss to the south, 1,651ft Whin Fell in the north-east, and 1,567ft Hawthornthwaite Fell in the distance.

Descend from the road summit of the Trough of Bowland to reach the village of Marshaw. After $1\frac{3}{4}$ miles reach a chapel and turn left on to the 'Preston' road and descend (1 in 5) to Abbeystead. Follow SP 'Preston' and in $3\frac{1}{4}$ miles reach Dolphinholme. After $\frac{1}{4}$ mile reach a church and bear right, then in $1\frac{1}{4}$ miles meet a T-junction and turn left SP 'Garstang'. The revolving restaurant tower of Forton Service Area can be seen on the left as the route reaches Forton village. After the village drive for $1\frac{1}{2}$ miles and turn left on to the A6 SP 'Preston', then continue for $2\frac{1}{4}$ miles. A detour from the main route to Garstang can be made by turning left here on to the B6430 and driving into the town itself.

The Forest of Bowland is a lonely area of great beauty.

GARSTANG, Lancs
Among the fine Georgian buildings in this little town, which stands on the Lancaster Canal, are the Town Hall and elegant St Thomas' Church.

On the main tour, continue along the A6 for another $2\frac{1}{2}$ miles and turn right on to the A586 SP 'Blackpool'. Follow the course of the River Wyre to St Michael's-on-Wyre.

ST MICHAEL'S-ON-WYRE, Lancs
Situated at the junction of the Rivers Calder, Brock, and Wyre, this pleasant village has a lovely church which preserves fragments of 14th-century wall paintings. The rural nature of the community is emphasized by a shearing scene in the church's 16th-century stained-glass window.

Continue along the A586 to reach Poulton-le-Fylde.

POULTON-LE-FYLDE, Lancs
Old fish stones where the prices of fish caught by local boats were once fixed survive here, and the old market place features a set of stocks. Alongside the latter is a whipping post and a stepped Jacobean pillar. Georgian St Chad's Church features a beautiful carved screen and chairs that are prime examples of the wood craftsman's art.

Continue along the A586 to re-enter Blackpool.

THE NORTH WOLDS

In this area of North Yorkshire and Humberside, lush green meadows, rich in wildlife and scattered with tiny villages, slope gently seawards beyond the resorts of Filey and Bridlington to the chalky cliffs of Flamborough Head

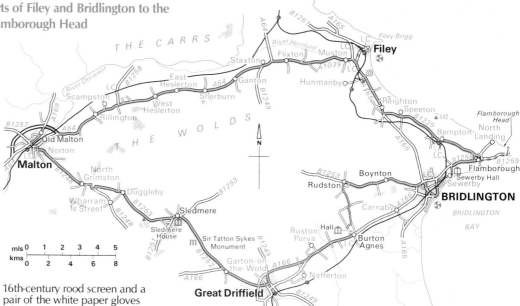

BRIDLINGTON, Humberside
Bridlington has less of the 'genteel' Yorkshire resort atmosphere of days gone by, but it is still a very popular seaside town boasting an attractive and historically interesting centre. The main point of interest in old Bridlington is the Priory Church of St Mary, which is particularly noted for its nave — the remains of an Augustinian priory founded here in the 12th century. The richly-decorated north porch, the 14th-century south aisle and the beautiful west doorway are also of note. Across the green is the priory's Bayle Gate which was built in 1388 and has, at various times since, served as the prior's courtroom, a sailors' prison, a barracks and a school, before being used in its present role of museum. Stones from the old priory were used in the building of 2 piers in the harbour which still services a small fishing fleet. The long stretches of fine sandy beach to the north and south of the harbour, on Bridlington Bay, enjoys a sheltered location protected by the great headland of Flamborough.

Leave by the Promenade for Flamborough Road. In 1¼ miles, at the roundabout, take the 3rd exit into Sewerby Road. Go over the level-crossing into Sewerby for Sewerby Hall.

SEWERBY HALL, Humberside
Sewerby Hall (OACT) was built between 1714 and 1720 and is surrounded by a fine park of 50 acres, which sweeps down to striking cliffs overlooking Bridlington Bay. The mansion has been turned into a museum, and included in this is the Amy Johnson Room, where many of the pilot's momentoes are kept. The grounds are also open to the public, and a miniature golf course, croquet lawns, a putting green and a children's corner provide entertainment.

At the entrance to the Hall keep left. In ½ mile turn right on to the B1255 (no SP) then bear right for Flamborough.

FLAMBOROUGH, Humberside
About 1,000 years ago the area around Flamborough was taken by the Vikings, and is still sometimes called 'Little Denmark'. The sprawling village stands 2 miles inland from Flamborough Head and the lighthouse, and boasts a much restored but delightful church, in which there is a fine

16th-century rood screen and a pair of the white paper gloves which were traditionally worn at the funeral of a maiden. There is also a monument of a man with his heart bared; he is Sir Marmaduke Constable who died in 1520, because, it is said, a toad which he swallowed ate his heart. Flamborough Head is where the Yorkshire Wolds meet the sea in glistening white 400ft cliffs. From here onlookers watched John Paul Jones, the Scottish-born American sailor who performed a number of daring naval exploits during his career, win a sea battle with 2 British men-of-war. The cliffs between Flamborough and Bempton are famous as a valuable breeding ground for seabirds, and here the only mainland gannetry in Britain is to be found.

Continue on the B1229, SP 'Filey', and at the end of the village turn right. Pass through Bempton, then in 4¼ miles turn right on to the A165, SP 'Scarborough', and enter Reighton. In 3 miles a detour along the A1039 (right) leads into Filey.

FILEY, N Yorks
Filey is now a popular holiday town, standing mostly on the cliff tops overlooking the bay. The old village has quaint streets and several houses dating from the 17th century, and the modern town boasts a fine promenade, a sandy beach and well-kept gardens. A lovely wooded road called the Ravine leads down to the beach, and at the top of it stands St Oswald's Church. The oldest parts are 12th century, and the great square medieval tower bears not a weathercock, but a 'weatherfish'. One of the windows commemorates all the Filey men

Cobles — open-decked fishing boats — run holiday fishing trips from Bridlington's harbour which is also still a working port

lost at sea. A great attraction nearby is Filey Brigg, a mile-long reef jutting out from the Carr Naze headland with caves, coves, cliffs and rock pools which are a delight to explore.

The main tour continues on the A165 for ¼ mile and turns left on to the A1039, SP 'Malton'. Pass through Flixton, then in 1 mile at the roundabout join the A64, SP 'York'. After 14 miles join the Malton Bypass and in 1¼ miles branch left, SP 'Malton B1257'. At the roundabout turn left for Old Malton and Malton.

MALTON, N Yorks
Malton is actually divided in half by the site of a Roman station which lies in between. New Malton is the busy market town serving a large farming community and its large market square is

always a hive of activity. The 18th-century town hall around the corner from the market square bears a plaque recording the fact that Edmund Burke was Malton's MP from 1780 to 1794. Other buildings of interest include the Cross Keys Inn in Wheelgate, which has a medieval crypt, and the former Hospital of St Mary Magdalene. The quaint old-fashioned cottages and inns of Old Malton lie a mile north-east of the town. Here, the Church of St Mary was built on the remains of a Gilbertine priory founded in the 12th century. South-east of Malton, at Langton Wold, is a famous training ground for race horses.

Above: the cliffs of Flamborough Head

Left: the elegant furnishings of King James's bedroom at Burton Agnes Hall are shown off by the Jacobean panelling

GT DRIFFIELD, Humberside
Driffield is a busy agricultural town on the edge of the Yorkshire Wolds, boasting an annual show and a regular Thursday cattle market. Anglers come to Driffield to fish for trout in the numerous streams which flow down from the Wolds.

Leave by the Bridlington road A166 to reach Burton Agnes.

BURTON AGNES, Humberside
The magnificent Elizabethan mansion, Burton Agnes Hall (OACT), is the main attraction in this sleepy village. The mellow redbrick exterior with stone trim is an impressive sight, distinguished by semi-octagonal bays on the south front. Octagonal towers are a feature of the gatehouse which was built a little later than the house. It provides an elegant entrance-way to the house via velvet lawns complemented by almost 100 clipped yew trees. The Hall is still owned by the Griffith family, whose ancestor, Sir Henry Griffith, built it more than 350 years ago. The splendid interior is just as impressive as the outside and visitors may require more than one trip to absorb all details of the richly-furnished rooms. Of special note are the stone and alabaster chimneypiece and oak and plaster screen of the great hall, the massive staircase and the beautifully-restored long gallery. The house also contains a fine collection of paintings.

The main tour turns left on to an unclassified road for Rudston.

RUDSTON, Humberside
In 1933 a ploughman uncovered a Roman villa at Rudston, and 3 fine mosaic pavements from the site are now on view in the Hull Transport Museum. The largest pavement measures 13ft by 10ft 6in and depicts a voluptuous Venus with flying hair, holding an apple and a mirror and surrounded by leopards, birds and hunters. An enormous monolith, a relic of earlier times, stands in the churchyard at Rudston.

At the far end of the village turn right on to the B1253, SP 'Bridlington'. In 2½ miles skirt the village of Boynton.

BOYNTON, Humberside
This small, picturesque village of whitewashed houses is set amidst woods on the slopes of the Gypsey Race valley. The Stricklands of Boynton Hall (not open) are thought to have introduced the turkey to England from America and there are monuments to the family in the church, rebuilt during the 18th century. Their family crest includes a turkey and a portrait.

Remain on the B1253 for 2 miles, then turn left on to the A165 for the return to Bridlington.

main road in the village stand 2 remarkable war memorials. One, known as the Waggoners' Memorial, is a tribute to the 1,200 men from the Wolds who died in World War I, and the other is a replica of the nationally famous Eleanor Crosses. The elegant 18th-century mansion, Sledmere House, was burnt down in 1911 but was rebuilt later in the same style. A great attraction at Sledmere is the beautifully-landscaped park designed by Capability Brown. A church within the park is reputedly one of the loveliest parish churches in England. Arguably the most famous member of the Sykes family was Sir Tatton. Born in 1823 and a legend in his own time, he excelled in the skills of farming, hunting, racing, boxing, building schools and breeding sheep. He also established the Sledmere stud before he died at the age of 91. Just outside the village, on Garton Hill, is a great spire dedicated to the celebrated Sir Tatton, which has a carving on the front depicting the great man on horseback. Garton Hill is a good vantage point from which to view the magnificence of the Wolds.

Continue on the B1252 Driffield road, and in 2¼ miles pass Sir Tatton Sykes's monument. After another 2 miles turn left on to the A166 for Great Driffield.

Leave Malton on the B1248, SP 'Beverley'. Cross the River Derwent then the level-crossing and keep left. In almost ½ mile turn right, still SP 'Beverley', then at the T-junction turn left. Beyond North Grimston ascend, then branch left on to the B1253, SP 'Driffield'. At Duggleby, bear right, then cross the Wolds to enter Humberside. In 2 miles turn left into Sledmere.

SLEDMERE, Humberside
This neat little village forms part of the Sledmere estate of which Sledmere House (OACT) is the centre. The estate is the property of the Sykes family who were largely responsible for the development of the Wolds from bare open wasteland into the richly-wooded agricultural land that exists here today. Beside the

BUXTON, Derbys

Situated just outside the boundaries of the national park, this is the highest town in England and an ideal base from which to tour the moors and dales of the Peak District. It is sheltered by hills even higher than its 1,007ft site, yet is able to offer gentle scenery more typical of the lowlands alongside sedate reaches of the lovely River Wye. Grinlow Woods lie to the south of the town, Corbar Woods are a mere ½ mile away, and 1 mile east is the enchanting valley of Ashwood Dale. The town itself is built round a spa whose medicinal properties were discovered by the Romans and exploited to the benefit of the town towards the end of the 18th century, when Buxton rivalled the elegant supremacy of Somerset's Bath. The growth of the town during this period was largely due to the efforts of the 5th Duke of Devonshire, who built the beautiful Crescent and Pump Rooms opposite the town's hot springs. The pale blue mineral water of the area still bubbles up from a mile underground at a rate of ¼ million gallons per day and a constant temperature of 82 degrees Fahrenheit and now feeds the local swimming pool. The Pavilion concert hall, theatre, and ballroom stand in 23 acres of lovely gardens featuring a boating lake, bowling and putting greens, tennis courts, and a children's play area. Spa treatment is available from the Devonshire Royal Hospital, which was originally built as the Great Stables and has a superb dome that was added in 1879. The former Pump Rooms now house the Micrarium, a unique opportunity to explore the world of nature using special microscopes. Poole's Cavern is an interesting show cave within the Buxton Country Park.

Leave Buxton on the A6 with SP 'Matlock' and descend through the wooded limestone gorge of the River Wye. Climb away from the valley, with Great Rocks Dale to the left, to reach the edge of Taddington. It is

THE PEAK DISTRICT DALES

Here the great River Wye and its tributaries have carved deep gorges in the soft limestone hills, making secluded pockets of outstanding beauty where the severity of naked rock is softened by water and foliage. The dales themselves are only accessible by foot.

possible to visit this village by turning right from the main route on to an unclassified road.

Buxton built its reputation as a spa, but today it provides facilities for all tastes. The Pavilion Gardens offer a varied and relaxing landscape which enhance the town's appeal.

TADDINGTON, Derbys

Taddington stands at an altitude of 1,130ft in attractive limestone country and is one of the highest villages in England. The slopes of Taddington Wood (NT) face lovely Monsal Dale some 1½ miles east, and to the south-west Taddington Moor rises to 1,500ft at the highest point in the hills south of the River Wye. Close to the summit of the moor is the Five Wells Tumulus, an unusual barrow with two burial chambers. Various interesting prehistoric remains can be found on the moors.

Descend wooded Taddington Dale, with Monsal Dale on the left, and pass Great Shacklow Wood and river valley on right. Take next junction, unclassified road, to enter Ashford-in-the-Water.

ASHFORD-IN-THE-WATER, Derbys

Two ancient bridges span the Wye in this delightful village, one dated 1664 and the other complete with a sheep-dipping enclosure at one end. An interesting well-dressing ceremony is held here on the Saturday before Trinity Sunday. Ashford marble was quarried near by.

Drive to the end of the village and turn right on to the B6465 then at T-junction turn right A6020 after a short distance rejoin the A6 to reach Bakewell.

Dramatic scenery found in the Peak District can be explored from Buxton by following the River Wye as it runs south through spectacular Chee Dale.

BAKEWELL, Derbys

A busy cattle market and the largest town in the national park, Bakewell stands on the wooded banks of the Wye and is sheltered by hills on three sides. Many of its attractive brownstone buildings bear witness to a historic past, and its beautiful 12th-century church is famous for the superb Saxon cross (AM) preserved in its churchyard. The 5-arched medieval bridge (AM) that spans the river was widened in the 19th century, but is basically one of the oldest structures of its type in Britain. Holme Hall and the Market Hall both date back to the 17th century, and the Old House Museum is an early-Tudor house with wattle-and-daub interior walls. Inside the latter are exhibitions of costumes and domestic utensils. The name of the town will always be associated with the Bakewell tart, a dish apparently created by accident when a harassed cook in the Rutland Arms mistakenly poured the egg mixture meant for the pastry of a jam tart into the jam. The unusual dish was very well received by guests, and the cook was instructed to continue making her delicious mistake.

Leave Bakewell on the A6 'Matlock' road to pass Haddon Hall.

HADDON HALL, Derbys

Although originally a fortified dwelling, exquisite 12th- to 15th-century Haddon Hall (open) was never fought over and survives as one of the finest examples of medieval architecture extant. Its peaceful history is reflected in its lovely wood and parkland setting on the River Wye, and its beauty is enhanced by the enchanting rose gardens that ornament its grounds. The romantic feeling of the place is supported by its history, for it was from here that Dorothy Vernon eloped with Sir John Manners in the 16th century.

Continue along the A6 and cross the Wye to enter Rowsley.

ROWSLEY, Derbys

This charming little greystone village stands on a tongue of land at the confluence of the rivers Wye and Derwent. The actual waters' meet is a delightful spot beloved of artists and anglers alike. Sir Joseph Paxton designed the earlier of two obsolete but charming station buildings here, and the beautiful old Peacock Inn was originally a 17th-century manor house.

Pass the Peacock Inn on the left, then in a short distance turn left on to the B6012 SP 'Baslow'. Continue to Beeley.

BEELEY, Derbys

From ancient times this little community was known for the grindstones fashioned by its craftsmen from the local hard grit. A tributary of the River Derwent, which is famous for its trout, runs close to the village.

Chatsworth's superb apartments include the State Bedroom of the ill-fated Mary Queen of Scots.

CALVER, Derbys
Anglers come here for the fine Derwent trout, and the village boasts a good 18th-century cotton mill.

In Calver meet traffic signals and turn left on to the B6001 'Bakewell' road. Continue to Hassop.

HASSOP, Derbys
Situated at the edge of wild Longstone Moor, this little village has a Jacobean hall that was the home of the Earls of Newburgh until 1853. Much of the local countryside has the tended appearance of parkland.

Paxton's Emperor Fountain boldly reflects the design of Chatsworth House.

Beyond Beeley skirt the grounds of Chatsworth House, then cross the River Derwent and enter the park to pass Chatsworth House itself.

CHATSWORTH HOUSE, Derbys
Popularly known as the Palace of the Peak, this magnificent mansion (open) stands in a superb park on the River Derwent and is backed by beautifully wooded slopes. It was built in the 17th century for the 1st Duke of Devonshire and is noted particularly for its superb state apartments and great art collection. An earlier house that stood on the same site was partly designed by the 1st Duke's ancestress Bess of Hardwick, and was occasionally visited by Mary Queen of Scots. Remains of the original Elizabethan park layout can be seen in the old Hunting Tower, which vies as the major focal point with a fountain that is the tallest in Britain. Features of the magnificent park include mature chestnut avenues and the charm of ornamental waters.

Beyond Chatsworth Park join the A619 and enter Baslow.

BASLOW, Derbys
This characteristic gritstone village stands on the River Derwent and is partly built round an old triangular goose green. Most through traffic is taken across the river by a recent bridge, but the old hump-backed crossing survives – complete with tollhouse.

In Baslow turn left SP 'Chapel-en-le-Frith' to join the A623. Continue to the village of Calver.

In Hassop turn right on to an unclassified road and drive to a T-junction in Great Longstone. Turn right for Monsal Head and continue to the Monsal Head Hotel, then turn right again on to the B6465 to pass a magnificent vantage point offering panoramic views across Monsal Dale.

MONSAL HEAD, Derbys
This great rocky prominence affords superb views into Monsal Dale, where the River Wye threads its way between lush slopes punctuated by rocky crags and overhangs of weathered stone. The head and dale together form one of the national park's loveliest beauty spots.

Continue through Wardlow, turn left on to the A623, and in 1¼ miles turn left again to join the B6049. Continue into Tideswell.

TIDESWELL, Derbys
Although this ancient town was granted a market as early as the 13th century, the only notable building to have survived the centuries is the superb Church of St John the Baptist. This is considered the finest building of its type in the county and is popularly known as The Cathedral of the Peak. Local wells and springs are dressed in a traditional ceremony held in Wakes Week, on the Saturday nearest June 24.

Continue with the 'Buxton' road, and after 1 mile pass the Tideswell picnic area (left). Descend into Miller's Dale.

MILLER'S DALE, Derbys
Threaded by a narrow road to Litton Mill, this part of the Wye Valley is enclosed by craggy limestone cliffs that rise high above the river behind dense screens of shrub and woodland. The mill was once used for processing silk.

Beyond a railway viaduct and just before a bridge over the Wye turn sharp right on to an unclassified road for Wormhill. Pass Chee Dale on the left and continue to Wormhill.

WORMHILL, Derbys
Situated high above the river curve that includes Chee Dale, this village is excellently situated for fine views across the River Wye and is popular with walkers. Narrow Chee Dale is only accessible on foot, but it is worth the exercise. One of the village's most notable buildings is a 17th-century hall with mullioned windows.

Pass Wormhill and bear left SP 'Peak Dale'. Continue for ½ mile and turn right for the village of Peak Forest.

PEAK FOREST, Derbys
The name of the medieval hunting ground that covered most of northern Derbyshire is preserved in this attractive little village. A chapel founded here in 1657 was extra-

Native ashwoods fringe the River Wye in picturesque Monsal Dale.

parochial and could issue marriage licences to anybody who applied. Before the building was demolished, Peak Forest gained something of a Gretna Green reputation as a goal for eloping couples. North of the village on the south side of Eldon Hill is a sheer-sided pothole known as Eldon Hole. For many years this was reputed to be bottomless, but modern potholers have discovered it to be a 186ft limestone shaft leading to two caverns which radiate from the bottom. On no account should an attempt be made to descend the hole without proper equipment.

Turn left on to the A623 SP 'Chapel-en-le-Frith', keep left at Sparrowpit, and within 1¼ miles turn left on to the A6. Proceed towards Buxton, passing limestone quarries on the left at Dove Holes. Black Edge rises to the right of the road.

DOVE HOLES, Derbys
Not to be confused with a natural rock formation of the same name north-west of Tissington, this area is the site of vast limestone workings that extend some 4 miles south-east along Doveholes Dale, Peak Dale, and Great Rocks Dale. The quarries are 1,086ft above sea level. A railway tunnel penetrates 1½ miles through bedrock deep beneath the main road here.

BLACK EDGE, Derbys
This high prominence rises to 1,662ft and affords excellent views over much of the national park's finest countryside.

Descend and return to Buxton.

BOUNDARY OF AN ANCIENT EMPIRE

Here the monumental ruins of Hadrian's Wall undulate across the rocky spine of Britain, still proclaiming the might of the Roman Empire many centuries after its collapse. South are the soft woodlands of the beautiful South Tyne Valley, the heart of rural Northumberland.

CARLISLE, Cumbria

During the Roman occupation Carlisle, then known as *Luguvalium*, was a strategic centre of the frontier that separated the largely Romanized peoples of the south from the wild northern tribes. Continued excursions from Scotland prompted William Rufus to build the town's sturdy castle (AM) in 1092; Queen Mary's Tower contains a fascinating museum devoted to the Border Regiments. During the Civil War the six western bays of Carlisle's small medieval cathedral were demolished to repair the town wall, but two surviving bays of the nave display Norman workmanship. The choir was restored in the 13th century and features a magnificent east window. In the cathedral grounds is a 13th-century pele tower known as the Prior's Tower. A museum occupies Tullie House a fine Jacobean mansion and contains exhibits relating to Hadrian's Wall.

Leave the centre of Carlisle with SP 'The South' on the A6 and in 3 miles reach the M6 junction roundabout. Take the 2nd exit SP 'Wetheral', and 1 mile beyond Cumwhinton pass a right turn leading to Wetheral Abbey. After a short distance enter the pleasant village of Wetheral.

WETHERAL, Cumbria

An ancient abbey gatehouse in this attractive village faces across the River Eden to the impressive pile of Corby Castle. Fine monuments by the sculptor Nollekens can be seen inside the local church.

Follow the main road through Wetheral village and in 1½ miles meet a T-junction. Turn right on to the A69 SP 'Newcastle' and cross the Eden. A detour from the main route to Corby Castle can be made by turning right immediately after the bridge on to an unclassified road and driving through pleasant countryside for 1½ miles.

CORBY CASTLE, Cumbria

In 1611 the local Howard family extended the old pele tower that had been guarding Great Corby since the 13th century, adding a long range that transformed it into a great L-shaped house. The present aspect of the building, set amid lovely grounds (open) in a particularly scenic area, owes much to further extension work carried out in the 19th century.

On the main tour, continue along the A69, skirt the grounds of Holme Eden Abbey, and enter Warwick Bridge.

WARWICK BRIDGE, Cumbria

The two small communities of Warwick and Warwick Bridge are separated by a fine bridge of 1837. Most of the notable buildings are off the main route in Warwick, including a superb Norman church with an outstanding 12th-century apse.

Leave Warwick Bridge and after a short distance meet crossroads. Turn right on to an unclassified road SP 'Castle Carrock' and in 50 yards turn left. Follow a quiet by-road and in 1 mile pass Toppin Castle, which incorporates a pele tower. In a further 1½ miles branch left SP 'Talkin', and 1 mile farther keep left, pass under a railway viaduct, and meet crossroads with the B6413. Drive forward over the main road and pass Talkin Fell on the right before entering Talkin.

TALKIN, Cumbria

Close to the high fells whose ownership was so hotly disputed for many centuries, this village has a lovely little church that has managed to preserve surprising evidence of its Norman origins. Work from that early period can be seen in the nave, bellcote, and chancel, and there are even traces in the pulpit and altar rail. Some 4 miles south-south-east of Talkin the summit of Cold Fell is surmounted by a cairn measuring 4ft high and 50ft in diameter.

Leave Talkin, and in ¼ mile turn right SP 'Hallbankgate'. Ascend, with views which extend left over the tree-bordered waters of Talkin Tarn and the great expanse of the Cumberland Plain. Reach Hallbankgate and turn right on to the A689 SP 'Alston'. Continue through Halton Lea Gate, then in just over 1 mile turn left on to an unclassified road SP 'Coanwood'. Descend to the steep wooded banks of the River South Tyne, cross the river, and ascend past Coanwood to meet crossroads. Turn left on to the 'Haltwhistle' road, in ¾ mile enter the hamlet of Rowfoot, and turn left SP 'Featherstone Park'. After ½ mile descend steeply to reach Featherstone Castle.

Carlisle Cathedral is impressive but small.

The River South Tyne chatters over its stony bed through the grounds of secluded Featherstone Castle.

FEATHERSTONE CASTLE, Northumb

Beautifully situated in large grounds beside the River South Tyne, this fine house dates from the 13th century and is now a children's activity holiday centre.

Leave Featherstone Castle on a secluded, picturesque road along the east bank of the River South Tyne. Meet a bridge and keep forward SP 'Haltwhistle', then in ¼ mile ascend to a T-junction and turn left. In 1¾ miles reach Bellister Castle on the right.

BELLISTER CASTLE, Northumb

In the 16th century the ruined tower attached to this 3-storey building was known as a bastell house, which perhaps gives a clue to the origin of the name. The house itself dates from 1669 and displays a number of good architectural features. Peel tower open by appointment.

Leave Bellister Castle and after a short distance turn left to cross a river bridge and reach the outskirts of Haltwhistle. Turn right on to the A69 to reach the town centre.

HALTWHISTLE, Northumb
William the Lion founded this old mining town's church in 1178, and as it stands today the building is considered a particularly fine example of early-English architecture. There is no tower, and the sanctuary preserves three carved coffin lids which are thought to date from the 14th century.

Return along the A69 'Carlisle' and follow the railway for 2¾ miles. Turn right on to the B630 to reach Greenhead.

GREENHEAD, Northumb
This little village lies south of Hadrian's Wall, close to a series of attractive ravines known as the Nine Nicks of Thirlwall. The route of a Roman track known as the Maiden Way extends from here to Penrith.

Leave Greenhead on the B6318 SP 'Gilsland'. In ½ mile pass a section of Hadrian's Wall on the left.

A section of Hadrian's Wall at Gilsland.

HADRIAN'S WALL, Cumbria
Between AD 122 and 139 the Roman Emperor Hadrian ordered that a defensive wall should be built to discourage the independent Scottish tribes from marauding into the largely pacified territory to the south. Today this major engineering achievement still stands as a remarkable monument to the Roman occupation of Britain, stretching 73 miles from Wallsend-on-Tyne to Bowness. Its course was plotted from one natural advantage to the next, and it was built of the materials most readily to hand – stone in the east and turf in the west. Along its length were 20 or so major forts, interspersed with milecastles and signal towers close enough together to allow the quick transference of a warning by fire beacon. Much of the surviving structure is protected under the Ancient Monuments scheme.

Continue along the B6318 to Gilsland, and on the nearside of a railway bridge reach a left turn leading to the Roman wall's Poltross Burn Milecastle.

GILSLAND, Northumb
Gilsland has natural sulphur and chalybeate springs that once made it a popular spa resort, though it never developed to the rarefied fashionable heights achieved by its southern contemporaries. Part of the Poltross Burn Milecastle (AM) is incorporated in a railway embankment near by, and a section of the Roman wall (AM) stands east of the school.

Meet a T-junction in Gilsland and turn right. A detour from the main tour can be made to Upper Denton by turning left at the T-junction.

UPPER DENTON, Cumbria
It is thought that the Saxon builders of this fascinating little church may have used stone from Hadrian's Wall in its construction. Of particular note is the reconstructed Roman arch in the chancel.

Leave Gilsland by crossing the River Irthing. In ¼ mile turn left, and ascend with views of the Roman wall to the left. After 1 mile turn left on to an unclassified road SP 'Birdoswald, Lanercost', and in a further ½ mile pass Harrow's Scar Milecastle (AM) to reach Birdoswald.

BIRDOSWALD, Cumbria
The Roman fort of *Camboglanna* (AM) occupies a 5-acre ridge-top site overlooking the gorge of the River Irthing near Birdoswald. Access to the remains, which include a particularly well-preserved angle tower and postern gate, is controlled by the farmer.

Leave Birdoswald and drive forward along the line of the Roman wall, passing two Roman turrets (AM) to reach Banks.

BANKS, Cumbria
Notable Roman sites in the area around Banks include Coombe Crag, Pike Hill (AM) and Boothby Castle Hill, and there is a milecastle (AM) with a section of the Roman wall here. One mile south-west lies the partly-ruined Augustinian, Lanercost Priory, founded in 1166. The nave is still in use. In the rebuilt Abbey mill is a craft workshop for the handicapped.

From Banks bear left, descend to the River Irthing, and continue to Lanercost.

LANERCOST, Cumbria
Extensive remains of a priory (AM) that was built with stones taken from the Roman wall can be seen here, including parts of a gatehouse showing 16th-century adaptations. The 12th-century nave serves as the parish church.

Pass the entrance to Lanercost Priory, cross the river, then immediately beyond the bridge turn left and ascend. After a short distance cross Naworth Park to reach Naworth Castle.

NAWORTH CASTLE, Cumbria
Pleasantly designed round a central courtyard, this 14th-century castle shows later additions and features a great hall, oratory, and rich tapestries. The building is open by arrangement.

At the castle entrance bear right and in ½ mile meet crossroads. Turn right on to the A69 SP 'Carlisle' to reach Brampton.

BRAMPTON, Cumbria
An unusual 8-sided moot hall stands in the cobble-flanked main street of Brampton, and the local church is the only ecclesiastical building known to have been designed by the inventive 19th-century architect, Philip Webb. The interior of the building is lit by a superb stained-glass window by the Victorian artist Burne-Jones.

Follow the A69 through Brampton, then keep forward on to the B6264 SP 'Carlisle Airport'. Proceed to Crosby-on-Eden.

CROSBY-ON-EDEN, Cumbria
The windows of the local church show the striking and original use of cut clear glass instead of stained glass. Other notable buildings here include Crosby House and High Crosby Farmhouse.

In 3½ miles turn left on to the A7 for the return to Carlisle.

BESIDE THE SOLWAY FIRTH

A coastal tour through small towns and hamlets not widely known, tracing the footsteps of Charles Dickens and his companion Wilkie Collins. Roman forts, Norman buildings and ecclesiastical art abound, a pleasing but complementary contrast to the dramatic coastline and marshlands along the Solway Firth.

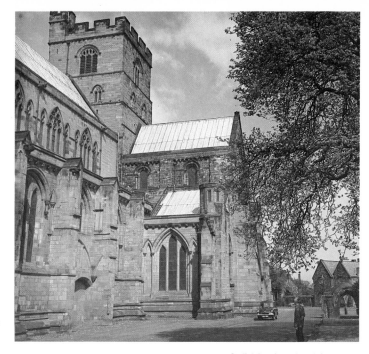

Carlisle's priory church became a cathedral in 1133

CARLISLE, Cumbria

Since early times Carlisle has been a strategically important city because of its position on the Anglo-Scottish border. The Romans occupied the town, calling it *Lugavulium*, and finding themselves repeatedly attacked by the Picts, they built Hadrian's Wall, parts of which can still be seen east of the city. Carlisle Castle (AM) was built by the Normans for the same reasons. It was founded in 1092 by William Rufus, strengthened by David I, and was for centuries the kingpin of conflicts between the Scottish and English, each often gaining the city, but never for long. Eventually, in 1745, the Scottish were finally ousted when Bonnie Prince Charlie's troops were driven from the town. Maintaining its military tradition, the castle's keep houses the former Border regiments' museum. Today Carlisle, known locally as 'Carel', is the chief administrative and agricultural centre of Cumbria and although the suburbs are industrialised, the centre has retained its ancient character. The red sandstone cathedral, where Sir Walter Scott was married in 1797, is England's 2nd smallest cathedral. Begun in the 12th century and rebuilt in the 13th century, it preserves one of the finest east windows in the country, superb carved choir stalls and a painted barrel-vault ceiling. Tullie House, the city's museum and art gallery, occupies a magnificent Jacobean mansion and contains Roman relics excavated from forts along Hadrian's Wall. The 15th-century Guildhall (OACT), a charming town house which became the meeting place for Carlisle's 8 Trade Guilds, is now a museum of Guild, Civic and local history. Exhibits include the great bell, pillory and stocks from the medieval castle.

Leave Carlisle on the A595 Workington road and ½ mile beyond the castle turn right on to the B5307. In 1 mile branch right into Burgh Road, SP 'Kirkandrews'. Pass through Kirkandrews-on-Eden and Monkhill to reach Burgh-by-Sands.

BURGH-BY-SANDS, Cumbria

Burgh-by-Sands boasts the strongly-fortified church of St Michael, built almost entirely from Roman stone. A monument to Edward I, who died in 1307 on his way to attack the Scots and lay in state here, may be found north of the village.

At the village end bear right, SP 'Port Carlisle'. NB: between here and Cardunock the road is liable to tidal flooding. Cross unfenced marshland, with views across the Solway Firth to reach Port Carlisle.

PORT CARLISLE, Cumbria

This was the brainchild of the Earl of Lonsdale, who built the harbour in 1819, and the canal to Carlisle in 1823. Unfortunately for him the harbour did not flourish and never grew beyond the row of terraced cottages and single detached house there is today. Over 140 acres of the Solway Firth lands here make up the Glasson Moss National Nature Reserve.

Continue to Bowness-on-Solway.

BOWNESS-ON-SOLWAY, Cumbria

The village of Bowness-on-Solway is situated on a low promontory overlooking the Solway Firth. At one time an iron trestle viaduct spanned the Firth here and carried a railway linking the iron manufacturing industries of west Cumbria with Annan and southern Scotland. The village is built on the site of a Roman settlement at the western end of Hadrian's Wall. The church, dedicated to St Michael, has 2 late-Norman doorways and in the porch rest 2 church bells, one of which is dated 1612. These were stolen from Scotland in the days of the Border raids by an English raiding party as reprisal for 2 bells removed from Bowness Church.

Continue forward, passing the embankment of the dismantled railway viaduct. Continue round the headland and through Cardurnock. 2 miles beyond Anthorn turn right SP 'Kirkbride', and cross the river. At the edge of Kirkbride turn right on the B5307 for the village centre.

KIRKBRIDE, Cumbria

Kirkbride is a pretty village, set amid trees on the tidal creek of the Wampol. Its ancient church, dedicated to St Bridget, is of Norman construction built with material from a Roman fort which stood in the area. There are wide areas of moss land in the parish which provide peat for many local hearths. On the marshes of Kirkbride and Whitrigg there grows a turf of remarkably fine quality which is cut and marketed to provide top-class bowling-greens.

Continue to Abbey Town.

ABBEY TOWN, Cumbria

The village of Abbey Town retains vestiges of a great ecclesiastical past. In approximately 1150, the Cistercian order founded Holme Cultram Abbey here, which soon prospered through the farming skills of its monks. However, over the years the abbey suffered considerably at the hands of Scottish raiders, and now all that remains is the 12th-century nave which forms the basis of today's parish church of St Mary. Abbot Robert Chambers built the west porch in the 16th century, and the church itself was restored many times during the 16th and 17th centuries.

At the crossroads go forward on to the B5302, SP 'Silloth' and 'Skinburness'. In 3¼ miles turn right, SP 'Skinburness', and shortly cross Skinburness Marsh. At Skinburness keep left and follow the coastal road to Silloth, joining the B5302 on entering the town.

SILLOTH, Cumbria
In the middle of the last century Silloth was transformed from a drowsy hamlet in to a busy port by the construction of the docks here, and today its pleasant lawns, putting green, children's amusements and sea-wall promenade (2 miles long), fill the town with holidaymakers during the summer months. West Beach, backed by sand dunes, is a fine expanse of sand where bathing and fishing are popular pastimes. The name 'Silloth' comes from a tithe barn built here by the monks of the great Cistercian abbey of Holme Cultram known as the 'sea lath'. From Silloth there are magnificent views of the Scottish hills across the Solway Firth.

At the crossroads turn left on to the B5300, SP 'Maryport', and shortly bear right. Continue through Greenrow and Blitterless to reach a pleasant coastal stretch with sand dunes, parking and picnic areas. Pass through Beckfoot and Mawbray to reach Allonby. Continue along the B5300 and in 4½ miles turn right on to the A596 for Maryport.

MARYPORT, Cumbria
Maryport was developed during the Industrial Revolution, and rose to prominence through coal mining, coal export and the great iron-making boom. The lord of the manor, Colonel H. Senhouse, was chiefly responsible for this development in 1748-9, and he named the port after his wife, Mary. The sea is Maryport's greatest attraction; miles of beach stretch north and south of the town and there is ample opportunity for sailing, fishing and safe bathing. On high ground to the north of the town are the remains of a Roman fort. This was defended by a double ditch which encloses 4½ acres. Outside the fort boundary there have been found the remnants of a considerable civilian settlement, with shops, workshops and taverns.

At the road junction by the church turn left on to the A594, SP 'Cockermouth'. In 6 miles, at a roundabout, take the 2nd exit and descend to cross the River Derwent into Cockermouth.

COCKERMOUTH, Cumbria
Cockermouth, famous as the birthplace of William Wordsworth, is a pleasant rural town that makes an ideal centre for touring the Lake District. See page 496.

Turn left into the main street and then keep forward. At the end bear left passing the castle (left) then turn left, SP 'Isel'. After 3¼ miles turn left again, SP 'Blindcrake, Isel'. Descend to cross the river then turn left. In ½ mile turn right, SP 'Bothel Sunderland'. Isel Hall,

Above: Scottish hills silhouetted against the Solway Firth

Right: the west door of Abbey Town's parish church, where an abbey once stood

Elizabethan, with a pele tower, is seen to the left at this point. In 1 mile turn left, continuing through Sunderland and in 1½ miles turn left on to the A591. At the roundabout, on the edge of Bothel, take the A595, SP 'Carlisle'. Later pass through Mealgate and in 3¾ miles turn left on to the B5304, SP 'Wigton'.

WIGTON, Cumbria
The town of Wigton, known locally as the 'Throstle Nest', is the market town of a wide area and has been for many centuries. In 1262 permission to hold the market was granted by King Henry III to Walter de Wigton. Popular for its market held on Tuesday; there are also cattle and sheep auctions. The red sandstone parish church of St Mary's was erected in 1788 on the site of an earlier church. The monument chest inside the church is thought to be pre-Reformation, and the church Registers date back to 1604. In the centre of the town is the memorial fountain erected in 1872 by George Moore, a merchant and philanthropist, in memory of his wife. The old parish pump and tall gas lamp which are to be found in West Road were immortalised by Charles Dickens in his book The Lazy Tour of Two Idle Apprentices. Dickens visited Wigton and the surrounding area with his friend Wilkie Collins, and as the many interesting nooks and crannies to be found in the town remain unchanged, it is easy to picture Wigton as he must have seen it.

In the town centre turn right on to the A596, SP 'Carlisle', and in 5¼ miles go forward on to the A595. In 5 miles re-enter the suburbs of Carlisle and keep forward for the castle and city centre.

TO THE VALLEY OF SONG

Walled Chester stands on the edge of England like the medieval guardian it once was. Across the border in Wales a natural wall of mountains encloses Llangollen, in a valley that rings with song during the International Eisteddfod.

Victorian architect W H Kelly designed this building, which stands in Park Street, Chester, in a convincing half-timbered style.

CHESTER, Cheshire

Founded nearly 2,000 years ago by the Romans, Chester boasts some of the richest archaeological and architectural treasures in Britain. It is the only city in England to have preserved its Roman and medieval walls in their entirety, and today they provide a 2-mile circular walk which affords excellent views of both the city and its surrounding countryside. At one point the walls overlook the Roodee, a racecourse where the Chester Cup has been run every May since 1824. Chester, or *Deva* as it was once known, remained a principal military station and trading town until the Romans withdrew from Britain, then was probably re-occupied by the Saxons to prevent the Danes from using it as a stronghold. It gradually regained its position as a place of importance, and after it had fallen to the Normans in 1070 became the capital of a county Palatine whose earls were almost as powerful as the king. The medieval town flourished as a port until silting of the Dee during the 15th century brought a decline in trade prosperity. The city continued as a commercial centre, however, and its fortunes largely revived during the rich 18th and 19th centuries. Much survives from all periods of Chester's history, but the source of its distinctive character is undoubtedly the galleried tiers of shops known as The Rows. The beautifully restored sandstone cathedral dates mainly from the 14th century. It incorporates extensive Benedictine monastic

remains, and is especially noted for its richly carved woodwork, the Lady Chapel, the refectory, and the cloisters. Partly ruined St John's Church retains excellent Norman workmanship. Most of Chester Castle now dates from the 19th century, but its 13th-century Agricola Tower is largely original. The castle contains the Cheshire Military Museum encompassing four separate regiments. Black-and-white buildings abound in Chester — God's Providence House, Bishop Lloyd's House and Old Leche House being outstanding — and there are also many timbered inns. The city's history is illustrated in the Heritage and Visitor Centres and the Grosvenor and Guildhall museums. Other museums located on the city walls are at the Water Tower and the King Charles Tower. There is also a Toy Museum in The Rows. Chester Zoo offers a variety of exhibits second only to London.

Leave Chester on the A483 SP 'North Wales' and cross the River Dee via Grosvenor Bridge. Reach a roundabout and take the 4th exit on to the A549 SP 'Saltney'. Reach Saltney and cross into Wales. In 2½ miles at Broughton roundabout take 2nd exit A5104 SP 'Corwen'. After ¾ mile turn left and 1¼ miles further left again. In 1 mile turn left into Penyffordd. In ¼ mile turn right and after 2 miles cross the River Alyn to pass through Portblyddyn.

The gates at the entrance to Chirk Castle are an outstanding example of wrought-iron work by the Davies brothers of Wrexham.

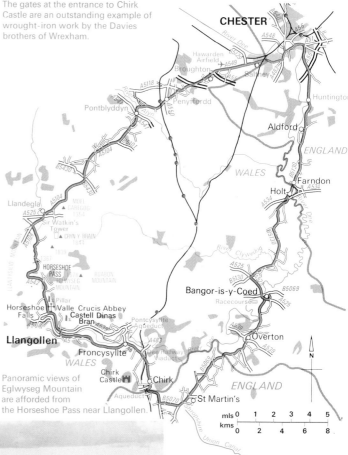

Panoramic views of Eglwyseg Mountain are afforded from the Horseshoe Pass near Llangollen.

At the Bridge Inn turn left then immediately right and ascend. Proceed, with mountain views, through the village of Llandegla.

Turn right then immediately left, then after ¾ mile reach a roundabout and take the 1st exit on to the A542 'Llangollen' road. Ascend to the Horseshoe Pass.

HORSESHOE PASS, Clwyd
Fine views of the surrounding mountain scenery can be enjoyed from this 1,367ft pass. North-east is 1,844ft Cyrn-y-Brain, topped by Sir Watkin's Tower, and west are the slopes of Llantysilio Mountain.

Descend along the Eglwyseg Valley to Valle Crucis Abbey.

VALLE CRUCIS ABBEY, Clwyd
Pleasantly wooded hills frame the view from the picturesque ruins of this ancient abbey, which was founded in 1201 and has left extensive remains (AM). 'Valle Crucis' means 'Vale of the Cross' and derives from nearby Eliseg's Pillar (AM), which was erected to commemorate a nobleman of ancient times.

After a short distance reach the Horseshoe Falls.

HORSESHOE FALLS, Clwyd
Not a natural cascade but a beautifully curving weir with a fall of 18 inches, this lovely River Dee feature was built to feed water into the Llangollen Canal.

Continue with Castell Dinas Bran to the left.

CASTELL DINAS BRAN, Clywd
Ramparts of an Iron-Age fort partly surround this ruined 13th-century stronghold, which occupies a hilltop site overlooking Llangollen.

Turn right to cross the Dee and enter Llangollen.

LLANGOLLEN, Clwyd
This small town's world-wide reputation as a centre of Welsh culture and music comes from the International Eisteddfod held here for one week in July. During this time the small streets are transformed by a riot of colourful national costumes and chatter of foreign tongues, while the surrounding hillsides echo to the sound of great international choirs and poets performing in a huge 1,000-seat marquee. Plas Newydd (open) is a black-and-white house on the edge of the town which was, for many years, the home of the 'Ladies

Valle Crucis Abbey was founded by Madog ap Gruffyd, a prince of Powys, during the 13th century.

of Llangollen' who arrived here in 1779, entertained a string of celebrities and generated endless gossip with their lifestyle. Transport enthusiasts are covered by the Canal Museum and Passenger Boat Trip Centre with horsedrawn trips along the Shropshire Union Canal, and by the Llangollen Railway.

Follow the A5 'Shrewsbury' road through the winding valley of the Dee to Froncysyllte.

FRONCYSYLLTE, Clwyd
Thomas Telford's amazing 120ft high Pontcysyllte Aqueduct and the longest in the United Kingdom, was built to carry the Shropshire Union Canal over the deep ravine of the River Dee. It can be seen by turning left. Downstream is a railway viaduct whose impressive design is almost as remarkable.

Continue to Chirk.

CHIRK, Clwyd
An interesting section of the Shropshire Union Canal in this well kept village includes a long, damp tunnel which opens into a wide basin before the canal is carried high across the Ceiriog Valley.

CHIRK CASTLE, Clwyd
Outside Chirk behind superb 18th-century wrought-iron gates (AM) is Chirk Castle, a 13th-century border

Poets, artists, and writers have praised Llangollen's hospitality since the early 19th century.

fortress in a commanding position above the Ceiriog Valley. Unlike many of its contemporaries this stronghold has been continuously inhabited since it was built, and considerable structural changes have been made to suit the tastes of successive owners.

Cross the River Ceiriog into England, and after 1¼ miles turn left on to the B5070 SP 'Overton'. In 1 mile reach St Martin's.

ST MARTIN'S, Salop
The interior of the beautiful 13th-century local church preserves Georgian furnishings which include boxpews and a double-decker pulpit. Attractive almshouses stand near by.

Join the B5069 and cross undulating countryside to re-enter Wales. Reach the A528 and turn left to enter Overton.

OVERTON, Clwyd
Very old churchyard yews in this pleasant small town are traditionally held to be among the 7 greatest wonders of Wales.

Keep forward on the B5059, SP 'Bangor' then turn right. Continue with views of the Dee and Bangor racecourse, to Bangor-is-y-Coed.

BANGOR-IS-Y-COED, Clwyd
An ancient stone bridge is the dominating feature of this picturesque village. At one time a monastery stood near by, but the buildings were destroyed and its monks slaughtered by order of King Aethelfrith of Northumbria in AD 615. Little survives today.

Turn right SP 'Wrexham' and shortly right again then in ¼ mile turn right on to the bypass A525. After 1¾ miles turn right on to the B5130 SP 'Wrexham Industrial Estate' then keep forward, no SP. In 5½ miles turn left then right across the bypass to enter Holt. Bear right then keep forward.

HOLT, Clwyd
Slight remains of a Norman castle can be seen near the 8-arched 15th-century bridge that spans the Dee here. The local church is a fine building which dates originally from the 13th century but was rebuilt in the 15th. Inside is an elaborately decorated font.

Cross the Dee on to the B5434 to Farndon and re-enter England.

FARNDON, Cheshire
In Farndon attractive houses group round a large church that was rebuilt after Civil War damage. An unusual feature of the church is a stained-glass window depicting a troop of Royalist soldiers.

Turn left on to the B5130 SP 'Chester' and continue through wooded scenery to Aldford.

ALDFORD, Cheshire
Earthworks of a Norman motte-and-bailey castle may be seen north of Aldford's Victorian church.

Return to Chester.

COCKERMOUTH, Cumbria

This attractive small town, situated at the point where the Rivers Cocker and Derwent meet, is rich in history and has the distinction of being one of 51 towns in Britain recommended by the British Council for preservation. The ruined Norman castle (OACT), which overlooks the River Derwent, was built of stone taken from a Roman fort at Papcastle. During the 16th century Cockermouth was a busy market town, and became the country's commercial centre in the 17th century. Today it is a rural town with a broad main street and a number of Georgian houses and squares and is a popular base for touring the Lake District. The most famous people in Cockermouth's history are, of course, the Wordsworths, and Wordsworth House (OACT) is internationally known as one of the 2 principal residences in the Lake District of Dorothy and her famous poet brother, William. The other is Dove Cottage at Grasmere. Their home in Cockermouth is a handsome house (NT) on Main Street which was built in 1745 and became the home of Wordsworth's father in 1766 when he was made steward to Sir James Lowther. William was born here in 1770 and his sister in 1771. Much of the house remains unchanged since Wordsworth's day, and he made reference to the garden in *The Prelude*. A stained-glass memorial window to him can be seen in the 19th-century Church of All Saints situated south of the market place.

From Cockermouth follow SP 'Workington', then in 1¼ miles turn right on to the A66 and follow the valley of the River Derwent to Workington.

NORTHERN LAKES AND THE SOLWAY FIRTH

This is Wordsworth's country, where the romance of majestic mountain scenery, flawless lakes and lush green valleys give way gently to flat pastoral farmland sprinkled with handsome Georgian farmhouses and tiny hamlets: a delicately-proportioned tapestry fringed with glittering stretches of golden sands and unspoilt resorts.

Above: the Norman doorway of the church at St Bees

WORKINGTON, Cumbria

A onetime Roman fort and town called *Gabrosentum,* Workington has an interesting history. It was from this port, where the River Derwent enters the Solway Firth, that the Lindisfarne monks fled from the Danes in the 9th century. In 1568 Mary, Queen of Scots, was received at the fine old mansion of Workington Hall (not open). An important industrial town in the area, Workington's main industries are iron and steel. An interesting museum known as the Helena Thompson Museum was bequethed to the town by the late Miss Thompson MBE, a native of Workington. Opened in 1948, it contains a fascinating collection of costumes, glass, ceramics and local history exhibits.

Leave on the A596, SP 'Barrow'. In 2¾ miles, at the T-junction, turn right on to the A595. Pass the edge of Distington, then in 3½ miles branch right on to the A5094 for Whitehaven town centre.

Left: Whitehaven's harbour and lighthouse date from the 18th century

WHITEHAVEN, Cumbria

Sir John Lowther was responsible for bringing industry to Whitehaven in 1690, transforming it from a cosy hamlet into the bustling seaport and coal-mining town it is today. During the 18th century, his son, Sir James Lowther, built Whitehaven Castle (now a hospital), and St James's Church was also built at this time. In 1701 George Washington's grandmother was buried in St Nicholas's Church, where she is commemorated by an inscribed tablet. The Washingtons were a Lancastrian family who later emigrated to America. The colourful American sailor John Paul Jones fired on Whitehaven in 1788.

Leave the one-way system on the B5345 for St Bees.

ST BEES, Cumbria

St Bees is a small coastal resort with fine cliffs and bathing sands. The 12th-century Benedictine priory church of SS Mary and Bega is reputed to be one of the most outstanding in Cumbria. It is thought that a princess, St Bega, came from Ireland in about AD650 to found a nunnery that preceded the priory. St Bees' church has an impressive Norman doorway, and a fine carved stone in the churchyard wall depicts St Michael fighting a dragon. A local man, who became Archbishop of Canterbury in 1576, founded St Bees Grammer School, which is now a public school.

Go over the level-crossing and at the end of the town keep left, SP 'Egremont'. After 2¾ miles go forward on to an unclassified road and continue to Egremont.

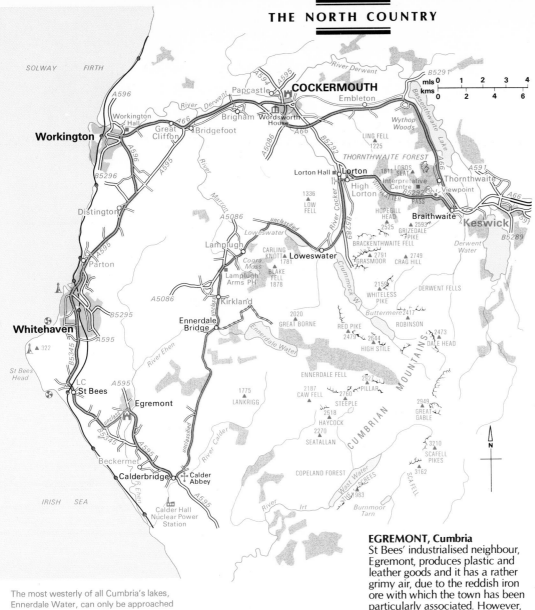

ENNERDALE BRIDGE, Cumbria
This tiny hamlet on the banks of the River Ehen is situated just a mile or so west of Ennerdale Water, amid breathtaking scenery. Its churchyard was the setting for Wordsworth's poem *The Brothers*.

The main tour turns left, SP 'Cockermouth', and proceeds to Kirkland. In 1 mile turn right on to the A5086, then in ½ mile right again, SP 'Loweswater'. Pass through the hamlet of Lamplugh and turn right. Follow this narrow road for 1 ¾ miles, then turn right and descend to pass Loweswater, and continue to the outskirts of Loweswater village.

LOWESWATER, Cumbria
A narrow road leads to this attractively-positioned village which lies halfway across the plains towards Crummock Water. Carling Knott rises to 1,781ft behind Loweswater lake and the great peak of Grasmoor (2,791ft) lies to the east. Opposite Grasmoor, the impressive screes of Mellbreak rise on the west side of Crummock Water.

Continue on the unclassified road then in ½ mile cross the River Cocker. Later join the B5289, SP 'Cockermouth', and continue to the edge of Lorton.

LORTON, Cumbria
Enjoying a pastoral situation beside the River Cocker in the Vale of Lorton, this village includes a church displaying a fine stained-glass window. The 17th-century Lorton Hall (not open) retains the ancient pele tower in which Malcolm III of Scotland and Queen Margaret stayed in 1089. Charles II visited Lorton Hall in 1650.

By the nearside of the village turn right, SP 'Keswick'. At High Lorton turn left into the village and at the end turn right, then at the T-junction turn right again on to the B5292. Continue across the Whinlatter Pass and at the bottom of the descent keep left to enter Braithwaite.

BRAITHWAITE, Cumbria
At the north-eastern end of the Coledale valley and the start of the Whinlatter Pass, this picturesque village is conveniently situated for the tourist. It enjoys great popularity among climbers as the starting point for an attack on Grisedale Pike, one of the northern peaks in the Grasmoor mountain group.

In Braithwaite turn left, SP 'Cockermouth (A66)', then turn left again to join the A66 and continue alongside the shore of Bassenthwaite Lake. At the north end the road veers away from the lake and continues through a wide valley. In 5 ½ miles turn right on to the A5086 for the return to Cockermouth.

The most westerly of all Cumbria's lakes, Ennerdale Water, can only be approached by road from the west side

EGREMONT, Cumbria
St Bees' industrialised neighbour, Egremont, produces plastic and leather goods and it has a rather grimy air, due to the reddish iron ore with which the town has been particularly associated. However, Wordsworth found sufficient inspiration here to write, in 1806, *The Horn of Egremont Castle* — which none could sound 'save he who came as rightful heir'. The castle he refers to was built in the 12th century to bolster Norman rule but was destroyed at the Reformation in the 16th century, leaving the ruins of today.

Follow the A595 Barrow road to Calderbridge.

CALDERBRIDGE, Cumbria
Here is the site of Britain's first nuclear power station which was opened in the autumn of 1956 by Queen Elizabeth II. Contrasting with this are the ruins of the 12th-century Calder Abbey (OACT) which was originally built by Savignac monks from Furness Abbey. Remains include the nave, the church aisles and parts of the cloister.

At Calderbridge turn left, SP 'Ennerdale'. In ¾ mile turn left then right, and ascend along a narrow moorland road. After 3 ¼ miles skirt Ennerdale Forest and later descend to a T-junction. Here turn right to reach Ennerdale Bridge.

AMONG THE HIGH PEAKS

Climbers and walkers come to this part of the national park for the stark ridges of weathered grit, towering rock outcrops, and refreshingly empty moorland. Villages of timbered cottages shelter in the valleys, making a contrast with the huge reflectors of Jodrell Bank's radio telescopes.

THE PEAK DISTRICT NATIONAL PARK
This tour starts west of the Peak District boundary and explores the brownstone towns and villages in the mid western part of the national park. In places massive limestone extraction has taken its toll on the landscape, but the sheep-cropped grass of high gritstone edges still rolls away to close horizons in areas of outstanding natural beauty that have been saved by the Peak Planning Board. Visitors should remember that although the region is protected it is not automatically accessible to the public. Some 40,000 people live and work in the park, and permission should always be sought from farmers and landowners before enclosed land is entered. Information centres are located in Buxton, Castleton, and Edale.

Leave Congleton via West Street and West Road to join the A34 'Newcastle' road. Proceed to Astbury.

ASTBURY, Cheshire
Notable Jacobean and earlier woodwork can be seen in Astbury's 14th- and 15th-century church, and the fine village Rectory dates from the 18th century.

Continue along the A34 to pass Little Moreton Hall.

An attractive aqueduct carries the Macclesfield Canal over the road near Congleton.

Little Moreton Hall is one of the finest medieval houses in Britain

CONGLETON, Cheshire
This market town stands on a bend on the River Dane and is a dormitory settlement for the vast industrial conurbations of Manchester and the Potteries. Its own industries include the manufacture of artificial yarn for the textile trade. Notable buildings in the town include three half-timbered inns and an 18th-century church with heavy woodwork that seems appropriate to Congleton's solid personality.

THE CLOUD, Cheshire
Some 3 miles east of Congleton a lofty hill known as The Cloud (NT) rises from farmed slopes to a 1,050ft summit offering magnificent all-round views. East are the Staffordshire hills, west the rolling Cheshire Plain, and south the towns and distinctively shaped chimneys of the Potteries.

LITTLE MORETON HALL, Cheshire
Beautiful carved gables and a distinctive black-and-white exterior of Elizabethan wood- and plasterwork have made this splendid 16th-century manor house (NT) one of the most famous examples in Britain. The dazzling effect of symmetrical timber patterns against brilliant white is increased by the reflection of the house in its own lovely moat. Inside are a long wainscoted gallery, a great hall, a chapel, and fine oak furniture.

Continue for ¾ mile to the edge of Scholar Green and turn left on to an unclassified road SP 'Mow Cop'. After ¼ mile turn left again, and after a further ¼ mile cross a canal bridge and drive beneath a railway before ascending Mow Cop.

MOW COP, Cheshire
Rough turf covers this stark limestone ridge for much of its 1,091ft height, but the rugged outcrop of rock known as the Old Man of Mow carries little but a sham ruin built in 1750. Known as Mow Cop Castle, this folly makes a picturesque addition to the distinctive outline of the Old Man.

Continue past a towered church and in 1 mile turn right (no SP) into Mow Lane. Descend through Gillow Heath to the main road and turn left, then in 300 yards turn right on to an unclassified road SP 'Biddulph Moor'. Climb to the village of Biddulph Moor and turn left SP 'Leek'. Take the next turning right, proceed for ½ mile to reach a T-junction, and turn left. Continue for 1 mile and turn right. After 2¼ miles glimpse Rudyard Reservoir on the left and descend to Rudyard.

RUDYARD, Staffs
Rudyard Kipling's parents courted and became engaged in this lovely village, and when their talented son was born they named him after it. Attractive woodlands to the north border a 2-mile reservoir formed in 1793 to provide water for the Trent and Mersey Canal. Today the banks of this attractive lake are skirted by a 5-mile footpath dotted with secluded picnic spots near the water's edge. A section of the path follows the trackbed of an abandoned railway, and its route passes caverns, unusual rock formations, and the remains of Roman copper workings.

Continue on the B5331 'Leek' road, meet a T-junction, and turn right on to the A523. Take the next turning left on to an unclassified road SP 'Meerbrook', continue for ½ mile, then turn left again. Approach Meerbrook with Tittesworth Reservoir right.

MEERBROOK, Staffs
Wild upland country popular with climbers and fell walkers surrounds this tiny moorland village. A curious aspect of the area is its naturalized colony of red-necked wallabies. This numbers some 30 strong and began when several of the animals – natives of Australia – escaped from a private estate.

Turn right SP 'Blackshaw Moor, Leek', and after ¼ mile meet a main road and turn left on to the A53 'Buxton' road. Climb on to open moors in the Peak District National Park, with a 2-mile stretch of rocky outcrops known as the Staffordshire Roaches to the left. The highest point of the Roaches is 1,658ft; Merryton Low rises to 1,603ft to the right. Pass the Royal Cottage Inn and reach an unclassified left turn leading to the village of Flash. A short detour can be made from the main route here.

FLASH, Staffs
Situated at 1,518ft, Flash is claimed to be the highest village in England and is itself dominated by 1,684ft Oliver Hill to the north.

Later enter Derbyshire and ascend to 1,631ft below the distinctive summit of Axe Edge.

AXE EDGE, Derbys
Rising from an area of fine walking country, this 1,810ft summit is the highest point in the moors from which the rivers Dove, Manifold, Wye, Dane, and Goyt spring.

Proceed to Buxton.

Extremely faint signals from outer space can be detected by the advanced Jodrell Bank radio telescopes.

BUXTON, Derbys
Situated some 1,007ft above sea level, this natural touring centre is the highest town in England and has been known as a spa resort of one sort or another since Roman times. A superb legacy of 18th-century architecture has been left from its most popular period, and the tourists of today are catered for by a large range of entertainment facilities.

Leave Buxton with SP 'Congleton' to return along the A53 'Leek' road, and after 1¼ miles turn right on to the A54. Make a winding ascent with 1,640ft Burbage Edge visible to the right, and after 1 mile enjoy views of 1,795ft Whetstone Edge on the same side. Below these ridges, in the deep Dane Valley, is a junction of Derbyshire, Cheshire, and Staffordshire boundaries in an area known as the Three Shire Heads. Descend from undulating moorland to Allgreave for distant views of a Post Office communications tower, and after passing close to the tower skirt Bosley Reservoir and turn right on to the A523 'Macclesfield' road. Continue for 2 miles to Oakgrove and turn left on to an unclassified road SP 'Gawsworth', immediately crossing the Macclesfield Canal. Proceed to Gawsworth.

GAWSWORTH, Cheshire
Spacious lawns and gardens watered by five lakes grace the grounds of Gawsworth Hall, a beautiful black-and-white timber-framed house (open) dating from Tudor times. Also in the park are rare traces of a tilting ground, where knights once displayed their prowess in jousts and mock battles. At one time the house was the seat of the Fytton family, whose daughter Mary was a favourite maid of Elizabeth I and may have been the 'Dark Lady' of Shakespeare's sonnets. Features of the village itself include the fine Old Rectory and an attractive church, both of the 15th century. The church carries quaint gargoyles and contains a notable range of monuments to the Fyttons. A nearby wood contains the tomb of 18th-century dramatist and eccentric Maggotty Johnson.

At Gawsworth turn left SP 'Gawsworth Church'. Continue to the end of the village and keep right, passing an attractive pond, with views of Gawsworth Hall. Continue along this unclassified road, pass the church, and at the Harrington Arms Inn turn right then right again on to the A536. After ½ mile meet crossroads and turn left on to an unclassified road for Marton.

MARTON, Cheshire
A famous oak tree in this village is said to be the largest in England. The local church is a quaint timbered structure dating from the 14th century.

Drive to a junction with the A34 and turn right SP 'Manchester'. Continue for 3¼ miles to reach the entrance to Capesthorne Hall.

Rudyard's extensive reservoir has been planned to cater for a wide variety of leisure pursuits.

CAPESTHORNE HALL, Cheshire
A chapel which adjoins this lovely 18th-century house (open) may be the earliest surviving work of the architect John Wood of Bath. The house itself contains various relics, including pictures, ancient vases, old furniture, and Americana.

Continue along the A34 for 1 mile, meet traffic signals, and turn left on to the A537 'Chester' road. Continue to the Chelford roundabout and turn left on to the A535 SP 'Holmes Chapel' to reach Jodrell Bank.

Ramshaw Rocks are among the most striking gritstone crags in the Peak District.

JODRELL BANK, Cheshire
Manchester University made the name Jodrell Bank internationally famous by building a giant steerable radio telescope here in 1957. Now known as Mark I, the instrument has a 250ft reflector and is still one of the largest of its type in the world. The Mark II was built in the early 1960s and has a 125ft reflector with an advanced form of digital control. Regular presentations of the stars and planets are given in the Planetarium (open), and there are fascinating working models of both the telescopes on view.

Keep forward on the A535. In 3¼ miles, near the outskirts of Holmes Chapel, turn left into unclassified Manor Lane (no SP). Continue to the A54 and turn left for the return to Congleton via Somerford.

GRANGE-OVER-SANDS, Cumbria

This quiet seaside resort is situated on Morecambe Bay. Its shingle and rock shore is scattered with fascinating rock pools at low tide, and is backed by lovely wooded fell scenery that sweeps right down to the sea. Bathing is dangerous. The mile-long promenade offers bracing walks, and the mild local climate has allowed the establishment of flourishing ornamental gardens throughout the town.

Leave Grange on the B5277 'Lindale, Kendal' road and drive through well-wooded countryside with views across Morecambe Bay to the right. Continue, with the Lakeland fells visible ahead, to Lindale.

LINDALE, Cumbria

John Wilkinson, the 18th-century iron master, is appropriately commemorated by a cast-iron obelisk in this pretty village.

In Lindale turn right SP 'Lancaster', and in 1¼ miles meet a roundabout. Take the 2nd exit on to the A590, later pass the craggy cliffs of Whitbarrow Scar on the left, and continue for 1¼ miles. Immediately before a river bridge turn left on to the A5074 SP 'Bowness' and follow the lovely Lyth Valley. Continue, with views of the Lakeland fells ahead, and ascend a winding road through picturesque countryside. Drive through Winster, continue for 2 miles to reach crossroads, and turn left on to the B5284. In ¼ mile turn right on to the A592 to reach the town of Bowness-on-Windermere.

LAKE WINDERMERE, Cumbria

The largest and one of the most beautiful lakes in England, Windermere measures 10½ miles long and is only 1 mile wide. Its surface is studded with charming little islands, and its steep banks are cloaked with dense masses of attractive woodland. Water-sports enthusiasts find it suitable for most of their requirements, and at one time it was the regular venue for world water-speed record attempts.

BOWNESS-ON-WINDERMERE, Cumbria

In summer the quaint narrow streets of this pleasant little Lakeland town are busy with anglers, sailors, walkers, and tourists who have come here just for the beauty of the surroundings. Its fine 15th- to 19th-century church has superb examples of medieval stained glass in the east window, and the picturesque quality of local stone can be seen everywhere. Motor launches operate from Bowness Pier to Belle Isle, an enchanting 38-acre island in the middle of Lake Windermere. The house (open) on this unusual estate was the first completely round building of its type erected in England and contains interesting collections of furniture, portraits, and miscellanea.

SOUTHERN LAKELAND

Characterized by narrow switchback lanes and tranquil lakes that recede far into the distance, this part of the Lake District was a favourite haunt of famous poets and artists. Relics of them remain, as does the timeless and indefinable quality of peace that first attracted them.

Return along the A592 SP 'Barrow' and in ¾ mile pass a right turn leading to Lake Windermere Ferry. An alternative route that shortens the tour by 15 miles can be followed by taking the ferry and rejoining the main route at Far Sawrey, on the other bank. On the main route, drive through thick woodland along the east shore of Lake Windermere to reach Fell Foot Park.

FELL FOOT PARK, Cumbria

Attractively situated on the shores of Lake Windermere, this 18-acre park (NT) offer facilities for bathing, boating, picnicking, and many other outdoor pursuits.

Meet a T-junction and turn right on to the A590 to reach Newby Bridge.

NEWBY BRIDGE, Cumbria

This unusual stone bridge dates from the 17th century and spans the River Leven at the southern extremity of Lake Windermere. It is an attractive ingredient of the beautiful local scenery.

Turn right on to an unclassified road SP 'Lakeside, Hawkshead' and follow a winding road along the west shore of Lake Windermere to Lakeside.

LAKESIDE, Cumbria

Steam locomotives run south from here to Haverthwaite on the Lakeside and Haverthwaite Railway, which connects with passenger ferries operating from Ambleside and Bowness-on-Windermere.

Lake Windermere is a popular centre for boating and sailing as well as being a magnetic scenic attraction.

Leave Lakeside and after ¾ mile bear right. In 2¼ miles reach Graythwaite Hall Gardens.

GRAYTHWAITE HALL GARDENS, Cumbria

In spring and summer the 7 acres of this landscape garden are glorious with the blooms and foliage of many different plants. The Elizabethan hall round which they were created was sympathetically re-modelled in the 19th century.

Leave Graythwaite Hall and branch right SP 'Sawrey'. In ¾ mile descend steeply, then in 1¾ miles bear left and ascend to Far Sawrey. If the alternative route via the ferry has been taken, resume the main tour here.

FAR SAWREY, Cumbria

This beautiful Lakeland village is situated between Lake Windermere and tranquil Esthwaite Water.

Keep left in Far Sawrey, then turn left on to the B5285 SP 'Hawkshead'. Continue to Near Sawrey.

NEAR SAWREY, Cumbria

In 1943 Beatrix Potter, creator of Peter Rabbit and a host of other engaging animals in her children's books, bequeathed Hill Top Farm (open) and about half the village to the National Trust. The 17th-century farmhouse was her home up until her death, and the lovely surroundings of the village must have influenced her enchanting and essentially rural tales.

Continue along the B5285 and follow the north shore of Esthwaite Water.

ESTHWAITE WATER, Cumbria

Rowing boats can be hired by those wishing to explore this picturesque small lake by water, and its shores offer mountain views in which the 2,631ft peak of the Old Man of Coniston is prominent.

Continue to the edge of Hawkshead. A detour can be made from the main tour route to the Grizedale Wildlife Centre by driving forward, turning left on to an unclassified road SP 'Newby Bridge', then continuing for ¼ mile and turning right SP 'Grizedale'; proceed across Hawkshead Moor to reach Grizedale.

GRIZEDALE, Cumbria

The variety of wildlife to be seen in this region is superbly illustrated in the Forestry Commission's Visitor and Wildlife Centre at Grizedale. The deer exhibit is of particular note, and among the best of several planned walks in the area is the 1-mile Millwood forest trail. Take care against fire in dry weather.

On the main tour, turn right to skirt the village of Hawkshead.

HAWKSHEAD, Cumbria

Hawkshead's distinctive charm comes from its unspoilt stone cottages, courtyards, and narrow winding alleys. The 16th-century grammar school numbers Wordsworth among its past pupils. The poet lodged in Ann Tyson's cottage while he studied there. The cottage still stands and is noted for its unusual outside staircase. The picturesque Courthouse (NT) houses the Folk Museum of Rural Crafts.

Keep forward on to the B5286 SP 'Ambleside' and follow a winding road that affords fine views of the local countryside. Drive through Out Gate, and in 2 miles reach an unclassified right turn offering a detour to impressive Wray Castle.

WRAY CASTLE, Cumbria

Lovely grounds (open) surround the 19th-century extravagance of Wray Castle (not open) on the banks of Lake Windermere, sweeping right down to the water's edge. The castle, estate, and much of the attractive local countryside are protected by the National Trust.

On the main route, continue to the village of Clappersgate.

CLAPPERSGATE, Cumbria

Magnificently situated at the northern end of Lake Windermere, Clappersgate is best known for the beautiful floral displays that can be enjoyed in the White Craggs Garden (limited opening) during spring and summer.

Leave Clappersgate and turn right on to the A593. Continue, with fine views of Wansfell and 1,581ft Wansfell Pike ahead, and cross a river bridge. Turn left to enter Ambleside.

Ambleside

Evening gives a dramatic aspect to Morecambe Bay.

AMBLESIDE, Cumbria
Features of this very popular Lakeland tourist centre include a National Trust information office in tiny Bridge House. Excellent walking and climbing areas are nearby.

The area around Skelwith Bridge is graced by several lovely waterfalls.

Return along the A593 SP 'Coniston' and pass through Clappersgate. Cross Skelwith Bridge and continue along an undulating road with all-round mountain views. Tilberthwaite High Fells rise to the right, dominated by the strangely-shaped peak of 2,502ft Wetherlam. Continue, later driving below the steep slopes of the Coniston Fells with the Old Man of Coniston towering in the background, to Coniston.

CONISTON, Cumbria
This cluster of whitewashed cottages at the tip of lovely Coniston Water is a bright spot in a landscape dominated in the west by the 2,631ft Old Man of Coniston. A little farther west is the 2,555ft peak of Dow Crag, whose testing faces are popular with climbers. Features of the village itself include Coniston Old Hall, with its typical round Lakeland chimneys, and the Ruskin Museum. John Ruskin, the 19th-century writer and artist, loved this area and is buried in the local churchyard. Although the museum is devoted mostly to him, parts of it recall the death of the famous Donald Campbell.

Leave Coniston and turn left on to the B5285 SP 'Hawkshead' to skirt the northern end of Coniston Water.

CONISTON WATER, Cumbria
One shore of this tranquil 5½-mile-long lake is cloaked in the woodlands of Grizedale Forest, and the lake itself is famous as the place where Sir Donald Campbell died while trying to better the world water-speed record in 1965. Conditions were not ideal during the attempt, but its failure may not have been entirely due to the choppy surface and is still a matter for conjecture.

Keep left and climb through woodland, then in 1¾ miles turn left on to an unclassified road SP 'Tarn Hows'. In ¾ mile turn left again and ascend steeply to reach Tarn Hows.

Marvellous views of the Langdale Pikes and other famous Lakeland features can be enjoyed from the peaceful shores of picturesque Tarn Hows.

TARN HOWS, Cumbria
Arguably the most outstanding of many beautiful areas in the Lakeland region, Tarn Hows (NT) is a group of lakes and woodland in an area ringed by the peaks of mountains. Visitors are catered for with carparks and picnicking facilities.

Descend steeply along a narrow road SP 'Coniston', meet a T-junction, and turn right on to the B5285. Take the next turning left on to an unclassified road SP 'East of Lake' and follow the eastern shore of Coniston Water. In 1¾ miles reach Brantwood.

BRANTWOOD, Cumbria
This house (open), once the home of writer and artist John Ruskin, is now a museum containing examples of his work and a variety of personal possessions. The grounds feature fine gardens, a deer trail, and one of the best nature trails in the Lake District.

Continue along a winding road that hugs the shore of the lake, with views of several waterfalls to the right. Above the road to the left are the steep wooded slopes of Grizedale Forest. On the far side of the lake descend into the Crake Valley, passing the wooded Furness Fells on the left, and meet a T-junction. Turn left to reach Spark Bridge, then turn left again and in ¼ mile drive forward over crossroads SP 'Newby Bridge', then bear right and at T-junction turn left on to the A590 SP 'Bowness', then in 1¼ miles meet crossroads and turn right on to the B5278 SP 'Cark'. A detour from the main route to Rusland can be made by turning left at the crossroads instead of right.

RUSLAND, Cumbria
Rusland Hall (open) was built in 1720 and nowadays houses a museum of mechanical musical instruments and early photographic equipment. Its elegant landscaped grounds are the home of white peacocks.

On the main tour, continue along the B5278 to reach Haverthwaite.

HAVERTHWAITE, Cumbria
Steam-hauled trains on the standard-gauge Lakeside and Haverthwaite Railway connect with passenger steamers on Lake Windermere, at the other end of the line, and run 3½ miles through some of Lakeland's finest scenery.

Drive beyond Haverthwaite and bear right, then continue along the B5278 through thickly wooded countryside to reach Holker Hall.

HOLKER HALL, Cumbria
Originally built in the 16th century, this house (open) contains fine furniture and exquisite woodcarvings by local craftsmen. A motor museum exhibits over 100 cars and motorcycles, and the grounds include a deer park featuring a number of different species. During the summer Holker Hall is the scene of many local shows and events.

Proceed to Cark.

CARK, Cumbria
One of the main features in this pleasant little village is its 16th-century hall, which has mullioned windows and a grand 17th-century doorway.

Drive to the Rose and Crown Hotel and branch left on to an unclassified road. Continue to Cartmel.

CARTMEL, Cumbria
Little remains of the great priory (NT) that made this pleasant old town one of the most important religious centres for miles around, but the exceptionally beautiful priory church has survived. This large building was extended at various times up until the dissolution of the monasteries, after which it was left to decay until its restoration in 1618.

Keep forward, pass a school, and turn right SP 'Grange'. In 1 mile turn left into Grangefell Road and descend, with fine views over Morecambe Bay, for the return to Grange-over-Sands.

HELMSLEY, N Yorks

Helmsley is an old stone market town with venerable houses gathered about the borders of its spacious market square, which has an old market cross as its focal point. Among the buildings is the modest town hall and several old inns; the Black Swan has 2 Georgian houses and a 16th-century timber-framed house incorporated in it. All Saints Church, just off the square, was rebuilt in the 1860s, but retained some Norman characteristics. Walter L'espec, founder of Rievaulx Abbey, built Helmsley Castle (AM) in the 12th century. Although the stronghold rarely saw action, perhaps because of the strength still evident in the ruins of the great keep, tower and curtain walls, it did suffer a 3-month seige during the Civil War before being taken by Parliamentary forces. In 1689 Sir Charles Duncombe, a banker, bought the town of Helmsley and built Duncombe Park (now a school) and the picturesque ruins of the old castle lie in the grounds of the park.

Leave Helmsley on the B1257, SP 'Stokesley'. In 1½ miles turn left, SP 'Sawton'. Later descend through woodland before turning right for Rievaulx Abbey.

RIEVAULX ABBEY, N Yorks

Rievaulx Abbey (AM), magnificent even in ruin, lies in the richly-wooded valley of the River Rye and is a favourite subject of artists. Walter L'espec gave the site to the Cistercians in 1131, and this was the first church they built in the north of England. The ruins consist of the choir and transepts of the church, the lower walls of the nave and its attendant chapels, and the chapter house. Other remains include the shrine of the first abbot and the refectory. One of the best views of the abbey can be obtained from Rievaulx Terrace (AM), high up to the south, where 18th-century garden temples were built to take advantage of the delightful landscape. It belonged to Duncombe Park and the gentry used to drive out and enjoy the magnificent views.

Continue on the unclassified road and ascend to the junction with the B1257. To the right is the entrance to Rievaulx Terrace. Here, turn left, SP 'Stokesley', and climb to over 800ft before the descent into Blisdale.

BLISDALE, N Yorks

It was said that a Blisdale man left his dale so rarely that when he did he was regarded as a foreigner in his own county. It is only in comparatively recent times that a proper road was laid along the valley floor, giving the outside world access to one of the wildest and most picturesque dales in this part of Yorkshire. Between

THE LESSER-KNOWN DALES

Solid little market towns of grey stone dot the dales, above which rise the heather-clad slopes of the Cleveland Hills. Medieval monks found the peace and solitude they sought in the secluded river valleys of the North Riding, and here still stand the ruins of their beautiful abbeys.

Helmsley and Chop Gate the bubbling River Selph flows through a dale luxuriously wooded with birch and aromatic pine, but northwards, through Great Broughton to Stokesley, a moorland landscape emerges. Up on the high moors above the road are old coal-workings and lime pits — all that remains of the iron-smelting activities of the monks from Rievaulx Abbey.

Continue on the B1257 and beyond the hamlet of Chop Gate reach the summit of Clay Bank — a fine viewpoint. Descend from the Cleveland Hills to Great Broughton. In 2 miles, at the roundabout, take the 2nd exit to enter Stokesley.

STOKESLEY, N Yorks

This old market town of narrow, cobbled streets lies at the foot of the Cleveland Hills. At each end of the long market place is a green, and standing on an island in the middle is the 19th-century town hall. The River Leven runs along one side of the town and is spanned at frequent intervals by footbridges. Stokesley's many trees were planted in memory of Miss Jane Page, who, in 1836, emigrated to become the first white woman to settle in Victoria, Australia. Every September this normally quiet town explodes into activity when its fair and major agricultural show takes place.

Follow SP 'Thirsk (A172)'. In ¾ mile turn right on to the A172 and continue along the foot of the Cleveland Hills.

CLEVELAND HILLS, N Yorks/Cleveland

This great mass of sandstone hills runs in high ridges separated by secluded valleys and patches of open moorland; one of these is Urra Moor, at 1,500ft the highest point in the hills. The moorlands are famous for the bilberries which grow here, possibly an important part of the diet of the lost civilisation which left their burial chambers, tumuli, scattered all over the region. In winter snow covers the hills in a blanket, in summer they are carpeted in the glowing colours of flowering heather.

Remain on the A172 for 8 miles then branch left to join the A19. In ½ mile a track (left) may be taken to visit Mount Grace Priory.

MOUNT GRACE PRIORY, N Yorks

The old Carthusian monastery (AM, NT) was built towards the end of the 14th century by an order which vowed to austerity, isolation and silence. Within the inner cloister the remains of 15 cells survive, one of which has been restored. Hermit-monks lived in these self-contained apartments, working each day in their own private gardens and only meeting for services in the church and for a Saturday meal. On other days of the week their food was passed to them through a right-angled hatch so that the monks could not see or touch the server. It is a peaceful place, and pleasant to wander in, but the architecture, though softened by time, still reflects the grim austerity of its former inhabitants.

In another ½ mile branch left on to the A684 for Northallerton.

Top: the Fauconberg Arms in Coxwold dates from the 17th century. It still has the right to graze 4 cows on village land

Above: the striking ruins of Byland Abbey still show something of the great rose window that was 26ft in diameter

NORTHALLERTON, N Yorks

This old posting station retains many of its old inns in which travellers stayed while waiting for the stage coaches, which were given romantic names like the *High Flyer* and the *Wellington*. The town is built along a curving street, which broadens in the middle to form a market square, and narrows again at its north end near the church. There is a lot of Georgian housing, and a town hall, built in 1873, stands in the square.

Leave on the A168, SP 'Thirsk'. In 7 miles turn right on to the B1448 to enter Thirsk.

Sutton Bank, a dramatic escarpment of the Hambleton Hills, is a famous viewpoint. The white horse was cut in 1857

THIRSK, N Yorks

As an important coaching station, Thirsk once boasted 35 pubs and 4 breweries; determined, it would seem, to send travellers merrily on their way. Many of these establishments still ply their trade, perhaps foremost among them is the Georgian Golden Fleece Inn, formerly the most important coaching inn, and now the hub of the town on market days and race days. The vast square is still cobbled as it was when bull-baiting was held here in the 18th century. The church is probably the finest Perpendicular church in the county. Begun in 1430, it was founded on a chantry built by Robert Thirsk, who died in 1419. He was a member of the ancient family which gave the town its name.

From the one-way system leave on the A170, SP 'Scarborough'. Beyond Sutton-under-Whitestonecliffe climb on to the Hambleton Hills by means of Sutton Bank (1 in 4). Continue for 3¾ miles before turning right, then immediately right again, SP 'Wass' and 'Coxwold'. To the south-west of Wass short detours can be made to visit Byland Abbey, Coxwold and Newburgh Priory.

BYLAND ABBEY, N Yorks

Here stood the largest Cistercian church in the county. The great west front, incorporating the broken circle of what must have been a magnificent rose window, stands starkly with a single turret as a reminder of its past glory. The monks of Furness who founded it searched for 43 years for a suitable site, and after several false starts settled in the village of Old Byland, only to discover this was too close to the existing abbey at Rievaulx for comfort, so they moved to this pleasant broad valley, drained the marshes, and began to build. Until the Dissolution they led an uneventful life, apart from a visit by Edward II. He stayed briefly while fleeing the Scots whose country he had tried to conquer. Unfortunately, after he left the Scots followed, sacked the abbey and ousted the indignant monks as further punishment.

COXWOLD, N Yorks

Coxwold, with a wide sloping street lined with cottages of golden stone set back beyond broad green verges and spreading trees could be called the 'perfect' village. At one end the 15th-century church, with an unusual octagonal tower, serenely stands as guardian. Its fame as a beauty spot has brought many tourists, but the inhabitants have resolutely kept the village community, which has evolved over the centuries, intact. Fame also came to Coxwold in the form of Thomas Sterne, author of *The Life and Opinions of Tristram Shandy*. Sterne was a rector here for 7 years, and although he died and was buried in London, the Sterne Trust brought his remains back to the village churchyard. The Trust also owns the house in which he lived, Shandy Hall (OACT). It is an old brick farmhouse with medieval timber-framing and a warren of rooms.

NEWBURGH PRIORY, N Yorks

This is essentially an 18th-century hall (OACT) built on a site where Augustinian canons settled in 1150. It is set amid pleasant gardens featuring a pond and striking ornamental hedges. At the Dissolution Henry VIII gave the property to Anthony Belayse, who rebuilt the house. In time it passed to Lord Fauconberg, who, it is said, married a daughter of Oliver Cromwell's who brought her father's heart to Newburgh and had it bricked-up in an attic room of the house to save it from desecration. The vault has never been opened so the story has never been proved.

At Wass the main tour turns left, SP 'Ampleforth', and follows the foot of the Hambleton Hills to Ampleforth.

AMPLEFORTH, N Yorks

Perched upon a shelf of the Hambleton Hills, this village was chosen in 1802 as the site of a Roman Catholic school by English Benedictine monks who had fled from France to escape the French Revolution. The college and abbey of St Lawrence stands at the eastern end of the street along which most of the stone-built houses of the village are ranked, overlooking magnificent views towards Gilling Castle 2 miles to the south. Within the college library are some of Robert Thompson's earliest pieces of furniture. His much sought-after work is easily recognisable by the handcarved mouse he always hid somewhere on his furniture as his signature.

At the end of the village bear right, SP 'Oswaldkirk', and pass Ampleforth College. At Oswaldkirk keep forward and join the B1363, SP 'Helmsley', then in ¼ mile turn left on to the B1257. Continue to Sproxton and turn right on to the A170, SP 'Scarborough', for the return to Helmsley.

mls 0 1 2 3 4 5
kms 0 2 4 6 8

Stokesley
River Leven
Great Broughton
Carlton in Cleveland
CLAY BANK
Faceby
Urra
Swainby
HILLS
Chop Gate
CLEVELAND
Mount Grace Priory (ruins)
Osmotherley
Brompton
Ellerbeck
BILSDALE
Northallerton
Thornton-le-Beans
HAMBLETON
NEWGATE BANK
Thornton-le-Moor
River Rye
Rievaulx Terrace
Rievaulx Abbey
HELMSLEY
Thirsk
Gormire Lake
HILLS
Castle (ruins)
Sutton Bank
Sproxton
Sutton-under-Whitestonecliffe
Wass Moor
Byland Abbey
Ampleforth
Wass
College
Oswaldkirk
Coxwold
Shandy Hall NT
Newburgh Priory
River Swale

HADRIAN'S WALL

Along the length of the great wall the Emperor Hadrian built to protect England from the fierce Picts is a wealth of Roman remains; temples to the god Mithras, great forts and little townships, all set in a magnificent countryside of sweeping views and desolate quiet.

HEXHAM, Northumb
Hexham grew up around the entrance to the abbey which St Wilfred founded in 674, and the buildings nearest the abbey are therefore some of Hexham's oldest. Opposite the abbey church is the Moot Hall, originally the gatehouse to a 12th-century castle. In its time this has served as a Bishop's Palace, and up until 1838 was the town court: now it is the borough library. The archway beneath the Moot Hall leads to the Manor Office. This former medieval prison dealt with all the business of the Manor of Hexham from Elizabeth I's reign up until about the 1870's. Close by, overlooking the Tyne valley, is an attractive whitewashed building which was the old grammer school. The plight of its predecessor was an unhappy one, for in 1296 200 scholars were burnt alive by Scottish raiders, who also destroyed the abbey. St. Wilfred's Church was built from Roman stones taken from *Corstopitum*, near Corbridge, and of this original church the foundations of the apse, piers of the nave and the crypt remain. An Augustinian priory took over the church from the Saxon bishops in 1116, and they built the beautiful choir and transept, including the survival of the almost unique canon's Night Stair to the dormitory. The nave, destroyed by the Scottish raid, was not rebuilt until 1908. Treasurers of the past within the church include the Frith Stool, thought to be the throne upon which Northumbrian kings were crowned, later also used as a sanctuary stool. In the south transept is a remarkable Roman memorial to Flavinius, a standard-bearer, depicted mounted upon a horse astride a cowering Briton with a drawn dagger.

Leave Hexham on the A6079, SP 'Carlisle', and cross the Tyne. At the roundabout take the A69 then in ¾ mile turn right on to the A6079, SP 'Rothbury', and pass the edge of Acomb to Wall. In 1 mile, at the crossroads, turn left on to the B6318, then recross the Tyne for Chollerford.

CHOLLERFORD, Northumb
Chollerford's fine bridge dating from 1771 lies with the rest of the village near the site of *Cilurnum*, an important Roman station on the banks of the North Tyne. It

stands in Chesters Park (not open), a stately mansion which was once the home of John Clayton, archaeologist and antiquary, who pioneered the excavation of *Cilurnum*. Today most of the plan of the camp has been unearthed, and at the entrance to the site is a fascinating museum. Artefacts which have been recovered from this site are displayed within, as well as relics found along Hadrian's Wall, ranging from coins to mill-stones and including jewellery and everyday objects of Roman life.

At the roundabout take the 1st exit, SP 'Carlisle', and pass Chesters Park (left). Follow the line of Hadrian's Wall to Carrawbrough.

HADRIAN'S WALL, Northumb
Stretching across the width of Britain between Solway and Tyne, Hadrian's Wall was begun in AD122 by Emperor Hadrian to keep the barbarians from the north at bay. It took 7 years to build and required some 15,000 men to defend it. On the north side of the wall a steep ditch was constructed and to the south a flat-bottomed ditch and a road. The southern defence was found necessary to prevent the conquered tribes pilfering from the well-fed Roman soldiers. Further fortification was provided by small forts, called milecastles, at 1 mile intervals, and watch-turrets at every ⅓ mile. In addition, 17 auxiliary forts were placed on or near the wall. The skill of the Roman engineers in taking advantage of the lie of the land resulted in the wall crossing some splendid countryside, with magnificent views from the many walks which can be taken along its length.

CARRAWBROUGH, Northumb
Although this fort was a later addition to the fortifications of Hadrian's Wall, there is little left to see apart from the grassy ramparts. However, what has been uncovered is a Mithraeum temple. For some reason the deity of Mithras was especially popular among soldiers, but although it was a wide-spread religion, the groups of its followers were small, and so the temple buildings were small. Carrawbrough is no exception, the whole building measuring no more than 35ft by 15ft. The central passage is guarded by statues of lesser gods,

Above: the precipitous crags beneath Hadrian's Wall near Housesteads meant there was no need to build ditch barriers

Right: Blanchland was named after the white canons who founded the abbey here

leading up to the 3 main carved alters. Angry Christians destroyed the temple, not so much disturbed by the morality of the religion as by its close parallels with Christian rites, such as its similar baptism and communion.

Continue on the B6318 and in 5 miles reach the car park for Housesteads.

HOUSESTEADS, Northumb
This was the ancient Roman fort of *Vercovicium*, set astride a ridge in wild frontier country with magnificent views to the north and south. What has been excavated within the fort walls show that here were granaries, a commandant's house, military headquarters, a hospital, latrines, baths and barracks — a miniature town in fact. Outside the walls a civilian settlement grew up, and here are the remains of long narrow shops and inns, which had sliding shutters to the street fronts. In one of these the bodies of a man and a woman of the 4th century were found. A dagger was

embedded in the man's ribs, which prompted the excavators to name the house Murder House. The site museum contains many finds from the excavation.

Continue on the B6138 and after 3 miles pass a Northumberland National Park Information Centre, next to the Twice Brewed Inn. In another 2½ miles, at a crossroads, turn left, SP 'Haltwhistle'. A mile farther descend into the South Tyne valley then turn right into Haltwhistle.

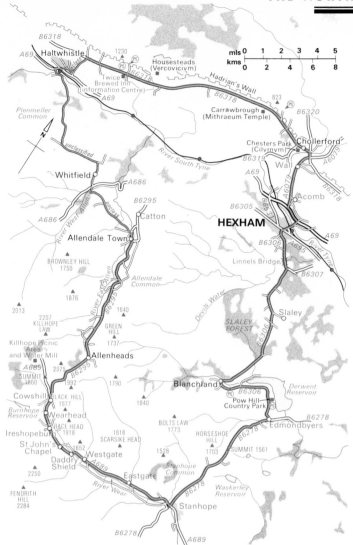

HALTWHISTLE, Northumb
This small industrial town lies between the junction of Haltwhistle Burn and the South Tyne, and is an excellent touring centre for Hadrian's Wall, which lies a little to the north. The towerless Holy Cross Church, hidden by trees and surrounded by houses, is considered a superb example of early English architecture.

Continue through the town and turn left, SP 'Carlisle', then turn right on to the A69. In ½ mile turn left on to the Plenmeller/ Whitfield road. Cross the River Tyne and turn left. After 4 miles turn left and 2¼ miles farther turn right, then descend into West Allen Dale for Whitfield.

WHITFIELD, Northumb
In all Allendale there is no prettier village than Whitfield, set amid trees by the banks of the West Allen River. Whitfield has 2 churches, known as the 'Old' and the 'New'. The 'Old' is St John's, a Georgian building with Victorian alterations, which lies hidden off the main road; the 'New' is all Victorian, rather out of character in the dales, looking as though it has been transplanted from the gentler landscape of southern England.

Turn right on to the A686, SP 'Alston', then in ¼ mile turn left, SP 'Allendale'. Cross the West Allen River and in 3½ miles go forward to join the B6295. In ½ mile cross the East Allen River and ascend to Allendale Town.

ALLENDALE TOWN, Northumb
A sundial, set in a wall near the 14th-century church high up on the wooded banks of the River East Allen, records longditude and latitude, for Allendale claims to be the centre of Britain. The solid little town has a stone-built market place, and an attractive main street enhanced by trees and greens. The many boarding houses and hotels attract the same visitors every year, for this pleasant village is set in fine hill and dale country, and is superbly situated as a touring centre. New Year's Eve is a big occasion here. It is celebrated with a huge bonfire at midnight, and by a procession of costumed men parading the streets carrying tubs of blazing tar on their heads — a curious custom thought to have originated from a form of fire worship introduced by the Norsemen.

Turn right on to the the Allenheads/ Cowshill road and follow East Allen Dale over the lofty and bleak Allendale Common to reach Allenheads.

Remains of the bath house at the Roman fort of *Cilurnum*. It was a complex of rooms consisting of changing rooms and a series of hot and cold baths

ALLENHEADS, Northumb
At one time a seventh of all lead mined in the Kingdom once came from near Allenheads, although now the workings are all long grown over, in some areas producing a strange irregular landscape. The hamlet of Allenheads lies snugly in a pine-covered enclave surrounded by bare moorland criss-crossed by stone walls at the head of wide East Allendale.

Continue on the B6295 and in 1½ miles, at the summit (1,860ft), enter the county of Durham. Descend and in 1¾ miles join the A689 Durham/Stanhope road. Continue through Cowshill, Wearhead and St Johns Chapel then Daddry Shield, Westgate and Eastgate. At the Grey Bull PH at the edge of Stanhope turn left on to the B6278, SP 'Edmondbyers'. In ½ mile a steep climb leads to Stanhope Common and 2 miles farther bear right. Later turn left on to the B6306, SP 'Blanchland', and after 1 mile a side road (right) leads to Pow Hill Country Park.

POW HILL COUNTRY PARK, Durham
This delightful park is set in beautiful countryside in a sheltered valley above Derwent Reservoir. Waders and waterfowl can be seen here, which are best observed from a specially constructed hide beside the reservoir. Car parks, a picnic area and other amenities have been provided for the convenience of visitors and the protection of the wildlife.

Continue on the B6306 and in 3½ miles cross the River Derwent to re-enter Northumberland and continue to Blanchland.

BLANCHLAND, Northumb
Blanchland has a neat, orderly appearance, its grey-stone cottages arranged around an L-shaped, gravelled 'square'. The village occupies the site of a 12th-century abbey; the square was previously the abbey courtyard and the Lord Crewe Arms was part of the abbey's guesthouse; the monastery gateway is still one of the entrances to the village. Hidden deep in wild moorland, a story tells of how in 1327 Scottish raiders bent on sacking the abbey got lost in a mist, and decided to return home. The monks, hearing of this, were so joyous they rang the abbey bells in celebration. Unfortunately the Scots heard the bells too and, guided by their sound, returned.

Turn right, SP 'Hexham', then ascend. There are more views of the Derwent Reservoir to the right. After 2 miles keep left and continue past the edge of Shaley and cross the Devil's Water at the narrow Linnels Bridge (care needed) before the return to Hexham.

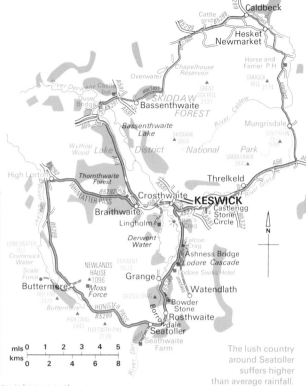

THE NORTHERN LAKE DISTRICT

This is a district of beautiful mountains and lakes, heathery slopes dotted with sheep and boulders between valley woodland and the misty blueness of windswept crags. Much of the countryside is owned or protected by the National Trust, whose codes of conduct should be respected.

KESWICK, Cumbria
This touring centre is close to some of Lakeland's finest scenery and attracts thousands of visitors every year. In Victorian times it was beloved of poets and artists, including such notables as Wordsworth, Coleridge, Southey, Ruskin, and Walpole. Many of their works and personal possessions are preserved in the fascinating Park Museum, which also features an impressive scale model of the Lake District and a variety of exhibits relating to the local area. Both Coleridge and Southey lived in Greta Park at different times, and there is a memorial to John Ruskin close to the town on the spectacular viewpoint of Friar's Crag (NT). Moot Hall is a handsome building that was reconstructed in the early 19th century. The superb 529ft viewpoint of Castle Head (NT) is within easy reach of Keswick.

Before starting the main route it is possible to take two rewarding detours to interesting areas close to the boundaries of Keswick. The first of these can be taken to Crosthwaite by driving through Keswick on the A5271 'Cockermouth' road before keeping forward on to the B5289 to reach the village.

CROSTHWAITE, Cumbria
Keswick's lovely 11th-century and later parish church is sited here, and is well worth a visit. Among its many treasures are several fine monuments, 21 consecration crosses, and the churchyard grave of poet and writer Robert Southey.

For the second detour, continue along the B5289 from Crosthwaite for ⅓ mile, bear left, then turn left to join the A66. Again a further ¼ mile turn left again on to an unclassified road SP 'Portinscale' to enter Portinscale village. Here turn right to reach Lingholm Gardens.

LINGHOLM GARDENS, Cumbria
The superb landscaped gardens of Lingholm (open), the home of Lord Rochdale, are laid out in a charming situation on the wooded western shores of Derwent Water. In spring the ground is golden with the famous Lakeland daffodils, and later in the year the banks of rhododendron bushes and azaleas blaze with colour.

DERWENT WATER, Cumbria
Typical of everything that is beautiful in the Lake District, this broad lake is ringed by mountain peaks and dotted with mysterious little tree-clad islands. It measures 3 miles long by 1½ miles wide at its widest point, and is best appreciated from the lofty Friar's Crag Viewpoint (NT), back along the route. At the foot of the crag is the start of a nature trail that runs for about 2 miles along the shoreline of the lake.

To start the main tour, leave Keswick on the B5289 'Borrowdale' road and pass the Friar's Crag Viewpoint (NT) on the right. Drive beneath Castle Head (NT) on the left and reach the eastern shores of Derwent Water. Steep wooded slopes rise to the left, and farther on the road runs beneath the cliffs of the Falcon Crag Viewpoint. A detour can be taken from the main route to Ashness Bridge and Watendlath by reaching Falcon Crag and then turning left on to a winding unclassified road.

ASHNESS BRIDGE, Cumbria
Thousands of visitors come here every year to admire the unique and enchanting combination of a single-arched packhorse bridge with beautiful falls on the little mountain stream which it spans.

Continue this detour by following the unclassified road to Watendlath.

Derwent Water is known as the queen of the lakes, deriving much of its beauty from the many islands.

WATENDLATH, Cumbria
A small beck which rises close to this delightful little hamlet (NT) threads its way through a pretty valley and joins Watendlath Tarn, which lies in the shadow of 1,588ft Armboth Fell.

On the main tour, drive forward on the B5289. Continue, with excellent views of the lake, and in 1 mile reach the Lodore Swiss Hotel and the impressive Lodore Cascade.

LODORE CASCADE, Cumbria
Views of this spectacular waterfall, which is situated at the southern extremity of Derwent Water, can be enjoyed from the carpark of the Lodore Swiss Hotel.

Drive through the short, green valley of Borrowdale, keeping to the left bank of the River Derwent, and in 1¾ miles pass Grange village on the righthand side of the road.

GRANGE, Cumbria
A double-arched bridge spans the River Derwent in this lovely little Borrowdale village. Superb views of the dale can be enjoyed from the summit of Grange Fell, which is known as King's How (NT).

Leave Grange and in ½ mile pass a track leading left to the Bowder Stone.

BOWDER STONE, Cumbria
Although this remarkable 2,000-ton boulder (NT) seems about to fall from its precarious perch at any moment, it is quite firm and makes a good vantage point from which to survey the surrounding countryside.

Continue through Borrowdale to Rosthwaite.

ROSTHWAITE, Cumbria
As Borrowdale opens out on the approach to this tiny village the views widen into a spectacular panorama of the mountains ahead. Massive Castle Crag (NT) dominates a narrow pass known as the Jaws of Borrowdale, rising high above the valley floor to a 900ft summit.

BORROWDALE, Cumbria
Much of Borrowdale, the beautiful valley through which the last section of tour has just passed, is owned or protected by the National Trust. Its impressive crags and fells offer a challenge which draws climbers and walkers from many parts of the country, and its tiny unspoilt villages are an essential part of the tranquillity that underlies its scenic grandeur. The southern end of the dale is dominated by the summits of 2,560ft Glaramara and 2,984ft Great End, and the north by high fells.

Continue along the B5289 to reach the village of Seatoller.

The lush country around Seatoller suffers higher than average rainfall.

mls 0 1 2 3 4 5

kms 0 2 4 6 8

SEATOLLER, Cumbria
During the 17th and 18th century this village was the centre of a busy mining industry. Seatoller is now known as a base from which walkers can ascend to the Sky Head Pass, in the south. Also south of the village is Seathwaite Farm (NT), one of England's wettest inhabited places.

A detour from the main route to Seathwaite Farm can be made by turning left in Seatoller on to an unclassified road and following a deep, steep-sided valley to the farm. On the main tour, continue along the B5289 and ascend Honister Pass.

HONISTER PASS, Cumbria
This part of the tour follows a steep, difficult road but offers some of the most spectacular scenery in the whole region. The summit of the pass is 1,176ft above sea level and affords distant eastern views of the craggy Helvellyn group, beyond the picturesque foreground of Borrowdale. Left towards Buttermere are the outstanding peaks of 2,479ft Red Pike and 2,644ft High Stile.

Descend between scree-covered slopes to the village of Buttermere.

BUTTERMERE, Cumbria
Well-situated between Crummock Water and the lake (NT) from which it derives its name, this pretty village stands in the heart of a spectacular landscape and is a popular base for walkers and climbers. Opposite the village curiously-named Sour Milk Ghyll tumbles down the flanks of lofty Red Pike. Scale Force, among the highest waterfalls in the Lake District, is nearby.

A detour from the main route to Newlands Hause and Moss Force can be made by driving to the outskirts of the village, turning right on to an unclassified road SP 'Keswick', and climbing steeply.

NEWLANDS HAUSE AND MOSS FORCE, Cumbria
Here the road climbs through the spectacular pass of Newlands Hause to a summit of 1,096ft, with an almost sheer drop plunging away into a deep valley on the left.

On the main tour, leave Buttermere village with the B5289 and follow the

Set amid mountains in one of Lakeland's most beautiful areas, Buttermere Lake is famous for the reflections that crowd its surface on calm days.

east shore of Crummock Water with views of the Loweswater Fell peaks on the far side of the lake. Leave the lakeside and after 2 miles meet a T-junction. Turn right SP 'Lorton, Cockermouth' and enter the broad expanse of Lorton Vale. Continue to the edge of Lorton and turn right on to an unclassified road SP 'Keswick'. Continue to High Lorton, turn left into the village, and at the end of the village turn right. Meet a T-junction and turn right again on to the B5292 and begin to ascend Whinlatter Pass.

WHINLATTER PASS, Cumbria
Drivers will find this one of the less taxing Lake District passes. Its gradients are reasonable and its bends are not quite as sharp as the others, but its 1,043ft summit affords views that are every bit as enjoyable as elsewhere.

THORNTHWAITE FOREST, Cumbria
Woodland walks planned by the Forestry Commission help the visitor to get the most out of this lovely area, the longest established national forest in the Lake District. Detailed information about all aspects of the forest is available from the Interpretative Centre near the summit of Whinlatter Pass.

Descend from the forest with fine views over Bassenthwaite Lake to the left. At the foot of the descent keep left into Braithwaite.

BRAITHWAITE, Cumbria
Climbers heading for the slopes and faces of 2,593ft Grisedale Pike generally start from this attractive village, which lies at the head of Coledale Valley.

Leave Braithwaite and take the 2nd turning left SP 'Cockermouth'. In ¼ mile turn left again on to the A66 and drive to the western shore of Bassenthwaite Lake.

BASSENTHWAITE LAKE, Cumbria
Opposite this wooded shore, towering above the peaceful waters of lovely Bassenthwaite Lake, are the stern slopes of 3,053ft Skiddaw.

After 2¼ miles turn right on to the B5291 SP 'Castle Inn', then turn right again to follow the northern end of Bassenthwaite Lake. In 1 mile turn right SP 'Bothel', cross Ouse Bridge, and continue to Castle Inn. Meet a T-junction and turn right on to the A591. Take the 2nd turning left on to an unclassified road SP 'Bassenthwaite' and approach that village.

BASSENTHWAITE, Cumbria
Close to the lake in charming surroundings is the village church, which was restored in Victorian times and has a Norman chancel arch.

Do not enter the village on the main tour, but on its approach keep left (no SP) on to a narrow road and drive through pretty woodland. In 1½ miles meet a T-junction and turn left SP 'Caldbeck', then ascend a winding road to pass Over Water and smaller Chapelhouse Reservoir on the left. After 2½ miles cross open moors and meet a T-junction. Turn right, and in ¾ mile keep forward on to the B5299. In 1¼ miles cross a cattle grid, and in ¼ mile keep left to reach Caldbeck.

CALDBECK, Cumbria
In 1854 the local folk hero of nursery song fame, John Peel, was buried in Caldbeck churchyard. According to tradition he was ruined by his obsessive love of fox hunting.

Drive forward on to an unclassified road and proceed to Hesket Newmarket.

HESKET NEWMARKET, Cumbria
At one time this charming village on the northern flanks of Skiddaw was an important market town. Nowadays it rests in quiet retirement as yet another of the Lake District's picturesque communities.

Drive to the end of the village and bear right SP 'Mungrisdale'. Continue through agricultural country and in ½ mile bear right. In 1 mile turn left on to a winding road and continue to the Horse and Farrier (PH). Just beyond the PH bear right on to moorland and drive below the sheer rock face of 2,174ft Carrock Fell. Continue through Mungrisdale, pass below Souther Fell, then meet a T-junction with the A66 and turn right SP 'Keswick'; 2,847ft Saddleback rises to the right. Continue to the outskirts of Threlkeld; the main village lies just off the main road to the right.

THRELKELD, Cumbria
No less than 35 local huntsmen are commemorated by a monument in the local churchyard, and it seems likely that the fanatical John Peel would have made many friends here. The village itself stands at the head of St John's Vale, on the banks of a stream that threads its way along the valley floor. North is the unusually shaped peak of Saddleback.

Continue along the A66 and pass the junction with the B5322. In ¼ mile turn left on to an unclassified road SP 'St John's in the Vale Church', and in 1 mile turn left again SP 'Stone Circle'. In ¼ mile turn left and ascend to the Castlerigg Stone Circle.

CASTLERIGG STONE CIRCLE, Cumbria
Situated in a superb mountain setting some 700ft above sea level, this prehistoric circle (AM, NT) measures over 100ft in diameter and is made up of 38 stones. An oblong space on the site contains another 10 stones.

Continue past the stone circle and descend to meet the A5271. Turn left and re-enter Keswick.

Castlerigg Stone Circle probably dates back to the bronze age.

MORECAMBE BAY AND THE LANCASHIRE MOORS

Between Morecambe Bay and the western edge of the Yorkshire Dales stretch the wild, remote moors of the Forest of Bowland, the haunt of grouse and hardy moorland sheep. North and west the steep fells drop down to one of the loveliest valleys in Lancashire, that of the River Lune, painted by Turner and extolled by Ruskin.

This lonely pass across the Forest of Bowland is called the Trough of Bowland

MORECAMBE, Lancs
Second in popularity only to Blackpool as a holiday resort for the north-west, Morecambe has excellent sands and a wealth of seaside entertainments, culminating in the famous 'illuminations' which take place every autumn. Its Marineland complex, billed as the first oceanarium ever built in Europe, boasts a vast swimming pool as well as a dolphinarium and fascinating aquaria displaying all types of marine life. The name Morecambe, as it applies to the town, is of very recent date. Until the railway era in the last century there was only a fishing village, Poulton-le-Sands, here. When the railway line was built, the new resort sprang up, engulfing not only Poulton but also the neighbouring villages of Bare and Torrisholme, and came to be known as Morecambe, which had formerly been simply the name of the bay.

Leave Morecambe on the A5105, SP 'The North and Hest Bank', and follow the seafront to Hest Bank.

HEST BANK, Lancs
From Hest Bank, there is a magnificent view of the bay to the hills of the Lake District. Morecambe Bay was, until the last century, the regular route to and from the Lake District. It was always a perilous journey, as there are shifting sands and 3 treacherous river estuaries to negotiate. Many people lost their lives, and the guides were even known to abandon travellers to their fate if they had not sufficient money to pay the charges. The 3-hour walk at low tide along the beach to Grange-over-Sands is still popular, but it must not be undertaken without an official guide, as the estuaries and shifting sands are a definite hazard.

Continue on the A5105 and in 1 mile turn left on to the A6, SP 'Kendal'. Pass through Bolton-le-Sands to reach Carnforth.

CARNFORTH, Lancs
To railway enthusiasts a visit to Steamtown, the railway museum that now occupies Carnforth's old locomotive sheds and marshalling yards, is a must. The *Flying Scotsman* is the most famous of the 30 steam engines from Great Britain, France and Germany that are maintained here. In the summer season, engines are in steam on Sundays (daily in July and August) and rides in vintage coaches are an added attraction.

On entering the town turn left (one-way), SP 'Warton', and shortly turn left again. Pass the railway museum (left) and continue to Warton.

WARTON, Lancs
The arms of the Washington family, ancestors of George Washington, once decorated the church tower and are now preserved inside the 15th-century church of this pleasant village. Although age has made it difficult to distinguish the symbols, it is said that this coat of arms was the inspiration of the stars and stripes motif of the United States flag. The last member of the English Washington family, Thomas, was the vicar of Warton until 1823.

Remain on the unclassified road for Yealand Conyers.

YEALAND CONYERS, Lancs
Tucked away in the far north of the county, Yealand Conyers is an outstandingly attractive village whose stone-built houses are fine examples of traditional architecture. An early Friends' Meeting House reminds the visitor that this is what the Quakers call '1652 country' because in that year the founder of the movement, George Fox (1624-91), first came into North Lancashire to preach.

From here a turning on the left leads to Leighton Hall.

LEIGHTON HALL, Lancs
Sheltering under Warton Crag, Leighton Hall (OACT) stands in extensive grounds. The Hall, built on the site of an earlier medieval one, dates from 1760-63, a Classical stone mansion with a charming Gothic façade that was added in the early 19th century. The home of the Gillow family for generations, their descendants still live here. In 1826 the estate was bought by Richard Gillow, a distinguished Lancaster furniture maker, and the house is a showplace for his artistry. There is a large collection of Birds of Prey with regular flying displays.

The main tour continues to Yealand Redmayne. Near the end of the village turn right, SP 'Kendal' on to a narrow byroad. In ¾ mile cross the M6 (no SP), then pass over the railway line, canal and M6 to reach the edge of Burton. Here turn left, then take the next turning right on to the Kirkby Lonsdale road. In 4¼ miles bear right and descend into Whittington. In the village turn left on to the B6254 and continue to Kirkby Lonsdale.

KIRKBY LONSDALE, Cumbria
Devil's Bridge (AM), 3-arched and possibly as old as the 13th century, spans the River Lune outside Kirkby. One of the finest ancient bridges in the country, it is now closed to traffic. Kirkby is a delightful small market town and it is an excellent centre for exploring the Lune valley. John Ruskin, the 19th-century writer and painter, was captivated by this, describing his favourite view as 'one of the loveliest scenes in England and therefore in the world'. Ruskin walks are signposted north of the churchyard.

Leave on the A65, SP 'Skipton', and re-enter Lancashire before reaching Cowan Bridge.

COWAN BRIDGE, Lancs
A few cottages mark the site of the Clergy Daughters' School to which Charlotte and Emily Brontë were sent as boarders from 1824-5. Later Charlotte was to describe the harsh treatment they suffered in her novel *Jane Eyre*, where the school appears under the name of Lowood.

In 1¾ miles enter North Yorkshire. In 2 miles a turning to the left may be taken to visit Ingleton.

INGLETON, N Yorks
Ingleton thrives as a centre for climbers, potholers and visitors to the Yorkshire Dales. The limestone hills of this region are honeycombed with caves, most of which are accessible only to experienced potholers, but the White Scar caves, with their stalactites, stalagmites, underground river and lake, are a noted tourist attraction. Above Ingleton loom the heights of Whernside (2,419ft) and Ingleborough (2,373ft). With Penyghent, these peaks are the most formidable in the Dales, and a walk taking in all 3 is a favourite feat of endurance for fell walkers. Even more gruelling are the 3-peaks races, one for runners and one for cyclists.

Continue on the A65 and after 4 miles pass the turning for Clapham.

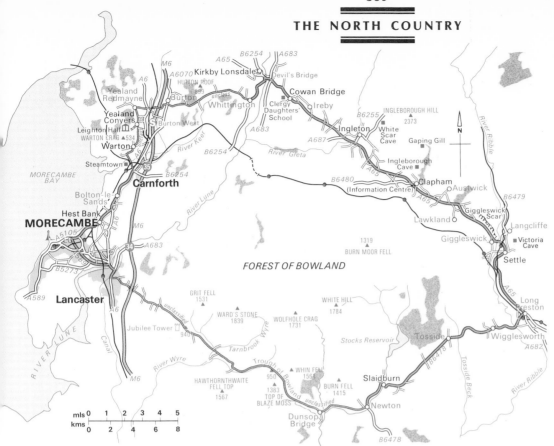

FOREST OF BOWLAND, Lancs
This wild region of grouse moor and high fells, dissected by deep, narrow valleys, was one of the ancient royal forests of Saxon England. There are no towns and few villages in the Forest, and no roads cross it, except for the lonely moorland road from Newton through the pass known as the Trough of Bowland to Lancaster. Parts of the Forest have now been designated an Area of Outstanding Natural Beauty and are therefore accessible, but much of the area remains a wilderness.

Continue on the unclassified road towards Lancaster. On entering the suburbs follow SP for city centre.

LANCASTER, Lancs
Lancaster, county town of the shire, was throughout the 18th century England's chief port for trade with America. St George's Quay, the elegant Customs House designed by Robert Gillow, whose family were famous furniture makers, and the many Georgian houses around the centre, are eloquent reminders of this prosperous era. The massive keep of the castle, 78ft high with walls 10ft thick, dates from the Norman era, when virtually the whole of Lancashire was given to Roger de Poitou by William the Conqueror. The castle was enlarged by King John and its magnificent gateway was built by John of Gaunt, 1st Duke of Lancaster, in the 14th century. The castle also served, and still does, as the county gaol. Among many distinguished prisoners was the Quaker leader George Fox, who was incarcerated in appalling conditions in the 17th century. Earlier in the same century, in 1612, the famous trial of the Lancashire Witches was held in Lancaster, and the iron rings by which they were chained can still be seen in the Well Tower. The City Museum in the Market Square is also the Museum of the Royal Lancashire Regiment.

Leave on the A589 for the return to Morecambe.

CLAPHAM, N Yorks
Stone-built cottages in trim little gardens straggling along the banks of a stream characterise this delightful Yorkshire village where a National Information Centre for the Yorkshire Dales is situated, and where the monthly *Dalesman* magazine is published. Like Ingleton, this is a noted potholing centre. To the north of the village is Ingleborough Cave (access by foot only). The famous Gaping Gill pothole, 378ft deep with a central chamber vast enough to hold a small cathedral, lies not far away.

Remain on the A65 for Settle.

SETTLE, N Yorks
Just outside Settle rises one of the most impressive natural features of the region, the massive rock wall of Giggleswick Scar. Settle itself is one of the most delightful towns in Ribblesdale, with picturesque narrow streets and Georgian houses, sometimes

Leighton Hall's façade, built of a white local limestone, was added in 1810

grouped around small courtyards. Castleberg Crag, 300ft high, dominates the town centre, and from the summit the visitor can enjoy panoramic views of the town and the surrounding dales. In 1838 a chance discovery of the feature now known as Victoria Cave led to the retrieval of many fascinating prehistoric remains, including the bones of animals long extinct in the British Isles.

Leave on the A65 Skipton road and follow Ribblesdale to Long Preston. Here turn right on to the B6478, SP 'Slaidburn'. Beyond Wigglesworth gradually climb through moorland countryside to Tosside. Re-enter Lancashire and later descend to reach Slaidburn.

Displays of heraldic shields and coats of arms of all sovereigns since Richard 1 adorn the Shire Hall in Lancaster Castle

SLAIDBURN, Lancs
Although only a village, Slaidburn was for centuries the administrative 'capital' of the Forest of Bowland, and boasted the only grammar school for miles around. The Forest 'court' next to the inn was in use until the outbreak of World War I. The inn itself bears the unique name of Hark to Bounty. The story goes that Bounty was a foxhound belonging to a local vicar and that whenever his master and other hunting friends were in the inn, Bounty's barking was easily distinguishable above the hullabaloo of the whole pack.

At the war memorial keep left, then turn left, SP 'Trough of Bowland'. At Newton continue forward to reach Dunsop Bridge. After crossing the river bridge turn right and later ascend the Trough of Bowland.

MORPETH, Northumb

Quiet prosperity came to Morpeth in the early 18th century as it was the last market in Northumberland on the cattle route down to the south. Although the railway age subsequently made such markets largely redundant, Morpeth has remained a busy country town. In the old market place there stands a 17th-century tower whose curfew bell is rung at 8 o'clock every evening. The town hall, an elegant structure dating from 1718, was designed by the architect Vanbrugh. The imposing bridge was built at a later date, 1831, across the River Wansbeck which intersects the town. It leads to the parish church, set well away from the town centre on high ground. The church has a refreshingly plain 14th-century interior and in the churchyard is a little watch tower, built in 1831 to help restrict the practice of body-snatching. Behind the church lie impressive earthworks of the castle which was built after the Conquest but little masonry is left of the noble fortress which looked over the river and town. Around Morpeth the banks of the river are pleasantly wooded, and in the town itself a park runs along part of it. Every year Northumberland miners mix pleasure and politics at the gala held in the park.

Leave on the A192, SP 'Alnwick'. In 1½ miles, at the roundabout, join the A1, then in ¼ mile branch left on to the A697, SP 'Coldstream'. Pass through Longhorsley and in 2¾ miles turn left on to the B6344, SP 'Rothbury', to enter the Coquet valley. In 1½ miles a short detour to the left leads to Brinkburn Priory.

BRINKBURN PRIORY, Northumb

Within a loop of the River Coquet in charmingly wooded parkland stands a possible rival in grandeur to the abbeys of Fountains and Tintern. Although Brinkburn (AM) is a 12th-century church, it has all the hallmarks of a great cathedral. It was a roofless ruin by 1858, but the architect Thomas Dobson restored it superbly in that year.

Continue along the B6344 and in 3½ miles pass the fine hillside grounds of the Cragside Estate on the right.

CRAGSIDE ESTATE, Northumb

The 1st Lord Armstrong commissioned architect Norman Shaw in 1863 to design this delightfully romantic house. However, the real attraction to Cragside (NT) is the gardens. The house is built high above the River Coquet on a plateau where rock gardens, artificial lakes and masses of rhododendrons and azaleas create an enchanting landscape. The house itself claims its place in history as being one of the first houses in the world to be powered by electricity.

NORTHUMBERLAND'S QUIET LOWLANDS

'Northumberland may claim to the least spoiled, least known, county of England' and this proves true as the tour travels through the remote countryside between the Cheviots and Hadrian's Wall, by way of peaceful valleys and stone-built villages.

Shortly join the B6341 to enter Rothbury.

ROTHBURY, Northumb

Hill and river country surrounds the little town of Rothbury, whose name means a clearing in the forest. It is typical of the Border towns; solid, stone-built houses lining, in this case, a steep wide street where the verges are planted with trees. This was a lawless town, and at the time of the Reformation thieving by the inhabitants of Rothbury was such an art that 'they could twist a cow's horn or mark a horse so that its owner would not know it'.

Keep forward through the town on the B6341, SP 'Otterburn', to Thropton.

THROPTON, Northumb

Built on either side of the River Coquet, Thropton lies in the stunning countryside of Simonside. This pretty but straggling village is dominated by Simonside itself, the 1409ft-high peak giving its name to the whole range of sandstone hills, which, it is said, can be seen from every corner of Northumberland. Here the heather-clad hills contrast strongly with the gentle arable land of the lower reaches of Coquetdale, especially in August when the hills are purple with the flowering heather and the lower fields are a carpet of golden corn.

Continue on the B6341 for 2¼ miles then turn right, SP 'Harbottle'. In 3 miles descend and cross the River Coquet, then turn left for Holystone.

7 million trees were planted on the Cragside Estate in the 19th century, which helped transform it from a barren hillside into a magnificent garden

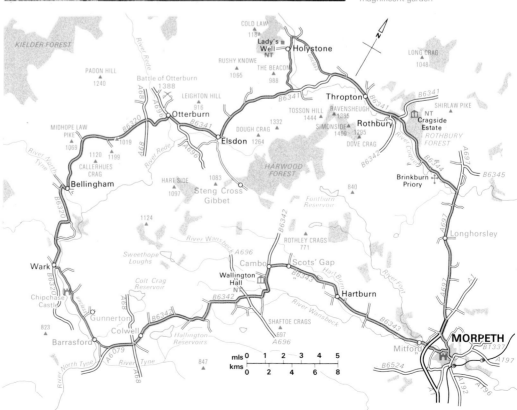

HOLYSTONE, Northumb

In the upper reaches of Coquetdale is the pleasing village of Holystone. Set within a circular enclosure surrounded by trees is the Lady's Well (NT), closely connected with St Ninian and St Paulinus. Paulinus is said to have come here to baptise the heathen Northumbrians and legend has it that on one Easter Day he baptised 3,000 souls. His statue stands in the centre of the well. Today the village has the holy water on tap, for the well supplies Holystone with its drinking water. Little remains of the priory that was built here for Augustinian canonesses, but the village, with its inn, church, and good stone houses, is one of the most attractive in Coquetdale.

Turn left at the edge of Holystone and continue along the valley, and in 2½ miles turn right to rejoin the B6341. Proceed through open and wilder countryside to reach Elsdon.

ELSDON, Northumb

Set among the rolling hills of Redesdale, Elsdon has a large triangular green with a few 18th-century houses gathered about it. By the church is a rare 14th-century fortified rectory, a reminder of more violent days, as is the Norman castle, c1080, nearby. When the chuch was restored 100 skeletons were found, and they are thought to be those of men who died at the Battle of Otterburn in 1388. Up above the village, on Steng Cross, are the remains of a gibbet. Here the body of one William Winter was hung after his execution in Newcastle for the murder of an old woman of Elsdon in 1791. In the hills hereabouts are many remnants and remains of prehistoric peoples — cairns, earthworks and hut circles.

Bear right through the village and in 2½ miles turn right on to the A696 for Otterburn.

OTTERBURN, Northumb

At the east end of Otterburn is Otterburn Tower — a largely Victorian building incorporating the remains of an old pele tower which withstood an assault by the Scottish army on its way to the Battle of Otterburn. This was fought 1½ miles north-west of the village in 1388 and was one of the many encounters between Scottish and English armies over this disputed territory. Today Otterburn is known for the textile mill by the bridge, where the famous Otterburn tweeds are made.

Turn left on to the B6320, SP 'Bellingham', and shortly cross River Rede. In 1½ miles cross the main road and ascend on to the moors, reaching 1,019ft before the long descent into the North Tyne valley and Bellingham.

BELLINGHAM, Northumb

Bellingham is a small market town, important in its own way as the capital of the North Tyne countryside and Redesdale. Its position also makes it an excellent base from which to explore this beautiful countryside. The church here has an unusual early stone roof. The story goes that the Scots, raiding from over the border, burnt the place so often it was decided a permanent, fireproof roof would be more economical in the long run. The inhabitants of this border country appear to have spent most of their time raiding the herds of their enemies over the border. Today, the farmers, many of them descendants of these lawless men, meet at Bellingham in autumn in a far more friendly fashion for the lamb sales, and again in September for the agricultural show.

Continue on the B6320, SP 'Hexham', and in ¼ mile turn left to cross the North Tyne River. In 5¼ miles enter Wark.

The kitchen at Wallington Hall is kept as if in daily use as it would have been at the turn of the century

WARK, Northumb

Now a few pleasant streets and a quadrangle of houses around a green, Wark was in medieval times the capital of North Tynedale; at the time this was a part of Scotland. It stands on a lovely stretch of the North Tyne River, near both Wark Forest and the Border Forest Park.

Turn left, SP 'Barrasford', recross the North Tyne and turn right. In 1½ miles pass (right) the 14th-century Chipchase Castle. Pass through Barrasford and in ½ mile turn left, SP 'Colwell'. In ¾ mile turn left again on to the A6079, SP 'Rothbury'. In 1½ miles bear left over the crossroads on to the B6342. Shortly pass the edge of Colwell. In 7½ miles turn right then immediately left across the A696. In 2 miles cross the River Wansbeck and pass through the grounds of Wallington Hall.

Tweed, being woven here at Otterburn Mill, is traditionally made with 2 or more colours of the same quality yarn

WALLINGTON HALL, Northumb

The exterior of Wallington Hall (NT) has hardly altered since Sir William Blackett built it in 1688. The house, which he demolished to make way for his building belonged to Sir John Fenwick, who was executed for treason by William III. However, Fenwick's famous house, which the king kept, brought him revenge when it stumbled on a mole hill and threw the sovereign, who consequently died. The modest façade of the Hall hides a sumptuous interior remodelled in the mid-18th century, when, among other things, the wonderful plaster decoration was added by Italian craftsmen. A century later, the architect John Dobson was employed to roof over the central courtyard to create the magnificent central hall. The gardens can be divided into 3 areas: the peaceful lawns and flowerbeds around the house, woodland and lakes, and an L-shaped walled garden and conservatory.

In 1 mile at Cambo turn right on to the B6343, SP 'Morpeth', and continue past Scots' Cap to Hartburn.

HARTBURN, Northumb

Hartburn lies in a superb position with steep, dramatic waterfalls on either side that drop down to the Hart Burn. In the village is a curious building known as Dr Sharpe's Tower. It is a castellated tower that was built to house the village schoolmaster on an upper floor reached by an exterior staircase, with a schoolroom below and stables for the village hearse. Next to it is the schoolhouse of 1844. There is also an elegant Georgian vicarage which has a 13th-century pele tower incorporated in to it. The church has a squat tower dating from the late 12th-century, and carved on a doorpost are 2 daggers and a Maltese cross.

Continue along the B6343 following the Wansbeck valley for the return via Mitford to Morpeth.

NB: The early part of this tour uses a Forestry Commission Forest Drive (toll). During periods of extremely dry weather the road may be closed owing to the high fire risk. If wishing to avoid this portion, leave Pickering on the A169, SP 'Whitby', and pick up the tour at the Saltersgate Inn (11 miles shorter).

PICKERING, N Yorks

This ancient market town, situated amidst beautiful countryside, is known as the Gateway to the Moors. The market place façades are mainly Georgian or Victorian, but older structures are often concealed behind them. The 12th century is evoked in the robust towers and ruined remains of Pickering Castle (AM), where Richard II was confined after his abdication. The Church of St Peter and St Paul, which stands above the main street, has retained fragments of a similar date. Its main attraction is the fine 15th-century wall paintings, depicting Bible stories with the figures in daily costumes of over 500 years ago. The Beck Isle Museum of Rural Life is housed in a fine Georgian house, formerly the home of William Marshall, a noted agriculturalist, and displays folk exhibits of local interest. Pickering is also the terminus of the North Yorkshire Moors Railway.

NORTH YORKSHIRE MOORS RAILWAY, N Yorks

The North Yorkshire Moors Railway operates over 18 miles of track between Pickering and Grosmont, taking in some superb panoramic views along the way. The private company which runs the railway was founded in 1967, and became a trust in 1972. Steam and diesel locomotives pull the trains, and at Grosmont there is a loco shed, viewing gallery, gift shop and catering facilities. At Pickering station there is an excellent bookshop and also a National Park information and audio-visual centre.

From the North Yorkshire Moors railway station at Pickering follow the Newton-on-Rawcliffe road to Newton-on-Rawcliffe.

NEWTON-ON-RAWCLIFFE, N Yorks

Newton-on-Rawcliffe stands close to the woodlands of Newton Dale on high ground overlooking a stupendous panorama of the Newton Dale canyon — a beautiful moorland glen bordered in places by crags and steep cliffs. The White Swan Inn in the village stands on one of the oldest hostelry sites in the district.

Continue to Stape.

STAPE, N Yorks

The hamlet of Stape was at one time the centre of besom-making; a besom being a kind of broom

NORTH YORKSHIRE'S MOORS AND DALES

Savage, desolate moorland, lush farmland and deep peaceful dales blend into an area of unique contrasts and beauty where picturesque grey-stone villages are centres for magnificent walks by streams and waterfalls.

made of a bundle of supple twigs tied to a handle. This little community is also the home of the Stape Silver Band — many of these northern villages boast their own bands, which are the objects of much fierce competition and pride. Closeby a footpath, near Mauley Cross, leads to Needle Point, where well-dressing ceremonies — the garlanding of wells with flowers once connected with pagan worship — and rural fairs used to be held.

Continue on the Stape road and in 1 mile descend (1 in 6). In 1¾ miles keep left then in ½ mile bear right to enter Cropton Forest and join the Newton Dale Forest Drive (toll). In 3 miles pass a picnic area and turn right. After another 2¼ miles leave the Forest Drive and continue to Levisham.

LEVISHAM, N Yorks

Levisham, high on open moorland, has a green and a Hall and a church with a Saxon chancel arch. This church, St Mary's, stands forlorn at the bottom of a glen beside Levisham Beck, with an old watermill for company. Because the descent from the village to the church is so steep, a new church, St John the Baptist, was built in the village in 1884. Levisham has a typical North Riding main street, with a wide lawn to the left and right, although the view at one end is obscured by a cottage. At the head of Levisham Beck is a great natural amphitheatre called the Hole of Horcum.

Continue to Lockton.

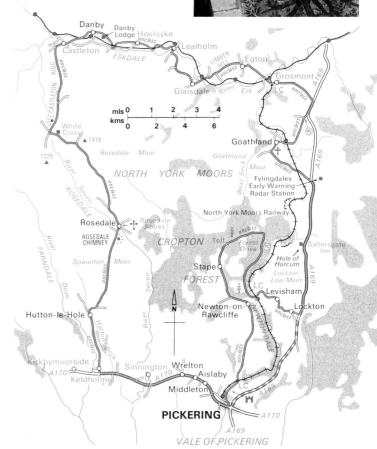

Part of the 15th-century wall paintings in Pickering's church

The Hole of Horcum, a great natural hollow, is the curious product of erosion during the Ice Age

LOCKTON, N Yorks

Lockton, across the dale from Levisham, is another moorland village with a spectacular view. The 13th-century Church of St Andrew and St Giles has been greatly modified over the years and has a Jacobean pulpit, reading desk and communion table. There is no village public house, but over Lockton Low Moor to the north, past the gorge known as the Hole of Horcum, is the picturesque Saltersgate Inn. Smugglers, running silk and gin inland from Robin Hood's Bay, are said to have used the inn as a refuge.

At Lockton keep left, SP 'Whitby', then in ½ mile turn left on to the A169. Climb on to Lockton Low Moor and later pass the Hole of Horcum before descending to the Saltersgate Inn. After 2¾ miles (right) there are views of the Fylingdales Radar Station.

FYLINGDALES EARLY WARNING RADAR STATION, N Yorks
A futuristic sight on the desolate Fylingdale Moor is the white domes of the Radar Station. This defence installation is a gaunt reminder of the consequences of technological development in an area which was previously uninhabited. The gruelling Lyke Wake Walk across the North Yorks Moors passes through Fylingdales Moor.

Turn left, SP 'Goathland', and cross Goathland Moor before descending to Goathland. Bear right to enter the village.

GOATHLAND, N Yorks
The grey-stone buildings of this delightful moorland village are set around a large village green where a group of sword dancers, the Plough Stotts, regularly perform traditional dances. Sheep graze between the houses scattered on the perimeter of the village. This is a marvellous centre for walking, and the local streams tumble over rocks forming spectacular waterfalls, some of which are named; for example: Mallyan Spout, Thomason Foss, Nelly Ayre Foss and Water Ark.

Follow SP 'Whitby' and cross the railway, then ascend. In 2 miles turn left on to the A169, then ¼ mile farther turn left again, SP 'Grosmont'. Cross Sleights Moor and later descend into Grosmont.

Hutton Beck tumbles down from the Yorkshire Moors through the enchanting village of Hutton-le-Hole to Westfield Wood which lies behind it

Continue over the level-crossing and the River Esk, then ascend to Egton. In the village bear right and at Wheatsheaf Inn turn left, SP 'Glaisdale'. In 1¼ miles descend (1 in 3), then cross the Esk and ascend through Glaisdale. Follow the Castleton road and in 1 mile bear right. In another ¾ mile turn right for Lealholm. Recross the Esk, then turn left, SP 'Danby'. Continue through Esk Dale and pass Danby Lodge before reaching Danby.

DANBY, N Yorks
Close to this village in the Esk valley is Danby Lodge, a former shooting lodge and now a visitor centre for the North Yorks Moors National Park. The village is also called Dale End, as it lies at the head of Danby Dale, which runs south into the moors. One mile south-east of the village is ruined 14th-century Danby Castle. The ruins have had a farmhouse added to them and are used as farm buildings. This was the home of the Latimers, and of their successors the Nevilles. Close to the castle is Duck Bridge, a packhorse bridge over the River Esk which dates from about 1386. All around are obscure circles and stones which are remnants of the Bronze and Iron Ages.

At Danby go over the staggered crossroads and continue to Castleton. Follow SP 'Rosedale' and in ½ mile bear left to climb along the 1,000ft-high Castleton Rigg. After 4 miles turn left (still SP 'Rosedale'). Cross the plateau of Rosedale Moor and after another 4 miles descend into Rosedale.

ROSEDALE, N Yorks
In the churchyard, near the attractive green of this main village in the dale of the same name, are a few stones which represent the remains of a 12th-century Cistercian abbey. South of the village, as the dale narrows, is the Rosedale Chimney, which is the remnant of an iron-ore working. What used to be the mineral railway at the head of the dale is now a walking trail with superb views of the countryside.

At the end of the village turn right and ascend Rosedale Chimney Bank (1 in 3). Beyond the summit cross Spaunton Moor and after 3 miles, at the T-junction, turn right for Hutton-le-Hole.

HUTTON-LE-HOLE, N Yorks
This attractive village was built randomly around wide greens dissected by 2 becks and various picturesque bridges, at the foot of a limestone escarpment. Grey-stone houses with red pantiled roofs complete the showplace-effect. Ryedale Folk Museum is housed here in an ancient cruck-type (timbered) building, once the home of prosperous Quakers. Craftsmen's tools, farm implements, an ancient dairy, Roman pottery and a reconstructed Elizabethan glass furnace are among the exhibits. The oldest building in the village, dating from 1695, belonged to John Richardson, who was a friend of William Penn the English Quaker who founded Pennsylvania. It is called, appropriately, Quaker Cottage.

Leave on the Kirkbymoorside road. In 2¾ miles, at the T-junction, turn left on to the A170, SP 'Scarborough', and continue to Wrelton.

WRELTON, N Yorks
The junction of the westward road from Pickering and the Roman Road is marked by the old village of Wrelton. The crossing is distinguished by a tiny green, set amidst sturdy Georgian farms and houses, and a substantial restored cruck building of 1665. An ancient alehouse, the Buck Inn, contains curios such as an old witness dock from Pickering magistrates' court. Back in 1779, the inn had its own brewhouse and served 'Old Tom' ale to passing stagecoach travellers.

Continue on the A170 to Aislaby.

AISLABY, N Yorks
One of the smallest villages on the main road, Aislaby was built by the Vikings. Among its most attractive buildings is the Georgian Hall (not open), with its lead statuettes and regal summer house which presides over a group of solid farmhouses.

Continue to Middleton.

MIDDLETON, N Yorks
A string of pleasant buildings lining the road make up the village of Middleton, with the early Georgian Middleton Hall (not open) just visible through the trees. Opposite the New Inn is the Church of St Andrew. The north aisle contains fragments of 3 fine Anglo-Danish crosses dating from the 10th century and the sculpted decorations include a dragon and an armed warrior.

Remain on the A170 for the return to Pickering.

Fylingdales Early Warning Radar Station was set up jointly by the British and United States governments in 1961

RICHMOND, N Yorks
Dramatically situated overlooking the River Swale, this attractive and historic town makes an excellent base from which to explore the lovely countryside of Swaledale. The dominant feature of the town is its massive Norman castle (AM), one of the earliest in Britain with 11th-century curtain walls round a splendid keep. In the shadow of its mighty presence are streets of lovely old buildings, all illustrative of important phases in Richmond's past. The cobbled Market Place is one of the largest in the country and is approached along little alleyways known as wynds. Greyfriars Tower is the remnant of an abbey that was founded here many centuries ago, and facing the Market Place is one of the strangest churches in England. Dedicated to the Holy Trinity, its main body and medieval tower are divided from each other by shops and offices actually built into its main structure. Other buildings in this area include several handsome Georgian and Victorian houses. The most outstanding Georgian building in the town is the Theatre Royal (open) of 1788, beautifully restored and the oldest theatre in the country to have survived in its original condition. A Green Howards' Museum displays the colourful and fascinating history of that regiment. Many fine walks can be enjoyed in and around Richmond, but one of the closest and best is along the banks of the Swale to spacious parklands at Lowenthwaite Bridge.

Leave Richmond on the A6108 SP 'Scotch Corner' at roundabout take 1st exit B6274 for Gilling West. Ascend to high ground, turn left on to the A66 'Brough' road, and continue along a pleasant road to Greta Bridge, on the Rivers Greta and Tees, with views across moors and valleys.

GRETA BRIDGE, Durham
Among the many artists and writers who have recognized and recorded the beauty of this charming little hamlet are Dickens, Scott, and Turner. Just to the north is the junction of the Greta with the Tees, and south-west of Greta Bridge the river runs through the lovely woodland of Brignall Banks. Features of the hamlet itself include a picturesque river bridge dating from the 18th century, and the Morrit Arms public house, whose site was once occupied by a Roman fort.

Continue along the A66 'Brough' road for ¼ mile and turn right on to an unclassified road SP 'Barnard Castle'. In 1¼ miles are views ahead of Egglestone Abbey.

EGGLESTONE ABBEY, Durham
The waters of the River Tees add an extra dimension to the picturesque quality of these lovely remains (AM).

Turn right and cross the River Tees to reach the Bowes Museum.

THE NORTHERN DALES
In the northern part of the Yorkshire Dales national park are the great ice-scoured valleys of Wharfedale and Swaledale, carved out to their present size by huge glaciers that flowed across the Pennines over a million years ago. On the moors above are greystone villages and steep, sheep-cropped slopes.

BOWES MUSEUM, Durham
Built in the style of a French château, the building that houses this museum is an architectural surprise to eyes that have come to expect the solid little stone houses of the area. Inside is one of the finest art collections in Britain, featuring fine European paintings, furniture, porcelain, tapestries, jewellery, and dolls.

Continue to Barnard Castle.

BARNARD CASTLE, Durham
Ancient houses and several inns line the main street of this enchanting town, which has grown up round the walls of its ruined medieval castle (AM) and is a busy market centre for its area.

Leave Barnard Castle with the A67 SP 'Brough, Bowes', re-cross the River Tees, and turn left on to the B6277 SP 'Scotch Corner'. Drive through woodland to meet the A66, turn right, and in ¼ mile turn left on to an unclassified road SP 'Reeth'. A short detour can be made from the main route to Bowes Castle by continuing along the A66.

Below the huge bulk of Richmond's 11th-century castle are picturesque streets displaying an attractive mixture of architectural styles. The abundance of Georgian design is particularly noticeable.

BOWES CASTLE, Durham
Close to the ruined keep of this Norman castle (AM) are the military remains of the Roman fort of *Lavatrae* (AM), which preceded it.

On the main tour, continue along an unclassified moorland road, with occasional steep hills (1 in 4), and drive through the pines of Stang Forest before climbing to a road summit of 1,677ft. Breathtaking views extend into lonely Arkengarthdale, in the vast and very beautiful Yorkshire Dales National Park.

YORKSHIRE DALES NATIONAL PARK
The boundaries of this national park encompass nearly 700 square miles of high dells scored by literally dozens of lovely river valleys that have collectivey come to be known as the Yorkshire Dales. Many great dales exist in the region, but Wharfedale and Airedale are probably the most famous. The

desolate rocky scenery in the high part of the first mentioned gradually softens towards its lower reaches, and Airdale opens out into spectacular limestone scenery as it drops towards the village of Malham. In the south are the Three Peaks, well known for their dangerous potholes, while the length of the park is threaded by the Pennine Way long-distance footpath. Movement and sound is brought to the region by delightful waterfalls and lakes fed by rapid streams that rise in the rocky countryside of the high fells. This is one of the many interesting dales tours.

ARKENGARTHDALE, N Yorks
Lead mining was carried on in this lovely valley from the 13th to 19th centuries, and traces can be seen today. The dale itself is a lovely valley that follows the course of the Arkle Beck to impressive Swaledale in the south-east.

Cross Arkle Beck and drive along Arkengarthdale, passing through Langthwaite to reach Reeth.

REETH, N Yorks
During the 19th century this one-time market town became a busy centre of the lead-mining industry of nearby Arkengarthdale. Nowadays it is a peaceful village charmingly grouped round its large green, within easy reach of some of the wildest country in the national park.

In Reeth turn left on to the B6270 'Richmond' road. Continue through pleasant countryside to Grinton.

GRINTON, N Yorks
Grinton Church is a splendid building that has come to be known as the Cathedral of the Dales. It was founded in Norman times and contains an ancient font that is probably its original. Other features include beautiful screenwork and a Jacobean pulpit.

Gradually descend along Swaledale, between moorland heights that rise steeply to over 1,400ft from the river.

SWALEDALE, N Yorks
Among the many relics of 18th- and 19th-century lead mining that still litter this wild and deep valley are remains of some of the 20 smelt mills that were used to process the ore. The valley itself is a deep cleft that runs west from Richmond, and is connected to Wensleydale via the bleak Buttertubs Pass.

Enter woodland and meet the A6108: turn right and follow SP 'Leyburn' to reach Downholme.

DOWNHOLME, N Yorks
This tiny village stands high above the River Swale and has an attractive church that features Norman workmanship.

Proceed along a winding moorland road, passing through Bellerby to reach Leyburn.

Arkengarthdale is one of Yorkshire's more secluded dales.

This 16th-century porcelain dish is one of many treasures in the Bowes Museum.

LEYBURN, N Yorks
The sloping market place in this old town is an appropriate example of the switchback landscape of the local countryside. Its Wensleydale position, above the River Ure, makes it an ideal touring base. Within easy walking distance of the town centre is a 2-mile limestone scar known as The Shawl, which affords excellent views into Wensleydale.

An exquisite setting adds to the enchantment of ruined Jervaulx Abbey, once a powerful monastic centre.

WENSLEYDALE, N Yorks
Dairy herds from the many farms scattered along the length of this fertile valley convert the freshness of its lush pastures into rich milk from which the distinctive Wensleydale cheese is made. The villages of the dale are generally small and without exception charming. Here and there its pastoral solitude is emphasized by the sound of falling water.

To leave Leyburn follow SP 'Middleham' to the end of the town and turn right on to the A6108. Descend and cross the River Ure via an unusual bridge to reach the village of Middleham.

MIDDLEHAM, N Yorks
Once the chief town of Wensleydale, this scenic village is now an important horse breeding and training centre and a good touring base. Its impressive ruined castle (AM) was the seat of the powerful Neville family, who controlled much of the area from the massive keep that still stands at its full height behind well-preserved 13th-century curtain walls. Close by is the curious Swine Cross.

Continue along the A6108 'Masham' road, with moorland to the right and gentle riverside pastures to the left. Continue to East Witton.

EAST WITTON, N Yorks
Most of the houses in this compact village are contained in two main rows facing two 19th-century churches and an attractive 17th-century bridge.

A detour can be made from the main route to Braithwaite Hall by turning right in East Witton and driving in partly-wooded country for 2 miles.

BRAITHWAITE HALL, N Yorks
Now in use as a farm, this fine 17th-century house (NT) stands in attractive pastoral countryside and is open by appointment. Near by a large hillfort occupies a 2½-acre site.

On the main tour, continue along the A6108 to reach Jervaulx Abbey.

JERVAULX ABBEY, N Yorks
Cistercian monks chose this beautiful riverside site as a fitting setting for their abbey in the 12th century. Although it was destroyed in the 15th century, enough remains to show today's visitors the exquisite proportions of their achievement. Particularly notable are the remains of the monks' dormitory, which features a hall and beautiful lancet windows of the period.

Continue along the A6108 and pass the Ellington Firth Picnic Site before entering Masham.

MASHAM, N Yorks
Masham's former importance as a market town can be judged from the huge square which is dominated by a Market Cross. In the churchyard of St Mary's are important remains of a Saxon cross, and the mainly-Norman church carries a beautiful 15th-century spire.

Leave Masham on the A6108 'Ripon' road. Cross the river, then immediately turn left on to the unclassified 'Bedale' road. Follow the river and in 1 mile turn right, then continue for ¾ mile and turn left on to the B6268. Continue to Bedale.

BEDALE, N Yorks
This mainly Georgian town features an old stepped market cross in the main street, and an unusual church whose first floor is reached by a stair guarded by a portcullis. These elaborate precautions were taken against the very real possibility of Scottish raids. Opposite the church is Georgian Bedale Hall (open), a fine house with a museum and a complete ballroom wing.

Continue along the A684 'Northallerton' road and later turn right, following SP 'Scotch Corner' to join the A1. Continue on a fast section of dual carriageway on the Great North Road. After 5 miles bear left, join the A6136 to reach Catterick.

CATTERICK, N Yorks
Known mainly for the military training area on its borders, this delightful little grey-stone village has a good church of c1500. Inside the church are two 15th-century brasses.

Drive through Catterick to Catterick Bridge, on the Swale.

CATTERICK BRIDGE, N Yorks
Most people come here to watch horse racing on the famous local course, but the lovely little local bridge that spans the Swale dates from 1422 and is worth attention. The local scenery is superb.

Turn right and cross the River Swale, then turn left SP 'Richmond' and meet the B6271. On the left are the river and Easby Abbey.

EASBY ABBEY, N Yorks
Picturesque ruins of an abbey founded in 1155 grace the beautiful surroundings of this Swaleside site. The remains (AM) are considerable.

Continue along the B6271 for the return to Richmond.

RIPON, N Yorks

Popularly known as the Gateway to the Dales, this attractive city stands at the meeting of the Rivers Ure, Skell, and Laver and boasts a small but impressive cathedral. The main features of this lovely 12th-century building include a Saxon crypt that may be the earliest Christian survival in England, a fine early-English west front, and a beautiful 15th-century screen. Excellent examples of local woodcarving are the finely worked misericords and curious Elephant and Castle bench. Every night Ripon's market square is the scene of a 1,000-year-old custom, when the town Hornblower or Wakeman strides out in his tricorn hat and sounds his ancient horn at each corner of a huge 18th-century obelisk. Years ago this sound indicated that the Wakeman had begun his night watch over the town, and that the townspeople could sleep secure in their beds. The half-timbered Wakeman's house, later used by the mayor, dates from the 13th century and now contains a museum. An interesting Prison and Police museum is housed in the old prison building dating from 1686.

Before Ripon is left on the main tour route, a short detour can be made to Newby Hall: follow the B6265 SP 'Boroughbridge' to pass Ripon Racecourse and cross the River Ure, then turn right on to an unclassified road and in ¼ mile turn right again to reach Newby Hall.

NEWBY HALL, N Yorks

Some of Robert Adam's finest work can be seen in his additions to this splendid Queen Anne House (open), which contains superb Gobelin tapestries and an important collection of classical sculpture. The beautiful grounds run down to the River Ure and contain a miniature railway.

To leave Ripon on the main tour follow SP 'Pateley Bridge B6265'. In 2¼ miles reach Studley Royal and Studley Royal Park.

STUDLEY ROYAL, N Yorks

The fine house that once graced this lovely park burned down in 1945, and the present owner lives in a converted stable block that dates from the 18th century. Attractive estate cottages cluster round a 19th-century church that is considered the ecclesiastical masterpiece of architect William Burges and has a very rich interior. The park (open), landscaped in the 18th century, features many of the conceits of the period, including a temple folly and various statues. Its lakes and woodland combine in a sylvan beauty which is enhanced by grazing herds of deer and livestock, and at one point adjoins the magnificent ruins of Fountains Abbey.

Leave Studley Royal on the B6265 and after ¾ mile turn left on to an unclassified road to reach the impressive ruins of Fountains Abbey.

ALONG THE EDGE OF THE DALES

Between York and the deep Dales country is a gentler area of farmland. Here the landscape is dotted with curiously-weathered rocks rising from deep vegetation, peaceful reservoirs, and ancient ruins beside enchanting rivers. A foretaste of the Dales is given in How Stean Gorge.

EXCEPT YE LORD KEEP * YE * CITTIE * YE * WAKEMAN WAKETH IN VAIN

Ripon's Town Hall reminds the citizens of the Wakeman's traditional role.

FOUNTAINS ABBEY, N Yorks

Generally considered to be the finest in England, the remarkably well-preserved ruins of this 12th- to 15th-century Cistercian abbey (NT) are part of the Studley Royal estate (open) and clearly demonstrate the layout of a Norman and medieval monastic foundation. Particularly notable are the nave, tower, and lay-brothers' quarters. Opposite the ruins is Fountains Hall, which was built with stone taken from the abbey in the 17th century.

Return to the B6265 and turn left, drive through wooded countryside, and emerge on to Pateley Moor for views over Nidderdale. A short detour from the main route to Brimham Rocks can be made by driving to the road summit on the moor and turning left.

Fountains Abbey was once the wealthiest Cistercian house in England.

BRIMHAM ROCKS, N Yorks

Thousands of years of wind and rain have sculpted the millstone grit of this group of rocks into a variety of weird and wonderful shapes. The surrounding moorland (NT) offers excellent views and is a popular site for picnics.

On the main tour, continue along the B6265 and later turn right to descend to Pateley Bridge.

PATELEY BRIDGE, N Yorks

Since ancient times this pleasant market town has been a focus for the everyday life of Nidderdale, but nowadays its steep main street is busy as much with tourists as with local traffic. The picturesque ruins of Old St Mary's Church occupy a lofty hillside site, and the Nidderdale Museum displays over 3,000 items relating to life in the Yorkshire Dales. Of particular note are the Victorian Room and a replica cobbler's shop. West of the town are the fascinating Stump Cross Caverns – more than ¼ mile of natural passages and caves featuring many strange rock formations (open).

Leave Pateley Bridge and cross the River Nidd, then take the next turning on the right SP 'Ramsgill' to join an unclassified road. Drive for 1 mile to reach Foster Beck Flax Mill.

FOSTER BECK FLAX MILL, N Yorks

Industrial archaeology enthusiasts will find this well-restored flax mill of considerable interest. Now a restaurant, it is built of local stone and features a huge 17th-century water wheel that is the second largest in the country.

Drive alongside Gouthwaite Reservoir and continue to Ramsgill and Lofthouse, at the head of Nidderdale.

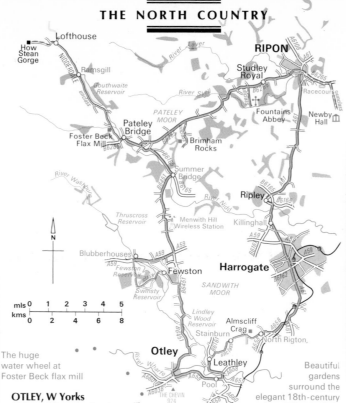

NIDDERDALE, N Yorks
Part of the lovely valley of the River Nidd, Nidderdale is rich in mineral deposits and has been mined for lead and iron for many centuries. Its stone has also been in great demand for building, and the landscape is pitted with the overgrown remains of worked-out quarries. All along the river, from its high source in the rugged fell country of Great Whernside to the lush lower parts of its valley, the scenery offers plenty of incentives for the motorist to leave his car and explore on foot.

LOFTHOUSE AND HOW STEAN GORGE, N Yorks
The pretty Upper Nidderdale village of Lofthouse is a good centre from which to explore the beautiful How Stean Gorge, a 70ft-deep cleft accessible by footpaths that thread their way along its rocky sides and over little bridges. The largest of two interesting caves here is Elgin's Hole, which penetrates nearly a mile into the roots of Middlesmoor Hill.

Return alongside Gouthwaite Reservoir to reach the B6265 and turn left to re-enter Pateley Bridge. Leave the town on the B6165 SP 'Harrogate' to reach Summer Bridge, then turn right on to the B6451 'Otley' road. Follow a long climb past Menwith Hill Wireless Station and turn right on to the A59 'Skipton' road, then proceed to Blubberhouses, at the north-west end of Fewston Reservoir. Drive to the village church, turn left on to the unclassified 'Timble' road, then take the next turning left SP 'Fewston'. Continue through pine forests, cross a dam separating Fewston and Swinsty Reservoirs, and continue to Fewston.

FEWSTON, W Yorks
This charming village faces across Fewston Reservoir to the historic lines of a 16th-century hall (not open). The lovely village church dates from the 17th century.

Keep right through Fewston and cross part of Swinsty Reservoir, then meet the B6451 'Otley' road and turn right to cross Sandwith Moor. Follow a long descent to Lindley Wood Reservoir and enter Otley.

The huge water wheel at Foster Beck flax mill

OTLEY, W Yorks
Although largely dominated by modern industry, this old market town on the River Wharfe retains several good buildings as reminders of its long history. Among these are old inns and a fine cruciform church containing fragments of Saxon crosses and a good Georgian pulpit. A curious memorial in the churchyard commemorates the men who lost their lives while working on the Bramhope railway tunnel between 1845 and 1849. Close to the town are the fine Elizabethan halls of Farnley, where the artist Turner was a visitor, and Western. Above the town is the 925ft summit of Otley Chevin, from which panoramic views over the lovely countryside of Lower Wharfedale can be enjoyed.

Leave Otley on the A659 'Tadcaster' road and follow the River Wharfe to reach Pool. Turn left on to the A658 SP 'Harrogate', then cross the river and turn left again on to the B6161 to reach Leathley.

LEATHLEY, N Yorks
Outside the Norman and later church in Leathley are the old village stocks and a mounting block. The local almshouses and hall date from the 18th century.

In Leathley turn right on to the unclassified 'Stainburn' road and follow SP 'Rigton' to reach lofty Almscliff Crag.

ALMSCLIFF CRAG, N Yorks
This high crag affords superb views and has been the training ground for some of Britain's best-known rock climbers. The climbing faces should not be attempted without proper experience and equipment.

Continue to North Rigton and turn left, then right, to meet a junction with the A658. Turn left SP 'Harrogate' and in 1¾ miles turn left again on to the A61 to reach Harrogate.

HARROGATE, N Yorks
One of the chief towns in Yorkshire's old West Riding, Harrogate achieved early fame as a spa resort and nowadays is an important conference centre. Its mineral springs were discovered in the 16th century, and the Royal Pump Room was built as the country's first public baths in 1842. From that time onwards the town's popularity steadily increased, resulting in a wealth of dignified stone buildings and beautiful gardens that have made it known as the Floral Resort of England. The Valley Gardens are particularly notable, and the Harlow Car Gardens contain 60 acres of ornamental and woodland gardens (open). Some 200 acres of commonland known as The Stray, a popular place for walking and picnics, borders the southern boundary of the town. An interesting museum of local history, Victoriana, and costumes is housed in the 19th-century Pump Room.

Leave Harrogate on the A61 SP 'Ripon' and drive to Killinghall. Continue for 1 mile beyond that village, cross the River Nidd, and meet a roundabout. Take the first exit on to an unclassified road and enter Ripley.

RIPLEY, N Yorks
Much of this attractive village was rebuilt during the 19th century, but it is largely unspoilt and retains an ancient market cross and stocks in its cobbled square. Ripley Castle (open), home of the Ingilby family since 1350, shows workmanship of mainly 16th- and 18th-century date and stands in beautiful grounds landscaped by Capability Brown. Its gatehouse is a fine building of c1450, and one of its floors was made from the timber of a British man-of-war. Oliver Cromwell stayed at the house on the eve of the Battle of Marston Moor in 1644, and armour from the opposing Royalist army is on view. Notable tombs and memorial brasses can be seen in the village church, and the churchyard features a curious weeping cross with eight niches in which sinners could kneel and repent.

Drive through Ripley, meet a roundabout, and take the 2nd exit to rejoin the A61. Return through undulating countryside to Ripon.

Beautiful gardens surround the elegant 18th-century mansion of Newby Hall.

Capability Brown landscaped the grounds of Ripley Castle.

FROM THE COAST TO THE MOORS

Every summer thousands of visitors flock to Scarborough and Whitby, bustling resorts with much to entertain the holidaymaker. Inland are the forest and heather-clad hills of the North Yorks Moors, where the colours are green and brown and silence is broken only by small natural sounds.

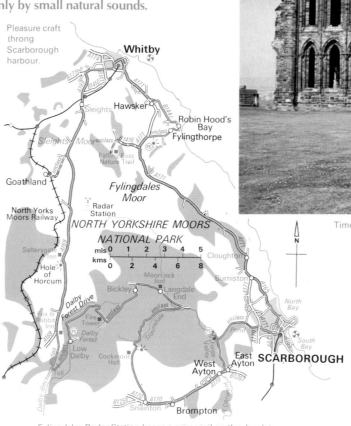

Time and war have desecrated Whitby Abbey.

Pleasure craft throng Scarborough harbour.

Fylingdales Radar Station keeps a grim vigil on the desolate moor.

SCARBOROUGH, N Yorks

An important conference centre and one of the most popular seaside resorts in Yorkshire, this charming old town overlooks two sandy bays divided by the massive bulk of a 300ft headland. In Roman times this excellent vantage point was the site of a signalling station, and the foundations of that ancient structure still exist amongst the magnificent 12th-century castle ruins (AM) that stand here today. Views from the 100-acre site, which is accessible through a 13th-century barbican, extend across the red roofs of the medieval old town to the harbour far below. Of particular note among the remains are the fine keep and three medieval chapels. During the 18th and 19th centuries the town became caught up in the fashion for seaside holidays and acquired several fine terraces of hotels and boarding houses, many of which still offer accommodation. The Natural History Museum, Art Gallery, and The Rotunda Museum are housed in notable Victorian buildings, and a museum of general interest can be visited in Woodend, the one-time holiday home of the Sitwell family. Typical resort facilities and amusements offered to the visitor include fine promenades and well-tended seafront gardens, plus a good zoo with a dolphinarium. Views can be enjoyed from pleasant clifftop walks and the 500ft eminence of nearby Oliver Hill.

Leave Scarborough with SP 'North Bay' and join the A165, then in 1 mile meet a roundabout and take the A165 to reach Burniston. Meet a junction with the A171 and turn right SP 'Whitby'. Continue to Cloughton, bear left with the A171, and drive through an afforested area to Fylingdales Moor.

FYLINGDALES MOOR AND RADAR STATION, N Yorks

The huge white domes of Fylingdales Early Warning Station seem a constant reminder of doom in the lonely desolation of the surrounding moor. At one time the area was inhabited, and the intrusive evidence of advanced technology contrasts strangely with prehistoric burial mounds and the Wade's Causeway, which is Roman.

Continue along the A171 for 8¾ miles. A detour from the main route can be made by turning left on to the B1416, driving 1¾ miles, then turning left again on to an unclassified road to reach Newton House and the start of the Falling Fosse Nature Trail. On the main route, continue along the A171 and in ¾ mile turn right on to an unclassified road SP 'Fylingthorpe' and 'Robin Hood's Bay'. Pass a viewpoint and picnic site on the right and

descend (1 in 4) through hairpin bends to reach Fylingthorpe.

FYLINGTHORPE, N Yorks

This residential area of Robin Hood's Bay boasts the fine 17th-century Old Hall, which was built by the Chomley family of Whitby Abbey.

Keep forward to Robin Hood's Bay.

ROBIN HOOD'S BAY, N Yorks

Considered one of the most picturesque villages in England, this charming collection of old houses, shops, and inns occupies a precarious cliff-top site and was once a favourite haunt of smugglers. Its steep flights of steps and narrow passages recall unlit boats at the bottom of the cliffs, and furtive movements between houses where well-disguised hiding places waited to be filled with contraband. It is difficult to establish any real connexion between the village and the folk hero after whom it is named, but it may be that the famous outlaw leader came here to escape by boat to Europe. During the last decade coastal erosion has destroyed two rows of houses, and the sea is so close that at high tide its waves lash the Bay Hotel. Superb sands are revealed at low tide.

Leave the village on the B1447 SP 'Whitby' and continue to Hawsker.

HAWSKER, N Yorks

It is thought that the well-preserved 10th-century cross shaft at Old Hall in Hawsker may mark the site of a medieval church. The intricate design of interlaced knot work and bird figures is typical of traditional Norse design.

Drive through the village, meet the A171, and turn right. Descend to Whitby.

WHITBY, N Yorks
Ruins (AM) of an abbey founded here by St Hilda in 657 can be seen above the town on the East Cliff. Close by is a huge carved cross that was erected in 1898 to commemorate Caedmon, the ancient poet whose *Song of Creation* is considered by some to mark the start of English literature. Below the abbey ruins the River Esk divides the old part of the settlement from the more recent West Cliff area, which is connected to the harbour via a rock-cut passage romantically named after the Khyber Pass. Whitby has always had a strong sea-going tradition and has been the home of many famous maritime figures, including Captain Cook. His house in Grape Street is identified by a plaque, and the stimulus that prompted his nautical career is still a persuasive element in the town's atmosphere – though the 18th-century colliers on which he worked have long since vanished. One of the finest buildings here is St Mary's Church, which stands at the top of a spectacular 199-step flight and contains superb 18th-century craftsmanship. The museum in Pannet Park illustrates fascinating episodes from the town's long history. Local craftsmen have been making ornaments and jewellery from jet, a particularly hard, shiny form of coal found in the area, for hundreds of years. One of the most unusual features of Whitby is a whalebone arch from Norway.

Leave Whitby on the A171 'Teesside' road and in 1½ miles turn left on to the A169 SP 'Pickering'. Drive through Sleights and climb on to Sleights Moor, in the North Yorks Moors National Park.

Several restored steam locomotives run on the North Yorks Moors Railway.

NORTH YORKS MOORS NATIONAL PARK
Heather-clad moors occasionally scored by fertile valleys are the main ingredients in the startlingly open landscape of this 553-square-mile national park. To the west are the rounded heights of the Cleveland and Hambledon Hills, east the rugged beauty of the Yorkshire coast, and south the lush woodlands of the Vale of Pickering.

Continue across Sleights Moor for 3 miles. A short detour from the main route to Goathland can be made by turning right on to an unclassified road and entering the village.

Old cottages line the hills on both sides of Whitby harbour.

GOATHLAND, N Yorks
All around this greystone moorland village are lovely walks leading past streams that suddenly plunge over rocky lips as spectacular waterfalls. Three superb examples in the immediate neighbourhood are Nelly Ayre Foss, Mallyan Spout, and Thomason Foss, and dozens of others in varying sizes can be visited by the rambler willing to venture a little farther. The village itself is well known for the Plough Stotts, a traditional group who perform sword dances in the area. A well-preserved stretch of Roman Road (AM) can be seen to the south, and the North Yorks Moors Railway is close by.

The Hole of Horcum is a vast bowl of rich grazing land.

NORTH YORKS MOORS RAILWAY
Steam railway enthusiasts have restored and re-opened the old British Rail link that connected Grosmont with Pickering, and in doing so have provided a superb mobile viewpoint from which 18 miles of beautiful national park countryside can be enjoyed in comfortable conditions.

On the main tour, follow the A169 over bleak moorland, with views of Fylingdales Early Warning Station, then pass the lovely Saltersgate Inn and ascend to the Hole of Horcum.

HOLE OF HORCUM, N Yorks
This vast natural hollow in the Yorkshire moorlands shelters the farms of High and Low Horcum, forming a lush oasis of pasture in the wilderness of Levisham Moor.

After 4 miles reach the Fox and Rabbit Inn, then turn left on to an unclassified road SP 'Thornton Dale'. After another 2 miles turn left SP 'Low Dalby (Forest Drive)' on to a Forestry Commission toll road. Proceed to the hamlet of Low Dalby and turn left on to the Forest Drive SP 'Bickley'.

DALBY FOREST DRIVE, N Yorks
Some 10 miles of well-surfaced roads offer the motorist a route through the beautiful woodlands of Dalby and Bickley Forests, where conifer plantations and stands of mature deciduous trees provide a vast haven for many species of wildlife. Red squirrels inhabit the conifers, the glades are full of wild flowers in spring and summer, and there is constant activity from such common woodland birds as jays, nuthatches, and the tiny goldcrest. A footpath which starts just beyond Staindale leads left to a curious formation of layered limestone known as the Bridestones. Amenities include numerous parking places, picnic sites, and forest trails, while many footpaths allow an uninhibited appreciation of the area. The Forest Drive is likely to be closed during periods of very dry weather, when the ever-present fire risk is abnormally high.

Continue along the Forest Drive to a fire tower and turn left, then drive for 2 miles to leave the Forestry Commission roads. Descend (1 in 8), and after ¾ mile meet a T-junction and turn right SP 'Scarborough'. Pass the Moorcock Inn at Langdale End and after 1 mile turn sharp right SP 'Troutsdale' and 'Snainton'. Continue along a winding road through Troutsdale; fine views can be enjoyed along the length of this valley, and there is a picnic site near a viewing spot at Cockmoor Hall (not open). Meet a T-junction in Snainton and turn left on to the A170 SP 'Scarborough'. Proceed to Brompton.

BROMPTON, N Yorks
Brompton's greystone Church of All Saints features fine stained glass.

Leave Brompton and continue along the A170 to West and East Ayton.

AYTON, WEST AND EAST, N Yorks
Situated on either side of the River Derwent, the twin villages of East and West Ayton are linked by an attractive 4-arched bridge which dates from 1775. The ruined pele tower of Ayton Castle makes a good counterpoint to the tower of East Ayton's church, on the other bank.

Immediately after crossing the Derwent to enter East Ayton turn left on to an unclassified road. In 2 miles turn right on to a road SP 'Private'. Keep forward at this junction to reach a picnic site and viewpoint. After 2 miles on the private road pass a pond on the right, then after another 1 mile meet a T-junction and turn right to re-enter Scarborough.

WAST WATER AND THE WESTERN DALES

The high fells sweep down almost to the sea and above Wast Water, deepest and wildest of the Cumbrian lakes, tower the formidable peaks of Scafell and Scafell Pike. In the shelter of the mountains lie 2 of the loveliest and quietest of the valleys, Eskdale and Dunnerdale, whose scenery inspired many of Wordsworth's poems.

Above: Eskdale, ideal for walking, is one of the few Lakeland valleys with no lake

Right: Scafell towers above the River Irt which flows through Wast Water

SEASCALE, Cumbria
Good sandy beaches and long rolling breakers, ideal for surfing, make Seascale a popular seaside resort. The village lies on a narrow coastal strip of flattish land, with the magnificent scenery of the distant fells of the Lake District as a backdrop. To the north loom the giant towers of Windscale and Calder Hall Nuclear Power Stations; the latter was the first atomic reactor in the world to generate electricity on a commercial scale. Recently, both plants were re-designated and are now known collectively as Sellafield. There is an information centre here open to the public.

Leave Seascale on the B5344 Gosforth road. In 2½ miles cross the main road on to an unclassified road and enter Gosforth.

GOSFORTH, Cumbria
In this remote Cumbrian village churchyard stands one of a very few survivals of the earliest Christian times in these islands, Gosforth Cross. This 1,000-year-old sacred monument is intricately carved with figures of men and beasts which may represent the pagan gods of Norse mythology, as well as orthodox Christian symbols, a sign that the 'new' religion had not yet completely supplanted the old beliefs of the Viking settlers.

Turn right, SP 'Wasdale Head', then in ¼ mile turn left. In ¾ mile bear right and continue to the shores of Wast Water.

WAST WATER, Cumbria
Bleak fells and cliffs of wild, grey scree sweep down to the shores of Wast Water. In places the water is more than 260ft deep, making this the deepest of the English lakes. To the east, dominating the surrounding hills, rise the towering jagged crags of Scafell and Scafell Pike, at 3,162ft and 3,206ft, the highest peaks in England. The mountain scenery of this remote stretch of water is incomparable.

From here a short detour to the left leads to Wasdale Head.

WASDALE HEAD, Cumbria
The only road through Wasdale ends abruptly at this small village, overshadowed by the massive bulk of Great Gable. From here the only way into the neighbouring valleys is on foot: over Black Sail Pass into Ennerdale, or by Sty Head into Borrowdale. The village is a famous centre for rock climbers: tracks lead up from Wasdale to climbs on Scafell, Napes ridges on Great Gable, and Pillar Rock. The first recorded ascent of Pillar was in 1826; Scafell Pinnacle and Lord's Rake were not climbed until the 1890s, and the Central Buttress not until 1914, but now climbers come from all over the country to tackle these ascents. In the graveyard of the tiny church at Wasdale Head several of the unsuccessful lie buried.

The main tour turns southwards alongside Wast Water, SP 'Santon Bridge'. In 1¾ miles turn left then left again and continue to Santon Bridge. Here turn left, SP 'Eskdale', and ascend through the Miterdale Forest, then continue to Eskdale Green.

ESKDALE GREEN, Cumbria
The easiest way to enjoy the scenery of this beautiful lakeland dale is to take the miniature railway, either at Irton Road, nestling in the shelter of Miterdale Forest, or at Eskdale Green station in the nearby village. The line runs from Ravenglass on the coast high up the valley to Dalegarth station at the foot of Hard Knott Pass, one of the highest and steepest motor roads in the Lake District. It was laid in 1875 to transport slate and minerals from the hills to the coast, but the steam locomotives, named after Lake District rivers, are not antique; they have been specially made by the railway company to carry passengers. The local name for the railway, 'Laal (little) Ratty', still sometimes used, comes from the name of the original contractor, Ratcliffe. From the top of the road leading from Eskdale Green into Ulpha can be seen one of the finest Lake District views, a panorama of the high fells, encompassing Harter Fell, Crinkle Crags, Bow Fell, Esk Pike, Scafell, Great Gable, Kirk Fell and Pillar.

Continue on the unclassified road and in ½ mile branch right, SP 'Ulpha'. Follow a narrow moorland road across Birker Fell then later descend and, at the T-junction, turn right into Ulpha.

Map

HAYCOCK 2618 / 2760 STEEPLE / 2630 KIRK FELL
2270 SEATALLON / 2649 LINGMELL / ▲3206 SCAFELL PIKE
Wasdale Head
SCA FELL 3162
Copeland Forest / BUCKBARROW
Wast Water
SCREES / Burnmoor Tarn
River Bleng
River Calder
Sellafield Nuclear Power Station
River Irt
Gosforth
THE ILLGILL HEAD 1983
WHINRIGG 1755
Beckfoot Station
CUMBRIAN MOUNTAINS
River Esk
A595
B5344
Santon Bridge
Miterdale Forest
Eskdale Green
SEASCALE
Dalegarth Station
The Ravenglass and Eskdale Railway
King George IV Inn
HARTER FELL 2129
Holmrook
Irton Road Station
BIRKER FELL
Muncaster Castle
LC
River Esk
Devoke Water
ULPHA FELL
Ravenglass
Glannaventa Roman Fort
unclass
A595
1632 STAINTON PIKE / 1566 HESK FELL
1735 CAW
Lane End
WHITFELL 1881
Ulpha
1790 BUCK BARROW
DUNNERDALE
A593
Broughton-in-Furness
Duddon Bridge
Bootle
1548
A5092
IRISH SEA
1361 / BLACK COMBE / WHITE COMBE / 1970
A595
A595
A5093
Whicham
Silecroft
LC
Duddon Sands
Millom
LC
N

mls 0 1 2 3 4
kms 0 2 4 6

Above: during medieval times the present entrance hall of Muncaster Castle was used as the great hall. It contains some intricate panelling and several family portraits of the Penningtons

ULPHA, Cumbria
Ulpha lies at the foot of the steep fell road out of Eskdale, looking across the River Duddon to the slopes of the Dunnerdale Fells. The poet Wordsworth wrote about the Chapel of St John, calling it the Kirk of Ulpha, in one of his sonnets. The chapel contains wall paintings dating from the 17th and 18th centuries.

In ¼ mile bear left across the river bridge, SP 'Broughton', and follow a winding road through Dunnerdale.

DUNNERDALE, Cumbria
Dunnerdale is the name given to the lower reaches of the lovely Duddon valley whose beautiful scenery inspired no less than 34 of Wordsworth's best-known sonnets. The poet had come to know the valley as a boy when staying with relations at Broughton. The River Duddon, which rises in the bleak moorland near Wrynose Pass, was until 1974 the old county boundary between Cumberland and Lancashire. It flows out to the sea beneath Duddon Bridge, into the deep estuary of Duddon Sands which washes the western shore of the Barrow-in-Furness peninsula.

After 3¼ miles turn right on to the A595, SP 'Workington,' cross Duddon Bridge, then continue to Whicham.

WHICHAM, Cumbria
A footpath from the village winds up the steep hillside to the summits of Black Crags and Black Combe with superb views on all sides. Black Combe, in the days before the postal service had established a reliable nationwide system of communications, was one of a chain of beacon hills stretching across the country, on which signal fires were lit to warn the people of danger or inform them of important events.

At the T-junction turn right and follow the foot of the fells to Bootle. Remain on the A595 and pass the edge of Waberthwaite, then in 1 mile descend into the River Esk valley. Cross the Esk and later pass the entrance to Muncaster Castle.

MUNCASTER CASTLE, Cumbria
The castle (OACT) stands on a superb site near Ravenglass, looking out westwards to the sea and eastwards to the high hills of Cumbria. The old medieval castle and pele tower still form part of the building which was enlarged and remodelled by Anthony Salvin in the 19th century. The Penningtons have lived here since the 13th century and there is a curious tradition associated with the family that dates back to 1461, when they gave shelter to King Henry VI after his defeat at the Battle of Towton. In gratitude, he gave them a bowl of greenish glass, enamelled and gilded, which has been known ever since as the 'Luck of Muncaster' because it is believed that while the bowl remains unbroken the Pennington succession at Muncaster will be assured. Among the other treasures of the castle is a fascinating collection of 17th-century miniature furniture. Muncaster is also famous for its bird gardens; small, brightly-coloured exotic species flit about the old courtyard and stately flamingoes, ibises and storks adorn the lakes.

½ mile beyond the castle keep forward on to an unclassified road for Ravenglass.

RAVENGLASS, Cumbria
Three rivers, the Irt, the Mite and the Esk, flow into the sea at Ravenglass, forming a sheltered, triple-pronged estuary, at the head of which lies the small resort. The town was granted a market charter in 1209, and flourished through the Middle Ages. In 1825 the beacon on the hill above the port was built as a lighthouse for the coastal traffic Ravenglass relied on, until alternative inland routes and the railway took this trade away. Today the sandy beaches, seafront and good bathing attract another trade — tourism. The village, as it now is, is the starting point of the Ravenglass and Eskdale Railway. On the north shore of the estuary, at Drigg Point, the Ravenglass Gullery and Nature Reserve (permit only) has the largest colony of black-headed gulls in Europe. Straight through the entrance of the harbour the Isle of Man can be seen 40 miles out to sea.

To the south of the village is Glannaventa.

GLANNAVENTA, Cumbria
Ruined walls, in places 13ft high, mark the site of a Roman fort, sometimes known as Walls Castle. The course of the old Roman road can still be traced along Eskdale to the site of another fort that once commanded the strategic heights of Hard Knott Pass, and thence by way of Wrynose Pass down to Ambleside.

Return to the A595 and turn left. At Holmrook turn left on to the B5344 for the return to Seascale.

AROUND THE THREE PEAKS

High fells and isolated dales sheltering the stone houses and outbuildings of hill farms surround Yorkshire's Three Peaks, rugged summits whose flanks are riddled with caves and pounded by the constant drop of lovely waterfalls. The roads are narrow and hilly, but the scenery is spectacular.

SEDBERGH, Cumbria
This market town lies below Howgill Fells, a range of rounded bracken-topped hills which links the Yorkshire Dales with the edge of the Lake District. A famous public school for boys was founded here in 1525, but the majority of the town's buildings are 19th-century and the general feel of the place is very Victorian. Permanent displays relating to the topography of the area can be seen in the National Park Centre.

Leave Sedbergh on the unclassified 'Dent' road and follow the River Dee through beautiful Dentdale. Continue through pleasant countryside to Den

DENTDALE, Cumbria
Lower Dentdale is a broad and well-wooded valley that narrows to a gorge and mountain pass beyond Dent village. Dent marble, a particularly hard form of limestone prized as a building material, is found in small quarries along its length, and beautiful fell scenery rises from both banks of the Dee.

DENT, Cumbria
In the heart of Dentdale is the attractive old village of Dent, a picturesque collection of houses and cottages centred on the twisting course of a cobbled main street. The village drinking fountain commemorates Alan Sedgwick, a pioneer geologist born here in the 19th century.

Drive to the George and Dragon Inn in Dent, turn right, and after 1 mile turn right again SP 'Ingleton'. Follow a narrow winding road into Deepdale, with Whernside rising on the left.

WHERNSIDE,
Cumbria & N Yorks
Whernside, the cave-riddled flanks of Pen-y-Ghent, and lofty Ingleborough are neighbouring summits of a massive millstone-grit formation known as the Three Peaks. The first-named rise to 2,419ft above sea level. The area's many potholes and tunnels should not be entered by any but the most experienced and well-equipped explorers.

Ascend steeply along a gated road to White Shaw Moss and a road summit of 1,553ft. Descend through Kingsdale, on either side of which runs a lofty limestone scar, and reach Thornton-in-Lonsdale. Turn left over a railway bridge, then left again. After a short distance turn left to enter the Dales centre of Ingleton.

INGLETON, N Yorks
This popular dales centre is a good rambling and touring base situated close to several beauty spots. Waterfalls in the area include 40ft Thornton Force and Pecca Falls, and lovely rock and river scenery can be enjoyed on a 2¼-hour round walk that follows the enchanting Doe Valley and returns alongside the River Twiss. The summit of Ingleborough is less than 4 miles from the village.

INGLEBOROUGH, N Yorks
Ingleborough is the second highest of the Three Peaks, and its 2,373ft summit forms a curious 15-acre plateau that was once guarded by an ancient stronghold. All that remains of the fortification today is a low rampart pierced by three openings. A well-known section of the massive cave systems that riddle the local limestone is known as the White Scar Caves (open). Potholers come from all parts of the country to explore its tunnels, where an underground river flows amongst strange rock formations into a sunless lake. Farther east is Gaping Gill, an awesome pothole whose 360ft shaft leads to a main chamber that extends a full 500ft below ground. It has the longest shaft in Britain and is a severe test of nerves and skill for the experienced climbers that attempt it.

Leave Ingleton and follow SP 'Settle' to join the A65. Drive through farming country and after 4 miles turn left on to the B6480 to enter Clapham.

CLAPHAM, N Yorks
A Yorkshire Dales National Park centre is based in this attractive little village, and the local caves attract potholing enthusiasts from all over Britain. About 1 mile north is the entrance to Ingleborough Cave (open), which runs for 900 yards and is noted for its splendid stalagmites and stalactites. The village is a charming collection of greystone houses and whitewashed cottages on the banks of Clapham Beck.

The windswept character of the Yorkshire Dales is particularly striking near Muker.

Leave Clapham on the 'Settle' road to join the A65, then in ¼ mile turn left on to an unclassified road for Austwick village. In ¾ mile reach Austwick.

AUSTWICK, N Yorks
Many of the Craven District's outstanding geological features lie close to this village. Of particular interest is a series of perched boulders, huge rocks left in precarious positions by the melting glaciers of the ice ages.

Great Shunner Fell towers over the village of Muker.

Leave Austwick by returning to the A65 and later pass beneath Giggleswick Scar to reach the edge of Giggleswick.

GIGGLESWICK, N Yorks
A well-known public school founded here in 1553 occupies impressive 19th-century buildings, but the early history of Giggleswick is best represented by its old market cross, stocks, and tithe barn. The local church features an ancient reading desk and a carved pulpit of 1680.

Leave Giggleswick and proceed to the town of Settle.

Adventurous visitors can follow a footpath behind the stupendous Hardrow Force waterfall.

HAWES, N Yorks

This sheep-marketing centre is the focal point of Upper Wensleydale life and a major supplier of the distinctive Wensleydale cheese. Within the old station buildings are a National Park Centre and the Upper Dales Folk Museum, which depicts life and trades in the dales.

In Hawes turn left on to the unclassified 'Muker' road and cross the River Ure. Reach a T-junction and turn left, then take the next turning right. A short detour can be made from the main route to Hardrow Force waterfall by keeping forward with SP 'Hardrow Force'.

HARDROW SCAR & FORCE, N Yorks

Considered one of the most spectacular in England, this magnificent waterfall plunges 90ft over the limestone rim of Hardrow Scar into a glen that was once used for brass band contests because of its superb acoustics. Access to the falls is by foot only, through the grounds of the Green Dragon Inn.

On the main tour, climb through the fine scenery of Buttertubs Pass.

BUTTERTUBS PASS, N Yorks

This 1,726ft pass links the lovely valleys of Swaledale and Wensleydale, and is named after deep limestone shafts that pock the countryside a short distance from the road. It is thought that these may have been dug by farmers and used to cool and harden butter that had got too warm on the way to market.

Continue along Buttertubs Pass and meet the B6270. A detour from the main route to Muker can be made by turning right here and driving for 1¼ miles through fell country.

Pen-y-Ghent, one of the impressive Three Peaks that rise above the national park.

MUKER, N Yorks

Set among the high moors and fells of Upper Swaledale, this remote little cluster of greystone houses is attractively set below the 2,340ft summit of Great Shunner Fell.

On the main tour, turn left on to the B6270 to Thwaite and later skirt the village of Keld.

KELD, N Yorks

Lovely Kisdon Force is one of several attractive waterfalls to be seen near this village, and the desolate area of Birkdale Common lies to the west.

Beyond Keld drive along a narrow hilly road through Birkdale Common, climbing to a road summit of 1,698ft on the Cumbrian border. Descend steeply (1-in-5) with views over the Eden Valley to reach Nateby, and turn right on to the B6259. Later turn right on to the A685 to enter Kirkby Stephen.

KIRKBY STEPHEN, Cumbria

This picturesque little market town is attractively set amongst moorland in the Eden Valley, and features a fine parish church containing several ancient carved stones. To the south the River Eden rises from its remote source in the wild Mallerstang Valley.

Leave Kirkby Stephen on the A685 SP 'Kendal' and after 2 miles turn left on to the A683 'Sedbergh' road. Continue among high fells along the attractive Rawthey Valley to reach the Cross Keys Inn.

CROSS KEYS INN, Cumbria

Originally built c1600, this inn (NT) was altered somewhat in the 18th and 19th centuries but is still a fine building. The impressive 600ft waterfall of Cautley Spout is accessible by footpath from here.

Leave the Cross Keys Inn and continue along the A683 to re-enter Sedbergh.

SETTLE, N Yorks

The charm of this small Ribblesdale market town is in its narrow streets of unpretentious buildings and secluded courtyards. Folly Hall, also known as Preston's Folly, is an unfinished 17th-century house with an elaborate front that contrasts severely with a very plain back. In many ways this sudden difference reflects the startling changes of the local countryside. In Victoria Street is an interesting museum of North Craven life.

Return through Settle along the A65 and turn right on to the B6479 SP 'Horton in Ribblesdale' to begin a drive through scenic Ribblesdale. After a short distance reach Langcliffe.

LANGCLIFFE, N Yorks

In 1838 a chance discovery of the feature now known as Victoria Cave led to the retrieval of many fascinating prehistoric remains, including the bones of animals long extinct in the British Isles.

Leave Langcliffe and proceed on the B6479 to reach Stainforth.

STAINFORTH, N Yorks

A 17th-century packhorse bridge that spans the River Ribble here is said to have replaced a similar structure built by monks in the 14th century. Some 300 yards downstream is the impressive waterfall of Stainforth Force. The lovely Ribblesdale Valley extends north and south along the river's rambling course.

From Stainforth, continue to Horton in Ribblesdale.

HORTON IN RIBBLESDALE, N Yorks

Alum Pot, one of the best-known potholes in the Craven district, lies 4 miles north-west of this picturesque moorland village.

Continue past Horton-in-Ribblesdale, with views of Pen-y-Ghent (right).

RIBBLESDALE, N Yorks

This long, wide valley of the Ribble cuts through a varied landscape and is popular with walkers, climbers, and potholers. The railway line from Settle to Carlisle runs through Ribblesdale and is considered one of the most scenic routes in the country.

PEN-Y-GHENT, N Yorks

One of the famous Three Peaks, this mountain rises to 2,273ft and is known for its potholes. In clear weather the views from its summit extend as far as Helvellyn, some 45 miles away.

Continue along the B6479 through desolate countryside beside the Leeds–Carlisle railway line to Ribblehead. A fine railway viaduct can be seen on the left, and 2,419ft Whernside rises straight ahead. Meet a T-junction and turn right on to the B6255 SP 'Hawes'. Ascend Redshaw Moss to a road summit of 1,434ft, then later descend through the steep fell country of Widdale. Meet the A684 and turn right to enter Hawes.

SHEFFIELD, S Yorks

Chaucer's *Canterbury Tales* refer to Sheffield cutlery as early as the 14th century, and when Flemish craftsmen settled here in the 16th century Sheffield began to specialise in cutlery in earnest. In about 1740 Benjamin Huntsman discovered how to produce steel, and Thomas Boulsover discovered how to roll silver plate; the 2 products for which Sheffield is world famous. Bomb damage in World War II necessitated the rebuilding of the city centre and there is little pre-Victorian building. The town hall, with a statue of Vulcan on the very top, was opened in 1897, and nearby the Cutlers Hall of 1832 contains a fine collection of silver from 1773 to the present. The City Museum in Weston Park, however, has the best collection, and the world's largest collection of Sheffield plate. There are 2 art galleries in Sheffield; the Graves, above the Central Library, which has an excellent collection of Chinese ivories and Mappin Art Gallery in Weston Park, specialising in English art.

Leave Sheffield on the A625, SP 'Chapel-en-le-Frith', and climb out of the suburbs on to Totley Moor (1,254 ft). To the left there are fine

THE PEAK DISTRICT

Great dams and small stone villages, bleak moorlands and narrow wooded valleys, fast-flowing rivers and placid lake waters; here is a mountain country in miniature, where ruined mills and tumbled stone walls testify to nature's supremacy. However, man has long inhabited the Peaks, and remnants of prehistoric cultures litter the hillsides.

views of the Derwent valley before entering Derbyshire and the well-known 'Surprise View', from where the entire Hope valley can be seen. Descend to Hathersage.

HATHERSAGE, Derbys

This small town in the Hope valley was well-known by the Brontë family, and nearby North Lees Hall and Moorseats Hall were depicted in Charlotte Brontë's novel *Jane Eyre*. Charlotte stayed with her friend Ellen Nussey in the vicarage, and her pearl inlaid writing desk is kept here. Over the church porch are the arms of the Eyre family, and within are fine brass portraits representing generations of Eyres. A grave in the churchyard is said to be that of Little John, Robin Hood's comrade.

Continue along the Hope valley and in 1¾ miles pass the junction with A6013, SP 'Glossop', which provides a short detour through Bamford to the Howden, Ladybower and Derwent reservoirs.

LADYBOWER, HOWDEN & DERWENT RESERVOIRS, Derbys

Howden, Derwent and Ladybower reservoirs lie in the valley of the Upper Derwent, forming a lovely landscape of tree-clad slopes and glittering lakes. Howden and Derwent, built in 1912 and 1916 with great castellated dams, were used for target practice during World War II by the famous Dambusters squadron. Ladybower was opened later, in 1945, at the cost of 10 farmhouses and 2 villages which lay in its path.

An unclassified road to the right immediately beyond the 2nd viaduct (A57) leads past an arm of the Ladybower reservoir up to the Derwent reservoir. The main tour continues for 2½ miles to Hope.

HOPE, Derbys

The village stands in the middle of a valley named after it, and was an important trading centre in medieval times. Today it is noted for the fishing and rough shooting to be had hereabouts. A weekly stock market is still held here and during late summer the Hope valley agricultural show with its popular sheepdog trials is a local highlight. Before this on Midsummer Day (25 June), a well-dressing ceremony takes place in which the village well is decked in flowers. The ceremony is pagan in origin and the flowers were offerings to the gods who supplied the spring water.

Continue on the A625 to Castleton.

The Mam Tor/Losehill ridge is a 3-mile barrier which separates Edale from the Hope valley

Inset: many Peak District villages ceremonially decorate their wells with clay panels inlaid with flower petals, such as this one at Hope

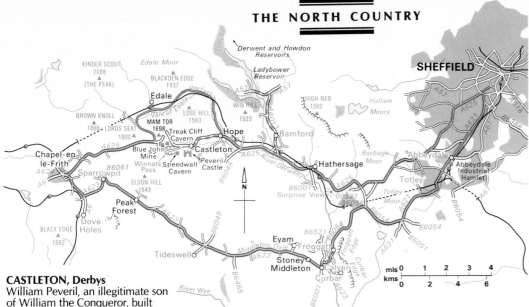

SHEFFIELD

CASTLETON, Derbys

William Peveril, an illegitimate son of William the Conqueror, built the castle (AM) around which this popular Peak District village grew. The keep which remains today was erected by Henry II in 1176, and is the most impressive medieval landmark in the Peak National Park. However, the feature which attracts the visitor most to this pleasant village is its group of limestone caverns (OACT): Peak, Speedwell, Treak Cliff and Blue John, the last named after the rare, blue semi-precious stone found in these hills. Speedwell Cavern is the most spectacular as it consists of one huge chamber and has to be toured in a boat. The nearest cavern to the village is Peak Cavern which is the largest and stretches 2,000ft into the hillsides. Castleton Garlanding, held on 29 May, is a strange custom, believed to be a fertility rite praising some long-forgotten god. A bell-like garland covers the wearer who is usually led through the village on horseback.

To visit Speedwell Cavern and the Winnats Pass, continue on the A625 (now closed at Mam Tor) and at the end of the village branch left on to the unclassified road. The Blue John Cavern can be reached by turning right beyond the end of the gorge, and Treak Cliff is reached by staying on the old A625 at the end of Castleton village. The main tour returns along the A625 to Hope and at the church turns left on to the Edale road.

EDALE, Derbys

In the shadow of the Kinder massif — the highest point in the peak District — is broad, green Edale valley. Along its length are hamlets known as booths (Upper Booth, Barber Booth, Grindsbrook Booth and so on), the name refers to the shelters used by cattle herdsmen in Elizabethan times when the valleys were divided into great ranches. Today sheep rather than cattle roam the valley pastures. On the other side of the valley from Kinder is a massive 3-mile-long ridge, with Mam Tor

(1,696ft) as the highest point. This is crowned by a great Iron-Age fort, which was once a sizeable town. Part of the earthworks have fallen away on the east side, giving rise to landslides which have given Mam Tor the nickname 'shivering mountain'. These slides have recently destroyed the main road running along its lower slopes. Mam Tor is a very old name, the 'Mam' referring to a pagan belief in a mother goddess.

Follow this unclassified road through the valley passing Edale village, and near the end bear left and later ascend to a 1,550ft pass, behind Mam Tor. Descend to the A625 and turn right and in 4¼ miles enter Chapel-en-le-Frith.

CHAPEL-EN-LE-FRITH, Derbys

The first church here was a chapel built in the 13th century by local foresters, and the site would then have been at the edge of the forest — hence, en-le-Frith. The present church dates from the early 14th century. The position of this small market town is high up in the Peak District and it is the gateway to the famous walking and climbing country for which the Peaks are renowned.

Follow SP 'Buxton' to join A6 and in 1½ miles turn left again on to the A623, SP 'Chesterfield'. At Sparrowpit turn sharp right, and in 2 miles pass through Peak Forest.

PEAK FOREST, Derbys

In high, exhilarating countryside this straggling village was once the 'Gretna Green' of the Peak District. The original church, dedicated to King Charles the Martyr in 1657, was extra-parochial, and therefore independent of episcopal jurisdiction, and so up until the early 19th century was able to hold marriage services outside usual church law.

In 2½ miles pass an unclassified road on the right for Tideswell. In 4 miles start the descent into Middleton Dale and in 1½ miles the B6521 to the left leads to Eyam.

EYAM, Derbys

One day in 1665 a clothes chest was delivered to a cottage in Eyam from plague-ridden London. The chest carried plague germs, and between 1665-1666 two-thirds of the population was wiped out. The villagers, led by their rector William Mompesson and his

predecessor Thomas Stanley, resolved to isolate themselves to prevent the plague spreading. Whether this heroic act saved or lost life is disputed by modern-day theorists, but either way it has earned Eyam an honoured place in history. The cottage which took delivery of the clothes chest still stands, and Cucklett Church, a nearby crag, where Mompesson held open-air services during the plague, is the scene of an annual commemorative service.

Shortly pass through Stoney Middleton.

STONEY MIDDLETON, Derbys

Stoney Middleton is as beautiful as Castleton, except for the white dust from the nearby limestone quarries, which covers trees for miles around and produces a most eerie landscape on a moonlit night. In the village is one of the few truly octagonal churches in the country. Two wells stand before the church, and are decorated every August with pictures from the Bible made from thousands of flower petals and bits of bark and moss which are pressed into soft clay.

Continue to Calver and turn left at the traffic signals on to the B6001, SP 'Grindleford', and in ¼ mile branch right on to the B6054, SP 'Sheffield'. Shortly turn left across the River Derwent and climb to Totley Moor. At the summit keep right. To the left is a ventilation shaft of the 3½ mile-long Totley railway tunnel which lies 650ft below the top of the moor. Further on join the A621 before reaching the Abbeydale Industrial Hamlet.

ABBEYDALE INDUSTRIAL HAMLET, S Yorks

Ranged round a large courtyard on a half-acre site on the banks of the River Sheaf, is a remarkable piece of industrial archaeology. This is the Abbeydale Industrial Hamlet, dating mainly from the 18th century, and consisting of workshops and workers' cottages. The main industry here was scything and there is a grinding shop, a tilt-hammer house, a steel melting shop and 6 hand forges. The hamlet has been restored to working order and opened to the public.

Continue on the A621 for the return to Sheffield.

THE PEAK NATIONAL PARK, Derbys

The National Park was the first to be designated as such in Britain, the green 'lung' of industrial England. Peak incidentally comes from Old English 'peac' for knoll or hill. The area comprises the White Peak central and southern limestone area, a gentle, rolling countryside of wooded slopes and rounded hills, and Dark Peak the northern gritstone region, hard, bleak and wild.

The cottage in Eyam where the plague, brought from London, broke out in 1665

SKIPTON, N Yorks

Attractively situated on the Airedale moorlands at the eastern edge of the Craven district, Skipton is dominated by a medieval castle (open) that was restored by Lady Anne Clifford in 1658. Founded in Norman times, the building was subsequently extended and was strong enough to resist a 3-year siege before falling into the hands of Cromwell's parliamentarian army in the Civil War. The Lord Protector dismantled the castle to make sure that it could never again be manned against him, but thanks to Lady Anne its six massive towers still punctuate the skyline of the town that grew beneath its walls. Opposite the massive castle gateway is the Craven Museum, where exhibits and displays illustrate the geology and folk history of the district. An old four-storey corn mill, on a site where similar buildings have operated since the 12th century, houses the George Leatt Industrial and Folk Museum, where working waterwheels and a collection of carts and horse traps can be seen.

Leave Skipton on the A59 'Harrogate' road. A detour from the main route to the Yorkshire Dales Railway can be made by taking the B6265 from Skipton and turning left on to an unclassified road to Embsay.

YORKSHIRE DALES RAILWAY, N Yorks

This small preserved steam railway with its centre at Embsay, runs on 1¼ miles of track and has over 20 locomotives at various stages of restoration. Existing facilities for visiting enthusiasts include access to the current work, a signal box, and a personalized saloon car.

On the main tour, leave Skipton via the A59 and drive through a countryside of drystone walls and quarries to Bolton Bridge. Reach the Devonshire Arms Hotel and turn left on to the B6160 SP 'Bolton Abbey', then continue to Bolton Abbey.

THE YORKSHIRE DALES

Some of England's most impressive scenery can be seen in the rocky clefts of Airedale and Wharfedale, the superb natural amphitheatre of Malham Cove, and the breathtaking gorge of Gordale Scar. Underground are miles of water-worn tunnels, many resplendent with rock and ice formations.

Augustinian monks selected a magnificent site for their abbey at Bolton.

BOLTON ABBEY, N Yorks

Woodlands and pastures in a bend of the River Wharfe make a fittingly peaceful setting for the remains of this once-powerful 12th-century priory (open). Most of the structure lies in ruins, but the nave has served as a parish church for hundreds of years and the old gatehouse was incorporated into a mansion during the 19th century. The little river can be crossed by stepping stones or a footbridge here, and attractive riverside walks extend from the ruins to The Strid.

Continue through a wooded stretch of Wharfedale to reach The Strid and later Barden Tower.

A man-made order is brought to parts of Wharfedale by a pattern of drystone walls.

THE STRID & BARDEN TOWER, N Yorks

The modern translation of the old English word Strid is Turmoil, which is an apt description of the way in which the River Wharfe boils through a 12ft constriction of its gorge at this point. Farther north are the picturesque ruins of Barden Tower, a 12th-century structure that was restored by Lady Anne Clifford of Skipton Castle in 1659.

Reach Barden Tower and turn right on to an unclassified road SP 'Appletreewick'. Cross the river, and turn sharp right on an ascent with SP 'Hazlewood' and 'Storiths'. Continue along a gated road beneath Barden Fell, descend (1 in 5), and cross a ford. Ascend steeply (1 in 4) from the ford,

passing The Strid again, and meet the A59. Turn left and ascend a winding road on to Blubberhouses Moor. Enter a narrow rocky valley and climb to the edge of Blubberhouses, at the end of Fewston Reservoir. Cross a river bridge and turn sharp left on to an unclassified road SP 'Pateley Bridge'. Continue over high moorland, and turn left on to the B6265. Stump Cross Caverns lie to the left of the road.

STUMP CROSS CAVERNS, N Yorks

Dramatic subterranean formations of ice and eroded rock can be appreciated from a pathway that extends ¼ mile into these caverns.

Continue, with views into beautiful Upper Wharfedale, to Grassington.

GRASSINGTON, N Yorks

The lovely area in which this Upper Wharfedale village stands has been mineral deposits and has been settled since very early times. Many iron-age camps and barrows survive, and during the Roman occupation the area was extensively mined for lead ore. The village itself is a popular tourist centre with a cobbled market square reached via a picturesque medieval bridge. A National Park Interpretation Centre is based here.

Leave Grassington and follow an unclassified road SP 'Conistone' through wooded country, occasionally passing close to the River Wharfe. Reach Conistone and keep left to meet the B6160. Turn right and continue to Kilnsey Crag.

KILNSEY, N Yorks

This village is completely dwarfed by the great limestone scar of Kilnsey Crag, one of the best-known landmarks in Yorkshire.

A pleasant detour can be made from the main route by continuing along the B6160 to Kettlewell.

KETTLEWELL, N Yorks

At one time this attractive Wharfedale village was a small oasis of civilization in a great tract of forest, but nowadays the drystone-scattered expanses of the open moor extend right to its boundaries. Great Whernside rises to 2,310ft in the north-east.

On the main tour, leave Kilnsey on the B6160 and drive north. In ¾ mile branch left on to an unclassified road SP 'Arncliffe' and drive through Littondale to reach Arncliffe.

ARNCLIFFE, N Yorks

Typical greystone houses of the Dales area nestle amongst clumps of mature sycamores in this secluded Littondale community. Evidence of long occupation is apparent in a clearly-defined Celtic field system in the immediate district, and the village church stands on the site of a building dated c1100. South of Arncliffe is the dramatic mile-long cliff of Yew Cogar Scar.

In Arncliffe turn right SP 'Halton Gill' and continue through Littondale.

LITTONDALE, N Yorks
Once a medieval hunting forest, this lovely dale in the national park has avoided the depredations of the early lead miners. It retains extensive areas of wild woodland, and its farmlands show signs of having been cultivated since early times.

Reach Halton Gill and turn left on to a gated unclassified road. Continue, following SP 'Stainforth' and 'Settle', and ascend (1 in 5) to a road summit of over 1,400ft, with views of Pen-y-Ghent to the right.

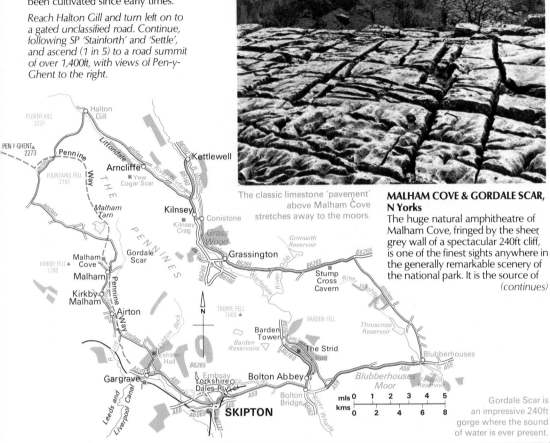

The classic limestone 'pavement' above Malham Cove stretches away to the moors.

MALHAM COVE & GORDALE SCAR, N Yorks
The huge natural amphitheatre of Malham Cove, fringed by the sheer grey wall of a spectacular 240ft cliff, is one of the finest sights anywhere in the generally remarkable scenery of the national park. It is the source of *(continues)*

the River Aire and forms part of a 22-mile fault that resulted from the intolerable stresses imposed by enormous glaciers during the ice ages. An energetic climb leads to the moorland above and Malham Tarn. Gordale Scar, a precipitous, winding gorge filled with the sound of waterfalls and dashing cascades, can be reached from the cove via a 1½-mile footpath.

MALHAM, N Yorks
In the height of the summer season this little stone village is inundated by visitors who flock to the area for its magnificent scenery. Information about the Malham district is available from the Yorkshire Dales National Park Interpretation Centre, which is based in the village.

THE PENNINE WAY
From its southern extremity in Derbyshire, this 250-mile footpath follows the mountainous spine of England and passes through Malham before crossing Pen-y-Ghent on its way to Kirk Yetholme in Scotland. Prospective walkers should realize that this is a fairly rugged route, particularly in its northern sections, and can be positively hazardous in bad weather.

Leave Malham with SP 'Skipton' and continue to Kirkby Malham.

KIRKBY MALHAM, N Yorks
Close to the local 17th-century vicarage is the charming village church, containing a 12th-century font and family box pews of the Georgian period.

Drive through the village to Airton.

AIRTON, N Yorks
Situated in Upper Airedale, this charming village is on the route of the Pennine Way and boasts several good 17th-century buildings. The most notable are the Manor House, the Friend's Meeting House, and the Post Office.

Leave Airton, continue for ¾ mile, and turn left. Drive through the grounds of Eshton Hall (not open) and turn right to reach Gargrave.

GARGRAVE, N Yorks
Although Gargrave's parish church is mostly Victorian, it retains a 16th-century tower and fragments of several Saxon crosses.

Meet the A65 in Gargrave and turn left to cross the Leeds and Liverpool Canal.

LEEDS & LIVERPOOL CANAL
Wonderful scenery that can only be guessed at by the road-bound tourist is revealed to anybody who takes the trouble to hire a boat on this 127-mile canal. It is one of the longest waterways in Britain, rising to 500ft above sea level as it crosses the high ridge of the Pennine Chain.

Continue along the A65 to re-enter Skipton.

PEN-Y-GHENT, N Yorks
Potholing enthusiasts come here to dare the uncertainties of aptly-named Hell Pot and Hunt Pot, two entrances to the cave system that riddles Pen-y-Ghent. Above ground, this 2,273ft summit, one of the famous Three Peaks, affords wide views that extend more than 40 miles to Helvellyn in clear weather.

Continue along the gated road and turn left on to the 'Malham' road. Ascend (1 in 5) to cross wild moorland, and in 3 miles bear right to meet crossroads. Drive forward on the gated 'Grassington' road to reach the Malham Tarn carpark.

MALHAM TARN, N Yorks
All around the isolated waters of Malham Tarn (NT) are heathery moorlands and unusual raised bogs. The tarn itself is the habitat of many species of aquatic wildlife, and the serious naturalist can familiarize himself with the area at the Field Centre in Malham Tarn House, on the northern shore. Above the field centre are the high white cliffs of Highfolds Scar and a natural limestone pavement.

Leave the Malham Tarn carpark and descend steeply to pass Malham Cove and Gordale Scar.

Gordale Scar is an impressive 240ft gorge where the sound of water is ever present.

| mls | 0 | 1 | 2 | 3 | 4 | 5 |
| kms | 0 | 2 | 4 | 6 | 8 | |

SOUTHPORT, Merseyside

Particularly well known for its beautifully laid out gardens, this attractive and elegant resort is also noted for its wide range of sporting facilities. It is the home of the Royal Birkdale Golf Club, which has been the venue for Ryder Cup competitions, and is host to county cricket matches, horse jumping trials, and lawn tennis matches. The annual flower show is also a popular event. Amenities for holiday-makers include 6 miles of excellent sands, the largest pier in England, a model village, and boat hire on the 91-acre Marine Lake. The Victorian heyday of seaside holidays is recalled by old salt-water swimming baths and a room of the Botanic Gardens Museum. An interesting collection of fine buildings and shops can be found in Lord Street, which is considered one of the finest thoroughfares in the north of England. Churches in Southport include St Cuthbert's, which displays fine woodwork and a clock of 1739, and a curious red and yellow building in the suburb of Crossens. The latter building shares its churchyard with a very ornate neo-Norman mausoleum. The expanding Steam Transport Museum boasts a fine collection of locomotives, buses, traction engines, and various commercial vehicles. It is planned to become the largest centre of its type in the north west of England, and will be a valuable aid to the understanding of industrial archaeology in transport.

Leave Southport on the A565 SP 'Preston', passing through Crossens. After 3 miles turn right on to the B5246 SP 'Rufford'. Continue through Mere Brow, Holmeswood, and Rufford, and meet the A59 SP 'Preston'. Turn left, and after ¼ mile reach the entrance to Rufford Old Hall on the right.

Unusual 17th-century windows at Astley Hall dominate the exterior.

TO THE WEST PENNINES

Between the elegant seaside resort of Southport and the wild western slopes of the Pennines is the Lancashire Plain, an area of farm and parkland where much of the county's folk history is preserved in picturesque villages, great houses in fine grounds, and fascinating small town museums.

The village cross guards a picturesque approach to St Michael's Church, Croston.

RUFFORD OLD HALL, Lancs

This superb timber-framed Tudor building (NT) stands in 14½ acres of beautiful grounds and is one of the finest examples surviving in England today. Built by the Hesketh family in the 15th century, it was slightly extended during Victorian times but has not been spoilt by 19th-century over restoration. The exterior is a startling combination of decorative black timbers infilled with brilliant white plaster, and the great hall carries an extremely ornate hammerbeam roof. Inside the house is a rare 15th-century screen, and one of the wings contains the Philip Ashcroft Museum of folk crafts and antiquities.

Leave Rufford Old Hall and continue along the A59 for 1 mile, then turn right on to the A581 'Chorley' road. Continue along the A581 to the Leeds and Liverpool Canal.

LEEDS AND LIVERPOOL CANAL, Lancs

As it crosses the rugged Pennine Chain this 127-mile waterway between two of northern England's major cities reaches an amazing 500ft above sea level. The canal took 40 years to build and has many features of interest to naturalists and industrial archaeologists.

Proceed along the A581, crossing the River Douglas, and later turn left over a bridge to reach Croston.

CROSTON, Lancs

Picturesque countryside following the twisting course of the River Yarrow makes a fine setting for this tiny village. Among its most notable buildings are 17th-century almshouses and a 15th-century church containing a curious memorial brass.

From Croston, turn right and in ¼ mile meet a war memorial. Turn left here and in 1 mile meet a T-junction. Turn right and continue along the A581 for 3½ miles. Cross the M6, then meet the A49 and turn left. Turn right on to the A581. Drive for a short distance to reach Astley Hall on the left.

ASTLEY HALL, Lancs

Charmingly set in nearly 100 acres of wood and parkland, this fine 16th-century and later house (open) has a drawing room with lovely tapestries depicting scenes from the legend of the Golden Fleece. Throughout the house are fine collections of furnishings, pottery and paintings, and special exhibitions are frequently mounted in its rooms.

Leave Astley Hall and proceed along the A581 into Chorley.

CHORLEY, Lancs

Industry is this old textile centre's way of life. It was once known for cotton weaving and calico printing, but in recent years these traditional concerns have been largely replaced by a variety of modern enterprises. The town stands at the edge of farming country close to the foot of the Pennines. The area is dominated by the imposing height of 682ft Healey Nab which rises to the east.

Meet traffic signals in Chorley and turn left on to the A6 SP 'Preston'. In 1 mile cross a railway bridge, meet a roundabout, and take the 2nd exit on to the A674 SP 'M61' and 'Blackburn'. Continue, with Healey Nab rising to the right, and drive through Higher Wheelton. In 2 miles meet a roundabout; a detour from the main route can be taken here by following the 1st exit on to the A675 to reach Hoghton Tower.

HOGHTON TOWER, Lancs

Ancestral home of what is claimed to be the oldest baronetcy in England, this fine 16th-century mansion occasionally opens its state rooms, ballroom, Tudor wellhouse, and dungeon to the public. The gardens can also be visited at certain times. In 1617 King James I stayed here, and is said to have been so taken with a loin of beef prepared by the house kitchen that he drew his sword and knighted it, ever since which that particular cut has been sirloin – a charming, if dubious, tale.

On the main tour, take the 2nd exit from the roundabout and continue for ½ mile to a T-junction. Turn right on to A6061 to Fensicowles, then meet the A6062 and turn right SP 'Darwen'. In ½ mile drive under a railway bridge and immediately turn right on to an unclassified road, then turn left. Continue for 1 mile to the Black Bull (PH), meet crossroads, and drive forward. In 1 mile meet the A666 and drive forward on to the B6231 SP 'Accrington'. In ½ mile pass a railway bridge and ascend to Guide, then meet crossroads by the King Edward VII (PH). Turn right on to the B6232 SP 'Bury', then keep left and after 2 miles reach the Grey Mare Inn; turn right on to an unclassified road SP 'Edgworth'. Drive to Edgworth, meet crossroads, and continue forward to reach Turton Bottoms. Meet a T-junction with the main road and turn sharp right on to the B6391 SP 'Darwen'. Turton Tower stands to the left.

Turton Tower features ornate 19th-century timbering.

BELMONT, Lancs

Belmont Church is a good example of 19th-century architecture that has been built to serve rather than impress. Its main feature is an attractive 6-light window.

At Belmont meet a T-junction and turn right on to the A675. Take the next turning left on to an unclassified road SP 'Rivington', and drive through open moorland with views of 1,498ft Winter Hill on the left. Descend to a T-junction and turn right, then meet another T-junction and turn left to reach Rivington.

TURTON TOWER, Lancs

The core of this L-shaped building (open) is a 15th-century pele tower, a type of fortified dwelling that was once common in the north of England. Two wings were added in the 16th century, and the house now contains fine collections of paintings and furnishings, plus a fascinating local history museum.

Good views of Turton and Entwhistle Reservoirs can be enjoyed from the Turton to Belmont road.

Continue north along the B6391 with views of the Turton and Entwhistle Reservoirs on the right. In 1 mile meet a T-junction and turn left on to the A666 SP 'Bolton'. In ¼ mile turn right on to an unclassified road SP 'Belmont', then take the next turning right and descend with views of Delph Reservoir to the left and Belmont Reservoir to the right. After 1 mile drive over crossroads to reach Belmont.

RIVINGTON, Lancs

Rivington Pike rises to a 1,190ft summit above this attractive little moorland village. It is crowned by an 18th-century stone tower and commands excellent views over miles of countryside. In the village itself is a good church housing a fine screen and a 16th-century pulpit. Rivington Hall, which stands in 400-acre Lever Park, was rebuilt in 1744 and contains a general interest museum. Close to the village are the Rivington and Anglezarke Reservoirs.

RIVINGTON AND ANGLEZARKE RESERVOIRS, Lancs

These broad sheets of water add an extra dimension of beauty to the somewhat severe moorland countryside around them. They were built in the 19th century to supply Liverpool with water, and have naturalized into perfect habitats for many types of wildlife.

Leave Rivington and drive forward SP 'Adlington', crossing the Rivington Reservoir. Meet a T-junction, turn left SP 'Horwich', and in ¾ mile meet a junction with the A673. Turn right on to the A673 and take the next turning left on to an unclassified road SP 'Blackrod'. In 1 mile meet the A6, drive forward, and in ¼ mile turn right. Continue for 1 mile, meet a T-junction with the B5239, and drive forward SP 'Standish'. In 1¼ miles meet a T-junction and turn right on to the A5106, then in 200 yards turn left on to the B5239 and continue to the town of Standish.

STANDISH, Gt Manchester

This colliery town stands on the line of a Roman road and features a good church that was rebuilt in the 16th century. Inside the building, particularly in the roof, are good examples of woodwork. The old village stocks are preserved on the steps of a modern town cross.

Meet traffic signals in Standish and drive forward on to the A5209. In 1¼ miles turn right to follow SP 'M6', then meet a roundabout and take the 2nd exit to cross the M6 motorway. Continue to Parbold.

PARBOLD, Lancs

Parbold Hall is a splendid stone-built Georgian house (not open) with a Venetian-style doorway. Excellent views of the surrounding countryside can be enjoyed from the summit of Parbold Hill, which is crowned by the impressive 19th-century building of Christ Church.

Leave Parbold and cross the Leeds and Liverpool Canal, then the River Douglas, to reach Newburgh. Continue to Burscough.

BURSCOUGH, Lancs

Slight remains of a priory lie to the south-west of Burscough, which has a Victorian church with four attractive pinnacled buttresses.

From Burscough, join the A59 SP 'Southport' and in ¾ mile turn right on to the B5242. Continue through Bescar, meet traffic signals, and turn right on to the A570 to reach Scarisbrick and its hall.

SCARISBRICK, Lancs

Designed by the architect Pugin in 1837, ornate Scarisbrick Hall (open on application) is an excellent example of the opulence favoured in the Victorian period. It is gothic in style and was the architect's first major work, taking 4 years to complete. The 150 rooms of the house are now occupied by a school.

Leave Scarisbrick and continue along the A570 for the return to Southport.

LAKES AND FELLS

Magnificent lakes, fells and mountains border the winding roads in this area beloved by poets, writers and painters, and immortalised by William Wordsworth. Some of the most dramatic scenery in England is here, including Kirkstone Pass — the highest pass open to motorists in Cumbria.

WINDERMERE, Cumbria

The quaint, crowded town of Windermere lies on the eastern shore of Lake Windermere which has been a well-known centre for sailing and boating since the 19th century, and a number of clubs are based on its shores. Lake Windermere, at 10½ miles, is the longest lake in England. It has 14 islands, including the delightful privately-owned 38-acre Belle Island which can be visited by steamer and has a historic round house (OACT) full of curios. The

Steamboat Museum has a collection of Victorian and Edwardian boats that were used on the lake in the days of steam. They are kept in working order in a covered dock and an exhibition recalls the development of navigation at Windermere. Casual visitors can travel up and down the lake by steamer and it is an ideal way to enjoy the scenery.

Leave Windermere on the A591, SP 'Kendal', and proceed to Staveley.

STAVELEY, Cumbria

This small village is set beside the second fastest-flowing river in England — the Kent. The Kentmere valley to the north of Staveley was once a lake, but it was drained a century ago for the mineral deposits on the bed. At the head of the valley, at Kentmere, is the 16th-century ruin of Kentmere Hall, birthplace in 1517 of the evangelist Bernard Gilpin. High fells dominate this lovely, lonely valley, with Ill Bell, to the north, the loftiest peak at 2,476ft.

In 3 miles, at the roundabout, take the A5284 for Kendal.

KENDAL, Cumbria

The largest of the south Lakeland towns, Kendal, known as the Auld Grey Town, is a blend of both ancient and modern architecture. Limestone buildings, their walls a dozen subtle shades of grey, dominate its narrow old streets and picturesque yards. The River Kent meanders through the town, its banks lined by well-tended

gardens and high on the hill in the centre of the town are the imposing ruins of Kendal Castle. Built during the 14th century, the castle was the birthplace of Catherine Parr, last of Henry VIII's 6 wives. A famous son of the town is George Romney, the portrait painter, born in 1734, and a collection if his works hangs in the Mayor's Parlour. Other collections can be viewed at Abbot Hall Art Gallery, close to the 12th-century parish church, and in the Borough Museum, which specialises in natural history. The Castle Dairy in William Street is a well-preserved example of vernacular Tudor architecture. Kendal has long been a centre of commerce and in 1331 a woollen industry was established and became famous for 'Kendal Green', mentioned by Shakespeare.

Leave on the A6, SP 'The North' then 'Penrith'. Later climb across Shap Fell and continue to Shap.

Ullswater, second largest lake in the Lake District, is a popular centre for boating and water sports

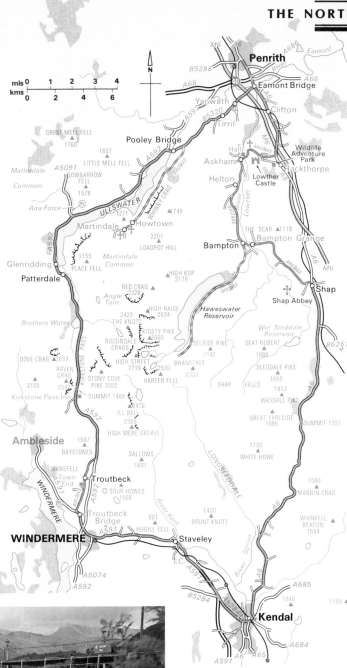

A British Rail steamer on Lake Windermere

At the end of the village turn left, SP 'Bampton'. In ½ mile bear right (passing the track to Shap Abbey) and continue to Bampton Grange. Cross the river bridge and turn right for Bampton.

BAMPTON & HAWESWATER RESERVOIR, Cumbria.

The small village of Bampton lies about 2 miles north-east of the spectacular Haweswater Reservoir which can be reached via an unclassified road from Bampton. The reservoir was created to supply Manchester with water and although the road to the north of the lake was submerged in the waterworks scheme, a footpath along the valley remains.

At Bampton turn right, SP 'Penrith', and later skirt Helton to reach Askham. At the crossroads turn right, SP 'Lowther'. Cross the river then pass through Lowther Park.

SHAP, Cumbria

Shap village, nearly 1,000ft above sea level, lies north of the wild, desolate Shap Summit which reaches to 1,300ft. The A6 crosses the summit and is frequently blocked by snowdrifts in winter. Hidden in the valley west of Shap village are the ruins of Shap Abbey (AM). Founded around 1191 by Premonstratensian canons (a French order) most of the ruins date from the early 13th century. There are dramatic views of the High Street group of peaks here.

LOWTHER PARK, Cumbria

This 3,000-acre park is sculpted out of beautiful countryside that surrounds the ruins of Lowther Castle (not open). This was once a grand house, home of the Earls of Lonsdale and visited by Mary, Queen of Scots. Also in the park is the 12th-century church of St Michael. This was considerably rebuilt during 1686 and outside it stands the mausoleum of the Earls of Lonsdale.

After 1 mile, at the crossroads, turn left, SP 'Lowther Wildlife Park', and in ½ mile reach the A6. At Hackthorpe (right) is the entrance to the Wildlife Adventure Park.

WILDLIFE ADVENTURE PARK, Cumbria

About 100 acres of parkland provide a natural setting for deer, rare breeds of sheep and cattle, and cranes. There are also special enclosures for many European mammals, including otters, badgers and wild pigs.

The main tour turns left on to the A6, SP 'Penrith', and continues through Clifton to Eamont Bridge.

EAMONT BRIDGE, Cumbria

The village of Eamont Bridge is distinguished by a triple-arched medieval bridge which carries traffic over the River Eamont. Nearby is a prehistoric earthwork, 300ft in diameter, called King Arthur's Round Table. It is nearly circular and originally had 2 entrances, one of which survives, and is surrounded by a ditch and a 5ft-high bank. Mayburgh, ¼ mile to the west, is another prehistoric site. This originally occupied 1½ acres and still has 15ft ramparts.

Continue from Eamont Bridge on the A6 and at the roundabout take the 2nd exit to enter Penrith.

PENRITH, Cumbria

Capital town of the old Cumbria in the 9th century, Penrith was probably initially occupied by the Celts c 500BC. Penrith Castle (AM), built in the 14th century as a defence against the Scots, is now just a ruin. The castle was enlarged by the Duke of Gloucester, later Richard III, who is said to have resided in The Gloucester Arms; dating from 1477, it is one of the oldest inns in England. Penrith town hall, built in 1791, is constructed from 2 houses designed by Richard Adam. In the graveyard of the partly-Norman church are 2 strange stone monuments named 'Giant's Grave' and 'Giant's Thumb'. They are believed to commemorate Owen, King of Cumbria c 920.

Return along the A6, SP 'Shap', and at the roundabout take the 3rd exit to re-enter Eamont Bridge. Here, turn right on to the B5320, SP 'Ullswater', for Yanwath. Continue on the B5320 and pass through Tirril to reach Pooley Bridge.

POOLEY BRIDGE & ULLSWATER, Cumbria

Pooley Bridge, a small village beside the River Eamont, is an ideal centre from which to explore the majestic, spectacular Ullswater lake and its surrounding fells and mountains. Boats may be hired from Pooley Bridge and passenger vessels sail regularly in summer. A small, unclassified road to the south of the lake ends at Martindale where there is a forest with red deer and 2 lonely old churches. The lake is 7 miles long, and about 5 miles from the east end is Gowbarrow Park, seen in spring as a sea of golden daffodils and immortalised by Wordsworth in his famous poem. Close by is Aira Force, a splendid waterfall. High mountains dominating the south-western end of the lake include some of the High Street peaks to the east and the Helvellyn range to the west. Glenridding is a hamlet towards the south-westerly tip of the lake, dominated by a large hotel; boats from Pooley Bridge put in here.

At Pooley Bridge cross the river bridge and in nearly ½ mile turn left on to the A592, SP 'Windermere'. Continue along the shore of Ullswater to Patterdale.

PATTERDALE, Cumbria

This attractive village at the head of Ullswater is encircled by mountains — Place Fell to the east is over 2,000ft and Helvellyn and Lower Man to the south and west are over 3,000ft. The summit of Helvellyn, the third highest peak in the Lake District, is a 3-mile walk along the mile-long Striding Edge, approached by the Grisedale valley. On a clear day, almost every peak in the Lakes is visible from the summit, with the mountains of Scotland rising to the north and the Pennines to the east.

The tour continues southwards and later ascends the dramatic Kirkstone Pass. Beyond the summit (1,489ft) there is an easier descent for 3 miles before turning right, SP 'Ambleside', to enter Troutbeck.

TROUTBECK, Cumbria

Spread along the side of a wild and beautiful valley of the same name, Troutbeck is dominated by lofty pikes of the Kirkstone Pass to the north. At the south end of the village is Townend — a typical yeoman's house (NT) of the early 17th century, with whitewashed walls and mullioned windows: it still retains much of the original oak furniture. At the north end farms and houses cluster around a 17th-century inn called The Mortal Man. The east window in the church was designed by the artist, Edward Burne-Jones.

Follow the Windermere road and in 1¼ miles turn right on to the A591 for the return to Windermere.

IN THE VALE OF YORK

Away from the gothic completeness of York's superb minster are the rolling farmlands of the Vale of York and dry limestone ridges of the Howardian Hills. Everywhere are monuments to the skills of past generations, and close by are the untamed tracts of the Yorkshire Moors and Dales.

YORK, N Yorks

Capital of a British province under the Romans in AD 71, this ancient centre is still the chief city of northern England and preserves many fascinating reminders of its historic past. The earliest surviving building is the Roman Multangular Tower, though parts of the city walls derive from the same period – particularly in the section south of Monk Bar. The walls themselves complete a 3-mile circuit round the medieval boundaries of the city and are among the finest examples of their type in Europe. Micklegate Bar, one of four main gates giving access through the defences, is traditionally the only one used by royalty. York's chief glory is its magnificent Minster, which towers over the little streets and houses of the old town. It is the largest gothic cathedral north of the Alps, and its fine windows contain more than half of all the medieval glass surviving in England. One reason for the purity of the Minster's architectural style is the speed with which it was built – between 1220 and 1470 – and the consequent absence of modifications brought about by changing ideas in church design. Many people consider the octagonal Chapter House to be the loveliest part of the overall medieval design. In 1984 the South Transept was seriously damaged by fire; fortunately it is now undergoing extensive restoration. As far as fine old churches are concerned, York probably has more than anywhere else in the country except perhaps Norwich. Holy Trinity is of 13th-century date and contains good box pews, All Saints' North Street has medieval glass and carries a beautiful 15th-century tower, and St Mary's Castlegate has a rare Saxon dedication stone. Many of the city's buildings have been standing for 500 years and more, including the lovely Guildhall (AM), the Merchant Adventurers' Hall and Chapel (open), Taylors' Hall (open), and the lovely timbered front and picturesque courtyard of William's College. The latter shows work from later periods, and the 17th-century Treasurer's House (NT) preserves good collections of painting and furniture. Elizabethan King's Manor (open), once the home of the Abbot of St Mary's Abbey, is now owned by York University. It is not surprising that a city with as rich and well-documented history as this should have as many museums as York. York's newest museum is the Jorvik Centre, where time cars take you back in time to a reconstruction of Jorvik 'a viking city'. Relics from the Roman occupation can be seen in the Yorkshire Museum, in the grounds of ruined St Mary's Abbey, and close to the 13th-century fragments of York Castle (AM) is the Castle Museum of Yorkshire life. Close by in the old Debtors' Prison are collections of dolls and militaria,

(continues)

York Minster's magnificent proportions are difficult to appreciate except from a distance.

The glorious architecture of the Minster can be glimpsed at the end of many of York's old streets and alleyways.

(continued)
and the National Steam Museum preserves great old locomotives such as the *Mallard*. St Mary's Heritage Centre, in Castlegate, uses audio-visual displays and the work of contemporary artists to describe the city's architectural development. Over all is a sense of permanence fostered by the mellow stone of a city that is more medieval than modern.

Leave York on the A1036 SP 'East Coast' and 'Malton', then in 3 miles at a roundabout take 2nd exit then 1st exit at next roundabout on to the A64 SP 'Malton'. Passing agricultural country and in 7½ miles pass the Spittle Beck Inn. In 1½ miles it is possible to make a short detour from the main route by turning right on to an unclassified road SP 'Kirkham Priory', descending over a level crossing and the River Derwent, and driving to the hamlet of Kirkham.

KIRKHAM, N Yorks

Ruined Kirkham Priory (AM) includes a beautiful 13th-century gatehouse and a lavatorium, where the monks used to wash.

On the main route, continue along the A64 and in 1 mile turn left on to an unclassified road SP 'Welburn, Castle Howard'. Pass through Welburn, meet crossroads and turn right, then drive through an arch and wall gateway to reach Castle Howard.

CASTLE HOWARD, N Yorks

One of the most spectacular houses in Britain, Castle Howard (open) dates from the 17th and 18th centuries and is considered to be the greatest achievement of the architect Vanbrugh. A central dome forms the focal point of the house and is echoed in the 1,000-acre grounds by a circular mausoleum designed by Hawksmoor. Other garden follies include the lovely Temple of the Four Winds, and the huge gatehouse is crowned by a pyramid. Among many treasures inside the house is an extensive collection of period costumes.

The square wooden tower of Raskelf Church, a most unusual feature in this part of England, contrasts pleasantly with the masonry body.

Leave Castle Howard, cross the Howardian Hills, and descend to meet a T-junction at the edge of Slingsby. It is possible to make a detour from the main route to Slingsby by driving forward at the village crossroads.

SLINGSBY, N Yorks

Misnamed and never completed, the 17th-century house known as Slingsby Castle is a picturesque ruin that adds an air of gothic mystery to the countryside round the village. It was originally started for the soldier, philosopher, and mathematician, Sir Charles Cavendish. A feature of the village itself is its maypole, the scene of great celebrations every May 1.

On the main tour, meet the aforementioned crossroads and turn left on to the B1257 SP 'Helmsley'. Continue to Hovingham.

HOVINGHAM, N Yorks

The stone cottages of this lovely little village cluster round the green under the Saxon tower of All Saints' Church and the stately presence of Hovingham Hall. The latter is an unusual building in distinctive yellow limestone, with a gatehouse that was designed as a riding school where horses could be exercised out of the rain (open by appointment only).

In Hovingham turn left on to an unclassified road SP 'Coulton' and 'Easingwold'. Drive through Hovingham High Wood and meet crossroads. Turn right SP 'Gilling' and follow a narrow road for 1½ miles. Meet a T-junction and turn right on to the B1363 to reach Gilling East.

GILLING EAST, N Yorks

It is thought that the architect Vanbrugh may have designed the west front of Gilling Castle (open), though most of the building is much too old for him to have had any hand in its construction. The keep dates from the 14th century, and a well-preserved ribbed plaster ceiling helps to make its dining room one of the finest in England. On either side of the village are the lovely Hambledon and Howardian Hills.

Return south along the B1363 to reach Brandsby.

BRANDSBY, N Yorks

Features of this harmonious hillside village include a woodcarver's shop, an 18th-century hall, and an unusual church with a stone cupola. Neat terraces of cottages complete the picture.

Continue to Stillington, in the Vale of York.

STILLINGTON, N Yorks

The 18th-century writer Laurence Sterne was vicar here for a time, and the lovely old church in which he served features a 12th-century priest's door.

VALE OF YORK, N Yorks

Numerous country lanes bordered by thick hedgerows criss-cross the fertile farmlands of the Vale of York, a large lowland expanse watered by the River Ouse and its many tributaries. Broad water meadows known as 'ings' border the rivers, providing an ideal habitat for marshland wildlife and water loving plants. Here and there large areas of heathland have survived uncultivated, providing ideal hunting grounds for nightjars and vipers.

The Devil's Arrows are a mysterious group of prehistoric standing stones near Boroughbridge.

Drive through Stillington village and pass the church. Keep forward on to an unclassified road SP 'Easingwold', then in 3½ miles meet the A19 and drive forward to enter Easingwold.

EASINGWOLD, N Yorks

An unusual bull ring can be seen in the market place of this pleasant town of red-brick houses and cobbled lanes. The local church contains an ancient parish coffin.

Meet crossroads in Easingwold and turn left on to an unclassified road to reach Raskelf.

RASKELF, N Yorks

The 15th-century tower of local St Mary's church is made of wood and is said to be unique in Yorkshire. Parts of the building's main body date back to Norman times.

In Raskelf bear left then right SP 'Boroughbridge', and drive to Brafferton.

Castle Howard is a superb example of Vanbrugh's architectural genius.

BRAFFERTON, N Yorks

Brafferton Church was extensively restored in Victorian times, but still displays good examples of 15th-century workmanship.

In Brafferton village turn right and after 1 mile cross the River Swale and turn left. In 2¾ miles turn left then immediately right, then in 1 mile meet a T-junction and turn left. Continue to a roundabout and take the 1st exit on to the B6265. Cross the River Ure and enter Boroughbridge.

BOROUGHBRIDGE, N Yorks

Three large monoliths known ominously as the Devil's Arrows stand a few hundred yards to the west of Boroughbridge. The largest rises to 22½ft, and it is thought that the group may be some 3,000 years old. On the town side of a fine bridge that spans the Ure is a market place with a 250ft-deep well.

Turn left then keep left through Boroughbridge with SP 'York', and at the far end of the town branch left on to an unclassified road to reach Aldborough.

ALDBOROUGH, N Yorks

This pretty village stands on the site of *Isurium*, the northernmost town to be built without any military motives during the Roman occupation. Remains (AM) revealed through excavation include sections of a boundary wall, two tessellated pavements, and a wide variety of coins, pottery, and artefacts on display in the small site museum. In the village itself are a striking maypole and a cross that probably commemorates the Battle of Boroughbridge, which was fought here in 1322.

Drive to the battle cross and bear right. Pass the church to reach the B6265, turn left to follow the old Ribchester Roman road, and continue to Green Hammerton. Join the A59, and in 1¾ miles cross the River Nidd. Drive through low-lying country for the return to York.

YORK, N Yorks

The many strands of York's proud history can be traced in its fascinating streets, its ancient buildings, superb museums and, above all, in the fabulous minster, the largest Gothic church in England. The Romans built *Eboracum* at this point on the River Ouse; the Anglo-Saxons made the city capital of their kingdom of Deira and, when the Vikings came, they named it Jorvic, from which we get the name of York. Sacked by the Normans, York rose again as a great medieval city, surrounded by massive walls within which a maze of narrow streets grew up around the towering minster. The medieval atmosphere is felt most vividly in the Shambles, the street of the butchers, where in places the overhanging storeys of the ancient houses almost touch across the narrow way. Old street scenes and exhibits of life in bygone times can be seen in the fascinating Castle Museum, and the power of the medieval guilds is displayed in the Merchant Adventurers' House, a restored 14th-century guild house in Fossgate. The minster reigns majestically over the city as it has done for more than 700 years, its beautiful interior lit by glowing stained-glass windows, created by medieval craftsmen at the height of their powers. The graceful design of the west window has earned it the title of the Heart of Yorkshire. The minster undercroft houses the cathedral treasury. In Jacobean and Georgian times York had 2 famous citizens, both of

THE VALE OF YORK

Yorkshire's mighty capital city looks out over the ancient kingdom of Elmet and the lowlands of the Vale of York where 3 great rivers, the Ouse, the Derwent and the Wharfe, meander through rich farmland sheltered by the rolling hills of the Yorkshire Wolds.

whom met a tragic fate: the first was Guy Fawkes, born at a house in Petergate and executed for treason in 1605; the second was Dick Turpin, a legendary hero of the ride from London, hanged as a highwayman in 1739 on the Knavemire, now York racecourse. At the Jorvik Viking Centre is one of Britain's newest and most exciting museums. Here visitors are transported — in 'time cars' — back to the sights, smells and sounds of 10th-century York. Providing a contrast is the National Railway Museum, which pays tribute to York's importance as a railway centre from the early days of steam. Here can be seen locomotives, rolling stock, models, films, and posters.

Leave York on the A1036, SP 'Leeds (A64)'. In 3¼ miles join the A64 and after 6 miles branch left on to the A659 for Tadcaster.

TADCASTER, N Yorks

Tadcaster is the home of traditional Yorkshire ales and the scent of the breweries pervades the old streets which are famous for the large number of public

houses. A restored 15th-century house called the Ark (OACT) has been converted into a museum of pubs and brewing, with a unique collection of fascinating relics of British drinking habits. The dignified stone church has an interesting past; it was completely dismantled in the last century and reconstructed on a site higher above the River Wharfe to save it from flooding. The limestone for the church was quarried locally, and much of this stone was used to build York minster.

In Tadcaster turn left on to the A162, SP 'Sherburn-in-Elmet', and continue to Towton.

TOWTON, N Yorks

One of the most savage battles in English history took place near this peaceful little village in wooded Wharfdale. A stone cross just outside Towton marks the place where more than 30,000 men were slaughtered on Palm Sunday, 1461, during the Wars of the Roses. The bodies were interred in a mass grave in a field nearby, and for centuries after ploughmen would often turn up bones.

At the end of the village turn right on to the B1217, SP 'Garforth'. After ½ mile pass (right) the War of the Roses memorial cross and continue for 2½ miles to reach the entrance to Lotherton Hall.

LOTHERTON HALL, N Yorks

Lotherton Hall (OACT), with its outstanding collection of European works of art, furniture and porcelain, was given to the city of Leeds by the Gascoigne family and is now a country house museum. In addition to the Gascoigne collection, there are superb Chinese ceramics, 20th-century pottery and a fascinating display of historical costumes, including examples of the best of the fashion designs of our own time.

Return along the B1217 for 200 yards and turn right on to an unclassified road, SP 'Sherburn-in-Elmet'. In 3¼ miles turn left on to the B1222 for Sherburn-in-Elmet.

SHERBURN-IN-ELMET, N Yorks

A white church stands like a beacon on the hill above Sherburn, once the eastern capital of the ancient Brigantine kingdom of Elmete. The church, built of local limestone, was the secret meeting place for loyal Catholics during the Reformation, when they are said to have made their way by night through underground passages, to worship according to their faith. The medieval Janus cross in the church, so called after the double-headed Roman deity because the carved figures face opposite directions, was buried for safety during the 16th-century Reformation; when it was later exhumed, a quarrel over its ownership caused it to be sawn in half vertically, but the 2 sections have finally been brought together. The old gabled grammar school dates from the 17th century.

At the crossroads turn right on to the A162, SP 'Ferrybridge', and proceed to South Milford. From here an unclassified road on the right may be taken to Steeton Hall Gatehouse.

STEETON HALL GATEHOUSE, N Yorks

Across the woods and meadows from the village of South Milford, stands the 14th-century gatehouse (AM) of a medieval castle, once owned by the Fairfax family. A forbear of the famous Cromwellian general is said to have ridden out from here to escape with his sweetheart, a wealthy heiress, who was incarcerated in Nun Appleton Priory.

York minster, one of England's best examples of Gothic architecture, has the largest lantern tower in Britain and contains more stained glass than any other cathedral in the country

Water lilies are the speciality of Burnby Hall's lovely gardens

Continue on the A162 and in 1¼ miles, at the roundabout, turn left on to the A63, SP 'Selby', for Monk Fryston.

MONK FRYSTON, N Yorks
This delightful little village with a Tudor Hall (not open) and old cottages around a small square was given to the monks of Selby Abbey in Norman times, hence the first part of its name. The village church predates the Norman Conquest and has preserved intact its Anglo-Saxon tower.

Remain on the A63 to Selby.

SELBY, N Yorks
Famous for its beautiful abbey church, Selby is an ancient town and port on the River Ouse, where small ships still put in and out of the small dock. When boats were built here they had to be launched sideways because the river was too narrow for the usual method. The abbey was founded in 1069 by a monk of Auxerre in France who, following a vision, came to England and sailed up the River Ouse, stopping at a place where 3 swans settled on the water. Here he built a hermitage and received permission from the king to found an abbey. Unfortunately he fell out with the authorities before work could begin, and the present church was started by Hugh de Lacy in 1100. Building went slowly and was not finally completed until the 14th century. The abbey stands, surrounded by lawns, in the attractive little market-place at the heart of the town.

Leave on the A19, SP 'York', and cross the River Ouse by a wooden toll bridge. Pass through Barlby and at the end turn right on to the A163, SP 'Market Weighton', then right again across the railway. Later cross the River Derwent for Bubwith and continue to Holme-upon-Spalding-Moor.

HOLME-UPON-SPALDING-MOOR, Humberside
Lonely Beacon Hill, crowned by Holme Church, looks out over the surrounding flat plain, once a marshland where travellers were guided by the welcome sight of the church tower. Monks kept a nightly vigil, tolling the church bell as a signal to anyone who might be lost. The church is a charming medieval structure, its walls whitewashed inside to show off the beautiful wood furnishings.

At the end of the village turn left, SP 'Bridlington'. In 1¾ miles, at the roundabout, turn left, and 2½ miles farther, at the next roundabout, turn left again on to the A1079, SP 'York'. Pass through Shiptonthorpe to Hayton, then in 1 mile turn right on to the B1247 for Pocklington.

POCKLINGTON, Humberside
This red-roofed little market town sits snugly in the shadow of the Yorkshire Wolds, with many attractive houses along the cheerful streets leading up to the medieval church, sometimes called the Cathedral of the Wolds. A memorial on the church wall commemorates an 18th-century flying man, Tom Pelling, who performed acrobatic tricks on a tightrope slung from the church tower to a nearby inn.

BURNBY HALL GARDENS, Humberside
These beautiful water gardens (OACT) on the outskirts of Pocklington were created by Major Stewart, a world-traveller in the old tradition, who gathered rare plants on his travels and brought home one of the finest collections of water lilies in Europe. Specimens of more than 50 varieties of lily bloom here all summer long. Nearby, in the Stewart Museum, is his collection of hunting trophies.

At the roundabout in Pocklington keep forward, SP 'Malton', then go over the crossroads. Nearly ½ mile farther turn right into Garth Ends, SP 'Millington'. At the next roundabout turn left, then in 1¾ miles keep forward, SP 'Givendale'. This byroad climbs on to the Wolds and passes the hamlet of Great Givendale. Continue for 1¾ miles and turn left on to the A166, SP 'York', to reach Stamford Bridge.

STAMFORD BRIDGE, Humberside
The first of the 2 decisive battles of English history was fought at this quiet village on the River Derwent in 1066. King Harold was threatened by 2 invading forces: across the North Sea were the combined fleets of Tostig of Northumbria and Harold Hardrada of Norway; on the French side of the channel lay the ships of William of Normandy. Both fleets were waiting for a favourable wind to bring them to England, and the Norsemen arrived first, obliging Harold to march his army north to Yorkshire, where he inflicted a crushing defeat on the invaders. In the meantime, however, William had landed in Kent and the Saxon army, exhausted from their long march south, were defeated at the Battle of Hastings and Harold was killed.

Beyond the town cross the River Derwent, then in 5 miles, at the roundabout, take the A1079 for the return to York.

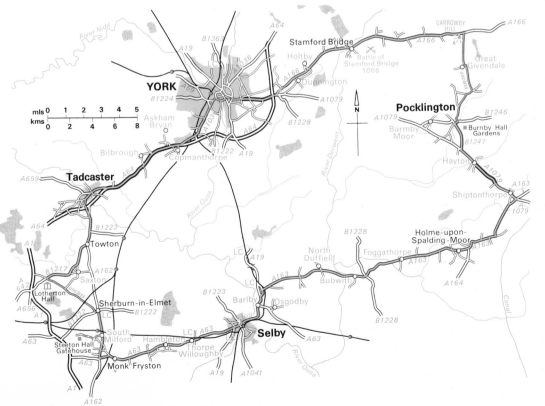

Key to Town Plans

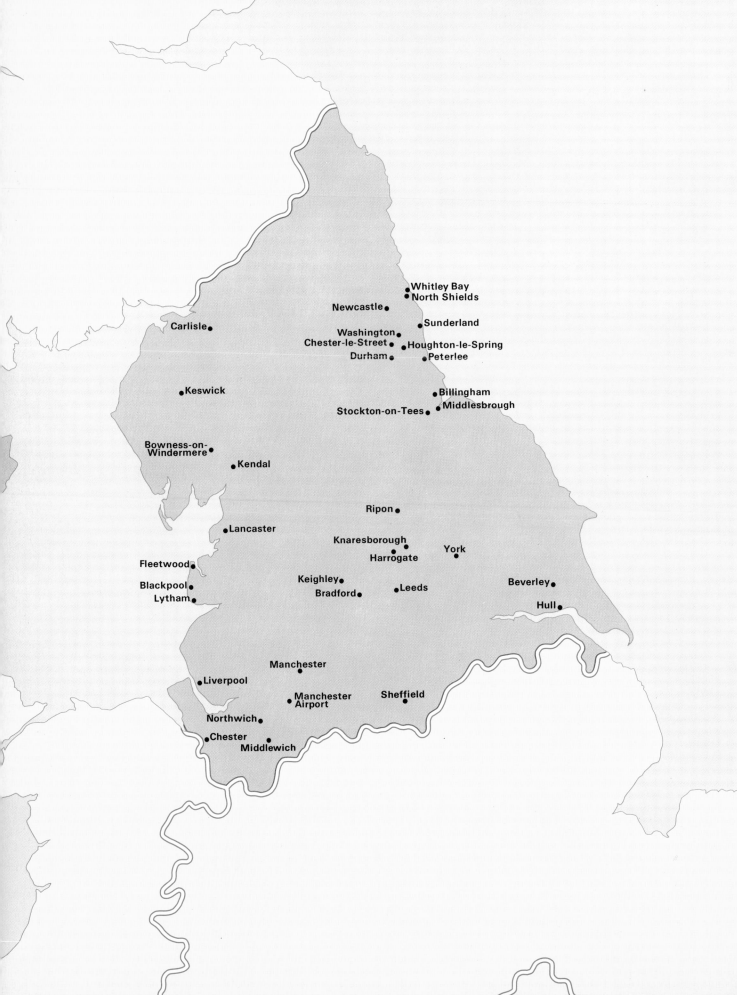

Whitley Bay
North Shields
Newcastle
Carlisle
Sunderland
Washington
Chester-le-Street
Houghton-le-Spring
Durham
Peterlee
Keswick
Billingham
Stockton-on-Tees
Middlesbrough
Bowness-on-Windermere
Kendal
Ripon
Lancaster
Knaresborough
York
Harrogate
Fleetwood
Keighley
Beverley
Blackpool
Bradford
Leeds
Lytham
Hull
Manchester
Liverpool
Manchester Airport
Sheffield
Northwich
Chester
Middlewich

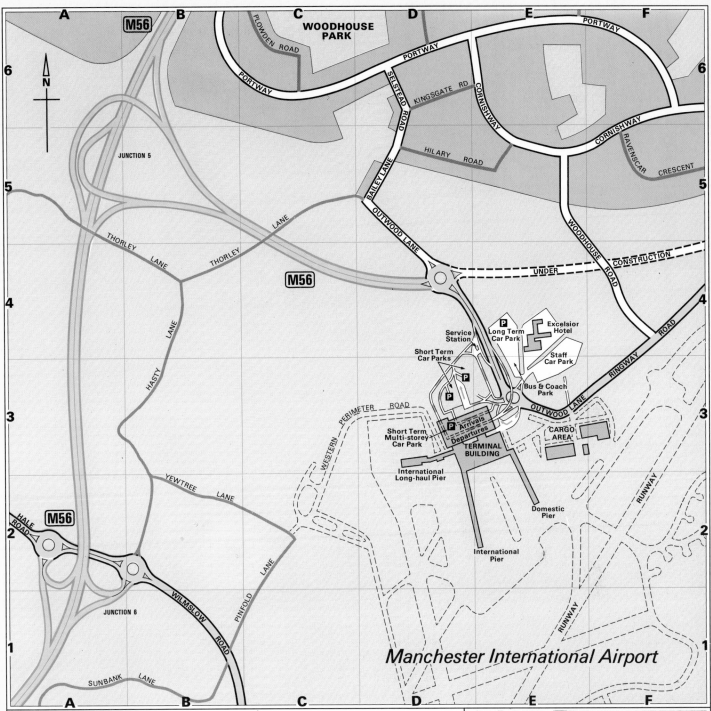

Manchester International Airport

Manchester International Airport

Nine miles south of the city of Manchester lies Manchester International Airport, operating flights to and from the Midlands, the north west, north east, Yorkshire and Wales. As well as flights within Britain, there are regular scheduled services operating to all the major business centres in Europe, the Far East and Australia. Charter and inclusive tour flights also operate from here to destinations world-wide.

The airport has been in use since just before World War II, and enjoys the distinction that its main buildings were opened by HRH Prince Philip. This was not until 1962, when the Prince became the first pilot to park an aircraft alongside the arrivals pier, and the first passenger to use the airport's facilities.

Today Manchester International has a spacious concourse area on the first floor of the terminal.

A bank, post office, bookstall, tobacconist and pharmacy are situated here. At the apron end of the concourse (and lying adjacent to the observation windows) is the Concourse Cafe, a self-service restaurant and bar. Also offering refreshments for travellers and other visitors to the airport is the 200-seat Lancaster restaurant and cocktail lounge, which overlooks International Pier B, and within just two minutes walk the Excelsior Hotel offers 300 bedrooms, a restaurant, a coffee shop and a bar.

The airport is well placed for passengers coming here by both road and rail. It offers easy access to the M56 and to the national motorway network. Greater Manchester Transport buses link the airport to Manchester and to Stockport all the year round, and also make a link to most towns in Greater Manchester during the summer months. Coach services also run to Birmingham, Liverpool, Lancaster, Leeds and Sheffield.

For railway travellers, the nearest station to the airport is Heald Green, which is about two miles away and has two bus services. Frequent trains go to Manchester (Piccadilly) and to Crewe.

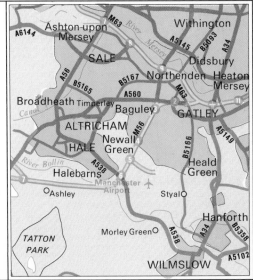

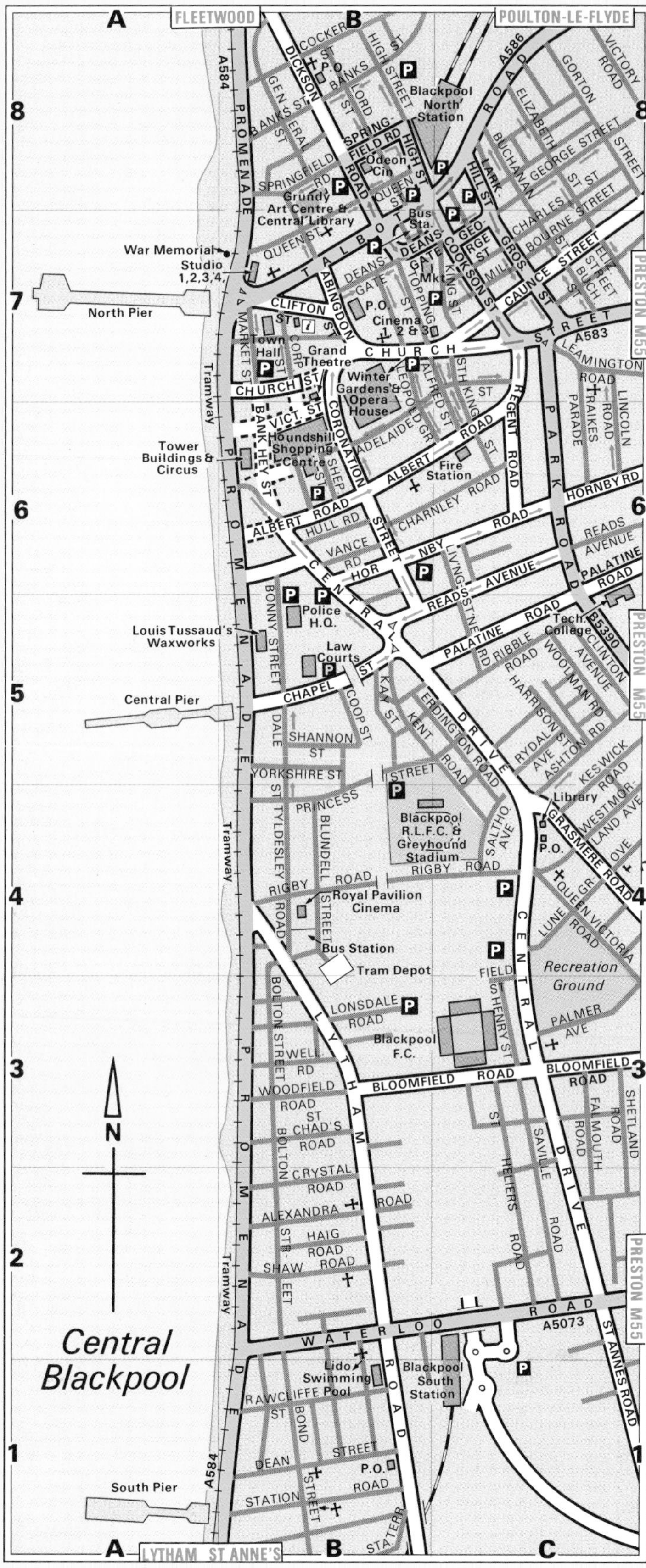

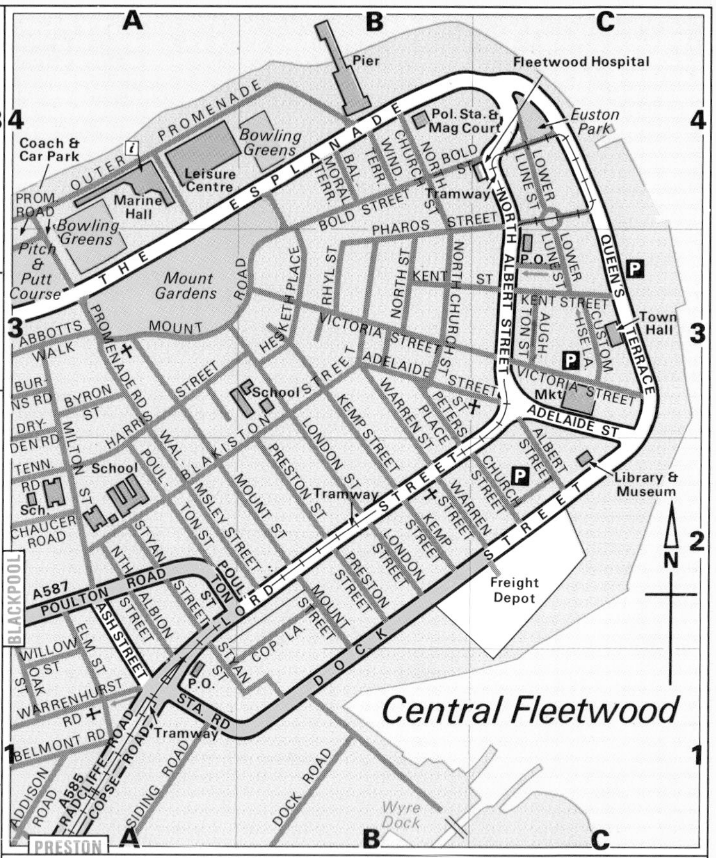

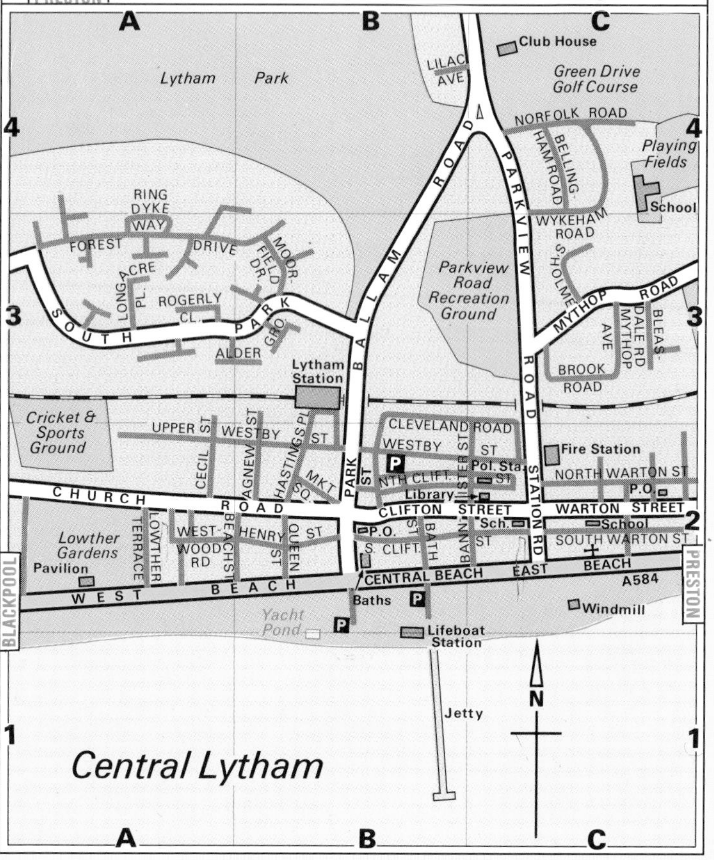

Central Blackpool

Central Fleetwood

Central Lytham

Blackpool

No seaside resort is regarded with greater affection than Blackpool. It is still the place where millions of North Country folk spend their holidays; its famous illuminations draw visitors from all over the world. It provides every conceivable kind of traditional holiday entertainment, and in greater abundance than any other seaside resort in Britain. The famous tower – built in the 1890s as a replica of the Eiffel Tower – the three piers, seven miles of promenade, five miles of illuminations, countless guesthouses, huge numbers of pubs, shops, restaurants and cafes play host to eight million visitors a year.

At the base of the tower is a huge entertainment complex that includes a ballroom, a circus and an aquarium. Other 19th-century landmarks are North Pier and Central Pier, the great Winter Gardens and Opera House and the famous trams that still run along the promenade – the only electric trams still operating in Britain. The most glittering part of modern Blackpool is the famous Golden Mile, packed with amusements, novelty shops and snack stalls. Every autumn it becomes part of the country's most extravagant light show – the illuminations – when the promenade is ablaze with neon representations of anything and everything from moon rockets to the Muppets. Autumn is also the time when Blackpool is a traditional venue for political party conferences.

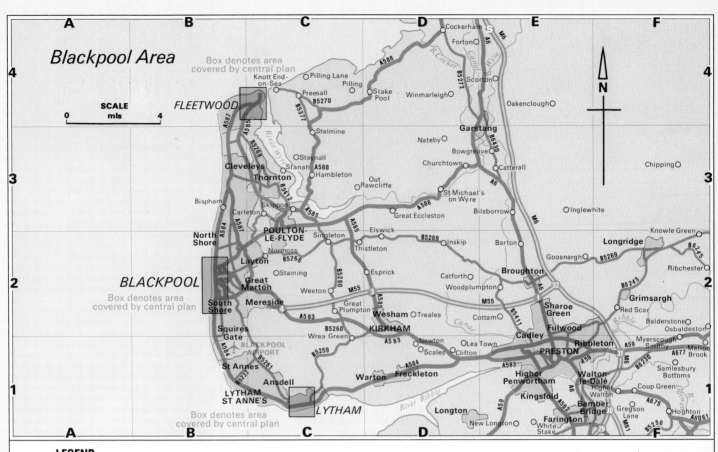

Blackpool Area

Box denotes area covered by central plan

SCALE
mls
0   4

FLEETWOOD

N

Knott End-on-Sea · Pilling Lane · Pilling · Preesall · Stake Pool · Winmarleigh · Cockerham · Forton · Scorton · Stalmine · Garstang · Nateby · Bowgreave · Oakenclough · Cleveleys · Staynall · Stanah · Hambleton · Out Rawcliffe · Churchtown · Catterall · Chipping · Thornton · Bispham · Carleton · Skippool · St Michael's on Wyre · Bilsborrow · Inglewhite · North Shore · POULTON-LE-FLYDE · Singleton · Elswick · Inskip · Barton · Goosnargh · Longridge · Knowle Green · Normoss · Thistleton · Ribchester · Layton · Staining · Esprick · Broughton · Grimsargh · BLACKPOOL · Great Marton · Weeton · Great Plumpton · Catforth · Woodplumpton · Sharoe Green · Red Scar · Balderstone · Osbaldeston · South Shore · Mereside · Wesham · Treales · Cottam · Fulwood · Ribbleton · Myerscough Smithy · Mellor Brook · Squires Gate · KIRKHAM · Newton · Scales · Lea Town · Cadley · PRESTON · BLACKPOOL AIRPORT · Wrea Green · Clifton · St Annes · Warton · Freckleton · Higher Penwortham · Walton-le-Dale · Coup Green · Ansdell · Higher Walton · Bamber Bridge · Gregson Lane · Houghton · LYTHAM ST ANNE'S · Kingsfold · Farington · LYTHAM · Longton · New Longton · White Stake

Box denotes area covered by central plan

LEGEND

Town Plan
AA recommended route
Restricted roads
Other roads
Buildings of interest — School
Car parks — P
Parks and open spaces

Area Plan
A roads
B roads
Locations — Wrea Green ○
Urban area

Street Index with Grid Reference

Blackpool

Abingdon Street	B7
Adelaide Street	B6-B7-C7
Albert Road	B6-C6
Alexandra Road	B2
Alfred Street	B7-C7-C6
Ashton Road	C4-C5
Bank Hey Street	B6-B7
Banks Street	B8
Bloomfield Road	B3-C3
Blundell Street	B4
Bolton Street	B2-B3-B4
Bond Street	B1-B2
Bonny Street	B5-B6
Buchanan Street	C7-C8
Caunce Street	C7-C8
Central Drive	B6-B5-C5-C4-C3-C2
Chapel Street	B5
Charles Street	C7-C8
Charnley Road	B6-C6
Church Street	B7-C7
Clifton Street	B7
Clinton Avenue	C5
Cocker Street	B8
Cookson Street	B8-B7-C7
Coop Street	B5
Coronation Street	B5-B6-B7
Corporation Street	B7
Crystal Road	B2
Dale Street	B4-B5
Deansgate	B7-C7
Dean Street	B1
Dickson Road	B7-B8
Erdington Road	B5-C5-C4
Elizabeth Street	C7-C8
Falmouth Road	C2-C3
Field Street	C3
General Street	B8
George Street	C7-C8
Gorton Street	C8
Grasmere Road	C4
Grosvenor Street	C7
Haig Road	B2
Harrison Street	C5
Henry Street	C3
High Street	B8
Hornby Road	B6-C6
Hull Road	B6
Kay Street	B5
Kent Road	B5-C5-C4
Keswick Road	C4-C5
King Street	C7
Larkhill Street	C8
Leamington Road	C7
Leopold Grove	B7-B6-C6
Lincoln Road	C6-C7
Livingstone Road	C5-C6
Lonsdale Road	B3
Lord Street	B8
Lune Grove	C4
Lytham Road	B1-B2-B3-B4
Market Street	B7
Milbourne Street	C7-C8
Palatine Road	B5-C5-C6
Palmer Avenue	C3
Park Road	C5-C6-C7
Princes Street	B4-B5-C5
Promenade	B1-B2-B3-B4-B5-B6-A6-A7-B7-B8
Queen Street	B7-B8
Queen Victoria Road	C3-C4
Raikes Parade	C6-C7
Rawcliffe Street	B1
Reads Avenue	B5-C5-C6
Regent Road	C6-C7
Ribble Road	C5
Rigby Road	B4-C4
Rydal Avenue	C5
St Annes Road	C1-C2
St Chad's Road	B3
St Heliers Road	C2-C3
Salthouse Avenue	C4
Saville Road	C2-C3
Shannon Street	B5
Shaw Road	B2
Sheppard Street	B6
Shetland Road	C2-C3
South King Street	C6-C7
Springfield Road	B8
Station Road	B1
Station Terrace	B1
Talbot Road	B7-B8-C8
Topping Street	B7
Tyldesley Road	B4
Vance Road	B6
Victoria Street	B6
Victory Road	C8
Waterloo Road	B2-C2
Wellington Road	B3
Westmorland Avenue	C4
Woodfield Road	B3
Woolman Road	C5
Yorkshire Street	B5

Fleetwood

Abbots Walk	A3
Adelaide Street	B3-C3-C2
Addison Road	A1
Albert Street	C2-C3
Ash Street	A1-A2
Aughton Street	C3
Balmoral Terrace	B4
Belmont Road	A1
Blakiston Street	A2-B2-B3
Bold Street	B4-C4
Burns Road	A3
Byron Street	A3

Chaucer Road	A2
Church Street	C2
Cop Lane	A1-B1-B2
Copse Road	A1
Custom House Lane	C3
Dock Road	B1
Dock Street	B1-B2-C2
Dryden Road	A2-A3
Elm Street	A1-A2
Harris Street	A2-A3-B3
Hesketh Place	B3
Kemp Street	B2-B3
Kent Street	B3-C3
London Street	B2-B3
Lord Street	A1-A2-B2-C2-C3
Lower Lune Street	C3-C4
Milton Street	A2-A3
Mount Road	A3-B3
Mount Street	A2-B2
North Albert Street	C3-C4
North Albion Street	A1-A2
North Church Street	B3-B4
North Street	B3
Oak Street	A1
Outer Promenade	A4-B4
Pharos Street	B3-C3-C4
Poulton Road	A2
Poulton Street	A2
Preston Street	B2
Promenade Road	A3-A4
Queen's Terrace	C3-C4
Radcliffe Road	A1
Rhyl Street	B3
St Peters Place	B2-B3
Siding Road	A1
Station Road	A1
Styan Street	A2-A1-B1
Tennyson Road	A2
The Esplanade	A3-A4-B4
Victoria Street	B3-C3
Walmsley Street	A3-A2-B2
Warrenhurst Road	A1
Warren Street	B3-B2-C2
Willow Street	A1
Windsor Terrace	B4

Lytham

Agnew Street	B2-B3
Alder Grove	A3-B3
Ballam Road	B2-B3-B4-C4
Bath Street	B2
Beach Street	B2
Bellingham Road	C4
Bleasdale Road	C3
Brook Road	C3
Cecil Street	A2-A3
Central Beach	B2-C2
Church Road	A2-B2
Cleveland Road	B3-C3
Clifton Street	B2-C2
East Beach	C2
Forest Drive	A3-B3
Hastings Place	B2-B3
Henry Street	B2
Lilac Avenue	B4
Longacre Place	A3
Lowther Terrace	A2
Market Square	B2
Moorfield Drive	B3
Mythop Avenue	C3
Mythop Road	C3
Norfolk Road	C2
North Clifton Street	B2-C2
North Warton Street	C2
Park Street	B2
Parkview Road	C2-C3-C4
Queen Street	B2
Ring Dyke Way	A3
Rogerly Close	A3
South Clifton Street	B2-C2
South-Holme	C3
South Park	A3-B3
South Warton Street	C2
Station Road	C2
Upper Westby Street	A2-B2
Warton Street	C2
West Beach	A2-B2
Westby Street	B2-C2
Westwood Road	A2
Wykeham Road	C3-C4

BLACKPOOL
Three piers, seven miles of promenade packed with entertainments galore and seemingly endless sandy beaches spread out beneath Blackpool's unmistakable tower which stands 518ft high in Britain's busiest and biggest holiday resort.

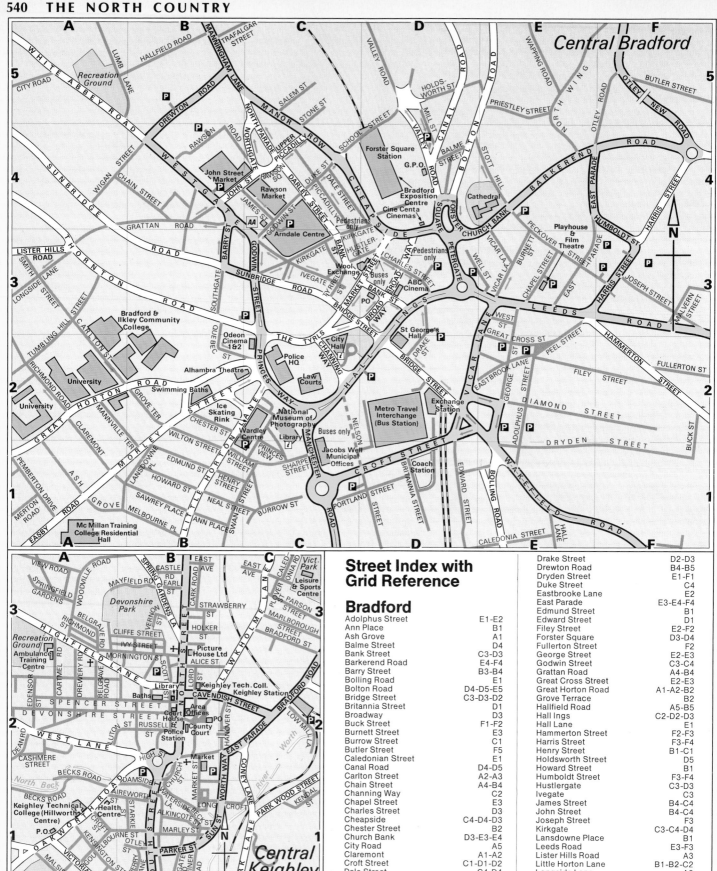

Central Bradford

Central Keighley

Street Index with Grid Reference

Bradford

Adolphus Street	E1-E2
Ann Place	B1
Ash Grove	A1
Balme Street	D4
Bank Street	C3-D3
Barkerend Road	E4-F4
Barry Street	B3-B4
Bolling Road	E1
Bolton Road	D4-D5-E5
Bridge Street	C3-D3-D2
Britannia Street	D1
Broadway	D3
Buck Street	F1-F2
Burnett Street	E3
Burrow Street	C1
Butler Street	F5
Caledonian Street	E1
Canal Road	D4-D5
Carlton Street	A2-A3
Chain Street	A4-B4
Channing Way	C2
Chapel Street	E3
Charles Street	D3
Cheapside	C4-D4-D3
Chester Street	B2
Church Bank	D3-E3-E4
City Road	A5
Claremont	A1-A2
Croft Street	C1-D1-D2
Dale Street	C4-D4
Darley Street	C3-C4
Diamond Street	E2-F2
Drake Street	D2-D3
Drewton Road	B4-B5
Dryden Street	E1-F1
Duke Street	C4
Eastbrooke Lane	E2
East Parade	E3-E4-F4
Edmund Street	B1
Edward Street	D1
Filey Street	E2-F2
Forster Square	D3-D4
Fullerton Street	F2
George Street	E2-E3
Godwin Street	C3-C4
Grattan Road	A4-B4
Great Cross Street	E2-E3
Great Horton Road	A1-A2-B2
Grove Terrace	B2
Hallfield Road	A5-B5
Hall Ings	C2-D2-D3
Hall Lane	E1
Hammerton Street	F2-F3
Harris Street	F3-F4
Henry Street	B1-C1
Holdsworth Street	D5
Howard Street	B1
Humboldt Street	F3-F4
Hustlergate	C3-D3
Ivegate	C3
James Street	B4-C4
John Street	B4-C4
Joseph Street	F3
Kirkgate	C3-C4-D4
Lansdowne Place	B1
Leeds Road	E3-F3
Lister Hills Road	A3
Little Horton Lane	B1-B2-C2
Longside Lane	A3
Lumb Lane	A5-B5
Malvern Street	F3

Bradford

Wool and Bradford are almost synonymous, such was its importance in the 19th century as a central market after the Industrial Revolution brought steam power to the trade. Like many small market towns that exploded into industrial cities almost overnight, Bradford's architecture is a mish-mash of grand civic buildings, factories and crowded housing. Among the former, the Wool Exchange is impressive, with its ornate tower adorned with stone busts of 13 famous men, and the massive town hall, also topped by a tower, 200ft high. Few traces remain of the town's past but one obvious exception is the cathedral. Set on a rise, its detailed carvings – particularly the 20 angels that support the nave roof – catch the eye.

Bradford boasts several parks – notably Lister Park where there is a boating lake, an open-air swimming pool, a botanical garden and a scented garden for the blind – and Bowling Park, on the other side of town. Cartwright Hall, named after the inventor of the power loom, stands in Lister Park. It now houses Bradford's permanent art collection.

Keighley The Brontë sisters used to walk from Haworth to this pleasant 19th-century town for their shopping sprees. Nowadays, the restored Keighley and Worth Valley Railway is a great attraction and passengers can travel to Oxenhope.

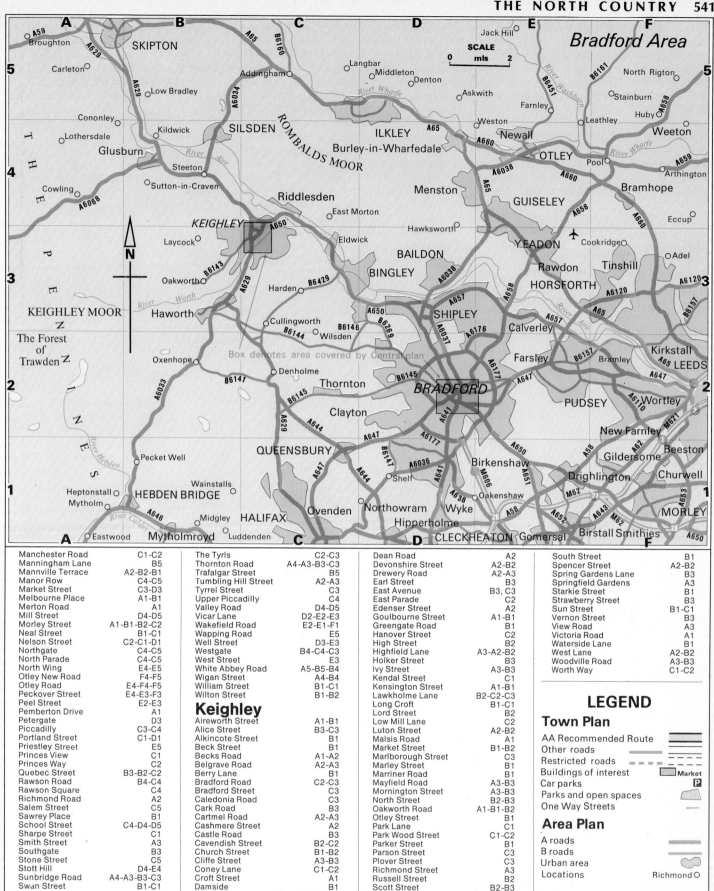

Bradford Area

SCALE
0   mls   2

Box denotes area covered by Central plan

Manchester Road	C1-C2
Manningham Lane	B5
Mannville Terrace	A2-B2-B1
Manor Row	C4-C5
Market Street	C3-D3
Melbourne Place	A1-B1
Merton Road	A1
Mill Street	D4-D5
Morley Street	A1-B1-B2-C2
Neal Street	B1-C1
Nelson Street	C2-C1-D1
Northgate	C4-C5
North Parade	C4-C5
North Wing	E4-E5
Otley New Road	F4-F5
Otley Road	E4-F4-F5
Peckover Street	E4-E3-F3
Peel Street	E2-E3
Pemberton Drive	A1
Petergate	D3
Piccadilly	C3-C4
Portland Street	C1-D1
Priestley Street	E5
Princes View	C1
Princes Way	C2
Quebec Street	B3-B2-C2
Rawson Road	B4-C4
Rawson Square	C4
Richmond Road	A2
Salem Street	C5
Sawrey Place	B1
School Street	C4-D4-D5
Sharpe Street	C1
Smith Street	A3
Southgate	B3
Stone Street	C5
Stott Hill	D4-E4
Sunbridge Road	A4-A3-B3-C3
Swan Street	B1-C1

The Tyrls	C2-C3
Thornton Road	A4-A3-B3-C3
Trafalgar Street	B5
Tumbling Hill Street	A2-A3
Tyrrel Street	C3
Upper Piccadilly	C4
Valley Road	D4-D5
Vicar Lane	D2-E2-E3
Wakefield Road	E2-E1-F1
Wapping Road	E5
Well Street	D3-E3
Westgate	B4-C4-C3
West Street	E3
White Abbey Road	A5-B5-B4
Wigan Street	A4-B4
William Street	B1-C1
Wilton Street	B1-B2

Keighley

Aireworth Street	A1-B1
Alice Street	B3-C3
Alkincote Street	B1
Beck Street	B1
Becks Road	A1-A2
Belgrave Road	A2-A3
Berry Lane	B1
Bradford Road	C2-C3
Bradford Street	C3
Caledonia Road	C3
Cark Road	B3
Cartmel Road	A2-A3
Cashmere Street	A2
Castle Road	B3
Cavendish Street	B2-C2
Church Street	B1-B2
Cliffe Street	A3-B3
Coney Lane	C1-C2
Croft Street	A1
Damside	B1

Dean Road	A2
Devonshire Street	A2-B2
Drewery Road	A2-A3
Earl Street	B3
East Avenue	B3, C3
East Parade	C2
Edenser Street	A2
Goulbourne Street	A1-B1
Greengate Road	B1
Hanover Street	C2
High Street	B2
Highfield Lane	A3-A2-B2
Holker Street	B3
Ivy Street	A3-B3
Kendal Street	C1
Kensington Street	A1-B1
Lawkholme Lane	B2-C2-C3
Long Croft	B1-C1
Lord Street	B2
Low Mill Lane	C2
Luton Street	A2-B2
Malsis Road	A1
Market Street	B1-B2
Marlborough Street	C3
Marley Street	B1
Marriner Road	B1
Mayfield Road	A3-B3
Mornington Street	A3-B3
North Street	B2-B3
Oakworth Road	A1-B1-B2
Otley Street	B1
Park Lane	C1
Park Wood Street	C1-C2
Parker Street	B1
Parson Street	C3
Plover Street	C3
Richmond Street	A3
Russell Street	B2
Scott Street	B2-B3

South Street	B1
Spencer Street	A2-B2
Spring Gardens Lane	B3
Springfield Gardens	A3
Starkie Street	B1
Strawberry Street	B3
Sun Street	B1-C1
Vernon Street	B3
View Road	A3
Victoria Road	A1
Waterside Lane	B1
West Lane	A2-B2
Woodville Road	A3-B3
Worth Way	C1-C2

LEGEND

Town Plan

AA Recommended Route	
Other roads	
Restricted roads	
Buildings of interest	Market
Car parks	P
Parks and open spaces	
One Way Streets	

Area Plan

A roads	
B roads	
Urban area	
Locations	Richmond O

BRADFORD
St George's, built with the profits of the wool trade, is one of Bradford's imposing Victorian buildings. It is once again being used for the purpose for which it was intended – a concert hall – and has exceptionally good acoustics.

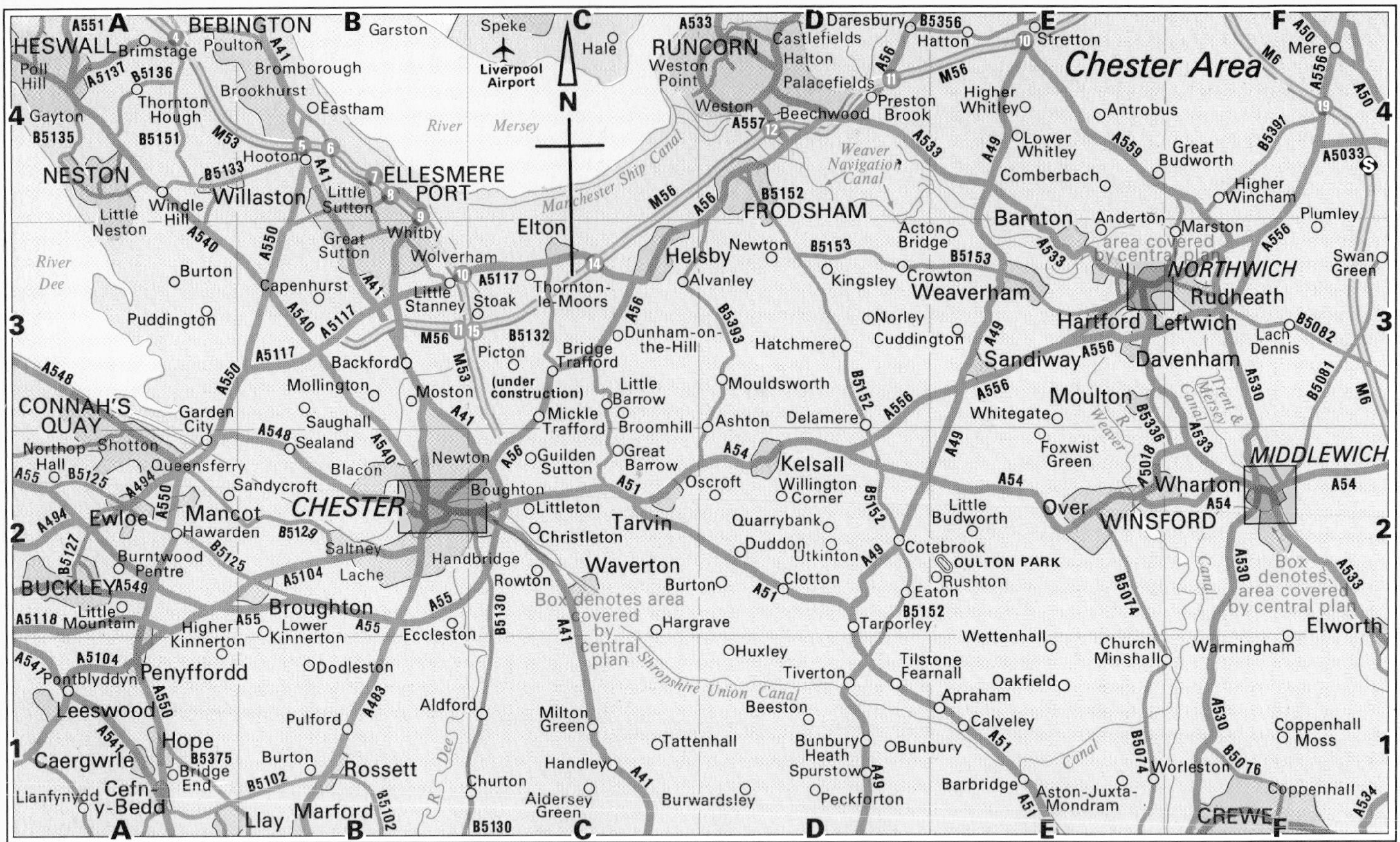

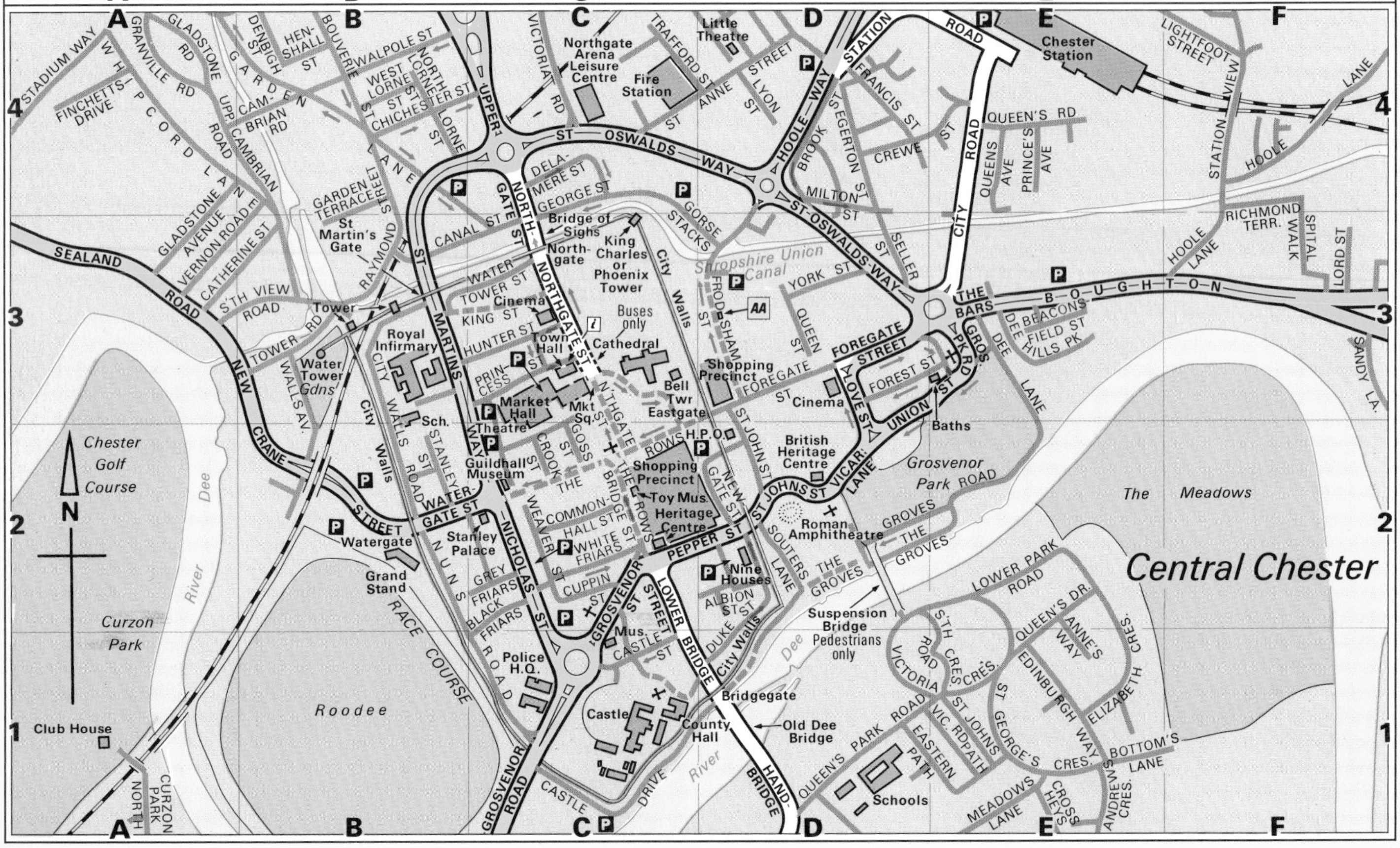

Chester

Chester is the only English city to have preserved the complete circuit of its Roman and medieval walls. On the west side, the top of the walls is now at pavement level, but on the other three sides the walk along the ramparts is remarkable. Two of the old watchtowers contain small museums: the Water Tower, built to protect the old river port, displays relics of medieval Chester; King Charles's Tower, from which Charles I watched the defeat of the Royalist army at the Battle of Rowton Moor in 1645, portrays Chester's role in the Civil War.

Looking down from the top of the Eastgate, crowned with the ornate and gaily-coloured Jubilee Clock erected in 1897, the view down the main street, the old Roman *Via Principalis*, reveals a dazzling display of the black-and-white timbered buildings for which Chester is famous. One of these, Providence House, bears the inscription 'God's Providence is Mine Inheritance', carved in thanks for sparing the survivors of the plague of 1647 that ravaged the city.

On either side of Eastgate, Watergate and Bridge Street are the Rows, a feature unique to Chester, and dating back at least to the 13th century. These covered galleries of shops, raised up at first-floor level, protected pedestrians from weather and traffic. Chester's magnificent cathedral has beautifully carved choir stalls.

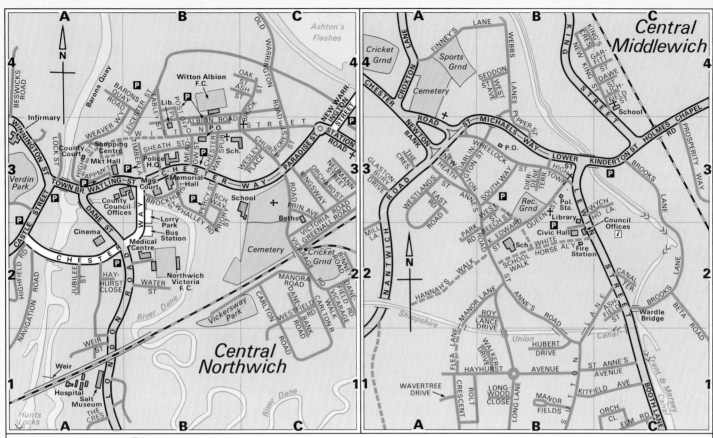

Central Northwich

Central Middlewich

Key to Town Plan and Area Plan

Town Plan

AA Recommended roads	
Other roads	
Restricted roads	
Buildings of interest	College
One Way Streets	←
Car Parks	P
Parks and open spaces	
Churches	+

Area Plan

A roads	
B roads	
Locations	Duddon O
Urban area	

Street Index with Grid Reference

Chester

Albion Street	D2
Andrews Crescent	E1
Anne's Way	E2-E1
Beaconsfield Street	E3
Black Friars	C1-C2
Bottom's Lane	E1-F1
Boughton	E3-F3
Bouverie Street	B4
Bridge Street	C2
Brook Street	D4
Cambrian Road	A4-B4
Canal Street	B3-C3
Castle Drive	C1
Castle Street	C1
Catherine Street	A3-B3
Chichester Street	B4-C4
City Road	E3-E4
City Walls Road	B3-B2
Commonhall Street	C2
Crewe Street	D4-E4
Crook Street	C2
Cross Heys	E1
Cuppin Street	C2
Curzon Park North	A1
Dee Hills Park	E3
Dee Lane	E3
Delamere Street	C4
Denbigh Street	B4
Duke Street	D1-D2
Eastern Path	D1-E1
Edinburgh Way	E1
Egerton Street	D4
Elizabeth Crescent	E1-E2
Finchetts Drive	A4
Foregate Street	D3

Forest Street	D3-E3
Francis Street	D4
Frodsham Street	D3
Garden Lane	A4-B4
Garden Terrace	B3-B4
George Street	C3-C4
Gladstone Avenue	A3-A4
Gladstone Road	A4
Gorse Stacks	C4-C3-D3
Goss Street	C2
Granville Road	A4
Grey Friars	C2
Grosvenor Park Road	E3
Grosvenor Road	C1
Grosvenor Street	C1-C2
Groves Road	D2-E2
Handbridge	D1
Henshall Street	B4
Hoole Lane	F3-F4
Hoole Way	D4
Hunter Street	B3-C3
King Street	B3-C3
Lightfoot Street	E4-F4
Lord Street	F3
Lorne Street	B4
Lower Bridge Street	C2-C1-D1
Lower Park Road	D2-E2
Love Street	D3
Lyon Street	D4
Meadows Lane	E1
Milton Street	D4
New Crane Street	A3-B3-B2
Newgate Street	D2
Nicholas Street	C2-C1
Northgate Street	C3-C2
North Lorne Street	B4
Nuns Road	B2-B1-C1
Pepper Street	C2-D2
Princess Street	C3
Prince's Avenue	E4
Queens Avenue	E4
Queen's Drive	E1-E2
Queen's Park Road	D1-E1
Queen's Road	E4
Queen Street	D3
Raymond Street	B3-B4
Richmond Terrace	F4
St Anne Street	C4-D4
St George's Crescent	E1
St Johns Road	E1
St Johns Street	D2
St John Street	D3-D2
St Martins Way	B4-B3-C3-B2-C2
St Oswalds Way	C4-D4-D3
Sealand Road	A3
Seller Street	D3
Souters Lane	D2
South Crescent Road	D2-E2-E1
South View Road	A3-B3
Spital Walk	F4-F3
Stadium Way	A4
Stanley Street	B2
Station Road	D4-E4
Station View	F4
The Bars	E3
The Groves	D2-E2
The Rows	C2
Tower Road	B3
Trafford Street	C4-D4
Union Street	D2-D3-E3
Upper Cambrian Road	A4-B4-B3

Upper Northgate Street	B4-C4-C3
Vernon Road	A3-B3-B4
Vicars Lane	D2
Victoria Crescent	D1-E1
Victoria Path	D1-E1
Victoria Road	C4
Walls Avenue	B3-B2
Walpole Street	B4
Watergate Street	B2-C2
Water Tower Street	B3-C3
Weaver Street	C2
West Lorne Street	B4
White Friars	C2
Whipcord Lane	A4-B4
York Street	D3

Northwich

Albion Road	B3
Apple Market	A3
Ash Street	B4-C4
Barons Quay Road	A4-B4
Beswicks Road	A4
Binney Road	C2
Brockhurst Street	B3
Brook Street	B3-C3-C4
Carlton Road	C2-C1
Castle Street	A2-A3
Chester Way	A2-B2-B3-C3
Chester Way Spur	B3
Church Road	C3
Danebank Road	C2-C1
Danefield Road	C2
Dane Street	A3-A2
Forest Street	C3
Greenall Road	C2-C3
Hayhurst Close	A2
Highfield Road	A2
High Street	A3
Jubilee Street	A2
Kingsway	C3
Leicester Street	B3-B4
Lock Street	A3
London Road	A1-A2-B2
Manora Road	C2
Meadow Bank	B3
Navigation Road	A1-A2
Neumann Street	C3
New Warrington Street	C3-C4
Oak Street	B4-C4
Old Warrington Road	C4-C3
Orchard Street	C3
Paradise Street	C3
Percy Street	B3
Post Office Place	B4-B3
Princes Avenue	C3
Priory Street	B2-B3
School Way	B3
Sheath Street	B3
Station Road	C3
The Crescent	A1
Tabley Street	B4-B3
Timber Lane	B3
Town Bridge	A3
Vicarage Road	C2
Vicarage Walk	C2
Victoria Road	C2-C3
Water Street	B2
Watling Street	A3-B3
Weaver Way	A3-B3-B4
Weir Street	A1

Wesley Place	C3
Westfield Road	C2
Whalley Road	B3-B2
Winnington Street	A3
Witton Street	B3-C3

Middlewich

Ashfield Street	C2
Beech Street	B2-B3
Beta Road	C2-C1
Booth Lane	C1
Brooks Lane	C3-C2
Canal Terrace	C2
Chester Road	A4-A3
Croxton Lane	A4
Darlington Street	A3-B3
Dawe Street	C4
Dierdene Terrace	B3
East Road	A3
Elm Road	C1
Finney's Lane	A4-B4
Flea Lane	A1
Garfitt Street	B4-C4
Glastonbury Drive	A3
Hannah's Walk	A2-B2
Hayhurst Avenue	A1-B1
High Town	B3
Holmes Chapel Road	C3-C4
Hubert Drive	B1
Kinderton Street	B3-C3
King Edward Street	B2
King's Crescent	B4-C4
King Street	B4-C4-C3
Kitfield Avenue	B1-C1
Lewin Street	B3-B2-C2-C1
Lichfield Street	C4
Long Lane	B1
Longwood Close	B2
Lower Street	B3
Manor Fields	B1
Manor Lane	A2-B2
Mill Lane	A2
Nantwich Road	A1-A2-A3
New King Street	B4-C4
Newton Bank	A4-A3
Newton Heath	A3
Orchard Close	C1
Park Road	A2-B2
Pepper Street	B4-B3
Prosperity Way	C3
Queen Street	B2-B3
Rolt Crescent	A1-B1
Roy Lance Drive	B2
St Anne's Avenue	B1-C1
St Anne's Road	A3-B3-B2-B1
St Michaels Way	A3-B3
School Walk	B2
Seddon Street	B4
Southway	B3
Sutton Lane	B1-B2-C2
The Crescent	A3
Walker Drive	B1
Wavertree Drive	A1
Webbs Lane	B4
West Avenue	B4
Westlands Road	A3-A2
West Street	B3
Wheelock Street	A3-B3
White Horse Alley	B2
Wych House Lane	B3-C3

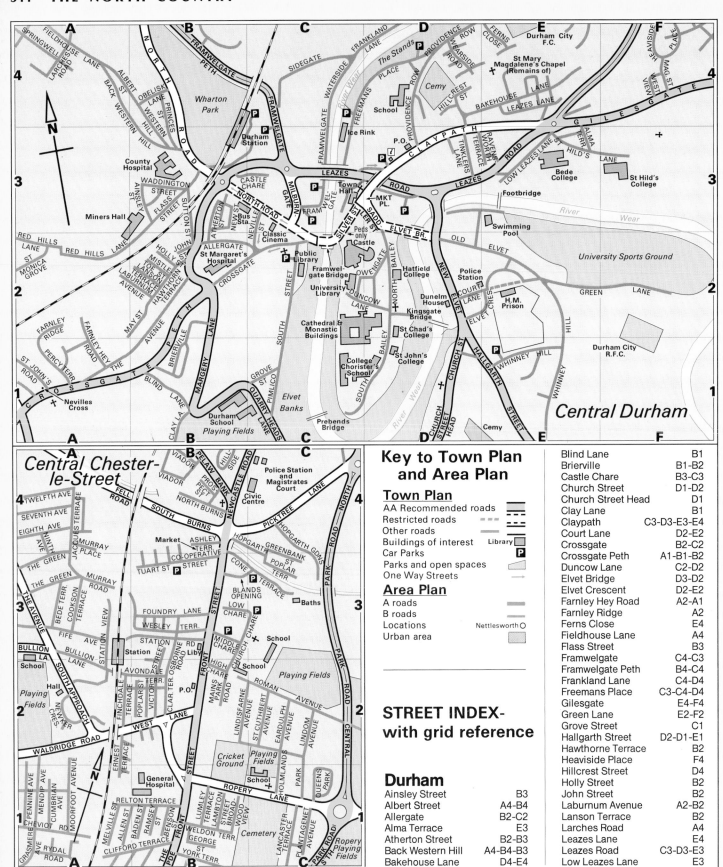

Central Durham

Central Chester-le-Street

Key to Town Plan and Area Plan

Town Plan
AA Recommended roads
Restricted roads
Other roads
Buildings of interest   Library
Car Parks   P
Parks and open spaces
One Way Streets

Area Plan
A roads
B roads
Locations   Nettlesworth ○
Urban area

STREET INDEX - with grid reference

Durham

Ainsley Street	B3
Albert Street	A4-B4
Allergate	B2-C2
Alma Terrace	E3
Atherton Street	B2-B3
Back Western Hill	A4-B4-B3
Bakehouse Lane	D4-E4
Blind Lane	B1
Brierville	B1-B2
Castle Chare	B3-C3
Church Street	D1-D2
Church Street Head	D1
Clay Lane	B1
Claypath	C3-D3-E3-E4
Court Lane	D2-E2
Crossgate	B2-C2
Crossgate Peth	A1-B1-B2
Duncow Lane	C2-D2
Elvet Bridge	D3-D2
Elvet Crescent	D2-E2
Farnley Hey Road	A2-A1
Farnley Ridge	A2
Ferns Close	E4
Fieldhouse Lane	A4
Flass Street	B3
Framwelgate	C4-C3
Framwelgate Peth	B4-C4
Frankland Lane	C4-D4
Freemans Place	C3-C4-D4
Gilesgate	E4-F4
Green Lane	E2-F2
Grove Street	C1
Hallgarth Street	D2-D1-E1
Hawthorne Terrace	B2
Heaviside Place	F4
Hillcrest Street	D4
Holly Street	B2
John Street	B2
Laburnum Avenue	A2-B2
Lanson Terrace	B2
Larches Road	A4
Leazes Lane	E4
Leazes Road	C3-D3-E3
Low Leazes Lane	E3

Durham

The castle and the cathedral stand side by side high above the city like sentinels, dramatically symbolising the military and religious power Durham wielded in the past. Its origins date from about 995 when the remains of St Cuthbert arrived from Lindisfarne and his shrine was a popular centre of pilgrimage. Soon after that early fortifications were built, later replaced by a stone castle which became the residence of the Prince-Bishops of Durham – powerful feudal rulers appointed by the King. Today the city's university, the oldest in England after Oxford and Cambridge, occupies the castle and most of the buildings around peaceful, secluded Palace Green. The splendid Norman cathedral, sited on the other side of the Green, is considered to be one of the finest in Europe. Its combination of strength and size, tempered with grace and beauty, is awe-inspiring.

Under the shadow of these giants the old city streets, known as vennels, ramble down the bluff past the 17th-century Bishop Cosin's House and the old grammar school, to the thickly-wooded banks of the Wear. Here three historic bridges link the city's heart with the pleasant Georgian suburbs on the other side of the river.

Although Durham is not an industrial city, it has become the venue for the North-East miners' annual Gala Day in July.

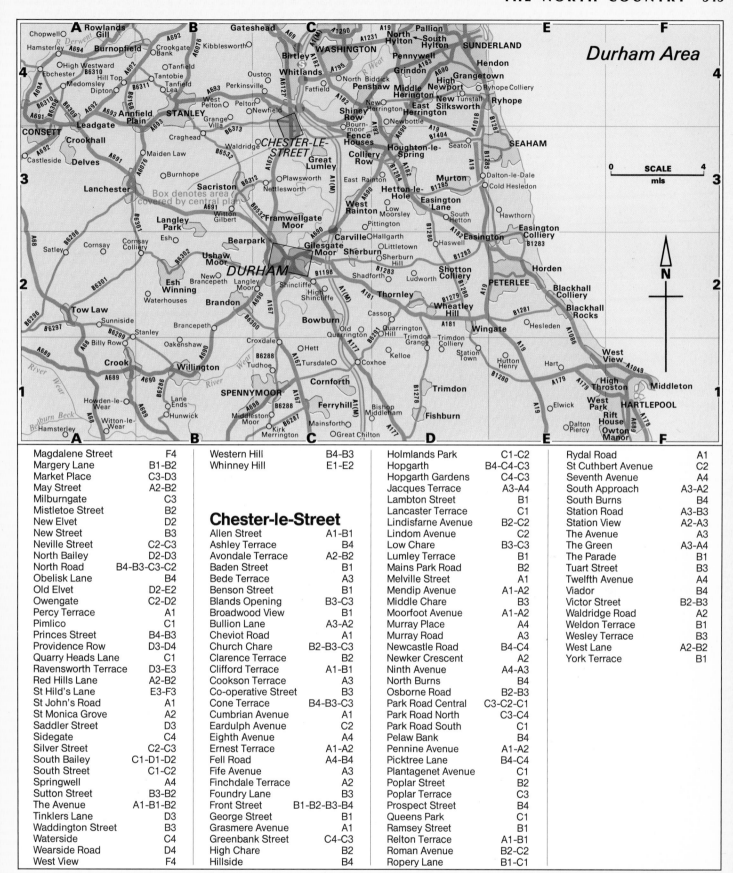

Durham Area

SCALE
0   4
mls

N

Box denotes area
covered by central plan

Magdalene Street	F4	Western Hill	B4-B3	Holmlands Park	C1-C2	Rydal Road	A1
Margery Lane	B1-B2	Whinney Hill	E1-E2	Hopgarth	B4-C4-C3	St Cuthbert Avenue	C2

DURHAM
High above the wooded banks of the River Wear, Durham's castle and cathedral crown the steep hill on which the city is built. They share the site with several of the university's attractive old buildings.

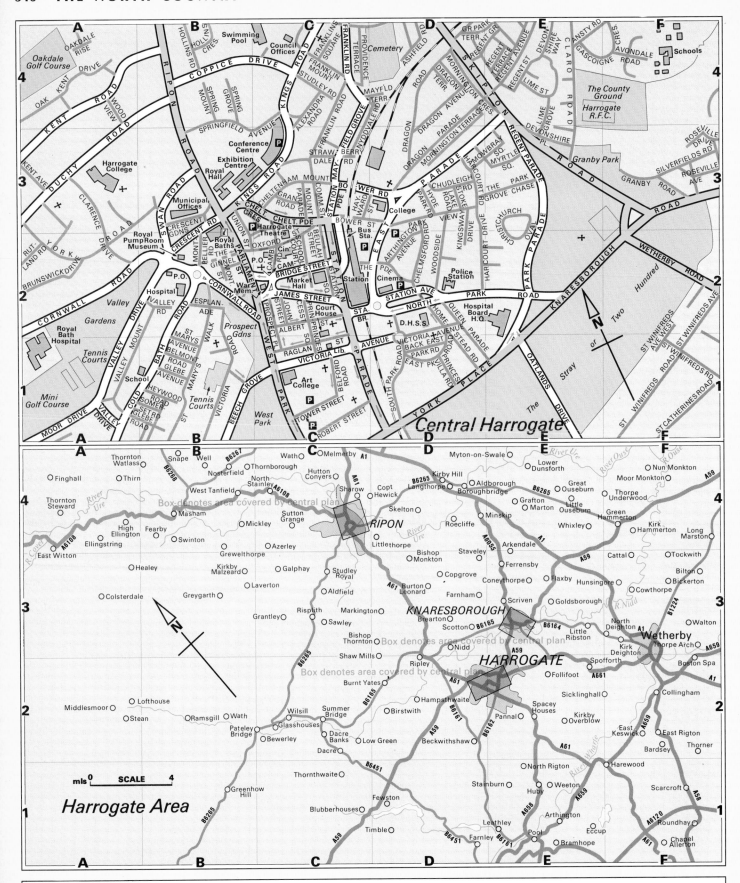

Central Harrogate

Harrogate Area

mls 0 SCALE 4

Harrogate

Dignified Victorian stone buildings and lovely gardens reflect Harrogate's 19th-century popularity as a spa town and its Royal Baths, opened in 1897, became one of the largest hydrotherapy establishments in the world. More recently the town has become a busy conference centre, the main venues being the Royal Hall and the elegant old Assembly Rooms. A glass-covered walkway in Valley Gardens leads to the Sun Pavilion and part of the lovely Harlow Car Gardens is used for experimental horticulture.

Ripon, known as the Gateway to the Dales, stands at the junction of three rivers; the Ure, the Skell and the Laver. Its small cathedral, a delightful 12th-century building occupying the site of an Anglo-Saxon church, has a small museum of church treasures in the original crypt. One corner of the town's rectangular market square is marked by the medieval Wakeman's house, now a local museum and tourist information centre.

Knaresborough Here buildings scramble higgledy-piggledy up a rocky outcrop from the banks of the River Nidd to the town's ruined 14th-century castle. The keep, two baileys and two gatehouses have survived, and there is a museum in the grounds. The town is able to claim two records; it has the oldest linen-mill and the oldest chemist's shop in England.

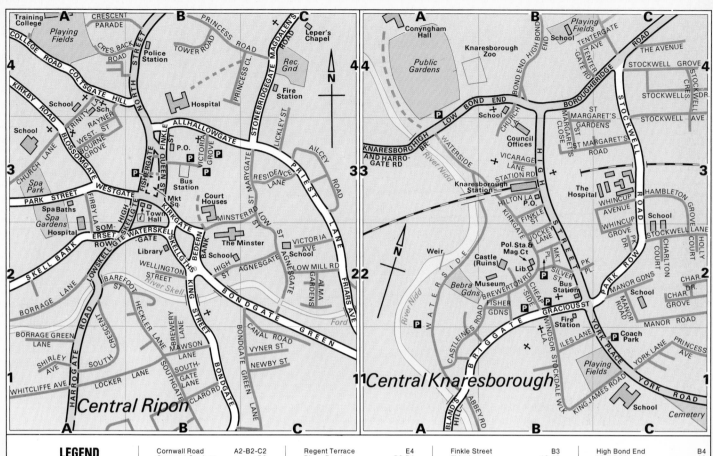

Central Ripon

Central Knaresborough

LEGEND

Town Plan

AA recommended route	
Restricted roads	
Other roads	
Buildings of interest	Station ☐
Car parks	🅿
Parks and open spaces	
One way streets	←

Area Plan

A roads	
B roads	
Locations	Nidd ○
Urban area	

Street Index with Grid Reference

Harrogate

Albert Street	C2
Alexandra Road	C4
Ansty Road	E4-F4
Arthington Avenue	D2
Ashfield Road	D4
Avondale Road	F4
BackEast Park Road	D1
Beech Grove	B1-C1
Belford Road	C1
Belmont Road	B1
Beulah Street	C2
Bower Road	C3-D3
Bower Street	C3-D3
Brunswick Drive	A2
Cambridge Road	C2
Cambridge Street	C2
Chelmsford Road	D2-D3
Cheltenham Crescent	B3-C3
Cheltenham Mount	C3
Cheltenham Parade	C3
Christchurch Oval	E2-E3
Chudleigh Road	D3
Clarence Drive	A2-A3
Claro Road	E3-E4
Cold Bath Road	A1-B1-B2
Commercial Street	C3
Coppice Drive	B4-C4

Cornwall Road	A2-B2-C2
Crescent Gardens	B3
Crescent Road	B2-B3
Devonshire Place	E3
Devonshire Way	E4
Dragon Avenue	D3-D4
Dragon Parade	D3-D4
Dragon Road	D3-D4
Dragon Terrace	D4
Duchy Road	A3-A4-B4
East Parade	D2-D3-E3-E4
East Park Road	D1-D2
Esplanade	B2
Franklin Mount	C4
Franklin Road	C3-C4
Franklins Square	C4
Gascoigne Crescent	E4-F4
Glebe Avenue	B1
Glebe Road	A1-B1
Granby Road	F3
Granville Road	C3
Grove Park Terrace	D4-E4
Harcourt Drive	D2-D3
Harcourt Road	D3
Hayward Street	C3-D3
Heywood Road	B1
Hollins Crescent	B4
Hollins Road	B4
Homestead Road	D1-D2
Hyde Park Road	D3
James Street	C2
John Street	C2
Kent Avenue	A3
Kent Road	A3-A4-B4
King's Road	B3-C3-C4
Kingsway Drive	D2-D3
Knaresborough Road	E1-E2-F2-F3
Lime Grove	E3-E4
Lime Street	E4
Mayfield Grove	C3-C4
Mayfield Terrace	C4-D4
Montpellier Road	B2
Montpellier Street	B2
Moor Drive	A1
Mornington Crescent	D4-E4
Mornington Terrace	D3-D4
Mount Parade	C3
Mowbray Square	D3-E3
Myrtle Square	E3
North Park Road	D2-E2
Nyddvale Road	C3-C4-D4
Oakdale Rise	A4
Oak Kent Drive	A4
Oatlands Drive	E1
Oxford Street	B2-C2-C3
Park Chase	E3
Park Parade	E1-E2-E3
Park View	D3
Parliament Street	B3-B2-C2
Princes Square	C1-C2
Princes Street	C2
Princes Villa Road	D1
Prospect Place	C1-C2
Providence Terrace	C1-C2
Queen Parade	D2-D1-E1
Raglan Street	C1-C2
Regent Avenue	E4
Regent Grove	D4-E4
Regent Parade	E3-E4
Regent Street	E4

Regent Terrace	E4
Ripon Road	B3-B4
Robert Street	C1
Roseville Avenue	F3
Roseville Drive	F3
Rutland Road	A2
St Catherine's Road	F1
St Marys Avenue	B1
St Mary's Walk	B1-B2
St Winifreds Avenue	F1-F2
St Winifreds Avenue West	F1-F2
St Winifreds Road	F1
School Court	C2
Silverfields Road	F3
Skipton Road	D4-E4-E3-F3
Somerset Road	A1-B1
South Park Road	D1
Springfield Avenue	B4-B3-C3-C4
Spring Grove	B4
Spring Mount	B4
Station Avenue	D2
Station Bridge	C2
Station Parade	C3-C2-C1-D1
Station Square	C2
Stoke Lake Road	D3
Strawberry Dale Road	C3
Studley Road	C4
Swan Road	B2-B3
The Ginnel	B2
The Grove	D3-E3
The Parade	C2-D2
Tower Street	C1
Union Street	B2-B3
Valley Drive	A1-A2-B2
Valley Mount	A1-B1-B2
Valley Road	B2
Victoria Avenue	C1-D1-D2
Victoria Road	B1-B2
West Park	C1-C2
Wetherby Road	F2
Woodside	D2-D3
Wood View	A4
York Place	D1-E1
York Road	A3-A2-A3-B3

Ripon

Agnesgate	B2-C2
Ailcey Road	C3
Allhallowgate	B3-C3
Alma Gardens	C2
Barefoot Street	A2-B2
Bedern Bank	B2
Blossomgate	A3
Bondgate	B1
Bondgate Green	B2-C2-C1
Bondgate Green Lane	C1-C2
Borrage Green Lane	A1
Borrage Lane	A2
Brewery Lane	B1-B2
Canal Road	C1-C2
Church Lane	A3
Claro Road	B1
College Road	A4
Coltsgate Hill	A4-B4
Crescent Back Road	A4-B4
Crescent Parade	A4-B4

Finkle Street	B3
Firby Lane	A2-A3
Fishergate	B3
Friars Avenue	C1-C2
Harrogate Road	A1-A2
Heckler Lane	B1-B2
High Skellgate	A3-A2-B2-B3
High Street	B2
King Street	B1-B2
Kirkby Road	A3-A4
Kirkgate	B2-B3
Lickley Street	C3-C4
Locker Lane	A1-B1
Low Mill Lane	C2
Lowskellgate	A2
Low Street	C2-C3
Magdalen's Road	C4
Mawson Lane	B1
Minster Road	B2-B3-C3
Newby Street	C1
North Street	B3-B4
Park Street	A3
Priest Lane	C2-C3
Princess Close	B4-C4
Princes Road	B4-C4
Queen Street	B3
Rayner Street	A3-A4
Residence Lane	C3
St Agnesgate	C2
St Marygate	C2
Shirley Avenue	A1
Skell Bank	A2
Skellgarths	B2
Somerset Row	A2
South Crescent	A1-A2
Southgate	B1
Southgate Lane	B1
Stonebridgegate	C3-C4
Tower Road	B4
Trinity Lane	A3-A4
Victoria Avenue	C2
Victoria Grove	B3
Vyner Street	C1
Waterskellgate	A2-B2
Wellington Street	B2
Westbourne Grove	A3
Westgate	A3-B3
Whitcliffe Avenue	A1

High Bond End	B4
High Bridge	A3
High Street	B2-B3-B4
Hilton Lane	B3
Holly Court	C2
Iles Lane	B1-C1
Jockey Lane	B2-B3
King James Road	B1-C1
Kirkgate	B2-B3
Knaresborough and Harrogate Road	A3
Low Bond End	A3-A4-B4
Manor Gardens	C2
Manor Road	C2
Market Place	B2
Park Drive	C2
Park Place	B2-C2
Park Row	C2
Princess Avenue	C1
St Margaret's Close	B3-B4
St Margaret's Gardens	B3-C3
St Margaret's Road	B3-C3
Silver Street	B2
Station Road	B3
Stockdale Walk	B1
Stockwell Avenue	C4
Stockwell Crescent	C4
Stockwell Drive	C4
Stockwell Grove	C4
Stockwell Lane	C4
Stockwell Road	C2-C3-C4
Tentergate Avenue	B4-C4
Tentergate Road	B4-C4
The Avenue	C4
Vicarage Lane	B3
Waterside	A1-A2-B2-B3-B3
Whincup Avenue	C3
Whincup Grove	C2-C3
Windsor Lane	B1-B2
York Lane	C1
York Place	B2-C2-C1
York Road	C1

Knaresborough

Abbey Road	A1-B1
Bland's Hill	A1
Bond End	B4
Boroughbridge Road	B4-B2
Brewerton Road	B2
Briggate	A1-B1-B2
Castleings Road	A1-B1-B2
Charlton Court	C2
Charlton Drive	C2
Charlton Grove	C2
Cheapside	B2
Church Lane	B3-B4
Finkle Street	B3
Fisher Gardens	B2
Gracious Street	B2
Hambleton Grove	C2-C3

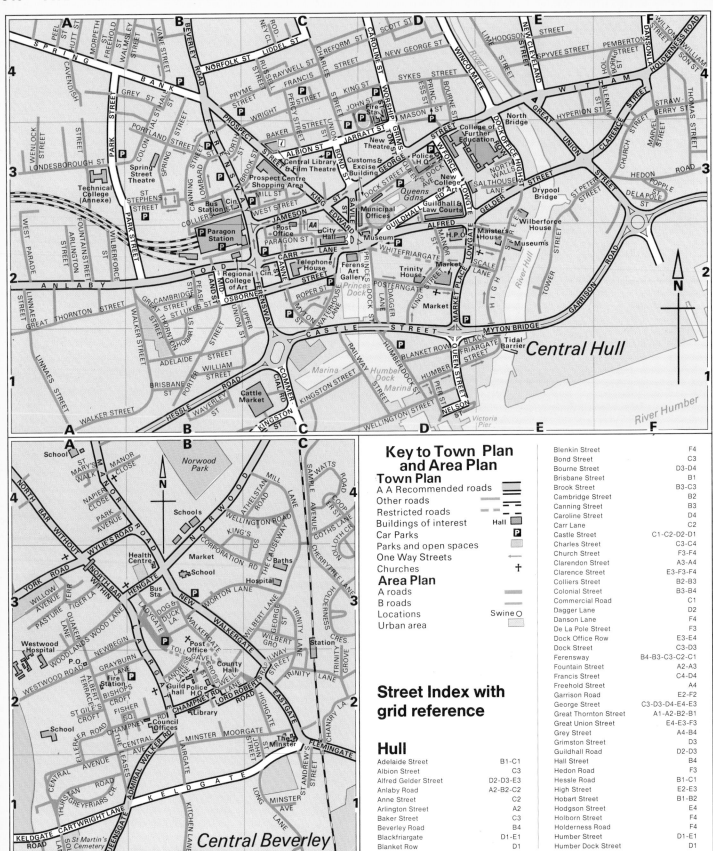

Central Hull

Central Beverley

Key to Town Plan and Area Plan

Town Plan

A A Recommended roads
Other roads
Restricted roads
Buildings of interest — Hall
Car Parks — P
Parks and open spaces
One Way Streets
Churches — +

Area Plan

A roads
B roads
Locations — Swine
Urban area

Street Index with grid reference

Hull

Adelaide Street	B1-C1
Albion Street	C3
Alfred Gelder Street	D2-D3-E3
Anlaby Road	A2-B2-C2
Anne Street	C2
Arlington Street	A2
Baker Street	C3
Beverley Road	B4
Blackfriargate	D1-E1
Blanket Row	D1
Blenkin Street	F4
Bond Street	C3
Bourne Street	D3-D4
Brisbane Street	B1
Brook Street	B3-C3
Cambridge Street	B2
Canning Street	B3
Caroline Street	D4
Carr Lane	C2
Castle Street	C1-C2-D2-D1
Charles Street	C3-C4
Church Street	F3-F4
Clarendon Street	A3-A4
Clarence Street	E3-F3-F4
Colliers Street	B2-B3
Colonial Street	B3-B4
Commercial Road	C1
Dagger Lane	D2
Danson Lane	F4
De La Pole Street	F3
Dock Office Row	E3-E4
Dock Street	C3-D3
Ferensway	B4-B3-C3-C2-C1
Fountain Street	A2-A3
Francis Street	C4-D4
Freehold Street	A4
Garrison Road	E2-F2
George Street	C3-D3-D4-E4-E3
Great Thornton Street	A1-A2-B2-B1
Great Union Street	E4-E3-F3
Grey Street	A4-B4
Grimston Street	D3
Guildhall Road	D2-D3
Hall Street	B4
Hedon Road	F3
Hessle Road	B1-C1
High Street	E2-E3
Hobart Street	B1-B2
Hodgson Street	E4
Holborn Street	F4
Holderness Road	F4
Humber Street	D1-E1
Humber Dock Street	D1

Hull

Officially Kingston-upon-Hull, this ancient port was specially laid out with new docks in 1293, on the decree of Edward I, and echoes of the town's past can be seen in the Town Docks Museum. The docks and the fishing industry are synonymous with Hull – it has Britain's busiest deep-sea fishing port – although flour-milling, vegetable oil extraction and petrochemical production are also important. The centre of Hull consists of broad streets and spacious squares and parks, such as Queen's Gardens, laid out on the site of what used to be Queen's Dock. The older part of the town which lies south-east of here between the docks and the River Hull is full of character, with a number of Georgian buildings and places of interest.

Beverley is one of England's most distinguished towns. Between its two principal buildings – the famous Minster and St Mary's Church – are medieval streets and pleasing market squares graced by redbrick Georgian houses built by the landed gentry of the East Riding during the town's heyday as a fashionable resort. The Minster's twin towers soar above the rooftops of the town as a constant reminder that here is one of the most beautiful pieces of Gothic architecture in Europe. The wealth of beauty and detail throughout is immense, but carving in both stone and wood is one of its most outstanding features.

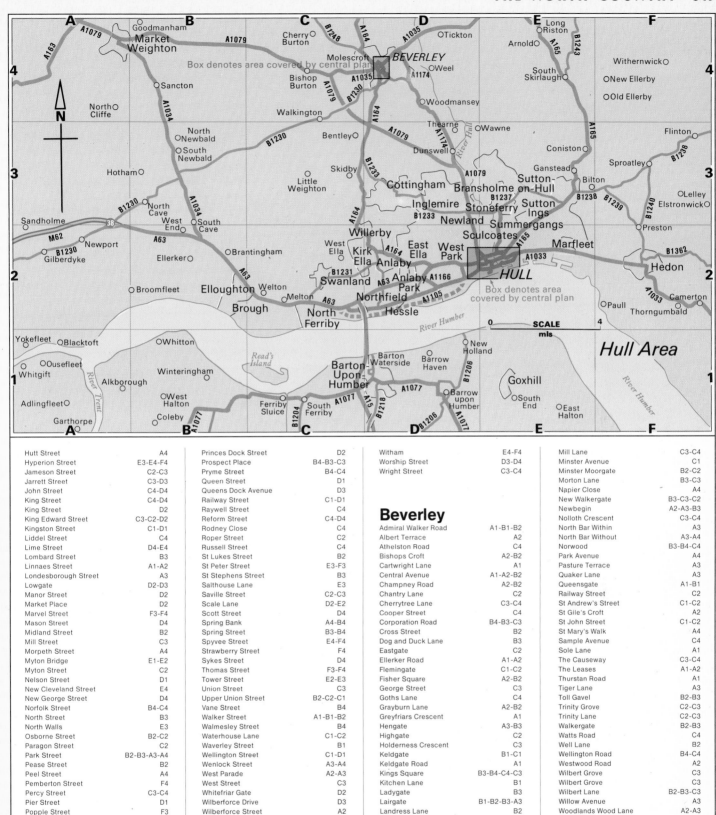

Box denotes area covered by central plan

BEVERLEY

Box denotes area covered by central plan

HULL

SCALE
mls

Hull Area

Hutt Street	A4
Hyperion Street	E3-E4-F4
Jameson Street	C2-C3
Jarrett Street	C3-D3
John Street	C4-D4
King Street	C4-D4
King Street	D2
King Edward Street	C3-C2-D2
Kingston Street	C1-D1
Liddel Street	C4
Lime Street	D4-E4
Lombard Street	B3
Linnaes Street	A1-A2
Londesborough Street	A3
Lowgate	D2-D3
Manor Street	D2
Market Place	D2
Marvel Street	F3-F4
Mason Street	D4
Midland Street	B2
Mill Street	C3
Morpeth Street	A4
Myton Bridge	E1-E2
Myton Street	C2
Nelson Street	D1
New Cleveland Street	E4
New George Street	D4
Norfolk Street	B4-C4
North Street	B3
North Walls	E3
Osborne Street	B2-C2
Paragon Street	C2
Park Street	B2-B3-A3-A4
Pease Street	B2
Peel Street	A4
Pemberton Street	F4
Percy Street	C3-C4
Pier Street	D1
Popple Street	F3
Porter Street	B1-B2
Portland Street	B3
Posterngate	D2
Princess Street	D4

Princes Dock Street	D2
Prospect Place	B4-B3-C3
Pryme Street	B4-C4
Queen Street	D1
Queens Dock Avenue	D3
Railway Street	C1-D1
Raywell Street	C4
Reform Street	C4-D4
Rodney Close	C4
Roper Street	C2
Russell Street	C4
St Lukes Street	B2
St Peter Street	E3-F3
St Stephens Street	B3
Salthouse Lane	E3
Saville Street	C2-C3
Scale Lane	D2-E2
Scott Street	D4
Spring Bank	A4-B4
Spring Street	B3-B4
Spyvee Street	E4-F4
Strawberry Street	F4
Sykes Street	D4
Thomas Street	F3-F4
Tower Street	E2-E3
Union Street	C3
Upper Union Street	B2-C2-C1
Vane Street	B4
Walker Street	A1-B1-B2
Walmesley Street	B4
Waterhouse Lane	C1-C2
Waverley Street	B1
Wellington Street	C1-D1
Wenlock Street	A3-A4
West Parade	A2-A3
West Street	C3
Whitefriar Gate	D2
Wilberforce Drive	D3
Wilberforce Street	A2
William Street	B1-C1
Williamson Street	F4
Wilton Street	F4
Wincolmlee	D4-E4

Witham	E4-F4
Worship Street	D3-D4
Wright Street	C3-C4

Beverley

Admiral Walker Road	A1-B1-B2
Albert Terrace	A2
Athelston Road	C4
Bishops Croft	A2-B2
Cartwright Lane	A1
Central Avenue	A1-A2-B2
Champney Road	A2-B2
Chantry Lane	C2
Cherrytree Lane	C3-C4
Cooper Street	C4
Corporation Road	B4-B3-C3
Cross Street	B2
Dog and Duck Lane	B3
Eastgate	C2
Ellerker Road	A1-A2
Flemingate	C1-C2
Fisher Square	A2-B2
George Street	C3
Goths Lane	C4
Grayburn Lane	A2-B2
Greyfriars Crescent	A1
Hengate	A3-B3
Highgate	B2
Holderness Crescent	C3
Keldgate	B1-C1
Keldgate Road	A1
Kings Square	B3-B4-C4-C3
Kitchen Lane	B1
Ladygate	B3
Lairgate	B1-B2-B3-A3
Landress Lane	B2
Long Lane	C1
Lord Roberts Road	B2-C2
Manor Close	A4-B4
Manor Road	A4-B4-B3

Mill Lane	C3-C4
Minster Avenue	C1
Minster Moorgate	B2-C2
Morton Lane	B3-C3
Napier Close	A4
New Walkergate	B3-C3-C2
Newbegin	A2-A3-B3
Nolloth Crescent	C3-C4
North Bar Within	A3
North Bar Without	A3-A4
Norwood	B3-B4-C4
Park Avenue	A4
Pasture Terrace	A3
Quaker Lane	A3
Queensgate	A1-B1
Railway Street	C2
St Andrew's Street	C1-C2
St Gile's Croft	A2
St John Street	C1-C2
St Mary's Walk	A4
Sample Avenue	C4
Sole Lane	A1
The Causeway	C3-C4
The Leases	A1-A2
Thurstan Road	A1
Tiger Lane	A3
Toll Gavel	B2-B3
Trinity Grove	C2-C3
Trinity Lane	C2-C3
Walkergate	B2-B3
Watts Road	C4
Well Lane	B2
Wellington Road	B4-C4
Westwood Road	A2
Wilbert Grove	C3
Wilbert Grove	C3
Wilbert Lane	B2-B3-C3
Willow Avenue	A3
Woodlands Wood Lane	A2-A3
Wylie's Road	A3-A4-B4
York Road	A3

HULL
Schemes to cross the Humber estuary were first discussed over 100 years ago, but it was not until 1981 that the mammoth project was sucessfully completed. At 4626ft, the Humber Bridge has the longest main span in the world.

Central Carlisle

Edenside Cricket Ground
Eden Bridge
THE SWIFTS (Miniature Golf Course)
Leisure Centre
BITTS PARK
Newark Terr.
DUKE'S ROAD
Trinity School
DACRE ROAD
Castle & Museum
CITY WALLS
Corporation Road
Civic Centre
Police Sta.
WARWICK ST.
RICKERGATE
DROVERS LANE
LOWTHER STREET
EAST TOWER ST.
GEORGIAN WAY
STRAND ROAD
Technical College
CHAPEL ST.
Sports Centre
COMPTON
CHATS-WORTH SQ.
BRIDGE STREET
ANNETWELL ST.
FINKLE FISHER STREET
Tullie Hse Museum & Art Gallery
PATER-NOSTER ROW
CASTLE STREET
MARKET ST.
Market Hall
SCOTCH ST.
ST. MARY'S GA.
VICTORIA PLACE
Prior Slee's Gateway
Cathedral & Priory Tower Museum
Guildhall Museum
T.I.C. Town Hall
Town Hall Square
BANK ST.
Bus Station
SPENCER STREET
CHISWICK ST.
ABBEY STREET
WEST WALLS
WEST WALLS
VIADUCT ESTATE
Tithe Barn
BLACKFRIARS ST.
ENGLISH ST.
LONSDALE ST.
CROSBY ST.
CECIL PL.
WARWICK ROAD
Cinema
County Offices
P.O.
MARY STREET
PORTLAND
TAIT ST.
MILBOURNE CRES.
LORNE CRES.
JUNCTION CHARLOTTE ST.
Swimming Pool
Crown Courts
Citadel Station
BOTCHERGATE
River Caldew
VIADUCT
VICTORIA
DAMSIDE
River Eden

Central Kendal

WINDERMERE RD.
County Hall
Cinema
Victoria Bridge
River Kent
Station
WEST-GATE
STATION RD.
LONG POOL
ANN ST.
WILDMAN ST.
Museum Castle Dairy
CASTLE STREET
CASTLE GARTH
THORNY HILLS
CASTLE CRES.
CASTLE ROAD
SANDES AVENUE
MAUDE STREET
Nobles Rest Park
District Council Offices
P.O.
Library
Bus Sta.
Stramongate Bridge
STRAMONGATE
STRICKLANDGATE
BLACKHALL ROAD
Parish Church
Footbridge
Kirkbie Kendal Lower School
MARKET PL.
FINKLE ST.
NEW ROAD
Recreation Ground
ALL HALLOWS LANE
Town Hall & T.I.C.
LOWTHER ST.
Miller Bridge
LITTLE AYNAM
BEAST BANKS
Sandes Hosp.
BRIDGE ST.
AYNAM ROAD
Castle Hill Ruins
Kendal Castle
Brewery Arts Centre
HIGHGATE
Footbridge
PARR STREET
SUNNYSIDE
Sunnyside Park
CAPTAIN FRENCH LANE
Abbot Hall Park
GILLING GATE
ANCHORITE FIELDS
KIRKBARROW
KIRKLAND
Abbot Hall
Church
Cemetery
Cricket Ground

Central Keswick

KESWICK BY PASS
VICARAGE HILL
GLEBE CLOSE
BRIAR
Cottage Hospital
RIGG
CROSTHWAITE ROAD
LIME POTS ROAD
HIGH HILL
BRUNDHOLME ROAD
River Greta
Pencil Museum
Lower Fitz Park
GRETA BRIDGE
STANGER ST.
School
GRETA SIDE
Museum & Art Gallery
STATION ROAD
Upper Fitz Park
River Greta
Council Offices
Bus Station
MAIN ST.
BANK ST.
Pol. Sta.
VICTORIA ST.
P.O.
Library
MKT. PL.
DERWENT ST.
PENRITH RD.
Rugby Ground
TITHEBARN ST.
THE CRESCENT
HEADS RD.
CLOSE
STATION ST.
ST. JOHN STREET
BLENCATHRA
SOUTHEY
GRETA ST.
WORDSWORTH ST.
HELVELLYN
HERBERT ST.
THE HEADLANDS
THE HEADS
HEADS ROAD
BORROWDALE ROAD
LAKE ROAD
Cinema
CHURCH ST.
ACORN ST.
HIGH ST.
ESKIN STREET
MANOR PARK
Miniature Golf Course
Cemetery
CASTLEHEAD CLOSE
AMBLESIDE ROAD
SPRING ROAD
Crow Park

Central Lancaster

MORECAMBE
Ryelands Park
OWEN ROAD
P.O.
MAIN WAY
ST. GEORGE'S
River Lune
Our Lady's R.C. High School
Old Custom House
Sports Ground
QUAY
Skerton Bridge
Kingsway Baths
CATON ROAD
LUNE ST.
ALBERT RD.
DERBY
River Lune
RIDGE LANE
GREEN STREET
DAMSIDE ST.
Greyhound Bridge
Lancaster Museum & King's Own Regimental Museum
PARLIAMENT STREET
BACK
BULK ROAD
DE VITRE STREET
WOLSELEY
The Judges Lodgings Museum
BRIDGE LA.
CABLE STREET
NORTH ROAD
Fire Station
Adult Education Centre
GATE
LODGE
ALFRED STREET
Lancaster Castle
CHURCH STREET
Music Room
Central Library
CASTLE HILL
CHINA LANE
CASTLE PARK
STONEWELL
ST. LEONARD'S
BREWARY LANE
MOOR LANE
EDWARD ST.
The Duke's Playhouse Theatre
Lancaster Station
LONG MARSH LANE
MEETING HOUSE LANE
P.O.
MARKET ST.
KING STREET
SULYARD ST.
DALTON SQ.
BULK ST.
ROAD
WILLIAMSON ROAD
MOORGATE
FENTON ST.
WHEATFIELD ST.
DALLAS RD.
Market Hall
Studio's 1 & 2
BROCK ST.
GEORGE STREET
NELSON STREET
EAST ROAD
SIBSEY STREET
BLADES STREET
HIGH ST.
MIDDLE ST.
Police H.Q.
Town Hall, County Court & Ashton Hall
BALMORAL ROAD
STIRLING RD.
ELGIN RD.
ABERDEEN RD.
PENNY STREET
THURNHAM STREET
QUEEN STREET
REGENT ST.
School
Gdns
LINDOW ST.
Playing Fields
QUARRY ROAD
ST. PETER'S ROAD
DALE ST.

Lake District

Keswick With the River Greta running through it and Skiddaw looming above, this is a charming, quiet market town set amid beautiful scenery at the southern end of Derwentwater. The Fitz Park Museum and Art Gallery houses a collection of manuscripts by the numerous authors and poets who took their inspiration from the Lakeland.

Windermere has remained unspoiled despite the enormous popularity it has won as a holiday resort. Centred around its extensive lake, it stands in a setting which has been exalted by poets and artists for years. Windermere's architecture is mainly Victorian, as a result of the railway coming in the mid-19th century and bringing prosperity to the town. But conservationists campaigned to stop the railway going any further, and so the natural peace of the area was preserved.

Lancaster Dominating the city from its hilltop site, Lancaster Castle was once the headquarters of the Duchy and is still in use today — as a prison. Its late Georgian courtrooms and the beautiful Shire Hall are open to visitors. Close by stands the Priory, an architectural gem, and also of interest is the early 17th-century Judge's Lodgings house, which provided accommodation for assize judges for 150 years. The building now houses a display of dolls, with beautiful

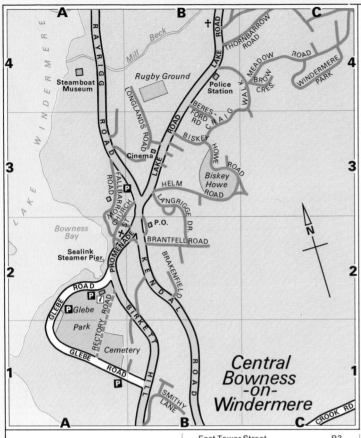

Central Bowness-on-Windermere

LEGEND

AA Recommended roads	
Restricted roads	
Other roads	
Buildings of interest	Library ▢
Car Parks	P
Parks and open spaces	▱
One Way Streets	←
Churches	✝

Street Index with Grid Reference

Carlisle

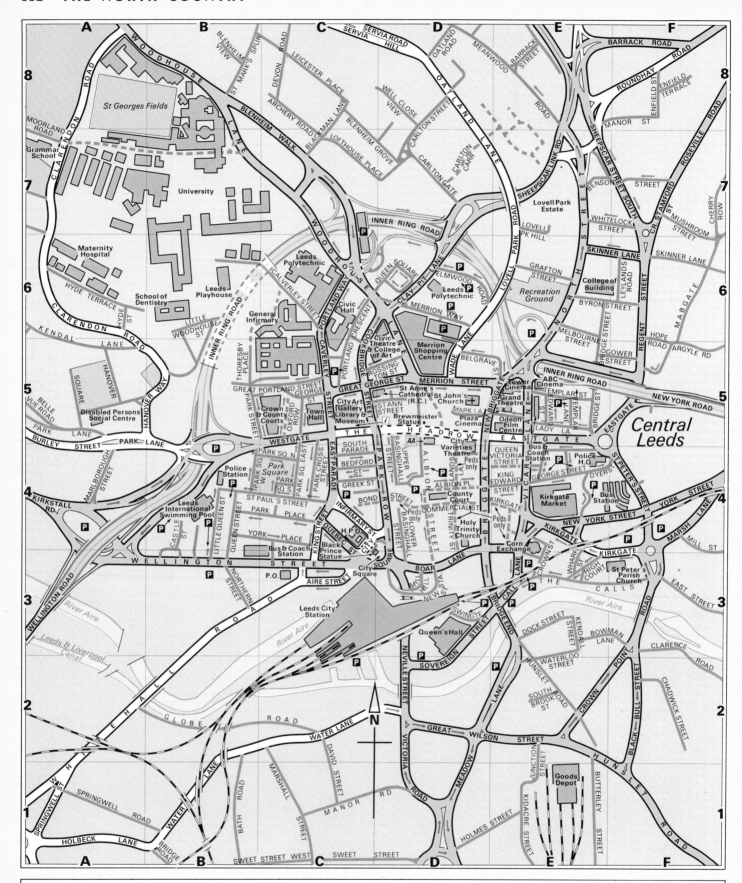

Leeds

In the centre of Leeds is its town hall – a monumental piece of architecture with a 225ft clock-tower. It was opened by Queen Victoria in 1858, and has been a kind of mascot for the city ever since. It exudes civic pride; such buildings could only have been created in the heyday of Victorian prosperity and confidence. Leeds' staple industry has always been the wool trade, but it

only became a boom town towards the end of the 18th century, when textile mills were introduced. Today, the wool trade and ready-made clothing (Mr Hepworth and Mr Burton began their work here) are still important, though industries like paper, leather, furniture and electrical equipment are prominent.

Across Calverley Street from the town hall is the City Art Gallery, Library and Museum. Its collections include sculpture by Henry Moore, who

was a student at Leeds School of Art. Nearby is the Headrow, Leeds' foremost shopping thoroughfare. On it is the City Varieties Theatre, venue for many years of the famous television programme 'The Good Old Days'. Off the Headrow are several shopping arcades, of which Leeds has many handsome examples. Leeds has a good number of interesting churches; perhaps the finest is St John's, unusual in that it dates from 1634, a time when few churches were built.

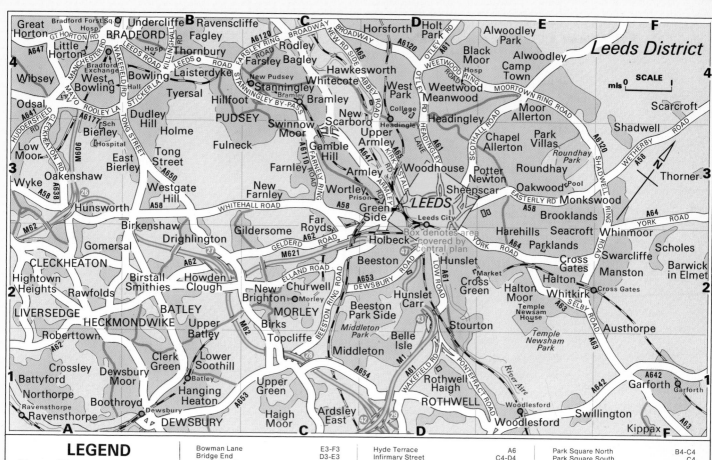

Leeds District

LEGEND

Town Plan

AA Recommended roads
Other roads
Restricted roads
Buildings of interset — Museum
AA Service Centre — AA
Parks and open spaces
Car Parks — P
Churches — †
One way streets

District Plan

A roads
B roads
Stations — Kirkgate
Urban area
Buildings of interest — Hospital

Street Index with Grid Reference

Leeds

LEEDS

Offices now occupy the handsome twin-towered Civic Hall which stands in Calverley Street in front of the new buildings of Leeds Polytechnic. This area of the city – the commercial centre – has been extensively redeveloped

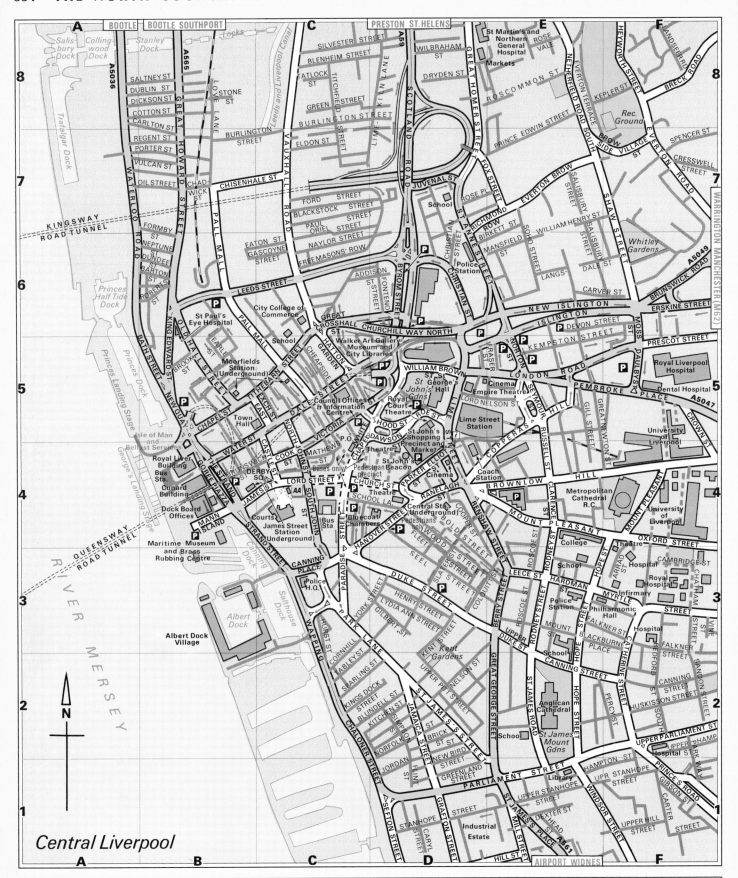

Central Liverpool

Liverpool

Although its dock area has been much reduced, Liverpool was at one time second only to London in pre-eminence as a port. Formerly the centrepiece of the docks area are three monumental buildings – the Dock Board Offices, built in 1907 with a huge copper-covered dome; the Cunard Building, dating from 1912 and decorated with an abundance of ornamental carving; and best-known of all, the world-famous Royal Liver Building, with the two 'liver birds' crowning its twin cupolas.

Some of the city's best industrial buildings have fallen into disuse in recent years, and have been preserved as monuments of the industrial age. One has become a maritime museum housing full-sized craft and a workshop where maritime crafts are demonstrated. Other museums and galleries include the Walker Art Gallery, with excellent collections of European painting and sculpture; Liverpool City Libraries, one of the oldest and largest public libraries in Britain, with a vast collection of books and manuscripts; and Bluecoat Chambers, a Queen Anne building now used as a gallery and concert hall. Liverpool has two outstanding cathedrals: the Roman Catholic, completed in 1967 in an uncompromising controversial style; and the Protestant, constructed in the great tradition of Gothic architecture, but begun in 1904 and only recently completed.

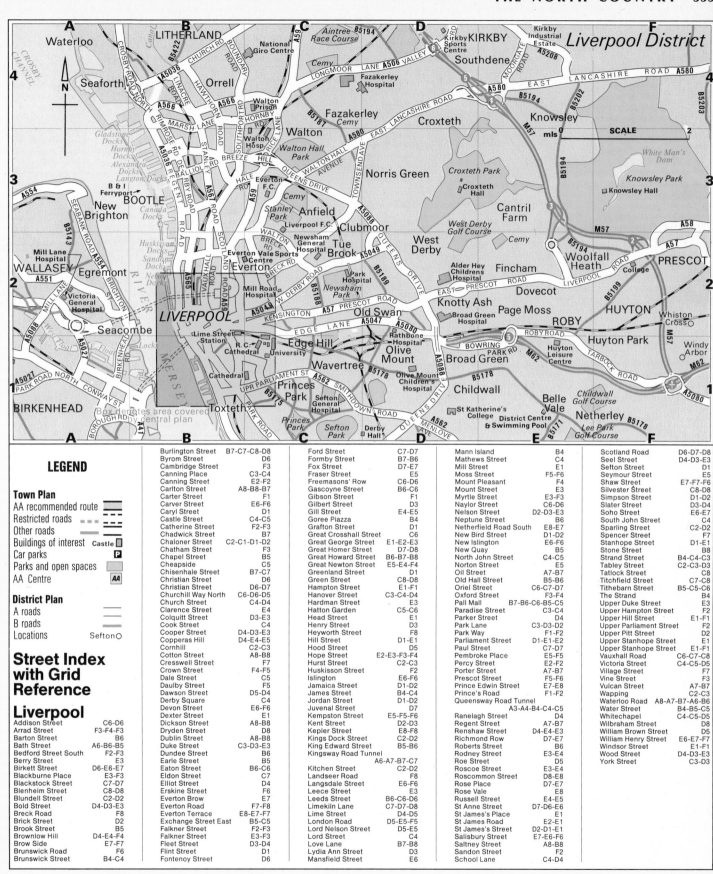

LEGEND

Town Plan

AA recommended route
Restricted roads
Other roads
Buildings of interest — Castle
Car parks — P
Parks and open spaces
AA Centre — AA

District Plan

A roads
B roads
Locations — Sefton○

Street Index with Grid Reference

Liverpool

Addison Street	C6-D6
Arrad Street	F3-F4-F3
Barton Street	B6
Bath Street	A6-B6-B5
Bedford Street South	F2-F3
Berry Street	E3
Birkett Street	D6-E6-E7
Blackburne Place	E3-F3
Blackstock Street	C7-D7
Blenheim Street	C8-D8
Blundell Street	C2-D2
Bold Street	D4-D3-E3
Breck Road	F8
Brick Street	D2
Brook Street	B5
Brownlow Hill	D4-E4-F4
Brow Side	E7-F7
Brunswick Road	F6
Brunswick Street	B4-C4
Burlington Street	B7-C7-C8-D8
Byrom Street	D6
Cambridge Street	F3
Canning Place	C3-C4
Canning Street	E2-F2
Carlton Street	A8-B8-B7
Carter Street	F1
Carver Street	E6-F6
Caryl Street	D1
Castle Street	C4-C5
Catherine Street	F2-F3
Chadwick Street	B7
Chaloner Street	C2-C1-D1-D2
Chatham Street	F3
Chapel Street	B5
Cheapside	C5
Chisenhale Street	B7-C7
Christian Street	D6
Christian Street	D6-D7
Churchill Way North	C6-D6-D5
Church Street	C4-D4
Clarence Street	E4
Colquitt Street	D3-E3
Cook Street	C4
Cooper Street	D4-D3-E3
Copperas Hill	D4-E4-E5
Cornhill	C2-C3
Cotton Street	A8-B8
Cresswell Street	F7
Crown Street	F4-F5
Dale Street	C5
Daulby Street	F5
Dawson Street	D5-D4
Derby Square	C4
Devon Street	E6-F6
Dexter Street	E1
Dickson Street	A8-B8
Dryden Street	D8
Dublin Street	A8-B8
Duke Street	C3-D3-E3
Dundee Street	B6
Earle Street	B5
Eaton Street	B6-C6
Eldon Street	C7
Elliot Street	D4
Erskine Street	F6
Everton Brow	E7
Everton Road	F7-F8
Everton Terrace	E8-E7-F7
Exchange Street East	B5-C5
Falkner Street	F2-F3
Falkner Street	E3-F3
Fleet Street	D3-D4
Flint Street	D1
Fontenoy Street	D6
Ford Street	C7-D7
Formby Street	B7-B6
Fox Street	D7-E7
Fraser Street	E5
Freemasons' Row	C6-D6
Gascoyne Street	B6-C6
Gibson Street	F1
Gilbert Street	D3
Gill Street	E4-E5
Goree Piazza	B4
Grafton Street	D1
Great Crosshall Street	C6
Great George Street	E1-E2-E3
Great Homer Street	D7-D8
Great Howard Street	B6-B7-B8
Great Newton Street	E5-E4-F4
Greenland Street	D1
Green Street	C8-D8
Hampton Street	E1-F1
Hanover Street	C3-C4-D4
Hardman Street	E3
Hatton Garden	C5-C6
Head Street	E1
Henry Street	D3
Heyworth Street	F8
Hill Street	D1-E1
Hood Street	D5
Hope Street	E2-E3-F3-F4
Hurst Street	C2-C3
Huskisson Street	F2
Islington	E6-F6
Jamaica Street	D1-D2
James Street	B4-C4
Jordan Street	D1-D2
Juvenal Street	D7
Kempston Street	E5-F5-F6
Kent Street	D2-D3
Kepler Street	E8-F8
Kings Dock Street	C2-D2
King Edward Street	B5-B6
Kingsway Road Tunnel	A6-A7-B7-C7
Kitchen Street	C2-D2
Landseer Road	F8
Langsdale Street	E6-F6
Leece Street	E3
Leeds Street	B6-C6-D6
Limekiln Lane	C7-D7-D8
Lime Street	D4-D5
London Road	D5-E5-F5
Lord Nelson Street	D5-E5
Lord Street	C4
Love Lane	B7-B8
Lydia Ann Street	D3
Mansfield Street	E6
Mann Island	B4
Mathews Street	C4
Mill Street	E1
Moss Street	F5-F6
Mount Pleasant	F4
Mount Street	E3
Myrtle Street	E3-F3
Naylor Street	C6-D6
Nelson Street	D2-D3-E3
Neptune Street	B6
Netherfield Road South	E8-E7
New Bird Street	D1-D2
New Islington	E6-F6
New Quay	B5
North John Street	C4-C5
Norton Street	E5
Oil Street	A7-B7
Old Hall Street	B5-B6
Oriel Street	C6-C7-D7
Oxford Street	F3-F4
Pall Mall	B7-B6-C6-B5-C5
Paradise Street	C3-C4
Parker Street	D4
Park Lane	C3-D3-D2
Park Way	F1-F2
Parliament Street	D1-E1-E2
Paul Street	C7-D7
Pembroke Place	E5-F5
Percy Street	E2-F2
Porter Street	A7-B7
Prescot Street	F5-F6
Prince Edwin Street	E7-E8
Prince's Road	F1-F2
Queensway Road Tunnel	A3-A4-B4-C4-C5
Ranelagh Street	D4
Regent Street	A7-B7
Renshaw Street	D4-E4-E3
Richmond Row	D7-E7
Roberts Street	B6
Rodney Street	E3-E4
Roe Street	D5
Roscoe Street	E3-E4
Roscommon Street	D8-E8
Rose Place	D7-E7
Rose Vale	E8
Russell Street	E4-E5
St Anne Street	D7-D6-E6
St James's Place	E1
St James Road	E2-E1
St James's Street	D2-D1-E1
Salisbury Street	E7-E6-F6
Saltney Street	A8-B8
Sandon Street	F2
School Lane	C4-D4
Scotland Road	D6-D7-D8
Seel Street	D4-D3-E3
Sefton Street	D1
Seymour Street	E5
Shaw Street	E7-F7-F6
Silvester Street	C8-D8
Simpson Street	D1-D2
Slater Street	D3-D4
Soho Street	E6-E7
South John Street	C4
Sparling Street	C2-D2
Spencer Street	F7
Stanhope Street	D1-E1
Stone Street	B8
Strand Street	B4-C4-C5
Tabley Street	C2-C3-D3
Tatlock Street	C8
Titchfield Street	C7-C8
Tithebarn Street	B5-C5-C6
The Strand	B4
Upper Duke Street	E3
Upper Hampton Street	F2
Upper Hill Street	E1-F1
Upper Parliament Street	F2
Upper Pitt Street	D2
Upper Stanhope Street	E1
Upper Stanhope Street	E1-F1
Vauxhall Road	C6-C7-C8
Victoria Street	C4-C5-D5
Village Street	F7
Vine Street	F3
Vulcan Street	A7-B7
Wapping	C2-C3
Waterloo Road	A8-A7-B7-A6-B6
Water Street	B4-B5-C5
Whitechapel	C4-C5-D5
Wilbraham Street	D8
William Brown Street	D5
William Henry Street	E6-E7-F7
Windsor Street	E1-F1
Wood Street	D4-D3-E3
York Street	C3-D3

LIVERPOOL
The Metropolitan Cathedral of Christ the King is one of Liverpool's most striking landmarks. Crowning the conical roof is a tower of stained glass which throws a pool of coloured light on to the altar below.

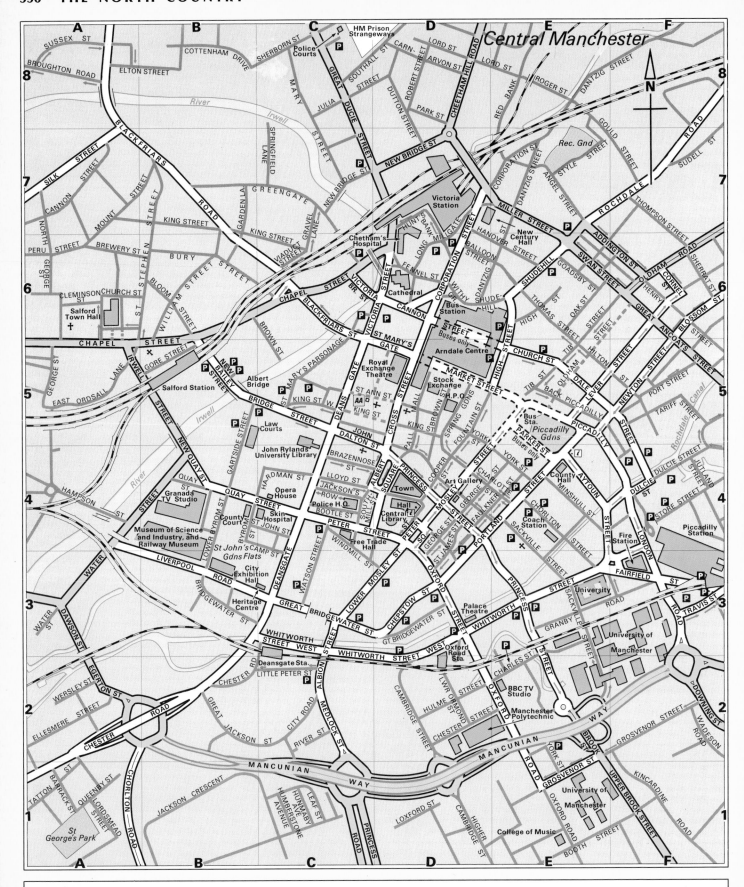

Central Manchester

Manchester

The gigantic conurbation called Greater Manchester covers a staggering 60 square miles, reinforcing Manchester's claim to be Britain's second city. Commerce and industry are vital aspects of the city's character, but it is also an important cultural centre – the Halle Orchestra has its home at the Free Trade Hall (a venue for many concerts besides classical music), there are several theatres, a library (the John Rylands) which houses one of the most important collections of books in the world, and a number of museums and galleries, including the Whitworth Gallery with its lovely watercolours.

Like many great cities it suffered badly during the bombing raids of World War II, but some older buildings remain, including the town hall, a huge building designed in Gothic style by Alfred Waterhouse and opened in 1877. Manchester Cathedral dates mainly from the 15th century and is noted for its fine tower and outstanding carved woodwork. Nearby is Chetham's Hospital, also 15th-century and now housing a music school. Much new development has taken place, and more is planned. Shopping precincts cater for the vast population, and huge hotels have provided services up to international standards. On the edge of the city is the Belle Vue centre, a large entertainments complex including concert and exhibition facilities, and a speedway stadium.

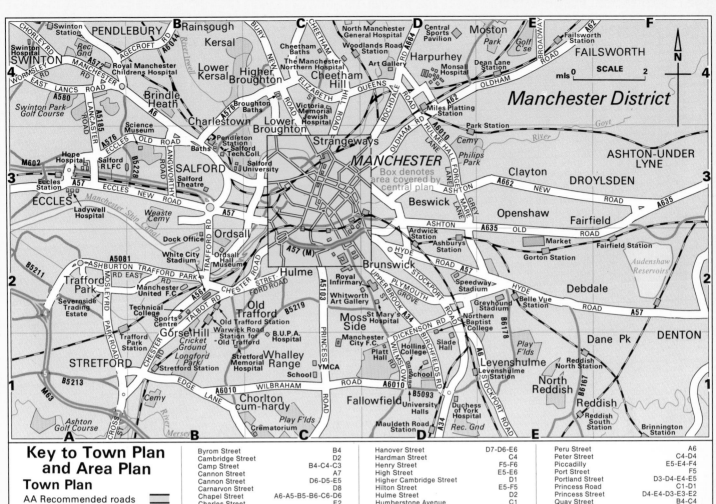

MANCHESTER
The Barton Swing Bridge carries the Bridgewater Canal over the Manchester Ship Canal, which links Manchester with the sea nearly 40 miles away. Completed in 1894, the canal is navigable by vessels up to 15,000 tons.

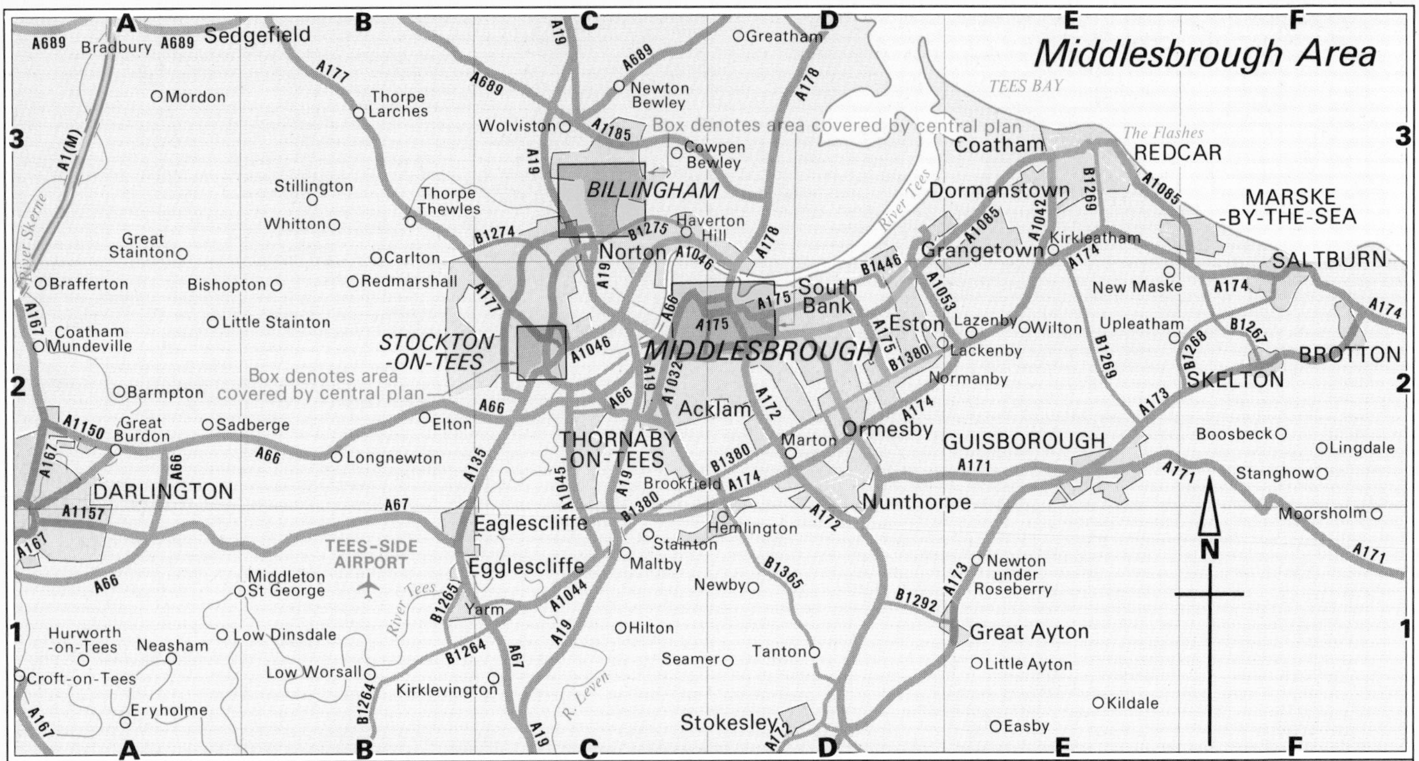

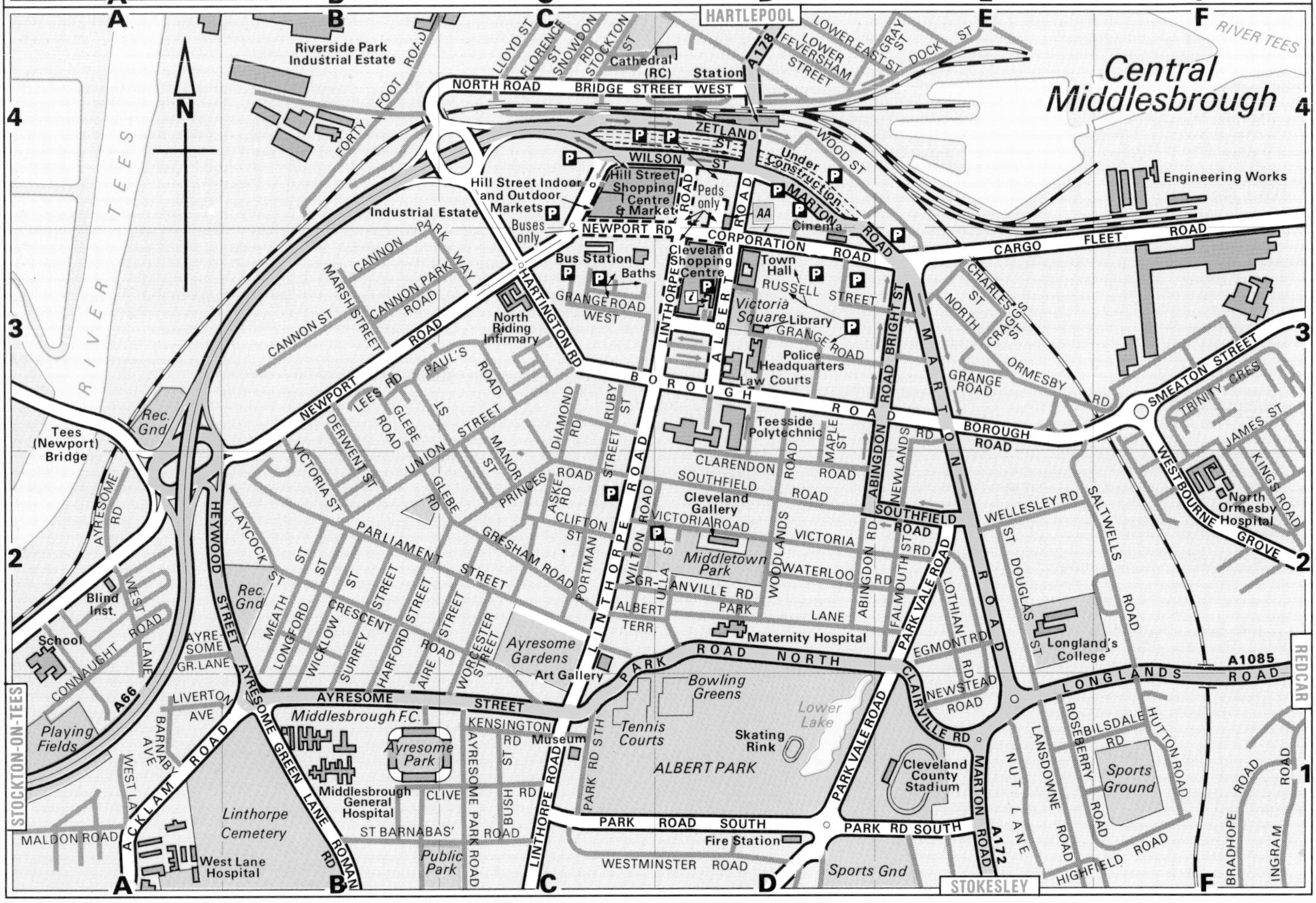

Middlesbrough Area

Central Middlesbrough

Middlesbrough

Heavy industry dominates Middlesbrough. It has been a centre of iron and steel manufacture since the 1840s although much of the steel-making has moved eastwards to a new works near Redcar. Its rise had begun ten years before, when the Stockton and Darlington Railway purchased land here and turned what had been a quiet riverside village into a busy coal exporting town. Middlesbrough's most notable structure is the Transporter Bridge, built across the Tees in 1911. It is one of only two bridges of its type left in Britain. The town centre is modern with spacious shopping areas and new public buildings. The Dorman Museum covers the region's history and there are two major art galleries.

Stockton has a place in transport history; it was here, on 27 September 1825, that the world's first steam passenger railway service began. The town, also situated on the River Tees, became an engineering and shipbuilding centre and is still an important industrial centre today. It has a town hall of 1763 standing in the middle of one of the widest main streets in England.

Billingham also stands on the Tees, and the river was one of the factors which encouraged various chemical industries to become established here. North Sea oil has given a boost to that industry, and the town centre has been completely rebuilt with every facility.

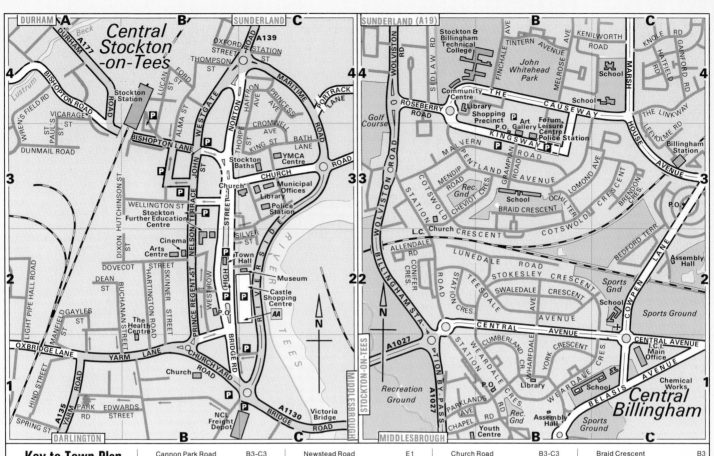

Key to Town Plan and Area Plan

Town Plan

AA Recommended roads
Other roads
Restricted roads
Buildings of interest
Car Parks   P
Parks and open spaces
AA Service Centre   AA

Area Plan

A roads
B roads
Locations   Aycliffe ○
Urban area

Street Index with Grid Reference

Middlesbrough

Abingdon Road	D2-E2-E3
Acklam Road	A1-B1
Aire Street	B1-B2-C2
Albert Road	D3-D4
Albert Terrace	C2-D2
Aske Road	C2
Ayresome Green Lane	A2-B2-B1
Ayresome Park Road	C1
Ayresome Road	A2
Ayresome Street	B1-C1
Barnaby Avenue	A1
Bilsdale Road	E1-F1
Borough Road	C3-D3-E3
Bradhope Road	F1
Bridge Street West	C4-D4
Bright Street	E3
Bush Street	C1
Cannon Park Road	B3-C3
Cannon Park Way	B3-C3
Cannon Street	B3
Cargo Fleet Road	E3-F3-F4
Charles Street	E3
Clairville Road	E1-E2
Clarendon Road	D2-D3
Clifton Street	C2
Clive Road	B1-C1
Connaught Road	A1-A2
Corporation Road	D4-D3-E3
Craggs Street	E3
Crescent Road	B2-C2-C1
Derwent Street	B2-B3
Diamond Road	C2-C3
Dock Street	E4
Egmont Road	E2
Falmouth Street	E2
Florence Street	C4
Forty Foot Road	B4-C4
Glebe Road	B3-B2-C2
Grange Road	D3-E3
Grange Road West	C3-D3
Granville Road	C2-D2
Gray Street	D4-E4
Gresham Road	C2
Harford Street	B1-B2
Hartinton Road	C3
Heywood Street	A2-B2
Highfield Road	E1-F1
Hutton Road	F1
Ingram Road	F1
James Street	F2-F3
Kensington Road	C1
Kings Road	F2-F3
Lansdowne Road	E1
Laycock Street	B2
Lees Road	B3
Linthorpe Road	C1-C2-C3-D3-D4
Liverton Avenue	A1-B1
Lloyd Street	C4
Longford Street	B1-B2
Longlands Road	E1-F1-F2
Lothian Road	E1-E2
Lower East Street	D4-E4
Lower Feversham Street	D4
Maldon Road	A1
Manor Street	C2-C3
Maple Street	D2-D3
Marsh Street	B3
Marton Road	D4-D3-E3-E2-E1
Meath Street	B2
Newlands Road	E2-E3
Newport Road	B2-B3-C3-C4-D4-D3
Newstead Road	E1
North Road	B4-C4
North Ormesby Road	E3-F3
Nut Lane	E1
Park Lane	D2-E2
Park Road North	C1-C2-D2-E2
Park Road South	C1-D1-E1
Park Vale Road	D1-E1-E2
Parliament Street	B2-C2
Portman Street	C2-C3
Princes Road	C2
Roman Road	B1
Roseberry Road	E1-F1
Ruby Street	C3
Russell Street	D3-E3
St Barnabas' Road	B1-C1
St Douglas Street	E1-E2
St Paul's Road	C3-B3-C3
Saltwells Road	E3-E2-F2
Smeaton Street	F3
Snowdon Road	C4
Southfield Road	C2-D2-E2
Stockton Street	C4
Surrey Street	B1-B2
Sussex Street	D4
Trinity Crescent	F2-F3
Ulla Street	D2
Union Street	B2-C2-C3
Victoria Road	C2-D2-E2
Victoria Street	B2-B3
Waterloo Road	D2-E2
Wellesley Road	E2
West Lane	A1-A2
Westbourne Grove	F2-F3
Westminster Road	C1-D1
Wicklow Street	B1-B2
Wilson Street	C4-D4
Wilton Road	C2-D2
Woodlands Road	D2-D3
Wood Street	D4
Worcester Street	C1-C2
Zetland Street	D4

Stockton-on-Tees

Alma Street	B3-B4
Bath Lane	C3
Bishopton Lane	A3-B3
Bishopton Road	A4-A3
Bridge Road	B2-B1-C1
Buchanan Street	A1-A2
Church Road	B3-C3
Church Yard Road	B1
Cromwell Avenue	C3
Dean Street	A2
Dixon Street	B2
Dovecot Street	A2-B2
Dunmail Road	A3
Durham Road	A4
Edwards Street	A1-B1
Ford Street	B4
Gayles Street	A2
Haffron Avenue	C3-C4
Hartington Road	B1-B2
High Street	B2-B3
Hind Street	A1
Hutchinson Street	B3
John Street	B3
King Street	C3
Light Pipe Hall Road	A1-A2
Lucan Street	B4
Manfield Street	A1-A2
Maritime Road	C3-C4
Nelson Terrace	B2-B3
Norton Road	B3-B4-C4
Oxbridge Lane	A1
Oxford Street	B4-C4
Park Road	A1
Portrack Lane	C4
Prince Regent Street	B1-B2
Princess Avenue	C4
Riverside	C1-C2-C3
St Paul's Street	A3-A4
Silver Street	B2-C2
Skinner Street	B1-B2
Spring Street	A1
Station Street	C4
Thompson Street	B4
Thorpe Street	C3
Vicarage Street	A4
Wellington Street	B3
Westbourne Street	A1-B1
Westgate	B3-B4
West Row	B2
Wren's Field Road	A3-A4
Yarm Lane	A1-B1-B2
Yarm Road	A1

Billingham

Allendale Road	A2
Bedford Terrace	C2-C3
Belasis Avenue	B1-C1
Billingham Station By-pass	A1-A2
Braid Crescent	B3
Brendon Crescent	C3
Central Avenue	A2-B2-B1-C1-C2
Chapel Road	A1-B1
Cheviot Crescent	A3-B3
Conifer Crescent	A2
Cotswold Crescent	A3-A2-B2-B3-C3
Cowpen Lane	C1-C2-C3
Cumberland Crescent	B1
Finchale Avenue	B4
Gainford Road	C4
Grampian Road	B3
Hatfield Road	C4
Kenilworth Road	B4-C4
Kingsway	A4-A3-B3-B4
Knole Road	C4
Leeholme Road	C3-C4
Lomond Avenue	B3-C3
Lunedale Road	A2-B2
Malvern Road	A3-B3
Marsh House Avenue	C4
Melrose Avenue	B4
Mendip Road	A3
Ochil Terrace	B3
Parklands Avenue	A1-B1
Pentland Avenue	A3-B3-B4-C3-C4
Roseberry Road	A4
Sidlaw Road	A4
Station Crescent	A2
Station Road	A3-A2-A1-B1
Stokesley Crescent	B2-C2
Swaledale Crescent	B2
Teesdale Avenue	A2-B2-C2
Tintern Avenue	B4
The Causeway	A4-B4-C4
The Linkway	C4
Weardale Crescent	A2-A1-B2-B1-C1
Wharfdale Avenue	B1-B2
Wolviston Road	A2-A3-A4
York Crescent	B1-C1

MIDDLESBROUGH
In 1911 the Transporter Bridge was built to replace the river ferry between Port Clarence and Middlesbrough. It is still used today and a special viewing platform has been built to enable visitors to watch the bridge in operation.

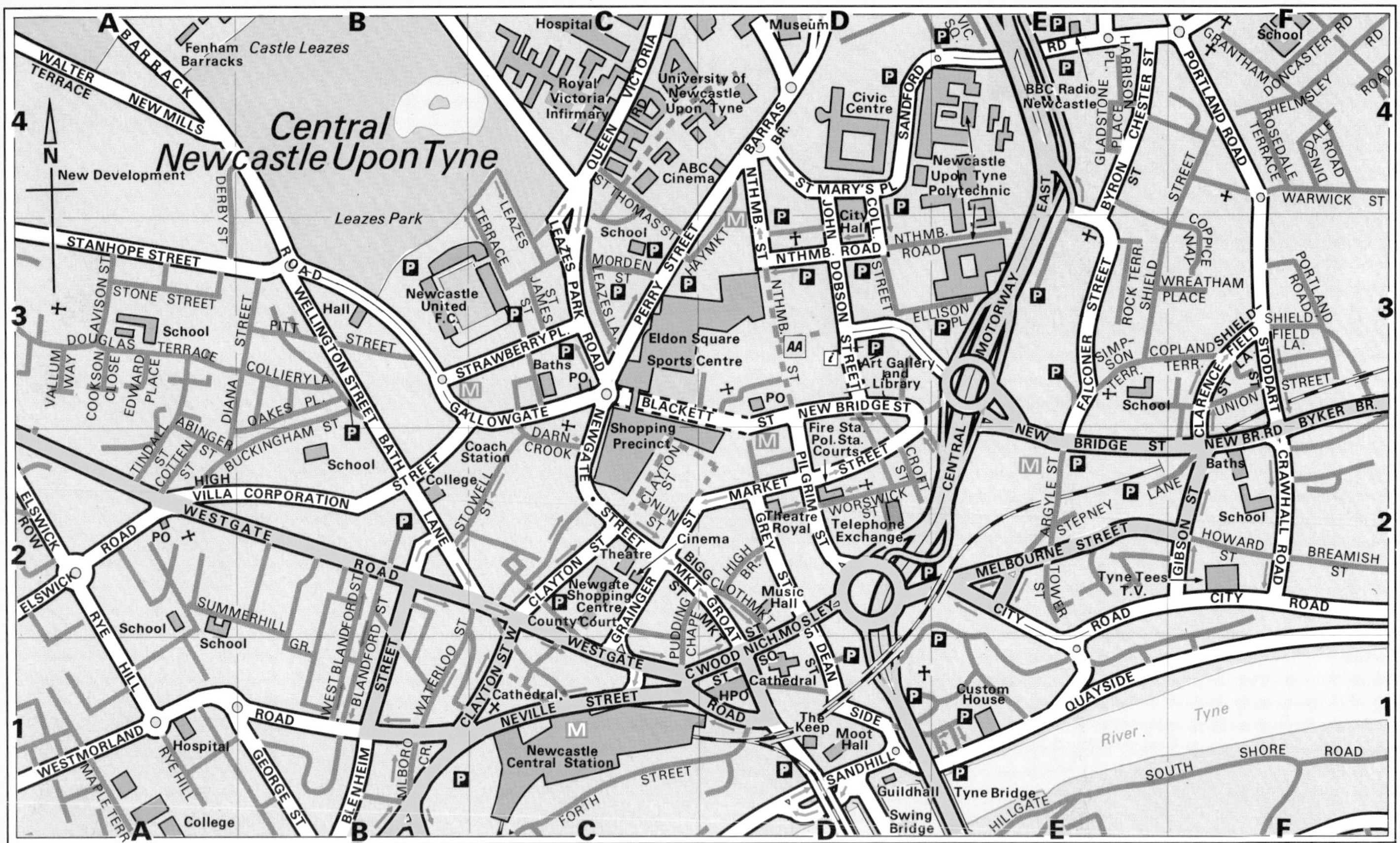

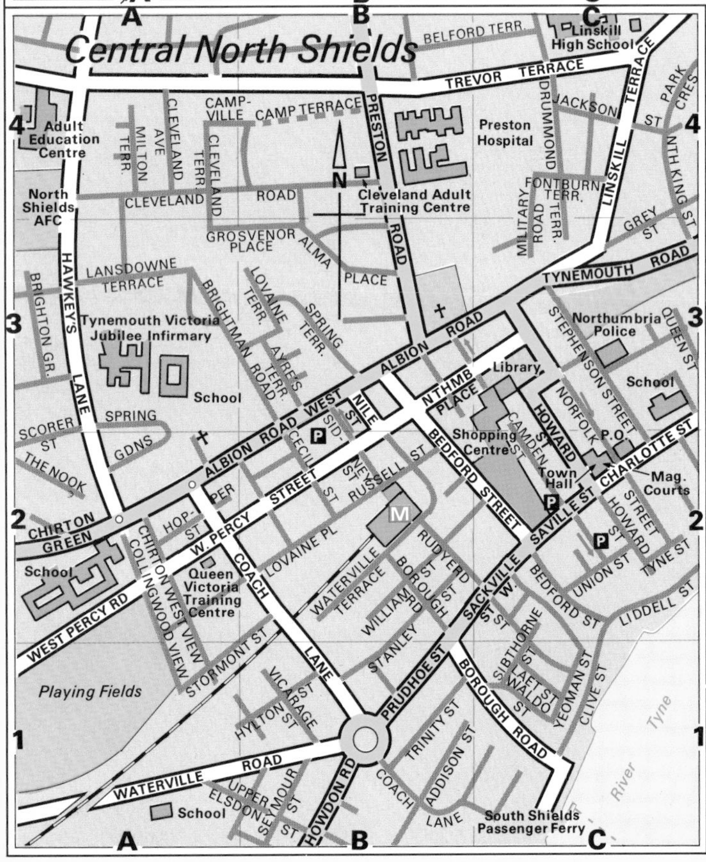

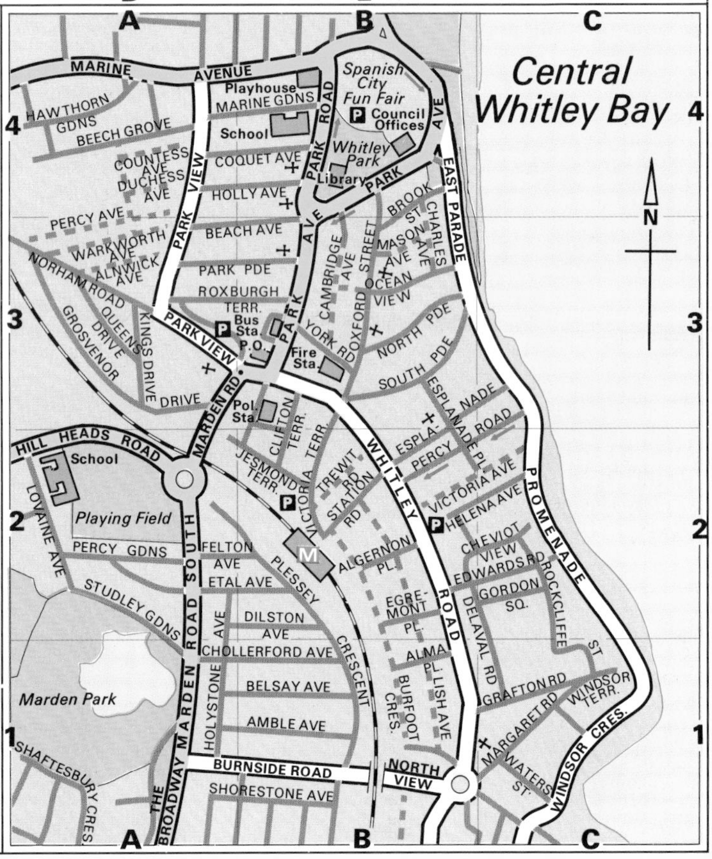

Central Newcastle Upon Tyne

Central North Shields

Central Whitley Bay

Newcastle

Six bridges span the Tyne at Newcastle; they all help to create a striking scene, but the most impressive is the High Level Bridge, built by Robert Stephenson in 1845-49 and consisting of two levels, one for the railway and one for the road. It is from the river that some of the best views of the city can be obtained. Grey Street is Newcastle's most handsome thoroughfare. It dates from the time, between 1835 and 1840, when much of this part of the city was replanned and rebuilt. Elegant façades curve up to Grey's Monument. Close to the Monument is the Eldon Centre, combining sports facilities and shopping centre to form an integrated complex which is one of the largest of its kind in Europe. Newcastle has many museums. The industrial background of the city is traced in the Museum of Science and Engineering, while the Laing Art Gallery and Museum covers painting, costumes and local domestic history. The Hancock Museum has an exceptional natural history collection and the John George Joicey Museum has period displays in a 17th-century almshouse. In Black Gate is one of Britain's most unusual museums – a collection of over 100 sets of bagpipes. Within the University precincts are three further museums. Of the city's open spaces, Town Moor is the largest. At nearly 1,000 acres it is big enough to feel genuinely wild.

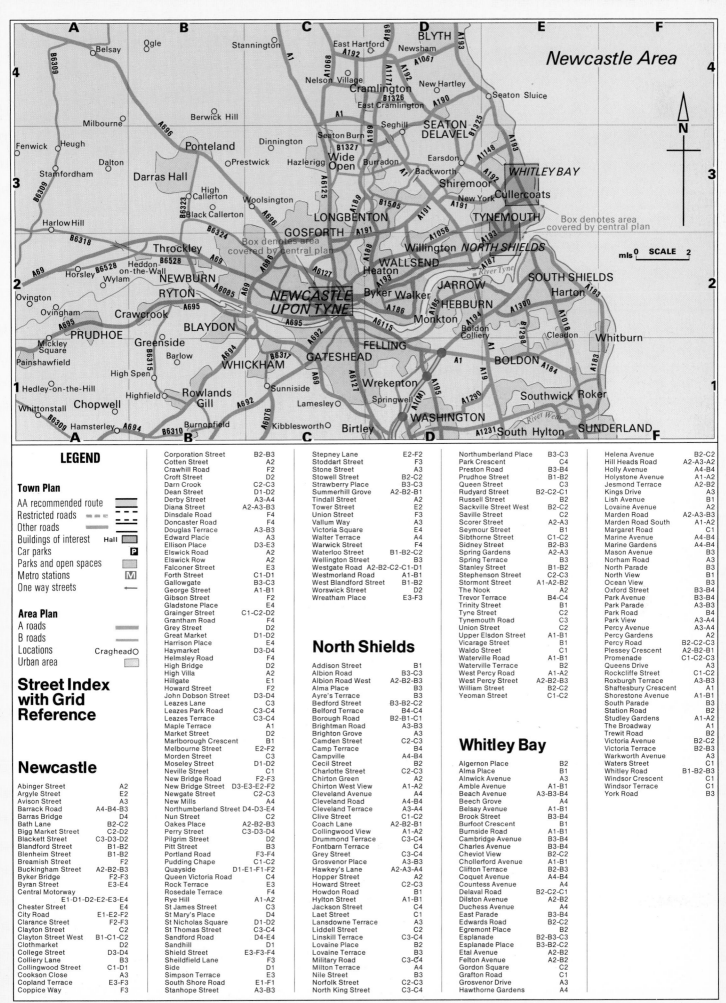

Newcastle Area

LEGEND

Town Plan

AA recommended route	
Restricted roads	
Other roads	
Buildings of interest	Hall
Car parks	P
Parks and open spaces	
Metro stations	M
One way streets	←

Area Plan

A roads	
B roads	
Locations	Craghead○
Urban area	

Street Index with Grid Reference

Newcastle

Abinger Street	A2
Argyle Street	E2
Avison Street	A3
Barrack Road	A4-B4-B3
Barras Bridge	D4
Bath Lane	B2-C2
Bigg Market Street	C2-D2
Blackett Street	C3-D3-D2
Blandford Street	B1-B2
Blenheim Street	B1-B2
Breamish Street	F2
Buckingham Street	A2-B2-B3
Byker Bridge	F2-F3
Byran Street	E3-E4
Central Motorway	
	E1-D1-D2-E2-E3-E4
Chester Street	E4
City Road	E1-E2-F2
Clarance Street	F2-F3
Clayton Street	C3-C4
Clayton Street West	B1-C1-C2
Clothmarket	D2
College Street	D3-D4
Colliery Lane	B3
Collingwood Street	C1-D1
Cookson Close	A3
Copland Terrace	E3-F3
Coppice Way	F3

Corporation Street	B2-B3
Cotten Street	A2
Crawhill Road	F2
Croft Street	D2
Darn Crook	C2-C3
Dean Street	D1-D2
Derby Street	A3-A4
Diana Street	A2-A3-B3
Dinsdale Road	F4
Doncaster Road	F4
Douglas Terrace	A3-B3
Edward Place	A3
Ellison Place	D3-E3
Elswick Road	A2
Elswick Row	A2
Falconer Street	E3
Forth Street	C1-D1
Gallowgate	B3-C3
George Street	A1-B1
Gibson Street	F2
Gladstone Place	E4
Grainger Street	C1-C2-D2
Grantham Road	F4
Grey Street	D2
Great Market	D1-D2
Harrison Place	E4
Haymarket	D3-D4
Helmsley Road	F4
High Bridge	D2
High Villa	A2
Hillgate	E1
Howard Street	F2
John Dobson Street	D3-D4
Leazes Lane	C3
Leazes Park Road	C3-C4
Leazes Terrace	C3-C4
Maple Terrace	A1
Market Street	D2
Marlborough Crescent	B1
Melbourne Street	E2-F2
Morden Street	C3
Moseley Street	D1-D2
Neville Street	C1
New Bridge Road	F2-F3
New Bridge Street	D3-E3-E2-F2
Newgate Street	C2-C3
New Mills	A3
Northumberland Street	D4-D3-E4
Nun Street	C2
Oakes Place	A2-B2-B3
Perry Street	C3-D3-D4
Pilgrim Street	D2
Pitt Street	B3
Portland Road	F3-F4
Pudding Chape	C1-C2
Quayside	D1-E1-F1-F2
Queen Victoria Road	C4
Rock Terrace	E3
Rosedale Terrace	F4
Rye Hill	A1-A2
St James Street	C3
St Mary's Place	D4
St Nicholas Square	D1-D2
St Thomas Street	C3-C4
Sandford Road	D4-E4
Sandhill	D1
Shield Street	E3-F3-F4
Sheildfield Lane	F3
Side	D1
Simpson Terrace	E3
South Shore Road	E1-F1
Stanhope Street	A3-B3

Stepney Lane	E2-F2
Stoddart Street	F3
Stone Street	A3
Stowell Street	B2-C2
Strawberry Place	B3-C3
Summerhill Grove	A2-B2-B1
Tindall Street	A2
Tower Street	E2
Union Street	F3
Vallum Way	A3
Victoria Square	E4
Walter Terrace	A4
Warwick Street	F4
Waterloo Street	B1-B2-C2
Wellington Street	B3
Westgate Road	A2-B2-C2-C1-D1
Westmorland Road	A1-B1
West Blandford Street	B1-B2
Worswick Street	D2
Wreatham Place	E3-F3

North Shields

Addison Street	B1
Albion Road	B3-C3
Albion Road West	A2-B2-B3
Alma Place	B3
Ayre's Terrace	B3
Bedford Street	B3-B2-C2
Belford Terrace	B4-C4
Borough Road	B2-B1-C1
Brightman Road	A3-B3
Brighton Grove	A3
Camden Street	C2-C3
Camp Terrace	B4
Campville	A4-B4
Cecil Street	B2
Charlotte Street	C2-C3
Chirton Green	A2
Chirton West View	A1-A2
Cleveland Avenue	A4
Cleveland Road	A4-B4
Cleveland Terrace	A3-A4
Clive Street	C1-C2
Coach Lane	A2-B2-B1
Collingwood View	A1-A2
Drummond Terrace	C3-C4
Fontbarn Terrace	C4
Grey Street	C3-C4
Grosvenor Place	A3-B3
Hawkey's Lane	A2-A3-A4
Hopper Street	A2
Howard Street	C2-C3
Howdon Road	B1
Hylton Street	A1-B1
Jackson Street	C4
Laet Street	C1
Lansdowne Terrace	A3
Liddell Street	C2
Linskill Terrace	C3-C4
Lovaine Place	B2
Lovaine Terrace	B3
Military Road	C3-C4
Milton Street	A4
Nile Street	B3
Norfolk Street	C2-C3
North King Street	C3-C4

Northumberland Place	B3-C3
Park Crescent	C4
Preston Road	B3-B4
Prudhoe Street	B1-B2
Queen Street	C3
Rudyard Street	B2-C2-C1
Russell Street	B2
Sackville Street West	B2-C2
Saville Street	C2
Scorer Street	A2-A3
Seymour Street	B1
Sibthorne Street	C1-C2
Sidney Street	B2-B3
Spring Gardens	A2-A3
Spring Terrace	B3
Stanley Street	B1-B2
Stephenson Street	C2-C3
Stormont Street	A1-A2-B2
The Nook	A2
Trevor Terrace	B4-C4
Trinity Street	B1
Tyne Street	C2
Tynemouth Road	C3
Union Street	C2
Upper Elsdon Street	A1-B1
Vicarage Street	B1
Waldo Street	C1
Waterville Road	A1-B1
Waterville Terrace	B2
West Percy Road	A1-A2
West Percy Street	A2-B2-B3
William Street	B2-C2
Yeoman Street	C1-C2

Whitley Bay

Algernon Place	B2
Alma Place	B1
Alnwick Avenue	A3
Amble Avenue	A1-B1
Beach Avenue	A3-B3-B4
Beech Grove	A4
Belsay Avenue	A1-B1
Brook Street	B3-B4
Burfoot Crescent	B1
Burnside Road	A1-B1
Cambridge Avenue	B3-B4
Charles Avenue	B3-B4
Cheviot View	B2-C2
Chollerford Avenue	A1-B1
Clifton Terrace	B2-B3
Coquet Avenue	A4-B4
Countess Avenue	A4
Delaval Road	B2-C2-C1
Dilston Avenue	A2-B2
Duchess Avenue	A4
East Parade	B3-B4
Edwards Road	B2-C2
Egremont Place	B2
Esplanade	B2-B3-C3
Esplanade Place	B3-B2-C2
Etal Avenue	A2-B2
Felton Avenue	A2-B2
Gordon Square	C2
Grafton Road	C1
Grosvenor Drive	A3
Hawthorne Gardens	A4

Helena Avenue	B2-C2
Hill Heads Road	A2-A3-A2
Holly Avenue	A4-B4
Holystone Avenue	A1-A2
Jesmond Terrace	A2-B2
Kings Drive	A3
Lish Avenue	B1
Lovaine Avenue	A2
Marden Road	A2-A3-B3
Marden Road South	A1-A2
Margaret Road	C1
Marine Avenue	A4-B4
Marine Gardens	A4-B4
Mason Avenue	B3
Norham Road	A3
North Parade	B3
North View	B1
Ocean View	B3
Oxford Street	B3-B4
Park Avenue	B3-B4
Park Parade	A3-B3
Park Road	B4
Park View	A3-A4
Percy Avenue	A3-A4
Percy Gardens	A2
Percy Road	B2-C2-C3
Plessey Crescent	A2-B2-B1
Promenade	C1-C2-C3
Queens Drive	A3
Rockcliffe Street	C1-C2
Roxburgh Terrace	A3-B3
Shaftesbury Crescent	A1
Shorestone Avenue	A1-B1
South Parade	B3
Station Road	B2
Studley Gardens	A1-A2
The Broadway	A1
Trewit Road	B2
Victoria Avenue	B2-C2
Victoria Terrace	B2-B3
Warkworth Avenue	A3
Waters Street	C1
Whitley Road	B1-B2-B3
Windsor Crescent	C1
Windsor Terrace	C1
York Road	B3

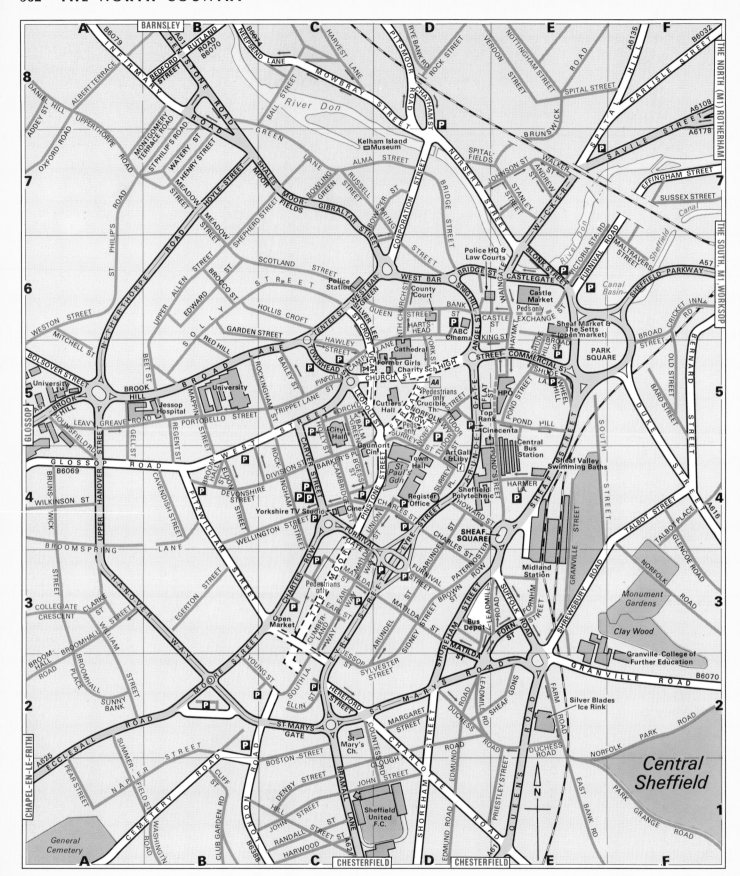

Central
Sheffield

Sheffield

Cutlery – which has made the name of Sheffield famous throughout the world – has been manufactured here since at least as early as the time of Chaucer. The god of blacksmiths, Vulcan, is the symbol of the city's industry, and he crowns the town hall, which was opened in 1897 by Queen Victoria. At the centre of the industry, however, is Cutlers' Hall, the headquarters of the Company of

Cutlers. This society was founded in 1624 and has the right to grant trade marks to articles of a sufficiently high standard. In the hall is the company's collection of silver, with examples of craftsmanship dating back every year to 1773. A really large collection of cutlery is kept in the city museum. Steel production, a vital component of the industry, was greatly improved when the crucible process was invented here in 1740. At Abbeydale Industrial Hamlet, 3½ miles south-west

of the city centre, is a complete restored site open as a museum and showing 18th-century methods of steel production. Sheffield's centre, transformed since World War II, is one of the finest and most modern in Europe. There are no soot-grimed industrial eyesores here, for the city has stringent pollution controls and its buildings are carefully planned and set within excellent landscaping projects. Many parks are set in and around the city, and the Pennines are within easy reach.

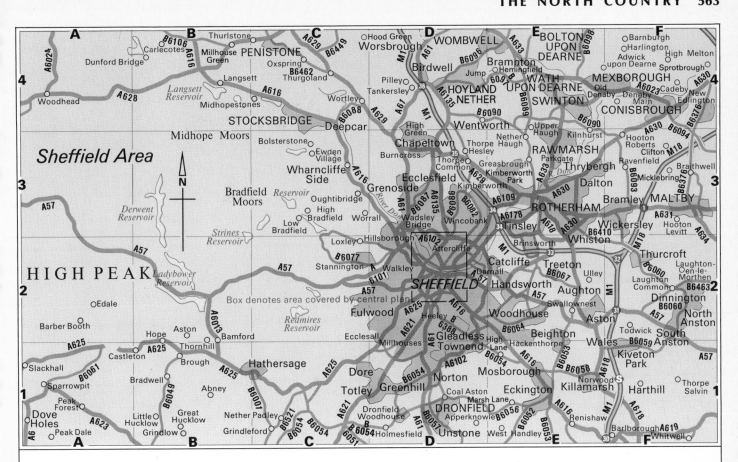

LEGEND

Town Plan

AA Recommended roads
Other roads
Restricted roads
Buildings of interest
AA Centre   **AA**
Car Parks   **P**
Parks and open spaces

Area Plan

A roads
B roads
Locations   Oakworth ○
Urban area

Street Index with grid reference

Sheffield

Street	Grid
Addey Street	A7-A8
Albert Terrace	A8
Alma Street	C7 D7
Andrew Street	E7
Angel Street	D5-D6
Arundel Gate	D4-D5
Arundel Street	C2-D2-D3-D4
Bailey Street	C5
Ball Street	C8
Balm Green	C4-C5
Bank Street	D6
Bard Street	F5
Barker's Pool	C4-C5-D5
Bedford Street	B8
Beet Street	B5
Bernard Street	F4-F5-F6
Blonk Street	E6
Bolsover Street	A5
Boston Street	C1-C2
Bower Street	C7-D7
Bowling Green	C7
Bramall Lane	C1-C2
Bridge Street	D7-D6-E6
Broad Lane	B5-C5-C6
Broad Street	E6-F5-F6
Brocco Street	B6
Brook Hill	A5-B5
Broomhall Place	A2
Broomhall Road	A2
Broomhall Street	A2-A3-B4
Broomspring Lane	A4-B4
Brown Street	D3

Street	Grid
Brunswick Street	A3-A4
Brunswick Road	E7-E8
Burgess Street	C4
Cambridge Street	C4
Campo Lane	C5-D5-D6
Carlisle Street	F8
Carver Street	C4-C5
Castle Street	D6-E6
Castlegate	E6
Cavendish Street	B4
Cemetery Road	A1-B1-B2
Charles Street	D3-D4
Charlotte Road	C2-D2-D1-E1
Charter Row	C3-C4
Chatham Street	D7-D8
Church Street	C5-D5
Clarke Street	A3
Cliff Street	B1
Clough Road	C1-D1-D2
Club Garden Road	B1
Collegiate Crescent	A3
Commercial Street	E5
Corporation Street	D6-D7
Countess Road	C2-D2-D1
Cricket Inn Road	F6
Cumberland Way	C3
Daniel Hill	A8
Denby Street	C1
Devonshire Street	B4-C4
Division Street	C4
Duchess Road	D2-E2
Duke Street	F4-F5
Earl Street	C3
Earl Way	C3
East Bank Road	E1-E2
Ecclesall Road	A1-A2-B2
Edmund Road	D1-D2
Edward Street	B5
Effingham Street	F7
Egerton Street	B3
Eldon Street	B4
Ellin Street	C2
Eyre Street	C2-C3-D3-D4
Exchange Street	E6
Fargate	D5
Farm Road	E2
Fitzwilliam Street	B4-B3-C3
Flat Street	E5
Fornham Street	E3
Furnival Gate	C3-C4-D3-D4
Furnival Road	E6-F6-F7
Furnival Street	D3
Garden Street	B6-C6-C5
Gell Street	A4-A5
Gibraltar Street	C7-C6-D6
Glencoe Road	F3-F4
Glossop Road	A4-B4
Granville Road	E2-F2
Granville Street	E3-E4
Green Lane	B8-C8-C7
Hanover Way	A3-B3-B2
Harmer Lane	A2
Hartshead	D6
Harwood Street	C1
Harvest Lane	C8

Street	Grid
Hawley Street	C5
Haymarket	E5-E6
Henry Street	B7
Hereford Street	C2
High Street	D5-E5
Hill Street	B1-C1
Hollis Croft	B6-C6
Holly Street	C4-C5
Hounsfield Road	A4-A5
Howard Street	D4-E4
Hoyle Street	B7
Infirmary Road	A8-B8 B7
Jessop Street	C2
John Street	C1-D1
Johnson Street	D7-E7
King Street	D5-E5-E6
Leadmill Road	D2-D3-E3
Leavy Greave Road	A5-B5
Lee Croft	C5-C6
Leopold Street	C5-D5
London Road	C1-B1-B2-C2
Maltravers Street	F6
Mappin Street	B4-B5
Margaret Street	D2
Matilda Street	C3-D3-D2
Matilda Way	C3
Meadow Street	B6-B7
Mitchell Street	A5-A6
Montgomery Terrace Road	A7-B7-B8
Moorfields	C7
Moore Street	B2-B3-C3
Mowbray Street	C8-D8-D7
Napier Street	A1-B1-B2
Neepsend Lane	B8-C8
Netherthorpe Road	A5-A6-B6-B7
Norfolk Park Road	E1-E2-F2
Norfolk Road	F3-F4
Norfolk Row	D5
Norfolk Street	D4-D5
North Church Street	D6
Nottingham Street	E8
Nursery Street	D7-E7-E6
Old Street	F5-F6
Orchard Lane	C5
Oxford Road	A7-A8
Park Grange Road	E1-F1
Park Square	E5-E6-F6-F5
Paternoster Row	D3-D4-E4
Pear Street	A1
Penistone Road	B7-B8
Pinfold Street	C5
Pinstone Street	C4-D4-D5
Pitsmoor Road	D8
Pond Hill	E5
Pond Street	E4-E5
Portobello Street	B5-C5
Priestley Street	D1-E1-E2
Queen Street	C6-D6
Queen's Road	E1-E2
Randall Street	C1
Red Hill	B5-B6
Regent Street	B4-B5
Rock Street	D8
Rockingham Street	B5-C5-C4
Russell Street	C7

Street	Grid
Rutland Road	B8
Rye Bank Road	D8
St Mary's Gate	C2
St Mary's Road	C2-D2-E2
St Philip's Road	A6-A7-B7-B8
Savile Street	E7-F7-F8
Scotland Street	B6-C6
Shales Moor	B7-C7
Sheaf Gardens	D2-E2
Sheaf Street	E4-E5
Sheffield Parkway	F6
Shepherd Street	B6-B7-C7
Shoreham Street	D1-D2-D3-E3
Shrewsbury Road	E3-E4-F3-F4
Shude Lane	E5
Shude Hill	E5-E6
Sidney Street	D3
Silver Street	C6
Snig Hill	D6
Solly Street	B5-B6-C6
South Lane	C2
South Street	E4-E5
Spital Hill	E7-E8-F8
Spital Street	E8-F8
Spitalfields	D7-E7
Spring Street	D6-D7
Stanley Street	E7
Suffolk Road	E3
Summerfield Street	A2-A1-B1
Sunny Bank	A2
Surrey Place	D4
Surrey Street	D4-D5
Sussex Street	F7
Sylvester Street	C2-D2
Talbot Place	F4
Talbot Street	F4
Tenter Street	C6
The Moor	C3-C4
Townhead Street	C5
Trippet Lane	C5
Tudor Street	D4-D5
Tudor Way	D5
Union Street	C4-D4
Upper Allen Street	B6
Upper Hanover Street	A3-A4-A5
Upperthorpe Road	A7-A8
Verdon Street	D8-E8
Vicar Lane	C5-D5
Victoria Station Road	E6-E7-F7
Waingate	E6
Walker Street	E7
Washington Road	B1
Watery Street	B7-B8
Wellington Street	B4-C4
West Bar	D6
West Bar Green	C6-D6
West Street	B4-B5-C5
Weston Street	A5-A6
Wheel Hill	E5
Wicker	E6-E7
Wilkinson Street	A4
William Street	A2-A3
York Street	D5-D6
Young Street	B2-C2

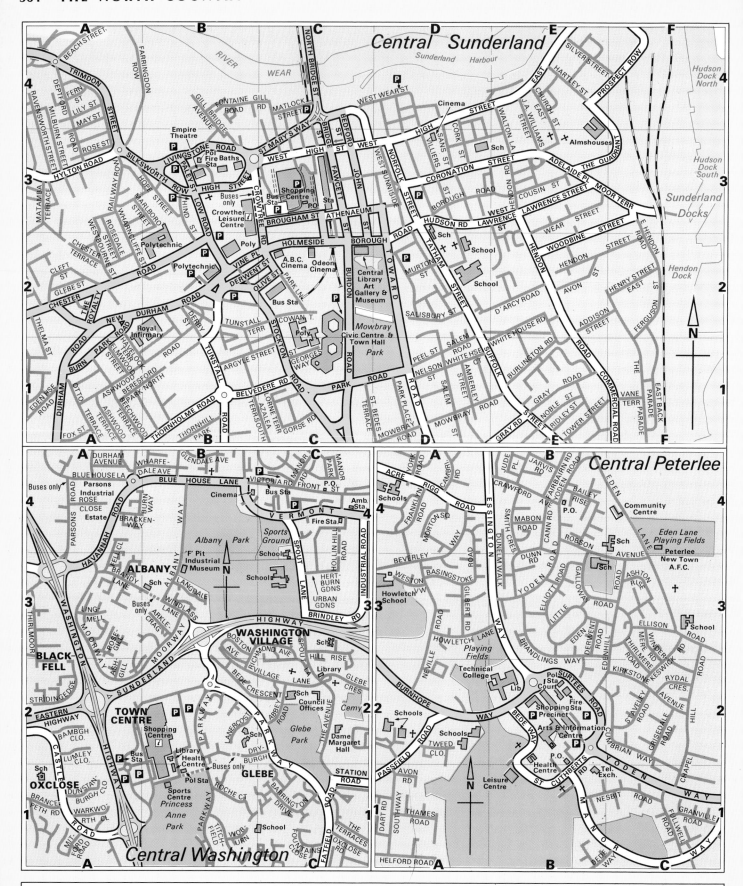

Central Sunderland

Central Washington

Central Peterlee

Sunderland

Renowned for its shipbuilding industry, Sunderland is also an important coal port. Its name is derived from the fact that it was 'sundered' from a monastery founded on the far bank of the River Wear in 674. Wearmouth Bridge, originally built in 1796, but replaced in 1929, was one of the first cast-iron bridges in the country. A modern Civic Centre and three museums feature among the town's amenities. Nearby are the fine beaches of Roker and Seaburn.

Peterlee, built to attract industry in the 1950s, is one of Durham's most successful New Towns. It is named after Peter Lee, who started work down the mines at the age of ten, and rose to become president of the Miners' Union. An unexpected but welcome feature of the town is Castle Eden Dene – a three-mile stretch of natural woodland kept as a nature reserve.

Washington is another New Town burgeoning in this industrial corner of north-east England. In the original village stands 17th-century Washington Old Hall, the former home of George Washington's ancestors. Now in the care of the National Trust, it has been fully restored in period style. Another far cry from industry is the Wildfowl Trust's 103-acre park on the north bank of the Wear, where visitors can observe a comprehensive collection of the world's waterfowl in landscaped surroundings.

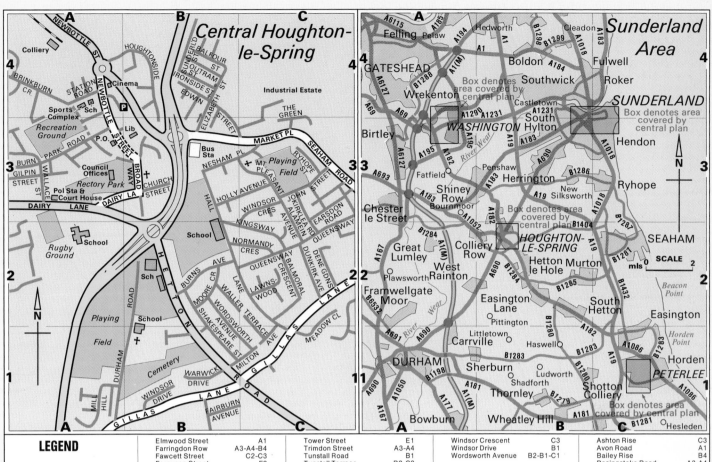

Central Houghton-le-Spring

Sunderland Area

LEGEND

Town Plan
AA recommended route
Restricted roads
Other roads
Buildings of interest   Cinema
Car parks
Parks and open spaces
One way streets

Area Plan
A roads
B roads
Locations   Haswell ○
Urban area

Street Index with Grid Reference

Sunderland

Addison Street	E2-F2
Adelaide Place	E3
Amberley Street	D1
Argyle Street	B1-C1
Ashwood Road	A1-B1-B2
Ashwood Terrace	C3-D3
Athenaeum	C3-D3
Avon Street	E2
Azalea Terrace South	B1-C1
Beach Street	A4
Beechwood Terrace	A1-B1
Bedford Street	C3-C4
Belvedere Road	B1-C1
Beresford Park North	A1-B1
Borough Road	C2-D2-D3-E3
Bridge Street	C3-C4
Brougham Street	C3
Burdon Road	C1-C2
Burlington Road	E1
Burn Park Road	A1-A2
Chester Road	A2-B2
Chester Terrace	A2
Church Street East	E3-E4
Cleft Street	A2
Commercial Road	E1-F1
Cork Street	D3-D4
Coronation Street	D3-E3
Cousin Street	E3
Cowan Terrace	C2
Crowtree Road	B3-C3-C2
D'Arcy Road	D2-E2
Deptford Road	A3-A4
Derby Street	B2
Derwent Street	B2-C2
Durham Road	A1-A2
East Back Parade	F1
East Hendon Road	F2-F3
Eden House Road	A1
Elmwood Street	A1
Farringdon Row	A3-A4-B4
Fawcett Street	C2-C3
Ferguson Street	F2
Fern Street	A4
Fontaine Road	B4
Fox Street	A1
Gill Bridge Avenue	B3-B4
Gill Road	B4-C4
Glebe Street	A2
Gorse Road	C1
Gray Road	D1-E1
Hartley Street	E4
Havelock Terrace	A2-A1-B1
Hendon Road	E1-E2-E3
Hendon Street	E2-F2
Henry Street East	F2
High Street East	D3-D4-E4
High Street West	B3-C3-D3
Hind Street	B2-B3
Holmeside	C2
Hope Street	A3-B3
Hudson Road	D3
Hylton Road	A3
J. A. Williams Street	E3-E4
John Street	C2-C3
Lawrence Street	E3
Lily Street	A4
Livingstone Road	B3
Lorne Terrace	C1
Low Road	B2-B3
Matamba Terrace	A3
Marlborough Street	A3-B3
Matlock Street	C4
May Street	A3-A4
Milburn Street	A3-A4
Moor Terrace	E3-F3
Mowbray Road	D1-E1
Murton Street	D2
Nelson Street	D1
New Durham Road	A2-B2
Noble Street	E1
Norfolk Street	D3
North Bridge Street	C4
Olive Street	B2-C2
Otto Terrace	A1
Paley Street	B3
Park Lane	C2
Park Road	C1-D1
Park Place	D1
Peel Street	D1
Prospect Row	E4-F4
Railway Row	A3
Ravensworth Street	A3-A4
Ridley Street	E1
Rosedale Street	A2-A3
Rose Street	A3
St Bedes Terrace	C1-D1
St George's Way	C1
St Mary's Way	C3-C4
Salisbury Street	D2
Sans Street	D3-D4
Salem Road	D1-D2
Salem Street	D1
Silksworth Row	A3-B3
Silver Street	E4-F4
Stockton Road	B2-C2-C1
Suffolk Street	D1-E1
Tatham Street	D2-D3
Thelma Street	A1-A2
Thornhill Park	B1
Thornholme Road	B1
Toward Road	D1-D2
Tower Street	E1
Trimdon Street	A3-A4
Tunstall Road	B1
Tunstall Terrace	B2-C2
The Parade	F1
The Royalty	A2
The Quadrant	E3-F3-F4-E4
Vane Terrace	F1
Villiers Street	D3
Vine Place	B2-C2
Walton Lane	E3-E4
Wear Street	E3
Westbourne Street	A2-A3
West Lawrence Street	D3-E3
West Sunniside	D3
West Wear Street	C4-D4
Wharncliffe Street	A2-A3
White House Court	D1
White House Road	D1-E1-E2
Woodbine Street	E2-E3-F3

Houghton-le-Spring

Alamein Avenue	C2-C3
Balfour Street	B4
Balmoral Crescent	C2
Brinkburn Crescent	A4
Broadway	B3
Burn Park Road	A3
Burns Avenue	B2
Church Street	B3
Dairy Lane	A3-B3
Dene Gardens	C2
Dunkirk Avenue	C2
Durham Road	A1-B1-B2
Earsdon Road	C3
Edwin Street	B4-B3-C3
Elizabeth Street	B3-B4
Fairburn Avenue	B1
Gillas Lane	A1-B1-C1-C2
Gilpin Street	A3
Hall Lane	B3-B2-C2
Hetton Road	B2-B1-C1
Holly Avenue	B3-C3
Houghtonside	A4-B4
Ironside Street	B4
John Street	C3
Kingsway	B2-C2
Kirklea Road	C2-C3
Lawnswood	C2
Market Place	C3
Meadow Close	C1-C2
Mill Hill	A1
Milton Avenue	B1-C1
Moore Crescent	B2
Mount Pleasant	C3
Nesham Place	B3-C3
Newbottle Street	A4-A3-B3
Normandy Crescent	B2-C2
Outram Street	B4
Queensway	B2-C2-C3
Ryhope Street	C3
Seaham Road	C3
Shakespeare Street	B1-B2
Station Road	A4
Sunderland Street	B4
The Green	C3-C4
Wallace Street	A3
Waller Terrace	B2-C2
Warwick Drive	B1

Washington

Abbey Road	C2
Albany Way	B3-B4
Arklecrag	B3
Ashgill	A2
Bamborough Close	A2
Barrington Drive	C1
Bede Crescent	B3-B2-C2
Blue House Lane	A4-B4
Boston Avenue	B2-B3
Bracken Way	A4
Brancepeth Road	A1
Brandy Lane	A3
Brindley Road	C3
Burn Way	A4-B4
Castle Road	A1-A2
Dryburgh	B2-C2
Dunstanburgh Close	A1
Durham Avenue	A4
Eastern Highway	A2
Fatfield Road	C1
Fell Close	A3-A4
Fountains Close	C1
Front Street	C4
Glebe Crescent	C2
Glendale Avenue	B4
Havannah Road	A3-A4
Hertburn Gardens	C3
Hill Rise	C3
Hollin Hill Road	C3-C4
Industrial Road	C3-C4
Lanercost	B2
Langdale	B3
Lingmell	A3
Lumley Close	A2
Manor Park	C4
Manor Road	C4
Mitford Road	A1
Moorway	A3-A2-B2-B3
Oxclose Road	C1
Parkway	B1-B2-C2-C1
Parsons Road	A3-A4
Richmond Avenue	B2-B3-C3
Roche Court	B1
Rose Close	A4
Rosegill	A3
Spout Lane	C2-C3-C4
Station Road	C1
Stridingedge	A2
Sunderland Highway	A2-A3-B2-B3-C3
The Avenue	C1-C2
The Terraces	C1
Thirlmoor	A3
Titchfield	B1
Urban Gardens	C3
Vermont	B4-C4
Victoria Road	B4-C4
Village Lane	B2-C2
Warkworth Close	A2
Washington Highway	A1-A2-A3-A4
Wharfedale Avenue	A4-B4
Windlass Lane	B3
Woburn	B1

Peterlee

Acre Rigg Road	A4
Ashton Rise	C3
Avon Road	A1
Bailey Rise	B4
Basingstoke Road	A3-A4
Bede Way	B2, B1-C1
Beverley Way	A3-A4
Brandlings Way	B3
Burnhope Way	A2-A3-B2
Cambridge Road	A4
Cann Road	B2
Chapel Hill Road	C1-C2-C3
Crawford Avenue	B4
Cumbrian Way	B2-C2-C1
Dart Road	A1
Derwent Road	B3
Dunelm Walk	B3-B4
Dunn Road	B3-B4
Edenhill Road	C2-C3
Eden Lane	B4-C4-C3
Elliot Road	B3
Ellison Road	C2
Essington Way	A4-B4-A3-B3-B2
Fairbairn Road	B4
Franklyn Road	A4
Fullwell Road	C1
Galloway Road	B4-B3-C3
Gilbert Road	A3
Granville Road	C1
Grisedale Road	C2
Helford Road	A1
Howletch Lane	A3-B3
Jarvis Road	B4
Jude Place	B4
Keswick Road	C2-C3
Kirkstone Avenue	C2
Little Eden	B3
Mabon Road	B4
Manor Way	B1-C1
Morton Square	A4
Nesbit Road	B1-C1
Neville Road	A2-A3
Passfield Road	A1-A2
Robson Avenue	B4-B3-C3
Rydal Crescent	C2
St Cuthberts Road	B1-B2
Smith Crescent	B4
Southway	A1
Staveley Road	C2
Surtees Road	B2
Thames Road	A1
Thirlmere Road	C2-C3
Tweed Close	A2
Weston View	A3
Windermere Road	C3
Yoden Road	B3-B4
Yoden Way	B2-C2-C1
York Road	A4

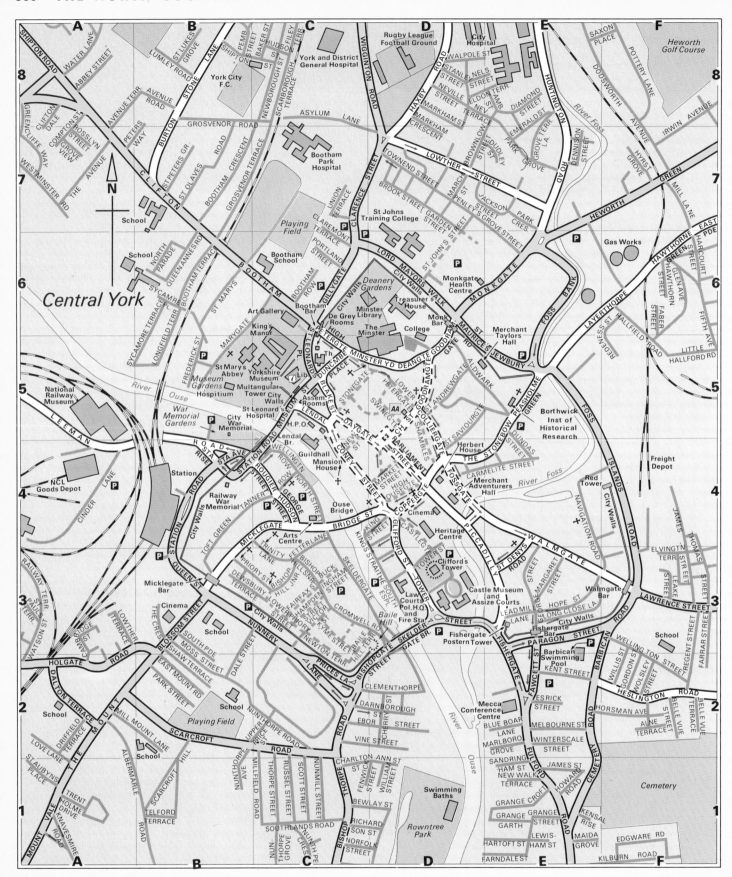

Central York

York

York Minster, unquestionably the city's outstanding glory, is considered to be one of the greatest cathedral churches in Europe. It is especially famous for its lovely windows which contain more than half the medieval stained glass in England.

Great medieval walls enclose the historic city centre and their three-mile circuit offers magnificent views of the Minster, York's numerous fine buildings,

churches and the River Ouse. The ancient streets consist of a maze of alleys and lanes, some of them so narrow that the overhanging upper storeys of the houses almost touch. The most famous of these picturesque streets is The Shambles, formerly the butchers' quarter of the city, but now colonised by antique and tourist shops. York flourished throughout Tudor, Georgian and Victorian times and handsome buildings from these periods also feature throughout the city.

The Castle Museum gives a fascinating picture of York as it used to be and the Heritage Centre interprets the social and architectural history of the city. Other places of exceptional note in this city of riches include the Merchant Adventurer's Hall; the Treasurer's House, now owned by the National Trust and filled with fine paintings and furniture; the Jorvik Viking Centre, where there is an exciting restoration of the original Viking settlement at York, and the National Railway Museum.

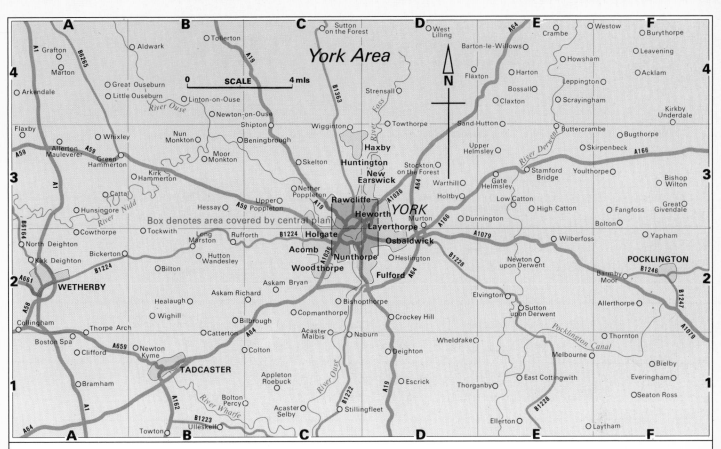

York Area

Box denotes area covered by central plan

SCALE 0 — 4 mls

Key to Town Plan and Area Plan

Town Plan

AA Recommended roads	
Other roads	
Restricted roads	
Buildings of interest	Station
Churches	+
Car Parks	P
Parks and open spaces	
AA Service Centre	AA
One Way Streets	→

Area Plan

A roads	
B roads	
Locations	Fangfoss O
Urban area	

Street Index with Grid Reference

York

Abbey Street	A8
Albermarle Road	A2-A1-B1
Aldwark	D5-E5
Alne Terrace	F2
Amber Street	E8
Ann Street	D1
Asylum Lane	C8-C7-D7
Avenue Road	B8
Avenue Terrace	A7-A8-B8
Baile Hill Terrace	C2-C3-D3
Baker Street	C8
Barbican Road	E2-F2-F3-E3
Belle Vue Street	F2
Belle Vue Terrace	F2
Bewlay Street	C1-D1
Bishopgate Street	C2-D2-D3
Bishophill Junior	C3
Bishophill Senior	C3
Bishop Thorpe Road	C1-C2
Blake Street	C5
Blossom Street	B2-B3
Blue Boar Lane	E2
Bootham	B6-C6
Bootham Crescent	B7-C7-C8
Bootham Row	C6
Bootham Terrace	B6
Bridge Street	C4-D4
Brook Street	D7
Brownlow Street	D7-E7-E8
Buckingham Street	C3
Burton Stone Lane	B7-B8
Cambridge Street	A2-A3
Carmelite Street	D4-E4
Castlegate	D3-D4
Cemetery Road	E1-E2
Charlton Street	C1-D1
Cherry Street	D2
Church Street	D5
Cinder Lane	A4
Claremont Terrace	C6-C7
Clarence Street	C6-C7-D7
Clementhorpe	C2-D2
Clifford Street	D3-D4
Clifton	A8-A7-B7
Clifton Dale	A7-A8
Colliergate	D4-D5
Compton Street	A7-A8
Coppergate	D4
Cromwell Road	C3-D3
Dale Street	B2-B3
Dalton Terrace	A2
Darnborough Street	C2-D2
Daygate	C5-C4-D4-D5
Deangate	D5
Dennison Street	E7
Dewsbury Terrace	B3-C3
Diamond Street	E8
Dodsworth Avenue	E8-F8-F7
Driffield Terrace	A2
Dudley Street	D7-E7
Duncombe Place	C5
Dundas Street	E4-E5
East Parade	F6-F7
East Mount Road	B2
Ebor Street	C2-D2
Edgware Road	F1
Eldon Terrace	D8-E8
Elvington Terrace	F3
Emerald Street	E7-E8
Escrick Street	E2
Faber Street	F6
Fairfax Street	C3
Farndale Street	E1
Farrar Street	F2-F3
Fawcett Street	E2-E3
Fenwick Street	C1-D1
Fetter Lane	C3-C4
Fifth Avenue	F5-F6
Filey Terrace	C8
Fishergate	E2-E3
Foss Bank	E5-E6
Fossgate	D4
Foss Islands Road	E4-E5-F5-F4
Frederick Street	B5
Fulford Road	E1-E2
Garden Street	D7
George Hudson Street	C4
George Street	E3-E4
Gillygate	C6
Glen Avenue	F6
Goodramgate	D5-D6
Gordon Street	F2
Grange Croft	E1
Grange Garth	E1
Grange Street	E1

Greencliffe Way	A7-A8
Grosvenor Road	B8-C8
Grosvenor Terrace	B6-B7-C7-C8
Grove Terrace Lane	E7-E8
Grove View	A7
Hallfield Road	F5-F6
Hampden Street	C3
Harcourt Street	E1
Harloft Street	E1
Hawthorne Green	F6
Hawthorn Street	F6
Haxby Road	D7-D8
Heslington Road	E2-F2
Heworth Green	E6-E7-F7
High Ousegate	D4
High Petergate	C5-C6
Holgate Road	A2-A3-B3
Hope Street	E3
Horsman Avenue	E2-F2
Howard Road	E1
Hudson Street	C8
Huntington Road	E6-E7-E8
Hyrst Grove	F7
Irwin Avenue	F7-F8
Jackson Street	D7-E7
James Street	E1
James Street	F3-F4
Jewbury	E5
Kensal Rise	E1
Kent Street	E2
Kilburn Road	E1-F1
Kings Straithe	C4-D4-D3
King Street	C4-D4
Knavesmire Road	A1
Kyme Street	C3
Lawrence Street	F3
Layerthorpe	E5-E6-F6
Lead Mill Lane	E3
Leake Street	F3
Leeman Road	A5-A4-B5-B4
Lendal Coney Street	C5-C4-D4
Lewisham Street	E1
Little Hallford Road	F5
Long Close Lane	E3-F3
Longfield Terrace	B5-B6
Lord Mayors Walk	C6-D6
Lumley Road	B8
Love Lane	A1-A2
Lower Petergate	D5
Lower Priory Street	C3
Lowther Street	D7-E7
Lowther Terrace	A3
Maida Grove	E1
March Street	D7
Margaret Street	E3
Market Street	D4
Markham Crescent	D7-D8
Markham Street	D7-D8
Marlborough Grove	E2
Marygate	B5-B6-C6
Melbourne Street	E2
Micklegate	B3-B4-C4
Millfield Road	C1-C2
Mill Lane	E1
Mill Mount Lane	A2-B2
Minster Yard	C5-D5
Monkgate	D6-E6
Moss Street	B2-B3
Mount Vale	A1
Museum Street	C5

Navigation Road	E4-E3-F3
Nelson Street	D8-E8
Neville Street	D8
Neville Terrace	D8-E8
Newborough Street	C8
New Street	C4-C5
Newton Terrace	C2-C3
New Walk Terrace	E1
Norfolk Street	C1-D1
North Parade	B6
North Street	C4
Nunmill Street	C1-C2
Nunnery Lane	B3-C3-C2
Nunthorpe Avenue	B1-B2
Nunthorpe Grove	C1
Nunthorpe Road	B2-C2
Paragon Street	E3-F3
Park Crescent	E7
Park Grove	E7-E8
Park Street	B2
Parliament Street	D4-D5
Peasholme Green	E5
Pembroke Street	B8
Penley's Grove Street	D7-E7-E6
Peters Way	A7-B7-B8
Piccadilly	D4-D3-E3-E4
Portland Street	C6
Pottery Lane	F8
Prices Lane	C1
Priory Street	B3-C3
Queen Annes Road	B6
Queen Street	B3
Railway Terrace	A3
Redness Street	F5-F6
Regent Street	F2-F3
Richardson Street	C1-D1
Rosslyn Street	A7
Rougier Street	C4
Russel Street	C1-C2
St Andrewgate	D5
St Aubyns Place	A1
St Denys Road	E3-E4
St Johns Street	D6-D7
St Leonards Place	D5-D6
St Lukes Grove	B8
St Marys	B6
St Maurices	D6-D5-E5
St Olaves Road	B7-B8
St Pauls Terrace	A3
St Peters Grove	B7
St Saviourgate	D4-D5-E5
Sandringham Street	E1
Saxon Place	E8-E7
Scarborough Terrace	C8
Scarcroft Hill	B1-B2
Scarcroft Road	A2-B2-C2-C1
Scott Street	C1-C2
Shambles	D4-D5
Shaw Terrace	B2-B3
Shipton Road	A8
Shipton Street	B8-C8
Skeldergate	C4-C3-D3
Skeldergate Bridge	D3
South Esplanade	D3
Southlands Road	C1
South Parade	B2-B3
Stanley Street	D8
Station Avenue	B4
Station Rise	B4
Station Road	B3-B4-C4-C5

Stonegate	C5-D5
Swinegate	D5
Sycamore Place	B6
Sycamore Terrace	A5-B5-B6
Tanner Row	B4-C4
Telford Terrace	B1
The Avenue	A7
The Crescent	B3
The Mount	A1-A2-B2
The Stonebow	D4-E4-E5
Thomas Street	F3-F4
Thorpe Street	C1-C2
Toft Green	B3-B4
Tower Street	D4-D3-E3
Townend Street	D7
Trent Holme Drive	A1
Trinity Lane	C3-C4
Union Terrace	C7
Upper Price Street	B2-C2
Victor Street	C3
Vine Street	C2-D2
Walmgate	D4-E4-E3-F3
Walpole Street	D8-E8
Water Lane	A8
Watson Street	A2-A3
Wellington Row	C4
Wellington Street	F2-F3
Westminster Road	A7
William Street	D1
Willis Street	F2-F3
Winterscale Street	E2
Wolsley Street	F2

Legend to Atlas

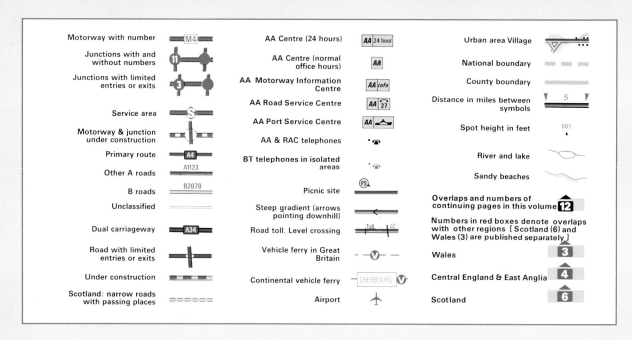

Motorway with number	M4
Junctions with and without numbers	11
Junctions with limited entries or exits	3
Service area	S
Motorway & junction under construction	
Primary route	A4
Other A roads	A1123
B roads	B2070
Unclassified	
Dual carriageway	A34
Road with limited entries or exits	
Under construction	
Scotland: narrow roads with passing places	

AA Centre (24 hours)	AA 24 hour
AA Centre (normal office hours)	AA
AA Motorway Information Centre	AA info
AA Road Service Centre	AA 27
AA Port Service Centre	AA
AA & RAC telephones	☎
BT telephones in isolated areas	☎
Picnic site	PS
Steep gradient (arrows pointing downhill)	
Road toll. Level crossing	Toll LC
Vehicle ferry in Great Britain	V
Continental vehicle ferry	CHERBOURG V
Airport	✈

Urban area Village	
National boundary	
County boundary	
Distance in miles between symbols	5
Spot height in feet	665
River and lake	
Sandy beaches	
Overlaps and numbers of continuing pages in this volume	12
Numbers in red boxes denote overlaps with other regions [Scotland (6) and Wales (3) are published separately]	
Wales	3
Central England & East Anglia	4
Scotland	6

Abbey or Cathedral	Coastal Launching Site	Nature Trail
Ruined Abbey or Cathedral	Surfing	Wildlife Park (mammals)
Castle	Climbing School	Wildlife Park (birds)
House and Garden	County Cricket Ground	Zoo
House	Gliding Centre	Forest Drive
Garden	Artificial Ski Slope	Lighthouse
Industrial Interest	Golf Course	Tourist Information Centre
Museum or Collection	Horse Racing	Tourist Information Centre (summer only)
Prehistoric Monument	Show Jumping/Equestrian Centre	Long Distance Footpath
Famous Battle Site	Motor Racing Circuit	AA Viewpoint
Preserved Railway or Steam Centre	Cave	Other Place of Interest
Windmill	Country Park	Boxed symbols indicate tourist attractions in towns
Sea Angling	Dolphinarium or Aquarium	

The National Grid

The National Grid provides a system of reference common to maps of all scales. The grid covers Britain with an imaginary network of 100 kilometre squares. Each square is identified by two letters, *eg* TR. Every 100 kilometre square is then sub-divided into 10 kilometre squares which appear as a network of blue lines on the map pages. These blue lines are numbered left to right 0-9 and bottom to top 0-9. These 10 kilometre squares can be further divided into tenths to give a place reference to the nearest kilometre.

Key to Road Maps

Thurso
Wick
Stornoway
Outer Hebrides
Ullapool
Portree
Banff
Inverness
Peterhead
Aberdeen
Fort William
Pitlochry
Oban
Perth
Dundee
Edinburgh

Shetland Islands

Orkney Islands

604/605
Berwick
Largs
Glasgow
Peebles
Ayr
600/601
602/603
Campbeltown
Dumfries
598/599
Newcastle upon Tyne
596/597
Stranraer
590/591
Workington
592/593
594/595
Middlesbrough
Isle of Man
Kendal
584/585
Scarborough
Douglas
Lancaster
586/587
588/589
York
Blackpool
Leeds
Hull
578/579
580/581
582/583
Grimsby
Liverpool
Manchester
Sheffield
Caernarfon
570/571
Chester
572/573
574/575
576/577
Lincoln
Stoke
Nottingham
King's Lynn
Shrewsbury
Leicester
Norwich
Great Yarmouth
Peterborough
Aberystwyth
Birmingham
Coventry
Northampton
Cambridge
Worcester
Fishguard
Carmarthen
Hereford
Felixstowe
Gloucester
Pembroke
Swansea
Chelmsford
Oxford
LONDON
Cardiff
Bristol
Reading
Maidstone
Barnstaple
Guildford
Dover
Salisbury
Folkestone
Taunton
Southampton
Brighton
Newhaven
Exeter
Weymouth
Bournemouth
Truro
Plymouth
Scilly Isles

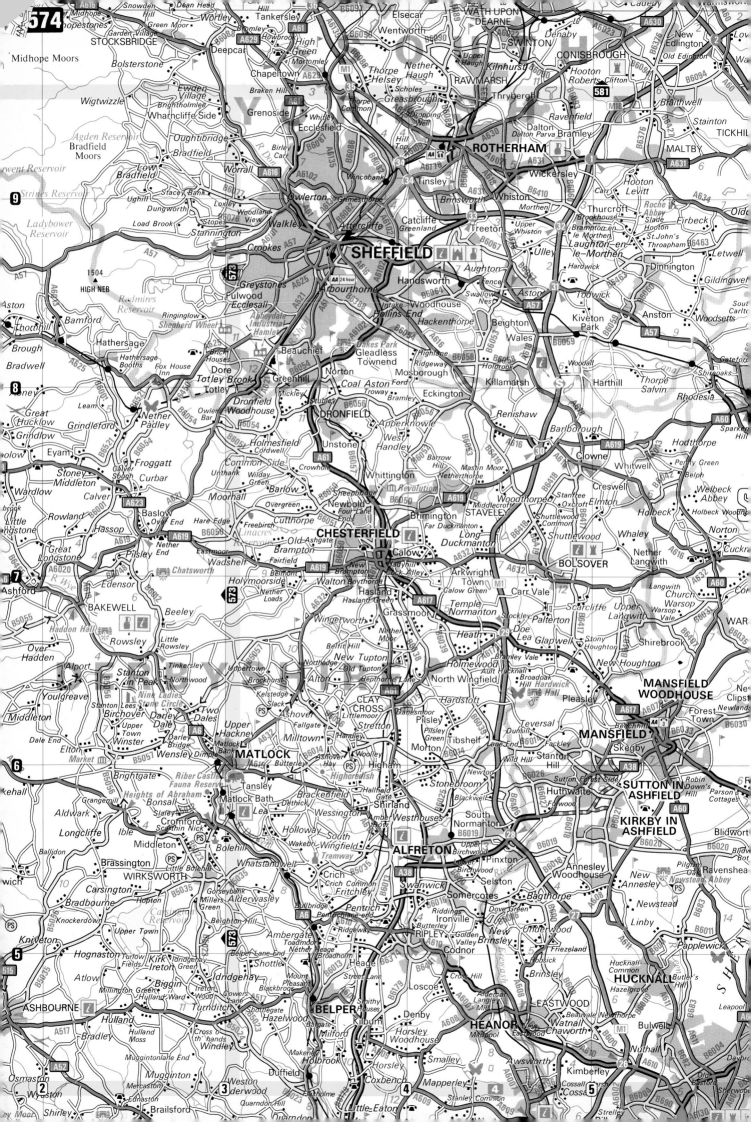

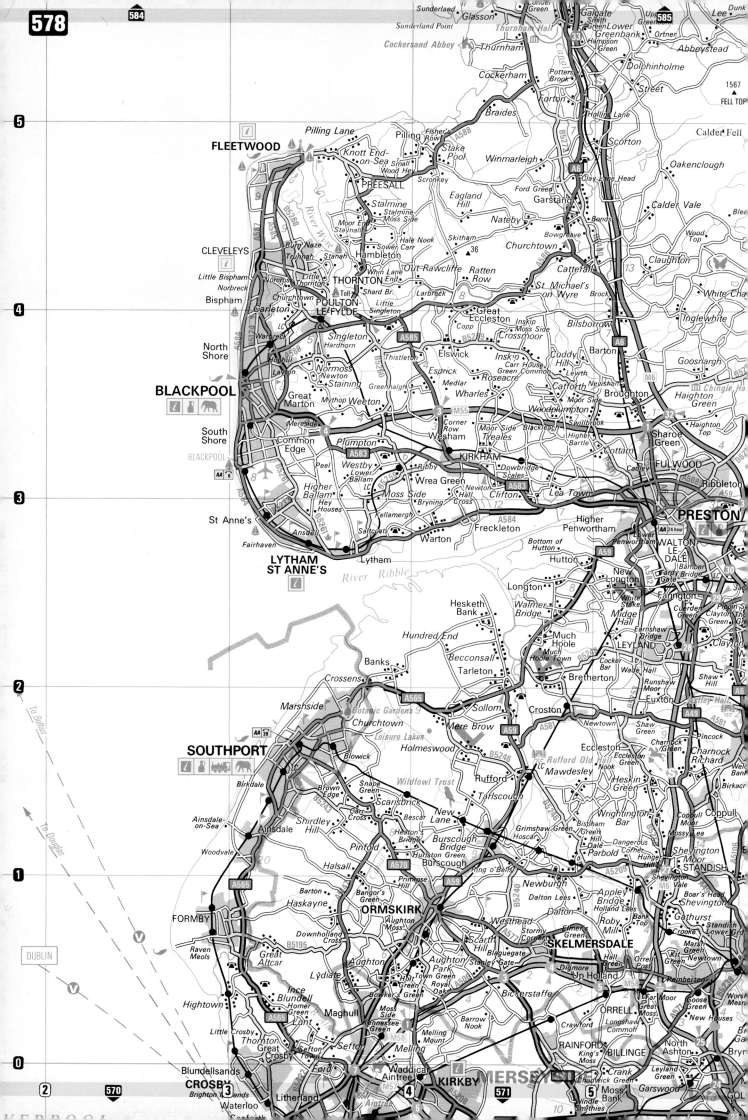

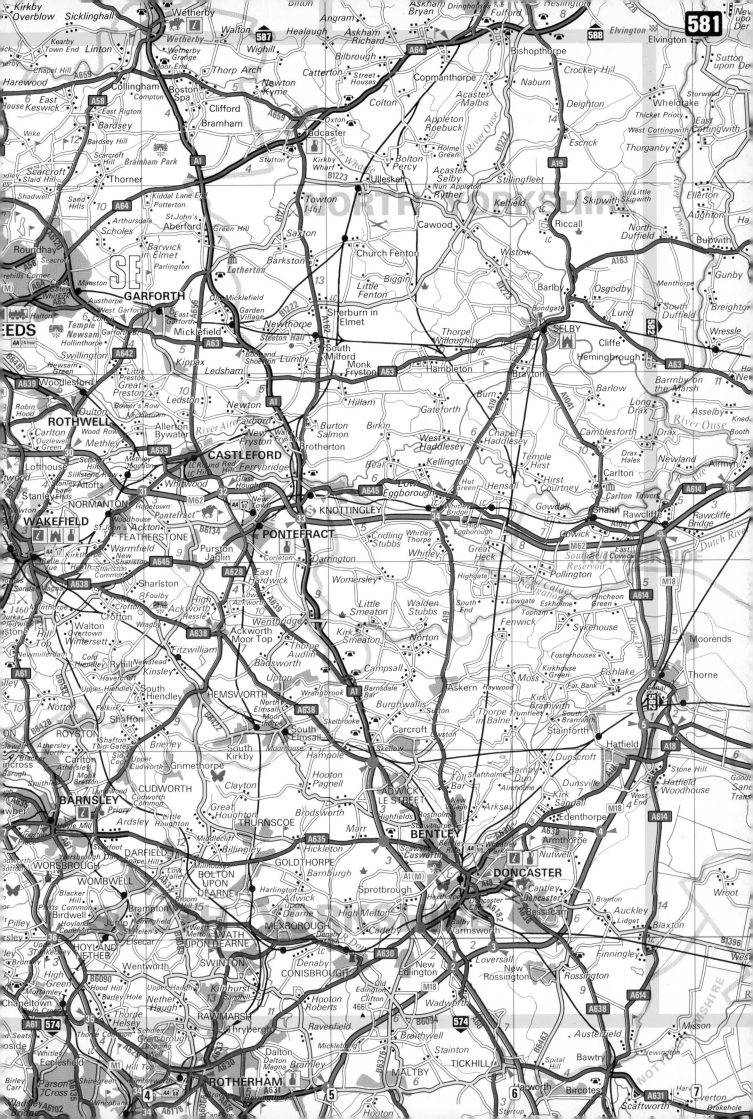

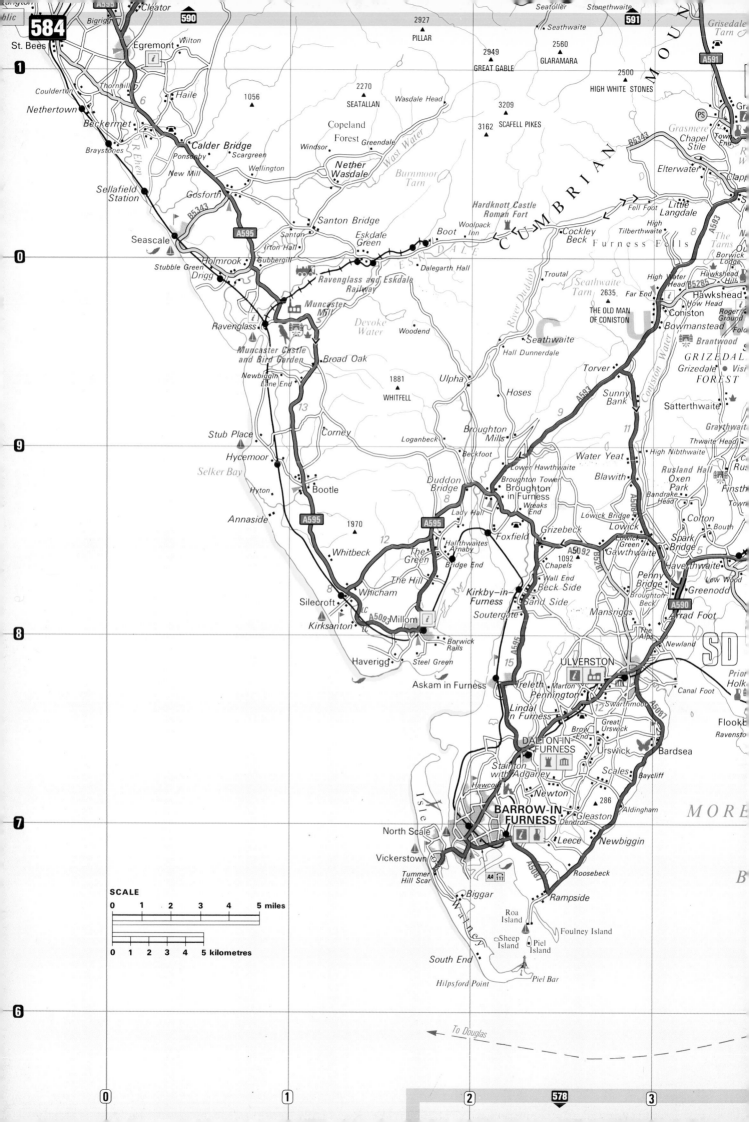

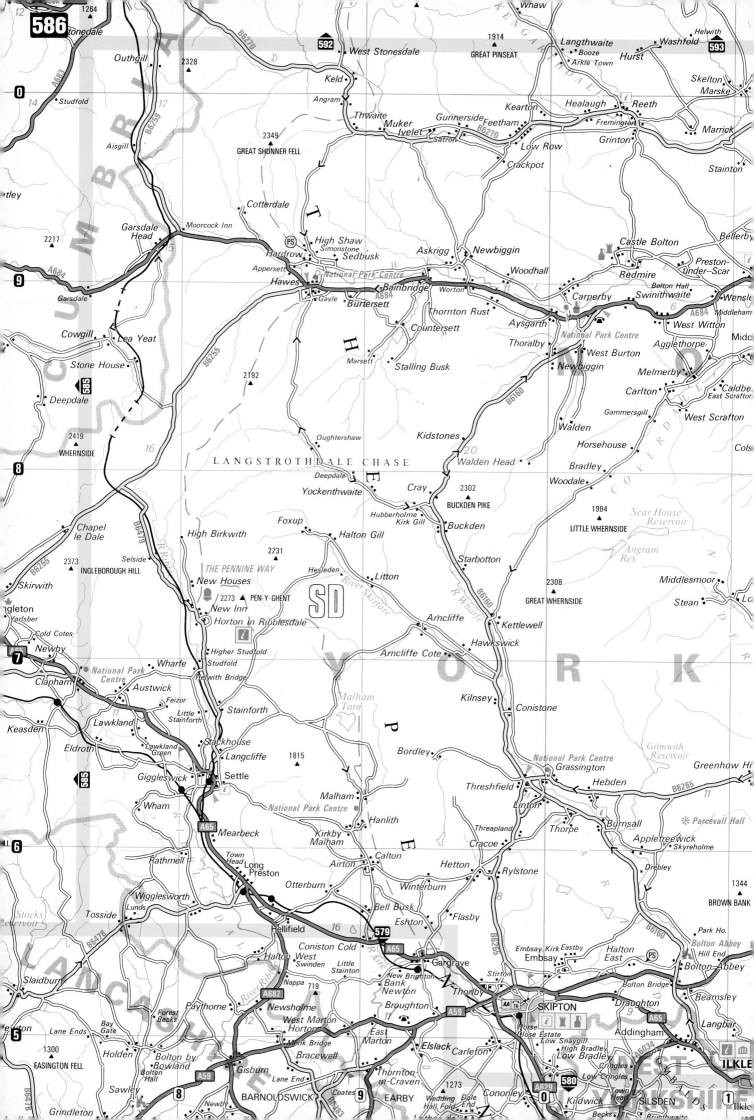

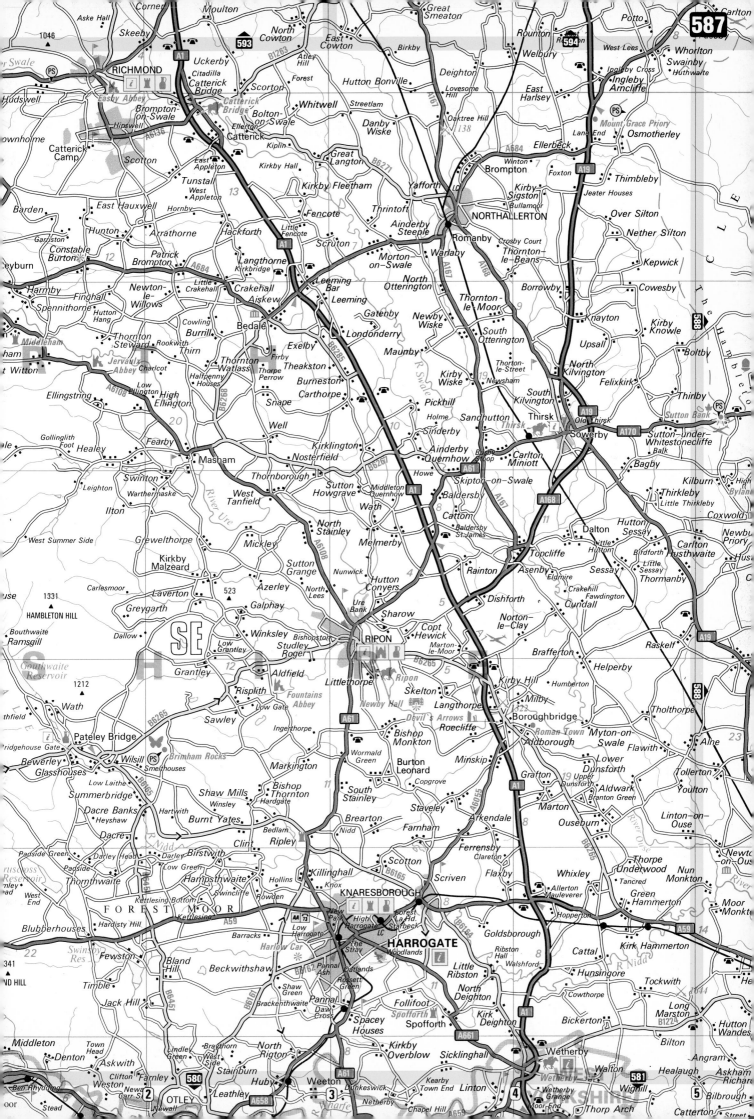

SCALE

0 1 2 3 4 5 miles

0 1 2 3 4 5 kilometres

Fylingthorpe
Old Peak or South Cheek
Low Flask
Ravenscar
Flask Inn
Falcon Inn
Staintondale
A171
Harwood Dale
20
Cloughton Newlands
Cloughton Wyke
Cloughton
Bickley
Langdale End
Silpho
Suffield
Burniston
Cromer Point
Hackness
A165
SCALBY
CLEVELAND WAY
Newby
Wrench Green
Everley
Barrowcliff
SCARBOROUGH
Sea Cut
River Derwent
Falsgrave
Oliver's Mount
AA
A165
A170
Ayton
Osgodby
Cayton Bay
Sawdon
Hutton Buscel
Irton
Eastfield
High Killerby
Ruston
Seamer
LC
The Wyke
Ebberston
A170
Snainton
Wykeham
Cayton
B1261
Gristhorpe
Brompton
Lebberston
LC
FILEY
Yedingham
Westfield
A64
River Hertford
Flixton
Folkton
LC
Filey Bay
Willerby
A1039
West Flotmanby
Muston
LC
Sherburn
Ganton
Staxton
PS
Hunmanby
Holiday Camp
TA
East Heslerton
Potter Brompton
Reighton
West Heslerton
16
Fordon
Speeton
Crab Rocks
B1249
Wold Newton
Burton Fleming
B1229
Buckton
Bempton
Foxholes
Grindale
North Moor
Flamborough
Weaverthorpe
Butterwick
Little Argam
West Huntow
Flamborough Head
Linton
Thwing
B1255
Sewerby
Sewerby Hall
West Lutton
East Lutton
Octon
Helperthorpe
B1253
Boynton
BRIDLINGTON
High Mowthorpe
14
Langtoft
Rudston
Low Caythorpe
BRIDLINGTON BAY
Kirby Grindalythe
Low Mowthorpe
Sledmere
Cowlam Manor
B1253
Cottam
Kilham
Burton Agnes Hall
Bessingby
Carnaby
Hilderthorpe
Sledmere
B1252
B1249
Ruston Parva
Burton Agnes
Carnaby
A165
Towthorpe
B1251
Harpham
Thornholme
North Kingsfield
Fraisthorpe
Garton-on-the-Wolds
Great Kendale
Lowthorpe
South Kingsfield
A166
Nafferton
Little Kelk
Gransmoor
Wetwang
Little Driffield
Elmswell
A166
Great Kelk
Allison Lane End
Lissett
Barmston
B1248
GREAT DRIFFIELD
LC
B1249
Wansford
Gembling Lane End
Gembling
Ulrome
B1242
Tibthorpe
Kirkburn
A163
Kelleythorpe
Skerne
Foston on the Wolds
West End
East End
Skipsea
Southburn
28
Hutton
Brigham
Church End
Beeford
B1249
Skipsea Brough
North Dalton
Bainton
Hutton Cranswick
Rotsea
North Frodingham
Upton
Dunnington
15
Watton
Hempholme
North End
Bewholme
Atwick
Middleton-on-the-Wolds
Kilnwick
Lund
Beswick
River Hull
Burshill
Nunkeeling
North Cliff
A163
Holme on the Wolds
Lockington
A164
Little Burton
Seaton
HORNSEA
Thorpe
A582
Brandesburton
Hornsea Mere
South Cliff
Leven
9
0
1
2
583

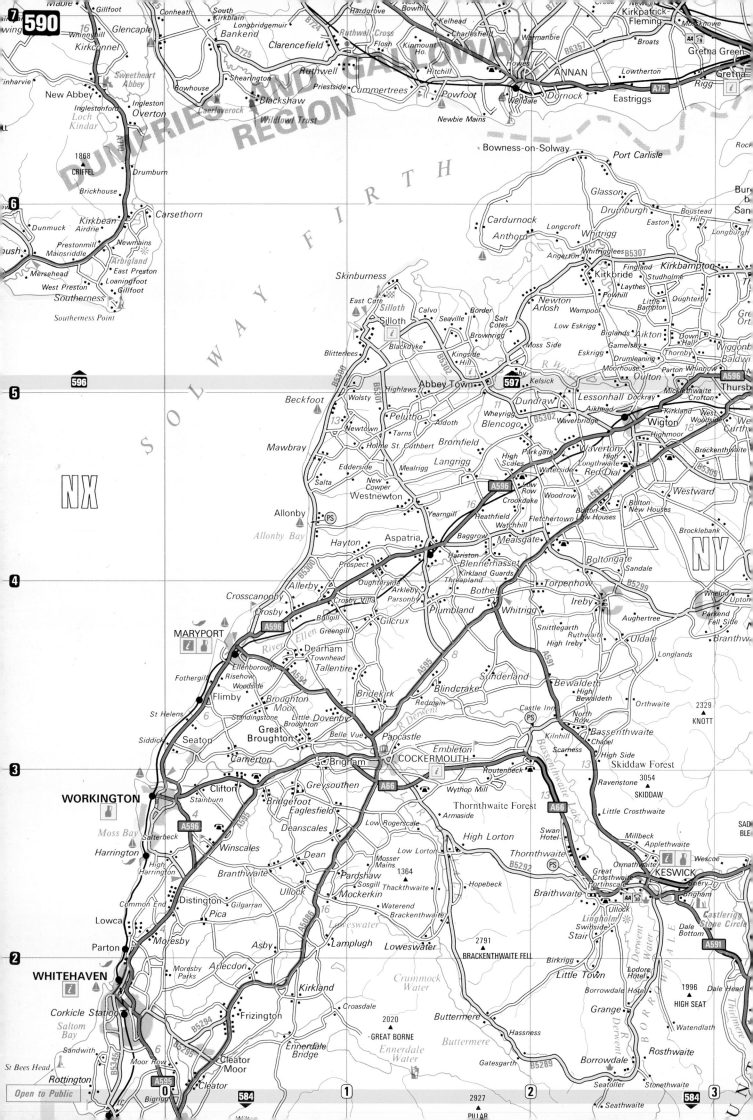

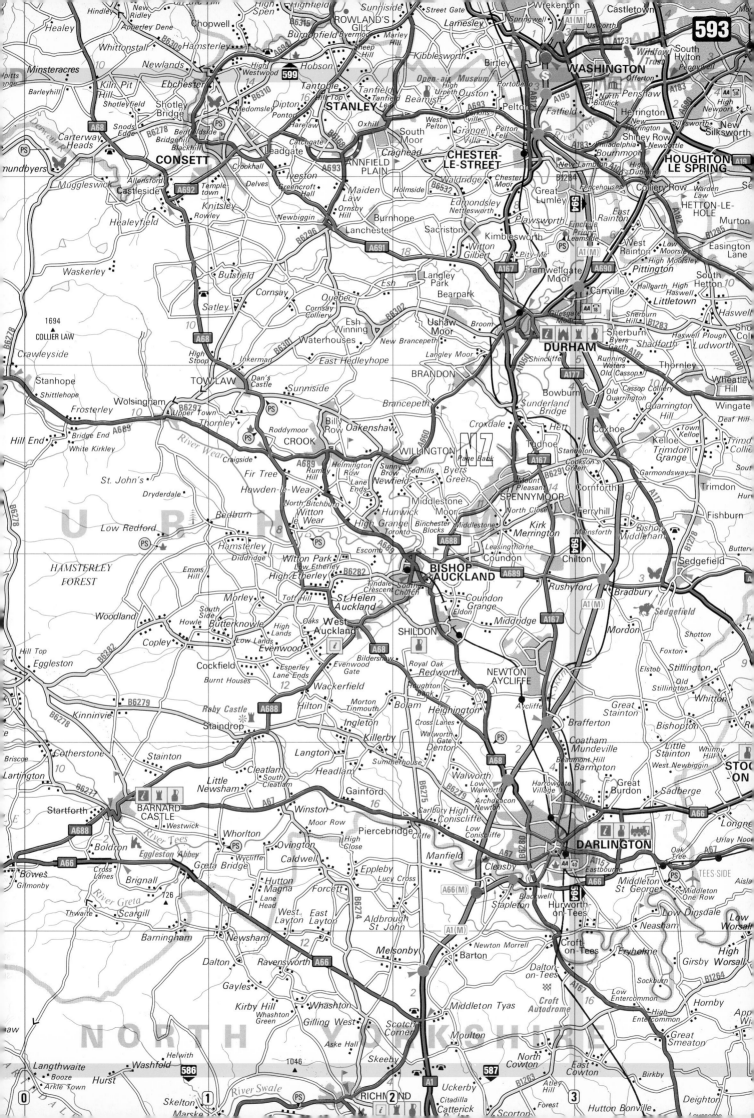

SCALE

0　1　2　3　4　5 miles

0　1　2　3　4　5 kilometres

OCAR
The Flashes

MARSKE-
BY-THE-SEA

New
Marske

SALTBURN-BY-THE-SEA

New Brotton

Skinningrove

Boulby

New
Skelton

Upleatham

BROTTON

Carlin How

Kilton

LOFTUS

Street
Houses

Cowbar

Staithes

A174

SKELTON

North Skelton

Kilton
Thorpe

East
Loftus

Easington

Dalehouse

Port Mulgrave

16

Boosbeck

Margrove
Park

Lingdale

Liverton
Mines

Handale

Hinderwell

Runswick

B1366

ough

Charlton

Stanghow

Liverton

Roxby

Borrowby

Newton
Mulgrave

CLEVELAND WAY

Goldsborough

1078

EVELAND WAY

Moorsholm

Ellerby

B1266

Lythe

Sandsend

A171

Gerrick

Scaling

A174

Open to Public

21

Scaling
Dam

Mickleby

A171

West
Barnby

East Barnby

Raithwaite

WHITBY

Saltwick Bay

Commondale

Ugthorpe

Hutton Mulgrave

Dunsley

Newholm

Selly Hill

Ruswarp

Stainsacre

Danby

Stonegate

Biggsgarth

Sneaton

Hawsker

Houlsyke

Lealholm
Side

Aislaby

e

Ainthorpe

Lealholm

PS

Iburndale

Sneatonthorpe

Ness Point or
North Cheek

Castleton

SK

The
Green

Sleights

Ugglebarnby

aysdale
Abbey

Westerdale

Low
Garth

Glaisdale

Egton

Grosmont

Robin Hood's Bay

HIRE

Danby
Botton

Street

Egton
Bridge

Esk Valley

Green End

Littlebeck

A169

B1416

Raw

Fylingthorpe

1422

588

Ralph Cross

7

Beck Hole

8

Goathland

PS

9

PS

589

Old Peak or
South Cheek

Low Flask

Rave**O**ar

Flask Inn

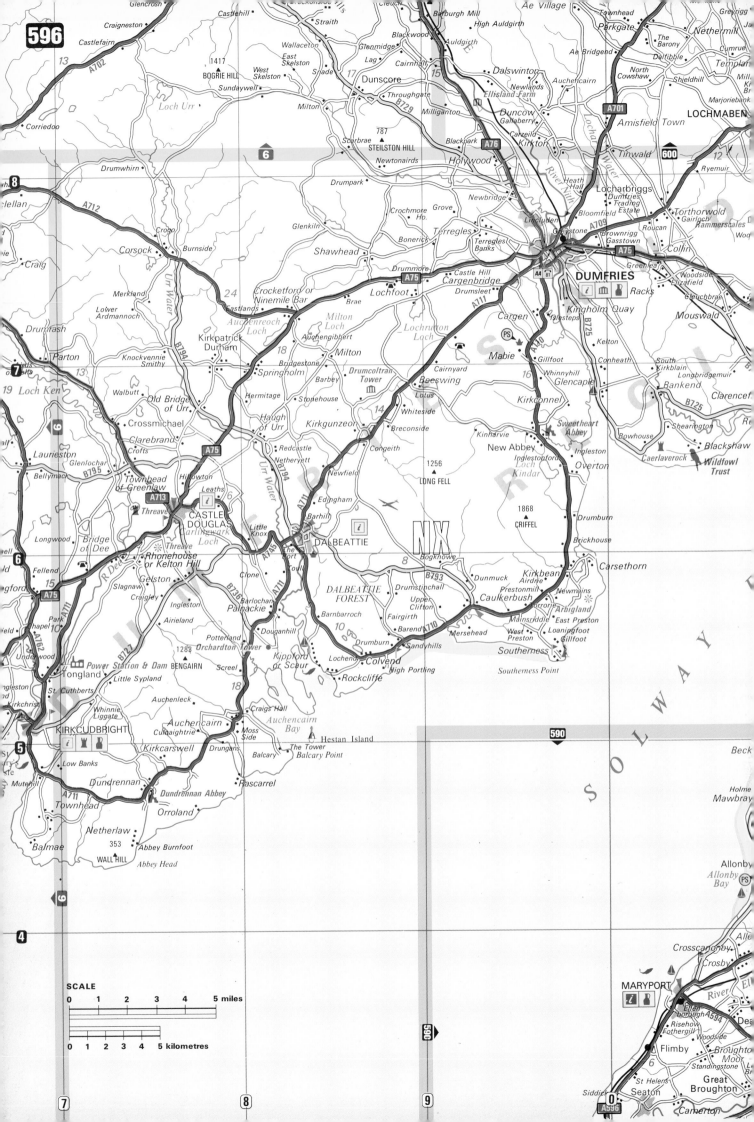

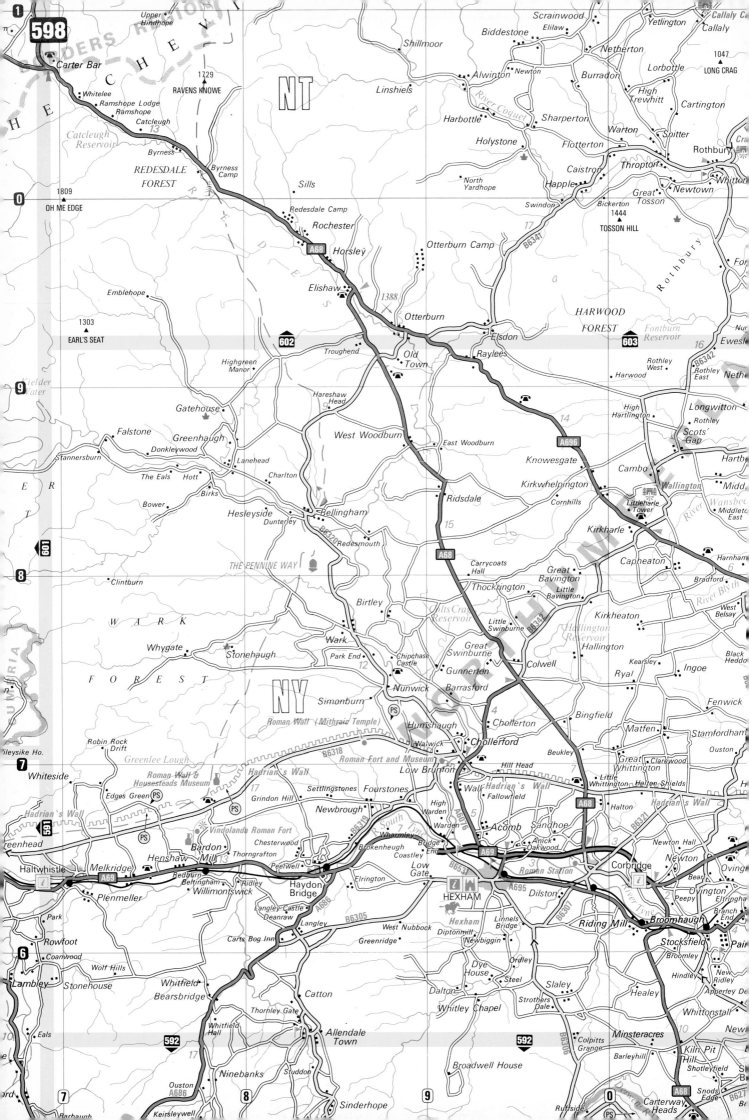

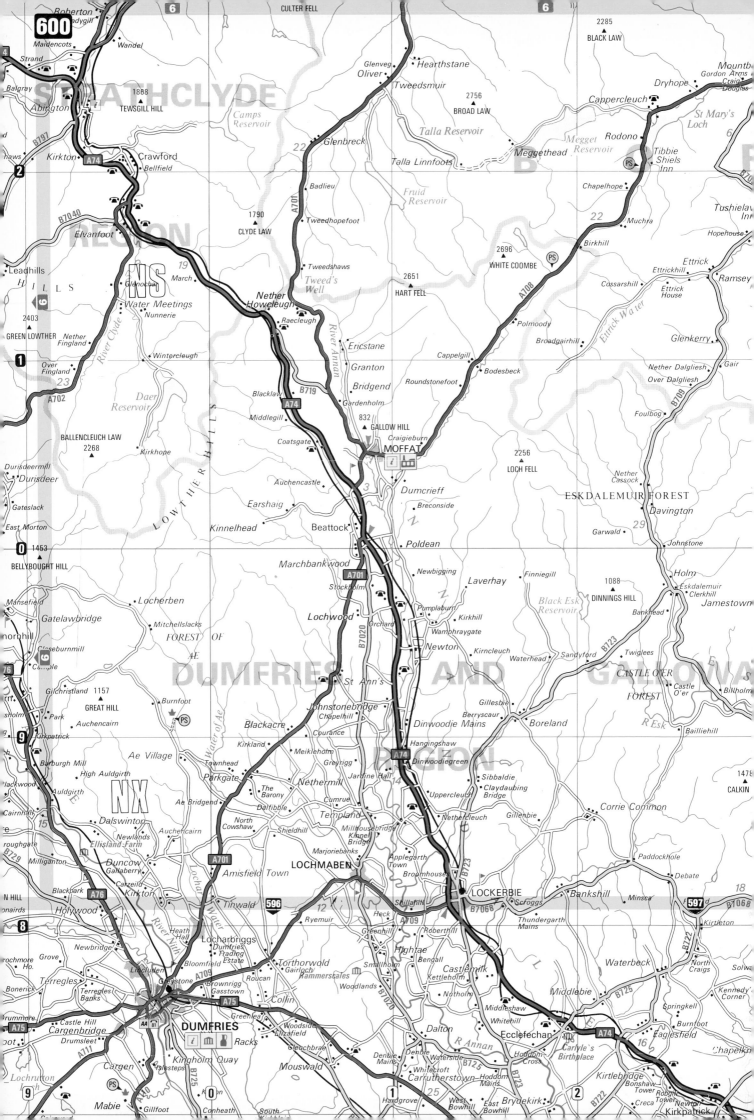

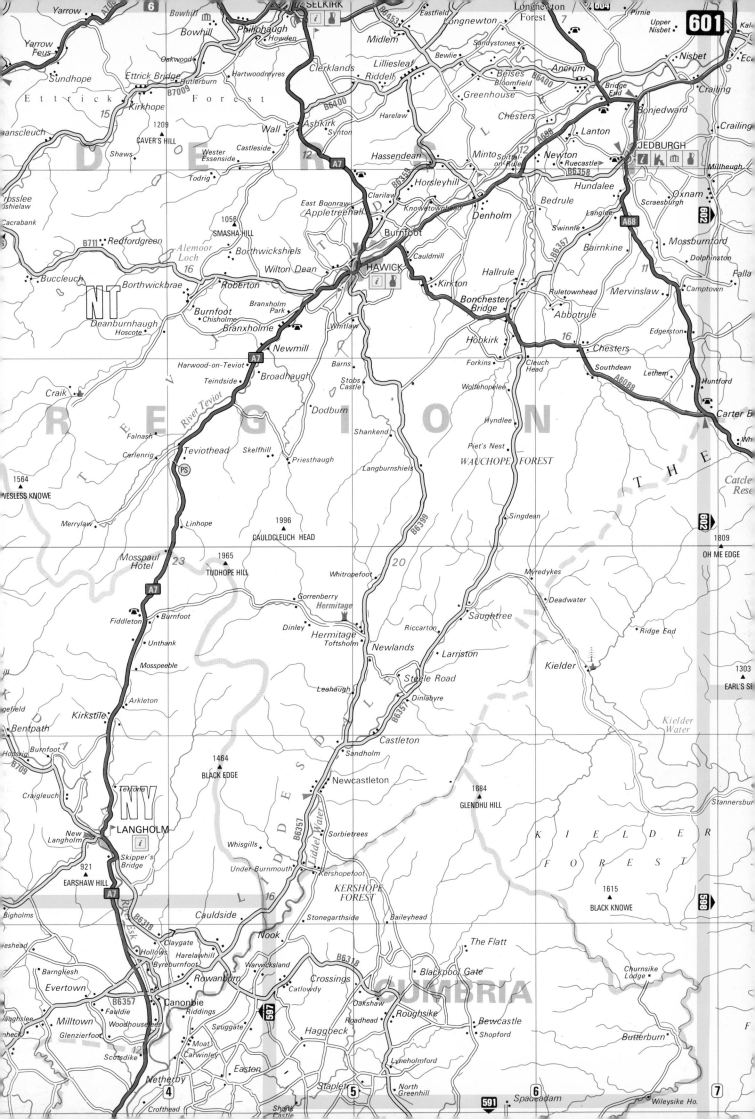

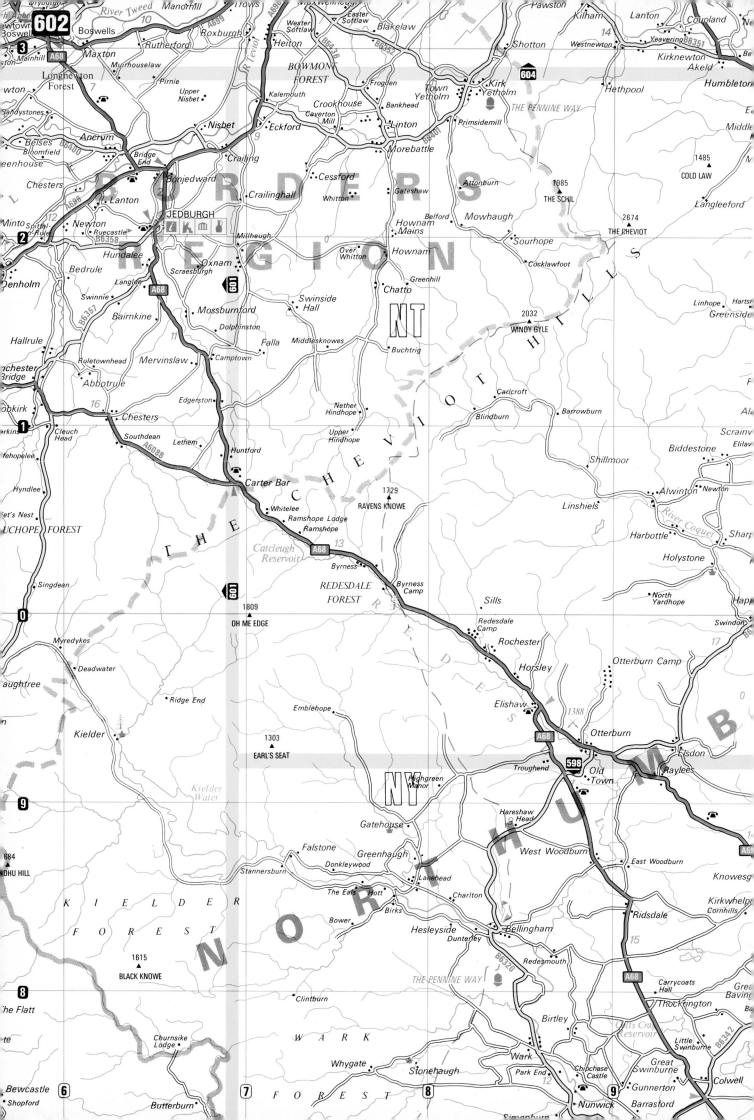

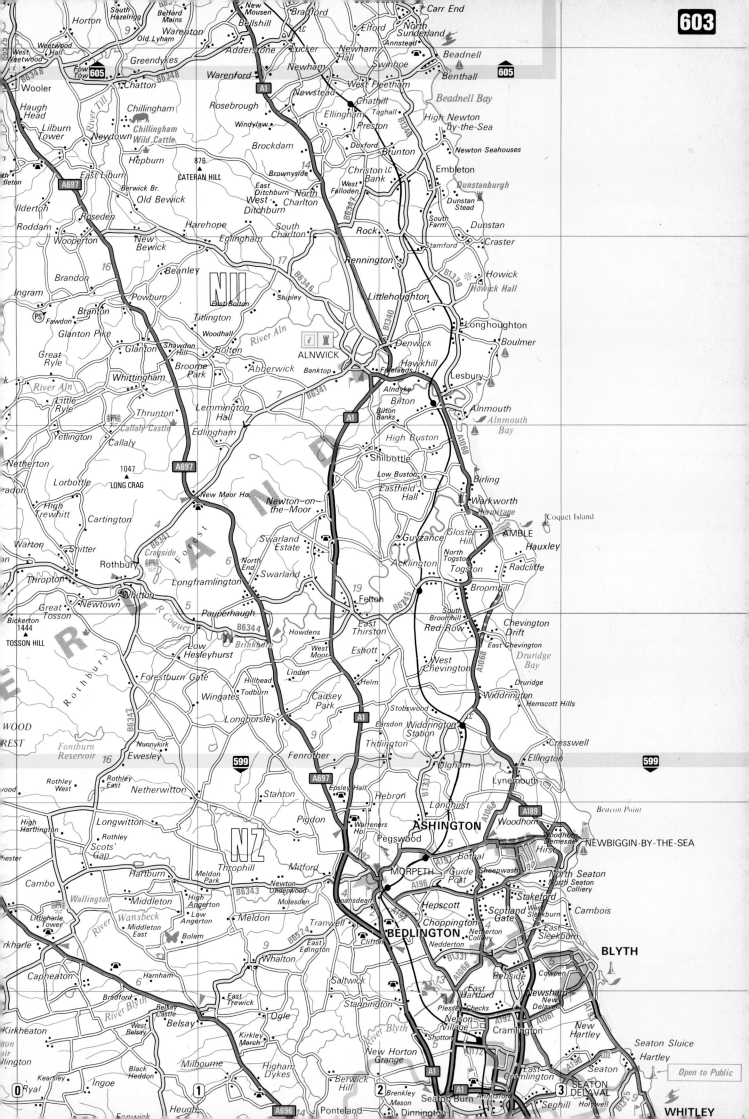

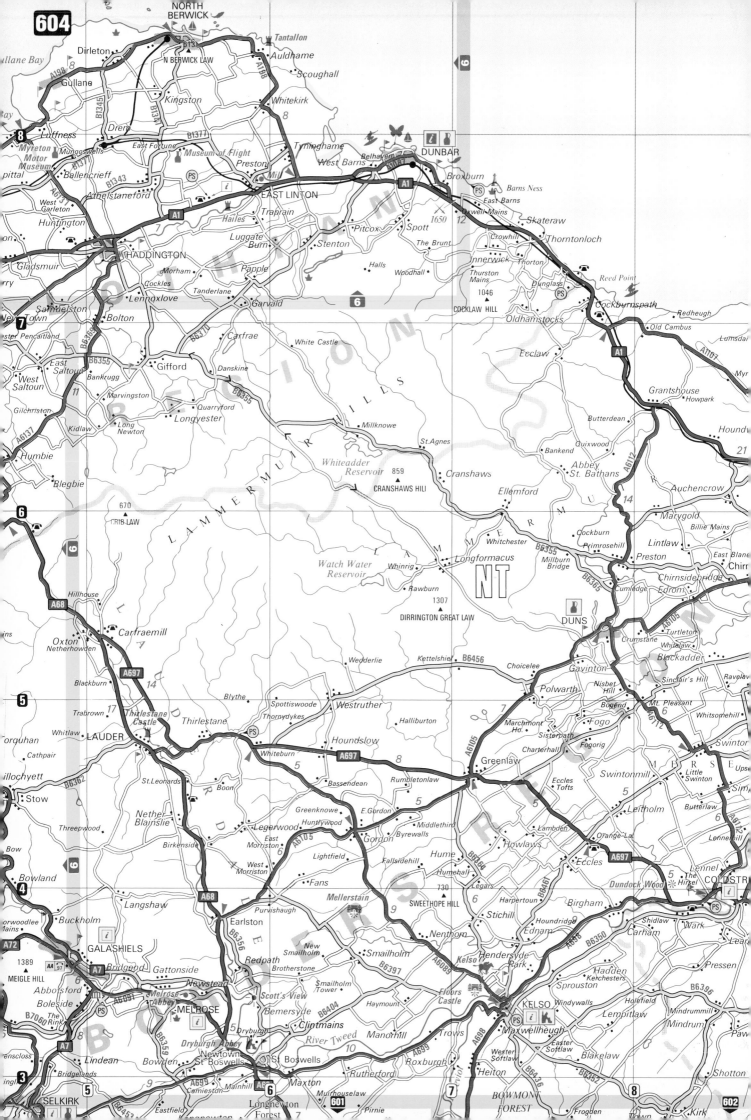

SCALE

0   1   2   3   4   5 miles

0   1   2   3   4   5 kilometres

ST ABB'S HEAD

Northfield

St Abbs

ngham

Whitecross

Acredale

Cairncross

EYEMOUTH

Biglawburn

Gunsgreenhill

ugh
ead

Reston   A1

Ayton   Burnmouth

Prenderguest

Causewaybank

Whiterig

NU

PS

B6355

Edington   Foulden

Lamberton

dhaugh
lanton

Clappers   1333   Conundrum

A1

Broomdykes

Foulden
Newton

A6105   Meadowhill

High Letham

roadykirk   Hutton   Paxton

B6461

BERWICK-UPON-TWEED

Hutton
Mains

Sunwick

Tweedmouth

Dykegatehead

Loanend   East Ord   Spittal

B6461   Fishwick

tsome
on   B6461

Horndean   West Longridge   Borewell

adykirk   Thorntonpark

Murton

Scremerston

Norham   Thornton   Unthank

Norham   Newburn   West
Allerdean   Cheswick

B6470

West
Newbiggin   Shoreswood   Shoresdean

adykirk
Ho.

Grindon   Ancroft   Goswick

CAUSEWAY
FLOODED
AT HIGH TIDE

HOLY ISLAND

eed
15   Shellacres   Grindonrigg

New
Haggerston   Haggerston

Beal

Twizel Bridge
lmouth Park   Till

Duddo   West Mains

Fenhamhill

Holy
Island

Lindisfarne Priory   Castle Point

Melkington

Bowsden   Kentstone

Fenham

Burrows Hole

Castle
Heaton

B6354   Etal   Kyloe   Fenwick

rnhill
Tweed

Heatherslaw Mill   B6353   Lowick   Buckton

Barelees   Crookham

The Lady Waterford Hall
Ford

Brownridge   Elwick   Ross

Staple
Sound   FARNE ISLANDS

Branxton   17   Smeafield

1513

Flodden   14   Kimmerston   Holburn   Detchant

Low Middleton   Budle
Bay   Inner
Sound   Bamburgh

NORTHUMBERLAND

A697   Hetton Steads

Middleton   Easington   Budle   Bamburgh

Open to Public

rnham

Howtel   Milfield   Nesbit   Hettonlaw

Belford

Waren
Mill
Glororum   Burton

B6352   Fenton
Town   Hettonhall   North
Hazelrigg   Sionside   Spindlestone   LC   Seahouses

Kilham   Doddington   Hetton   South
Hazelrigg   Horton   Belford
Mains   B6349   New
Mousen   Bradford   Carr End

Lanton   Coupland   Newtown   Warenton   Bellshill   Elford   North
Sunderland

14   Yeavering   B6351   Weetwood
Hall   Old Lyham   LC   Newham
Hall   Annstead

stnewton   Kirknewton   Bendor   West
twood   9   Adderstone   Lucker   Beadnell

Akeld   B6125   Fowl
Town   603   Warenford   Newham   2   nhoe   Benthall

Humbleton   B6348   Chatton   West Fleetham

NORTH COUNTRY INDEX
As well as the page number of each place name the index also includes an appropriate atlas page number together with a four figure map reference (see National Grid explanation at start of atlas section).

In a very few instances place names appear without a map reference. This is because either they are not shown on the atlas or they lie just outside the mapping area of the region. However, each tour does include a detailed map which highlights the location of all places mentioned on the route.